ADVANCES IN

REAL-TIME SYSTEMS

ADVANCES IN
REAL-TIME SYSTEMS

Edited by

John A. Stankovic and Krithi Ramamritham

IEEE Computer Society Press
Los Alamitos, California

Washington ● Brussels ● Tokyo

Library of Congress Cataloging-in-Publication Data

Stankovic, John A.
  Advances in real-time systems / John A. Stankovic, Krithi Ramamritham.
    p. cm.
  "April 1992."
  Includes bibliographical references.
  ISBN 0-8186-3792-7. -- ISBN 0-8186-3790-0 (paper)
    1. Real-time data processing.   I. Ramamritham, Krithi.
II. Title.
QA76.54.S73   1993
004' .33--dc20   93-2243
                                                      CIP

Published by the
IEEE Computer Society Press
10662 Los Vaqueros Circle
PO Box 3014
Los Alamitos, CA 90720-1264

IEEE Computer Society Press Order Number 3792-01
Library of Congress Number 93-2243
IEEE Catalogue Number EH0374-9
ISBN 0-8186-3791-9 (microfiche)
ISBN 0-8186-3792-7 (case)

Additional copies can be ordered from

IEEE Computer Society Press
Customer Service Center
10662 Los Vaqueros Circle
P.O. Box 3014
Los Alamitos, CA 90720-1264

IEEE Service Center
445 Hoes Lane
P.O. Box 1331
Piscataway, NJ 08855-1331

IEEE Service Center
13, avenue de l'Aquilon
B-1200 Brussels
BELGIUM

IEEE Computer Society
Ooshima Building
2-19-1 Minami-Aoyama
Minato-ku, Tokyo 107
JAPAN

Technical Editor: Ajit Singh
Editorial production: Penny Storms
Copy Editor: David Sims
Cover Design: Joseph Daigle/Schenk-Daigle Studios
Printed in the United States of America by Braun-Brumfield, Inc.

 THE INSTITUTE OF ELECTRICAL AND ELECTRONICS ENGINEERS, INC.

Table of Contents

Chapter 1:   Introduction

Motivation

Real-time systems depend not only on the logical results of computation, but also on the timeliness of those results. Examples include command and control, process control, flight control, the space shuttle's avionics, flexible manufacturing applications, and future systems planned for the space station or space-based defense systems. These systems can integrate with expert systems and other AI applications, creating additional requirements and complexities. Most real-time systems are special purpose and complex, require a high degree of fault tolerance, and are typically embedded in a larger system. They also include substantial knowledge about the application and its environment.

Most of today's systems assume that much of this knowledge is available a priori, and hence are based on *static* designs. This static nature contributes to their high cost and inflexibility. Next-generation real-time systems must be designed to be *dynamic* and *flexible* while providing guarantees for the safety-critical components of the system.

We wrote this text for several audiences. We expect that engineers, computer scientists and all researchers involved in the design, analysis, and development of real-time systems will benefit from the technical material contained here. Articles in this tutorial cover the current state of the art as well as new technologies. We also try to show how the current state of the art is emerging in its attempt to handle the next-generation systems. Obviously, there are less results for these future systems, but the work is beginning and we present some of it.

We also want to address project managers and government contract monitors who need to understand the complexities and scientific aspects related to real-time constraints. We believe they will appreciate the introduction and the papers on common misconceptions about real-time computing, on detailed descriptions of predictability, and on the difficulties encountered in evaluating safety-critical software.

Our third audience is the university research community. The scientific and engineering problems relating to real-time systems are many and complex. We hope that this text entices more university researchers to tackle some of these problems so that more efficient, more flexible, and better integrated solutions can be generated for the next generation systems.

Outline

This tutorial text on real-time computing is divided into 10 chapters:

- *Introduction*. In this opening section we define and discuss real-time systems. We also provide an overview of current practices and itemize emerging views in each of the nine subject areas covered in the rest of the tutorial. The introduction includes three papers that discuss common misconceptions, the meaning of predictability, and the difficulties in building and evaluating safety-critical software. Some of the material found in this introduction is adapted from Hard Real-Time Systems by Stankovic and Ramamritham, published in 1988 by the IEEE Computer Society Press. However, this tutorial text includes an entirely different set of papers, primarily published since that time. Both books, taken together, provide close to 90 papers containing basic to advanced material.
- *Scheduling*. This section presents scheduling results in two parts: those dealing with uniprocessors and those dealing with multiprocessor or distributed scheduling. Between them they cover many different performance metrics and task characteristics. A paper summarizing results from operations research (OR) is also included to give an OR perspective on scheduling.
- *Operating system kernels*. Good operating system support forms the basis for real-time application development. Contrary to popular myth, they have to be designed with explicit time constraints in mind. Should you believe that all real-time operating systems are the same, we present three very different real-time operating systems in this section.

- *Programming languages.* Programming languages for real-time applications must provide the flexibility to express various timing requirements and the generality of general-purpose languages. However, restrictions may have to be imposed on the programs to ensure predictable systems. This section gives three complementary approaches to programming real-time systems as embodied in real-time concurrent C, in an object-oriented language, and in FLEX.
- *Design and analysis techniques.* Design and analysis techniques for real-time systems span a very wide spectrum. We include three papers, two dealing with computing execution times of programs and one dealing with performance evaluation in the presence of failures.
- *Communication.* Communication is the backbone of distributed real-time systems. We present four papers that, in total, provide deterministic guarantees for message transmission, provide a best effort approach for transmitting messages so that they meet deadlines, propose a real-time local area network architecture, and discuss a synchronous atomic broadcast protocol.
- *Architecture and fault tolerance.* Real-time systems must also be fault tolerant. Fault tolerance is achieved via replication of components along with an efficient management of the redundancy. This section presents four papers that address architecture and fault tolerance for real-time systems. The architectures span the spectrum from bus-connected components to a mesh. The targeted applications are also quite varied from process control to air traffic control.
- *Clock synchronization.* All distributed real-time systems must have a global time base, so clock synchronization is very important. This section includes three clock synchronization papers. We discuss deterministic approaches, which guarantee a required bound on clock deviation, as well as probabilistic approaches, which guarantee the bound but with a (small) probability of error.
- *Databases.* Real-time databases must preserve not only the logical consistency of the data, but the temporal validity of data as well. This section includes five papers representing recent work on real-time databases. These papers cover locking-based as well as optimistic concurrency control protocols for real-time databases, span several models for a real-time database, and present a set of real-time disk scheduling algorithms.
- *Artificial intelligence.* Very complex real-time systems of the future are likely to contain expert systems or real-time AI components. This section presents three papers from this emerging field. They discuss ways that traditional AI approaches can be tailored to deal with time constraints and to be more predictable.

One of the areas of real-time computing that, due to space limitations, we have not included here is formal specification and verification. A lot of research is in progress in this area, much of it involved with extending formalisms developed to deal with non-real-time systems. Readers can get an idea of the current approaches by reading the third section of our previous tutorial text, *Hard Real-Time Systems*, and a recent book by van Tilborg and Koob, *Foundations of Real-Time Computing: Formal Specifications and Methods*, published by Kluwer in 1991.

An extensive bibliography at the end of this tutorial represents the state of the art in the areas covered, as well as in formal specification and verification. You may also find the references at the end of the included papers very useful, as well as the annual *Proceedings from the Real-Time Systems Symposium*, published by the IEEE.

What is a real-time system?

Real-time systems are characterized by the fact that severe consequences will result if logical as well as timing correctness properties of the system are not satisfied. Typically, a real-time system consists of a *controlling* system and a *controlled* system. For example, in an automated factory the controlled system is the factory floor with its robots, assembling stations, and the assembled parts. The controlling system is the computer and human interfaces that manage and coordinate the activities on the factory floor. Thus, the controlled system can be viewed as the *environment* with which the computer interacts.

The controlling system interacts with its environment based on the information available about the environment, say from various sensors attached to it. It is imperative that the state of the environment, as perceived by the controlling system, be consistent with the actual state of the environment. Otherwise, the effects of the controlling systems' activities may be disastrous. Hence, periodic monitoring of the environment as well as timely processing of the sensed information is necessary.

Timing correctness requirements in a real-time system also arise because of the *physical impact* of the controlling systems' activities upon its environment. For example, if the computer controlling a robot does not command it to stop or turn on time, the robot might collide with another object on the factory floor. Needless to say, such a mishap can result in a major catastrophe.

Real-time systems span many application areas. In addition to automated factories, applications can be found in avionics, undersea exploration, process control, robot and vision systems, as well as military applications such as command and control. The complexity of real-time systems also spans the gamut from very simple control of laboratory experiments, to process control applications, to very complicated projects such as the space station.

In most of these systems, activities that have to occur in a timely fashion coexist with those that are not time-critical. An accounting application or a long-term planning activity running on an automated factory's computer is an example of the latter. Let's call both types of activities *tasks* and a task with a timeliness requirement a *real-time task*. In the literature, real-time tasks are sometimes called *time-critical tasks*. Ideally, the computer should execute time-critical tasks so that each task meets its deadline, and it should execute the non time-critical tasks so as to minimize their average response time. One of the difficulties of designing a real-time system is meeting the requirements of individual time-critical requirements. Other issues include fault tolerance and the need to operate in uncertain environments. However, in the remainder of this introduction we concentrate on the timing issue, as it permeates all systems and environment issues.

Timing constraints for tasks can be arbitrarily complicated but the most common timing constraints for tasks are either *periodic* or *aperiodic*. An aperiodic task has a deadline by which it must finish or start, or it may have a constraint on both start and finish times. In the case of a periodic task, a period might mean "once per period T" or "exactly T units apart."

Low-level application tasks, such as those that process information from sensors or those that activate elements in the environment, typically have stringent timing constraints dictated by the environment's physical characteristics. Most sensory processing is periodic. For example, a radar that tracks flights produces data at a fixed rate. A temperature monitor of a nuclear reactor core should be read periodically to detect any changes promptly. Some of these periodic tasks may exist from the point of system initialization, while others may come into existence dynamically. A reactor's temperature monitor is an instance of a permanent task. An example of a dynamically created task is a (periodic) task that monitors a particular flight; the task begins when the aircraft enters an air traffic control region and ends when the aircraft leaves the region.

More complex types of timing constraints also occur. For example, spray painting a car on a moving conveyor must be started after time t_1 and completed before time t_2. Aperiodic requirements can arise from dynamic events, such as an object falling in front of a moving robot or a human operator pushing a button on a console.

In addition, time-related requirements may also be specified in indirect terms. For example, a value may be attached to the completion of each task where the value may increase or decrease with time; or a value may be placed on the *quality* of an answer whereby an inexact but fast answer might be considered more valuable than a slow but accurate answer. In other situations, missing X deadlines might be tolerated, but missing $X+1$ deadlines cannot be tolerated.

This brings us to the question of what happens when timing constraints are not met. The answer depends, for the most part, on the type of application. Needless to say, a real-time system that controls a nuclear power plant or one that controls a missile, cannot afford to miss timing constraints of the critical tasks. Resources needed for critical tasks in such systems have to be preallocated so that the tasks can execute without delay. Many situations, however, offer some leeway. For example, on an automated factory floor, if a system estimates that the correct command to a robot cannot be generated on time, it may be appropriate to command the robot to stop (provided it will not cause other moving objects to collide with it and cause a different type of disaster). This is an instance of a real-time task producing a lower quality result, but on time. In the case of a periodic task monitoring an aircraft, depending on the aircraft's trajectory, missing the processing of one or two radar readings may not cause any problems.

In summary, real-time systems differ from traditional systems in that deadlines or other explicit timing constraints are attached to tasks, the systems are in a position to make compromises, and faults including timing faults may cause catastrophic consequences. This implies that, unlike many systems which separate correctness and performance, real-time systems tightly interrelate correctness and performance. Thus, real-time systems solve the problem of missing deadlines in ways specific to the requirements of the target application. The sooner a system determines it will miss a deadline, the more flexibility it will have in dealing with the exception.

In addition to timing constraints, a task can have the following types of constraints and requirements.

- *Resource constraints.* A task may require access to certain resources other than the CPU such as I/O devices, data structures, files, and databases.
- *Precedence relationships.* A complex task (for example, one requiring access to many resources) is better handled by breaking it up into multiple subtasks related by precedence constraints and each requiring a subset of the resources.
- *Concurrency constraints.* Tasks should be allowed concurrent access to resources providing the consistency of the resources is not violated.
- *Communication requirements.* Sets of cooperating tasks will be the norm for distributed, hard real-time systems. The semantics of the communications will vary, as will the interconnection structure between the communicating tasks and their timing requirements.
- *Placement constraints.* When multiple instances of a task are executed for fault-tolerance, the different instances should be executed on different processors.
- *Criticalness.* Depending on the functionality of a task, meeting the deadline of one task may be considered more critical than another. For example, a task that reacts to an emergency situation, such as fire on the factory floor, probably will be more critical than the task that controls the movements of a robot under normal operating conditions.

Characteristics of the various application tasks are usually known a priori and may be scheduled statically or dynamically. Whereas static specification of schedules is typically the case for periodic tasks, the opposite is true for aperiodic tasks. When the temperature monitor a nuclear reactor senses a problem in the core, it can invoke another (aperiodic) task to activate the appropriate elements of the reactor to correct the problem – for example, to force more coolant into the reactor core. In this case, the deadline for the aperiodic task can be statically set depending on the physical characteristics of the reactions within the core. On the other hand, the deadline of a task that controls a robot in a factory floor can be determined dynamically, depending on the speed and direction of the robot. The command to the robot forcing it to turn right, left, or stop should be generated before this time.

In a static system, the characteristics of the controlled system are assumed to be known a priori, and hence the nature of activities and the sequence in which they take place can be determined off-line before the system begins operation. Needless to say, such systems are quite inflexible even though they may incur lower runtime overheads. In practice, most applications involve several components that can be statically specified along with many dynamic components. If handled appropriately, a system with high resource utilization and low overheads can be produced for such applications.

Whereas a large proportion of currently implemented real-time systems are static in nature, by necessity, next-generation systems will have to adopt solutions that are more dynamic and flexible. This is because we believe that such systems will be large and complex and they will function in environments that are dynamic and physically distributed. More importantly, they will have to be maintainable and extensible due to their evolving nature and projected long lifetimes.

Because of these characteristics, real-time systems in general, and systems with the above characteristics in particular, need to be *fast* and *predictable, reliable* and *adaptive*.

A popular misconception about real-time computing is that these systems only need to be fast. The article "Misconceptions About Real-Time Computing," included later in this section, discusses this and other misconceptions. Speed is necessary, but it is not enough. A system has to be fast *and* predictable. Predictability has many meanings. (See the article in this introduction, "What is Predictability for Real-Time Systems?") For now, let's define predictability as the ability to determine a task's completion time with certainty. This must be done taking into account the state of the system (including the state of the operating system and the state of the resources controlled by the operating system) and the task's resource needs. For a system with predictability, given a particular situation, the question "Will task T meet its timing requirements?" is answerable. Other possible questions are:

- How many tasks will complete before their deadline?
- What will be the maximum utilization of a given resource?
- When will a task complete?

Reliability is a prerequisite for real-time systems. Real-time constraints cannot be achieved if system components are not reliable. The level of reliability should be specifiable and predictability will involve determining system performance under different levels of reliability.

A real-time system should be adaptive to changes in

- system state, that is, system dynamics including overloads and failures (short-term),
- system configuration (long-term), and
- input specifications, in particular, task specifications (long-term).

Adaptability is particularly important for real-time systems because if a task's deadlines can be met only under a restricted system state and configuration, reliability and performance may be compromised. If a system is adaptive, one does not have to redefine the system or recompute resource and task allocation for every small change. This reduces development and maintenance costs. To be predictable and adaptive at the same time we need carefully designed schemes. Maintainability and expandability follow from being adaptive. A real-time system's timing properties, specifically task execution times, are very tightly related to the system's hardware; thus the logical functions are often bound to the hardware early in the design process. The point at which this binding occurs, in part determines the system's adaptability and predictability.

Clearly, design and implementation strategies adopted will vary depending on the complexity of a controlled system, the static versus dynamic nature of the activities of the environment, the complexity of the tasks executed by the controlling system, and the system's goals. This tutorial looks at a wide variety of real-time systems and introduces readers to the currently available and emerging solutions to tackle problems inherent in these systems.

Current practices

Existing practices for designing, implementing, and validating real-time systems are still rather ad hoc. Software engineering practices that advocate modularity and the use of abstract data types are not usually pursued in real-time software production due to their perceived conflict with real-time requirements. Before we discuss why this is the case, let us study some salient features of today's real-time systems.

Real-time systems are often supported by stripped-down and optimized versions of time-sharing operating systems. To reduce the runtime overheads incurred by the kernel and to make the system fast, the kernel underlying a current real-time system

- has a fast context switch,
- is small (with associated minimal functionality),
- responds to external interrupts quickly,
- minimizes intervals during which interrupts are disabled,
- provides fixed- or variable-sized partitions for memory management (in other words, no virtual memory), as well as the ability to lock code and data in memory, and
- provides special sequential files that can accumulate data at a fast rate.

To deal with timing requirements, the kernel

- maintains a real-time clock,
- provides a priority scheduling mechanism,
- provides for special alarms and time-outs, and
- allows tasks the ability to invoke primitives to delay and to pause and resume execution.

In general, the kernels perform multitasking; intertask communication and synchronization are achieved via standard, well-known primitives such as mailboxes, events, signals, and semaphores.

In real-time kernels these features are also designed to be fast. However, fast is a relative term and, as pointed out earlier, not sufficient when dealing with real-time constraints. Nevertheless, many real-time system designers believe that these features provide a good basis upon which to build real-time systems. Others believe that such features provide almost no *direct* support for solving the difficult timing problems and would rather see more sophisticated kernels that directly address timing and fault tolerance constraints. For example, see the paper on the Spring kernel in Chapter 3.

Two examples of current technology and the problems associated with it are priority scheduling and cyclic scheduling. In task scheduling, primary consideration must be given to execution times, timing constraints, and criticalness factors of tasks. Task execution times are, in general, stochastic: The worst-case execution time of a task may be much higher than its average execution time. Whereas the timing constraints are an indication of the *level of urgency* of a real-time task, the *criticalness* of a task is indicative of the *level of importance* attached to that task relative to the other tasks. Providing enough processing power so that even at peak loads (worst-case situations) all tasks will meet their timing requirements will result in a highly underutilized system. However, real-time systems such as those used in air traffic control and military command and control are called upon to perform efficiently and correctly, especially in overloaded situations. The solution then lies in scheduling tasks such that the highly critical tasks are always guaranteed to meet their timing constraints. However, because task deadlines and criticalness do not normally correlate, scheduling tasks to maximize the number of highly critical tasks that meet their deadlines is a nontrivial problem and using fixed priorities to solve the problem has difficulties, as we describe next.

Now consider that, as is done in many of today's real-time systems, we use *priority-driven* mechanisms for scheduling tasks with the above timing and importance characteristics. This is a carry-over from the approach taken in kernels of time-sharing systems. The first problem in using priorities is that two competing considerations, namely, time constraints and criticalness values of tasks, have to be mapped into one factor, namely, a task's priority. This creates two subsequent problems: how to choose the priorities and anomalies that can arise. Choosing priorities is done through an iterative process involving extensive simulation studies: Initially, task priorities reflect just their criticalness values and the system is tested. Task priorities are adjusted if some critical tasks miss their deadlines or if the resource utilization is poor. Optimization of task code is often performed. The changes to task code as well as task priorities continues until a satisfactory performance is achieved. Any minor changes require the entire process to be repeated.

Even with such tuning, anomalies can occur. In particular, after tuning, a low importance task with high frequency usually ends up having an assigned high priority, while an important task with a low frequency is given a low priority. This results from the goal of all tasks meeting their deadlines under normal conditions. However, upon failures or overloads, the more important task is dropped.

A second main problem is that priority scheduling has a fixed number of levels, so tasks with different deadlines can get mapped to the same level. Third, there is no on-line support for how to adjust priorities to meet deadlines if conditions change from the original assignment. Fourth, assuming that some policy does exist to dynamically readjust priorities, then in some cases it may be necessary to readjust *all* the priorities to maintain a proper relationship among active tasks. This can be very expensive and can subsequently cause missed deadlines either because it adds overhead that occurs at an inopportune time or because scheduling anomalies can occur during the transition period. In spite of these significant problems, priority scheduling is so prevalent in current real-time systems that it is becoming a standard through efforts like the real-time extensions to POSIX and in many commercial offerings of RT-UNIX.

One policy for priority assignment, the rate monotonic priority assignment, assigns task priorities that are inversely proportional to task periods. Various extensions to this basic policy have appeared (see Chapter 2).

Either separately or in conjunction with priority-based scheduling, many of today's real-time systems also use a small set of cyclical executives, each executing at a different frequency. Tasks execute in the major cycle (the cycle with the highest frequency) or in one of the minor cycles (of lower frequency). The major cycle is assigned the highest priority and hence the high frequency periodic tasks as well as the highly critical (but lower frequency) tasks are associated with the major cycle. Tasks execute in an order specified in a table. The table's construction requires several iterations involving the adjustment of cycle frequencies, reordering of tasks, and task code optimization. Cyclic scheduling faces the same problems we described for priority scheduling. In addition, cyclic scheduling is much more inflexible than priority scheduling; any changes may require a complete restructuring of the table and unexpected events or events arriving at the wrong time are difficult to handle.

A good example of application of the above priority-based and table-driven techniques is the space shuttle Primary Avionics Software System discussed in the paper by Carlow et al. in Section 9 of our previous tutorial text, *Hard Real-Time Systems*.

In summary, today's priority-based scheduling technology involves a lot of code and priority tuning accompanied by extensive simulations to gain confidence in the system. Even though the above scheduling techniques have been successfully used in many real-time embedded systems, they are costly and inflexible. Because the scheduling technique is not algorithmic, it is error-prone. For example, it is difficult to predict how tasks invoked dynamically interact with other active tasks, where blocking over resources will occur, and the subsequent effect of this interaction and blocking on the timing constraints of all the tasks. In addition, even a small change is subject to another extensive round of testing. Overall, this design philosophy forces designers and implementers to deviate from structured system development techniques whereby the resulting system is neither adaptive nor extensible. This makes maintenance and upgrading very expensive. But since typical embedded systems, such as automated factories and air traffic control systems, have long lifetimes during which the systems evolve, incremental development and dynamic maintainability are important to these systems.

Emerging views

We organized the remaining tutorial text into nine areas. A perusal of current work in each of these areas reveals a set of emerging views. In this section we summarize those views by area. More detailed descriptions of such views are found in the introduction of each section and in the included papers.

Scheduling. Real-time scheduling results have been extensive over the past five years. Theoretical results have identified worst case bounds for dynamic on-line algorithms and complexity results have been produced for scheduling tasks with various characteristics and for different performance metrics. Queueing theoretic analysis has been applied to soft real-time systems covering algorithms based on real-time variations of first-come-first-served, earliest deadline, and least laxity. We have seen the development of scheduling results for imprecise computation (where tasks obtain a greater value the longer they execute up to some maximum value). More applied results have also been produced with an extensive set of improvements to the rate monotonic algorithm (this includes extensions to deal with tasks that have different levels of importance, shared resource requirements, multiprocessors and aperiodic tasks), techniques to address the problem of priority inversion, and algorithms for dynamic on-line planning. We have also seen practical applications of a priori calculation of static schedules to provide what is called 100-percent guarantees for critical tasks. While these a priori analyses are very valuable, system designers better not be lulled into thinking that 100-percent guarantees mean that no scheduling error can occur. It is important to know that these 100-percent guarantees are based on many – often unrealistic – assumptions. If the assumptions are a poor match for what can be expected from the environment, then even with 100-percent guarantees the system will miss deadlines. Hence, a key issue is to choose an algorithm whose assumptions provide the greatest coverage over what really happens in the environment.

For all these scheduling results outlined above, the trend has been to deal with more complicated task set and environment characteristics, such as multiprocessing and distributed computing, and tasks with precedence constraints. While many interesting scheduling results have been produced, the state of the art still provides piecemeal solutions. Many realistic issues have not yet been addressed.

We still need comprehensive and integrated scheduling approaches, possibly a collection of algorithms. For example, the overall approach must be comprehensive enough to handle:

- preemptable and nonpreemptable tasks,
- periodic and nonperiodic tasks,
- tasks with multiple levels of importance (or value function),
- groups of tasks with a single deadline,
- end-to-end timing constraints,
- precedence constraints,
- communication requirements,
- resource requirements,
- placement constraints,
- fault tolerance needs,
- tight and loose deadlines, and
- normal and overload conditions.

The solution must be integrated enough to handle the interfaces between

- CPU scheduling and resource allocation,
- I/O scheduling and CPU scheduling,
- CPU scheduling and real-time communication scheduling,
- local and distributed scheduling, and
- static scheduling of safety-critical tasks and dynamic scheduling of less critical tasks.

Operating system kernels. In our discussion of real-time operating systems kernels and next-generation real-time operating systems, we see the need to provide predictability. Predictability requires bounded operating system primitives, some knowledge of the application, proper scheduling algorithms (see previous discussion), and a viewpoint based on a *team* attitude between the operating system and the application. For example, simply having a very primitive kernel that is itself predictable is only the first step. We need more direct support for developing predictable and fault-tolerant real-time applications.

One aspect of this support is scheduling algorithms. For example, design and analysis of applications is easier if the operating system schedules CPU time and allocates resources in a planning mode, so that cooperating tasks get the resources they need when they need them. Further, if the operating system retains information about a task's importance and alternative actions if the task will miss its deadline, then it can make more intelligent decisions about alternative actions and can better support a graceful degradation of the system's performance (rather than a possible catastrophic collapse of the system if no such information is available). Kernels that support retaining and using semantic information about the application are sometimes called reflective kernels.

Real-time kernels are also being extended to operate in highly cooperative multiprocessor and distributed system environments. This means there is an end-to-end timing requirement, in the sense that a set of communication tasks must complete before a deadline. In other words, a collection of activities must occur (possibly with complicated precedence constraints) before a deadline.

Much research is being done on developing time-constrained communication protocols to serve as a platform for supporting this user level, end-to-end timing requirement. However, while communication protocols are being developed to support host-to-host bounded delivery time, using the current operating system paradigm of allowing arbitrary waits for resources or events, or treating the operation of a task as a *random process*, will cause great uncertainty in accomplishing the application level end-to-end requirements. The Mars project, the Spring project, and a project at the University of Michigan are among the research efforts attempting to solve this problem. The Mars project uses an a priori analysis and then statically schedules and reserves resources so that distributed execution can be guaranteed to make its deadline. The Spring approach supports dynamic requests for real-time virtual circuits (guaranteed delivery time) and real-time datagrams (best effort delivery) integrated with CPU scheduling to guarantee the application level end-to-end timing requirements. The Spring project uses a distributed replicated memory based on a fiber optic ring to achieve the lower level predictable communication properties. The Michigan work also supports dynamic real-time virtual circuits and datagrams, but their work is based on a general multi-hop communication subnet.

Research is also being done on developing real-time object-oriented kernels to support object-oriented applications. As far as we know, no commercial products of this type are available.

An important realistic and complicating factor to the on-line support of real-time applications is the need for predictability in the presence of faults; we need a merging of real-time scheduling and fault tolerance research. This issue must receive more attention. It is also important to avoid having to rewrite the operating system for each application area that may have differing timing and fault tolerance requirements. A library of real-time operating system objects might provide the level of functionality, performance, and portability required. We envision a Smalltalk-like system for hard real-time, so that a designer can tailor the operating system to an application without having to write everything from scratch. In particular, a library of real-time scheduling algorithms should be available that can be plugged in, depending on the runtime task model being used and the load and timing requirements of the system.

The standards community is creating an extension to POSIX for real-time systems and since many commercial RT-UNIX systems now exist, RT-UNIX also will become a de facto standard. We believe that these standards contain most of the problems of current kernels that we identified in this introduction (and elsewhere). The standards do not address the need for supporting the new ideas and emerging principles being developed by the research community to carefully address timing issues. On the other hand, the standards will certainly have several significant advantages of portability and ease of use, especially for soft real-time systems.

Programming languages. Future languages for real-time systems should satisfy certain minimal requirements. First, the languages should be high-level so that users need only minimal knowledge of the underlying hardware architecture – details of the implementation should be the task of the compiler and other design and analysis tools.

Second, the language should allow the specification of requirements and semantics of applications such as deadlines and fault-tolerant properties. As mentioned earlier in the section on kernels, more and more such information is being used by new, research-oriented kernels to provide more direct support for predictable applications. This information comes from two main sources: the application programmer supplies it via language level statements, or the compiler automatically computes the information (such as calculating the worst case execution time or identifying resource requirements). Using the high-level properties of real-time languages, it should then be possible to use some of the many formal analysis techniques and tools that are applicable to high-level programs. However, such high-level analysis cannot assess detailed timing properties of the system. This gives rise to the third requirement that detailed timing properties must be analyzable.

Detailed timing analysis requires several features. Modules should be programmable such that they have (a priori determinable) bounded execution times. Hence, the use of dynamic structures, recursion, and unbounded loops should be disallowed or carefully controlled. All program constructs and modules should be analyzable with respect to the schedulability of modules and availability of resources. To accomplish this, some researchers are carefully separating the programming representation (designed for ease of programming) from the runtime representation (designed for facilitating analysis of timing requirements). The runtime representation can then specifically deal with the implementation details and enable detailed timing analysis.

The analyzability of programs written in a real-time programming language is an important criterion in choosing a language for constructing real-time systems. Further, the analyzability requirement implies that there must be a much tighter interaction between the language level and the runtime system including the kernel and hardware. However, in the absence of good, automatic analysis techniques, a lower-level view of programming languages for real-time systems prevails. By low level we mean that the programmer explicitly controls parallelism, priority, and timing.

While many languages, including Ada, have been purportedly designed with real-time systems in mind, few have the requisite features to program *predictable* real-time systems. Ada, for instance, permits one to write concurrent programs but the only time-related feature it provides is a delay statement which, when invoked, suspends a process for the given (minimum) amount of time. Clearly, given the complex needs of next-generation real-time systems, these are insufficient.

Design and analysis techniques. The problem of design and analysis of real-time programs is made difficult by the parallelism inherent in real-time applications and is exacerbated further by the presence of real-time constraints. Thus, one is interested not only in the logical properties of safety and liveness, but also in the physical property of timeliness.

The specification for a real-time system is a kind of contract between the system and the environment. Based on certain assumed properties of the environment, the system guarantees to provide the specified performance. The design of the system should not only meet the specifications but also guard the system against faults in the behavior of the environment, that is, against deviations from its assumed behavior.

Design tools must support descriptions of the system at multiple levels:
- the conceptual level, where high-level requirements and environmental considerations are stated,
- the logical level where functional and behavioral descriptions are given; and
- the implementation level where details of the actual implementation are provided.

Some of the available tools support different levels of analysis related to these levels of descriptions. Many of these design tools were developed in the context of commercial operating system kernels (for instance, Reddy Systems' VRTX). However, more sophisticated design tools are required as real-time systems become complex, functioning in uncertain and complex environments, possessing fault tolerance properties, and requiring intricate timing guarantees. Many tools are now beginning to address some of these needed extensions (see RT-QUASE or Structured Analysis for Real-Time Systems), but much work is still required.

There are several ways to determine whether a real-time system meets its requirements. Today's real-time systems are tested in extensive simulations of scenarios in which the system is expected to function. As is well known, testing only reveals the bugs that exist in a system and is fraught with many problems. First, the confidence one can achieve is limited by the coverage obtained by the scenarios tested. Second, even a small change to the system can affect the results of the simulations and hence the tests have to be repeated. This is especially true with regard to timing requirements because changing even one instruction may impact many of the system's timing characteristics. In large systems, this approach is known to have caused delays in missions and an enormous increase in the cost of the project. Clearly, we need alternatives.

Another approach is based on direct measurement of a system's performance. This involves the introduction of probes into a system to monitor system behavior. The concomitant changes to system performance are unavoidable. Finding problems at this stage of system development also implies possibly expensive and time-consuming redesign and reimplementation efforts. Furthermore, recreating worst case behavior, a situation in which a real-time system is especially called upon to work as per requirements, is likely to be difficult since it may not be possible to deploy the system to conduct the measurements.

Both simulation-based and experimentation-based approaches provide a developer with some confidence that, in a probabilistic or stochastic sense, the system works. Analytical or queuing-theoretic approaches work towards this goal as well. However, they can be employed much earlier in the development process and therein lies their attraction. Furthermore, if analysis indicates that the probabilities of system failure are smaller than, say the system being hit by a meteor, then, for all practical purposes, we have a system that meets its requirements (unless of course, it is supposed to withstand meteor hits!).

Contrasting probabilistic approaches are those that use constructive means or verification to show that the system will function correctly, even under worst case scenarios. These techniques obviously need information about worst-case arrival patterns, worst case execution times, and worst-case fault hypotheses. Such worst case based approaches are especially essential to verify the correctness of the safety-critical parts of a real-time system. When applied to other parts of a real-time system, they are likely to produce over-designed and over-configured systems.

In verifying a real-time system both *logical* and *timeliness* properties must be taken into account. Traditional verification approaches have been concerned with the properties of a concurrent application assuming a *fair* scheduler. However, to ensure timely behavior of real-time activities, time-constraint driven scheduling algorithms are used in real-time systems. Thus, verification techniques for real-time systems must consider the interplay between the system scheduler as well as the logical components of the application.

Scheduling algorithms for real-time systems use task execution time information in making the scheduling decisions. Here again, we have the differences arising from the use of stochastic vs. worst-case execution times. If the former is used, one has to provide for the exceptional situation in which there is a time overrun. In the latter case, resource utilization is likely to be very small if resources are allocated with respect to worst-case execution times. However, as we have noted before, there may be no choice but to use worst-case times when designing safety-critical components.

Communication. Distributed real-time systems need to use communication protocols that provide deterministic behavior (guarantees) for the communicating components and a best effort service to deliver on deadline. Deterministic service requires protocols that result in bounded message communication delays where the bound is low compared to timing requirements. Protocols providing such service are sometimes called real-time virtual circuits. Such protocols are being developed or exist for arbitrary mesh networks, rings, TDMA-like busses, and globally replicated memory. Most of the work in this area assumes that messages requiring the deterministic service are periodic or occur rarely (such as alarms), and are statically specifiable. These requirements are likely to prove inadequate for autonomous real-time systems of the future. For example, these new systems will be highly dynamic and have strong cooperation requirements typical of distributed problem solving software inducing richer communication patterns than simple periodic messages. The dynamics might require that a task dynamically seek a guarantee that a particular message will arrive in time, before that task commits to beginning an action.

For the best effort service (sometimes called real-time datagrams), several advances have been made as extensions to collision-based protocols. These extensions provide time *aware* scheduling and are more predictable than pure CSMA protocols. However, this service is unreliable in that the timing constraint of a message may be missed. These protocols work by attempting to transmit messages that would minimize the number of messages whose deadlines are not met. Usually, systems use a protocol that mimics earliest-deadline-first or least-laxity-first scheduling. These protocols only approximate these algorithms, because no single node has a complete picture of all pending messages.

Complicating factors in developing both types of services include the need to support high-speed networks, the integration of the low-level protocols with the operating system kernel, I/O modules, and application modules, as well as the inclusion of fault-tolerant features. Generally, the protocols for real-time communication must be supported at the kernel level and deep and expensive protocol stacks are avoided. Along these lines, researchers are proposing various local area network architectures for communication in distributed real-time systems that are efficient, allow specification of service requirements, and provide mechanisms to achieve those service requirements.

There has also been significant work in developing reliable atomic broadcasts with varying semantics and performance characteristics. For example, some broadcast protocols support FIFO semantics, others a causal ordering, and yet others are tailored to determine group membership. However, all of these protocols are expensive and do not adequately support predictable timing properties. Since broadcasting is such an important underlying facility for many things including fault tolerance, application cooperation, and state consistency, it is important to develop such solutions for real-time systems.

Architecture and fault tolerance. Many hard real-time systems are very specialized. Architectures to support such applications tend to be specialized, too. However, the current trend is to develop more general real-time architectures. Several general concepts and principles have emerged from various architecture developments. Not all of these principles will always apply, so the reader should be careful and not apply these rules of thumb blindly. These rules include the following.

- Avoid, if possible, hardware features that are difficult to analyze for worst case execution time (see discussion below on this point).

- Develop special-purpose configurations of off-the-shelf, general components.
- Do not change the problem to fit the hardware. (Too many designers choose hardware first, which results in difficulty getting this hardware to execute fast and predictably enough.)
- Design fault tolerance and real-time capability at the outset.
- Accommodate the need for multiple busses.
- Growth limitations are strongly influenced by the growth in overhead as modules are added.
- Code might have to be in ROM to withstand harsh environments.
- Perform functional partitioning – but too rigid a partitioning and static scheduling will prove cumbersome.
- Provide on-line testability.
- Off-load system overhead onto system processors to keep application tasks free from interference. (This point may be controversial, but many architectures use it, and we believe more will use it in the future.)
- Private memories can be used for read only code, and global memory can contain shared data.
- Dynamically loaded local memories and caches cause many problems difficult to deal with under timing constraints because they may violate a principle that repeatability of timings is crucial.

Most real-time systems are based on the premise that the worst case execution time of a program is known. Worst case execution times of programs are dependent on the system hardware, the operating system, the compiler used, and the programming language used. Many hardware features that have been introduced to speed-up the average case behavior of programs pose problems when information about worst case behavior is sought. For instance, the ubiquitous caches, pipelining, dynamic RAMs, and virtual (secondary) memory, lead to highly nondeterministic hardware behavior. Similarly, compiler optimizations tailored to make better use of these architectural enhancements as well as techniques such as constant folding contribute to poor predictability of code execution times. System interferences due to interrupt handling, shared memory references, and preemptions further complicate the situation. In summary, any approach to the determination of execution times of real-time programs must contend with many complexities.

In general, prediction of execution times is easier if compiled code follows the parsing structure. However, the complexities in the implementation of machine instructions on the one hand and complex program construction on the other exacerbate the problem. For instance, most implementations of the simple multiplication operator are optimized for different types of operands. Hence, seemingly straight-line code can involve branches. Introducing the use of go-to's, pointers (to functions), recursion, and loops creates problems, not only in determining execution times, but also in predetermining the program's resource requirements, such as memory. Many real-time system architectures employ multiprocessors, networks of uniprocessors, or networks of uni- and multiprocessors. Such architectures have potential for high fault tolerance, but are also much more difficult to manage in a way that predictably meets deadlines. Much new research is beginning in this area.

Fault tolerance must be included in the initial design, must encompass hardware and software, and must be integrated with timing constraints. In many situations, the fault-tolerant design must be static due to extremely high data rates and severe timing constraints. Ultrareliable systems need to employ proof-of-correctness techniques to ensure fault tolerance properties. Primary and backup schedules computed off-line are often found in hard real-time systems. We also see new approaches where on-line schedulers predict that timing constraints will be missed, enabling early action on such faults. Dynamic reconfigurability is needed, but little progress has been reported in this area. Also, while considerable advance has been made in the area of software fault-tolerance, techniques that explicitly take timing into account are lacking.

Since fault tolerance is difficult, the trend is to let experts build the proper underlying support for it. For example, implementing checkpointing, reliable atomic broadcasts, logging, lightweight network protocols, synchronization support for replicas, and recovery techniques, and having these primitives available to applications, then simplifies creating fault tolerant applications. However, many of these techniques have not carefully addressed timing considerations. Many real-time systems that require a high degree of fault tolerance have been designed with significant architectural support, but the design and scheduling to meet deadlines is done statically, with all replicas functioning in lock step. This may be too restrictive for many future applications. What is required is the integration of fault tolerance and real-time scheduling to produce a much more flexible system. For example, the use of the imprecise computation model, or a planning scheduler (such as the Spring scheduling algorithm), gives rise to a more flexible approach to fault tolerance than static schedules and fixed backup schemes.

Clock synchronization. In systems with multiple processing elements, such as fault-tolerant systems, distributed systems, and multiprocessor systems, each node in the system or each processor on a node may maintain its own clock. Even if these clocks are initialized with the same time, since physical clocks drift, due to changes in physical conditions like temperature, sooner or later, individual clocks will indicate different times. A clock's *drift rate* is typically on the order of 1 μsec/sec; thus, an initially synchronized fault-free clock could drift away from the reference time by a few seconds every few days, in the worst case. This introduces the problem of clock synchronization.

There are two types of clock synchronization problems. One is external synchronization, wherein each clock in a system must be synchronized with the real-world clock. The other problem is internal synchronization, which relates to the synchronization among the multiple clocks within a system so as to keep the relative deviation between individual clock values small. The typical solution is for one or more clocks to maintain external synchronization (by listening for example, to the WWV signal of NIST) while other clocks maintain internal synchronization among themselves as well as with these clocks.

Clearly, to achieve internal synchronization, clocks must be in a position to read each other's values so that they can determine the amount by which they are out of synchrony. Since this reading involves communication delays, there is a limit to the synchronization that can be achieved. This limit can be reduced if the difference between the maximum and minimum end-to-end delays for clock synchronization messages is small. Clock synchronization has been a very active research area with numerous papers discussing algorithms that show how clocks synchronize by reading each other's clocks in the presence of communication delays, clock drifts, and failures. Almost all of them assume a maximum communication delay and provide *deterministic clock synchronization*, that is, the worst case clock skew can be known with certainty.

More recently, some have advocated *probabilistic clock synchronization* algorithms. These capitalize on the observation that most messages incur communication delays shorter than the worst case delay, because the delay depends on many stochastic phenomena, such as the current computations at the sending and receiving nodes, the actual transmission delay, and the messages contending for transmission. This delay can hence be affected by random events, such as, transmission errors, page faults, and context switches. Many real-time systems use special hardware support for clock synchronization to reduce the impact of these factors. Even with such hardware support, the delays can lie in a wide range if the actual communication delays vary.

However, if we relax the certainty requirement and permit an algorithm to provide a probabilistic guarantee (that is, the guarantee may fail sometimes, but its *failure probability* is known or has a known bound), then we can find algorithms that guarantee much smaller clock deviations. These algorithms achieve synchronization by balancing the maximum clock synchronization error, the probability of not achieving synchronization, and the maximum number of attempts one clock makes at reading another clock. One interesting thing about these algorithms is that the probability of achieving clock synchronization can be used at the system's higher levels to achieve a high system-wide timing and performance guarantee. This is especially important given that many ultrareliable systems demand extremely low probability (for example, 10^{-10}) of system failures.

Databases. In a real-time database, some transactions have deadlines. Transaction processing must satisfy not only the database consistency constraints, but also timing constraints. Real-time database systems can be found, for instance, in program trading in the stock market, radar-tracking systems, battle management systems, and computer-integrated manufacturing systems. Some of these systems (such as program trading) are *soft* real-time systems — soft, because missing a deadline is not catastrophic. Usually, research into algorithms and protocols for such systems explicitly address deadlines and make a best effort at meeting them. But they do not guarantee that tasks will make their deadlines. By contrast, in *hard* real-time systems (such as controlling a nuclear power plant) missing deadlines can cause catastrophe. These systems need a priori guarantees for critical tasks or transactions.

Most current real-time database work deals with soft real-time systems, where the need for an integrated approach that includes time-constrained protocols for concurrency control, conflict resolution, CPU and I/O scheduling, transaction restart and wake-up, deadlock resolution, buffer management, and commit processing have been identified. Many protocols based on locking, optimistic, and time-stamped concurrency control have been developed and evaluated in testbed or simulation environments. In most cases the optimistic approaches seem to work best, although some reported work shows the opposite. At this time it seems that the significantly different system assumptions including transaction parameters made by these studies create the different performance results.

Most hard real-time database systems are small, main-memory databases with predefined transactions, and hand-crafted for efficient performance. The metrics for hard real-time database systems are different than for soft real-time databases. For example, in a typical database system a transaction is a sequence of operations performed on a database. Normally, consistency (serializability), atomicity and permanence are properties supported by the transaction mechanism. Transaction throughput and response time are the usual metrics. In a soft real-time database, such as trading on the stock market, transactions have similar properties, but, in addition, have soft real-time constraints. Metrics include response time and throughput, but also include percentage of transactions that meet their deadlines, or a weighted value function that reflects the value imparted by a transaction completing on time. On the other hand, in a hard real-time database, not all transactions have serializability, atomicity, and permanence properties. These requirements need to be supported only in certain situations. For example, hard real-time systems are characterized by their close interactions with the environment they control. This is especially true for subsystems that receive sensory information or that control actuators. Processing involved in these subsystems are such that it is typically not possible to *rollback* a previous interaction with the environment. While the notion of consistency is relevant here (for example, the interactions of a real-time task with the environment should be consistent with each other), traditional approaches to achieving consistency, involving waits, rollbacks, and abortions, are not directly applicable. Instead, compensating transactions may have to be invoked to nullify the effects of previously committed transactions. The transaction property of *permanence* is of limited applicability in this context. This is because real-time data, such as those arriving from sensors, have limited lifetimes – they become obsolete after a certain time. Data received from the environment by the lower levels of a real-time system undergoes a series of processing steps (filtering, integration, and correlation). We expect the traditional transaction properties to be less relevant at the lowest levels and become more relevant at higher levels in the system.

While the hard real-time system should guarantee all critical transaction deadlines and strive to meet all other transaction deadlines, this is not always possible. It must, however, meet the deadlines of the more important transactions. Hence, metrics such as maximizing the value imparted by completed transactions and maximizing the percentage of transactions that complete by their deadline are primary metrics. Throughput and response time are secondary metrics, if they are used at all.

Outstanding questions in real-time database work include the following.
- Should all the data be integrated in one uniform database?
- Should several subsystems exist, each better tailored to the specific needs of transactions that comprise that subsystem? If so, what are good interfaces between those subsystems?
- What is the relevance of traditional properties of transactions to hard real-time databases? In some real-time systems, it's better to get an *incomplete* result on time than to get a complete result late. In the context of transactions, this implies that committing a (partially completed) transaction that is expected to be *lost* may be acceptable, depending on the nature of the transaction and on the consistency of the data modified by it.
- What distributed operating system and communication primitives are required to support predictability in such systems?
- What form should active databases take when used in a real-time setting, when an active base's triggers can be initiated by timing requirements and where other triggers must complete by a deadline?

14

Current real-time database research has focused on database systems with flat, soft real-time transactions operating on centralized databases with read/write objects. Extensions to real-time database research is needed along four dimensions:

- enhancing the *data model* from a simple read/write data model to an abstract data type model,
- enhancing the *transaction model* to nested transactions,
- enhancing the *system model* to include distributed database systems, and
- enhancing the *nature of timing constraints* to include hard real-time constraints.

Artificial intelligence. Many complex real-time applications now require or will require in the near future knowledge-based on-line assistance operating in real-time. This requires a major change to some of the paradigms and implementations previously used by AI researchers. For example, AI systems must be made to

- run much faster (a necessary but not sufficient condition),
- allow preemption to reduce latency for responding to new stimuli,
- attain predictable memory management via incremental garbage collection or by explicit management of memory,
- include deadlines and other timing constraints in search techniques,
- develop anytime algorithms (algorithms where a non-optimal solution is available at any point in time),
- develop time-driven inferencing, and develop time-driven planning and scheduling.

Rules and constraints may also have to be imposed on the design, models, and languages used to facilitate predictability, for example, limit recursion and backtracking to some fixed bound. Coming to grips with what predictability means in such applications is very important.

In addition to these changes within AI, real-time AI (RTAI) techniques must be interfaced with lower-level real-time systems technology to produce a functioning, reliable, and carefully analyzable system. Should the higher-level RTAI techniques ignore the system level, or treat it as a black box with *general* characteristics, or be developed in an integrated fashion with it so as to best build these complex systems? What is the correct interface between these two (to this point in time) separate systems? Integrating RTAI and low-level real-time systems software is quite a challenge because these RTAI applications are operating in nondeterministic environments, there is missing or noisy information, some of the control laws are heuristic at best, objectives may change dynamically, partial solutions are sometimes acceptable so that a trade-off between the quality of the solution and the time needed to derive it can be made, the amount of processing is significant and highly data dependent, and the execution time of tasks may be difficult to determine. These sets of demanding requirements will drive real-time research for many years to come.

Not only is it important to develop real-time AI techniques, but it is also necessary to determine what must change at the low levels to provide adequate support for the higher level, more application-oriented tasks? Answers to these questions have been somewhat arbitrarily chosen on an application by application basis. It is too early to synthesize the general principles and ideas from these experiments, as sufficient evaluative data is not available.

Competing software architectures for real-time AI include production rule architectures, blackboard architectures, and a process trellis architecture. Some real-time AI systems have been built by carefully and severely restricting how production rules and blackboard systems are built and used. Research is ongoing to relax the restrictions so that the power of these architectures can be used, while providing a high degree of predictability. The process trellis architecture, used in the medical domain, is a highly static approach while the other two are much more dynamic. The trellis architecture (because it is static) has potential to provide static real-time guarantees for those applications characterized by enough time to completely compute results from a set of inputs before the next set of inputs arrive. This approach is suitable for certain types of real-time AI monitoring systems, but no one has demonstrated its generality for complex real-time AI systems.

Introductory articles

As part of the introductory material for this text we include three papers from the literature. The first paper, "Misconceptions About Real-Time Computing" by Stankovic, defines various terms, discusses popular misconceptions about real-time systems, and itemizes research problems facing the field. These misconceptions include
- there is no science in real-time systems,
- advances in supercomputers will take care of real-time requirements,
- real-time computing is equivalent to fast computing,
- real-time computing is assembly language coding, priority interrupt programming, and writing device drivers,
- the hard problems for real-time systems have been solved in operations research, and
- real-time systems are static.

For most of the research problems and areas discussed in the paper, the reader will find more detailed papers in the remaining parts of this tutorial text.

One key concept that arises in almost every paper presented in this tutorial text is predictability. However, this term is often misused or only implicitly defined, leaving the reader to guess what it means. The second paper, "What is Predictability for Real-Time Systems" by Stankovic and Ramamritham, carefully defines the term. The complexity of assigning a meaning to this term is introduced and examples are given to illustrate its use in various contexts. To achieve predictability two approaches are outlined, the layer-by-layer approach and the top-level approach. We believe that it will be very instructive for the reader to keep the information from this paper in mind when reading all the other papers.

The third paper, "Evaluation of Safety-Critical Software" by Parnas, van Schouwen, and Kwan, serves as an introduction to the complexities involved in building safety-critical systems. In particular, they discuss how safety-critical software (often found in real-time systems) is different from other software. They stress the need for extreme discipline in design, documentation, testing, and review. They indicate that it is essential for operating conditions and requirements to be well understood. It is interesting to contrast this view with the real-time AI papers in Chapter 10. A large part of the paper deals with making the system reliable and obtaining measurements to verify that it is indeed reliable. Before placing a safety critical system into operation the safety and trustworthiness of the system must be determined. Of course, satisfying real-time constraints are part of this verification process.

Misconceptions About Real-Time Computing

A Serious Problem for Next-Generation Systems

John A. Stankovic*

University of Massachusetts

Real-time computing is a wide-open research area of intellectually challenging computer science problems with direct payoffs to current technology. But results have been few, and designers presently have little that would enable them to handle the timing constraints of real-time systems effectively. Furthermore, not enough emphasis is being placed on building the proper scientific underpinnings to achieve the needed results.[1] Worse yet, many researchers, technical managers, and government contract monitors have serious misconceptions about real-time computing—misconceptions with serious ramifications.

This article has three major objectives:

- to state and then dispel the most common misconceptions about real-time computing,
- to briefly discuss the fundamental scientific issues of real-time computing, and
- to encourage increased research in real-time systems.

Development of next-generation real-time systems must be highly focused and coordinated because their failure to meet timing constraints will result in economic, human, and ecological catastrophes.

*The author uses ideas presented at the Carnegie Mellon University Workshop on Fundamental Issues in Distributed Real-Time Systems, March 1987, and subsequently elaborated on by many individuals (see Acknowledgments).

What is real-time computing?

In real-time computing the correctness of the system depends not only on the logical result of the computation but also on the time at which the results are produced. Real-time computing systems play a vital role in our society, and they cover a spectrum from the very simple to the very complex. Examples of current real-time computing systems include the control of laboratory experiments, the control of automobile engines, command-and-control systems, nuclear power plants, process control plants, flight control systems, space shuttle and aircraft avionics, and robotics. The more complicated real-time systems are expensive to build and their timing constraints are verified with ad hoc techniques, or with costly and extensive simulations. Minor changes in the system result in another round of extensive testing. Different system components are extremely difficult to integrate and consequently add to overall system cost. Millions (even billions) of dollars are being spent (wasted) by industry and government to build today's real-time systems. Current brute force techniques will not scale to meet the requirements of guaranteeing real-time constraints of next-generation systems.

Next-generation real-time systems will be in application areas similar to those of current systems. However, the systems will be more complex: They will be distributed and capable of exhibiting intelligent, adaptive, and highly dynamic behavior. They will also have long lifetimes. Moreover, catastrophic consequences will result if the logical or timing constraints of the systems are not met. Examples of these more sophisticated systems are the autonomous land rover, controllers of robots with elastic joints, and systems found in intelligent manufacturing, the space station, and undersea exploration.

Two major forces are pushing real-time systems into the next generation: their need for artificial intelligence capabilities and the rapid advance in hardware. These forces are exacerbating the difficult scientific and engineering problems faced in building real-time systems. They add complex entities that must be integrated into current and future applications, but the required design, analysis, and verification techniques for such integration have not kept pace. For example, hardware (and software) technology has made distributed computing and multiprocessing a reality, and soon there will be many networks of multiprocessors. However, almost no fundamental or scientific work has been done in designing and verifying a real-time application's timing requirements when that application is distributed across a network.

As another example, AI systems exhibit a great deal of adaptability and complexity, making it impossible to precalculate all possible combinations of tasks that might occur. This precludes use of static scheduling policies common in today's real-time systems. We need new approaches for real-time scheduling in such systems, including on-line guarantees and incremental algorithms that produce better results as a function of available time.

Common misconceptions

Real-time-system design has not attracted the attention from academic computer scientists and basic-research funding agencies that it deserves. This lack of adequate attention is due, at least in part, to some common misconceptions about real-time systems. Let's look at some of them.

There is no science in real-time-system design.

It is certainly true that real-time-system design is mostly ad hoc. This does not mean, however, that a scientific approach is not possible. Most good science grew out of attempts to solve practical problems, and there is plenty of evidence that engineers of real-time systems need help. For example, the first flight of the space shuttle was delayed, at considerable cost, because of a subtle timing bug that arose from a transient CPU overload during system initialization. Can we then develop a scientific basis for verifying that a design is free of such subtle timing bugs? Indeed, the purpose of this article is to introduce some of the technical problems involved in designing reliable real-time systems and point out where a scientific basis is emerging. We are starting to understand what the important problems are in real-time scheduling of resources.[2] Investigations are beginning into the subtleties of including a time metric in system specification methods and semantic theories for real-time programming languages.[3]

Advances in supercomputer hardware will take care of real-time requirements.

Advances in supercomputer design will likely exploit parallel processors to improve system throughput, but this does not mean that timing constraints will be met automatically. Unless the architecture of the computing system is carefully tailored to match that of the application, the processors and their communication subsystems may not be able to handle all of the task load and time-critical traffic. In fact, real-time task-and-communication scheduling problems will likely get worse as more hardware is used.

Realistically, the history of computing shows that the demand for more computing power has always outstripped the supply. If the past is any guide to the future, the availability of more computing power will only open up real-time applications requiring greater functionality, thus exacerbating the timing problems. There is no substitute for intelligent deployment of finite resources. Other important issues exist in real-time-systems design that cannot be resolved by supercomputer hardware alone, as we will see.

Real-time computing is equivalent to fast computing.

The objective of fast computing is to minimize the average response time of a given set of tasks. However, the objective of real-time computing is to meet the individual timing requirement of each task. Rather than being fast (which is a relative term anyway), the most important property of a real-time system should be predictability; that is, its functional and timing behavior should be as deterministic as necessary to satisfy system specifications. Fast computing is helpful in meeting stringent timing specifications, but fast computing alone does not guarantee predictability.

Other factors besides fast hardware or algorithms determine predictability. Sometimes the implementation language may not be expressive enough to prescribe certain timing behavior. For example, the delay statement of Ada puts only a lower bound on when a task is next scheduled; there is no language support to guarantee that a task cannot be delayed longer than a desired upper bound. The scheduling of (or the lack of programmer control over) nondeterministic constructs such as the select statement in Ada is especially troublesome, since timing properties that involve upper bounds cannot be guaranteed by the usual fairness semantics defining such constructs.

Perhaps the best response to those who claim that real-time computing is equivalent to fast computing is to raise the following question: Given a set of demanding real-time requirements and an implementation using the fastest hardware and software possible, how can one show that the specified timing behavior is indeed being achieved? Testing is not the answer. Indeed, for all the laborious testing and simulation effort on the space shuttle, the timing bug that delayed its first flight was discovered the hard way; there was only a 1 in 67 probability that a transient overload during initialization could put the redundant processors out of sync, but it did nevertheless. Predictability, not speed, is the foremost goal in real-time-system design.

Since testing is not the answer to our problems, do we know the answer? Not completely. We do know that a formal verification procedure coupled with testing would be significantly better than what we have now. However, that is not the entire answer either. In fact, most of the problems enumerated in the upcoming section on the challenge of real-time computing systems must be solved and then used in an integrated fashion.

Real-time programming is assembly coding, priority interrupt programming, and device driver writing.

To meet tight timing constraints, current practice in real-time programming relies heavily on machine-level optimization techniques. These techniques are labor intensive and sometimes introduce additional timing assumptions (unwisely, but as a last resort) on which the correctness of an implementation depends. Reliance on clever hand-coding and difficult-to-trace timing assumptions is a major source of bugs in real-time programming, especially in modifying large real-time programs. A primary objective in real-time-systems research is in fact to automate, by exploiting optimizing transforms and scheduling theory, the synthesis of highly efficient code and customized resource schedulers from timing-constraint specifications. On the other hand, while assembly language programming, interrupt programming, and device driver writing are aspects of real-time computing, they do not constitute open scientific problems—except in their automation.

Real-time-systems research is performance engineering.

An important aspect of real-time-systems research is to investigate effective resource allocation strategies so as to satisfy stringent timing-behavior requirements. The synthesis aspects of real-time-system research can indeed be regarded as performance engineering (but see the next misconception below). The proper design of a real-time system, however, requires solutions to many other interesting problems—for example, specification and verification of timing behavior, and programming-language semantics dealing with time. Certain theoretical problems also involve the use of timing constraints, sometimes implicitly, to ensure correctness. For example, the well-known Byzantine generals problem is unsolvable for totally asynchronous systems but is solvable if the generals can vote in rounds. That a good general must deliver a number of messages within a round according to the voting protocol is a form of timing constraint.

Indeed, the correct functioning of many systems often depends on having an implementation that can perform an operation requiring the satisfaction of certain timing constraints, albeit implicitly specified (for example, in the form of testing an atomic predicate such as determining whether a communication channel is empty). An important problem in real-time-systems research is to investigate the role time plays as a synchronization mechanism; for example, what is the logical power of different forms of timing constraints in solving various coordination problems? If a system must depend on the satisfaction of some timing constraints for its correctness, is there a least-restrictive set of timing constraints sufficient for the purpose? Does the imposition of various timing constraints facilitate more efficient solutions to distributed coordination problems? Such questions certainly go beyond traditional performance engineering.

The problems in real-time-system design have all been solved in other areas of computer science or operations research.

While real-time-system researchers should certainly try to exploit the problem solution techniques developed in more established research areas, there are unique problems in real-time systems that have not been solved in any other area. For example, performance engineering in computer science has been concerned mostly with analyzing the average values of performance parameters, whereas an important consideration in real-time-system design is whether or not some stringent deadlines can be met. Queueing models traditionally use convenient stochastic assumptions that are justified by large populations and stable operating conditions. Analytical results based on these assumptions may be quite useless for some real-time applications. For example, the hot-spot contention phenomenon (a highly nonlinear performance degradation due to slight deviations from uniform traffic in multistage interconnection networks) is likely to be catastrophic for time-critical communication packets. Likewise, the combinatorial scheduling problems in operations research deal mostly with one-shot tasks, that is, each task needs to be scheduled only once, whereas in real-time systems the same task may recur infinitely often, either periodically or at irregular intervals, and may have to synchronize or communicate with many other tasks. The general synthesis problem of arbitrary timing behavior will certainly require new techniques not found in existing literature.

It is not meaningful to talk about guaranteeing real-time performance, because we cannot guarantee that the hardware will not fail and the software is bug free or that the actual operating conditions will not violate the specified design limits.

It is a truism that one can only hope to minimize the probability of failure in the systems one builds (assuming a belief in quantum mechanics). The relevant question, of course, is how to build systems in such a way that we can have as much confidence as possible that they will meet specifications at acceptable costs. In real-time-system design, one should attempt to allocate resources judiciously to make certain that any critical timing constraint can be met with the available resources, assuming that the hardware/software functions correctly and the external environment does not stress the system beyond what it is designed to handle. The fact that the hardware/software may not function correctly or that the operating conditions imposed by the external world may exceed the design limits with a nonzero probability does not give the designer license to *increase* the odds of failure by not trying to allocate resources carefully so as to meet critical timing constraints. We certainly cannot guarantee anything outside our control, but what we can guarantee, we should.

Real-time systems function in a static environment.

Depending on the operating mode, a real-time system may have to satisfy different sets of timing constraints at different times. Thus, an important topic in real-time-systems research is the design of hierarchical or selectable schedulers to make resource allocation decisions for different time granularities. A particularly vexing industrial problem is how to reconfigure systems to accommodate changing requirements so as to create minimal disruption to ongoing operation. It is not uncommon for some real-time-system hardware to be in the field 15 or more years; hence, any design methodology for such systems must not assume a static environment. On the other hand, if the real-time application is small, inexpensive, and unlikely to change, then current static solution techniques work well. However, such real-time applications are trivial compared with those addressed in this article.

The challenge of real-time computing systems

An important approach used in managing large-scale systems is to hierarchically decompose the system into modules that are realizations of the abstract data type model. Although this methodology allows us to reason about the correctness of computation at each level of abstraction, it has no provisions to support reasoning about time and reliability abstractions, two vital aspects of real-time systems. To develop a scientific underpinning for real-time systems, we face the difficult scientific challenge of creating a set of unified theories and technologies that will allow us to reason about the correctness, timeliness, and reliability at each level of abstraction and to combine the results of each level into results for the integrated system.

Building a science of large-scale real-time systems will require new research efforts in many distinct and yet related areas. While each of these areas contains well-developed theories and technologies, none currently contains theories and methods addressing the central issue in real-time systems: a coherent treatment of correctness, timeliness, and fault tolerance in large-scale distributed computations.

The following subsections briefly identify the main research areas that need to be better addressed if we are to solve the problems facing developers of next-generation real-time systems. Of course, many of the problems in these areas are difficult to solve even without worrying about real-time constraints. This article emphasizes the special problems that real-time constraints cause. This material is intended for those not familiar with research in real-time computing, so it is necessarily high level. Readers can find a more detailed and technical discussion of each area in a companion report.[1]

Specification and verification. The fundamental challenge in the specification and verification of real-time systems is how to incorporate the time metric. Methods must be devised for including timing constraints in specifications and for establishing that a system satisfies such specifications. The usual approaches for specifying computing system behavior entail enumerating events or actions that the system participates in and describing orders in which these can occur. It is not clear how to extend such approaches for

> **A great challenge lies ahead in the modeling and verification of systems that are subject to timing constraints.**

real-time constraints. Neither is it clear how to extend programming notations to allow the programmer to specify computations that are constrained by real time.

In general, inclusion of a time metric can create subtleties in the semantics of concurrency models (see Reed and Roscoe,[4] for example) and complicate the verification problem. Whereas proof of noninterference is the major verification task in extending sequential systems to concurrent systems on the basis of interleaving, verification of real-time systems will require the satisfaction of timing constraints where those constraints are derived from the environment and implementation.[3] Consequently, a major challenge is to solve the dilemma that verification techniques abstract away from the implementation even though it is the implementation and environment which provide the true timing constraints. The result is that we need a quantitative analysis (deadlines, repetition rates) rather than the qualitative analysis (eventual satisfaction) that is typically handled by current verification techniques. On the other hand, the partial synchrony of real-time systems that results from the presence of timing constraints may open up a whole new class of distributed control algorithms and inspire novel verification techniques. Real-time systems lie somewhere between the relatively well studied fully synchronous and fully asynchronous systems, and there is a great challenge ahead in the modeling and verification of systems that are subject to timing constraints.

In addition, to deduce properties of the whole system from properties of its parts and the way these parts are combined, we must characterize a way to compose the real-time constraints and properties of parts to synthesize them for the whole. For real-time properties, the parts interact in ways that depend on resource constraints.

Thus, aspects of the system that are usually ignored when real time is not of concern come into play. This again suggests that a new set of abstractions must be devised for real-time systems. For example, *fairness*, which is frequently used when reasoning about concurrent and distributed systems, is no longer an appropriate abstraction of the way processes are scheduled when real time is a concern.

Another problem that will be encountered is dealing with the state explosion found in verification techniques. Hundreds or even thousands of states are usually required to formally express the state of even a relatively simple system in enough detail so that correctness can be proved. Techniques for abstracting many states into a higher level state are necessary to tackle this problem, which is a difficult one even when timing constraints are not included.

Real-time scheduling theory. While specification and verification concern the integrity of the system with respect to the specification, scheduling theory addresses the problem of meeting the specified timing requirements. Satisfying the timing requirements of real-time systems demands the scheduling of system resources according to some well-understood algorithms so that the timing behavior of the system is understandable, predictable, and maintainable.

Scheduling theory is not restricted to the study of real-time systems or even general computer systems. It also arises in the study of manufacturing systems, transportation systems, process control systems, and so on. However, it is important to realize that real-time-system scheduling problems are different from the scheduling problems usually considered in areas of operations research.[5,6] In most operations research scheduling problems, there is a fixed system having completely specified and static service characteristics. The goal is to find optimal static schedules that minimize the response time for a given task set. Many real-time computing systems lack an incentive for minimizing the response time other than for meeting deadlines. The system is often highly dynamic, requiring on-line, adaptive scheduling algorithms. Such algorithms must be based on heuristics, since these scheduling problems are NP-hard.[2] In these cases the goal is to schedule as many jobs as possible, subject to meeting the task timing requirements. Alternative schedules and/or error handlers are required and must be integrated with the on-line scheduler.

One primary measure of a scheduling algorithm is its associated processor utilization level below which the deadlines of all the tasks can be met.[7] There are other measures too, such as penalty functions defined according to the number of jobs that miss their deadlines, and a weighted success ratio, which is the percentage of tasks that meet their deadlines weighted by the importance of those tasks. The next subsection discusses some additional real-time scheduling issues in the context of operating systems.

Real-time operating systems. One major focal point for developing next-generation real-time systems is the operating system.[8-10] The operating system must provide basic support for guaranteeing real-time constraints, supporting fault tolerance and distribution, and integrating time-constrained resource allocations and scheduling across a spectrum of resource types, including sensor processing, communications, CPU, memory, and other forms of I/O. Given that the system is distributed, we face a complicated end-to-end timing analysis problem (see Figure 1). In other words, time constraints are applied to collections of cooperating tasks, labeled T_i in the figure, and not *only* to individual tasks.

For example, assume that a given node processes sensor hits and determines that a vehicle has entered its area of concern. This node may have to communicate that information to one or more remote nodes and receive replies indicating the appropriate action. The time by which this node must act depends on a time constraint imposed by the velocity of the incoming vehicle. Such a system is distributed, highly dynamic, and operates under strict time constraints. The entire collection of tasks dealing with sensor processing, communication between tasks, and application logic must be accomplished under a single end-to-end timing constraint.

To develop next-generation real-time distributed operating systems suitable for complicated applications such as the space station, teams of robots working in a hazardous environment, or command-and-control applications, at least three major scientific innovations are required.

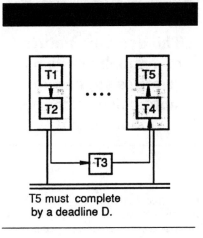

T5 must complete by a deadline D.

Figure 1. The end-to-end timing problem.

(1) The *time dimension* must be elevated to a central principle of the system. Time requirements and properties cannot be an afterthought. An especially perplexing aspect of this problem is that most system design and verification techniques are based on abstraction, which ignores implementation details. This is obviously a good idea; however, in real-time systems, timing constraints are derived from the environment and the implementation. Solving this dilemma is a key scientific issue.

(2) The basic paradigms found in today's general-purpose distributed operating systems must change. The current basis, with the notion of application tasks requesting resources as if they were random processes and the operating system being designed to expect such random inputs, is unacceptable. A new, more deterministic paradigm is needed. In such a paradigm, each operating-system primitive, along with application tasks and their interactions, would be well understood, bounded, and predictable. The interaction between tasks includes invocation interactions, communication interactions, and resource conflict interactions. In the new paradigm the system must be flexible enough to react to a highly dynamic and adaptive environment, but at the same time able to predict and possibly avoid resource conflicts so that timing constraints can be (predictably) met. In other

words, the environment may cause an unpredictable combination of events to occur, but the system must be carefully constructed to enable it to react in such a way that at any time during execution the system can predict its capabilities in meeting its deadline. The new paradigm must be based on the delicately balanced notions of flexibility and predictability. One such paradigm is being investigated in the Spring kernel.[9]

(3) A highly integrated and time-constrained resource allocation approach[2] is necessary to adequately address timing constraints, predictability, adaptability, and fault tolerance. Most current scheduling algorithms typically account for one resource at a time and ignore fault tolerance. This is especially true in the present state of real-time scheduling. Independent scheduling of unique resources is not sufficient when attempting to perform time-constrained scheduling. For a task to meet its deadline, we must ensure that resources are available to it *in time* and that the sequencing of events meets precedence constraints.

One can identify many other issues (at all levels of detail) that are critical to real-time operating systems. The need for a global time reference and the ability to scale to larger and larger systems are just two examples.

Real-time programming languages and design methodology. As the complexity of real-time systems increases, high demand will be placed on the programming abstractions provided by languages. Currently available abstractions and languages must evolve with future advances in the specification techniques, logic, and theory underlying real-time systems. Unfortunately, this goal has not been fulfilled in the past. For example, Ada is designed for embedded hard real-time applications and is intended to support static priority scheduling of tasks. However, the definition of Ada tasking allows a high-priority task to wait for a low-priority task for an unpredictable duration. Consequently, when processes are programmed in the form of Ada tasks, the resulting timing behavior is likely to be unpredictable. Building the next generation of real-time systems will require a programming methodology that gives due consideration to the needs of meeting real-time requirements. The important research issues include

• Support for the management of time. First, language constructs should support the expression of timing constraints. For example, Ada tasking should have supported the raising of an exception when a task's deadline is missed. Second, the programming environment should provide the programmer with the primitives to control and to keep track of the resource utilization of software modules. This includes being able to develop programs with predictable performance in terms of absolute time. Finally, language constructs should support the use of sound scheduling algorithms.

• Schedulability check. Given a set of well-understood scheduling algorithms, schedulability analysis allows us to determine if the timing requirements can be met. With proper support for the management of time, it may be possible to perform schedulability checks at compile time. This idea is similar to the type-checking concept.

• Reusable real-time software modules. An added difficulty with reusable real-time software modules is meeting different timing requirements for different applications.

• Support for distributed programs and fault tolerance. The problem of predicting the timing behavior of real-time programs is further exacerbated in the context of distributed systems. Special fault-tolerance features might be added to the semantics of the language—for example, various recovery mechanisms subject to timing considerations.

Distributed real-time databases. In a real-time database system, a significant portion of data is often highly perishable in the sense that it has value to the mission only if used quickly. Satisfying the timing requirements involves two key issues: First, the degree of concurrency in transaction processing must be increased; second, concurrency control protocols and real-time scheduling algorithms must be integrated.

The characteristics of a real-time database, such as a tracking database, are distinct from commercial database systems. In a real-time database, transactions often must perform statistical operations—correlation, for example—over a large amount of data that is continuously updated, and they must satisfy stringent

The dynamic nature of symbolic systems requires support for automated memory management.

timing requirements. As observed by Bernstein et al.,[11] serializability is not a good criterion for concurrency control of such databases because of the limitation of concurrency allowed by serializable concurrent executions. Several approaches designed to obtain a high degree of concurrency by exploring application-specific semantic information have been proposed. In addition, a modular decomposition approach for nonserializable concurrency control and failure recovery has been proposed.[12] This approach assumes that global serialization is too strong a condition. Instead it uses a setwise serializability notion, which is shown to apply to the database associated with a cluster of tracking stations.

While concurrency control of transactions and hard real-time process scheduling have both progressed, very little is known about the integration between concurrency control protocols and hard real-time process-scheduling algorithms. In concurrency control we do not typically address the meeting of hard deadlines. The objective is to provide a high degree of concurrency and thus faster average response time. On the other hand, in the schedulability analysis of real-time process scheduling—for example, processes for signal processing and feedback control—it is customary to assume that tasks are independent, or that the time spent synchronizing their access to shared data is negligible compared with execution time and deadlines. The objective here is to maximize resources, such as CPU utilization, subject to meeting timing constraints. The fundamental challenge of real-time databases seems to be the creation of a unified theory that will provide us with a real-time concurrency-control protocol that maximizes both concurrency and resource utilization subject to three constraints at the same time: data consistency, transaction correctness, and transaction deadlines.

Artificial intelligence. Real-time AI research currently emphasizes reasoning about time-constrained processes and using heuristic knowledge to control or schedule these processes. A key consideration in robust problem solving is to provide the best available solution within a dynamically determined time constraint. Many of the current issues in real-time-systems research are applicable to such a system, but additional considerations exist. For example, the dynamic nature of symbolic systems requires support for automated memory management. Current garbage collection techniques make it difficult, if not impossible, to guarantee a maximum system latency.

Other features of symbolic systems that exacerbate the predictability problem include the ability to create and execute a function at runtime and the ability to execute a runtime-selected function passed as an argument. In addition, opportunistic control strategies provide the ability to dynamically direct program execution in response to real-time events. This contrasts sharply with the current real-time-systems assumption of a statically determined "decision tree" control sequence. The implication here is that the sequences of processing cannot be predetermined.

This is by no means a comprehensive list of the issues involved in real-time symbolic systems. No doubt additional research issues will arise as real-time AI applications evolve and attempts are made to solve problems in severely time-constrained domains.

Fault tolerance. A real-time computer system and its environment form a synergistic pair. For example, most commercial and military aircraft cannot fly without digital-control computers. In such systems it is meaningless to consider on-board control computers without considering the aircraft itself. The tight interaction between the environment and a real-time computer arises from time and reliability constraints. Unless the computer can provide "acceptable" services to its environment, its role will be lost and thus viewed as failed or nonexistent. Failure can result from massive loss of components (static failure) or from failure to respond fast enough to environmental stimuli (dynamic failure).[13] This interplay must be carefully characterized for various real-time applications, in which even the determination of deadlines is by itself a relatively unexplored problem. On the basis of this characterization of a real-time problem, a vast number of design and analysis problems for real-time computers remain to be solved—for example, optimal error handling, redundancy management, and tuning of architectures.

Certain research issues are important in making real-time systems fault tolerant and reliable. Specifically,

• The formal specification of the reliability requirement and the impact of timing constraints on such a requirement is a difficult problem.

• Error handling is usually composed of an ordered sequence of steps: error detection, fault location, system reconfiguration, and recovery. All these steps must be designed and analyzed in the context of combined performance (including timing constraints) and reliability. Interplay between these steps must be carefully studied. Hardware and operating-system support, together with their effects on performance and reliability, are important research subjects.

• The effects of real-time work loads on fault tolerance has not been adequately addressed. It is well known that the reliability of a computer system depends heavily on its work load. Characterizing the effects of "representative" real-time work loads on fault tolerance is essential.

Real-time-system architectures. Many real-time systems can be viewed as a three-stage pipeline: data acquisition from sensors, data processing, and output to actuators and/or displays.[14] Next-generation systems will often be distributed such that each node may be a multiprocessor (see Figure 2). A real-time system's architecture must be designed to support these components with high fidelity. For data acquisition and for actuators, the architecture must provide extensive I/O capabilities while providing fast, timely, and reliable operations for the data-processing stage.

Conventional real-time architectures are based on dedicated hardware and software: The architecture usually must change with a change in applications. Such architectures are neither cost effective nor well utilized. Because of advances in VLSI technology, it is becoming possible to develop a new distributed architecture suitable for broader classes of real-time applications. Important issues in this new architecture include interconnection topology, interprocess communications, and support of operating-system and fault-tolerance functions.

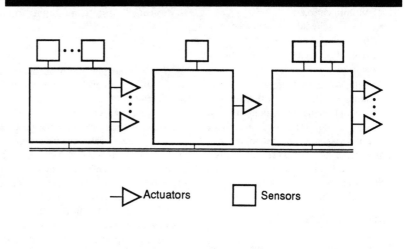

Figure 2. A distributed real-time architecture.

Some open research topics in real-time architecture are

• Interconnection topology for processors and I/O. The need for extensive I/O and high-speed data processing in real-time applications makes it important to develop an integrated interconnection topology for both processors and I/O. Although the processing topology has been studied extensively, little attention has been paid to the distribution of I/O data.

• Fast, reliable, and time-constrained communications.

• Architectural support for error handling.

• Architectural support for scheduling algorithms.

• Architectural support for real-time operating systems.

• Architectural support for real-time language features.

Ideally, any architectural design should adopt a synergistic approach wherein theory, operating system, and hardware are all developed with the single goal of achieving the real-time constraints in a cost-effective and integrated fashion.

Real-time communication. The communication media for next-generation distributed real-time systems will be required to form the backbone upon which predictable, stable, and extensible system solutions will be built. To be successful, the real-time communication subsystem must

be able to predictably satisfy individual message-level timing requirements. The timing requirements are driven not only by applications' interprocess communication, but also by time-constrained operating-system functions invoked on behalf of application processes. Networking solutions for this context are distinguished from the standard nonreal-time solutions with the introduction of *time*. In a nonreal-time setting, it is sufficient to verify the logical correctness of a communications solution; however, in a real-time setting it is also necessary to verify timing correctness. Software engineering practices have helped in determining the logical correctness of systems solutions but have not addressed timing correctness. Timing correctness includes ensuring the schedulability of synchronous and sporadic messages as well as ensuring that the response time requirements of asynchronous messages are met. Ensuring timing correctness for static real-time communications systems using current technology is difficult; ensuring timing correctness in the next generation's dynamic environment will be a substantial research challenge.

Additional research is needed to develop technologies that support the unique challenges of real-time communications. These include

• Dynamic routing solutions with guaranteed timing correctness.
• Network buffer management that

supports scheduling solutions.
- Fault-tolerant and time-constrained communications.
- Network scheduling that can be combined with processor scheduling to provide system-level scheduling solutions.

Meeting these challenges will require substantial research effort with associated breakthroughs in network control theory. With the network forming the backbone of many next-generation distributed real-time systems, a system will be no stronger than the communications solution that supports it.

Conclusions

Many real-time systems of tomorrow will be large and complex and will function in distributed and dynamic environments. They will include expert system components and will involve complex timing constraints encompassing different granules of time. Moreover, economic, human, and ecological catastrophes will result if these timing constraints are not met. Meeting the challenges imposed by these characteristics very much depends on a focused and coordinated effort in all aspects of system development, such as

- Specification and verification techniques that can handle the needs of real-time systems with a large number of interacting components.
- Design methodologies that can be used to synthesize systems with the specified timing properties where these timing properties are considered from the beginning of the design process.
- Programming languages with explicit constructs to express—with unambiguous semantics—the time-related behavior of modules.
- Scheduling algorithms that can, in an integrated and dynamic fashion, handle (1) complex task structures with resource and precedence constraints, (2) resources (such as the communication subnet and I/O devices), and (3) timing constraints of varying granularity.
- Operating-system functions designed to deal with highly integrated and cooperative time-constrained resource management in a fast and predictable manner.
- Communication architectures and protocols for dealing efficiently with messages that require timely delivery.

- Architecture support for fault tolerance, efficient operating-system functioning, and time-constrained communication.

Real-time systems have brought about unmet challenges in a wide range of computer science disciplines. Each of these challenges must be overcome before a science of large-scale real-time systems can become a reality. The task is formidable, and success will require a concerted effort by many different participants in the computer science community. It will require the enticement of new researchers into the field, especially in academia, where relatively little work of this nature is being done. We must coordinate interaction between research efforts in universities and development efforts in industry so that academic researchers will be familiar with key problems faced by system developers, and system developers will be aware of relevant new theories and technologies.

The solution to developing a theory of large-scale real-time systems does not lie in the current methodologies of operations research, database theory, scheduling theory, or operating-systems theory. Rather, it lies in well-coordinated and expanded efforts of universities, industry, and government laboratories directed toward the distinct problems that this topic introduces. The need for such cooperation was also emphasized in a report to the Executive Office of the President, Office of Science and Technology Policy.[15] While that report dealt with problems in high-performance computing, software technology and algorithms, networking, basic research, and human resources, our general conclusions are the same. However, this article is much more detailed in its emphasis on the basic research needs of a single important research topic: real-time computing. □

Acknowledgments

This article incorporates ideas presented at the Carnegie Mellon University Workshop on Fundamental Issues in Distributed Real-Time Systems and represents the work of many individuals. Those who contributed significantly to the ideas presented here include Lui Sha, John Lehoczky, Hide Tokuda, Jay Strosnider, and Ragunathan Rajkumar, Carnegie Mellon University; Al Mok, University of Texas at Austin; Andre van Tilborg, Office of Naval Research; Krithi Ramamritham and Zhao Wei, University of Massachusetts; Kang Shin, University of Michigan; David C.L. Liu, University of Illinois; Pat Watson, IBM; and Karen Johnson and Ellen Waldrum, Texas Instruments.

A longer and more technical version of this article,[1] produced in concert with the individuals listed above, is available from J. Stankovic. This work has been partially supported by the Office of Naval Research under contract 048-716/3-22-85.

References

1. J. Stankovic, "Real-Time Computing Systems: The Next Generation," Tech. Report TR-88-06, COINS Dept., Univ. of Massachusetts, Jan. 1988.

2. W. Zhao, K. Ramamritham, and J. Stankovic, "Scheduling Tasks with Resource Requirements in Hard Real-Time Systems," *IEEE Trans. Software Eng.*, Vol. SE-13, No. 5, May 1987, pp. 564-577.

3. F. Jahanian and A.K. Mok, "Safety Analysis of Timing Properties in Real-Time Systems," *IEEE Trans. Software Eng.*, Vol. SE-12, No. 9, Sept. 1986, pp. 890-904.

4. G.M. Reed and A.W. Roscoe, "A Timed Model for Communicating Sequential Processes," *Proc. ICALP 86*, Springer LNCS 226, 1986, pp. 314-323.

5. S.K. Dhall and C.L. Liu, "On a Real-Time Scheduling Problem," *Operations Research*, Vol. 26, No. 1, Feb. 1978, pp. 127-140.

6. M.R. Garey and D.S. Johnson, "Two-Processor Scheduling with Start-Times and Deadlines," *SIAM J. Computing*, Vol. 6, 1977, pp. 416-426.

7. C.L. Liu and J.W. Layland, "Scheduling Algorithms for Multiprogramming in a Hard Real-Time Environment," *J. ACM*, Vol. 20, No. 1, Jan. 1973, pp. 46-61.

8. K. Schwan et al., "High Performance Operating System Primitives for Robotics and Real-Time Control Systems," *ACM Trans. Computer Systems*, Vol. 5, No. 3, Aug. 1987, pp. 189-231.

9. J. Stankovic and K. Ramamritham, "The Design of the Spring Kernel," *Proc. Real-Time Systems Symp.*, CS Press, Los Alamitos, Calif., Dec. 1987, pp. 146-155.

10. H. Tokuda, J. Wendorf, and H. Wang, "Implementation of a Time Driven Scheduler for Real-Time Operating Systems," *Proc. Real-Time Systems Symp.*, CS Press, Los Alamitos, Calif., Dec. 1987, pp. 271-280.

11. P.A. Bernstein, V. Hadzilacos, and N. Goodman, *Concurrency Control and Recovery in Database Systems*, Addison-Wesley, Reading, Mass., 1987.

12. L. Sha, J. Lehoczky, and E.D. Jensen, "Modular Concurrency Control and Failure Recovery," *IEEE Trans. Computers*, Vol. 37, No. 2, Feb. 1988, pp. 146-159.

13. K.G. Shin, C.M. Krishna, and Y.-H. Lee, "A Unified Method for Evaluating Real-Time Computer Controllers and Its Application," *IEEE Trans. Automatic Control*, Vol. AC-30, No. 4, Apr. 1985, pp. 357-366.

14. C.M. Krishna, K.G. Shin, and I.S. Bhandari, "Processor Trade-offs in Distributed Real-Time Systems," *IEEE Trans. Computers*, Vol. C-36, No. 9, Sept. 1987, pp. 1,030-1,040.

15. *A Research and Development Strategy for High Performance Computing*, Report, Executive Office of the President, Office of Science and Technology Policy, Nov. 20, 1987.

John A. Stankovic is an associate professor in the Computer and Information Science Department at the University of Massachusetts at Amherst. His research interests include investigating various approaches to scheduling on local area networks and multiprocessors, and developing flexible, distributed, hard real-time systems. He is currently building a hard real-time kernel called Spring, based on a new scheduling paradigm and on ensuring predictability. He is also doing research on a distributed database testbed called CARAT, which has been operational for several years.

Stankovic has held visiting positions in the Computer Science Department at Carnegie Mellon University and at INRIA in France. He is an editor for *IEEE Transactions on Computers* and a member of ACM and Sigma Xi. Stankovic received a BS in electrical engineering and MS and PhD degrees in computer science, all from Brown University, in 1970, 1976, and 1979, respectively.

Readers may contact the author at COINS Dept., Lederle Graduate Research Center, Univ. of Massachusetts at Amherst, Amherst, MA 01003.

Editorial

What is Predictability for Real-Time Systems?*

JOHN A. STANKOVIC AND KRITHI RAMAMRITHAM
Department of Computer and Information Science, University of Massachusetts, Amherst, MA 01003, U.S.A

1. Introduction

Real-time systems span a broad spectrum of complexity from very simple microcontrollers (such as a microprocessor controlling an automobile engine) to highly sophisticated, complex and distributed systems (such as air traffic control for the continental United States). Some future systems will be even more complex (Stankovic 1988). These complex future systems include the space station, integrated vision/robotics/AI systems, collections of humans/robots coordinating to achieve common objectives (usually in hazardous environments such as undersea exploration or chemical plants), and various command and control applications. To further complicate the problem there are many dimensions along which real-time systems can be categorized. The main ones include:

- the granularity of deadlines and the laxities for tasks,
- the strictness of the deadlines,
- reliability requirements of the system,
- the size of the system and the degree of interaction (coordination) among components, and
- the characteristics of the environment in which the system operates.

The characteristics of the environment, in turn, seem to give rise to how static or dynamic the system has to be. As can be imagined, depending on the above considerations many different system designs occur. However, one common denominator seems to be that all designers want their real-time system to be *predictable*. But what does predictability mean? It means that it should be possible to show, demonstrate, or prove that requirements are met subject to any assumptions made, for example, concerning failures and workloads. In other words, predictability is always subject to the underlying assumptions being made.

In this editorial we concentrate on predictability with respect to the timing requirements. We use examples to show that, in the current literature, predictability in real-time systems means different things depending on the requirements with respect to the above five dimensions. We then suggest two approaches for achieving predictability in complex real-time systems.

*This work was supported by ONR under contract N00014-85-K-0389 and NSF under grants DCR-8500332 and IRI-8908693.

We encourage readers to submit comments on this editorial, or to present their own definitions and views. Selected submissions will be published in future issues.

2. Categorizing real-time systems

Real-Time systems are those systems in which the correctness of the system depends not only on the logical results of computations, but also on the time at which the results are produced. However, the full meaning of this definition takes on various subtleties depending on the five system dimensions listed above. Let us now briefly discuss each of these dimensions in turn.

2.1. Granularity of the deadline and laxity of the tasks

In a real-time system some of the tasks have deadlines and/or periodic timing constraints. If the time between when a task is activated (required to be executed) and when it must complete execution is short, then the deadline is tight (i.e., the granularity of the deadline is small, or alternatively said, the deadline is close). This implies that the operating system reaction time has to be short, and the scheduling algorithm to be executed must be fast and very simple. Tight time constraints may also arise when the deadline granularity is large (i.e., from the time of activation), but the amount of computation required is also great. In other words even large granularity deadlines can be tight when the laxity (deadline minus computation time) is small. In many real-time systems tight timing constraints predominate and consequently designers focus on developing very fast and simple techniques to react to this type of task activation.

2.2. Strictness of deadline

The strictness of the deadline refers to the value of executing a task after its deadline. For a *hard real-time task* there is no value to executing the task after the deadline has passed. A *soft real-time task* retains some diminished value after its deadline so it should still be executed. Very different techniques are usually used for hard and soft real-time tasks. In many systems hard real-time tasks are preallocated and prescheduled resulting in 100% of them making their deadlines. Soft real-time tasks are often scheduled either with non-real-time scheduling algorithms, or with algorithms that explicitly address the timing constraints but aim only at good average case performance, or with algorithms that combine importance and timing requirements (for example, cyclic scheduling).

2.3. Reliability

Many real-time systems operate under severe reliability requirements. That is, if certain tasks, called critical tasks, miss their deadline then a catastrophe may occur. These tasks are usually guaranteed to make their deadlines by an off-line analysis and by schemes that reserve resources for these tasks even if it means that those resources are idle most of the time. In other words, the requirement for critical tasks should be that all of them always make their deadline (a 100% guarantee), subject to certain failure and workload assumptions. However, it is our opinion that too many systems treat all the tasks that have hard timing constraints as critical tasks (when, in fact, only some of those tasks are truly critical). This can result in erroneous requirements and an overdesigned and inflexible system. It is also common to see hard real-time tasks defined as those with both strict deadlines and of critical importance. We prefer to keep a clear separation between these notions because they are not always related.

2.4. Size of system and degree of coordination

Real-time systems vary considerably in size and complexity. In most current real-time systems the entire system is loaded into memory, or if there are well defined phases, each phase is loaded just prior to the beginning of the phase. In many applications, subsystems are highly independent of each other and there is limited cooperation among tasks. The ability to load entire systems into memory and to limit task interactions simplifies many aspects of building and analyzing real-time systems. However, for next generation large, complex, real-time systems, having completely resident code and highly independent tasks will not always be practical. Consequently, increased size and coordination give rise to many new problems that must be addressed and complicates the notion of predictability.

2.5. Environment

The environment in which a real-time system is to operate plays an important role in the design of the system. Many environments are very well defined (such as a lab experiment, an automobile engine, or an assembly line). Designers think of these as deterministic environments (even though they may not be intrinsically deterministic, they are forced to be). These environments give rise to small, static real-time systems where all deadlines can be guaranteed a priori. Even in these simple environments we need to place restrictions on the inputs. For example, the assembly line can only cope with five items per minute; given more than that, the system fails. Taking this approach enables an off-line analysis where a quantitative analysis of the timing properties can be made. Since we know exactly what to expect given the assumptions about the well defined environment we can consider these systems to be predictable.

The problem is that the approaches taken in relatively small, static systems do not scale to other environments which are larger, much more complicated, and less controllable. Consider a next generation real-time system such as a team of cooperating mobile robots on Mars. This next generation real-time system will be large, complex, distributed, adaptive, contain many types of timing constraints, need to operate in a highly nondeterministic environment, and evolves over a long system lifetime. It is much more difficult to force this environment to look deterministic—in fact, that is exactly what you do not want to do because the system would be too inflexible and would not be able to react to unexpected events or combinations of events. We consider this type of real-time system to be a dynamic real-time system operating in a nondeterministic environment. Such systems are required in many applications. It is much more difficult to define predictability for these systems and the typical semantics (all tasks make their deadlines 100% of the time) associated with the term for small static real-time systems is not sufficient. Many advances are required to address predictability of these next generation systems in a scientific manner. For example, one of the most difficult aspects will be in demonstrating that these systems meet both their overall performance requirements (which are generally average case statistics but with respect to meeting deadlines and maximizing value of executed tasks), as well as specific deadline and periodicity timing requirements of individual tasks or groups of tasks, or instances thereof. If both types of timing requirements can be demonstrated, then we can refer to the system as being predictable.

3. Predictability

For tutorial purposes, let us consider a series of examples of systems which are called predictable in the literature.

3.1. Predictability in a simple system

System A has a fixed worst case interrupt response time of 30 microseconds. This system is called predictable because you can guarantee that any new interrupt is *begun* to be serviced within 30 microseconds. Any overlapping interrupt is also guaranteed to begin to be processed in 30 microseconds, but this may impact the completion of the previous task. Consequently, there is no guarantee that a task will *finish* by its deadline. That requirement must be handled in some other manner. In other words, the system is predictable *only* with respect to the requirement that interrupts are to begin being processed in 30 microseconds. Consequently, in System A, the claim of predictability is an extremely tenuous one and offered at a microscopic level. However, assume that you have a very simple system where at most two overlapping interrupts are possible, where interrupts of the same type do not occur within 100 microseconds of each other, and all tasks that execute in response to an interrupt need five microseconds and that deadlines for these tasks are 100 microseconds. Then you can a priori show the macroscopic predictability, that is, the system level predictability. Note that here predictability means that all tasks make their deadlines with 100% guarantee. We emphasize again that often requiring 100% guarantees for all tasks is unnecessary. Implicit in this guarantee are assumptions such as no failures occur and various execution times and deadlines are correct.

3.2. Predictability in systems with only periodic tasks

In system B there are 100 periodic tasks, they are all hard real-time tasks and 25 are critical. The designers decide to treat all 100 as critical and produce a fixed cyclic schedule for these tasks. An underlying assumption in producing the schedule is that the worst case execution times for the tasks are known which means that the hardware instruction times must be known. To facilitate this computation the designers eliminate caches and virtual memory from their design. All operating system primitives needed by these 100 tasks must also be accounted for, hence the execution time of each OS primitive must be bounded. Any precedence constraints between the tasks and conflicts over shared resources must be accounted for. At this point the system is completely fixed and inflexible, but there is a 100% guarantee that all deadlines will be met. The system meets its timing requirements. This is again subject to no failures and to the worst case times being accurate including maximum delays in waiting for shared resources.

In system C there are 25 independent periodic tasks. Suppose that the designers can show that the maximum cpu utilization ever required by these 25 tasks is less than 69%. Hence, they use the rate monotonic algorithm which guarantees that all tasks will make their deadlines if utilization is less than 69%. An underlying assumption behind the rate monotonic algorithm is that preemption costs are zero. However, since the number of preemptions is bounded it is possible to take the preemption costs into account. Consequently, we have 100% predictable performance even though a dynamic scheduling algorithm is used.

3.3. Predictability in a next generation, complex real-time system

System D is a large, complex, real-time system operating in a nondeterministic environment. It has both tight time constraints and loose time constraints; it has hard and soft real-time tasks; some of its tasks are critical; parts of the system may be highly static but many parts require a dynamic approach. In other words all dimensions of real-time systems are found simultaneously in this system. Designers cannot focus on just one predominant feature of the system such as tight time constraints, or simply bound the interrupt latency, or assume a fixed set of periodic tasks. It is this type of system for which it is difficult to define and demonstrate predictability. The notion that you obtain a 100% guarantee (as found in all the previous examples) must be relaxed.

We believe that you must demonstrate that the requirements are met at two levels of detail and for each class of task. At the macroscopic (system-wide) level we need to show first that all critical tasks will always make their deadline (100% guarantee) and that all non-critical tasks (both hard and soft deadline tasks) meet overall requirements. As an example, these overall requirements might be stated in the following way: 97% of noncritical hard real-time tasks, and 95% of soft real-time tasks must make their deadlines. Alternatively, the requirements might be to maximize the value of noncritical hard and soft real-time tasks executed by the system. At the microscopic level (on an individual task or task group basis) we also would like some level of predictability. For the critical tasks we already know that they will always make their deadline. For the other real-time tasks their performance will depend on the current state of the system. However, using scheduling algorithms in a planning mode (as done in Stankovic and Ramamritham 1989) can provide an instantaneous snapshot of the current predictability of this set of tasks. In other words, at any point in time the system can identify exactly which tasks will make their deadlines. This provides many advantages including graceful degradation, the ability to handle overloads, and the ability to make more intelligent decisions concerning the overall operation of the system (Stankovic and Ramamritham 1989).

4. Achieving predictability

We now consider two alternative ways to achieve predictability in complex real-time systems. The first we call the *layer-by-layer* approach and the second we call the *top layer* approach. In the first case we require both microscopic and macroscopic predictability, while in the second case we only require macroscopic predictability. It is important to note that these approaches can be merged.

Before we discuss each of these approaches we have a few preparatory remarks. A real-time system can be considered to be composed of entities at various hardware and software layers. Broadly speaking these levels are: semiconductor components, the hardware/architecture layer, the operating system layer, and the application layer. The layer-by-layer method assumes that a higher layer is predictable, if and only if, the lower layer is predictable. The top layer approach challenges this statement.

4.1. Layer-by-layer approach

In this approach, in order to obtain a predictable system, it is necessary to have a tight interaction between all aspects of the system starting from the design rules and constraints used, to the programming language, to the compiler, to the operating system, and to the hardware. Then, based on a careful software and hardware design we believe that it is possible to achieve both microscopic and macroscopic predictability. In the microscopic view, we can compute the worst case execution time of any task. This is not as simple as it first may seem. First, we require a simplified architecture so that instruction times are well-defined. Second, we must be able to account for resource requirements and calls to system primitives made on behalf of this task. This can be accomplished via various techniques including a *planning* scheduler such as found in the Spring system (Ramamritham, Stankovic and Shiah 1990; Stankovic and Ramamritham 1987; Stankovic and Ramamritham 1989; Zhao, Ramamritham and Stankovic 1987). In this way, the execution time of a particular invocation of a task with its resource needs can be accurately computed. In many other approaches predictability breaks down here because they have no good method for dealing with delays for resources.

Further, the layer-by-layer approach enables a macroscopic view of predictability. That is, first, we require the *macroscopic* view that *all* critical tasks will *always* make their deadlines (subject to the assumptions of the analysis). In other words, for critical tasks the requirement is a 100% guarantee. As mentioned above some systems force all their tasks to be critical. This has a number of disadvantages and will not scale to next generation, large, and dynamic systems. Second, by planning and through microscopic predictability, at any point in time we know *exactly* which noncritical but hard real-time tasks in the entire system will make their deadlines given the current load. In other words we have a dynamic and macroscopic picture of the capabilities of the current state of the system with respect to timing requirements. This has several advantages with respect to fault tolerance and graceful degradation. Third, it is also possible to develop an overall quantitative, but probabilistic assessment of the performance of noncritical hard real-time tasks given expected normal and overload workloads. For example, via simulation one might compute the average percentage of noncritical tasks that make their deadlines or the expected value of tasks that make their deadline. We then would need to show that on the average these tasks meet the system requirements or add resources until this is true. Fourth, we require the macroscopic view of the capabilities of the I/O front ends. For example, it may be possible to state that the tasks on the I/O processor, scheduled according to the rate monotonic algorithm, will always make all their deadlines because the load is less than 69% and because there are no resource conflicts.

In some circles this four pronged macroscopic view may seem unsatisfying because *everything* is not 100% guaranteed. However, we believe that this is necessary and unavoidable given that we are operating in a complex, nondeterministic environment. In these environments it seems necessary to *carefully* develop the requirements as actually needed, and then to employ different means to meet the different types of requirements.

4.2. Top layer approach

In the top layer approach we concentrate on the fact that what is really important is the *application layer* predictability requirements. Deadlines imposed on activities other than those that occur at the application layer are artifacts. The lower layers need not be predictable, but only provide services so that the application layer is predictable.

This approach also recognizes that in the layer-by-layer approach, even if everything has been predicted—at each of the layers—to work as required, error handlers have to be provided for fail-safe and fail-soft behavior. This is just in case assumptions made to derive predictability figures do not hold, or the algorithms used to derive predictability are in error.

Let us first consider the requirements for hard real-time tasks. Suppose the requirement imposed is that either an activity with a hard deadline D is done completely by its deadline, or some alternative action is taken that is guaranteed to take the system to a safe state. The alternative action should also be completed by the deadline. The alternative action can be thought of as an error handler.

Assuming that the computation time C for the error handler is easier to determine than for the original activity, the system can do the following: Before the activity begins, it guarantees with 100% that the error handler, when started at time D' ($D' \leq D - C$) will run and complete prior to D. The lower layers run as fast as they can to provide the services required so that the activity is completed by D'. If this fails, the error handler is invoked.

To use this approach, it must be possible to demonstrate that the error handler can execute by its deadline with 100% guarantee. To guarantee this, some of the techniques used in the layer-by-layer approach may be necessary, although applied to a small subset of the system (the error handlers) rather than to the entire system. It might even be possible to allocate a separate subsystem dedicated for the error handlers, so that the various layers of this subsystem are carefully designed using the layer-by-layer approach to provide the needed guarantees.

Now consider the requirements for the critical tasks. Critical activities, by the semantics given earlier, must be completed by their deadlines. So, for such activities, the layer-by-layer approach has to be used to provide 100% guarantees.

The top-layer approach is most suited when the activities are complex. For instance, it may not be possible to "break" a complex activity at one layer into activities/tasks assumed at the lower layers. Further, the uncertainties caused by the environment in which an activity is being performed may make it impossible to quantitatively describe the behavior of components of that activity.

Another situation where the top layer approach will be called for is where the bounds found at one layer, based on bounds at the lower layers, may be so high so as not to be of any practical value. Let us look at an example. Suppose an activity A is made up of A1 that happens on node p, A2 that happens on node q and communication C between them. Say A1 and A2 are subproblems such that if A1 takes more time, then A2 takes less, and vice versa. If A1 does more work, C takes more time. Whether or not A1 takes more time depends on various factors not all of which are known at the time the activity begins. However, A1 and A2 are bounded. So is C. Here all the component activities are bounded. So the overall activity is also bounded. However, this bound may be too large to be useful in making any prediction, say, whether A will meet its timing requirement.

5. Conclusion

In summary, predictability in real-time systems has been defined in many ways. For static real-time systems we can predict the overall system performance over large time frames (even over the life of the system) as well as predict the performance of individual tasks. If the prediction is that 100% of all tasks over the entire life of the system will meet their deadlines, then the system is predictable without resorting to any stochastic evaluation. In dynamic real-time systems we must resort to a stochastic evaluation for part of the performance evaluation. Predictability for these systems should mean that we are able to satisfy the timing requirements of critical tasks with 100% guarantee over the life of the system, be able to assess overall system performance over various time frames (a stochastic evaluation), and be able to assess individual task and task group performance at different times and as a function of the current system state. If all these assessments meet the timing requirements, then the system is predictable with respect to its timing requirements.

References

Ramamritham, K., Stankovic, J., and Shiah, P. 1990. Efficient scheduling algorithms for real-time multiprocessor systems. *IEEE Trans. on Parallel and Distributed Systems*, vol. 1, 184–194.

Stankovic, J. and Ramamritham, K. 1987. The design of the Spring kernel. *Proc. 1987 Real-Time Systems Symposium*, Dec.

Stankovic, J. and Ramamritham, K. 1989. The Spring kernel: A new paradigm for real-time operating systems. *ACM Operating Systems Review*, vol. 23, 54–71.

Stankovic, J. 1988. Misconceptions about real-time computing. *IEEE Computer*, vol. 21.

Zhao, W., Ramamritham, K., and Stankovic, J. 1987. Scheduling tasks with resource requirements in hard real-time systems. *IEEE Transactions on Software Engineering*.

Dependable
Computing

John Rushby
Editor

Evaluation of Safety-Critical Software

Methods and approaches for testing the reliability and trustworthiness of software remain among the most controversial issues facing this age of high technology. The authors present some of the crucial questions faced by software programmers and eventual users.

David L. Parnas, A. John van Schouwen, and Shu Po Kwan

It is increasingly common to use programmable computers in applications where their failure could be life-threatening and could result in extensive damage. For example, computers now have safety-critical functions in both military and civilian aircraft, in nuclear plants, and in medical devices. It is incumbent upon those responsible for programming, purchasing, installing, and licensing these systems to determine whether or not the software is ready to be used. This article addresses questions that are simple to pose but hard to answer. What standards must a software product satisfy if it is to be used in safety-critical applications such as those mentioned? What documentation should be required? How much testing is needed? How should the software be structured?

This article differs from others concerned with software in safety-critical applications, in that it does not attempt to identify *safety* as a property separate from reliability and trustworthiness. In other words, we do not attempt to separate safety-critical code from other code in a product used in a safety-critical application. In our experience, software exhibits *weak-link* behavior, that is failures in even the unimportant parts of the code can have unexpected repercussions elsewhere. For a discussion of another viewpoint, we suggest the work of N. G. Leveson [6, 7, 8].

We favor keeping safety-critical software as small and simple as possible by moving any functions that are not safety critical to other computers. This further justifies our assumption that all parts of a safety-critical software product must be considered safety critical.

WHY IS SOFTWARE A SPECIAL CONCERN?
Within the engineering community software systems have a reputation for being undependable, especially in the first years of their use. The public is aware of a few spectacular stories such as the Space Shuttle flight that was delayed by a software timing problem, or the Ve-

nus probe that was lost because of a punctuation error. In the software community, the problem is known to be much more widespread.

A few years ago, David Benson, professor of Computer Science at Washington State University, issued a challenge by way of several electronic bulletin board systems. He asked for an example of a real-time system that functioned adequately when used for the first time by people other than its developers for a purpose other than testing. Only one candidate for this honor was proposed, but even that candidate was controversial. It consisted of approximately 18,000 instructions, most of which had been used for several years before the "first use." The only code that had not been used before that first use was a simple sequence of 200 instructions that simulated a simple analogue servomechanism. That instruction sequence had been tested extensively against an analogue model. All who have looked at this program regard it as exceptional. If we choose to regard this small program as one that worked in its first real application, it is the proverbial "exception that proves the rule."

As a rule software systems do not work well until they have been used, and have failed repeatedly, in real applications. Generally, many uses and many failures are required before a product is considered reliable. Software products, including those that have become relatively reliable, behave like other products of evolution-like processes; they often fail, even years after they were built, when the operating conditions change.

While there are errors in many engineering products, experience has shown that errors are more common, more pervasive, and more troublesome, in software than in other technologies. This information must be understood in light of the fact it is now standard practice among software professionals to have their product go through an extensive series of carefully planned tests before real use. The products fail in their first real use because the situations that were not anticipated by the programmers were also overlooked by the test planners. Most major computer-using organizations, both

This work was supported by the National Science and Engineering Research Board of Canada as well as the Atomic Energy Control Board of Canada.

military and civilian, are investing heavily in searching for ways to improve the state of the art in software. The problem remains serious and there is no sign of a "silver bullet." The most promising development is the work of Harlan Mills and his colleagues at IBM on a software development process known as "clean room" [3, 9, 12]. Mills uses randomly selected tests, carried out by an independent testing group. The use of randomly generated test data reduces the likelihood of shared oversights. We will discuss this approach in more detail later in this article.

WHY IS SOFTWARE USED?

If software is so untrustworthy, one might ask why engineers do not avoid it by continuing to use hard-wired digital and analogue hardware. Here, we list the three main advantages of replacing hardware with software:

1. Software technology makes it practical to build more *logic* into the system. Software-controlled computer systems can distinguish a large number of situations and provide output appropriate to each of them. Hard-wired systems could not obtain such behavior without prohibitive amounts of hardware. Programmable hardware is less expensive than the equivalent hard-wired logic because it is regular in structure and it is mass produced. The economic aspects of the situation also allow software-controlled systems to perform more checking; reliability can be increased by periodic execution of programs that check the hardware.
2. Logic implemented in software is, in theory, easier to change than logic implemented in hardware. Many changes can be made without adding new components. When a system is replicated or located in a physical position that is hard to reach, it is far easier to make changes in software than in hardware.
3. Computer technology and software flexibility make it possible to provide more information to operators and to provide that information in a more useful form. The operator of a modern software-controlled system can be provided with information that would be unthinkable in a pure hardware system. All of this can be achieved using less space and power than was used by noncomputerized systems.

These factors explain the replacement of hard-wired systems with software-controlled systems in spite of software's reputation as an unreliable technology.

HOW ARE SOFTWARE CONTROLLERS LIKE OTHER CONTROLLERS?

In the next section we will argue that software technology requires some refinements in policies and standards because of differences between software and hardware technology. However, it is important to recognize some common properties of software and hardware control systems.

In the design and specification of control systems,

engineers have long known how to use a black box mathematical model of the controller. In such models, (1) the inputs to the controller are described as mathematical functions of certain observable environmental state variables, (2) the outputs of the controller are described as mathematical functions of the inputs, (3) the values of the controlled environmental variables are described as mathematical functions of the controller's outputs, and (4) the required relation between the controlled variables and observed variables is described. It is then possible to confirm that the behavior of the controller meets its requirements.

It is important to recognize that, in theory, software-implemented controllers can be described in exactly the same way as black box mathematical models. They can also be viewed as black boxes whose output is a mathematical function of the input. In practice, they are not viewed this way. One reason for the distinction is that their functions are more complex (i.e. harder to describe) than the functions that describe the behavior of conventional controllers. However, [4] and [17] provide ample evidence that requirements for real systems can be documented in this way. We return to this theme later.

HOW IS SOFTWARE DIFFERENT FROM OTHER CONTROLLER TECHNOLOGIES?

Software problems are often considered growing pains and ascribed to the adolescent nature of the field. Unfortunately there are fundamental differences between software and other approaches that suggest these problems are here to stay.

Complexity: The most immediately obvious difference between software and hardware technologies is their complexity. This can be observed by considering the size of the most compact descriptions of the software. Precise documentation, in a reasonably general notation, for small software systems can fill a bookcase. Another measure of complexity is the time it takes for a programmer to become closely familiar with a system. Even with small software systems, it is common to find that a programmer requires a year of working with the program before he/she can be trusted to make improvements on his/her own.

Error Sensitivity: Another notable property of software is its sensitivity to small errors. In conventional engineering, every design and manufacturing dimension can be characterized by a tolerance. One is not required to get things exactly right; being within the specified *tolerance* of the right value is good enough. The use of a tolerance is justified by the assumption that small errors have small consequences. It is well known that in software, trivial clerical errors can have major consequences. No useful interpretation of tolerance is known for software. A single punctuation error can be disastrous, even though fundamental oversights sometimes have negligible effects.

Hard to Test: Software is notoriously difficult to test

adequately. It is common to find a piece of software that has been subjected to a thorough and disciplined testing regime has serious flaws. Testing of analogue devices is based on interpolation. One assumes that devices that function well at two close points will function well at points in-between. In software that assumption is not valid. The number of cases that must be tested in order to engender confidence in a piece of software is usually extremely large. Moreover, as Harlan Mills has pointed out, "testing carried out by selected test cases, no matter how carefully and well-planned, can provide nothing but anecdotes" [3, 9, 12].

These properties are fundamental consequences of the fact that the mathematical functions implemented by software are not continuous functions, but functions with an arbitrary number of discontinuities. The lack of continuity constraints on the functions describing program effects makes it difficult to find compact descriptions of the software. The lack of such constraints gives software its flexibility, but it also allows the complexity. Similarly, the sensitivity to small errors, and the testing difficulties, can be traced to fundamental mathematical properties; we are unlikely to discover a miracle cure. Great discipline and careful scrutiny will always be required for safety-critical software systems.

Correlated Failures: Many of the assumptions normally made in the design of high-reliability hardware are invalid for software. Designers of high-reliability hardware are concerned with manufacturing failures and wear-out phenomena. They can perform their analysis on the assumption that failures are not strongly correlated and simultaneous failures are unlikely. Those who evaluate the reliability of hardware systems should be, and often are, concerned about design errors and correlated failures; however in many situations the effects of other types of errors are dominant.

In software there are few errors introduced in the manufacturing (compiling) phase; when there are such errors they are systematic, not random. Software does not wear out. The errors with which software reliability experts must be concerned are design errors. These errors cannot be considered statistically independent. There is ample evidence that, even when programs for a given task are written by people who do not know of each other, they have closely related errors [6, 7, 8].

In contrast to the situation with hardware systems, one cannot obtain higher reliability by duplication of software components. One simply duplicates the errors. Even when programs are written independently, the oversights made by one programmer are often shared by others. As a result, one cannot count on increasing the reliability of software systems simply by having three computers where one would be sufficient [6, 7, 8].

Lack of Professional Standards: A severe problem in the software field is that, strictly speaking, there are no software engineers. In contrast to older engineering fields, there is no accrediting agency for professional software engineers. Those in software engineering have not agreed on a set of skills and knowledge that should be possessed by every software engineer. Anyone with a modicum of programming knowledge can be called a software engineer. Often, critical programming systems are built by people with no postsecondary training about software. Although they may have useful knowledge of the field in which the software will be applied, such knowledge is not a substitute for understanding the foundations of software technology.

SOFTWARE TESTING CONCERNS
Some engineers believe one can design black box tests without knowledge of what is inside the box. This is, unfortunately, not completely true. If we know that the contents of a black box exhibit linear behavior, the number of tests needed to make sure it would function as specified could be quite small. If we know that the function can be described by a polynomial of order "N," we can use that information to determine how many tests are needed. If the function can have a large number of discontinuities, far more tests are needed. That is why a shift from analogue technology to software brings with it a need for much more testing.

Built-in test circuitry is often included in hardware to perform testing while the product is in use. Predetermined values are substituted for inputs, and the outputs are compared to normative values. Sometimes this approach is imitated in software designs and the claim is made that built-in online testing can substitute for black box testing. In hardware, built-in testing tests for decay or damage. Software does not decay and physical damage is not our concern. Software can be used to test the hardware, but its value for testing itself is quite doubtful. Software self-testing does increase the complexity of the product and, consequently, the likelihood of error. Moreover, such testing does not constitute adequate testing because it usually does not resemble the conditions of actual use.

The fundamental limitations on testing mentioned earlier have some very practical implications.

We cannot test software for correctness: Because of the large number of states (and the lack of regularity in its structure), the number of states that would have to be tested to assure that software is correct is preposterous. Testing can show the presence of bugs, but, except for toy problems, it is not practical to use testing to show that software is free of design errors.

It is difficult to make accurate predictions of software reliability and availability: Mathematical models show that it is practical to predict the reliability of software, provided that one has good statistical models of the actual operating conditions. Unfortunately, one usually gains that information only after the system is installed. Even when a new system replaces an existing one, differences in features may cause changes in the input distribution. Nonetheless, in safety-critical situations, one must attempt to get and use the necessary statistical data. The use of this data is discussed later in this article.

Predictions of availability are even more difficult; estimates of availability depend on predictions of the time it will take to correct a bug in the software. We never know what that amount of time will be in advance; data from earlier bugs is not a good predictor of the time it will take to find the next bug.

It is not practical to measure the trustworthiness of software: We consider a product to be trustworthy if we believe that the probability of it having a potentially catastrophic flaw is acceptably low. Whereas reliability is a measure of the probability of a problem occurring while the system is in service, trustworthiness is a measure of the probability of a serious flaw remaining after testing and review. In fact, inspection and testing can increase the trustworthiness of a product without affecting its reliability.

Software does not need to be correct in order to be trustworthy. We will trust imperfect software if we believe its probability of having a serious flaw is very low. Unfortunately, as we will show, the amount of testing necessary to establish high confidence levels for most software products is impractically large. The number of states and possible input sequences is so large that the probability of an error having escaped our attention will remain high even after years of testing. Methods other than testing must be used to increase our trust in software.

There is a role for testing: A number of computer scientists, aware of the limitations on software testing, would argue that one should not test software. They would argue that the effort normally put into testing should, instead, be put into a form of review known as mathematical verification. A program is a mathematical object and can be proven correct. Unfortunately, such mathematical inspections are based on mathematical models that may not be accurate. No amount of mathematical analysis will reveal discrepancies between the model being used and the real situation; only testing can do that. Moreover, errors are often made in proofs. In mature engineering fields, mathematical methods and testing are viewed as complementary and mutually supportive.

There is a need for an independent validation agency: It is impossible to test software completely and difficult to test one's own design in an unbiased way. A growing number of software development projects involve independent verification and validation (V&V). The V&V contractor is entirely independent of the development contractor. Sometimes a competitor of the development contractor is given the V&V contract. The testers work from the specification for the software and attempt to develop tests that will show the software to be faulty. One particularly interesting variation of this approach has been used within the IBM Federal Systems Division. In IBM's *clean room* development approach the authors of the software are not allowed

to execute their programs. All testing is done by an independent tester and test reports are sent to the developer's supervisors. The test cases are chosen using random number generators and are intended to yield statistically valid data. It was hypothesized that the software would be written far more carefully under these conditions and would be more reliable. Early reports support the hypothesis [3, 9, 12].

It is important that these validation tests not be made available to the developers before the software is submitted for testing. If the developers know what tests will be performed, they will use those tests in their debugging. The result is likely to be a program that will pass the tests but is not reliable in actual use.

SOFTWARE REVIEWABILITY CONCERNS

Why is reviewability a particular concern for software?

Traditionally, engineers have approached software as if it were an art form. Each programmer has been allowed to have his own style. Criticisms of software structure, clarity, and documentation were dismissed as "matters of taste."

In the past, engineers were rarely asked to examine a software product and certify that it would be trustworthy. Even in systems that were required to be trustworthy and reliable, software was often regarded as an unimportant component, not requiring special examination.

In recent years, however, manufacturers of a wide variety of equipment have been substituting computers controlled by software for a wide variety of more conventional products. We can no longer treat software as if it were trivial and unimportant.

In the older areas of engineering, safety-critical components are inspected and reviewed to assure the design is consistent with the safety requirements. To make this review possible, the designers are required to conform to industry standards for the documentation, and even the structure, of the product. The documentation must be sufficiently clear and well organized that a reviewer can determine whether or not the design meets safety standards. The design itself must allow components to be inspected so the reviewer can verify they are consistent with the documentation. In construction, inspections take place during the process—while it is still possible to inspect and correct work that will later be hidden.

When software is a safety-critical component, analogous standards should be applied. In software, there is no problem of physical visibility but there is a problem of clarity. Both practical experience and planned experiments have shown that it is common for programs with major flaws to be accepted by reviewers. In one particularly shocking experiment, small programs were deliberately flawed and given to a skilled reviewer team. The reviewers were unable to find the flaws in spite of the fact they were certain such flaws were present. In theory, nothing is invisible in a program—

it is all in the listing; in practice, poorly structured programs hide a plethora of problems.

In safety-critical applications we must reject the "software-as-art-form" approach. Programs and documentation must conform to standards that allow reviewers to feel confident they understand the software and can predict how it will function in situations where safety depends on it. However, we must, equally strongly, reject standards that require a mountain of paper that nobody can read. The standards must insure clear, precise, and concise documentation.

It is symptomatic of the immaturity of the software profession that there are no widely accepted software standards assuring the reviewability essential to licensing of software products that must be seen as trustworthy. The documentation standards name and outline certain documents, but they only vaguely define the contents of those documents. Recent U.S. military procurement regulations include safety requirements; while they require that safety checks be done, they neither describe how to do them nor impose standards that make those checks practicable. Most standards for code documentation are so vague and syntactic in nature that a program can meet those standards in spite of being incomprehensible.

In the next section we derive some basic standards by considering the reviews that are needed and the information required by the reviewers.

What reviews are needed?

Software installed as a safety-critical component in a large system should be subjected to the following reviews:

a. Review for correct intended function. If the software works as the programmers intend, will it meet the actual requirements?
b. Review for maintainable, understandable, well documented structure. Is it easy to find portions of the software relevant to a certain issue? Are the responsibilities of the various modules clearly defined? If all of the modules work as required, will the whole system work as intended? If changes are needed in the future, can those changes be restricted to easily identified portions of the code?
c. Review each module to verify the algorithm and data structure design are consistent with the specified behavior. Is the data structure used in the module appropriate for representing the information maintained by that module? If the programs are correctly coded, will the modules perform as required? Will the algorithms selected perform as required? These reviews must use mathematical methods; one cannot rely on intuitive approaches. We have found a formal review based on functional semantics, [10], to be practical and effective.
d. Review the code for consistency with the algorithm and data structure design. Is the actual source code consistent with the algorithms and data structures described by the designers? Have the assemblers,

compilers, and other support tools been used correctly?
e. Review test adequacy. Was the testing sufficient to provide sound confidence in the proper functioning of the software?

The structure of this set of reviews is consistent with modern approaches to software engineering. Because we are unable to comprehend all the critical details about a software product at once, it is necessary to provide documentation that allows programmers and reviewers to focus on one aspect at a time and to zoom in on the relevant details.

Developing and presenting these views in the sequence listed is the analogue of providing inspections during a construction project. Just as construction is inspected before further work obscures what has been done, the early specifications should be reviewed before subsequent coding hides the structure in a sea of detail.

The set of reviews also reflects the fact that reviewers of a software product have a variety of skills. Those who have a deep understanding of the requirements are not usually skilled software designers. It follows that the best people to review the functional behavior of the software are not the ones who should study the software. Similarly, within the software field we have people who are good at algorithm design, but not particularly good finding an architecture for software products. Skilled algorithm designers are not necessarily experts on a particular compiler or machine language. Those intimately familiar with a compiler or assembly language are not always good at organizing large programs. When the software is safety critical, it is important that each of the five reviews be conducted by those best qualified to review that aspect of the work.

Within this framework, all code and documentation supplied must be of a quality that facilitates review and allows the reviewers to be confident of their conclusions. It is the responsibility of the designers to present their software in a way that leaves no doubt about their correctness. It is not the responsibility of the reviewers to guess the designers' intent. Discrepancies between code and documentation must be treated as seriously as errors in the code. If the designers are allowed to be sloppy with their documentation, quality control will be ineffective.

In the following sections of this article, we will describe the documentation that must be provided for each of these reviews. This documentation should not be created merely for review purposes. It should be used throughout the development to record and propagate design decisions. When separate review documents are produced, projects experience all the problems of keeping two sets of books. Because of the complexity of software products, it is unlikely that both records would be consistent. Moreover, the documents described below from the reviewers' viewpoint are invaluable to the designers as well [5, 13, 16].

What documentation is required to review the functional requirements?

The software can be viewed as a control system whose output values respond to changes in the states of variables of interest in its environment. For many real-time systems, the desired outputs approximate piece-wise continuous functions of time and the history of the relevant environmental parameters. For other systems, the outputs are functions of a snapshot of the environmental parameters taken at some point in time. Some systems provide both reports and continuous outputs.

The reviewers at this stage should be engineers and scientists who understand the situation being monitored and the devices to be controlled. They may not be computer specialists and should not be expected to read and understand programs. Because the requirements could, in theory, be fulfilled by a completely hardware design, the description should use the mathematics of control systems, not the jargon and notation of computer programming. The functional requirements can be stated precisely by giving three mathematical relations: (1) The required values of the controlled environmental variables in terms of the values of the relevant observable environmental parameters, (2) the computer inputs in terms of those observable environmental variables, and (3) the values of the controlled environmental variables in terms of the computer outputs.

These requirements can be communicated as a set of tables and formulae describing the mathematical functions to be implemented [4]. We should not describe a sequence of computations anywhere in this document. The use of natural language, which inevitably introduces ambiguity, should be minimized. Documents of this form have been written for reasonably complex systems and are essential when safety-critical functions are to be performed. Our experience has shown that documents written this way can be thoroughly and effectively reviewed by engineers who are not programmers. Some suggestions for organizing the reviews are contained in [19]. A complete example of such a document has been published as a model for other projects [17].

What documentation is required to review the software structure?

For this review we require documents that describe the breakdown of the program into modules. Each module is a unit that should be designed, written and reviewed independently of other modules. Each module is a collection of programs; the programs that can be invoked from other modules are called access programs. The purpose of this review is to make sure that: (1) the structure is one that allows independent development and change; (2) all programs that are needed are included once and only once in the structure; (3) the interfaces to the modules are precisely defined; (4) the modules are compatible and will, together, constitute a system that meets the functional requirements.

For this review three types of documents are required. The first is the requirements specification, which should have been approved by an earlier review. The second is an informal document describing the responsibilities of each module. The purpose of this *module guide* is to allow a reviewer to find all the modules relevant to a particular aspect of system design [1]. The third type of document is known as a module specification. It provides a complete black box description of the module interface. There should be one specification for each module mentioned in the module guide [2, 14].

Reviewers of these documents must be experienced software engineers. Some of them should have had experience with similar systems. This experience is necessary to note omissions in the module structure. Discussions of these documents and how to organize the reviews are contained in [14, 19].

What documentation is required to review the module's internal design?

The first step in designing the module should be to describe the data structures that will be used and each proposed program's effect on the data. This information can be described in a way that is, except for the data types available, independent of the programming language being used.

The design documentation is a description of two types of mathematical functions: program functions and abstraction functions. This terminology was used in IBM's Federal Systems Division, the IBM branch responsible for U.S. Government systems. These concepts are described more fully elsewhere [11, 13]. The program functions, one for each module access program, give the mapping from the state before the program is executed to the state after the program terminates. The abstraction functions are used to define the "meaning" of the data structure; they give the mapping between the data states and abstract values visible to the users of the module. It is well-known that these functions provide sufficient information for a formal review of correctness of the design before the programs are implemented.

Programs that cannot be described on a single page must be presented in a hierarchical way; each page must present a small program, calling other programs whose functions are specified on that page. This type of presentation allows the algorithm to be understood and verified one page at a time.

If the module embodies a physical model (i.e., a set of equations that allows us to compute nonobservables from observables), the model must be described and its limitations documented.

If the module performs numerical calculations in which accuracy will be a concern, numerical analysis justifying the design must be included.

If the module is hardware-dependent, the documentation must include either a description of the hardware or a reference to such a description.

If the module is responsible for certain parts of the functional specification, a cross reference must be provided.

The reviewers of each internal module design document will include experienced software engineers and other specialists. For example, if a physical model is involved, a physicist or engineer with expertise in that area must be included as a reviewer. If the information is presented in a notation that is independent of the programming language, none of the reviewers needs to be an expert in the programming language involved. Numerical analysts will be needed for some modules, device specialists for others.

What documentation is required to review the code?

While it is important that the algorithms and data structures be appropriate to the task, this will be of little help if the actual code is not faithful to the abstract design. Because of the previous reviews, those who review the code do not need to examine the global design of the system. Instead, they examine the correspondence between the algorithms and the actual code. These reviewers must be experienced users of the hardware and compilers involved; of course, they must also understand the notation used to specify the algorithms.

What documentation is required for the Test Plan Review?

Although these reviews, if carried out rigorously, constitute a mathematical verification of the code, testing is still required. Sound testing requires that a test plan (a document describing the way test cases will be selected) be developed and approved in advance. In addition to the usual engineering practice of normal case and limiting case checks, it is important that the reliability of safety-critical systems be estimated by statistical methods. Reliability estimation requires statistically valid random testing; careful thought must be given to the distribution from which the test cases will be drawn. It is important for the distribution of inputs to be typical of situations in which the correct functioning of the system is critical. A more detailed discussion of statistical testing can be found in the upcoming section, Reliability Assessment for Safety-Critical Software.

The test plan should be described in a document that is not available to the designers. It should be reviewed by specialists in software testing, and specialists in the application area, who compare it with the requirements specification to make certain the test coverage is adequate.

Reviewing the relationship between these documents

The hierarchical process described is designed to allow reviews to be conducted in an orderly way, focusing on one issue at a time. To make this "separation of concerns" work, it is important that the required relationships between the documents be verified.

a. The module guide must show clearly that each of the mathematical functions described in the re-

quirements specification is the responsibility of a specific module. There must be no ambiguity about the responsibilities of the various modules. The module specifications must be consistent with the module guide and the requirements specification.

b. Each module design document should include argumentation showing that the internal design satisfies the module specification. If the module specification is mathematical [18], mathematical verification of the design correctness is possible [11].

c. The module design document, which describes the algorithms, must be clearly mapped onto the code. The algorithms may be described in an abstract notation or via hierarchically structured diagrams.

d. The test plan must show how the tests are derived and how they cover the requirements. The test plan must include black box module tests as well as black box system tests.

Why is configuration management essential for rigorous reviews?

Because of the complexity of software, and the amount of detail that must be taken into consideration, there is always a tremendous amount of documentation. Some of the most troublesome software errors occur when documents are allowed to get out-of-date while their authors work with pencil notes on their own copies.

For the highly structured review process outlined earlier to succeed, all documents must be kept consistent when changes are made. If a document is changed, it, and all documents related to it, must be reviewed again. A careful review of the software may take weeks or months. Each reviewer must be certain that the documents given to him are consistent and up-to-date. The time and energy of reviewers should not be wasted, comparing different versions of the same document.

A process known in the profession as *configuration management*, supported by a configuration control mechanism, is needed to ensure that every designer and reviewer has the latest version of the documents and is informed of every change in a document that might affect the review.

We should be exploiting computer technology to make sure that programmers, designers, and reviewers do not need to retain paper copies of the documents at all. Instead, they use online documentation. If a change must be made, all who have used the affected document should be notified of the change by the computer system. When a change is being considered, but is not yet approved, users of the document should receive a warning. The online versions must be kept under strict control so they cannot be changed without authorization. Every page must contain a version identifier that makes it easier for a reviewer to verify that the documents he has used represent a consistent snapshot.

MODULAR STRUCTURE

Modern software engineering standards call for software to be organized in accordance with a principle

40

known variously as "Information Hiding," "Object-Oriented Programming," "Separation of Concerns," "Encapsulation," "Data Abstraction," etc. This principle is designed to increase the cohesion of the modules while reducing the "coupling" between modules. Several new textbooks, well-known programming languages such as ADA, practical languages such as MESA, PROTEL, and MODULA, are designed to support such an organization.

Any large program must be organized into programmer work assignments known as modules. In information-hiding designs, each module hides a secret, a fact, or closely related set of facts, about the design that does not need to be known by the writers and reviewers of other modules. Each work assignment becomes much simpler than in an old-fashioned design because it can be completed and understood without knowing much about the other modules. When changes are needed, they do not ripple through an unpredictable number of other modules, as they frequently do in more conventional software designs.

A number of practical systems illustrate the benefits of information hiding even when the designers did not use that abstract principle but depended on their own intuition. For example, the widely used UNIX operating system gains much of its flexibility from hiding the difference between files and devices.

The thought of hiding information from others often strikes engineers as unnatural and wrong. In engineering projects, careful scrutiny by others working on the project is considered an important part of quality control. However, information hiding occurs naturally in large multidisciplinary projects. An electrical engineer may use a transformer without understanding its molecular structure or knowing the size of the bolts that fasten it to a chassis. The circuit designer works with a specification that specifies such abstractions as voltage ratio, hysteresis curve, and linearity. Designers of large mechanical structures work with abstract descriptions of the girders and other components, not with the detailed molecular structures that are the concern of materials engineers. Large engineering projects would be impossible if every engineer on the project had to be familiar with all the details of every component of the product.

Large software projects have the complexity of huge multidisciplinary projects, but there is only one discipline involved. Consequently, information hiding does not occur naturally and must be introduced as an engineering discipline. Software engineers should be trained to provide and use abstract mathematical specifications of components just as other engineers do.

The criterion of information hiding does not determine the software structure. Software engineers try to minimize the information that one programmer must have about another's work. They also try to minimize the expected cost of a system over the period of its use. Both information and expected cost are probabilistic measures. For maximum benefit, one should hide those details most likely to change but does not need to hide facts that are fundamental and unlikely to change. Further, decisions likely to be changed and reviewed together should be hidden in the same module. This implies that to apply the principle, one must make assumptions about the likelihood of various types of changes. If two designers apply the information-hiding principle, but make different assumptions about the likelihood of changes, they will come up with different structures.

RELIABILITY ASSESSMENT FOR SAFETY-CRITICAL SOFTWARE

Should we discuss the reliability of software at all?

Manufacturers, users, and regulatory agencies are often concerned about the reliability of systems that include software. Over many decades, reliability engineers have developed sophisticated methods of estimating the reliability of hardware systems based upon estimates of the reliability of their components. Software is often viewed as one of those components and an estimate of the reliability of that component is deemed essential to estimating the reliability of the overall system.

Reliability engineers are often misled by their experience with hardware. They are usually concerned with the reliability of devices that work correctly when new, but wear out and fail as they age. In other cases, they are concerned with mass-produced components where manufacturing techniques introduce defects that affect only a small fraction of the devices. Neither of these situations applies to software. Software does not wear out, and the errors introduced when software is copied have not been found to be significant.

As a result of these differences, it is not uncommon to see reliability assessments for large systems based on an estimated software reliability of 1.0. Reliability engineers argue that the correctness of a software product is not a probabilistic phenomenon. The software is either correct (reliability 1.0) or incorrect (reliability 0). If they assume a reliability of 0, they cannot get a useful reliability estimate for the system containing the software. Consequently, they assume correctness. Many consider it nonsense to talk about "reliability of software."

Nonetheless, our practical experience is that software appears to exhibit stochastic properties. It is quite useful to associate reliability figures such as MTBF (Mean Time Between Failures) with an operating system or other software product. Some software experts attribute the apparently random behavior to our ignorance. They believe that all software failures would be predictable if we fully understood the software, but our failure to understand our own creations justifies the treatment of software failures as random. However, we know that if we studied the software long enough, we could obtain a complete description of its response to inputs. Even then, it would be useful to talk about the MTBF of the product. Hence, ignorance should not satisfy us as a philosophical justification.

When a program first fails to function properly, it is because of an input sequence that had not occurred before. The reason that software appears to exhibit random behavior, and the reason that it is useful to talk about the MTBF of software, is because the input sequences are unpredictable. When we talk about the failure rate of a software product, we are predicting the probability of encountering an input sequence that will cause the product to fail.

Strictly speaking, we should not consider software as a component in systems at all. The software is simply the initial data in the computer and it is the initialized computer that is the component in question. However, in practice, the reliability of the hardware is high and failures caused by software errors dominate those caused by hardware problems.

What should we be measuring?

What we intuitively call "software reliability" is the probability of not encountering a sequence of inputs that leads to failure. If we could accurately characterize the sequences that lead to failure we would simply measure the distribution of input histories directly. Because of our ignorance of the actual properties of the software, we must use the software itself to measure the frequency with which failure-inducing sequences occur as inputs.

In safety-critical applications, particularly those for which a failure would be considered catastrophic, we may wish to take the position that design errors that would lead to failure are always unacceptable. In other technologies we would not put a system with a known design error in service. The complexity of software, and its consequent poor track record, means we seldom have confidence that software is free of serious design errors. Under those circumstances, we may wish to evaluate the probability that serious errors have been missed by our tests. This gives rise to our second probabilistic measure of software quality, *trustworthiness*.

In the sequel we shall refer to the probability that an input will not cause a failure as the reliability of the software. We shall refer to the probability that no serious design error remains after the software passes a set of randomly chosen tests as the trustworthiness of the software. We will discuss how to obtain estimates of both of these quantities.

Some discussions about software systems use the terms *availability* and *reliability* as if they were interchangeable. Availability usually refers to the fraction of time that the system is running and assumed to be ready to function. Availability can depend strongly on the time it takes to return a system to service once it has failed. If a system is truly safety-critical (e.g., a shutdown system in a nuclear power station), we would not depend on it during the time it was unavailable. The nuclear reactor would be taken out of service while its shutdown system was being repaired. Con-

sequently, reliability and availability can be quite different.

For systems that function correctly only in rare emergencies, we wish to measure the reliability in those situations where the system must take corrective action, and not include data from situations in which the system is not needed. The input sequence distributions used in reliability assessment should be those that one would encounter in emergency situations, and not those that characterize normal operation.

Much of the literature on software reliability is concerned with estimation and prediction of error-rates, the number of errors per line of code. For safety purposes, such rates are both meaningless and unimportant. Error counts are meaningless because we cannot find an objective way to count errors. We can count the number of lines in the code that are changed to eliminate a problem, but there usually are many ways to alleviate that problem. If each approach to repairing the problem involves a different number of lines (which is usually the case), the number of errors in the code is a subjective, often arbitrary, judgment. Error counts are unimportant because a program with a high error count is not necessarily less reliable than one with a low error count. In other words, even if we could count the number of errors, reliability is not a function of the error count. If asked to evaluate a safety-critical software product, there is no point in attempting to estimate or predict the number of errors remaining in a program.

Other portions of the literature are concerned with reliability growth models. These attempt to predict the reliability of the next (corrected) version on the basis of reliability data collected from previous versions. Most assume the failure rate is reduced whenever an error is corrected. They also assume the reductions in failure rates resulting from each correction are predictable. These assumptions are not justified by either theoretical or empirical studies of programs. Reliability growth models may be useful for management and scheduling purposes, but for safety-critical applications one must treat each modification of the program as a new program. Because even small changes can have major effects, we should consider data obtained from previous versions of the program to be irrelevant.

We cannot predict a software failure rate from failure rates for individual lines or subprograms.

The essence of system-reliability studies is the computation of the reliability of a large system when given the reliability of the parts. It is tempting to try to do the same thing for software, but the temptation should be resisted. The lines or statements of a program are not analogous to the components of a hardware system. The components of a hardware system function independently and simultaneously. The lines of a computer program function sequentially and the effect of one execution depends on the state that results from the earlier executions. One failure at one part of a program may lead to many problems elsewhere in the code.

When evaluating the reliability of a safety-critical software product, the only sound approach is to treat the whole computer, hardware and software, as a black box.

The finite state machine model of programs

The following discussion is based on the simplest and oldest model of digital computing. Used for more than 50 years, this model recognizes that every digital computer has a finite number of states and there are only a finite number of possible input and output signals at any moment in time. Each machine is described by two functions: *next-state*, and *output*. Both have a domain consisting of (state, input) pairs. The range of the next-state function is the set of states. The range of the output function is a set of symbols known as the output alphabet. These functions describe the behavior of a machine that starts in a specified initial state and periodically selects new states and outputs in accordance with the functions.

In this model, the software can be viewed as part of the initial data. It determines the initial state of the programmed machine. Von Neumann introduced a machine architecture in which program and data could be intermixed. Practicing programmers know they can always replace code with data or vice versa. It does not make sense to deal with the program and data as if they were different.

In effect, loading a program in the machine selects a terminal submachine consisting of all states that can be reached from the initial state. The software can be viewed as a finite state machine described by two very large tables. This model of software allows us to define what we mean by the number of faults in the software; it is the number of entries in the table that specify behavior that would be considered unacceptable. This fault count has no simple relation to the number of errors made by the programmer or the number of statements that must be corrected to remove the faults. It serves only to help us to determine the number of tests that we need to perform.

Use of hypothesis testing

In most safety-critical applications we do not need to know the actual probability of failure; we need to confirm the failure probability is very likely to be below a specified upper bound. We propose to run random tests on the software, checking the result of each test. Since we are concerned with safety-critical software, if a test fails (i.e., reveals an error in the software), we will change the software in a way that we believe will correct the error. We will again begin random testing. We will continue such tests until we have sufficient data to convince us that the probability of a failure is acceptably low. Because we can execute only a very small fraction of the conceivable tests, we can never be sure that the probability of failure is low enough. We can, however, calculate the probability that a product with unacceptable reliability would have passed the test that we have carried out.

TABLE I. Probability That a System With Failure Probability of .001 Will Pass N Successive Tests

N	$M = (1 - 1/h)^N$
500	0.60638
600	0.54865
700	0.49641
800	0.44915
900	0.40639
1000	0.3670
1500	0.22296
2000	0.13520
2500	0.08198
3000	0.04971
3500	0.03014
4000	0.01828
4500	0.01108
4700	0.00907
5000	0.00672

$h = 1000.$

Let us assume the probability of a failure in a test of a program is $1/h$ (i.e., the reliability is $1 - 1/h$). Assuming that N randomly selected tests (chosen, with replacement, from a distribution that corresponds to the actual usage of the program) are performed, the probability there will be no failure encountered during the testing is

$$(1 - 1/h)^N = M. \qquad (1)$$

In other words, if we want the failure probability to be less than $1/h$, and we have run N tests without failure, the probability that an unacceptable product would pass our test is no higher than M. We must continue testing, without failure, until N is large enough to make M acceptably low. We could then make statements like, "the probability that a product with reliability worse than .999 would pass this test is less than one in a hundred." Table I provides some sample values of M for $h = 1000$ and various values of N.

Table I shows that, if our design target was to have the probability of failure be less than 1 in 1000, performing between 4500 and 5000 tests (randomly chosen from the appropriate test case distribution) without failure would mean that the probability of an unacceptable product passing the test was less than 1 in a hundred.

Because the probability of failure in practice is a function of the distribution of cases encountered in practice, the validity of this approach depends on the distribution of cases in the tests being typical of the distribution of cases encountered in practice.

We can consider using the same approach to obtain a measure of the trustworthiness of a program. Let the total number of cases from which we select tests be C. Assume we consider it unacceptable if F of those cases results in faulty behavior; (F might be 1). By substituting F/C for $1/h$ we obtain

$$(1 - F/C)^N = M. \qquad (2)$$

We now assume that we have carried out N randomly selected tests without finding an error. If, during that testing, we had found an error, we would have corrected the problem and started again. We can estimate the value of C, and must determine whether to use $F = 1$ or some higher value. We might pick a higher number if we thought it unlikely that there would be only 1 faulty (state, input) pair. In most computer programs, a programming error would result in many faulty pairs, and calculations using $F = 1$ are unnecessarily pessimistic. After choosing F, we can determine M as above. (F, M) pairs provide a measure of trustworthiness. Note that systems considered trustworthy would have relatively low values of M and F.

As a result of such tests we could make statements like, "The probability that a program with more than five unacceptable cases would pass this test is one in a hundred." Since we are not concerned with the frequency of failure of those cases in practice, the tests should be chosen from a distribution in which all state input combinations are equally likely. Because C is almost always large and F relatively small, it is not practical to evaluate trustworthiness by means of testing. Trustworthiness, in the sense that we have defined it here, must be obtained by means of formal, rigorous inspections.

It is common to try to achieve high reliability by using two or more programs in an arrangement that will be safe if one of their specified subsets fails. For example, one could have two safety systems and make sure that each one could alone take the necessary actions in an emergency. If the system failures are statistically independent, the probability of the joint system failing is the product of the probability of individual failures. Unfortunately, repeated experiments have shown that, even when the programs for the two systems are developed independently, the failures are correlated [6, 7, 8]. As a result, we should evaluate the probability of joint failure experimentally.

The hypothesis testing approach can be applied to the evaluation of the probability of joint failures of two (or more) systems. Both systems must be subjected to the same set of test conditions. Joint failures can be detected. However, because the permitted probability of failures for joint systems is much lower than for single systems, many more tests will be needed. Table II shows some typical values.

In this table, we have been quite vague about the nature of a single test and have focused on how many tests are needed. Next we will discuss what constitutes a test and how to select one or more tests.

Three classes of programs

The simplest class of programs to test comprises

TABLE II. Probability That a System With Failure Probability of .000001 Will Pass N Successive Tests

$h = 1000000.$		$h = 1000000.$	
N	$M = (1 - 1/h)^N$	N	$M = (1 - 1/h)^N$
1000000.	0.36788	4000000.	0.01832
2000000.	0.13534	4100000.	0.01657
3000000.	0.04979	4200000.	0.01500
4000000.	0.01832	4300000.	0.01357
5000000.	0.00674	4400000.	0.01228
6000000.	0.00248	4500000.	0.01111
7000000.	0.00091	4600000.	0.01005
8000000.	0.00034	4700000.	0.00910
9000000.	0.00012	4800000.	0.00823
10000000.	0.00005	4900000.	0.00745

those that terminate after each use and retain no data from one run to the next. These memoryless batch programs are provided with data, executed, and return an answer that is independent of any data provided in earlier executions.

A second class consists of batch programs that retain data from one run to the next. The behavior of such programs on the nth run can depend on data supplied in any previous run.

A third class contains programs that appear to run continuously. Often these real-time programs are intended to emulate or replace analogue equipment. They consist of one or more processes; some of those processes run periodically, others run sporadically in response to external events. One cannot identify discrete runs, and the behavior at any time may depend on events arbitrarily far in the past.

Reliability estimates for memoryless batch programs: For memoryless batch programs a test consists of a single run using a randomly selected set of input data. If we are concerned with a system required to take action in rare circumstances, and one in which action in other circumstances is inconvenient rather than unsafe, the population of possible test cases should be restricted to those in which the system should take action. It is essential that one know the reliability under those circumstances. Of course, additional tests can be conducted, using other data, to determine the probability of action being taken when no action is required.

Reliability estimates for batch programs with memory: When a batch program has memory, a test consists of a single run. However, a test case is selected by choosing both input data and an internal state. For reliability estimates, the distribution of internal states must match that encountered in practice. It is often more difficult to determine the appropriate distribution of internal states than to find the distribution of inputs. Determining the distribution of internal states requires an understanding of, and experience with, the program.

An alternative to selecting internal states for the test would be to have each test consist of a sequence of executions. The system must be reinitialized before each new sequence. Again, the distribution of these cases must match that found in practice if the reliability estimates are to be meaningful. In addition, it is difficult to determine the length of those sequences. The sequences must be longer than the longest sequence that would occur in actual use. If the sequences are not long enough, the distribution of internal states that occur during the test may be badly skewed. In effect, this means that in actual use, the system must be reinitialized frequently so that an upper bound can be placed on the length of each test.

Reliability estimates for real-time systems: In real-time systems, the concept of a batch run does not apply. Because the real-time system is intended to simulate or replace an analogue system, the concept of an input sequence must be replaced by a multidimensional trajectory. Each such trajectory gives the input values as continuous functions of time. Each test involves a simulation in which the software can sample the inputs for the length of that trajectory.

The question of the length of the trajectory is critical in determining whether or not statistical testing is practical. In many computer systems there are states that can arise only after long periods of time. Reliability estimates derived from tests involving short trajectories will not be valid for systems that have been operating for longer periods. On the other hand, if one selects lengthy trajectories, the testing time required is likely to be impractical.

Statistical testing can be made practical if the system design is such that one can limit the length of the trajectories without invalidating the tests. To do this, one must partition the state. A small amount of the memory is reserved for data that must be retained for arbitrary amounts of time. The remaining data are reinitialized periodically. The length of the period becomes the length of the test trajectory. Testing can then proceed as if the program were a batch program with (memory-state, trajectory) pairs replacing input sequences.

If the long-term memory has a small number of states, it is best to perform statistically significant tests for each of those states. If that is impractical, one must select the states randomly in accordance with a predicted distribution. In many applications, the long-term memory corresponds to operating modes and a valid distribution can be determined.

Picking test cases for safety-critical real-time systems

Particular attention must be paid to trajectory selection if the system is required to act only in rare circumstances. Since the reliability is a function of the input distribution, the trajectories must be selected to provide accurate estimates under the conditions where performance matters. In other words, the population from which trajectories are drawn must include only trajectories in which the system must take action. Similarly,

the states of the long-term memory should be restricted to those in which the system will be critical to safety.

Determining the population of trajectories from which the tests are selected can be the most difficult part of the process. It is important to use one's knowledge of the physical situation to define a set of trajectories that can occur. Tests on impossible trajectories are not likely to lead to accurate reliability estimates. However, there is always the danger that the model used to determine these trajectories overlooks the same situation overlooked by the programmer who introduced a serious bug. It is important that any model used to eliminate *impossible* trajectories be developed independently of the program. Most safety experts would feel more comfortable if, in addition to the tests using trajectories considered possible, some statistical tests were conducted with *crazy* trajectories.

CONCLUSIONS

There is no inherent reason that software cannot be used in certain safety-critical applications, but extreme discipline in design, documentation, testing, and review is needed. It is essential that the operating conditions and requirements be well understood, and fully documented. If these conditions are not met, adequate review and testing are impossible.

The system must be structured in accordance with information hiding to make it easier to understand, review, and repair. The documentation must be complete and precise, making use of mathematical notation rather than natural language. Each stage of the design must be reviewed by independent reviewers with the specialized knowledge needed at that stage. Mathematical verification techniques must be used to make the review systematic and rigorous.

An independent agency must perform statistically valid random testing to provide estimates of the reliability of the system in critical situations. Deep knowledge and experience with the application area will be needed to determine the distribution from which the test cases should be drawn.

The vast literature on random testing is, for the most part, not relevant for safety evaluations. Because we are not interested in estimating the error rates or conducting reliability growth studies, a very simple model suffices. Hypothesis testing will allow us to evaluate the probability that the system meets our requirements. Testing to estimate reliability is only practical if a real-time system has limited long-term memory.

Testing to estimate trustworthiness is rarely practical because the number of tests required is usually quite large. Trustworthiness must be assured by the use of rigorous mathematical techniques in the review process.

The safety and trustworthiness of the system will rest on a tripod made up of testing, mathematical review, and certification of personnel and process. In this article, we have focused on two of those legs, testing and review based on mathematical documentation. The third leg will be the most difficult to implement. While there are authorities that certify professional engineers in other areas, there is no corresponding authority in software engineering. We have found that both classical engineers and computer science graduates are ill-prepared for this type of work. In the long term, those who are concerned about the use of software in safety-critical applications will have to develop appropriate educational programs [15].

Acknowledgments. Conversations with many people have helped to develop these observations. Among them are William Howden, Harlan Mills, Jim Kendall, Nancy Leveson, B. Natvik, and Kurt Asmis. In addition, we are thankful to the anonymous *Communications* referees and the editor for their constructive suggestions.

REFERENCES

1. Britton, K., and Parnas, D. A-7E software module guide. NRL Memo. Rep. 4702, December 1981.
2. Clements, P., Faulk, S., and Parnas, D. Interface specifications for the SCR (A-7E) application data types module. NRL Rep. 8734, August 23, 1983.
3. Currit, P.A., Dyer, M., and Mills, H.D. Certifying the reliability of software. *IEEE Trans. Softw. Eng. SE-12*, 1 (Jan. 1986).
4. Heninger, K. Specifying software requirements for complex systems: New techniques and their applications. *IEEE Trans. Softw. Eng. SE-6*, (Jan. 1980), 2–13.
5. Hester, S.D., Parnas, D.L., and Utter, D.F. Using documentation as a software design medium. *Bell Syst. Tech. J. 60*, 8 (Oct. 1981), 1941–1977.
6. Knight, J.C., and Leveson, N.G. An experimental evaluation of the assumption of independence in multi-version programming. *IEEE Trans. Softw. Eng. SE-12*, 1 (Jan. 1986), 96–109.
7. Knight, J.C., and Leveson, N.G. An empirical study of failure probabilities in multi-version software. Rep.
8. Leveson, N. Software safety: Why, what and how. *ACM Comp. Surveys 18*, 2 (June 1986), 125–163.
9. Mills, H.D. Engineering discipline for software procurement. COMPASS '87—Computer Assurance, June 29–July 3, 1987. Georgetown University, Washington, D.C.
10. Mills, H.D. The new math of computer programming. *Commun. ACM 18*, 1 (Jan. 1975), 43–48.
11. Mills, H.D., Basili, V.R., Gannon, J.D., and Hamlet, R.G. *Principles of Computer Programming—A Mathematical Approach.* Allyn and Bacon, Inc., 1987.
12. Mills, H.D., and Dyer, M. A formal approach to software error removal. *J. Syst. Softw.* (1987).
13. Mills, H.D., Linger, R.C., and Witt, B.I. *Structured Programming: Theory and Practice.* Addison-Wesley, Reading, Mass., 1979.
14. Parker, A., Heninger, K., Parnas, D., and Shore, J. Abstract interface specifications for the A-7E device interface module. NRL Memo. Rep. 4385, November 20, 1980.
15. Parnas, D.L. Education for computing professionals. *IEEE Comp. 23*, 1 (Jan. 1990), 17–22.
16. Parnas, D.L., and Clements, P.C. A rational design process: How and why to fake it. *IEEE Trans. Softw. Eng. SE-12*, 2 (Feb. 1986), 251–257.
17. Parnas, D.L., Heninger, K., Kallander, J., and Shore, J. Software requirements for the A-7E aircraft. NRL Rep. 3876, November 1978.
18. Parnas, D.L., and Wang, Y. The Trace assertion method of module-interface specification. Tech. Rep. 89-261. Queen's University, TRIO (Telecommunications Research Institute of Ontario). October 1989.
19. Parnas, D.L., and Weiss, D.M. Active design reviews: Principles and Practices. In *Proceedings of the 8th International Conference on Software Engineering* (London, August 1985).

ABOUT THE AUTHORS:

DAVID L. PARNAS is professor of Computing and Information Science at Queen's University in Kingston, Ontario. His work interests involve most aspects of computer system engineering. His special interests include precise abstract specifications, real-time systems, safety-critical software, program semantics, language design, software structure, process structure, and process synchronization.

A. JOHN VAN SCHOUWEN, currently completing his master's thesis at Queen's University, is a research associate at the Telecommunications Research Institute of Ontario. His research interests include formal and precise software documentation.

Authors' Present Address: Dept. of Computing and Information Science, Queen's University, Kingston, Ontario, Canada K7L 3N6.

SHU PO KWAN is a specialist in nuclear reaction and nuclear structure. He has also done research work in computer simulation and modelling. Author's Present Address: 1118 Avenue Rd., Toronto, Ontario, Canada M5N 2E6.

Chapter 2: Scheduling

Scheduling involves allocating resources and time to activities so that a system meets certain performance requirements. Scheduling is perhaps the most widely researched topic in real-time systems, because many researchers believe that deadlines are the key factor that distinguishes real-time systems from non-real-time systems. Thus they reason that the basic problem in real-time systems is ensuring that tasks meet their deadlines. Scheduling is also a well-structured and conceptually demanding problem — the sort of problem that academics like.

Two different research communities have examined scheduling problems from their own perspectives. The operations research (OR) community has focussed on job shop and flow-shop scheduling problems, with and without deadlines. These researchers assume very different resources (for example, machines and factory cells) from those assumed by computer science researchers (CPU cycles, memory). Factory floor activities typically have larger time granularities than those studied by computer scientists. Also, OR techniques are geared towards static (off-line) techniques, whereas those developed in computer science focus more on dynamic techniques. In spite of these differences, the abstract problems studied by the two communities have much in common. In this section, we examine scheduling problems mainly from the perspective of computer science. However, we have included a paper that reviews results from an OR view.

The metrics that guide scheduling decisions depend on the application areas. The need to minimize the schedule length pervades static non-real-time systems; in dynamic non-real-time systems, the primary metrics are minimizing response times and increasing the throughput. However, in static and dynamic real-time systems, the main goal is to achieve timeliness, which introduces quite different metrics.

The variety of metrics suggested for real-time systems indicates the different types of real-time systems that exist in the real world, as well as the types of requirements imposed on them. This sometimes makes it hard to compare different scheduling algorithms. Another difficulty arises from the fact that different types of task characteristics occur in practice. Tasks can be associated with computation times, resource requirements, importance levels (sometimes also called priorities or criticalness), precedence relationships, communication requirements, and of course, timing constraints. If a task is periodic, its period becomes important; if it is aperiodic, its deadline becomes important. A periodic task may have a deadline by which it must be completed. This deadline may or may not be equal to the period. Both periodic and aperiodic tasks may have start time constraints.

Let us consider some performance metrics. In the static case, an off-line schedule must be found that meets all deadlines. If many such schedules exist, a secondary metric, such as maximizing the average *earliness,* is used to choose one among them. If no such schedule exists, one that minimizes the average *tardiness* may be chosen. Since most dynamic real-time systems cannot guarantee that all deadlines will be met, maximizing the number of arrivals that meet their deadlines is often used as a metric.

Related to metrics is the level of predictability afforded by scheduling approaches. That is, using a particular approach, how well can we predict that the tasks will meet their deadlines? (We comment on this when we examine the different scheduling paradigms.)

There are several scheduling paradigms currently in vogue. The *table-driven* approach is often encountered in static systems. It applies to periodic tasks. Given task characteristics, a table is constructed that identifies the start and completion times of each task, and tasks are dispatched according to this table. This approach is highly predictable, but also highly inflexible since any change to the tasks and their characteristics may require a complete overhaul of the table.

The traditionally adopted dynamic approach is *priority-based preemptive scheduling.* In this approach, tasks have priorities that may be statically or dynamically assigned. At any given time, the task with the highest priority executes. This latter requirement necessitates preemption: if a low-priority task is executing and a higher-priority task arrives, the former is preempted and the processor is given to the new arrival. If priorities are assigned systematically — say, using the rate-monotonic approach [Liu and Layland 73] — utilization bounds can be derived. If a set of tasks do not exceed the bound, they can be scheduled without missing any deadlines.

An important problem that has received a lot of attention recently concerns *priority inversion*, wherein a higher-priority task cannot execute because a lower-priority task is holding a resource that it currently needs. If care is not taken, a task may block for an unbounded length of time. The rate-monotonic framework has been extended (see the papers in the next section on uniprocessor scheduling) to bound the duration of priority inversion so that schedulability analysis is still possible. Cyclic scheduling, ubiquitous in large-scale dynamic real-time systems [Carlow84], is a combination of both table-driven scheduling and priority scheduling. Here, tasks are assigned one of a set of harmonic periods. Within each period, tasks are dispatched according to a table that just lists the order in which the tasks execute. It is slightly more flexible than the table-driven approach because no start times are specified and it is amenable to a priori bound analysis — if maximum requirements of tasks in each cycle are known beforehand. However, pessimistic assumptions are necessary for determining these requirements. Rather than making worst case assumptions, confidence in a cyclic schedule is obtained by very elaborate and extensive simulations of typical scenarios, which are both error-prone and expensive.

Another approach that provides the flexibility of dynamic approaches with some of the predictability of static approaches is based on the notion of dynamic guarantees. Here, after a task arrives but before its execution begins, an attempt is made to create a schedule that contains the previously guaranteed tasks as well as the new arrival. If the attempt fails and if the attempt is made sufficiently ahead of the deadline, time is available to take alternative actions. This approach provides for predictability with respect to individual arrivals. In contrast, if a system uses a purely priority-driven preemptive approach — say, using task deadlines as priorities — a task could be preempted any time during its execution. In this case you cannot know whether a timing constraint will be met until the deadline arrives or until the task finishes, whichever comes first.

Another dimension to the scheduling problem has been added recently with the approach of trading quality of a task's results for its timely production of results. This is variously called *imprecise computations* or *anytime algorithms*. In this case, improving the interrelated requirements of timeliness and quality becomes important and, as we will see later, leads to further performance metrics and further scheduling approaches.

Different scheduling algorithms are also necessitated by the nature of the processing resources used. Approaches for dealing with tasks on a single processor do not always work well when applied to multiple processors. A completely different approach is often necessary when a distributed system is considered. For the most part, real-time scheduling work has focussed on single-processor systems; multiprocessors and distributed systems have more recently attracted attention. Hence the rest of this section is divided into two subsections, one that deals with single processor systems, one that examines work on parallel and distributed systems.

Uniprocessor scheduling

Priority-driven preemptive-scheduling is used most often in time-sharing systems. In non-real-time systems, a job's priority changes depending on whether it is CPU-bound or I/O-bound. In real-time systems, priority assignment is related to the time constraints associated with a job or task, and this assignment can be either static or dynamic.

Static priorities are attractive because a task's priority is assigned once it arrives and does not have to be reevaluated as time progresses. The rate-monotonic (RM) priority assignment is a static priority-based policy applicable to periodic tasks — the smaller the period, the higher the priority of a task. This assignment is also intuitively easy to understand. A dynamic priority assignment policy, however, can be applied to both periodic and aperiodic tasks — the smaller a task's deadline, the higher its priority. This again is an intuitive priority assignment policy. In contrast to static priorities, a task's dynamic priority may change, for example, when a new task with an earlier deadline arrives. This makes using dynamic priorities more expensive in terms of runtime overheads.

The advantage of either of these two priority assignment policies is that they offer schedulability bounds on resource utilization for periodic tasks. That is, as long as the total resource utilization does not exceed the bound, a given set of tasks can be scheduled to meet their deadlines. In the case of the RM policy the bound is 0.69 in the worst case. Better bounds based on more exact characterization of the RM policy can be found in [Lehoczky et al. 89]. If the periods are harmonics of the smallest period, the bound is 1.00. In the case of the deadline-based policy, the bound is always 1.00.

NASA used the RM policy in its software for Apollo missions, but Liu and Layland were the first to publish a formal characterization and analysis of the policy, in 1973. After a long hiatus, it was picked up again by Sha, Lehoczky, and their colleagues, as well as by Baker and others who extended it in a variety of ways to deal with shared resources, aperiodic tasks, tasks with different importance levels, and mode changes. Four papers in this section describe these extensions.

When tasks with different priorities access shared resources, priority inversion can occur. Suppose task t_1 is currently accessing a shared resource S in exclusive mode and a new higher priority task t_2 arrives. Even though t_1 is preemptable, t_2 cannot access S unless it is released by t_1. This implies that a higher priority task is now waiting for a lower priority task to complete — a phenomenon antithetic to priority driven scheduling, called priority inversion. In fact, the presence of shared resources leads to other problems such as chained blocking and, even worse, deadlocks. The former has the problem of producing very long priority inversion intervals and with the latter, no bounds on task execution times can be found. Clearly, the presence of shared exclusive resources introduces problems that need careful and thoughtful handling.

Obviously, unless all the shared resources themselves are also preemptable, some amount of priority inversion is unavoidable. (Making all shared resources preemptable has its own problems: all the changes to a resource have to be undone, which may or may not be possible. Even if it is possible, the resource is unavailable during this time.) The key is to place a bound on the priority inversion interval. In "Priority Inheritance Protocols: An Approach to Real-Time Synchronization," Sha, Rajkumar, and Lohoczky describe and analyze a class of protocols that bound the priority inversion interval for any task. This interval is the length of the longest critical section within which a shared resource is accessed. The crux of the protocol lies in allowing a task (t_1 in the example above) that blocks a higher priority task (t_2) to *inherit* the (higher) priority (that is, the priority of t_2). The authors use this basic idea and, combined with the notion of priority ceilings of resources, develop the Priority Ceiling Protocol (PCP) for which the priority inversion interval is bounded and resource utilization bounds exist. These bounds preserve the attractive features of an RM algorithm (namely, a priori determinable predictability and static priority assignment) even when tasks access shared resources.

A variant of PCP, called the stack resource policy (SRP) is described in "Stack-Based Scheduling of Real-Time Processes" by Ted Baker. Unlike PCP, SRP uses two task attributes. A *preemption level* is computed using *static* task parameters and is used in the determination of worst case blocking times. A task also has a priority level that can be dynamic; for instance, it can be assigned based on the task's deadline. Priority levels and preemption levels are required to satisfy the following requirement: If a task T has a higher priority than T' but arrives after T', then T must have a higher preemption level than T'. A task cannot begin execution without a guarantee that it will not block for further resources. In SRP, the runtime stack is explicitly treated as a resource. This reduces the number of context switches, but can result in reduced concurrency, since resource usage is based on pessimistic assumptions. SRP also provides for the use of resources for which multiple units are available.

A typical real-time system moves from one mode of execution to another. For example, the space shuttle has different requirements and different sets of tasks and resources for the different phases of its flight [Carlow84]. The following questions then arise: How do you model a mode change so that schedulability analysis can be carried out even in the presence of mode changes? How can you move from one mode of execution to another smoothly, keeping the consistency of the resources intact? How long does it take to complete the transition from one mode to another? These are the questions answered by Sha, Rajkumar, Lehoczky, and Ramamritham in "Mode Change Protocols for Priority-Driven Preemptive Scheduling." Specifically, they focus on the RM priority assignment policy. A mode change is modeled as the deletion of existing tasks and the introduction of new tasks. Modification to task parameters — for example, periods, resource needs, and so on — are modeled as the deletion of an existing task and the introduction of a new task with the changed parameters. The paper derives the conditions under which a new task can be introduced and determines the worst case mode change delay to be the largest of the periods of the tasks involved in the mode change.

This paper as well as the one that follows discuss other extensions that have been carried out with respect to the RM algorithms. In particular, they discuss the extensions that relate to the following three aspects of real-time systems: First, the method is extended to accommodate dynamically arriving (aperiodic) tasks for which the performance metric is response time. The approach is based on providing servers that execute aperiodic tasks. It discusses different types of servers, of varying responsiveness. Second, tasks with different importance levels are handled by performing *period transformations* such that a task with a higher importance is (artificially) assigned a lower period. However, the overall functionality of a task remains the same. Third, rate-monotonic theory is applied to multiprocessor systems. The idea is to first allocate tasks and resources to processors and then analyze the influence, on the schedulability, of shared access to local and global resources.

The last in the series of papers here on RM scheduling is the one by Sha and Goodenough titled "Real-Time Scheduling Theory and Ada." As the title indicates, the authors discuss how the algorithms presented in the previous two papers and the extensions just discussed can be incorporated in the programming language Ada. They first highlight several restrictions imposed by and limitations inherent in Ada's tasking model and scheduling philosophy. Subsequently they show that with an *enlightened* interpretation of Ada's scheduling rules, with appropriate modifications to the runtime support system, and with suitable guidelines for real-time programming in Ada, you can accommodate the needs of RM-based scheduling algorithms. (Based on the work proposed here, proposed extensions for Ada — in Ada-9x — include those needed to incorporate SRP.)

The penultimate paper in this section deals with the imprecise model of computation, trading off solution quality for timeliness. In "Algorithms for Scheduling Imprecise Computation," Liu et al. succinctly discuss the imprecise model of computation, give examples of its applicability, present several scheduling problems related to this model, and review several algorithms. They also discuss some of the overheads of different formulations of imprecise computations. These overheads can take the form of increased computation costs (for example, to prepare intermediate or partial results) and increased scheduling costs (for example, in determining which inputs to look at, or in selecting the appropriate version of a computation that can be accommodated in a given situation).

The papers we have discussed focus on scheduling independent tasks, with perhaps access to shared resources. In "Scheduling Processes with Release Times, Deadlines, Precedence, and Exclusion Relations," Xu and Parnas examine the scheduling problem for an extended task model. Processes are divided into segments and exclusion and precedence relations are specified among segments. If an exclusion relation exists between two segments s_1 and s_2, then s_1's execution can not be interrupted by s_2 and vice versa. Exclusion relations can be used to model resource access conflicts. The algorithm uses a branch and bound technique in which an initial schedule, which orders processes by their deadlines, is modified at each step to reduce the maximum lateness of the processes. A schedule with a maximum lateness of zero or negative meets all deadlines. If a feasible schedule is not found then the algorithm at least derives a schedule with the smallest maximum lateness. The authors compare the performance of their algorithm with another that schedules *processes* that exclude each other and show that their algorithm reduces the number of nodes examined in the search tree for the sample problems studied. This algorithm is designed to be applied off-line.

Multiprocessor and distributed scheduling

The first paper in this section reviews the state of the art in scheduling multiple machines from an operations research perspective. As mentioned earlier, the scheduling problems tackled in OR have a slightly different flavor than scheduling in the CS literature. For instance, manpower scheduling, project scheduling, and scheduling of machines are some of the topics studied in OR. This paper reviews work in the scheduling of machines. It looks at scheduling involving identical, uniform, and unrelated machines. It also examines job shop and flow-shop scheduling problems. Different types of optimization problems are examined with a focus on polynomially bound algorithms. Some of the metrics of interest are: minimizing maximum cost, minimizing the sum of completion times, minimizing schedule length, minimizing tardiness, and minimizing the number of tardy jobs. Many significant NP-completeness results are also included.

Given an application made up of multiple (precedence-related) communicating tasks, how should the modules be allocated to nodes in a distributed system such that the *response time* of each invocation of the application is minimized? This is the question posed by Chu and Lan in "Task Allocation and Precedence Relations for Distributed Real-Time Systems." Precedence relations among tasks, task computation times, and the cost of intertask communication are the factors studied. The authors base their solution on two observations: 1) it is important to minimize the load on the bottleneck processor, which is the processor with the maximum load on it, and 2) the computation time of two communicating tasks should be considered in deciding whether they must be allocated to the same node. Intertask communication is assumed to occur through shared, and perhaps replicated, files. The paper uses a combination of analytical techniques and heuristic approaches to allocate tasks in an application to a distributed system. They show that an approach that takes the precedence constraints into account does better than one that does not.

The next two papers in this section deal with algorithms used with the guarantee notion introduced earlier. A task is guaranteed by constructing a plan for task execution whereby all guaranteed tasks meet their timing constraints. A task is guaranteed subject to a set of assumptions, for example, about its worst-case execution time, and the nature of faults in the system. If these assumptions hold, once a task is guaranteed it *will* meet its timing requirements. A guarantee algorithm must consider many issues including the presence of periodic tasks, preemptable tasks, precedence constraints (which are used to handle task groups), multiple importance levels for tasks, and fault tolerance requirements. In a distributed system, when a task arrives at a node, the scheduler at that node attempts to guarantee that the task will complete execution before its deadline, on that node. If the attempt fails, the scheduling components on individual nodes cooperate to determine which other node in the system has sufficient resource surplus to guarantee the task. The two papers included here discuss the basic approaches to these two aspects of the guarantee approach. Other details can be found in [Ramamritham and Stankovic 91].

In "Distributed Scheduling of Tasks with Deadlines and Resource Requirements," Ramamritham, Stankovic, and Zhao propose and evaluate four algorithms for cooperation. The algorithms differ in the way a node treats a task that cannot be guaranteed locally. In the *random scheduling algorithm*, the task is sent to a randomly selected node. In the *focussed addressing algorithm*, the task is sent to a node that is estimated to have sufficient surplus resources and time to complete the task before its deadline. In the *bidding algorithm*, the task is sent to a node based on the bids received for the task from nodes in the system. And, in the *flexible algorithm*, the task is sent to a node based on a technique that combines bidding and focussed addressing.

Through simulations, the authors compare these algorithms to each other and to two baselines. The first baseline is the non-cooperative algorithm where a task that cannot be guaranteed locally is not sent to any other node. The second is an (ideal) algorithm that behaves exactly like the bidding algorithm but incurs no communication overheads. The fact that distributed scheduling improves the performance of a hard real-time system is attested by the better performance of the flexible algorithm compared to the non-cooperative baseline under all load distributions. The performance of the flexible algorithm is better than both the focussed addressing and bidding algorithms. However, the performance difference between the bidding algorithm and the flexible algorithm under small communication delays is negligible. The same can be said about the performance difference between the focussed addressing algorithm and the flexible algorithm at large communication delays. The random algorithm performs quite well compared to the flexible algorithm, especially when system load is low, as well as when system load is high and the load is unevenly distributed. Under moderate loads, its performance falls short by a few percentage points which may be significant in a hard real-time system. Overall, the studies show that no algorithm outperforms all others in all system states. Though the flexible algorithm performs better than the rest in most cases, it is more complex than the other algorithms. Other details of the distributed scheduling algorithms can be found in [Ramamritham and Stankovic 84], [Ramamritham et al. 89], and [Stankovic et al. 85]. The stability of these algorithms is discussed in [Stankovic 85].

Note that in the context of guarantees, the metric of interest is the percentage of arriving tasks that are guaranteed. The manner in which resources and task (code) are allocated to the individual nodes affects the performance of the guarantee algorithms. The second paper in this section deals with such an allocation problem, albeit in a different context.

In "Efficient Scheduling Algorithms for Real-Time Multiprocessor Systems," Ramamritham, Stankovic, and Shiah describe the basic version of the guarantee algorithm that handles non-preemptable tasks given their arrival time, deadline or period, worst case computation time, and resource requirements. A task uses a resource either in shared mode or in exclusive mode and holds a requested resource as long as it executes. Using heuristics, a full feasible schedule for a set of tasks is constructed in the following way. Starting at the root of the search tree which is an empty schedule the algorithm tries to extend the schedule (with one more task) by moving to one of the vertices at the next level in the search tree until a full feasible schedule is derived. To this end, a heuristic function H synthesizes various characteristics of tasks affecting real-time scheduling decisions to actively direct the scheduling to a plausible path. H is applied to, at most, k tasks that remain to be scheduled at each level of search. The task with the smallest value of function H is selected to extend the current partial schedule. If a partial schedule is found to be infeasible, it is possible to backtrack and then continue the search. If the value of k is constant (and in practice, k will be small when compared to the task set size n), the complexity is linearly proportional to n, the size of the task set [Ramamritham et al. 89]. While the complexity is proportional to n, the algorithm is programmed so that it incurs a fixed worst case cost by limiting the number of H function evaluations permitted in any one invocation of the algorithm. The paper also discusses how to choose k. Extensive simulation studies of the algorithm show that a heuristic that combines deadline and resource requirement information works very well (see also [Zhao et al. 87], [Zhao and Ramamritham 87], and [Ramamritham et al. 90]). [Wang et al. 90] derives another dimension of the heuristic algorithm: the bound on the length of the schedule compared to an optimal algorithm.

Priority Inheritance Protocols: An Approach to Real-Time Synchronization

LUI SHA, MEMBER, IEEE, RAGUNATHAN RAJKUMAR, MEMBER, IEEE, AND JOHN P. LEHOCZKY, MEMBER, IEEE

Abstract— A direct application of commonly used synchronization primitives such as semaphores, monitors, or the Ada rendezvous can lead to uncontrolled priority inversion, a situation in which a higher priority job is blocked by lower priority jobs for an indefinite period of time. In this paper, we investigate two protocols belonging to the class of *priority inheritance protocols*, called the *basic priority inheritance protocol* and the *priority ceiling protocol*. We show that both protocols solve this uncontrolled priority inversion problem. In particular, the priority ceiling protocol reduces the worst case task blocking time to at most the duration of execution of a single critical section of a lower priority task. In addition, this protocol prevents the formation of deadlocks. We also derive a set of sufficient conditions under which a set of periodic tasks using this protocol is schedulable.

Index Terms— Priority inheritance, priority inversion, real-time systems, scheduling, synchronization.

I. INTRODUCTION

THE SCHEDULING of jobs with hard deadlines has been an important area of research in real-time computer systems. Both nonpreemptive and preemptive scheduling algorithms have been studied in the literature [3], [4], [6]–[8], [10], [11]. An important problem that arises in the context of such real-time systems is the effect of blocking caused by the need for the synchronization of jobs that share logical or physical resources. Mok [9] showed that the problem of deciding whether it is possible to schedule a set of periodic processes is NP-hard when periodic processes use semaphores to enforce mutual exclusion. One approach to the scheduling of real-time jobs when synchronization primitives are used is to try to dynamically construct a feasible schedule at run-time. Mok [9] developed a procedure to generate feasible schedules with a kernelized monitor, which does not permit the preemption of jobs in critical sections. It is an effective technique for the case where the critical sections are short. Zhao, Ramamritham, and Stankovic [14], [15] investigated the use

of heuristic algorithms to generate feasible schedules. Their heuristic has a high probability of success in the generation of feasible schedules.

In this paper, we investigate the synchronization problem in the context of priority-driven preemptive scheduling, an approach used in many real-time systems. The importance of this approach is underscored by the fact that Ada, the language mandated by the U.S. Department of Defense for all its real-time systems, supports such a scheduling discipline. Unfortunately, a direct application of synchronization mechanisms like the Ada rendezvous, semaphores, or monitors can lead to uncontrolled priority inversion: a high priority job being blocked by a lower priority job for an indefinite period of time. Such priority inversion poses a serious problem in real-time systems by adversely affecting both the schedulability and predictability of real-time systems. In this paper, we formally investigate the priority inheritance protocol as a priority management scheme for synchronization primitives that remedies the uncontrolled priority inversion problem. We formally define the protocols in a uniprocessor environment and in terms of binary semaphores. In Section II, we review the problems of existing synchronization primitives, and define the basic concepts and notation. In Section III, we define the basic priority inheritance protocol and analyze its properties. In Section IV, we define an enhanced version of the basic priority inheritance protocol referred to as the priority ceiling protocol and investigate its properties. Section V analyzes the impact of this protocol on schedulability analysis when the rate-monotonic scheduling algorithm is used and Section VI examines the implication considerations as well as some possible enhancements to the priority ceiling protocol. Finally, Section VII presents the concluding remarks.

II. THE PRIORITY INVERSION PROBLEM

Ideally, a high-priority job J should be able to preempt lower priority jobs immediately upon J's initiation. Priority inversion is the phenomenon where a higher priority job is blocked by lower priority jobs. A common situation arises when two jobs attempt to access shared data. To maintain consistency, the access must be serialized. If the higher priority job gains access first then the proper priority order is maintained; however, if the lower priority job gains access first and then the higher priority job requests access to the shared data, this higher priority job is blocked until the lower priority job completes its access to the shared data. Thus, *blocking* is a form of priority inversion where a higher priority job must wait for the processing of a lower priority job. Prolonged du-

Manuscript received December 1, 1987; revised May 1, 1988. This work was supported in part by the Office of Naval Research under Contract N00014-84-K-0734, in part by Naval Ocean Systems Center under Contract N66001-87-C-0155, and in part by the Federal Systems Division of IBM Corporation under University Agreement YA-278067.

L. Sha is with the Software Engineering Institute and the Department of Computer Science, Carnegie Mellon University, Pittsburgh, PA 15213.

R. Rajkumar is with IBM Thomas J. Watson Research Center, Yorktown Heights, NY 10598.

J. P. Lehoczky is with the Department of Statistics, Carnegie Mellon University, Pittsburgh, PA 15213.

IEEE Log Number 9037197.

0-8186-3792-7/93 $03.00 © 1990 IEEE

rations of blocking may lead to the missing of deadlines even at a low level of resource utilization. The level of resource utilization attainable before a deadline is missed is referred to as the *schedulability* of the system. To maintain a high degree of schedulability, we will develop protocols that would minimize the amount of blocking. It is also important to be able to analyze the performance of any proposed protocol in order to determine the schedulability of real-time tasks that use this protocol.

Common synchronization primitives include semaphores, locks, monitors, and Ada rendezvous. Although the use of these or equivalent methods is necessary to protect the consistency of shared data or to guarantee the proper use of non-preemptable resources, their use may jeopardize the ability of the system to meet its timing requirements. In fact, a direct application of these synchronization mechanisms can lead to an indefinite period of priority inversion and a low level of schedulability.

Example 1: Suppose that J_1, J_2, and J_3 are three jobs arranged in descending order of priority with J_1 having the highest priority. We assume that jobs J_1 and J_3 share a data structure guarded by a binary semaphore S. Suppose that at time t_1, job J_3 locks the semaphore S and executes its critical section. During the execution of job J_3's critical section, the high priority job J_1 is initiated, preempts J_3, and later attempts to use the shared data. However, job J_1 will be blocked on the semaphore S. We would expect that J_1, being the highest priority job, will be blocked no longer than the time for job J_3 to complete its critical section. However, the duration of blocking is, in fact, unpredictable. This is because job J_3 can be preempted by the intermediate priority job J_2. The blocking of J_3, and hence that of J_1, will continue until J_2 and any other pending intermediate jobs are completed.

The blocking period in Example 1 can be arbitrarily long. This situation can be partially remedied if a job in its critical section is not allowed to be preempted; however, this solution is only appropriate for very short critical sections, because it creates unnecessary blocking. For instance, once a low priority job enters a long critical section, a high priority job which does not access the shared data structure may be needlessly blocked. An identical problem exists in the use of monitors. The priority inversion problem was first discussed by Lampson and Redell [2] in the context of monitors. They suggest that the monitor be executed at a priority level higher than all tasks that would ever call the monitor. In the case of the Ada rendezvous, when a high priority job (task) is waiting in the entry queue of a server job, the server itself can be preempted by an independent job J, if job J's priority is higher than both the priority of the server and the job which is currently in rendezvous with the server. Raising the server priority to be higher than all its callers would avoid this particular problem but would create a new problem: a low priority job may unnecessarily block the execution of independent higher priority jobs via the use of the server.

The use of *priority inheritance protocols* is one approach to rectify the priority inversion problem in existing synchronization primitives. Before we investigate these protocols, we first define the basic concepts and state our assumptions. A *job* is a sequence of instructions that will continuously use the processor until its completion if it is executing alone on the processor. That is, we assume that jobs do not suspend themselves, say for I/O operations; however, such a situation can be accommodated by defining two or more jobs. In addition, we assume that the critical sections of a job are *properly* nested and a job will release all of its locks, if it holds any, before or at the end of its execution. In all our discussions below, we assume that jobs J_1, J_2, $\cdots$, J_n are listed in descending order of priority with J_1 having the highest priority. A *periodic task* is a sequence of the same type of job occurring at regular intervals, and an *aperiodic task* is a sequence of the same type of job occurring at irregular intervals. Each task is assigned a fixed priority, and every job of the same task is initially assigned that task's priority. If several jobs are eligible to run, the highest priority job will be run. Jobs with the same priority are executed in a FCFS discipline. When a job J is forced to wait for the execution of lower priority jobs, job J is said to be "blocked." When a job waits for the execution of high priority jobs or equal priority jobs that have arrived earlier, it is not considered as "blocked." We now state our notation.

Notation:

- J_i denotes a job, i.e., an instance of a task τ_i. P_i and T_i denote the priority and period of task τ_i, respectively.
- A binary semaphore guarding shared data and/or resource is denoted by S_i. $P(S_i)$ and $V(S_i)$ denote the indivisible operations *lock* (wait) and *unlock* (signal), respectively, on the binary semaphore S_i.
- The jth critical section in job J_i is denoted by $z_{i,j}$ and corresponds to the code segment of job J_i between the jth P operation and its corresponding V operation. The semaphore that is locked and released by critical section $z_{i,j}$ is denoted by $S_{i,j}$.
- We write $z_{i,j} \subset z_{i,k}$ if the critical section $z_{i,j}$ is entirely contained in $z_{i,k}$.
- The duration of execution of the critical section $z_{i,j}$, denoted $d_{i,j}$, is the time to execute $z_{i,j}$ when J_i executes on the processor alone.

We assume that critical sections are properly nested. That is, given any pair of critical sections $z_{i,j}$ and $z_{i,k}$, then either $z_{i,j} \subset z_{i,k}$, $z_{i,k} \subset z_{i,j}$, or $z_{i,j} \cap z_{i,k} = \varnothing$. In addition, we assume that a semaphore may be locked at most once in a single nested critical section.

Definition: A job J is said to be blocked by the critical section $z_{i,j}$ of job J_i if J_i has a lower priority than J but J has to wait for J_i to exit $z_{i,j}$ in order to continue execution.

Definition: A job J is said to be blocked by job J_i through semaphore S, if the critical section $z_{i,j}$ blocks J and $S_{i,j} = S$.

In the next two sections, we will introduce the concept of priority inheritance and a priority inheritance protocol called the priority ceiling protocol. An important feature of this protocol is that one can develop a schedulability analysis for it in the sense that a schedulability bound can be determined. If the utilization of the task set stays below this bound, then the deadlines of all the tasks can be guaranteed. In order to create such a bound, it is necessary to determine the worst case duration of priority inversion that any task can encounter. This worst case blocking duration will depend upon the particular protocol in use.

Notation: $\beta_{i,j}$ denotes the set of all critical sections of the lower priority job J_j which can block J_i. That is, $\beta_{i,j} = \{z_{j,k} | j > i \text{ and } z_{j,k} \text{ can block } J_i\}$.[1]

Since we consider only properly nested critical sections, the set of blocking critical sections is partially ordered by set inclusion. Using this partial ordering, we can reduce our attention to the set of maximal elements of $\beta_{i,j}$, $\beta_{i,j}^*$. Specifically, we have $\beta_{i,j}^* = \{z_{j,k} | (z_{j,k} \in \beta_{i,j}) \wedge (\sim \exists z_{j,m} \in \beta_{i,j} \text{ such that } z_{j,k} \subset z_{j,m})\}$.

The set $\beta_{i,j}^*$ contains the longest critical sections of J_j which can block J_i and eliminates redundant inner critical sections. For purposes of schedulability analysis, we will restrict attention to $\beta^* = \bigcup_{j>i} \beta_{i,j}^*$, the set of all longest critical sections that can block J_i.

III. THE BASIC PRIORITY INHERITANCE PROTOCOL

The basic idea of priority inheritance protocols is that when a job J blocks one or more higher priority jobs, it ignores its original priority assignment and executes its critical section at the highest priority level of all the jobs it blocks. After exiting its critical section, job J returns to its original priority level. To illustrate this idea, we apply this protocol to Example 1. Suppose that job J_1 is blocked by job J_3. The priority inheritance protocol requires that job J_3 execute its critical section at job J_1's priority. As a result, job J_2 will be unable to preempt job J_3 and will itself be blocked. That is, the higher priority job J_2 must wait for the critical section of the lower priority job J_3 to be executed, because job J_3 "inherits" the priority of job J_1. Otherwise, J_1 will be indirectly preempted by J_2. When J_3 exits its critical section, it regains its assigned lowest priority and awakens J_1 which was blocked by J_3. Job J_1, having the highest priority, immediately preempts J_3 and runs to completion. This enables J_2 and J_3 to resume in succession and run to completion.

A. The Definition of the Basic Protocol

We now define the basic priority inheritance protocol.

1) Job J, which has the highest priority among the jobs ready to run, is assigned the processor. Before job J enters a critical section, it must first obtain the lock on the semaphore S guarding the critical section. Job J will be blocked, and the lock on S will be denied, if semaphore S has been already locked. In this case, job J is said to be blocked by the job which holds the lock on S. Otherwise, job J will obtain the lock on semaphore S and enter its critical section. When job J exits its critical section, the binary semaphore associated with the critical section will be unlocked, and the highest priority job, if any, blocked by job J will be awakened.

2) A job J uses its assigned priority, unless it is in its critical section and blocks higher priority jobs. If job J blocks higher priority jobs, J inherits (uses) P_H, the highest prior-

ity of the jobs blocked by J. When J exits a critical section, it resumes the priority it had at the point of entry into the critical section.[2]

3) Priority inheritance is transitive. For instance, suppose J_1, J_2, and J_3 are three jobs in descending order of priority. Then, if job J_3 blocks job J_2, and J_2 blocks job J_1, J_3 would inherit the priority of J_1 via J_2. Finally, the operations of priority inheritance and of the resumption of original priority must be indivisible.[3]

4) A job J can preempt another job J_L if job J is not blocked and its priority is higher than the priority, inherited or assigned, at which job J_L is executing.

It is helpful to summarize that under the basic priority inheritance protocol, a high priority job can be blocked by a low-priority job in one of two situations. First, there is the *direct* blocking, a situation in which a higher priority job attempts to lock a locked semaphore. Direct blocking is necessary to ensure the consistency of shared data. Second, a medium priority job J_1 can be blocked by a low priority job J_2, which inherits the priority of a high priority job J_0. We refer to this form of blocking as *push-through* blocking, which is necessary to avoid having a high-priority job J_0 being indirectly preempted by the execution of a medium priority job J_1.

B. The Properties of the Basic Protocol

We now proceed to analyze the properties of the basic priority inheritance protocol defined above. In this section, we assume that deadlock is prevented by some external means, e.g., semaphores are accessed in an order that is consistent with a predefined acyclical order. Throughout this section, β_i^* refers to the sets of the longest critical sections that can block J_i when the basic priority inheritance protocol is used.

Lemma 1: A job J_H can be blocked by a lower priority job J_L, only if J_L is executing within a critical section $z_{L,j} \in \beta_{H,L}^*$, when J_H is initiated.

Proof: By the definitions of the basic priority inheritance protocol and the blocking set $\beta_{H,L}^*$, task J_L can block J_H only if it directly blocks J_H or has its priority raised above J_H through priority inheritance. In either case, the critical section $z_{L,j}$ currently being executed by J_L is in $\beta_{H,L}^*$. If J_L is not within a critical section which cannot directly block J_H and cannot lead to the inheritance of a priority higher than J_H, then J_L can be preempted by J_H and can never block J_H.

Lemma 2: Under the basic priority inheritance protocol, a high priority job J_H can be blocked by a lower priority job J_L for at most the duration of one critical section of $\beta_{H,L}^*$ regardless of the number of semaphores J and J_L share.

Proof: By Lemma 1, for J_L to block J_H, J_L must be currently executing a critical section $z_{L,j} \in \beta_{H,L}^*$. Once J_L exits $z_{L,j}$, it can be preempted by J_H and J_H cannot be blocked by J_L again.

---

[1] Note that the second suffix of $\beta_{i,j}$ and the first suffix of $z_{j,k}$ correspond to job J_j.

[2] For example, when J executes $V(S_2)$ in $\{P(S_1), \cdots, P(S_2), \cdots, V(S_2), \cdots, V(S_1)\}$, it reverts to the priority it had before it executed $P(S_2)$. This may be lower than its current priority and cause J to be preempted by a higher priority task. J would, of course, still hold the lock on S_1.

[3] The operations must be indivisible in order to maintain internal consistency of data structures being manipulated in the run-time system.

Theorem 3: Under the basic priority inheritance protocol, given a job J_0 for which there are n lower priority jobs $\{J_1, \cdots, J_n\}$, job J_0 can be blocked for at most the duration of one critical section in *each* of $\beta^*_{0,i}$, $1 \leq i \leq n$.

Proof: By Lemma 2, each of the n lower priority jobs can block job J_0 for at most the duration of a single critical section in each of the blocking sets $\beta^*_{0,i}$.

We now determine the bound on the blockings as a function of the semaphores shared by jobs.

Lemma 4: A semaphore S can cause push-through blocking to job J, only if S is accessed both by a job which has priority lower than that of J and by a job which has or can inherit priority equal to or higher than that of J.

Proof: Suppose that J_L accesses semaphore S and has priority lower than that of J. According to the priority inheritance protocol, if S is not accessed by a job which has or can inherit priority equal to or higher than that of J, then job J_L's critical section guarded by S cannot inherit a priority equal to or higher than that of J. In this case, job J_L will be preempted by job J and the lemma follows.

We next define $\zeta^*_{i,j,k}$ to be the set of all longest critical sections of job J_j guarded by semaphore S_k and which can block job J_i either directly or via push-through blocking. That is, $\zeta^*_{i,j,k} = \{z_{j,p} | z_{j,p} \in \beta^*_{i,j} \text{ and } s_{j,p} = S_k\}$.

Let $\zeta^*_{i,\cdot,k} = \bigcup_{j \geq i} \zeta^*_{i,j,k}$ represent the set of all longest critical sections corresponding to semaphore S_k which can block J_i.

Lemma 5: Under the basic priority inheritance protocol, a job J_i can encounter blocking by at most one critical section in $\zeta^*_{i,\cdot,k}$ for each semaphore S_k, $1 \leq k \leq m$, where m is the number of distinct semaphores.

Proof: By Lemma 1, job J_L can block a higher priority job J_H if J_L is currently executing a critical section in $\beta^*_{H,L}$. Any such critical section corresponds to the locking and unlocking of a semaphore S_k. Since we deal only with binary semaphores, only one of the lower priority jobs can be within a blocking critical section corresponding to a particular semaphore S_k. Once this critical section is exited, the lower priority job J_L can no longer block J_H. Consequently, only one critical section in β^*_i corresponding to semaphore S_k can block J_H. The lemma follows.

Theorem 6: Under the basic priority inheritance protocol, if there are m semaphores which can block job J, then J can be blocked by at most m times.

Proof: It follows from Lemma 5 that job J can be blocked at most once by each of the m semaphores.

Theorems 3 and 6 place an upper bound on the *total* blocking delay that a job can encounter. Given these results, it is possible to determine at compile-time the worst case blocking duration of a job. For instance, if there are four semaphores which can potentially block job J and there are three other lower priority tasks, J may be blocked for a maximum duration of three longest subcritical sections. Moreover, one can find the worst case blocking durations for a job by studying the durations of the critical sections in $\beta^*_{i,j}$ and $\zeta^*_{i,\cdot,k}$.

Still, the basic priority inheritance protocol has the following two problems. First, this basic protocol, by itself, does not prevent deadlocks. For example, suppose that at time t_1, job

J_2 locks semaphore S_2 and enters its critical section. At time t_2, job J_2 attempts to make a nested access to lock semaphore S_1. However, job J_1, a higher priority job, is ready at this time. Job J_1 preempts job J_2 and locks semaphore S_1. Next, if job J_1 tries to lock semaphore S_2, a deadlock is formed.

The deadlock problem can be solved, say, by imposing a total ordering on the semaphore accesses. Still, a second problem exists. The blocking duration for a job, though bounded, can still be substantial, because a *chain* of blocking can be formed. For instance, suppose that J_1 needs to sequentially access S_1 and S_2. Also suppose that J_2 preempts J_3 within the critical section $z_{3,1}$ and enters the critical section $z_{2,2}$. Job J_1 is initiated at this instant and finds that the semaphores S_1 and S_2 have been respectively locked by the lower priority jobs J_3 and J_2. As a result, J_1 would be blocked for the duration of two critical sections, once to wait for J_3 to release S_1 and again to wait for J_2 to release S_2. Thus, a blocking chain is formed.

We present in the next section the priority ceiling protocol that addresses effectively both these problems posed by the basic priority inheritance protocol.

IV. The Priority Ceiling Protocol

A. Overview

The goal of this protocol is to prevent the formation of deadlocks and of chained blocking. The underlying idea of this protocol is to ensure that when a job J preempts the critical section of another job and executes its own critical section z, the priority at which this new critical section z will execute is guaranteed to be higher than the inherited priorities of all the preempted critical sections. If this condition cannot be satisfied, job J is denied entry into the critical section z and suspended, and the job that blocks J inherits J's priority. This idea is realized by first assigning a priority ceiling to each semaphore, which is equal to the highest priority task that may use this semaphore. We then allow a job J to start a new critical section only if J's priority is higher than all priority ceilings of all the semaphores locked by jobs other than J. Example 2 illustrates this idea and the deadlock avoidance property while Example 3 illustrates the avoidance of chained blocking.

Example 2: Suppose that we have three jobs J_0, J_1, and J_2 in the system. In addition, there are two shared data structures protected by the binary semaphores S_1 and S_2, respectively. We define the *priority ceiling* of a semaphore as the priority of the highest priority job that may lock this semaphore. Suppose the sequence of processing steps for each job is as follows.

$$J_0 = \{\cdots, P(S_0), \cdots, V(S_0), \cdots\}$$

$$J_1 = \{\cdots, P(S_1), \cdots, P(S_2), \cdots, V(S_2), \cdots, V(S_1), \cdots\}$$

$$J_2 = \{\cdots, P(S_2), \cdots, P(S_1), \cdots, V(S_1), \cdots, V(S_2), \cdots\}.$$

Recall that the priority of job J_1 is assumed to be higher than that of job J_2. Thus, the priority ceilings of both semaphores S_1 and S_2 are equal to the priority of job J_1.

The sequence of events described below is depicted in Fig. 1. A line at a low level indicates that the corresponding job

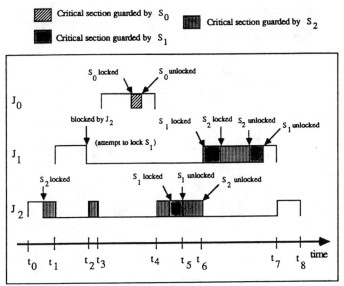

S_0 locked S_0 unlocked

J_0

blocked by J_2 S_1 locked S_2 locked S_2 unlocked S_1 unlocked

(attempt to lock S_1)

J_1

S_2 locked S_1 locked S_1 unlocked S_2 unlocked

J_2

time

t_0 t_1 t_2 t_3 t_4 t_5 t_6 t_7 t_8

Fig. 1.   Sequence of events described in Example 2.

is blocked or has been preempted by a higher priority job. A line raised to a higher level indicates that the job is executing. The absence of a line indicates that the job has not yet been initiated or has completed. Shaded portions indicate execution of critical sections. Suppose that

- At time t_0, J_2 is initiated and it begins execution and then locks semaphore S_2.
- At time t_1, job J_1 is initiated and preempts job J_2.
- At time t_2, job J_1 tries to enter its critical section by making an indivisible system call to execute $P(S_1)$. However, the run-time system will find that job J_1's priority is *not* higher than the priority ceiling of *locked* semaphore S_2. Hence, the run-time system suspends job J_1 without locking S_1. Job J_2 now *inherits* the priority of job J_1 and resumes execution. Note that J_1 is blocked outside its critical section. As J_1 is not given the lock on S_1 but suspended instead, the potential deadlock involving J_1 and J_2 is prevented.
- At time t_3, J_2 is still in its critical section and the highest priority job J_0 is initiated and preempts J_2. Later, J_0 attempts to lock semaphore S_0. Since the priority of J_0 is higher than the priority ceiling of locked semaphore S_2, job J_0 will be granted the lock on the semaphore S_0. Job J_0 will therefore continue and execute its critical section, thereby effectively preempting J_2 in its critical section and not encountering any blocking.
- At time t_4, J_0 has exited its critical section and completes execution. Job J_2 resumes, since J_1 is blocked by J_2 and cannot execute. J_2 continues execution and locks S_1.
- At time t_5, J_2 releases S_1.
- At time t_6, J_2 releases S_2 and resumes its assigned priority. Now, J_1 is signaled and having a higher priority, it preempts J_2, resumes execution, and locks S_2. Then, J_1 locks S_1, executes the nested critical section, and unlocks S_1. Later it unlocks S_2 and executes its noncritical section code.
- At t_7, J_1 completes execution and J_2 resumes.

- At t_8, J_2 completes.

Note that in the above example, J_0 is never blocked because its priority is higher than the priority ceilings of semaphores S_1 and S_2. J_1 was blocked by the lower priority job J_2 during the intervals $[t_2, t_3]$ and $[t_4, t_6]$. However, these intervals correspond to part of the duration that J_2 needs to lock S_2. Thus, J_1 is blocked for no more than the duration of one critical section of a lower priority job J_2 even though the actual blocking occurs over disjoint time intervals. It is, indeed, a property of this protocol that any job can be blocked for at most the duration of a single critical section of a lower priority job. This property is further illustrated by the following example.

Example 3: Consider the example from the previous section where a chain of blockings can be formed. We assumed that job J_1 needs to access S_1 and S_2 sequentially while J_2 accesses S_2 and J_3 accesses S_1. Hence, the priority ceilings of semaphores S_1 and S_2 are equal to P_1. As before, let job J_3 lock S_1 at time t_0. At time t_1, job J_2 is initiated and preempts J_3. However, at time t_2, when J_2 attempts to lock S_2, the run-time system finds that the priority of J_2 is *not* higher than the priority ceiling P_1 of the *locked* semaphore S_1. Hence, J_2 is denied the lock on S_2 and blocked. Job J_3 resumes execution at J_2's priority. At time t_3, when J_3 is still in its critical section, J_1 is initiated and finds that only one semaphore S_1 is locked. At time t_4, J_1 is blocked by J_3 which holds the lock on S_1. Hence, J_3 inherits the priority of J_1. At time t_5, job J_3 exits its critical section $z_{3,1}$, resumes its original priority, and awakens J_1. Job J_3, having the highest priority, preempts J_3 and runs to completion. Next, J_2 which is no longer blocked completes its execution and is followed by J_3.

Again, note that J_1 is blocked by J_3 in the interval $[t_4, t_5]$ which corresponds to the single critical section $z_{3,1}$. Also, job J_2 is blocked by J_3 in the disjoint intervals $[t_2, t_3]$ and $[t_4, t_5]$ which also correspond to the same critical section $z_{3,1}$.

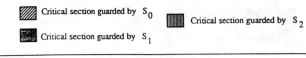

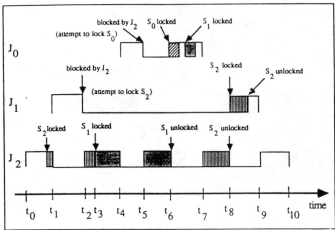

Fig. 2. Sequence of events described in Example 4.

B. Definition

Having illustrated the basic idea of the priority ceiling protocol and its properties, we now present its definition.

1) Job J, which has the highest priority among the jobs ready to run, is assigned the processor, and let S^* be the semaphore with the highest priority ceiling of all semaphores currently locked by jobs other than job J. Before job J enters its critical section, it must first obtain the lock on the semaphore S guarding the shared data structure. Job J will be blocked and the lock on S will be denied, if the priority of job J is not higher than the priority ceiling of semaphore S^*.[4] In this case, job J is said to be blocked on semaphore S^* and to be blocked by the job which holds the lock on S^*. Otherwise, job J will obtain the lock on semaphore S and enter its critical section. When a job J exits its critical section, the binary semaphore associated with the critical section will be unlocked and the highest priority job, if any, blocked by job J will be awakened.

2) A job J uses its assigned priority, unless it is in its critical section and blocks higher priority jobs. If job J blocks higher priority jobs, J inherits P_H, the highest priority of the jobs blocked by J. When J exits a critical section, it resumes the priority it had at the point of entry into the critical section.[5] Priority inheritance is transitive. Finally, the operations of priority inheritance and of the resumption of previous priority must be indivisible.

3) A job J, when it does not attempt to enter a critical section, can preempt another job J_L if its priority is higher than the priority, inherited or assigned, at which job J_L is executing.

We shall illustrate the priority ceiling protocol using an example.

[4] Note that if S has been already locked, the priority ceiling of S will be at least equal to the priority of J. Because job J's priority is not higher than the priority ceiling of the semaphore S locked by another job, J will be blocked. Hence, this rule implies that if a job J attempts to lock a semaphore that has been already locked, J will be denied the lock and blocked instead.

[5] That is, when J exits the part of a critical section, it resumes its previous priority.

Example 4: We assume that the priority of job J_i is higher than that of job J_{i+1}. The processing steps in each job are as follows:

Job J_0 accesses $z_{0,0}$ and $z_{0,1}$ by executing the steps

$$\{\cdots, P(S_0), \cdots, V(S_0), \cdots, P(S_1), \cdots, V(S_1), \cdots\},$$

job J_1 accesses only $z_{1,2}$ by executing

$$\{\cdots, P(S_2), \cdots, V(S_2), \cdots\},$$

and job J_2 accesses $z_{2,2}$ and makes a nested semaphore access to S_1 by executing

$$\{\cdots, P(S_2), \cdots, P(S_1), \cdots, V(S_1), \cdots, V(S_2), \cdots\}.$$

Note that the priority ceilings of semaphores S_0 and S_1 are equal to P_0, and the priority ceiling of semaphore S_2 is P_1. Fig. 2 depicts the sequence of events described below. Suppose that

- At time t_0, job J_2 begins execution and later locks S_2.
- At time t_1, job J_1 is initiated, preempts J_2, and begins execution.
- At time t_2, while attempting to access S_2 already locked by J_2, job J_1 becomes blocked. Job J_2 now resumes the execution of its critical section $z_{2,2}$ at its inherited priority of J_1, namely P_1.
- At time t_3, job J_2 successfully enters its nested critical section $z_{2,1}$ by locking S_1. Job J_2 is allowed to lock S_1, because there is no semaphore S^* which is locked by other jobs.
- At time t_4, job J_2 is still executing $z_{2,1}$ but the highest priority job J_0 is initiated. Job J_0 preempts J_2 within $z_{2,1}$ and executes its own noncritical section code. This is possible because P_0, the priority of J_0, is higher than P_1, the inherited priority level at which job J_2's $z_{2,1}$ was being executed.
- At time t_5, job J_0 attempts to enter its critical section $z_{0,0}$

58

by locking S_0, which is not locked by any job. However, since the priority of job J_0 is not higher than the priority ceiling P_0 of the locked semaphore S_1, job J_0 is blocked by job J_2 which holds the lock on S_1. This is a new form of blocking introduced by the priority ceiling protocol in addition to the direct and push-through blocking encountered in the basic protocol. At this point, job J_2 resumes its execution of $z_{2,1}$ at the newly inherited priority level of P_0.

- At time t_6, job J_2 exits its critical section $z_{2,1}$. Semaphore S_1 is now unlocked, job J_2 returns to the previously inherited priority of P_1, and job J_0 is awakened. At this point, J_0 preempts job J_2, because its priority P_0 is higher than the priority ceiling P_1 of S_2. Job J_0 will be granted the lock on S_0 and will execute its critical section $z_{0,0}$. Later, it unlocks S_0 and then locks and unlocks S_1.
- At time t_7, job J_0 completes its execution, and job J_2 resumes its execution of $z_{2,2}$ at its inherited priority P_1.
- At time t_8, job J_2 exits $z_{2,2}$, semaphore S_2 is unlocked, job J_2 returns to its own priority P_2, and job J_1 is awakened. At this point, J_1 preempts job J_2 and J_1 is granted the lock on S_2. Later, J_1 unlocks S_2 and executes its noncritical section code.
- At time t_9, job J_1 completes its execution and finally job J_2 resumes its execution, until it also completes at time t_{10}.

The priority ceiling protocol introduces a third type of blocking in addition to direct blocking and push-through blocking caused by the basic priority inheritance protocol. An instance of this new type of blocking occurs at time t_5 in the above example. We shall refer to this form of blocking as *ceiling* blocking. Ceiling blocking is needed for the avoidance of deadlock and of chained blocking. This avoidance approach belongs to the class of pessimistic protocols which sometimes create unnecessary blocking. Although the priority ceiling protocol introduces a new form of blocking, the worst case blocking is dramatically improved. Under the basic priority inheritance protocol, a job J can be blocked for at most the duration of $\min(n, m)$ critical sections, where n is the number of lower priority jobs that could block J and m is the number of semaphores that can be used to block J. On the contrary, under the priority ceiling protocol a job J can be blocked for at most the duration of one longest subcritical section.

C. The Properties of the Priority Ceiling Protocol

Before we prove the properties of this protocol, it is important to recall the two basic assumptions about jobs. First, a job is assumed to be a sequence of instructions that will continuously execute until its completion, when it executes alone on a processor. Second, a job will release all of its locks, if it ever holds any, before or at the end of its execution. The relaxation of our first assumption is addressed at the end of this section. Throughout this section, the sets $\beta_{i,j}$, $\beta_{i,j}^*$, and β_i^* refer to the blocking sets associated with the priority ceiling protocol.

Lemma 7: A job J can be blocked by a lower priority job J_L, only if the priority of job J is no higher than the highest priority ceiling of all the semaphores that are locked by all lower priority jobs when J is initiated.

Proof: Suppose that when J is initiated, the priority of job J is higher than the highest priority ceiling of all the semaphores that are currently locked by all lower priority jobs. By the definition of the priority ceiling protocol, job J can always preempt the execution of job J_L, and no higher priority job will ever attempt to lock those locked semaphores.

Lemma 8: Suppose that the critical section $z_{j,n}$ of job J_j is preempted by job J_i which enters its critical section $z_{i,m}$. Under the priority ceiling protocol, job J_j cannot inherit a priority level which is higher than or equal to that of job J_i until job J_i completes.

Proof: Suppose that job J_j inherits a priority that is higher than or equal to that of job J_i before J_i completes. Hence, there must exist a job J which is blocked by J_j. In addition, J's priority must be higher than or equal to that of job J_i. We now show the contradiction that J cannot be blocked by J_j. Since job J_i preempts the critical section $z_{j,n}$ of job J_j and enters its own critical section $z_{i,m}$, job J_i's priority must be higher than the priority ceilings of all the semaphores currently locked by all lower priority jobs. Since J's priority is assumed to be higher than or equal to that of J_i, it follows that job J's priority is also higher than the priority ceilings of all the semaphores currently locked by all lower priority jobs. By Lemma 7, J cannot be blocked by J_j. Hence, the contradiction and the lemma follows.

Definition: Transitive blocking is said to occur if a job J is blocked by J_i which, in turn, is blocked by another job J_j.

Lemma 9: The priority ceiling protocol prevents transitive blocking.

Proof: Suppose that transitive blocking is possible. Let J_3 block job J_2 and let job J_2 block job J_1. By the transitivity of the protocol, job J_3 will inherit the priority of J_1 which is assumed to be higher than that of job J_2. This contradicts Lemma 8, which shows that J_3 cannot inherit a priority that is higher than or equal to that of job J_2. The lemma follows.

Theorem 10: The priority ceiling protocol prevents deadlocks.

Proof: First, by assumption, a job cannot deadlock with itself. Thus, a deadlock can only be formed by a cycle of jobs waiting for each other. Let the n jobs involved in the blocking cycle be $\{J_1, \cdots, J_n\}$. Note that each of these n jobs must be in one of its critical sections, since a job that does not hold a lock on any semaphore cannot contribute to the deadlock. By Lemma 9, the number of jobs in the blocking cycle can only be two, i.e., $n = 2$. Suppose that job J_2's critical section was preempted by job J_1, which then enters its own critical section. By Lemma 8, job J_2 can never inherit a priority which is higher than or equal to that of job J_1 before job J_1 completes. However, if a blocking cycle (deadlock) is formed, then by the transitivity of priority inheritance, job J_2 will inherit the priority of job J_1. This contradicts Lemma 8 and hence the theorem follows.

Remark: Lemma 1 is true under the priority ceiling protocol.

Remark: Suppose that the run-time system supports the

priority ceiling protocol. Theorem 10 leads to the useful result that programmers can write arbitrary sequences of properly nested semaphore accesses. As long as each job does not deadlock with itself, there will be no deadlock in the system.

Lemma 11: Let J_L be a job with a lower priority than that of job J_i. Job J_i can be blocked by job J_L for at most the duration of one critical section in $\beta_{i,L}^*$.

Proof: First, job J_i will preempt J_L if J_L is not in a critical section $z_{L,m} \in \beta_{i,L}^*$. Suppose that job J_i is blocked by $z_{L,m}$. By Theorem 10, there is no deadlock and hence job J_L will exit $z_{L,m}$ at some instant t_1. Once job J_L leaves this critical section at time t_1, job J_L can no longer block job J_i. This is because job J_i has been initiated and J_L is not within a critical section in $\beta_{i,L}^*$. It follows from Lemma 1 that job J_L can no longer block job J_i.

Theorem 12: A job J can be blocked for at most the duration of at most one element of β_i^*.

Proof: Suppose that job J can be blocked by $n > 1$ elements of β_i. By Lemma 11, the only possibility is that job J is blocked by n different lower priority jobs. Suppose that the first two lower priority jobs that block job J are J_1 and J_2. By Lemma 1, in order for both these jobs to block job J, both of them must be in a longest blocking critical section when job J is initiated. Let the lowest priority job J_2 enter its blocking critical section first, and let the highest priority ceiling of all the semaphores locked by J_2 be ρ_2. Under the priority ceiling protocol, in order for job J_1 to enter its critical section when J_2 is already inside one, the priority of job J_1 must be higher than priority ceiling ρ_2. Since we assume that job J can be blocked by job J_2, by Lemma 7 the priority of job J cannot be higher than priority ceiling ρ_2. Since the priority of job J_1 is higher than ρ_2 and the priority of job J is no higher than ρ_2, job J_1's priority must be higher than the priority of job J. This contradicts the assumption that the priority of job J is higher than that of both J_1 and J_2. Thus, it is impossible for job J to have priority higher than both jobs J_1 and J_2 and to be blocked by both of them under the priority ceiling protocol. The theorem follows immediately.

Remark: We may want to generalize the definition of a job by allowing it to suspend during its execution, for instance, to wait for I/O services to complete. The following corollary presents the upper bound on the blocking duration of a generalized job that might suspend and later resume during its execution.

Corollary 13: If a generalized job J suspends itself n times during its execution, it can be blocked by at most $n + 1$ not necessarily distinct elements of β_i^*.

V. SCHEDULABILITY ANALYSIS

Having proved the properties of the priority ceiling protocol, we now proceed to investigate the effect of blocking on the schedulability of a task set. In this section, we develop a set of *sufficient* conditions under which a set of periodic tasks using the priority ceiling protocol can be scheduled by the rate-monotonic algorithm, which assigns higher priorities to tasks with shorter periods and is an optimal static priority algorithm when tasks are independent [8]. To this end, we will use a simplified scheduling model. First, we assume that

all the tasks are periodic. Second, we assume that each job in a periodic task has deterministic execution times for both its critical and noncritical sections and that it does not synchronize with external events, i.e., a job will execute to its completion when it is the only job in the system. Finally, we assume that these periodic tasks are assigned priorities according to the rate-monotonic algorithm. Readers who are interested in more general scheduling issues, such as the reduction of aperiodic response times and the effect of task stochastic execution times, are referred to [4] and [12].

We quote the following theorem also due to Liu and Layland which was proved under the assumption of independent tasks, i.e., when there is no blocking due to data sharing and synchronization.

Theorem 14: A set of n periodic tasks scheduled by the rate-monotonic algorithm can always meet their deadlines if

$$\frac{C_1}{T_1} + \cdots + \frac{C_n}{T_n} \leq n(2^{1/n} - 1)$$

where C_i and T_i are the execution time and period of task τ_i, respectively.

Theorem 14 offers a sufficient (worst case) condition that characterizes the rate-monotonic schedulability of a given periodic task set. The following exact characterization was proved by Lehoczky, Sha, and Ding [5]. An example of the use of this theorem will be given later in this section.

Theorem 15: A set of n periodic tasks scheduled by the rate-monotonic algorithm will meet all their deadlines for all task phasings if and only if

$$\forall i, \ 1 \leq i \leq n, \qquad \min_{(k,l) \in R_i} \sum_{j=1}^{i} C_j \frac{1}{lT_k} \left\lceil \frac{lT_k}{T_j} \right\rceil$$

$$= \min_{(k,l) \in R_i} \sum_{j=1}^{i} U_j \frac{T_j}{lT_k} \left\lceil \frac{lT_k}{T_j} \right\rceil \leq 1$$

where C_j, T_j, and U_j are the execution time, period, and utilization of task τ_j, respectively, and $R_i = \{(k,l)|1 \leq k \leq i, l = 1, \cdots, \lfloor T_i/T_k \rfloor\}$.

When tasks are independent of one another, Theorems 14 and 15 provide us with the conditions under which a set of n periodic tasks can be scheduled by the rate-monotonic algorithm.[6] Although these two theorems have taken into account the effect of a task being preempted by higher priority tasks, they have not considered the effect of a job being blocked by lower priority jobs. We now consider the effect of blocking. Each element in β_i is a critical section accessed by a lower priority job and guarded by a semaphore whose priority ceiling is higher than or equal to the priority of job J_i. Hence, β_i^* can be derived from β_i. By Lemma 7 and Theorem 12, job J_i of a task τ can be blocked for at most the duration of a single element in β_i^*. Hence, the worst case blocking time for J is at most the duration of the longest element of β_i^*. We denote this worst case blocking time of a job in task τ_i by B_i. Note that given a set of n periodic tasks, $B_n = 0$, since there is no lower priority task to block τ_n.

---

[6] That is, the conditions under which all the jobs of all the n tasks will meet their deadlines.

Theorems 14 and 15 can be generalized in a straightforward fashion. In order to test the schedulability of τ_i, we need to consider both the preemptions caused by higher priority tasks and blocking from lower priority tasks along with its own utilization. The blocking of any job of τ_i can be in the form of direct blocking, push-through blocking, or ceiling blocking but does not exceed B_i. Thus, Theorem 14 becomes

Theorem 16: A set of n periodic tasks using the priority ceiling protocol can be scheduled by the rate-monotonic algorithm if the following conditions are satisfied:

$$\forall i, \ 1 \le i \le n, \qquad \frac{C_1}{T_1} + \frac{C_2}{T_2} + \cdots + \frac{C_i}{T_i} + \frac{B_i}{T_i} \le i(2^{1/i} - 1).$$

Proof: Suppose that for each task τ_i the equation is satisfied. It follows that the equation of Theorem 14 will also be satisfied with $n = i$ and C_i replaced by $C_i^* = (C_i + B_i)$. That is, in the absence of blocking, any job of task τ_i will still meet its deadline even if it executes for $(C_i + B_i)$ units of time. It follows that task τ_i, if it executes for only C_i units of time, can be delayed by B_i units of time and still meet its deadline. Hence, the theorem follows.

Remark: The first i terms in the above inequality constitute the effect of preemptions from all higher priority tasks and τ_i's own execution time, while B_i of the last term represents the worst case blocking time due to *all* lower priority tasks for any job of task τ_i. To illustrate the effect of blocking in Theorem 16, suppose that we have three harmonic tasks: $\tau_1 = (C_1 = 1, T_1 = 2)$, $\tau_2 = (C_2 = 1, T_2 = 4)$, $\tau_3 = (C_3 = 2, T_3 = 8)$. In addition, $B_1 = B_2 = 1$. Since these tasks are harmonic, the utilization bound becomes 100%. Thus, we have "$C_1/T_1 + B_1/T_1 = 1$" for task τ_1. Next, we have "$C_1/T_1 + C_2/T_2 + B_2/T_2 = 1$" for task τ_2. Finally, we have "$C_1/T_1 + C_2/T_2 + C_3/T_3 = 1$" for task τ_3. Since all three equations hold, these three tasks can meet all their deadlines.

Corollary 17: A set of n periodic tasks using the priority ceiling protocol can be scheduled by the rate-monotonic algorithm if the following condition is satisfied:

$$\frac{C_1}{T_1} + \cdots + \frac{C_n}{T_n} + \max\left(\frac{B_1}{T_1}, \cdots, \frac{B_{n-1}}{T_{n-1}}\right) \le n(2^{1/n} - 1).$$

Proof: Since $n(2^{1/n} - 1) \le i(2^{1/i} - 1)$ and $\max(B_1/T_1, \cdots, B_{n-1}/T_{n-1}) \ge B_i/T_i$, if this equation holds then all the equations in Theorem 16 also hold.

Similar to the sufficient condition in Theorem 16, the conditions in Theorem 15 can be easily generalized. Specifically,

Theorem 18: A set of n periodic tasks using the priority ceiling protocol can be scheduled by the rate-monotonic algorithm for all task phasings if

$$\forall i, \ 1 \le i \le n,$$

$$\min_{(k,l) \in R_i} \left[\sum_{j=1}^{i-1} U_j \frac{T_j}{lT_k} \left\lceil \frac{lT_k}{T_j} \right\rceil + \frac{C_i}{lT_k} + \frac{B_i}{lT_k} \right] \le 1$$

where C_i, T_i, and U_i are defined in Theorem 15, and B_i is the worst case blocking time for τ_i.

Proof: The proof is identical to that of Theorem 16.

Remark: The blocking duration B_i represents the worst case conditions and hence the necessary and sufficient conditions of Theorem 15 become sufficient conditions in Theorem 18.

The following example helps clarify the use of Theorem 18. Consider the case of three periodic tasks:

- Task τ_1: $C_1 = 40$; $T_1 = 100$; $B_1 = 20$; $U_1 = 0.4$
- Task τ_2: $C_2 = 40$; $T_2 = 150$; $B_2 = 30$; $U_2 = 0.267$
- Task τ_3: $C_3 = 100$; $T_3 = 350$; $B_3 = 0$; $U_3 = 0.286$.

Task τ_1 can be blocked by task τ_2 for at most 20 units, while τ_2 can be blocked by task τ_3 for at most 30 time units. The lowest priority task, τ_3, cannot be blocked by any lower priority tasks. The total utilization of the task set ignoring blocking is 0.952, far too large to apply the conditions of Theorem 16. Theorem 18 is checked as follows:

1) Task τ_1: Check $C_1 + B_1 \le 100$. Since $40 + 20 \le 100$, task τ_1 is schedulable.
2) Task τ_2: Check whether either

$$C_1 + C_2 + B_2 \le 100 \qquad 80 + 30 > 100$$

$$\text{or} \quad 2C_1 + C_2 + B_2 \le 150 \qquad 120 + 30 \le 150.$$

Task τ_2 is schedulable and in the worst case phasing will meet its deadline exactly at time 150.

3) Task τ_3: Check whether either

$$C_1 + C_2 + C_3 \le 100 \qquad 40 + 40 + 100 > 100$$

$$\text{or } 2C_1 + C_2 + C_3 \le 150 \qquad 80 + 40 + 100 > 150$$

$$\text{or } 2C_1 + 2C_2 + C_3 \le 200 \qquad 80 + 80 + 100 > 200$$

$$\text{or } 3C_1 + 2C_2 + C_3 \le 300 \qquad 120 + 80 + 100 = 300$$

$$\text{or } 4C_1 + 3C_2 + C_3 \le 350 \qquad 160 + 120 + 100 > 350.$$

Task τ_3 is also schedulable and in the worst case phasing will meet its deadline exactly at time 300.

VI. Applications of the Protocol and Future Work

In this section, we briefly discuss the implementation aspects of the protocol as well as the possible extensions of this work.

A. Implementation Considerations

The implementation of the basic priority inheritance protocol is rather straightforward. It requires a priority queueing of jobs blocked on a semaphore and indivisible system calls *Lock_Semaphore* and *Release_Semaphore*. These system calls perform the priority inheritance operation, in addition to the traditional operations of locking, unlocking, and semaphore queue maintenance.

The implementation of the priority ceiling protocol entails further changes. The most notable change is that we no longer maintain semaphore queues. The traditional ready queue is replaced by a single job queue *Job_Q*. The job queue is a priority-ordered list of jobs ready to run or blocked by the ceiling protocol. The job at the head of the queue is assumed to be currently running. We need only a single prioritized job queue because under the priority ceiling protocol, the job with the highest (inherited) priority is always eligible to execute. Finally, the run-time system also maintains *S_List*, a list of currently locked semaphores ordered according to their priority ceilings. Each semaphore S stores the information of the job, if any, that holds the lock on S and the ceiling of S. Indivisible system calls *Lock_Semaphore* and *Release_Semaphore* maintain *Job_Q* and *S_List*. An example of the implementation can be seen in [13].

The function *Lock_Semaphore* could also easily detect a self-deadlock where a job blocks on itself. Since the run-time system associates with each semaphore the job, if any, that holds the lock on it, a direct comparison of a job requesting a lock and the job that holds the lock determines whether a self-deadlock has occurred. If such a self-deadlock does occur, typically due to programmer error, the job could be aborted and an error message delivered.

Suppose monitors are used for achieving mutual exclusion. We again assume that a job does not suspend until its completion when it executes alone on the processor. We also assume that the job does not deadlock with itself by making nested monitor calls. A job inside a monitor inherits the priority of any higher priority job waiting on the monitor. To apply the priority ceiling protocol, each monitor is assigned a priority ceiling, and a job J can enter a monitor only if its priority is higher than the highest priority ceiling of all monitors that have been entered by other jobs. Since the priority ceiling protocol prevents deadlocks, nested monitor calls will not be deadlocked. The implications of priority ceiling protocol to Ada tasking are more complicated and are beyond the scope of this paper. Readers who are interested in this subject are referred to [1].

B. Future Work

The priority ceiling protocol is an effective real-time synchronization protocol for it prevents deadlock, reduces the blocking to at most one critical section, and is simple to implement. Nonetheless, it is still a suboptimal protocol in that it can cause blocking to a job that can be avoided by enhancements to the protocol. Although a formal treatment of possible enhancements is beyond the scope of this paper, we would like to present the ideas of some possible enhancements to stimulate more research on this subject.

For example, we can define the *priority floor* of a semaphore, analogous to its priority ceiling, as the priority of the lowest priority job that may access it. Then, a job J can lock a semaphore S if its priority is higher than the priority ceiling of S *or* if the following conditions are true. The lock on S can also be granted if the priority of J is equal to the priority ceiling of S and the priority floor of S is greater than the highest priority preempted job. This latter condition, called the *priority floor condition*, ensures that neither a preempted job nor a higher priority job accesses S. This guaran-

tees that deadlocks and chaining will be avoided. This protocol is called the *priority limit protocol*. The priority limit protocol eliminates the ceiling blocking that J_0 encounters at time t_5 in Example 4. Moreover, this protocol requires identical information as does the priority ceiling protocol and can be implemented with equal ease. However, the priority limit protocol does not improve the worst case behavior and hence the schedulability.

It is also possible to enhance the priority limit protocol by replacing the priority floor condition by the following condition. A job J can also be allowed to lock a semaphore S if the priority of J is equal to the priority of S and no preempted lower priority job accesses the semaphore S. This condition also guarantees avoidance of deadlock and chaining. This protocol is called the *job conflict protocol* and is better than the priority ceiling and priority limit protocols.[7] The job conflict protocol is, however, still a suboptimal protocol. It will be an interesting exercise to develop an optimal priority inheritance protocol, and then compare it to the priority ceiling protocol for both performance and implementation complexity.

VII. Conclusion

The scheduling of jobs with hard deadlines is an important area of research in real-time computer systems. In this paper, we have investigated the synchronization problem in the context of priority-driven preemptive scheduling. We showed that a direct application of commonly used synchronization primitives may lead to uncontrolled priority inversion, a situation in which a high priority job is indirectly preempted by lower priority jobs for an indefinite period of time. To remedy this problem, we investigated two protocols belonging to the class of *priority inheritance protocols*, called the *basic priority inheritance protocol* and the *priority ceiling protocol* in the context of a uniprocessor. We showed that both protocols solve the uncontrolled priority inversion problem. In particular, the priority ceiling protocol prevents deadlocks and reduces the blocking to at most one critical section. We also derived a set of sufficient conditions under which a set of periodic tasks using this protocol is schedulable by the rate-monotonic algorithm. Finally, we outlined implementation considerations for and possible extensions to this protocol.

Acknowledgment

The authors wish to thank D. Cornhill for his contributions on the priority inversion problems in Ada, J. Goodenough for his many insightful and detailed comments on this paper that helped us to clarify some of the key issues, and K. Ramamritham for his suggestions on the possible enhancements of this protocol. We would also like to thank H. Tokuda, T. Ess, J. Liu, and A. Stoyenko for their helpful comments. Finally, we want to thank the referees for their many fine suggestions.

References

[1] J. B. Goodenough and L. Sha, "The priority ceiling protocol: A method for minimizing the blocking of high priority Ada tasks," in *Proc. 2nd ACM Int. Workshop Real-Time Ada Issues*, 1988.
[2] B. W. Lampson and D. D. Redell, "Experiences with processes and monitors in Mesa," *Commun. ACM*, vol. 23, no. 2, pp. 105–117, Feb. 1980.

This enhancement was suggested by Krithi Ramamritham.

[3] J. P. Lehoczky and L. Sha, "Performance of real-time bus scheduling algorithms," *ACM Perform. Eval. Rev.*, Special Issue, vol. 14, no. 1, May 1986.

[4] J. P. Lehoczky, L. Sha, and J. Strosnider, "Enhancing aperiodic responsiveness in a hard real-time environment," in *Proc. IEEE Real-Time Syst. Symp.*, 1987.

[5] J. P. Lehoczky, L. Sha, and Y. Ding, "The rate monotonic scheduling algorithm—Exact characterization and average case behavior," in *Proc. IEEE Real-Time Syst. Symp.*, 1989.

[6] D. W. Leinbaugh, "Guaranteed response time in a hard real-time environment," *IEEE Trans. Software Eng.*, Jan. 1980.

[7] J. Y. Leung and M. L. Merrill, "A note on preemptive scheduling of periodic, real time tasks," *Inform. Processing Lett.*, vol. 11, no. 3, pp. 115–118, Nov. 1980.

[8] C. L. Liu and J. W. Layland, "Scheduling algorithms for multiprogramming in a hard real time environment," *J. ACM*, vol. 20, no. 1, pp. 46–61, 1973.

[9] A. K. Mok, "Fundamental design problems of distributed systems for the hard real time environment," Ph.D. dissertation, M.I.T., 1983.

[10] K. Ramamritham and J. A. Stankovic, "Dynamic task scheduling in hard real-time distributed systems," *IEEE Software*, July 1984.

[11] L. Sha, J. P. Lehoczky, and R. Rajkumar, "Solutions for some practical problems in prioritized preemptive scheduling," in *Proc. IEEE Real-Time Syst. Symp.*, 1986.

[12] L. Sha, R. Rajkumar, and J. P. Lehoczky, "Task scheduling in distributed real-time systems," in *Proc. IEEE Industrial Electron. Conf.*, 1987.

[13] ——, "Priority inheritance protocols: An approach to real-time synchronization," Tech. Rep., Dep. Comput. Sci., CMU, 1987.

[14] W. Zhao, K. Ramamritham, and J. A. Stankovic, "Scheduling tasks with resource requirements in hard real-time systems," *IEEE Trans. Software Eng.*, Apr. 1985.

[15] ——, "Preemptive scheduling under time and resource constraints," *IEEE Trans. Comput.*, Aug. 1987.

Lui Sha (S'76-M'84) received the B.S.E.E. (Hons.) degree from McGill University, Montreal, P.Q., Canada in 1978 and the M.S.E.E. and Ph.D. degrees from Carnegie-Mellon University (CMU), Pittsburgh, PA, in 1979 and 1985.

He was an engineer in the CMU Department of Computer Science from 1979 to 1984 and was a member of the Research Faculty in CMU CS department from 1985 to 1987. Since 1988 he has been a member of the Technical Staffs in the CMU's Software Engineering Institute, a member of Research Faculty in the CMU CS department, and a senior member of the Advanced Real-Time Technology (ART) project at CMU CS department. He is interested in developing analytical solutions for the problems in the construction of distributed real-time systems.

Dr. Sha is a member of the IEEE Computer Society.

Ragunathan Rajkumar (M'90) received the B.E. (Hons.) degree from the P.S.G. College of Technology, Coimbatore, India, and the M.S. and Ph.D. degrees from Carnegie Mellon University in 1986 and 1989, respectively.

He has been a Research Staff Member at the IBM Thomas J. Watson Research Center, Yorktown Heights, NY, since 1989. His interests lie in the area of real-time systems.

Dr. Rajkumar is a member of the IEEE Computer Society and the Association for Computing Machinery.

John P. Lehoczky (M'88) received the B.A. degree in mathematics from Oberlin College, Oberlin, OH, in 1965, and the M.S. and Ph.D. degrees in statistics from Stanford University, Stanford, CA, in 1967 and 1969, respectively.

He was an Assistant Professor of Statistics at Carnegie Mellon University, Pittsburgh, PA, from 1969 to 1973, Associate Professor from 1973 to 1981, and Professor from 1981 to the present. He has served as Head of the Department of Statistics since 1984. His research interests involve applied probability theory with emphasis on models in the area of computer and communication systems. In addition, he is a senior member of the Advanced Real-Time Technology (ART) Project in the Carnegie Mellon University Computer Science Department and is doing research in distributed real-time systems.

Dr. Lehoczky is a member of Phi Beta Kappa, a fellow of the Institute of Mathematical Statistics, and the American Statistical Association. He is a member of the Operations Research Society of America and the Institute of Management Science. He served as area editor of *Management Science* from 1981 to 1986.

Stack-Based Scheduling of Realtime Processes

T.P. BAKER*

Department of Computer Science, Florida State University, Tallahassee, FL 32306-4019 U.S.A.

Abstract. The Priority Ceiling Protocol (PCP) of Sha, Rajkumar and Lehoczky is a policy for locking binary semaphores that bounds priority inversion (i.e., the blocking of a job while a lower priority job executes), and thereby improves schedulability under fixed priority preemptive scheduling. We show how to extend the PCP to handle: multiunit resources, which subsume binary semaphores and reader-writer locks; dynamic priority schemes, such as earliest-deadline-first (EDF), that use static "preemption levels"; sharing of runtime stack space between jobs. These extensions can be applied independently, or together.

The Stack Resource Policy (SRP) is a variant of the SRP that incorporates the three extensions mentioned above, plus the conservative assumption that each job may require the use of a shared stack. This avoids unnecessary context switches and allows the SRP to be implemented very simply using a stack. We prove a schedulability result for EDF scheduling with the SRP that is tighter than the one proved previously for EDF with a dynamic version of the PCP.

The Minimal SRP (MSRP) is a slightly more complex variant of the SRP, which has similar properties, but imposes less blocking. The MSRP is *optimal* for stack sharing systems, in the sense that it is the least restrictive policy that strictly bounds priority inversion and prevents deadlock for rate monotone (RM) and earliest-deadline-first (EDF) scheduling.

1. Introduction

Hard realtime computer systems are subject to absolute timing requirements, which are often expressed in terms of deadlines. They are often subject to severe resource constraints; in particular, limited memory. They are also expected to be reliable in the extreme, to that it is necessary to verify *a priori* that a system design will meet timing requirements within the given resource constraints.

Verifying timing and resource utilization properties of programs is inherently difficult. In fact, it is impossible without some constraints on program structure. This is a consequence of the Halting Problem, which is known to be undecidable. To get around the Halting Problem, it is customary to assume the program is divided into a set of *jobs*, whose arrival times, execution times, and other resource requirements are known. Verification that the program satisfies timing and resource constraints then reduces to a scheduling problem. However, scheduling is also difficult. Specifically, determining whether a set of jobs can be scheduled so as to complete execution by a fixed deadline is known to be NP-hard (Garey and Johnson 1979; Leung and Merrill 1980) unless severe restrictions are placed on the problem.

Practical schedulability analysis requires a simple model of software architecture. Liu and Layland (1973) were able to obtain very strong results from such a simple model. They assumed that for jobs with hard deadlines:

*This work is supported in part by grant N00014-87-J-1166 from the U.S. Office of Naval Research.

1. there is a fixed set of such jobs;
2. requests for job executions are periodic, with a constant interval between requests;
3. relative deadlines are the same as the respective periods, i.e., a job need only complete by the arrival of the next request for it;
4. no synchronization or precedence requirements exist between jobs;
5. there is no control over phasing of periodic jobs;
6. processor time is the only resource that needs to be scheduled;
7. execution times are constant.

Subject to these assumptions, they proved that rate monotone (RM) scheduling, in which the job with the shortest period is given highest priority, is optimal among static priority policies, and that earliest-deadline-first (EDF) scheduling is optimal among dynamic priority policies. They also derived conditions for schedulability under these two policies, and for a mixture of the two.

Other researchers have discovered that some of the restrictive assumptions made by Liu and Layland can be relaxed, generally without much change to the schedulability results or their proofs. Most of these extensions have been to the RM policy: Sha, Lehoczky, and Rajkumar (1986) outline approaches to dealing with transient overloads due to variable execution times; Sprunt, Sha, and Lehoczky (1989) describe techniques for handling an aperiodic *server* job; Sha, Rajkumar, and Lehoczky (1987) show that the schedulability results can be adapted to tolerate bounded blocking, such as may be due to scheduling exclusive access to shared data. The problem of bounded blocking has also been addressed for EDF scheduling, by Chen and Lin (1989).

Liu and Layland's Theorem 5 (1973) says that a set of n periodic jobs can be scheduled by the RM policy if

$$\sum_{i=1}^{n} \frac{C_i}{T_i} \leq n \cdot (2^{1/n} - 1).$$

Here T_i and C_i denote the period and execution time of the ith job, respectively, and the jobs are ordered by increasing period.

Sha, Rajkumar, and Lehoczky's Theorem 15 (1987) generalizes this result, showing that the jobs are schedulable by the RM priority assignment if

$$\forall k \atop k=1,\ldots,n \left(\sum_{i=1}^{k} \frac{C_i}{T_i} \right) + \frac{B_k}{T_k} \leq k \cdot (2^{1/k} - 1).$$

Here B_k is an upper bound on the duration of blocking that the kth job may experience due to resources held by lower priority jobs. The authors introduce the term *priority inversion* to describe this sort of blocking.

Liu and Layland's Theorem 7 (1973) says that a set of n periodic jobs can be scheduled by the EDF policy iff[1]

$$\sum_{i=1}^{n} \frac{C_i}{T_i} \leq 1.$$

Chen and Lin's Theorem 4 (1989) extends the *if* part of this result to show that the jobs are schedulable using the dynamic PCP for semaphore locking if

$$\sum_{i=1}^{n} \frac{C_i + B_i}{T_i} \leq 1.$$

In Section 5, we will tighten this result.

For these results to be useful, the priority inversion bound, B_i, of each job must be small. This requirement has motivated the study of resource allocation policies that can strictly bound priority inversion.

A great deal of effort has been spent studying the extreme forms of unbounded blocking that are of interest to conventional operating systems designers, such as deadlock and starvation (Bic and Shaw 1988). Unfortunately, conventional operating systems techniques do not provide a tight enough bound on blocking to be suitable for realtime schedulability analysis. For example, the ordered resource allocation technique of Havender (1968) still allows a job to be blocked by up to n lower priority jobs.

Sha, Rajkumar, and Lehoczky (1987) have devised a locking protocol for binary semaphores, cxalled the Priority Ceiling Protocol (PCP), for which priority inversion is bounded by the execution time of the longest critical section of a lower-priority job. This protocol has since been extended in several directions, including reader-writer resources (Sha, Rajkumar and Lehoczky 1989), mode changes (Sha, Rajkumar and Lehoczky 1989), and multiple processors (Rajkumar, Sha and Lehoczky 1988). Several variations have been defined, including one which is optimal in the sense of avoiding unnecessary blocking (Baker 1989; Rajkumar, Sha and Lehoczky 1988). Chen and Lin have also extended the PCP to use dynamically recomputed priority ceilings, so that it can be applied with EDF as well as RM priorities (1989).

This article describes three more extensions to the PCP. These are:

1. Multi-unit resources.
   This extension is based on treating the priority ceiling of a resource as a function of the number of units that are currently available. It permits us to subsume binary semaphores and reader-writer locks.
2. Simpler support for EDF scheduling.
   This extension is based on separating the priority of a job, which may be dynamic, from its *preemption level*, which is required to be static. Preemption levels are based on the deadlines of jobs, relative to their request times. So long as these do not change, ceilings do not need to be recomputed. This extension supports EDF, RM, deadline-monotone, and combinations of these policies.
3. Sharing runtime stack resources.
   This extension is based on treating the shared runtime stack as a resource, with ceiling zero, which is requested at the time each job starts executing.

Although these three extensions can be applied independently, they work very well together. We present them here in a combined form, which we call the *Stack Resource Policy*, or *SRP*. The SRP takes one step further away from the PCP, by treating every job as if it requires the use of a shared stack. This means that if it is necessary to block a job to wait for a shared resource held by another job, this is done at the time the job attempts to preempt (and thereby occupy runtime stack space), rather than later, when it actually may need the shared resource. At the cost of some reduction in concurrency, this earlier blocking saves unnecessary context switches, and allows us to implement the SRP very simply using a stack.

We are also able to prove a schedulability result for EDF scheduling with the SRP that is tighter than the one proved in (Chen and Lin 1989) for EDF with the dynamic PCP. This proof appears to be independent of the early blocking, so that it could also apply to the dynamic PCP.

The idea of using early blocking based on preemption levels, with a shared stack, has been around for a long time. It is the way many machines handle hardware interrupts, and has been used in real-time executives for at least 15 years. However, the use of this technique appears to have been limited to fixed-priority scheduling, without consideration for locking of individual resources. Moreover, the problem of predicting schedulability of periodic task systems using this technique does not appear to have been formally addressed.

The rest of this article is organized as follows. Section 2 defines the elements of our formal model, including jobs, featherweight processes, and resources. Section 3 outlines the general reasoning underlying the SRP. Section 4 defines the SRP, and proves that it works. Section 5 gives the schedulability result for earliest-deadline-first (EDF) scheduling with the SRP. Section 6 explains the idea of stack sharing, how it leads to interactions with allocation of other resources, and how the SRP solves these interactions. Section 7 compares the SRP to the Priority Ceiling Protocol, and includes a comparative example. Section 8 describes the MSRP, which is a slightly more complex variant of the SRP, and proves that it is optimal with respect to minimizing unnecessary blocking under certain assumptions. Section 9 very briefly discusses the implementation of the SRP and its relation to more complex process models, such as Ada tasking. Section 10 summarizes the results and mentions some ongoing research.

2. Definitions

This section establishes notation, and defines the elements of our formal model. These elements include jobs, featherweight processes, resources, priorities, and preemption levels.

2.1. Jobs and processes

A *job* is a finite sequence of instructions to be executed on a single processor. It may have some branching control flow, but its maximum execution time and its other resource requirements must be fixed. A job might correspond to a subprogram in some programming language. Jobs are considered to be the lowest level of schedulable activity in a system. A job may be preempted, but never intentionally waits. (Here waiting means suspending execution until a specified time or event, as opposed to blocking because a needed resource is busy.) Names of the forms J, J', J'', ... and J_i denote jobs.

A *job execution* is an instance of execution of a specific job, in response to a *job execution request*. Each job execution request *arrives* at some time, $Arrival(\mathcal{J})$. The execution of J in response to request $\mathcal{J}$ starts at some time, $Start(\mathcal{J})$, where $Arrival(\mathcal{J}) \leq Start(\mathcal{J})$. Requests that have arrived, but for which the corresponding executions have not yet completed are called *pending*. (Note that the pending jobs include both those that have not started and those that have started execution but have not finished yet.) Names of the forms $\mathcal{J}$, $\mathcal{J}'$, $\mathcal{J}''$, ... and $\mathcal{J}_i$ denote both job execution requests and job executions.

A *featherweight process* (*process* for short) is a higher level abstraction. Every job belongs to one of a fixed finite set of processes, $\mathcal{P}_1$, ..., $\mathcal{P}_n$. Each process $\mathcal{P}_i$ is characterized by an (infinite) sequence of job execution requests $\mathcal{J}_{i,1}$, $\mathcal{J}_{i,2}$, ... A process is *periodic* if the interval between successive execution requests is a constant (called the *period*); otherwise it is *aperiodic*. The jobs requested by each process are assumed to belong to a finite set, which are known *a priori*. Names of the forms $\mathcal{P}$ and $\mathcal{P}_i$ always denote processes.

There should be no more than one execution of any job going on at the same time. This may be taken as an assumption, or as a consequence of other assumptions we will make: that each job has a static preemption level and that there is only one processor. Thus, it is usually not necessary to be very careful about distinguishing jobs from job executions and job execution requests. The current execution of job J may be referred to by the same name as the job, i.e., J. In particular, if we say *job J is actively doing something* (such as holding or requesting a resource), we mean *the current execution of job J*.

2.2. Resources

An execution of a job requires the use of a processor and runtime stack space, and may require certain other serially reusable nonpreemptable resources. Allocation of processor time, stack space, and nonpreemptable resources to jobs is governed by *processor and resource allocation policies*.

We assume there is a single processor, which is preemptable, and a finite set of *resources*, R_1, ..., R_m. These resources are all nonpreemptable and serially reusable. For each resource R there is a fixed number of units in the system, N_R. Names of the forms R and R_i always denote resources.

A job acquires an allocation of a nonpreemptable resource by executing a request instruction. Formally, an *allocation* is a triple (J, R, m), where J is a job, R is a nonpreemptable resource, and m is the number of units requested. The number of units being requested must be less than or equal to N_R. The job making a request must wait to execute its next instruction until the allocation is granted. While a job is waiting for a resource allocation the job (and the request) are said to be *blocked*. After the allocation is granted, the job holds it until the job executes an instruction that releases it. While the job holds an allocation the allocation is said to be *outstanding*.

The sequence of instructions performed by the job between the request and release operations for a resource allocation is called a *critical section* of the job for that resource. Note that there is no implication of serialization between critical sections for the same resource, if the resource has more than one unit. Each job is required to request and release resources in Last-In-First-Out (LIFO) order; so critical sections of the same job can only overlap if they are properly nested.

A critical section is *trivial* if it involves a resource that cannot cause any blocking. (For example, in Section 6, we will show shared stack resources are trivial under the SRP.) An *outermost nontrivial* critical section is nontrivial and is not nested within any other nontrivial critical section. For bounding priority inversion, we will only be interested in the execution times of *outermost nontrivial* critical sections.

Without loss of generality, semaphores and reader/writer locks can be treated as special cases of multiunit resources. For a binary semaphore, $N_R = 1$. For a reader/writer lock, N_R can be any number greater than or equal to the number of jobs that may request R. While writing, a job needs to hold all N_R units, thus blocking both readers and writers. While reading, a job needs to hold an allocation of one unit, which blocks writers but does not block any other readers.

Example. Suppose J_1, J_2, and J_3 are jobs, where the relationships of the jobs' critical sections are as shown by Figure 1. Here, an operation of the form *request* (J_i, R_j, m) means the job J_i is requesting m units of resource R_j. A *release* operation releases the most recently acquired resource allocation. (Since we assume resources are released in LIFO order, the resource and number of units are uniquely determined.) The relationship of jobs to resources in this example is also shown, schematically, in Figure 2. The arrows indicate the *may request* relationship between jobs and resources, and are labeled with the number of units the jobs may request. We are supposing $N_{R_1} = 3$, $N_{R_2} = 1$, $N_{R_3} = 3$, resource R_2 behaves as a binary semaphore, R_3 behaves as a reader/writer lock, and R_1 behaves as a more general multiunit resource.

J_1	J_2	J_3
... request $(J_1, R_2, 1)$; ... request$(J_1, R_1, 3)$; ... release; ... release; ... request$(J_1, R_3, 1)$; ... release; ...	... request$(J_2, R_3, 3)$; ... request$(J_2, R_2, 1)$; ... release; ... release; ... request$(J_2, R_1, 2)$; ... release; ...	... request$(J_3, R_3, 1)$; ... request$(J_3, R_1, 1)$; ... release; ... release; ...

Figure 1. The critical sections of J_1, J_2 and J_3.

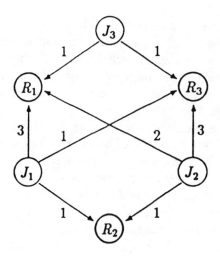

Figure 2. The resource graph for J_1, J_2 and J_3.

2.3. Blocking

The resource allocation policy is constrained to block a request (at least) when there are insufficient resources available to satisfy the request. We call such a conflict a *direct blockage*. Since we are assuming a job never makes a request that exceeds the total resources in the system, a job execution $\mathcal{J}$ can only be directly blocked if there is an identifiable set of other jobs that are *directly blocking J*, in the sense that there will be sufficient resources available to satisfy $\mathcal{J}$'s request as soon as one or more of these other jobs releases an allocation.

For a multiunit nonpreemptable resource, a request (J, R, m) is blocked directly iff $\nu_R < m$, where ν_R denotes the number of units of R that are currently available (i.e., not outstanding). As a consequence of this definition, if R is a binary semaphore, any request for an allocation of R is blocked directly by any outstanding allocation of R to another job. Similarly, if R is a reader/writer lock, any request for an allocation of R is blocked directly by any outstanding write-allocation of R to another job, and any request for a write-allocation of R is blocked by any outstanding read-allocation of R to another job.

In addition to direct blocking, there may be other blocking. The resource allocation policy may choose to block some requests that are not blocked directly. In particular, it may do this to insure priority inversion is bounded. However, we will assume that the resource policy preserves the property that whenever a job J is blocked there is an identifiable set of other jobs that are *blocking J*; i.e., if some (or all) of the jobs blocking J released their current allocations J would become unblocked.

2.4. Priorities

Each job execution request $\mathcal{J}$ has a *priority*, $p(\mathcal{J})$. Priorities are values from some ordered domain, where $\mathcal{J}$ has higher priority than $\mathcal{J}'$ iff $p(\mathcal{J}) > p(\mathcal{J}')$. $\mathcal{J}$ having higher priority than $\mathcal{J}'$ means that expediting $\mathcal{J}$ is sufficiently important that completion of $\mathcal{J}'$ is permitted to be delayed. For concreteness in our examples, we will use numeric priorities, where *larger values indicate greater urgency*. Examples of priority assignments of interest in real-time systems include RM and EDF.

A *processor allocation policy* determines which one of the pending unblocked jobs is allowed to use the processor. The primary objective of the processor and resource allocation policies is to expedite the highest priority pending job execution request. Normally, expediting the highest priority pending job means allocating the processor to that job, but this is not possible when the job is blocked. If a job J is blocked, the only way to expedite it is to expedite another (lower-priority) job that is blocking J, until the resources released by such jobs remove the cause of the blocking. This rule, which is called *priority inheritance* in (Sha, Rajkumar and Lehoczky 1987), can be applied transitively to expedite any directly blocked job that is not involved in a deadlock.

The rest of this article assumes that use of the processor is allocated to jobs preemptively, according to the priorities of requests and First-In-First-Out (FIFO) among jobs of equal priority, with priority inheritance. More precisely, let $\mathcal{J}_{cur}$ denote the currently executing request, and $\mathcal{J}_{max}$ denote the oldest highest priority pending job execution request. (Note that $\mathcal{J}_{cur}$ may, but need not, be the same as $\mathcal{J}_{max}$.) Under the priority inheritance policy, either $\mathcal{J}_{cur} = \mathcal{J}_{max}$ or there is a chain of job executions $\mathcal{J}_1, \ldots, \mathcal{J}_k$ such that $\mathcal{J}_1 = \mathcal{J}_{max}$, $\mathcal{J}_k = J_{cur}$, and $\mathcal{J}_i$ is blocked by $\mathcal{J}_{i+1}$ for $i = 1, \ldots, k - 1$. For there to be no multiple priority inversion, the resource allocation policy must insure that there is at most one such chain and the length of this chain never exceeds one.

2.5. Preemption levels

In addition to the priorities which are attached to individual requests for job executions, there are *preemption levels* (*level* for short), which are attached to jobs. Each job J has a preemption level $\pi(J)$. The level of a job is statically assigned to the job and applies to all execution requests for the job. The essential property of preemption levels is that a job J' is not allowed to preempt another job J unless $\pi(J) < \pi(J')$. This is also true for priorities. The reason for distinguishing preemption levels from priorities is to enable us to predict potential blocking, in the presence of dynamic priority schemes such as EDF scheduling.

2.5.1. Relative deadlines. For the specific priority assignments mentioned in this article, the preemption level of a job is based on the *relative deadline* of the job. The relative deadline of a job J is a fixed value, $D(J)$, such that if a request for execution of J arrives at time t, that execution must be completed by time $t + D(J)$. In other words, the relative deadline of a job is the size of the scheduling *window* in which each execution of the job must fit.

We define the *preemption levels* of jobs, $\pi(J)$, so that they are ordered inversely with respect to the order of relative deadlines; that is:

$$\pi(J) < \pi(J') \Leftrightarrow D(J') < D(J).$$

Suppose there are two jobs, J and J', with relative deadlines $D(J) = D$ and $D(J') = D'$, respectively. Suppose $\mathcal{J}$ is a job execution request of J such that $Arrival(\mathcal{J}) = t$, and $\mathcal{J}'$ is a request of J' such that $Arrival(\mathcal{J}') = t'$. In order for $\mathcal{J}'$ to preempt $\mathcal{J}$, we must have:

i. $t < t'$ (so $\mathcal{J}$ can get started);

ii. $p(\mathcal{J}) < p(\mathcal{J}')$ (so $\mathcal{J}'$ can preempt).

This is illustrated in Figure 3.

With EDF scheduling, $p(\mathcal{J}) < p(\mathcal{J}')$ iff $t' + D' < t + d$, so the essential property of preemption levels is satisfied; i.e., job J' is not allowed to preempt J unless $\pi(J) < \pi(J')$.

Example. An example will emphasize the difference between EDF priority and preemption level. Let $\mathcal{P}$ and $\mathcal{P}'$ be two periodic processes, each of which has a single job. Let the jobs be J and J', with relative deadlines 20 and 10, respectively. Preemption level 1 is assigned to J and preemption level 2 is assigned to J', since the relative deadline of J' is shorter than the relative deadline of J.

J' can never be preempted by J. This does not mean that requests for J' always have higher priority than those for J, or that we are allowing enforcement of preemption levels to cause priority inversion. It is just that the only way a request for J can have higher priority than a request for J' is if it arrived earlier, before the request for J' could have started, in which case it will have *no need* to preempt J.

Suppose request $\mathcal{J}$ arrives at time t, and a request $\mathcal{J}'$ arrives at time $t + 11$, as shown in Figure 4. Since the absolute deadline of $\mathcal{J}$ is $t + 20$ and the absolute deadline of $\mathcal{J}'$ is $t + 21$, $\mathcal{J}$ will have higher priority than $\mathcal{J}'$, and so $\mathcal{J}$ will not be preempted. On the other hand, if $\mathcal{J}'$ had arrived at time $t + 9$ its deadline would have been $t + 19$ and we would have had $p(\mathcal{J}) < p(\mathcal{J}')$, so $\mathcal{J}$ would be preempted. Thus preemption level is different from priority, but there is no priority inversion.

In addition to EDF scheduling, our preemption levels based on relative deadlines can be used with RM, *deadline monotone* (Leung and Whitehead 1982) (where $p(J) < p(J')$ iff $D(J') < D(J)$), and *static least-slack time* scheduling (where $p(J) < p(J')$ iff $D(J') - C(J') < D(J) - C(J)$, and $C(J)$ is the maximum execution time of job J).

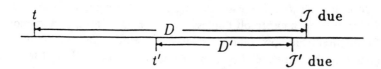

Figure 3. Preemption. in EDF scheduling.

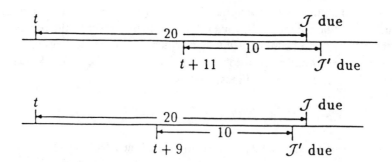

Figure 4. Preemption level *vs.* priority with EDF.

2.5.2. Abstract preemption levels. Although relative deadlines are the basis for preemption levels for all these examples, the theoretical results proven in this article do not depend on this. The only property of preemption levels on which these results do depend is the following condition:

$$p(\mathcal{J}) \leq p(\mathcal{J}') \text{ or } Arrival(\mathcal{J}) \leq Arrival(\mathcal{J}') \text{ or } \pi(J) > \pi(J'). \qquad (2.1)$$

This is equivalent to requiring that if $\mathcal{J}$ has higher priority than $\mathcal{J}'$, but $\mathcal{J}$ arrives after $\mathcal{J}'$, then J must have a higher preemption level than J'. Note that our preemption levels based on relative deadlines do satisfy condition (2.1) above for all the priority assignments mentioned in this article, and condition (2.1) is sufficient to guarantee that J can preempt J' only if $\pi(J') < \pi(J)$.

Condition (2.1) and the other definitions enable us to prove the following lemma, which characterizes the relationships between allocation of processor time, preemption levels, priorities, and arrival times.

LEMMA 1. For every preempted job execution $\mathcal{J}$:

1. $p(\mathcal{J}) < p(\mathcal{J}_{cur})$;
2. $\pi(J) < \pi(J_{cur})$;
3. $Start(\mathcal{J}) < Arrival(\mathcal{J}_{cur})$.

Moreover, if $\mathcal{J}_{cur} \neq \mathcal{J}_{max}$, for every preempted or executing request $\mathcal{J}$, including $\mathcal{J}_{cur}$:

1. $p(\mathcal{J}) < p(\mathcal{J}_{max})$;
2. $\pi(J) < \pi(J_{max})$;
3. $Start(\mathcal{J}) < Arrival(\mathcal{J}_{max})$.

Proof. Recall from Section 2 that $\mathcal{J}_{cur}$ stands for the currently executing request and $\mathcal{J}_{max}$ stands for the oldest highest priority pending request. A request $\mathcal{J}$ cannot preempt another request $\mathcal{J}'$ unless $\mathcal{J}$ arrives after $\mathcal{J}'$ has started execution and $\mathcal{J}$'s priority is higher than $\mathcal{J}'$'s. By condition (2.1) this means the preemption level of J must also be higher than that of J'. These relations are transitive. It follows that $p(\mathcal{J}) < p(\mathcal{J}_{cur})$, $\pi(J) < \pi(J_{cur})$, and $Start(\mathcal{J}) < Arrival(\mathcal{J}_{cur})$. From the definition of $\mathcal{J}_{max}$, $p(\mathcal{J}) \leq p(\mathcal{J}_{max})$, for every pending $\mathcal{J}$. If $\mathcal{J}_{cur} \neq \mathcal{J}_{max}$ we have $p(\mathcal{J}) < p(\mathcal{J}_{max})$. If $\mathcal{J}_{max}$ arrived before $\mathcal{J}_{cur}$ started, it would have been chosen to execute ahead of $\mathcal{J}_{cur}$, so $Start(\mathcal{J}_{cur}) < Arrival(\mathcal{J}_{max})$. Given these two facts, from condition (2.1), we have $\pi(J_{cur}) < \pi(J_{max})$. These three relations then apply to jobs preempted by $\mathcal{J}_{cur}$, transitively.

3. Preventing deadlock and multiple priority inversion

To strictly bound priority inversion, we want to require that the resource management policy not allow deadlock or *multiple priority inversion*—that is, situations where a job is blocked for the duration of more than one outermost nontrivial critical section of a lower priority

73

job. Given the model and assumptions described above, it is possible to derive general conditions that are sufficient to guarantee there is no deadlock or multiple priority inversion. (Moreover, we will show in Section 6 that these conditions are necessary if all jobs share a single stack.) The conditions are:

> To prevent deadlock, a job should not be permitted to start until the resources currently available are sufficient to meet the maximum requirements of the job. (3.1)

> To prevent multiple priority inversion, a job should not be permitted to start until the resources currently available are sufficient to meet the maximum requirement of any single job that might preempt it. (3.2)

Note that condition (3.1) above is similar to Havender's collective allocation approach to avoiding deadlock (1968), but Havender proposes to actually allocate all the resources to the job before it starts. In contrast, condition (3.1) only requires that the resources be *available*. They need only be allocated to the job during the critical sections in which it actually needs to use them. A higher-priority job may preempt and use the resources between these critical sections, if the available quantities are sufficient to meet its requirements.

LEMMA 2. Condition (3.1) guarantees that a job cannot block after it starts.

Proof. Suppose condition (3.1) is enforced. We have assumed there are only finitely many jobs, and that a second execution of a job is not permitted to start while an execution of the same job is active. Thus, an executing job can be preempted by only finitely many other jobs. We will prove by induction on N that if $\mathcal{J}$ is preempted by no more than N other jobs, $\mathcal{J}$ executes to completion without blocking.

Suppose the induction hypothesis fails for some N; that is, suppose $\mathcal{J}$ is blocked making request (J, R, m), and N is the number of other jobs that preempt $\mathcal{J}$ during its lifetime. By the condition (3.1), at least m units of R were available when $\mathcal{J}$ started. If $N = 0$, no other job preempts $\mathcal{J}$, so these resources will still be available when $\mathcal{J}$ requests them, and $\mathcal{J}$ will execute to completion without blocking. If $N > 0$, suppose job $\mathcal{J}_H$ preempts $\mathcal{J}$. By condition (2), all the resources required by $\mathcal{J}_H$ are available when $\mathcal{J}_H$ preempts. Since any job that preempts $\mathcal{J}_H$ also preempts $\mathcal{J}$, the induction hypothesis guarantees that $\mathcal{J}_H$ executes to completion without blocking, as will any job that preempts $\mathcal{J}_H$, transitively. Since all of the jobs that preempt $\mathcal{J}$ execute to completion without blocking, the priority inheritance policy will not permit $\mathcal{J}$ to resume execution until there are no higher priority pending jobs. At this point, since the completing jobs must have released all their resource holdings, the only resources outstanding will be those held by $\mathcal{J}$ and jobs preempted by $\mathcal{J}$. It follows that $\mathcal{J}$ cannot be blocked.

THEOREM 3. Condition (3.1) is sufficient for preventing deadlock.

Proof. Observe that a job cannot hold resources until it starts, and by Lemma 2 it cannot be blocked after it starts. Since a job cannot be blocked while holding resources, there can be no deadlock.

THEOREM 4. Assuming condition (3.1) is enforced, condition (3.2) is sufficient to prevent multiple priority inversion.

Proof. Suppose there is multiple priority inversion. By Lemma 2, the only way a job $\mathcal{J}_H$ can be subject to such multiple priority inversion is if there are two or more lower priority jobs, $\mathcal{J}$ and $\mathcal{J}'$, that execute while $\mathcal{J}_H = \mathcal{J}_{max}$. The priority inheritance policy only allows such lower priority jobs to execute if they are blocking $\mathcal{J}_H$. Both $\mathcal{J}$ and $\mathcal{J}'$ must have started executing before $\mathcal{J}$ arrives, and one of them must have preempted the other. Without loss of generality, suppose $\mathcal{J}$ preempted $\mathcal{J}'$. Condition (3.2) must have been violated when $\mathcal{J}$ was allowed to start.

The Stack Resource Policy enforces conditions (3.1) and (3.2) indirectly, by imposing stronger conditions, that are simpler to check.

4. Stack resource policy

This section defines the SRP, and proves that it *works*; that is, it enforces direct blocking requirements, without allowing multiple priority inversion or deadlock.

4.1. Ceilings

4.1.1. Abstract ceilings. The SRP enforces conditions (3.1) and (3.2) in terms of *preemption ceilings* (*ceilings*). Each resource R is required to have a *current ceiling*, $\lceil R \rceil$, which is an integer-valued function of the set of outstanding allocations of R. The correctness of the SRP does not depend on the exact definition of $\lceil R \rceil$, but only requires that ceilings be related to priorities and preemption levels by the following condition:

> If J is currently executing or can preempt the currently executing job, and may request an allocation of R that would be blocked directly by the outstanding allocations of R, then $\pi(J) \leq \lceil R \rceil$.
>
> (4.1)

The SRP will work with any definition of ceiling that satisfies these conditions. One specific definition of ceiling, that satisfies condition (4.1), is given below. However, freedom to choose a slightly different definition is a convenience when one implements the SRP. For this reason, the definition and proofs of the SRP are based on abstract ceilings, characterized only by condition (4.1).

4.1.2. Specific ceilings. For a multiunit nonpreemptable resource R, $\lceil R \rceil$ may be defined to be $\lceil R \rceil_{\nu_R}$, where ν_R denotes the number of units of R that are currently available and $\lceil R \rceil_{\nu_R}$ denotes the maximum of zero and the preemption levels of all the jobs that may be blocked directly when there are ν_R units of R available. That is:

$$\lceil R \rceil_{\nu_R} = max(\{0\} \cup \{\pi(J) \mid \nu_R < \mu_R(J)\}),$$

R	N_R	$\mu_R(1)$	$\mu_R(2)$	$\mu_R(3)$	$\lceil R \rceil_0$	$\lceil R \rceil_1$	$\lceil R \rceil_2$	$\lceil R \rceil_3$
R_1	3	3	2	1	3	2	1	0
R_2	1	1	1	0	2	0	0	0
R_3	3	1	3	1	3	2	2	0

Figure 5. Ceilings of resources.

where μ_R is the maximum requirement of job J for R. (Note that this definition satisfies condition (4.1).)

Example. The ceilings of the resources for the example shown in Figures 1 and 2 are shown in Figure 5, under the assumption that $\pi(J_i) = p(\mathcal{J}_i) = i$ for $i = 1, 2, 3$.

4.1.3. Ceilings and deadlock prevention. Given condition (4.1), the following relationships can be established between the current ceiling of a resource and conditions (3.1) and (3.2) of Section 3.

LEMMA 5. Suppose $\mathcal{J} = \mathcal{J}_{max}$, $\mathcal{J}$ is not executing, and R is a resource.

(a) If $\lceil R \rceil < \pi(J)$ then there are sufficiently many units of R available to meet the maximum requirement of J. (Condition (3.1) is satisfied for J and R.)
(b) If $\lceil R \rceil \leq \pi(J)$ then there are sufficiently many units of R available to meet the maximum requirement of every job that can preempt $\mathcal{J}$. (Condition (3.2) is satisfied for J and R.)

Proof. To show (a), suppose $\lceil R \rceil < \pi(J)$ but the maximum request of J for R cannot be satisfied. By condition (4.1), $\pi(J) \leq \lceil R \rceil$ —a contradiction.

To show (b), suppose $\lceil R \rceil \leq \pi(J)$, but for some job $\mathcal{J}_H$ that can preempt $\mathcal{J}$ the maximum requirement of $\mathcal{J}_H$ for R cannot be satisfied. By condition (4.1), $\pi(J_H) \leq \lceil R \rceil$, but for $\mathcal{J}_H$ to preempt $\mathcal{J}$ we must have $\pi(J) < \pi(J_H)$—a contradiction.

THEOREM 6. If no job J is permitted to start until $\lceil R_i \rceil < \pi(J)$, for every resource R_i, then:

(a) no job can be blocked after it starts;
(b) there can be no deadlock;
(c) no job can be blocked for longer than the duration of one outermost nontrivial critical section of a lower priority job.

Proof. Part (a) follows directly from part (a) of Lemma 5 and Lemma 2. Part (b) follows directly from part (a) of Lemma 5 and Theorem 3. Part (c) follows from part (b) of Lemma 5 and Theorem 4.

4.2. Definition of the SRP

The Stack Resource Policy is defined as follows: Each job execution request $\mathcal{J}$ is blocked from starting execution (i.e., from receiving its initial stack allocation) until $\mathcal{J}$ is the oldest highest priority pending request, and if $\mathcal{J}$ would preempt an executing job,

$$\forall R_i \atop i=1,\ldots,m \quad \lceil R_i \rceil_{\nu_{R_i}} < \pi(J). \tag{4.2}$$

Thereafter, once $\mathcal{J}$ has started execution, all its resource requests are granted immediately, without blocking.

This can be stated more simply, by introducing the concept of a system-wide *current ceiling*. At any instant of time, let the *current ceiling* of the system, $\bar{\pi}$, be the maximum of the current ceilings of all the resources. That is,

$$\bar{\pi} = max\{ \lceil R_i \rceil \mid i = 1, \ldots, m\}.$$

The SRP preemption test (4.2) then reduces to

$$\bar{\pi} < \pi(J). \tag{4.3}$$

If $\mathcal{J}$ is blocked, it is blocked by the preemption test. The other jobs holding resources R such that $\pi(J) \leq \lceil R \rceil$ are said to be *blocking* $\mathcal{J}$.

Note that the SRP does not restrict the order in which resources may be acquired, in contrast to the ordered resource allocation approach of (Havender 1968). It is also less restrictive than another approach of (Havender 1968), collective allocation. That is, even though the condition $\bar{\pi} < \pi(J)$ is tested before the job J starts to execute, the SRP does not at that time actually allocate all the resources that may ever be requested by J. They are only allocated when requested, and are released as soon as they are not needed. Thus, even if J will later request some allocation of R that would block a higher level job J_H, J_H is free to preempt until J actually requests enough of R to block J_H directly.

Note also that the SRP preemption test (4.2) has the effect of imposing priority inheritance (that is, an executing job that is holding a resource resists preemption as though it inherits the priority of any jobs that might need that resource), though the effect is accomplished without modifying the formal priority of the job, $p(\mathcal{J})$. This is important for understanding the meaning of the preemption test, above, and the rest of this article.

Example. Two possible executions of jobs J_1, J_2, and J_3 under the SRP are shown in Figure 6 and Figure 7. The solid horizontal lines indicate which job is executing, while the barred lines indicate the relative value of the current ceiling, $\bar{\pi}$. Figure 6 shows what happens if J_1 acquires R_2 before J_2 and J_3 arrive. Since $\lceil R_2 \rceil_0 = 2$, J_2 is unable to preempt J_1 after it acquires R_2, and since $\lceil R_1 \rceil_0 = 3$, J_3 is unable to preempt J_1 after it acquires all of R_1. J_3 preempts J_1 as soon as J_1 releases R_1, and J_2 preempts J_1 as soon as J_1 releases R_2. Figure 7 shows what happens if J_3 arrives before J_1 acquires R_1; it is able to preempt immediately, but J_2 still has to wait for J_1 to release R_2. (Note that in both cases the current ceiling happens not to change when J_3 acquires R_3; that is because J_3 only needs one unit, and $\lceil R_3 \rceil_2 = 2$ in our example.)

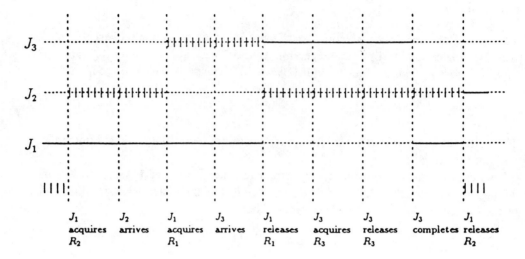

Figure 6. J_3 arrives after J_1 acquires R_1.

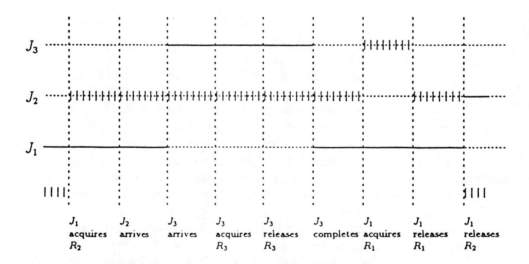

Figure 7. J_3 arrives before J_1 acquires R_1.

4.3. Blocking properties of the SRP

The SRP enforces direct blocking, prevents deadlock, and strictly bounds priority inversion. We shall prove this.

COROLLARY 7. If no job J is permitted to start until $\bar{\pi} < \pi(J)$, then:

(a) no job can be blocked after it starts;
(b) there can be no deadlock;

(c) no job can be blocked for longer than the execution time of one outermost nontrivial critical section of a lower priority job.

Proof. This follows from Theorem 6, since $\lceil R \rceil \leq \bar{\pi}$ for every resource R.

Since no job is blocked after it starts executing, there can be no transitive blocking. A consequence of this and priority inheritance is that whenever the processor is not idle it is executing either the oldest highest-priority request, $\mathcal{J}_{max}$, or a job that is directly blocking $\mathcal{J}_{max}$. These facts and Lemma 1 enable us to prove the following theorem, which says that the current job, J_{cur}, is the only job that may block $\mathcal{J}_{max}$.

THEOREM 8. If $\mathcal{J}_{max}$ is blocked, it will become unblocked no later than the first instant that $\mathcal{J}_{cur}$ is not holding any nonpreemptable resources.

Proof. Suppose $\mathcal{J}_{max}$ is blocked. Since $\mathcal{J}_{max}$ is not executing, it must have arrived after $\mathcal{J}_{cur}$, and so by condition (2.1), $\pi(J_{cur}) < \pi(J_{max})$.
Consider the moment that $\mathcal{J}_{cur}$ releases the last resource allocation it was holding when $\mathcal{J}_{max}$ arrived. Suppose $\mathcal{J}_{max}$ remains blocked. Since such resources are required to be requested and released in LIFO order, the same resource allocations are outstanding as when $\mathcal{J}_{cur}$ started, and $\bar{\pi}$ is the same as it was then. Since $\mathcal{J}_{cur}$ was not blocked then, $\bar{\pi} < \pi(J_{cur})$. It follows that $\mathcal{J}_{max}$ is not blocked now.

THEOREM 9. The SRP never grants a request that is directly blocked.

Proof. This is true because the SRP never allows a job to start unless it can be guaranteed not to block, as shown by Corollary 7. More directly, suppose J makes a request for resource R that is directly blocked. By condition (4.1), $\pi(J) \leq \lceil R \rceil$. By definition of $\bar{\pi}$, $\lceil R \rceil \leq \bar{\pi}$, but the SRP would not let J start unless $\bar{\pi} < \pi(J)$—a contradiction.

5. Schedulability with the SRP

Corollary 7 is sufficient to support the schedulability results for RM and EDF scheduling cited in Section 1. We can also derive a tighter schedulability test for the EDF policy with semaphores than the one proved in (Chen and Lin 1989). To show this, we restrict our process model so that it more closely resembles that used in previous work (Liu and Layland 1973). In particular, let there be a one-to-one correspondence between processes and jobs. Suppose there are n (periodic or aperiodic) processes, $\{\mathcal{P}_1, \ldots, \mathcal{P}_n\}$, ordered by increasing relative deadlines of the corresponding jobs, $\{J_1, \ldots, J_n\}$. Let the relative deadlines all be positive, and let each be less than or equal to the period of the corresponding process. Let T_i denote the period or minimum interarrival time of $\mathcal{P}_i$, let D_i denote the relative deadline of J_i, and let C_i denote the maximum execution time of J_i. Let B_i denote the maximum execution time of the longest nontrivial critical section of every job J_k such that $D_i < D_k$ and $i \neq k$, or zero if there is no such J_k. (This maximum includes all the critical section of other jobs that might subject J_i to priority inversion.) Assume there is a system start time, before which no jobs are requested, and that $D_i \leq T_i$ for every process.

THEOREM 10. A set of n (periodic and aperiodic) processes is schedulable by EDF sheduling with SRP semaphore locking if

$$\forall k \atop k=1,\ldots,n \left(\sum_{i=1}^{k} \frac{C_i}{D_i} \right) + \frac{B_k}{D_k} \leq 1.$$

Proof. Assume the theorem is false. Let t be the first time a job misses its deadline. Let t' be the last time before t such that there are no pending job execution requests with arrival times before t' and deadlines before or at t. Since no requests can arrive before system start time, t' is well defined. Since deadlines are all positive, $t' < t$. By choice of t and t', there is no idle time in $[t', t]$.

Let $\mathcal{Q}$ be the set of jobs that arrive in $[t', t]$ and have deadlines in $[t', t]$. By choice of t', there are pending requests of jobs in $\mathcal{Q}$ at all times during the interval $[t', t]$. Thus, by the EDF priority assignment, the only jobs that will be allowed to start in $[t', t]$ will be in $\mathcal{Q}$. These jobs can only be preempted by other jobs in $\mathcal{Q}$.

If a job not in $\mathcal{Q}$ executes in $[t', t]$ it must have started before t' and have been preempted while holding some resource allocation that is blocking a job in $\mathcal{Q}$. Once such a job releases the resources that are causing the blocking, it cannot execute further in $[t', t]$.

Suppose there are two such jobs, $\mathcal{J}_b$ and $\mathcal{J}_c$. Both of these jobs must have been holding resources when they were preempted, and since they are blocking some job(s) in $\mathcal{Q}$, these resources must have current ceilings higher than or equal to $\pi(J_i)$ for some $\mathcal{J}_i$ in $\mathcal{Q}$. (If they are not both blocking the same job in $\mathcal{Q}$, we can choose the $\mathcal{J}_i$ with lower preemption level.) Since both $\mathcal{J}_b$ and $\mathcal{J}_c$ are in nontrivial critical sections at time t', one must have preempted the others; say $\mathcal{J}_b$ preempts $\mathcal{J}_c$. For some resource R held by $\mathcal{J}_b$, we have $\pi(J_i) < \lceil R \rceil$. Since $\mathcal{J}_i$ is capable (transitively) of preempting $\mathcal{J}_c$, we also have $\pi(J_c) < \lceil R \rceil$, but then $\mathcal{J}_c$ should not have been able to preempt $\mathcal{J}_b$—a contradiction.

It follows that there can be at most one job, $\mathcal{J}_j$, that blocks any job in $\mathcal{Q}$, and that this job can only execute for as long as it takes to exit its outermost nontrivial critical section. Therefore J_j is the only job not in $\mathcal{Q}$ that can execute in $[t', t]$. (Actually, by Theorem 8, we know that $\mathcal{J}_j$ must be the job that is executing at time t', if it exists.) If there is no such job J_j, only the jobs in $\mathcal{Q}$ can execute in $[t', t]$.

Note that if J_j uses more than one nonpreemptable resource simultaneously it may execute more than once, since it may unblock several jobs in stages, as it releases successive resources. However, the total execution time of J_j in $[t', t]$ cannot be any longer than it takes J_j to release its last resource, since after that J_j will be preempted continuously by jobs in $\mathcal{Q}$.

Let $\Delta = t' - t$. By choice of t', $D_i \leq \Delta$, for every J_i in $\mathcal{Q}$. If a job J_j is executing at time t', then $\Delta < D_j$. Since the jobs are ordered by increasing value of D_i it follows that there exists a k such that $\mathcal{Q} \subseteq \{J_1, \ldots, J_k\}$, $D_k \leq \Delta$, and $k < j$.

The total length of time that J_j executes in $[t', t]$ is bounded by the longest time J_j uses a resource. This is bounded by B_i for each job J_i in $\mathcal{Q}$, since $D_i < D_j$. In particular, the maximum execution time of J_j in $[t', t]$ is bounded by B_k.

For every J_i in $\mathcal{Q}$, the demand for CPU time in $[t', t]$ is not more than KC_i, where

$$K = \left\lfloor \frac{\Delta - D_i}{T_i} \right\rfloor + 1.$$

In $[t', t]$ there is no idle time and the only jobs executing are J_j and those in $\mathcal{Q}$. Since there is an overflow, the total demand for processor time in $[t', t]$ exceeds Δ, so

$$B_k + \sum_{i=1}^{k} \left(\left\lfloor \frac{\Delta - D_i}{T_i} \right\rfloor + 1 \right) C_i > \Delta.$$

Since $\lfloor X \rfloor \leq X$, we have

$$\frac{B_k}{\Delta} + \sum_{i=1}^{k} \frac{\Delta - D_i + T_i}{T_i \Delta} C_i = \frac{B_k}{\Delta} + \sum_{i=1}^{k} \left(1 + \frac{T_i - D_i}{\Delta} \right) \frac{C_i}{T_i} > 1,$$

and since $D_i \leq \Delta$ for $i = 1, \ldots, k$,

$$\frac{B_k}{D_k} + \sum_{i=1}^{k} \left(1 + \frac{T_i - D_i}{D_i} \right) \frac{C_i}{T_i} = \frac{B_k}{D_k} + \sum_{i=1}^{k} \frac{C_i}{D_i} > 1.$$

COROLLARY 11. A set of n (periodic and aperiodic) jobs with relative deadlines equal to their respective periods is schedulable by EDF scheduling if

$$\forall k \atop k=1,\ldots,n \left(\sum_{i=1}^{k} \frac{C_i}{T_i} \right) + \frac{B_k}{T_k} \leq 1.$$

Proof. Since $D_i = T_i$, $T_i/D_i = 1$.

Note that this result is tighter than Chen and Lin's Theorem 4 (quoted in Section 1), since there is only one blocking term in the sum. However, the proof does not appear to depend on the use of preemption levels or early blocking. Thus, we believe it can also be applied to the dynamic SRP as described in (Chen and Lin 1989).

6. Stack sharing

This section discusses the sharing of runtime stack space between jobs, and shows that the SRP supports stack sharing without allowing unbounded priority inversion or deadlock. Supporting stack sharing was the original motivation for the development of the SRP, and in particular for the choice of early blocking.

6.1. The motivation for stack sharing

In a conventional process-based model of concurrent programming, such as Ada tasking, each process needs its own runtime stack. The region allocated to each stack must be large enough to accommodate the maximum stack storage requirement of the corresponding process. Storage is reserved for the stack continuously, both while the process is executing and between executions.

In some hard realtime applications there may be thousands of actions that are to be performed at different times in response to appropriate triggering events. In a conventional process model each action would be implemented by a process, which waits for a triggering event and then executes the action. A problem with this kind of design is that a great deal of storage may be required for the stacks of all the waiting processes—storage which is unused most of the time.

For example, suppose that there are four processes $\mathcal{P}_1$, $\mathcal{P}_2$, $\mathcal{P}_3$, and $\mathcal{P}_4$, with respective priorities 1, 2, 2, and 3 (3 is the highest priority). Figure 8 shows the stack usage of these processes during a possible execution sequence, assuming each process is allocated its own stack space. In the figure, $\mathcal{P}_1$ is running at time t_1; $\mathcal{P}_2$ preempts at time t_2, and completes at time t_3, allowing $\mathcal{P}_1$ to resume; $\mathcal{P}_3$ preempts at time t_4; $\mathcal{P}_4$ preempts at time t_5, and completes at time t_6, allowing $\mathcal{P}_3$ to resume; $\mathcal{P}_3$ completes at time t_7, allowing $\mathcal{P}_1$ to resume. The top of each process's stack varies during the process's execution, as indicated by the solid lines. The regions of storage reserved for each stack remain constant, as indicated by the dashed lines.

The requirement for stack space can be dramatically reduced by using the *featherweight* processes described in this article. A key feature of the featherweight process model is that when a job execution completes, all resources required by that execution may be released. In particular, stack space may be allocated when the job begins execution and completely freed when it completes.

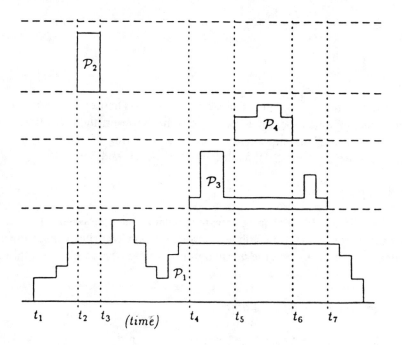

Figure 8 One stack per process.

6.2. How stack sharing works

One obvious way to allocate stack space is to partition jobs into groups that cannot preempt one another, and allocate a stack to each group. The SRP provides a more elegant solution than this, by allowing even jobs that preempt one another to share a single stack.

Suppose all jobs share a single stack. When a job J is preempted by a job J', J continues to hold its stack space and J' is allocated space immediately above it on the stack. Figure 9 shows what would happen to the jobs of Figure 8 if they shared a single stack. The space between the two dashed horizontal lines represents space that will no longer be needed, since the priorities of $\mathcal{P}_2$ and $\mathcal{P}_3$ guarantee they will never need to occupy stack space at the same time.

Stack sharing may result in very large storage savings if there are many more processes than preemption levels. For example, suppose we have 100 jobs, with 10 jobs at each of 10 preemption levels, and each job needs up to 10 kilobytes of stack space. Using a stack per job, 1000 kilobytes of storage would be required. In contrast, using a single stack, only 100 kilobytes of storage would be required (since no more than one job per preemption level could be active at one time). The space savings is 900 kilobytes; that is, 90%.

6.3. Stack usage assumptions

Let us now assume stack sharing is allowed, and consider how it affects scheduling. Each job may either have its own individual runtime stack, or share the use of a runtime stack

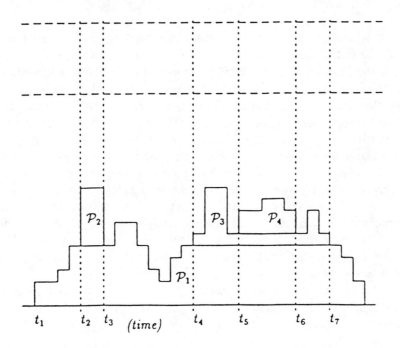

Figure 9. Single stack, for all processes.

with a collection of other jobs. Although runtime stack space is a nonpreemptable resource, it must be treated differently from the other multiunit nonpreemptable resources we have considered so far. The big difference is that the location of the requested space, rather than the quantity, is what matters.

Based on the way in which programming language implementations typically use the runtime stack, we make the following assumptions:

1. Every job requires an initial allocation of at least one cell of stack space before it can start execution, and cannot relinquish that space until it completes execution. This means the entire execution of each job is a *critical section* with respect to the stack which it is using.
2. After a job starts execution, if it makes any request that is blocked it must continue to hold its stack space while it is blocked.
3. A stack storage request can be granted to a job if and only if the job is not yet holding any stack space or it is at the top of the stack it is using.
4. Only a job at the top of a stack may execute, since an executing job may need to increase its stack size at any time.

Due to these assumptions, the request for the initial stack allocation of each job may be treated as part of the request for job execution, and subsequent use of the stack by that job may be allowed without explicit request and release operations.

6.4. How the SRP avoids stack blocking

The problem with stack sharing is that it can cause blocking. For a shared stack, a job J is *directly blocked* iff there is another job J' holding the space immediately above J on the stack, so that J's part of the stack cannot grow without overflowing into the holdings of J'. For this situation to occur, J' must have preempted J; J will be blocked until J' completes and releases all of its stack space. That is, once a job is preempted by another job on the same stack it cannot be resumed until the preempting job completes. Such *stack blocking* effectively requires that use of the processor be allocated according to a LIFO policy. Fortunately, since any job that preempts must have higher priority than the job it preempts, this requirement is consistent with priority preemptive scheduling.

When there are other nonpreemptable resources, stack blocking can easily lead to deadlock. For example, suppose jobs $\mathcal{J}_H$ and $\mathcal{J}_L$ both use a nonpreemptable resource (e.g., binary semaphore) R. Suppose $\mathcal{J}_H$ preempts while $\mathcal{J}_L$ is holding R. Job $\mathcal{J}_H$ will start to execute, occupying the stack space above $\mathcal{J}_L$, but will eventually try to obtain R. It cannot do this, since $\mathcal{J}_L$ is still holding R. Unfortunately, $\mathcal{J}_H$ is now also blocking $\mathcal{J}_L$, by sitting on top of its stack space.

Note that it is possible to solve the problem of stack deadlock without bounding priority inversion very strictly. For example, reconsider the jobs $\mathcal{J}_H$ and $\mathcal{J}_L$ described above. Suppose a deadlock prevention scheme is used, that prevents job $\mathcal{J}_H$ from preempting while R is in use. Now suppose there is an intermediate priority job $\mathcal{J}_M$, which preempts while $\mathcal{J}_L$ is holding resource R, but before $\mathcal{J}_H$ arrives. Since $\mathcal{J}_L$ cannot execute while $\mathcal{J}_M$ is sitting on its stack, $\mathcal{J}_H$ will suffer priority inversion until $\mathcal{J}_M$ completes its whole execution, and then until $\mathcal{J}_L$ completes the section in which it is using R.

We showed in Section 4.3 that the SRP will prevent deadlock and bound priority inversion to the duration of a single critical section. It does this by enforcing conditions (3.1) and (3.2), using the preemption ceilings for all resources that can cause blocking. The only requirement for preemption ceilings is condition (4.1). If we can define the ceiling of a stack in a way that satisfies (4.1), the SRP will handle stack blocking.

Because of the assumptions we have made about stack usage, the stack space held by a job J can only block jobs that it might preempt; that is, jobs with lower preemption levels. It follows that condition (4.1) imposes no restriction on the current ceiling of a stack. Therefore, the ceiling of a stack can be defined to be anything we want. We define it to be zero.

By defining the ceiling of a shared stack to be zero, we can ignore stack usage in computation of $\bar{\pi}$, and so stack usage can never cause blocking. *Critical sections* with respect to stack usage are therefore trivial, and can be ignored in the computation of the priority inversion bound, B_i. Note, however, that this does not mean stack resources can be ignored completely; where there is stack sharing, the preemption operation must be treated as a request for stack resources, and may block.

7. Comparison to PCP

Since the SRP is a refinement of the PCP it is natural to compare the two techniques, to see what the differences are and what consequences they have.

7.1. Review of the PCP

As a basis for the comparison, we review the definition of the PCP. Each job is assumed to be requested cyclically, with a fixed priority. There is a fixed set of semaphores, each of which has a priority ceiling.

Sha, Rajkumar, and Lehoczky (1987) define the priority ceiling of a semaphore to be "the priority of the highest priority job that may lock this semaphore." They refine this concept for readers and writers in (Sha, Rajkumar and Lehoczky 1988), defining the "absolute priority ceiling" of an object to be the priority of the highest priority job that may lock the object for reading or writing, and the "write priority ceiling" of an object to be the priority of the highest priority job that may lock it for writing. Chen and Lin (1989) define the "dynamic priority ceiling" of a semaphore to be "the priority of the highest priority task that may lock S in the current effective task set."

If S is a semaphore, let $c(S)$ denote its priority ceiling. Let S^* be the semaphore that has the highest priority ceiling among all semaphores locked by jobs other than $\mathcal{J}_{cur}$, if there are any. For notational simplicity, let $c(S^*)$ be defined to be zero when S^* is undefined (i.e., when there are no locked semaphores).

The Priority Ceiling Protocol consists of the following policy: When a job $\mathcal{J}$ requests a semaphore S it will be blocked unless

$$c(S^*) < p(\mathcal{J}).$$

(That is, $\mathcal{J}$ is blocked until it has strictly higher priority than all the priority ceilings of all the semaphores locked by jobs other than $\mathcal{J}$.) If $\mathcal{J}$ blocks, the job that holds S^* is said to be blocking $\mathcal{J}$ and inherits $\mathcal{J}$'s priority. A job $\mathcal{J}$ can always preempt another job executing at a lower priority level as long as $\mathcal{J}$ does not request any semaphore.

7.2. Differences of the SRP

In most respects, the SRP is a consistent extension of the PCP. The SRP relaxes restrictions of the PCP in the following ways:

1. The PCP assumes that the preemption level of each job is the same as its priority, which is fixed, except for mode changes (Sha, Rajkumar and Lehoczky 1989). With the SRP, the preemption level of a job may be different from its priority, and while the preemption level of a job is required to be static, the priority may be dynamic. Ceilings are based on preemption levels, rather than priorities. This allows the SRP to be applied directly to EDF scheduling without resort to dynamic recomputation of ceilings.
2. The PCP model views each process as a sequence of requests for the same *type* of job. We make the same assumption for the purposes of EDF schedulability analysis, but do not make this assumption in the other proofs. Thus, an SRP process may consist of requests for several different jobs, with different preemption levels.
3. The original PCP handles binary semaphores, and has been extended to handle reader-writer locks by distinguishing two kinds of priority ceilings. The SRP allows multiunit resources, by treating the ceiling of a resource as a function of the number of units currently available.
4. The PCP does not allow stack sharing. The SRP treats a shared stack as a resource with ceiling zero.

The only way in which the SRP is not a consistent extension of the PCP is in earlier blocking. When the PCP blocks a job it does so at the time it makes its first resource request, which is some time after it has started execution. In contrast, the SRP schedules every job as though it starts by requesting use of a shared stack (whether or not it actually does). This eliminates the possiblity of a job blocking after it has started execution, and eliminates the extra context switches associated with blocking and unblocking. (This issue of context switches is discussed further in Section 7.5.)

A technical difference between the SRP and PCP is Theorem 8, which says that if a job is blocked by the SRP, it is blocked while trying to preempt, and only by the one job it is trying to preempt. In contrast, the PCP only guarantees that if a job is blocked it will be blocked at its first resource request and then will not be blocked again.

7.3. A comparative example

To illustrate the differences between the PCP and SRP, we present an example, involving three jobs with the structure shown in Figure 10. Consider the following scenario, in which the jobs execute under the PCP:

J_H	J_M	J_L
... request($J_H, S, 1$); ... release; ...	...	... request($J_L, S, 1$); ... release; ...

Figure 10. The jobs J_H, J_M, J_L.

1. A high priority job, J_H preempts the processor from a lower priority job, J_M, and executes for a while.
2. J_H is forced to allow a lower priority job J_L (preempted earlier by J_M) to resume execution, because J_L is holding a resource needed by J_H.
3. J_L releases the resource needed by J_H, and J_H resumes execution.
4. J_H completes, and J_M resumes execution.

This is illustrated in Figure 11. The solid horizontal lines indicate which job is executing. The barred horizontal lines indicate the relative value of $c(S^*)$, the current ceiling as defined for the PCP.

For comparison, consider the corresponding scenario under the SRP:

1. J_H waits until $\pi(J_H) > \bar{\pi}$, then begins execution, preempting J_L. (Note that J_M and J_H are forced to wait until J_L releases S, since $\pi(J_H) \leq \bar{\pi}$.)
2. J_H completes and J_M resumes execution.

This is illustrated in Figure 12. The solid horizontal lines indicate which job is executing. The barred horizontal lines indicate the relative value of $\bar{\pi}$.

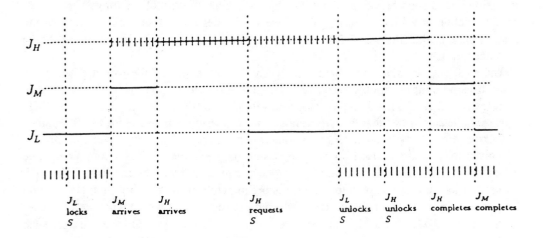

Figure 11. Execution with PCP.

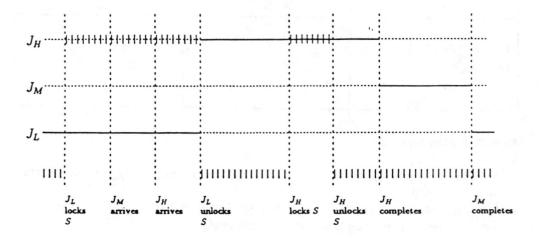

Figure 12. Execution with SRP.

Note that the two ceilings, $c(S^*)$ and $\bar{\pi}$, differ slightly, since $c(S^*)$ does not include the semaphores held by the current job. However, this makes no practical difference, since for both the PCP and SRP, whenever a job performs its first potentially blocking operation $c(S^*) = \bar{\pi}$. That is, it would be a valid optimization of the PCP to ignore $c(S^*)$ after the first potentially blocking operation, just as the SRP does.

7.4. Priority inversion

One weakness of the SRP is that it will block a job in some situations where the PCP would not. This is a consequence of early blocking, and consequent pessimistic assumptions about resource usage. It is not a major problem, since we have shown that the priority inversion due to such blocking is bounded by the execution time of the longest nontrivial critical section of a lower priority job. However, it does mean that a comparison of the effectiveness of the SRP and PCP in preventing unbounded priority inversion must take into account the characteristics of specific jobs.

The most obvious situation where the SRP will block and the PCP would not is when a job uses no nonpreemptible resources. This is illustrated by job J_M in the example of Figures 11 and 12. J_M is subject to priority inversion with the SRP, but not with the PCP. The example also shows that this difference is not a clear-cut advantage for the PCP, since the extra priority inversion for J_M can sometimes reduce the priority inversion for J_H.

This problem cannot arise if there is stack sharing, since the stack is a nonpreemptable resource. If there is no stack sharing, the defect can be reduced by modifying the SRP to exempt jobs that are known to use no nonpreemptable resources from the preemption requirement $\bar{\pi} < \pi(J)$. However, there will remain some cases where whether a job uses such resources is decided by data dependent logic within the job. On the average, such a job may suffer less priority inversion with the PCP than with the SRP. Moreover, if the data-dependent control flow of the job causes it to have the longest execution time in the cases where it uses no nonpreemptable resources, the unnecessary blocking may cause the worst-case combined execution and blocking time of that job to be longer with SRP than PCP, reducing schedulability.

The comparison is simpler if we assume every job uses at least one nonpreemptable resource. We can prove that in this case the SRP doesn't allow any longer priority inversion than the PCP.

THEOREM 12. Under the SRP the maximum priority-inversion time of any job that uses a nonpreemptable resource is no longer than it would be under the PCP.

Proof. Suppose a set of jobs and a sequence of job execution requests is given. We will compare the maximum priority-inversion time of some job J under both policies. Since we are comparing against the PCP, which only supports binary semaphores and static priorities, we will assume that the only resources are semaphores and that the priority of each job execution request is the same as the preemption level of the job. Under these assumptions, the only significant difference between the SRP and the PCP is that the SRP blocks earlier.

Let $\mathcal{J}$ be a request for J that achieves the maximum priority inversion under the SRP. From Theorem 8 we know that $\mathcal{J}$ can only be subject to priority inversion from the current job, $\mathcal{J}_{cur}$. Thus, $\mathcal{J}_{cur}$ is holding a semaphore S that blocks $\mathcal{J}$ from preempting. That is, $\pi(J) \leq \lceil S \rceil$. Since we are assuming preemption level equals priority, $p(\mathcal{J}) \leq \lceil S \rceil$.

The same order of events may happen with the PCP. That is, a higher-priority job execution request for J may arrive while J_{cur} is holding S. Under the PCP, J would preempt. Suppose J later requests some resource. We have $p(\mathcal{J}) \leq \lceil S \rceil \leq \lceil S^* \rceil$. Since this is the blocking condition for the PCP, this request by J would be blocked. $\mathcal{J}$ would therefore be subject to priority inversion until J_{cur} releases S, which is at least as long as under the SRP.

7.5. Context switches

A positive consequence of the early blocking policy of the SRP is a reduction in unnecessary context switches, as compared with the PCP. The cost of context switches can be significant for certain processors. Architectural features that increase the relative cost of context switching include large register sets, address-translation lookaside buffers, instruction pipelining, prefetching, and cache memory for data and instructions. For such architectures, the early blocking property of the SRP may be important, because it reduces the need for context switches.

For comparison, consider resource allocation policies that bound priority inversion but allow late blocking, such as the PCP and the Priority Limit Protocol (Sha, Rajkumar and Lehoczky 1987). These policies all permit the scenario shown in Figures 10, 11, and 12. The diagrams reveal that with the PCP the execution of J_H requires four context switches, but with the SRP it only requires two context switches. This generalizes.

THEOREM 13. The SRP requires at most two context switches for a job execution request.

Proof. This is a consequence of early blocking, and can be seen immediately from the definition of the SRP. Since a job cannot be blocked after it starts execution, the only context switches are one switch from the job that is preempted to the job that is requested and one switch back when the preempting job completes.

THEOREM 14. The PCP, and any other policy that waits to block a job until it makes a resource request, may require four context switches for a job execution request, for any job that shares a nonpreemptable resource with some lower-priority job.

Proof. Let J be any job such that there is a lower-priority job J_L and a resource R such that both J and J_L lock R. If J is requested while J_L is running and has locked R, there will be four context switches: (1) from J to J_L, when J preempts; (2) from J_L to J, when J tries to lock R; (3) from J_L to J, when J_L unlocks R; (4) from J back to J_L, when J completes.

Together, Theorem 13 and Theorem 14 say that the upper bound on the number of context switches caused by a request with the SRP is half of the maximum for the PCP. This improvement is due to earlier blocking.

Note that this improvement is dependent on the preempting job being one that requires a nonpreemptable resource—which we are assuming to be the normal case. If the job uses no nonpreemptable resources, there would be no extra context switch with the PCP. Moreover, it is possible that whether a job uses such resources is determined by data-dependent control flow. If the control flow causes the job to have the longest execution time in the cases where it uses no nonpreemptable resources, the cost of the extra context-switches may not contribute to the worst-case combined execution and context-switching time of that job, and so it may not be considered significant with respect to schedulability.

8. Minimal SRP

The SRP was designed to solve the problem of stack blocking, but it is not an optimal solution to that problem, in the sense of causing no unnecessary blocking. If we are willing to make the blocking test more complicated, we can define such an optimal resource management policy. The Minimal SRP (MSRP) imposes the minimum blocking necessary to insure there is no deadlock or multiple priority inversion, assuming there is a single stack and RM or EDF priorities are used.

8.1. Definition of the MSRP

The Minimal SRP is defined as follows: Each job execution request $\mathcal{J}$ is blocked from starting execution (i.e., from receiving its initial stack allocation) until $\mathcal{J}$ is the oldest highest priority pending request, and if $\mathcal{J}$ would preempt an executing job, one of the following conditions is satisfied:

$$\bar{\pi} < \pi(J); \tag{8.1}$$

$$\bar{\pi} = \pi(J) \text{ and the presently available resources are sufficient for } J \text{ to}$$
execute to completion without direct blocking. \hfill (8.2)

Once J has started execution, all subsequent resource requests by J are granted immediately, without blocking.

Note that for the specific definitions of ceilings given here, condition (8.2) is equivalent to

$$\bar{\pi} = \pi(J) \text{ and } \forall R \; (\mu_R(J) \leq \nu_R).$$

8.2. Blocking properties of the MSRP

Outside of the extra complexity of its preemption test, the MSRP has the same desirable properties as the SRP.

THEOREM 15. The MSRP prevents deadlock and multiple priority inversion.

Proof. To show that the MSRP prevents deadlock and multiple blocking, we need to show that it enforces conditions (3.1) and (3.2). Lemma 5 shows that condition (8.1) enforces conditions (3.1) and (3.2). The second part of condition (8.2) is equivalent to (3.1), so the only remaining question is whether (8.2) enforces (3.2).

Suppose (8.2) is satisfied by J_{max}, but (3.2) is not. Let J_H be a job that might preempt J_{max}, such that there are not sufficient resources available for J_H to execute to completion without direct blocking. That means J_H may request an allocation of some resource R that is blocked directly by currently outstanding allocations. Since J_H must also be able to preempt the current job, by condition (4.1), $\pi(J_H) \leq \lceil R \rceil$. By definition of $\bar{\pi}$, $\lceil R \rceil \leq \bar{\pi}$. It follows that $\pi(J_H) \leq \pi(J_{max})$, but then J_H would not be able to preempt J_{max}—a contradiction.

Theorems 8 and 9 also apply to the MSRP, with the same proofs, except that the relation $\bar{\pi} < \pi(J)$ is replaced by $\bar{\pi} \leq \pi(J)$.

8.3. Minimality of the SRP

We will show that the MSRP imposes the minimal blocking necessary to prevent unbounded priority inversion and deadlock under conditions of stack sharing. We will start by showing that the conditions (3.1) and (3.2), which were shown in Section 3 to be sufficient to prevent deadlock, are necessary to prevent deadlock if there is stack sharing.

THEOREM 16. Deadlock prevention condition (3.1) is necessary if there is a single stack.

Proof. To see that condition (3.1) is necessary, suppose there is a single stack, and $\mathcal{J}$ is allowed to start execution while there are insufficient resources to meet its maximum requirements. If $\mathcal{J}$ makes its maximum requests for all resources, it will be blocked for some request. The resources required to unblock $\mathcal{J}$ will be held by jobs that sit below $\mathcal{J}$ on the stack, and these jobs are in turn blocked by the stack allocations of the jobs above them, culminating in $\mathcal{J}$—a deadlock.

THEOREM 17. Assuming condition (3.1) is enforced, deadlock prevention condition (3.2) is necessary if there is stack sharing.

Proof. To see that condition (3.2) is necessary, suppose there is a single stack and $\mathcal{J}$ is permitted to start while there are insufficient resources available to meet the maximum requirements of some job $\mathcal{J}_H$ that can preempt $\mathcal{J}$. Condition (3.1) guarantees that $\mathcal{J}_H$ will be blocked if it attempts to preempt $\mathcal{J}$. Due to stack blocking, no other job may execute to release resources until $\mathcal{J}$ completes, but then $\mathcal{J}_H$ will still be blocked. Thus, $\mathcal{J}_H$ will be forced to wait for at least two lower priority jobs—a multiple priority inversion situation.

Up to now, the only assumption made about preemption levels is condition (2.1), from which it follows that J can preempt J' only if $\pi(J') < \pi(J)$. With RM or EDF scheduling, if preemption levels of jobs are assigned based on relative deadlines, we also have

$$\pi(J') < \pi(J) \Leftrightarrow \text{some execution of } J \text{ can preempt some execution of } J'. \quad (8.3)$$

The *only if* direction follows directly from (2.1). To see that the *if* direction holds, suppose $\mathcal{J}$ arrives after $\mathcal{J}'$ has started and J has a shorter relative deadline that J'. By RM, EDF, or deadline monotone scheduling, $\mathcal{J}$ will have higher priority than $\mathcal{J}'$ and preempt. This will happen unless J and J' have harmonic periods and there is precise control over phasing of requests.

THEOREM 18. Under the assumption of a single shared runtime stack, and condition (8.3), any resource allocation policy that does not permit deadlock or multiple blocking must block every request that is blocked by the MSRP.

Proof. Suppose a resource allocation policy is given, and it does not block some request that would be blocked by the MSRP. We will show that a job may be blocked by more than one other job, or be deadlocked. Like the SRP, the MRSP only blocks jobs before they start. Suppose job J is allowed to start when one of the two MSRP blocking conditions is true and job J_{cur} is executing. We know that $p(\mathcal{J}_{cur}) < p(\mathcal{J})$, and since $\mathcal{J}_{cur}$ is executing we know $\mathcal{J}$ arrives after $\mathcal{J}_{cur}$ starts. By condition (2.1), this means $\pi(J_{cur}) < \pi(J)$. Since J is blocked from preempting by the MSRP, we have two cases:

1. $\pi(J) < \bar{\pi}$. There is some outstanding resource R and a job J_H such that $\pi(J) < \pi(J_H)$, and J_H can be blocked directly by the currently outstanding allocations of R. By condition (8.3), J_H may preempt J and be blocked directly by R. Since the allocations outstanding when J started were already enough to block J_H directly, J_H will be blocked until some job J', below J, resumes execution and releases its allocation of R. J' cannot resume execution until J completes, due to stack blocking. Thus, J_H will be blocked by both J and J'. This is at least double blocking, and if J_H is allowed to start before blocking, it will deadlock, since it will be blocking J's stack.
2. $\pi(J) = \bar{\pi}$ and J may make a request, for some resource R, that is blocked directly. Since we are assuming stack sharing, we know that J_{cur} will be blocked by J's stack allocation if it tries to resume execution before J completes. By assumption, J's request

92

for R may be blocked directly. The resource allocations blocking J must be held by jobs that are on the stack. J_{cur} must complete before any of these jobs can resume and release their allocations of R. There is deadlock.

9. Practical considerations

9.1. Implementation of the SRP

The SRP can be implemented very simply and efficiently. The implementation is similar to that of the PCP (Sha, Rajkumar and Lehoczky 1987), but the locking operations are simpler, since they cannot block, do not require any blocking test, and never require a context switch. The blocking test is also simplified slightly, since it does not need to distinguish the ceilings of resources held by the current job from those of resources held by other jobs. The ceilings are static, and so may be precomputed and stored in a table. A stack may be used to keep track of the current ceiling. When a resource R is allocated its current state, ν_R, is updated, and $\bar{\pi}$ is set to $\lceil R \rceil_{\nu_R}$ iff $\bar{\pi} < \lceil R \rceil_{\nu_R}$. The old values of ν_R and $\bar{\pi}$ are pushed onto the stack. When resource R is released, the values of $\bar{\pi}$ and ν_R are restored from the stack. If the restored ceiling is lower than the previous ceiling, a dispatching procedure is invoked to check whether a waiting higher level job should be allowed to preempt.

The dispatching procedure checks the priority queue to see if $\mathcal{I}_{max}$ is different from $\mathcal{I}_{cur}$ and satisfies the preemption criterion, $\bar{\pi} < \pi(J_{max})$. If $\mathcal{I}_{max}$ passes this test, the identity of $\mathcal{I}_{cur}$ is pushed on the stack, runtime stack space is allocated to $\mathcal{I}_{max}$, and $\mathcal{I}_{max}$ starts execution. If $\mathcal{I}_{max}$ fails the test, the dispatcher simply returns. Whenever a job completes, $\mathcal{I}_{cur}$ is restored from the stack. The dispatcher is called whenever $\mathcal{I}_{max}$ changes, due to arrival of a higher priority request or completion of the old $\mathcal{I}_{max}$.

9.2. Relationship to conventional process models

As realtime systems grow in complexity they strain the limits of existing software technology. One response to this increasing complexity has been movement toward process-based models of concurrent programming. Such models have been very successful in the design of operating systems and interactive computer applications. One manifestation of this movement is the multitasking model of the Ada programming language (Military Standard Ada Programming Language 1983). Ada has been mandated by the U.S. Department of Defense for all mission-critical software. Another manifestation is the development by the IEEE of a proposed realtime extension to its standard POSIX operating system interface (IEEE Computer Society 1988), which is derived from the UNIX[2] process model.

Unfortunately, these conventional process models are too general to permit direct application of the SRP. The SRP is based on a *featherweight* process model. We view this model as an *alternative*, which is superior to conventional process models for hard realtime applications, because it allows better *a priori* schedulability analysis. However, there are situations where other considerations may dictate the use of a less restricted model.

This problem of mismatching models has already been addressed by people who have attempted to apply the PCP to Ada (Borger and Rajkumar 1989). Their approach has been to identify a set of restrictions that define a subset of the more general model that can be mapped into the PCP's model. This same approach can be applied with the SRP, with very little difference.

A conventional process can be viewed as a featherweight process if the sequence of instructions between each blocking operation (e.g., rendezvous, delay) and the next is bounded, no nonpreemptable resources are retained while the process is blocked, and resources are released in LIFO order. Such a process can use the SRP to synchronize with other processes, if no attempt is made to share stack space. The SRP preemption test is applied each time a process becomes unblocked; that is, the next sequence of instructions executed by the process from that point to the next blocking operation is viewed as a new *job*.

The SRP appears to be applicable to the same range of Ada task systems as the PCP. Passive tasks, sometimes also called *monitor* or *server* tasks, may be implemented as collections of procedures, interlocked via semaphores. Other tasks can be treated as featherweight processes, if they satisfy the restrictions stated in the previous paragraph. Stack sharing may be possible between such tasks, if further restrictions are imposed, such as that the tasks do not block within any subprogram calls or *declare* blocks. In this fashion, a sufficiently simple Ada task system may be transformed into a system of featherweight processes and semaphores.

This idea of doing optimizing transformations on special kinds of Ada tasks, based on *idioms*, is well known and has been discussed by several authors (Borger and Rajkumar 1989; Habermann and Nassi 1989; Hilfinger 1982; Giering and Baker 1989). However, it has not yet been widely implemented. It is not yet clear how far it will be practical to go with this approach for the SRP.

10. Conclusions and further research

Starting from the motivation of supporting stack sharing, we have shown that the PCP can be extended in three ways, and that earlier blocking may be advantageous in some situations. We have defined the SRP and MSRP, two extensions of the PCP that incorporate these extensions and early blocking.

One strength of the SRP and MSRP is that they support EDF priorities, as well as fixed priorities. EDF scheduling permits higher utilization than fixed-priority scheduling, but fixed-priority scheduling has an advantage of *stability*—that is, it guarantees lower priority jobs will not prevent higher priority jobs from meeting their deadlines during periods of processing overload. Since the SRP supports both fixed and EDF priorities, it is possible to run EDF jobs as *background* in a system where the critical jobs are scheduled in *foreground* according to a RM policy. In particular, it appears that the schedulability result of (Liu and Layland 1973) on using a mixture of RM and EDF policies can be applied to this situation, if B_k is subtracted from the processor availability function.

The SRP has been implemented. In continuing research, we plan to conduct some empirical studies of the SRP versus other scheduling and resource allocation policies. We also hope to extend the theory in several directions.

Several of the ideas presented in this article, which are embodied in the SRP, appear to have wider applicability. These ideas are:

1. Distinguishing preemption level from priority.
2. Early blocking.
3. Stack sharing.

Further research, to explore wider application of these ideas, seems warranted. More specifically, it seems that the concepts of preemption level and early blocking can be applied to much of the work that has been done on RM scheduling and the PCP, including the multiprocessor version of the PCP. Already, we have observed that the SRP is compatible with the aperiodic server concepts of (Sprunt, Sha and Lehoczky 1989).

While this article was being reviewed, Ghazalie (Ghazalie 1990) has shown that the deferred and sporadic server models can be adapted to improve average response times with EDF scheduling, as they are known to do with RM scheduling. The basic idea is to associate a deadline with each replenishment of server execution time. This enables the server to be scheduled within the EDF paradigm. For a sporadic server, there is no reduction in schedulability. For a deferred server, a special term must be added to the schedulability test, to account for the effect of the server.

Acknowledgments

This article is a more formal development of ideas first proposed in (Baker, Malec and Wilson 1989). The motivation to reduce wasted space for stacks of inactive tasks came from discussions with Russ Wilson of Boeing Aerospace and Electronics (BAE), regarding a BAE project which involved thousands of tasks. The importance of avoiding unnecessary context switches, due to the increasingly high relative cost of context switches in recent generations of 32-bit microprocessors, also came from conversations at BAE, with Russ Wilson, Carl Malec, and Greg Scallon. The idea of modifying the idea of the PCP to address these two issues crystalized during a discussion of the need for lighter-weight alternatives to Ada tasking at the July 1989 meeting of the Ada Runtime Environment Working Group, in Seattle.

Mike Victor, of Raytheon, pointed out that an executive based on the basic stack-sharing model described here has been in use at Raytheon for over fifteen years, though there are apparently no published descriptions of that executive. Lui Sha pointed out the possible advantage of the PCP in the case where there is no stack sharing and resource usage depends on data-dependent control flow. Ted Giering pointed out that the proof of Theorem 10 does not require early blocking.

The author is indebted to the referees for their careful readings of this article and their constructive criticisms. In particular, the author is especially thankful to the referees for suggesting that the applicability to multiunit resources be made more explicit, and that schedulability results such as Theorem 10 should be explicitly included.

Notes

1. The abbreviation "iff" is used for "if and only if."
2. UNIX is a registered trademark of AT&T.

References

U.S. Department of Defense. 1983. *Military Standard Ada Programming Language*, ANSI/MILSTD1815A, Ada Joint Program Office.

Baker, T.P., and Scallon, G.L. 1986. An Architecture for Real-Time Software Systems. *IEEE Software*. 50–59; reprinted in *Hard-Real-Time Systems*, Washington, DC: IEEE Press (1988).

Baker, T.P. 1989. A Fixed-Point Approach to Bounding Blocking Time in Real-Time Systems. Technical Report, Department of Computer Science, Florida State University, Tallahassee, FL 32306.

Baker, T.P., Malec, C., and Wilson, R. 1989. Practical Tasking. Boeing Aerospace and Electronics Company white paper.

Baker, T.P. 1990. Preemption vs. Priority, and the Importance of Early Blocking. *Proceedings of the Seventh IEEE Workshop on Real-Time Operating Systems and Software*, Charlottesville, VA (May): 44–48.

Baker, T.P. 1990. A Stack-Based Resource Allocation Policy for Realtime Processes. *Proceedings of the IEEE Real-Time Systems Symposium*.

Borger, M.W., and Rajkumar, R. 1989. Implementing Priority Inheritance Algorithms in an Ada Runtime System. Technical report, Software Engineering Institute, Carnegie Mellon University, Pittsburgh, PA.

Chen, M.I., and Lin, K.J. 1989. Dynamic Priority Ceilings: A Concurrency Control Protocol for Real-Time Systems. Technical report UIUCDCS-R-89-1511, Department of Computer Science, University of Illinois at Urbana-Champaign.

Coffman, E.G. Jr., and Denning, P.J. 1973. *Operating Systems Theory*. Englewood Cliffs, NJ: Prentice-Hall.

Garey, M.R., and Johnson, D.S. 1979. *Computers and Intractability*. New York: W.H. Freeman.

Ghazalie, T. 1990. Improving Aperiodic Response with Deadline Scheduling. Master's Thesis, Florida State University.

Giering, E.W. III, and Baker, T.P. 1989. Toward the Deterministic Scheduling of Ada Tasks. *Proceedings of the IEEE Real-Time Systems Symposium*, 31–40.

Habermann, A.N., and Nassi, I.R. 1980. Efficient Implementation of Ada Tasks. Technical report, Department of Computer Science, Carnegie Mellon University.

Havender, J.W. 1968. Avoiding Deadlock in Multitasking Systems. *IBM Systems Journal* 7, 2: 74–84.

Hilfinger, P.N. 1982. Implementation Strategies for Ada Tasking Idioms. *Proceedings of the AdaTEC Conference on Ada*, Arlington, VA: 26–30.

Holt, R.C. 1971. On Deadlock in Computer Systems. Ph.D. Thesis, TR 71-91, Department of Computer Science, Cornell University.

IEEE Computer Society. 1988. IEEE Standard Portable Operating System Interface for Computer Environments, Washington, DC: IEEE Press.

Leung, J.Y.-T., and Merrill, M.L. 1980. A Note on Preemptive Scheduling of Periodic, Real-Time Tasks. *Information Processing Letters* 11, 3: 115–118.

Leung, J.Y.-T., and Whitehead, J. 1982. On the Complexity of Fixed-Priority Scheduling of Periodic Real-Time Tasks. *Performance Evaluation* 2: 237–250.

Liu, C.L., and Layland, J.W. 1973. Scheduling Algorithms for Multiprogramming in a Hard-Real-Time Environment. *JACM* 20.1: 46–61.

Mok, A.K.-L. 1983. Fundamental Design Problems of Distributed Systems for the Hard Real-Time Environment. Ph.D. Thesis, MIT.

Rajkumar, R., Sha, L., Lehoczky, J.P., and Ramamritham, K. 1989. An Optimal Priority Inheritance Protocol for Real-Time Synchronization. Technical report, Carnegie Mellon University (submitted for publication).

Rajkumar, R., Sha, L., and Lehoczky, J.P. 1988. Real-Time Synchronization Protocols for Multiprocessors. *Proceedings of the Real-Time System Symposium*, IEEE, 259–272.

Sha, L., Lehoczky, J.P., and Rajkumar, R. 1986. Solutions for Some Practical Problems in Prioritized Preemptive Scheduling. *Proceedings of the IEEE Real-Time Systems Symposium*, 181–191.

Sha, L., Rajkumar, R., and Lehoczky, J.P. 1987. Priority Inheritance Protocols, An Approach to Real-Time Synchronization. Technical report CMU-CS-87-181, Carnegie Mellon University.

Sha, L., Rajkumar, R., and Lehoczky, J. 1988. A Priority Driven Approach to Real-Time Concurrency Control. Technical report, Carnegie Mellon University.

Sprunt, B., Sha, L., and Lehoczky, J. 1989. Aperiodic Task Scheduling for Hard-Real-Time Systems. *Real Time Systems* 1, 1: 27–60.

Sha, L., Rajkumar, R., and Lehoczky, J. 1989. Mode Change Protocols for Priority-Driven Preemptive Scheduling. *Real Time Systems* 1, 3: 243–264.

Bic, L., and Shaw, A.C. 1988. The Logical Design of Operating Systems. Englewood Cliffs NJ: Prentice-Hall.

Mode Change Protocols for Priority-Driven Preemptive Scheduling

LUI SHA
Software Engineering Institute, Carnegie Mellon University, Pittsburgh, PA 15213

RAGUNATHAN RAJKUMAR
Department of Computer Engineering, Carnegie Mellon University, Pittsburgh, PA 15213

JOHN LEHOCZKY
Department of Statistics, Carnegie Mellon University, Pittsburgh, PA 15213

KRITHI RAMAMRITHAM
Department of Computer and Information Science, University of Massachusetts, Amherst, MA 01003

Abstract. In many real-time applications, the set of tasks in the system, as well as the characteristics of the tasks, change during system execution. Specifically, the system moves from one mode of execution to another as its mission progresses. A mode change is characterized by the deletion of some tasks, addition of new tasks, or changes in the parameters of certain tasks, for example, increasing the sampling rate to obtain a more accurate result. This paper discusses how mode changes can be accommodated within a given framework of priority driven real-time scheduling.

1. Introduction

To successfully develop a large-scale real-time system, we must be able to manage both the logical complexity and timing complexity by using a disciplined approach. The logical complexity is addressed by software engineering methodology, while the timing complexity is addressed by research in real-time scheduling algorithms (Lehoczky and Sha 1986; Lehoczky, Sha and Strosnider 1987; Leinbaugh 1980; Leung and Merrill 1980; Liu and Layland 1973; Rajkumar, Sha and Lehoczky 1987; Ramamritham and Stankovic 1984; Sha, Rajkumar and Lehoczky 1987; Zhao, Ramamritham and Stankovic 1987). An important class of scheduling algorithms is known as static priority scheduling algorithms. These algorithms have several attractive properties. First, they are simple to implement. Second, they have good performance. In a uni-processor, the CPU utilization bound of a randomly chosen periodic task set is 88 percent (Lehoczky, Sha and Ding 1987), while the worst-case bound for any task set is 69 percent (Liu and Layland 1973). In many applications, periodic tasks are often harmonic or nearly harmonic, and this leads to utilization bounds at or near 100 percent.

In addition to good performance found in practice, static priority scheduling algorithms are analyzable for a wide variety of practical conditions such as: (a) the scheduling of a mixture of periodic and aperiodic tasks (Lehoczky, Sha and Strosnider 1987), (b) the handling of transient overloads (Sha, Lehoczky and Rajkumar 1986), and (c) the effect of using semaphores (Sha, Rajkumar and Lehoczky 1987) and Ada rendezvous (Goodenough and Sha 1986) for task synchronization. From a software engineering point of view, these algorithms translate complex timing constraints into simple resource utilization constraints. As long as the utilization constraints of the CPU, I/O channels and communication media are observed, the deadlines of periodic tasks and the response time requirements of aperiodic tasks will both be met (Lehoczky and Sha 1986). This means that the real-time software can be modified freely as long as the utilization bounds are observed. Furthermore, should there be a transient overload, the tasks that will miss deadlines will miss them in reverse order of importance, and the number of tasks missing their deadlines will be a function of the overload (Sha, Lehoczky and Rajkumar 1986).

However, in many applications neither the task set nor the task parameters can remain static throughout the mision. A change in operational mode often leads to the modification of task parameters (for example, task period and execution time) as well as the addition of some new tasks and deletion of some existing tasks. For example, a phase array radar can adjust its sampling rate for the tracking task. Generally speaking, there are two types of mode change issues: application issues and runtime management issues. Application issues deal with the semantics of mode change: the condition for initiating a mode change, the set of tasks to be replaced or modified, and the sequence to delete, add and modify tasks. In this paper, we do not address the application issues of mode change. We assume that when a mode change is initiated, we are given a list of tasks to be modified, added or deleted, and the sequence to do so.

The focus of this paper is on the runtime management of the mode change process. Specifically, we focus upon the scheduling of mode change activities and of tasks during the transition period of mode change. Our objective is to accomplish the mode change process quickly, subject to keeping the consistency of shared data and to meeting the deadlines of tasks that must execute before, during, and after a mode change. This paper is intended to provide an overview on rate-monotonic based scheduling methods and to show how mode changes can be accommodated within this framework. In addition, we analyze the time delay associated with using the mode change protocol presented in this paper.

This paper is organized as follows. In Section 2, we first review the rate-monotonic algorithm and the priority ceiling protocol for scheduling periodic tasks since our mode change protocol will be designed to be compatible with them. In Section 3, we develop the basic mode change protocol and analyze the properties of the basic protocol. In Section 4, we first examine some possible alternatives to the basic protocol. Next, we consider the interplay between this basic protocol and other scheduling issues, namely, the period transformation method for maintaining stability under transient overload and the server algorithms for scheduling both periodics and aperiodics. Finally in Section 5, we present the concluding remarks.

2. Scheduling periodic tasks

In this section, we first review the rate-monotonic scheduling algorithm for independent periodic tasks and then review the priority ceiling protocol designed for the synchronization of periodic tasks using the rate-monotonic scheduling approach. We shall first define the basic concepts and state our assumptions before presenting a review of the scheduling algorithms. A *job J* with execution time *C* is a sequence of instructions that will continuously use the processor until its completion if it is executing alone on the processor. That is, we assume that a job *J* does not suspend itself, say for I/O operations; however, such a situation can be accommodated by defining two or more jobs. In addition, we assume that the critical section of a job is *properly* nested, that is, semaphores will be unlocked in the reversed order of locking. A job will release all of its locks, if it holds any, before or at the end of its execution. In all our discussions below, we assume that jobs $J_1, J_2, \ldots, J_n$ are listed in descending order of priority with J_1 having the highest priority. A *periodic task τ* is a sequence of the same type of job *J* occurring at regular intervals, $\{kT, k = 0, 1, 2, \ldots\}$, where *T* is the period of task τ. An *aperiodic task* is a sequence of the same type of job occurring at irregular intervals. Each task is assigned a fixed priority *P*, and every job of the same task is initially assigned that task's priority. If several jobs are eligible to run, the highest priority job will be run. Jobs with the same priority are executed according to a first-come first-serve discipline. When a job *J* is forced to wait for the execution of lower priority jobs, job *J* is said to be *blocked*. When a job waits for the execution of higher priority jobs or equal priority jobs that have arrived earlier, it is not considered blocked.

In the following, we first review the scheduling of independent periodic tasks. Next, we review the synchronization of periodic tasks and illustrate the issues with an example.

2.1. Scheduling independent periodic tasks

From a scheduling point of view, tasks are considered independent if they do not need to synchronize their executions with each other. Given a set of independent tasks, the scheduler can always preempt the execution of a lower priority task whenever a high priority task is ready to execute. Given a set of independent periodic tasks, the rate-monotonic scheduling algorithm gives a fixed priority to each task and assigns higher priorities to tasks with shorter periods. A task set is said to be *schedulable* if all its deadlines are met, that is, if every periodic task finishes its execution before the end of its period. Any set of independent periodic tasks is schedulable by the rate-monotonic algorithm if the condition of Theorem 1 is met (Liu and Layland 1973).

THEOREM 1:   A set of *n* independent periodic tasks scheduled by the rate-monotonic algorithm will always meet its deadlines, for all task phasings, if

$$\frac{C_1}{T_1} + \ldots + \frac{C_n}{T_n} \leq n(2^{1/n} - 1)$$

where C_i and T_i are the execution time and period of task τ_i respectively.

Theorem 1 offers a sufficient (worst-case) condition that characterizes the schedulability of the rate-monotonic algorithm. This bound converges to 69 percent (*ln* 2) as the number of tasks approaches infinity. Table 1 shows values of the bound for 1 to 10 tasks.

Table 1. Worst-case scheduling bounds as a function of number of tasks.

Scheduling Bounds	
Number of Tasks	Utilization Bound
1	1.0
2	0.828
3	0.779
4	0.756
5	0.743
6	0.734
7	0.728
8	0.724
9	0.720
10	0.718

The utilization bound of Theorem 1 is pessimistic because the worst-case task set is contrived and rather unlikely to be encountered in practice. For a randomly chosen task set, the likely bound is 88 percent (Lehoczky, Sha and Ding 1987). To know if a set of given tasks with utilization greater than the bound of Theorem 1 can meet its deadlines, the conditions of Theorem 2 can be checked (Lehoczky, Sha and Ding 1987).

THEOREM 2: A set of n independent periodic tasks scheduled by the rate-monotonic algorithm will always meet its deadlines, for all task phasings, if and only if

$$\forall i, \ 1 \le i \le n, \ \min_{(k,l) \in R_i} \sum_{j=1}^{i} C_j \frac{1}{lT_k} \left\lceil \frac{lT_k}{T_j} \right\rceil \le 1$$

where C_j and T_j are the execution time and period of task τ_j respectively and $R_i = \{(k, l) \mid 1 \le k \le i, l = 1, \ldots \lfloor T_i/T_k \rfloor \}$.

Theorem 2 provides the exact criterion for testing the schedulability of independent periodic tasks using the rate-monotonic algorithm. In effect, the theorem checks if each task can complete its execution before its first deadline by checking all the scheduling points.[1] The scheduling points for task τ are τ's first deadline and the end of periods of higher priority tasks within τ's first deadline. In each application of the formula, i corresponds to the task τ_i whose deadline is to be checked, and k corresponds to each of the tasks that affects the completion time of task τ, that is, task τ_i itself and the higher priority tasks. For given i and k, l represents the scheduling points of task τ_k. For example, suppose that we have tasks τ_1 and τ_2 with periods $T_1 = 5$ and $T_2 = 14$. For task (τ_i, $i = 1$) we have only *one* scheduling point, the end of task τ_1's first period, that is, $i = k = 1$ and ($l = 1$, ..., $\lfloor T_i/T_k \rfloor = \lfloor T_1/T_1 \rfloor = 1$). The scheduling point is, of course, τ_1's first deadline ($lT_k = 5$, $l = 1$, $k = 1$). For task (τ_i, $i = 2$), there are *two* scheduling points from all higher priority tasks, (τ_k, $k = 1$), that is, ($l = 1$, ..., $\lfloor T_i/T_k \rfloor = \lfloor T_2/T_1 \rfloor = 2$). The two scheduling points correspond to the two end-points of task τ_1's period within the first deadline of task τ_2 at 14, that is, $(lT_k = 5, l = 1, k = 1)$ and $(lT_k = 10, l = 2, k = 1)$. Finally, there is the scheduling point from τ_2's own first deadline, that is, $(lT_k = 14, l = 1, k = 2)$. At each scheduling point, we check if the task in question can complete its execution at or before the scheduling point. A detailed illustration of the application of this theorem and its generalization is given in Example 3 in Section 2.3.

2.2. Task synchronization

In the previous sections we have discussed the scheduling of independent tasks. Tasks, however, do interact and hence need to be synchronized. Common synchronization primitives include semaphores, locks, monitors, and Ada rendezvous. Although the use of these or equivalent methods is necessary to protect the consistency of shared data or to guarantee the proper use of non-preemptable resources, their use may jeopardize the ability of the system to meet its timing requirements. In fact, a direct application of these synchronization mechanisms may lead to an indefinite period of priority inversion and low schedulability. However, the discussion is limited to scheduling within a uniprocessor. Readers who are interested in the multiprocessor synchronization problem are referred to (Rajkumar, Sha and Lehockzy 1988).

Example 1: Suppose J_1, J_2, and J_3 are three jobs arranged in descending order of priority with J_1 having the highest priority. Let jobs J_1 and J_2 share a data structure guarded by a binary semaphore S. Suppose that at time t_1, job J_3 locks the semaphore S and executes its critical section. During the execution of job J_3's critical section, the high priority job J_1 is initiated, preempts J_3 and later attempts to use the shared data. However, job J_1 will be blocked on the semaphore S. One might expect that J_1, being the highest priority job, is blocked no longer than the time for job J_3 to complete its critical section. However, the duration of blocking is, in fact, unpredictable. This is because job J_3 can be preempted by the intermediate priority job J_2. The blocking of J_3, and hence that of J_1, will continue until J_2 and any other pending intermediate jobs are completed.

The blocking period in this example can be arbitrarily long. One way to deal with the priority inversion problem is to let the critical section of each task to run to completion without interruption. This is know as the *kernelized monitor approach* (Mok 1983), which is an effective approach for short critical sections. Another approach is to properly manage task interactions. The *priority ceiling protocol* is a scheme designed for the use of binary semaphores. This protocol ensures (1) freedom from mutual deadlock and (2) that a high priority task will be blocked by lower priority tasks for the duration of at most one critical section (Goodenough and Sha 1988; Sha, Rajkumar and Lehoczky 1987).

Two ideas underlie the design of this protocol. First is the concept of priority inheritance: when a task τ blocks the execution of higher priority tasks, task τ should execute at the highest priority level of all the tasks blocked by τ. Secondly, we must guarantee that each newly started critical section executes at a priority level that is higher than the (inherited) priority levels of the preempted critical sections. It was shown in (Sha, Rajkumar, and Lehoczky 1987) that such a prioritized total ordering in the execution of critical sections leads to the two properties mentioned above. To achieve such prioritized total ordering, we define the concept of the priority ceiling of a binary semaphore S to be equal to the highest priority task that may lock S. When a job J attempts to execute one of its critical sections, it will be blocked unless its priority is strictly higher than all the priority ceilings of semaphores currently locked by jobs other than J. If job J blocks, the job that holds the lock on the highest priority ceiling semaphore is said to be blocking J and hence inherits J's priority. A job J can, however, always preempt another job executing at a lower priority level as long as J does not attempt to enter a critical section.

Example 2: Suppose that we have two jobs J_1 and J_2 in the system. In addition, there are two shared data structures protected by binary semaphores S_1 and S_2 respectively. Suppose the sequence of processing steps for each job is as follows:

$$J_1 = \{\ldots, \mathbf{P}(S_1), \ldots, \mathbf{P}(S2), \ldots, \mathbf{V}(S_2), \ldots, \mathbf{V}(S_1), \ldots\}$$

$$J_2 = \{\ldots, \mathbf{P}(S_2), \ldots, \mathbf{P}(S_1), \ldots, \mathbf{V}(S_1), \ldots \mathbf{V}(S_2), \ldots\}\ .$$

Recall that the priority of job J_1 is assumed to be higher than that of job J_2. Thus, the priority ceilings of both semaphores S_1 and S_2 are equal to the priority of job J_1. Suppose that at time t_0, J_2 is initiated and it begins execution and then locks semaphore S_2. At time t_1, job J_1 is initiated and preempts job J_2 and at time t_2, job J_1 tries to enter its critical section by making an indivisible system call to execute $\mathbf{P}(S_1)$. However, the runtime system will find that job J_1's priority is *not* higher than the priority ceiling of *locked* semaphore S_2. Hence, the runtime system suspends job J_1 without locking S_1. Job J_2 now *inherits* the priority of job J_1 and resumes execution. Note that J_1 is blocked outside its critical section. As J_1 is not given the lock on S_1 but suspended instead, the potential deadlock involving J_1 and J_2 is prevented. Once J_2 exits its critical section, it will return to its assigned priority and immediately be preempted by job J_1. The J_1 will execute to completion, and finally J_2 will resume and run to completion.

Let B_i be the longest duration of blocking that can be experienced by a job of task τ_i. The following two theorems indicate whether the deadlines of a set of periodic tasks can be met if the priority ceiling protocol is used.

THEOREM 3: A set of n periodic tasks using the priority ceiling protocol can be scheduled by the rate-monotonic algorithm if the following condition is satisfied (Sha, Rajkumar and Lehoczky 1987):

$$\frac{C_1}{T_1} + \ldots + \frac{C_n}{T_n} + max\left(\frac{B_1}{T_1}, \ldots, \frac{B_{n-1}}{T_{n-1}}\right) \le n(2^{1/n} - 1)\ .$$

THEOREM 4: A set of n periodic tasks using the priority ceiling protocol can be scheduled by the rate-monotonic algorithm for all task phasings if the following condition is satisfied (Sha, Rajkumar and Lehoczky 1987).

$$\forall i, \ 1 \leq i \leq n, \ \min_{(k,l)\epsilon R_i} \left(\sum_{j=1}^{i-1} C_j \frac{1}{lT_k} \left\lceil \frac{lT_k}{T_j} \right\rceil + \frac{C_i}{lT_k} + \frac{B_i}{lT_k} \right) \leq 1$$

where C_i, T_i and R_i are defined in Theorem 2, and B_i is the worst-case blocking time for a job of task τ_i.

Remark: Theorems 3 and 4 generalize Theorems 1 and 2 by taking the blocking duration of a job into consideration. The B_i's in Theorems 3 and 4 can be used to account for any delay caused by resource sharing. Note that the upper limit of the summation in the theorem is $(i-1)$ instead of i, as in Theorem 2.

In the application of Theorems 3 and 4, it is important to realize that under the priority ceiling protocol, a task τ can be blocked by a lower priority task τ_L if τ_L may lock a semaphore S whose priority ceiling is higher than or equal to the priority of task τ, even if τ and τ_L do not share any semaphore. For example, suppose that τ_L locks S first. Next, τ is initiated and preempts τ_L. Later, a high priority task τ_H is initiated and attempts to lock S. Task τ_H will be blocked. Task τ_L now *inherits* the priority of τ_H and executes. Note that τ has to wait for the critical section of τ_L even τ and τ_L do not share any semaphore. We call such blocking, *push-through blocking*. Push-through blocking is the price for avoiding unbounded priority inversion. If task τ_L does not inherit the priority of τ_H, task τ_H can be indirectly preempted by task τ and all the tasks that have priority higher than that of τ_L. Finally, we want to point out that even if task τ_H does not attempt to lock S but attempts to lock another unlocked semaphore, τ_H will still be blocked by the priority ceiling protocol because τ_H's priority is not higher than the priority ceiling of S. We call this form of blocking, *ceiling blocking*. Ceiling blocking is the price for ensuring the freedom of deadlock and the property of a task being blocked at most once. Both ceiling blocking and push-through are accounted for by B_i in Theorems 3 and 4.

2.3. An example

In this section, we give a simple example to illustrate the application of the scheduling theorems.

Example 3: We would like to check the schedulability of the following task set.

1. Periodic task τ_1: execution = 40 msec; period = 100 msec; deadline is at the end of each period.
   In addition, τ_3 may block τ_1 for 10 msec through the use of a shared communication server and task τ_2 may block τ_1 for 20 msec through the use of a shared data object.
2. Periodic task τ_2: execution time = 40 msec; period = 150 msec; deadline is 20 msec before the end of each period.
3. Periodic task τ_3: execution time = 100 msec; period = 350 msec; deadline is at the end of each period.

Since under the priority ceiling protocol a task can be blocked by lower priority tasks at most once, the maximal blocking time for task τ_1 is $B_1 = \max(10, 20)$ msec = 20 msec. Since τ_3 may lock the semaphore S_c associated with the communication server and the priority ceiling of S_c is higher than that of task τ_2, task τ_2 can be blocked by task τ_3 for 10 msec.[2] Finally, task τ_2 has to finish 20 msec earlier than the nominal deadline of a periodic task. This is equivalent to saying that τ_2 will always be blocked for additional 20 msec but its deadline is at the end of the period. Hence, $B_2 = (10 + 20)$ msec = 30 msec.[3] Using Theorem 4:

1. Task τ_1: Check $C_1 + B_1 \leq 100$. Since $40 + 20 \leq 100$, task τ_1 is schedulable.
2. Task τ_2: Check whether either

$$C_1 + C_2 + B_2 \leq 100 \qquad 40 + 40 + 30 > 100$$
$$\text{or} \qquad 2C_1 + C_2 + B_2 \leq 150 \qquad 80 + 40 + 30 = 150$$

Task τ_2 is schedulable and in the worst-case phasing will meet its deadline exactly at time 150.
3. Task τ_3: Check whether either

$$C_1 + C_2 + C_3 \leq 100 \qquad 40 + 40 + 100 > 100$$
$$\text{or} \qquad 2C_1 + C_2 + C_3 \leq 150 \qquad 80 + 40 + 100 > 150$$
$$\text{or} \qquad 2C_1 + 2C_2 + C_3 \leq 200 \qquad 80 + 80 + 100 > 200$$
$$\text{or} \qquad 3C_1 + 2C_2 + C_3 \leq 300 \qquad 120 + 80 + 100 = 300$$
$$\text{or} \qquad 4C_1 + 3C_2 - C_3 \leq 350 \qquad 160 + 120 + 100 > 350$$

Task τ_3 is also schedulable and in the worst-case phasing will meet its deadline exactly at time 300. If follows that all the three periodic tasks can meet their deadlines.

3. Mode change protocols

We now discuss the protocols needed to support mode changes in the context of our scheduling algorithms for periodic tasks. First, we discuss the characteristics of mode change. This is followed by a simple protocol when only independent tasks are involved. Finally, we discuss the mode change problems in the presence of task interactions.

3.1. Mode changes for independent tasks

From a scheduling point of view, typical mode change operations can be classified into two types:

1. Operations that increase a task set's processor utilization:
   a. Adding a task
   b. Increasing the execution time of a task
   c. Increasing the frequency of execution of a task.

2. Operations that decrease a task set's processor utilization:
   a. Deleting a task
   b. Decreasing the execution time of a task
   c. Decreasing the frequency of a task.

A simple mode change protocol can be defined in terms of the deletion of existing tasks and the addition of a new task. If a task modifies its parameters, that is, changes its sampling rate, it is modeled as the deletion of the original task and the addition of a new task. In addition, we assume that all the tasks are periodic and that a task which has started its execution will not be deleted until it has completed its execution in the current period. We will relax these assumptions later in this paper, however.

When tasks are independent, the addition, deletion, or modification of a task's parameters is merely an application of Theorems 1 or 2.

THEOREM 5:   At any time t, a task τ can be added, or its computation time C increased or its frequency increased without causing any task to miss their deadlines if the conditions of Theorems 1 or 2 are satisfied.

Proof: It directly follows from the fact that a task set is schedulable if it satisfies the conditions of Theorems 1 or 2.

THEOREM 6:   At any time t, a task τ can be deleted, or its computation time C reduced or its frequency reduced without causing any task to miss their deadlines.

Proof: It directly follows the fact that if a given task set satisfies the conditions of Theorems 1 or 2, then the modified task set will also satisfy the conditions in question.

It may seem that once a task is deleted, its allocated processor capacity can be immediately reused by other tasks. However, this is not true. The schedulability of a set of tasks using the rate-monotonic algorithm is determined under the assumption that once a job J of a task τ is initiated, task τ cannot request additional processing until the beginning of τ's next period. Thus, even if job J has finished its execution m units before the end of τ's current period, task τ has used up the processor capacity for the given period. Hence, task τ must be included in the application of Theorems 1 and 2, 3 and 4 until the end of the current period. In other words, the processor capacity allocated to τ cannot be used by new tasks until the end of τ's current period.

3.2. The basic mode change protocol

In this section, we will develop a basic mode change protocol for periodic tasks using binary semaphores for synchronization. There are two basic concepts in the design of this protocol. The first is the notion of sufficient processor capacity to add a task *on the fly* when synchronization is involved. The second is the preservation of the characteristic of the priority ceiling protocol: each newly started critical section is guaranteed to execute at a priority level that is higher than the maximum priority that any of the preempted critical sections can inherit.

Definition: Processor capacity is said to be sufficient for adding a task τ, if the resulting n tasks, including τ, can meet all their deadlines using the rate-monotonic algorithm and the priority ceiling protocol.

Theorems 3 and 4 provide us with sufficient conditions for processor capacity to be sufficient. Theorem 4 allows for a higher degree of processor utilization while Theorem 3 is easier to apply.

We have defined the concept of having sufficient capacity to add a task. A related concept is the deletion of a task τ and reclaiming the processor capacity used by τ.

Definition: The processor capacity used by a deleted task τ is said to be reclaimed at time t if after t task τ does not need to be included in the application of Theorems 3 and 4.

We now define the basic mode change protocol. We assume that during mode transition, tasks are deleted/added in an order that is consistent with the semantics of the application.

1. The addition and/or the deletion of tasks in mode change may lead to the modification of the priority ceiling of some semaphores across the mode change. Upon the initiation of mode change,
   - For each of the unlocked semaphores S, whose priority ceiling needs to be raised, S's ceiling is raised immediately and indivisibly.
   - For each locked semaphore S, whose priority ceiling needs to be raised, S's priority ceiling is raised immediately and indivisibly after S is unlocked.
   - For each semaphore S, whose priority ceiling needs to be lowered, S's priority ceiling is lowered when all the tasks which may lock S and which have priorities greater than the new priority ceiling of S are deleted.
2. A task τ, which needs to be deleted, can be deleted immediately upon the initiation of mode change, if τ has not yet started its execution in its current period. In addition, the processor capacity used by τ is reclaimed immediately. On the other hand, if τ has started execution, τ can be deleted after the end of its execution and before its next initiation time. The processor capacity allocated to τ will, however, not be reclaimed until the next initiation time.
3. A task τ can be added into the system if the following two conditions are met:
   - If task τ's priority is higher than the priority ceiling of locked semaphores $S_1, \ldots$ S_k, then the priority ceiling of $S_1, \ldots S_k$ must be first raised before adding task τ.
   - There must be sufficient processor capacity for adding task τ.

We now illustrate the mode change protocol using an example.

Example 4: Suppose that the task set $\{\tau_1, \tau_2, \tau_2\}$ is replaced by the task set $\{\tau_0, \tau_3^*, \tau_4, \tau_5\}$. In other words, tasks τ_1 and τ_2 are to be deleted and replaced with τ_0, τ_4 and τ_5 in the new task set. The task τ_3 is to be modified to τ_3^* resulting in a change of parameters. Suppose that τ_0 cannot be added until τ_1 is deleted because of insufficient processor capacity or semantic requirements. Similarly, suppose that τ_4 and τ_5 cannot be added until τ_2 is deleted and its processor capacity reclaimed. We assume that we add tasks τ_0, τ_4 and τ_5

in that order when a mode change is initiated. In addition, we assume that tasks that need to be deleted can be deleted in any order.

Let the jobs of each task execute the following sequences of instructions in the current task set.

$$J_1 = \{\ldots, P(S_1), \ldots, V(S_1), \ldots\}$$
$$J_2 = \{\ldots, P(S_1), \ldots, P(S_2), \ldots, V(S_2), \ldots, V(S_1), \ldots\}$$
$$J_3 = \{\ldots, P(S_2), \ldots, V(S_2), \ldots\} \ .$$

Let the jobs in the new mode execute the following sequences of events:

$$J_0 = \{\ldots, P(S_2), \ldots, V(S_2), \ldots\}$$
$$J_3^* = \{\ldots, P(S_2), \ldots, V(S_2), \ldots\}$$
$$J_4 = \{\ldots, P(S_2), \ldots, P(S_1), \ldots, V(S_1), \ldots, V(S_2), \ldots\}$$
$$J_5 = \{\ldots, P(S_1), \ldots, V(S_1), \ldots\} \ .$$

As before, we assume that the priority of J_{i+1} is lower than the priority of J_i. Before the mode change, the priority ceilings of S_1 and S_2 are the priorities of τ_1 and τ_2 respectively. However, after the mode change, the priority ceilings of S_1 and S_2 are the priorities of τ_4 and τ_0 respectively. Thus, after the mode change, the priority ceiling of S_1 is lowered, while that of S_2 is raised.

Consider the following sequence of events depicted in Figure 1. A line at a low level indicates that the corresponding job is blocked or has been preempted by a higher priority job. A line raised to a higher level indicates that the job is executing. The absence of a line indicates that the job has not yet been initiated or has completed. Shaded portions indicate execution of critical sections.

- At time t_0, the task set that is being run is $\{\tau_1, \tau_2, \tau_3\}$. J_3 arrives and begins execution.
- At time t_1, J_3 locks S_2 and enters its critical section.
- At time t_2, J_2 arrives and preempts J_3.
- At time t_3, J_2 attempts to lock S_1 and is blocked by the priority ceiling protocol. J_3 inherits J_2's priority and resumes execution.
- At time t_4, J_1 arrives and preempts J_3.
- At time t_5, J_1 successfully locks S_1, since its priority is higher than the priority ceiling of locked semaphore S_2.
- At time t_6, J_1 releases the semaphore S_1. At the same time, a mode change is initiated due to external requirements. τ_0 is the first task to be added at the mode change and it cannot be added until the processing capacity is reclaimed from τ_1. Hence, τ_0 cannot be added until the end of J_1's current period (at t_{12}). Similarly, τ_4 and τ_5 cannot be added until the end of J_2's current period (at t_{17}). The priority ceiling of S_2 gets raised in the new mode but cannot be raised until it is unlocked.
- At time t_7, J_1 completes execution and J_3 resumes execution at its inherited priority of J_2.
- At time t_8, J_3 releases the semaphore S_2 and resumes its original priority. The priority ceiling of S_2 is raised now. J_2 immediately preempts J_3 and locks S_1.
- At time t_9, J_2 makes a nested access to S_2 and locks S_2.

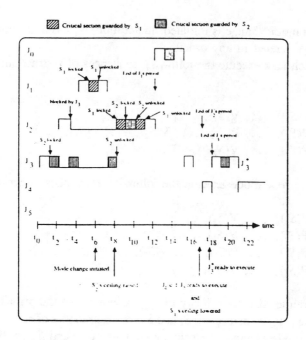

Figure 1. Sequence of events described in example 4.

- At time t_{10}, J_2 releases the semaphore S_2.
- At time t_{11}, J_2 releases the semaphore S_1.
- At time t_{12}, J_2 completes execution. The current period τ_1 ends here and τ_1 is deleted. Hence, τ_0 is added into the system and immediately becomes eligible for execution.
- At time t_{13}, J_0 locks semaphore S_2 since there is no other locked semaphore in the system.
- At time t_{14}, J_0 releases S_2.
- At time t_{15}, J_0 completes execution and J_3 resumes execution.
- At time t_{16}, J_3 completes execution.
- The processor remains idle during the interval $[t_{16}, t_{17}]$.[4]
- At time t_{17}, the current period of τ_2 ends and it can be deleted from the system. The priority ceiling of S_1 is lowered and τ_0 was added into the system. Now, τ_4 and τ_5 can also be added into the system. Having the highest priority among tasks ready to run. J_4 begins execution.
- At time t_{18}, τ_3's current period ends and τ_3 can be replaced with τ_3^*. The mode change is now complete. Job J_3 preempts J_4 and begins execution.
- At time t_{21}, J_3^* completes execution, locking and releasing S_2 at t_{19} and t_{20} respectively. Now, J_4 resumes execution.
- Processing proceeds normally in the new mode.

The above example illustrates the following properties of the mode change protocol. First, tasks can be added as long as they are schedulable in the resulting task set. However, a task to be added may have to wait for the deletion of an existing task even though there is idle capacity available. We shall further study this mode change delay in Section 3.4. Task modifications, such as the modification of τ_3 into τ_3^* can be carried out relatively easily.

3.3. *Properties of the basic mode change protocol*

The Mode Change Protocol is designed to keep the properties of the priority ceiling protocol valid. Under the priority ceiling protocol, there is no mutual deadlock, and a job can be blocked by lower priority jobs for at most the duration of a single critical section (Sha, Rajkumar and Lehoczky 1987). We shall now prove that both these properties are preserved under the mode change protocol.

Lemma 7: Under the mode change protocol, when a job J enters its critical section and preempts job J_i while J_i is in its critical section, the priority of J is higher than the priority that can be inherited by J_i.

Proof: Under the definition of the mode change protocol, the priority ceiling of a semaphore S will not be lower than the priority of any job that may lock S. When job J enters its critical section, its priority will be higher than the (inherited) priority of the jobs preempted by J. since (1) a job J is allowed to enter its critical section only if J's priority is higher than the priority ceilings of all the semaphores locked by jobs other than J, and (2) the highest priority that a job can inherit is bounded by the priority ceiling of the semaphores locked by this job.

THEOREM 8: There is no mutual deadlock under the mode change protocol.

Proof: Suppose that there is a mutual deadlock. Let the highest priority of all the jobs involved in the deadlock be P. Due to the transitivity of priority inheritance, all the jobs involved in the deadlock will eventually inherit the same highest priority P. This contradicts Lemma 7.

Lemma 9: A job J can be blocked by a lower priority job J_L at most for the duration of executing one critical section.

Proof: First. if job J_L is not already in its critical section when job J arrives, then job J_L will be preempted by J and cannot block J. Suppose that J_L is in its critical section when J arrives and that J_L blocks J. J_L inherits the priority of J and continues its execution. Once J_L exits its critical section, by the definition of the priority ceiling protocol, J_L will be assigned its original priority and be immediately preempted by J. Hence, J_L cannot block J again.

THEOREM 10: Under the mode change protocol, a job J can be blocked by lower priority jobs for at most the duration of a single (outermost) critical section.

Proof: Suppose that job J is blocked by lower priority jobs more than once. By Lemma 9. job J must be blocked by n different lower priority jobs, $J_1, \ldots, J_n$, where the priority of J_i is assumed to be higher than or equal to that of J_{i+1}. Since a lower priority job cannot block a higher priority job unless it is already in its critical section, jobs $J_1, \ldots, J_n$ must be in their critical sections when J arrives. By assumption, J is blocked by J_n and J_n

inherits the priority of J. It follows that job J's priority cannot be higher than the highest priority P that can be inherited by J_n. On the other hand, by Lemma 7, job J_{n-1}'s priority is higher than P. It follows that job J_{n-1}'s priority is higher than that of job J. This contradicts the assumption that J's priority is higher than that of jobs $J_1, \ldots, J_n$.

Remark: It is important to point out that the property of a job being blocked for at most one critical section depends upon our model of a job, an instance of a periodic task. We assume that when a job executes alone on the processor, input data from I/O devices will be ready when the job is initiated and it will continue to execute until it completes without suspension for I/O activities. In some applications, an instance of a periodic task may need to suspend itself for I/O. In this case, we have the following corollary:

Corollary 11: If a generalized job J suspends itself n times during its execution, it can be blocked for the duration of at most $n + 1$ critical sections.

3.4. Mode change delays.

In this section, we analyze the delays that can occur before a mode change is completed. In the following analysis, we assume that the given task set is schedulable using the rate-monotonic algorithm and the priority ceiling protocol.

Notation: Let t_0 denote the time at which the mode change is initiated. Let D_s be the delay in elevating semaphore priority ceilings, that is, the delay between t_0 and the time at which all the semaphores whose ceilings need to be raised are raised. Let D_c be the delay in reclaiming processor capacity, that is, the delay between t_0 and the time at which all the tasks that need to be deleted are deleted and their allocated processor capacity becomes available. Finally, let D be the *mode change delay*, that is, the duration between t_0 and the time at which the mode change is completed.

The following lemmas and theorems are based on the assumption that the task sets before and after a mode change are schedulable.

Lemma 12: Let S_i be a semaphore whose priority ceiling needs to be raised during a mode change. Let τ be a task whose priority is equal to the priority ceiling of semaphore S_i. The delay in elevating the priority ceiling of S_i is bounded by the period of task τ, T.

Proof: The priority ceiling of a semaphore S can be raised only if it is not locked. Semaphore S may have been locked when the mode change is initiated. However, under the assumption that task τ can meet its deadline, the locking of S cannot be longer than T and the lemma follows.

Lemma 13: Let S^* be the semaphore that has the lowest priority ceiling of all the semaphores whose ceilings need to be raised. The ceiling elevation delay for mode change, D_s is bounded by T^*, the period of a task whose priority is equal to the priority ceiling of S^*.

Proof: It directly follows from Lemma 12 and from the fact that a task associated with a lower priority ceiling has a longer period under the rate-monotonic scheduling algorithm.

Lemma 14: Let task τ be the lowest priority task needed to be deleted. The delay due to the reclamation of processor capacity, D_b, is bounded by the period of task τ.

Proof: Let the periods of the tasks that need to be deleted be $\{T_j, \ldots, T_m\}$, where $T_k \geq T_j$ if $k > j$. Under the assumption that the set of given tasks is schedulable, each of the tasks needed to be deleted can be deleted by the end of its current period, and its allocated processor capacity can be reclaimed. Hence, we have $D_c = max\{T_j, \ldots, T_m\}$. Under the rate-monotonic scheduling algorithm, a task with a longer period has lower priority. It follows that the delay due to reclaiming all the processor capacity is bounded by the period of task τ_m, T_m.

THEOREM 15: The mode change delay D is bounded by $max(D_s, D_c)$.

Proof: Suppose that the mode change request occurs at time t_0. By $(t_0 + D_s)$, all the semaphore priority ceilings that need to be raised have been raised. By $(t_0 + D_c)$, all the tasks in the current mode that need to be deleted are deleted. That is, the processor capacity needed for the new tasks is available by $(t_0 + D_c)$. It follows that all the new tasks can be added by the time $(t_0 + max(D_s, D_c))$. Finally, by the definition of the basic mode change protocol, all the semaphore priority ceilings that need to be lowered have been lowered by $(t_0 + D_c)$. Hence, the mode change delay is bounded by $max(D_s, D_c)$.

Remark: Under the mode change protocol, the maximal mode change delay is bounded by the longest period in a task set, which is generally much shorter and will never be longer than the least common multiple (LCM) of all the periods. In the cyclical executive approach, the major cycle is the LCM of all the periods and a mode change will not be initiated until the current major cycle completes. Hence, the delay to complete a mode change using the mode change protocol would typically be much shorter than the delay using the cyclical executive approach. In addition, the mode change protocol also provides the flexibility of adding the most urgent task in the new mode first.

4. Extensions of the basic mode change protocol

In this section, we will examine some design alternatives to the mode change protocol as well as the integration of our basic mode change protocol with other scheduling algorithms.

4.1. Variations of the basic protocol

The objective in the design of the mode change protocol is to minimize the mode change delay subject to keeping the shared data consistent and to meeting all the deadlines of tasks that must be continuously executing. We also made an implicit assumption that the mode change protocol should not lower the system schedulability in any given mode.

However, assumptions and objectives are, of course, application dependent. Generally, there is relatively little that one can do about mode change delay caused by reclaiming processor capacity, because a task could have started its execution when the mode change is initiated. Once a task begins execution, it may well be desirable to let it complete because the abortion of a task may lead to complications that makes later correction and/or recovery time-consuming. There is an exception to this general observation, however. In certain applications, one can define a set of tasks that constitutes an atomic configuration unit. Such a unit encapsulates all the shared variables for the task set in question. In this case, the application semantic may allow the entire unit to be deleted immediately and indivisibly at the initiation of mode change.

Generally, when $D_s > D_c$, there is an incentive to minimize D_s. We can minimize the mode change delay associated with elevating the priority ceilings if we are willing to pay a schedulability cost. For example, we define the *global ceiling* mode change protocol as follows. In this protocol, the priority ceiling of a semaphore S is defined as the priority of the highest priority task that may access S across *all* modes. The disadvantage of this mode change protocol is rather obvious. In any mode, the *actual* ceiling of a semaphore can be much lower than the *global* priority ceiling. As a consequence, the blocking duration is longer and it translates into schedulability cost, causing some otherwise schedulable task sets to become unschedulable. The priority ceiling elevation cost can be fine-tuned, however. Since D_s is determined solely by the period of the task whose priority equals the lowest priority ceiling that needs to be raised, D_s can be shortened by deliberately assigning a higher priority ceiling to the semaphore with this lowest priority ceiling that needs to be raised in mode changes.

Finally, we may want to emphasize the simplicity of managing a mode change process. In this case, we do not raise the semaphore priority ceiling of any semaphore until all the tasks that need to be deleted are deleted and the priority ceilings of associated semaphores are lowered. New tasks will be added at time $t_{add} = t_0 + (D_s + D_c)$. We need apply neither Theorem 3 nor Theorem 4 during runtime as long as tasks are known to be schedulable in each mode. This is because at time t_{add} all the deleted tasks' processor capacity have already been reclaimed and the priority ceilings are at the correct level. That is, the condition under which we may apply Theorem 3 or 4 is the same as in the new mode.

4.2. Stability under transient overload

In this section, we discuss the integration between the mode change protocol and the solution to the stability problem. In the previous sections, the computation time of a task is assumed to be constant. However, in many applications, task execution times are often stochastic, and the worst-case execution time can be significantly larger than the average execution time. In order to have a reasonably high average processor utilization, we must deal with the problem of transient overload. We consider a scheduling algorithm to be *stable* if there exists a set of *critical* tasks such that all tasks in the set will meet their deadlines even if the processor is overloaded. This means that under worst-case conditions, tasks outside the critical set may miss their deadlines. The rate-monotonic algorithm is stable in the sense that the set of tasks that never miss their deadlines does not change as the processor gets more overloaded or as task phasings change. Of course, which tasks are in the critical task set depends on the worst-case utilizations of the particular tasks being considered. The important point is that the rate-monotonic theory guarantees that if such a set exists, it always consists of tasks with the highest priorities. This means that if a transient overload should develop, tasks with longer periods will miss their deadlines.

Of course, a task with a longer period could be more critical to an application than a task with a shorter period. One might attempt to ensure that the critical task always meets its deadline by assigning priorities according to a task's importance. However, this approach can lead to poor schedulability, that is, with this approach, deadlines of critical tasks might be met only when the total utilization is low.

The *period transformation* technique can be used to ensure high utilization while meeting the deadline of an important, long-period task. Period transformation means turning a long-period important task into a high priority task by splitting its work over several short periods. For example, suppose task τ with a long period T is not in the critical task set and must never miss its deadline. We can make τ simulate a short period task by giving it a period of $T/2$ and suspending it after it executes half its worst-case execution time, $C/2$. The task is then resumed and finishes its work in the next execution period. It still completes its total computation before the end of period T. From the viewpoint of the rate-monotonic theory, the transformed task has the same utilization but a shorter period, $T/2$, and its priority is raised accordingly. It is important to note that the most important task does not have to have the shortest period. We only need to make sure that it is among the first n high priority tasks whose worst-case utilization is within the scheduling bound. A systematic procedure for period transformation with minimal task partitioning can be found in (Sha, Lehoczky and Rajkumar 1986).

Period transformation allows important tasks to have higher priority while keeping priority assignments consistent with rate-monotonic rules. This kind of transformation should be familiar to users of cyclic executives. The difference here is that we don't need to adjust the code segment sizes so different code segments fit into shared time slots. Instead, τ simply requests suspension after performing $C/2$ amount of work. Alternatively, the runtime scheduler can be instructed to suspend the task after a certain amount of computation has been done, without affecting the application code.[5]

The period transformation approach has another benefit—it can raise the rate-monotonic utilization bound. Suppose the rate-monotonic utilization bound is $U_{max} < 100$ percent, that is, total task utilization cannot be increased above U_{max} without missing a deadline. When a period transformation is applied to the task set, U_{max} will rise. For example:

Example 4: Let

- Task τ_1: $C_1 = 4$; $T_1 = 10$; $U_1 = .400$
- Task τ_2: $C_2 = 6$; $T_2 = 14$; $U_1 = .428$.

The total utilization is .828, which just equals the bound of Theorem 1, so this set of two tasks is schedulable. If we apply Theorem 2, we find:

$$C_1 + C_2 \le T_1 \qquad 4 + 6 = 10 \qquad l = 1, k = 1$$
$$\text{or} \qquad 2C_1 + C_2 \le T_2 \qquad 8 + 6 = 14 \qquad l = 1, k = 2.$$

So Theorem 2 says the task set is just schedulable. Now suppose we perform a period transformation on task τ_1, so $C_1' = 2$ and $T_1' = 5$. The total utilization is the same and the set is still schedulable, but when we apply Theorem 2 we find:

$$
\begin{array}{llll}
 & C_1 + C_2 \leq T_1 & 2 + 6 > 5 & l = 1, k = 1 \\
\text{or} & 2C_1 + C_2 \leq 2T_1 & 4 + 6 = 10 & l = 2, k = 1 \\
\text{or} & 3C_1 + C_2 < T_2 & 6 + 6 < 14 & l = 1, k = 2.
\end{array}
$$

The third inequality shows that the compute times for tasks τ_1 and/or τ_2 can be increased without violating the constraint. For example: the compute time of Task τ_1 can be increased by 2/3 units to 2.667, giving an overall schedulable utilization of 2.667/5 + 6/14 = .961; or the compute time of Task τ_2 can be increased to 8, giving an overall schedulable utilization of 2/5 + 8/14 = .971. So the effect of the period transformation has been to raise the utilization bound from .828 to at least .961 and at most .971. Indeed, if periods are uniformly harmonic, that is, if each period is an integral multiple of each shorter period, the utilization bound of the rate-monotonic algorithm is 100 percent.[6] So the utilization produced by the rate-monotonic approach is only an upper bound on what can be achieved if the periods are not transformed. Of course, as the periods get shorter, the scheduling overhead utilization increases, so the amount of useful work that can be done decreases. For example, before a period transformation, the utilization for a task, including scheduling overhead, is $(C + 2S)/T$, where $2S$ is the context switching time due to the preemption and resumption of a task. After splitting the period into two parts, the utilization is $(.5C + 2S)/.5T$, so scheduling overhead is a larger part of the total utilization. However, the utilization bound is also increased, in general. If the increase in utilization caused by the scheduling overhead is less than the increase in the utilization bound, then the period transformation is a win— more useful work can be done while meeting all deadlines.

Period transformation does not affect the mode change protocol except that to delete a transformed task that has already started execution, we must wait for its completion which may take several *transformed periods*. In addition, we cannot reclaim the processor capacity of a transformed task until the end of the last transformed period, which is also the end of the task's original period.

4.3. Scheduling both aperiodic and periodic tasks

It is important to meet the regular deadlines of periodic tasks *and* the response time requirements of aperiodic events. We now review the scheduling of both aperiodic and periodic tasks within the rate monotonic framework.[7] As we will see, the mode change protocol can easily accommodate the aperiodic scheduling algorithms. Let us begin with a simple example.

Suppose that we have two tasks. Let τ_1 be a periodic task with period 100 and execution time 99. Let τ_2 be an aperiodic task that appears once within a period of 100 but the arrival time is random. The execution time of task τ_2 is one unit. If we let the aperiodic task wait for the periodic task, then the average response time is about 50 units. The same can be said for a polling server, which provides one unit of service time in a period of 100. On the other hand, we can deposit one unit of service time in a *ticket box* every 100 units of time; when a new ticket is deposited, the unused old tickets, if any, are discarded. With this approach, no matter when the aperiodic event arrives during a period of 100, it will find there is a ticket for one unit of execution time at the ticket-box. That is, τ_2 can use the ticket to preempt τ_1 and execute immediately when the event occurs. In this case, τ_2's response time is precisely one unit and the deadlines of τ_1 are still guaranteed. This is the idea behind the *deferrable* server algorithm (Lehoczky, Sha and Strosnider 1987), which reduces aperiodic response time by a factor of about 50 in this example.

In reality, there can be many periodic tasks whose periods can be arbitrary. Furthermore, aperiodic arrivals can be very bursty, as for a Poisson process. However, the idea remains unchanged. We should allow the aperiodic tasks to preempt the periodic tasks subject to not causing their deadlines to be missed. It was shown in (Lehoczky, Sha and Strosnider 1987) that the deadlines of periodic tasks can be guaranteed provided that during a period of T_a units of time, there are no more than C_a units of time in which aperiodic tasks preempt periodic tasks. In addition, the total periodic and aperiodic utilization must be kept below $(U_a + ln[(2 + U_a)/(2U_a + 1)])$, where $U_a = C_a/T_a$. And the server's period must observe the inequality $T_a \leq (T - C_a)$, where T is the period of a periodic task whose priority is just lower than that of the server.

Compared with background service, the deferrable server algorithm typically improves aperiodic response time by a factor between 2 and 10 (Lehoczky, Sha and Strosnider 1987). Under the deferrable server algorithm, both periodic and aperiodic task modules can be modified at will as long as the utilization bound is observed.

A variation of the deferrable server algorithm is known as the *sporadic* server algorithm (Sprunt, Sha and Lehoczky 1987). As for the deferrable server algorithm, we allocate C_a units of computation time within a period of T_a units of time. However, the C_a of the server's budget is not refreshed until the budget is consumed.[8] From a capacity planning point of view, a sporadic server is equivalent to a periodic task that performs polling. That is, we can place sporadic servers at various priority levels and use only Theorems 1 and 2 to perform a schedulability analysis. Sporadic and deferrable servers have similar performance gains over polling because any time an aperiodic task arrives, it can use the allocated budget immediately. When polling is used, however, an aperiodic arrival generally needs to wait for the next instant of polling. The sporadic server has the least runtime overhead. Both the polling and the deferrable servers have to be serviced periodically, even if there are no aperiodic arrivals.[9] There is no overhead for the sporadic server until its execution budget has been consumed. In particular, there is no overhead if there are no aperiodic arrivals. Therefore, the sporadic server is especially suitable for handling emergency aperiodic events that occur rarely but must be responded to quickly.

Simulation studies of the sporadic server algorithm (Sprunt, Sha and Lehoczky 1989) show that given a lightly loaded server, aperiodic events are served 5–10 times faster than with background service, and 3–6 times faster than with polling. Figure 2, from (Sprunt, Sha and Lehoczky 1989), shows one example of the relative performance between background execution, the deferrable server algorithm (DS), the sporadic server algorithm (SS), polling, and another algorithm, not explained here, called the priority exchange algorithm (PE). The analysis underlying these results assumes a Poisson arrival process with exponentially distributed service time. In addition, each server (other than the background server)

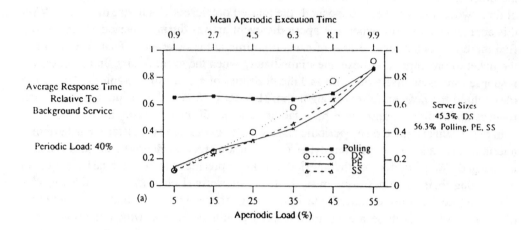

Figure 2. Scheduling both aperiodic and periodic tasks.

is given a period that allows it to execute as the highest priority task.[10] Aperiodic requests can therefore preempt the execution of periodic tasks as long as server execution time is available.

The maximum amount of aperiodic service time allowed before periodic tasks will miss their deadline is called the *maximum server size.* In this example, aperiodic tasks can preempt periodic tasks for at most 56.3 percent of the sporadic or polling server's period without causing the deadlines of periodic tasks to be missed. For the deferrable server, only a smaller amount of service time is possible: 43.6 percent. In either case, the server is not allowed to execute at its assigned priority once its computation budget is exhausted, although it can continue to execute at background priority if time is available. A server's budget is refreshed at the end of its period, at which time execution can resume at the server's assigned priority.

Figure 2 shows the average response times of the different scheduling algorithms as a function of average aperiodic workload. When the average aperiodic workload is small compared with the sporadic server size, randomly arriving requests are likely to find the server available and can successfully preempt the periodic tasks. This results in good performance. For example, when the average aperiodic workload is 5 percent,[11] the deferrable and sporadic server response time is about 10 percent of the average background response time, while the average polling response time is about 65 percent of background time. (This means the sporadic server gives about 6 times faster response than polling and 10 times faster than background service.) When the aperiodic workload increases, the likelihood of server availability decreases and the resulting performance advantage also decreases. For example, when the apersiodic load is 55 percent, the different server algorithms do not give significant performance improvement over background service.

From a mode change point of view, sporadic server effectively transforms the service of aperiodic events into periodic tasks. We can add or delete a server and increase or decrease its capacity as if it were a normal periodic task.

5. Conclusions

In many real-time applications, neither the task set nor the task priorities remain static throughout the mission. A change in operational mode often leads to the modification of task parameters as well as the addition of new tasks and deletion of old tasks. In this paper, we have developed a simple mode change protocol in a prioritized preemptive scheduling environment. We have shown that under this mode change protocol, there cannot be mutual deadlocks, and a high priority job can be blocked by lower priority jobs for at most the duration of one critical section, despite the addition and deletion of tasks during the mode change. We have shown that the worst-case mode change delay under this protocol is bounded and is generally much shorter than that possible in a commonly used cyclical executive.

Acknowledgement

The authors wish to thank John Goodenough for his helpful comments.

Notes

1. It was shown in (Liu and Layland 1973) that when all the tasks are initiated at the same time, if the first job of a task meets its deadline, that task will never miss a deadline.
2. This may occur if τ_3 blocks τ_1 and inherits τ_1's priority.
3. Note that the blocked-at-most-once result does not apply here. It only applies to blocking caused by task synchronization using the priority ceiling protocol.
4. Idling of the processor can occur for two reasons: the rate-monotonic algorithm does not guarantee a 100 percent schedulability level for all task sets. Secondly, task sets in some modes may have lower processor utilization levels than task sets in other modes.
5. The scheduler must ensure that τ is not suspended while in a critical region since such a suspension can cause other tasks to miss their deadlines. If the suspension time arrives but the task is in a critical region, then the suspension should be delayed until the task exits the critical region. To account for this effect on the schedulability of the task set, the worst-case execution time must be increased by ϵ, the extra time spent in the critical region, that is, τ's utilization becomes $(0.5C + \epsilon)/0.5T$.
6. For example, by transforming the periods in Example 3 so τ_1' and τ_2' both have periods of 50, the utilization bound is 100 percent, that is, 4.7 percent more work can be done without missing a deadline.
7. Aperiodic tasks are used to service aperiodic events.
8. Early refreshing is also possible under certain conditions. See (Sprunt, Sha and Lehoczky 1989).
9. The ticket box must be refreshed at the end of each deferrable server's period.
10. This means each server's period must not be greater than the shortest period of all the periodic tasks. The sporadic server and polling server can have a period equal to that of the shortest period task. As mentioned earlier in this section, however, the deferrable server must have an even shorter period.
11. A 5 percent average aperiodic workload means that in the long run, the aperiodic requests consume about 5 percent of the CPU cycles, although the number of requests and their execution time vary from period to period and from request to request.

References

Goodenough, J. B., and L. Sha 1988. The Priority Ceiling Protocol: A Method for Minimizing the Blocking of High Priority Ada Tasks. *The Proceedings of the 2nd ACM International Workshop on Real-Time Ada Issues*.

Lehoczky, J. P. and L. Sha 1986. Performance of Real-Time Bus Scheduling Algorithms. *ACM Performance Evaluation Review, Special Issue*. 14, (1) (May).

Lehoczky, J. P., L. Sha, and J. Strosnider 1987. Enhancing Aperiodic Responsiveness in a Hard Real-Time Environment. *IEEE Real-Time System Symposium*.

Lehoczky, J. P., L. Sha, and Y. Ding 1987. *The Rate Monotonic Scheduling Algorithm—Characterization and Average Case Behavior*. Technical Report, Department of Statistics, Carnegie Mellon University.

Leinbaugh, D. W. 1980. Guaranteed Response Time in a Hard Real-Time Environment. *IEEE Transactions on Software Engineering*, (Jan).

Leung, J. Y. and M. L. Merrill 1980. A Note on Preemptive Scheduling of Periodic Real-Time Tasks. *Information Processing Letters* 11 (3) (Nov.): 115-118.

Liu, C. L. and J. W. Layland 1973. Scheduling Algorithms for Multiprogramming in a Hard Real-Time Environment. *JACM* 20 (1): 46-61.

Mok, A. K. 1983. *Fundamental Design Problems of Distributed Systems for the Hard-Real-Time Environment*. Ph.D. thesis, Massachusetts Institute of Technology.

Rajkumar, R., L. Sha, and L. Lehoczky 1987. On Countering the Effect of Cycle Stealing in A Hard Real-Time Environment. *IEEE Real-Time System Symposium*.

Rajkumar, R., L. Sha, and J. P. Lehockzy 1988. Real-Time Synchronization Protocols for Multiprocessors. *Proceedings of the IEEE Real-Time Systems Symposium*.

Ramaritham, K. and J. A. Stankovic 1984. Dynamic Task Scheduling in Hard Real-Time Distributed Systems. *IEEE Software* (July).

Sha, L., J. P. Lohoczky, and R. Rajkumar 1986. Solutions for Some Practical Problems in Prioritized Preemptive Scheduling. *IEEE Real-Time Systems Symposium*.

Sha, L., R. Rajkumar, and J. P. Lehoczky 1987. Priority Inheritance Protocols: An Approach to Real-Time Synchronization. Technical Report, Department of Computer Science, Carnegie Mellon University (To appear in *IEEE Transactions on Computers*).

Sprunt, B., L. Sha, and J. P. Lehoczky 1989. Scheduling Sporadic and Aperiodic Events in a Hard Real-Time System. *Real-Time Systems* 1 (1) (June).

Zhao, W., K. Ramamritham, and J. Stankovic 1987. Preemptive Scheduling Under Time and Resource Constraints. *IEEE Transactions on Computers*, (Aug).

Real-Time Scheduling Theory and Ada*

Lui Sha and John B. Goodenough

Software Engineering Institute, Carnegie Mellon University

I n real-time applications, the correctness of computation depends on not only the results of computation but also the time at which outputs are generated. Examples of real-time applications include air traffic control, avionics, process control, and mission-critical computations.

The measures of merit in a real-time system include

- Predictably fast response to urgent events.
- High degree of schedulability. Schedulability is the degree of resource utilization at or below which the timing requirements of tasks can be ensured. You can think of it as a measure of the number of timely transactions per second.
- Stability under transient overload. When the system is overloaded by events and meeting all deadlines is impossible, we must still guarantee the deadlines of selected critical tasks.

Traditionally, many real-time systems use cyclical executives to schedule concurrent threads of execution. Under this approach, a programmer lays out an execution timeline by hand to serialize the execution of critical sections and to meet task deadlines.

While such an approach is manageable for simple systems, it quickly becomes

---

Rate monotonic scheduling theory puts real-time software engineering on a sound analytical footing. Here, we review the theory and its implications for Ada.

---

unmanageable for large systems. It is a painful process to develop application code so that it fits the time slots of a cyclical executive while ensuring that the critical sections of different tasks do not interleave. Forcing programmers to schedule tasks by fitting code segments on a time-

* This article is a modified version of a technical report, CMU/SEI-89-TR-14, sponsored by the US Dept. of Defense and bearing the same title.

line is no better than the outdated approach of managing memory by manual memory overlay.

Under the cyclical executive approach, meeting the responsiveness, schedulability, and stability requirements has become such a difficult job that practitioners often sacrifice program structure to fit the code into the "right" time slots. This results in real-time programs that are difficult to understand and maintain.

The Ada tasking model represents a fundamental departure from the cyclical executive model. To reduce the complexity of developing a concurrent system, Ada tasking allows software engineers to manage concurrency at an abstract level divorced from the details of task executions. Indeed, the dynamic preemption of tasks at runtime generates nondeterministic timelines at odds with the very idea of a fixed execution timeline.

This nondeterminism seems to make it impossible to decide whether real-time deadlines will be met. However, Ada's tasking concepts are well-suited to the rate monotonic theory being considered in our project.

In essence, this theory ensures that as long as the CPU utilization of all tasks lies below a certain bound and appropriate scheduling algorithms are used, all tasks will meet their deadlines without the programmer knowing exactly when any given task will be running. Even if a transient

Reprinted from *IEEE Computer*, Vol. 23, No. 4, April 1990, pp. 53-62.

0-8186-3792-7/93 $03.00 © 1990 IEEE

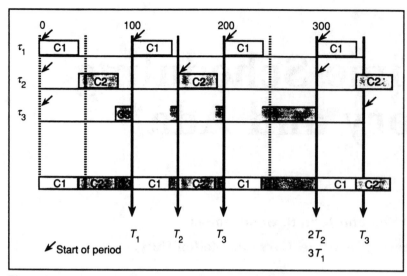

Figure 1. Application of the critical zone theorem to Task τ_3.

overload occurs, a fixed subset of critical tasks will still meet their deadlines as long as their CPU utilizations lie within the appropriate bound.

In short, the scheduling theory allows software engineers to reason about timing correctness at the same abstract level used by the Ada tasking model. Applying this theory to Ada makes Ada tasking truly useful for real-time applications while also putting the development and maintenance of real-time systems on an analytic, engineering basis, making these systems easier to develop and maintain.

The next section reviews some of the basic results in the rate monotonic scheduling theory, although the theory also deals with mode changes and multiprocessing.[1,2] In the final section, we review the Ada tasking model and scheduling policies, and suggest some workarounds that permit us to implement rate monotonic scheduling algorithms within the framework of existing Ada rules.

Scheduling real-time tasks

This section contains an overview of some of the important issues of real-time scheduling theory, beginning with the problem of ensuring that independent periodic tasks meet their deadlines. Then, we show how to ensure that critical tasks will meet their deadlines even when a system is temporarily overloaded, address the problem of scheduling both periodic and aperi-odic tasks, and review real-time synchronization and communication issues.

Periodic tasks. Tasks are independent if their executions need not be synchronized. Given a set of independent periodic tasks, the rate monotonic scheduling algorithm gives each task a fixed priority and assigns higher priorities to tasks with shorter periods. A task set is said to be *schedulable* if all its deadlines are met, that is, if every periodic task finishes its execution before the end of its period. Any set of independent periodic tasks is schedulable by the rate monotonic algorithm if the condition of Theorem 1 is met.[3]

> *Theorem 1*: A set of n independent periodic tasks scheduled by the rate monotonic algorithm will always meet its deadlines, for all task phasings, if
>
> $$\frac{C_1}{T_1} + \dots + \frac{C_n}{T_n} \le n(2^{1/n} - 1) = U(n)$$
>
> where C_i and T_i are the execution time and period of task τ_i, respectively.

Theorem 1 offers a sufficient (worst-case) condition that characterizes schedulability of a task set under the rate monotonic algorithm. This bound converges to 69 percent (*ln* 2) as the number of tasks approaches infinity. The values of the scheduling bounds for one to nine independent tasks are as follows: U(1) = 1.0, U(2) = 0.828, U(3) = 0.779, U(4) = 0.756, U(5) = 0.743, U(6) = 0.734, U(7) = 0.728, U(8) = 0.724, and U(9) = 0.720.

Example 1: Consider the case of three periodic tasks, where $U_i = C_i/T_i$.

- Task τ_1: $C_1 = 20$; $T_1 = 100$; $U_1 = 0.2$
- Task τ_2: $C_2 = 40$; $T_2 = 150$; $U_2 = 0.267$
- Task τ_3: $C_3 = 100$; $T_3 = 350$; $U_3 = 0.286$

The total utilization of these three tasks is 0.753, which is below Theorem 1's bound for three tasks: $3(2^{1/3} - 1) = 0.779$. Hence, we know these three tasks are schedulable, that is, they will meet their deadlines if τ_1 is given the highest priority, τ_2 the next highest, and τ_3 the lowest.

The bound of Theorem 1 is very pessimistic because the worst-case task set is contrived and unlikely to be encountered in practice. For a randomly chosen task set, the likely bound is 88 percent.[4] To know if a set of given tasks with utilization greater than the bound of Theorem 1 can meet its deadlines, we can use an exact schedulability test based on the *critical zone* theorem (rephrased from Liu and Layland[3]):

> *Theorem 2*: For a set of independent periodic tasks, if each task meets its first deadline when all tasks are started at the same time, then the deadlines will always be met for any combination of start times.

This theorem provides the basis for an exact schedulability test for sets of independent periodic tasks under the rate monotonic algorithm. In effect, the theorem requires that we check to see if each task can complete its execution before its first deadline. To do so, we need to check the *scheduling points* for a task. The scheduling points for task τ are τ's first deadline and the ends of periods of higher priority tasks prior to τ's first deadline. The process is illustrated by Figure 1, which applies to the task set in the next example.

Example 2: Suppose we replace τ_1's algorithm in Example 1 with one that is more accurate and computationally intensive. Suppose the new algorithm doubles τ_1's computation time from 20 to 40, so the total processor utilization increases from 0.753 to 0.953. Since the utilization of the first two tasks is 0.667, which is below Theorem 1's bound for two tasks, $2(2^{1/2} - 1) = 0.828$, the first two tasks cannot miss their deadlines. For task τ_3, we use Theorem 2 to check whether the task set is schedulable. Figure 1 shows the scheduling points relevant to task τ_3, that is, the ends of periods of higher priority tasks for times less than or equal to τ_3's period. To check against the critical zone theorem, we check whether all tasks have completed their execution at any of the scheduling points. For example, to see if all tasks have met their deadlines at time 350, we can see that task τ_1 will have had to start executing four times; task τ_2, three times; and task τ_3, once. So we check to see if all these executions can complete in 350 milliseconds:

$$4C_1 + 3C_2 + C_3 \leq T_3$$
$$160 + 120 + 100 > 350$$

This test fails, but that doesn't mean the task set can't meet its deadlines; the theorem requires that all the scheduling points be checked. If all tasks meet their deadlines for at least one scheduling point, the task set is schedulable. The equations to be checked are shown below, for each scheduling point:

$$C_1 + C_2 + C_3 \leq T_1$$
$$40 + 40 + 100 > 100$$

$$2C_1 + C_2 + C_3 \leq T_2$$
$$80 + 40 + 100 > 150$$

$$2C_1 + 2C_2 + C_3 \leq 2T_1$$
$$80 + 80 + 100 > 200$$

$$3C_1 + 2C_2 + C_3 \leq 2T_3$$
$$120 + 80 + 100 = 300$$

$$4C_1 + 3C_2 + C_3 \leq T_3$$
$$160 + 120 + 100 > 350$$

The equation for scheduling point $2T_2$ is satisfied. That is, after 300 units of time, τ_1 will have run three times, τ_2 will have run twice, and τ_3 will have run once. The required amount of computation just fits within the allowed time, so each task meets its deadline. Liu and Layland[3] showed that since the tasks meet their deadlines at least once within the period T_3, they will always meet their deadlines. Hence, we can double the utilization of the first task in Example 1 from 20 percent to 40 percent and still meet all the deadlines. Since task τ_3 just meets its deadline at time 300, we cannot add any tasks with a priority higher than that of task τ_3, although a task of lower priority could be added if its period is sufficiently long.

The checking required by Theorem 2 can be represented by an equivalent mathematical test[4]:

Theorem 3: A set of n independent periodic tasks scheduled by the rate monotonic algorithm will always meet its deadlines, for all task phasings, if and only if

$\forall i, 1 \leq i \leq n,$

$$\min_{(k,l) \in R_i} \sum_{j=1}^{i} C_j \frac{1}{lT_k} \left\lceil \frac{lT_k}{T_j} \right\rceil \leq 1$$

where C_j and T_j are the execution time and period of task τ_j, respectively, and

$$R_i = \{(k,l) \mid 1 \leq k \leq i, l = 1, ..., \lfloor T_i / T_k \rfloor \}.$$

A major advantage of using the rate monotonic algorithm is that it allows us to follow the software engineering principle of separation of concerns. In this case, the theory allows systems to separate concerns for logical correctness from concerns for timing correctness.

Suppose a cyclical executive is used for this example. The major cycle must be the least common multiple of the task periods. In this example, the task periods are in the ratio 100:150:350 = 2:3:7. A minor cycle of 50 units would induce a major cycle of 42 minor cycles, which is an overly complex design.

To reduce the number of minor cycles, we can try to modify the periods. For example, it might be possible to reduce the period of the longest task, from 350 to 300. The total utilization is then exactly 100 percent, and the period ratios are 2:3:6; the major cycle can then be six minor cycles of 50 units.

To implement this approach and minimize the splitting of computations belonging to a single task, we could split task τ_1 into two parts of 20 units computation each. The computation of task τ_2 similarly could be split into at least two parts such that task τ_3 need only be split into four parts. A possible timeline indicating the amount of computation for each task in each minor cycle is shown in Table 1, where 20_1 on the first line indicates the first part of task τ_1's computation, which takes 20 units of time.

When the processor utilization level is high and many tasks need to be performed, fitting code segments into time slots can be a time-consuming iterative process. In addition, a later modification of any task may overflow a particular minor cycle and require the entire timeline to be redone.

But more importantly, the cyclic executive approach has required us to modify the period of one of the tasks, increasing the utilization to 100 percent without in fact doing more useful work. Under the rate monotonic approach for this example, all deadlines are met, but total machine utilization must not exceed 95.3 percent instead of 100 percent.

This doesn't mean the rate monotonic approach is less efficient. The capacity not needed to service real-time tasks in the rate monotonic approach can be used by background tasks, for example, for built-in-test purposes. With the cyclic executive approach, no such additional work can be done in this example.

Control applications typically require that signals be sent and received at fixed intervals with minimal *jitter*, that is, with precise timing in sending or receiving data. Jitter requirements are a special kind of deadline requirement.

One way of meeting an output jitter requirement using rate monotonic scheduling is to have a normal periodic task compute a result and place it in a memory-mapped I/O buffer before it is time to send the value. Rate monotonic scheduling theorems can be used to ensure the value is computed in time. A hardware timer or the operating system clock interrupt handler routine can then initiate the device I/O precisely at the required time. A similar approach can be used for input jitter requirements.

Stability under transient overload. So far, we have assumed that the computation time of a task is constant. However, in many applications, task execution times

Table 1. Minor cycle timeline for Example 2. Each minor cycle is 50.

	1	2	3	4	5	6
τ_1	20_1	20_2	20_1	20_2	20_1	20_2
τ_2	30_1	10_2		30_1	10_2	
τ_3		20_1	30_2		20_3	30_4

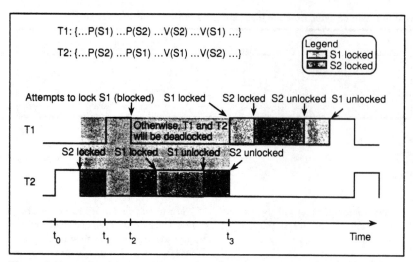

Figure 2. Example of deadlock prevention. The gray section shows the interval of time when the priority ceiling protocol prevents task T1 from locking semaphore S1 or semaphore S2.

are often stochastic, and the worst-case execution time can be significantly larger than the average execution time.

To have a reasonably high average processor utilization, we must deal with the problem of transient overload. We consider a scheduling algorithm to be *stable* if a set of tasks exists such that all tasks in the set will meet their deadlines even if the processor is overloaded.

This means that, under worst-case conditions, tasks outside the set may miss their deadlines. The rate monotonic algorithm is stable — the tasks guaranteed to meet their deadlines under worst-case execution times are always the n highest priority tasks. These tasks form the schedulable task set. Software designers, therefore, must be sure that all tasks whose deadlines must be met under overload conditions are in the schedulable set.

Since task priorities are assigned according to the period of each task, a critically important task might not be in the schedulable set. A task with a longer period could be more critical to an application than a task with a shorter period. You might try to ensure that such a task always meets its deadline simply by increasing its priority to reflect its importance. However, this approach makes it more likely that other tasks will miss their deadlines, that is, the schedulability bound is lowered.

The *period transformation* technique can be used to ensure high utilization while meeting the deadline of an important, long-period task. For example, suppose task τ with a long period T is not guaranteed to

meet its deadline under transient overload conditions, but nonetheless, the work performed by the task is critical, and it must never miss its deadline.

We need to ensure that task τ belongs to the schedulable task set. Since the rate monotonic priority of a task is a function of its period, we can raise task τ's priority only by having it act like a task with a shorter period. We can do so by giving it a period of $T/2$ and suspending it after it executes half its worst-case execution time, $C/2$.

The task is then resumed and finishes its work in the next execution period. It still completes its total computation before the end of period T. From the viewpoint of the rate monotonic theory, the transformed task has the same utilization but a shorter period, $T/2$, and its priority is raised accordingly. Note that the most important task need not have the shortest period. We only need to make sure that it is in the schedulable set. A systematic procedure for period transformation with minimal task partitioning can be found in Sha, Lehoczky, and Rajkumar.[5]

Period transformation resembles the task slicing found in cyclic executives. The difference here is that we don't need to adjust the code segment sizes so different code segments fit into shared time slots. Instead, τ simply requests suspension after performing $C/2$ amount of work. Alternatively, the runtime scheduler can be instructed to suspend the task after $C/2$ work has been done, without affecting the application code.

Scheduling both aperiodic and periodic tasks. It is important to meet both the regular deadlines of periodic tasks and the response time requirements of aperiodic requests. Aperiodic servers are tasks used to process such requests. Here is a simple example.

Example 3: Suppose we have two tasks. Let τ_1 be a periodic task with period 100 and execution time 99. Let τ_2 be a server for an aperiodic request that randomly arrives once within a period of 100. Suppose one unit of time is required to service one request.

If we let the aperiodic server execute only in the background, that is, only after completing the periodic task, the average response time is about 50 units. The same can be said for a polling server that provides one unit of service time in a period of 100.

On the other hand, we can deposit one unit of service time in a "ticket box" every 100 units of time; when a new "ticket" is deposited, the unused old tickets, if any, are discarded. With this approach, no matter when the aperiodic request arrives during a period of 100, it will find a ticket for one unit of execution time at the ticket box. That is, τ_2 can use the ticket to preempt τ_1 and execute immediately when the request occurs. In this case, τ_2's response time is precisely one unit and the deadlines of τ_1 are still guaranteed.

This is the idea behind a class of aperiodic server algorithms[6] that can reduce aperiodic response time by a large factor (a factor of 50 in this example). We allow the aperiodic servers to preempt the periodic tasks for a limited duration allowed by the rate monotonic scheduling formula.

A good aperiodic server algorithm is known as the *sporadic* server.[7] Instead of refreshing the server's budget periodically, at fixed points in time, replenishment is determined by when requests are serviced. In the simplest approach, the budget is refreshed T units of time after it has been exhausted, but earlier refreshing is also possible.

A sporadic server is only allowed to preempt the execution of periodic tasks as long as its computation budget is not exhausted. When the budget is used up, the server can continue to execute at background priority if time is available. When the server's budget is refreshed, its execution can resume at the server's assigned priority.

There is no overhead if there are no

requests. Therefore, the sporadic server is especially suitable for handling emergency aperiodic events that occur rarely but must be serviced quickly.

From a schedulability point of view, a sporadic server is equivalent to a periodic task that performs polling. That is, we can place sporadic servers at various priority levels and use only Theorems 1 and 2 to perform a schedulability analysis. With this approach, both periodic and aperiodic task modules can be modified at will, as long as the rate monotonic utilization bound is observed.

When the average aperiodic workload is no more than 70 percent of the CPU capacity allocated for the sporadic server, randomly arriving requests are likely to find the server available and can successfully preempt the periodic tasks. This results in about 6 times faster response than polling and 10 times faster response than background service.[7]

When the aperiodic workload is about equal to the server's budget, the likelihood of server availability decreases and the resulting performance advantage also decreases. The performance of such an overloaded server is essentially that of a polling server.

Finally, sporadic servers can be used to service hard-deadline aperiodic requests. An example will be given in the section "An example of application of the theory."

Task synchronization. In previous sections, we discussed the scheduling of independent tasks. Tasks, however, do interact. In this section, we discuss how the rate monotonic scheduling theory can be applied to real-time tasks that must interact. The discussion is limited in this article to scheduling within a uniprocessor. Readers interested in the multiprocessor synchronization problem should see Rajkumar, Sha, and Lehoczky.[1]

Common synchronization primitives include semaphores, locks, monitors, and Ada rendezvous. Although the use of these or equivalent methods is necessary to ensure the consistency of shared data or to guarantee the proper use of non-preemptable resources, their use may jeopardize the ability of the system to meet its timing requirements. In fact, a direct application of these synchronization mechanisms may lead to an indefinite period of *priority inversion*, which occurs when a high-priority task is prevented from executing by a low-priority task. Unbounded priority inversion can occur as shown in the following example:

Example 4: Suppose periodic tasks T1, T2, and T3 are arranged in descending order of priority (high, medium, and low). Suppose tasks T1 and T3 share a data structure guarded by semaphore S1. During the execution of the critical section of task T3, high-priority task T1 starts to execute, preempts T3, and later attempts to use the shared data. However, T1 is blocked on the semaphore S1.

We would prefer that T1, being the highest priority task, be blocked no longer than the time it takes for T3 to complete its critical section. However, the duration of blocking is, in fact, unpredictable. This is because T3 can be preempted by the medium priority task T2. T1 will be blocked, that is, prevented from executing, until T2 and any other pending tasks of intermediate priority are completed.

The problem of unbounded priority inversion can be partially remedied in this case if a task is not allowed to be preempted while executing a critical section. However, this solution is only appropriate for very short critical sections because it creates unnecessary priority inversion. For instance, once a low-priority job enters a long critical section, a high priority job that does not access the shared data structure may be needlessly blocked.

The *priority ceiling protocol* is a real-time synchronization protocol with two important properties:

(1) freedom from mutual deadlock and
(2) bounded priority inversion. Namely, at most one lower priority task can block a higher priority task.[8,9]

There are two ideas in the design of this protocol. First is the concept of priority inheritance: when a task τ blocks the execution of higher priority tasks, task τ executes at the highest priority level of all the tasks blocked by τ. Second, we must guarantee that a critical section is allowed to start execution only if the section will always execute at a priority level higher than the (inherited) priority levels of any preempted critical sections.

It was shown in Sha, Rajkumar, and Lehoczky[9] that such a prioritized total ordering in the execution of critical sections leads to the two desired properties. To achieve such a prioritized total ordering, we define the *priority ceiling* of a binary semaphore S to be the highest priority of all tasks that may lock S.

When a task τ attempts to execute one of its critical sections, it will be suspended unless its priority is higher than the priority ceilings of all semaphores currently locked by tasks other than τ. If task τ is unable to enter its critical section for this reason, the task that holds the lock on the semaphore with the highest priority ceiling is said to be blocking τ and, hence, inherits the priority of τ. As long as a task τ is not attempting to enter one of its critical sections, it will preempt every task that has a lower priority.

The priority ceiling protocol guarantees that a high-priority task will be blocked by at most one critical region of any lower priority task. Moreover, the protocol prevents mutual deadlock, as shown in the following example:

Example 5: Suppose we have two tasks T1 and T2 (see Figure 2). In addition, there are two shared data structures protected by binary semaphores S1 and S2, respectively. Suppose task T1 locks the semaphores in the order S1, S2, while T2 locks them in the reverse order. Further, assume that T1 has a higher priority than T2.

Since both T1 and T2 use semaphores S1 and S2, the priority ceilings of both semaphores are equal to the priority of task T1. Suppose that at time t_0, T2 begins execution and then locks semaphore S2. At time t_1, task T1 is initiated and preempts task T2, and at time t_2, task T1 tries to enter its critical section by attempting to lock semaphore S1. However, the priority of T1 is not higher than the priority ceiling of locked semaphore S2. Hence, task T1 must be suspended without locking S1. Task T2 now inherits the priority of task T1 and resumes execution. Note that T1 is blocked outside its critical section. Since T1 is not given the lock on S1 but instead is suspended, the potential deadlock involving T1 and T2 is prevented. At time t_3, T2 exits its critical section; it will return to its assigned priority and immediately be preempted by task T1. From this point on, T1 will execute to completion, and then T2 will resume its execution until its completion.

Let B_i be the longest duration of blocking that can be experienced by task τ_i. The following theorem determines whether the deadlines of a set of periodic tasks can be met if the priority ceiling protocol is used:

Theorem 4: A set of n periodic tasks using the priority ceiling protocol can be scheduled by the rate monotonic algorithm for all task phasings, if the

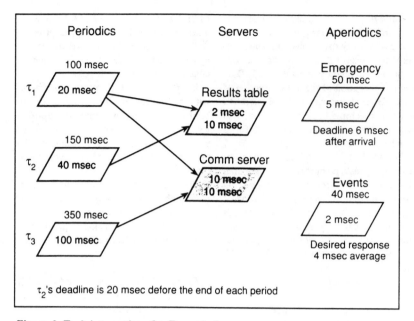

Figure 3. Task interactions for Example 6.

following condition is satisfied[9]:

$$\frac{C_1}{T_1} + \ldots + \frac{C_n}{T_n}$$
$$+ \max\left(\frac{B_1}{T_1}, \ldots, \frac{B_{n-1}}{T_{n-1}}\right) \le n(2^{1/n} - 1)$$

This theorem generalizes Theorem 1 by taking blocking into consideration. A similar extension can be given for Theorem 3. The B_i's in Theorem 4 can be used to account for any delay caused by resource sharing. Note that B_n is always zero, since the lowest priority task cannot, by definition, be blocked by a task of lower priority, and hence, B_n is not included in the theorem's formula.

In the priority ceiling protocol, a task can be blocked even if it does not lock any semaphores. For example, in Figure 2, any task, τ, with a priority between that of T1 and T2 could be prevented from executing while T2 has semaphore S2 locked. This can happen because S2's priority ceiling is greater than the priority of τ. Therefore, if T1 tries to lock S1 while T2 has locked S2, T2 will inherit T1's priority and will prevent any tasks of intermediate priority from executing. Since the low priority task T2 prevents the execution of the intermediate priority tasks, these tasks suffer priority inversion, or blocking. This source of blocking is the cost of avoiding unbounded priority inversion. It must be taken into account when applying Theorem 4.

An example application of the theory.
A simple example illustrates how to apply

the scheduling theory.

Example 6: Consider the following task set (see Figure 3):

(1) Emergency handling task: execution time = 5 milliseconds; worst case interarrival time = 50 milliseconds; deadline is 6 milliseconds after arrival.

(2) Aperiodic event handling tasks: average execution time = 2 milliseconds; average interarrival time = 40 milliseconds; fast response time is desirable, but there are no hard deadlines.

(3) Periodic task τ_1: worst-case execution time = 20 milliseconds (which includes service time for accessing a shared data object and a shared communication server); period = 100 milliseconds; deadline is at the end of each period. In addition, τ_1 may block τ_1 for 10 milliseconds by using a shared communication server, and task τ_2 may block τ_1 for 20 milliseconds by using a shared data object.

(4) Periodic task τ_2: execution time = 40 milliseconds (including 20 milliseconds spent accessing the shared data object); period = 150 milliseconds; deadline is 20 milliseconds before the end of each period.

(5) Periodic task τ_3: execution time = 100 milliseconds (including 10

milliseconds for accessing the communications server); period = 350 milliseconds; deadline is at the end of each period.

Solution: First, we create a sporadic server for the emergency task, with a period of 50 milliseconds and a service time of 5 milliseconds. Since the server has the shortest period, the rate monotonic algorithm will give this server the highest priority. It follows that the emergency task can meet its deadline.

Since the aperiodic event handling activities have no deadlines, they can be assigned a low priority. However, since fast response time is desirable, we create a sporadic server executing at the second highest priority. The size of the server is a design issue. A larger server (that is, a server with higher utilization) needs more processor cycles but will give better response time. In this example, we choose a large server with a period of 100 milliseconds and a service time of 10 milliseconds. We now have two tasks with a period of 100 milliseconds — the aperiodic event server and periodic task τ_1. The rate monotonic algorithm allows us to break the tie arbitrarily, and we let the server have the higher priority.

We now have to check if the three periodic tasks can meet their deadlines. Since, under the priority ceiling protocol, a task can be blocked at most once by lower priority tasks, the maximal blocking time for task τ_1 is B_1 = maximum (10 milliseconds, 20 milliseconds) = 20 milliseconds. Since τ_3 may lock the semaphore S_c associated with the communication server and the priority ceiling of S_c is higher than that of task τ_2, task τ_2 can be blocked by task τ_3 for 10 milliseconds. (This may occur if τ_3 blocks τ_1 and inherits the priority of τ_1.) Finally, task τ_2 has to finish 20 milliseconds earlier than the nominal deadline for a periodic task. This is equivalent to saying that τ_2 will always be blocked for an additional 20 milliseconds, but its deadline is at the end of the period. Hence, $B_2 = (10 + 20)$ milliseconds = 30 milliseconds.* At this point, we can directly apply the appropriate theorems. However, we can also reduce the number of steps in the analysis by noting that period 50 and 100 are harmonics, so we can treat the emergency server

---

* Note that the blocked-at-most-once result does not apply here. It only applies to blocking caused by task synchronization using the priority ceiling protocol.

mathematically as if it had a period of 100 milliseconds and a service time of 10 milliseconds. We now have three tasks with a period of 100 milliseconds and an execution time of 20 milliseconds, 10 milliseconds, and 10 milliseconds, respectively. For the purpose of analysis, these three tasks can be replaced by a single periodic task with a period of 100 milliseconds and an execution time of 40 milliseconds (20 + 10 + 10). We now have the following three equivalent periodic tasks for analysis:

- Task τ_1: $C_1 = 40$; $T_1 = 100$; $B_1 = 20$; $U_1 = 0.4$
- Task τ_2: $C_2 = 40$; $T_2 = 150$; $B_2 = 30$; $U_2 = 0.267$
- Task τ_3: $C_3 = 100$; $T_3 = 350$; $B_3 = 0$; $U_3 = 0.286$

Note that B_3 is zero, since a task can only be blocked by tasks of lower priority. Since τ_3 is the lowest priority task, it can't be blocked.

When Theorem 3 is extended to account for blocking, we simply check to be sure that each task will meet its deadline if it is blocked for the maximal amount of time:

(1) Task τ_1: Check $C_1 + B_1 \leq T_1$. If this inequality is satisfied, τ_1 will always meet its deadline. Since $40 + 20 < 100$, task τ_1 is schedulable.

(2) Task t_2: Check each of the following:

$$C_1 + C_2 + B_2 \leq T_1$$
$$40 + 40 + 30 > 100$$

$$2C_1 + C_2 + B_2 \leq T_2$$
$$80 + 40 + 30 = 150$$

These equations reflect the two scheduling points applicable to task τ_2, and take into account the fact that task τ_2 will be blocked at most B_2 milliseconds. Moreover, we don't need to consider the blocking time for task τ_1 because this time only affects the completion time for τ_1; it cannot affect τ_2's completion time. Hence, task τ_2 is schedulable and in the worst-case phasing will meet its deadline exactly at time 150.

(3) Task τ_3: The analysis here is identical to the analysis for Task 3 of Example 2. Hence, task τ_3 is also schedulable and in the worst-case phasing will meet its deadline exactly at time 300. It follows that all three periodic tasks can meet their deadlines.

Next, we determine the response time for the aperiodics. The server capacity is 10 percent and the average aperiodic workload is 5 percent (2/40). Because most of the aperiodic arrivals can find tickets, we would expect a good response time. Indeed, using a M/M/1 approximation[10] for the lightly loaded server, the expected response time for the aperiodics is $W = E[S]/(1 - \rho) = 2/(1 - (0.05/0.10)) = 4$ milliseconds where $E[S]$ is the average execution time of aperiodic tasks and ρ is the average server utilization. Finally, although the worst-case total periodic and server workload is 95 percent, we can still do quite a bit of background processing, since the soft deadline aperiodics and the emergency task are unlikely to fully utilize the servers.

The results derived for this example show how the scheduling theory puts real-time programming on an analytic engineering basis.

Real-time scheduling in Ada

Although Ada was intended for use in building real-time systems, its suitability for real-time programming has been widely questioned. Many of these questions concern practical issues, such as fast rendezvous and interrupt handling.

These problems are being addressed by compiler vendors aiming at the real-time market. More important are concerns about the suitability of Ada's tasking model for dealing with real-time programming. For example, tasks in Ada run nondeterministically, making it hard for traditional real-time programmers to decide whether any tasks will meet their deadlines.

In addition, the scheduling rules of Ada don't seem to support priority scheduling well. Prioritized tasks are queued in FIFO order rather than by priority; high priority tasks can be delayed indefinitely when calling low priority tasks (due to priority inversion); and task priorities cannot be changed when application demands change at runtime.

Fortunately, solutions exist within the current language framework, although some language changes would be helpful to ensure uniform implementation support.

Whether or not language changes are made, we must be careful to use Ada constructs in ways that are consistent with rate monotonic principles. The Real-Time Scheduling in Ada Project at the Carnegie Mellon University Software Engineering

Institute is a cooperative effort between CMU, the SEI, system developers in industry, Ada vendors, and government agencies. It aims to specify coding guidelines and runtime system support needed to use rate monotonic scheduling theory in Ada programs. The guidelines are still evolving and being evaluated, but so far it seems likely they will meet the needs of a useful range of systems.

The remainder of this section summarizes the approach being taken by the project and shows how Ada's scheduling rules can be interpreted to support the requirements of rate monotonic scheduling algorithms.

Ada real-time design guidelines. Since Ada was not designed with rate monotonic scheduling algorithms in mind, it is not surprising to find some difficulties in using these algorithms. There are basically two ways of using rate monotonic algorithms in Ada:

(1) follow coding guidelines that take into account the scheduling policy that must be supported by every real-time Ada implementation or

(2) take advantage of the fact that Ada allows rate-monotonic scheduling algorithms to be supported directly by a special-purpose runtime system.

There are several Ada usage issues that must be addressed:

(1) how to code Ada tasks that must share data,
(2) how to use sporadic server concepts for aperiodic tasks, and
(3) how to ensure precise scheduling of periodic tasks.

We discuss the first two issues in this article. For data sharing among periodic Ada tasks (client tasks), our first guideline is that these tasks must not call each other directly to exchange data. Instead, whenever they must read or write shared data or send a message, they call a monitor task. Each monitor task has a simple structure — an endless loop containing a single select statement with no guards (see Figure 4). (The prohibition against guards simplifies the schedulability analysis and the runtime system implementation, but otherwise is not essential.)

This structure models the notion of critical regions guarded by a semaphore; each entry is a critical region for the task calling the entry. By using this coding style, we

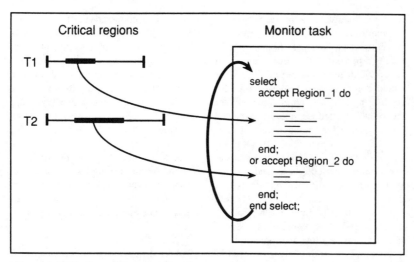

Figure 4. Modeling critical regions with an Ada task. T1 and T2 are two periodic tasks with critical regions guarded by a single semaphore. The corresponding monitor task acts as the semaphore guarding the critical regions. Each entry of the monitor task is the critical region for one of the periodic tasks.

have a program structure that can be analyzed directly in rate monotonic terms.

Client tasks are assigned priorities according to the rate monotonic algorithm. There are two options when assigning a priority to a monitor. If the Ada runtime system supports the priority ceiling protocol directly, then give the monitor task an undefined priority. In addition, tell the runtime system the priority ceiling of the monitor — that is, the highest priority of all its clients — using an implementation-defined pragma or system call.

If the ceiling protocol is not supported directly, the same schedulability effect can be emulated by giving the monitor task a priority that is just higher than the priority of any client task. This artificial priority assignment is consistent with the priority ceiling protocol.

To see this, note that once a high-priority client task starts to execute, it cannot be blocked by any lower priority client that has called an entry of the monitor; if the low-priority client is in rendezvous with the monitor before the high-priority client is ready to execute, the low-priority client will complete its rendezvous before the higher priority client is allowed to execute. If the low-priority task is not in rendezvous with a monitor task and the high-priority client becomes eligible to run, the low-priority task will be preempted and won't be allowed to execute until the high-priority-client task has finished its work.

Therefore, a high-priority client task can be blocked by at most one lower priority client task. The effect on system performance of giving the monitor task a high priority is simply that the worst-case blocking time is more frequently experienced; when rendezvous times are short, this effect is negligible.

Giving monitor tasks a high priority is not an acceptable implementation of the ceiling protocol if the monitor task suspends itself while in rendezvous, for example, while waiting for an I/O device to complete. Suspension allows other tasks to execute, meaning first-in, first-out (that is, unprioritized) entry queues could build up or critical sections could be entered under conditions inconsistent with the requirements of the priority ceiling protocol. If such a suspension is a possibility, the ceiling protocol should be supported directly in the Ada runtime implementation.

We have shown how the effect of the priority ceiling protocol can be provided at the application code level. A simple version of the sporadic server algorithm can also be supported at the application code level by creating a server task with the following structure:

```
task body Server is
    Tickets := Initial_Budget;
    -- set initial execution time budget
begin
    loop
```

```
        accept Aperiodic_Request;
        Set_Replenishment_Time;
        -- do work
        Decrement_Ticket_Count;
        -- one ticket per request
        if No_More_Tickets then
        Delay_Until_Replenishment_Time;
            Replenish_Tickets;
        end if;
    end loop;
end Server;
```

In essence, this task refuses to accept work unless it has a ticket to complete a request. The algorithm for deciding when to replenish tickets can be considerably more complicated, and a single server can be structured to accept a variety of service requests with different execution times.

If the runtime system supports the sporadic server algorithm directly, then the budget and replenishment period are specified by system calls or by implementation-dependent pragmas, and the loop simply accepts an entry call and does the work. Execution time management and task suspension is then handled directly by the runtime.

On Ada scheduling rules. The most general solution to the problem of using rate monotonic scheduling algorithms in Ada, within the constraints of the language, is simply to not use pragma PRIORITY at all.

If all tasks in a program have no assigned priority, then the runtime system is free to use any convenient algorithm for deciding which eligible task to run. An implementation-dependent pragma could then be used to give "Rate_Monotonic_Priorities" to tasks.

This approach would even allow "priorities" to be changed dynamically at runtime because, in a legalistic sense, there are no Ada priorities at all. The only problem with this approach is Ada's requirement that calls be queued in order of arrival, independent of priority.

However, even this problem can be solved efficiently. To get the effect of prioritized queueing, the runtime scheduler should ensure that no calls "arrive" until they can be accepted. This can be achieved by a legalistic trick — keeping the Count attribute zero (because logically, no entry calls are queued), and correspondingly suspending tasks making entry calls at the point of the call if the priority ceiling protocol requires that the call be blocked.

The elimination of entry queues also

126

makes the runtime more efficient. However, we must emphasize here that this treatment of entry calls is only allowed if no tasks have a priority specified by Ada's pragma PRIORITY.

Of course, telling programmers to assign "Rate_Monotonic_Priorities" to tasks but not to use pragma PRIORITY surely says we are fighting the language rather than taking advantage of it. But, the important point is that no official revisions to the language are needed.

Now, let us consider in more detail the specific Ada scheduling rules that cause difficulties and the appropriate ways of getting around the problems. When we describe these workarounds, we don't intend to suggest that Ada is therefore completely satisfactory for use with rate monotonic theory, but rather, to show that software designers need not wait for a revision to the Ada standard before trying out these ideas.

• *CPU allocation: Priorities must be observed.* Ada requires that, in a uniprocessor environment, the highest priority task eligible to run be given the CPU. For applications using the rate monotonic theory, this scheduling rule is correct as far as it goes. The only problem arises when determining the priority at which a task rendezvous should be executed. This is discussed below.

• *Hardware task priority: Always higher than software task priorities.* This Ada rule reflects current hardware designs, but hardware interrupts should not always have the highest priority from the viewpoint of the rate monotonic theory.

Solution: When handling an interrupt that, according to the rate monotonic theory, should have a lower priority than the priority of some application task, keep the interrupt handling actions short (which is already a common practice) and include the interrupt handling duration as blocking time in the rate monotonic analysis. In other words, use the scheduling theory to take into account the effect of this source of priority inversion.

• *Priority rules for task rendezvous.* The priority of a task can only be increased while executing a rendezvous, and any increase is based only on the priorities of the rendezvousing tasks. In particular, the priority is not increased based on the priority of blocked tasks, as required by the priority ceiling protocol.

Solution: We have already discussed the two solutions to this problem: (1) give monitor tasks a high priority, or (2) implement the priority ceiling protocol directly in the runtime system. If a monitor task is given a priority higher than that of its callers, then no increase in priority is ever necessary, so the problem is side-stepped. Alternatively, give the monitor task no priority at all. An implementation can then use priority ceiling rules to increase the priority of the called task to the necessary level since, in this case, the Ada rules say a rendezvous is executed with "at least" the priority of the caller, that is, the rendezvous can be executed at the priority of a blocked task.

• *FIFO entry queues.* Ada requires that the priority of calling tasks be ignored; calls must be serviced in their order of arrival, not in order of priority. Using FIFO queues rather than prioritized queues usually has a serious negative effect on real-time schedulability. FIFO queues must be avoided.

Solution: As noted earlier, it is possible to avoid FIFO queueing by giving monitor tasks a high priority or by using an implementation-defined scheduler to ensure that calls do not arrive unless they can be accepted. In either case, no queues are formed.

• *Task priorities: Fixed.* This rule is inappropriate when task priorities need to be changed at runtime. For example, when a new mode is initiated, the frequency of a task and/or its criticality may change, implying its priority may change. In addition, the scheduling rules for a certain class of aperiodic servers demand that the priority of such a server be lowered when it is about to exceed the maximum execution time allowed for a certain interval of time and be raised when its service capacity has been restored.

Solution: When an application needs to adjust the priority of a task at runtime, this task should be declared as having no Ada priority. The runtime system can then be given a way of scheduling the task appropriately by, in effect, changing its priority.

• *Selective wait.* Priority can be ignored. That is, the scheduler is allowed, but not required, to take priorities into account when tasks of different priorities are waiting at open select alternatives.

Solution: If a monitor task is given a priority higher than that of any of its callers and is not suspended during a rendezvous (for example, by executing a delay statement), this rule doesn't matter because there will never be more than one caller at any given time. Otherwise, the implementation should select the highest priority waiting task.

Summing up. From what our project has learned so far, it seems to be possible in practice to support analytic scheduling algorithms in Ada by using an enlightened interpretation of Ada's scheduling rules together with a combination of runtime system modifications and appropriate coding guidelines. Of course, it would be better if the language did not get in the way of rate monotonic scheduling principles. The future revision of Ada should reword some of these rules so that support for rate monotonic scheduling is more clearly allowed.

I n this article, we have reviewed some important results of rate monotonic scheduling theory. The theory allows programmers to reason with confidence about timing correctness at the tasking level of abstraction. As long as analytic scheduling algorithms are supported by the runtime system and resource utilization bounds on CPU, I/O drivers, and communication media are observed, the timing constraints will be satisfied. Even if there is a transient overload, the tasks missing deadlines will be in a predefined order.

Rate monotonic scheduling theory puts real-time system design on a firmer, analytical, engineering basis than has been possible before now. Moreover, the theory is not just an academic curiosity. It has been used in the design of several production systems. Interestingly, none of the systems actually supported the theory in an ideal way.

The theory has proven to be quite robust in giving insight into the behavior of existing systems that are failing to meet their performance requirements and to suggest remedies. It promises to be even more useful when used at the outset in designing real-time systems.

The ideas have been applied to uniprocessor systems and to a real-time local area network. Currently, work is actively underway to apply the ideas to distributed systems in a more integrated fashion.

Although the treatment of priorities by the current Ada tasking model can and should be improved, the scheduling algorithms can be used today within the existing Ada rules if an appropriate coding and design approach is taken and if runtime systems are written to take full advantage of certain coding styles and the existing flexibility in the scheduling rules. DDC-I, Verdix, Telesoft, and Ready Systems are among the Ada compiler vendors working on supporting rate monotonic algorithms. In particular, DDC-I and Verdix currently support the priority inheritance protocol,[9] whose performance for practical purposes is quite similar to that of the priority ceiling protocol. Verdix also provides special optimizations for monitor tasks. The SEI is providing technical reports showing how to implement the algorithms, and we will be providing test programs to check the correctness and the performance of the implementations. ∎

Acknowledgments

The authors thank Mark Klein and Mark Borger for pointing out why the priority ceiling protocol cannot be correctly simulated simply by giving a monitor task a high priority when the monitor can suspend itself during a rendezvous. In addition, we thank Anthony Gargaro for catching an error in an early draft of Example 2. Finally, we thank the referees for their helpful comments.

References

1. R. Rajkumar, L. Sha, and J.P. Lehoczky, "Real-Time Synchronization Protocols for Multiprocessors," *Proc. IEEE Real-Time Systems Symp.*, CS Press, Los Alamitos, Calif., Order No. 894, 1988, pp. 259-269.

2. L. Sha et al., "Mode Change Protocols for Priority-Driven Preemptive Scheduling," *J. Real-Time Systems*, Vol. 1, 1989, pp. 243-264.

3. C.L. Liu and J.W. Layland, "Scheduling Algorithms for Multiprogramming in a Hard Real Time Environment," *J. ACM*, Vol. 20, No. 1, 1973, pp. 46-61.

4. J.P. Lehoczky, L. Sha, and Y. Ding, "The Rate Monotonic Scheduling Algorithm — Exact Characterization and Average Case Behavior," *Proc. IEEE Real-Time System Symp.*, CS Press, Los Alamitos, Calif., Order No. 2004, 1989, pp. 166-171.

5. L. Sha, J.P. Lehoczky, and R. Rajkumar, "Solutions for Some Practical Problems in Prioritized Preemptive Scheduling," *Proc. IEEE Real-Time Systems Symp.*, CS Press, Los Alamitos, Calif., Order No. 749, 1986, pp. 181-191.

6. J.P. Lehoczky, L. Sha, and J. Strosnider, "Enhancing Aperiodic Responsiveness in a Hard Real-Time Environment," *Proc. IEEE Real-Time Systems Symp.*, CS Press, Los Alamitos, Calif., Order No. 815, 1987, pp. 261-270.

7. B. Sprunt, L. Sha, and J. Lehoczky, "Aperiodic Task Scheduling for Hard Real-Time Systems," *J. Real-Time Systems*, Vol. 1, No. 1, 1989, pp. 27-60

8. J.B. Goodenough and L. Sha, "The Priority Ceiling Protocol: A Method for Minimizing the Blocking of High Priority Ada Tasks," *Ada Letters, Special Issue: Proc. 2nd Int'l Workshop on Real-Time Ada Issues VIII*, Vol. 7, Fall 1988, pp. 20-31.

9. L. Sha, R. Rajkumar, and J.P. Lehoczky, "Priority Inheritance Protocols: An Approach to Real-Time Synchronization," tech. report, Dept. of Computer Science, Carnegie Mellon Univ., 1987. To appear in *IEEE Trans. Computers*.

10. L. Kleinrock, *Queueing Systems*, Vol. I. John Wiley and Sons, 1975.

Lui Sha is a senior member of the technical staff at the Software Engineering Institute, Carnegie Mellon University, and a member of the research faculty at the School of Computer Science at CMU. His interests lie in real-time computing systems. He has authored and coauthored a number of articles in this area.

Sha co-chaired the 1988 IEEE and Usenix Workshop on Real-Time Software and Operating Systems; chairs the Real-Time Task Group on the IEEE Futurebus+ and is the architect of the Futurebus+ Real-Time System Configuration guide; is vice chair of the 1990 10th International Conference on Distributed Computing Systems and a reviewer of NASA Space Station Freedom's data management system design; and is a member of the IEEE Computer Society. He received his BSEE from McGill University in 1978, and his MSEE and PhD from Carnegie Mellon University in 1979 and 1985, respectively.

John B. Goodenough is a senior member of the technical staff at the Software Engineering Institute at Carnegie Mellon University. His technical interests include programming languages, with special emphasis on Ada, real-time methods, software engineering, and software reuse. He was heavily involved in the design of Ada as a distinguished reviewer and led the Ada compiler validation test effort.

Goodenough is chair of the group responsible for providing interpretations of the Ada standard and has the title of distinguished reviewer for the Ada revision effort. He has published papers on software testing, exception handling, and software engineering principles. He earned his MA and PhD in applied mathematics at Harvard University in 1962 and 1970, respectively. He is a member of the IEEE Computer Society.

The authors can be contacted at the Software Engineering Institute, Carnegie Mellon University, Pittsburgh, PA 15213-3890.

Algorithms for Scheduling Imprecise Computations

Jane W.S. Liu, Kwei-Jay Lin, Wei-Kuan Shih, and Albert Chuang-shi Yu,
University of Illinois at Urbana-Champaign

Jen-Yao Chung, IBM T.J. Watson Research Center

Wei Zhao, Texas A&M University

I n a hard real-time system, every time-critical task must meet its timing constraint, typically specified as its deadline. (A task is a granule of computation treated by the scheduler as a unit of work to be allocated processor time, or scheduled.) If any time-critical task fails to complete and produce its result by its deadline, a timing fault occurs and the task's result is of little or no use. Such factors as variations in the processing times of dynamic algorithms make meeting all deadlines at all times difficult.

The imprecise computation technique[1-3] can minimize this difficulty. It prevents timing faults and achieves graceful degradation by giving the user an approximate result of acceptable quality whenever the system cannot produce the exact result in time. Image processing and tracking are examples of real-time applications where the user may accept timely approximate results: Frames of fuzzy images and rough estimates of location produced in time may be better than perfect images and accurate location data produced too late.

In this article, we review workload models that quantify the trade-off between result quality and computation time. We also describe scheduling algorithms that exploit this trade-off.

Imprecise computation techniques provide scheduling flexibility by trading off result quality to meet computation deadlines. We review imprecise computation scheduling problems: workload models and algorithms.

Imprecise computation technique

A basic strategy to minimize the bad effects of timing faults is to leave the less important tasks unfinished if necessary.

The system schedules and executes to completion all mandatory tasks before their deadlines, but may leave less important tasks unfinished.

The imprecise computation technique uses this basic strategy but carries it one step further. In addition to dividing tasks into mandatory and optional, programmers structure every time-critical task so it can be logically decomposed into two subtasks: a mandatory subtask and an optional subtask. The mandatory subtask is required for an acceptable result and must be computed to completion before the task deadline. The optional subtask refines the result. It can be left unfinished and terminated at its deadline, if necessary, lessening the quality of the task result.

The result produced by a task when it completes is the desired *precise* result, which has an error of zero. If the task is terminated before completion, the intermediate result produced at that point is usable as long as the mandatory subtask is complete. Such a result is said to be *imprecise*. A programming language in which imprecise computations can be easily implemented is Flex,[1] an object-oriented language that supports all C++ constructs along with timing-constraint and imprecision primitives.

Reprinted from *IEEE Computer*, Vol. 24, No. 5, May 1991, pp. 58-68.

0-8186-3792-7/93 $03.00 © 1991 IEEE

Monotone time-critical computations provide maximum flexibility in scheduling. A task is monotone if the quality of its intermediate result does not decrease as it executes longer. Underlying computational algorithms enabling monotone tasks are available in many problem domains, including numerical computation, statistical estimation and prediction, heuristic search, sorting, and database query processing.[4]

To return an imprecise result of a monotone task, the intermediate results produced by the task are recorded at appropriate instances of its execution. Flex provides language primitives with which the programmer can specify the intermediate result variables and error indicators, as well as the time instants to record them. The latest recorded values of the intermediate result variables and error indicators become available to the user if the task prematurely terminates. The user can examine these error indicators and decide whether an imprecise result is acceptable. This method for returning imprecise results is called the *milestone method*.

For some applications, making all computations monotone is not feasible. In this case, result quality can be traded off for processing time through *sieve functions* — computation steps that can be skipped to save time. In radar signal processing, for example, the step that computes a new estimate of the noise level in the received signal can be skipped; an old estimate can be used.

In applications where neither the milestone method nor the sieve method is feasible, the *multiple version* method[5] almost always works. The system has two versions of each task: the primary version and the alternate version. The primary version produces a precise result but has a longer processing time. The alternate version has a shorter processing time but produces an imprecise result. During a transient overload, the system executes a task's alternate version instead of its primary version.

Programmers can easily implement both the milestone and sieve methods in any existing language. Tools and environments have been developed to support the multiple-version method in real-time computing and data communication.

The cost of the milestone technique is the overhead in recording intermediate results. The cost of the sieve technique is the higher scheduling overhead. Since there is no benefit in completing part of a sieve, while incurring the cost in processing that part, the execution of such an optional subtask must satisfy the *0/1 constraint:*

The system must either execute it to completion before its deadline or not schedule it at all. Algorithms for scheduling tasks with the 0/1 constraints are more complex than the ones for monotone tasks.[2]

The cost of the multiple-version method is the overhead to store multiple versions, as well as the relatively high scheduling overhead. Scheduling tasks that have two versions is the same as scheduling tasks with the 0/1 constraint. For scheduling purposes, we can view the primary version of a task as consisting of a mandatory subtask and an optional subtask, and the alternate version as the mandatory subtask. The processing time of the mandatory subtask is the same as the processing time of the task's alternate version. The processing time of the optional subtask in the primary version is equal to the difference between the processing times of the primary and alternate versions. Thus, scheduling the primary version corresponds to scheduling the mandatory subtask and the entire optional subtask, while scheduling the alternate version corresponds to scheduling only the mandatory subtask.

To ensure that imprecise computation works properly, we need to make sure that all the mandatory subtasks have bounded resource and processing time requirements and are allocated sufficient processor time to complete by their deadlines. The system can use leftover processor time to complete as many optional subtasks as possible. For guaranteed performance and predictable behavior, we can use a conservative scheduling discipline such as the rate-monotone algorithm[6] to schedule the mandatory subtasks. To schedule optional subtasks for optimal processor use, we can use more dynamic disciplines, such as the earliest-deadline-first algorithm,[6] which may have unpredictable behavior. Because a monotone task can be terminated any time after it has produced an acceptable result, the system can decide — on line or nearly on line — how much of each optional subtask to schedule.

Basic workload model

The problems in scheduling imprecise computations are at least as complex as the corresponding classical real-time-scheduling problems. Almost all problems beyond scheduling unit-length, dependent tasks on two processors are NP-hard, and most known heuristic algorithms for multiprocessor scheduling of dependent tasks have poor worst-case performance.[7] For this

reason, a better approach to scheduling dependent tasks is first to assign the tasks statically to processors and then schedule the tasks on each processor using an optimal or near-optimal uniprocessor scheduling algorithm. When the tasks are independent, optimal preemptive multiprocessor schedules can be obtained by transforming an optimal uniprocessor schedule using McNaughton's rule.[8]

All the imprecise computation models are extensions and variations of the following basic model. We have a set of preemptable tasks $\mathbf{T} = \{T_1, T_2, ..., T_n\}$. Each task T_i is characterized by parameters, which are rational numbers:

- Ready time r_i' at which T_i becomes ready for execution

- Deadline d_i' by which T_i must be completed

- Processing time τ_i, the time required to execute T_i to completion in the traditional sense on a single processor

- Weight w_i, a positive number that measures the relative importance of the task

Logically, we decompose each task T_i into two subtasks: the *mandatory* subtask M_i and the *optional* subtask O_i. Hereafter, we refer to M_i and O_i simply as tasks rather than subtasks: M_i and O_i mean the mandatory task and the optional task of T_i. We use T_i to refer to the task as a whole. The processing times of M_i and O_i are m_i and o_i, respectively. Here m_i and o_i are rational numbers, and $m_i + o_i = \tau_i$. The ready times and deadlines of the tasks M_i and O_i are the same as those of T_i.

A schedule on a uniprocessor system is an assignment of the processor to the tasks in $\mathbf{T}$ in disjoint intervals of time. A task is scheduled in a time interval if the processor is assigned to the task in the interval. A valid schedule assigns the processor to at most one task at any time, and every task is scheduled after its ready time. Moreover, the total length of the intervals in which the processor is assigned to T_i, referred to as the total amount of processor time assigned to the task, is at least equal to m_i and at most equal to τ_i. A task is completed in the traditional sense at an instant t when the total amount of processor time assigned to it becomes equal to its processing time at t.

A mandatory task M_i is completed when it is completed in the traditional sense. The optional task O_i depends on the mandatory task M_i and becomes ready for execution when M_i is completed. The system can terminate O_i at any time; no processor time is assigned to it after it is terminated.

A task T_i is completed in a schedule whenever its mandatory task is completed. It is terminated when its optional task is terminated. Given a schedule S, we call the earliest time instant at which the processor is assigned to a task the *start time* of the task and the time instant at which the task is terminated its *finishing time*.

The traditional workload model of hard real-time applications is a special case of this model in which all the tasks are mandatory, that is, $o_i = 0$ for all i. Similarly, the traditional soft real-time workload model is also a special case in which all tasks are optional, that is, $m_i = 0$ for all i.

Precedence constraints specify the dependences between the tasks in **T**. The constraints are given by a partial-order relation "<" defined over **T**. $T_i < T_j$ if the execution of T_j cannot begin until the task T_i is completed and terminated. T_j is a *successor* of T_i, and T_i is a *predecessor* of T_j, if $T_i < T_j$. For a schedule of **T** to be valid, it must satisfy the precedence constraints between all tasks. A set of tasks is independent if the partial-order relation is empty, and the tasks can be executed in any order. A valid schedule is *feasible* if every task is completed by its deadline. A set of tasks is *schedulable* if it has at least one feasible schedule.

The given deadline of a task can be later than that of its successors. Rather than working with the given deadlines, we use modified deadlines consistent with the precedence constraints and computed as follows. The modified deadline d_i of a task T_i that has no successors is equal to its given deadline d_i'. Let A_j be the set of all successors of T_j. The modified deadline d_j of T_j is

$$\min\left\{d_j', \min_{T_i \in A_j}\{d_i\}\right\}$$

Similarly, the given ready time of a task may be earlier than that of its predecessors. We modify the ready times of tasks as follows. The modified ready time r_i of a task T_i with no predecessors is equal to its given ready time r_i'. Let B_j be the set of all predecessors of T_j. The modified ready time r_j of T_j is

$$\max\left\{r_j', \max_{T_i \in B_j}\{r_i\}\right\}$$

A feasible schedule on a uniprocessor system exists for a set of tasks **T** with the given ready times and deadlines if and only if a feasible schedule of **T** with the modified ready times and deadlines exists.[7] Working with the modified ready times and deadlines allows the precedence constraints to be ignored temporarily. If an algorithm finds an invalid schedule in which T_i is assigned a time interval later than some intervals assigned to T_j but $T_i < Tj$, it can construct a valid schedule by exchanging the time intervals assigned to T_i and T_j to satisfy their precedence constraint without violating their timing constraints. In our subsequent discussion, the terms ready times and deadlines mean *modified* ready times and deadlines. We call the time interval $[r_i, d_i]$ the *feasibility interval* of the task T_i.

When the amount of processor time σ_i assigned to O_i in a schedule is equal to o_i, the task T_i is precisely scheduled. The error $\in_i$ in the result produced by T_i (or simply the error of T_i) is zero. In a precise schedule, every task is precisely scheduled. Otherwise, if σ_i is less than o_i, we say that a portion of O_i with processing time $o_i - \sigma_i$ is discarded, and the error of T_i is equal to

$$\in_i = E_i(o_i - \sigma_i) \qquad (1)$$

where the error function $E_i(\sigma_i)$ gives the error of the task T_i as a function of σ_i. We assume throughout this article that $E_i(\sigma_i)$ is a monotone nonincreasing function of σ_i.

Imprecise scheduling problems

Depending on the application, we use different performance metrics as criteria for comparing different imprecise schedules. Consequently, there are many different imprecise scheduling problems. We describe some in this section.

Minimization of total error. In practice, the exact behavior of error functions $E_i(x)$ is often not known. A reasonable choice is the simplest one:

$$\in_i = o_i - \sigma_i \qquad (2a)$$

for all i. For a given schedule, the total error of the task set **T** is

$$\in = \sum_{i=1}^{n} w_i \in_i \qquad (2b)$$

Again, $w_i > 0$ are the weights of the tasks. Sometimes, we also refer to $\in$ as the total error of the schedule. The basic imprecise scheduling problem is, given a set **T** of n tasks, to find a schedule that is optimal in that it is feasible and has the minimum total error given by Equations 2a and 2b. An optimal scheduling algorithm always finds an optimal schedule whenever feasible schedules of **T** exist. In later sections, we consider this problem for dependent tasks on uniprocessor systems or independent tasks on multiprocessor systems.

Minimization of the maximum or average error. Two straightforward variations of the minimization of total error performance metric are concerned with the average error and the maximum error. Given a schedule of the task set **T** and the errors $\in_i$ of the tasks, the maximum error of the task set is

$$\max_i[w_i \in_i]$$

For some applications, we may want to find feasible schedules with the smallest maximum error, rather than the total error. There are polynomial-time, optimal algorithms for solving this scheduling problem. (We are preparing a manuscript describing them.)

Minimization of the number of discarded optional tasks. In a schedule that satisfies the 0/1 constraint, σ_i is equal to o_i or 0 for every task. The general problem of scheduling to meet the 0/1 constraint and timing constraints, as well as to minimize the total error, is NP-complete when the optional tasks have arbitrary processing times. Often — for example, when scheduling tasks with multiple versions — we are concerned only with the number of discarded optional tasks. A reasonable strategy for scheduling to minimize the number of discarded optional tasks is the shortest-processing-time-first strategy, which tries to schedule the optional tasks with shorter processing times first. Given a set **T** of n tasks, N_s and N_o are the numbers of optional tasks discarded in a schedule produced using this strategy and discarded in an optimal schedule, respectively. Our conjecture is that $N_s \leq 2N_o$.

When optional subtasks have identical processing times, tasks with 0/1 constraints and identical weights can be optimally scheduled in $O(n \log n)$ time or $O(n^2)$ time, depending on whether the tasks have identical or different ready times. Optimal algorithms for this case can be found elsewhere.[2]

Minimization of the number of tardy tasks. As long as the total error of the tasks is lower than a certain acceptable limit, its value is often not important. We may then want to minimize the number of tasks that are tardy — that is, tasks that complete and terminate after their deadlines — for a given maximum, tolerable total error. Leung and Wong[9] presented a pseudopolynomial time algorithm and a fast heuristic algorithm for preemptive uniprocessor scheduling of tasks whose feasibility intervals include each other. In the worst case, the number of tardy tasks in a schedule found by the heuristic algorithm is approximately three times the number in an optimal schedule.

Minimization of average response time. Given a schedule S and the finishing time $f(T_i, S)$ of every task, the *mean flow time* of the tasks according to the schedule is equal to

$$F = \sum_{i=1}^{n} f(T_i, S) / n$$

The mean flow time of the tasks measures the average response time, the average amount of time a task waits until it completes. The goal of scheduling is to minimize the mean flow time, subject to the constraint that the total error is less than an acceptable value. Unfortunately, all but the simplest special cases of this scheduling problem are NP-hard.[10] In a later section, we discuss the queuing-theoretical formulation, a more fruitful approach to this problem.

Scheduling to minimize total error

Two optimal algorithms for scheduling imprecise computations to meet deadlines and minimize total error use a modified version of the classical earliest-deadline-first algorithm.[7] This is a preemptive, priority-driven algorithm that assigns priorities to tasks according to their deadlines. Tasks with earlier deadlines have higher priorities. In our version, every task is terminated at its deadline even if it is not completed at the time. We call this algorithm the *ED algorithm*. Its complexity is $O(n \log n)$. In any ED algorithm schedule, every task is scheduled in its feasibility interval.

We use the ED algorithm to test whether a task set **T** can be feasibly scheduled. In the feasibility test, we schedule the mandatory set **M** using the ED algorithm. If the resultant schedule of **M** is precise, then the task set **T** can be feasibly scheduled. Otherwise, no feasible schedule of **T** exists.

Figure 1. An example showing the need for step 3 in algorithm F.

Identical-weight case. An ED schedule of a set of entirely optional tasks is, by definition, a feasible schedule of the set. Moreover, because such a schedule is priority-driven, the processor is never left idle when there are schedulable tasks. A portion of an optional task is discarded only when necessary. Therefore, the ED algorithm is optimal when used to schedule optional tasks that have identical weights.[2]

The optimality of the ED algorithm provides the basis of algorithm F, which schedules a set $\mathbf{T} = \{T_1, T_2, ..., T_n\}$ of n tasks with identical weights on a uniprocessor system. We decompose the set **T** into two sets, the set **M** of mandatory tasks and the set **O** of optional tasks. Algorithm F works as follows:

(1) Treat all mandatory tasks in **M** as optional tasks. Use the ED algorithm to find a schedule S_t of the set **T**. If S_t is a precise schedule, stop. The resultant schedule has zero error and is, therefore, optimal. Otherwise, carry out step 2.

(2) Use the ED algorithm to find a schedule S_m of the set **M**. If S_m is not a precise schedule, **T** is not schedulable. Stop. Otherwise, carry out step 3.

(3) Using S_m as a template, transform S_t into an optimal schedule S_o that is feasible and minimizes the total error.

The example in Figure 1 shows the need for step 3. The task set in Figure 1a consists of six tasks of identical weights. Figure 1b shows the schedules S_t and S_m generated in steps 1 and 2, respectively. S_m of the mandatory set **M** is precise. Therefore, feasible schedules of **T** exist.

The schedule S_t is, in general, not a feasible schedule of **T**. Because step 1 treats all the tasks as entirely optional, some tasks may be assigned insufficient processor time for their mandatory tasks to complete. In this example, step 1 assigns T_4 only two units of processor time in S_t, which is less than the processing time of M_4. In step 3, we transform S_t into a feasible schedule of **T** by adjusting the amounts of processor time assigned to the tasks, so every task T_i is assigned at least m_i units of processor time in the transformed schedule.

The transformation process in step 3 has as inputs the schedules S_m and S_t. Let a_1 and a_{k+1} be, respectively, the earliest start time and the latest finishing time of all tasks in the schedule S_m. We partition the time interval $[a_1, a_{k+1}]$ according to S_m into k disjoint intervals $[a_j, a_{j+1}]$, for $j = 1, 2, ..., k$, so in S_m the processor is assigned to only one task in each of these intervals and is assigned to different tasks in adjacent intervals. In the example in Figure 1, k is equal to 6, and the time instants $a_1, a_2, ..., a_7$ are

```
begin
    Use the ED algorithm to find a schedule S_m of M.
    If S_m is not precise, stop; the task set T cannot be feasibly scheduled.
    else
        The mandatory set M' (= {M_1', M_2',..., M_n' }) = M
        i = 1
        while (1 ≤ i ≤ n)
            Use algorithm F to find an optimal schedule S_o^i of M' ∪ {O_i};
                O_i' = the portion of O_i with processing time σ_i'' scheduled in S_o^i
            M_i' = M_i ∪ O_i'
            i = i + 1
        endwhile
        The optimal schedule sought is S_o^n
    endif
end algorithm LWF
```

Figure 2. Pseudocode for the LWF algorithm.

	r_i	d_i	τ_i	m_i	o_i	w_i
T_1	6	20	10	4	6	4
T_2	2	12	9	2	7	3
T_3	0	14	8	3	5	2
T_4	5	17	13	1	12	1

(a)

(b)

Figure 3. An illustration of the LWF algorithm.

0, 3, 7, 9, 13, 15, and 16, respectively. Let $M(j)$ denote the mandatory task scheduled in the interval $[a_j, a_{j+1}]$ in S_m, and let $T(j)$ be the corresponding task.

Step 3 adjusts the amounts of processor time assigned to the tasks in S_t, using S_m as a template. In this step, we scan the schedule S_t backward from its end a_{k+2}. The segment of S_t after a_{k+1} is left unchanged. We compare in turn, for $j = k, k - 1, ..., 1$, the total amounts $L_t(j)$ and $L_m(j)$ of pro- cessor time assigned to the tasks $T(j)$ and $M(j)$ after a_j according to S_t and S_m, re- spectively. If $L_t(j) \geq L_m(j)$, the segment of S_t in $[a_j, a_{j+1}]$ is left unchanged. Otherwise, let $\Delta = L_m(j) - L_t(j)$. We assign Δ additional units of processor time in $[a_j, a_{j+1}]$ to $T(j)$. These units may be originally assigned to other tasks in S_t. Arbitrarily, we choose some of these tasks. We decrease the amounts of processor time assigned to them in this interval by a total of Δ units and update accordingly the values of $L_t(l)$ (for $l = 1, 2, ..., j$) for all the tasks affected by this re- assignment. This reassignment can always be done because Δ is less than or equal to $a_{j+1} - a_j$ and $T(j)$ is ready in the interval.

In the example in Figure 1, $L_t(6)$ and $L_t(5)$ are left unchanged because they are equal to $L_m(6)$ and $L_m(5)$, respectively. $L_t(4)$ is 2 while $L_m(4)$ is 4; therefore, we assign two additional units of processor time to $T(4)$, which is T_4. These two units of time are taken from T_2. T_2 has three units of proces- sor time in the interval [9, 13] before the reassignment and only one unit after the reassignment. The new values of $L_t(j)$ are 5, 5, 2, and 4 for $j = 1, 2, 3$, and 4, respec- tively. Similarly, we compare $L_t(3)$ and $L_m(3)$, and so on. The result of step 3 is the optimal schedule S_o.

The complexity of algorithm F is the same as that of the ED algorithm, that is, $O(n \log n)$. Algorithm F always produces a feasible schedule of T as long as T can be feasibly scheduled — this follows directly from the algorithm's definition. The schedule S_t obtained in step 1 achieves the minimum total error for any set of tasks with identical weights. Since step 3 intro- duces no additional idle time, the total error remains minimal. Hence, algorithm F is optimal for scheduling tasks with identi- cal weights to minimize total error.[2] With McNaughton's rule,[8] it can be modified to optimally schedule independent tasks with identical weights on a multiprocessor sys- tem containing v identical processors. Then its complexity is $O(vn + n \log n)$.

Different-weight case. When tasks in T have different weights, we can number them according to their weights: $w_1 \geq w_2 \geq ... \geq w_n$. Algorithm F is not optimal for scheduling tasks with different weights. We use the largest-weight-first algorithm, which is optimal. Figure 2 shows the LWF algorithm in pseudocode.

Starting from the task with the largest weight, in the order of nonincreasing weights, the LWF algorithm first finds for each task T_i in turn the maximum amounts of processor time σ_i'' that can be assigned to its optional task O_i. An optimal schedule is a feasible schedule in which the amount of processor time assigned to each optional task T_i is σ_i''.

The LWF algorithm makes use of the fact that the amount of processor time σ_i'' assigned to the only optional task in the set $M \cup \{O_i\}$ in an optimal schedule of this set is as large as possible. (In Figure 2, the notation for the optimal schedule of the set is S_o^i.) It uses algorithm F to schedule the tasks in the set $\mathbf{M} \cup \{O_1\}$. Again, T_1 is the task with the largest weight. In the resultant schedule S_o^1, the optional task O_1 is assigned the maximum possible amount of processor time σ_1^o. There are optimal schedules of $\mathbf{T}$ in which O_1 is assigned σ_1^o units of processor time.[2] We commit ourselves to finding one of these schedules by combining M_1 and the portion O_1' of O_1 that is scheduled in S_o^1 into a task M_1'. We treat the task M_1' as a mandatory task in the subsequent steps.

In the next step, we again use algorithm F to schedule the task set $\{M_1', M_2, ..., M_n\} \cup \{O_2\}$. Let O_2' be the portion of the optional task O_2 that is scheduled in the resultant optimal schedule S_o^2. O_2' has the maximum possible amount of processor time σ_2^o. There are optimal schedules of $\mathbf{T}$ in which the amounts of processor time assigned to O_1 and O_2 are σ_1^o and σ_2^o, respectively. We commit ourselves to finding one of these schedules by combining M_2 and O_2' into the mandatory task M_2'.

We repeat these steps for $i = 3, 4, ..., n$ until all σ_i^o are found. The schedule S_o^n found in the last step is an optimal schedule of $\mathbf{T}$ with minimum total error.

The time complexity of the first step when algorithm F is used is $O(n \log n)$, but in subsequent steps, algorithm F requires only $O(n)$ time. Hence, the time complexity of the LWF algorithm is $O(n^2)$.

Figure 3 shows how the LWF algorithm works. Figure 3a lists four tasks and their weights. Figure 3b shows the schedule S_m of $\mathbf{M} \cup \{O_1\}$ produced by algorithm F. We commit ourselves to finding an optimal schedule in which the amount of processor time assigned to O_1 is 6. This is an earliest-deadline-first schedule, and we use it in the second step as a template to find an optimal schedule of the task set $\{M_1', T_2, M_3, M_4\}$. Figure 3b shows the resultant schedule S_o. The total error of the tasks is 25. Also shown is a schedule S_u, which minimizes the unweighted total error.

Scheduling periodic jobs

In the well-known periodic-job model,[3,6] there is a set $\mathbf{J}$ of n periodic jobs. Each job consists of a periodic sequence of requests for the same computation. The period π_i of a job J_i in $\mathbf{J}$ is the time interval between two consecutive requests in the job. In terms of our basic model, each request in job J_i is a task whose processing time is τ_i. The ready time and deadline of

the task in each period are the beginning and the end of the period, respectively. Therefore, we can specify each job J_i by the two-tuple (π_i, τ_i). In the extended-workload model used to characterize periodic imprecise computations,[3] each task in J_i consists of a mandatory task with processing time m_i and an optional task with processing time $\tau_i - m_i$. The optional task is dependent on the mandatory task. In other words, we decompose each job $J_i = (\pi_i, \tau_i)$ into two periodic jobs: the mandatory job $M_i = (\pi_i, m_i)$ and the optional job $O_i = (\pi_i, \tau_i - m_i)$. The corresponding sets of mandatory jobs and optional jobs are denoted by $\mathbf{M}$ and $\mathbf{O}$, respectively. Let

$$U = \sum_{i=1}^{n} \tau_i / \pi_i$$

denote the *utilization factor* of the job set $\mathbf{J}$. U is the fraction of processor time required to complete all the tasks in $\mathbf{J}$ if every task is completed in the traditional sense. Similarly, let

$$u = \sum_{k=1}^{n} m_k / \pi_k$$

Here, u is the utilization factor of the mandatory set $\mathbf{M}$.

Because the worst-case performance of priority-driven strategies for scheduling periodic jobs on multiprocessor systems is unacceptably poor, it is common to assign jobs once and for all to processors, and schedule the jobs assigned to each processor independently of the jobs assigned to the other processors. We can formulate the problem of finding an optimal assignment of jobs to processors and using a minimum number of processors as a bin-packing problem.

A heuristic job-assignment algorithm with reasonably good worst-case performance is the rate-monotone next-fit (or first-fit) algorithm. According to this algorithm, jobs in $\mathbf{J}$ are sorted in the order of nonincreasing rates and are assigned to the processors on the next-fit (or first-fit) basis. A job fits on a processor if it and the jobs already assigned to the processor can be feasibly scheduled according to the rate-monotone algorithm.[6] (The rate-monotone algorithm is a preemptive, priority-driven algorithm that assigns priorities to jobs according to their rates: the higher the rate, the higher the priority.) When deciding whether an imprecise job fits on a processor, the algorithm considers only the mandatory set $\mathbf{M}$. Let $u_i = m_i/\pi_i$. Suppose that k jobs are already assigned to a processor, and their mandatory jobs have a total utilization factor

$$u = \sum_{i=1}^{k} u_i$$

If an additional job J_{k+1} is also assigned to this processor, the total utilization factor of the $k+1$ mandatory jobs is $u + m_{k+1}/\pi_{k+1}$. J_{k+1} is assigned to the processor only if

$$u + m_{k+1}/\pi_{k+1} \leq (k+1)(2^{1/(k+1)} - 1) \quad (3)$$

Hereafter, $\mathbf{J}$ denotes the set of n jobs assigned to one processor in this manner. The utilization factor U of the job set $\mathbf{J}$ may be larger than $n(2^{1/n} - 1)$. Consequently, $\mathbf{J}$ may not be precisely schedulable to meet all deadlines according to the rate-monotone algorithm. However, the utilization factor u of the mandatory set is less than $n(2^{1/n} - 1)$. Hence, the mandatory set $\mathbf{M}$ is always precisely schedulable.[6] Since the value of u is less than 1 (for example, 0.82 for $n = 2$ and ln 2 for large n), a fraction of processor time is always available to execute tasks in the optional set $\mathbf{O}$.

Depending on the kind of undesirable effect that errors cause, applications can be classified as either *error-noncumulative* or *error-cumulative*. Different performance metrics are appropriate for each.

For an error-noncumulative application, only the average effect of errors in different periods is observable and relevant. Optional tasks are truly optional because none need to be completed. Image enhancement and speech processing are examples of this type of application.

In contrast, for an error-cumulative application, errors in different periods have a cumulative effect. The optional task in one period among several consecutive periods must be completed within that period and, hence, is no longer optional. Tracking and control are examples of this type of application.

The complexity of scheduling error-cumulative jobs and an approximate algorithm for scheduling them with identical periods have been discussed elsewhere.[3] Much work remains in finding effective algorithms and schedulability criteria for scheduling error-cumulative jobs that have arbitrary periods and error characteristics. The workload on practical systems typically is a mixture of error-cumulative jobs, error-noncumulative jobs, aperiodic jobs, and dependent jobs. Programmers need good heuristic algorithms for scheduling such complex job mixes.

Error-noncumulative jobs. Now, we focus on error-noncumulative jobs. Since each periodic job can be viewed as an

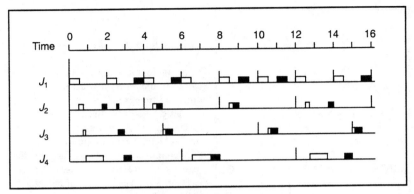

Figure 4. Scheduling error-noncumulative jobs.

infinite chain of tasks, the total error defined in Equations 2a and 2b is infinite for an imprecise schedule. A more appropriate performance metric of the overall result quality is the average error in the results produced in several consecutive periods. While the duration over which the average error is computed can be arbitrary, a convenient choice of this duration is π, the least common multiple of all the periods in **J**. For this duration, the average error ϵ_i of J_i at any time is the average value of $E_i(o_i - \sigma_{i,j})$ over the past π/π_i periods, where $\sigma_{i,j}$ is the amount of processor time assigned to the task in the jth period of J_i. Again, the error function $E_i(\sigma_{i,j})$ is a nonincreasing function of $\sigma_{i,j}$. The average error over all jobs in **J** is

$$\epsilon = \sum_{i=1}^{n} w_i \, \epsilon_i$$

where w_i is a nonnegative constant weight and

$$\sum_{i=1}^{n} w_i = 1$$

A class of heuristic algorithms for scheduling error-noncumulative periodic jobs on uniprocessors to minimize the average error has been designed and evaluated.[3] All the algorithms in this class are preemptive and priority-driven, and all use the same strategy: They execute optional tasks only after all the ready mandatory tasks have completed. Specifically, given a job set **J** and its associated mandatory set **M** and optional set **O**, all the jobs in **M** have higher priorities than all the jobs in **O**. Moreover, the rate-monotone algorithm schedules jobs in **M** precisely. Because of the condition given by Equation 3, the set **M** can always be feasibly scheduled.[6] Such algorithms meet all the deadlines, regardless of how jobs in **O** are scheduled.

Figure 4 shows an example in which the

job set **J** consists of four jobs. They are (2, 1), (4, 0.5), (5, 0.5), and (6, 1.5), and their mandatory tasks have processing times 0.5, 0.2, 0.1, and 1.0, respectively. The utilization factor of the job set **J** is 0.975. **J** is not precisely schedulable according to the rate-monotone algorithm. In a rate-monotone schedule, the task in the first period of J_4 misses its deadline. However, the mandatory set **M** consists of (2, 0.5), (4, 0.2), (5, 0.1), and (6, 1.0) with a utilization factor 0.4867. It is precisely schedulable according to the rate-monotone algorithm.

White boxes in the timing diagram in Figure 4 show the time intervals when the processor is assigned to tasks in **M** in a rate-monotone schedule of **M**. Black bars indicate the time intervals during which the processor is assigned to jobs in the optional set **O**, consisting of (2, 0.5), (4, 0.3), (5, 0.4), and (6, 0.5).

Types of heuristic algorithms. The heuristic algorithms[3] differ only in how they assign priorities to optional jobs. Some make priority assignments to optional tasks on the basis of error function behavior. Examples include the least-utilization algorithm, the least-attained-time algorithm, and the first-come-first-serve algorithm.

The *least-utilization algorithm* statically assigns higher priorities to optional jobs with smaller weighted utilization factors: $(\tau_i - m_k)/\pi_i w_i$. It minimizes the average error when the error functions $E_i(x)$ are linear and when all jobs have identical periods and weights.

At any time, the *least-attained-time algorithm* assigns the highest priority to the optional task that has attained the least processor time among all the ready optional tasks. This algorithm tends to perform well when the error functions $E_i(x)$ are

convex, that is, when the error in the result decreases faster earlier and more slowly later, as the computation proceeds.

The *first-come-first-serve algorithm* performs well when the error functions $E_i(x)$ are concave, that is, when the underlying procedure converges more slowly earlier and faster later, as the computation proceeds.

When we do not know the exact behavior of the error function, we can use an algorithm that ignores the error functions in assigning priorities to optional tasks. The *shortest-period algorithm*, which also assigns priorities to optional jobs on a rate-monotone basis, is such an algorithm.

Another example is the *earliest-deadline algorithm*. This algorithm assigns priorities dynamically to optional tasks according to their deadlines: the earlier the deadline, the higher the priority. If any of the heuristic algorithms we have described here can precisely schedule a set of jobs, the earliest-deadline algorithm can precisely schedule it, too.[3]

Quantitative data on achievable average errors with the algorithms described above for different values of the utilization factors of **M** and **J** are available elsewhere.[3] These algorithms have the advantage of the rate-monotone algorithm: Tasks miss deadlines in a predictable manner during a transient overload. Like the classical earliest-deadline-first algorithm, these algorithms also use the processor to its fullest extent. They are ideal for applications where transient overloads occur frequently or actual task processing times vary widely. Usually the average error remains tolerably small when U becomes larger than 1 and no classical algorithm can schedule the tasks satisfactorily.

The advantages are realized at the expense of not being optimal. For example, these algorithms may lead to schedules with a nonzero average error for job sets that can be precisely scheduled to meet deadlines by the classical rate-monotone or earliest-deadline-first algorithms.

Scheduling parallelizable tasks

A task is parallelizable if it can be executed in parallel on a number of processors to complete in less time. The degree of concurrency of any task in an interval refers to the number of processors on which the task executes in parallel in the interval. In our model of parallelizable tasks, the degree of concurrency of any task may change during its execution.

The parameters that characterize each parallelizable task T_i in a set $\mathbf{T}$ of n tasks include its ready time r_i, deadline d_i, processing time τ_i, and weight w_i — in short, the parameters that characterize any sequential task. A parallelizable task also has the following two parameters:

- Maximum degree of concurrency C_i, the number of processors on which T_i can execute in parallel
- Multiprocessing overhead factor θ_i, a proportional constant used to compute the overhead in the parallel execution of T_i

Like sequential tasks, each parallelizable task T_i is logically composed of a mandatory task M_i and an optional task O_i, whose processing times on a single processor are m_i and o_i, respectively. In this section we use task to refer to a parallelizable task. We consider only cases where the tasks are independent.

A parallel schedule of the task set $\mathbf{T}$ on a system containing v identical processors assigns no more than one task to any processor at any time and assigns each task T_i to at most C_i processors. For a given a task set $\mathbf{T}$, let $\mathbf{a} = \{a_1, a_2, ..., a_{k+1}\}$ be an increasing sequence of distinct numbers obtained by sorting the list of ready times and deadlines of all the tasks in $\mathbf{T}$ and deleting duplicate entries in the list. (Here $k + 1 \leq 2n$.) This sequence divides the time between the earliest ready time a_1 and latest deadline a_{k+1} into k intervals $I_j = [a_j, a_{j+1}]$ for $j = 1, 2, ..., k$.

We divide the problem of finding feasible parallel schedules of $\mathbf{T}$ into two subproblems: the time allocation problem and the schedule construction problem. To solve the time allocation problem, we decide how many units of processor time in each of the k intervals I_j should be allocated to each task T_i, so the tasks meet their timing constraints and the total error is minimized. Given this solution, we then solve the second problem to obtain a parallel schedule on v processors.

Time allocation problem. When a system executes a task in parallel on more than one processor, it wastes some processor time in interprocessor communication and synchronization. This multiprocessing overhead Θ_i of a task T_i in any time interval depends on the task's degree of concurrency c_i and, consequently, on the amount of

$$minimize \sum_{i=1}^{n} w_i \{ \tau_i - \sum_{j=1}^{k} [x_i(j) - \theta_i(j)] \}$$

$$\sum_{j=1}^{k} x_i(j) \leq \tau_i + \sum_{j=1}^{k} \theta_i(j) \quad i = 1, 2, ..., n$$

$$\sum_{j=1}^{k} x_i(j) \geq m_i + \sum_{j=1}^{k} \theta_i(j) \quad i = 1, 2, ..., n$$

$$v t_j \geq \sum_{i=1}^{n} x_i(j) \quad j = 1, 2, ..., k$$

$$(C_i - 1) \geq Y(x_i(j)) \geq 0 \quad i = 1, 2, ..., n$$

$$x_i(j) \geq 0 \quad \begin{matrix} i = 1, 2, ..., n \\ j = 1, 2, ..., k \end{matrix}$$

Figure 5. Linear programming formulation.

processor time allocated to the task in the interval.

Studies on scheduling parallelizable (precise) tasks typically assume that for c_i larger than 1, Θ_i is either a positive constant or a monotone nondecreasing function of c_i. We present a special case where the multiprocessing overhead is a linear function of the degree of concurrency. This assumption allows us to formulate the time allocation problem as a linear programming problem and solve it using any of the well-known techniques.[11]

To calculate the multiprocessing overhead, we suppose that a task T_i is allocated a total of x units of processor time on all processors in an interval of length t. If $x \leq t$, this task is not parallelized in this interval, and its multiprocessing overhead in this interval is zero. If $x > t$, the minimum degree of concurrency of the task in this interval is $\lceil x / t \rceil$. Rather than make the multiprocessing overhead proportional to this nonlinear function of x, we let the multiprocessing overhead of T_i in this interval be proportional to $Y(x) = \max(x/t - 1, 0)$. Then $\theta_i Y(x)$ units of processor time is wasted as the multiprocessing overhead.

The actual amount of processor time available to the task in this interval for its execution toward completion is $x - \theta_i Y(x)$. We say that this amount of processor time is actually assigned to the task T_i. Again, Equations 2a and 2b give us the error ϵ_i of a task T_i in terms of the amount σ_i of processor time actually assigned to its optional task O_i in all k intervals.

Let t_j denote the length of the interval I_j, and $x_i(j)$ denote the amount of processor time allocated to the task T_i in I_j. Here $x_i(j)$ is zero if the feasibility interval of T_i does

not include the interval I_j. Let

$$\Theta_i(j) = \theta_i Y(x_i(j)) = \theta_i \max(x_i(j)/t - 1, 0)$$

be the multiprocessing overhead of T_i incurred in this interval when its allocated processor time is $x_i(j)$.

Figure 5 gives the linear programming formulation of the processor time allocation problem. We want to find the set $\{x_i(j)\}$ that minimizes the objective function, the total (weighted) error expressed here in terms of $x_i(j)$. The first set of constraints specifies that the total processor time allocated to every task in all k intervals is no more than its processing time τ_i plus its total multiprocessing overhead. These constraints ensure that no task gets more processor time than its processing time. The second set of constraints specifies that the total processor time allocated to every task T_i in all k intervals is no less than the sum of the processing time m_i of the mandatory task M_i and the total multiprocessing overhead. These constraints ensure that the schedule assigns sufficient processor time to every mandatory task for it to complete in the traditional sense. Together, they ensure that we can construct a valid schedule from the resultant set $\mathbf{X} = \{x_i(j)\}$ of processor time allocations.

The third set of constraints requires that the total processor time allocated to all tasks in every interval I_j is no greater than the total amount of processor time available on all v processors. The fourth set of constraints ensures that the degree of concurrency of each task is at most equal to its maximum degree of concurrency. The fifth set states that every $x_i(j)$ is nonnegative.

The optimal solution of this linear program, if one exists, gives a set $\mathbf{X}$ of processor time allocations from which we can construct a feasible parallel schedule of $\mathbf{T}$ with the minimum total error. The complexity of the processor time allocation problem is the same as the complexity of the most efficient algorithm for linear programming.[11] One efficient algorithm for linear programming requires $O((\alpha + \beta)\beta^2 + (\alpha + \beta)^{1.5}\beta)$ operations, where α is the number of inequalities and β is the number of variables. For our problem, α is equal to $3n + k$, and β is at most equal to nk.

In the example in Figure 6, there are three tasks; Figure 6a lists their parameters. Their ready times and deadlines divide the time between 0 to 14 into four intervals beginning at 0, 4, 6, and 12. The values of t_j for $j = 1, 2, 3$, and 4 are 4, 2, 6, and 2, respectively. Figure 6b shows the solution of the corresponding linear pro-

136

	r_i	d_i	τ_i	m_i	o_i	w_i	C_i	θ_i
T_1	0	6	8	3	5	3	2	2
T_2	4	12	13	10	3	2	2	2
T_3	0	14	17	7	10	1	2	2

(a)

	$x_i(1)$	$x_i(2)$	$x_i(3)$	$x_i(4)$	$\sum x_i(j)$	Y_1	Y_2	Y_3	Y_4	$\sum Y_i$	$w_i\epsilon_i$
a_i	0	4	6	12		0	4	6	12		
T_1	6	2			8	0.5	0			0.5	3
T_2		2	9		11		0	0.5		0.5	6
T_3	2	0	3	2	7	0	0	0	0	0	10

(b)

Figure 6. An example of processor time allocation.

gram. A blank entry at a row T_i and a column $x_i(j)$ indicates that the feasibility interval of T_i does not include the interval $[a_j, a_{j+1}]$. To save space in the tabulation, Figure 6b lists $Y(x_i(j))$ simply as Y_j. The total error of the feasible schedule is 19.

Schedule construction. The solution of the linear program is the set $\mathbf{X} = \{x_i(j)\}$ of processor time allocations, which gives us the amounts of processor time allocated to the n tasks in $\mathbf{T}$ in each time interval I_j. Given $\mathbf{X}$, we need to decide which task is to run on which processor(s) in each interval I_j, so we can construct a parallel schedule. A straightforward approach is first to construct independently a segment of the parallel schedule in each interval I_j on the basis of the processor time allocations $x_i(j)$ for the interval. After constructing the schedule segments in all k intervals, we rearrange the order in which tasks are assigned in adjacent segments to reduce the total number of preemptions and migrations. If a task is scheduled in two adjacent segments on two different processors, in this rearrangement step we move them whenever possible so they are scheduled contiguously on the same processor(s) in these segments. To do this, we can use an $O(n^2 \log n)$ algorithm based on a solution of the bipartite matching problem.

Returning to how to construct a parallel schedule segment from the processor time allocations of an interval I_j, we consider now the first interval I_1. Segments in the other

intervals can be constructed in the same manner. Without loss of generality, let T_1, T_2, ... T_l be all the tasks allocated nonzero processor time in this interval. The portion of each task T_i assigned in I_1 is divided into $v_i = \lfloor x_i(1)/t_1 \rfloor$ subtasks with processing time t_1 and a fractional subtask with processing time $\psi_i = t_1 - \lfloor x_i(1)/t_1 \rfloor t_1$. After all the subtasks with processing time t_1 are assigned on

$$\sum_{i=1}^{l} v_i$$

processors, we try to pack the l fractional subtasks on the remaining processors. We can use a pseudopolynomial algorithm for this knapsack problem.

Queuing-theoretical formulation

A performance metric common in many applications is the *average response time* of tasks, that is, the average amount of time between the instant when a task is ready and the instant at which the task is completed (and leaves the system). The section on imprecise scheduling briefly describes the deterministic formulation of the problem: Find optimal schedules with the minimum average response time, subject to the constraint of a maximum acceptable total error. This problem is NP-hard[10] for most practical cases, so the queuing-theoretical

approach is more fruitful than the deterministic formulation. Here we briefly describe two queuing-theoretical formulations.

The simplest model of an imprecise multiprocessor system with v identical processors is an open v-server Markov queue. Tasks arrive and join a common queue according to a Poisson process with an average rate of λ. They are serviced (that is, executed) on a first-come-first-serve basis. The processing times (that is, service times) of all tasks are exponentially distributed. (Later, we say more about this assumption.) This simple Markov multi-server queue is analytically tractable. For most practical cases, however, it models imprecise computation systems in sufficient detail to provide the performance data we need to choose design parameters of imprecise service disciplines.

First, we consider imprecise computations implemented by providing two versions of each task. A task is serviced at the full level when its primary version is scheduled and executed, or at reduced level when its alternate version is scheduled and executed. When the system has a light load and the response time is small, it services every task at the full level. When the load becomes heavy, the system reduces the overall response time by servicing some tasks at the reduced level. Such a scheduling scheme is called a *two-level scheduling discipline*.[12] The full-level processing times of all tasks are statistical-

137

ly independent, exponentially distributed with a mean of $1/\mu$. The reduced-level processing time of a task is a constant fraction γ of its full-level processing time, where γ is a real number between 0 and 1. Let $\rho = \lambda/\nu\mu$ denote the *offered load* of a processor in the system, that is, the fraction of time each processor is busy if all tasks are serviced at their full level. It is easy to see that the system is not saturated as long as $\rho < 1/\gamma$.

Here γ is a design parameter of an imprecise computation system. We assume that the larger γ is, the better the result quality of the tasks that are serviced at the reduced level. A design parameter of the two-level service discipline is the threshold H: As long as the number of tasks in the system is less than H, the system load is light. For a given γ, we choose the value of H to achieve a desired trade-off between the average waiting time and the average result quality. The trade-off reduces the average waiting time W of tasks — the average time a task spends in the queue before its execution begins.

Thus W plus the average processing time of the tasks corresponds to the mean flow time F defined in the section on imprecise scheduling problems. We can minimize it easily by servicing every task at the reduced level. Therefore, we must consider the cost of this trade-off. Studies on the two-level scheduling discipline[12] measure this cost in terms of the average result quality, the average fraction G of tasks serviced at the full level. G measures the system's quality of service. In the steady state, $G = (U - \gamma\rho)/(1 - \gamma)\rho$, where U is the average utilization of each processor.

We choose H on the basis of the performance data on W and G. Such data on two-level scheduling in uniprocessor systems are available elsewhere.[12] More recently, we evaluated the performance of imprecise multiprocessor systems. The results indicate that an appropriate choice of H makes an imprecise system with a two-level scheduling discipline perform almost as well as the corresponding precise system in terms of the average service quality, when the offered load of the system is small. When the offered load is high, the two-level scheduling scheme can significantly improve the average task waiting time by sacrificing service quality. This trade-off is most effective when the offered load per processor is near 1. While the average waiting time in a precise system approaches infinity, the two-level scheduling scheme keeps the average waiting time in an imprecise system small,

with a reasonably small decrease in the average service quality.

An imprecise computation system that uses monotone tasks is more appropriately modeled as an open $M/E_{K+1}/\nu$ queue. Each task T_i is composed of a mandatory task M_i followed by K optional tasks $O_{i,j}$. (In the deterministic models discussed in earlier sections, K is at most equal to 1.) Let $o_{i,j}$ denote the processing time of $O_{i,j}$. The processing time τ_i of the task T_i is given by

$$\tau_i = m_i + \sum_{j=1}^{K} o_{i,j}$$

The processing times m_i of the mandatory tasks, as well as the $o_{i,j}$, are all statistically independent and exponentially distributed random variables.

When a monotone imprecise system is overloaded, it may discard a number x ($x \le K$) of optional tasks in some task or tasks in the system. The decrease in result quality can be quantified in part by the fraction of optional tasks that the system discards. The expected value of this fraction gives a rough measure of the average error ε in the task results.

Since the system can discard a variable number of optional tasks in each task, the average error does not give us a complete picture of the incurred cost. Another cost function is the imprecision probability, the probability of any task being imprecise because the system discarded some of its optional tasks. We are studying the dependence of these cost factors on parameters K, x, and H of the monotone imprecise system.

A direction of our future study concerns the way a system determines the kind of service each task receives. Past studies on two-level scheduling disciplines assume that the system checks the number of its tasks at each instant immediately before a processor begins to execute a task.[12] The system services the task at the head of the queue at full level if its load is light, and at the reduced level otherwise. In other words, the system is reasonably responsive to overload conditions.

Similarly, we have proposed that in monotone imprecise systems, the system could check the total number of tasks in the queue at each instant when a new task arrives and immediately before it begins to service a task. As long as the queue length is equal to or greater than H, the system discards x optional tasks in the tasks being served. This scheme, called the *responsive service scheme*, is highly responsive to overloads: The system does very well in reducing its backlog and clearing up the

overload whenever such a condition occurs. However, it cannot guarantee service quality. A task that arrives when the system is lightly loaded may have its optional tasks discarded if the system becomes overloaded during the time the task waits in the system.

With the *guaranteed-service scheme*, on the other hand, the system checks its total number of tasks at each arrival instant. It tags for reduced service a task arriving when H or more tasks are in the queue. The tasks already in the system before the overload are fully serviced to completion. With this scheme, an imprecise system does not respond as quickly as possible to correct an overload. However, the quality of results produced by tasks arriving to the system when it is not overloaded is guaranteed to be good. This scheme is good for applications in which overloads can be cleared quickly.

We have reviewed different approaches for scheduling imprecise computations in hard real-time environments. We also described several imprecise computation models that explicitly quantify the costs and benefits in the trade-off between result quality and computation time requirements. An imprecise computation scheduler must balance the benefit in enhanced system response with the cost in reduced result quality.

Because the criteria for measuring costs and benefits vary according to application, there are many different imprecise scheduling problems. We have presented our recent progress toward solving some of these problems, and the directions we plan to take in our future work on each of these problems. ∎

Acknowledgments

We thank Susan Vrbsky for her comments and suggestions. This work was partially supported by US Navy Office of Naval Research contracts NVY N00014 87-K-0827 and NVY N00014 89-J-1181.

References

1. K.-J. Lin and S. Natarajan, "Expressing and Maintaining Timing Constraints in Flex," *Proc. Ninth IEEE Real-Time Systems Symp.*, IEEE CS Press, Los Alamitos, Calif., Order No. 894, 1988, pp. 96-105.

2. W.K. Shih, J.W.S. Liu, and J.Y. Chung, "Algorithms for Scheduling Imprecise Computations with Timing Constraints," to be published in *SIAM J. Computing*, July 1991.

3. J.Y. Chung, J.W.S. Liu, and K.-J. Lin, "Scheduling Periodic Jobs That Allow Imprecise Results," *IEEE Trans. Computers*, Vol. 19, No. 9, Sept. 1990, pp. 1,156-1,173.

4. S. Vrbsky and J.W.S. Liu, "An Object-Oriented Query Processor That Returns Monotonically Improving Answers," *Proc. Seventh IEEE Int'l Conf. Data Eng.*, IEEE CS Press, Los Alamitos, Calif., Order No. 2138, 1991.

5. K. Kenny and K.J. Lin, "Structuring Real-Time Systems with Performance Polymorphism," *Proc. 11th IEEE Real-Time Systems Symp.*, IEEE CS Press, Los Alamitos, Calif., Order No. 2112, 1990, pp. 238-246.

6. C.L. Liu and J.W. Layland, "Scheduling Algorithms for Multiprogramming in a Hard Real-Time Environment," *J. ACM*, Vol. 20, No. 1, Jan. 1973, pp. 46-61.

7. E.L. Lawler et al., "Sequencing and Scheduling: Algorithms and Complexity," tech. report, Centre for Mathematics and Computer Science, Amsterdam, 1989.

8. R. McNaughton, "Scheduling with Deadlines and Loss Functions," *Management Science*, Vol. 12, No. 1, Oct. 1959, pp. 1-12.

9. J.Y.-T. Leung and C.S. Wong, "Minimizing the Number of Late Tasks with Error Constraints," *Proc. 11th IEEE Real-Time Systems Symp.*, IEEE CS Press, Los Alamitos, Calif., Order No. 2112, 1990, pp. 32-40.

10. J.Y.-T. Leung et al., "Minimizing Mean Flow Time with Error Constraints," *Proc. 10th IEEE Real-Time Systems Symp.*, IEEE CS Press, Los Alamitos, Calif., Order No. 2004, 1989, pp. 2-11.

11. N. Karmarker, "A New Polynomial-Time Algorithm for Linear Programming," *Combinatorica*, Vol. 4, No. 4, 1984, pp. 373-395.

12. E.K.P. Chong and W. Zhao, "Task Scheduling for Imprecise Computer Systems with User Controlled Optimization," *Computing and Information*, Elsevier Science Publishers, North Holland, 1989.

Readers many write to Jane W.S. Liu, Department of Computer Science, University of Illinois at Urbana-Champaign, 1304 W. Springfield Ave., Urbana, IL 61801.

Jane W.S. Liu is a professor of computer science and of electrical and computer engineering at the University of Illinois at Urbana-Champaign. Her research interests include real-time systems, distributed systems, and computer networks.

Liu received a BS in electrical engineering from Cleveland State University. She received her masters of science and electrical engineering degrees and her doctor of science degree from MIT. She is a member of the IEEE Computer Society and the ACM, and chairs the Computer Society Technical Committee on Distributed Processing.

Kwei-Jay Lin is an assistant professor in the Department of Computer Science at the University of Illinois at Urbana-Champaign. His research interests include real-time systems, distributed systems, programming languages, and fault-tolerant systems. He was program chair for the Seventh IEEE Workshop on Real-Time Operating Systems and Software in May 1990.

Lin received his BS in electrical engineering from the National Taiwan University in 1976, and his MS and PhD in computer science from the University of Maryland in 1980 and 1985. He is a member of the IEEE Computer Society.

Wei-Kuan Shih is a PhD student in computer science at the University of Illinois at Urbana-Champaign, where his research interests include real-time systems, scheduling theory, and VLSI design automation. From 1986 to 1988, he was with the Institute of Information Science, Academia Sinica, Taiwan.

Shih received his BS and MS in computer science from the National Taiwan University.

Albert Chuang-shi Yu is a doctoral candidate in the Department of Computer Science at the University of Illinois at Urbana-Champaign. His research interests include all aspects of real-time systems, parallel processing, and artificial intelligence. He is currently supported by the NASA graduate student researcher program.

Yu received a BA in computer science and physics from the University of California, Berkeley, and an MS in computer science from the University of Illinois. He is a member of the IEEE Computer Society and Sigma Xi.

Jen-Yao Chung is a research staff member at the IBM T.J. Watson Research Center. His research interests include job scheduling and load balancing in hard real-time system, object-oriented programming environments, and operating system design.

Chung received his BS in computer science and information engineering from the National Taiwan University, and his MS and PhD in computer science from the University of Illinois at Urbana-Champaign. He is a member of the IEEE Computer Society, IEEE, ACM, Tau Beta Pi, Sigma Xi, and Phi Kappa Phi.

Wei Zhao is an associate professor in the Department of Computer Science at Texas A&M University. His research interests include distributed real-time systems, concurrency control for database systems, and resource management in operating systems and knowledge-based systems. He was a guest editor for a special issue of *Operating System Review* on real-time operating systems.

Zhao received his diploma in physics from Shaanxi Normal University, Xian, China, and his MS and PhD in computer science from the University of Massachusetts, Amherst. He is a member of the IEEE Computer Society and ACM.

Scheduling Processes with Release Times, Deadlines, Precedence, and Exclusion Relations

JIA XU AND DAVID LORGE PARNAS

Abstract—We present an algorithm that finds an optimal schedule on a single processor for a given set of processes such that each process starts executing after its release time and completes its computation before its deadline, and a given set of precedence relations and a given set of exclusion relations defined on ordered pairs of process segments are satisfied. This algorithm can be applied to the important and previously unsolved problem of automated pre-run-time scheduling of processes with arbitrary precedence and exclusion relations in hard-real-time systems.

Index Terms—Automated pre-run-time scheduler, deadlines, exclusion, hard-real-time systems, precedence, scheduling algorithms.

I. INTRODUCTION

WE present an algorithm for solving the following problem: we are given a set of processes, where each process consists of a sequence of segments. Each segment is required to precede a given set of other segments. Each segment also excludes a given set of other segments, i.e., once a segment has started its computation it cannot be preempted by any segment in the set that it excludes. For each process, we are given a release time, a computation time, and a deadline. It is also assumed that we know the computation time and start time of each segment relative to the beginning of the process containing that segment.

Our problem is to find a schedule on a single processor for the given set of processes such that each process starts executing after its release time and completes its computation before its deadline, and all the precedence and exclusion relations on segments are satisfied.

Note that if we can solve the problem stated above, then we can also solve the special case where the release times and deadlines of each process are periodic, by solving the above problem for the set of processes occurring within a time period that is equal to the least common multiple of the periods of the given set of processes.

The algorithm presented here was designed to be used by a pre-run-time scheduler for scheduling processes with arbitrary precedence and exclusion relations in hard-real-

Manuscript received April 3, 1989; revised July 1, 1989. Recommended by P. A. Ng. This work was supported in part by Natural Sciences and Engineering Research Council of Canada operating grants to D. L. Parnas and K. C. Sevcik.

J. Xu is with the Department of Computer Science, York University, 4700 Keele Street, North York, Ont. M3J 1P3, Canada.

D. L. Parnas is with the Department of Computing and Information Sciences, Queens University, Kingston, Ont. K7L 3N6, Canada.

IEEE Log Number 8933204.

time systems [3]. In such systems, precedence relations may exist between process segments when some process segments require information that is produced by other process segments. Exclusion relations may exist between process segments when some process segments must exclude interruption by other process segments to prevent errors caused by simultaneous access to shared resources, such as data, I/O devices, etc.

It has been observed that in many hard-real-time applications, the bulk of the computation can be confined to periodic processes where the sequencing and timing constraints are known in advance. That is, the release times and deadlines of processes besides the precedence and exclusion relations defined on them are known in advance. General techniques also exist for transforming a set of asynchronous processes into an equivalent set of periodic processes [16], [17]. Thus it is possible to use a pre-run-time scheduler to make scheduling decisions before run time. Pre-run-time scheduling has many advantages compared to run time scheduling: precious run time resources required for run time scheduling and context switching can be greatly reduced, and more importantly, it is easier to guarantee in advance that real-time deadlines will be met.

However, up to the present time, the automated pre-run-time scheduler for processes with arbitrary precedence and exclusion relations has remained "an unsolved problem" [3]. As will be discussed below, no algorithm previously existed for solving the problem of finding an optimal schedule for a set of processes with arbitrary release times, deadlines, precedence and exclusion relations. In the past, designers of safety-critical hard-real-time systems have had to resort to ad hoc methods and perform pre-run-time scheduling by hand. Except for very simple problems, ad hoc and manual methods are prone to errors, time consuming, and they often fail to find a feasible schedule even when one exists.

The algorithm presented here makes it possible to completely automate the task of pre-run-time scheduling processes with arbitrary precedence and exclusion relations. Currently we are working on producing a practical system that uses this algorithm to systematically search for a feasible schedule when given a set of release time, deadline, precedence, and exclusion relation parameters. Such a system would greatly facilitate the task of pre-run-time scheduling. It would virtually eliminate any possibility of errors in the computation of schedules. Not only would it

0-8186-3792-7/93 $03.00 © 1990 IEEE

be capable of finding a feasible schedule whenever one exists, it would also be capable of informing the user whenever no feasible schedule exists for a given set of parameters much faster and reliably than any ad hoc or manual method. In the latter case, it could also provide the user with useful information on which parameters should be modified in order to obtain a feasible schedule. Such a system would be particularly useful for applications in which changes in the system often occur and schedules have to be frequently recomputed.

In [16], Mok treats in detail techniques which allow one to use a pre-run-time scheduler to make scheduling decisions before run time for both periodic and synchronous processes by replacing asynchronous processes with an equivalent set of periodic processes. Extensive surveys of scheduling problems and algorithms can be found in [2], [8], and [10]. For solving the problem of finding a feasible schedule for a set of processes where each process must execute between a given release time and deadline, all previously reported algorithms either solve the special case where each process consists of a single segment that does not allow preemptions, or, solve the special case where each process consists of a single segment that can be preempted by any other process. The latter case can be solved in polynomial time, even if n processors are used [11], [13]. In the former case, the problem is NP-complete in the strong sense, even if only one processor is used [6], which effectively excludes the possibility of the existence of a polynomial time algorithm for solving the problem. For special cases where all processes have unit computation time, and no preemptions are allowed, polynomial time algorithms have been obtained [4], [5], [7], [18]. Several heuristics have also been proposed or studied for the former case [12], [9]. For solving the case where each process consists of a single segment that does not allow preemptions, and a single processor is used, an elegant implicit enumeration algorithm was presented in [14]. Another implicit enumeration algorithm of comparable efficiency is described in [1].

We do not know of any published algorithm that solves the more general problem where some portions of a process are preemptable by certain portions of other processes, while other portions of a process are not preemptable by certain portions of other processes. Such problems occur frequently in many real world situations. Since the major concern in a hard-real-time environment is meeting deadlines, none of the previously published algorithms were applicable to our problem, since assuming all processes are completely preemptable would allow simultaneous access to shared resources which could have disastrous consequences; whereas assuming all processes are completely nonpreemptable would seriously affect our ability to meet deadlines.

The problem as stated above can easily be proved to be NP-hard (even the special case where each process is composed of a single segment that excludes all other single segment processes is NP-hard). The objective of the work reported here was to find a feasible schedule whenever one exists for a given set of problem parameters. This requirement together with the fact that the problem to be solved is NP-hard, effectively excludes all other types of solutions except solutions that implicitly enumerates all possible feasible schedules.

Although it is possible to construct pathological problem instances where the algorithm would require an amount of computation time that is exponentially related to the problem size, it is extremely unlikely that such pathological problem instances would occur in practical hard-real-time system applications. Our experience has shown that even with difficult problems of very large size, the algorithm can still provide an optimal solution within reasonable time.

One can easily see that our algorithm is also applicable to a wide range of practical problems that are not directly related to the field of computer science. Although we have adopted the terminology commonly used in computer science, readers familiar with the terminology of operations research may substitute the terms "job" or "task" for "process," "machine" for "processor," "processing time" for "computation time," and "portions of a job that cannot be interrupted by portions of other jobs" for "segments that exclude other segments."

A very useful property of this algorithm is that at each intermediate stage of the algorithm a complete schedule is constructed. At the beginning, the algorithm starts with a schedule that is obtained by using an earliest-deadline-first strategy. Then it systematically improves on that initial schedule until an optimal or feasible schedule is found. Thus, even if we have to terminate the algorithm prematurely, it would still provide a complete schedule that is at least as good as any schedule obtained by using an earliest-deadline-first heuristic. Schedules obtained by using an earliest-deadline-first heuristic have the best known upperbound on lateness among all previously proposed heuristics for scheduling nonpreemptable process with arbitrary release times and deadlines [9]. The earliest-deadline-first strategy is also optimal for scheduling processes that are completely preemptable [15]. Under any circumstance, for solving the problem of scheduling processes with arbitrary release times, deadlines, and precedence and exclusion relations defined on process segments, this algorithm should outperform any previously proposed heuristic.

In the next section, we provide an overview of the algorithm. Basic notation and definitions are introduced in Section III. In Section IV we show how to improve on a valid initial solution. In Section V we describe the strategy used to search for an optimal or feasible solution. The empirical behavior of the algorithm is described in Section VI. Finally, conclusions are presented in Section VII.

II. Overview of the Algorithm

From the computation time and start time of each segment relative to the beginning of the process containing that segment, and the release time, computation time, and deadline of each process, one should be able to compute the release time, computation time, and the deadline for each segment.

Our algorithm finds a valid schedule in which the lateness of all segments in the schedule is minimized, while satisfying a given set of "*EXCLUDE*" relations and a given set of "*PRECEDE*" relations defined on ordered pairs of segments. The set of *EXCLUDE* relations and the set of *PRECEDE* relations are initialized to be identical with those exclusion and precedence relations required in our original problem.

If the minimum lateness of all schedules is greater than zero, then no feasible schedule exists that will satisfy all deadline constraints. Otherwise, the algorithm will find a feasible schedule that meets all deadline constraints.

Our algorithm uses a branch-and-bound technique. It has a search tree where at its root node we use an earliest-deadline-first strategy to compute a schedule called a "valid initial solution" that satisfies the release time constraints and all the initial *EXCLUDE* and *PRECEDE* relations.

At each node in the search tree, we find the latest segment in the valid initial solution computed at that node. We identify two "expand" sets of segments G_1 and G_2 such that the valid initial solution can be improved on if either the latest segment is scheduled before a segment in the expand set G_1; or, the latest segment preempts a segment in the expand set G_2.

For each segment in the expand sets G_1 and G_2, we create a successor node in which we add appropriate *PRECEDE* or "*PREEMPT*" relations, such that if a valid initial solution for the successor node is computed using those new additional relations, then the latest segment in the parent node would be scheduled before a segment in G_1, or preempt a segment in G_2 whenever possible.

For each node in the search tree, we also compute a lower bound on the lateness of any schedule leading from that node. The node that has the least lower bound among all unexpanded nodes is considered to be the node that is most likely to lead to an optimal solution—we always branch from the node that has the least lower bound among all unexpanded nodes. In case of ties, we choose the node with least lateness among the nodes with least lower bound.

We continue to create new nodes in the search tree until we either find a feasible solution, or, until there exists no unexpanded node that has a lower bound less than the least lateness of all valid initial solutions found so far. In the latter case, the valid initial solution that has the least lateness is an optimal solution.

The ways in which we use *PRECEDE* and *PREEMPT* relations to either schedule the latest segment before a segment in the expand set G_1 or let the latest segment preempt a segment in the expand set G_2 cover *all* possible ways of improving on a valid initial solution. This guarantees that in the latter case, the solution is globally optimal rather than locally optimal.

In the following section, we shall formally define all the terms mentioned above.

III. Notation and Definitions

In order to solve the problem stated above, we first introduce the following definitions and notations.

Let the *set of processes* be denoted by P.

Each process $p \in P$ consists of a finite sequence of *segments* $p[0], p[1], \cdots, p[n[p]]$, where $p[0]$ is the first segment and $p[n[p]]$ is the last segment in process p.

For each segment i, we define:
- a release time $r[i]$;
- a deadline $d[i]$;
- a computation time $c[i]$;

It is assumed that $r[i]$, $d[i]$, and $c[i]$ have integer values.

Let the *set of all segments* belonging to processes in P be denoted by $S(P)$. Each segment i consists of a sequence of *segment units* $(i, 0), (i, 1), \cdots, (i, c[i] - 1)$, where $(i, 0)$ is the first segment unit and $(i, c[i] - 1)$ is the last segment unit in segment i.

We define the *set of segment units of* $S(P)$:

$$U = \left\{ (i, k) \mid i \in S(P) \wedge 0 \le k \le c[i] - 1 \right\}.$$

Intuitively, a segment unit is the smallest indivisible granule of a process. Each segment unit requires unit time to execute, during which it cannot be preempted by any other process. The total number of segment units in each segment is equal to the computation time required by that segment.

A *schedule* of a set of processes P is a total function π: $U \to [0, \infty)$ satisfying the following properties:

1) $\forall t \in [0, \infty): \left| \left\{ (i, k) \in U \mid \pi(i, k) = t \right\} \right| \le 1$.

2) $\forall (i, k_1), (i, k_2) \in U: (k_1 < k_2) \Rightarrow (\pi(i, k_1)$
$< \pi(i, k_2))$.

3) $\forall p, i, j, p \in P, 0 \le i, j \le n[p]$:
$$(i < j) \Rightarrow \left(\pi\left(p[i], c[p[i]] - 1\right) < \pi\left(p[j], 0\right)\right)$$

Above, condition 1) states that no more than one segment can be executing at any time. Condition 2) states that a schedule must preserve the ordering of the segment units in each segment. Condition 3) states that a schedule must preserve the ordering of the segments in each process.

We say *segment i executes at time t* iff $\exists k, 0 \le k \le c[i] - 1: \pi(i, k) = t$.

We say *segment i executes from t_1 to t_2* iff $\exists k, \forall t, 0 \le k \le c[i] - 1, 0 \le t \le t_2 - t_1 - 1: \pi(i, k + t) = t_1 + t$.

We define the *start time* of segment i to be $s[i] = \pi(i, 0)$;

We define the *completion time* of segment i to be $e[i] = \pi(i, c[i] - 1) + 1$.

The *lateness of a segment i* in a schedule of P is defined by $e[i] - d[i]$.

The *lateness of a schedule of P* is defined by $\max \{ e[i] - d[i] \mid i \in S(P) \}$.

We define a *latest segment* to be a segment that realizes the value of the lateness of the schedule.

We introduce the *PRECEDE* relation and *EXCLUDE* relation on ordered pairs of segments together with the notion of a "valid schedule."

A *valid schedule* of a set of processes P is a schedule of P satisfying the following properties.

$\forall i, j \in S(P)$:

1) $s[i] \geq r[i]$

2) $(i\ PRECEDES\ j) \Rightarrow (e[i] \leq s[j])$

3) $(i\ EXCLUDES\ j \land s[i] < s[j])$
   $\Rightarrow (e[i] \leq s[j])$

Above, condition 1) states that each process can only start execution after its release time. Condition 2) states that in a valid schedule, if segment i *PRECEDES* segment j, then under all circumstances, segment j cannot start execution before segment i has completed its computation. Condition 3) states that in a valid schedule, if segment i *EXCLUDES* segment j, then segment j is not allowed to preempt segment i. That is, if segment i started execution before segment j, then segment j can only start execution after segment i has completed its computation.

We initialize the set of *PRECEDE* relations and the set of *EXCLUDE* relations to be identical with the precedence and exclusion relations that must be satisfied in the original problem. In addition, in order to enforce the proper ordering of segments within each process, we let $p[k]$ *PRECEDE* $p[k+1]$ for all $p \in P$, and for all k, $0 \leq k \leq n[p] - 2$. Thus, a valid schedule would satisfy all the release time, exclusion, and precedence constraints in the original problem.

A *feasible schedule* of a set of processes P is a valid schedule of P such that its lateness is less than or equal to zero.

An *optimal schedule* of a set of processes P is a valid schedule of P with minimal lateness.

The *adjusted release time* $r'[i]$ of segment i is defined by

1) $r'[i] = r[i]$, if $\nexists j: j\ PRECEDES\ i$;

else

2) $r'[i] = \max \{r[i], r'[j] + c[j] \mid j\ PRECEDES\ i\}$

At any time t, $t \in [0, \infty]$, we say segment "j is *ELIGIBLE at* t" iff:

1) $t \geq r'[j] \land \neg (e[j] \leq t)$

2) $\nexists i: i\ PRECEDES\ j \land \neg (e[i] \leq t)$

3) $\nexists i: i\ EXCLUDES\ j \land s[i] < t \land \neg (e[i] \leq t)$

The above definition guarantees that at any time t, if segment j is *ELIGIBLE at* t, then j can be put into execution at t, while satisfying all the properties of a valid schedule.

We also introduce a third relation that will be used in our algorithm—the *PREEMPT* relation on pairs of segments together with the notion of a "valid initial solution."

A *valid initial solution* for a set of processes P is a valid schedule of P satisfying the following properties:

$\forall t \in [0, \infty)$:

'1) $\forall j: \big(\exists i: ((i\ PREEMPTS\ j \land i\ is\ ELIGIBLE\ at\ t)$

$\lor (d[i] < d[j] \land \neg (j\ PREEMPTS\ i)$

$\land i\ is\ ELIGIBLE\ at\ t)$

$\lor (d[i] = d[j] \land c[i] > c[j]$

$\land \neg (j\ PREEMPTS\ i) \land i\ is\ ELIGIBLE\ at\ t))$

$\Rightarrow \neg (j\ executes\ at\ t) \big)$

2) $\exists i: i\ is\ ELIGIBLE\ at\ t$
   $\Rightarrow \exists i: i\ executes\ at\ t$

Above, condition 1) states that in a valid initial solution, if at least one segment i *PREEMPTS* segment j and i is *ELIGIBLE* at time t; or if at least one segment i has a shorter deadline than j and i is *ELIGIBLE* at time t and j does NOT *PREEMPT* i; or if at least one segment i has the same deadline but a longer computation time than j and i is *ELIGIBLE* at time t and j does NOT *PREEMPT* i, then segment j cannot execute at time t. Condition 2) states that in a valid initial solution, at any time t, if at least one segment is *ELIGIBLE*, then one segment should execute at time t. Condition 2) effectively guarantees that all segments will eventually be completed in a valid initial solution, provided that all relations on segments are "consistent" as defined below.

We define each pair of relations on segments indicated by an "x" in the following table to be *inconsistent*. All other pairs of relations on segments are *consistent*.

	i PC j	j PC i	i EX j	j EX i	i PM j	j PM i
i PC j:		x				x
i EX j:						x
i PM j:		x			x	x

i PC j : i *PRECEDES* j
i EX j : i *EXCLUDES* j
i PM j : i *PREEMPTS* j
x : inconsistent

In addition to satisfying release time, exclusion and precedence constraints, a valid initial solution also satisfies execution priority constraints defined by the set of *PREEMPT* relations and deadlines.

Initially, we set the set of *PREEMPT* relations to be empty. New *PREEMPT* relations as well as new *PRECEDE* relations will be defined and used by the algorithm to reschedule the latest segment earlier in order to improve on existing valid initial solutions.

The following (simplified) procedure uses an earliest-deadline-first strategy to compute a valid initial solution in which release time constraints and a given set of *EX-CLUDE*, *PRECEDE*, and *PREEMPT* relations are enforced:

$t \leftarrow 0$
while $\neg (\forall i : e[i] \leq t)$ **do**
   begin
     if $(\exists i : t = r'[i] \vee t = e[i])$ **then**
       begin
          Among the set
          $\{ j \mid j$ *is ELIGIBLE at t*
              $\wedge (\nexists i : i$ *is ELIGIBLE at t* $\wedge i$ *PREEMPTS*
                $j)$
          $\}$
          select the segment j that has min $d[j]$.
          in case of ties, select the segment j that has
             max $c[j]$.
          put j into execution.
       end
     $t \leftarrow t + 1$
   end

A more detailed implementation of the procedure for computing a valid initial solution can be found in Appendix 1.

See Examples 1–5 in Appendix 3 for examples of schedules corresponding to valid initial solutions.

IV. How to Improve on a Valid Initial Solution

Let j be the latest segment in a valid initial solution. (If there exists more than one segment that have maximum lateness, then let j be the segment that completed last among those segments.)

Any nonoptimal schedule may be improved on only if j can be rescheduled earlier.

We define the set of segments $Z[i]$ recursively as follows:

1) $i \in Z[i]$;

2) $\forall k$:

   if $\exists l, l \in Z[i]$:

     $\big(e[k] = s[l] \wedge (\exists l', l' \in Z[i] : r'[l']$

     $< e[k])$

     $\vee (s[l] < e[k] < e[i])$

   then $k \in Z[i]$

The properties of a valid initial solution imply that in any schedule that corresponds to a valid initial solution:

• $Z[i]$ is the set of segments that precede (and include) i in a period of continuous utilization of the processor;

• $e[i]$ is the earliest possible completion time for the entire set of segments $Z[i]$.

• any nonoptimal schedule may be improved on only by scheduling some segment $k \in Z[j]$ such that $d[j] < d[k]$ later than the latest segment j.

As an example, in the valid initial solution of the root node of the search tree of Example 5: $D \in Z[D]$ from 1);

$A \in Z[D]$ because $e[A] = s[D] \wedge r'[D] < e[A]$; $B, C \in Z[D]$ because $s[A] < e[B], e[C] < e[D]$. Thus $Z[D] = \{A, B, C, D\}$. $e[D]$ is the earliest possible completion time for the entire set of segments $Z[D]$—if any other order for the segments in $Z[D]$ is chosen, the last segment in that new order cannot complete before $e[D]$.

We define two *expand sets* G_1 and G_2 as follows:

$$G_1 = \big\{ i \mid i \in Z[j] \wedge d[j] < d[i]$$
$$\wedge\ i\ EXCLUDES\ j$$
$$\wedge\ \neg\ (i\ PRECEDES\ j)$$
$$\wedge\ \neg\ (i\ PREEMPTS\ j) \big\}$$
$$G_2 = \big\{ i \mid i \in Z[j] \wedge d[j] < d[i]$$
$$\wedge\ \neg\ (i\ EXCLUDES\ j)$$
$$\wedge\ \neg\ (i\ PRECEDES\ j)$$
$$\wedge\ \neg\ (i\ PREEMPTS\ j)$$
$$\wedge\ \nexists l : (\exists k, t : 0 \leq k \leq c[l] - 1, 0$$
$$\leq t < \infty : s[i] \leq \pi(l, k) \leq e[j])$$
$$\%\ \text{an execution of } l \text{ occurs between}$$
$$i \text{ and } j \%$$
$$\wedge\ (i\ PRECEDES\ l\ \vee\ i\ PREEMPTS\ l) \big\}$$

G_1 is the set of segments that, if scheduled after j, may reduce the maximum lateness.

G_2 is the set of segments that, if preempted by j, may reduce the maximum lateness.

As examples, the valid initial solution of the root node of the search tree in Example 1 can be improved on by scheduling $A \in G_1$ after the latest segment C. The valid initial solution of the root node of the search tree in Example 4 can be improved on if the latest segment E preempts $A \in G_2$. In Example 4 $B \notin G_2$ because there exists D such that $B\ PRECEDES\ D$ and an execution of D occurs between B and E.

By making use of the fact that $e[i]$ is the earliest possible completion time of the entire set of segments $Z[i]$, we can compute a lower bound on the lateness of any valid initial solution satisfying a given set of *EXCLUDE*, *PRECEDE*, and *PREEMPT* relations with the following formula:

let $K[i] = \big\{ k \mid k \in Z[i] \wedge k \neq i \wedge d[i]$
$$< d[k] \wedge \neg (k\ PRECEDES\ i)$$
$$\wedge\ \neg (k\ PREEMPTS\ i) \big\}$$
if $K[i] = \varnothing$
then $LB[i] = e[i] - d[i]$
else $LB[i] = e[i] + \min \{ GAP[k, i]$
$$-\ d[k] \mid k \in K[i] \}\ \text{where}$$
if $\neg (k\ EXCLUDES\ i)$ then $GAP[k, i] = 0$

144

else $GAP[k, i] = \max \left\{ 0, -s[k] + \min \left\{ r'[l] \mid \right. \right.$

$$l \in Z[i] \wedge k \neq l$$

$$\wedge \, s[k] < s[l] \leq s[i]$$

$$\left. \left. \wedge \, \neg \, (k \text{ } PRECEDE \text{ } l) \right\} \right\}$$

$$LB_1[i] = \min \left\{ LB[i], e[i] - d[i] \right\}$$

$$LB_2[i] = r'[i] + c[i] - d[i]$$

$$\text{lowerbound} = \max \left\{ LB_1[i], LB_2[i] \mid i \in S(P) \right\}$$

The lower bound function can be derived by observing the following: if the set $K[i]$ is empty then the lateness of i, i.e., $e[i] - d[i]$ cannot be improved on. This is because if any other segment $k \in Z[i]$ where $d[k] \leq d[i]$ is scheduled last, then k would be at least as late as the lateness of i. If k EXCLUDEs i and $s[k] < \min \left\{ r'[l] \mid s[k] < s[l] \leq s[i] \right\}$, then from the properties of a valid initial solution, scheduling k after i would leave a gap in the new schedule that starts at $s[k]$ and ends at $\min \left\{ r'[l] \mid s[k] < s[l] \leq s[i] \right\}$. (Note that l could be equal to i), and the lateness of the new schedule would be at least $e[i] - d[k]$ plus the gap size. $LB_2[i]$ is a trivial lowerbound on the lateness of any segment i.

V. Searching for an Optimal or Feasible Solution

We now define a search tree that has as its root node the valid initial solution that satisfies all the EXCLUDE and PRECEDE relations in the original problem specification.

At each node in the search tree we compute the lower bound and two expand sets G_1 and G_2. Let segment j be the latest segment in the valid initial solution computed at that node.

For each segment $k \in G_1$, we create a successor node that corresponds to a new problem, in which we assign a new relation j PRECEDES k. If we apply the procedure above and compute a new valid initial solution in which the new relations are enforced, then segment k will be scheduled later than segment j in the new schedule.

For each segment $k \in G_2$, we create a successor node that corresponds to a new problem, in which for all segments l such that k EXCLUDES l and an execution of l occurs between k and j, we assign the relation l PRECEDES k, and for all segments q such that k does NOT EXCLUDE q and an execution of q occurs between k and j, we assign the relation q PREEMPTS k and the relation j PREEMPTS k. We let each successor node inherit all relations assigned to any of its predecessor nodes. If we apply the procedure above and compute a new valid initial solution in which the new relations are enforced, then segment k will be preempted by segment j in the new schedule if possible. After generating the valid initial solution for each new successor node, we test it for optimality. If the optimal solution is not discovered among any of the resulting problems, then we proceed to create new successor nodes in a similar manner. We use a strategy of branching from the node with the least lower bound. In case of ties, we choose the node with least lateness among the nodes with least lower bound.

The steps of the algorithm are as follows:
(For a more detailed implementation of the algorithm see Appendix 2.)

Step 0: Compute an initial valid solution and the corresponding lowerbound. Find the latest segment j and its lateness. If its lateness equals its lowerbound then stop—the schedule is optimal. Otherwise, call the node corresponding to the schedule of the parent node.

Step 1: Find the expand sets G_1 and G_2 and create $|G_1| + |G_2|$ new child nodes. For each node corresponding to a segment k in G_1, assign a new relation j PRECEDES k. For each node corresponding to a segment k in G_2, for all segments l such that k EXCLUDES l and an execution of l occurs between k and j, assign a new relation l PRECEDES k, and, for all segments q such that k does NOT EXCLUDE q and an execution of q occurs between k and j, assign the relation q PREEMPTS k and the new relation j PREEMPTS k.

Let each child node inherit all relations assigned to any of its predecessor nodes.

Recompute a valid initial solution, lowerbound and find the latest segment and its lateness for each child node.

Step 2: If Steps 3 and 4 have been performed for all child nodes then close the parent node and go to Step 5.

Otherwise, select the child node with the least lateness.

Step 3: Set minlateness $\leftarrow$ min {minlateness, lateness (childnode)}.

If minlateness is less than or equal to the least lowerbound of all open nodes then **stop**—the solution is optimal.

Step 4: If lateness (childnode) = lowerbound (childnode) then close this child node and return to step 2—this solution is locally optimal.

If minlateness is less than lowerbound (childnode) then close this childnode—this node will never lead to a solution that is better than the current minlateness.

Return to step 2.

Step 5: Select among all open nodes the node with the least lower bound, in case of ties, select the node with least lateness. Call this node the parent node and goto step 1. $\square$

(See Examples 1–5 in Appendix 3.)

If a feasible schedule is considered sufficient, to achieve more efficiency, instead of terminating the algorithm only when a minimum lateness schedule has been found, one may terminate the algorithm as soon as a feasible schedule in which all deadlines are met is found. One could also adopt a strategy of terminating the search whenever a schedule has been found such that its lateness is within a prespecified ratio of optimal. An upperbound on that ratio can be computed with the formule (lateness $- L$)$/L$ where L is the least lower bound of all nodes belonging to the open node set.

VI. Empirical Behavior of the Algorithm

We have written a program in Pascal that implements the algorithm described above.

Observation of the empirical behavior of the algorithm indicated that this algorithm consistently generated significantly fewer nodes than one of the best algorithms reported so far that solves the special case where each process consists of only one segment that excludes all other segments [14].

We restricted ourselves to comparing the number of nodes generated for an identical problem sample, because this is the major factor that determines the size of the problem that can be effectively computed—it is basically this number that will grow exponentially when the problem size increases.

By comparing the two algorithms on sample problems corresponding to the special case where each process consists of only one segment that excludes all other segments, we found that for problem sizes of 25 (number of segments), our algorithm frequently generated 25% fewer nodes than the algorithm reported in [14]. When the problem size doubled to 50, our algorithm frequently generated 44% (approximately $1 - (1 - 0.25)^2$) fewer nodes. When we doubled the problem size again, the difference became even greater—their algorithm was unable to terminate after generating several tens of thousands of nodes, while our algorithm terminated on the same problem sample after generating only a few thousand nodes. It was also observed that for all problem samples of the general case (arbitrary exclusion relations defined on segments) that we constructed, solving them with our algorithm always generated fewer nodes before an optimal schedule was found than if all segments excluded each other (which corresponds to the special case).

Thus the performance of our algorithm on the general case in terms of the number of nodes generated should be much better than the performance reported in [14] when solving the special case.

VII. Conclusions

The major contribution of our algorithm is that it solves a very general and important problem that no other reported algorithm is capable of solving. It is the first algorithm that is able to systematically search for an optimal or feasible schedule that satisfies a given set of release time, deadline, precedence, and exclusion constraints defined on process segments. The algorithm can be applied to the important and previously unsolved problem of automated pre-run-time scheduling of processes with arbitrary precedence and exclusion relations in hard-real-time systems.

With our algorithm it is possible to take into account the cost of context switching. All we need to do is add to the computation time of each segment the following: 1) the time required to save the status of a preempted segment, 2) the time required to load a new segment, and 3) the time required to restart a preempted segment. This is because the only possible time where a process switch may take place is either at the adjusted release time or at the completion time of a segment. Furthermore, each segment can only preempt any other segment once. Hence we can always "charge" the cost of a context switch to the preempting segment so that all deadlines will be met. (See [15] for a similar argument for the earliest-deadline-first strategy.)

When implementing this algorithm, it may be advantageous to make space-time tradeoffs to match available resources. If our major constraint is space instead of time, we might consider only storing at each node partial information that is different from the information stored at its ancestor nodes, then whenever we need complete information to proceed at a certain node, we use the information stored at its ancestor nodes to reconstruct the complete information required at that node. For example, we only stored new *PRECEDE* and *PREEMPT* relations at each node when implementing our algorithm, which resulted in a significant saving of space without seriously affecting computation time.

One may also include an initial problem parameter verification stage that performs a preliminary analysis of all the initial problem parameters and modifies or rejects if necessary any problem parameters that are either redundant or inconsistent with other parameters prior to using this algorithm.

We note that this algorithm can be easily generalized to the case where exclusion regions within each process overlap or are embedded within each other.

For future work, we will explore ways of generalizing this algorithm to solve the problem of scheduling processes with release times, deadlines, precedence and exclusion relations on n processors. Another interesting direction for future work would be to explore ways of generalizing this algorithm to solve the problem with additional resource constraints [19].

Appendix 1
An Implementation of the Procedure for Computing a Valid Initial Solution

The following procedure computes a valid initial solution in which the release time constraints and a set of *EXCLUDE*, *PRECEDE*, and *PREEMPT* relations are satisfied:

```
lastt := ⟨ any negative value ⟩;
lastseg := ⟨ any segment index ⟩;
idle := true;
for each segment i do
    begin
        started[i] := false;
        completed[i] := false;
        comptimeleft[i] := c[i];
        s[i] := -1;
    end;
t := 0;
while not(for all segments i: completed[i] = true) do
begin
    t := min { t | t > lastt and ((exists i: t = r'[i]) or
            ((idle = false) and (comptimeleft[lastseg] = t - lastt)))
        };
    if idle = false then
```

```
begin
    % in the valid initial solution computed by the procedure: %
    let segment lastseg execute from lastt to t;
    comptimeleft[ lastseg ] := comptimeleft[ lastseg ] − (t −
    lastt );
    if comptimeleft[ lastseg ] = 0 then
        begin
            completed[ lastseg ] := true;
            e[ lastseg ] := t;
        end;
end;
S ← { j | j is ELIGIBLE and no other segment i exists
        such that i is also ELIGIBLE and i
        PREEMPTS j
    }
if S is empty then idle := true
    else
        begin
            idle := false;
            S1 ← { j | d[ j ] = min { d[ i ] | i in S } }
            select segment x such that c[ x ] = max { c[ i ] | i in S1
            };
            if not started[ x ] then
                begin
                    started[ x ] := true;
                    s[ x ] := t;
                end;
            lastseg := x;
        end;
    lastt := t;
end;
```

Above, "lastt" is the last time that the procedure tried
to select a segment for execution. "lastseg" is the segment that was last selected for execution. "idle" indicates whether there was any segment selected at lastt.
"started[i]" indicates whether segment i had started execution. "completed[i]" indicates whether segment i had
completed execution. "comptimeleft[i]" is the remaining computation time of segment i.

APPENDIX 2
AN IMPLEMENTATION OF THE MAIN ALGORITHM

```
begin { main }
    nodeindex := 0
    initialize ( PC ( nodeindex ), EX )
    PM ( nodeindex ) ← ∅
    optimal := false;
    feasible := false;
    opennodeset ← ∅
    if consistent ( PC ( nodeindex ), EX, PM ( nodeindex )) then
    begin
        schedule ( nodeindex ) ← validinitialsolution ( PC ( nodeindex ),
        EX, PM ( nodeindex ))
        leastlowerbound := lowerbound ( nodeindex )
        if lateness ( nodeindex ) = least lowerbound then
            optimal := true;
        if lateness ( nodeindex ) ≤ 0 then
            feasible := true;
        if not (optimal or feasible) then
        begin
            opennodeset ← { nodeindex }
            minlateness := lateness ( nodeindex );
            minlatenode := nodeindex;
            while not ( optimal or feasible or spacetimelimitsexceeded )
                do
            begin
                lowestboundset ← { l | lowerbound ( l ) = leastlower-
                    bound }
                select parentnode such that:
                    lateness ( parentnode ) = min { lateness ( i ) | i ∈ low-
                        estboundset }
                j := latestsegment ( schedule ( parentnode ))
                firstchildnode := nodeindex + 1
```

```
                for each segment k ∈ G₁ ( parentnode )
                begin
                    nodeindex := nodeindex + 1
                    PC ( nodeindex ) ← PC ( parentnode ) ∪ {(j,k)}
                end
                for each k ∈ G₂ ( parentnode )
                begin
                    nodeindex := nodeindex + 1
                    PC ( nodeindex ) ← PC ( parentnode )
                    for all l such that:
                        k EX l and an execution of l
                        occurs between k and j in sched-
                        ule ( parentnode ):
                        begin
                            PC ( nodeindex ) ← PC ( nodeindex ) ∪
                            {(l,k)}
                        end
                    PM ( nodeindex ) ← PM ( parentnode ) ∪ {(j,k)
                    for all q such that:
                        not ( k EX q ) and an execution of q
                        occurs between k and j in sched-
                        ule ( parentnode ):
                        begin
                            PM ( nodeindex ) ← PM ( nodeindex ) ∪
                            {(q,k)
                        end
                end
                opennodeset ← opennodeset - { parentnode }
                if not ( optimal or feasible ) then
                for childnode := firstchildnode to nodeindex do
                begin
                    if consistent ( PC ( childnode ), EX, PM ( childnode ))
                        then
                    begin
                        schedule ( childnode ) ←
                            validinitialsolution ( PC ( childnode ),     EX,
                            PM ( childnode ))
                        if lateness ( childnode ) < minlateness then
                        begin
                            minlateness := lateness ( childnode );
                            minlatenode := childnode;
                        end;
                        if lateness ( childnode ) ≤ 0 then
                            feasible := true
                        else
                            if minlateness > lowerbound ( childnode ) then
                                opennodeset ← opennodeset ∪ { child-
                                    node }
                    end;
                end;
                leastlowerbound ← min { lowerbound ( i ) | i ∈ openno-
                    deset }
                if opennodeset = ∅ or ( minlateness ≤ leastlowerbound )
                    then
                        optimal := true;
            end;
            minlateschedule := schedule ( minlatenode )
        end;
    end;
end.
```
(end of algorithm)

In the algorithm above, a node in the "opennodeset"
is a node that does not have successors, but may be selected as the node to be branched from next.
"PC(nodeindex)" and "PM(nodeindex)" are respectively the set of *PRECEDE* relations and the set of
PREEMPT relations associated with the node identified
by "nodeindex." "EX" is the (constant) set of *EX-
CLUDE* relations. "schedule(nodeindex)" is the valid
initial solution computed using PC(nodeindex), EX and
PM(nodeindex). "lateness(nodeindex)" is the lateness
of schedule(nodeindex). "lowerbound(nodeindex),
G_1(nodeindex), and G_2(nodeindex)" are, respectively,

the lowerbound and the two expand sets computed from schedule (nodeindex).

To achieve more efficiency, instead of terminating the algorithm only when a minimum lateness schedule has been found, the algorithm terminates as soon as a feasible schedule in which all deadlines are met is found; or, when a predefined space/time limit is exceeded.

APPENDIX 3

EXAMPLES 1–5

Example 1.

$r[A] = 40$	$r[B] = 60$	$r[C] = 50$	$r[D] = 0$	**A EXCLUDES B** **C EXCLUDES A**
$c[A] = 20$	$c[B] = 20$	$c[C] = 20$	$c[D] = 20$	**B EXCLUDES A** **B EXCLUDES C**
$d[A] = 110$	$d[B] = 90$	$d[C] = 91$	$d[D] = 120$	**A EXCLUDES C** **C EXCLUDES B**

Root node of search tree:

latest segment: C
lateness = $e[C] - d[C] = 100 - 91 = 9$
$Z[C] = \{A, B, C\}$
lowerbound = $LB[C] = e[C] + (r[C] - s[A] - d[A]) = 100 + (50 - 40 - 110) = 0$

$G1 = \{A\}$ $G2 = \emptyset$

C PRECEDES A

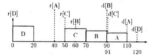

latest segment: A, B
lateness = $e[A] - d[A] = e[B] - d[B] = 0$
$Z[A] = \{C, B, A\}$
$Z[B] = \{C, B\}$
lowerbound = $LB[A] = e[A] - d[A]$
$= LB[B] = e[B] - d[B] = 0$
(globally optimal since lateness equal to least lower bound of all open nodes)

Example 2.

$r[A] = 0$	$r[B] = 10$	$r[C] = 60$	**A EXCLUDES B**
$c[A] = 50$	$c[B] = 20$	$c[C] = 30$	**B EXCLUDES C**
$d[A] = 110$	$d[B] = 101$	$d[C] = 90$	

Root node of search tree:

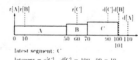

latest segment: C
lateness = $e[C] - d[C] = 100 - 90 = 10$
$Z[C] = \{A, B, C\}$
lowerbound = $LB2[C] = r[C] + c[C] - d[C] = 60 + 30 - 90 = 0$

$G1 = \{B\}$ $G2 = \{A\}$

C PRECEDES B **C PREEMPTS A**
B PRECEDES A

latest segment: B
lateness = $e[B] - d[B] = 110 - 101 = 9$
$Z[B] = \{C, B\}$
lowerbound = $LB[B] = e[B] - d[B] = 110 - 101 = 9$
(locally optimal since lateness equal to lower bound - close this node)

latest segment: A, C
lateness = $e[A] - d[A] = e[C] - d[C] = 0$
$Z[A] = \{A, B, C\}$
$Z[C] = \{C\}$
lowerbound = $LB[A] = e[A] - d[A]$
$= LB[C] = e[C] - d[C] = 0$
(globally optimal since lateness equal to least lower bound of all open nodes)

Example 3.

$r[A] = 0$	$r[B] = 20$	$r[C] = 40$	**B EXCLUDES C**
$c[A] = 30$	$c[B] = 20$	$c[C] = 30$	
$d[A] = 80$	$d[B] = 81$	$d[C] = 70$	

Root node of search tree:

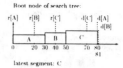

latest segment: C
lateness = $e[C] - d[C] = 80 - 70 = 10$
$Z[C] = \{A, B, C\}$
lowerbound = $LB2[C] = r[C] + c[C] - d[C] = 40 + 30 - 70 = 0$

$G1 = \{B\}$ $G2 = \{A\}$

C PRECEDES B **C PREEMPTS A**
B PREEMPTS A

latest segment: B
lateness = $e[B] - d[B] = 90 - 81 = 9$
$Z[B] = \{C, B\}$
lowerbound = $LB[B] = e[B] - d[B] = 90 - 81 = 9$
(locally optimal since lateness equal to lower bound - close this node)

latest segment: A, C
lateness = $e[A] - d[A] = e[C] - d[C] = 0$
$Z[A] = \{A, B, C\}$
$Z[C] = \{C\}$
lowerbound = $LB[A] = e[A] - d[A]$
$= LB[C] = e[C] - d[C] = 0$
(globally optimal since lateness equal to least lower bound of all open nodes)

Example 4.

$r[A] = 0$	$r[B] = 1$	$r[C] = 60$	$r[D] = 40$	$r[E] = 90$	**A EXCLUDES D** **C EXCLUDES E**
$c[A] = 30$	$c[B] = 40$	$c[C] = 30$	$c[D] = 10$	$c[E] = 50$	**A EXCLUDES B** **C EXCLUDES D**
$d[A] = 161$	$d[B] = 51$	$d[C] = 90$	$d[D] = 91$	$d[E] = 140$	**B EXCLUDES C** **D EXCLUDES E**
					B PRECEDES D

Root node of search tree:

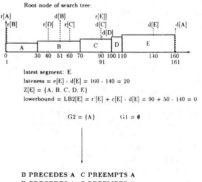

latest segment: E
lateness = $e[E] - d[E] = 160 - 140 = 20$
$Z[E] = \{A, B, C, D, E\}$
lowerbound = $LB2[E] = r[E] + c[E] - d[E] = 90 + 50 - 140 = 0$

$G2 = \{A\}$ $G1 = \emptyset$

B PRECEDES A **C PREEMPTS A**
D PRECEDES A **E PREEMPTS A**

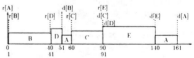

latest segment: A, C, E
lateness = $e[A] - d[A] = e[C] - d[C] = e[E] - d[E] = 0$
$Z[A] = \{B, D, C, E, A\}$
$Z[C] = \{C\}$
$Z[E] = \{E\}$
lowerbound = $LB[A] = e[A] - d[A] = LB[C] = e[C] - d[C]$
$= LB[E] = e[E] - d[E] = 0$
(globally optimal since lateness equal to least lower bound of all open nodes)

148

Example 5.

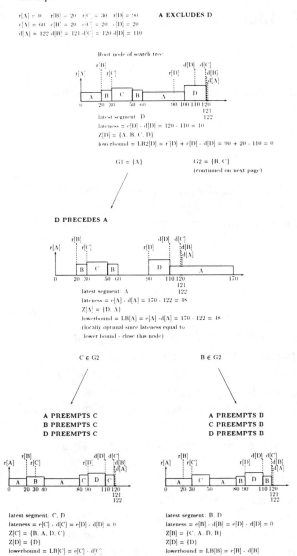

r[A] = 0   r[B] = 20   r[C] = 30   r[D] = 90   **A EXCLUDES D**
c[A] = 60 c[B] = 20   c[C] = 20   c[D] = 20
d[A] = 122 d[B] = 121 d[C] = 120 d[D] = 110

Root node of search tree

latest segment: D
lateness = $c[D] - d[D] = 120 - 110 = 10$
$Z[D] = \{A, B, C, D\}$
lowerbound = $LB2[D] = r[D] + c[D] - d[D] = 90 + 20 - 110 = 0$

G1 = {A}   G2 = {B, C}
(continued on next page)

D PRECEDES A

latest segment: A
lateness = $c[A] - d[A] = 170 - 122 = 48$
$Z[A] = \{D, A\}$
lowerbound = $LB[A] = c[A] - d[A] = 170 - 122 = 48$
(locally optimal since lateness equal to
lower bound - close this node)

C ∈ G2   B ∈ G2

A PREEMPTS C   A PREEMPTS B
B PREEMPTS C   C PREEMPTS B
D PREEMPTS C   D PREEMPTS B

latest segment: C, D   latest segment: B, D
lateness = $c[C] - d[C] = c[D] - d[D] = 0$ lateness = $c[B] - d[B] = c[D] - d[D] = 0$
$Z[C] = \{B, A, D, C\}$ $Z[B] = \{C, A, D, B\}$
$Z[D] = \{D\}$ $Z[D] = \{D\}$
lowerbound = $LB[C] = c[C] - d[C]$ lowerbound = $LB[B] = c[B] - d[B]$
       $= LB[D] = c[D] - d[D] = 0$ $= LB[D] = c[D] - d[D] = 0$
(locally optimal since lateness equal to   (globally optimal since lateness equal to
lower bound - close this node)   least lower bound of all open nodes
                                      Note that the schedule resulting from
                                      C ∈ G2 is also globally optimal)

ACKNOWLEDGMENT

We are grateful to E. Margulis and K. C. Sevcik for helpful comments on earlier drafts. Helpful comments and suggestions from the anonymous referees are gratefully acknowledged.

REFERENCES

[1] J. Carlier. "Probleme a une machine." Institute de Programmation, Univ. Paris VI, manuscript, 1980.
[2] E. G. Coffman, Jr., *Computer and Jobshop Scheduling Theory*. New York: Wiley-Interscience, 1976.
[3] S. R. Faulk and D. L. Parnas. "On synchronization in hard-real-time systems," *Commun. ACM*, vol. 31, Mar. 1988.
[4] M. R. Garey and D. S. Johnson. "Scheduling tasks with non-uniform deadlines on two-processors," *J. ACM*, vol. 23, July 1976.
[5] —. "Two-processor scheduling with start-times and deadlines," *SIAM J. Comput.*, vol. 6, Sept. 1977.
[6] —. *Computers and Intractability: A Guide to the Theory of NP-Completeness*. San Francisco, CA: Freeman, 1979.
[7] M. R. Garey, D. S. Johnson, B. B. Simons, and R. E. Tarjan.
"Scheduling unit-time tasks with arbitrary release times and deadlines," *SIAM J. Comput.*, vol. 10, May 1981.
[8] M. J. Gonzalez, Jr., "Deterministic processor scheduling," *Comput. Surveys*, vol. 9, Sept. 1977.
[9] D. Gunsfield. "Bounds for naive multiple machine scheduling with release times and deadlines," *J. Algorithms*, vol. 5, 1984.
[10] E. L. Lawler, J. K. Lenstra, and A. H. G. Rinnooy Kan. "Recent developments in deterministic sequencing and scheduling: A survey," in *Proc. NATO Advanced Study and Research Institute on Theoretical Approaches to Scheduling Problems*, Durham, England, July 1981; also in *Deterministic and Stochastic Scheduling*, M. A. H. Dempster *et al.*, Eds. Dordrecht, The Netherlands: D. Reidel.
[11] C. L. Lui and J. W. Layland. "Scheduling algorithms for multiprogramming in a hard-real-time environment," *J. ACM*, vol. 20, Jan. 1973.
[12] G. K. Manacher. "Production and stabilization of real-time task schedules," *J. ACM*, vol. 14, July 1967.
[13] C. Martel. "Preemptive scheduling with release times, deadlines, and due dates," *J. ACM*, vol. 29, July 1982.
[14] G. McMahon and M. Florian. "On scheduling with ready time and due dates to minimize maximum lateness," *Oper. Res.*, vol. 23, 1975.
[15] A. K. Mok and M. L. Detouzos. "Multiprocessor scheduling in a hard real-time environment," in *Proc. 7th IEEE Texas Conf. Computing Systems*, Nov. 1978.
[16] A. K. Mok. "Fundamental design problems of distributed systems for the hard-real-time environment," Ph.D. dissertation, Dept. Elec. Eng. Comput. Sci., Massachusetts Inst. Technol., Cambridge, MA, May 1983.
[17] —. "The design of real-time programming systems based on process models," in *Proc. IEEE Real-Time Systems Symp.*, Dec. 1984.
[18] B. Simons. "Multiprocessor scheduling of unit-time jobs with arbitrary release times and deadlines," *SIAM J. Comput.*, vol. 12, May 1983.
[19] W. Zhou, K. Ramamrithan, and J. Stankovic. "Preemptive scheduling under time and resource constraints," *IEEE Trans. Comput.*, Aug. 1987.

Jia Xu received the Docteur en Sciences Appliquées degree in computer science from the Université Catholique de Louvain, Belgium, in 1984.

He is presently an Assistant Professor in the Department of Computer Science at York University, North York, Ont., Canada. From 1984 to 1985 he was a postdoctoral fellow at the University of Victoria, Victoria, B.C., Canada. From 1985 to 1986 he was a postdoctoral fellow at the University of Toronto, Toronto, Ont., Canada. His research interests include real-time systems, scheduling, and database management systems.

Dr. Xu is a member of the Association for Computing Machinery.

David Lorge Parnas, born February 10, 1941, is a Professor at Queen's University in Kingston, Ont., Canada, where he is a project leader and principal investigator for the Telecommunications Research Institute of Ontario. He is interested in all aspects of computer systems engineering. His special interests include program organization, program semantics, precise computer system documentation, process structure, process synchronization, and precise abstract specifications. He initiated and led an experimental redesign of a hard-real-time system, the on-board flight program for the U.S. Navy's A-7 aircraft, in order to evaluate a number of software engineering principles. More recently he has advised the Atomic Energy Control Board on the use of safety-critical real-time software in a new nuclear plant. Previously, he was Lansdowne Professor of Computer Science at the University of Victoria, Victoria, B.C., Canada. He was also Principle Investigator of the Software Cost Reduction Project at the Naval Research Laboratory in Washington, DC. He has also taught at Carnegie-Mellon University, the University of Maryland, the Technische Hochschule Darmstadt, and the University of North Carolina at Chapel Hill.

Dr. Parnas was the first winner of the "Norbert Wiener Award for Professional and Social Responsibility," given annually by Computing Professionals for Social Responsibility, and has an honorary doctorate from the ETH in Zurich.

Recent Results in the Theory of Machine Scheduling

E.L. Lawler

University of California, College of Engineering, Computer Science Division, 591 Evans Hall, Berkeley, CA 94720, USA

Abstract. The state of the art of deterministic machine scheduling is reviewed. Emphasis is placed on efficient, i.e. polynomial-bounded, optimization algorithms. A few of the more significant NP-hardness results are highlighted, and some open problems are mentioned.

I. Introduction

The theory of sequencing and scheduling encompasses a bewilderingly large variety of problem types. In the present paper, I shall not attempt to survey more than a small part of this active and rapidly growing area of research. In particular, I shall confine my attention to *machine* scheduling problems, excluding from consideration such worthy topics as project scheduling, timetabling, and cyclic scheduling of manpower. I shall concentrate on strictly *deterministic* models, with emphasis on *efficient*, i.e. polynomial-bounded, algorithms for *optimization*, as opposed to approximation. I shall mention certain significant NP-completeness results and point out several open problems.

This selection of topics reflects my own interests in the field, which I have pursued since the early 1960's but most vigorously since 1974 when I began working with Jan Karel Lenstra and Alexander Rinnooy Kan. One of the objectives of our collaboration has been to delineate, as closely as possible, the boundary between those machine scheduling problems which are *easy* (solvable in polynomial time), and those which are *NP-hard*. We have produced two surveys (Graham, et al, 1977), (Lawler, Lenstra & Rinnooy Kan, 1982 A), and a detailed tabulation of the status of problem types (Lageweg, et al, 1981). The reader is referred to (Lawler, Lenstra & Rinnooy Kan, 1982 B), for an anecdotal account of our collaboration, which will eventually result in a book.

The present paper differs from the surveys mentioned above in that I have chosen to emphasize only those algorithms which I believe are most interesting, elegant or important. Moreover, I have tried to provide something of a historical perspective, in that for each type of problem considered. I first try to state a "classical" algorithm (usually meaning one obtained prior to 1960) and then show how this algorithm has been generalized or improved (or how generalization has been blocked by NP-hardness). There are four principal parts to the paper dealing respectively with single machines, identical and uniform parallel machines, open shops and unrelated parallel machines, and flow shops and job shops.

It greatly facilitates any discussion of machine scheduling to have an appropriate notation for problem types. Such a notation is detailed in the references mentioned above, and is of the form $\alpha|\beta|\gamma$, where α indicates *machine environment* (single machine, parallel machine, open shop, flow shop, job shop), β indicates *job characteristics* (independent vs. precedence constrained, etc.), and γ indicates the *optimality criterion* (makespan, flow time, maximum lateness, total tardiness, etc.). Instead of defining this notation at the outset, I shall introduce it a bit at a time, and hope that the reader will find this natural and not distracting.

II. Single-Machine Scheduling

1. Minimizing Maximum Cost

Consider the following simple sequencing problem. There are n jobs to be processed by a *single machine* which can execute at most one job at a time. Each job j requires a *processing time p_j* and has a specified *due date d_j*. If the jobs are executed without interruption and without idle time between them, with the first job beginning at time $t = 0$, then any given sequence induces a well defined *completion time C_j* and *lateness $L_j = C_j - d_j$* for each job j. What sequence will minimize maximum lateness? That is, minimize

$$L_{\max} = \max_j \{L_j\}.$$

The "earliest due date" or EDD rule of (Jackson, 1955) provides a simple and elegant solution to this problem: Any sequence is optimal that puts the jobs in order of nondecreasing due dates. This result can be proved by a simple interchange argument. Let π be any sequence and π^* be an EDD sequence. If $\pi \neq \pi^*$ then there exist two jobs j and k such that j immediately precedes k in π, but k precedes j in π^*. Since $d_k \leqslant d_j$, interchanging the positions of j and k in π cannot increase the value of $L_{\max}$. A finite number of such transpositions transforms π to π^*, showing that π^* is optimal.

One generalization of this problem is to allow a monotone nondecreasing *cost function f_j* to be specified for each job j, and to attempt to minimize $f_{\max}$, where

$$f_{\max} = \max_j \{f_j(C_j)\}.$$

Another generalization is to allow *precedence constraints* to be specified in the form of a partial order $\rightarrow$; if $j \rightarrow k$ then job j has to be completed before job k can start. (In the original problem, jobs were *independent*, i.e. the relation $\rightarrow$ was assumed to be empty.)

We denote the problem solved by Jackson by $1\|L_{\max}$ and the generalized problem by $1|prec|f_{\max}$ ("1" for single machine; "*prec*" for arbitrary precendence constraints; $f_{\max}$ for the objective function). The problem $1|prec|f_{\max}$ is solved by the following simpe rule (Lawler, 1973): From among all jobs that are eligible to be sequenced last, i.e. that have no successors under $\rightarrow$, put that job last which will incur the smallest cost in that position. Then repeat on the set of $n-1$ jobs remaining, and so on. (For $1\|L_{max}$, this rule says, "Put that job last which has largest due date. Then repeat.")

The correctness of this rule is proved as follows. Let $N=\{1, \ldots, n\}$ be the set of all jobs, let $L\subseteq N$ be the set of jobs without successors, and for any $S\subseteq N$ let $f^*(S)$ be the maximum job completion cost in an optimal schedule for S. We know that the last job of any sequence is completed at time $P=p_1+p_2+\ldots+p_n$. If job $l\in L$ is chosen such that

$$f_l(P)=\min_{j\in L}\{f_j(P)\},$$

then the optimal value of a sequence subject to the condition that job l is processed last is given by

$$\max\{f^*(N-\{l\}), f_l(P)\}.$$

Since both $f^*(N-\{l\})\leqslant f^*(N)$ and $f_l(P)\leqslant f^*(N)$, the rule is proved.

The algorithm can be implemented to run in $O(n^2)$ time, under the assumption that each f_j can be evaluated in unit time for any value of the argument. This contrasts with $O(n\log n)$ time for sorting due dates under Jackson's rule.

A further natural generalization is obtained by specifying a *release time* r_j for each job j, prior to which the job cannot be performed. (Prior to this we have assumed each job is available at time zero, i.e. $r_j=0$ for all j.) If it is required that jobs be executed without interruption, then the introduction of release dates makes things quite difficult. It is an NP-complete problem even to determine if a set of independent jobs can be completed by specified due dates. However, if *preemption* is permitted, i.e. the processing of any job may arbitrarily often be interrupted and resumed at a later time without penalty, then the problem is much easier, and the procedure of (Lawler, 1973) has been further generalized in (Baker, et al, 1982) to apply to the problem $1|pmtn, prec, r_j|f_{max}$ ("pmtn" for preemption, "r_j" for release dates). For brevity we do not describe this algorithm here, but mention that it can be implemented to run in $O(n^2)$ time.

We should mention that although the nonpreemptive problem $1|r_j|L_{max}$ is NP-hard, the special case of unit-time jobs, $1|r_j, p_j=1|L_{max}$ is easy. Moreover, it remains easy even if release dates and due dates are not integers (Simons, 1978).

2. Smith's Rule and Interchange Arguments

Now suppose that we have a single-machine scheduling problem in which each job has a specified *processing time* p_j and *weight* w_j, and the objective is to find a sequence minimizing the *weighted sum of job completion times*, $\Sigma w_j C_j$. This problem, $1\|\Sigma w_j C_j$ in our notation, is solved by another classical result of scheduling theory, the "ratio rule" of (Smith, 1956): Any sequence is optimal that puts the jobs in order of nondecreasing ratios $\rho_j=p_j/w_j$. As a corollary, if all jobs have equal weight, any sequence is optimal which places the jobs in nondecreasing order of processing times. (This is known as the "shortest processing time"or SPT rule.)

Let us pose a very general type of sequencing problem that includes $1\|L_{max}$ and $1\|\Sigma w_j C_j$ as special cases. Given a set of n jobs and a real-valued function f which assigns a value $f(\pi)$ to each permutation π of the jobs, find a permutation π^* such that

$$f(\pi^*) = \min_\pi \{f(\pi)\}.$$

If we know nothing of the structure of the function f, there is clearly nothing to be done except to evaluate $f(\pi)$ for each of the $n!$ permutations π. However, we may be able to find a transitive and complete relation $\leqslant$ (i.e. a quasi-total order) on the jobs with the property that for any two jobs b, c and any permutation of the form $\alpha b c \delta$ we have

$$b \leqslant c \Rightarrow f(\alpha b c \delta) \leqslant f(\alpha \overset{c b}{b c} \delta).$$

Such a relation is called a *job interchange relation*. It says that whenever b and c occur as adjacent jobs with c before b, we are at least as well off to interchange their order. Hence, this relation is sometimes referred to as the "adjacent pairwise interchange property." It is a simple matter to verify the following.

Theorem 1. If f admits of a job interchange relation $\leqslant$, then an optimal permutation π^* can be found by ordering the jobs according to $\leqslant$, with $O(n \log n)$ comparisons of jobs with respect to $\leqslant$.

Note that both Jackson's rule and Smith's rule are based on job interchange relations. Job interchange realtions have been found for a number of other sequencing problems. There is such a relation for the weighted sum of *discounted* job completion times (Rothkopf, 1966), for the "least cost testing sequence" problem (Garey, 1973), and for the two-machine flow shop problem (Johnson, 1954; Mitten, 1958). More will be said about such problems in the next section in the context of precedence constraints.

Let us now consider the generalization of $1\|\Sigma w_j C_j$ to allow release dates and deadlines. It turns out that $1|r_j|\Sigma C_j$ (and a fortiori, $1|r_j|\Sigma w_j C_j$) is NP-hard (Lenstra, 1977), as is $1|pmtn, r_j|\Sigma w_j C_j$ (Labetoulle, et al, 1979). However, $1|pmtn, r_j|\Sigma C_j$ admits of a very simple solution (Baker, 1974): Schedule over time, starting at the first release date. At each decision point (whenever a job is released or a job is completed) choose to process next from among the available jobs (those whose release dates have been met and for which processing is not yet complete) a job whose remaining processing time is minimal. Only $O(n \log n)$ time is required to construct an optimal schedule in this way.

A *deadline* d_j (as opposed to a due date, which is used for computing the cost of a schedule) imposes a constraint that $C_j \leqslant \bar{d}_j$. In (Smith, 1956), a solution is offered to the problem $1|\bar{d}_j|\Sigma C_j$: From among all jobs that are eligible to be sequenced last, i.e. are such that $d_j \geqslant p_1 + \ldots + p_n$, put that job last which has the largest possible processing time. Then repeat on the set of $n-1$ jobs remaining, and so on. This rule yields an $O(n \log n)$ algorithm. (It is left to the reader to verify that if there exists any sequence in which all jobs meet their deadlines, then Smith's algorithm produces such a sequence.)

Although $1|\bar{d}_j|\Sigma C_j$ is easy, $1|\bar{d}_j|\Sigma w_j C_j$ is NP-hard (Lenstra, 1977). (An incorrect algorithm is proposed in (Smith, 1956).) It is easily shown that there is no advantage to preemption, in that any solution that is optimal for $1|\bar{d}_j|\Sigma w_j C_j$ is optimal for $1|pmtn, \bar{d}_j|\Sigma w_j C_j$. It follows that $1|pmtn, \bar{d}_j|\Sigma C_j$ is easy and $1|pmtn, \bar{d}_j|\Sigma w_j C_j$ is NP-hard.

The cited results leave us with one unresolved issue in this area.

Open Problem: What is the status of $1|pmtn, r_j, \bar{d}_j|\Sigma C_j$? Easy or NP-hard?

3. Series Parallel Scheduling

Over a period of years, investigators considered the effect of precedence constraints on the $1\|\Sigma w_j C_j$ problem. In (Conway, et al, 1967) precedence constraints in the form of parallel chains were dealt with, but only subject to the condition that all $w_j = 1$. In (Horn, 1972), an $O(n^2)$ algorithm was proposed for precedence constraints in the form of rooted trees. In (Adolphson & Hu, 1973) an $O(n \log n)$ algorithm was proposed for the same case. In (Lawler, 1978 A), an $O(n \log n)$ algorithm was given for "series parallel" precedence constraints (with rooted trees as a special case), and the problem was shown to be NP-hard for arbitrary precedence constraints, even if all $w_j = 1$ or if all $p_j = 1$. Other contributions to the problem were made by (Sidney, 1975) and (Adolphson, 1977).

The concept of series parallelism, as introduced in (Lawler, 1978 A), may be unfamiliar to the reader. A digraph is said to be *series-parallel* if its transitive closure is *transitive series-parallel*, as given by the recursive definition below:
(1) A digraph $G = (\{j\}, \phi)$ with a single vertex j and no arcs is transitive series-parallel.
(2) Let $G_1 = (V_1, A_1)$, $G_2 = (V_2, A_2)$ be transitive series-parallel digraphs with disjoint vertex sets. Both the *series composition* $G_1 \rightarrow G_2 = (V_1 \cup V_2, A_1 \cup A_2 \cup (V_1 \times V_2))$ and the *parallel composition* $G_1 \| G_2 = (V_1 \cup V_2, A_1 \cup A_2)$ are transitive series-parallel digraphs.
(3) No digraph is transitive series-parallel unless it can be obtained by a finite number of applications of Rules (1) and (2).

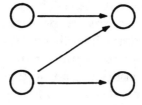

Fig. 1. Z-diagraph

A variety of interesting and useful digraphs (and their corresponding partial orders) are series-parallel. In particular, rooted trees, forests of such trees and level digraphs are series-parallel. The smallest acyclic digraph which is not series-parallel is the *Z-digraph* shown in Figure 1. An acyclic digraph is series-parallel if and only if its transitive closure does not contain the Z-diagraph as an induced subgraph. It is possible to determine whether or not an arbitrary digraph $G = (V, A)$ is series-parallel in $O(|V| + |A|)$ time (Valdes, et al, 1982).

The structure of a series-parallel digraph is displayed by a *decomposition tree* which represents one way in which the transitive closure of the digraph

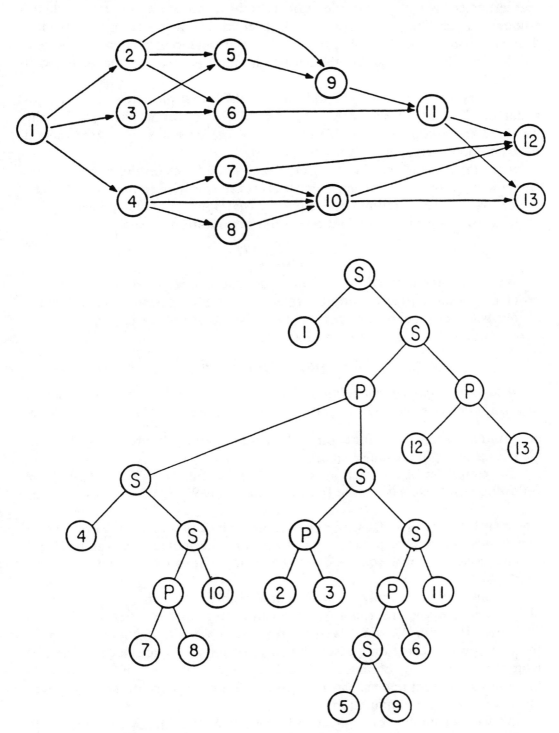

Fig. 2. Series-parallel diagraph and decomposition tree

can be obtained by successive applications of Rules (1) and (2). A series-parallel digraph and its decomposition tree are shown in Figure 2. Each leaf of the decomposition tree is identified with a vertex of the digraph. An S-node represents the application of series composition to the subdigraphs identified with its children; the ordering of these children is important: We adopt the convention that left precedes right. A P-node represents the application of parallel composition to the subdigraphs identified with its children; the ordering of these children is unimportant. The series or parallel relationship of any pair of vertices can be determined by finding their least common ancestor in the decomposition tree.

It was observed by (Monma and Sidney, 1979) that the series-parallel algorithm of (Lawler, 1978 A) has much broader application than just to the weighted completion time problem. We now indicate this by a very general problem formulation, as in (Lawler, 1978 B).

As in the previous section let f be a real-valued function of permutations. But now suppose that precedence constraints are specified in the form of a partial order $\rightarrow$. A permutation π is *feasible* if $j \rightarrow k$ implies that job j precedes job k under π. The objective is to find a feasible permutation π^* such that

$$f(\pi^*) = \min_{\pi \text{ feasible}} \{f(\pi)\}.$$

We need something stronger than a job interchange relation to solve this problem. A transitive and complete relation $\leqslant$ on subpermutations or *strings* of jobs with the property that for any two disjoint strings of jobs β, γ and any permutation of the form $\alpha\beta\gamma\delta$ we have

$$\beta \leqslant \gamma \Rightarrow f(\alpha\beta\gamma\delta) \leqslant f(\alpha\gamma\beta\delta)$$

is called a *string interchange relation*. Smith's rule generalizes to such a relation in a fairly obvious way: For any string α we define $\rho_\alpha = \sum_{j \in \alpha} p_j / \sum_{j \in \alpha} w_j$. However, it is not true that every function f which admits of a job interchange relation also has a string interchange relation.

The remainder of this section is devoted to an intuitive justification of the following result. Details can be found in (Lawler, 1978 B).

Theorem 2. If f admits of a string interchange relation $\leqslant$ and if the precedence constraints $\rightarrow$ are series-parallel, then an optimal permutation π^* can be found by an algorithm which requires $O(n \log n)$ comparisons of strings with respect to $\leqslant$.

Suppose we are to solve a sequencing problem for which a string interchange relation $\leqslant$ exists and a decomposition tree for the series-parallel constraints $\rightarrow$ is given. We can solve the problem by working from the bottom of the tree upward, computing a set of strings of jobs for each node of the tree from the sets of strings obtained for its children. Our objective is to obtain a set of strings at the root node such that sorting these strings according to $\leqslant$ yields an optimal feasible permutation.

We will accomplish our objective if the sets S of strings we obtain satisfy two conditions:

(i) Any ordering of the strings in a set S according to $\leqslant$ is feasible with respect to the precedence constraints $\rightarrow$.

(ii) At any point in the computation, let $S_1, \ldots, S_k$ be the sets of strings computed for nodes such that sets have not yet been computed for their parents. Then some ordering of the strings in $S_1 \cup \ldots \cup S_k$ yields an optimal feasible permutation.

If we order the strings computed at the root according to $\leqslant$, then condition (i) ensures that the resulting permutation is feasible and condition (ii) ensures that it is optimal.

For each leaf of the tree, we let $S = \{j\}$, where j is the job identified with the leaf. Condition (i) is satisfied trivially and condition (ii) is clearly satisfied for the union of the leaf-sets.

Suppose S_1 and S_2 have been obtained for the children of a P-node in the tree. There are no precedence constraints between the strings in S_1 and the strings in S_2. Accordingly, conditions (i) and (ii) remain satisfied if for the P-node we let $S = S_1 \cup S_2$.

Suppose S_1 and S_2 have been obtained for the left child and the right child of an S-node, respectively. Let

$$\sigma_1 = \max_< S_1, \quad \sigma_2 = \min_< S_2.$$

If $\sigma_2 \not\leqslant \sigma_1$, then conditions (i) and (ii) are still satisfied if for the S-node we let $S = S_1 \cup S_2$. If $\sigma_2 \leqslant \sigma_1$, we assert that there exists an optimal feasible permutation in which σ_1 and σ_2 are replaced by their concatenation $\sigma_1 \sigma_2$. (The proof of this assertion involves simple interchange arguments; see (Lawler, 1978 B).) This suggests the following procedure:

```
begin
    σ₁ := max< S₁; σ₂ := = min< S₂;
    if σ₂ ≰ σ₁
    then S := S₁ ∪ S₂
    else σ := σ₁σ₂
        S₁ := S₁ − {σ₁}; σ₁ := max< S₁;
        S₂ := S₂ − {σ₂}; σ₂ := min< S₂;
        while σ ≤ σ₁ ∨ σ₂ ≤ σ
        do if σ ≤ σ₁
            then σ := σ₁σ;
                S₁ := S₁ − {σ₁}; σ₁ := max< S₁
            else σ := σσ₂;
                S₂ := S₂ − {σ₂}; σ₂ := min< S₂
        fi
        od;
        S := S₁ ∪ {σ} ∪ S₂
    fi
end.
```

(We make here the customary assumption that $\max_< \phi$ and $\min_< \phi$ are very small and large elements, respectively.) It is not difficult to verify that conditions (i) and (ii) remain satisfied if for an S-node we compute a set of strings according to the above procedure.

The entire algorithm can be implemented so as to require $O(n \log n)$ time plus the time for the $O(n \log n)$ comparisons with respect to $\leqslant$.

In addition to the total weighted completion time problem, several other sequencing problems admit of a string interchange relation and hence can be solved efficiently for series-parallel precedence constraints. Among these are the problems of minimizing *total weighted discounted completion time* (Lawler & Sivazlian, 1978), *expected cost of fault detection* (Garey, 1973; Monma & Sidney, 1979), *minimum initial resource requirement* (Abdel-Wahab & Kameda, 1978; Monma & Sidney, 1979), and the *two-machine permutation flow shop problem with time lags* (Sidney, 1979).

4. The Total Tardiness Problem

The *tardiness* of job j with respect to due date d_j is $T_j = \max\{0, C_j - d_j\}$. It is a far more difficult task to minimize total tardiness than to minimize total completion time. (Note that $\Sigma C_j = \Sigma L_j + \Sigma d_j$, where Σd_j is a constant.) Over the years a large number of papers have been written about the problem $1 \| \Sigma T_j$, among the most important of which is (Emmons, 1969), in which certain "dominance" conditions were established. These are conditions under which there exists an optimal sequence in which one job j precedes another job k. (A simple case is that in which $p_j \leqslant p_k$ and $d_j \leqslant d_k$.)

In (Lawler, 1977), a "pseudopolynomial" algorithm with running time $O(n^4 \Sigma p_j)$ was described, and a "strong" NP-hardness proof (due to M. R. Garey and D. S. Johnson) was presented for $1 \| \Sigma w_j T_j$. This pseudopolynomial algorithm also serves as the basis for a fully polynomial approximation scheme for the problem $1 \| \Sigma T_j$ (Lawler, 1982B).

The existence of a pseudopolynomial algorithm rules out the possibility that the total tardiness problem is NP-hard in the "strong" sense (unless $P = NP$). However, it leaves unresolved the foolowing question.

Open Problem: What is the status of $1 \| \Sigma T_j$? Easy or NP-hard (in the "ordinary" sense)?

5. Minimizing the Number of Late Jobs

Another possible objective of single-machine scheduling is to find a sequence minimizing the number of jobs j which are late with respect to specified due dates d_j. We let

$$U_j(C_j) = \begin{cases} 0 & \text{if } C_j \leqslant d_j \\ 1 & \text{if } C_j > d_j \end{cases}$$

and denote this problem $1 \| \Sigma U_j$.

The problem $1 \| \Sigma U_j$ is clearly equivalent to that of finding a subset $S \subseteq N = \{1, \ldots, n\}$ such that all the jobs in S can be completed on time and $|S|$ is maximal. An optimal sequence then consists of the jobs in S, in EDD order, followed by the jobs in $N - S$ in arbitrary order. (Note that once a job is late it does not matter how late it is.) An elegant algorithm for finding a maximum subset S is given in (Moore, 1968). We state this without proof.

```
begin
    order the jobs so that d₁ ≤ ... ≤ dₙ.
    S:= φ
    P:= 0
    for j:= 1 to n
        do  S:= S ∪ {j}
            P:= P + p_j
            if  P > d_j
            then let p_l = max {p_i|i ∈ S}
                 S:= S − {l}
                 P:= P − p_l
        fi
    od
end.
```

This algorithm can be easily implemented to run in $O(n \log n)$ time.

The weighted version of this problem, $1||\Sigma w_j U_j$, is easily shown to be NP-hard, but can be solved in pseudopolynomial time $O(n \max\{d_j\})$ by a dynamic-programming computation similar to that used for the knapsack problem (Lawler & Moore, 1969). However, if job weights are *agreeable*, i.e. there is an ordering of the jobs so that

$$p_1 \leq p_2 \leq ... \leq p_n,$$

$$w_1 \geq w_2 \geq ... \geq w_n,$$

then the problem can be solved in $O(n \log n)$ time by a simple modification of Moore's algorithm (Lawler, 1976).

If $1||\Sigma U_j$ is generalized to allow arbitrary release dates, it immediately becomes NP-hard. If release dates and due dates are *compatible*, i.e. there is an ordering of the jobs so that

$$r_1 \leq r_2 \leq ... \leq r_n,$$

$$d_1 \leq d_2 \leq ... \leq d_n,$$

then the problem is easy. An $O(n^2)$ algorithm was proposed in (Kise, et al, 1978). An $O(n \log n)$ algorithm, generalizing Moore's procedure, has been provided for this case in (Lawler, 1982C).

If preemption is permitted, then introducing arbitrary release dates does not cause NP-hardness. In (Lawler, 1982C) a rather complicated dynamic programming procedure for $1|pmtn, r_j|\Sigma w_j U_j$ is presented. This procedure has running time $O(n^3 W^3)$ where $W = \Sigma w_j$. (Job weights are assumed to be integers.) Thus for $1|pmtn, r_j|\Sigma U_j$ the running time becomes $O(n^6)$.

We should also mention the case in which each job has both a due date d_j and a deadline $\bar{d}_j$ (where without loss of generality $d_j \leq \bar{d}_j$). The problem $1|\bar{d}_j|\Sigma U_j$ is shown to be NP-hard in (Lawler, 1982C).

6. Minimizing the Sum of Cost Functions

Suppose, as in Section 1, for each job j there is specified a cost function f_j. Except that now we wish to find a sequence that minimizes the sum of the costs, $\sum_j f_j(C_j)$, instead of the maximum of the costs. A general dynamic programming procedure for this problem, which we denote by $1\|\Sigma f_j$, was suggested in (Held & Karp, 1962) and (Lawler, 1964):

For any subset $S \subseteq N$, let $p(S) = \sum_{j \in S} p_j$ and let $F(S)$ denote the minimum total cost for a sequence of the jobs in S. Then we have

$$F(\phi) = 0$$
$$F(S) = \min_{j \in S} \{ F(S - \{j\}) + f_j(p(S)) \}. \tag{1}$$

The optimum value for the complete set of jobs N is $F(N)$ and this value can be obtained in $O(n2^n)$ time.

Note that this solution method does not require that the functions f_j be nondecreasing. It is only necessary to assume that jobs are performed without preemption and without idle time between them.

Interestingly, precedence constraints can only make the dynamic programming computation easier, not harder. In solving $1|prec|\Sigma f_j$, it is necessary to solve equations (1) only for subsets S that are *initial* sets of the partial order $\rightarrow$, in the sense that $j \rightarrow k$, $k \in S$ imply that $j \in S$. Moreover, the minimization in (1) need be carried out only over jobs $j \in S$ that have no successors in S. If the precedence constraints $\rightarrow$ are at all significant, then the number of initial sets is likely to be *very much* smaller than 2^n. One can then hope to solve much larger problems than in the absence of such constraints.

Dominance relations, such as those given by (Emmons, 1969) for the total tardiness problem, can be viewed as precedence constraints. Thus there is real motivation for finding dominance relations for various types of problems. This approach has been taken by (Fisher, et al, 1981) and others for solving the total tardiness problem and other related problems.

It should be noted that it is a nontrivial problem to devise suitable data structures for solving $1|prec|\Sigma f_j$ by dynamic programming. In (Baker, & Schrage, 1978), various "labeling" schemes have been proposed for assigning addresses to initial sets. The difficulty with these schemes is that the address space is not necessarily fully utilized and that memory may be wasted. In (Lawler, 1979), a time- and memory-efficient procedure is proposed for generating the necessary data structures, and tests by (Kao & Queyranne, 1980) seem to confirm its advantages.

There have been many proposals for solving problems of the form $1\|\Sigma f_j$ and $1|prec|\Sigma f_j$, by other dynamic programming schemes (Fisher, 1976), and by branch-and-bound, using a variety of bounding methods. Some bounding techniques, are quite sophisticated, as in (Fisher, 1976), where Lagrangean techniques are applied to problem relaxations. The author believes that "hybrid" techniques, combining the best features of branch-and-bound and dynamic programming have potential.

III. Identical and Uniform Parallel Machines

1. Introduction

As before, there are n jobs to be scheduled and job j has a *processing requirement* p_j. But we now suppose there are m *parallel machines* available to do the processing. Each job can be worked on by at most one machine at a time and each machine can work on at most one job at a time. Machine i processes job j with *speed* s_{ij}. Hence if machine i does all the work on job j, it requires a total amount of time p_j/s_{ij} for its processing.

We distinguish three types of parallel machines:

(P) *Identical Machines:* All s_{ij} are equal. In this case we may assume, without loss of generality, that $s_{ij} = 1$, for all i, j.

(Q) *Uniform Machines:* $s_{ij} = s_{ik}$, for all i, j, k. In other words, each machine i performs all jobs at the same speed s_i. Without loss of generality, we assume $s_1 \geqslant s_2 \geqslant \ldots \geqslant s_m$.

(R) *Unrelated Machines:* There is no particular relationship between the s_{ij} values.

In the next several sections, we shall consider problems involving identical and uniform machines. Unrelated machines, which require rather different algorithmic techniques, are dealt with in Part IV of this paper.

The difficulty of parallel machine problems is profoundly affected by whether or not preemption is permitted. It is easy to see that even the problem of nonpreemptively scheduling two identical machines so as to minimize makespan, $P2\|C_{max}$, in our notation, is NP-hard. However, in recent years there have been many new good algorithms developed for preemptive scheduling of parallel machines.

2. Nonpreemptive Scheduling to Minimize the Sum of Completion Times

The solution to the problem $P\|\Sigma C_j$ is quite easy (Conway, et al, 1967): Order the jobs so that $p_1 \leqslant p_2 \leqslant \ldots \leqslant p_n$. Having scheduled jobs $1, 2, \ldots, j$, find the earliest available machine and schedule job $j+1$ on that machine, thereby completing it as soon as possible. This greedy approach, clearly a variant of the SPT rule, yields a schedule like that indicated by the Gannt chart in Figure 3.

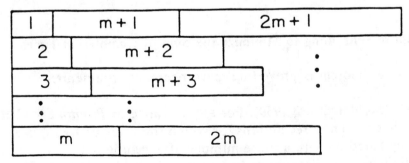

Fig. 3. Gannt chart for SPT schedule

As justification, consider the jobs to be performed on any single machine and for simplicity let these be $1, 2, ..., k$ in that order. For these jobs we have

$$\Sigma C_j = kp_1 + (k-1)p_2 + ... + 2p_{k-1} + p_k. \qquad (2)$$

Considering all m machines, it is apparent that we have available as coefficients m $1's$, m $2's$, ..., m $n's$, and the n smallest of these mn coefficients should be assigned to the n jobs, with the smallest coefficients being assigned to the largest jobs. This is precisely what the SPT rule accomplishes.

Now consider $Q\|\Sigma C_j$, and suppose jobs $1, 2, ..., k$ are performed on machine i. Then instead of (2) we have

$$\Sigma C_j = \frac{k}{s_i}p_1 + \frac{(k-1)}{s_i}p_2 + ... + \frac{2}{s_i}p_{k-1} + \frac{1}{s_i}p_k.$$

It is now apparent that what we have are mn coefficients of the form k/s_i, $k = 1, 2, ..., n$; $i = 1, 2, ..., m$ and our task is to assign the n smallest of these coefficients to the n jobs, with the smallest coefficients being assigned to the largest jobs. This can be done in $O(n \log n)$ time with the algorithm of (Howowitz & Sahni, 1976):

begin
    order the jobs so that $p_1 \leqslant p_2 \leqslant ... \leqslant p_n$
    initialize a priority queue Q with the values $\frac{1}{s_i}$, $i = 1, 2, ..., m$.

    for $j = n$ **to** 1
        do let $\frac{k}{s_i}$ be a smallest value in Q
        assign $\frac{k}{s_i}$ as the coefficient of p_j
        replace $\frac{k}{s_i}$ in Q by $\frac{k+1}{s_i}$
    od
end

Unfortunately, the problem of nonpreemptively scheduling identical parallel machines so as to minimize *weighted* total completion time, i.e. $P\|\Sigma w_j C_j$, is NP-hard.

3. Preemptive Scheduling to Minimize the Sum of Completion Times

The following theorem is proved by rearrangement arguments.

Theorem 3. (McNaughton, 1959). For any instance of $P\|pmtn|\Sigma w_j C_j$ there exists a schedule with no preemptions for which the value of $\Sigma w_j C_j$ is as small as that for any schedule with a finite number of preemptions.

(The finiteness restriction can be removed by results implicit in (Lawler & Labetoulle, 1978).)

From McNaughton's theorem it follows immediately that the procedure of the previous section solves $P|pmtn|\Sigma C_j$, since there is no advantage to preemption. Also, from the fact that $P||\Sigma w_j C_j$ is NP-hard, it follows that $P|pmtn|\Sigma w_j C_j$ (and *a fortiori* $Q|pmtn|\Sigma w_j C_j$) is NP-hard.

A simple example suffices to show that there *is* advantage to preemption in $Q|pmtn|\Sigma C_j$, i.e. the procedure of (Horowitz & Sahni, 1976) does not necessarily yield an optimal solution. We now state a lemma which is also proved by rearrangement arguments.

Lemma 4. (Lawler & Labetoulle, 1978). Let $p_1 \le p_1 \le \ldots \le p_n$. Then there is an optimal schedule for $Q|pmtn|\Sigma C_j$ in which $C_1 \le C_2 \le \ldots \le C_n$.

This lemma is essential to prove the validity of a solution to $Q|pmtn|\Sigma C_j$ presented in (Gonzalez, 1977). Let $p_1 \le p_2 \le \ldots \le p_n$. Having scheduled jobs $1, 2, \ldots, j$, schedule job $j+1$ to be completed as easily as possible. This variant of the SPT rule yields a schedule as shown in Figure 4.

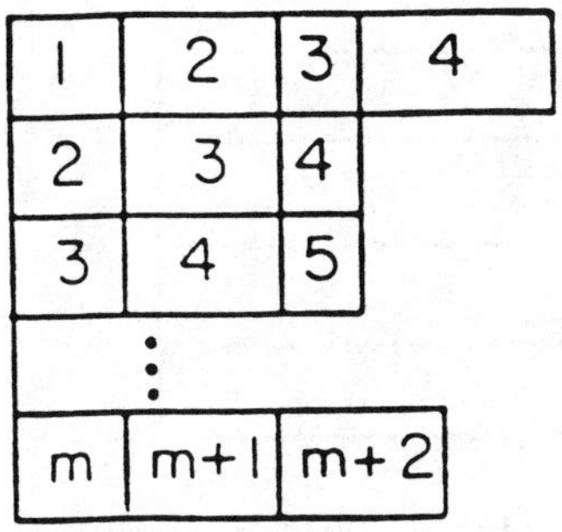

Fig. 4. SPT rule for preemptive scheduling of uniform machines

We comment that the same strategy is optimal for certain stochastic scheduling problems. Cf. (Weiss & Pinedo, 1980).

In (Gonzalez, 1977), a procedure is presented for minimizing total completion time, subject to a common deadline for all jobs. It seems quite feasible to extend the same ideas to the situation in which the deadlines d_j and the processing times p_j are *compatible*. i.e. there is a numbering of the jobs so that

$$p_1 \le p_2 \le \ldots \le p_n$$
$$\bar{d}_1 \le \bar{d}_2 \le \ldots \le \bar{d}_n.$$

However, the status of the problem for arbitrary deadlines is open.

Open Problem: What is the status of $Q|pmtn, \bar{d}_j|\Sigma C_j$? Easy or NP-hard?

Perhaps even more perplexing, almost nothing is known about the case of release dates.

Open Problem: What is the status of $Q|pmtn, r_j|\Sigma C_j$? (Or, for that matter, $P2|pmtn, r_j|\Sigma C_j$?) Easy or NP-hard?

4. Preemptive Scheduling to Minimize Makespan

The problem of preemptively scheduling m identical parallel machines so as to minimize makespan is quite easy. Clearly we must have

$$C_{max} \geq \max \left\{ \max_j \{p_j\}, \frac{1}{m} \Sigma p_j \right\}.$$

Yet one can achieve the lower bound given by the right hand side of the inequality by applying the "wraparound" rule of (McNaughton, 1959). Imagine the processing times of the n jobs are laid out end-to-end, in arbitrary order, in a strip. Now cut the strip at intervals whose length is given by the lower bound. Each of the shorter strips becomes a row of the Gannt chart for an optimal schedule, as shown in Figure 5.

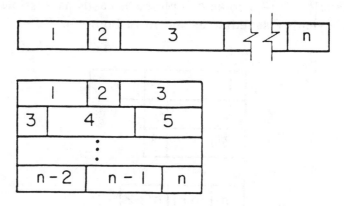

Fig. 5. McNaughton's "wraparound" rule

It is easy to see that this procedure requires $O(n)$ time and creates at most $m - 1$ preemptions.

Now let us consider the case of uniform machines. Assuming $s_1 \geq s_2 \geq \ldots \geq s_m$, it is clear that we must have

$$C_{max} \geq \max \left\{ \max_{1 < k < m-1} \left\{ \sum_{j=1}^{k} p_j \bigg/ \sum_{i=1}^{k} s_i \right\}, \ \sum_{j=1}^{n} p_j \bigg/ \sum_{i=1}^{m} s_i \right\} \tag{3}$$

It is possible to achieve the lower bound given by the right-hand size of this inequality, and to show this most easily, we now generalize the problem a bit.

Let us suppose that the speeds of the machines are time-varying and that the speed of machine i at time t is $s_i(t)$. Assume $s_1(t) \geq s_2(t) \geq \ldots \geq s_m(t)$, for all t. Define the *capacity* of machine i in the interval $[0, d]$ as

$$S_i = \int_0^d s_i(u) \, du.$$

Assume $p_1 \geq p_2 \geq \ldots \geq p_n$. Then, by the same reasoning behind (3), a necessary condition for there to exist a feasible schedule of length d is that all of the following inequalities be satisfied:

164

$$S_1 \qquad\qquad\qquad\qquad \geqslant p_1$$
$$S_1 + S_2 \qquad\qquad\qquad \geqslant p_1 + p_2$$
$$\vdots$$
$$S_1 + S_2 + \ldots S_{m-1} \qquad \geqslant p_1 + p_2 + \ldots + p_{m-1}$$
$$S_1 + S_2 + \ldots S_{m-1} + S_m \geqslant p_1 + p_2 + \ldots + p_{m-1} + \ldots + p_n .$$

$$(4)$$

The inequalities simply assert that, for $k = 1, 2, \ldots, m-1$, the sum of the capacities of the k fastest machines is at least as large as the sum of the processing requirements of the k largest jobs, and that the sum of the capacities of all m machines is at least as large as the sum of the requirements of all n jobs. Satisfaction of inequalities (4) is also a sufficient condition for the existence of a feasible schedule. Our proof is based on ideas of (Gonzalez & Sahni, 1978).

Let us choose an arbitrary job j to schedule in the interval $[0, d]$. Find the largest index k such that $S_k \geqslant p_j$. If $k = m$, then let machine $m+1$ be a dummy machine with zero speed in the discussion which follows. Let

$$f(t) = \int_0^t s_k(u)\,du, \qquad g(t) = \int_t^d s_{k+1}(u)\,du .$$

From $f(0) = 0$, $f(d) \geqslant p_j$, $g(0) < p_j$, $g(d) = 0$, and the fact that f and g are continuous functions, it follows that there exists a t', $0 < t' \leqslant d$, such that $f(t') + g(t') = p_j$. Accordingly, schedule job j for processing by machine k in the interval $[0, t]$ and by machine $k+1$ in the interval $[t', d]$.

Next replace elementary machines k and $k+1$ by a *composite* machine formed from the remaining available time on those machines. This new machine has speed $s_{k+1}(t)$ in the interval $[0, t']$, speed $s_k(t)$ in $[t', d]$, and total processing capacity $S_k + S_{k+1} - p_j$ in the interval $[0, d]$. If $k < m$, create a dummy machine with zero speed. (We already created such a machine if $k = m$.) This gives us m machines with capacities S_i' as follows. If $k < m$, then

$$S_i' = \begin{cases} S_i & \text{for } i = 1, \ldots, k-1, \\ S_k - S_{k+1} - p_j & \text{for } i = k, \\ S_{i+1} & \text{for } i = k+1, \ldots, m-1, \\ 0 & \text{for } i = m. \end{cases}$$

And if $k = m$, then

$$S_i' = \begin{cases} S_i & \text{for } i = 1, \ldots, m-1 \\ S_m - p_j & \text{for } i = m. \end{cases}$$

The problem thus reduces to one involving m machines and $n-1$ jobs. The new machine capacities S_i', $i = 1, 2, \ldots, m$, and processing requirements $p_1, p_2, \ldots, p_{j-1}, p_{j+1}, \ldots, p_n$ satisfy inequalities (4). (This can be verified by an analysis of the cases $j \leqslant k < m$, $k < j \leqslant m$, $k = m$, which we omit.) Induction on the number of jobs proves that repeated application of the scheduling rule yields a schedule in which all jobs are completed on time. (It can also be shown that such a schedule requires no more than $2(m-1)$ preemptions.) Satisfaction of inequalities (4) is thus a sufficient condition for the existence of a feasible schedule and we have proved the following result.

Theorem 5. Satisfaction of inequalities (4) is a necessary and sufficient condition for the existence of a schedule in which all n jobs are completed within the interval $[0, d]$.

5. Preemptive Scheduling with Due Dates

Now suppose the n given jobs have arbitrary due dates. Is it possible to schedule the jobs so that they are are all completed on time? The procedure we shall describe for solving this problem is adapted from (Sahni & Cho, 1980).

Let $d_0 = 0$, assume $d_0 < d_1 \leqslant d_2 \leqslant \ldots \leqslant d_n$ and let S_i denote the processing capacity of machine i in the interval $[0, d_1]$. If there exists a schedule in which all jobs are completed on time, then in any such schedule *all* of the processing requirement of job 1 and some amount $p_j' \leqslant p_j$ of the requirement of each job $j, j = 2, 3, \ldots, n$, is processed in the interval $[0, d_1]$. The unknown values $p_j', j \neq 2$, together with the known value p_1 (appropriately reordered) satisfy inequalities (4). It follows that, if there exists a feasible schedule, there exists a feasible schedule in which job 1 is scheduled in accordance with the rule presented in the previous section.

So suppose we find the largest index k such that $S_k \geqslant p_1$, determine the value t', $0 < t' \leqslant d_1$, and schedule job 1. This leaves us with m machines with processing capacities S_i', $i = 1, 2, \ldots, m$, in the interval $[0, d_1]$. We now also have m (composite) machines with well-defined speeds $s_i'(t)$, in the interval $[0, d_n]$, as follows. If $k < m$, then

$$
s_i'(t) = \begin{cases}
s_i(t) & (0 \leqslant t \leqslant d_n) \quad \text{for } i = 1, \ldots, k-1, \\[1mm]
\left.\begin{array}{ll} s_{k+1}(t) & (0 \leqslant t \leqslant t') \\ s_k(t) & (t' < t \leqslant d_n) \end{array}\right\} & \text{for } i = k, \\[3mm]
\left.\begin{array}{ll} s_{i+1}(t) & (0 \leqslant t \leqslant d_1) \\ s_i(t) & (d_1 < t \leqslant d_n) \end{array}\right\} & \text{for } i = k+1, \ldots, m-1 \\[3mm]
\left.\begin{array}{ll} 0 & (0 \leqslant t \leqslant d_1) \\ s_m(t) & (d_1 < t \leqslant d_n) \end{array}\right\} & \text{for } i = m.
\end{cases}
$$

And if $k = m$, then

$$
s_i'(t) \begin{cases}
s_i(t) & (0 \leqslant t \leqslant d_n) \quad \text{for } i = 1, \ldots, m-1, \\[1mm]
\left.\begin{array}{ll} 0 & (0 \leqslant t \leqslant t') \\ s_m(t) & (t' < t \leqslant d_n) \end{array}\right\} & \text{for } i = m.
\end{cases}
$$

The problem thus reduces to one involving m machines and $n - 1$ jobs: There exists a feasible schedule for the n jobs $1, 2, \ldots, n$ on machines with speeds $s_i(t)$, $i = 1, 2, \ldots, m$, if and only if there exists a feasible schedule for the $n - 1$ jobs $2, 3, \ldots, n$ on machines with speeds $s_i'(t)$, $i = 1, 2, \ldots, m$.

6. Preemptive Scheduling to Minimize the Number of Late Jobs

The algorithm described in the previous section provides a key to the solution of the problem of minimizing the weighted number of jobs that do not meet their deadlines, i.e. the problem $Q|pmtn\Sigma w_j U_j$. The algorithm is rather complicated to explain and details can be found in (Lawler, 1979). We state only that the running time is $O(W^2 n^2)$ for $m=2$ and $O(W^2 n^{3m-5})$ for $m \leq 3$, where $W = \Sigma w_j$.

Note that for *fixed* m the algorithm is pseudopolynomial and that for fixed m and unweighted jobs, i.e. $W=n$, the algorithm is strictly polynomial This is probably the best that we can hope for, since the problem of minimizing the (unweighted) number of jobs is NP-hard, even for *identical* machines, if m is *variable*, i.e. specified as part of the problem instance.

Theorem 6. The problem $P|pmtn|\Sigma U_j$ is NP-hard.

Proof: An instance of the scheduling problem consists of n pairs of positive integers (p_j, d_j), $j=1, 2, \ldots, n$, representing processing requirements and due dates of n jobs, a positive integer m, representing the number of identical machines, and a positive integer $k \leq n$. The question asked is: Does there exist a feasible preemptive schedule in which k (or more) jobs are on time?

We shall describe a polynomial transformation from the known NP-complete problem PARTITION. An instance of this problem consists of t positive integers a_i, $i=1, 2, \ldots, t$, with $\sum a_i = 2b$. Is there a subset S such that

$$\sum_{i \in S} a_i = \sum_{i \notin S} a_i = b?$$

Given an instance of PARTITION, create an instance of the scheduling problem with $n = 5t - 2$ jobs as follows:
(1) t jobs with $p_j = b + a_j$, $d_j = b + 2a_j$ $(j = 1, \ldots, t)$;
(2) t jobs with $p_j = b$, $d_j = b$ $(j = t+1, \ldots, 2t)$;
(3) $3t-2$ jobs with $p_j = b$, $d_j = 4b$ $(j = 2t+1, \ldots, 5t-2)$.
Let $m = t$ and $k = 4t - 1$.

If there exists a solution S to PARTITION, then there exists a solution to the scheduling problem. Let $|S| = s$ and construct a set of jobs consisting of the s jobs of type (1) whose indices are in S, any $t - s + 1$ jobs of type (2), and all $3t-2$ jobs of type (3). We assert htat there is a feasible schedule for this set of $4t-1$ jobs, by the following argument.

Each of the s jobs of type (1) and $t-s$ of the jobs of type (2) can be scheduled on a separate machine. Each type (2) job is processed continuously in the interval $[0, b]$. Each type (1) job j is processed continuously in the interval $[b, b+2a_j]$, leaving a_j units of idle time on its machine in the interval $[0, b]$. The idle time remaining in $[0, b]$ can be distributed so that the $(t+1)st$ type (2) job can be scheduled. For example, if $S = \{1, 2, 3\}$, with $a_1 + a_2 + a_3 = b$, the last type (2) job can be scheduled on one machine in the interval $[0, a_1]$, on a second machine in the interval $[a_1, a_1 + a_2]$, and on a third machine in the interval $[a_1 + a_2, b]$. After the $t+1$ jobs of type (1) and type (2) are scheduled, a total of

167

$(3t-2)b$ units of idle time remain on the t machines in the interval $[b, 4b]$, with at least $3b-2\max_j\{a_j\}\geqslant b$ units of idle time on each machine. The $3t-2$ jobs of type (3) can be scheduled in "wrap-around" fashion in the idle time in the interval $[b, 4b]$.

Conversely, if there exists a solution to the scheduling problem, then there exists a solution to PARTITION, by the following argument. Suppose there exists a feasible set of size $4t-1$. Type (3) jobs have later due dates and no greater processing requirements than jobs of type (1) or (2). Hence by a simple substitution argument we may assume, without loss of generality, that the feasible set contains all $3t-2$ of the type (3) jobs. Let S denote the set of indices of the type (1) jobs. There are s, where $s=|S|$, type (1) jobs and $t-s+1$ type (2) jobs. The type (1) jobs require at least $sb-\sum_{j\in S} a_j$ units of processing in the interval $[0, b]$. It follows that the type (2) jobs can be scheduled only if $\sum_{i\in S} a_i \geqslant b$. The total amount of processing required by the type (1) and type (2) jobs is $(t+1)b+\sum_{j\in S} a_j$, which leaves $3(t-1)b-\sum_{j\in S} a_j$ units in the interval $[0, 4b]$ for the type (3) jobs. It follows that the type (3) jobs can be scheduled only if $\sum_{i\in S} a_i \leqslant b$ and we have $\sum_{j\in S} a_j = b$.

This NP-hardness proof differs significantly from previous proofs of NP-hardness for other preemptive scheduling problems. Virtually all other such proofs have proceeded by first showing that there is "no advantage" to preemption for the problem at hand, or for a restricted set of instances of the problem. That is, if there exists a feasible preemptive schedule there must also exist a feasible nonpreemptive schedule. The proof then proceeds by showing that the corresponding nonpreemptive scheduling problem (or an appropriately restricted set of instances of it) is NP-hard. We did not do this. And, in fact, there *is* advantage to preemption in our problem and the nonpreemptive version is well known to be NP-hard even if the number of identical machines is fixed at two.

7. A "Nearly On-Line" Algorithm for Preemptive Scheduling with Release Dates

The algorithm of Section 5 can be applied to solve the problem $Q|pmtn, r_j|C_{max}$. (Simply turn the problem around and deadlines assume the role of release dates.) However, the algorithm is then "off line"; full knowledge of all problem parameters must be known in advance of computation. It can be shown that there is no fully "on-line" algorithm for the problem. However a "nearly" on-line algorithm is possible. By this we mean that at each release date r_j, the next release date r_{j+1} is known. However, there need be no knowledge of the processing times $p_{j+1}, \ldots, p_n$ nor the release dates $r_{j+2}, \ldots, r_n$.

What we want to accomplish in this. At time r_n we want the remaining processing requirements of jobs $1, 2, \ldots, n-1$, together with the processing requirement of job n, to be such that the value of C_{max} can be minimized. This will clearly be the case if the k longest of these requirements, for $k = 1, 2, \ldots, m - 1$, and for $k = n$, is as small as possible. The interesting fact is that this objective can be achieved at each release date $r_j, j = 1, 2, \ldots, n$.

So the strategy is as follows. Having determined the schedule up to time r_j, we then determine the schedule for the interval $[r_j, r_{j+1}]$ so that the remaining processing requirements of jobs $1, 2, \ldots, j$ at time r_{j+1} are as "uniform" as possible. Without going into details, we simply indicate that at time r_j we have a "staircase" of remaining processing times, from longest to shortest, as indicated in Figure 6. We then choose to process an amount of each job in the interval $[r_j, r_{j+1}]$, as indicated by the shaded region in the figure. These amounts are chosen to satisfy the requirement that the sum of the k longest remaining processing requirements be as small as possible, for all k.

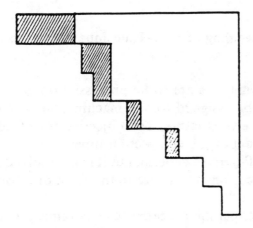

Fig. 6. "Staircase" of remaining processing times

Details may be found in (Sahni & Cho, 1979; and Labetoulle, et al, 1979). The nearly on-line algorithm requires $O(n \log n + mn)$ time. At most $O(mn)$ preemptions are introduced into the schedule.

8. Preemptive Scheduling with Release Dates and Due Dates

Consider the problem of preemptively scheduling jobs on identical parallel machines subject to release dates and deadlines. This was given a network flow formulation in (Horn, 1974).

Let $E = \{r_j\} \cup \{d_j\}$ and order the numbers in E. This yields at most $2n - 1$ time intervals $[e_h, e_{h+1}]$. Now create a flow network with a node for each job j, a node for each time interval $[e_h, e_{h+1}]$, a dummy source s and a dummy sink t. There is an arc (s, j) from the source to each job node j, and the capacity of this arc is p_j. There is an arc from job node j to the node for interval $[e_h, e_{h+1}]$ if and only if job j can be processed in the interval, i.e. $r_j \leqslant e_h$ and $e_{h+1} \leqslant d_j$, and the capacity of this arc is $e_{h+1} - e_h$. There is an arc from each interval node $[e_h, e_{h+1}]$ to the sink, and the capacity of this arc is $m(e_{h+1} - e_h)$. We assert that there exists a feasible preemptive schedule if and only if there exists a flow of value $P = \Sigma p_j$ in this network.

In the case of uniform parallel machines, it is not possible to give such a simple formulation to the problem. What are needed are capacity constraints on *sets* of arcs into a given interval node $[e_h, e_{h+1}]$. In particular, it is necessary that the sum of the k largest flows not exceed $\left(\sum_{i=1}^{k} s_i\right)(e_{h+1} + e_h)$ for

$k = 1, 2, \ldots, m-1$, and the arc to the sink is given capacity $\left(\sum_{i=1}^{m} s_i\right)(e_{h+1} - e_h)$.

What is interesting is that these capacity constraints are *submodular* and the network is an example of a so-called "polymatroidal" flow network. See (Martel, 1981) for a solution to the specific scheduling problem and (Lawler & Martel, 1982 A, B) for a discussion of polymatroidal network flows in general.

9. Nonpreemptive Scheduling of Unit-Time Jobs Subject to Precedence Constraints

Suppose that n unit-time jobs are to be processed on m identical parallel machines. Each job can be assigned to any machine, and the schedule has to respect given precedence constraints. The objective is to find a schedule which minimizes the maximum of job completion times.

This problem is NP-hard in general, but it can be solved in polynomial time if either the precedence constraints are in the form of a rooted tree or if there are only two machines.

First, let us assume that the precedence constraints are in the form of an *in-tree*, i.e. each job has exactly one immediate succesor, except for one job which has no successors and which is called the *root*. It is possible to minimize the maximum completion time in $O(n)$ time by applying an algorithm due to Hu (Hu, 1961). The *level* of a job is defined as the number of jobs in the unique path to the root. At the beginning of each time unit, as many available jobs as possible are scheduled on the m machines, where highest priority is granted to the jobs with the largest levels. Thus, Hu's algorithm is a *list scheduling* algorithm, whereby at each step the available job with the highest ranking on a priority list is assigned to the first machine that becomes available. It can also be viewed as a *critical path scheduling* algorithm: the next job chosen is the one which heads the longest current chain of unexecuted jobs.

To validate Hu's algorithm, we will show that, if it yields a schedule of length t^*, then no feasible schedule of length $t < t^*$ exists.

Choose any $t < t^*$ and define a label for each job by subtracting its level from t; note that the root has label t and that each other job has a label one less than its immediate sucessor. The algorithm gives priority to the jobs with the smallest labels. Since it yields a schedule of length larger than t, in some unit-time interval s a job is scheduled with a label smaller than s. Let s be the earliest such interval and let there be a job with label $l < s$ scheduled in it. We claim that there are m jobs scheduled in each earlier interval $s' < s$. Suppose there is an interval $s' < s$ with fewer than m jobs scheduled. If $s' = s - 1$, then the only reason that the job with label l was not scheduled in s' could have been that an immediate predecessor would have label $l-1 < s-1$; which contradicts the definition of s. If $s' < s-1$, then there are fewer jobs scheduled in s' than in $s'+1$, which is impossible from the structure of the intree. Hence, each interval $s' < s$ has m jobs scheduled. Since each of these jobs has a label smaller than s, at least one job with a label smaller than s must be scheduled in interval s, so that there is no feasible schedule of length $t < t^*$ possible. This completes the correctness proof of Hu's algorithm.

An alternative linear-time algorithm for this problem has been proposed by Davida and Linton (Davida & Linton, 1976). Assume that the precedence constraints are in the form of an *outtree*, i.e. each job has at most one immediate predecessor. The *weight* of a job is defined as the total number of its successors. The jobs are now scheduled according to decreasing weights.

If the problem is to minimize the *maximum lateness* with respect to given due dates rather than the maximum completion time, then the case that the precedence constraints are in the form of an *intree* can be solved by an adaptation of Hu's algorithm, but the case of an *outtree* turns out to be NP-hard (Brucker, et al, 1977). Polynomial-time algorithms and NP-hardness results for the maximum completion time problem with various other special types of precedence constraints are reported in (Dolev, 1981; Garey, et al, 1981; Warmuth, 1980).

Next, let us assume that there are *arbitrary precedence constraints* but only *two machines*. It is possible to minimize the maximum completion time by a variety of algorithms.

The earliest and simplest approach is due to Fujii, Kasami and Ninomiya (Fujii, et al, 1969, 1971). A graph is constructed with vertices corresponding to jobs and edges $\{j, k\}$ whenever jobs j and k can be executed simultaneously, i.e. $j \nrightarrow k$ and $k \nrightarrow j$. A *maximum cardinality matching* in this graph, i.e. a maximum number of disjoint edges, is then used to derive an optimal schedule; if the matching contains c pairs of jobs, the schedule has length $n - c$. Such a matching can be found in $O(n^3)$ time.

A completely different approach (Coffman & Graham, 1972) leads to a *list scheduling* algorithm. The jobs are labeled in the following way. Suppose labels $1, \ldots, l$ have been applied and S is the subset of unlabeled jobs all of whose successors have been labeled. Then a job in S is given the label $l+1$ if the labels of its immediate successors are *lexicographically minimal* with respect to all jobs in S. The priority list is formed by ordering the jobs according to decreasing labels. This method requires $O(n^2)$ time.

Recently, an even more efficient algorithm has been developed by Gabow (Gabow, 1980). His method uses labels, but with a number of rather sophisticated embellishments. The running time can be made strictly linear in $n + a$, where a is the number of arcs in the precedence graph (Gabow, 1982 B).

If the problem is to find a *feasible* two-machine schedule under arbitrary precedence constraints when each job becomes available at a given integer *release date* and has to meet a given integer *deadline*, polynomial-time algorithms exist (Garey & Johnson, 1976, 1977). These algorithms can be applied to minimize *maximum lateness* in polynomial time.

It was shown in (Ullman, 1975) that the problem of minimizing maximum completion time for n unit-time jobs on m identical parallel machines is NP-hard. (Cf. (Lenstra & Rinnooy Kan, 1978) or (Lawler & Lenstra, 1982) for a simpler proof.) However, this NP-completeness proof requires that the number of machines m be specified as part of the problem instance. The status of the problem for any *fixed* number of machines, in particular three, is open.

Open Problem: What is the status of the problem $P3|prec, p_i = 1|C_{max}$? (Scheduling unit-time jobs on three identical parallel machines subject to arbitrary precedence constraints, so as to minimize maximum completion time.) Easy or NP-hard?

10. Preemptive Scheduling Subject to Precedence Constraints

In the previous section we discussed problems involving the *nonpreemptive* scheduling of *unit-time* jobs. There has been a parallel investigation of problems concerning *preemptive* scheduling of jobs of *arbitrary length*. Interesting, there is a preemptive counterparts for virtually all of the unit-time scheduling algorithms. In particular, in (Gonzalez & Johnson, 1980), a preemptive algorithm is given which is analogous to that of (Davida & Linton, 1976). In (Lawler, 1982A) algorithms are proposed that are the preemptive counterparts of those found in (Brucker, et al, 1977) and (Garey & Johnson, 1976, 1977). These preemptive scheduling algorithms employ essentially the same techniques for dealing with precedence constraints as the corresponding algorithms for unit-time jobs. However, they are considerably more complex, and we shall not deal with them here.

IV. Open Shops and Unrelated Parallel Machines

1. Introduction

Problems involving unrelated parallel machines have been solved primarily by linear programming techniques, the validity of which depends on results from the theory of open shops. Moreover, it turns out that it is possible to solve scheduling problems for models that generalize both open shops and unrelated parallel machine shops (Lawler, Luby & Vazirani, 1982). Accordingly, we shall consider these two types of shops together.

2. Open Shops

In an *open shop* there are n jobs, to be scheduled for processing by m machines. Each machine is to work on job j for a total *processing time* p_{ij}. A machine can work on only one job at a time and a job can be worked on by only one machine at a time. There is no restriction on the order in which a given job can be worked on by the different machines or on the order in which a machine can work on different jobs. (Hence the term "open shop".)

We let the letter "O" denote an open shop. It is easily established that $O\|C_{max}$ is NP-hard. However, the two-machine problem, $O2\|C_{max}$, can be solved in $O(n)$ time. Moreover, it can be established that there is no advantage to preemption in the two-machine case, so the linear time algorithm of (Gonzalez & Sahni, 1978) for $O2\|C_{max}$ solves $O2\|pmtn\|C_{max}$ as well.

We shall now describe the algorithm of (Gonzalez & Sahni, 1978) for $O|pmtn|C_{max}$. The description is adapted from (Lawler & Labetoulle, 1978).

As noted, an instance of the $O|pmtn|C_{max}$ problem is defined by an $m \times n$ matrix $P = (p_{ij})$. It is evident that a lower bound on the length of a feasible schedule is given by

$$C_{max} = \max\left\{ \max_i \left\{ \sum_j p_{ij} \right\},\ \max_j \left\{ \sum_i p_{ij} \right\} \right\}. \tag{5}$$

We shall show how to construct a feasible schedule with this value of C_{max}. Since no schedule can be shorter, the constructed schedule will clearly be optimal.

Let us call row i (column j) of matrix P tight if $\sum_j p_{ij} = C_{max}$ $\left(\sum_i p_{ij} = C_{max} \right)$, and slack otherwise. Suppose we are able to find a subset of strictly positive elements of P, with exactly one element of the subset in each tight row and in each tight column and no more than one element in any slack row or column. We shall call such a subset a *decrementing set*, and use it to construct a *partial schedule* of length δ, for some suitably chosen $\delta > 0$. In this partial schedule processor i works on job j for $\min\{p_{ij}, \delta\}$ units of time, for each element p_{ij} in the decrementing set. We then replace p_{ij} by $\max\{0, p_{ij} - \delta\}$, for each element in the decrementing set, thereby obtaining a new matrix P', for which $C'_{max} = C_{max} - \delta$ satisfies condition (5).

For example, suppose $C_{max} = 11$ and

$$P = \begin{pmatrix} 3 & ④ & 0 & 4 \\ ④ & 0 & 6 & 0 \\ 4 & 0 & 0 & ⑥ \end{pmatrix} \begin{matrix} 11 \\ 10 \\ 10 \end{matrix},$$
$$\begin{matrix} 11 & 4 & 6 & 10 \end{matrix}$$

with row and column sums as indicated on the margins of the matrix. One possible decrementing set is indicated by the encircled elements. Choosing $\delta = 4$, we obtain $C'_{max} = 7$ and P' as shown below, with the partial schedule indicated to the right:

$$P' = \begin{pmatrix} ③ & 0 & 0 & 4 \\ 0 & 0 & ⑥ & 0 \\ 4 & 0 & 0 & ② \end{pmatrix} \begin{matrix} 7 \\ 6 \\ 6 \end{matrix} \quad \begin{array}{|c|} \hline 2 \\ \hline 1 \\ \hline 4 \\ \hline \end{array}$$
$$\begin{matrix} 7 & 0 & 6 & 6 \end{matrix} \qquad\qquad 4$$

A decrementing set of P' is indicated by the encircled elements.

There are various constraints that must be satisfied by δ, in order for $C'_{\max} = C_{\max} - \delta$ to satisfy condition (5) with respect to P'. First, if p_{ii} is an element of the decrementing set in a tight row or column, then clearly it is necessary that $\delta \leqslant p_{ii}$, else there will be a row or column sum of P which is strictly greater than $C_{\max} - \delta$. Similarly, if p_{ij} is an element of the decrementing set in a slack row (slack column), then it is necessary that

$$\delta \leqslant p_{ij} + C_{\max} - \sum_k p_{ik} \quad \left(\delta \leqslant p_{ij} + C_{\max} - \sum_k p_{kj}\right).$$

And if row i (column j) contains no element of the decrementing set (and is therefore necessarily slack), it is necessary that

$$\delta \leqslant C_{\max} - \sum_j p_{ij} \quad \left(\delta \leqslant C_{\max} - \sum_i p_{ij}\right).$$

Thus for the example above we have

$$\delta \leqslant p_{12} = 4, \quad \delta \leqslant p_{21} = 4,$$
$$\delta \leqslant p_{34} + C_{\max} - \sum_k p_{3k} = 7, \quad \delta \leqslant t_{34} + C_{\max} - \sum_k p_{k4} = 7$$
$$\delta \leqslant C_{\max} - \sum_k p_{k3} = 5.$$

Suppose δ is chosen to be maximum, subject to conditions indicated above. Then either P' will contain at least one less strictly positive element than P or else P' will contain at least one more tight column or tight row (with respect to $C'_{\max}$) than P. It is thus apparent that no more than $r + m + n$ iterations, where r is the number of strictly positive elements in P, are necessary to construct a feasible schedule of length $C_{\max}$.

To illustrate this point, we continue with the example. Choosing $\delta = 3$, we obtain from P' the matrix P', with the augmented partial schedule shown to the right:

$$P'' = \begin{pmatrix} 0 & 0 & 0 & ④ \\ 0 & 0 & ③ & 0 \\ ④ & 0 & 0 & 0 \end{pmatrix} \begin{matrix} 4 \\ 3 \\ 4 \end{matrix}$$

2	1	
1	3	
4	4	0

4 0 3 4   4 6 7

(The symbol "ϕ" indicates idle time.) The final decrementing set yields the following complete schedule:

2	1	4	
1	3	3	0
4	4	0	1

4   6   7   10   11

To complete our proof, we need the following lemma.

Lemma 7. For any nonnegative matrix P and $C_{\max}$ satisfying condition (5), there exists a decrementing set.

Proof: From the $m \times n$ matrix P construct an $(m+n) \times (m+n)$ matrix U, as indicated below:

$$U = \left(\begin{array}{c|c} P & D_m \\ \hline D_n & P' \end{array} \right)$$

Here P' denote the transpose of P, D_m and D_n are $m \times m$ and $n \times n$ diagonal matrices of nonnegative "slacks", determined in such a way that each row sum and column sum of U is equal to C_{max}. It follows that $(1/C_{max})\, U$ is a doubly stochastic matrix. The well-known Birkhoff-von Neumann theorem states that a doubly stochastic matrix is a convex combination of permutation matrices. It is easily verified that any one of the permutation matrices in such a convex combination is identified with a decrementing set of P. $\square$

There are several possible ways to construct a decrementing set. For our purposes, it is sufficient to note that one can construct the matrix U from P and then solve an assignment problem over U, which can be done in polynomial time. This observation, together with the observation that no more than a polynomial number of such assignment problems need be solved, is sufficient to establish a polynomial bound for the schedule construction procedure. In (Gonzalez & Sahni, 1976) time bounds of $O(r^2)$ and $O(r(\min\{r, m^2\} + m \log n))$, are obtained, where r is the number of strictly positive elements in P.

3. Preemptive Scheduling of Unrelated Parallel Machines

Let us now consider $R|pmtn|C_{max}$, the problem of finding a minimum-length preemptive schedule for unrelated parallel machines. Let p_{ij} denote the total amount of time that machine i is to work on machine j. We assume that the processing requirements have been normalized so that for each job j we must have $\sum_i s_{ij} p_{ij} = 1$. It is evident that the values of C_{max} and p_{ij} for any feasible schedule must constitute a feasible solution to the following linear programming problem (Lawler & Labetoulle, 1978):

$$\text{minimize } C_{max}$$
$$\text{subject to}$$
$$\sum_i s_{ij} p_{ij} = 1 \qquad j = 1, \ldots, n$$
$$\sum_i p_{ij} \leq C_{max} \qquad j = 1, \ldots, n$$
$$\sum_j p_{ij} \leq C_{max} \qquad i = 1, \ldots, m$$
$$p_{ij} \geq 0.$$

It follows from the results of the previous section that the converse is also true: For any feasible solution to this linear programming problem there is a feasible preemptive schedule with the same values of p_{ij} and C_{max}. Moreover, such a schedule can be constructed in polynomial time.

Because of the existence of the ellipsoid method for linear programming, the linear programming formulation of $R|pmtn|C_{max}$ can be regarded yielding a polynomial-bounded algorithm for the problem. In the case of two machines, $R2|pmtn|C_{max}$, the linear programming problem can be solved in $O(n)$ time by special techniques (Gonzalez, et al, 1982).

It is a fairly straightforward matter to formulate a linear programming problem for $R|pmtn|L_{max}$ and $R|r_j, pmtn|C_{max}$. Moreover, $R|r_j, pmtn|L_{max}$ can be solved as a series of linear programming problems.

Open Problem: An upper bound of $4m^2 - 5m + 2$ on the number of preemptions required for an optimal schedule for $R|pmtn|C_{max}$ is established in (Lawler & Labetoulle, 1978). However, this upper bound is certainly not tight. It is known that no more than two preemptions are required for the case $m = 2$ (Gonzalez, et al, 1981), and no example is known to require more than $2(m-1)$ preemptions. What is a tight upper bound?

4. Minimizing the Sum of Completion Times

The problem $R||\Sigma C_j$ is solved by the technique of (Bruno & Coffman, 1976). Note that if jobs $1, \ldots, k$ are performed by machine i in that order, we have for the sum of the completion times of the jobs performed on that machine,

$$\Sigma C_j = \frac{k}{s_{i1}} + \frac{(k-1)}{s_{i2}} + \ldots + \frac{2}{s_{i,k-1}} + \frac{1}{s_{ik}}.$$

In other words, if job j is the last job performed on machine i, its contribution to the objective function is $\frac{1}{s_{ij}}$, if j is the second-to-last job on machine i, its contribution $\frac{2}{s_{ij}}$, and so forth. A little reflection shows that we can formulate the problem $R||\Sigma C_j$ as follows.

Let $S' = \left(\frac{1}{s_{ij}}\right)$ and let S'' be the matrix obtained by stacking multiples of S', as shown in Figure 7. A solution to the problem is obtained by finding a subset of elements of S'' of minimum total value, subject to the conditions that at least one element is chosen from each column of S'' (each job is performed by some machine) and at most one element is chosen from each row (no two jobs are

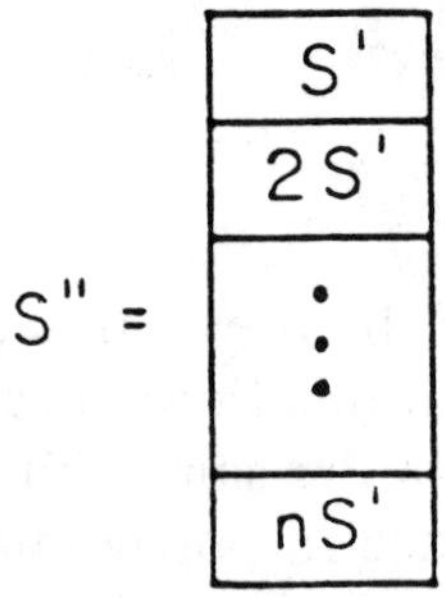

Fig. 7. Matrix S''

176

performed in the same position on a given machine). In other words, the problem reduces to a simple transportation problem.

Curiously, no good algorithm is known for $R|pmtn|\Sigma C_i$. If a "birdie" were to tell us the order in which jobs are to be completed in an optimal schedule, we could easily formulate and solve a linear programming problem to find such an optimal schedule. But this observation is not much help.

Open Question: What is the status of $R|pmtn|\Sigma C_j$? Easy of NP-hard? (If this problem is NP-hard, it will be the first such problem known to the author in which the nonpreemptive version is easy.)

V. Flow Shops and Job Shops

1. Introduction

Flow shops and *job shops* are much like open shops, except that for each job there is a prescribed order in which the job must be processed by the m machines. In a flow shop this order is the same for all jobs, i.e. each job must first be processed by machine 1, then machine 2, ... and finally by machine m. In a job shop, the prescribed order may differ from job to job. (Quite commonly, job shops are defined in terms of "operations" which must be performed on a given job in a prescribed order, and two or more operations may be performed by the same machine. However, we are not concerned with this distinction here.)

We shall not have much to say about flow shops or job shops in this survey paper, because nearly all flow shops and job shop problems are NP-hard. Essentially the only known polynomial algorithms are for special cases of the two-machine flow shop problem. Moreover, empirical work has shown that flow shop and job shop problems, other than these special cases, are extremely difficult to solve.

2. The Two-Machine Flow Shop

One of the most significant pioneering works of scheduling theory is (Johnson, 1954), in which an $O(n \log n)$ procedure was given for minimizing makespan in the two-machine flow shop. Johnson's results have been extended to encompass "time-lags" (Mitten, 1958), and series parallel precedence constraints (Sidney, 1979).

3. The "No-Wait" Two-Machine Flow Shop

The "no wait" flow shop is one in which each job must start its processing on machine $i+1$ the instant its processing is completed on machine i. Interestingly, the two-machine "no wait" problem is actually a special case of the traveling salesman problem that can be solved efficiently (Reddi & Ramamoorthy, 1972; Gilmore & Gomory, 1964).

4. The General Job Shop Problem

The general job shop problem is one of the most computationally intractable combinatorial problems existing. One indication of this is given by the fact that a certain 10-job, 10-machine problem formulated in 1963 (Muth & Thompson, 1963) still has not been solved, despite the efforts of many investigators. This challenge for future research perhaps provides us with an appropriate note on which to end this survey.

References

D. L. Adolphson, "Single Machine Job Scheduling With Precedence Constraints", *SIAM J. Comput.*, 6 (1977) 40-54.

D. L. Adolphson, T. C. Hu, "Optimal Linear Ordering", *SIAM J. Appl. Math.*, 25 (1973) 403-423.

H. M. Abdel-Wahab, T. Kameda, "Scheduling to Minimize Maximum Cumulative Cost Subject to Series Parallel Precedence Constraints", *Operations Res.*, 26 (1978) 141-158.

K. R. Baker, *Introduction to Sequencing and Scheduling*, Wiley, New York, 1974.

K. R. Baker, L. E. Schrage, "Finding an Optimal Sequence by Dynamic Programming: An Extension to Precedence-Constrained Tasks", *Operations Res.*, 26 (1978) 111-120.

K. R. Baker, E. L. Lawler, J. K. Lenstra, A. H. G. Rinnooy Kan, "Preemptive Scheduling of a Single Machine to Minimize Maximum Cost Subject to Release Dates and Precedence Constraints", (1982) to appear in *Operations Res.*

P. Brucker, M. R. Garey, D. S. Johnson, "Scheduling Equal-Length Tasks under Tree-Like Precedence Constraints to Minimize Maximum Lateness", *Math. Operations Res.*, 2 (1977) 275-284.

E. G. Coffman, Jr., R. L. Graham, "Optimal Scheduling for Two-Processor Systems", *Acta Informat.*, 1 (1972) 200-213.

R. W. Conway, W. L. Maxwell, L. W. Miller, *Theory of Scheduling*, Addison-Wesley, Reading, Mass. 1967.

G. I. Davida, D. J. Linton, "A New Algorithm for the Scheduling of Tree Structured Tasks", *Proc. Conf. Inform. Sci. and Systems*, Baltimore, MD., 1976.

D. Dolev, "Scheduling Wide Graphs", (1981), unpublished manuscript.

H. Emmons, "One-Machine Sequencing to Minimize Certain Functions of Job Tardiness", *Operations Res.*, 17 (1969) 701-715.

M. L. Fisher, "A Dual Algorithm for the One-Machine Scheduling Problem", *Math. Programming*, 11 (1976) 229-251.

M. L. Fisher, B. J. Lageweg, J. K. Lenstra, A. H. G. Rinnooy Kan, "Surrogate Duality Relaxation for Job Shop Scheduling", Report, *Mathematisch Centrum*, Amsterdam, 1981.

M. Fujii, T. Kasami, K. Ninomiya, "Optimal Sequencing of Two Equivalent Processors", *SIAM J. Appl. Math.*, 17 (1969) 784–789; *Erratum*, 20 (1971) 141.

H. N. Gabow, "An Almost-Linear Algorithm for Two-Processor Scheduling", *J. Assoc. Comput. Mach.*, 29 (1982 A) 766–780.

H. N. Gabow, private communication, 1982 B.

M. R. Garey, "Optimal Task Sequencing with Precedence Constraints", *Discrete Math.*, 4 (1973) 37–56.

M. R. Garey, D. S. Johnson, "Scheduling Tasks with Nonuniform Deadlines on Two Processors", *J. Assoc. Comput. Mach.*, 23 (1976) 461–467.

M. R. Garey, D. S. Johnson, "Two-Processor Scheduling with Start-Times and Deadlines", *SIAM J. Comput.*, 6 (1977) 416–426.

M. R. Garey, D. S. Johnson, R. E. Tarjan, M. Yannakakis, "Scheduling Opposing Forests", unpublished manuscript, (1981).

P. C. Gilmore, R. E. Gomory, "Sequencing a One-State Variable Machine: A Solvable Case of the Traveling Salesman Problem", *Oper. Res.*, 12 (1964) 655–679.

T. Gonzalez, "Optimal Mean Finish Time Preemptive Schedules", Technical Report 220, (1977) Computer Science Department, Pennsylvania State University.

T. Gonzalez, "A Note on Open Shop Preemptive Schedules", *IEEE Trans. Computers.* C-28 (1979) 782–786.

T. Gonzalez, D. B. Johnson, "A New Algorithm for Preemptive Scheduling of Trees", *J. Assoc. Comput. Mach.*, 27 (1980) 287–312.

T. Gonzalez, E. L. Lawler, S Sahni, "Optimal Preemptive Scheduling of Two Unrelated Processors in Linear Time", (1981), to appear.

T. Gonzalez, S. Sahni, "Open Shop Scheduling to Minimize Finish Time", *J. Assoc. Comput. Mach.*, 23 (1976) 665–679.

T. Gonzalez, S. Sahni, "Preemptive Scheduling of Uniform Processor Systems", *J. Assoc. Comput. Mach.*, 25 (1978) 92–101.

R. L. Graham, E. L. Lawler, J. K. Lenstra, A. H. G. Rinnooy Kan, "Optimization and Approximation in Deterministic Sequencing and Scheduling : A Survey", *Ann. Discrete Math.*, 5 (1979) 287–326.

M. Held, R. M. Karp, "A Dynamic Programming Approach to Sequencing Problems", *SIAM J. Appl. Math.*, 10 (1972) 196–210.

W. A. Horn, "Single-Machine Job Sequencing with Treelike Precedence Ordering and Linear Dealy Penalties", *SIAM J. Appl. Math.*, 23 (1972) 189–202.

W. A. Horn, "Minimizing Average Flow Time with Parallel Machines", *Oper. Res.*, 21 (1973) 846–847.

W. A. Horn, "Some Simple Scheduling Algorithms", *Naval Res. Logist. Quart.*, 21 (1974) 177–185.

E. Horowitz, S. Sahni, "Exact and Approximate Algorithms for Scheduling Nonidentical Processors", *J. Assoc. Comput. Mach.*, 23 (1976) 317–327.

T. C. Hu, "Parallel Sequencing and Assembly Line Problems", *Oper. Res.*, 9 (1961) 841–848.

J. R. Jackson, "Scheduling a Production Line to Minimize Maximum Tardiness", Research Report 43, (1955) Management Science Research Project, University of California, Los Angeles.

J. R. Jackson, "An Extension of Johnson's Results on Job Lot Scheduling", *Naval Res. Logist. Quart.*, 3 (1956) 201–203.

S. M. Johnson, "Optimal Two- and Three-Stage Production Schedules with Setup Times Included", *Naval Res. Logist. Quart.*, 1 (1954) 61–68.

S. M. Johnson, "Discussion: Sequencing *n* Jobs on Two Machines with Arbitrary Time Lags", *Management Sci.*, 5 (1958) 299–303.

E. P. C. Kao, M. Queyranne, "On Dynamic Programming Methods for Assembly Line Balancing", working paper, Dept Quantitative Management Sci., University of Houston, Texas, (1980).

H. Kise, T. Ibaraki, H. Mine, "A Solvable Case of the One-Machine Scheduling Problem with Ready and Due Times", *Oper. Res.*, 26 (1978) 121–126.

J. Labetoulle, E. L. Lawler, J. K. Lenstra, A. H. G. Rinnooy Kan, "Preemptive Scheduling of Uniform Machines Subject to Release Dates", Report BW 99, (1979) Mathematisch Centrum, Amsterdam.

B. J. Lageweg, E. L. Lawler, J. K. Lenstra, A. H. G. Rinnooy Kan, "Computer Aided Complexity Classification of Deterministic Scheduling Problems", Report BW 138, (1981) Mathematisch Centrum, Amsterdam.

E. L. Lawler, "On Scheduling Problems with Deferral Costs", *Management Science*, 11 (1964) 270–288.

E. L. Lawler, "Optimal Sequencing of a Single Machine Subject to Precedence Constraints", *Management Sci.*, 19 (1973) 544–546.

E. L. Lawler, "Sequencing to Minimize the Weighted Number of Tardy Jobs", *RAIRO Rech. Oper.*, 10 suppl. (1976) 27–33.

E. L. Lawler, "A 'Pseudopolynomial' Algorithm for Sequencing Jobs to Minimize Total Tardiness", *Ann. Discrete Math.*, 1 (1977) 331–342.

E. L. Lawler, "Sequencing Jobs to Minimize Total Weighted Completion Time Subject to Precedence Constraints", *Ann. Discrete Math.*, 2 (1978 A) 75–90.

E. L. Lawler, "Sequencing Problems With Series Parallel Precedence Constraints", to appear in *Proc. Confer. on Combinatorial Optimization*, (N. Christofides, ed.), Urbino, Italy, 1978 B.

E. L. Lawler, "Efficient Implementation of Dynamic Programming Algorithms for Sequencing Problems", Report BW 106/79, (1979 A) Mathematisch Centrum, Amsterdam.

E. L. Lawler, "Preemptive Scheduling of Uniform Parallel Machines to Minimize the number of Late Jobs", Report BW 105, (1979 B) Mathematisch Centrum, Amsterdam.

E. L. Lawler, "Preemptive Scheduling of Precedence-Constrained Jobs on Parallel Machines", in *Deterministic and Stochastic Scheduling*, (M. A. H. Dempster, et al., eds.), D. Reidel, Dordrecht, Holland, 1982 A, pp. 101–124.

E. L. Lawler, "A Fully Polynomial Approximation Scheme for the Total Tardiness Problems", (1982 B), submitted for publication.

E. L. Lawler, "On Scheduling a Single Machine to Minimize the Number of Late Jobs", (1982 C), submitted for publication.

E. L. Lawler, J. Labetoulle, "On Preemptive Scheduling of Unrelated Parallel Processors by Linear Programming", *J. Assoc. Comput. Mach.*, 25 (1978) 612–619.

E. L. Lawler, J. K. Lenstra, A. H. G. Rinnooy Kan, "Minimizing Maximum Lateness in a Two-Machine Open Shop, *Math. Oper. Res.*, 6 (1981) 153–158.

E. L. Lawler, C. U. Martel, "Scheduling Periodically Occurring Tasks on Multiple Processors", *Info. Proc. Letters*, 12 (1981) 9–12.

E. L. Lawler, C. U. Martel, "Computing 'Polymatroidal' Network Flows", *Math. of Operations Res.*, 7 (1982 A) 334–347.

E. L. Lawler, C. U. Martel, "Flow Network Formulations of Polymatroid Optimization Problems", *Annals Discrete Math.*, 16 (1982 B) 189–200.

E. L. Lawler, J. K. Lenstra, "Machine Scheduling with Precedence Constraints", in *Ordered Sets*, (I. Rival, ed.), D. Reidel, Dordrecht, Holland, 1982, pp. 655–675.

E. L. Lawler, J. K. Lenstra, A. H. G. Rinnooy Kan, "Recent Developments in Deterministic Sequencing and Scheduling: A Survey", in *Deterministic Sequencing and Sched-*

uling. (M. A. H. Dempster, et al., eds.), D. Reidel Co., Dordrecht, Holland, 1982 A, pp. 35–74.

E. L. Lawler, J. K. Lenstra, A. H. G. Rinnooy Kan, "A Gift for Alexander!: At Play in the Fields of Scheduling Theory", *OPTIMA*, Mathematical Programming Society Newsletter, No. 7, (1982 B).

E. L. Lawler, M. G. Luby, V. V. Vazirani, "Scheduling Open Shops with Parallel Machines", (1982), to appear in *Operations Res. Letters*.

E. L. Lawler, J. M. Moore, "A Functional Equation and Its Application to Resource Allocation and Sequencing Problems", *Management Sci.*, 16 (1969) 77–84.

E. L. Lawler, B. D. Sivazlian, "Minimization of Time Varying Costs in Single Machine Scheduling", *Operations Res.*, 26 (1978) 563–569.

J. K. Lenstra, *Sequencing by Enumerative Methods*, Mathematical Centre Tracts 69, Mathematisch Centrum, Amsterdam, 1977.

J. K. Lenstra, A. H. G. Rinnooy Kan, "Complexity of Scheduling under Precedence Constraints", *Operations Res.*, 26 (1978) 22–35.

C. Martel, "Scheduling Uniform Machines With Release Times, Deadlines and Due Times", *J. Assoc. Comput. Mach.*, (1981), to appear.

R. McNaughton, "Scheduling With Deadlines and Loss Functions", *Management Sci.*, 6 (1959) 1–12.

L. G. Mitten, "Sequencing n Jobs On Two Machines With Arbitrary Time Lags", *Management Sci.*, 5 (1958) 293–298.

C. L. Monma, A. H. G. Rinnooy Kan, "Efficiently Solvable Special Cases of the Permutation Flow-Shop Problem", Report 8105, (1981) Erasmus University, Rotterdam.

C. L. Monma, J. B. Sidney, "Sequencing With Series-Parallel Precedence Constraints", *Math. Oper. Res.*, 4 (1979) 215–224.

J. M. Moore, "An n Job, One Machine Sequencing Algorithm for Minimizing the Number of Late Jobs", *Management Sci.*, 15 (1968) 102–109.

J. F. Muth, G. L. Thompson, eds., *Industrial Scheduling*, Prentice Hall, Englewood Cliffs, N. J., 1963, p. 236.

S. S. Reddi, C. V. Ramamoorthy, "On the Flow-Shop Sequencing Problem With No Wait in Process", *Oper. Res. Quart.*, 23 (1972) 323–331.

M. H. Rothkopf, "Scheduling Independent Tasks on Parallel Processors", *Management Sci.*, 12 (1966) 437–447.

S. Sahni, Y. Cho, "Nearly On Line Scheduling of a Uniform Processor System With Release Times", *SIAM J. Comput.*, 8 (1979) 275–285.

S. Sahni, Y. Cho, "Scheduling Independent Tasks With Due Times on a Uniform Processor System", *J. Assoc. Comput. Mach.*, 27 (1980) 550–563.

J. B. Sidney, "An Extension of Moore's Due Date Algorithm", in *Symposium on the Theory of Scheduling and Its Applications*, Lecture Notes in Economics and Mathematical Systems 86, (S. E. Elmaghraby, ed.), Springer, Berlin, 1973, pp. 393–398.

J. B. Sidney, "Decomposition Algorithms for Single-Machine Sequencing With Precedence Relations and Deferral Costs", *Oper. Res.*, 23 (1975) 283–298.

J. B. Sidney, "The Two-Machine Maximum Flow Time Problem With Series Parallel Precedence Relations", *Oper. Res.*, 27 (1979) 782–791.

B. Simons, "A Fast Algorithm for Single Processor Scheduling", *Proc. 19th Annual IEEE Symp. Foundations of Computer Science*, (1978) 50–53.

W. E. Smith, "Various Optimizers for Single-Stage Production", *Naval Res. Logist. Quart.*, 3 (1956) 59–66.

J. D. Ullman, "NP-Complete Scheduling Problems", *J. Comput. System Sci.*, 10 (1975) 384–393.

J. Valdes, R. E. Tarjan, E. L. Lawler, "The Recognition of Series Parallel Digraphs", *SIAM J. Computing*, 11 (1982) 298–313.

M. K. Warmuth, "M Processor Unit-Execution-Time Scheduling Reduces to M-1 Weakly Connected Components", M. S. Thesis, (1980) Department of Computer Science, University of Colorado, Boulder.

G. Weiss, M. Pinedo, "Scheduling Tasks with Exponential Service Times on Non Identical Processors to Minimize Various Functions", *J. Appl. Probab.*, 17 (1980) 187–202.

Task Allocation and Precedence Relations for Distributed Real-Time Systems

WESLEY W. CHU, FELLOW, IEEE, AND LANCE M-T. LAN, MEMBER, IEEE

Abstract—In a distributed processing system with the application software partitioned into a set of program modules, allocation of those modules to the processors is an important problem. This paper presents a method for optimal module allocation that satisfies certain performance constraints. An objective function that includes the intermodule communication (IMC) and accumulative execution time (AET) of each module is proposed. It minimizes the bottleneck-processor utilization—a good principle for task allocation. Next, the effects of precedence relationship (PR) among program modules on response time are studied. Both simulation and analytical results reveal that the program-size ratio between two consecutive modules plays an important role in task response time. Finally, an algorithm based on PR, AET, and IMC and on the proposed objective function is presented. This algorithm generates better module assignments than those that do not consider the PR effects.

Index Terms—Distributed processing, intermodule communication (IMC), interprocessor communication (IPC), minimum bottleneck, module assignment, parallel processing, precedence relationship (PR), real-time systems, response time, task allocation algorithms.

I. Introduction

ALTHOUGH computer speed has been increased by several orders of magnitude in recent decades, the demand for computing capacity increases at an even faster pace. The required processing power for many real-time applications cannot be achieved with a single processor. One approach to this problem is to use distributed data processing (DDP) that concurrently processes an application program on multiple processors. If properly designed and planned, DDP provides a more economical and reliable approach than that of centralized processing systems.

Task partitioning and task allocation are two major steps in the design of DDP systems. If these steps are not done properly, an increase in the number of processors in a system may actually result in a decrease of the total throughput [5]. Assuming the software for an application (a *task*) has been partitioned into a set of program *modules* (or subroutines), in this paper we study how to optimally allocate these modules to the set of processors in the DDP system.

Manuscript received September 10, 1985; revised August 11, 1986. This work was supported by the Ballistic Missile Defense Advanced Technology Center under Contracts DASG60-79-C-0087 and DASG60-83-C-0019.

W. W. Chu is with the Department of Computer Science, University of California, Los Angeles, CA 90024.

L. M-T. Lan was with the Department of Computer Science, University of California, Los Angeles, CA 90024. He is now with the Cellular Telecommunications Laboratory, AT&T Bell Laboratories, Whippany, NJ 07981.

IEEE Log Number 8713985.

First, we shall present two important parameters for task allocation: intermodule communication (IMC) and accumulative execution time (AET) of each module. The load of a processor consists of AET and IMC. We propose an objective function for task allocation that is based on minimizing the load on the most heavily loaded processor ("bottleneck"). The precedence relation (PR) among program modules, that specifies the execution sequence of the modules, is another parameter that affects module assignment. It is studied analytically and experimentally. A series of experiments are presented which reveal that the *program-size ratio* between two consecutive modules plays an important role in determining whether two modules should be colocated. An analytical model is developed that enables us to decide whether to assign consecutive modules to the same processor. Finally, a heuristic algorithm is developed that considers PR, IMC, and AET to search for the minimum-bottleneck assignment. Examples are given to illustrate the performance of the algorithm and also the improvement that may be obtained when considering PR in task allocation.

II. A New Objective Function for Task Allocation

In this section we shall first describe the two important parameters, AET and IMC, for task allocation. An objective function based on these parameters that minimizes system bottleneck is proposed. Then, we present the behavior of the proposed objective function.

A. IMC and AET

The AET for module M_j during time interval (t_h, t_{h+1}) is the total execution time incurred for this module during that time interval, i.e.,

$$T_j(t_h, t_{h+1}) = N_j(t_h, t_{h+1}) y_j(t_h, t_{h+1})$$

where $N_j(t_h, t_{h+1})$ = number of times module M_j executes during (t_h, t_{h+1}), and $y_j(t_h, t_{h+1})$ = average execution time of M_j during (t_h, t_{h+1}). Both the y_j and the AET T_j can be expressed in units of machine language instructions (MLI). Although the execution time of a machine language instruction varies from one instruction to another, based on a given instruction mix we can use the *mean* instruction execution time. Our study reveals that both the number of module executions and the AET are almost independent of module assignments when the load offered to the system is fixed. For example, the AET's produced by five different assignments for a module in a space-defense application, the Distributed

Reprinted from *IEEE Transactions on Computers*, Vol. C-36, No. 6, June 1987, pp. 667-679. Copyright © 1987 by The Institute of Electrical and Electronic Engineers, Inc. All rights reserved.

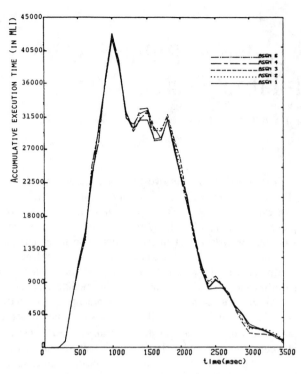

Fig. 1. Accumulative execution time of module M_8, $T_8(t, t + 100$ ms$)$.

Processing Architecture Design (DPAD) system, are almost identical (Fig. 1).

IMC is the communication between program modules and file modules. When a module on a processor writes to or reads from a shared file on *another* processor, such IMC incurs IPC (interprocessor communication) and requires processing overhead. *Control IMC* is another type of IMC. As discussed in [8], it can be treated in the same way as the file-access IMC when we consider the *control files*, as opposed to the application files. The importance of IPC minimization has been recognized by many researchers [5], [14]. IPC can be reduced by assigning a pair of heavily communicating modules to the same processor. Like AET, the IMC can also be assumed to be independent of module assignments [16]. A method for estimating both IMC and AET has been reported in [8].

IPC occurs only when two communicating modules are assigned to different processors. If two modules reside on different processors and communicate through a *replicated* shared file, then the file is assumed to be replicated on each processor. When a module updates the file, it updates the copy on its local processor and sends the updates to the remote processor. This results in IPC, which requires processing load on both the sending and receiving processors. Even if the actual transfer of the update words is done in the background by some I/O processors, the sending processor still needs to spend time on message formatting and address initialization for the I/O processor. The receiving processor, on the other end, will spend time on extracting the message contents and notifying the destination module. Such IPC overhead is eliminated if the two modules are assigned to the same processor since both modules would share the same local file

copy. Module assignments also effect IPC for other file structures such as partitioned files or single-copy files.

B. The Objective Function

Assuming each module is assigned to one and only one processor, then there are S^J different ways to assign J modules to S processors. This can be represented by an assignment tree. This tree has J levels, each representing a module. At each nonleaf node there are S downward branches, each representing the choice of a processor to host the particular module. Therefore, the tree has S^J leaves, each leaf corresponding to a possible assignment.

An *exhaustive search* approach for module assignment is to search every *leaf* of the assignment tree. The optimal module assignment is the one that minimizes (or maximizes, e.g., throughput) a given objective function. Exhaustive search is usually undesirable because of the prohibitive time requirement. For example, if the computation time for a leaf is 250 μs on a computer system, then the enumeration for a tree with 3^{20} leaves requires about 10 days of processing time.

Existing approaches to task allocation can be divided into three categories: graph-theoretic [15], [20], [2], [3], integer 0-1 programming approach [4], [6], [18], and the heuristic approach [13], [10]. Many of these methods try to minimize a task's total cost which is defined as the sum, over all processors, of both the processing cost (i.e., AET) and the IPC cost of that task. This might be acceptable for a distributed system *shared* by multiple simultaneous nonreal-time applications (tasks), each having program modules running on some or all of the multiple processors. Such applications attempt to maximize the total throughput. For a distributed system with identical processors, this formulation is equivalent to the minimization of IPC since the total AET is fixed.

For real-time systems, *response time* is the most important performance measure. A computer system is designated solely for a specific application, i.e., the system is *not* shared by any other application. The system is required to finish a certain task within a specified time limit. Minimizing IPC alone may not produce a good assignment. In fact, in a homogeneous system where all processors are identical, a minimum-IPC assignment will assign all program modules to a single processor (thus, zero IPC) which will saturate that processor and thus yield poor response time.

The processor with the heaviest loading in a distributed system is the one that causes the *bottleneck*. For instance, for a system with three processors, an assignment resulting in 58, 60, and 61 percent of processor utilizations might have a better response time than another assignment yielding 20, 40, and 90 percent utilizations, although the total processor utilization of the first assignment is higher than the second. This is mainly due to the fact that the second assignment has a *bottleneck processor* more heavily loaded than the first assignment, and queueing delay is a nonlinear function that rises rapidly with the level of bottleneck (processor load).

The *processor load* consists of the loads due to program module execution and IPC. Therefore, both AET and IPC play important roles in module assignment and influence task response time. AET is usually represented in machine language instruction (MLI). The number of transferred IPC words can be converted into the MLI's spent by both the processor that sends the IPC and the processor that receives it.

For a given assignment X, the workload $L(r; X)$ on a given processor r is

$$L(r; X) = \sum_{j=1}^{J} \chi_{jr} T_j + \sum_{\substack{s=1 \\ s \neq r}}^{S} [\text{IPC}(r, s; X) + \text{IPC}(s, r; X)]$$

$$= \text{AET}(r; X) + \text{IPC}(r; X) \qquad (1)$$

where $X = [x_{jr}]$ is the assignment matrix in which $x_{jr} = 1$ or 0 indicates whether module M_j is assigned to processor r. The first term in the equation is the AET for all modules assigned to processor r. The second term is IPC overhead due to both the IPC originated from processor r to other processors, and incoming IPC destined to processor r from other processors. For a system whose file-update messages dominate the IPC traffic, we can ignore other types of IPC such as module-enablement messages and system-control messages. The total overhead due to outgoing IPC at processor r is

$$\sum_{\substack{s=1 \\ s \neq r}}^{S} \text{IPC}(r, s; X) = \omega \sum_{j=1}^{J} \chi_{jr} \sum_{k=1}^{K} V_{jk} \sum_{\substack{s=1 \\ s \neq r}}^{S} \delta_{ks} \qquad (2)$$

where K is the number of files used in the distributed system; V_{jk} is the IMC message volume sent from M_j to update the replicated file F_k; δ_{ks} indicates whether a replicated copy of F_k resides at processor s; the term $\sum_{\substack{s=1 \\ s \neq r}}^{S} \delta_{ks}$ gives the number of remote copies of F_k that must be updated; and ω is a weighting constant for converting the message volume into MLI's. For a system with message-broadcasting capability, a file update need only be sent out *once*; thus, the term $\sum_{\substack{s=1 \\ s \neq r}}^{S} \delta_{ks}$ in (2) should be replaced by the constant *one*.

The AET, T_j, for a module M_j is represented as a single value in (1). Also, the IMC between a module and a file, V_{jk}, in (2) is represented as a single value. However, the measured T_j and V_{jk} vary from one time interval to another (e.g., see Fig. 1). Since we are concerned with system performance during the peak-load period, we shall use the *average* T_j and V_{jk} values during the peak-load period for the terms T_j and V_{jk} in (1) and (2) to compute our objective function.

Similar to (2), the total overhead at processor r for incoming IPC from all remote sites is

$$\sum_{\substack{s=1 \\ s \neq r}}^{S} \text{IPC}(s, r; X) = \omega \sum_{\substack{s=1 \\ s \neq r}}^{S} \sum_{j=1}^{J} \chi_{js} \sum_{k=1}^{K} V_{jk} \delta_{kr}. \qquad (3)$$

Based on the above discussion, we propose to use the *workload of the bottleneck processor* (in unit of MLI) as the objective function for module assignment, i.e.,

$$\text{Bottleneck}(X) = \max_{1 \leq r \leq S} \{L(r; X)\}. \qquad (4)$$

We want to find the assignment that yields the *minimum*

bottleneck [7] among all possible assignments in the assignment tree, i.e.,

$$\min_{X} \{\text{Bottleneck}(X)\}. \qquad (5)$$

Substituting (1) and (4) into (5) yields

$$\min_{X} \left\{ \max_{1 \leq r \leq S} [\text{AET}(r; X) + \text{IPC}(r; X)] \right\} \qquad (6)$$

where $\text{AET}(r; X)$ and $\text{IPC}(r; X)$ are the total module execution time and total IPC overhead incurred at processor r.

A good assignment can be obtained by reducing IPC while balancing processor loads among the set of processors. A minimum-bottleneck assignment generally has low IPC and fairly balanced processor loads because of the following.

1) If the given assignment resulted in a large volume of IPC, the sum of processor loads over all processors would be high, which would yield high bottleneck.

2) If the loads were not fairly balanced for an assignment, the bottleneck (highest load of all processors) would be high which would not yield a minimum-bottleneck assignment.

Our minimum-bottleneck approach, (6), is different from the commonly used measure of minimizing the *sum* of processor loads (e.g., [20]),

$$\min_{X} \left\{ \sum_{r=1}^{S} [\text{AET}(r; X) + \text{IPC}(r; X)] \right\}. \qquad (7)$$

An assignment obtained from (7) can be quite unbalanced. In a homogeneous system all modules will be assigned to a single processor as discussed before. Our minimax principle [7] is also used in [21] which considers only the *single execution* of a task, instead of using the processor load. Since each external stimulus causes a task execution in our formulation, the processing load is based on *multiple* executions of a task.

C. Behavior of the Proposed Objective Function

To illustrate the characteristics and performance of the proposed objective function, we apply the objective function to the Distributed Processing Architecture Design (DPAD) system. The DPAD system was developed to manage the data processing and radar resources for a space-defense application [11], [12], [18], [19]. The control-and-data-flow graph (similar to Fig. 12) consists of 23 modules which are to be assigned to three processors.

The average AET (T_j) and IMC (V_{jk}) during the peak-load period (from 1.0 to 2.0 s of mission time) for all modules of the DPAD system are calculated. For example, $T_8 = 32\,055$ MLI is the average of ten measured AET values for M_8 within the period at each increment of 100 ms.

A program was developed to compute the proposed objective function for *every* assignment (corresponding to a leaf of the assignment tree), performing an exhaustive search for the minimum-bottleneck assignment. When an assignment yields a bottleneck value lower than the smallest bottleneck obtained so far, that assignment is recorded. The last ten recorded assignments, denoted as assignment 1–10, are shown in Table I. The 23 digits under the "assignment" column represent the

TABLE I
TOP TEN ASSIGNMENTS FROM EXHAUSTIVE SEARCH

	ASSIGNMENT	LOAD-1	LOAD-2	LOAD-3	BOTTLENECK	TOTAL LOAD
10th	11111 11121 00330 12322 123	75612	75546	70420	75612	221579
9th	11111 11121 00330 12322 323	75323	75546	70709	75546	221579
8th	11112 11121 00330 13222 223	75413	75352	73643	75413	224408
7th	11112 12131 00220 13231 132	75178	74275	73829	75178	223282
6th	11112 12131 00220 13231 232	75013	74564	73829	75013	223406
5th	11112 32333 00220 33211 112	74414	74275	74023	74414	222712
4th	11112 32333 00220 33211 312	74249	74275	74312	74312	222836
3rd	12123 23212 00330 21322 113	74308	73873	74275	74308	222456
2nd	12123 23212 00330 21322 213	74019	74038	74275	74275	222332
MINIM. BOTTLE-NECK	12213 13121 00330 11322 223	74004	73805	74275	74275	222084

NOTE: 1. LOAD-i IS EACH PROCESSOR'S LOAD PER 100 MSEC (IN UNIT OF MLI).

2. AN ASSIGNMENT WITH THE MINIMUM TOTAL LOAD

IS NOT THE ASSIGNMENT WITH THE MINIMUM BOTTLENECK.

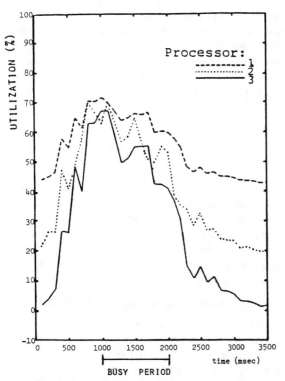

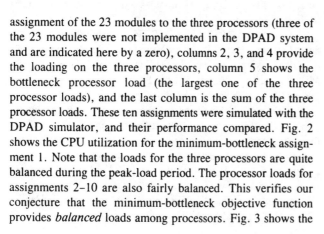

Fig. 2. Processor utilization for the best module assignment selected by exhaustive search.

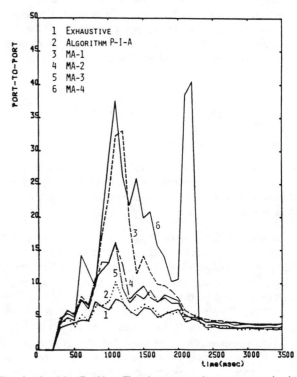

Fig. 3. Precision-Tracking Thread response times—compare the best assignment from exhaustive search, Algorithm P-I-A, and the four assignments from Ma *et al.* [18].

assignment of the 23 modules to the three processors (three of the 23 modules were not implemented in the DPAD system and are indicated here by a zero), columns 2, 3, and 4 provide the loading on the three processors, column 5 shows the bottleneck processor load (the largest one of the three processor loads), and the last column is the sum of the three processor loads. These ten assignments were simulated with the DPAD simulator, and their performance compared. Fig. 2 shows the CPU utilization for the minimum-bottleneck assignment 1. Note that the loads for the three processors are quite balanced during the peak-load period. The processor loads for assignments 2–10 are also fairly balanced. This verifies our conjecture that the minimum-bottleneck objective function provides *balanced* loads among processors. Fig. 3 shows the

Precision-Tracking *port-to-port time* (response time for a task thread) for assignment 1 (curve 1). The assignments MA-1–MA-4, reported in [18] for the DPAD system, minimize the sum of AET and IPC and, thus, do not generate balanced-load assignments as discussed in Section II-B. As a result, their response times (curves 3–6) are higher than that generated by our objective function. (Curve 2 will be discussed later.)

III. PRECEDENCE RELATIONSHIP AND MODULE ASSIGNMENT

The precedence relationship (PR) among program modules is another important factor that needs to be considered in task allocation. In this section we shall present several experiments to illustrate the effect of PR on response time. These experiments provide us with enough insight to formulate an analytical model to quantitatively study the PR effect on task allocation. The quantitative PR effect will be used in module grouping in our module-assignment algorithm.

A. PR Experiments

In experiment 1, we compare three assignments of a task, consisting of nine modules, to three processors. The control-flow graph [Fig. 4(a)] shows the strong PR relationship among the modules. Assume that the task arrival is a Poisson process with rate λ. When a module completes its execution, it enables its succeeding module according to the control-flow graph. The enabled module is placed at the end of the *ready queue* of its residence processor in a first-come-first-served manner. Let the execution times for all modules be identical and equal to *one* time unit. To clearly observe the PR effect on response time we further assume there is no IMC between the modules and thus there is no IPC overhead among the processors. Three assignments [Fig. 4(b), (c) and (d)] were simulated using the PAWS simulator [1]. The results are presented in Fig. 5. Note that assignment 2 (pipelined) yields the best task response time. The vertical bars in the figure represent 90 percent confidence intervals for each simulation point. The response time varies substantially among these assignments in spite of the fact that all the three assignments have equal and balanced loads and there is no IPC overhead. This discrepancy is solely due to the PR effect among modules.

In experiment 2, the execution time of each module is *exponentially distributed* (instead of being a constant), with an *average* of one time unit. All other parameters remain unchanged from experiment 1. Experimental results reveal that the task response times for the three assignments are comparable (Fig. 5). Due to the memoryless property of the exponential distribution, the job queue at each processor can be approximated by an M/M/1 queue. Since the service-time distributions of all modules are identical and all modules are invoked for execution at identical arrival rate, the three load-balanced processors can be represented as three identical queueing systems. Thus, the wait-time is the same for all modules and all three assignments yield the same response times.

Experiment 1 reveals that precedence relationship *does* have an impact on task response time. Experiment 2 shows that the PR effect on response time is also influenced by module-execution-time distributions. In experiment 3, we shall study the effect of module size on response time. We assume that every module's execution time is exponentially distributed, but with a different mean value, as shown in Fig. 6. The simulation results for the three assignments reveal that assigning two consecutive modules to the same processor yields good response times *if the execution time of the second module is much larger than that of the first module* (Fig. 7). We shall denote this as PR Principle 1. For example, because y_2 is considerably greater than y_1, M_1 and M_2 should be assigned to the same processor. This principle was used in assignment 1 (Fig. 6) which yielded the best performance. Likewise, in assignment 1 module pairs (M_3, M_4) and (M_5, M_6) are allocated to processors 2 and 3, respectively.

If the second module is much smaller than the first one,

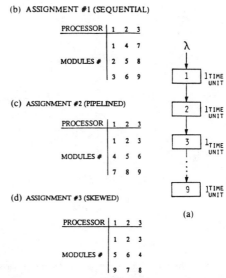

Fig. 4. Precedence-relationship experiment 1. (a) Task control-flow graph. (b) Sequential assignment. (c) Pipelined assignment. (d) Skewed assignment.

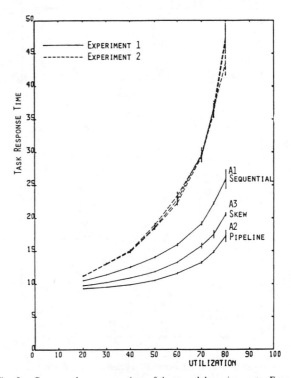

Fig. 5. Compare the response time of three module assignments. Experiment 1 uses deterministic execution time. Experiment 2 uses exponential execution time.

separating the two consecutive modules and assigning them to two different processors yields better response time. We shall denote this as PR Principle 2. Since y_3 is much less than y_2 in this example, M_2 and M_3 should be assigned to different processors. Assignment 1 satisfies the PR Principles for all pairs of consecutive modules. Therefore, it yields the best response time. Assignment 2 is the worst of the three assignments because it violates the PR Principles for all module pairs. Assignment 3 violates PR Principle 1 for some

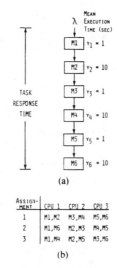

(a)

ASSIGN-MENT	CPU 1	CPU 2	CPU 3
1	M1,M2	M3,M4	M5,M6
2	M1,M6	M2,M3	M4,M5
3	M1,M4	M2,M5	M3,M6

(b)

Fig. 6. (a) Task control-flow graph and (b) module assignments for PR experiment 3.

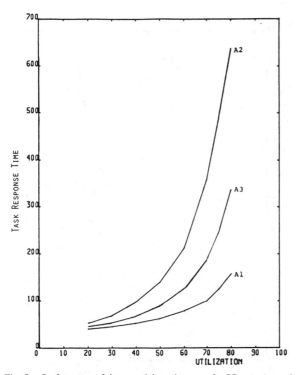

Fig. 7. Performance of three module assignments for PR experiment 3.

assigned to the same processor and if the execution time of the second module is much larger than that of the first, the second one will act as a *regulating valve* which controls the task flow into the next processor. This makes the arrival process at the next processor *more deterministic* than the arrival process of the first module at the first processor. It is well known from queueing theory that for a given queueing system with a given arrival rate, the deterministic-arrival case yields less wait time than that of the bursty arrival case.

We can explain the results of experiment 3 based on the above reasoning. In assignment 1, M_2 at processor 1 has a large execution time, regulating the task flow into processor 2. Therefore, even though there are bursty arrivals for M_1, the invocation arrivals for M_3 at processor 2 are spread fairly evenly over time. As a result, the queue that contains invocations for M_3 and M_4 at processor 2 would be short and thus yield short wait times for M_3 and M_4. Likewise, M_4 acts as a regulating valve for the task flow into processor 3.

Assignment 2 yields poor response time. Since the size of M_1 is small, each group of bursty invocation arrivals for M_1 results in bursty arrivals for M_2 at processor 2 (i.e., there is no regulating valve between processors 1 and 2). As a result, there is a high probability of having many arrivals for M_2 waiting in the queue at processor 2. A newly arrived invocation for M_2 (called M_2 invocation) at processor 2 has a high probability of finding other previously arrived M_2 invocations in the queue. Execution of the first M_2 invocation in the queue generates an invocation for M_3 which is placed *at the end* of the queue at processor 2. There is a *long* wait time for the execution of this M_3 invocation due to the large number of M_2 invocations in front of it. This process is repeated with the execution of other M_2 invocations in the queue, thus contributing to the large response time. Furthermore, since M_3 (at processor 2) is small, the consecutive M_3 invocations finish their execution *rapidly* (although they each have a long wait time). This generates bursty invocations for M_4 at processor 3, again causing long wait time for those modules assigned at processor 3.

From these experiments, we note that module-size (service time) distribution and the *module-size ratios* of consecutive module pairs influence response time. In the following, we shall use analytical methods to derive quantitative guidelines for determining whether or not a consecutive module pair M_i and M_j, with given module-size distributions and average sizes y_i and y_j, should be colocated in the same processor.

B. PR Analysis

Consider the control-flow graph with two separate threads in Fig. 8(a) where all modules have deterministic execution times. Assume no IMC exists among modules. Let $y_1 = y_3$, $y_2 = y_4$. Thus, the module-size ratio $r = r_{1,2} = y_2/y_1 = r_{3,4} = y_4/y_3$. Furthermore, let the job arrival rates $\lambda_1 = \lambda_2 = \lambda$. Under the above condition, both assignments 1 and 2 [Fig. 8(b)] yield equal processor loads. However, they yield different response times. We wish to derive analytical results so that the module-size ratio r can be used as a parameter for determining whether M_1 and M_2 (also M_3 and M_4) should be colocated; that is, if r is greater than some threshold value, M_1

module pairs (e.g., separation of M_1 from M_2) and satisfies PR Principle 2 for some other pairs (e.g., separation of M_2 from M_3), therefore its performance lies between that of assignments 1 and 2. We repeated these experiments with deterministic execution times and obtained similar results.

Let us now discuss the reasons why good response time can be obtained from following the PR Principles. When a job arrival process is deterministic, the workload is *evenly spread* over time. The average queue length at every processor and thus, the average module wait time, should be smaller than that of a bursty arrival process. If two consecutive modules are

188

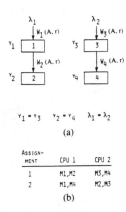

Fig. 8. PR analytical study. Two threads of consecutive modules for studying wait-time ratio between assignments 1 and 2 as a function of size ratio between the consecutive modules.

and M_2 should be assigned to the same processor; otherwise they should be separated.

The response time for the left control thread in Fig. 8(a) is $w_1(A, r) + y_1 + w_2(A, r) + y_2$ while the response time for the right thread is $w_3(A, r) + y_3 + w_4(A, r) + y_4$, where $w_i(A, r)$ is the queueing wait time experienced by module M_i. The queueing wait time is a function of both the assignment A and the module-size ratio r. Because of the symmetry of the two threads and the balanced loading on both processors, both threads have the same response time for assignment 1, denoted as A_1. The two threads also have the same response time for A_2. Therefore, it is sufficient to compare A_1 and A_2 using the response time of only one thread. The left thread is chosen for the following analysis.

The thread response times for A_1 and A_2 are $w_1(A_1, r) + y_1 + w_2(A_1, r) + y_2$ and $w_1(A_2, r) + y_1 + w_2(A_2, r) + y_2$, respectively. Since the values of y_1, y_2, y_3, and y_4 are fixed and independent of module assignment, they need not be considered. Thus, the *wait-time ratio* between assignments 1 and 2 is defined as

$$R = R(r) = \frac{w_1(A_1, r) + w_2(A_1, r)}{w_1(A_2, r) + w_2(A_2, r)}. \tag{8}$$

If $R < 1$, then assignment 1 yields better response time than assignment 2. The response-time improvement is due to better handling of the PR effect. Under such conditions, we should assign the pair of consecutive modules M_1 and M_2 to the same processor, and the other pair M_3 and M_4 to the alternate processor. If $R > 1$, then assignment 2 has better response time than assignment 1 and the consecutive modules should be assigned to different processors. Thus, R [see (8)] allows us to select the better module assignment.

Let us now discuss how to compute $w_i(A, r)$ and thus, R. For a given control-flow graph, module assignment, and module-size distributions, the wait-time w_i's for all modules can be estimated via the analytical model reported in [9]. The Appendix shows how to use the model to derive the numerator and denominator for (8). Therefore, we are able to determine the wait-time ratio R for various module-size ratios r. When all the modules have *constant* service times, we can compute R as a function of processor utilization ρ for executing M_1 and M_2 [Fig. 9(a) and (b)]; $\rho = \rho_1 + \rho_2$, $\rho_1 = \lambda_1 y_1$ and $\rho_2 = \lambda_1 y_2$. Note that R increases as r decreases from 100 to 0.4 [Fig. 9(a)]. As r further decreases from 0.4, R then reverses the trend and starts to decrease [Fig. 9(b)]. Note that $R = 1$, occuring at $r = 2.5$, is the threshold value that determines whether two consecutive modules should be colocated. R varies slightly with processor utilization. In the same manner, when the module execution times are exponentially distributed, we can derive the relationship between the wait-time ratio R and the module-size ratio r, as shown in Figs. 9(c) and (d). In this case, the threshold value $R = 1$ occurs at $r = 1$.

Note from Fig. 9 that when each module execution time is exponentially distributed, R is less sensitive to r, as compared to the case of deterministic module execution time. Results from the analytical model also confirm our observation in experiments 1 and 2 that response time is more sensitive to precedence relationship when module service times are deterministic than when they are exponentially distributed.

We have extended the above analysis to encompass the case where each control thread consists of *three* consecutive modules. M_1, M_2, M_3 are consecutive modules in one thread and M_4, M_5, M_6 in another. Let $y_1 = y_4, y_2 = y_5, y_3 = y_6$, and $\lambda_1 = \lambda_2$. Assignment 1 allocates all the consecutive modules to the same processors, i.e.,

Processor 1: M_1, M_2, M_3

Processor 2: M_4, M_5, M_6.

Assignment 2 allocates the consecutive modules to different processors, i.e.,

Processor 1: M_1, M_5, M_3

Processor 2: M_4, M_2, M_6.

Note that both assignments yield balanced loads. The wait-time ratio can be expressed similar to (8). The analytical results show that if we hold $y_1(= y_4)$ fixed, then as module-size ratio $r_{2,3} = y_3/y_2(= y_6/y_5)$ decreases, the wait-time ratio R between assignments 1 and 2 increases to a point and then reverses the trend and starts to decrease. This is similar to the case with two-module threads (Fig. 9). Similar relationships are observed for a control-flow graph consisting of four consecutive modules in a thread. All of these suggest that one way to handle the cases with more than two consecutive modules is to treat *each* pair of consecutive modules in a control-flow graph independently. Using the PR relation (Fig. 9) one can decide whether to allocate the two modules to the same processor. Our experience shows that assignments generated by such an approach yield good task response time.

IV. Module Assignment Algorithm

A. The Algorithm

Using exhaustive search to select an assignment from an entire assignment tree is prohibitively time consuming. Therefore, we shall propose a heuristic algorithm for module

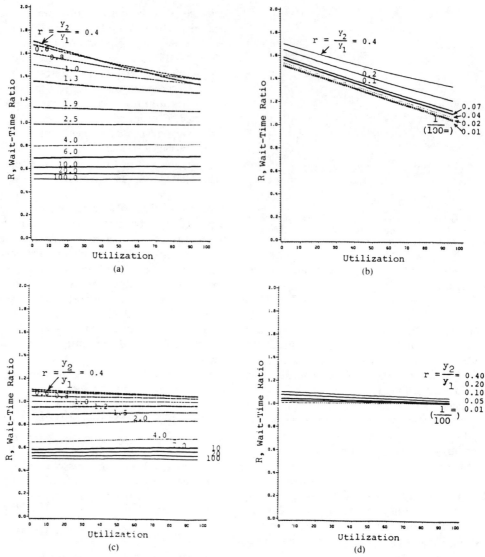

Fig. 9.   Wait-time ratio between two assignments as a function of program-
module-size ratio, for (a) and (b) deterministic execution times and (c) and
(d) exponentially distributed execution times.

assignment (Fig. 10) that considers PR, IMC, and AET. We shall call it Algorithm P–I–A. This algorithm assumes that

1) there are J modules, $M_1, M_2, \cdots, M_J$, and S processors;
2) the AET (an average during the peak-load period) for each module M_j, T_j, ($j = 1, \cdots, J$) is given;
3) the IMC (an average during the peak-load period) between each module pair M_i and M_j, IMC_{ij}, ($i = 1, \cdots J; j = 1, \cdots J$) is given. Each IMC_{ij} can be derived from the V_{jk}'s [8].

The algorithm consists of two phases. Phase I reduces J modules to G groups ($G < J$) which corresponds to a much smaller assignment tree for Phase II. This grouping can be done with very little computation. Each group generated at the end of Phase I is a *set* of modules which will be assigned *as a single unit* to a processor. In Phase II these groups are assigned to the processors such that the bottleneck (in the most heavily utilized processor) is minimized.

The grouping of modules in Phase I is based on several factors. To reduce IPC, heavily communicating modules may be combined into groups. To do this, communicating module pairs are listed in descending order of the IMC volume (Step 1.1). Module pairs with large IMC are considered first.

Next, the PR effects are considered. The decision of whether to group two consecutive modules should be based on the two possibly conflicting factors: IMC volume and the effect of PR (i.e., module-size ratios). For a module pair (M_i, M_j), we propose to use *IMC index* $\gamma_{\text{IMC}}(i, j) = \text{IMC}_{ij}/\overline{\text{AET}}$ and *PR index* $\gamma_{\text{PR}}(i, j) = 1 - R(r_{ij})$, as defined in the initialization in the algorithm, to evaluate these conflicting factors. The IMC index indicates the relative IMC size normalized by the average module size in terms of the execution time. The typical index value should be between 0.1 and 0.5. An IMC with an index value below 0.1 may be considered negligible. Grouping two modules with the small IMC saves little IPC. The wait-time ratio R in the PR-index

Initialization:

0. Compute average AET, $\overline{AET}$, and average processor load, $\overline{PL}$:

$$\overline{AET} \leftarrow \sum_{j=1}^{J} T_j / J$$

$$\overline{PL} \leftarrow \sum_{j=1}^{J} T_j / S$$

Compute the IMC index and the PR index:

$$\gamma_{IMC}(i,j) = \frac{IMC_{ij}}{\overline{AET}} \quad i=1,...,J; \quad j=1,...,J$$

$$\gamma_{PR}(i,j) = 1 - R(r_{ij}) \quad i=1,...,J; \quad j=1,...,J$$

Do $\alpha = \alpha_1$ to α_2; with increment $\Delta\alpha$
Do $\beta = \beta_1$ to β_2; with increment $\Delta\beta$

Phase I — Combine modules with large IMC into groups to reduce total system load (i.e., to reduce the sum of processor loads):

1.1 List all module pairs (M_i, M_j) in the *descending* order of IMC volume.

    Let each program module form a distinct group (a set):
        $G_j \leftarrow \{ M_j \} \quad j = 1,...,J$

1.2 If no more pairs exist in the module-pair list
      go to Phase II.
    Pick the next pair of modules, M_i and M_j, and delete this pair from the list.

1.3 If $\alpha \times \gamma_{IMC}(i,j) + \gamma_{PR}(i,j) \leq 0$
      go to Step 1.2.

1.4 Find the group G_s that contains M_i, and the group G_t that contains M_j (i.e., $M_i \in G_s$, $M_j \in G_t$).
    If $s = t$ (i.e., if M_i and M_j are already in the same group)
      go to Step 1.2.

1.5 If $T_s + T_t > (\overline{PL} \times \beta)$
      go to Step 1.2.

1.6 Combine the two groups G_s and G_t into a single one:
        $G_s \leftarrow G_s \cup G_t$
        $G_t \leftarrow \emptyset$
        $T_s \leftarrow T_s + T_t$
        $T_t \leftarrow 0$

1.7 Go to Step 1.2.

Phase II — Assign module groups to processors:

2.1 Perform an exhaustive search through the new assignment tree for the assignment that has the smallest bottleneck.

2.2 Record the minimum-bottleneck assignment.

  end;
end;

Fig. 10. The Algorithm P-I-A.

can be computed from (8). For deterministic and exponential module execution times, from Fig. 9, R ranges between 0 and 2. $R = 1$ is the threshold value for deciding whether to group two consecutive modules. The condition $R < 1$ corresponds to a positive PR index $\gamma_{PR}(i, j)$, which favors the grouping of modules M_i and M_j. Likewise, $R > 1$ indicates a negative PR index favoring separation of M_i and M_j. Since the IMC index has a range between 0.1 and 0.5 and the PR index has a range between -1 and 1, a *scaling factor* α is introduced to combine the two indexes (Step 1.3). The α value can range from 1 to 10 and thus is a variable in Algorithm P-I-A.

Another factor to be considered is the size of a new group. If the new group, resulting from combining two subgroups, becomes too large, it would be impossible to obtain a balanced-load assignment during Phase II. Therefore, the concept of *processor-load threshold* $(\overline{PL} \times \beta)$ is introduced (Step 1.5), where $\overline{PL}$ is the average processor load and β is a scale constant. If the size of a candidate new group is greater than the threshold, the two subgroups should not be combined. Note that a too small β would retard proper beneficial module grouping while a too large β makes it impossible to balance processor loads during Phase II. Our experiences on DPAD

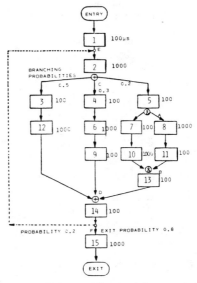

Fig. 11. Task control-flow graph for example 1.

and other systems reveal that a good range for β is between 0.6 and 1.2 times of the average processor load.

For each pair of α and β values the algorithm generates a minimum-bottleneck assignment. We should select the assignment which corresponds to the *smallest* minimum-bottleneck among all sets of (α, β). If several assignments yield the same smallest minimum-bottleneck value, then we select the one with the smallest *total* processor load.

B. Examples

In this section, we shall use an example (denoted "example 1") to show that significant response-time improvement can be achieved when PR is considered in module assignment. Consider the control-flow graph in Fig. 11 where each program module has a deterministic execution time of either 100 or 1000 μs. Thus, the size ratios of most consecutive module pairs are either 0.1 or 10 (except for four pairs whose size ratios are 1.0). The job interarrival time is assumed to be exponentially distributed, with a rate of one hundred arrivals per *unit* interval. Each arrival makes an invocation to the entire control-flow graph. Some modules are executed more frequently than the others. Using the model presented in [8], the AET can be estimated for a specified time interval for each module. The estimated AET for each unit interval is shown in column 2 of Table II. Let us assume that the IMC sizes for all communicating module pairs are about equal, either 1400 or 1500 μs (see Table II and Fig. 12) which implies that IMC plays a lesser role than PR does. Given the PR, IMC, and AET, the module assignment generated by Algorithm P-I-A is shown in Table III along with the processor loads. In order to compare the PR effect, we generate a second assignment (also shown in Table III) which excludes the PR effect by replacing the Step 1.3 of Algorithm P-I-A with

1.3 If $\gamma_{IMC}(i, j) \leq 0.1$

go to Phase II.

TABLE II
AET T_j AND FILE-UPDATE IMC V_{jk} FOR EXAMPLE 1

Write-Module j	AET* T_j (in μs)	File k Updated	IMC* V_{jk} (in μs)	Read-Modules
1	10,000	101	1400	2
2	125,000	102	1400	3,4,5
3	6,250	103	1400	12
4	3,750	104	1400	6
5	2,500	107	1400	7,8
6	37,500	106	1500	9
7	2,500	108	1400	10
8	25,000	109	1500	11
9	3,750	110	1400	14
10	25,000	111	1500	13
11	2,500	112	1500	13
12	62,500	105	1500	14
13	2,500	113	1400	14
14	12,500	114	1400	15
15	100,000	--	--	--

* AET and Total IMC during a 100-arrival period

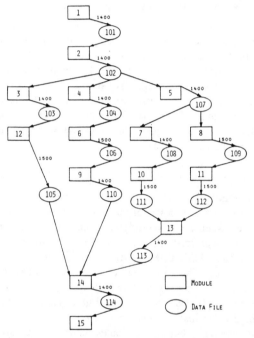

Fig. 12. Data-flow graph for example 1.

When $\gamma_{\text{IMC}}(i, j) \leq 0.1$, the IMC effect is negligible. We called this Algorithm I–A.

Note that in the assignment generated by Algorithm P–I–A, most module pairs are assigned (either colocated or separated) according to our PR Principles rather than the IMC sizes. For example, the module-size ratio $r_{4,6} = y_6/y_4 = 10$, thus M_4 and M_6 are colocated on processor 3. On the other hand, $r_{6,9} = 0.1$, thus M_6 is separated from M_9 although $\text{IMC}_{6,9}$ is larger than $\text{IMC}_{4,6}$.

These two assignments are simulated via the PAWS simulator. The average response time for each job arrival is measured from when the job arrives at the system until it finishes the execution of M_{15}. Fig. 13 portrays the response time for the two assignments. Note that the assignment generated by Algorithm P–I–A yields better response time

than that generated by Algorithm I–A, with 10.8 percent improvement at processor utilization $\rho = 0.2$ and 25.7 percent improvement at $\rho = 0.8$ percent. Both assignments yield fairly balanced processor loads with similar bottleneck values. The difference in response time is due to the consideration of PR in module assignment.

We have applied both Algorithms P–I–A and I–A to the DPAD module assignment problem. The assignment generated from Algorithm P–I–A is the same as that generated from Algorithm I–A. This is due to the fact that there are very few consecutive modules in the DPAD system. Note that if a module is enabled by another through an OR branch with a low probability (say less than 0.5), the PR effect of such a module pair is greatly reduced. Therefore, they can logically be viewed as nonconsecutive modules because the second module is *not* always invoked for execution after the first module finishes its execution. Many module pairs in the DPAD belong to this type. The result also reveals that the performance of the best assignment obtained from Algorithm P–I–A is comparable with that of the exhaustive search (see Fig. 3). This demonstrates that the heuristic Algorithm P–I–A can generate an assignment which yields response time comparable to that of using the time-prohibitive exhaustive search method.

V. SUMMARY

The three important parameters that influence task allocation are accumulative execution time (AET) of each module, intermodule communication (IMC), and precedence relationship (PR) among program modules. AET contributes to processor load and is independent of task allocation. IMC is the communication between program modules through shared files. When a module on a processor writes to or reads from a shared file on *another* processor, IMC becomes IPC (interprocessor communication) which requires extra processing and communication overhead. A task-allocation algorithm should minimize the IPC by assigning heavily communicating modules to the same processor.

An objective function for minimizing the bottleneck processor load (consisting of IMC and AET) has been proposed for task allocation. It is shown to generate load-balanced assignments with small IPC.

The third parameter for task allocation is the *precedence relationship* (PR). Due to PR, a program module cannot be enabled before its predecessor(s) finish executing. Both simulation and analytical study revealed that the module-size ratio of two consecutive modules affects task response time. Two principles were observed: 1) assigning two consecutive modules to a same processor yields good response times if the execution time of the second module is much larger than that of the first module; 2) if the second module is much smaller than the first one, the two consecutive modules should be separated and assigned to two different processors.

An analytical model was proposed to study the PR effect on response time which quantitatively determines whether two consecutive modules should be colocated in a processor. Our study reveals that this depends on the size ratio of the two consecutive modules, module-execution-time distribution, and processor load.

TABLE III
MODULE ASSIGNMENTS FOR EXAMPLE 1

MODULES	ASSIGNMENT I-A (W/O CONSIDERING PR)			ASSIGNMENT P-I-A (CONSIDERING PR)		
	CPU1	CPU2	CPU3	CPU1	CPU2	CPU3
	1	6	3	1	7	3
	2	9	5	2	10	4
	4	15	7	9	13	5
			8		14	6
			10		15	8
			11			11
			12			12
			13			
			14			
PROCESSOR LOADS	141550	144050	146850	143050	148300	147300
PERCENTAGE OF LOADS	32.73%	33.31%	33.96%	32.61%	33.81%	33.58%

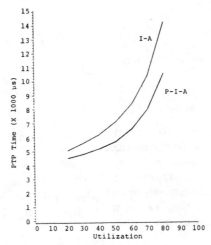

Fig. 13. Task-response-time comparison between assignments with and without PR consideration for example 1.

A heuristic algorithm that considers PR, IMC, and AET was developed for task allocation. In determining whether two consecutive modules should be colocated on the same processor, the effect of PR on response time may be in conflict with the effect of IMC. Therefore, the allocation algorithm jointly considers the effect of IMC and PR. Using the minimum bottleneck as an objective function, the algorithm was applied to two example systems. The results revealed that module assignments considering PR may yield better response time than assignments without PR consideration.

Further investigation is needed to generalize the algorithm to handle the assignment of replicated program modules. This could have a significant effect on task response time [22].

GLOSSARY

F_k—the kth file in the system
IMC—intermodule communication
IPC—interprocessor communication
J—number of program modules
K—number of files
L—processor loading
MLI—machine language instruction
M_j—the jth program module
$N_j(t_h, t_{h+1})$—number of times module M_j executes during (t_h, t_{h+1})
R—wait-time ratio of two assignments
S—number of processors (sites)
$T_j(t_h, t_{h+1})$—accumulative execution time (AET) for module M_j during (t_h, t_{h+1})
V_{jk}—IMC message volume sent from M_j to update the file F_k
$X = [x_{jr}]$—module assignment matrix in which $x_{jr}(= 1$ or $0)$ indicates whether module M_j is assigned to processor r
$r_{i,j}$—size ratio between modules M_j and M_i
$w_j(A, r)$—the queueing wait-time of module M_j for assignment A and module-size ratio, r
y_j—average execution time of module M_j per execution
δ_{ks}—indicating function to specify whether a copy of F_k resides at processor s

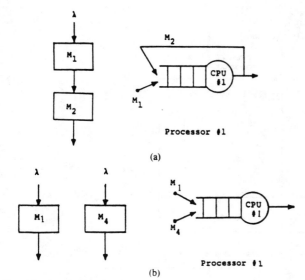

(a)

(b)

Fig. 14. Queuing model for computing module waiting time for (a) Assigment 1 and (b) Assignment 2.

λ—task arrival rate
ρ—processor utilization
ω—a normalizing constant for converting IMC to MLI's.

APPENDIX

I. DERIVATION OF THE NUMERATOR FOR (8) (ASSIGNMENT 1)

According to [9], the average wait-time $w_1(A_1, r)$ and $w_2(A_1, r)$ at Processor 1 for Assignment 1 can be obtained as follows. The mean wait-time for a given invocation of M_1 under FCFS scheduling policy is the average time to complete the executions of *both* the module invocation currently being served by the processor *and* all module invocations waiting in the job queue when the given M_1 invocation arrives. [See Fig. 14(a)]. Thus, we have

$$w_1(A_1, r) = w_{r1} + \overline{n_1}\,\overline{y_1} + \overline{n_2}\,\overline{y_2} \qquad (A\text{-}1)$$

where

w_{r1} = mean residual module-execution time at processor 1 for assignment 1.

$$= \frac{1}{2}\,(\lambda\overline{y_1^2} + \lambda\overline{y_2^2})$$

$$= \frac{1}{2}\,\lambda[(1 + c_1^2)\,\bar{y}_1^2 + (1 + c_2^2)\,\bar{y}_2^2]$$

c_i = coefficient of variation for the execution time of M_i
$\overline{n_i}$ = average number of M_i invocations waiting in the job queue.

To find the waiting time for M_2, we need to keep track of the queueing behavior starting from the arrival of the invocation for M_1. Let us consider a particular tagged invocation for M_1. After the completion of this tagged M_1 execution, its succeeding tagged invocation for M_2 is placed at the end of the job queue. The waiting time for this tagged M_2 invocation consists of three components. The first component is the total

execution time of the new invocations for M_1 that arrive during the waiting and execution time of the tagged M_1 invocation. The second component is due to the executions of all the M_2 invocations which are enabled by the M_1 invocations that wait in the job queue when the tagged M_1 invocation arrives at processor 1. The last component is due to the execution of a M_2 invocation (with a probability of $\rho_1 = \lambda\overline{x_1}$). This M_2 invocation is enabled if module M_1 is in execution at the arrival of the tagged M_1 invocation. By adding these components, we have

$$w_2(A_1, r) = [w_1(A_1, r) + \overline{y_1})\lambda]\,\overline{y_1} + \overline{n_1}\,\overline{y_2} + \rho_1\overline{y_2}. \quad (A\text{-}2)$$

Since $\overline{n_i} = \lambda w_i$ (Little's result [23]) and $\rho_i = \lambda y_i$, (A-1) and (A-2) become

$$w_1(A_1, r) = w_{r1} + \rho_1 \cdot w_1(A_1, r) + \rho_2 \cdot w_2(A_1, r) \quad (A\text{-}3)$$

and

$$w_2(A_1, r) = (w_1(A_1, r) + \overline{y_1})\rho_1 + \rho_2 \cdot w_1(A_1, r) + \rho_1\overline{y_2}. \quad (A\text{-}4)$$

From (A-3) and (A-4), $w_1(A_1, r)$ and $w_2(A_1, r)$ can be solved as

$$w_1(A_1, r) = \frac{w_{r1} + \rho_1\rho_2(\overline{y_1} + \overline{y_2})}{1 - \rho_1 - \rho_2(\rho_1 + \rho_2)} \qquad (A\text{-}5)$$

and

$$w_2(A_1, r) = \frac{w_{r1} + \rho_1\rho_2(\overline{y_1} + \overline{y_2})}{1 - \rho_1 - \rho_2(\rho_1 + \rho_2)}\,(\rho_1 + \rho_2) + \rho_1(\overline{y_1} + \overline{y_2}). \quad (A\text{-}6)$$

Therefore, the numerator of (8) is the sum of (A-5) and (A-6).

II. DERIVATION OF THE DENOMINATOR FOR (8) (ASSIGNMENT 2)

With Assignment 2, Processor 1 can be treated as an M/G/1 queueing system with two types of "customers," M_1 and M_4. [See Fig. 14(b)]. The mean wait-time for these customers is given by

$$w_1(A_2, r) = w_4(A_2, r) = \frac{w_{r2}}{1 - \rho} = \frac{w_{r2}}{1 - \rho_1 - \rho_4} = \frac{w_{r2}}{1 - \lambda\overline{y_1} - \lambda\overline{y_4}} \quad (A\text{-}7)$$

where

ρ_i = processor utilization due to module i

w_{r2} = mean residual module execution time at processor 1 for assignment 2

$$= \frac{1}{2}\,(\lambda\overline{y_1^2} + \lambda\overline{y_4^2})$$

$$= \frac{1}{2}\,\lambda[(1 + c_1^2)\,\bar{y}_1^2 + (1 + c_4^2)\,\bar{y}_4^2].$$

Due to the symmetry in module threads (See Fig. 8), $w_2(A_2, r) = w_4(A_2, r)$. Thus, the denominator of (8) is equal to $2w_1(A_2, r) = 2w_{r2}/(1 - \lambda\overline{y_1} - \lambda\overline{y_4})$.

ACKNOWLEDGMENT

The formulation of the wait-time ratio as a function of module assignment and module-size ratio, was first proposed and studied by K. K. Leung at UCLA. The Appendix is

194

adapted from his dissertation [17]. The authors would also like to thank the referees for their comments which improved the organization of this paper.

References

[1] R. Berry, K. M. Chandy, J. Misra, and D. Neuse, *PAWS 2.0—Performance Analyst's Workbench System: User's Manual*, Inform. Res. Ass., Austin, TX, Dec. 1982.

[2] S. H. Bokhari, "Dual processor scheduling with dynamic reassignment," *IEEE Trans. Software Eng.*, vol. SE-5, pp. 341–349, July 1979.

[3] T. C. K. Chou and J. A. Abraham, "Load balancing in distributed systems," *IEEE Trans. Software Eng.*, vol. SE-8, pp. 401–412, July 1982.

[4] W. W. Chu, "Optimal file allocation in a multiple computer system," *IEEE Trans. Comput.*, vol. C-18, pp. 885–889, Oct. 1969.

[5] W. W. Chu, D. Lee, and B. Iffla, "A distributed processing system for naval data communication networks," in *Proc. AFIPS Nat. Comput. Conf.*, vol. 47, 1978, pp. 783–793.

[6] W. W. Chu, L. J. Holloway, M. T. Lan, and K. Efe, "Task allocation in distributed data processing," *Computer*, vol. 13, pp. 57–69, Nov. 1980.

[7] W. W. Chu, J. Hellerstein, M. T. Lan, J. M. An, and K. K. Leung, "Database management algorithms for advanced BMD applications," Dep. Comput. Sci., Rep. UCLA-ENG-84-07 (CSD-840031), Univ. California, Los Angeles, Apr. 1984.

[8] W. W. Chu, M-T. Lan, and J. Hellerstein, "Estimation of intermodule communication (IMC) and its applications in distributed processing systems," *IEEE Trans. Comput.*, vol. C-33, pp. 691–699, Aug. 1984.

[9] W. W. Chu and K. K. Leung, "Task-response-time model and its applications for real-time distributed processing systems," in *Proc. 5th Real-Time Syst. Symp.*, Austin, TX, Dec. 1984, pp. 255–236.

[10] K. Efe, "Heuristic models of task assignment scheduling in distributed systems," *Computer*, vol. 15, pp. 50–56, June 1982.

[11] M. L. Green, E. Y. S. Lee, S. Majumdar, and D. C. Shannon, "A distributed real-time operating system," in *Proc. Symp. Distributed Data Acquisition, Comput. Contr.*, Dec. 1980, pp. 175–184.

[12] ——, *Phase III of Distributed Processing Architecture Design (DPAD) System—The DDP Underlay Simulator Experiment: Tactical Applications and d-RTOS Models*, TRW Defense Space Syst. Group, Special Rep. 35010-79-A005, May 15, 1980.

[13] V. B. Gylys and J. A. Edwards, "Optimal partitioning of workload for distributed systems," in *Proc. COMPCON Fall 76*, Sep. 1976, pp. 353–357.

[14] K. B. Irani and K-W. Chen, "Minimization of interprocessor communication for parallel computation," *IEEE Trans. Comput.*, vol. C-31, pp. 1067–1075, Nov. 1982.

[15] C. J. Jenny, "Process partitioning in distributed systems," in *Proc. NTC 1977*, pp. 31:1-1-31:1-10.

[16] L. M-T. Lan, "Characterization of intermodule communications and heuristic task allocation for distributed real-time systems," Ph.D. dissertation, Rep. CSD-850012, Univ. California, Los Angeles, Mar. 1985.

[17] K. K. Leung, "Task response time and module assignment for real time distributed processing systems," Ph.D. dissertation, UCLA, Dec. 1985.

[18] P. Y. R. Ma, E. Y. S. Lee, and M. Tsuchiya, "A task allocation model for distributed computing systems," *IEEE Trans. Comput.*, vol. C-31, pp. 41–47, Jan. 1982.

[19] D. Palmer, "On the design of distributed data processing systems," in *Proc. COMPSAC 78*, Chicago, IL, invited paper.

[20] G. S. Rao, H. S. Stone, and T. C. Hu, "Assignment of tasks in a distributed processing system with limited memory," *IEEE Trans. Comput.*, vol. C-28, pp. 291–299, Apr. 1979.

[21] C. C. Shen and W. H. Tsai, "A graph matching approach to optimal task assignment in distributed computing systems using a minimax criterion," *IEEE Trans. Comput.*, vol. C-34, pp. 197–203, Mar. 1985.

[22] W. W. Chu and K. K. Leung, "Module replication and assignment for real-time distributed processing systems," *Proc. IEEE*, May 1987.

[23] J. D. C. Little, "A proof of the queueing formula $L = \lambda W$," *Oper. Res.*, vol. 9, pp. 383–387, 1961.

Wesley W. Chu (S'62-M'67-SM'74-F'78) received the B.S. and M.S. degrees from the University of Michigan, Ann Arbor, in 1960 and 1961, respectively, and the Ph.D. degree in electrical engineering from Stanford University, Stanford, CA, in 1966.

From 1961 to 1962 he worked on switching circuit design at the General Electric Computer Department (now Honeywell), Phoenix, AZ. From 1964 to 1966 he worked on the design of large-scale computers at IBM, Menlo Park and San Jose, CA, and from 1966 to 1969 he researched on computer communications at Bell Laboratories, Holmdel, NJ. He joined the University of California, Los Angeles, in 1969, and is currently a Professor in the Department of Computer Science. He directs a research group at UCLA in the areas of computer communications and networking, distributed processing, and distributed databases. He is also a consultant to government agencies and private industries. He has authored or coauthored more than 80 articles on information processing systems and computer communications and has edited three textbooks: *Advances in Computer Communications* (Artech House, first ed., 1974 and 2nd rev. ed., 1977), *Centralized and Distributed Database Systems*, coedited with P. P. Chen, (IEEE Computer Society, 1979), and *Distributed Systems, Vol. I: Distributed Processing Systems, Vol. II: Distributed Database Systems* (Artech House, 1986).

Dr. Chu is a member of Tau Beta Pi, Eta Kappa Nu, Phi Tau Phi, and Sigma Xi. He was Chairman of the ACM SIGCOMM from 1973 to 1977, Chairman of the 1975 ACM Interprocess Communication Workshop, Technical Program Chairman of the Fourth Data Communication Symposium in 1975, and Chairman of the IEEE Lake Arrowhead Workshop on Computer Networking and Distributed Databases in 1977. He was the program cochairman for the First International Conference on Data Engineering, 1984, and the program cochairman for the 12th International Conference on VLDB, 1986. He was an associate editor for the IEEE TRANSACTIONS ON COMPUTERS for the field of computer networking and distributed processing systems (1978–1982) and received a meritorious award for his service to the IEEE in 1983. He is currently a member of the Editorial Board of *Computer Networks* and the *International Journal on Computers and Electrical Engineering* and an associate editor for the *Journal of Data and Knowledge Engineering*.

Lance M-T. Lan (S'79-M'85) received the B.S. degree in electrical engineering from National Taiwan University in 1974, the M.S. degree in computer science from the University of Nebraska, Lincoln (UNL), in 1977, and the Ph.D. degree in computer science from the University of California, Los Angeles (UCLA), in 1985.

He was a Computer System Engineer with China Steel Corp., Taiwan from 1974 to 1976 and a System Analyst with the Nebraska State Department of Labor in 1978. As a Research Assistant at UNL, from 1976 to 1977, he performed a comparative study of text editors. In 1979, while working for the Technology Service Corp., Santa Monica, CA, he designed a parallel-processing database machine for a defense project. From 1980 to 1985 he was a Research Assistant at UCLA and worked on a Ballistic Missile Defense Distributed Processing Contract. He also held part-time positions with the OAO Corp., Los Angeles, designing an Ada programs complexity analyzer, and the RFA Associates, Los Angeles, consulting on the B-1 Bomber Logistics Database design. He joined AT&T Bell Laboratories, Whippany, NJ in 1985 and is involved in capacity studies of AUTOPLEX cellular telecommunication systems and in the design of future mobile-phone systems. His research interests include system architecture, performance modeling, simulation, and analysis for distributed processing systems.

Distributed Scheduling of Tasks with Deadlines and Resource Requirements

KRITHI RAMAMRITHAM, JOHN A. STANKOVIC, SENIOR MEMBER, IEEE, AND WEI ZHAO, MEMBER, IEEE

Abstract—In the design of distributed computer systems, the scheduling problem is considered to be an important one and has been addressed by many researchers. However, most approaches have not dealt with tasks' *timing and resource requirements*. In this paper, we describe a set of heuristic algorithms to schedule tasks that have deadlines and resource requirements, in a distributed system. These algorithms are dynamic and function in a decentralized manner. When a task arrives at a node, the local scheduler at that node attempts to guarantee that the task will complete execution before its deadline, on that node. If the attempt fails, the scheduling components on individual nodes cooperate to determine which other node in the system has sufficient resource surplus to guarantee the task. In this paper, four algorithms for cooperation are evaluated. They differ in the way a node treats a task that cannot be guaranteed locally.

• The *random scheduling algorithm*: The task is sent to a randomly selected node.

• The *focused addressing algorithm*: The task is sent to a node that is estimated to have sufficient surplus to complete the task before its deadline.

• The *bidding algorithm*: The task is sent to a node based on the bids received for the task from nodes in the system.

• The *flexible algorithm*: The task is sent to a node based on a technique that combines *bidding* and *focused addressing*.

Simulation studies were performed to compare the performance of these algorithms relative to each other as well as with respect to two baselines. The first baseline is the noncooperative algorithm where a task that cannot be guaranteed locally is not sent to any other node. The second is an (ideal) algorithm that behaves exactly like the bidding algorithm but incurs no communication overheads. The simulation studies examine how communication delay, task laxity, load differences on the nodes, and task computation times affect the performance of the algorithms. The results show that distributed scheduling is effective even in a hard real-time environment and that the relative performance of these algorithms is a function of the system state.

Index Terms—Deadlines, distributed scheduling, real-time systems, resource constraints, simulation studies.

I. INTRODUCTION

DISTRIBUTED real-time systems are becoming more prevalent in applications such as avionics, process control, and command and control systems. These applications contain many tasks that have execution deadlines that must be met. Tasks in these applications are typically categorized as being critical, essential, and nonessential. *Critical tasks* are defined as those which must meet their deadlines under all circumstances, otherwise the result could be catastrophic. Resources needed to meet the deadlines of critical tasks are typically preallocated. Also, these tasks are usually statically scheduled such that their deadlines will be met even under worst case conditions. *Essential* tasks are tasks that have deadlines and are important to the operation of the system, but will not cause a catastrophe if they are not finished on time. If essential tasks miss their deadlines, the performance of the system will seriously degrade. It is necessary to treat such tasks in a dynamic manner as it is impossible to reserve enough resources for all contingencies with respect to these tasks. Our approach applies an on-line, dynamic guarantee to this collection of tasks. Strategies for dynamically scheduling essential tasks in a distributed system form the subject of this paper. *Nonessential tasks* are defined as those whose deadlines if missed will not affect the system in the near future but may have an effect in the long term. Maintenance and bookkeeping activities fall in this category.

Many solutions used today for scheduling tasks are static in that they assume complete and prior knowledge of *all* tasks and make static scheduling and allocation decisions for the tasks. These solutions suffer from inflexibility and poor resource utilization. On the other extreme are solutions that assign priorities to tasks and design the system to perform preemptive priority-based scheduling. This approach suffers from a number of problems. First, one figure, namely a task's priority, has to reflect a number of characteristics of the task including its deadline and level of importance. This assignment is error prone and causes several well-known anomalies because deadline and importance are not always compatible. Second, that a task has missed its deadline is known only when the deadline occurs. This does not allow time for any corrective actions. Third, priority scheduling (as commonly defined) only addresses the CPU resource. This is a mistake. What value is there to immediately scheduling a task with a close deadline if the first thing that the task does is ask for a locked resource and therefore must wait? What is required is an integrated approach to CPU scheduling and resource allocation. Our work addresses this very important need.

The scheduling decisions made by the schemes discussed in this paper are based on task deadline *and* resource requirements. Also, the notion of *guarantee* underlies all scheduling decisions: when a task arrives at a node, the local scheduler at that node attempts to guarantee that the task will complete execution before its deadline, on that node. If the attempt fails, the scheduling components on individual nodes cooperate to determine which other node in the system has sufficient

Manuscript received November 1, 1988; revised April 6, 1989. This work is part of the Spring Project at the University of Massachusetts and is funded in part by the Office of Naval Research under Contract N00014-85-K-0398 and by the National Science Foundation under Grant DCR-8500332.

The authors are with the Department of Computer and Information Science, University of Massachusetts, Amherst, MA 01003.

IEEE Log Number 8928531.

Reprinted from *IEEE Transactions on Computers*, Vol. 38, No. 8, August 1989, pp. 1110-1123. Copyright © 1989 by The Institute of Electrical and Electronic Engineers, Inc. All rights reserved.

resource surplus to guarantee the task. If such a node is not found, corrective action can be attempted before the deadline is missed. This guarantee-based scheme significantly improves the predictability and fault-tolerance properties of the system.

Designing good distributed scheduling algorithms that meet task deadlines is our goal. The performance metric used to evaluate the competing algorithms is the *guarantee ratio* defined as the ratio of the number of tasks which can be guaranteed to complete before their deadlines compared to the number of tasks which are invoked.[1] The goal of the scheduling algorithms presented in this paper will be to *maximize the guarantee ratio*.

Due to the real-time constraints on tasks, the scheduling algorithm itself should be very efficient. That is, the *scheduling delay must be minimized* and the *scheduling overheads incurred by the system should be minimized*. This implies that the decisions, such as whether a task can be completed before its deadline as well as which node the task should be sent, must be made efficiently. The problem of determining an optimal schedule even in a multiprocessor system is known to be NP-hard [7]. A distributed system introduces further problems due to communication delays. All of these factors necessitate a *heuristic* approach to scheduling.

Our basic strategy for scheduling hard real-time tasks in a loosely coupled distributed system is as follows. Assume that when a task arrives at a node of a distributed system, the task's deadline, computation time, and resource requirements are known. When the task arrives, the scheduler component local to that node decides if the new task can be *guaranteed* at this node. The guarantee means that no matter what happens (except failures) this task will finish execution by its deadline and that all previously guaranteed tasks will still meet their deadlines.[2] If the new task cannot be guaranteed locally, then the scheduling components on individual nodes cooperate to determine whether another node has sufficient surplus in all those resources required by the task to guarantee the task and if such a node exists, the task is sent to that node; otherwise, the task is rejected.

Algorithms for local guarantee under resource and timing requirements have already been studied [24], [25], [19] and will not be repeated here. Rather, this paper focuses on the algorithms for selecting a *remote node* to which a task should be sent when the task cannot be guaranteed locally.

A number of approaches are possible for distributed scheduling. A simple approach, called the *random scheduling* algorithm, sends the task to another randomly selected node. Two other cooperative approaches, that utilize system state information, may be taken for selecting a remote node [17], [21]: *bidding* and *focused addressing*. In focused addressing, a node with the highest estimated surplus is selected. In bidding, a node is selected if the node offers the best bid. Both bidding and focused addressing utilize information on the state

of other nodes and hence incur more overheads than random scheduling. The communication costs involved in bidding are high, but selection is made based on relatively accurate state information of nodes. Focused addressing entails less communication costs and delay than bidding, although the use of incomplete, inaccurate, and out-of-date state information increases the risk of making wrong decisions. In addition to these algorithms, a *flexible algorithm* that combines bidding and focused addressing is described and studied. It is designed to reap the benefits of both and to overcome the shortcomings inherent in using each by itself.

We also compare these algorithms with two baseline algorithms. One is the *noncooperative* algorithm. Here a task that is not guaranteed locally is not sent to any other node. The second is the *perfect-state-information* algorithm. This algorithm behaves exactly like the bidding algorithm, but it incurs no communication overheads.

One major contribution of this work is that it extends the state of the art in scheduling for real-time systems because it deals with algorithms that explicitly take into account the deadlines and resource needs of tasks. Besides proposing these algorithms, a major contribution of this paper is that the algorithms are evaluated to determine their effectiveness for scheduling tasks with hard real-time constraints and general resource requirements. The simulations compare the algorithms with different loads, different communication delays, different laxities, and different loads at the nodes in the system which causes an unbalanced system if no distributed scheduling is performed. The effects of a computation time reclaim policy that several of the algorithms have, as well as the effects of erroneously specifying worst case computation times of tasks (which is one of the inputs to the scheduling algorithms), are also studied.

Most related work on scheduling tasks with hard real-time constraints is restricted to CPU resources only [16], [11], [3], [8], [6], [15], [22]. Perhaps the only exception is the work reported in [9] wherein, given the general resource requirements of each task, the worst case response time of each task is determined. In Leinbaugh's model, a task is divided into multiple segments and the segments of a task can be executed concurrently on different nodes. His approach is useful at system design time to statically determine the upper bounds on response times.

In other work, Efe [4] and Ma [14] use *heuristic approaches* for related task allocation problems. According to Lenat [10], heuristics are informal, judgmental rules of thumb which come in two types: those that *actively* guide the system toward plausible paths to follow and those that guide the system away from implausible ones. Both Ma and Efe use heuristics to guide their systems away from implausible paths. This approach of only using the second type of heuristic is limited because in the worst case, the exponential search problem cannot be avoided. In our algorithm, both types of heuristics are used to prevent the exponential search problem [24].

The remainder of this paper is organized as follows. Section II defines the system model adopted in this paper. Section III describes the algorithms for dynamic scheduling in hard real-

---

[1] If tasks belong to different categories, such as essential and nonessential, or have different levels of importance, it is possible to define a suitable *weighted guarantee ratio*. We do not consider this case in this paper.

[2] If a task's execution has to be guaranteed in spite of failures, a guarantee should be obtained from multiple nodes. We do not discuss such multiple guarantees in this paper.

time distributed systems while Section IV discusses the details of the steps involved in bidding and focused addressing. The simulation results are presented and discussed in Section V. Section VI summarizes the work.

II. THE SYSTEM MODEL

There are n nodes, N_1, N_2, $\cdots$, N_n in a loosely coupled distributed system. Let each *node* contain a set of *distinct* resources, R_1, R_2, $\cdots$, R_r. A resource is an abstraction and can include CPU, I/O devices, files, data structures, etc. A resource is *active* if it has processing power, otherwise, it is *passive*. For example, a CPU or a physical device is active, but a file is passive. Thus, a passive resource must always be used with some active resource. Some resources can be (simultaneously) shared by multiple tasks while others, such as a CPU, have to be assigned exclusively to one task. Furthermore, if a sharable resource, such as a file, is modified by a task, the resource should be exclusively assigned to the task.

A *task* is a scheduling entity and its execution cannot be preempted. The following characteristics of a task T are assumed known when it arrives:

• The worst case computation time $C(T)$: Tasks in real-time system have to be designed so that the difference between their worst case and normal execution times is not large. Otherwise, when resources are assigned to a task for its worst case execution time, poor resource utilization will result. In this regard, a dynamic scheduling scheme has advantages since based on the input parameters of a dynamically invoked task, a lower worst case computation time can be determined (compared to a statically determined worst case computation time).

• The deadline $D(T)$ by which the task must complete: (The *laxity* of a task T is defined to be $(D(T) - C(T) -$ current time).)

• The resource requirements of the task: It is assumed that a task needs all its resources throughout its execution. A task will request at least one active resource and zero or more passive resources.

There are two types of tasks: *nonperiodic tasks* and *periodic tasks*. A *nonperiodic task* arrives at any node dynamically and has to be executed before its deadline. An instance of a *periodic task* with period P should be executed once every P units of time. Periodic tasks are assigned to nodes at system initialization time and their timely execution is guaranteed when nonperiodic tasks are scheduled. Since periodic tasks remain on the node where they are initially assigned, this paper focuses on the distributed scheduling of nonperiodic tasks. The effect of periodic tasks on local scheduling is, however, taken into account.

In addition to resource requirements and timing constraints, tasks in real-time systems are also characterized by their *priority* and *precedence constraints*. The priority of a task encodes its *level of importance* relative to other tasks. Precedence constraints enter the picture when tasks communicate or when a complex task is viewed in terms of a number of subtasks related by precedence constraints. Whereas distributed scheduling of tasks with precedence constraints is the subject of [2] and prioritized tasks are considered in [1], this paper focuses on tasks that are independent and have equal priority. This focus was chosen in order to carefully study a set of algorithms that vary in their complexity but have general applicability. Consideration of precedence and priority would have added to the (already) large number of variables that can affect the results.

On each node, there are three components involved in the task. The *local scheduler* handles scheduling of tasks that arrive at a given node. The *dispatcher* invokes the next task to be executed based on the schedule determined by the local scheduler. The *global scheduler* interacts with the schedulers on other nodes in order to perform distributed scheduling.

Nodes are connected by a communication network. In describing the algorithms, no specific communication topology is assumed. However, depending on the topology of a given network, an algorithm could be optimized. Some of the algorithms presented here implicitly take topology information into account, for instance, in determining the nodes to which local state information is sent.

III. ALGORITHMS FOR GLOBAL SCHEDULING

When a local task T arrives at a node N_i, the *local scheduler* of N_i is invoked to try to guarantee the newly arrived task on the node. If the task can be guaranteed, it will be added to the *schedule* which contains all the guaranteed tasks on the node. Details of the local scheduling algorithm can be found in [24], [25], and [19]. This section discusses five algorithms for dealing with a task that is not guaranteed locally.

The first plausible algorithm is the *noncooperative algorithm* (NC). When a task cannot be guaranteed locally, it is rejected. No attempt is made to send the task to other nodes. One can see that if all nodes are heavily loaded, a noncooperative strategy is the best. This algorithm is used as a baseline in the simulation studies.

The second algorithm is the *random scheduling algorithm* (RSA). In this algorithm, when a task cannot be locally guaranteed, the node sends the task to a *randomly* selected node. The advantage of this algorithm is that it uses minimum communication overhead to determine the node to which a task should be sent. The disadvantage is that it is easy to send a task to an *improper* node because of the randomness.

A more informed choice can be made by a node if it has information about the state of other nodes, in particular, about the resources available on a node as well as the node's surplus resources. The three algorithms to be discussed next consider a remote node as a candidate for receiving a task only if that node contains the resources needed by this task. Among the nodes that meet this criterion, a node is chosen based on the surplus information with respect to the required resources.

Each node periodically calculates the *node surplus* and sends it to a subset of the nodes in the system. The node surplus provides information about the available time on resources, after taking into account resource utilization of *local* tasks, i.e., the tasks that directly arrived at a node from the external environment and not from other nodes. A node's surplus is a vector, with one entry per resource on that node. Each entry indicates the total amount of time, in a (past) window, during which a resource is not used by the local tasks. The window is a time interval $[(t - WL), t]$ where t is the current time, and WL is the length of the window which is an adjustable parameter of the algorithm. For example, within the recent window, suppose 400 time units is the sum of the length of all the time intervals during which a resource R on a node is not used by any task. Then the surplus on that node for resource R is said to be 400 time units. WL should not be too short—in this case, it may reflect the transient behavior of a node, and not too long—in this case, it may not reflect the changes that are of legitimate interest to other nodes.

A node sorts other nodes according to the number of tasks received from them that were guaranteed on this node in the past time window. Then, according to this sorted node list, the node selects a subset of nodes to send information on its own current node surplus. The subset is chosen such that nodes in the subset will potentially use this information in deciding whether or not to send a task to this node. Hence, the nodes which recently sent more tasks to this node will more likely be selected. The above strategy minimizes the overheads of exchanging surplus information. One effect of this is that not all nodes will have the same state information about other nodes. If the network is small, the surplus information can be sent to all the other nodes.

Recall that a node has the estimate of the surplus of a given resource on other nodes. Thus, knowing the resources needed by a task and the computation time of the task the node can determine whether one or more nodes are in a position to meet the task's needs. The three algorithms discussed next differ in the way they select the node to which the task should be sent.

The three algorithms are the *bidding algorithm*, the *focused addressing algorithm*, and the *flexible algorithm*. In this section, we provide a very high-level overview of the algorithms. All the details necessary to fully understand the workings of these algorithms are provided in Section IV. Section IV also shows how the bidding algorithm and the focused addressing algorithm are special cases of the flexible algorithm.

The *focused addressing* (FA) algorithm works as follows. When N_i has a task that is not locally guaranteed, it determines the node with the highest surplus in the resources needed by the task. If this surplus is greater than *focused addressing surplus* (FAS), a tunable system parameter, the task is immediately sent to that node. If no such node is found, the task is rejected.

In the *bidding* algorithm, k nodes with sufficient surplus in the resources needed by this task are selected. The value of k is chosen to maximize the chances of finding a node for the task. A request-for-bid message is sent to these nodes. When a node receives the request-for-bid message, it calculates a bid, indicating the likelihood that the task can be guaranteed on the node, and if it is higher than MB, the minimum required bid, it sends the bid to the node which issued the request-for-bid. After receiving the bids, N_i sends the task to the node which offers the best bid. If there is no good bid available for the task, it is assumed that no node in the network is able to guarantee the task.

Here are the steps involved in the *flexible* algorithm for a task T that is not locally guaranteed.

- N_i selects k nodes with sufficient surplus in the resources needed by T. If the largest value of the surplus of these k nodes is greater than FAS, then the node with that surplus is chosen as the *focused* node. If a focused node is found, T is immediately sent to that node. In addition to sending the task to the focused node, node N_i sends in parallel, a request-for-bid message to the remaining $k - 1$ nodes. The request-for-bid message also contains the identity of the focused node if there is one.

- When a node receives the request-for-bid message, it calculates a bid, indicating the likelihood that T can be guaranteed on the node, and sends the bid to the focused node if there is one, otherwise, to the original node which issued the request-for-bid.

- When a task reaches a focused node, it first invokes the local scheduler to try to guarantee T. If it succeeds, all the bids for T will be ignored. If it fails, the bids for T are evaluated and T is sent to the node responding with the "highest bid." A message about whether and where T is finally guaranteed is sent to the original node. The original node then modifies its surplus information about other nodes accordingly.

- In case there is no focused node, the original node will receive the bids for T and will send T to the node which offers the best bid.

- If the focused node cannot guarantee T and if there is no good bid available for T, then corrective actions as described Section IV-C can be taken.

IV. Details of Bidding and Focused Addressing

This section deals with the estimation and proper use of node surplus, the heuristics for choosing focused nodes, the strategies for making bids, and the evaluation of the bids. The details provided are in the context of the flexible algorithm. We also discuss the conditions under which the flexible algorithm behaves like the focused addressing and the bidding algorithm.

A. Focused Addressing and Requesting Bids

The global scheduler at each node of the distributed system is responsible for doing focused addressing and requesting bids. For $j = 1, \cdots, n$ and $j \neq i$, the global scheduler on node N_i estimates

$$ES(T, j) = \text{number of instances of task } T$$
$$\text{that node } N_j \text{ can guarantee.} \quad (1)$$

This estimation is made according to the node surplus information of resources available on node N_i and provides a good indication of the likelihood of a site being able to guarantee a given task. The global scheduler then uses this estimate to decide whether or not to try focused addressing and/or bidding.

For example, assume that the computation time of task T is 250 time units. Suppose node N_s is estimated to have a minimum surplus of 400 time units on *each* of the resources needed by T in the time interval in which task T must run. We say that the surplus of N_i with respect to the resources needed by task T is 400. Then $\mathrm{ES}(T, s) = 400/250 = 1.6$. The global scheduler on node N_i sorts the nodes according to their $\mathrm{ES}(T, j)$, in descending order. The first k nodes are selected to participate in focused addressing and bidding. The value of k is decided such that the sum of $\mathrm{ES}(T, j)$ of the k nodes is larger than or equal to SGS, the *systemwide guarantee surplus*. This is a tunable parameter of the system. If the first node N_f among the k nodes has its $\mathrm{ES}(T, f)$ larger than FAS, the *focused addressing surplus*, node N_f is selected as the focused node. The task is immediately sent to that node. The remaining $k - 1$ nodes are sent request-for-bid messages in parallel, to handle the case where the focused node cannot guarantee the task. A request-for-bid message includes information about the deadline and computation time of the task as well as the latest bid arrival time, i.e., time by which bids should reach the focused/requesting node to be eligible for further consideration. The latest bid arrival time for a task T, $L(T)$, is estimated as follows:

$$L(T) = D(T) - C(T) - (\mathrm{TD} + \mathrm{SD}) \qquad (2)$$

where $D(T)$ is the deadline of T, $C(T)$ is the computation time of T, TD is the (networkwide) average transmission delay between two nodes, and SD is the average scheduling delay on a *bidder node*. Thus, on the average, at or before $L(T)$ there will be sufficient time to send the task to a bidder node, for it to be scheduled there, and then be executed before its deadline.

System performance is sensitive to the values assigned to SGS and FAS. FAS should be such that the chance of a focused node guaranteeing a task will be high. SGS should not be too high, otherwise too many messages will be transmitted in the network. It should not be too low since this may result in too many *remote* tasks (i.e., tasks that were not locally scheduled) not being guaranteed, because request-for-bid messages may not be sent to the nodes that can guarantee a task.

B. Bidding, Bid Evaluation, and Response to Task Awarded

When a node receives a request-for-bid message for a task, it calculates a bid for the task. The *bid* indicates the number of instances of the task the bidder node can guarantee. The calculation is done in two steps. First, an upper bound of the bid, Max-Bid, is determined by

The second step calculates the actual bid. In this step, a binary search between 0 and Max-Bid is performed. In each stage of the binary search, a given number of instances of task T are temporarily inserted into the current schedule of this node, and it is checked whether the inserted instances can also be guaranteed. The maximum number of instances of the remote task T that this node can actually guarantee without jeopardizing previously guaranteed tasks is obtained at the end of the search. This number, if above *minimum bid* (MB), a tunable parameter, becomes the bid. The bid is sent to the node selected for focused addressing if there is one. Otherwise, the bid is sent to the original node which issued the request-for-bid message. The inserted instances of the remote task are removed from the schedule on a bidder's node. Hence, the schedule on the bidder's node is not affected by the bid it makes. This implies that a node does not reserve the resources needed by the tasks for which it bids. Since a node will typically bid for multiple tasks and multiple bids will be received for a task, reservation of resources will result in pessimistic bids and hence may reduce system performance.

When a node receives a bid for a given task, and the bid is higher than *high bid* (HB), a tunable parameter, the node awards the task to the bidding node immediately and all other bids for this task, that arrived earlier or may arrive later, are discarded. If all the bids that have arrived for a given task are lower than HB, the node postpones making the awarding decision until $L(T)$, the latest bid arrival time of the task. At time $L(T)$, the task will be awarded to the highest bidder, if any.

When the awarded task arrives at the highest bidder, the local scheduler on that node is invoked to see if the task can be guaranteed. Clearly, the state of the node may have changed after making a bid and since resources needed by the task were not reserved, the task may or may not be guaranteed. If the task is not guaranteed, it is rejected.

Note that this algorithm requires five tunable parameters: WL, FAS, SGS, MB, and HB. Section V-B discusses these parameters in more depth.

C. Dealing with Unguaranteed Tasks

In all these algorithms, the action to be taken when a task is not guaranteed depends on the application requirements as well as on the characteristics of the task. If the task has sufficient laxity, then another attempt at global scheduling may

$$\mathrm{Max\text{-}Bid} = \frac{\mathrm{Min(Free\ Time\ of\ Each\ Resource\ Required\ by\ the\ Task)}}{\mathrm{Computation\ Time\ of\ the\ Task}}. \qquad (3)$$

The free time is calculated to be the sum of the lengths of the free time slots between the estimated earliest task arrival time on this node and the task's deadline. The earliest arrival time is estimated in an optimistic manner to be the sum of current time, the minimum message delay in transmitting the bid, and the minimum message delay in sending the task to the bidder. Max-Bid is also calculated optimistically to be the best possible bid that this node can make assuming ideal availability of resources that the task needs, i.e., assuming that all the time slots when a resource is idle appear together and that all the needed resources are concurrently idle.

be made. However, this will increase the scheduling and communication overheads. In general, the invoker of a task that is not guaranteed may invoke the same task with an increased deadline or may invoke another task that produces less precise results but with lower computational costs.

D. Relationship Between the Algorithms

Note that if FAS is small and SGS is equal to FAS, then k will be at most 1 and the flexible algorithm will behave like the focused addressing algorithm. If FAS is large, it behaves like the bidding algorithm. Thus, the flexible algorithm combines features from focused addressing and bidding, utilizing them in an opportunistic manner. The advantage of the flexible algorithm lies in the fact that its choice of focused addressing, bidding, or both is made *on a per-task basis*. For example, for a particular task, if a focused node cannot be found, a rather large subset of nodes, perhaps all the nodes in the network, will be sent the request-for-bid message. In this case, the scheme converges to the bidding scheme. On the other hand, if the surplus of the focused node is sufficiently large, the subset of the nodes to which the request-for-bid message is sent can be relatively small, perhaps even empty. In this case, the scheme converges to focused addressing.

V. EVALUATION OF THE ALGORITHMS THROUGH SIMULATION

In this section, simulation results are presented for the algorithms discussed in the previous sections. We will see how different variables, such as the network communication delay, the task laxity, the load distribution among nodes, and the task computation times affect the performance of the algorithms. Due to space limitations, not all results of the simulation studies are included here. The reader is referred to [19] for a complete presentation and discussion of the results.

A. Simulation Model

The simulation is made with a system having six nodes where each node has two active resources and three passive resources. (Were it not for the excessive CPU time and memory requirements needed for this simulation we would have experimented with a larger set of nodes and with more resources.) There is one periodic task per node. It has a period of 2000 time units and a computation time of 400 units. The periodic task needs all the resources.

Unless specified otherwise, both the computation time and laxity of nonperiodic tasks are normally distributed. The mean of tasks' computation time and laxity are 400 and 600 time units, respectively, with respective standard deviations being 100 and 300.

The nonperiodic tasks arrive as a Poisson process. The arrival rates of nonperiodic tasks on different nodes may be different, resulting in differences in the node loads. Let us define the term *systemwide nonperiodic task arrival rate* (abbreviated as R) as the sum of the nonperiodic task arrival rates of all the nodes. To normalize the arrival rate, in the rest of this section let us define the task arrival rate to be the average number of arrivals per 400 time units (400 is the mean task computation time). Because of this normalization, the specific value chosen for the computation time, namely 400, is not very important. Also, even though we have chosen the nominal value for the mean laxity to be 600, we also study the effect of different laxity values.

Each nonperiodic task requires at least one active resource and zero or more passive resources. A task's resource requirements are chosen randomly. A nonperiodic task requests each of the two active resources with a probability of 2/3 and each passive resource with a probability of 0.5. (This choice is arbitrary. It affects the performance via its effect on the system load L.) For a given system nonperiodic task arrival rate R, L is measured as the average load on the active

resources. It can be determined by

$$L = (2/3)(R/n) + 0.20 \qquad (4)$$

where n is the number of nodes. The first term gives the average load on an active resource of a node caused by the nonperiodic tasks. The second term is due to periodic tasks (since periodic tasks take 400/2000, i.e., 20 percent, of computation power in each node).

The simulation model assumes that the global scheduler and the local scheduler are executed on a specially designed coprocessor dedicated to scheduling and other system support tasks. Such a coprocessor isolates application tasks from external interrupts and from the overheads caused by the execution of kernel modules and thus contributes to predictable behavior. Since real-time systems are characterized by the specialized hardware, for example, to process information from sensors, dependence on an additional piece of specialized hardware is not unreasonable, especially because of the additional benefits that it offers. The presence of the coprocessor does not imply the absence of the time delay involved in guaranteeing a task. These delays, proportional to the square of the size of the task set processed by the guarantee routine [24], are taken into account. In the simulation studies, the constant of proportionality is taken to be 2. Thus, if the maximum number of tasks processed at any given time by the guarantee routine is 5 (as was the case in our simulation scenarios), then a task incurs a worst case guarantee overhead of a little over 10 percent of the average computation time of a task.

Nodes communicate with each other through a *star* communication network (see Fig. 1). Each channel is associated with a node. One end of a channel is connected to the node it is associated with. The other ends of all channels are connected together.

Messages, sent by a node to another, will pass the sender's channel first, then the receiver's channel. Messages pass a channel in a first-come-first-served fashion with only one message occupying a channel at a given time. When a message is in a channel, if another message needs to be transmitted through the channel (in either direction), the latter must wait until the first has left the channel. The total time for transmitting a message from one node to another without any waits is denoted as *conflict-free message delay* (MD). Because a message from one node to another passes two channels, the time taken by a message to pass a channel is half of its message delay.

Communication delays are also incurred for transferring tasks. In real-time systems, the set of tasks that execute in the system is known before the system begins operation. Because of this, it is feasible to store the code of the task at one or more nodes (in particular, those that have the resources needed by the task), or all nodes if the number of nodes is not large. Thus, when one node wants another to execute a task, it needs to provide the other with information identifying the task as well as inputs relevant to the task. In this case, sending the task implies sending this required information. Only when task code is not available at the receiving node is it necessary for the sender to send the code for the task as well.

For the purpose of the simulation studies, we assume that

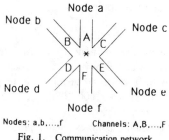

Node a
Node b Node c
B A C
*
D E
F
Node d Node e
Node f

Nodes: a,b,...,f   Channels: A,B,...,F

Fig. 1. Communication network.

the delay involved in transferring a task to another node is equal to the message delay plus 10 percent of the computation time of the task. Whereas the choice of the figure 10 percent is arbitrary, a fixed percentage of the task's computation time can be justified: since the sender of a task sends the data needed for the execution of a task, it is plausible to assume that the amount of data processed by a task is proportional to the amount of processing done by the task. Another, but perhaps less plausible, explanation is that the longer a task executes, the larger its code is.

Overall, the above network topology, the communication protocol, and the models for the communication overheads were chosen for simulation because they accentuate the effect of communication overhead on the performance of the algorithms.

It is often the case that the performance of a distributed scheduling algorithm depends on the differences in the node loads. In order to quantify the differences in the node loads, and for the sake of simplicity, let us assume that the nonperiodic task arrival rates of the six nodes form an equal-rate sequence, and the rate is denoted as the *load distribution factor* (B). That is, if the load distribution factor takes a value of B, and if at the first node, on average, N tasks arrive per unit time, then the ith node has an arrival rate of NB^{i-1}. For example, if $B = 0.5$, and $N = 2$, then nodes 1–6 experience an arrival rate of 2, 1, 0.5, 0.25, 0.125, and 0.0625, respectively. The balance rate is between 0 and 1, and the closer to 1 it is, the more balanced the node loads will be.

Clearly, the value assigned to the different tunable parameters will affect the system performance. This is attested by the simulation studies; results of only some of these are reported here due to space limitations. These studies indicate that the algorithms studied here are *relatively stable* in the sense that the percentage change in system performance for a given change in parameter value is very small. In practice, this implies that the system performance will not change drastically when the parameters do not deviate much from the "best value"—the value at which the best system performance is achieved for a given application. We return to the issue of stability further at the end of Section V-B.

For the simulation studies, the values for the tunable parameters are set as follows. Simulation studies (not reported here) indicated that an "optimum" WL value lies in the range of 30–70 times the mean task interarrival time, depending on task characteristics. So the window length is set to be 50 times the mean of the task interarrival times. Surplus information is transmitted to other nodes periodically where the period is also set to be 50 times the mean task interarrival times. Since the network has only six nodes, suprlus information is sent to all the nodes in the network.

The message traffic created by the transmission of surplus information as well as *all* other messages generated in the course of scheduling is included in the simulation model.

Systemwide guarantee surplus (SGS) is 2.0. Focused addressing surplus (FAS) is 1.2. Minimum bid (MB) is 1.0, and high bid (HB) is 2.0.

Each data point in the simulation results reported in the following sections indicates the average of three runs where each run was made to last for (at least) 3000 times the mean task interarrival time. The 95 percent confidence intervals for these data points are less than 2 percent.

Before presenting the simulation results, let us define the following terms to describe the system's performance. Since meeting task deadlines is the goal of any hard real-time system, the guarantee ratio is a good measure of the performance of scheduling algorithms.

$$G = \text{System Task Guarantee Ratio}$$

$$= \frac{\text{Total Number of Tasks Guaranteed}}{\text{Total Number of Task Arrivals}} \qquad (5)$$

$$G_{\text{NP}} = \text{System Nonperiodic Task Guarantee Ratio}$$

$$= \frac{\text{Total Number of Nonperiodic Tasks Guaranteed}}{\text{Total Number of Nonperiodic Task Arrivals}} \qquad (6)$$

$$G_{\text{NP-local}} = \text{System Nonperiodic Local Task Guarantee Ratio}$$

$$= \frac{\text{Total Number of Local Nonperiodic Tasks Guaranteed}}{\text{Total Number of Nonperiodic Task Arrivals}} \qquad (7)$$

$$G_{\text{NP-remote}} = \text{System Nonperiodic Remote Task Guarantee Ratio}$$

$$= \frac{\text{Total Number of Remote Nonperiodic Tasks Guaranteed}}{\text{Total Number of Nonperiodic Task Arrivals}} \qquad (8)$$

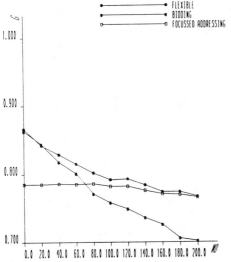

Fig. 2. Performance of bidding, focused addressing, and flexible algorithms—heavy load.

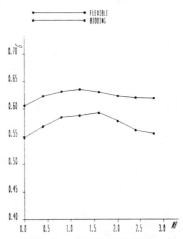

Fig. 3. Stability of flexible and bidding algorithms with respect to MB.

B. Comparison of Focused Addressing, Bidding, and the Flexible Algorithms

The first set of simulation results show how the communication delay affects the performance (G) of the three algorithms that utilize state information.

In this simulation, three of the six nodes have equal loads which are higher than the remaining three nodes which also have equal loads. The load on the latter was set to be 0.3 times that of the former. Note that for a given system arrival rate R and the ratio of the node loads in the two sets, the arrival rate for each node can be determined. Fig. 2 shows the performance when the system load is heavy (the system nonperiodic task arrival rate R is equal to 6 per 400 time units, and the system load $L = 0.87$). We study the performance under different conflict-free message delays (MD) from 0, with increments of 20 time units, up to 200 time units. The performance of the flexible algorithm is compared to the bidding algorithm and the focused addressing algorithm. From the figure, the following are observed.

• The communication overhead has explicit effect on the performance of the flexible algorithm as well as the bidding algorithm. For example, when the load is heavy, the performance of the flexible algorithm degrades by about 10 percent when MD increases from 0 to 200.

• The performance of the focused addressing algorithm is not as sensitive to MD as the other two algorithms. But, when MD is small, the difference in the performances between the focused addressing algorithm and the flexible algorithms is higher than when MD is large.

• The performance curve of the flexible algorithm follows the "envelope" of the curves for the bidding and the focused addressing algorithms, indicating that the flexible algorithm performs well over almost the entire range of MD's. In fact, for most communication delays, the flexible algorithm does better than bidding and focused addressing. This is because, unlike these algorithms (that use one scheme for all tasks), the flexible algorithm chooses to do bidding, focused addressing,

or both on a per-task basis, depending on the system state and task characteristics at the time the choice is made.

• The performance of the bidding algorithm is close to the flexible one when MD is small (below 40). As MD increases, the difference in the performance between the two schemes increases.

• When MD is very high, focused addressing is a better choice than bidding. This is because bidding involves more message traffic. Also, the overhead of processing the request-for-bid messages and bids affects the performance of the bidding algorithm. The performance of the flexible algorithm is equal to the focused addressing algorithm for MD above 160, showing the adaptability of the flexible algorithm.

The flexible algorithm uses a number of tunable parameters: WL, FAS, SGS, HB, MB. Of these, FAS and MB are expected to have more impact on the performance than the others. This is because FAS is used to determine a focused node, and MB determines whether or not a node is going to offer a bid. Figs. 3 and 4 show the effect of these two parameters on the performance of the bidding, focused addressing, and the flexible algorithms. The figures show that with respect to these two parameters, the algorithms are *relatively stable*, that is, their performance does not vary widely when the parameter value is varied. In addition, while producing better performance, the flexible algorithm also displays better stability compared to bidding and focused addressing algorithms. Similar observations have also been made for other parameters such as WL, SGS, and HB. They are not reported here due to space limitations. We believe that five tunable parameters for a distributed scheduling algorithm that takes deadlines and resource allocation into account is not unreasonable. For example, the VAX VMS uniprocessor scheduling algorithm is a multilevel feedback queue that has many tunable parameters including the base level priority of a task, the highest priority level, the rate at which a priority is increased for an I/O, the rate at which the priority is dropped for using up a whole time slice, the length of the time slice, etc.

Since the flexible algorithm performs better than bidding and focused addressing based algorithms, in the remainder of this section we focus on the flexible algorithm.

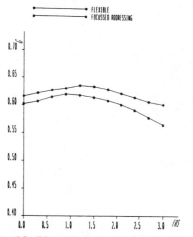

Fig. 4. Stability of flexible and focused addressing algorithms with respect to FAS.

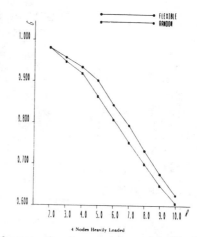

Fig. 6. Performance of random scheduling and flexible algorithms—four nodes heavily loaded.

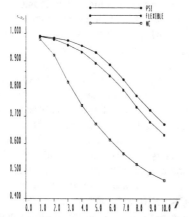

Fig. 5. Performance of noncooperative (NC), perfect-state-information (PSI), and flexible algorithms—$B = 0.50$.

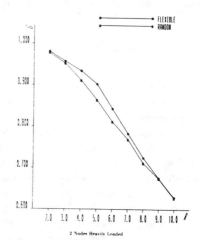

Fig. 7. Performance of random scheduling and flexible algorithms—two nodes heavily loaded.

C. Comparison of Flexible Algorithm to the Baselines

We now compare the performance of the flexible algorithm to that of the noncooperative algorithm and the *perfect state information scheduling algorithm* (PSI). The PSI algorithm behaves like the bidding algorithm except for the following differences. Communication overheads are zero, i.e., the system overheads to obtain surplus information is assumed to be zero and the cost of sending request for bids as well as bids is also assumed to be zero. The performance of this algorithm should be better than all practical algorithms, thus serving as an upper bound for a distributing scheduling algorithm.

Here we report on the case when $B = 0.50$. The system nonperiodic task arrival rate R varies from 1.00 to 10.00. MD is 30 time units. Fig. 5 plots the guarantee ratio G versus system nonperiodic task arrival rate R. It depicts the performance of the flexible algorithm, the noncooperative algorithm (NC), and the perfect state information algorithm (PSI).

These simulation results indicate that the performance of the flexible algorithm is much better than the lower bound offered by the noncooperative algorithm, and is close to the upper bound achieved by the perfect state information algorithm, irrespective of values of the load distribution factor.

D. Comparison of Flexible and Random Algorithms

We now show the simulation results that compare the performance of the flexible algorithm to that of the random scheduling algorithm. The simulation parameters are set as before.

Two cases were tested. In each case, the flexible scheduling algorithm and the random scheduling algorithm are studied with nonperiodic task arrival rate from 2 to 10 per 400 time units. In the first case, there are four nodes which are relatively heavily loaded, and two nodes which are relatively lightly loaded. In the second, there are two nodes relatively heavily loaded, two nodes moderately loaded, and another two nodes lightly loaded. MD is 30 time units.

Figs. 6 and 7 show the results.

• In general, the flexible algorithm performs better than the random focused addressing algorithm, especially at moderate loads. This is expected, since the decisions of the flexible algorithm are made by using the networkwide surplus information, but in the random focused addressing algorithm, they are made randomly.

• However, because the flexible algorithm uses much more

communication than the random scheduling algorithm, the nonnegligible communication delay may hurt the flexible algorithm, resulting in a poor performance, especially when the system load is very high. However, the flexible algorithm contains mechanisms to avoid sending messages which are not necessary, for example, by choosing to do just focused addressing. From the simulation results shown above, it can be seen that even in the cases when the system load is very high, the flexible algorithm performs better than the random scheduling algorithm. This fact indicates that the mechanisms in the flexible algorithm to prevent the transmission of unnecessary messages have a positive effect.

• When the system load is very low, the performance difference between the flexible algorithm and the random scheduling algorithm is negligible. This is because when the load is light, most of the nodes have enough surplus so that any node selected randomly is as good as any other. For a similar reason, when the nodes are well balanced and the system load is high, the random algorithm should perform as well as the flexible algorithm. When the system is overloaded (say $R >$ 8), the performance difference between the flexible algorithm and the random algorithm is very small. The minimal communication overheads incurred by the random algorithm play an important role here.

It is important to note that the above results were obtained after including the overheads incurred by the flexible algorithm and thus its complexity has been taken into account. Even with this, it performs better than the simpler random scheduling although the performance difference is less than 5 percent in the cases studied. As was discussed in the Introduction, in a hard real-time system, every task that misses its deadline can seriously degrade the performance of the system. Hence, even a small performance improvement may be considered significant in the context of hard real-time systems.

E. Effect of Task Laxity on the Performance of the Flexible Algorithm

This study examines how the laxity of tasks affects the performance of the flexible algorithm. Three nodes have heavier loads compared to the remaining three nodes. The load of the latter is 0.3 times that of the former. We study the performance of three cases.

1) The laxity is relatively small with a normal distribution having a mean of 300 and a standard deviation of 150, denoted as $N(300, 150^2)$;

2) The laxity is moderate with a distribution of $N(600, 300^2)$; and

3) The laxity is large with a distribution of $N(900, 450^2)$.

All the laxities are larger than 0. In each case, the system nonperiodic task arrival rate R varies from 1 to 9 per 400 time units. From the simulation results (Fig. 8), the following observations can be made.

• The task laxity affects the system performance. When the laxity increases from $N(300, 150^2)$ to $N(900, 450^2)$, the number of tasks guaranteed increases significantly. For example, when $R = 5.0$, the system task guarantee ratio increases substantially from 76.3 to 92.6 percent.

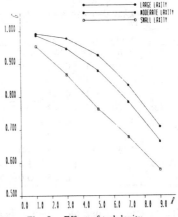

Fig. 8.   Effect of task laxity.

• The system performance, measured as the system task guarantee ratio, is not a linear function of the mean of the laxity. For example, when the nonperiodic task arrival rate is 5.0 and the mean of the laxity increases from 300 to 600, the system task guarantee ratio increases from 76.3 to 87.9 percent, i.e., 12.6 percent. While the laxity increases from 600 to 900, and the system task guarantee ratio increases from 87.9 to 92.6 percent, i.e., 4.7 percent. When the arrival rate is small, this increase is more obvious than when the rate is high.

F. Effect of Load Distribution on the Flexible Algorithm

The purpose of this study is to examine how the differences in the loads of nodes affects the performance of the flexible algorithm.

Nine cases were studied (Cases $A-I$). For MD = 10 time units, the system load is varied from 3, 6, to 9 (Cases $A-C$). This is repeated for MD = 60 time units (Cases $D-F$) and 120 time units (Cases $G-I$). In each case, the load distribution factor (B) takes values of 0.1, 0.3, 0.5, 0.7, 0.9, and 1.0.

For convenience of discussion, the simulation results of these nine cases are summarized in Table I. The table lists the differences between the best and worst performance in each case (under the column of ''diff''), and points out when (in terms of load distribution factor B) the maximum performance occurs (under the column of ''max'').

Based on these simulation studies, the following observations can be made.

• The node balance has a great effect on the local nonperiodic task guarantee ratios. The difference due to the node imbalance may be as high as 50 percent (Cases A, D, and G). That is, in the case where the system is heavily unbalanced, the tasks guaranteed locally may be 50 percent less than in the case where the system is well balanced.

• Consequently, the node balance affects $G_{NP-remote}$, the percentage of nonperiodic tasks which are remotely guaranteed. This percentage typically has its maximum at the load distribution factor of 0.1. This is because at that time some nodes are very heavily loaded while others are very lightly loaded and hence the system has the most number of tasks which cannot be guaranteed locally. However, it is interesting to see that sometimes $G_{NP-remote}$ does not have its maximum at the load distribution factor of 0.1, but at the load distribution

TABLE I
SUMMARY OF CASE A–CASE I

Case	$G_{NP-local}$		$G_{NP-remote}$		G_{NP}		G	
	diff	max	diff	max	diff	max	diff	max
A	0.499	1.0	0.459	0.1	0.045	0.9	0.038	0.9
B	0.448	1.0	0.386	0.1	0.060	0.9	0.051	0.9
C	0.348	1.0	0.310	0.1	0.078	0.7	0.069	0.7
D	0.502	1.0	0.426	0.1	0.087	0.9	0.063	0.9
E	0.476	1.0	0.362	0.1	0.113	1.0	0.095	1.0
F	0.366	1.0	0.184	0.3	0.214	0.9	0.189	0.9
G	0.501	1.0	0.389	0.1	0.103	1.0	0.085	1.0
H	0.474	1.0	0.341	0.1	0.150	1.0	0.126	1.0
I	0.387	1.0	0.221	0.3	0.255	0.9	0.225	0.9

factor of 0.3. This happens when the system is heavily loaded and the MD is not small (Cases F and I). One explanation is that when the system is heavily unbalanced and MD is not small, too many remote tasks and the messages for scheduling them are transmitted in the network such that the overall network delay increases.

• The node balance has an explicit effect on system performance—the total task guarantee ratio G. For example, in Case I it causes a difference of 22.5 percent in the total task guarantee ratios.

• However, it is interesting to notice that in only three out of nine cases the maximum performance is achieved at the best balanced situation (node load distribution factor = 1.0). This is because when the nodes are slightly unbalanced, the benefit, gained from sending nonperiodic tasks which cannot be locally guaranteed to other nodes (where their resource requirements match with other tasks there), may be larger than the loss due to the imbalance. Also, since resource requirements are also considered, a balanced arrival rate across all nodes does not imply a balanced load on all resources of a node. The tables show that in most cases as soon as the load distribution factor B reaches 0.7, the system performance is very close to the maximum it can achieve. Consequently, a perfect node balance is not necessary with the flexible algorithm.

The results show that although a perfect node balance is not necessary, an extremely unbalanced situation should be avoided. To prevent such a situation, algorithms discussed in this paper can be augmented to balance loads by transfering guaranteed tasks from highly loaded nodes to nodes that are lightly loaded. Of course, such transfers should be attempted only after ensuring that the task will remain guaranteed even after the transfer.

G. Effect of Task Computation Times on the Flexible Algorithm

In the simulation discussed so far, it was assumed that no matter what the real computation time is, the system allocates the resources needed by the task for the worst case computation time. Obviously, under this policy, resources are wasted if a task completes before its worst case computation time.

In the simulation results reported in this subsection, each time when a task finishes (in many cases, before its worst case computation time) the resources are allocated to the task which needs these resources and is waiting to be dispatched. The simulation results show that the system performance can be improved significantly under this *reclaim policy*.

Tasks are normally guaranteed with respect to their worst case computation times. In practice, it is often very difficult to predict precisely the computation time for a task. That is, the estimation of task computation times in practice always has some error. Consequently, the worst computation time claimed by the task must be the estimated computation time plus the maximum error under the estimation. We will show by simulation that although the maximum error affects the system performance, the flexible algorithm can tolerate a certain amount of this error.

MD in the simulation is set to be 60 time units. $B = 0.6$.

Effect of Reclaim Policy: In this part of the simulation, we will see how the reclaim policy improves the system performance under different cases.

The worst case computation for a nonperiodic task is a random number from $N(400, 100^2)$. The real computation time of a task is assumed to be a uniform random number taken from the interval which is centered by the mean computation time and right-bounded by the claimed worst case computation time. For example, if the mean computation time = 360 and the claimed worst computation time = 400, then the real computation time is randomly taken from [320, 400].

For a given worst case computation time of a task, the mean computation time of the task is determined by a parameter K which is defined as

$$K = \frac{\text{Mean of Nonperiodic Task Computation Time}}{\text{Worst Case Nonperiodic Task Computation Time}}. \qquad (9)$$

Note that when K equals 1.0, the system reflects the original policy. To testify that the system performs better under the reclaim policy, we should show that the system guarantee ratio G is higher when $K < 1$ than when $K = 1$.

We test three cases for the system nonperiodic task arrival rates to be 3, 6, and 9 per 400 time units, respectively. In each case, we let K vary from 0.5 to 1.0. The simulation results are shown in Fig. 9. As expected, the new policy does improve the system performance, i.e., the system task guarantee ratio G. When the system load increases, the improvement increases. In the overload case, if K is 0.5, the improvement can be as high as 14 percent.

It should be pointed out that the flexible algorithm can be enhanced to take into account the fact that many tasks do not execute up to their worst case computation times. For instance, higher bids can be made by a node if it expects guaranteed tasks to finish sooner than is indicated by their worst case computation times. The results reported here do not include the effect of any such enhancement.

Effect of the Maximum Error: Here, we will examine how the maximum error in estimating the computation time for a task may affect the system performance. We assume that it is possible to know the value of the maximum error rate.

For simplicity, we fix the mean computation time for all tasks to be 400 time units. The worst case computation time, which a task claims when it arrives, will be (1 + maximum error rate) × 400. The actual computation time of a task is

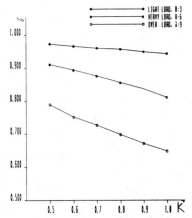

Fig. 9.   Effect of reclaiming unused task computation times.

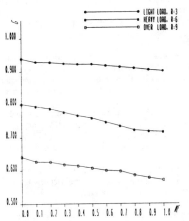

Fig. 10.   Effect of the maximum error in the estimation of task computation times.

randomly chosen from the interval of [(1 − maximum error rate) × 400, (1 + maximum error rate) × 400]. The reclaim policy is used.

We test three cases with the system nonperiodic task arrival rate R being 3, 6, and 9 per 400 time units, respectively. In each case, we let the maximum error rate (ME) vary from 0.0 to 1.0. From Fig. 10, the following can be observed.

• The maximum error in estimating computation time of tasks can affect the system performance. When the error increases, the system performance decreases in all three cases. Specifically, when the system load is high (heavy load or overload) and the error is large (> 50 percent), the system performance will degrade significantly. However, when the maximum error is small (< 20 percent), in all three cases the task guarantee ratios reduce by at most 1.5 percent, compared with the error rate of 0. We conclude that the flexible algorithm can tolerate small amounts of error of this kind.

• The difference between the maximum and minimum guarantee ratios for light load is 93.9 − 90.1 = 2.8 percent; for heavy load is 80.1 − 71.6 = 8.5 percent; and for overload is 64.1 − 57.1 = 7.0 percent. It is interesting to observe that when the system load is heavy, the effect of the maximum error is larger than when the system is lightly loaded or overloaded. This is probably because when the system load is light, a task may be guaranteed anyway; consequently, the

effect is small. When the system load is very heavy (overload), if a task finishes before its claimed worst case computation time, it is more likely that there are tasks waiting to be executed, resulting in the noted performance improvement.

One aspect of algorithm behavior that merits attention is the fairness of a scheduling algorithm to tasks of different lengths. Data obtained in the course of the simulation studies indicate that distributed scheduling algorithms that utilize resource surplus information are likely to have better success with tasks that have smaller computation times than algorithms that do not use state information, for example, random scheduling. This is to be expected: since resources are almost always scarce, in general, it is easier to find a node for a task that needs a set of resources for a shorter duration than another task. One way to "correct" this bias may be to choose a local scheduling algorithm that has a bias towards tasks that have long execution times. Clearly, the issue of bias requires further study.

Another topic for future studies is the effect of the topology of a network on the performance of a specific algorithm. The additional message traffic produced varies from one distributed scheduling algorithm to another. Also, depending on the specifics of a particular network, a given algorithm can be optimized for that network. This issue deserves further study.

VI. Conclusions

Many interesting real-time scheduling problems are known to be NP-hard [7]. The problems are further complicated when, in addition to computation times and deadlines of tasks, their resource requirements need to be taken into account. It is impossible to find an optimal schedule for a dynamic distributed system given the inherent communication delay.

In this paper, we discussed and evaluated different heuristic schemes for solving this problem. The algorithms perform on-line scheduling of tasks that arrive dynamically and handle nonperiodic tasks even in the presence of periodic tasks, i.e., tasks that are known to occur at regular intervals. They work in conjunction with a heuristic local scheduling algorithm—one that determines a schedule for tasks that will execute on a node given that those tasks have dealines to meet and require multiple resources (not just the CPU) [24]. The cooperation among the nodes, needed when a node is unable to guarantee a task, can occur in a number of ways as illustrated by the algorithms discussed in this paper. On the one extreme is an algorithm that does not cooperate with other nodes. On the other extreme is an algorithm that utilizes bidding and focused addressing techniques in a flexible manner.

Bidding and focused addressing techniques discussed here are refined forms of the traditional source-initiated and server-initiated scheduling techniques [5], [20], [23]. The two most important refinements are the manner in which the two techniques are combined in the flexible algorithm to give the benefits of both, and how timing and general resource requirements are included. Neither of these has been done before. Other differences also exist. For example, in focused addressing, a source node regularly sends to other nodes its surplus information. A large surplus is an implicit request for tasks. This is unlike the approach in [23] where a node requests for a task only when it is idle. The surplus information is also used in bidding. Using this information, a server node selects a subset of nodes to send the request-for-bid messages, eliminating the transmission of unnecessary messages and hence reducing the network traffic. As shown by the simulation studies, properly combining these two improved techniques has the potential to make use of their positive features while overcoming their shortcomings, resulting in an algorithm with improved performance.

Results of the simulation studies can be used to make several observations regarding the relative performance of the various algorithms with respect to the system state, specifically, the system load, the load distribution among nodes, and the communication delays.

• Distributed scheduling improves the performance of a hard real-time system. This is attested by the better performance of the flexible algorithm compared to the noncooperative baseline under all load distributions.

• The performance of the flexible algorithm is better than both the focused addressing and bidding algorithms. However, the performance difference between the bidding algorithm and the flexible algorithm under small communication delays is negligible. The same can be said about the performance difference between the focused addressing algorithm and the flexible algorithm at large communication delays.

• Random algorithm performs quite well compared to the flexible algorithm, especially when system load is low as well as when system load is high and the load is unevenly distributed. Under moderate loads, its performance falls short by a few percentage points which may be significant in a hard real-time system.

In summary, no algorithm outperforms all others in all system rates. Although the flexible algorithm performs better than the rest in most cases, it is more complex than the other algorithms.

References

[1] S. Biyabani, "The integration of deadlines and criticalness in hard real-time scheduling," Masters Thesis, Univ. of Massachusetts, May 1988.
[2] S. Cheng, J. A. Stankovic, and K. Ramamritham, "Dynamic scheduling of groups of tasks with precedence constraints in distributed hard real-time systems," in Proc. Real-Time Syst. Symp., Dec. 1986.
[3] M. Dertouzos, "Control robotics: The procedural control of physical process," in Proc. IFIP Congress, 1974.
[4] K. Efe, "Heuristic models of task assignment scheduling in distributed systems," IEEE Computer, June 1982.
[5] D. C. Farber and K. C. Larson, "The distributed computer system," in Proc. Symp. Comput. Commun. Networks, Teletraffic, 1972.
[6] M. R. Garey and D. S. Johnson, "Complexity results for multiprocessor scheduling under resource constraints," SIAM J. Comput., vol. 4, 1975.
[7] R. L. Graham et al., "Optimization and approximation in deterministic sequencing and scheduling: A survey," Ann. Discrete Math., vol. 5, 1979.
[8] H. H. Johnson and M. S. Madison, "Deadline scheduling for a real-time multiprocessor," in Proc. NTIS (N76-15843), Springfield, VA, May 1974.
[9] D. W. Leinbaugh and M. Yamini, "Guaranteed response times in a distributed hard real-time environment," IEEE Trans. Software Eng., pp. 1139–1144, Dec. 1986.
[10] D. B. Lenat, "Theory formation by heuristic search—The nature of heuristics II: Background and examples," Artif. Intell., vol. 21, 1983.
[11] C. L. Liu and J. Layland, "Scheduling algorithms for multiprogramming in a hard real-time environment," J. ACM, vol. 20, Jan. 1973.
[12] M. Livny and M. Melman, "Load balancing in homogeneous broadcast distributed systems," in Proc. ACM Comput. Network Perform. Symp., Apr. 1982.
[13] R. P. Ma, E. Y. S. Lee, and M. Tsuchiya, "A task allocation model for distributed computing systems," IEEE Trans. Comput., vol. C-31, Jan. 1982.
[14] P. Ma, "A model to solve timing-critical application problems in distributed computer systems," IEEE Computer, Jan. 1984.
[15] A. K. Mok and M. L. Dertouzos, "Multiprocessor scheduling in a hard real-time environment," in Proc. Seventh Texas Conf. Comput. Syst., Nov. 1978.
[16] R. R. Muntz and E. G. Coffman, "Preemptive scheduling of real-time tasks on multiprocessor systems," J. ACM, vol. 17, Apr. 1970.
[17] K. Ramamritham and J. A. Stankovic, "Dynamic task scheduling in distributed hard real-time systems," IEEE Software, vol. 1, May 1984.
[18] K. Ramamritham, J. Stankovic, and W. Zhao, "Distributed scheduling of tasks with deadlines and resource requirements," COINS Tech. Rep. 88-92, Univ. of Massachusetts, Oct. 1988.
[19] K. Ramamritham, J. Stankovic, and P. Shiah, "O(n) scheduling algorithms for real-time multiprocessor systems," in Proc. Int. Conf. Parallel Processing Syst., Aug. 1989.
[20] R. G. Smith, "The contract net protocol: High level communication and control in a distributed problem solver," IEEE Trans. Comput., vol. C-29, Dec. 1980.
[21] J. A. Stankovic, K. Ramamritham, and S. Cheng, "Evaluation of a flexible task scheduling algorithm for distributed hard real-time systems," IEEE Trans. Comput., Dec. 1985.
[22] T. Teixeira, "Static priority interrupt scheduling," in Proc. Seventh Texas Conf. Comput. Syst., Nov. 1978.
[23] Y. Wang and R. Morris, "Load sharing in distributed systems," IEEE Trans. Comput., vol. C-34, Mar. 1985.
[24] W. Zhao, K. Ramamritham, and J. A. Stankovic, "Scheduling tasks with resource requirements in hard real-time systems," IEEE Trans. Software Eng., May 1987.
[25] W. Zhao and K. Ramamritham, "Simple and integrated heuristic algorithms for scheduling tasks with time and resource constraints," J. Syst. Software, 1987.

Krithi Ramamritham received the Ph.D. degree in computer science from the University of Utah, Salt Lake City, in 1981.

Since then he has been with the Department of Computer and Information Science University of Massachusetts, Amherst, where he is currently an Associate Professor. During 1987–1988, he was a Science and Engineering Research Council (U.K.) visiting fellow at the University of Newcastle upon Tyne, U.K., and a Visiting Professor at the Technical University of Vienna, Austria. His primary research interests lie in the areas of real-time systems, and distributed computing. He co-directs the Spring project whose goal is to develop scheduling algorithms, operating system support, architectural support, and design strategies for real-time applications. In addition, he directs the Gutenberg project which deals with structuring distributed computations through the control of interprocess communication and with enhancing concurrency in distributed applications through the use of semantic information.

Dr. Ramamritham is an editor for the new *Journal on Real-Time Systems*, and is the co-author of an IEEE tutorial text on hard real-time systems. He is a member of the Association for Computing Machinery.

John A. Stankovic (S'77–M'79–SM'86) received the B.S. degree in electrical engineering, and the M.S. and Ph.D. degrees in computer science, all from Brown University, Providence, RI, in 1970, 1976, and 1979, respectively.

He is an Associate Professor in the Department of Computer and Information Science, the University of Massachusetts, Amherst. His current research interests include investigating various approaches to scheduling on local area networks and multiprocessors, developing flexible, distributed, hard real-time systems, and performing experimental studies on distributed database protocols. He is currently building a hard real-time kernel, called Spring, which is based on a new scheduling paradigm and on ensuring predictability. The distributed database work is being performed on the CARAT testbed. The CARAT testbed has been operational for several years and now includes

protocols for real-time transactions. He has held visiting positions in the Department of Computer Science, at Carnegie-Mellon University, Pittsburgh, PA and at INRIA in France.

Dr. Stankovic received an Outstanding Scholar Award from the School of Engineering, University of Massachusetts. He is an editor-in-chief for *Real-Time Systems* and an editor for IEEE TRANSACTIONS ON COMPUTERS. He also served a Guest Editor for a special issue of IEEE TRANSACTIONS ON COMPUTERS on Parallel and Distributed Computing. He is a member of ACM and Sigma Xi.

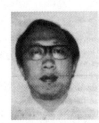

Wei Zhao (S'85–M'86) received the Diploma in physics from Shaanxi Normal University, Xian, China in 1977, and the M.S. and Ph.D. degrees in computer science from the University of Massachusetts, Amherst, in 1983 and 1986, respectively.

His current research interests include scheduling algorithms, communication protocols, performance analysis and simulation studies of distributed real-time systems, concurrency control for database systems, resource management in operating systems and knowledge-based systems.

Dr. Zhao was a Guest Editor for a special issue of *Operating System Review* on real-time operating systems. He is a member of the Association for Computing Machinery and the IEEE Computer Society.

Efficient Scheduling Algorithms for Real-Time Multiprocessor Systems

KRITHI RAMAMRITHAM, JOHN A. STANKOVIC, SENIOR MEMBER, IEEE,
AND PERNG-FEI SHIAH

Abstract—Hard real-time systems require both functionally correct executions and results that are produced on time. This means that the task scheduling algorithm is an important component of these systems. In this paper, efficient scheduling algorithms based on heuristic functions are developed to schedule a set of tasks on a multiprocessor system. The tasks are characterized by worst case computation times, deadlines, and resources requirements. Starting with an empty partial schedule, each step of the search extends the current partial schedule with one of the tasks yet to be scheduled. The heuristic functions used in the algorithm actively direct the search for a feasible schedule, i.e., they help choose *the* task that extends the current partial schedule. Two scheduling algorithms are evaluated via simulation. For extending the current partial schedule, one of the algorithms considers, at each step of the search, *all* the tasks that are yet to be scheduled as candidates. The second focuses its attention on a small subset of tasks with the shortest deadlines. The second algorithm is shown to be very effective when the maximum allowable scheduling overhead is fixed. This algorithm is hence appropriate for dynamic scheduling in real-time systems.

Index Terms—Deadlines, heuristics, multiprocessors, real-time systems, scheduling algorithms.

I. INTRODUCTION

HARD real-time systems require both functionally correct executions and results that are produced on time. Nuclear power plants, flight control, and avionics are examples of such systems. In these systems, many tasks have explicit deadlines. This means that the task scheduling algorithm is an important component of these systems. In general, a scheduling algorithm in a hard real-time system is used to determine a schedule for a set of tasks so that the tasks' deadlines and resource requirements are satisfied.

Many practical instances of scheduling algorithms have been found to be NP-complete, i.e., it is believed that there is no optimal polynomial-time algorithm for them [15], [16]. A majority of scheduling algorithms reported in the literature perform static scheduling and hence have limited applicability since not all task characteristics are known *a priori* and further, tasks arrive dynamically. For dynamic scheduling, in [4] Dertouzos points out that for a single processor system with independent preemptable tasks, the earliest deadline first algorithm is optimal. Later, Mok and Dertouzos in [7], [9] further

Manuscript received April 21, 1989; revised December 19, 1989. This work is part of the Spring Project at the University of Massachusetts and is funded in part by the Office of Naval Research under Contract N00014-85-K-0398 and by the National Science Foundation under Grant DCR-8500332.

The authors are with the Department of Computer and Information Science, University of Massachusetts, Amherst, MA 01003.

IEEE Log Number 8934120.

show that the least laxity first algorithm is also optimal for the same system. For dynamic systems with more than one processor, and/or tasks that have mutual exclusion constraints, Mok and Dertouzos in [7]–[9] show that an optimal scheduling algorithm does not exist. These negative results point out the need for heuristic approaches to solve scheduling problems in such systems.

Many scheduling algorithms developed so far only take processor requirements into consideration [11], [1], [5], [6], [3]. As a result, contention among tasks over other resources, such as buffers and data structures, might cause locking and waiting and thus presents a problem for predictability in real-time systems. In this paper, scheduling algorithms based on heuristic functions are developed to dynamically schedule a set of tasks with deadlines and resources requirements. Specifically, the algorithms schedule a set of tasks with given computation times, deadlines, and resource requirements. Previously, in [17] and [18] we have shown that for uniprocessors a simple heuristic which accounts for resource requirements significantly outperforms heuristics, such as scheduling based on earliest-deadline-first, that ignore resource requirements. Here, we show that an extension of this ($O(n^2)$) heuristic algorithm also works well for multiprocessors. Furthermore, we develop an $O(n)$ version of this algorithm, called the *myopic algorithm* and show that

- For a given maximum scheduling cost, the myopic algorithm works as well as the original algorithm in the cases when tasks have tight deadlines or resource contentions are high.

- For a given maximum scheduling cost, the myopic algorithm can work better than the original algorithm for the cases when tasks have loose deadlines or resource contentions are low.

- In general, the myopic algorithm incurs substantially less computational cost than the original algorithm and thus can work more effectively during dynamic scheduling.

The algorithms discussed in this paper are being incorporated into the Spring System, a distributed hard real-time system where each node is a multiprocessor [13]. In the Spring System, tasks can arrive dynamically at any node in the system. The local scheduler on a node tries to guarantee that the task will complete before its deadline. It does so by determining if the new task plus all the previously guaranteed tasks on this node can be scheduled to complete before their deadlines. If such a schedule exists, the new task is guaranteed; otherwise not. In either case, previously guaranteed tasks remain guaranteed. A task that is not guaranteed can be sent to another node if appropriate. The distributed scheduler [10] on each node makes the decision connected with this case. In this paper, we focus on the local scheduler, specifically the component which dynamically determines if a feasible schedule can be found for a set of tasks.

The rest of this paper is organized as follows. Section II introduces our model of multiprocessor systems and the characteristics of real-time tasks. Section III discusses the heuristic scheduling algorithms. In Section IV, simulation results are presented and discussed. Section V summarizes the work.

II. SYSTEM AND TASK MODELS

Broadly speaking, two types of multiprocessor models exist:

- a shared memory model, and
- a local memory model.

In the *shared memory model*, tasks are loaded into the shared global memory and the next scheduled task to run is dispatched to the first available processor. This case does not impose any relationships between processors and tasks, and models homogeneous multiprocessor systems. On the other hand, in the *local memory model*, each processor has its own memory and a task can be loaded into the memory of one of the processors. A task is thus eligible to be executed on a specific processor. (In general, code for certain tasks may reside on more than one processor's memory, offering greater flexibility during scheduling. We do not study this alternative here.) The second model can be used either in homogeneous multiprocessor systems, or in heterogeneous systems.

In multiprocessor scheduling, processors can be represented either by multiple processor resource items each with a single instance (corresponding to the local memory model), or by one processor resource item with multiple instances (corresponding to the shared memory model). In our simulation study, we assume that all the processors are identical.

In addition to processor resources, a multiprocessor system also has resources such as files, data structures, buffers, etc., that will be used by tasks. One of the strengths of our scheduling algorithm is that it takes into account the requirements of tasks for these nonprocessor resources.

Tasks are the dispatchable entities and are characterized by the following:

- Task arrival time T_A;
- Task deadline T_D;
- Task worst case processing time T_P;
- Task resource requirements $\{T_R\}$;
- Tasks are independent, nonperiodic and nonpreemptive.
- A Task uses a resource either in shared mode or in exclusive mode and holds a requested resource as long as it executes.

In the process of scheduling, the algorithm determines the earliest start time of a task, T_{est}. This is the earliest time at which a task can begin execution, i.e., the time when resources required by a task are available. The value of T_{est} depends on the tasks in execution, their processing times, and their resource requirements. For a schedule to be feasible, the following condition should be true for every task T being scheduled: $0 \leq T_A \leq T_{est} \leq T_D - T_P$.

III. OVERVIEW OF THE SCHEDULING STRATEGY

At any given time, a node N is said to have *guaranteed* a set of tasks by generating a full feasible schedule for this set of tasks. This means that each task will finish execution no later than its deadline. In the following, we compare scheduling to searching and present heuristic functions used to direct the search for a full feasible schedule. The data structures used in the heuristic algorithm are also described.

A. A Heuristic Scheduling Algorithm

Scheduling a set of tasks to find a full feasible schedule is actually a search problem. The structure of the search space is a search tree. An intermediate vertex of the search tree is a partial schedule, and a leaf, a terminal vertex, is a complete schedule. It should be obvious that not all leaves, each a complete schedule, correspond to feasible schedules. If a feasible schedule is to be found, it might cause an exhaustive search which is computationally intractable in the worst case. Since in many real applications, a feasible schedule is time consuming to find and we need to find a feasible schedule quickly, we take a heuristic approach.

The heuristic scheduling algorithm tries to determine a full feasible schedule for a set of tasks in the following way. It starts at the root of the search tree which is an empty schedule and tries to extend the schedule (with one more task) by moving to one of the vertices at the next level in the search tree until a full feasible schedule is derived. To this end, we use a heuristic function H which synthesizes various characteristics of tasks affecting real-time scheduling decisions to actively direct the scheduling to a plausible path. The heuristic function H is applied to each of the tasks that remain to be scheduled at each level of search. The task with the smallest value of function H is selected to extend the current schedule.

While extending the partial schedule at each level of search, the algorithm determines if the current partial schedule is *strongly-feasible* or not. A partial feasible schedule is said to be *strongly-feasible* if all the schedules obtained by extending this current schedule with any one of the remaining tasks are also feasible. Thus, if a partial feasible schedule is found not to be *strongly-feasible* because, say, task T misses its deadline when the current schedule is extended by T, then it is appropriate to stop the search since none of the future extensions involving task T will meet its deadline. In this case, a set of tasks cannot be scheduled given the current partial schedule. (In the terminology of branch-and-bound techniques, the search path represented by the current partial schedule is *bound* since it will not lead to a feasible complete schedule.)

However, it is possible to backtrack to continue the search even after a nonstrongly-feasible schedule is found. Backtracking is done by discarding the current partial schedule, returning to the previous partial schedule, and extending it by a different task. The task chosen is the one with the *second* smallest H value. Even though we allow backtracking, the overheads of backtracking are restricted either by restricting the maximum number of possible backtracks or by restricting the total number of evaluations of the H function.

In summary, given a particular H function, the algorithm works as follows. The algorithm starts with an empty partial schedule. Each step of the algorithm involves 1) determining that the current partial schedule is strongly-feasible, and if so 2) extending the current partial schedule by one task. This task is chosen by first applying the H function to all the tasks that are not in the current partial schedule and then determining the one with the least H value. This algorithm has a total of n steps, where the complexity of each step is given by the complexity of determining strong-feasibility and the complexity of H function evaluations. Both of these are linearly proportional to the number of tasks that remain to be scheduled. Hence, the overall complexity of the algorithm is $n + (n-1) + \cdots + 2 = O(n^2)$.

Henceforth, for ease of discussion, the $O(n^2)$ algorithm described in this section is called *the original algorithm*.

The following is a list of potential H functions that can be used in conjunction with the original algorithm as well as the myopic algorithm developed in the next section.

- Minimum deadline first (Min_D): $H(T) = T_D$;
- Minimum processing time first (Min_P): $H(T) = T_P$;
- Minimum earliest start time first (Min_S): $H(T) = T_{est}$;
- Minimum laxity first (Min_L): $H(T) = T_D - (T_{est} + T_P)$;
- Min_D + Min_P: $H(T) = T_D + W * T_P$;
- Min_D + Min_S: $H(T) = T_D + W * T_{est}$;

The first four heuristics are simple heuristics and the last two are integrated heuristics. W is a weight used to combine two simple heuristics. Min_L and Min_S need not be combined because the heuristic Min_L contains the information in Min_D and Min_S. Note that Min_P, Min_D, and (Min_P + Min_D) heuristics do not consider task resource requirements. Our simulation results show that they perform poorly. The other heuristics do consider resource requirements. Our simulation studies show that (Min_D + Min_S) has very good performance.

B. The Myopic Scheduling Algorithm

Before we describe this algorithm, let us define some terms to facilitate the presentation of the algorithm.

- {*Tasks_remaining*}: The tasks that remain to be scheduled. Tasks in {*Tasks_remaining*} are arranged in the order of increasing deadlines.
- N_r: Number of tasks in {*Tasks_remaining*}.
- k: *Maximum* number of tasks in *Tasks_remaining* considered by the myopic algorithm.
- N_k: *Actual* number of tasks in {*Tasks_remaining*} considered by the myopic algorithm at each step of scheduling.

$$N_k = \min(k, N_r)$$

- {*Tasks_considered*}: The first N_k tasks in {*Tasks_remaining*}.

Recall that at a certain search step, the original algorithm first checks whether the current partial schedule is *strongly-feasible* and if so, it applies the H function to all the remaining tasks. In the original algorithm, strong-feasibility is

determined with respect to all the remaining tasks. Instead, the myopic algorithm considers only the first N_k tasks in a task set (where $0 < N_k \le k$) both for checking strong-feasibility and for determining the task with the lowest H value. The algorithm works as follows:

Tasks in the task set are maintained in the order of increasing deadlines.[1] When attempting to extend the schedule by one task, 1) strong-feasibility is determined with respect to the first N_k tasks in the task set, 2) if found to be strongly-feasible, the particular H function being used is applied to the first N_k tasks in the task set, and 3) that task which has the smallest H value is chosen to extend the current schedule. Since only N_k tasks are considered at each step, the complexity incurred in the myopic algorithm is smaller than the original scheduling algorithm where *all* the remaining tasks are considered all the time. Let us elaborate upon this. Consider a task set which has n tasks; the complexity for the original algorithm to schedule this task set was shown to be $O(n^2)$. On the other hand, the complexity is $O(nk)$ for the myopic algorithm since only the first N_k tasks (where $N_k \le k$) are considered each time. If the value of k is constant (and in practice, k will be small when compared to the task set size n), the complexity of the myopic algorithm is linearly proportional to n, the size of the task set.

By now, the reason for calling this algorithm *myopic* should be clear. It is short-sighted in each decision-making step. In choosing the next task to extend the current partial schedule, it focuses only on the N_k tasks with the shortest deadlines.

It should be pointed out that in the integrated heuristic (Min_D + Min_S), the effect of the simple heuristic Min_D is always taken into account. The myopic algorithm preserves this flavor by working with tasks in a task set that are ordered according to increasing deadlines. The fact that the myopic algorithm applies the heuristic (Min_D + Min_S) only to N_k tasks with the earliest deadlines implies that it places less emphasis on the heuristic Min_S than the original scheduling algorithm. Thus, the myopic algorithm uses less information in making scheduling decisions and hence one would expect degraded performance. In order to study the performance of the myopic algorithm, we resort to simulation. As the simulation results presented in Section IV will show, it achieves the same performance as the original algorithm at a lower run-time cost and it achieves better performance than the original algorithm for a given run-time cost.

C. Data Structures

When resources are taken into account (e.g., in the Min_S heuristic) in the heuristic function, several data structures are required. To simplify discussions, we first present the data structures when the system has one instance of each resource. Subsequently, extensions to handle multiple instances are discussed. When only one instance exists for each resource, the algorithm maintains two vectors EAT^s and EAT^e, to indi-

---

[1] This is realized in the following way. When a task arrives at a node, it is *inserted*, according to its deadline, into a (sorted) list of tasks that remain to be executed. This insertion takes at most $O(n)$ time.

cate the earliest available times of resources for shared and exclusive modes respectively:

$$EAT^s = (EAT^s_1, EAT^s_2, \cdots, EAT^s_r) \text{ and}$$

$$EAT^e = (EAT^e_1, EAT^e_2, \cdots, EAT^e_r).$$

Here EAT^s_i (or EAT^e_i) is the earliest time when resource R_i will become available for shared (or exclusive) usage.

At each level of the search, using the EAT^s and EAT^e vectors the algorithm calculates the earliest start time T_{est} for each remaining task to be scheduled. An example of the computation for T_{est} will be illustrated later in this section. After the task with the smallest value of heuristic function is chosen to add to the partial schedule, the algorithm updates EAT^s and EAT^e using the new task's start time, computation time, and resource requirements. Because a task T can start running only after all the resources it needs are available, it is clear that

$$T_{est} = \text{MAX}(EAT^u_i).$$

Here $u = s$, for shared use of R_i and $u = e$, for exclusive use of R_i.

After a task T is selected to extend the current partial schedule, its scheduled start time T_{sst} is equal to T_{est}. After the EAT^s and EAT^e vectors are updated according to currently selected task T's computation time and resource requirements, other remaining tasks' earliest start time will be recomputed at the next level using the newly updated EAT^s and EAT^e.

Here is a simple example to illustrate the computation of new EAT^s and EAT^e values: Assume a system has five resources, $R_1, R_2, \cdots, R_5$. Let current EAT^s and EAT^e be

$$EAT^s = (EAT^s_1, EAT^s_2, EAT^s_3, EAT^s_4, EAT^s_5)$$
$$= (5, 25, 10, 5, 10), \text{ and}$$

$$EAT^e = (EAT^e_1, EAT^e_2, EAT^e_3, EAT^e_4, EAT^e_5)$$
$$= (5, 25, 10, 10, 15).$$

Suppose task T is being selected by the scheduler at the current level. Assume T has processing time $T_P = 10$, and requests R_1, R_4 for exclusive use and R_5 for shared use. Then the earliest time when T can start is the earliest available time of the resources needed by task T. So,

$$T_{est} = \text{MAX}(EAT^e_1, EAT^e_4, EAT^s_5)$$
$$= \text{MAX}(5, 10, 10)$$
$$= 10 \text{ and}$$

the scheduled start time T_{sst} of task T is 10.

The algorithm updates the EAT^s and EAT^e vectors:

$$EAT^s = (EAT^s_1, EAT^s_2, EAT^s_3, EAT^s_4, EAT^s_5)$$
$$= (20, 25, 10, 20, 10), \text{ and}$$

$$EAT^e = (EAT^e_1, EAT^e_2, EAT^e_3, EAT^e_4, EAT^e_5)$$
$$= (20, 25, 10, 20, 20).$$

Note that for R_5, both EAT^s_5 and EAT^e_5 need to be updated. $EAT^s_5 = 10$ because task T uses R_5 in shared mode and it is therefore possible for some other task to utilize R_5 in parallel, in shared mode. However, $EAT^e_5 = 20$ because another task which requires R_5 in exclusive mode cannot be permitted to execute in parallel with T.

Based on the above discussion, it is easy to observe that given a task's earliest start time, its finish time can be determined and thus the scheduling algorithm can decide if a task will finish by its deadline.

Now, we discuss our extensions to allow each distinct resource to have multiple instances. In this case, a vector no longer suffices to represent the two EAT's. EAT^s and EAT^e have to be matrices so that we can represent the earliest available time for every instance of each resource.

$$EAT^s = \begin{matrix} (EAT^s_{11}, EAT^s_{12}, \cdots, EAT^s_{1n}) \\ (EAT^s_{21}, EAT^s_{22}, \cdots, EAT^s_{2m}) \\ \vdots \\ (EAT^s_{r1}, EAT^s_{r2}, \cdots, EAT^s_{rp}) \end{matrix}$$

and

$$EAT^e = \begin{matrix} (EAT^e_{11}, EAT^e_{12}, \cdots, EAT^e_{1n}) \\ (EAT^e_{21}, EAT^e_{22}, \cdots, EAT^e_{2m}) \\ \vdots \\ (EAT^e_{r1}, EAT^e_{r2}, \cdots, EAT^e_{rp}) \end{matrix}$$

where n, m, and p are the number of instances of resource items 1, 2, and r, respectively.

After we extend our representations for EAT^s and EAT^e into a matrix format, we need to revise the formula for determining T_{est}: $T_{est} = \text{MAX}_{i=1\cdots r} (\text{MIN}_{j=1\cdots q} (EAT^u_{ij}))$ where u is s when R_i is used in shared mode or e when R_i is used in exclusive mode and q is the number of instances of R_i.

In summary, the EAT vectors are used in the Min_S, Min_L, and the (Min_D + Min_S) heuristics and they need to be matrices to account for multiprocessing and for multiple instances of other nonprocessor resources.

IV. RESULTS OF SIMULATION STUDIES

In this section, we first introduce the task set generation and simulation method and then present the simulation results.

A. Task Generation

Clearly, what we are striving for is a scheduling algorithm that is able to find a feasible schedule for a set of tasks, if such a schedule exists. Obviously, a heuristic algorithm cannot be guaranteed to achieve this. However, one heuristic algorithm can be considered better than another, if given a number of task sets for which feasible schedules exist, the former is able to find feasible schedules for more task sets than the latter. This is the basis for our simulation study. Ideally, we would like to come up with a number of task sets, each of which is known to have a feasible schedule. Unfortunately, given an arbitrary task set, only an exhaustive search can reveal whether the tasks in this task set can be feasibly scheduled.

Given m distinct processor resource items, the complexity of an exhaustive search to find a feasible schedule for n tasks in the worst case can be $O(m^n * n!)$. Although we can use techniques like branch and bound to cut down the complexity, we consider it impractical and inefficient to find the feasible schedule in the worst case. Therefore, we take a different approach in our study here. We develop a task set generator that can generate schedulable task sets where the number of tasks in a task set can be very large without imposing much complexity on the task generation. Also, the tasks are generated to guarantee the (almost) total utilization of the processors. The schedule generated by the task generator is used only for the purpose of generating a feasible set of tasks which are then input to the scheduling algorithm, i.e., the scheduling algorithms have no knowledge of the schedule itself but are only given the tasks and their requirements. The following are the parameters used to generate the task sets:

1) Probability that a task uses a resource, Use_P.
2) Probability that a task uses a resource in shared mode, Share_P.
3) The minimum processing time of tasks, Min_C.
4) The maximum processing time of tasks, Max_C.
5) The schedule length, L;

The cost of accessing resources is assumed to be accounted for in the computation time of a task.

The schedule generated by this task set generator is in the

So far we have discussed how task resource requirements and computation times are determined. The issue of choosing task deadlines without any bias is addressed now. In order to exercise the scheduling algorithms in scenarios that have different levels of scheduling difficulty, we choose the deadline of each task in the task set randomly between the task set's SC (shortest completion time) and $(1 + R)$*SC, where R is a simulation parameter indicating the tightness of the deadlines. (Thus, the deadline of each task is chosen independently.) In most cases, if R is 0, a scheduler must be capable of finding the same schedule as that found by the task generator, in order to have a task set completion time of SC. This means that there is little leeway for the scheduler. As we increase the value of R, it is not difficult to see that the scheduler has a better and better chance to guarantee a task set. Because of this unbiased generation of task sets we believe that the resulting task sets can be used to evaluate the heuristic algorithms in a rigorous manner.

B. Simulation Method

In the simulation, N task sets are generated and each task set is known to be schedulable, given the task set generation procedure. Performance of various heuristics are compared according to how many of the N feasible task sets are found schedulable when the heuristics are used. In the simulation, we are interested in whether or not all the tasks in a task set can finish before their deadlines. Therefore, the most appropriate performance metric is the schedulability of task sets. This metric called the success ratio SR is defined as

$$SR = \frac{\text{total number of task sets found schedulable by the heuristic algorithm}}{N, \text{ the total number of task sets}}.$$

form of a matrix M which has r columns and L rows. Each column represents a resource and each row represents a time unit. In order to illustrate the process of task set generation, we assume that there are n processors and m other resources, i.e., the total number of resources is $n + m$. Resource items $1 \cdots n$ represent the n processors. The task set generator starts with an empty matrix, it then generates a task by selecting one of these n processors with the earliest available time and then requests the m resources according to the probabilities specified in the generation parameters. The generated task's processing time is randomly chosen using a uniform distribution between the minimum processing time and the maximum processing time. The task set generator then marks on the matrix that the processor and resources required by the task are used up for a number of time units equal to the task's computation time starting from the aforementioned earliest available time of the processor. The task set generator generates tasks until the remaining unused time units of each processor, up to L, is smaller than the minimum processing time of a task, which means that no more tasks can be generated to use the processors. Then the largest finish time of a generated task in the set t_f becomes the task set's *shortest completion time*, SC. As a result, we generate tasks according to a very tight schedule without leaving any usable time units on the n processors between 0 and SC. However, there may be some empty time units in the m resources.

Other possible performance metrics not considered in this paper include minimizing schedule length [2] and maximizing resource utilization. Recall that simulation parameter Use_P determines, at task set generation time, the probability that a task will use a nonprocessor resource R_i; if a task chooses to use R_i, then another simulation parameter Share_P determines the probability that this task will use R_i in shared mode. The system tested consists of three processors and 12 nonprocessor resources. Share_P is 0.5. A Task's computation time is randomly chosen between Min_C (10) and Max_C (40). Except for the studies done in Section IV-C5, each task set has between 20 and 30 tasks.

All the simulation results shown in this section are obtained from the average of five simulation runs. For each run, we generate 200 task sets. Recall that our major performance metric is the task set success ratio, therefore, we present the results in plot form where we plot the SR on the Y-axis and R on the X-axis (where R is related to laxity). Simulation parameters include R, W (the weight used in the H function), and Use_P (resource utilization probability). Running the simulation with different values of R helps us investigate the sensitivity of each heuristic algorithm to the change of laxities. Generating task sets with different resource requirements, by changing the value of Use_P, can be used to evaluate the heuristic algorithms under different resource conflict situations.

C. Simulation Results

In [12], we report on the performance of the algorithm for both shared and local memory models. The results show that all the observations we make in this paper for the local memory model are also applicable to the shared memory model. Because of this, we do not present the results of the shared memory model here.

In Section IV-C1, we explore the basic performance characteristics of different heuristics for the $O(n^2)$ algorithm. We find that the integrated heuristic (Min_D + Min_S) has superior performance when compared to other heuristics including the best simple heuristic, namely Min_D. Besides, it is more stable under different levels of resource contention. Also the results show that the performance is not sensitive to the specific value of W as long as the value of W is ≥ 4 and ≤ 20.

Therefore, in the following sections, we focus our attention on the integrated heuristic (Min_D + Min_S) applied to the myopic algorithm. The value of the weight W used to combine the two factors is set to 8. We work for the most part with Use_P = 0.7, which represents a situation where there is high contention for resources since the probability of a task requiring a resource is high. We have experimented with other resource contention situations and many more results have been obtained than those reported here. These can be found in [12]. Here only salient graphs are included.

We first discuss the effect of the value of k on the performance of the myopic algorithm. As one would expect, the simulation results of Section IV-C2 show that the larger the values of k, the better the performance of the myopic algorithm. Following this, simulation results with backtracking are discussed. Note that a step in the myopic algorithm incurs less costs (i.e., total cost of determining strong feasibility and evaluating the H functions) than a step in the original algorithm. This makes it difficult to compare the cost–performance properties of the two algorithms for a given number of backtracks. Therefore, we adopt the following scheme. We fix the maximum number of times the H function can be applied by a given algorithm. In general, this will allow the myopic algorithm to backtrack a larger number of steps than the original algorithm but for the same total cost. The simulation results, reported in Section IV-C3, show that the myopic algorithm works very effectively when compared to the original algorithm unless the task deadlines are tight or the resource contention is high.

Hence, in Section IV-C4, we formulate an adaptive strategy for determining the value of k according to current resource contention and the tightness of deadlines. When using an adaptive value for k, the myopic algorithm works *as well as or better than* the original algorithm in all the cases.

Clearly, the amount of scheduling costs allowed will affect the performance of the heuristics. To study the effect, in Section IV-C5, we evaluate the performance when a maximum of $(p \times n)$ H function evaluations are permitted for $p = 12$, 16, and 20. Also we study the behavior for two different task set sizes. As the number of tasks being scheduled increases, the performance of the original algorithm deteriorates while that of the myopic algorithm displays little change. The reason is that the myopic algorithm focuses its computations on the most likely candidates. Therefore, *for a fixed cost of execu-*

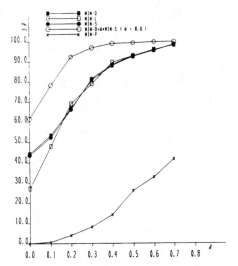

Fig. 1. Effect of different heuristics on the original algorithm, Use_P = 0.1

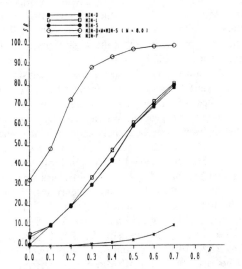

Fig. 2. Effect of different heuristics on the original algorithm, Use_P = 0.7.

tion, it is able to try more alternatives among more likely candidates rather than squandering computation time on unlikely candidates.

1) Performance of the Original Algorithm with Different Heuristics: In this section, we first explore the basic performance characteristics of the original algorithm when it employs different heuristics. We show the results in Figs. 1 and 2 with respect to two levels of resource contention (Use_P = 0.1 and 0.7) when no backtracking is allowed.

As can be seen from the results in these figures with different levels of R and Use_P, we find that Min_P is not a good heuristic since the SR's remain very low even when the laxity is relaxed, i.e., with increasing values of R. This is an important observation because in nonreal-time environments, the simple heuristic Min_P is the best algorithm for minimizing average response time. Here we see that Min_P is totally inadequate in a real-time environment. As for other simple heuristics, we find that Min_D and Min_S have ap-

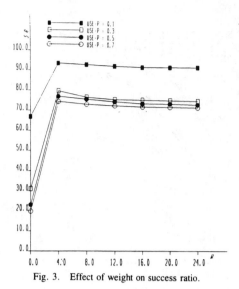

Fig. 3. Effect of weight on success ratio.

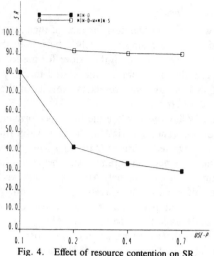

Fig. 4. Effect of resource contention on SR.

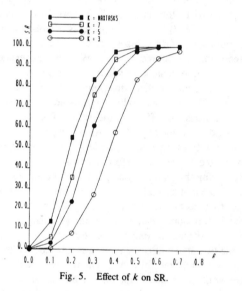

Fig. 5. Effect of k on SR.

proximately the same performance and Min_L works slightly better than Min_D and Min_S in the cases when tasks' timing constraints are relaxed, i.e., with increasing value of R. After a little thought, we perceive that the slightly better performing simple heuristic Min_L, formed by $T_D-T_P-T_{est}$, actually combines the information of a task's deadline constraint T_D and earliest start time T_{est}. As a result, the additional information helps Min_L to perform better than Min_D and Min_S. However, in general, we can say that none of the simple heuristics works substantially better than the others.

Now let us move our focus to the integrated heuristic Min_D + W^*Min_S. It should be clear in Figs. 1 and 2 that the integrated heuristic Min_D + W^*Min_S has substantially better performance than all the simple heuristics. For example, in the tightest case when $R = 0$ from Fig. 1, we see that the integrated heuristic Min_D + W^*Min_S works better than the simple heuristics Min_D, Min_S, Min_L, and Min_P by 18%, 17%, 35%, and 61%, respectively. The integrated heuristic Min_D + W^*Min_S also performs better for different Use_P values as reported in Figs. 1 and 2. This shows that a well-formed integrated heuristic does help in achieving higher SR's.

However, since an integrated heuristic combines more than one simple heuristic by different weight values W, we investigate the sensitivity of the integrated heuristic Min_D + W^*Min_S to the changes of weight values W. We show one instance of the results when $R = 0.2$ in Fig. 3. In the case when $W = 0$, the integrated heuristic Min_D + W^*Min_S degrades to the simple heuristic Min_D and does not perform well. We see a substantial performance increase when W is increased from 0 to 4. After that, when we vary the value of weight W from 4 to 24, we see that different weights affect the performance only slightly. This implies that the algorithm is robust with respect to this weight. If we use a very large value of weight W (say much greater than 24), the factor Min_S becomes the decisive part and as a result we can predict that the performance will drop to what the simple heuristic Min_S exhibits.

Another interesting question concerning the integrated

heuristic Min_D + W^*Min_S is its sensitivity to the increase in resource contention. To get an answer, we plot the simulation results in Fig. 4 with respect to different levels of Use_P. We see that for a fixed value of R, as the value of Use_P increases, the performance of the integrated heuristic Min_D + W^*Min_S remains more stable than the simple heuristic Min_D. This is because the integrated heuristic Min_D + W^*Min_S not only accounts for the timing constraints of tasks but also explicitly addresses the resource conflict. Again, this shows another promising aspect of a well-formed integrated heuristic.

2) Effect of the Value of k on SR: In this section, we investigate the performance of the myopic algorithm when considering k tasks where $k = 3, 5, 7$, and N_r (indicated by *maxtasks* in the figures). We show the simulation results in Fig. 5 for Use_P = 0.7. It should be easy to see that $k = maxtasks$ corresponds to the original algorithm and hence serves as a baseline in the performance comparisons. As can be seen in this figure, when $k = 3$, the myopic algorithm does not perform well in tight deadline cases. This implies that the value of k should not be too small. Considering more tasks is one way to obtain better performance in general.

However backtracking can also potentially improve the performance. Also, the more backtracks we allow, the more performance improvement we can get. However it is not appropriate to compare the two algorithms when each is allowed to backtrack for a fixed maximum number of times. This is because, as we mentioned earlier, the complexity incurred in scheduling is dependent on the number of tasks considered at each step. Therefore, the computation cost to schedule a task set, say, with ten maximum backtracks, when using the original algorithm which considers all the tasks in {*Tasks_remaining*} is likely to be higher than with the myopic algorithm which considers only N_k tasks at a time. This is likely to be the case especially if N_k is much smaller than N_r. Hence, we study backtracking from another perspective where we compare the performance of the original algorithm and the myopic algorithm given a maximum allowable scheduling cost.

3) Effect of Limited Scheduling Cost: In this section, we rerun the simulation with bounds on the overheads allowed for scheduling. Note that the cost of the heuristic scheduling algorithm is incurred in calculating H values, and in the determination of strong feasibility. Recall that at each level of the search, the myopic algorithm works with N_k tasks—both for determining strong feasibility as well as for extending the current partial schedule. Thus, if we limit the maximum number of times the H function is evaluated, we also limit the overheads due to the determination of strong feasibility.

The original algorithm and the myopic algorithm are compared when each is allowed to backtrack as long as the total number of H calculations is within the maximum. We study the effect when the maximum allowable H function calculations is set to two different values: 300 and 400.

As can be seen in Fig. 6, the myopic algorithm with $k = 7$ works better than the original algorithm for the case when $H = 300$. The extremely low performance of the original algorithm when $H = 300$ is because the original algorithm considers all the tasks in {*Tasks_remaining*} and as a result runs out of the maximum allowed number of H calculations faster. When the maximum allowed H calculations is increased from 300 to 400, we see a large increase in the performance of the original algorithm. However, it is interesting to observe in Fig. 6 that the performance of the myopic algorithm with $k = 7$ does not vary too much as the value of H is increased from 300 to 400. This implies that when $R \geq 0.3$, the myopic algorithm with $H = 300$ works better than the original algorithm with $H = 400$. This indicates that for large laxities, the myopic algorithm has better performance than the original algorithm even with a smaller computational cost. The reason for this is that it focuses on tasks with earlier deadlines, i.e., tasks that are more likely to produce the smallest H value.

Our simulation studies showed that for the tight deadline cases, i.e., when the value of R is small, the performance of the myopic algorithm drops as the value of Use_P increases. That is, for tighter deadline and higher resource contention cases, more tasks should be considered to obtain better performance. Therefore, our problem now is to choose a value of k

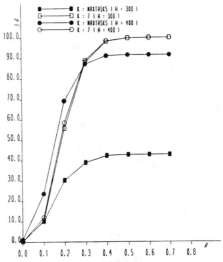

Fig. 6.   Effect of limited H calculations.

in the myopic scheduling algorithm by which we can have lower computational cost while still keeping good performance. It is not difficult to see that the value of k needs to adapt to different levels of resource contention and task deadline constraints.

4) Adapting the Value of K: In this section, we present an adaptive myopic algorithm. In order to have an effective way for choosing the value of k, we reexamine the simulation results and find that for $k = 7$, the performance of the myopic algorithm drops significantly lower than the original algorithm when Use_P is higher than 0.3 and R is smaller than 0.3. This implies that, for the loads tested, when Use_P is higher than 0.3 or R is lower than 0.3, we should use a bigger value of k to consider more tasks in making scheduling decisions. Therefore, we construct a function to determine the value of k as

$$k = W_1 + W_2 * f_1(R) + W_3 * f_2(\text{Use\_P}).$$

Based on the discussion of the previous paragraph,

$$f_1(R) = 0.3 - R, \qquad \text{if } R \leq 0.3, \text{ else } 0.$$

$$f_2(\text{Use\_P}) = \text{Use\_P} - 0.3, \qquad \text{if Use\_P} > 0.3, \text{ else } 0.$$

Again, for the loads tested here, we choose $W_1 = 7$, $W_2 = W_3 = 10$. According to this heuristic, for the cases when R is smaller than 0.3 or Use_P is greater than 0.3, the value of k will be greater than W_1, which means that scheduling decisions are made based on information about more tasks. However, for the cases when the task deadlines are not tight, i.e., $R \geq 0.3$, and resource contentions are not high, i.e., Use_P ≤ 0.3, the value of k will still be W_1. We rerun the simulation for the adaptive myopic algorithm and show the simulation results in Fig. 7.

The figure shows that the adaptive myopic algorithm with $H = 400$ performs better than the original algorithm for all values of R. For example, consider the case again when $R = 0.1$ and $H = 400$. Recall that in the last section, the original algorithm has a 12% higher performance than the myopic algorithm with $k = 7$. But now, the adaptive myopic

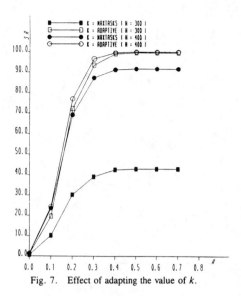

Fig. 7. Effect of adapting the value of k.

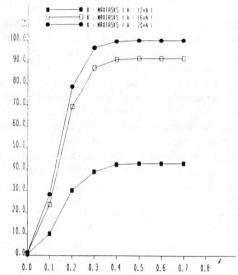

Fig. 8. Effect of linear scheduling costs—original algorithm with 20–30 tasks per set.

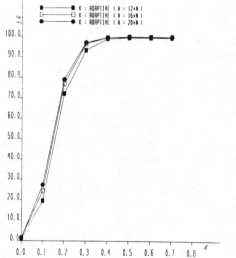

Fig. 9. Effect of linear scheduling costs—myopic algorithm with 20–30 tasks per set.

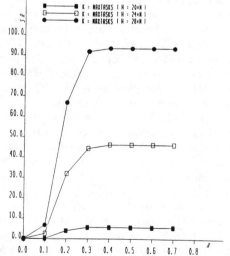

Fig. 10. Effect of linear scheduling costs—original algorithm with 45–55 tasks per set.

algorithm works better than the original algorithm by 1%. Thus, an overall improvement of 13% is achieved by using the adaptive algorithm. This implies that the adaptive myopic algorithm is more robust under high resource contention than the original algorithm. Generally speaking, the performance of the adaptive myopic algorithm is very promising. The good point of the adaptive myopic algorithm is that *for a fixed overhead*, it is as effective as the original algorithm at high resource contention and tight deadline constraint cases. Furthermore, it has higher performance than the original algorithm when resource contentions are not high and tasks have loose deadline constraints. Under such conditions, it has the same or even less computational cost than the original algorithm. This is shown by the fact that for the adaptive myopic algorithm case, when $R \geq 0.4$, evaluating H a maximum of 300 times is sufficient to achieve a 100% SR.

5) Effect of Different Scheduling Costs: In the last section, we worked with task sets with between 20 and 30 tasks and allowed a maximum of 300 and 400 H function evaluations. In this section, we examine the effect of this maximum number on tasks sets of different sizes. Specifically, we allow a maximum of $(p \times n)$ H evaluations for $p = 12$, 16, and 20, and where n is the average number of tasks in a task set. We experiment with two types of task sets. One contains between 20 and 30 tasks, and the second between 45 and 55 tasks. We investigate both the original algorithm and the myopic algorithm. Again, we focus on Use_P $= 0.7$. The simulation results are shown in Figs. 8–11.

For tasks sets with between 20 and 30 tasks the results of the original algorithm are shown in Fig. 8 and for the myopic algorithm in Fig. 9. When the value of $p = 12$, the original algorithm shows very poor performance. Besides, the performance of the original algorithm changes substantially when the value of p increases from 12 to 16 and from 16 to 20. However, for the myopic algorithm, the performance does not vary too much as the value of p changes from 12 to 20. In addition, when the value of $p = 12$ and 16, the myopic algorithm has much higher performance than the original algorithm. For example, for $R = 0.2$ and $p = 12$ and 16, the

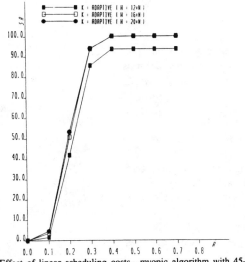

Fig. 11. Effect of linear scheduling costs—myopic algorithm with 45-55 tasks per set.

myopic algorithm has higher performance than the original algorithm by 41% and 9%, respectively. This shows that the smaller the allowable overhead, i.e., smaller the p, the bigger the performance difference between the myopic algorithm and the original algorithm. It also implies that the myopic algorithm works much more effectively than the original algorithm in the low overhead cases.

The second case we investigated is for large task sets—with 45-55 tasks. It is to be pointed out that in Figs. 10 and 11, we had to investigate the original algorithm by using the value of p from 20 to 28 instead of 12 to 20 because the original algorithm shows 0% SR when $p = 12$ and 16. Even when $p = 20$, the original algorithm has no more than a 5% SR. Therefore, clearly, the myopic algorithm performs much better than the original algorithm when $p = 12$, 16, and 20. This again says that the myopic algorithm has a relatively stable performance for a given allowable overhead. For example, for the case when $R = 0.2$ and $p = 20$, the performance of the myopic algorithm is 78% and 52% for task sets with 20-30 tasks and 45-55 tasks, respectively. However, for the same case, the performance of the original algorithm drops from 79% to 3% as the task sets size increases. This shows that the myopic algorithm is more suitable for dynamic scheduling given its better performance even under a low allowable overhead. This observation is also corroborated by our tests involving even larger task sets with around 100 tasks [12].

D. Summary

The simulation results show that the myopic algorithm which adapts the value of k to the system state and task characteristics works very effectively when compared to the original algorithm even when the maximum allowable overheads is fixed to be linearly proportional to the number of tasks. This makes the myopic algorithm an $O(n)$ algorithm.

The fact that in dynamic situations scheduling costs have to be restricted, favors the myopic algorithm. This is exemplified by the results portrayed in Section IV-C5. They show that when the task size is large, for a given maximum cost, the myopic algorithm performs very well while the original algorithm has very poor performance.

To apply the myopic algorithm in practice, a number of questions have to be considered.

1) In general, what should be the values of W_1, W_2, and W_3 be in the function used to determine k?

2) What should be the maximum number of H computations allowed in a given situation, i.e., what should be the value of p when $(p \times n)$ H calculations are allowed?

The results of this section can be seen as providing guidelines for answering the above questions. In general, the answer to 1) depends on the characteristics of a given task set as well as the number of tasks in this set. The answer to 2) depends on the allowable scheduling overhead and the number of tasks that need to be scheduled. The advantage of the myopic algorithm lies in its ability to perform better than the original algorithm for a given maximum cost.

Before we conclude this section, we would like to point out that we have implemented the myopic algorithm developed in this paper on a hardware prototype of the Spring System, a network of (Motorola 68020 processor based) multiprocessor nodes. k was set to 5 and at most 100 H calculations were allowed. Initial measurements show that the scheduling overheads are of the order of 40 ms for guaranteeing task sets of size 12.

V. CONCLUSIONS

In this paper, we investigated the performance of very efficient heuristic algorithms when applied to multiprocessor systems.

• We evaluated the heuristic approach when tasks with deadlines and resource requirements are scheduled on multiprocessors.

• We allowed multiple instances of a resource item.

• We evaluated two kinds of multiprocessor models, a shared memory model and a local memory model. Due to space limitations, only the results of the local memory model were presented here. The results of the shared memory model are similar to those presented here.

- The heuristic (Min_D + Min_S) that integrates information about tasks deadlines and resource requirements performs better than simple heuristics such as Min_D, Min_P, Min_S, and Min_L.

- For a given maximum scheduling cost, the myopic algorithm works as well as the original algorithm in the cases when tasks have tight deadlines or resource contentions are high.

- For a given maximum scheduling cost, the myopic algorithm can work better than the original algorithm for the cases when tasks have loose deadlines or resource contentions are low.

- In general, the myopic algorithm incurs less computational cost than the original algorithm and thus can work more effectively during dynamic scheduling.

ACKNOWLEDGMENT

Development of some of the details of the myopic algorithm benefited from discussions with C. Shen.

REFERENCES

[1] J. Blazewicz, "Deadline scheduling of tasks with ready times and resource constraints," *Inform. Process. Lett.*, vol. 8, no. 2, Feb. 1979.
[2] J. Blazewicz, M. Drabowski, and J. Weglarz, "Scheduling multiprocessor tasks to minimize schedule length," *IEEE Trans. Comput.*, pp. 389–393, May 1986.
[3] H. Chetto and M. Chetto, "Some results of the earliest deadline scheduling algorithm," *IEEE Trans. Software Eng.*, pp. 1161–1169, Oct. 1989.
[4] M. Dertouzos, "Control robotics: The procedural control of physical process," in *Proc. IFIP Congress*, 1974.
[5] W. A. Horn, "Some simple scheduling algorithms," *Naval Res. Log. Quart.*, vol. 21, 1974.
[6] C. Martel, "Preemptive scheduling with release times, deadlines, and due times," *J. ACM*, vol. 29, no. 3, pp. 812–829, July 1982.
[7] A. K. Mok and M. L. Dertouzos, "Multiprocessor scheduling in a hard real-time environment," in *Proc. Seventh Texas Conf. Comput. Syst.*, Nov. 1978.
[8] A. K. Mok, "The design of real-time programming systems based on process models," in *Proc. IEEE Real-Time Syst. Symp.*, Dec. 1984.
[9] ——, "Fundamental design problems of distributed systems for the hard real-time environment," Ph.D. dissertation, Dep. Elec. Eng. Comput. Sci., Mass. Inst. Technol., Cambridge, MA, May 1983.
[10] K. Ramamritham, J. A. Stankovic, and W. Zhao, "Distributed scheduling of tasks with deadlines and resource requirements," *IEEE Trans. Comput.*, pp. 1110–1123, Aug. 1989.
[11] S. Sahni and Y. Cho, "Nearly on line scheduling of a uniform processor system with release times," *Soc. Industrial Appl. Math. J. Comput.*, vol. 8, no. 2, pp. 275–285, May 1979.
[12] P. F. Shiah, "A heuristic approach on real-time scheduling for multiprocessors," M.S. thesis, Dep. Elec. Comput. Eng., Univ. Massachusetts, Amherst, MA, Jan. 1989.
[13] J. A. Stankovic and K. Ramamritham, "The design of the spring kernel," in *Proc. Real-Time Syst. Symp.*, San Jose, CA, Dec. 1987.
[14] J. A. Stankovic and K. Ramamritham, P. F. Shiah, and W. Zhao, "Real-time scheduling algorithms for multiprocessors," Tech. Rep. Univ. Massachusetts, Nov. 1988.
[15] J. D. Ullman, "Polynomial complete scheduling problems," *Oper. Syst. Rev.*, vol. 7, no. 4, Oct. 1973.
[16] ——, "NP-complete scheduling problems," *J. Comput. Syst. Sci.*, Oct. 1975.
[17] W. Zhao, K. Ramamritham, and J. A. Stankovic, "Scheduling tasks with resource requirements in hard real-time systems," *IEEE Trans. Software Eng.*, vol. SE-12, May 1987.
[18] W. Zhao and K. Ramamritham, "Simple and integrated heuristic algorithms for scheduling tasks with time and resource constraints," *J. Syst. Software*, 1987.

Krithi Ramamritham received the Ph.D. degree in computer science from the University of Utah in 1981.

Since then he has been with the Department of Computer and Information Science at the University of Massachusetts, Amherst where he is currently an Associate Professor. During 1987–1988, he was a Science and Engineering Research Council (U.K.) Visiting Fellow at the University of Newcastle upon Tyne, U.K., and a Visiting Professor at the Technical University of Vienna, Austria. His primary research interests lie in the areas of real-time systems, and distributed computing. He co-directs the Spring project whose goal is to develop scheduling algorithms, operating system support, architectural support, and design strategies for real-time applications. His other research activities deal with enhancing concurrency in distributed applications through the use of semantic information.

Dr. Ramamritham is an associate editor of the *Real-Time Systems* journal and is the co-author of an IEEE tutorial text on hard real-time systems. He is a member of the Association for Computing Machinery.

John A. Stankovic (S'77–M'79–SM'86) received the B.S. degree in electrical engineering, and the M.S. and Ph.D. degrees in computer science, all from Brown University, Providence, RI, in 1970, 1976 and 1979, respectively.

He is an Associate Professor in the Computer and Information Science Department at the University of Massachusetts, Amherst. His current research interests include investigating various approaches to scheduling on local area networks and multiprocessors, developing flexible, distributed, hard real-time systems, and performing experimental studies on distributed database protocols. He is currently building a hard real-time kernel, called Spring, which is based on a new scheduling paradigm and on ensuring predictability. The distributed database work is being performed on the CARAT testbed. The CARAT testbed has been operational for several years and now includes protocols for real-time transactions. He has held visiting positions in the Computer Science Department at Carnegie-Mellon University and at INRIA in France. He received an Outstanding Scholar Award from the School of Engineering, University of Massachusetts.

Dr. Stankovic is an editor-in-chief for *Real-Time Systems* and an editor for IEEE TRANSACTIONS ON COMPUTERS. He also served a Guest Editor for a special issue of IEEE TRANSACTIONS ON COMPUTERS on Parallel and Distributed Computing. He is a member of the Association for Computing Machinery and Sigma Xi.

Perng-Fei Shiah received the diploma in electrical engineering from Taipei Institute of Technology, Taiwan, in 1982 and the M.S. degree in electrical and computer engineering from the University of Massachusetts, Amherst, in 1989.

His interests lie in real-time computing and distributed processing, with emphasis on multiprocessor systems.

Mr. Shiah is a member of the IEEE Computer Society.

Chapter 3: Operating System Kernels

We have seen a proliferation of commercial real-time operating systems (and kernels). They generally fall into one of two categories: small, fast, proprietary kernels, and those based on real-time versions of UNIX. The fast proprietary kernels, such as VRTX [Ready 86], VxWorks (Wind River Systems), and OS-9 (Microware), are often used to guarantee very fast and highly predictable execution time. In these systems the kernel primitives are generally designed to provide functions with well-defined execution times. RT-UNIX systems include LynxOS [Gallmeister and Lanier 91] and REAL/IX [Furth et al. 91]. These systems provide a UNIX-like environment but are generally slower and less predictable (depending on the implementation) than the proprietary kernels. An interesting question is, Why are the RT-UNIX systems slower and less predictable? Is there a fundamental reason based on the UNIX paradigm and interface, or is it due to the extra functionality one finds in RT-UNIX over the proprietary kernels, or is it simply that no one has yet designed a detailed, highly efficient and predictable RT-UNIX implementation?

RT-UNIX's main advantage is that it is based on a set of familiar interfaces (standards) that speed development and facilitate portability. However, since many variations of UNIX have evolved, a new standards effort, called POSIX, has been creating a common set of user-level interfaces for operating systems. In particular, the POSIX P.1003.4, subcommittee is defining standards for real-time operating systems. To date, the effort has focussed on 10 important real-time related functions:

- timers,
- priority scheduling,
- shared memory,
- real-time files,
- semaphores,
- interprocess communication,
- asynchronous event notification,
- process memory locking,
- asynchronous I/O, and
- synchronized I/O.

For more details on these standards, read the POSIX 1003.4 report from the IEEE [POSIX 89]. While many real-time systems will be constructed with these commercial operating systems, we do not detail these systems in this text. Rather, this text is intended to identify research issues and new ideas. In this regard we present two papers on research-oriented kernels, and due to the increasing popularity of Real-Time UNIX, one paper on the problems and solutions in building a real-time UNIX system. For more details on Real-Time UNIX, see the excellent text [Furth et al. 91].

The first paper, "UNIX For Real-Time Control: Problems and Solutions," by Salkind is an interesting summary of the problems encountered when applying UNIX to real-time systems. These problems exist at the system interface and in the implementation. For example, interface problems exist in process scheduling due to the *nice* and *setpriority* primitives and the round robin scheduling policy. In addition, the timer facilities are too coarse, memory management (of some versions) contains no method for locking pages into memory, and interprocess communication facilities don't support fast and predictable communication. The implementation is shown to have intolerable overhead and excessive latency in responding to interrupts, partly (but very importantly) because the kernel is non-preemptable and the internal queues are FIFO. These and other problems are described and then proposed solutions are presented in the form of a new kernel called SAGE. For readers very interested in real-time UNIX see [Furth et al. 91] for a much more detailed description of how UNIX might be converted to support real-time computing. Many real-time systems are large and complex. More support is required from real-time kernels for such environments. The paper by Tokuda, Nakajima, and Rao entitled "Real-Time MACH: Towards a Predictable Real-Time System" addresses these issues by describing extensions to the MACH operating system that can support networks of multiprocessors and uniprocessors. The paper describes a real-time thread model, real-time synchronization primitives, a scheduling algorithm, and support for memory resident objects. Real-time threads can have soft or hard deadlines and be periodic or aperiodic. An RT-lock includes a waiting policy based on priority or deadlines and supports a mechanism to avoid unbounded priority inheritance. The scheduling approach allows a partitioning of the processors (of a multiprocessor) into sets where each set can have its own scheduling policy. The policies can be dynamically changed. Memory support allows locking of pages (objects) into memory. The features presented take MACH toward predictable real-time computing, but it is unclear what obstacles still remain, if any, in truly achieving predictability in MACH.

In the last paper of this section, "The Spring Kernel: A New Paradigm for Real-Time Systems," Stankovic and Ramamritham outline some of the problems with today's real-time operating systems. The paper then presents a design for a kernel to support complex real-time multiprocessor systems. It offers a set of ideas (some well known and some new) that, in total, constitute a new paradigm for developing predictable execution in non-deterministic environments. Main ideas in this paper include the need for next-generation kernels to provide more direct support for dealing with timing issues rather than a simple priority scheduler, the need to incorporate (in a general manner) semantic information concerning the application, the need for on-line, dynamic planning, the need for an integrated strategy that includes design, programming languages, compilers, loaders, operating systems and hardware, and the need to have scheduling support predictable execution of groups of tasks with differing values and precedence constraints. A scheduling algorithm is presented in the paper. More details on this algorithm can be found in the previous section on Multiprocessor and distributed scheduling. Further, the Spring kernel has also addressed predictable distributed communication, but this work is not described in the paper. See [Ramamritham and Stankovic 84], [Ramamritham et al. 89], and [Stankovic et al. 91] for details on the distributed aspects of the Spring kernel.

UNIX for Real-Time Control:
Problems and Solutions

by

Lou Salkind

Technical Report No. 400
Robotics Report No. 171
September, 1988

New York University
Dept. of Computer Science
Courant Institute of Mathematical Sciences
251 Mercer Street
New York, New York 10012

Work on this paper has been supported by Office of Naval Research Grant N00014-87-K-0129 National Science Foundation CER Grant DCR-83-20085, National Science Foundation Grant subcontract CMU-406349-55586, and by grants from the Digital Equipment Corporation and the IBM Corporation.

UNIX For Real-Time Control: Problems and Solutions

Lou Salkind
Robotics Group
New York University

October 18, 1988

Abstract

UNIX is often said to be a poor real-time system, but rarely are its weaknesses identified. In this paper, we describe some of UNIX's real-time problems in the context of millisecond level control applications. We find that such problems are due to both the system interface and the implementation.

We also describe how some of these problems were solved in the SAGE operating system, a small system specifically designed for such control applications. Although SAGE is not a UNIX system, it has many similarities, and hence many of the solutions can be applied to UNIX.

1 Introduction

In a time-sharing environment, where response time on the order of seconds can be tolerated, UNIX performs ably. But in a supervisory control environment, where a number of devices and their controlling processes must be serviced within milliseconds, UNIX does not work well. Indeed, neither System V nor Berkeley UNIX can reliably support a real-time application with millisecond time constraints, even though the underlying hardware can provide the needed computational power.

Nevertheless, there are several reasons why real-time capabilities should be added to UNIX:

- UNIX already supports many of the facilities needed for writing sophisticated real-time applications. Besides a rich development environment, it has a simple system interface, runs on a wide range of hardware, and supports many different communication disciplines.

- Other commercially available real-time systems also tend to have shortcomings. Many are missing a significant number of facilities that UNIX provides, e.g. [1], while others run only on vendor specific hardware, e.g. [2]. In most cases, software problems cannot be overcome because source code is either unobtainable or prohibitively expensive.

- By using the same system for program development and real-time control, both software development and hardware costs can be reduced.

- Time-sharing applications will also benefit from the additional real-time capabilities, since the system will have greater functionality and performance.

In this paper, we describe why existing UNIX system interfaces and implementation techniques cannot reliably support real-time applications with millisecond time constraints. We also describe how some of these problems were resolved in SAGE, a real-time operating system designed specifically for supervisory control applications. Although SAGE is not a UNIX system, it has a similar internal structure and emulates many of the UNIX system calls. Therefore, SAGE and UNIX are quite similar at both the kernel and programmer levels, and many of the techniques used in SAGE can be directly applied to UNIX.

2 UNIX Deficiencies

In this section we describe some of the deficiencies that arise in both the UNIX system interface and implementation. For the most part we consider only the two major variants of UNIX: Berkeley 4.3 BSD and System V UNIX. However, since most UNIX systems are ported from one of these two bases, the discussion should be relevant to most other UNIX systems as well.

2.1 Interface Problems

Interface problems are due to either inadequate, incomplete, or missing functionality in the system facilities available to the application. For real-time applications running under UNIX, interface problems arise in many areas, including the scheduler, timer, memory management, and IPC facilities.

2.1.1 Process Scheduling

In UNIX, process priority is set through either the nice (System V) or setpriority (Berkeley) system call. Unfortunately, neither call guarantees that the process with the highest assigned priority will be running at any given instant, since the system's round-robin scheduling algorithm preempts processes that have been using extensive amounts of CPU time.

This presents a problem for many real-time applications, which are structured on a fixed priority basis. Typically, the most time-critical processes are (statically) assigned the highest priorities, with the understanding that at any instant the scheduler should run the highest priority process that is ready. For such real-time applications, UNIX must provide some range of priorities that are not subject to round-robin preemption.

Another useful facility the system can provide is to allow one process to change the priority of another process. Then a sophisticated application could conveniently perform its own scheduling (such as run the process with the nearest deadline first). Unfortunately, there is no way to change the priority of another process in System V UNIX. Note, however, that the Berkeley UNIX setpriority call does provide this capability.

2.1.2 Timer Facilities

As a rule of thumb, timer services should provide a resolution of at least two orders of magnitude smaller than the period at which events occur, to avoid quantization error. Thus, for example, if events occur on the order of seconds (such as in a general time-sharing system), system time services should be accurate to roughly 1/100 of a second. Likewise, when dealing with real-time events on the order of milliseconds, the timers should be accurate to tens of microseconds.

Unfortunately, UNIX timers are much too coarse for real-time applications. System V UNIX, for instance, only provides for second granularity on alarms and time of day, and (using streams) millisecond resolution for polling and sleep functions.

These problems are corrected by the Berkeley UNIX interface, which specifies all time values with microsecond resolution. In reality, however, implementation problems (to be described later) reduce the effective resolution of the Berkeley timers to hundreths of a second, which again is inadequate for real-time.

UNIX timer facilities are also lacking some needed functionality. Because the timer values are interpreted relative to the current time, there is no way to atomically perform such operations as "sleep until a given time." Thus all timer events are subject to an unpredictable amount of clock skew, which is unacceptable if events should be generated at specific times. Berkeley UNIX addresses this problem in a limited way, by providing a second "repeat" argument to the setitimer command. But it is still impossible to generate a single event without skew, or to generate multiple events with non-uniform periods.

2.1.3 Memory Management

The memory management facilities provided by UNIX are inadequate for many real-time applications. The most glaring deficiency, perhaps, occurs in Berkeley UNIX, where there is no way to lock a process into memory. Therefore, a page fault taken at an inopportune moment could easily cause a process to miss a real-time deadline. System V UNIX addresses this problem with a system call that can lock an entire program text or data segment. This is adequate but wasteful, since only certain pages generally need to be locked.

For a finer grain of memory locking control in a demand paged real-time system, two system calls seem appropriate. The first returns the status for a range of pages (locked, in-core, etc.); the second forces the system to bring (and perhaps lock) these pages into core. Similar calls have been proposed for other UNIX systems [5,6].

Shared memory is another real-time facility that is missing in Berkeley UNIX. Although the relative merits of shared memory (as opposed to message passing) have been debated for many years, shared memory can often provide significantly faster (indeed, optimal) inter-process communication in many cases.

Of course, shared memory is generally useful for non real-time applications as well, e.g. to provide shared libraries. However, the main reason for providing shared memory is performance. In this way, the system can accommodate real-time applications that push the limits of the underlying hardware. Fortunately, many UNIX systems (including System V UNIX) have implemented some form of shared memory.

For similar reasons, memory mapped I/O is also useful for real-time applications, since it allows a process to efficiently interface to other devices and computers on a shared bus. Memory mapped I/O is also attractive since it allows devices to be programmed without resorting to kernel modifications or special purpose device drivers. Neither System V nor Berkeley UNIX provides such a memory mapping capability, although the Berkeley UNIX interface does propose an mmap system call which can handle memory mapped I/O. Indeed, because of its utility, mmap has been partially implemented in several vendor supplied systems.

Even with memory mapped I/O, no existing UNIX system provides an application level facility to map bus addresses to process memory (needed for DMA applications) or allows the user to supply a per-application interrupt handler. Therefore, the value of memory mapped I/O is greatly diminished, and device control typically remains relegated to kernel device drivers. In turn, this causes the application to incur greater overhead and reduces device programmability by fixing the system interface.

2.1.4 User-Level Synchronization

Existing UNIX systems provide process synchronization through either message passing or (System V) semaphores. Both mechanisms have fairly high overhead, however. Message passing implies at least two system calls (for reading and writing the message) and a context switch to the monitor process for every synchronization operation. System V semaphores have better performance, but still require at least one system call for every synchronization operation.

Inefficient synchronization primitives greatly diminish the performance benefits of shared memory, since short critical sections are frequently performed when accessing shared variables. Therefore, more efficient synchronization methods must be provided by a real-time UNIX.

Synchronization, like many performance problems, can be viewed as either an interface problem or an implementation problem: it is an interface problem if we plan to add new mechanisms, but it is an implementation problem if we plan to speed up existing mechanisms. Indeed for many problems, both the interface and the implementation will have to be modified to achieve the desired level of performance.

2.1.5 Serial Lines

Since RS-232 is an ubiquitous device interface, a real-time system should be able to support a number of high speed tty lines efficiently. One major problem with the UNIX tty driver interface is the high overhead incurred running in "raw" mode. Because the interface returns as soon as characters are present, the process rapidly context switches between kernel and user mode.

To avoid context switches, the usual workaround is to delay for an appropriate period before reading from the line. In general, however, this solution either encounters needless delays (by waiting too long) or generates extra context switches (by waiting too little). Another approach is to construct a special purpose kernel line discipline such as used for Berknet or SLIP in 4.3 BSD, but once again this does not address the general problem.

Another problem with the serial line interface is that it does not support the full range of UART capabilities: parity, stop bits, variable data bits, etc. For example, UNIX does not support eight bit data with parity, a configuration which is becoming more common.

2.1.6 Interprocess Communication

Current UNIX systems provide a variety of IPC facilities, including signals, pipes, sockets (Berkeley), named pipes, and messages (System V). These different styles of communication are particularly useful for providing client-server based applications.

Although the client-server model is a useful one for structuring distributed and modular applications, a potential problem arises for real-time applications. Because the client's service request is executed in the context of the server process, the client's priority effectively becomes that of the server. If the server and client have different priorities, the request will either assume a greater or lesser importance when processed by the server. Usually, however, we want the server to run at the same priority as the client.

This example points out that the system should be able to propagate priorities across communication streams; neither Berkeley nor System V UNIX addresses this issue. While it is possible for much of this work to be done by the application (by passing priorities in messages), some amount of system support still seems required. For instance, the system needs to be able to recognize when a high priority request for the server is pending, in order that the process be scheduled promptly.

In the distributed environment the problem is more pervasive, since it extends beyond the operating system to the underlying communication subnet: communications resources should be allocated on a priority basis, and the associated protocols must recognize different classes of service. Unfortunately such priority service is rarely provided in existing networks.

2.2 Implementation

The main implementation problems in UNIX are due to:

- Latency Effects. In many cases, there can be a significant amount of delay between the time a process is supposed to run and when it actually does run, potentially causing real-time deadline to be missed.

- Intolerable Overhead. Some facilities are so costly in terms of time that they cannot be used. This renders the facility useless.

- Partial Implementations. Although the system service should theoretically provide the necessary functionality, it has not been completely implemented.

We now describe some of the more severe implementation problems.

2.2.1 Process Latency

The two major causes of process latency in UNIX are the non-preemptibility of the kernel and the lengthy amount of time spent in the interrupt handlers. Because the kernel is non-preemptible, a newly readied higher priority process must wait until an active kernel process completes a system call or voluntarily gives up the processor. Since system calls such as read and write often perform block copies of several kilobytes, these delays can amount to milliseconds.

Interrupt handlers or code that disables hardware interrupts also contributes to latency in two ways. First, rescheduling is delayed, since rescheduling events are effectively disabled while processor priority is raised. Secondly, an interrupt handler steals cycles from the currently executing process. Therefore a process may not receive enough time to be able to meet a real-time deadline. Lengthy interrupt handlers are especially common in both the Berkeley networking and System V streams code, where checksums and block copies are done at software interrupt level.

Clearly to avoid latency effects, kernel processes need to be preemptible, and interrupt routines need to queue work for later processing by kernel-resident preemptible processes.

2.2.2 Signal Latency

Signal delivery experiences latency effects similar to process scheduling, since once a process is running inside the kernel, it only checks for signals before it returns to user mode or (for interruptible kernel sleeps) when it gives up the processor.

Since signals simulate software interrupts, they are useful for communicating exceptional conditions. However, if such a facility is going to be used in real-time applications, the implementation must allow processes to respond to such signals immediately. In particular, when a signal is delivered to a process running inside the kernel, the kernel stack needs to be unwound. Therefore the kernel must have some exception handling capability.

2.2.3 Timer Problems

As mentioned before, Berkeley UNIX allows interval timers to be specified in microseconds. Internally, however, such values are rounded up to the nearest tick of the line clock, so the effective resolution of the timer is really the line clock frequency. In Berkeley UNIX the line clock frequency is 1/100 of a second, much too coarse for the real-time domain.

Profiling time values generally suffer the same resolution problem, since these counters are only updated from the line clock interrupt. Indeed in most UNIX implementations, time of day is also only accurate to the nearest clock tick (although the 4.3 BSD VAX distribution does return reasonably accurate values).

2.2.4 Copy Overhead

In any real-time system, reducing overhead is an important goal. In UNIX, one major cause of system overhead is the time spent copying data back and forth between the kernel and user address spaces. In particular, it takes roughly a millisecond to copy a page on a standard 32-bit microprocessor. In many cases, however, these copies can be avoided by mapping the data pages into and out of the kernel. Systems such as Mach have shown that such an approach is feasible and implementable in UNIX [5].

Unfortunately, the Mach scheme may cause problems for real-time applications. When the same page is mapped into two different address spaces, and one process attempts to modify the page, a page fault is generated, and a copy of the page is made. In many cases, this would cause the process to experience unacceptable latencies. Ideally, the system should avoid copying data where possible, while at the same time insuring that processes cannot generate unpredictable page faults.

2.2.5 Queueing Delays

Queues are useful in real-time systems, since they increase the potential concurrency of the system. However, because most of the internally maintained system queues obey a FIFO queueing discipline, a queued request can experience unpredictable delays before it is serviced. Therefore, there is no guarantee that such queued requests will be performed in a timely fashion. This is especially true when performing I/O on heavily shared devices such as network interfaces and disk drives.

To eliminate unwanted queueing delays, the UNIX kernel should be modified to support internal queueing disciplines based on process priority. In other words, a priority should be associated with each message in the queue, equal to the priority of the process that generated the message. If the system then services the queue in priority order, the highest priority requests will always be handled in a timely fashion.

3 SAGE Overview

Many of the UNIX problems we have just described have been directly addressed in SAGE, a real-time operating system that is being developed for robotics control applications.

The SAGE system architecture is quite similar to that of the BLIT or DMD. Programs are developed and cross-compiled on a UNIX workstation, and then dynamically downloaded to the SAGE host, which consists of a resident kernel running on a 68000 processor board. SAGE programs invoke operating system services by trapping to the executive.

The SAGE kernel provides many of the facilities needed for real-time supervisory control: multitasking, a preemptive scheduler, precise timing facilities, and a number of supported devices. More novel features of the system include extensive use of memory management facilities and support of real-time network communications, things that are rarely found in other real-time systems.

Many aspects of the SAGE design were based on previous experiences with NRTX, a real-time operating system developed at AT&T Bell Laboratories [7]. In fact, the original SAGE kernel was bootstrapped from the NRTX development tools, and the two systems have a similar architecture. However, the current SAGE kernel bears little resemblance to NRTX.

3.1 Design Goals

The main design goals of SAGE were to:

- Support real-time supervisory control applications. Such applications require millisecond response time, and must interface to a diverse number of devices and systems. Therefore the kernel must be responsive and provide extensive I/O capabilities.

- Provide a friendly development environment. SAGE was intended to be used for research in robotics control. Therefore, good system support for program development and debugging was required.

- Maintain a large degree of UNIX compatibility. UNIX was already a familiar and friendly environment, and a degree of compatibility would allow us to avoid learning a entirely new system. Furthermore, modules could be partially debugged in the UNIX environment.

Perhaps the most important design goal was an implicit requirement: that a working system be ready quickly for use in other research projects. This led to incorporating only those facilities essential to our real-time applications, and making every effort to take advantage of existing code where possible, especially since the development of the system was a one-man effort.

The desire for a quick implementation is reflected in two ways. First, by relegating program development functions to the UNIX host, the SAGE kernel can be made considerably simpler. Secondly, SAGE is internally structured in a similar fashion to UNIX. This has allowed us to rapidly develop a working system, since a large amount of UNIX code could be reused in SAGE. In fact, the device structure entries of both systems are nearly identical, so standard Multibus and VMEbus UNIX device drivers only need minor changes to run under SAGE.

Although SAGE is similar in many ways to UNIX, SAGE is most definitely not a UNIX system. At the system interface level, for example, process creation is handled completely differently (there is no equivalent of fork, for example), and all processes share the same virtual address space (although one process, in general, cannot overwrite another process's address space). Also, a few major subsystems, such as filesystem support, have been removed. Instead, SAGE provides file operations through remote procedure calls to a UNIX system serving as a fileserver.

Furthermore, the SAGE kernel does not support the standard UNIX user interface. Neither the shell, nor most of the standard UNIX utilities, run under the SAGE kernel. Rather, the SAGE kernel is intended solely to provide a good execution environment for real-time programs, with most program development and user interface issues handled through the UNIX machine.

4 SAGE Facilities

We now describe a few of the real-time facilities provided by SAGE that are not in standard UNIX systems, including the real-time scheduler, extended timer facilities, process synchronization primitives, and memory management facilities.

4.1 Scheduler

The SAGE scheduler always runs the highest priority ready process, and it will not adjust process priorities dynamically. In particular, the scheduler does not provide round-robin preemption, and so is much simpler than the UNIX scheduler. In spite of this simplicity, the SAGE scheduler is better suited for real-time applications than the UNIX scheduler because processes cannot be unexpectedly preempted. Therefore, the most time critical operations are guaranteed to be run first.

Process priorities are specified by 64 bit integers. By default, SAGE processes execute at the processor's base priority, so all interrupt handlers effectively have a higher priority than any process. However, a SAGE process can elevate its processor priority as needed to mask out interrupts.

SAGE also allows one process to modify the priority of another (known) process. This allows an application to efficaciously schedule a group of related processes.

4.2 Process Latency

The single most important goal in the implementation of SAGE was to minimize process scheduling latency. Therefore, it was important to maximize the amount of preemptible kernel code. It is mostly for this reason that the internal structure of SAGE differs from that of a standard UNIX system, where the kernel is non-preemptible.

Two techniques were used to make the kernel preemptible. First, all critical sections of the kernel were identified and suitably protected against rescheduling interrupts. This was tedious but straight forward, and has been done in many multiprocessor UNIX systems.

Secondly, every effort was made to minimize the amount of time spent in the kernel interrupt handlers. Where ever possible, the interrupt handlers were written to queue work for later execution rather than directly executing the code. In some cases callouts (described below) were used to execute subroutines at software interrupt level, while in other cases kernel resident processes were used to perform preemptible lengthy operations.

Queueing work in the interrupt handler also reduced the need to protect many critical sections against hardware interrupts, since the shared data was now being accessed by code running at a lower priority. Therefore the overall system latency was once again reduced, since the critical sections only needed to mask out lower priority interrupts.

4.2.1 Callouts

To support the SAGE style of callouts, the UNIX-style callout code had to be extended to accept multiple arguments, allow untimed callout events to be queued, and provide separate queues for timed callouts waiting to expire and callouts that need to be executed. The hardware clock routine then consists mostly of moving expired timer events from the wait queue to the execute queue, and generating a software interrupt.

In general, SAGE uses a callout for executing short subroutines that cause a process state transition. However, because callouts currently run from a software interrupt handler, they are non-preemptible. Therefore for lengthier operations, SAGE uses a kernel process instead.

4.2.2 Kernel Processes

Kernel processes in SAGE are functionally equivalent to the kernel-half of a UNIX process. In particular, a kernel process occupies a slot in the process table and has its own stack. Because the kernel is mapped into each process's address space, a context switch to a kernel process requires little more than saving and restoring its registers. Therefore a kernel process is extremely lightweight.

SAGE uses kernel processes to implement many of the network input modules, including those which support the Internet protocols IP, UDP, and ARP. In this way, the system allows lengthy network operations such as checksums and packet reassembly to be preempted.

In addition, kernel processes are used by some device drivers to avoid extensive copy operations at interrupt time. For example, the device driver for a non-DMA ethernet controller uses two kernel processes, one for receiving and one for transmitting. The receiver process copies packets out of the controller's on-board memory into a system buffer, while the transmitter process copies buffers from higher level protocols into device memory. SAGE also insures that the more important communication streams are serviced first, because the higher level protocols are careful to queue buffers for the driver in priority order.

4.3 Timer Facilities

SAGE extends the UNIX timer facilities to provide both relative and absolute timers, the main ones being:

pauseabsolute	pause a process until a certain time
pauserelative	pause a process for a given amount of time
alarmabsolute	send an alarm signal at a certain time
alarmrelative	send an alarm signal after a given amount of time
gettimeofday	return the current time
settimeofday	set the current time

In addition, a few profiling and instrumentation timers are provided.

All time arguments are specified to microsecond resolution. Absolute time values are specified in terms of the number of microseconds elapsed since the system has booted. In addition, the kernel maintains a global time offset, which when added to the absolute time, gives the current Greenwich Mean Time. This offset, along with the absolute time, is returned by the gettimeofday call. The offset can also be changed by the settimeofday call.

To achieve high resolution on the alarm and time of day functions, SAGE uses two hardware timers, with one timer providing time of day information, and the other timer providing an event timer interrupt. Conceptually then, the time of day function is provided by simply reading the time of day register. In practice, however, the register is a counter clocked at a fast frequency, and so can wrap around quickly. Thus we must also maintain an additional counter in kernel memory to record the overflow.

Internally, all alarm events are stored on the callout wait queue, sorted in increasing absolute time. The interval timer is then programmed to interrupt at a time given by the first queue entry. The hardware clock handler removes all expired entries from the queue (as determined by a simple comparison), and reprograms the interval timer to interrupt at the next timer event given by the new entry at the head of the wait queue.

In the current implementation, an AMD 9513 timer chip is used, and both the time of day and interval timers are accurate to better than 5 microseconds. However, system call and context switching overhead effectively increase this value an order of magnitude as far as the application is concerned. Furthermore, because the number of hardware timers is limited, profiling timers are still performed by a "line-clock" routine called at a configuration-dependent frequency, which is usually set at 50 HZ. Therefore, the profiling timers still have very coarse resolution.

4.4 User-Level Synchronization

SAGE provides two basic facilities for process synchronization: a locking facility, whereby processes can temporarily raise their priority, and a scheduling facility, whereby processes can suspend and resume themselves. The facilities are intended to allow application dependent synchronization primitives to be built with a minimum of system overhead. Variations of these calls were first proposed in [10].

```
lock(sharedvar}
{
        word1 = 31;  /* non-preemptible */
        while (testandset(sharedvar) == TRUE)
                continue;  /* multiprocessor busy-wait */
}

unlock(sharedvar)
{
        sharedvar = FALSE;  /* multiprocessor */
        word1 = 0;
        if (word2)
                reschedule();
}
```

Figure 1: Lock and unlock

4.4.1 Locking

A test-and-set operation is often used in conjunction with busy-waiting to insure that small critical sections are atomically executed. For a fixed priority scheduler, however, such a technique by itself will not work. This is easily seen in the case where a process, running on a uniprocessor, has been preempted inside a critical section. If a higher priority process now attempts to enter the critical section, the busy-wait will always fail, and both processes will deadlock.

What is really needed is a locking facility, whereby a process can insure it is not preempted once inside a critical section. In SAGE, this facility is provided by two words (herein denoted as word1 and word2) that are shared between the process and the kernel scheduler. word1 is set by the process, and is interpreted by the scheduler as the process's temporary priority. By setting this priority to a suitably high value, the process can insure it will not be preempted. word2 is set by the scheduler, and informs the process that other processes are waiting to run.

Figure 1 shows in detail how a SAGE process can lock and unlock a critical section in a multiprocessor environment. When the process wants to enter a critical section, it calls lock, which temporarily raises the process's priority by setting word1. Likewise when leaving the critical section, the process calls unlock, which restores the process's base priority by clearing word1. Instructions involving sharedvar are used to implement a multiprocessor busy-wait, which can no longer deadlock because the process holding the lock cannot be preempted. Of course, these particular instructions can be eliminated in a uniprocessor system.

The scheduler performs a complimentary action. If the scheduler is about to preempt the process, it checks word1, which is the process's temporary priority. If the temporary priority is still too low, the process is preempted. However, if the temporary priority is now high enough, the process is allowed to continue, and word2 is set to indicate that preemption has been deferred. unlock will eventually check if word2 is set, and if it is, request that the processor be rescheduled.

In the usual case, neither rescheduling nor busy-waiting is required, and only a few instructions are required to lock and unlock a critical section. In particular, system calls are avoided.

4.4.2 Scheduling Control

Two primitives are provided for scheduling control which are analogous to the kernel's sleep and wakeup mechanism:

```
        P(sem)
        {
                lock(sem.mutex);
                while (sem.value == BUSY) {
                        enqueue(sem.queue, getpid());
                        unlock(sem.mutex);
                        suspendproc(getpid(), 0);
                        lock(sem.mutex);
                }
                sem.value = BUSY;
                unlock(sem.mutex);
        }

        V(sem)
        {
                lock(sem.mutex);
                pid = dequeue(sem.queue);
                sem.value = FREE;
                unlock(sem.mutex);
                if (pid)
                        resumeproc(pid);
        }
```

Figure 2: Binary semaphore

suspendproc(pid, flag)	suspend process pid if flag != 0 or flag == 0 and the RESUME_CALLED flag has not been set for process pid. In any case, clear the RESUME_CALLED flag for pid.
resumeproc(pid)	resume pid if it is suspended, otherwise set the RESUME_CALLED flag for pid

suspendproc and resumeproc can be used with lock and unlock to implement a wide range of synchronization primitives. For instance, a binary semaphore can be implemented as in Figure 2. Note that the RESUME_CALLED flag associated with suspendproc and resumeproc is used here in an essential way, since another process can call resumeproc in between the time a process has placed itself on sem.queue and called suspendproc.

Again, this code is quite fast in the usual non-blocking case.

4.5 Memory Management

SAGE attempts to provide several memory management facilities needed for real-time work, including shared memory and memory mapped I/O. At the same time, other generally useful facilities, such as swapping or demand paging, have not been implemented. The net result is that the SAGE virtual memory system is radically different from that of UNIX in both its interface and implementation.

4.5.1 Segments

SAGE memory management operations center around the notion of a segment, which is simply a range of virtual addresses. Segments are referred to by UNIX style pathnames, and can be mapped into a process's address space using the open system call:

        open("/dev/seg/name", flags);

where the name part of the pathname identifies the particular segment. Similarly, a segment can be created by using the O_CREAT flag in open.

Shared memory is provided by having several processes open the same segment simultaneously. The open call also returns a handle to the segment, which can be used in future ioctl calls for performing control operations.

The first control operation that must be performed on a segment is virtual memory allocation. Usually the application just specifies the desired segment size, and the system selects the segment's virtual addresses. However, an application allocating virtual memory can force the virtual addresses to reside at a particular location. In this way, SAGE can accommodate ROM and other statically-bound address programs.

After virtual addresses have been allocated, the segment consists of a set of invalidated virtual pages. In particular, no physical memory has yet been allocated to the segment. Therefore, another ioctl call is required before a process can reference the segment's addresses. Usually this additional call allocates physical memory for the segment. SAGE implements this call by mapping the segment's virtual addresses to valid physical pages.

Other operations allow more complicated mappings but are performed similarly. The map-out operation allows a segment to reference bus memory or I/O space, and thus provides memory mapped I/O. The map-in operation, on the other hand, allows segment addresses to be referenced by other DMA bus masters.

Another control operation allows the process to set segment protections such as read-only, read-write, etc. The typical process will create at least three segments for itself: a read-only text segment, a read-write data segment, and a read-write stack segment. Segment protection, combined with the ability to invalidate individual pages, allows a SAGE process to set firewalls in its address space.

4.5.2   Address Sharing

All SAGE segments currently allocate virtual memory from the same pool. In general this is quite safe, since part of the process's context is a list of mapped in segments. The system makes sure that a process can only access its mapped in segments.

Because all processes share the same virtual addresses, there is no context-dependent addressing. In other words, a virtual address always refers to the same physical location, independent of the process that dereferences the address. Therefore, the kernel, by mapping all segments into its address space, can always reference any process without changing any hardware MMU maps.

Context-independent addressing allows the system to support user-supplied interrupt handlers in a simple way. A system call is provided to set an interrupt vector to a handler inside the process's address space. Because the kernel can always access every process, the interrupt handler can always access its shared variables, regardless of which process is currently running.

SAGE also provides two other system calls to support user-supplied interrupt handlers. The first allows a process to modify the processor status word, in order to mask interrupts. The second call allows a process to resume a process that has suspended itself awaiting an event.

One drawback of address sharing is that a process cannot always anticipate what virtual addresses it will occupy. Therefore, the executable image either has to be relocated before it is loaded into memory, or it has to be written using position independent code. Currently, relocation on demand is performed in a similar way to that done in the BLIT or DMD systems.

4.5.3   Page Copies

Page mapping is also used by SAGE to avoid copying data in and out of the kernel. To do this, SAGE provides special versions of the read and write system calls, pgswapread and pgswapwrite, that swap pages with the kernel instead of copying data between address spaces.

When performing a pgswapread call, the kernel maps the pages containing data into the process's address space. The overwritten pages in the process's address space are released back to the kernel.

The pgswapwrite call works similarly. The pages in the process containing the data to be written are remapped into the kernel's address space. The original pages in the process are then replaced with new physical pages allocated by the kernel.

Since neither of these calls preserve copy semantics, they are much simpler to implement than the "lazy evaluation" techniques used in Accent [11] and Mach [5]. However, because the SAGE calls

Function	SAGE	SUN 3/160 (3.2)
System Call	50-80 usecs	120 usecs
Null Process	1 msec	12 msec
UDP 4K writes	367K bytes/sec	374K bytes/sec
Context Switch	60 usecs	

Table 1: SAGE vs. UNIX

are destructive, they are somewhat less convenient to use than the Mach equivalents. Nevertheless, the SAGE calls have proved useful for real-time work, since copying can still be avoided in most cases, and page faults are guaranteed not be taken at inappropriate times.

4.6 Serial Lines

In order to improve support for high speed serial lines, several extensions were made to the Berkeley UNIX tty driver. First, the SAGE driver now allows character buffering capacity and water marks to be specified on a per-line basis. Next, the driver has been expanded (hardware permitting) to support most UART configurations. Finally, the SAGE driver has added a "block mode" discipline. In block mode, a read will return only when the given number of characters are read, or when one of a given set of characters is read. Any eight-bit character can be a member of this set, which is specified by a bit string.

5 Current Status

SAGE is now running on several different Pacific Microsystems 68000-based processor boards, including both Multibus and VMEbus systems. The essential hardware components used by SAGE include the memory management unit (for protection and memory mapped I/O), dual ported memory, two high resolution timers, and on-board software interrupts. These components are found in most minicomputers and many microcomputers.

Extensive benchmarks have yet to be performed for the SAGE system. However, preliminary figures illustrated in Table 1 show SAGE's performance is competitive with UNIX systems for common functions. Here both SAGE and the SUN are using 68020 processors clocked at 16.7MHz.

Of course, the benchmarks should not be taken too seriously, since the systems are totally different in many respects. Indeed, SAGE's only performance goal has been to support the type of supervisory control applications performed in our laboratory. In this regard, SAGE has been successful. In particular, one 68020-based system simultaneously handles several thousand interrupts a second and a number of active network connections, all while still providing real-time response on the order of milliseconds.

6 Conclusion

Interestingly enough, many of UNIX's real-time problems, such as providing shared memory, efficient synchronization, and minimal latency, are now being dealt with in multiprocessor UNIX implementations. This is probably due to the common desire to provide high performance. In addition, several commercially available UNIX ports have also addressed some of these real-time issues. For instance, MASSCOMP [8] provides page locking, shared memory, memory-mapped I/O, a real-time scheduler, and some degree of kernel preemption.

The author knows of no UNIX system, however, which (running on comparable hardware) can handle the type of applications currently handled by SAGE. In particular, little attention has been paid in UNIX to reducing interrupt latency or providing network communications compatible with real-time goals. Hopefully, future UNIX systems will be able to handle such applications.

Many of the ideas appearing in SAGE were inspired by work done elsewhere. The user-level synchronization techniques are similar to those in Mach [9] and the NYU Ultracomputer. Page mapping techniques were first made prominent in Accent. Many of the ideas for timers and callouts came from VMS. The SAGE segment, process, and IPC interface was inspired by Version 8 UNIX [12], which allows objects to be referred to by pathnames and accessed through the open system call. User-level interrupt handlers were taken from NRTX.

In the future, we hope to port SAGE to several other types of processor boards and to build a multiprocessor system. We would also like the extend the kernel in several ways, including adding the ability to handle signals and exceptions in a timely fashion.

References

[1] *pSOS-68k User's Manual*, Software Components Group, Santa Clara, Cal., 1986

[2] *VAX/VMS 4.0 Reference Manual*, Digital Equipment Corporation, Maynard, Mass., 1987

[3] *UNIX Programmer's Manual*, 4.3 Berkeley Software Distribution, University of California Berkeley, 1986

[4] *UNIX Programmer's Manual, System V Release 3.0*, AT&T, 1986

[5] A. Tevanian Jr. et. al., *A UNIX Interface fo Shared Memory and Memory Mapped Files Under Mach*, USENIX Summer Conference Proceedings, pp. 53-67, June 1987

[6] R. A. Gingell, J. P. Moran, W. A. Shannon, *Virtual Memory Architecture in SunOS*, USENIX Summer Conference Proceedings, pp. 81-94, June 1987

[7] D. A. Kapilow, *Real-Time Programming in a UNIX Environment*, Proceedings of the Symposium on Factory Automation and Robotics, Courant Institute of Mathematical Sciences, New York University, September 1985

[8] *MASSCOMP RT-2000 UNIX Reference Manual*, MASSCOMP Corp., 1986

[9] A. Tevanian Jr. et. al., *Mach Threads and the UNIX Kernel: The Battle for Control*, USENIX Summer Conference Proceedings, pp. 185-197, June 1987

[10] J. Edler, A. Gottlieb, J. Lipkis, *Considerations for Massively Parallel UNIX Systems on the NYU Ultracomputer and IBM RP3*, USENIX Winter Conference Proceedings, pp. 193-210, January 1986

[11] R. P. Fitzgerald, R. F. Rashid, *The Integration of Virtual Memory Management and Interprocess Communication in Accent*, ACM Transactions on Computer Systems, 4(2), May 1986

[12] T. J. Killian, *Processes as Files*, USENIX Summer Conference Proceedings, pp. 203-207, June 1984

Real-Time Mach:
Towards a Predictable Real-Time System

Hideyuki Tokuda, Tatsuo Nakajima, Prithvi Rao
School of Computer Science
Carnegie Mellon University
Pittsburgh, Pennsylvania 15213
hxt@cs.cmu.edu

Abstract

Distributed real-time systems play a very important role in our modern society. They are used in aircraft control, communication systems, military command and control systems, factory automation, and robotics. However, satisfying the rigid timing requirements of various real-time activities in distributed real-time systems often requires *ad hoc* methods to tune the system's runtime behavior

The objective of Real-Time Mach is to develop a real-time version of the Mach kernel which provides users with a predictable and reliable distributed real-time computing environment. In this paper, we describe a real-time thread model, real-time synchronization, and the ITDS scheduler in Real-Time Mach. We also discuss the implementation issues, a real-time toolset, and the current status of the system.

1 Introduction

Distributed real-time systems are becoming more common as real-time technology is applied to many real-time applications[20]. However, satisfying the rigid timing requirements of various real-time activities in distributed real-time systems is getting more complex due to the distributed nature of the system.

In many cases, system designers of such complex systems lack systematic development methods and analysis tools, so they resort to *ad hoc* methods to develop, test, and verify real-time systems. For processor scheduling, for instance, the cyclic executive model which uses time line analysis to schedule real-time activities is not suitable for a distributed

environment. It is very difficult to test and tune the executive based on some changes in the task set or its timing requirements for complex real-time systems [9]. Message communication scheduling in a network is also difficult since some communication media such as Ethernet do not guarantee bounded communication delay at media access level and do not provide priority-based arbitration.

A new challenge in such real-time systems is to develop a real-time kernel which can provide users with a predictable and reliable distributed real-time computing environment. In particular, the kernel should allow a system designer to analyze the runtime behavior at the design stage and predict whether the given real-time tasks having various types of system and task interactions (e.g., memory allocation/deallocation, message communications, I/O interactions, etc) can meet their timing requirements.

CMU's ART (Advanced Real-Time Technology) group has been working on a real-time version of the Mach as well as a real-time toolset for system design and analysis. Real-Time Mach is being developed based on a version of the pure kernel [1, 7] using a network of SUN, SONY workstations, and single board target machines. Unlike the standard release 2.5 Mach, this kernel includes new real-time thread management, an integrated time-driven scheduler (ITDS), real-time synchronization, and memory resident objects. The real-time thread model is based on the ARTS real-time thread model [21, 25] and our real-time scheduling theories. Real-Time Mach was also integrated with our real-time toolset, *Scheduler 1-2-3*[23] and Advanced Real-Time Monitor, *ARM*[22].

In this paper, we describe new system facilities in Real-Time Mach and the current status. In Section 2, we first introduce the real-time thread model, real-time synchronization primitives, integrated time-driven scheduler, and support for memory resident objects. Section 3 discusses implementation issues and our solution to priority inversion problems. In Section 4, we also compare our approach and real-time thread model to other operating systems. Section 5 summarizes the development status and considers future work.

---

1   This research was supported in part by the U.S. Naval Ocean Systems Center under contract number N66001-87-C-0155, by the Office of Naval Research under contract number N00014-84-K-0734, by the Defense Advanced Research Projects Agency, ARPA Order No. 7330 under contract number MDA72-90-C-0035, by the Federal Systems Division of IBM Corporation under University Agreement YA-278067, and by the SONY Corporation. The views and conclusions contained in this document are those of the authors and should not be interpreted as representing official policies, either expressed or implied, of NOSC, ONR, DARPA, IBM, SONY, or the U.S. Government.

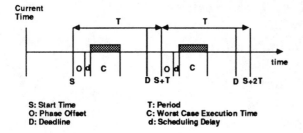

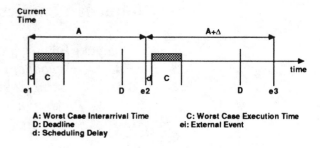

Figure 1: Timing attributes of a periodic thread

Figure 2: Timing attributes of an aperiodic thread

2 Real-Time Mach

The objective of Real-Time Mach (RT-Mach) is to develop a real-time version of Mach which can support a predictable real-time computing environment together with a real-time toolset. Because of the high portability of Mach, RT-Mach should be able to provide a common real-time computing environment in various machine architectures including single board computer-based targets.

In this section, we will describe the new features of RT-Mach. The current version of RT-Mach supports a real-time thread model, integrated real-time thread scheduler, policy/mechanism separation in the scheduler, real-time synchronization mechanisms, and memory resident objects.

2.1 RT-Thread Model

The objective of the RT-thread model is to support a predictable real-time scheduler and provide a uniform system interface to both real-time and non-real-time threads. Unlike the traditional real-time systems which often use a cyclic executive model, the RT-Mach supports an integrated time-driven scheduler [26] based on a rate monotonic scheduling paradigm [12, 13].

A thread can be defined for a real-time or non-real-time activity. Each thread is specified by at least a procedure name and a stack descriptor which specifies the size and address of the local stack region. For a real-time thread, additional *timing attributes* must be defined by a timing attribute descriptor. A real-time thread can be also defined as a *hard* real-time or *soft* real-time thread. By hard real-time thread, we mean that the thread must complete its activities by its *hard* deadline time, otherwise it will cause undesirable damage or a fatal error to the system. The soft real-time thread, on the other hand, does not have such a hard deadline, and it still makes sense for the system to complete the thread even if it passed its critical (i.e. *soft* deadline) time.

A real-time thread can be also defined as a *periodic* or *aperiodic* thread based on the nature of its activity. A periodic thread P_i is defined by the worst case execution time C_i, period T_i, start time S_i, phase offset O_i, and task's semantic importance value V_i. In a periodic thread, a new instantiation of the thread will be scheduled at S_i and then repeat the activity in every T_i. The phase offset is used to adjust a ready time within each period. If a periodic thread is a soft real-time thread, it may need to express the abort time which tells the scheduler to abort the thread. Figure 1 depicts the timing attributes of a hard periodic real-time thread.

An aperiodic thread AP_j is defined by the worst case execution time C_j, the worst case interarrival time A_j, deadline D_j, and task's semantic importance value V_i. In the case of soft real-time threads, A_j indicates the average case interarrival time and D_j represents the average response time. Abort time can be also defined for the soft real-time thread. Figure 2 depicts the timing attributes of a hard aperiodic real-time thread[2].

2.2 RT-Thread Creation and Termination

A thread can be created, within a task, by using the *rt_thread_create* primitive. As we described in the model, it can be a periodic or aperiodic thread depending on its timing attributes. The timing attributes are specified in the corresponding time descriptor, and the user and kernel stack regions are also given by the stack descriptor. If a creation is successful, a unique thread id will be returned. A thread can be terminated by calling *rt_thread_exit* primitive. If a thread is a periodic thread, a new instantiation of the thread will be scheduled for the next start time and a new thread id will be assigned. The

---

[2]When a hard real-time thread is aperiodic, we call it a *sporadic* thread where consecutive requests of the task initiation are kept at least Q units of time apart [15].

rt_thread_kill primitive terminates the specified thread while the *rt_thread_wait* primitive blocks the caller thread until the target thread terminates. The *rt_thread_self* primitive returns the thread id of the caller. The *rt_thread_set_attribute* and *rt_thread_get_attribute* primitive are used to assign or get the value of the attribute respectively. The brief description of the thread attribute is shown in below.

```
kval_t = rt_thread_create( parent, child_thread,
                                    thread_attr, entry_point, arg )
kval_t = rt_thread_exit( )
kval_t = rt_thread_kill( thread )
kval_t = rt_thread_wait( thread )
thread_t = rt_thread_self( )
kval_t = rt_thread_set_attribute( thread, thread_attr )
kval_t = rt_thread_get_attribute( thread, thread_attr )
```

```
typedef stuct time_desc {
  int rt_type;                    /* periodic or aperiodic thread */
  union {
    struct rt_Periodic {
      time_value_t rt_start;      /* start time */
      time_value_t rt_period;     /* period or response time info */
      time_value_t rt_offset;     /* phase offset */
    } rt_periodic;
    struct rt_Aperiodic {
      time_value_t rt_wcia;       /* worst case interarrival time */
    } rt_aperiodic;
  } rt_attribute;
  time_value_t rt_wcec;           /* worst case exec time */
  time_value_t rt_deadline;       /* deadline */
  time_value_t rt_abort;          /* abort time */
  int rt_value;                   /* semantic_value */
  . . .
} time_desc_t

typedef struct stack_desc {
  vm_address_t rt_stack_addr;
  vm_size_t rt_stack_size;
  . . .
} stack_desc_t

typedef struct thread_attribute {
  time_desc_t time_desc;
  stack_desc_t stack_desc;
  . . .
} thread_attr_t;
```

2.3   RT-Thread Synchronization

Synchronization among threads is necessary since all threads within a task share the task's resources. The synchronization mechanism in RT-Mach is based on mutual exclusion using a lock variable. A thread can allocate, deallocate, and initialize a lock variable. A simple pair of *rt_mutex_lock* and *rt_mutex_unlock* primitives is used to specify mutual exclusion. The *rt_mutex_trylock* primitive is used for acquiring the lock conditionally. A modified version of the condition variable is also created for specifying a conditional critical region. A pair of *rt_condition_signal* and *rt_condition_wait* primitives is used to synchronize over a condition variable. RT-Mach uses the earliest deadline first (or highest priority first) policy as a queueing policy in both the *rt_mutex* and *rt_condition* primitives. A caller can also control its priority inheritance policy by setting the proper mutex's or condition variable's attribute.

```
kval_t = rt_mutex_allocate( lock, lock_attr )
kval_t = rt_mutex_deallocate( lock )
kval_t = rt_mutex_lock( lock, timeout )
kval_t = rt_mutex_unlock( lock )
kval_t = rt_mutex_trylock( lock )

kval_t = rt_condition_allocate( cond, cond_attr )
kval_t = rt_condition_deallocate( cond )
kval_t = rt_condition_wait( cond, lock, cond_attr, timeout )
kval_t = rt_condition_signal( cond, cond_attr )
```

Unlike the ordinary mutual exclusion mechanism, the *rt_mutex_lock* and *rt_mutex_unlock* pair provide a priority inheritance mechanism in order to avoid an unbounded *priority inversion* problem. Priority inversion occurs when a high priority task must wait indefinitely for a lower priority task to execute.

Suppose that a low priority thread τ_L is in the critical region. While thread τ_L is executing, a high priority thread τ_H attempts to enter the critical region by executed the *rt_mutex_lock* primitive. Since τ_L is in the critical region, τ_H must wait for τ_L to exit. Now suppose that other threads $\tau_{M_1} \cdots \tau_{M_k}$ become active. These threads can begin their computation and will preempt thread τ_L, thus we cannot bound the worst case blocking time of τ_H.

In order to bound the worst case blocking time of threads, our group has developed priority inheritance protocols including *Priority Ceiling Protocol* [18]. In this example, once τ_H executes *rt_mutex_lock*, then τ_L will inherit the high priority from τ_H. In this way, the highest priority thread's worst case blocking time is bounded by the size of critical region (See Section 2.5).

2.4 RT-Thread Scheduling

In real-time operating systems, thread scheduling plays an important role in managing the system resources in a timely fashion. However, traditional operating systems do not provide us a flexible and a adaptable scheduling management. We have developed a novel scheduling model, Integrated Time-Driven Scheduler(ITDS) for the ARTS kernel[24], and have extended the model for RT-Mach. This section describes the Mach scheduling mechanism and an extended ITDS model.

2.4.1 Mach Scheduling Mechanism

Mach provides a flexible processor allocation facility. The facility uses two objects: *processor* and *processor set*. A processor object represents a physical processor and a processor set object corresponds to a set of processors. A thread belongs to a processor set and similarly a processor belongs to a processor set. A special processor set called a *default processor set* exists. Before a new processor set is created, all processors belong to a default processor set.

The most important data structure to manage scheduling of thread is the *run queue*. All processor sets have their own respective run queues. When a thread becomes runnable, it is enqueued into the run queue of the processor set to which the thread belongs. Also, when the current running thread in a processor is blocked or preempted, the new thread is chosen from the processor set where the blocked thread belongs. Because threads do not migrate between processor sets, we can choose a suitable scheduling policy for each processor set. However, the current Mach scheduler has only *round-robin* and *fixed priority* policies and manages 32-levels of thread priorities. Mach's fixed priority policy preempts the running thread if there are runnable threads with same priority and its quantum is expired. In real-time computing, such preemption decreases schedulability and we need other scheduling policies, for example, rate monotonic policy, and various aperiodic servers[19].

2.4.2 ITDS Scheduling in RT-Mach

The objective of the integrated time-driven scheduler is to provide predictability, flexibility, and modifiability for managing both *hard* and *soft* real-time activities. The ITDS scheduler allows the system designer to predict whether the given task set can meet its deadlines or not.

The ITDS scheduler adopted a *capacity preservation* scheme to cope with hard and soft types of real-time activities. By bandwidth preservation we mean that we divide the necessary processor cycles between the two types. We first analyze the necessary processor cycles by accumulating the total computation time for the hard periodic and sporadic activities. Then, we will assign the remaining schedulable amount of the unused processor cycles to the soft real-time tasks.

The ITDS scheduler was designed and implemented using an object model and layered structure. The scheduling policy

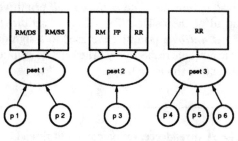

P i : Processor i
Pset i : Processor Set i

RM : Rate Monotonic
FP : Fixed Priority
RR : Round Robin
RM/DS : RM with Deferrable Server
RM/SS : RM with Sporadic Server

Figure 3: ITDS for RT-Mach

used by the scheduler object is a self-contained object and separated from the mechanism layer used to actually switch threads within the kernel. Using the ITDS scheduler, we can assign five different polices for each processor set in RT-Mach (See Figure 3).

The low level mechanism layer is divided into two sublayers: a processor set management sublayer and a thread dispatching management layer. The processor set management sublayer manages context switching, preemptions of threads and assignment of processors. The thread dispatching management layer controls idle threads and aperiodic servers: the polling server, deferrable server, and sporadic server[19].

Each processor set can have a scheduling policy since each processor set maintains its own run queue and operations for controlling the run queue. Therefore, we can configure the system for the various real-time applications. For example, let us consider the multiprocessor with six processors, and three processor sets: $pset_1$, $pset_2$, and $pset_3$. $pset_1$ has two processors: p_1 and p_2, $pset_2$ has one processor: p_3, and $pset_3$ has a three processors: p_4, p_5 and p_6. $pset_1$ executes real-time applications using two processors using rate monotonic with deferrable server or rate monotonic with sporadic server. $pset_2$ executes real-time and non real-time applications, so the application program may change scheduling policies from rate monotonic, fixed priority, or round-robin. $pset_3$ executes non real-time applications using three processors by round-robin algorithm.

We can change scheduling policies by using the following primitives. The policy attribute is used to pass policy specific arguments such as a server's period, capacity of the server, etc. to the specified policy module in the system.

```
kval_t = rt_get_sched_policy( policy, policy_attr )
kval_t = rt_set_sched_policy( policy, policy_attr )
```

2.5 Memory Object Management

The kernel must also avoid unbounded delay while it manages memory objects for real-time threads. In general, Mach's resource allocation policy is based on *lazy* evaluation technique. For instance, if a thread allocates a region of memory, the system does not allocate the physical memory object unless the thread touches the region and cause a page fault.

In order to eliminate such unpredictable page fault handing delay, a real-time thread can "pin-down" any region of its parent task's virtual address space by using the following *vm_wire* primitive.

```
kval_t = vm_wire(task, start_addr, size, access_type)
```

2.6 Schedulability Analysis

In the RT-Thread Model, our goal is to provide a better interface to adopt the well-known schedulability analysis techniques. For instance, given a set of periodic, independent tasks in a single processor environment, with the rate monotonic scheduling algorithm the worst case schedulable bound is 69%[13], the average case is 88% [12], and the best case, where threads have harmonic periods, is up to 100% of the CPU utilization.

In the case of a more general task set where threads can synchronize via critical regions, we can also bound the synchronization (blocking) time for each task by using the priority ceiling protocol. Using these inheritance protocols, we can also check schedulable bound for n periodic threads as follows.

$$\forall i, 1 \leq i \leq n, \frac{B_i}{T_i} + \sum_{j=1}^{i} \frac{C_j}{T_j} \leq i(2^{\frac{1}{i}} - 1)$$

where C_i, T_i, B_i represents the total computation time, the period, and the worst case blocking time of $Thread_i$ respectively.

These techniques are integrated with our real-time toolset. However, providing end-to-end schedulability analysis for a given task set which communicates over a real-time network still remains as a future challenge[3].

3 Implementation

The current version of RT-Mach is being developed using a network of SUN, SONY workstations and single board target machines. We first experimented with our real-time thread model using a modified version of Release 2.5 Mach kernel which can support fixed priority thread scheduling, a cpu server (i.e., processor set), and a *vm_wire* call. We then moved to the current pure kernel based environment. The pure kernel provided us much better execution environment where we can reduce unexpected delays in the kernel and can run real-time threads without having a UNIX server, if necessary. The preemptability of the kernel was also improved significantly since many device drivers are no longer in the kernel.

A platform for RT-Mach has slightly different requirements in terms of its execution environment. For embedded real-time applications, we need to support not only various types of workstations, but also a wide variety of single-board or multiple-board based target machine environments. Booting the target machines also requires a different booting procedure via the system's backplane-bus or via a network. For instance, we are working on a VME-bus based target environment. For real-time communication, we are also supporting a FDDI network in addition to the IEEE 802.5 token ring network.

In this section, we will describe some implementation issues encountered in our first version of the pure kernel-based RT-Mach. We also discuss the capability of the real-time toolset and the current status of RT-Mach.

3.1 Implementation Issues

Our primary focus in the current implementation was to remove unbounded delay in the system and provide better preemptability among real-time threads. However, there are many places we encountered problems in managing system resources in Mach. In many cases, we can recognize differences in resource allocation policy between the time-sharing paradigm and the real-time computing paradigm. Major policy differences are

- "lazy" evaluation vs. "eager" evaluation policy

- FIFO ordering vs. deadline-driven ordering (starvation-free vs. no missed deadlines)

- unbounded delay vs. bounded delay

---

[3]Using the latest processor architecture such as various RISC chips, it becomes an interesting practical problem in determining the worst case execution time for sections of code (which must take into account cache management and pipelined architectures).

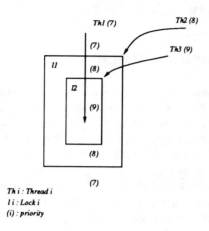

Figure 4: Priority Inheritance in Nested Lock

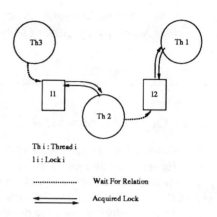

Figure 5: Cascaded Priority Inheritance

In many resource allocation cases, Mach takes advantage in deferring the actual allocation of resources until the requester needs it. *Copy-on-write* and *map-on-reference* techniques are good examples of the lazy evaluation scheme. On the other hand, this type of memory management policy often creates an unpredictable delay in getting the actual resources that the requester needs. For instance, if a thread needs to allocate memory, it calls *vm_alloc* routine, but the actual physical memory may not be allocated unless the thread actually touches that region and causes a page fault. However, if the thread is a real-time thread, it cannot afford to wait for unpredictable page fault service time. Rather, we would like to allocate memory resources in eager fashion. We can then estimate the worst case time for the allocation delay.

Mach uses many queues to manage various system resources such as ready queues, message queues, and free memory list queues. FIFO queuing is often used in these queues since the system can easily avoid the starvation among waiting threads. However, in a real-time environment, FIFO queueing often creates a priority inversion problem. If all of real-time threads can meet their deadlines, then there will be no starvation among these threads.

Similarly, in real-time synchronization, we do not treat waiting threads in FIFO order. For instance, when a real-time thread attempts to enter a critical region, it will be queued in its waiting queue in earliest deadline first (or the highest priority first) order. Then, when a thread exits from the critical region, the highest priority real-time thread will be chosen rather than the oldest waiting thread in the waiting queue.

In RT-Mach, we also use a basic priority inheritance protocol to avoid priority inversion problem in real-time synchronization. Let us describe three interesting cases where priority inheritance requires an additional mechanism.

In the first example, when a priority inversion occurs in a nested critical region, the propagation of the effective priority has to be performed carefully. Let us consider three threads: th_1, th_2, and th_3, and two locks: l_1 and l_2. We assume that th_1 has priority 7, th_2 has priority 8, and th_3 has priority 9. The larger value means higher priority. th_1 acquires l_1 and then l_2. th_3 then tries to acquire l_2, and th_2 tries to acquire l_1. The priority inheritance protocol makes th_1 inherit a priority of th_3, then the priority of th_1 becomes 9. After th_1 unlocks l_2, the priority of th_1 must become 8 because th_2's priority is 8 and th_2 waits for th_1 for unlocking l_1. When th_1 unlocks l_1, the priority of th_1 goes back to the base priority 7.

The second case is where the *waiting for* relation must be maintained among threads so that we can propagate the proper priority to a target thread. Let us consider three threads: th_1, th_2, and th_3, and two locks l_1 and l_2. th_3 has the highest priority, th_2 has middle priority, and the priority of th_1 is the lowest. th_1 acquires l_2. th_2 acquires l_1 and waits for unlocking l_2. When th_3 tries to acquired l_1, th_1 must inherit the priority of th_3. To manage this type of blocking case, the effect of priority inheritance is cascaded[4].

The third case is where the highest priority thread is timed out while waiting for a lock. For instance, in Figure 5, th_3 is inherits the priority of th_1. However, if th_1 is timed out while waiting for l_1, the priority of th_3 must be changed back to the priority of th_2.

The above problems can be solved by maintaining a relation between the lock variables and the threads. In RT-Mach, each thread maintains a pointer to lock variables, and the lock variable also keeps track of the nesting relation to the other locks and the holding thread. For example, in Figure 4, when

---

[4]The similar cascading problem and its solution was also described in [8]

th_1 acquires l_1, th_1 points to l_1. Next, when th_1 acquires l_2, l_2 points to l_1, and th_1 points to l_2. Then, if th_1 unlocks l_2, the priority of th_1 can degrade to the priority of $th2$ because l_2 knows l_1, and l_1 knows the priority of th_2.

We can solve the timeout problem mentioned above, the following way. From Figure 5, th_1 points to l_1, l_1 points to th_2, th_2 points to l_2, and l_2 points to th_3. So, th_1 can inherit the priority of th_3. If th_1 is timed out while waiting to acquire l_1, the priority of th_2 reverts to its base priority, and th_3 inherit that priority.

3.2 Real-Time Toolset

We have also developed a set of tools which we can use in conjunction with Real-Time Mach for predicting the behavior of the system and for runtime monitoring and debugging. The goal of the toolset is to incorporate a system-wide scheduling analysis which includes communication and synchronization among real-time threads. The toolset consists of *Scheduler 1-2-3* and *ARM*.

Scheduler 1-2-3 is a schedulability analyzer and is an X11-window based interactive tool for creating, manipulating, and analyzing real-time task sets. It employs methods ranging from closed form analysis to simulation to determine whether a feasible schedule exists for a given task set and what the schedulable bound is for that set.

ARM (Advanced Real-Time Monitor) is also an X11-window based tool designed to analyze and visualize the runtime behavior of the target nodes in real time. The ARM allows us to reach into a remote target and view the scheduling events which are extracted using event taps in RT-Mach.

3.3 Current Status

In the current version of RT-Mach, the RT-thread model and extended ITDS scheduler have been implemented. RT-Mach has also been integrated with the real-time tool set. In Figure 6, we show the snapshot of ARM with three periodic threads, and ten aperiodic threads. ARM is useful for monitoring the occurrences of preemption and the order in which threads are executed. Timing bugs can also be deleted easily using ARM.

Figure 7 demonstrates the RT-thread model. In the gmol demo, seven periodic threads are created and every thread represents an atom of a molecule. The threads, while executing, cause the molecule to rotate about an axis passing through the atom at the center. If scheduled correctly, the molecule maintains its integrity, otherwise the atoms move in a random fashion. Gmol visually demonstrates lack of schedulability, when the molecule's rotation is random. If we use a proper scheduling policy, we can ensure schedulability with high CPU utilization and each molecule rotates in a completely synchronized way (the left figure). However, if the scheduling policy is inappropriate, some deadlines are missed, so the synchronized rotation of the molecules is violated, and each molecule rotates

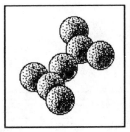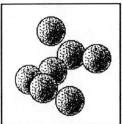

Figure 7: The Snapshot of Gmol

Null Argument Trap	0.03 ms
Null Argument MIG	0.30 ms
Context Switch	0.26 ms
vm_alloc 1KB (no wiring)	0.59 ms
vm_alloc 1KB (wiring)	2.67 ms
Port Allocate/Deallocate	1.2 ms
RT-Thread Creation/Termination	4.258 ms
RT-Lock and Unlock	0.146 ms

Table 1: The Basic Performance of RT-Mach

in chaotic manner (the right figure). Gmol further demonstrates the importance of the RT-thread model in preserving the schedulability of RT-thread. The traditional system offers the *delay* primitive for representing time description. However, the calculation of delay time and the execution of delay primitives may not be atomic giving rise to invalid time values, resulting in non synchronized rotation of the molecule.

Table 1 summarizes the basic performance of the current version of RT-Mach.

All measurements are performed on a Sun3/60 workstation with 12 Mbytes by repeating the target function more than 10,000 times. The trap interface to the kernel is about 10 times faster than MIG [5]. The context switch time between threads is acceptable in our application, and we can assume this number as the worst case since all resources are wiring down for these threads. Allocation of memory is normally done without wiring, thus the overhead is relatively small. However, additional wiring cost is not reduce to negligible yet, since we simply reused the original wiring facility in Mach. The creation and termination cost are mainly due to allocation and deallocation of system resources which belongs to a thread. The total cost should be reduced further by re-

---
[5]Mach uses a MIG(Mach Interface Generator) [10] to call kernel primitives in a object-oriented fashion and generates stubs for user programs.

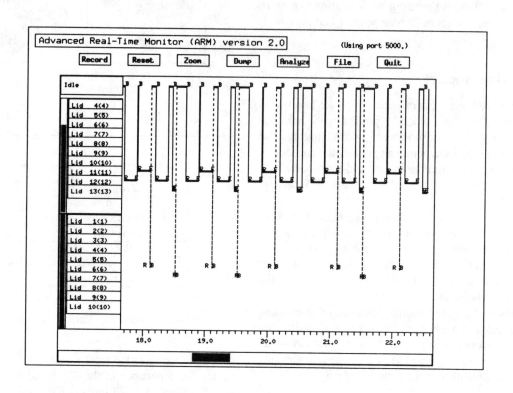

This figure shows an example of the history execution diagram. The top six boxes indicate the action menus. The top half of threads correspond to the periodic threads and the bottom half correspond to the aperiodic threads. Character 'R' shown in the execution history diagram indicates a periodic thread which becomes runnable and 'E' indicates that it terminates with its deadline being met; 'A' or 'C' indicate that the thread is aborted or canceled due to a missed deadline. 'B' indicates that the thread is blocked waiting for some event, or for preemption. The bottom window shows the various statistical information.

Figure 6: An Example of the ARM Snapshot

lacing the allocation and deallocation policies. The current version of the *rt_thread_create*, *rt_thread_exit*, *rt_mutex_lock*, and *rt_mutex_unlock* primitives are implemented using a trap mechanism, rather than MIG.

4   Related Work

The pure kernel-based approach is gaining popularity and several pure (or micro) kernel-based operating systems have been developed for the distributed computing environment [3, 16, 17]. Advantages of using a pure kernel instead of a standard monolithic kernel is that the preemptability of the kernel will be inherently better, the size of the kernel becomes much smaller, and modification of the kernel will be easier. However, only a few micro-kernels were designed for supporting distributed real-time applications.

In many commercially available real-time operating systems and executives, a fixed priority-based preemptive scheduling policy has been used. Emphasis was placed on fast interrupt latency, fast context switching, and small kernel size [6]. Although these factors are important properties for real-time operating systems, users were often forced to create an *ad hoc* scheduling module for each particular application. Furthermore, under a transient overload, users may loose control over which tasks should complete their computations and which should be aborted or canceled. It is also difficult to remove priority inversion problems in the kernel and bound the worst case blocking time for threads.

The proposed real-time thread model is different from many other thread models. In particular, our model

- distinguishes between real-time and non real-time threads,

- assumes explicit timing constraints for each real-time thread, and

- provides a priority inheritance protocol to avoid unbounded priority inversion.

The POSIX-Thread proposal[11] is very similar to Mach's C-Thread package[5] and it also does not distinguish between real-time threads and non-real-time threads. This poses a problem of identifying the type of threads that can "pinned down" its memory objects. However, it can dynamically select the thread scheduling policy and a thread also contains the thread attributes such as "inherit priority", "scheduling priority", "scheduling policy", and "minimum stack size". Thus, adding the timing attributes would be very simple.

The Ultrix-Thread model[4] does not address real-time thread issues, however, the designer intended to create much lighter threads by leaving the context information of thread at the process level as much as possible. Thus, creation of a new thread can be done by specifying thread's stack page and guard page address: **tfork**(stack_ptr, guard_ptr).

The Topaz-Thread model[14]provides a clean thread interface library at the Modula-2+ language level, however, it does not address real-time thread issues.

5   Summary

The objective of Real-Time Mach is to develop a real-time version of Mach which can support a predictable real-time computing environment together with a real-time toolset. In particular, the kernel should allow a system designer to predict the schedulability of *hard* and *soft* real-time tasks which communicate over a real-time network.

In this paper, we described a real-time thread model, real-time synchronization, integrated time-driven scheduler, and memory resident objects for Real-Time Mach. We also discussed the implementation issues, real-time toolset, and the current status of the system.

We are still improving the system capability in order to provide a system-wide schedulability analysis in Real-Time Mach. In particular, we are working on predictable real-time communication support, priority inversion problems in Mach IPC, and multi-board based multiprocessor targets.

6   Acknowledgments

We would like to thank the members of the ART Project and the Mach group for their valuable comments and inputs to the development of Real-Time Mach.

References

[1] M.J. Accetta, W. Baron, R.V. Bolosky, D.B. Golub, R.F. Rashid, A. Tevanian, and M.W. Young, "Mach: A new kernel foundation for unix development", *In Proceedings of the Summer Usenix Conference,*, July, 1986.

[2] David L. Black, "Scheduling support for concurrency and parallelism in the Mach operating system", *IEEE Computer,* Vol.23, No.5, 1990

[3] D.R. Cheriton, G.R. Whitehead and E.D. Sznyter, "Binary emulation of UNIX using V Kernel", *In proceedings of Summer Usenix Conference*, June, 1990.

[4] D. S Conde, F. S. Hsu, and U. Sinkewicz, "Ultrix threads", In *Proceedings of Summer Usenix Conference*, June, 1989.

[5] E. C. Cooper, and R. P. Draves, "C threads", Technical report, Computer Science Department, Carnegie Mellon University, CMU-CS-88-154, March, 1987.

[6] B. Furht, J. Parker, and D. Grostick, "Performance of *REAL/IX*^{TM} - Fully Preemptive Real Time UNIX", *Operating System Review*, Vol.23, No.4, April, 1989

[7] D. Golub, R. Dean, A. Forin, and R. Rashid, "Unix as an application program", *In the proceedings of Summer Usenix Conference*, June, 1990.

[8] Mark Heuser, "An implementation of real-time thread synchronization", *In Proceedings of Usenix Summer Conference,* June, 1990.

[9] P. Hood and V. Grover, "Designing real time systems in ADA", Tech Report 1123-1, SofTech, Inc., January, 1986.

[10] M.B. Jones, and R.F. Rashid, "Mach and Matchmaker: Kernel and language support for object-oriented distributed system", *In proceedings of the first conference of OOPSLA*, September, 1986

[11] IEEE, "Realtime Extension for Portable Operating Systems", P1003.4/Draft6, February, 1989.

[12] J. P. Lehoczky, L. Sha, and Y. Ding, "The rate-monotonic scheduling algorithm: Exact characterization and average case behavior", Department of Statistic, Carnegie Mellon University, 1987.

[13] C. L. Liu and J. W. Layland, "Scheduling algorithms for multiprogramming in a hard real time environment", *Journal of the ACM*, Vol.20, No.1, 1973.

[14] P. McJones and Swart P, "Evolving the unix system interface to support multithreaded programs", Technical report, Tech Report 21, Part I, DEC SRC, September, 1987.

[15] A. K. Mok, "Fundamental Design Problems of Distributed Systems for the Hard-Real-Time Environment", *PhD thesis*, Massachusetts Institute of Technology, May 1983.

[16] S.J. Mullender, G.V. Rossum, A.S. Tanenbaum, R. Renesse and H. Staveren, "Amoeba: A Distributed Operating System for the 1990s", *IEEE Computer* Vol.23, No.5, May, 1990

[17] M. Rozier, V. Abrossimov, F. Armand, I. Boule, M. Gien, M. Guillemount, F. Herrmann, C. Kaiser, S. Langlois, P. Léonard, and W. Neuhauser, "Chorus distributed operating system", *Computing Systems Journal*, The Usenix Association, December, 1988

[18] L. Sha, R. Rajkumar, and J. P. Lehoczky, "Priority inheritance protocols: An approach to real-time synchronization", Technical Report CMU-CS-87-181, Carnegie Mellon University, November 1987

[19] B. Sprunt, L. sha and J. P.Lehoczky, "Aperiodic Task Scheduling for Hard-Real-Time Systems", *The Journal of Real-TIme Systems*, Vol.1, No.1, 1989.

[20] J. A. Stankovic, "Misconceptions about real-time computing: A serious problem for next-generation systems", *IEEE Computer*, Vol.21, No.10, October, 1988.

[21] H. Tokuda and M. Kotera, "A real-time tool set for the ARTS kernel", Proceedings of 9th IEEE Real-Time Systems Symposium, December, 1988.

[22] H. Tokuda and M. Kotera, "Scheduler1-2-3: An interactive schedulability analyzer for real-time systems", *In Proceedings of Compsac88*, October 1988.

[23] H. Tokuda, M. Kotera, and C. W. Mercer, "A real-time monitor for a distributed real-time operating system", *In Proceedings of ACM SIGOPS and SIGPLAN workshop on parallel and distributed debugging*, May, 1988.

[24] H. Tokuda, M. Kotera, and C. W. Mercer, "An integrated time-driven scheduler for the ARTS kernel", *In Proceedings of 8th IEEE Phoenix Conference on Computers and Communications*, March, 1989.

[25] H. Tokuda and C. W. Mercer, "ARTS: A distributed real-time kernel", *ACM Operating Systems Review*, Vol.23, No.3, July, 1989.

[26] H. Tokuda, C. W. Mercer, Y. Ishikawa, and T. E. Marchok, "Priority inversions in real-time communication", In *Proceedings of 10th IEEE Real-Time Systems Symposium*, December, 1989.

THE SPRING KERNEL: A NEW PARADIGM FOR REAL-TIME SYSTEMS

Current real-time operating systems use the wrong paradigm to handle hard deadlines. The Spring kernel uses an alternative paradigm to address this need.

JOHN A. STANKOVIC
KRITHI RAMAMRITHAM
University of Massachusetts at Amherst

Real-time computing systems play a vital role in our society — controlling laboratory experiments, automobile engines, nuclear power plants, flight systems, and manufacturing processes — and the spectrum of their complexity varies widely from the very simple to the very complex.

Next-generation systems will include autonomous land rovers, teams of robots operating in hazardous environments like chemical plants and undersea exploration, intelligent manufacturing systems, and the proposed space station. These next-generation real-time systems will be large, complex, distributed, and adaptive. They will contain many types of timing constraints, operate in nondeterministic environments, and evolve over a long lifetime.

Many advances are required to address these next-generation systems. One of the most difficult aspects will be in demonstrating that these systems meet their performance requirements, including satisfying specific deadline and periodicity constraints.

To address this need, we have developed a new real-time operating system kernel, called the Spring kernel, that provides some of the basic support required for next-generation real-time systems, especially in meeting timing constraints. In developing this new operating system, our research approach challenged several basic assumptions on which most real-time operating systems are built. Our approach handles the need to build predict-

Reprinted from *IEEE Software*, Vol. 8, No. 3, May 1991, pp. 62-72.

247

able, yet flexible real-time systems. Although some current real-time kernels are themselves predictable, they provide no direct support for application-level predictability. The Spring kernel does. The Spring kernel is not meant for all types of real-time systems, but for large, complex, real-time systems.

CURRENT SYSTEMS

Most current real-time operating systems contain the same basic paradigms found in time-sharing operating systems. These kernels are simply stripped-down and optimized versions of time-sharing operating systems. For example, while they stress fast mechanisms like a fast context switch and the ability to respond to external interrupts quickly, they retain the main abstractions of time-sharing operating systems, including:

♦ Viewing the execution of a task as a random process where a task could be blocked at arbitrary points during its execution for an indefinite time. While this view is necessary in a general-purpose time-sharing environment, in critical real-time environments each task in the system is well defined and can be analyzed beforehand. Furthermore, how tasks cooperate via communication and contend for shared resources must be carefully controlled to bound blocking times. In the random-process model, the arbitrary blocking that occurs causes tremendous difficulty in predicting whether timing constraints will be met.

♦ Assuming that little is known about the tasks beforehand so little (or no) semantic information about tasks is used at runtime. This assumption is false for real-time systems. In real-time systems, the system software should be able to use important semantic information about the application tasks, rather than ignoring it.

♦ Trying to maximize throughput or minimize average response time. Throughout and average response time are not the primary metrics for real-time systems — a system could have a good average response time and miss every deadline, resulting in a useless system. The metrics must specifically address the timing constraints: maximizing the percentage of tasks that meet their deadline and guaranteeing that all critical tasks always meet their deadline.

Also, today's real-time kernels very often use a basic priority-scheduling mechanism that provides no direct support for meeting timing constraints. For example, current technology burdens the designer with the task of mapping the requirements of tasks, like their time constraints and importance, into task priorities so all tasks will meet their deadlines. Thus, when using current paradigms with priority scheduling, it is difficult to predict how dynamically invoked tasks interact with other active tasks, where blocking over resources will occur, and what the effects of this interaction and blocking are on the timing constraints of all the tasks.

Current kernels are inadequate for three main reasons:

♦ timing constraints are not considered explicitly,

♦ predictable task executions are difficult to ensure, and

♦ tasks with complex characteristics (like those with precedence constraints and resource requirements) are not handled explicitly.

SPRING KERNEL OVERVIEW

We believe that next-generation, critical, real-time systems should be based on the following considerations:

♦ Tasks are part of a single application with a system-wide objective. The types of tasks that occur in a real-time application are known beforehand and thus can be analyzed to determine their characteristics. This information should be used at runtime.

♦ The value imparted to the system by tasks should be maximized. While value can be defined in many ways, in this article, the value of a task that completes before its deadline is its full value (depends on what the task does) and is a diminished value (a negative value or zero) if it does not meet its deadline.

♦ Predictability should be ensured so the timing properties of both individual tasks and the system can be assessed.

♦ Flexibility should be ensured so system modifications and on-line dynamics are more easily accommodated.

Environment. Real-time systems interact heavily with their environments. We assume that the environment is dynamic, large, complex, and evolving. In a system interacting with such an environment, there are many types of tasks. Our kernel treats the different classes of tasks differently, reducing the overall complexity.

Our approach categorizes the types of tasks by their interaction with and effects on the environment. This results in two main criteria for classifying tasks: importance and timing requirements.

♦ The importance of a task signifies the value imparted to the system when the task satisfies its timing constraint.

♦ Tasks' timing requirements may range over a wide spectrum, including hard deadlines, soft deadlines, and periodic execution requirements, while other tasks may have no explicit timing requirements.

Based on importance and timing requirements, we define three types of tasks: critical tasks, essential tasks, and unessential tasks.

♦ Critical tasks are those tasks that must meet their deadline, otherwise a catastrophic result might occur (missing their deadlines will contribute a $-\infty$ value to the system). You must show beforehand that these tasks will always meet their deadlines subject to some specified number of failures. You must reserve resources for such tasks. The number of truly critical tasks (even in very large systems) will be small compared to the total number of tasks in the system.

♦ Essential tasks are those tasks that are necessary to the operation of the system, have specific timing constraints, and will degrade the system's performance if their timing constraints are not met. However, essential tasks will not cause a catastrophe if they do not finish on time.

> Our kernel uses two criteria to classify tasks' interaction with and effects on the environment: importance and timing requirements.

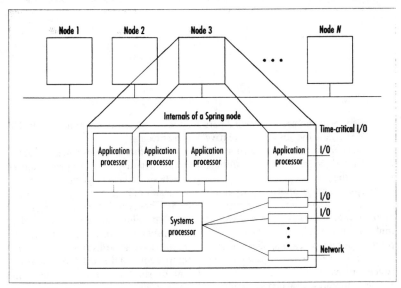

Figure 1. *The Springnet distributed system. Each processor uses the Spring real-time kernel.*

There are many such tasks and the importance of each may differ. You must treat such tasks dynamically because it is impossible to reserve enough resources for all of their contingencies. Our approach applies an on-line, dynamic guarantee algorithm to this collection of tasks.

♦ Unessential tasks may or may not have deadlines, and they execute when they do not affect critical or essential tasks. Many background tasks, long-range planning tasks, and maintenance functions fall into this category.

Tasks handled by the Spring kernel may have characteristics that are complicated in many other ways as well. For example, a task may be preemptable or periodic; it may have a variety of timing constraints, precedence constraints, communication constraints, and fault-tolerance constraints.

Another timing issue relates to the closeness of the deadline. Some tasks may have extremely tight deadlines. These tasks usually occur in the data-acquisition front ends of the real-time system. Given the overheads of the dynamic guarantees of the Spring kernel, such front-end tasks must be treated differently. For example, they might execute using a very-low-overhead technique like cyclic scheduling or rate-monotonic priority scheduling. Current real-time kernels can be appropriate for these front ends because they can guarantee overall timing properties given the small number and static nature of tasks in the front ends. In this type of partitioning, you can precisely quantify the timing properties of each front-end subsystem. Front-end tasks may invoke higher level tasks with deadlines. These tasks are handled by the Spring kernel.

Springnet node. Springnet (shown in Figure 1) is a physically distributed system composed of a network of multiprocessors each running the Spring kernel. Each multiprocessor contains application processors, system processors, and an I/O subsystem (front end):

♦ Application processors execute previously guaranteed and relatively high-level application tasks.

♦ System processors (which could be specifically designed to offer hardware support to our system activities like guaranteeing tasks) offload the scheduling algorithm and other operating-system overhead from the application tasks both to increase speed and to remove external interrupts and operating-system overhead so they do not cause uncertainty in executing guaranteed tasks.

♦ The I/O subsystem is partitioned from the Spring kernel and it handles noncritical I/O, slow I/O devices, and fast sensors. (The Spring kernel is being developed for multiprocessor-based real-time systems, but it can be tailored for uniprocessors. In this case, even though system tasks are scheduled to execute on the same processor as application tasks, the time for both are explicitly scheduled.)

Not surprisingly, the main components of the kernel can be grouped into task management, scheduling, memory management, and intertask communication. (Intertask communication falls outside the scope of this article, so we do not detail it here.) While this sounds similar to many other kernels, the abstractions supported are very different. One significant aspect is that system primitives have bounded worst-case execution times. Another is that some primitives execute as iterative algorithms where the number of iterations they will perform for a particular call depends on its bounded execution time and on other state information, including available time.

Task management. Tasks arise when the compiler decomposes real-time programs — specified in the form of communicating processes — into schedulable entities (tasks) with precedence relationships, resource requirements, fault-tolerance requirements, importance levels, and timing constraints. The task-management primitives support executable and guaranteeable entities called tasks and task groups.

A task consists of reentrant code, local data, global data, a stack, a task descriptor, and a task-control block. Each task acquires resources before it begins and releases the resources upon completion. This is reasonable in our system because the compiler takes resource needs into account when creating relatively small, but predictable, tasks from the larger but functional processes written by the programmer. This approach then lets the scheduling algorithm avoid unpredictable blocking over a resource because all required resources for a task are assigned at the start of its planned execution. You may invoke multiple instances of a task; in this case, the (reentrant) code and task descriptor are shared.

A task group is a collection of simple tasks that have precedence constraints among themselves but share a single group deadline. For task groups, we assume that all tasks in the group can be sized when the task group is invoked (this means that the compiler can determine worst-case computation time and resource requirements of each task at invocation time). We are investigating more flexible types of task groups.

Tasks are characterized by

♦ a worst-case execution time, which may be a formula that depends on various input data or state information about a specific task invocation,

♦ a deadline, period, or other real-time constraint,

♦ a preemptive or nonpreemptive property,

♦ the maximum number and type of resources needed (including memory segments and ports),

♦ its type (critical, essential, or unessential),

♦ its importance level (for essential and unessential tasks),

♦ whether it is an incremental task (an incremental task computes an initial answer quickly and then continues to refine the answer for the rest of its requested computation time),

♦ the location of task copies indicating the various nodes in the distributed system and on which processor of each node the task resides,

♦ a precedence graph, which describes the required precedence among tasks in a task group, and

♦ a communication graph, which lists the tasks with which a task communicates, and the type of communication (asynchronous or synchronous).

The task descriptor maintains all this information. We have plans for adding information concerning a task's fault-tolerance requirements to the task descriptor. The task control block also maintains much of this information. The difference between the two sets of information is that the information in the task control block is specific to a particular instance of the task.

For example, a task descriptor might indicate that the worst-case execution time for task A is $5z$ ms, where z is the number of input data items when the task is invoked. At invocation time, a short procedure is executed to compute the actual worst-case time for this module, and this value is then inserted into the task control block. The guarantee is then performed for this task instance. All the other fields dealing with time, computation, resources, and importance are handled similarly.

Scheduling. Scheduling is an integral part of the kernel, and the abstraction we have provided is one of a currently guaranteed task set. It is the single most distinguishing feature of the kernel.

Our scheduling approach separates policy from mechanism and is composed of four levels. At the lowest level, there are multiple dispatchers: one type of dispatcher running on each application processor and another type executing on the system processors.

The application dispatchers simply remove the next (ready) task from a system task table that contains previously guaranteed tasks arranged in the proper order for each application processor. The dispatcher on the system processor allows the periodic execution of systems tasks (and asynchronous invocation when it can determine that allowing these extra invocations will not affect guaranteed tasks) or the minimum guaranteed periodic rate of other system tasks. Asynchronous invocation of system tasks are ordered by importance. For example, the local scheduler is more important than the metalevel controller.

The system processor also executes the three higher level scheduling modules:

♦ The second level is a local scheduler, which is responsible for dynamically guaranteeing that, given the current guaranteed task set, a new task or task group can be scheduled locally so it meets its deadline. The local scheduler orders the tasks in the system task table to reflect the order of their execution. The box on pp. 68-69 details the logic in this algorithm. When the kernel is fully operational, the local scheduler will not only schedule essential tasks but also schedule unessential tasks in idle time slots.

♦ The third scheduling level is the distributed scheduler that tries to find a node to execute any task or components of a task group that must execute on different

> **Our scheduling approach separates policy from mechanism. It is the single most distinguishing feature of the Spring kernel.**

nodes[1] because they cannot be locally guaranteed.

♦ The fourth level is a metalevel controller that adapts various parameters or switches scheduling algorithms by noticing significant changes in the environment. These capabilities support some of the adaptability and flexibility needed by next-generation real-time systems. We are still refining the distributed scheduling component and the metalevel controller, both of which are not part of the Spring kernel itself.

When a task is activated, the kernel computes any dynamic information about its resource requirements or timing constraints and writes it into the task control block; the guarantee routine then determines if it can meet its deadline. The execution of the guarantee algorithm ensures that the task will get the necessary segments like the ports and data segments at its scheduled start time. Again, at activation time, essential tasks always identify their maximum resource requirements.

Memory management. Memory-management primitives create various well-defined resource segments like code, stacks, task control blocks, task descriptors, local data, global data, ports, virtual disks, and unsegmented memory.

Memory-management techniques must not introduce erratic delays into a task's execution time. Because page faults and page replacements in demand-paging schemes create large and unpredictable delays, these memory-management techniques (as currently implemented) are not suitable for real-time applications that must guarantee timing constraints.

Tasks require a maximum number of memory segments of each type, but at activation time a task may request fewer segments. The kernel allocates all the required segments when the task starts execution; the segments are completely memory-resident. The allocation is part of the integrated scheduling and allocation scheme we use. If a task is programmed to dynamically request segments, the worst-case time for this task must include time to invoke the bounded kernel primitives to acquire these resources, which the local scheduling algorithm has already allocated.

NEW PARADIGM

In light of the complexities of real-time systems, the key to next-generation real-time operating systems is finding the correct approach to make the systems predictable enough — yet flexible enough — to assess system performance with respect to requirements, especially timing requirements. The Spring kernel stresses the real-time and flexibility requirements and contains several features to support fault tolerance. Our new paradigm is composed of the following ideas:

- ♦ resource segmentation/partitioning,
- ♦ functional partitioning,
- ♦ selective preallocation,
- ♦ *a priori* guarantee for critical tasks,
- ♦ an on-line guarantee for essential tasks,
- ♦ integrated CPU scheduling and resource allocation,
- ♦ use of the scheduler in a planning mode,
- ♦ the separation of importance and timing constraints,
- ♦ end-to-end scheduling, and
- ♦ the use of significant information about tasks at runtime, including timing, task importance, fault-tolerance requirements, and the ability to dynamically alter this information.

Resource segmentation. All resources in the system are partitioned into well-defined entities. Tasks and task groups are segmented and bound by both time and resources, meaning that they are com-

> **The key to next-generation systems is to make them predictable enough, yet flexible enough, to assess performance against timing requirements.**

posed of well-defined segments and that both the worst-case execution times and the worst-case resource requirements for these tasks are known. Kernel primitives are also segmented and bound by time and resources.

Resource segmentation provides the scheduling algorithm with a clear picture of all the resources that must be allocated and scheduled. This contributes to microscopic predictability: On activation, each task is bounded in time and resource requirements. Microscopic predictability is a necessary but insufficient condition for overall system predictability.

Functional partitioning. Functional partitioning manifests itself in two ways on a Spring node.

First, each Springnet node is structured to handle four types of processing:

- ♦ processing of data acquired from the environment on the I/O front ends,
- ♦ processing of higher level application tasks on the application processors,
- ♦ processing of system functions on the system processors, and
- ♦ processing of communication to and from other nodes.

This type of partitioning lets you tailor each subsystem to the functions it is intended for. For example, this allows different solutions for different levels of granularity of timing constraints. Also, this partitioning shields the guaranteed tasks running on the application processors from external interrupts. The shielding from external interrupts is extremely important and, with our guarantee algorithm, lets you construct a more macroscopic view of predictable performance because the collection of tasks currently guaranteed to execute by their deadline are not subject to unknown, environment-driven interrupts.

Second, we partitioned the application processors so critical tasks are separated from essential and unessential tasks. This

shields the critical tasks from noncritical tasks.

Selective preallocation. The Spring kernel preallocates resources needed for critical tasks and for tasks on I/O front ends. Furthermore, the Spring kernel has task-management primitives that use preallocation where possible to improve speed and to eliminate unpredictable delays. For example, an essential task is made memory-resident on one or more processors to improve flexibility during dynamic scheduling, or it is made memory-resident before it can be invoked. In addition, a system-initialization program loads code and sets up stacks, task control blocks, task descriptors, local data, global data, ports, virtual disks, and unsegmented memory. You can create multiple instances of a task or task group at initialization time, as well as multiple free task control blocks, task descriptors, ports, and virtual disks. Subsequently, the system needs only to free and allocate these segments dynamically rather than create them.

While the Spring kernel also has facilities to dynamically create new segments of any type, such facilities should not be used under hard real-time constraints. This combined approach lets our system be fast and predictable, yet still be flexible enough to accommodate major changes, but without hard deadlines.

A priori guarantee. The notion of guaranteeing timing constraints is central to our approach. However, because we are dealing with large, complex systems in nondeterministic environments, the guarantee is separated into two main parts: an *a priori* guarantee for critical tasks and an on-line guarantee for essential tasks.

All critical tasks are guaranteed beforehand and resources are reserved for them either in dedicated processors or as a dedicated collection of resource slices on the application processors (this is part of Spring's selective preallocation policy). Resources are provided under specified failure assumptions. For example, if t processor failures should be accommodated, resources are provided for $2t+1$ replicates of a task.

Typically, a real-time system undergoes mode changes during its execution. The set of critical tasks may change from mode to mode. Thus, when executing in a particular mode, critical tasks for that mode should be guaranteed for the entire duration of that mode. While dedicating resources to critical tasks beforehand is, of course, not flexible, we have no other choice because of these tasks' importance. Fortunately, the ratio of critical tasks to essential tasks is typically very small.

On-line guarantee. Because of the many essential tasks and their many possible invocation orders, preallocation of resources to essential tasks costs too much and is too inflexible. Thus, this class of tasks is guaranteed on line via the algorithm presented in the box on pp. 68-69. This lets many task-invocation scenarios be handled dynamically (partially supporting the flexibility requirement). The basic notion and properties of guarantee for essential tasks have the following characteristics (which we have detailed elsewhere[2]):

♦ It allows the unique abstraction that, at any time, the operating system knows exactly which tasks have been guaranteed to meet their deadlines; what, where, and when spare resources exist or will exist; a complete schedule for the guaranteed tasks; and which tasks are running under unguaranteed assumptions. (By contrast, current real-time scheduling algorithms, like earliest deadline, have no global knowledge of the task set nor of the system's ability to meet deadlines; they know only which task to run next.)

Because of the nondeterministic environment, the system's capabilities may change over time, so the on-line guarantee for essential tasks is an instantaneous guarantee that refers to the current state. Thus, at any time, our system provides the macroscopic view that all critical tasks will meet their deadlines, and you know exactly which essential tasks will meet their deadlines given the current load. (You could also develop an overall quantitative, but probabilistic, assessment of the performance of essential tasks. For example, given expected normal and overload workloads, you can compute the average

percentage of essential tasks that are guaranteed — that meet their deadlines.)

♦ Conflicts over resources are avoided, thus eliminating the random nature of waiting for resources found in time-sharing operating systems (this same feature also minimizes context switches because tasks are not being context-switched to wait for resources). Basically, resource conflicts are solved by scheduling tasks at different times if they contend for a given resource.

♦ Dispatching and guarantees are separated, letting these system functions run in parallel. The dispatcher is always working with a set of tasks that have been previously guaranteed to meet their deadlines; the guarantee routine operates on the current set of guaranteed tasks plus any newly invoked tasks.

♦ Spring provides early notification. By performing the guarantee calculation when a task arrives, there may be time to reallocate the task to another host via the distributed-scheduling module of the scheduler. Early notification also has fault-tolerance implications in that you can now run alternative error-handling tasks early — before a deadline is missed.

♦ This approach supports the notion of *possibly* meeting the deadline even if the task is not guaranteed: If a task is not guaranteed, it could receive idle cycles at this node. In parallel, there can be an attempt to get the task guaranteed on another host subject to location-dependent constraints. Or, based on the task's fault-tolerance semantics, the kernel could invoke various alternatives.

♦ The guarantee routine supports the coexistence of real-time and non-real-time tasks. This is significant when non-real-time tasks might use some of the same resources as real-time tasks.

♦ The guarantee can be subject to computation-time requirements, deadline or periodic time constraints, resource requirements where resources are seg-

> **Preallocation of resources to essential tasks costs too much and is too inflexible, so Spring guarantees them on line.**

mented, importance levels for tasks, precedence constraints, and I/O requirements, depending on the specific guarantee algorithm used in the system.

♦ Even though a task is guaranteed for its worst-case time and resource requirements, the kernel can reclaim the unused time and resources if the task finishes early.[3]

Integrated CPU scheduling and resource allocation. Current real-time scheduling algorithms schedule the CPU independently of other resources. For example, consider a typical real-time scheduling algorithm: earliest deadline first. Scheduling a task that has the earliest deadline does no good if it later blocks and misses its deadline because a resource it requires is unavailable. Our approach integrates CPU scheduling and resource allocation so this blocking never occurs. Scheduling is an integral part of the kernel, and the abstraction we provide is that of a currently guaranteed task set.

Because real-time scheduling with hard deadlines in a multiprocessor with resource constraints is NP-hard, we use a heuristic approach. Scheduling a set of tasks to find a feasible schedule is actually a search problem. The structure of the search space is a search tree. An intermediate vertex of the search tree is a partial schedule, and a leaf (a terminal vertex) is a complete schedule. Not all leaves (each of which is a complete schedule) correspond to feasible schedules.

The heuristic scheduling algorithm we use try to determine a full feasible schedule for a set of tasks works as follows: It starts at the root of the search tree (an empty schedule) and tries to extend the schedule (with one more task) by moving to one of the vertices at the next level in the tree until a full feasible schedule is derived.

To do this, we use a heuristic function that synthesizes various characteristics of tasks affecting real-time scheduling deci-

THE SPRING SCHEDULING ALGORITHM

The goal of our scheduling algorithm is to dynamically guarantee new task arrivals in the context of the current load. Specifically, if a set of tasks has been previously guaranteed and a new task arrives, the task is guaranteed if and only if a feasible schedule can be found for tasks in the set formed by the union of the tasks in the current schedule and the new task. Thus, determining whether a feasible schedule exists for a set of tasks — whether all the tasks in the set can be scheduled to meet their timing constraints — is the crux of the problem.

In practice, the actual algorithm that determines a feasible schedule must consider many issues, including whether tasks are preemptive, precedence constraints (used to handle task groups), multiple importance levels for tasks, and fault-tolerance requirements. Here, we focus on the essential features of the algorithm by presenting a simple version of the algorithm that deals with tasks characterized by

♦ a task-arrival time of T_A,

♦ a task deadline of T_D or a period of T_P,

♦ a task worst-case computation time of T_C,

♦ task-resource requirements $\{T_R\}$,

♦ the fact that tasks are not preemptive,

♦ the use of a resource either in shared mode or in exclusive mode and the holding of a requested resource as long as it executes, and

♦ an earliest start time, T_{est}, at which the task can begin execution that is calculated when the task is scheduled and that accounts for resource contention among tasks. It is a key ingredient in our scheduling strategy.

Scheduling a set of tasks to find a feasible schedule is a search problem, and the structure of the search space is a search tree. An intermediate vertex of the search tree is a partial schedule, and a leaf, a terminal vertex, is a complete schedule. In the worst case, finding a feasible schedule requires an exhaustive search. Thus, we take a heuristic approach.

The heuristic scheduling algorithms we use try to determine a full feasible schedule for a set of tasks as follows: It starts at the root of the search tree that is an empty schedule and tries to extend the schedule (with one more task) by moving to one of the vertices at the next level in the search tree until a full feasible schedule is derived. We use a heuristic function that synthesizes various characteristics of tasks affecting real-time scheduling decisions to actively direct the scheduling to a plausible path. The task with the smallest value determined by the heuristic function is selected to extend the current schedule.

While extending the partial schedule at each level of search, the algorithm determines if the current partial schedule is strongly feasible or not. A partially feasible schedule is strongly feasible if all the schedules obtained by extending this current schedule with any of the remaining tasks are also feasible. Thus, if a partially feasible schedule is found not to be strongly feasible because, say, a task misses its deadline when the current schedule is extended by that task, it is appropriate to stop the search because none of the future extensions involving the task will meet its deadline. In this case, a set of tasks can not be scheduled given the current partial schedule. (In the terminology of branch-and-bound techniques, the search path represented by the current partial schedule is bound because it will not lead to a feasible complete schedule.)

However, it is possible to backtrack to continue the search even after a schedule is found that is not strongly feasible. The algorithm backtracks by discarding the current partial schedule, returning to the previous partial schedule, and extending it by a different task. The task chosen is the one with the second smallest heuristic value. Even though we allow backtracking, you can restrict the overheads of backtracking either by restricting the maximum number of possible back-

---

sions to actively direct the scheduling to a plausible path. The heuristic function (in a straightforward approach) is applied to each task that remains to be scheduled at each level of search. The task with the smallest value of the heuristic function is selected to extend the current schedule.

As the box above shows, a more efficient scheme that we use allows application of the heuristic function to only k tasks at each level.

The heuristic that we use combines a task's deadline (or other timing constraint) and its resource requirements into a relatively simple weighted formula that quantifies the needs of each task. An innovation in our work is how we quantify the resource requirements: We quantify resource requirements by computing an earliest start time. The earliest start time considers both resource requirements and worst-case computation time. Other con-

siderations, like precedence constraints, are handled by additional logic in the algorithm and not directly in the heuristic function.

An important and unique aspect of this work is that we model resource use in two modes — exclusive mode and shared mode — in addition to considering resource requirements. By modeling two access modes, we can schedule more task sets than if we used only exclusive mode.

By integrating CPU scheduling and resource allocation at runtime, you can understand (at each point in time) the current resource contention and completely control it so you can predict task performance with respect to deadlines, rather than letting resource contention occur randomly, resulting in an unpredictable system.

Scheduler in planning mode. Another im-

portant feature of our scheduling approach is how and when we use the scheduler: We use it in a planning mode when a new essential task is invoked. (We do not use this scheme for critical tasks or for front-end tasks.) When a new task is invoked, the scheduler tries to plan a schedule for it so all tasks can meet their deadlines. This lets our system understand the total system load and make intelligent decisions when a guarantee cannot be made (making the system more flexible).

This is at odds with other real-time scheduling algorithms, which have a myopic view of the set of tasks, since these algorithms know only which task to run next and have no understanding of the total load or current system capabilities. This planning is done on the system processor in parallel with the previously guaranteed tasks, so it must account for those tasks that may be completed before it itself

tracks or by restricting the total number of evaluations of the heuristic function. In Spring, we used the latter scheme because we found it to be more effective.

The algorithm works as follows:

The algorithm starts with an empty partial schedule. Each step of the algorithm involves first determining that the current partial schedule is strongly feasible and, if so, then extending the current partial schedule by one task. In addition to the data structure maintaining the partial schedule, tasks in the task set S are maintained in the order of increasing deadlines. When a task arrives at a node, it is inserted, according to its deadline, into a (sorted) list of tasks that remain to be executed. This insertion takes at most $O(N)$ time, where N is the task set's size. Then when trying to extend the schedule by one task, the algorithm must take three steps:

♦ Strong feasibility is determined with respect to the first N_k tasks (still remaining to be scheduled) in the task set.

♦ If the partial schedule is found to be strongly feasible, the heuristic function is applied to the first N_k tasks in the task set (the k remaining tasks with the earliest deadlines).

♦ The task that has the smallest heuristic value is chosen to extend the current schedule.

Given that only N_k tasks are considered at each step, the complexity incurred is $O(Nk)$ because only the first N_k tasks (where N_k is less than or equal to k) are considered each time. If the value of k is constant (and in practice, k will be small when compared to the task set size of N), the complexity is linearly proportional to N, the size of the task set. While the complexity is proportional to N, the algorithm is programmed so it incurs a fixed worst-case cost by limiting the number of heuristic-function evaluations permitted in any one invocation of the algorithm.

While aperiodic tasks are typically invoked with a deadline for completion and can be started any time after they are invoked, the deadline and start times of periodic tasks can be computed from the period of the tasks. (There are more efficient ways to deal with periodic tasks, by generating, for example, a separate scheduling template applicable to them, but we do not go into that here.)

Given a partial schedule, the algorithm can determine, for each resource, the earliest time the resource is available. This is denoted by EAT. The earliest time that a task that is yet to be scheduled can begin execution is given by

$$T_{est} = Max(T\text{'s start time}, EAT_i^u)$$

where u equals s if T needs resource R_i in shared mode or where u equals e if T needs resource R_i in exclusive mode.

You can construct the heuristic function by simple or integrated heuristics. The following is a list of potential simple and integrated heuristics that we have tested:

♦ Minimum deadline first (Min_D): $H(T) = T_D$

♦ Minimum processing time first (Min_C): $H(T) = T_C$.

♦ Minimum earliest start time first (Min_S): $H(T) = T_{est}$.

♦ Minimum laxity first (Min_L): $H(T) = T_D - (T_{est} + T_C)$.

♦ $Min_D + Min_C$: $H(T) = T_D + W * T_C$.

♦ $Min_D + Min_S$: $H(T) = T_D + W * T_{est}$.

The first four heuristics are simple heuristics because they treat only one dimension at a time — only deadlines, or only resource requirements. The last two are integrated heuristics. W is a weight used to combine two simple heuristics. H is the heuristic function. Min_L and Min_S need not be combined because the heuristic Min_L contains the information in Min_D and Min_S.

Our extensive simulation studies of the algorithm for uniprocessor and multiprocessors show that the simple heuristics do not work well and that the integrated heuristic ($Min_D + Min_S$) works very well and has the best performance among all these possibilities, as well as compared to many other heuristics we tested. For example, combinations of three heuristics did not improve performance over the ($Min_D + Min_S$) heuristic. Thus, the Spring kernel uses the ($Min_D + Min_S$) heuristic.

---

completes. Several race conditions had to be solved to make this approach work.[4]

Separating importance and deadline. A major advantage of our approach is that it separates deadlines from importance. This is necessary because importance and deadline are distinct task characteristics. All critical tasks are of the utmost importance and are guaranteed beforehand. Essential tasks are not critical, but each is assigned a level of importance that may vary as system conditions change. To maximize the value of executed tasks, all critical tasks should meet their deadlines, and as many essential tasks as possible should also meet their deadlines. Ideally, if any essential tasks cannot meet their deadline, those tasks that do not execute should be the least important ones.

The first phase of the guarantee algorithm ignores importance when scheduling. If all tasks are guaranteed then the importance value plays no part. But when a newly invoked essential task is not guaranteed, the guarantee routine will remove the least important tasks from the system task table if those removals contribute to the guarantee of the new task. As a result, either the original task (if it is not guaranteed) or the set of preempted tasks (if the original task is guaranteed) is then subject to the fault semantics related to that task or set of tasks. For example, you might try to guarantee an error-handling version of the task or perform distributed scheduling. There are several algorithms to handle this combination of deadlines and importance.[5]

Our approach is much more flexible at handling the combination of timing and importance than a static priority-scheduling mechanism typically found in real-time systems. For example, with static priority scheduling, a designer may have a task with a short deadline and low importance and another task with a long deadline and high importance. For average loads, it is usually acceptable to assign the short-deadline task the higher priority, and under these loads all tasks will probably meet their deadlines. But if there is overload, it will be the high-importance task that ends up missing its deadline. This condition would not occur with our scheme.

(We are now investigating an alternative strategy where the schedule produced by the guarantee routine is biased so the more important tasks are toward the front of the schedule. In this case, when a new task arrives, it is more likely that the more important tasks have already completed execution.)

End-to-end scheduling. Most application-level functions (like "stop the robot before it hits the wall") that must be accomplished under a timing constraint are actually composed of a set of smaller dispatchable tasks. Previous real-time kernels do not support a collection of tasks with a single deadline. The Spring kernel supports tasks and task groups, and we are developing support for dependent task groups.

A dependent task group is the same as a task group except that computation time and resource requirements of only those tasks with no precedence constraints are known at invocation time. The needs of the remaining tasks can be known only when all preceding tasks are completed. The dependent task group requires some special handling with respect to guarantees that we have not yet done.

We use precedence constraints to model end-to-end timing constraints both for a single node and across nodes, and the scheduling heuristic we use can account for precedence constraints.

Dynamic use of task information. The Spring kernel retains information about tasks and task groups. This information includes formulas describing worst-case execution time, deadlines, or other timing requirements; importance level; precedence constraints; resource requirements; fault-tolerance requirements; task-group information; and so on. The kernel then uses this information dynamically to guarantee timing and other system requirements. The kernel has primitives to inquire about this information and to dynamically alter the information. This enhances the system's flexibility.

IMPLEMENTATION EXPERIENCE

Our preliminary implementation of the Spring kernel focused on one Spring (multiprocessor) node consisting of four Motorola 68020-based MVME136A boards. One board is a system board that executes the scheduler and other system tasks, and the other three boards are application boards. The application dispatchers, one per application board, are responsible for the dispatching of application tasks. The scheduler and application dis-

patcher processes are thus designed to run in parallel. When a task is invoked, the scheduler tries to dynamically guarantee that the new task will meet its deadline. As tasks are guaranteed, the scheduler adds them to a system task table and links them into dispatcher queues. Because the system task table resides on the system board, a dispatch queue reference performed by a dispatcher accesses the shared bus.

The MVME136A boards support features typical of shared bus multiprocessors: an asynchronous bus interface, architectural support for test-and-set-like operations, and a local memory. This memory can be accessed remotely over the VME bus by another processor or locally by the processor that has mapped this local memory. The Spring kernel's memory model represents multiprocessor systems where each processor has local memory for task code and private resources, while at the same time letting other resources — like shared data structures, files, and communication ports — be used by tasks residing on different processors. The assignment of tasks to processors, done statically, determines on which processors' memory the task code is resident.

Additional support for multiprocessing is provided through the use of the Multiprocessor control/status registers. These registers let the kernel generate interrupts on a selected board or a simultaneous interrupt on multiple boards.

Scheduler and dispatchers. The predictability of the underlying real-time operating system is necessary to predict the application behavior.

To ensure predictability of application tasks, both the scheduler cost and the dispatching costs must be bounded. Version 1 of Spring supports the scheduler described in the box on pp. 68-69 that executes in time $O(N)$ where N is the number of tasks at the node. But the scheduler has a fixed worst-case

execution time per invocation. The dispatching cost is bounded by a constant.

In addition to being predictable, the Spring operating system is concurrent. Multiple dispatchers operate concurrently with no interdispatcher interference. Dispatchers and the scheduler require concurrent access to the system task table. Correctness of this access is maintained by the use of critical sections, while predictability is ensured by constructing all critical sections to execute in constant time.

The kernel achieves concurrent execution of dispatchers by partitioning the system task table based on the processor to which tasks are assigned.

Figure 2 shows the system task table and the dispatch queues. Consider seven tasks: T_1 and T_2 on application processor 1, T_3 and T_4 on application processor 2, and T_5, T_6, and T_7 on application processor 3. Because a task is scheduled to be executed by exactly one processor, the multiple dispatcher processes can concurrently access their dispatch queues without interference. To facilitate correct and efficient dispatching, the system task table is sorted according to the scheduled start time of each task. This design provides a dispatcher with a constant time access to its dispatch queue to determine which task to execute next.

We achieved concurrent execution of the scheduler and the multiple dispatchers by reserving a set of tasks for each dispatcher, where the scheduler is not free to reschedule the tasks reserved for the dispatchers. Thus, each dispatcher has tasks to execute while the scheduler is trying to reschedule the remaining tasks to guarantee the new task.

This reservation involves the calculation of a cutoff line. Once the kernel has determined an upper bound of the scheduler's cost for guaranteeing a task, it adds this cost to the current time to determine the cutoff line. All tasks having a scheduled start time before the cutoff line

> Previous real-time kernels did not support a collection of tasks with a single deadline. The Spring kernel supports tasks and tasks groups.

are reserved for the dispatchers and thus cannot be rescheduled.

Furthermore, the on-line guarantee does not alter the current schedule. Instead, it operates on *copies* of the task-invocation information. This convention facilitates the return to the original system task table if the guarantee fails.

Periodic scheduler invocation. Because the system processor is used for some system tasks, the scheduler is invoked periodically to ensure a minimum responsiveness for those system-level activities. In addition, if the kernel determines that an asynchronous invocation of the scheduler can occur without violating the minimum responsiveness of all the system tasks, it permits additional invocations of the scheduler immediately upon the arrival of new tasks.

Given that the scheduler has execution time of $O(N)$ and knowing the constant of proportionality and the fixed overheads, you can determine how many tasks the scheduler can guarantee during each periodic invocation. Suppose this is N_{max}, which we call the cap on the system task table's length. Suppose that, at a given time, the number of tasks in the system task table is S. Then at most $N_{max}-S$ newly arrived tasks can be considered for guarantee at this time.

It is likely that invoking a task will impose a deadline not only on the invoked task but also on the guarantee. In addition, some invokers may want to know how long to wait to find out if the invoked task has been guaranteed. In imposing a deadline on both the task and the guarantee, the scheduler must check whether the deadline on the guarantee can be met. For an invoker to know how long to wait, it can determine the scheduler's response time based on the length of the system task table.

Maximizing concurrency. While the scheduler's execution time is a function of N (capped by N_{max}), the dispatcher execution time need not depend on N. Because the worst-case dispatching costs must be included in each task's worst-case computation time, an efficient worst-case design of the dispatcher is very important. Version 1 of the Spring kernel uses dispatchers with

constant worst-case computation times — the time is not affected by the number of tasks in the system.

When an application task completes its execution, it must be deleted from the system. The most natural implementation is to have the local dispatcher delete the finished task. But this is not the best implementation because it increases dispatching costs by requiring mutual exclusive access to the system task table by the dispatchers. In this case, if the scheduler locks the dispatch queue immediately before a dispatcher, the dispatcher will be forced to wait. Given that scheduling costs are a function of the number of tasks in the system, the dispatcher wait times will be affected by the number of tasks in the system. This is unacceptable.

By having the scheduler — not the dispatcher — delete tasks from the system task table, we made the worst-case computation time of the dispatcher constant. This involves two dispatch-queue pointers: one modified by the scheduler and another by the dispatchers. When a task completes execution, the dispatcher modifies the head of the appropriate dispatch queue to point to the next task on the queue. The scheduler maintains a separate shadow copy of the dispatch queue head that is never altered by the dispatcher. When the scheduler is invoked, it first deletes all tasks that lie between the dispatch-queue head and its shadow. Mutual exclusion is reduced to constant time — only modifications of the dispatch-queue head need be done inside a critical section.

Performance evaluation. Each Spring board requires 1 µs to read or write local memory, and, on an unsaturated VME bus, 2 µs to access another board's memory. We input several synthetic workloads, each consisting of hundreds of tasks, to the system. The workloads consisted entirely of aperiodic tasks so we could evaluate the cost of the on-line scheduling algorithm. Each task required as many as seven non-CPU resources. We measured the execution times with a clock accurate to 0.5 µs.

These experiments focused on two kernel costs: the scheduler cost and the dispatcher cost. Figure 3 shows the cost of

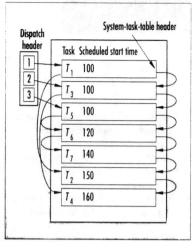

Figure 2. *The system task table and dispatch queues.*

the scheduler process on the system processor as a function of the number of tasks in the system. The cost of the scheduler consists of the Spring $O(N)$ guarantee algorithm and the overhead required to update the system task table once the guarantee algorithm has produced a new schedule. These costs are for unoptimized code. The fact that the dynamic-guarantee costs on a 0.5-MIPS machine are tens of milliseconds implies that the deadlines should be large enough to permit these overheads.

The cost of the dispatcher was 150 µs for the best case, 170 µs for the average case, and 410 µs for the worst case. These costs include three components: code executed at task start, at task finish, and to suspend waiting for new work. Although the reported dispatcher costs do not include context-switch overhead, it does include the cost of reading and writing information into shared memory (the system task table).

For example, to execute the next task, the dispatcher reads the scheduled start time, the worst-case computation time, and the event number (for bookkeeping) from the system task table. If the scheduled start time has arrived, the task can start execution. But if the start time has not arrived, the dispatcher waits for the scheduled start time to arrive. At task completion, the head of the dispatch queue must be updated to point to the next task in the application processor's dispatch queue. In addition, per-task status information is updated (also stored in the system task table) to indicate the state of a task (ready, executing, or completed).

The variance between the worst-case

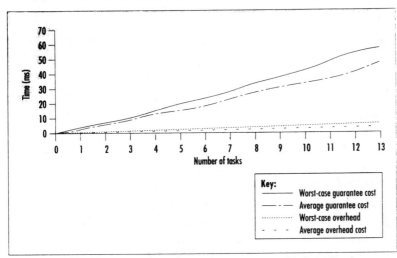

Figure 3. *Guarantee costs and overheads in experimental implementations of the Spring kernel.*

and average dispatcher times can be explained by variances inherent in the hardware architecture and by the fact that our dispatcher is implemented as a user-level process. As a user process, the dispatcher is subject to unmaskable interrupts and must poll to determine when to execute a task. We expect a marked performance improvement in the dispatcher when it is moved into the kernel proper.

Most critical, real-time computing systems require that many competing requirements be met, including hard and soft real-time constraints, fault tolerance, protection, and security. In this list of requirements, the real-time requirements have received the least formal attention. We believe that it is necessary to raise the real-time requirements to a central, focusing issue. This includes the need to formally state the metrics and timing requirements (which are usually dynamic and depend on many factors, including the system state) and to then be able to show that the system indeed meets the timing requirements.[6,7]

Achieving this goal is not easy and will require research breakthroughs in many aspects of system design and implementation. For example, good design rules and constraints must be used to guide real-time system developers to aid later implementation and *analysis*. Language features must be tailored to these rules and constraints, must limit system features to enhance predictability, and must provide the ability to specify timing, fault tolerance, and other information for subsequent use at run-time. The execution time of each primitive of the kernel must be bounded and predictable, and the operating system should provide explicit support for all the requirements, including the real-time requirements.

The hardware must also adhere to the rules and constraints and be simple enough so you can get predictable timing information — caching, memory refresh, wait states, pipelining, and some complex instructions all contribute to timing-analysis difficulties.

An insidious aspect of critical real-time systems, especially for the real-time requirements, is that the weakest link in the entire system can undermine careful design and analysis at other levels.

Our research is trying to address all of these issues in an integrated fashion by adopting a new paradigm that avoids the pitfalls inherent in the current paradigm.◆

John A. Stankovic is a professor of computer and information science at the University of Massachusetts at Amherst. His research interests include scheduling on local area networks and multiprocessors, developing flexible, distributed, hard real-time systems, and experimental studies of distributed-database protocols.

Stankovic received a BS in electrical engineering and an MS and PhD in computer science from Brown University. He is editor-in-chief of *Real-Time Systems* and a member of the IEEE executive committee for distributed systems and an advisory board member for the Computer Society of India's *Journal of Computer Science and Informatics*.

ACKNOWLEDGMENTS
Many people have worked on various parts of the kernel. We thank Krishnamoorthy Arvind, Sara Biyabani, Sheng-Chang Cheng, Elizabeth Gene, Chung-Huei Kuan, Lory Molesky, Douglas Niehaus, Chia Shen, Fuxing Wang, Wei Zhao, and Goran Zlokapa for their work on the kernel development.

REFERENCES
1. K. Ramamritham, J. Stankovic, and W. Zhao, "Distributed Scheduling of Tasks with Deadlines and Resource Requirements," *IEEE Trans. Computers*, Aug. 1989, pp. 1,110-1,123.
2. K. Ramamritham, J. Stankovic, and P. Shiah, "Efficient Scheduling Algorithms for Real-Time Multiprocessor Systems," *IEEE Trans. Parallel and Distributed Systems*, April 1990, pp. 184-194.
3. C. Shen, K. Ramamritham, and J. Stankovic, "Resource Reclaiming in Real Time," *Proc. Real-Time System Symp.*, CS Press, Los Alamitos, Calif., 1990, pp. 41-50.
4. L. Molesky, C. Shen, and G. Zlokapa, "Predictable Synchronization Mechanisms for Real-Time Systems," *Real-Time Systems*, Sept. 1990, pp. 163-180.
5. S. Biyabani, J. Stankovic, and K. Ramamritham, "The Integration of Criticalness and Deadline in Scheduling Hard Real-Time Tasks," *Proc. Real-Time Systems Symp.*, CS Press, Los Alamitos, Calif., 1988, pp. 152-160.
6. K. Schwan, A. Geith, and H. Zhou, "From Chaos^{base} to Chaos^{arc}: A Family of Real-Time Kernels," *Proc. Real-Time Systems Symp.*, CS Press, Los Alamitos, Calif., 1990, pp. 82-91.
7. H. Tokuda and C. Mercer, "Arts: A Distributed Real-Time Kernel," *ACM Operating Systems Rev.*, July 1989, pp. 29-53.

Krithi Ramamritham is an associate professor of computer and information science at the University of Massachusetts at Amherst and codirector of the Spring project. His research interests include real-time systems, distributed computing, and semantics-based database transaction management.

Ramamritham received a PhD in computer science from the University of Utah. He is an associate editor of *Real-Time Systems* and is a member of the IEEE and ACM.

Address questions about this article to the authors at Computer and Information Science Dept., University of Massachusetts, Amherst, MA 01003; Internet stankovic@cs.umass.edu.

Chapter 4:   Programming Languages

While many languages, including Ada, purportedly were designed with real-time systems in mind (see [Burns and Wellings 89] and [Halang and Stoyenko 90] for surveys), few have the requisite features to program predictable real-time systems. Ada, for instance, lets you write concurrent programs, but the only explicit time-related feature it provides is a delay statement which when invoked suspends a process for the given (minimum) amount of time. Clearly, given the complex needs of next-generation real-time systems, these are insufficient, to say the least.

Hence, some researchers have noted the inadequacy of existing programming languages and begun to design programming languages explicitly aimed at the needs of complex real-time systems. These efforts have produced various types of languages. Some languages (for example, [Lee and Gehlot 85]) have focused on identifying time-related constructs without expressly being concerned with their realization or with the general applicability of the language. Many efforts, however, have resulted in languages as well as support tools.

An early example of these endeavors is Real-Time Euclid [Klingerman and Stoyenko 86], which has constructs designed to support *static* real-time systems, specifically, those that require static guarantees of specified timing properties. In conjunction, a schedulability analyzer has been built for Real-Time Euclid programs to check, a priori, whether the specified timing requirements can be met.

Most of the remaining efforts aim at real-time systems that have different types of predictability requirements (see Chapter 1 and the paper there by Stankovic and Ramamritham). Specifically, they allow some of the activities to demand design-time or compile-time guarantees that certain timing constraints will be met, some to demand dynamic guarantees, and some to possess nominal deadlines. The three papers included in this section belong to this latter category. They share another commonality in that they are all extensions of existing general-purpose languages, all of which are extensions of C. The three languages are Real-Time Concurrent C, RTC++, and FLEX. Their design philosophies are closely tied to three different schools of real-time system design. Real-Time Concurrent C is founded on the notion of statically or dynamically guaranteed timing constraints, with activities scheduled using time and resource constrained algorithms. RTC++ assumes a system run by a preemptive static priority driven scheduler based on the rate-monotonic paradigm. FLEX uses the notion of *real-time computations with imprecise results* as its driving force.

Real-Time Concurrent C, a language designed by Gehani and Ramamritham, extends Concurrent C by providing facilities that are tailored to build complex real-time systems. Specifically, Real-Time Concurrent C allows processes to execute activities with specified periodicity or deadline constraints, to seek guarantees that timing constraints will be met, and perform alternative actions when either the timing constraints cannot be met or the guarantees are not available. One of the novel aspects of Real-Time Concurrent C is the incorporation of *guarantee* as a language concept. The approach to guarantees is based on the Spring paradigm [Stankovic and Ramamritham 91]. Once guaranteed, an activity can be depended upon to finish before its deadline. When a guarantee is not possible, the approach provides more leeway for the process to take alternative actions. For instance, if a guarantee is not possible for the *best* version of a function, it might be possible to guarantee another version which has a lower computation time but produces a lower quality result. This is similar in flavor to that of the imprecise computations in FLEX. Unlike RTC++, guarantees can be sought for both periodic as well as aperiodic activities. The paper also discusses scheduling and other runtime facilities needed to support the real-time features. A prototype implementation of Real-Time Concurrent C is in its final stages.

RTC++, the language discussed by Ishikawa, Tokuda, and Mercer, makes explicit use of the object-orientedness of C++, unlike FLEX. Specifically, some of the objects can be declared to be *active* and timing constraints can be attached not only to code segments but also to specific operations. Active objects are multithreaded with each thread executing an operation invoked on that object. The thread *inherits* the priority of the invoker. As we mentioned earlier, RTC++ is built on the rate-monotonic scheduling framework [Liu and Layland 73] extended by Sha, Lehoczky, Rajkumar, and others to deal with resources, mode changes, aperiodic tasks, and multiprocessors (see papers in Chapter 2) as well as

[Lehoczky et al. 87]). Thus, periodic code segments can be pre-analyzed to determine if they are schedulable. For aperiodic code segments, deadlines can be attached and exception handling is done if the deadlines are missed. That is, guarantees are provided only to periodic activities. Clearly, to determine schedulability for periodic activities, one has to know beforehand the execution time and resource requirements of these activities so as to conduct schedulability analysis. For this reason, the number of threads that an active object can have is defined at object creation time thereby bounding the resource requirements of an object and hence its threads at the time it is created.

Real-time Mentat [Grimshaw et al. 90], is another real-time language extension to C++ in which the active entities are objects. However, unlike RTC++, Real-Time Mentat does not provide for the preemption of these active objects.

While all three languages attempt to provide the programmer with a language for implementing flexible real-time systems, FLEX derives its name from this requirement. The paper by Kenny and Lin discusses the design philosophy and the language constructs of FLEX. The incorporation of imprecise computations in FLEX is based on the observation that, quite often, one is called upon to trade off performability and quality. If we assume that the longer you perform a computation, the better the quality of the results produced, then we see a direct correlation between the ability to meet timing constraints and the quality of computations. FLEX provides two facilities to program this trade-off. The first allows a computation to provide imprecise results as the computation progresses; the computation terminates when its deadline expires or when it completes. The second allows the specification of *performance polymorphic* functions. Associated with each such function are several candidates that have the same functionality, but possess different performance characteristics. (A similar feature is also available in the real-time programming language GARTL [Marlin et al. 90]). FLEX determines the timing characteristics of these functions by *measuring* the execution time under different invocations and by combining these to produce a parameter-dependent formula. At runtime, given the values of the parameters to a specific function call, one of the candidates is chosen to compute the function such that timing constraints will be met. No a priori restrictions, such as (bounded) loops and recursion, are placed on FLEX code. This is because, FLEX uses measurement to determine code execution times, as opposed to using analysis (see [Shaw 89] and [Puschner and Koza 89] in Chapter 5 as well as [Mok 89] for some approaches to analysis). Such restrictions are enforced by Real-Time Euclid, and by Real-Time Concurrent C, for code segments requiring guarantees, to produce the worst-case computation times for code segments. As a result, the guarantees provided in FLEX are probabilistic in nature whereas in Real-Time Euclid and Real-Time Concurrent C, they hold even under worst-case assumptions.

Only by programming nontrivial real-time systems will the adequacy and expressiveness of the proposed new constructs and concepts in the above languages become clear. Each of these languages has features suitable for designing (parts of) a complex real-time system. Within a system, different components or subsystems will probably find their best match with different approaches. So ideally what is needed is a way to mix and match the languages for programming different subsystems, along with an integrated set of loading-time and runtime tools. Another alternative is to design a language that combines the flexibility-enhancing features from each of these. But further experience in using these and other languages is necessary before these projects can be undertaken.

Real-Time Concurrent C: A Language for Programming Dynamic Real-Time Systems

NARAIN GEHANI
AT&T Bell Labs, Murray Hill, NJ 07974, U.S.A.

KRITHI RAMAMRITHAM
University of Massachusetts, Amherst, MA 01003, U.S.A.

Abstract. *Concurrent C*, is a parallel superset of C (and of C++) that provides facilities such as specifying timeouts during process interactions, delaying program execution, accepting messsages in a user-specified order, and asynchronous messages that can be used for writing real-time programs. However, Concurrent C does not provide facilities for specifying strict timing constraints, e.g., Concurrent C only ensures that the lower bounds on the specified delay and timeout periods are satisfied.

Real-Time Concurrent C extends Concurrent C by providing facilities to specify periodicity or deadline constraints, to seek guarantees that timing constraints will be met, and to perform alternative actions when either the timing constraints cannot be met or the guarantees are not available.

In this paper, we will discuss requirements for a real-time programming language, briefly summarize Concurrent C, and motivate and describe the real-time extensions to Concurrent C. We also discuss scheduling and other run-time facilities that have been incorporated to support the real-time extensions. A prototype implementation of Real-Time Concurrent C is nearing completion.

1. Introduction

Real-time systems are systems in which activities must take place such that the results are not only logically correct, but also meet the timing requirements. Timing constraints typically take the form of periodicity requirements or deadline constraints. While periodic activities occur during the processing of sensory information or in the control of actuators, aperiodic activities are triggered by periodic activities or are triggered in response to exceptional situations.

An important requirement of systems with time-constrained activities is timing predictability; specifically, it should be possible to predict whether or not an activity or a set of activities will meet their timing requirements. A prerequisite for predictable executions is the ability to determine the execution time of code segments. In order to ensure the existence of an execution time bound, bounded loops and bounded recursion should be used. Ensuring existence of execution time bounds also implies that interprocess interactions that delay or suspend a process for unbounded time periods should be disallowed. Thus, decisions must be made to restrict the use of language facilities while retaining the flexibility of the language. These are some of the issues that a language designer has to be cognizant of in designing a programming language to express real-time systems.

Concurrent C (Gehani and Roome 1986), (Gehani and Roome 1989) is a superset of C (and of C++) that provides parallel programming facilities. Concurrent C supports writing real-time programs by providing facilities for specifying, changing and querying process priorities, accepting process interaction requests in a user-specified order, asynchronous messages, specifying timeouts during process interactions, and delaying (suspending) execution.

Real-Time Concurrent C extends Concurrent C by providing facilities for building systems with strict timing constraints. Real-Time Concurrent C allows processes to execute activities with specified periodicity or deadline constraints, to seek guarantees that timing constraints will be met, and to perform alternative actions when either the timing constraints cannot be met or the guarantees are not available. With these extensions, Real-Time concurrent C can serve as a platform for programming real-world real-time systems.

We are targeting at dynamic real-time systems, i.e., systems in which activities may be spawned dynamically. We are also aiming at systems in which some activities have deadlines which have to be *guaranteed*, some activities for whom a "best effort" approach is sufficient, and some which have no deadlines associated with them.

A point to remember while reading the rest of the paper is that if a new real-time programming language is being designed, then we can ensure that the language contains only facilities that are appropriate for real-time programming and analysis. But if real-time programming facilities are being added to an existing programming language, as is the case here, then a programming discipline may need to be used or enforced.

The rest of the paper is organized as follows. A quick overview of Concurrent C is provided in Section 2. Features necessary to program real-time systems are discussed in Section 3. The real-time extensions to Concurrent C and the rationale for these extensions are discussed in Section 4. We also present an example from robotics to illustrate the use of the real-time features. A prototype implementation of the compiler and run-time support system for Real-Time Concurrent C is nearing completion. Some salient aspects of the prototype are discussed in Section 5. Section 6 summarizes the paper and discusses outstanding issues.

2. Overview of concurrent C

Concurrent C extends C for parallel programming by providing facilities for

- specifying process types,
- creating processes,
- specifying the processor on which a process is to run,
- specifying, querying and changing process priorities,
- synchronous transactions (synchronous message sends),
- asynchronous transactions (asynchronous message sends),
- delays and timeouts,
- interrupt handling,
- waiting for a set of events such as transactions,
- accepting transactions in a user-specified order,
- process abortion, and
- collective termination.

We now briefly describe Concurrent C facilities that may be used in programming real-time systems. But these are not sufficient to ensure strict timing requirements.

Transactions. Processes interact through transaction calls. Two forms of transactions exist. In the synchronous case, the caller waits for the callee to accept the call and return the results. In the asynchronous case, the caller "posts" the call and continues with its execution.

Timed synchronous transaction calls. Concurrent C provides facilities for timed synchronous transaction calls. This allows a process to withdraw a transaction call if it is not *accepted* within the specified period. A process can also time out if a transaction call does not arrive within a specified period. Timeouts prevent a process from being blocked for an unduly long period. However, the specified time-out period is only a lower bound on the duration for which the caller waits.

Asynchronous transactions. Asynchronous transactions provide maximum flexibility because processes can compute and send and receive messages in parallel and in any way they want. Asynchronous message passing is especially important in situations where the inter-process communication time is high (as in the case of distributed systems). Asynchronous message passing also allows pipelining of multiple messages from the same process and allows the receiving process to accept the messages in the most appropriate order.

Flexibility in accepting transaction calls. Concurrent C allows transactions (messages) to be accepted in a user-specified order (through the use of the by and suchthat clauses). Thus, if the deadline of a call is passed as parameter, a process can accept transaction calls in earliest-deadline-first order. In general, transaction call acceptance can be based on the transaction name, the order in which transaction calls are received, the transaction arguments, its priority, and the state of the called process.

Process priorities. Concurrent C provides facilities for specifying process priorities, and for querying and changing process priorities. Process priorities are specified when creating a process, but the priority can be changed at any time. Processes that need to respond quickly to events such as interrupts, which need immediate attention, are usually given high priorities. Such priorities can be used to implement the traditionally used priority-based scheduling mechanisms used in real-time systems.

Handling interrupts. An important aspect of real-time programming is interrupt handling. The implementation-dependent function c_associate is used to indicate that the specified interrupt should be converted to a call to the specified transaction. To avoid losing interrupts, it is important that they (the associated transactions) be handled quickly. Delay in handling interrupts can occur because of the

1. overhead in converting the interrupt to a transaction call,
2. delay in scheduling the interrupt handling process, and
3. delay in accepting the call.

These delays may not be bounded if traditional process scheduling algorithms, that allow preemptions at arbitrary points, are used.

3. Characteristics of real-time systems

In general, activities with different types of deadline semantics occur in real-time systems.

- *Critical activities.* Activities for which deadlines cannot be missed under any circumstances. Such activities typically come in the form of critical periodic activities. In most systems, a separate subsystem or front end is allocated for such activities so that other activities do not interfere with such critical activities. Resources needed for these activities may be preallocated and activities may be scheduled according to a table-driven schedule. Alternatively, static priorities may be associated with these activities and a priority-driven execution of the activities may occur.
- *Guaranteed activities.* Activities that need not always execute but, if executed, should be completed by their deadlines. Guaranteed activities are motivated by the fact that in some cases, recovering from a partially completed activity can be complicated especially if it involves inter-process interactions. In such cases, it might be better to allow an activity to take place only if the activity ccan be guaranteed to complete by its deadline. If a guarantee cannot be provided, then the program can perform an alternative action. To provide sufficient time for executing the alternative action, a deadline may be imposed on the determination of the guarantee. A generalization of this is to have N versions of the activity and try to guarantee the best version possible (Marlin, Zhao, Doherty and Bohonis 1990). "Best" refers to the quality of the results produced by a particular version; typically, the better the quality of the results, the longer the execution time.
- *Activities with nominal deadlines.* Activities for which deadlines can be missed. Such a deadline can have two connotations. On the one hand, the activity may be allowed to continue beyond the deadline to complete even if it is delayed. The other possibility is that once the deadline is past, a timing-error handler is executed after terminating the original activity. Clearly, the error handler may be complicated in general and abnormal termination may produce inconsistent system states. It is precisely in such situations that we believe the guarantee concept will prove useful.

A static real-time system, i.e., one in which all activities are critical, is a system in which all activities are guaranteed a priori. Real-Time Concurrent C can be used for such systems. However, here our focus is on dynamic real-time systems, i.e., systems whose activities have to be guaranteed dynamically, or whose activities execute with nominal deadlines.

To guarantee whether or not an activity can complete within a specified deadline, the worst-case execution time of the activity must be known prior to the start of the activity. There are two aspects to the problem of determining the worst-case execution time of an activity: (1) its execution must be bounded and (2) the variance in the execution time should not be large. The latter need arises from the fact that to guarantee an activity, resources (including time) needed for it must be found with respect to worst case needs. In general, the larger the worst case needs, the less likely it will be to give a guarantee. Further, even if a guarantee can be given, it is likely to have an adverse effect on future guarantees. Hence, code for activities requiring guarantees should be written to minimize the variance in execution time.

As was mentioned in the introduction, to ensure predictable executions, certain restrictions have to be placed on the statements used within guaranteed code segments. Given these restrictions, using a timing analysis tool, such as the one described in (Lavoie 1991), we can determine the execution times of individual pieces of code. We will discuss this further in Section 6.2.

As alluded to earlier, traditional real-time systems adopt preemptive priority-driven scheduling algorithms. To obtain predicability, processes should be assigned static priorities or, at the very least, they should be modified only when the system moves from one *mode* to another. A static priority-driven approach (Sha, Rajkumar and Lehoczky 1990) based on the rate-monotonic priority assignment (Liu and Layland 1973) provides such predictability. However, these are applicable primarily to periodic processes. We want to accommodate the different types of real-time activities such as periodic and aperiodic activities that may require execution guarantees. Even though schemes exist for accommodating aperiodic activities within the (rate-monotonic) priority driven approach (Lehoczky, Sha and Strosnider 1987), they are not geared towards providing guarantees for the aperiodic activities.

Hence, activities in Real-Time Concurrent C will be scheduled based on their deadlines. Thus, we will be employing a deadline-driven scheduling scheme. In addition, to meet the needs of activities that require guarantees, a variant of the scheme proposed in (Ramamritham, Stankovic and Shiah 1990) is used. Some of the essential details are discussed in Section 6.1.

Suppose activities have deadlines as well as priorities where the latter signify the importance of activities. An issue that needs to be resolved concerns how process priorities and deadlines relate. There are a number of questions that need to be explored. Suppose a process makes a transaction call with a deadline. How do the priorities of the caller, the callee, and the urgency (the deadline) specified by the caller relate? How should the scheduler take deadlines and priorities into account? We do not tackle these issues in the current version of Real-time Concurrent C. We will instead be assuming that all Concurrent C processes have the same priority and that activities have just deadlines. (This implies that the priority inversion problem (Sha, Rajkumar and Lehoczky 1990) does not have to be addressed.) Also, we will be assuming that all the resources, such as memory, needed by an activity are available, and hence will not be concerned with resource-constrained scheduling of activities with deadlines.

Real-time systems are expected to be fault-tolerant and hence the programming languages used should allow fault tolerance requirements to be specified. Whereas we do not explicitly address fault tolerance in this paper, we would like to note that it should be possible to utilize aspects from Fault Tolerant Concurrent C (Cmelik, Gehani and Roome 1988) for this purpose.

4. Real-time concurrent C

While designing Real-Time Concurrent C, we kept the following factors in perspective:

- Upward compatibility with Concurrent C.
- Simplicity of semantics. Even though simplicity is a subjective consideration, we were wary of facilities whose semantics would be difficult to understand or articulate.

265

- Separating performance-oriented implications from the semantics of a construct. This is a challenge in the context of real-time systems since performance (timing) issues and correctness issues are highly intertwined in such systems.
- Ease of implementation.
- Flexibility in expressing timing requirements.

Turning to the last point, Real-Time Concurrent C was designed to address the following types of real-time needs:

- In a real-time program, some components may be executed periodically. Others may have to be executed within a deadline.
- A periodic activity may have to be terminated when some condition becomes true or when a transaction call (interrupt) arrives.
- If it is not possible to meet the periodicity requirement or a deadline, then it should be possible to take alternative action ("timing-error handler"). This will enable a program to take some corrective action to address the fact that the periodicity requirement or the deadline constraint was not met.
- Before initiating an activity, if desired, it should be possible to get a guarantee from the run-time system that the activity will be completed within the specified deadline (*a la* the *guarantee* notion used in Spring (Stankovic and Ramamritham 1991)). If the system cannot give the guarantee—the guarantee itself may have a deadline—then the programmer should be able to specify the execution of alternative code.

  An activity can be guaranteed to complete execution within its deadline if a schedule can be created for the activity being guaranteed and other activities that have been previously guaranteed such that all these activities will meet their timing constraints. If such a schedule cannot be created, the new activity is not guaranteed.

The rest of this section is devoted to a description of the timing constructs of Real-Time Concurrent C. A complete example is given in Section 5 to illustrate the timing constructs. The necessary run-time support for achieving the semantics of the constructs is presented in Section 6.

Sections 4.1 through 4.4 are devoted to the extensions made to Concurrent C to meet the above needs. As we discuss the extensions, we also present our rationale for choosing them and motivations for the choices made. Finally, in Section 4.5 we discuss further possible extensions.

In what follows, terminals in the language are shown in typewriter font. [and] indicates optional items while | denotes alternatives. The unit of time is seconds. All deadlines are relative to current time, thus a deadline of 10 implies an absolute deadline of (current time + 10).

We use the term *activity* to refer to a Real-Time Concurrent C statement. A real-time activity is an activity with a time constraint attached to it, i.e., a statement with a periodicity requirement or a deadline.

4.1. Activities with deadlines

Timeouts can be associated with any statement using the within deadline statement which has the form

within deadline (*d*) *statement*₁
[else *statement*₂]

Suppose control reaches the within deadline statement at time *t*. If *statement*₁ is not completed by (*t* + *d*), then its execution is terminated and *statement*₂, if specified, is executed. The effects of this abnormal termination depend upon the nature of *statement*₁. If *statement*₁ does not involve any transaction calls or accept statements, then the effect of termination is local to the process. Otherwise, other interacting processes may be affected. We discuss these effects when we discuss transactions in Section 4.4.

Deadline example. An air-traffic control system should provide final clearance for a pilot to land within 60 seconds after clearance is requested. Otherwise the pilot will abort the landing procedure.

within deadline (60) *get clearance*;
else *abort landing*;

4.2. Periodic activities

Periodic activities are specified using the every statement which has the form

every (*p*) [until *expression* | until accept statement]
    *statement*₁
[else *statement*₂]

expression is a Boolean condition. *statement*₁ will be repeated once every *p* seconds subject to the following semantics:

- If control reaches the every statement at time *t*, the ith period will begin at time *t* + (i-1) × *p*.
- Typcally, a periodic activity executes until some condition becomes true. After the execution of an instance of the activity, the condition should be checked before the execution of another instance is undertaken. In Real-Time Concurrent C, this takes two forms:
  - If the "until *expression*" clause is given, then the *expression* is evaluated at the beginning of each period. The every statement terminates if this expression evaluates to true.
  - If an "until accept_statement" clause is given, then at the beginning of each period, the every statement attempts to accept the specified transaction. If a transaction can be accepted, then the every statement terminates after the transaction is accepted.

Note that interrupts manifest themselves as transactions in Concurrent C (and hence also in Real-Time Concurrent C). Thus, the provision of the until accept_statement clause allows termination of a periodic activity upon the arrival of an interrupt.

- If execution of *statement*₁ is not completed within the period, then the every statement executes *statement*₂, if given, and terminates. Any inconsistencies that result from the abrupt termination must be handled independently. The termination of the every statement can affect other processes, e.g., if *statement*₁ contains a synchronous transaction call. We discuss this in Section 4.4.

The every statement terminates if any execution of the periodic activity does not complete within the specified period. If it is necessary to resume execution of the periodic activity, then the following paradigm can be used:

```
while(...) {
    every (p) [until expression | until accept_statement]
        statement₁
    else statement₂
}
```

Here, for each instance that is terminated because its deadline is not met, *statement*₂ will be executed and the periodic activity will continue.[1]

Periodic activity example. Consider a telephone network in which switches periodically monitor other switches to detect node failures. Each switch sends an "I am alive" message to a subset of switches in the network. We will refer to this subset as "cohorts" of a switch. If a switch does not receive an "I am alive" message once every period, of duration p seconds, from each of its cohorts, it suspects that the cohort may be down and initiates fault detection and recovery. If, for any reason, a switch is shutdown, a "shutdown" message is sent to all its cohorts. Each switch creates processes, one per cohort, to monitor the cohorts. These processes execute a code segment of the form

```
every (p) until accept shutdown(id) {...}
    accept I_am_alive(id) {...}
else initiate fault detection and recovery;
```

Robotics example. This illustrates the nesting of time constraints. Suppose that a robot driver must provide the robot with a new move position every 10 seconds. Assume that communication with the robot takes 2 seconds. Hence within the first 8 seconds of each 10 second interval the controller has to compute the new position. If this computation is not completed within 8 seconds, the robot is asked to stay at its current position by sending position values equal to those of its current position.

```
every (10) {
    within deadline (8) compute new_position
```

```
else { new position is same as old }
robot.move(new_position);
}
```

A more elaborate robotics example is given in Section 5.

4.3. Guaranteed activities

The guarantee statement is used to ensure, before an activity is started, that the activity can be completed within the specified time-constraints. It has the form

```
[within deadline (gd)] guarantee
    time_constrained_statement
[else statement]
```

where *gd* is the guarantee deadline and a time-constrained statement is either an every or a within deadline statement.

When control reaches the guarantee statement, the Real-Time Concurrent C run-time system attempts to determine, within *gd* if specified, whether or not the time-constrained statement can be guaranteed to complete within its time-constraints. If the guarantee is not possible, or if the guarantee cannot be given within *gd*, then the else statmement, if any, is executed. Otherwise, the time-constrained statement is executed.

For the guarantee to be provided, the execution time of the statement must be a priori determinable (at least at the time of the guarantee). Under some circumstances, it may not be possible to determine the total execution time required for executing the time-constrained statement, e.g., if the time-constrained statement contains a while loop, an arbitrary accept statement of a synchronous transaction call. For while loops, the loop count should be bounded. As discussed in Section 4.4, execution times can be computed only if synchronous transaction calls and accept statements have associated time-constraints.

Guaranteed activities with deadlines. The following statement attempts to guarantee that *statement₁* will be completed within *d* seconds after it has started execution:

```
within deadline (gd) guarantee
    within deadline (d) statement₁
    [else ;]
[else statement₂]
```

Statement₂ will be executed if it is not possible to give the guarantee by *gd*. If guaranteed, *statement₁* will be executed between *st* and $(t + d)$ where *st* lies in the interval $(t, t + gd)$.[2]

A simple railroad crossing example. Suppose a process that controls a railroad signal has to determine whether a certain track will be clear by the time a train is expected to reach the track. It has to make this determination early enough so as to give itself enough time to stop the train in case it is determined that the track is not expected to be clear. The train will not reach the track before *d* seconds and it takes at most *s* seconds to stop the train ($s < d$).

```
within deadline (d-s) guarantee
     within deadline (d) clear track;
     else ;
else stop train;
```

Guaranteed periodic activities. Execution of a periodic activity can be guaranteed by using the guarantee statement in conjunction with the every statement:

```
within deadline (gd) guarantee
     every (p) [until condition] statement₁
     [ else ; ]
[else statement₂]
```

attempts to guarantee that *statement*₁ will execute once every *p* seconds. If guaranteed, the first period will begin at *st* and end at $(st + p)$ where *st* lies in the interval $(t, t + gd)^2$.

Recall that at the beginning of every instance of a periodic activity, *condition* is first checked to determine if it satisfied and only if it is, *statement*₁ is executed. Thus the execution time of each instance of the periodic activity should include both the time required to check the condition as well as the time to execute *statement*₁.

Switching example revisited. Returning to our switching example in which switches monitor each other by periodically transmitting "I am alive" messages, we would like to guarantee that it is possible for a switch to send such messages, once every period, to its cohorts.

```
within deadline (gd) guarantee
     every (p)
          for(i=1; i=num_cohorts; ++i)
               cohort[i].I_am_alive(my_id);
     else ;
else
     try alternative set of cohorts for each switch;
```

gd is the deadline by which the guarantee must be made available; I_am_alive is an asynchronous transaction. cohort[i] contains the id of the ith cohort process.

4.4. Transactions and time-constraints

We will now discuss two complications that happen as a result of a time-constrained activity containing interactions with other processes. The first deals with the duration of such interactions. This is important when the execution time of the activity must be known for the purpose of guaranteeing execution of the activity within its time-constraints. The second deals with the effects on other processes when a time-constrained activity is terminated when the specified time-constraint is not met. We examine these two issues in order.

Assuming that buffers/queues do not overflow, asynchronous transactions do not pose any problem. From a caller's point of view, the time taken to execute an asynchronous transaction is the time needed to "post" the transaction. The caller does not wait for the callee to respond to it. Hence an asynchronous call takes a bounded amount of time.

However, the same is not true of synchronous transaction calls since the calling process is suspended until the callee responds. This suspension can be unbounded. However, in case of a timed transaction call (these are synchronous transactions), the maximum time that a process may wait for the call to complete is bounded. Since an activity that is guaranteed must have a bounded execution time, in Real-Time Concurrent C, only timed transaction calls should be used in activities that have to be guaranteed to execute within a specified deadline.

Recall that the execution of a statement with an associated deadline is abandoned if the deadline expires. We now examine the consequences of this when a synchronous transaction call is withdrawn by the caller or execution of an accept statement is abandoned by the callee.

- Suppose a transaction call is abandoned. If the call is withdrawn before the call has been accepted, it clearly will not affect the callee. If the call is withdrawn during the execution of the accept statement, the call is withdrawn *without* affecting the callee. To help the caller determine if the call had been accepted or if the call was withdrawn while it was in the process of being accepted, a special variable t_interrupted is associated with each process. t_interrupted is set to one if the last transaction call made by a process was withdrawn during the accept; otherwise, it is set to zero.
- Suppose the execution of an accept statement is abandoned. We allow the calling process to determine if its call was abandoned by examining another special variable t_abandoned associated with each (calling) process. This variable is set to one if the execution of the accept statement was abandoned by the callee; otherwise, it is set to zero.

Termination during process interaction example. Suppose a resource is managed by a process called Manager. Any process that needs the resource waits for an amount of time max_wait. If the Manager does not provide the resource within max_wait seconds, the resource is to be requested from another provider:

```
within deadline (max_wait)
    Manager.get(pid);
else get resource from another provider;
```

where pid is the id of the calling process.

The Manager process can be in the middle of accepting transaction get when the specified time limit max_wait expires. In this case, although the transaction call is withdrawn, the process accepting the call, i.e., (the Manager), continues executing as if nothing happened. As a result, Manager will continue with the resource allocation. It is the caller's responsibility to free the resource after examining the value of variable t_interrupted:

For example, the above code should be written as

```
within deadline (max_wait)
    Manager.get(pid);
else {
    if (t_interrupted)
        Manager.free(pid);
    get resource from another provider;
}
```

Let us now examine what is involved in guaranteeing whether or not a synchronous call can be completed within a deadline. For instance, consider

```
within deadline (d) guarantee
        within deadline (max_wait) Manager.get(pid);
    else get resource from another provider;
```

To provide this guarantee however, the scheduler must be able to determine when the callee will get around to accepting the call. In some special cases, e.g., in the case of a server process which handles only one transaction, it may be possible to determine this time. In general, however, the delay involved depends on the current outstanding calls, the control flow in the callee's code, the execution times of the various code segments within the callee, the times these code segments will be scheduled, etc. These factors make it all but impossible for the caller to determine when the callee will get around to accepting the call in the general case. Hence, in such situations, the else clause which requests the resource from another provider will be executed since we cannot give the guarantee.

4.5. Future extensions

We present two extensions that we plan to incorporate in subsequent versions of Real-Time Concurrent C. One involves a more flexible notion of deadlines, and another involves the specification of start time constraints.

4.5.1. Flexible time-constraints. The semantics of time-constraints thus far has been that if an activity is not completed within the specified time, it is terminated and timing-error handling is done. This is appropriate for activities where there is no value to completing the task past the specified time.

In many real-time systems, a more flexible semantics is associated with time-constrained activities. Specifically, while the system should strive to meet the timing constraints, for some activities, it is better, and sometimes necessary, to complete the activity even if it is delayed. We call such time-constraints *flexible*. More generally, an activity may have a value even past its deadline, but no value beyond a certain point past its deadline. If this point is not bounded, the activity should be completed regardless of how long it takes. If it is bounded, it can be terminated past this point. If this point is the same as the deadline, we obtain the semantics originally assumed.

To express flexible time-constraints, we allow the association of a *slop* with a time-constraint: An activity should be terminated only after the interval corresponding to the slop expires.

The counterpart of the above situation is one where a negative value for *slop* is specified. This corresponds to requesting the following from the system: Attempt to complete the activity within *slop* units before the deadline but if this is not possible, within the specified deadline. This is akin to asking the system to be "nice" to this activity by trying to complete it before the deadline.

The deadline-constrained activity *statement$_1$*, specified as,

```
within deadline (d) [(slop)] statement₁
[else statement₂]
```

has the following semantics:

- If *statement$_1$* is not completed by max(d, d + *slop*), the processing of *statement$_1$* is terminated and *statement$_2$*, if provided, is executed.
- If *slop* is not specified, it is assumed to be zero.
- If a guarantee is requested, the guarantee algorithm will first attempt to guarantee *statement$_1$* with respect to min(d, d + *slop*) and if unsuccessful, with respect to max(d, d + *slop*). If the latter attempt is also unsuccessful, the `else` clause, if specified, will be executed.
- A time-constrained component of *statment$_1$* can have a slop. This can increase the worst-case execution time of *statement$_1$*.

Example. An air-traffic control system should preferably provide final clearance for a pilot to land within `t1` seconds after the request has been made and, if this is not possible, within another `t2` seconds. Otherwise the pilot will abort the landing procedure.

```
within deadline (t1) (t2) clear landing;
else abort landing
```

It should be easy to see that specifying a large slop (say, equal to infinity, e.g., `maxint`) corresponds to specifying that the activity has a *nominal* deadline where the activity should be allowed to complete even if the deadline is past.

Whereas the addition of a slop to a deadline does not unduly complicate the semantics of the `within deadline` statement, this is not the case when a slop is added to a periodicity requirement. Suppose, for example, a periodic activity *statement$_1$* is specified as

```
every (p) (slop) [until condition]
    statement₁
[else statement₂]
```

This statement has the following semantics:

- Suppose the first period begins at time t. Lt c_{i-1} be the completion/termination time of the $(i - 1)^{th}$ instance of *statement*$_1$. The ith instance can begin execution after b_i where b_i $(t + (i - 1) \times p)$ or c_{i-1}, whichever is later.
- If a particular instance of the periodic activity *statement*$_1$ is not completed by b_i + *slop*, the processing of *statement*$_1$ is terminated and *statement*$_2$, if given, will be executed. And this terminates the execution of the every statement.

While a number of variations of the above semantics exist, it is easy to see that, once the potential for execution beyond a period is introduced, it is difficult to meet the requirements one typically associates with a periodicity constraint. In addition, we believe that most of these *weakened periodicity constraints* are implementable using the for loop in conjunction with the delay statement that are already part of Concurrent C. Hence, we prefer not to allow a slop in conjunction with a period.

4.5.2. Specification of start-time-constraints. Consider the following modification to the specification of activities with deadlines:

```
start at (s) within deadline (d) statement₁
[else statement₂]
```

Suppose control reaches the within deadline statement at time t. This statement should be started at or after $(t + s)$ and completed by $(t + d$ with $d > s)$.

Consider the following extension to the specification of activities with periodicity constraints:

```
start at (s) every (p) [until expression]
    statement₁
[else statement₂]
```

This requests the first period to begin at time $(t + s)$.

It is easy to picture the guaranteed versions of the above statements. So we do not present them here.

Start time-constraints demand slightly more complex scheduling and guarantee algorithms that we have incorporated in the current prototype. Hence their incorporation is deferred to subsequent versions of Real-Time Concurrent C.

5. A robot control example

In order to illustrate Real-Time Concurrent C facilities, we will discuss a simple robot control system organized as four processes: the operator, the planner, the joint controller, and the motor controller.

The operator sends a *move* command to the planner specifying the end point *ep* and t, the absolute time by which that point should be reached. If the planner is unable to come up with a plan that meets the timing constraint, it notifies the operator of failure. Otherwise, it returns the plan to the operator which in turn sends it to the joint controller.

Here is the body of the main, i.e., the operator process:

```
                                                                    cc/robot.cc

#include "robot.h"
main()
{
    process planner pl;
    process joint_controller jc;
    process motor_controller mc;
    plan p;
    float t;
    point sp, ep;

    pl = create planner();
    mc = create motor_controller();
    jc = create joint_controller(mc);

    sp = start point;
    ep = end point;
    t = time by which ep should be reached;

    p = pl.move(sp, ep, t);
    if (!p.n) {
        fprintf(stderr, "error, insufficient time to compute plan!\n");
        exit(1);
    }
    jc.newplan(p);
}
```

The specification of the planner process is:

```
                                                                    cc/plan.h

process spec planner()
{
    trans plan move(point initial, point final, float t);
};
```

The body of the planner process is:

```
                                                          cc/plan.cc

#include "robot.h"
process body planner()
{
    float limit1, limit2;
    plan p;
        accept move(initial, final, t) {
            split(localtime(), t, &limit1, &limit2);
            within deadline (limit1)
                efficient_plan_alg(initial, final, &p);
            else within deadline (limit2)
                plan_alg(initial, final, &p);
            else {
                p.n = 0;
            }
            treturn p;
        }
}
```

The planner first accepts the *move* command. It has two different types of planning algorithms built into it. The first develops an "efficient plan" but takes longer. The second produces a less efficient plan but takes less time for planning. The planner works as follows. It divides the interval between the current time and t into three subintervals. The last subinterval is earmarked for the robot to carry out the actual move. The planner uses the efficient algorithm to plan the move within the first subinterval. If the planning activity does not complete within the specified time, it uses the second algorithm to produce a less efficient plan. The length of the second interval is chosen such that the second algorithm is highly likely to come up with such a plan within this interval. In the event that the planner fails again, it informs the operator and terminates. If it succeeds, it sends the plan to the operator.

The plan consists of a sequence of $(n + 1)$ joint angle and end time pairs (j_i, t_i). Value t_0 specifies the motion start time and j_0 the current joint angle. The robot arm should be at angle j_i by time t_i ($1 <= i <= n$).

The specification of the joint_controller process is:

```
                                                        cc/joint.h

process spec joint_controller(process motor_controller mc)
{
    trans async newplan(plan p1);
};
```

The body of the `joint_controller` process is:

```
                                                        cc/joint.cc

#include "robot.h"
process body joint_controller(mc)
{
    plan p;
    velocity v; int i;

        select {
            accept newplan(p1)
                p = p1;
            for (i=0; i<p.n; i++) {
                within deadline
                        (p.pos[i+1].time - p.pos[i].time - trans_delay) {
                    v = find_velocity(p.pos[i].time, p.pos[i].angle,
                                        p.pos[i+1].time, p.pos[i+1].angle);
                    mc.newvelocity(v, p.pos[i].time);
                }
                else {
                    fprintf(stderr,
                    "insufficient time to compute velocity and move!\n");
                    mc.halt();
                }
            }
        }
}
```

277

The joint controller handles one plan element at a time. For each j_i ($1 <= i <= n$), it computes a motor velocity such that given that the joint is at j_{i-1} at t_{i-1}, with the new motor velocity, joint angle j_i will be reached at t_i.

Specifically, given ($0 <= i <= n - 1$), within time (t_i-*trans-delay*), the joint controller computes the motor velocity v_i required to achieve j_{i+1} and sends it to the motor controller. t_i, the time when v_i becomes effective, is also sent to the motor controller. *trans-delay* is the maximum time it takes the joint controller to transmit the velocity to the motor controller.

The specification of the motor_controller process is:

```
                                                          cc/motor.h


process spec motor_controller()
{
    trans async newvelocity(velocity v, float t);
    trans async halt();
};
```

The body of the motor_controller process is:

```
                                                    ┌──────────────┐
                                                    │  cc/motor.cc │
                                                    └──────────────┘

#include "robot.h"
process body motor_controller()
{
    process motor_controller me = c_mypid();
    velocity v, vnext, vin;
    float t, tnext, tin;
    int new_vel_available = 0;

    v.xvel = v.yvel = t = new_vel_available = 0;
    c_associate(me.halt, 50);  /* interrupt address = 50 */

    guarantee
            every (MSCP) until accept halt() break; {
                select {
                    (current_time() >= t && new_vel_available==0):
                        accept newvelocity(vin, tin) {
                                vnext = vin;
                                tnext = tin;
                            }
                        new_vel_available = 1;
                    or
                        ;
                }
                if (current_time() >= t && new_vel_available) {
                    t = tnext; v = vnext;
                    new_vel_available = 0;
                }
                  move arm according to v;
            }
            else ;
    else
        fprintf(stderr, "motor controller guarantee not possible!\n");
}
```

The motor controller executes a periodic activity with period MSCP until told to halt.
The period is determined by the servo control algorithms used by the motor controller.
It should be a priori guaranteed that this period can be sustained by the system. In our
case, such a guarantee will be obtained when the motor controller begins execution. If
a guarantee is not possible, the motor controller notifies the operator and halts.

Suppose the motor controller is taking the arm to point $i + 1$, i.e., the current motor velocity is v_i and this will remain in effect from t_i until t_{i+1}. At the beginning of the next period, if v_{i+1} has not yet been received, the motor controller checks if velocity v_{i+1} is available and accepts it if it is. This becomes the motor velcoty at t_{i+1}.

The robot example shows how Real-Time Concurrent C facilities such as deadlines and periods can be specified, and how guarantees are requested. It also shows how different versions of an algorithm can be tried depending on the time available to solve a problem.

6. Implementing Real-Time Concurrent C

A prototype implementation of Real-Time Concurrent C is nearing completion. This implementation is based on a Concurrent C complier and run-time support system. This section describes some of the salient aspects of these extensions along the following three dimensions (Pedregal-Martin, forthcoming).

1. Scheduling support for time-constrained activities.
2. Determining worst-case execution time for guaranteed time-constrained activities.
3. Implementing the real-time constructs.

Before discussing these three issues, we would like to note that the run-time system of the existing Concurrent C implementation time-slices the execution of the Concurrent C processes for fairness. This is achieved by doing a context switch when interrupted by the timer. Context switching can also occur at process interaction points.[3]

6.1. Scheduling support for time-constrained activities

A single scheduling algorithm that handles periodic and aperiodic activities, guaranteed or otherwise, will be complex. We therefore use different scheduling algorithms for the different activities. In case of multiprocessor systems, a subset of the processors is allocated for periodic (guaranteed or otherwise) activities and a different subset for aperiodic (guaranteed or otherwise) activities. In case of a single processor system, the target of our current implementation, a *processor sharing* model is implemented. That is, time is partitioned into slots. A fixed part of each slot is dedicated for executing periodic activities and the rest of the slot for aperiodic activities. The percentage of each slot earmarked for each category will depend on the mix of periodic and aperiodic activities in the system. The length of the slot and the percentage allocated for each category can be fixed or changed by a system call. While this call is most likely to be made when a Real-Time Concurrent C program begins execution, under certain circumstances (not to be detailed here), the call can be made as the program executes. Timers are set to ensure the switch from the execution of periodic activities to aperiodic activities and vice versa.

A (a)periodic activity is guaranteed by allocating certain specific time intervals for the activity in the (a)periodic portion of the slots. Barring processor failure, these guarantees are absolute. Thus, a time-constrained activity without guarantees should be executed only if it does not jeopardize existing guarantees. In a simlar vein, it is more important to execute a time-constrained activity than executing one without timing constraints. Thus, within the portion of a slot earmarked for periodic activities, time for guaranteed periodic activities is allocated; in the remaining time within this portion, nonguaranteed periodic activities can be executed; if further time remains, activities without any time-constraints can be executed. A similar strategy applies to the portion of a slot earmarked for aperiodic activities.

Given this scheme, the Real-Time Concurrent C scheduler incorporates five separate algorithms:

1. An algorithm for guaranteeing deadline-constrained activities.
2. An algorithm for guaranteeing periodicity-constrained activities.
3. An algorithm for executing nonguaranteed activites with deadlines.
4. An algorithm for executing nonguaranteed activities with periodicity requirements.
5. An algorithm for executing activities without constraints.

Guaranteeing aperiodic activities. A schedule ordered according to the deadlines is maintained for guaranteed aperiodic activities. As mentioned earlier, the time intervals assigned to the aperiodic activities fall within the portions earmarked for aperiodic activities. When a new aperiodic activity that requires a guarantee arrives, it is inserted into this schedule as per its deadline. If this new activity will cause one or more existing guaranteed activities to miss their deadlines, then this activity is not guaranteed and is removed from the schedule. Note that it may be necessary to preempt the execution of a guaranteed activity and resume it in the following slot. The guarantee algorithm handles such situations and also accounts for the preemption overheads. Other considerations underlying the guarantee are detailed in Section 6.2.

Guaranteeing periodic activities. A template of length equal to the least common multiple (LCM) of the guaranteed periodic tasks, is maintained. It is formed by ordering (LCM/period) instances of each of the periodic activities according to their deadlines (which are derived from the periods). This template has information about the time intervals allocated for periodic activities. As mentioned earlier, these time intervals fall within the portions earmarked for periodic activities. A new periodic activity is guaranteed provided a new template can be constructed with the previous guaranteed periodic activities and the new one. Instances of periodic activities are dispatched based on information in this table.

Executing nonguaranteed aperiodic activities. Aperiodic activities that are not guaranteed are maintained in a queue, earliest-deadline-first. Within the portion earmarked for aperiodic activities, if no guaranteed activity is slated to execute or if the slated activity has already completed (perhaps earlier than expected given that execution times are based on worst-case assumptions) then the activity in front of this queue is executed. Its execution continues until it completes, until its deadline arrives, or until the end of the portion, whichever comes first.

Executing periodic activities that do not require guarantees. Instances of ready periodic activities that are not guaranteed are placed in another queue, also earliest-deadline-first.

In a time interval earmarked for periodic activities, if no guaranteed activity is slated to execute, then the first entry in this queue is dispatched. It will execute until the portion expires, until a guaranteed periodic activity has to execute, until the activity completes, or until the end of the period, whichever comes first.

Executing activities without timing constraints. If no activities with time-constraints are eligible to execute, the program's execution will be as though it were a Concurrent C program.

The above implementation applies to the most general Real-Time Concurrent C program, one which has guaranteed as well as nonguaranteed periodic and nonperiodic activities. If only some of these combinations exist, the implementation can be optimized. Let us consider a case that we expect to encounter quite often, namely, one where activities require no guarantees. In this case, all that is required is a single queue of ready periodic and aperiodic activities ordered according to the earliest-deadline-first scheme. Whenever the processor is idle, it executes the first activity, if one exists, in front of this queue; otherwise it executes a non time-constrained activity.

Note that a deadline may be explicitly imposed on the guarantee. Even otherwise, the deadline of the guaranteed activity imposes an implicit deadline on the guarantee. In other words, the guarantee itself is a nonguaranteed aperiodic activity and hence will be dealt with like any other nonguaranteed aperiodic activity. This implies that all guarantees occur under timing constraints and further, the overheads of guarantees will not jeopardize guaranteed activities.

Our final remark concerns the detection of timing errors. An activity that is not guaranteed must be terminated[4] if its deadline expires before it completes execution. To achieve this, the run-time system ensures, before beginning (or resuming) a nonguaranteed time-constrained activity that its deadline has not expired. In addition, in case no other timer is set to occur before the deadline, a timer is set. If the activity is in progress when the timer interrupt occurs, the activity is terminated; the e l se clause associated with the activity, if any, is executed next.

6.2. Determining the execution time of a code segment

Code whose execution is to be guaranteed should have a bounded execution time. The guaranteed algorithm utilizes this bound to decide whether or not the activity can be guaranteed. Note that execution times will invariably depend on processor speeds. Determining execution time of a code segment has been the subject of ongoing research (Puschner and Koza 1989; Mok 1989; Shaw 1990). While the tools described in (Mok 1989) and (Puschner and Koza 1989) work with object code segments, (Shaw 1990) is aimed at source code segments. They all handle code with (bounded) loops and conditionals for programs written in (a subset of) C-like languages.

The tool used by our implementation is based on the one described in (Lavoie 1991) which itself is based on (Mok 1989). (Lavoie 1991) determines worst-case execution times for C code executing on 68020 processors. The code can have loops, with user-specified loop bounds. Recursion is disallowed.

In the context of the execution model assumed here, the cost of preemptions (to switch from executing periodic to aperiodic activities and vice versa) must be accounted for. Also, since a guaranteed activity can make system calls or calls to library routines, it is important to design the system calls to have bounded execution times. In addition, since some calls, such as malloc, return condition codes that reflect success or failure of the call, it is important for the calling process to check the returned condition codes and act accordingly. Otherwise, incorrect program executions are highly likely, just as in nonreal-time systems. It is our assumption that even if a process makes a dynamic request for a resource, such as memory, the system responds to the request within a bounded amount of time. The process should be designed to react to a negative outcome. In other words, no unbounded blocking occurs for resources.

Not all requests for dynamic memory allocations are visible to a process. For instance, storage allocation done when a function/procedure call is made, or when an asynchronous transaction call is made may fail. Here we are assuming that given the abundance of memory, such failures do not occur. A more appropriate alternative is to determine the worst-case resource requirements of an activity and guarantee a task only if the required resources are available (Ramamritham, Stankovic and Shiah 1990).

Concurrent C introduces the following additional demands. In addition to sequential (C or C++) code, Concurrent C involves the use of transaction calls and the select statement. As was mentioned earlier, the time for executing an asynchronous transaction call is the time needed to "post" a transaction which can be determined a priori. Only timed synchronous transaction calls are allowed within guaranteed activities and so the worst-case delays on their completion are known. Similarly, an accept used as an alternative of a select statement with at least one delay alternative or an *immediate* alternative with a true guard has a known worst-case execution time. The worst-case execution time of the select statement is the smallest of the execution times of the delay or *immediate* alternatives with guards that are true. Such select statements, are *acceptable* as activities to be guaranteed.

Thus two Concurrent C constructs that are disallowed within an activity to be guaranteed are:

- A synchronous transaction call without a timeout.
- A select statement without a delay or *immediate* alternative with true guards.

select statements that utilize the by and suchthat clauses are more complicated to analyze since they examine the parameters of the waiting calls. Allowing their use within Real-Time Concurrent C forms part of our future work.

One final issue is related to *when* execution time bounds should be determined. If they are determined at compile time, the run-time guarantee overheads can be reduced substantially. On the other hand, the bounds are likely to be quite pessimistic since they will be based on the absolute worst-case scenario. Run-time determination may increase guarantee overheads to such an extent that guarantee requests with deadlines will invariably fail; on the other hand, the bounds will not be as pessimistic.

A *via media* is to express execution times as functions of the variables of individual activities. These functions can be determined at compile time; the functions can be evaluated at run-time knowing the values of the variables.

Such an approach is needed if the full power of Concurrent C is to be employed, for example, if pointer and function variables are to be used. Clearly, we can allow these features within code that requires guarantees only as long as it is still possible to derive worst-case bounds for computation times. Whereas this requires further study, it can be said that a certain amount of dynamics can still be captured if what we need is not a statically determined absolute computation time but a function that encodes the computation time.

Given the simplicity of compile-time determination of bounds, our prototype adopts this approach. We envisage subsequent extensions to incorporate more dynamic variations.

6.3. Implementing Real-Time Concurrent C facilities

Interface between a Real-Time Concurrent C process and the run-time system occurs, basically, via three calls:

declare-request. This function is called at the beginning of a time-constrained activity to provide the run-time system with the information needed to schedule the (timed) activity. The run-time system records the information and attempts to schedule the activity. If it is impossible to schedule, the process is informed so that it can take alternative actions.

A *guaranteed aperiodic* activity is declared providing its *worst-case execution time* and its *deadline*. A *guaranteed periodic* activity is delcared by giving the *worst-case execution time* and its *period*. In both these cases, the guarantee routine is involked in turn to construct a schedule, if possible.

A *nonguaranteed aperiodic* activity is declared by providing its *deadline*. A *nonguaranteed periodic* activity is declared by supplying its *period*.

wait-start. If the decl call is successful, this call is made and it returns when the scheduler deems that it is time for the actual activity to start.

Note that in the *periodic* cases, wait-start is called for each instance of the activity.

complete. This function is called to notify the run-time system that the activity has completed successfully. The run-time system turns off any timers asociated with this activity,[5] records that it has completed normally (i.e., the else alternative will not be taken), for guaranteed activities, frees the activity's remaining time in the schedule for other activities.

We now turn to express the Real-Time Concurrent C facilities in terms of the primitives just described.

6.3.1. Implementing the within deadline *statement.* The declare-request only involves the run-time system taking note of the deadline, and it can be combined with the wait-start. The combined call wd_decl_wait(d) informs the run-time system of the deadline, and suspends the process until its turn in the schedule comes up. (The prefix wd identifies that the primitive is used to implement the within deadline statement. A similar convention is used later also.) It may return at or after the deadline with a false value if there is no chance to start the activity before then. A return with true means that the activity can *start*. In this case, before returning, the run-time system sets the timer to go off at the activity's deadline.

Termination of the activity and execution of the else clause is realized using UNIX system setjmp/longjmp primitives: when the timer interrupt (corresponding the activity's deadline) occurs, the run-time system terminates the activity and returns control to the starting point of the activity (remembered via setjmp).[6] This, in turn, transfers control to *statement*$_2$. Since the abortion of the ongoing activity followed by the transfer of control takes some (known) time, the timer interrupt is set to occur ahead of the deadline so as to complete the transfer of control by the deadline.

Thus, the within deadline statement is translated into the following:

```
if (wd_decl_wait(d) && !setjmp(env)) {
    statement₁; cmplt() }
[else statement₂]
```

(We are assuming that terms within a condition are evaluated left to right.)

6.3.2. Implementing the every statement.
The every statement is realized by first invoking e_decl to inform the run-time system about the period. Subsequently, e_wait is invoked, before each instance of the loop, which suspends the activity until it is resumed by the run-time system.

We show how to implement the every construct for the until *expression* case. The until accept_statement case is similar.

```
e_decl (p);
if (!setjmp(env)) {
    while (e_wait() && !expression)
        statement₁
    cmplt();
}
[else statement₂]
```

If an instance is not executed within its corresponding period, the scheduler issues a longjmp which causes the loop to be ignored and the alternative statement to be executed.

6.3.3. Implementing the guarantee within deadline statement.
We will first consider the case in which *no* deadlines are imposed on the guarantee.

From the viewpoint of code generation, the *guaranteed aperiodic* activity is the simplest construct to translate. In this case the first two actions are combined. gwd_decl_wait takes as arguments the worst-case execution time of the activity and the deadline for the activity, and returns false if the activity cannot be guaranteed. If the activity is guaranteed, the process *is suspended on this call*, and gwd_decl_wait returns true when the process can proceed with the execution of the activity.

285

```
if (gwd_decl_wait(wcxt(p_statement_1), d))
    statement_1; cmplt()
[else statement_2]
```

where $p_{statement_1}$ points to *statement₁* and wcxt returns the worst-case execution time for the specified code segment. The time required to execute cmplt should be included in the worst-case execution time that is guaranteed; otherwise, guaranteed activities that are scheduled to execute subsequently will be jeopardized.

Recall that, in the situation just considered, since no deadlines are imposed on the guarantee, the guarantee itself can be carried out without time constraints, i.e., as an untimed activity. However, d-$p_{statement_1}$ is the implicit deadline on the guarantee. We return to guarantees with time constraints at the end of this section.

6.3.4. Implementing the guarantee every *statement*.
The declare-request function call for giving a guarantee is perhaps the most expensive since it entails building a template.

Function ge_decl takes as arguments the worst-case execution time for the loop body and the period of the activity. It returns true if the run-time system is able to guarantee the activity, false otherwise. If successful, this call is immediately followed by ge_wait which suspends the process until it is awakened by the run-time system when it is time for it to execute an instance of the activity. It is invoked before every cycle of the every loop.

```
if (ge_decl(wcxt(p_statement_1), p)) {
    while (ge_wait() && !expression)
        statement_1;
    cmplt(); }
[else statement_2]
```

For textual clarity, the worst-case execution time of *expression* was omitted. It should be added in the call to wcxt.

Finally, let us consider the situation where a deadline is imposed on the guarantee. Note that within deadline *gd* guarantee ... combines already known constructs. However, there are some details to keep in mind. In the other (nonguaranteed) time constrained statements, when a deadline is not met, the system just aborts the user code and, if provided, transfers control to the process in such a way that the else clause is executed when the process is scheduled next. In the case we are considering now, the code that is to complete before the deadline is *run-time system* code. It cannot be aborted on timeout in the same way user code would be, because granting a guarantee involves manipulating run-time data structures whose consistency would be compromised by a "dirty" termination. So, rather than directly manipulating the relevant data structure, the current version of the data structure is retained, to be returned to in case the run-time receives a timer interrupt signaling a missed deadline on the task of getting guarantee. It is important to reiterate that the guarantee itself is done during time that lies in the portion earmarked for aperiodic activities and only if no guaranteed activities are eligible to execute during that time. Thus, the time overheads of guarantees do not conflict with guaranteed activities themselves.

7. Conclusions

Real-Time Concurrent C, an extension to Concurrent C was motivated by a desire to provide facilities in Concurrent C to express real-time considerations explicitly. The facilities that have been added to Concurrent C allow a programmer to specify deadline and periodicity constraints associated with code segments. One of the novel aspects of Real-Time Concurrent C is the incorporation of *guarantee* as a language concept. In particular, it allows a process to obtain a commitment from the system that a certain activity will be completed on time. When such a commitment is not available, it provides more leeway for the process to take alternative actions.

While many languages have also been purportedly designed with real-time systems in mind (e.g., Ada (Baker 1990), see also (Burns and Wellings 1989) and (Halang and Stoyenko 1990) for surveys), few have the requisite features to program predictable real-time systems. Among recent work, the work on Real-Time Euclid (Klingerman and Stoyenko 1986) had concerns similar to ours. However, its features were designed to support *static* real-time systems, specifically, those that required static guarantees of specified timing properties. Even in cases where a language has been designed explicitly for dynamic real-time systems (e.g., Lee and Gehlot 1985)), they lack the general-purpose facilities required to make them serious candidates. Other real-time language definitions have also appeared in the literature, for instance, RTC++ (Ishikawa, Tokuda and Mercer 1990) and Real-Time Mentat (Grimshaw, Silberman and Liu 1990), both of which are language extensions to C++. Whereas processes are the active entities in Real-Time Concurrent C, in both of these, the active entities are objects. We have not only defined Real-Time Concurrent C, a language for programming dynamic predictable real-time systems, but are about to complete a prototype implementation. This has given us confidence about the viability of the constructs that have been designed to express real-time constraints.

In designing Real-Time Concurrent C, several compromises were made and decisions taken in order to meet the needs of compatibility with Concurrent C, simplicity of semantics, and ease of implementation. Only by programming nontrivial real-time systems will the adequacy and expressiveness of the new constructs become clear. Further, a number of issues still have to be addressed in order to implement the necessary run-time support for Real-Time Concurrent C. These include

- More flexible and efficient tools to determine computation times of code whose timing constraints have to be guaranteed. Work on these tools will suggest those aspects of the language that must be avoided in order to compute worst-case execution times.
- Techniques for providing guarantees in the context of synchronous transaction calls. Here again, since such guarantees cannot be provided in general, canonical structures for programming server processes are needed, such that the calls that they serve can be guaranteed.

Also, note that the guarantee statement in Real-Time Concurrent C, is designed to support dynamic guarantees where each activity is an independent piece of code local to a process. When guarantees are sought, say for an activity that involves multiple (communicating) processes, the above language constructs need to be extended. Specifically, such processes have to be identified as a process group which has to be guaranteed as a whole. While the language extensions required are quite straightforward, the necessary algorithms to map the processes into schedulable tasks and the required system support are not. This is part of ongoing work (Niehaus 1991).

Acknowledgments

Our thanks to Cristobal Pedregal-Martin for implementing the prototype and to Jack Stankovic, Lory Molesky, Ed Ferguson, and Amar Diwan for comments on previous versions of this paper.

Notes

1. We would like to point out that the every statement can be functionally implemented using the Concurrent C select statement and without using the until clause. For instance, an every statement with the until *expression* clause can be realized as follows:

```
every (p)
      select {
      (expression):
            break;
      or
            statement₂
      }
[else statement₃]
```

We preferred to add an until clause to the every statement instead of advocating use of the above simulation because the until clause reflects typical use of the every statement and because it facilitates determination of upper bounds on execution time.
2. This implies that no specific start time constraints are imposed by the above statement. We return to this issue in Section 4.5.2.
3. Even though Concurrent C implementations that execute on bare machines exist, for expediency, we have built the current Real-Time Concurrent C on top of UNIX™-based implementation of Concurrent C in which a Concurrent C program runs as a single UNIX process. Within this single process, the Concurrent C scheduler schedules the Concurrent C processes that form the concurrent program. Thus, assuming that the Concurrent C program is the only one running, and ignoring the effects of any background UNIX-specific processes, the effect is one of several concurrent C processes sharing a single processor.
4. Without "rolling-back," i.e., whatever effects the unfinished activity had, must be explicitly nullified by the process (e.g., in the else clause).
5. To avoid terminating the activity incorrectly on timeout.
6. More specifically, UNIX system provides a pair of system calls, setjmp(3C) and longjmp(3C) to deal with errors enountered at a low level. setjmp(*env*) stores the environment at its place of invocation, and returns a zero (on its first invocation). longjmp(*env, val*) causes a pseudo return, so that execution resumes where setjmp was called (with the environment restored), with setjmp returning a nonzero value *val*.

References

Baker, T. 1990. The Use of Ada for Real-Time Systems. *Real-Time Systems Newletter* 6, 1: 3–8.

Burns, A. and Wellings, A. 1989. *Real-Time Systems and their Programming Languages*. Reading, MA: Addison-Wesley.

Gehani, N.H. and Roome, W.D. 1986. Concurrent C. *Software—Practice & Experience*, 16, 9: 821–844.

Gehani, N.H. and Roome, W.D. 1989. *Concurrent C*. Summit, NJ: Silicon Press.

Cmelik, R.G., Gehani, N.H., and Roome, W.D. 1988. Fault Tolerant Concurrent C: A Tool for Writing Fault Tolerant Distributed Programs. *The 18th International Symposium on Fault-Tolerant Computing*, Tokyo, Japan, pp. 56–61.

Grimshaw, A.S., Silberman, A., and Liu, J.W.S. 1990. Real-Time Mentat Programming Language and Architecture. *Seventh Workshop on Real-Time Operating Systems and Software*, pp. 82–87.

Halang, W.A. and Stoyenko, A.D. 1990. Comparative Evaluation of High-Level Real-Time Programming Languages. *Real-Time Systems* 2, 4: 365–382.

Ishikawa, Y., Tokuda, H. and Mercer, C.W. 1990. Object-Oriented Real-Time Language Design: Constructs for Timing Constraints. *Proceedings of OOPSLA/ECOOP 90*, pp. 289–298.

Klingerman and Stoyenko. 1986. Real-Time Euclid: A Language for Reliable Real-Time Systems. *IEEE Transaction on Software Engineering* 12, 9: 941–949.

Lavoie, P. 1991. A Tool to Analyze Timing on a 68020 Processor. Master's Project Report, Department of Computer Science, University of Massachusetts, Amherst.

Lee, I. and Gehlot, V. 1985. Language Constructs for Distributed Real-Time Programming Systems. *Real-Time Systems Symposium*.

Lehoczky, J.P., Sha, L. and Strosnider, J. 1987. Enhancing Aperiodic Responsiveness in a Hard Real-Time Environment. *IEEE Real-Time Systems Symp.*

Liu, C.L. and Layland, J. 1973. Scheduling Algorithms for Multiprogramming in a Hard Real-Time Environment. *J. ACM* 20, 1.

Marlin, C., Zhao, W., Doherty, G. and Bohonis, A. 1990. GARTL: A Real-Time Programming Language Based on Multi-Version Computation. *Proc. International Conference On Computer Languages*, pp. 107–115.

Pedregal-Martin, C. (forthcoming). *A Real-Time Concurrent C Prototype*, Master's Project Report, Department of Computer Science, University of Massachusetts, Amherst.

Puschner, P. and Koza, Ch. 1989. Calculating Maximum Execution Time of Real-Time Programs. *The Journal of Real-Time Systems*, pp. 159–176.

Mok, A. 1989. Evaluating Tight Execution Time Bounds of Programs by Annotations. Proc. IEEE Workshop on Real-Time Operating Systems and Software, pp. 74–80.

Ramamritham, K., Stankovic, J. and Shiah, P. 1990. Efficient Scheduling Algorithms for Real-Time Multiprocessor Systems. *IEEE Transactions on Parallel and Distributed Systems*, pp. 184–194.

Sha, L., Rajkumar, R. and Lehoczky, J.P. 1990. Priority Inheritance Protocols: An Approach to Real-Time Synchronization. *IEEE Transactions on Computers*.

Shaw, A. 1990. Deterministic Timing Schema for Parallel Programs. Technical Report #90-05-06, Department of Computer Science, University of Washington.

Stankovic, J.A. and Ramamritham, K. 1991. The Spring Kernel: A New Paradigm for Real-Time Systems. *IEEE Software*, pp. 62–72.

Object-Oriented Real-Time Language Design:
Constructs for Timing Constraints

Yutaka Ishikawa†, Hideyuki Tokuda‡, Clifford W. Mercer‡

†Electrotechnical Laboratory
1-1-4 Umezono, Tsukuba,
Ibaraki, 305, JAPAN

‡Carnegie Mellon University
Pittsburgh, PA 15213 USA
yisikawa@etl.go.jp, hxt@cs.cmu.edu, cwm@cs.cmu.edu

Abstract

We propose a new object-oriented programming language called RTC++ for programming real-time applications. RTC++ is an extension of C++ and its features are to specify i) a real-time object which is an active entity, ii) timing constraints in an operation as well as in statements, and iii) a periodic task with rigid timing constraints.

In this paper, we first discuss real-time programming issues and what language support should be provided for building real-time applications. Then, the key features of RTC++ are described. Some programming examples are shown to demonstrate RTC++'s expressive power. A comparison to other programming languages are also discussed.

1   Introduction

Real-time computer systems play a very important role in our society. They are used in multimedia systems, robotics, factory automation, telecommunication systems, and in air traffic control systems. The object-oriented concept and programming languages make it easier to design and develop such complex real-time application programs. However, unlike non real-time programs, real-time programs must satisfy the *timing* correctness as well as *logical* correctness. Satisfying the timing correctness of a real-time program is difficult because of the lack of explicit specification of the timing constraints in a program and the lack of schedulability analysis techniques.

For example, a real-time task must start at a specified time and complete its activity by its deadline. However, in a conventional real-time program, such timing constraints are not explicitly described in its program, rather described in a separate timing chart or document. Thus, it is very difficult to enforce timing constraints or detect timing errors during compile time or/and runtime. Although the data encapsulation in object-oriented programming languages will help us to confine *logical errors* in a program, *timing errors* often penetrate the module boundary.

The schedulability analysis of a real-time program is also a difficult problem. By the schedulability analysis, we mean that a program designer should be able to analyze or predict whether the given real-time tasks having various types of system and task interactions (e.g., memory allocation/deallocation, message communications, I/O interactions, etc) can meet their timing constraints. For instance, if real-time tasks are interacting via shared resources, prediction of the worst case blocking time is difficult due to a possibility of having unbounded blocking delay.

In order to eliminate such unbounded blocking delay, a real-time system must avoid *priority inversion* problems. A priority inversion problem occurs when a higher task must wait indefinitely for a lower priority task to execute. For example, priority inversion may occur in task scheduling: when a task attempts to get a shared resource, it is blocked if another task is keeping the resource. If the task keeping the resource has a lower priority and a middle priority task can run under priority-based preemptive scheduling, then the blocked task has to wait for unbounded time. Thus, the system cannot guarantee to satisfy rigid timing constraints when priority inversion occurs.

We have designed and implemented a real-time distributed operating system kernel called the ARTS kernel and programming languages ARTS/C and ARTS/C++ both of which are running on the kernel[11]. The ARTS kernel provides primitives of remote object invocation with timing constraints, methods for specifying periodic execution, and mechanisms for avoiding priority inversion. ARTS/C and ARTS/C++ are an extension of C and C++ respectively. Those have a capability of defining a special object called a *real-time object*. A real-time object has a set of operation with timing constraints and threads each of which is an execution unit. Languages do not have linguistic support for avoiding priority inversion but they can call kernel primitives for that purpose.

Our experiment with those languages leads to design more suitable object-oriented programming language which copes with real-time issues easily and efficiently. What capabilities we need in a real-time language are: i) expressions for timing constraints for statement level in addition to operation timing constraints, ii) linguistic support for avoiding priority inversion problem, and iii) an inheritance mechanism in a real-time object.

In this paper, first we discuss real-time programming issues and describe what language supports are required. Then, a new object-oriented programming language called RTC++ is proposed in section 3. In section 4, some programming examples are shown in order to demonstrate the RTC++ programming power. In section 5, we compare RTC++ with other object-oriented programming languages and real-time programming languages.

2   Real-Time Programming Issues

2.1   Timing Specification

Both ARTS/C and ARTS/C++ allow us to specify timing constraints of each operation in a real-time object. The objective of this support is as follows[11]: In traditional real-time systems which use a cyclic executive, a timing error often penetrates the task or module boundary, so that it is very difficult to capture the error at run-time. By using the timing specification, we can bound the timing error at run-time as well as compile-time.

Furthermore, we need to specify timing constraints for statement by statement in order to control execution depending on an external behavior. That is, when a part of statements (or transaction) in an operation cannot finish within the specified time, the current execution (or transaction) is aborted and then alternative statements are executed in order to satisfy timing constraint of the operation.

Another construct we need is the capability of describing a periodic task. Such capability is often realized as the duration of the waiting time by a language or an operating system. However, this leads to the unbounded waiting time. For example, the following program written in Ada is considered:

```
1    loop
2         -- ... body of cyclic activity ...
3         dtime := nexttime - currenttime;
4         delay dtime;
5    end loop
```

In this example, because the execution of the statement at line 3 is not an atomic action the `dtime` variable may have wrong value. That is, if the execution of the program is suspended after the `currenttime` is evaluated and then the execution is resumed later, the `dtime` is calculated with the wrong value of `currenttime`. So the program might sleep for wrong time at the `delay` statement.

2.2   Priority Inversion Problem

Using object-oriented paradigm, the client-server model is suitable in a distributed application. This model introduces a priority inversion problem in a real-time application. For example, suppose that there are server S and clients A and B where A's priority is higher than B's one. Suppose that when the client A sends a message to the server S, the server is performing for a request of the client B. In that case the request of client A is postponed until the server's execution for client B is finished. Because A's priority is higher than B's one but processing for B is prior to A, we call this phenomena *priority inversion* in the server. In order to avoid the priority inversion in a server, three methods can be considered: i) *preemption*, ii) *abort*, and iii) *priority inheritance*.

In the preemption method, the server's execution is preempted at the request of client A. Then, the server turns to perform for client A. After finishing the service for client A the service for client B is resumed.

In the abort method, the server's execution is aborted at the request of client A and then the server turns to perform for client A. At the abort of the execution the server must be responsible for maintaining the consistency. The principle of the recovery scheme in ARTS appeared in [9].

If the server's execution cannot be preempted and the cost of the abort procedure is too high compared with waiting for finishing the current server's execution, waiting is the best method.

However, this is not true when the server is running with other tasks. Suppose that the server's priority depends on the client's priority [1] and there is another task C whose priority is lower than the client A's priority but higher than the client B's priority. In this assumption, when C is ready to run, C begins to run while the server S performing for B is suspended. Thus, priority inversion occurs.

---

[1] This assumption is reasonable since the server has to serve for many clients whose priorities are different.

To avoid such priority inversion, we use the notion of priority inheritance [8] to propagate priority. That is, if a task provides a service on behalf of a client, the server should inherit the priority of the client. Furthermore, the server should inherit the priority of the highest priority task which is waiting for the service. Also, it is important to use priority queue instead of FIFO queue for a message queue.

If we apply the priority inheritance mechanism to the above example, the server S's priority is changed to client A's priority at the request from A. Thus, C could not run even when it becomes ready to run.

2.3 Single vs Multiple Threaded Object Model

Most object-oriented concurrent programming languages such as Actor[1], ABCL/1[14], ConcurrentSmalltalk[13], and Orient84/K[4] provide an object with a single thread model [2]. The idea of an object-oriented concurrent language is that an object is a sequential execution entity and concurrency is expressed by means of various message passing forms such as synchronous and asynchronous communication. The concept of sequential objects and message passing allows us to reduce programming complexity in a parallel application. Let us call this model the single threaded object model.

As described in the previous subsection, a highly preemptable server is required in a real-time application. The mechanism we need is that if a request message is coming at a server from a client during the server's execution for a lower priority's client, the server's execution is preempted or aborted and then performs for the higher priority's client. However, if the lower priority's client requests a service to the server, the request should be enqueued.

In object-oriented concurrent languages such a server can be implemented as follows. A server object consists of a root object and a set of objects each of which is responsible for one of the server's operation with a priority. Objects have to share the server's internal data so that each object can access the same data. For example, if two operations are defined in a server and the number of possible different priorities is three, then three objects each of which has a different priority are responsible for an operation and other three objects are responsible for the other operation. When a client sends a request message to the root object, the root object forwards the message to an object according to the client's request and priority.

Another approach to describing a preemptable server is that the server is implemented based on the multiple threaded object model. In the multiple threaded object model, there are some threads of control in an object so

---

[2] Actor and ABCL/1 support a reentrant object if the object has no internal data.

that a thread is invoked at the new client request whose priority is higher than the current client's priority. Because the object has multiple threads, the concurrency control has to be employed.

Conceptually the single threaded model and multiple threaded model have the same capability. So we have to consider the implementation of those models. The implementation of a highly preemptable server in the single threaded model needs more resources than one in the multiple threaded model because there are so many objects required. Moreover, if the internal data is primitive data such as integer or character, the compiler can generate an optimum code in the multiple threaded model while message passing forms are always needed in the single threaded model.

Based on the above observation, we choose the multiple threaded model to describe a real-time application. In the multiple threaded model, no restrictions on dynamically creating threads in an object may lead to increasing the complexity of concurrency control. Thus, the restriction we choose is that each operation may be executed concurrently but an operation has to be executed by one thread at a time. Moreover, the execution may be preempted to realize a highly preemptable server.

3 RTC++

In this section, we propose an object-oriented real-time language called RTC++ which is an extension of C++. RTC++ is designed based on the previous discussion. The syntax and semantics are described with examples.

3.1 Real-Time Object

In addition to C++ objects, RTC++ introduces an active object. If an active object is defined with timing constraints, it is called a real-time object. In the following example, the active class **Example1** is defined.

```
active class Example1 {
private:
    char    buf[BUF_SIZE];
    int     count;
    int     background();
public:
    int     read(char* data, int size) when(count > siz
    int     write(char* data, int size);
    int     open();
    int     close();
activity:
    slave[5]    read(char*, int);
    slave[5]    write(char*, int);
    slave       open(), close();
    master      background() cycle(;;0t30m;);
}
```

An active object definition is almost the same as an original C++ object definition except for adding the keyword **active** before the **class** keyword in RTC++. An active object has a single thread of control in default. A user can specify multiple threads of control which we call *member threads* in an active object. Member threads are defined in an *activity part* of a class definition. There are two types of member threads, *slave* and *master*.

A *slave thread* is an execution unit related to a member function or a group of member functions [3] . In the following definition, one slave thread is only responsible for the **open** and **close** requests.

```
slave                open(), close();
```

A slave thread inherits the priority from a sender. If there are some waiting messages, the priority of the slave thread is set to the highest priority of those messages. When a new message for those functions is comming and the sender's priority is higher than the current thread's priority, the thread's priority is changed to the higher priority. This mechanism is called the *priority inheritance mechanism in an object*.

In the following definition, the processing of the member function **read** can be preempted by up to five clients whose priorities are higher than the current execution of the **read** function. We call ``**slave[5]**'' a slave thread group.

```
slave[5]     read(char*, int);
```

A slave thread group does not realize just an interrupt mechanism. In order to illustrate the concept of the slave thread group, the following example is considered:

```
read(char* b, int s)
{
    <non-critical region A>
    <critical region B>
    <non-critical region C>
}
```

In this example, the read function consists of the sequence of the non-critical region, critical region, and non-critical region. Suppose that one of the thread group enters the critical region B and at that time a new **read** request where the sender's priority is higher than the previous sender's one is coming. Another new thread begins to execute the **read** function with the higher priority while the former thread is suspended. Since the critical region B is captured by the former thread, the higher priority's thread cannot enter the region B and is blocked. So the former thread executes again until the exiting critical region B. After that, the higher priority's thread is resumed. In this way, a slave thread group does not just realize an interrupt mechanism but supports a preemption mechanism.

The priority inheritance in a slave thread group is as follows: When all slave threads of a group are employed for clients' requests and at that time a higher priority's request than those threads' priorities is comming, then the highest priority's thread of the group changes its priority to the new highest priority.

A master thread is intended to use a background thread within an active object. For example, we want to specify the background thread which saves its internal data into a back up disk every 30 minute [4]:

```
master          background() cycle(;;0t30m;);
```

In this example, the **cycle** expression specifies that the **background** thread is a cyclic task. The following is the syntax of the **cycle** expression:

```
cycle(<start-time>; <end-time>; <period>; <deadline>);
```

In the example, `<start-time>`, `<end-time>`, and `<deadline>` are omitted so that those constraints are free.

In RTC++, a guard expression[2] may be defined in a member function definition in order to control concurrency. A guard expression may consist of primitive data types such as integer, primitive operations such as addition, internal variables (or instance variables in Smalltalk terminology), and message variables. For example, the following definition specifies that iff the expression ``count > size'' is true, the ``read(...)'' member function is invoked by a request, otherwise the invocation for the request is postponed until the expression becomes true:

```
int     read(char* data, int size) when(count > size);
```

In addition to a guard expression, we can specify a function which is invoked when a request is postponed. For example, the definition below specifies that if the guard expression is false then the *busy* function is invoked. If the function returns 0 the request is rejected, otherwise it is enqueued to the message queue.

```
int     read(char* data, int size) when(count > size)
                                    onwait(busy);
```

An expression for creating an active object is the same as an original C++ **new** expression except for adding priority. For example, the following expression means that an instance of class **Example1** is created with priority 4 [5]:

```
Example1 *v = new Example1 priority 4;
```

When an instance object is created in the above expression, threads in the object have priority 4 at the first.

---

[3] A member function is called a method in Smalltalk terminology.

[4] An example of the notation of time is that 8 hour 20 minute 30 second and 10 millisecond 10 microsecond is specified as "0t8h20m30s10.10".

[5] Priority is defined as number. Larger number represents higher priority.

3.2 Inheritance

Unlike the previous language ARTS/C++, RTC++ supports the inheritance mechanism in an active object. An example below defines the **Example2** active class derived from class **Example1** which we call a base class in C++ terminology [6]. In class **Example2** member functions **read** and **write** are redefined and the **control** member function is defined. The activity parts of among a class and its base classes are merged consistently. That is, an instance of class **Example2** has two slave thread groups defined in class **Example1** and one slave thread defined in class **Example2**.

```
active class Example2 : public Example1 {
public:
    int     read(char* data, int size);
    int     write(char* data, int size);
    int     control(...);
activity:
    slave   open(), close(), control(...);
}
```

It should be noted that if there are no activity parts of among an active class and its base classes, an instance of the class has only one thread which is responsible for all member functions.

3.3 Communication

RTC++ supports synchronous communication. The syntax of communication among active objects is the same as C++ syntax. An example is shown below:

```
Example1  *v;
...;
n = v->read(buf, size);
...;
```

RTC++ provides two means of sending a reply message, *return* and *reply* statements. The semantics of a *return* statement is that a reply message is sent to the sender and the execution of the function is finished. The semantics of a *reply* statement is that a reply message is sent and the subsequent statements are executed instead of finishing the execution of a member function.

It should be mentioned that a message has a priority which is the same as the thread's priority of a sender.

3.4 Exception Handling

A block started with the **except** keyword is called an *exception handling block*. An exception handling block is led by *do*, *within*, *cycle*, or *region* blocks. The *within*, *cycle*, and *region* blocks are described later. In an exception handling block, we can catch and handle an exception from an object, a thread, or a kernel. In the following example, *timeout* and *abort* exceptions can be handled during the execution of "<do region>":

---

[6] In Smalltalk terminology, class **Example2** is a subclass of **Example1** while class **Example1** is the superclass of **Example2**.

```
do {
    <do region>
} except {
case abort:
    ...;
    break;
case timeout:
    ...;
    break;
}
```

In order to protect a sequence of statements from exceptions such as *timeout* and *abort*, a protect region is supported in RTC++. In the following example, a block started with the **protect** keyword is a protect region. That is, even if *timeout* or *abort* occurs while the region is executed, the exception is postponed until exiting the region.

```
protect {
    ...;
}
```

The following example specifies that the **read** function is a protected region:

```
active class Example {
    protect int read(....);
};
```

3.5 Timing Facilities

As described in Section 2.1, a real-time programming language should support i) timing specification in each operation, ii) timing constraints for statement by statement, and iii) specifying a periodic task. RTC++ supports those requirements.

3.5.1 Time Encapsulation

The time encapsulation mechanism allows us to specify timing specification in an operation. The following definition specifies that the **read** function has to be finished within 20 milliseconds, otherwise the **read_abort()** function is called.

```
active class Example1 {
private:
    ...;
    int     read_abort();
    int     write_abort();
public:
    int     read(char* data, int size)
                when(count > size)
                within(0t20) timeout(read_abort());
    int     write(char* data, int size)
                within(0t20) timeout( write_abort());
    ...;
}
```

3.5.2 Within, At, Before Statements

Statements *within*, *at*, and *before* express statement-level timing constraints. A *within* statement expresses the duration of execution. An *at* statement expresses the constraint of starting time while a *before* statement expresses the constraint of ending time.

For example, an example of a *within* statement is as follows:

```
within(time) {
    ...;
} except {
case timeout:
    ...;
}
```

The *time* variable keeps an instance of the **Time** class which is supported by the ARTS kernel. We can specify the duration of a time [7]. When the execution of statements surrounded by ''within(time) {'' and ''}'' cannot be finished within the time specified by the **time** value, statements led by ''case timeout:'' are executed.

3.5.3 Cycle Statement

A cycle statement is to specify a periodic task. As shown below, a cycle statement can be followed by an exception handling block:

```
cycle(starttime; endtime; period; deadline) {
    ...;
} except {
case timeout:
    ...;
}
```

In this example, **starttime**, **endtime**, and **deadline** specify starting time, ending time, period, and the deadline time of the execution respectively. Those are instances of class **Time**.

3.6 Critical Region

A critical region is realized by implementing an object with a guard expression. In a critical region we need a mechanism that a thread entering a critical region can be aborted or inherit a priority from another thread trying to enter the region. RTC++ introduces a special class called **ActiveEntity** which supports the abort and priority inheritance mechanism.

The **ActiveEntity** keeps an active object and member thread information. All member functions in an active object can refer to special variables **myentity** and **sender** which are instances of **ActiveEntity**. The **myentity** variable keeps own object and thread information while the **sender** variable keeps the sender object and thread information. Class **ActiveEntity** has

---

[7] For example, 0t1s20.10 means that the duration of a time is second 20 milliseconds 10 microseconds.

the **pinherit** member function to propagate priority, the **prelinquish** member function to cancel the propagated priority, and the **abort** member function to abort a member thread of an object.

The **ActiveEntity** class allows us to define a **Region** class which realizes a critical region with the abort and priority inheritance mechanisms. The following is a part of the class **Region** definition

```
active class Region {
private:
    int            flag;
    ActiveEntity   *user;
public:
    protect int    use()     when(flag == USED)
                                 onwait(check());
    protect int    release();
    protect int    who();
    protect int    abort();
activity:
    slave          use(), release(), who(), abort();
}
Region::check()
{
    if (sender->prio() > user->prio()) {
        user->pinherit(sender->prio);
    }
}
Region::use()
{
    flag = USED;
    user = sender;
}
Region::release()
{
    user->prelinquish();
    flag = FREE;
}
```

The **Region** class defines **use**, **release**, **who**, and **abort** member functions. The **use** and **release** functions are equivalent to the P and V operations in a semaphore, respectively. The **who** function returns who is currently occupying. The **abort** function is to abort the execution of a thread which is currently occupying the region.

Class **Region** supports the priority inheritance mechanism as follows. If a thread of an object has entered the region, another thread will wait for changing the **flag** variable at the **use** function. On waiting a message at the **use** function, the **check** function is called. If the waiting sender's priority is higher than the priority of the thread entering the region, the higher priority is propagated to the thread by the **check** function.

The thread leaving the region sends the **release** message to the region. The **release** function cancels the propagated priority to the thread so that the thread's priority becomes the previous priority. In a complex case, the **prelinquish** function in the **ActiveEntity** class must decide the new priority of the thread because the thread may have been inherited priorities from other threads.

An example of a critical region is shown below:

```
active class aClass {
    Region    *rr;
    ...;
}

aClass::aFunction() {
    do {
        t = rr->use();
        ...;
        t = rr->release();
    } except {
    case abort:
        ...;
        if (t == USED) {
            t = rr->release();
        }
        break;
    }
}
```

The reader may wonder if this example is too complex and a programmer forgets to call the **release** function. We also think many critical regions are used in order to realize a preemptable object. Thus, RTC++ provides a critical region statement which is a kind of macro:

```
region (rr) {
    ...;
} except {
case abort:
    ...;
}
```

The following critical region statement expresses that if the region **rr** cannot be entered within **tt**, the **timeout** exception occurs:

```
within(tt) region (rr) {
    ...;
} except {
case timeout:
    ...;
case abort:
    ...;
}
```

It should be noted that RTC++ predefines class **Region** which is the same semantics described above but the implementation is different. That is, functions are almost implemented by the ARTS kernel because of the efficient execution. However, a programmer can program an object which has the same semantics of class **Region** described above by using instances of class **ActiveEntity**.

4   Examples

In this section, we demonstrate capabilities of RTC++ by three examples. One is called *Dining Touchy Philosophers* problem and another one is called *Gluttons-Chef in Restaurant*. The other one is called *Dining Faithful Philosophers problem*. The full programs of examples appear in [6].

4.1   Dining Touchy Philosophers

Dining Touchy Philosophers problem is an extension of the dining philosophers problem stated by Dijkstra. The philosophers share a common dining room where there are a side table and a circular table surrounded by five chairs. There are four set of chopsticks in the side table. In the center of the circular table there is a large bowl of spaghetti, and the table is laid with five forks. On feeling hungry, a philosopher enters the dining room, sits in his own chair, and tries to eat spaghetti. He prefers to use forks but he can use chopsticks. He needs to pick up forks on the both side. He can wait for getting both forks for a while depending on his feeling. If he could not get them, he gives up using forks and goes to the side table to pick up chopsticks. When he has finished to eat, he puts down forks or chopsticks, and leaves the room.

The following is a part of the program written in RTC++:

```
78    for(;;) {
79        room.enter();
80        left = right = STATUS_WAITING;
81        method = FORK;
82        within(wait_t) {
83            /* gettting right fork */
84            right = fork[n].use();
85            /* gettting left fork */
86            left = fork[(n + 1)%N].use();
87        } except {
88        case timeout:
89            if(right == STATUS_GETTING) {
90                right = fork[n].release();
91            }
92            if(left == STATUS_GETTING) {
93                left = fork[(n + 1)%N].release();
94            }
95            ch = chopstick.use();
96            method = CHOPSTICK;
97        }
98        /* eating */
99        if(method == FORK) {
100           left = fork[(n + 1)%N].release();
101           right = fork[n].release();
102       } else {
103           ch = chopstick.release();
104       }
105       room.exit();
106       /* thinking */
107   }
```

In order to wait for getting both forks for the specified time, the **within** statement is used in lines 82 to 87. If the timeout occurs, lines 89 to 96 are executed to give up using forks and try to use chopsticks.

4.2   Gluttons-Chef in Restaurant

An example called *Gluttons-Chef in Restaurant* is considered in order to show a highly preemptable object written in RTC++.

Two gluttons go to a restaurant to eat stir-fry vegetables or pork stir-fry every lunch. They always have seats.

Table 1: Recipe

menu	instructions	time(min)
Stir-Fry Vegetables	chopping tomato	1
	chopping onion	1
	chopping green pepper	1
	chopping cucumbers	1
	getting fry pan	
	making stir-fry	6
	releasing fry pan	
Pork Stir-Fry	chopping pork	1
	chopping mushrooms	1
	chopping onion	1
	chopping green pepper	1
	getting fry pan	
	making stir-fry	9
	releasing fry pan	

Table 2: Faithful Philosophers Action

	period(min)	eating(min)	thinking(min)
P	15	3	10
Q	30	5	20
R	60	10	40

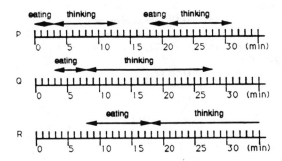

Figure 1: Timing Chart of Faithful Philosophers

```
93   switch(req) {
94   case V_STIR_FRY:
95       region(fp) { fproc->chopping(0t1m, "tomato"); }
96       region(fp) { fproc->chopping(0t1m, "onion"); }
....
103  case P_STIR_FRY:
104      region(fp) { fproc->chopping(0t1m, "pork"); }
105      region(fp) { fproc->chopping(0t1m, "mushrooms"); }
....
112  }
```

Unfortunately only one chef is cooking for them. Gluttons A and B's action patterns are as follows: Glutton A's lunch time is only 25 minutes and he decides his order within 2 minutes. Glutton B's lunch time is 50 minutes and he decides his order within 1 minute.

The recipe of stir-fry vegetables and pork stir-fry is shown in Table1. There are one poor food processor, one fry pan, and seasoning. The food processor is capable of chopping one stuff at a time.

If the chef is only cooking for one order at a time without preemption, the worst case cooking time is 23 minutes (i.e., 13 + 10). In this case, glutton A could not eat. Suppose that the chef can suspend cooking while he is using the food processor but he cannot suspend cooking when he is using the fry pan. If the chef can suspend to cook when glutton A orders, he starts to cook for glutton A. In this case, the worst case cooking time is 19 minutes.

The **Chef** class is defined below. The **request** function is to accept entree from gluttons and cook it. The activity part specifies that the **request** function can be executed by two threads.

```
71   active class Chef {
72   public:
73                       Chef();
74       void            request(menu req);
75   private:
76       Foodprocessor   *fproc;
77       Fpan            *fpan;
78       Region          *fp;
79   activity:
80       slave[2]        request(menu req);
81   };
```

The following list is a part of the definition of the **request** function. Each request to an instance of the food processor **fproc** is performed inside the critical region **fp** so that another thread cannot request the food processor even if the thread's priority is higher than the running thread's priority.

4.3 Dining Faithful Philosophers

In order to demonstrate how to use the abort method, another extension of the dining philosophers problem is considered. We call it the *Dining Faithful Philosophers* problem.

For simplicity, suppose only three philosophers. They are so faithful that their action is strictly decided shown in Table 2. For example, philosopher P eats spaghetti for 3 minutes and then thinks for 10 minutes every 15 minutes. He doesn't complaint even if someone disturbs his eating. However, because he is so faithful to his decision, when he could not perform his action on his schedule he might get angry and break the dining room.

As shown in Figure 1, philosopher P could not finish his second action within that period if a traditional program is used. This is because a philosopher is always keeping forks until finishing eat. In this example, we may preempt a fork which philosopher R is using because philosophers are so kind not to complain. This example should be implemented by using the abort method because the philosopher R has to give up eating by requesting from philosopher P.

The **Tool** class which is the base class of the **Fork** class is implemented so that if an object tries to use a tool while another object having a lower priority is keeping the tool, the keeping object is aborted. The following list is a part of the Tool class definition. The function abort is invoked when an object has to wait for getting the tool. In the abort function, if the sender's priority is higher than the current user's priority, then the current user is aborted:

```
8   active class Tool {
9    public:
10      protect int use()  when(used == 0)
11                         onwait(abort);
12      protect int release();
13    private:
14      protect void abort();
15      ActiveEntity *user;
16      int          used = 0;
17   };


31   Tool::abort()
32   {
33       if(sender->prio() > user->prio()) {
34           user->abort();
35       }
36       return 1;
37   }
```

The following program is a part of the Philosopher class. In order to catch the abort exception, the exception handling block is defined:

```
67   cycle(start_t; end_t; period; worst_t) {
68       room.enter();
69       do {
70           left = right = STATUS_WAITING;
71           do {
72               /* gettting right fork */
73               right = fork[n].use();
74               /* gettting left fork */
75               left = fork[(n + 1)%N].use();
76               /* eating */
77               right = fork[n].release();
78               left = fork[(n + 1)%N].release();
79           } except {
80           case abort:
81               if(right == STATUS_GETTING) {
82                   right = fork[n].release();
83               }
84               if(left == STATUS_GETTING) {
85                   left = fork[(n + 1)%N].release();
86               }
87           }
88       } while (/* if he needs to eat more spaghetti
89           because someone disturbs him, continue */ );
90       room.exit();
91       /* thinking */
92   }
```

5   Comparison

RTC++ has two profiles, an object-oriented concurrent language and a real-time language. We compare RTC++ with those languages in this section.

In object-oriented concurrent languages such as ABCL/1[14], Actor[1], and Orient84/K[4], all objects are active entities each of which may have a thread of execution. That is, there are no distinction between active and passive objects. In contrast with those languages, RTC++ introduces the notion of the active object which is distinct from an original C++ object. The major reason is that we want to bound the memory resource and kernel resources statically when a program is written without dynamic properties such as the dynamic creation of active objects. If all objects are active entities, it is impossible to assign resources for a thread of execution to all objects. So a run-time routine must decide whether or not an object needs new resources for a thread of the execution[4]. In this case, it is difficult to bound the amount of the resource statically. In such an unbounded behavior, it is very complex to analyse the schedulability of a system because an object may wait for an unbounded time to get a resource from a resource pool when all resources are used by other objects.

In terms of communication primitives, many object-oriented concurrent languages support both asynchronous and synchronous communication facilities which imply the reliable facilities. In RTC++, asynchronous communication is not supported. This is because it is difficult for recovery from aborting in asynchronous communication. Moreover, in the underlying system only supporting reliable communication, asynchronous communication is equivalent to a function which is realized by a communication buffer object using synchronous communication. If unreliable asynchronous communication is required in a distributed environment, the language and its kernel may support such semantics.

Real-Time languages such as Real-Time Euclid[7] and real-time Mentat[3] provide facilities for rigid timing constraints such as specifying a periodic task. Real-Time Mentat is an object-oriented real-time language which is also an extension of C++. In Real-Time Mentat, a programmer may specify timing constraints in statement level. There are two ways of specifying timing constraints, *soft* and *hard* deadlines. In a block with *soft* deadline, the execution may be optionally skipped if the hard real-time tasks cannot meet their deadlines. The *soft* deadline constraint is currently not supported in RTC++. In contrast with RTC++, the facilities for a preemptable object are not supported in Real-Time Mentat.

Real-Time Euclid is an extension of Euclid. In order to bound the resources statically, Real-Time Euclid restricts language constructs such as recursion and dynamic memory allocation. In addition to specifying starting time of a task, Real-time Euclid supports facilities signal and wait to control concurrency. The wait statement is extended to specify a time bound. In RTC++, the statement "within() region() {}" provides the same functionality which is a kind of macro and realized by the timeout mechanism in an object.

Real-Time Euclid is a system rather than just a language. The system consists of the language compiler, schedulability analyzer, and run-time system. The schedulability analyzer allows a programmer to find if a system is schedulable or not before the execution. This is one of the key issues in the real-time system research field.

In this paper, we have described on the language features of RTC++, but we also have been developing a schedulability analysis tool and monitoring tool for distributed real-time systems[10]. In particular, a schedulability analyzer called *Scheduler123* which takes the timing specification of a real-time task set and analyzes its schedulability based on various scheduling algorithms, and *ARM*, advanced real-time monitor, have been in use for a few years. We are currently extending the toolset for coping with the end-to-end schedulability analysis and designing a new timing analysis tool which extracts timing information from a RTC++ source code and transfers the information to Scheduler123. In order to extract timing information statically, the language constructs will be used restrictively or more language features will be added.

6 Conclusion

In this paper, we have proposed an object-oriented real-time language called RTC++ which supports explicit timing constraints, highly preemptable object, periodic task creation, and priority inheritance. We think, however, that the constructs we proposed are not only for the extension of C++ language, but also those can be adapted in many other object-oriented languages. We also introduced interesting real-time concurrent programs and demonstrated the usefulness of RTC++ features.

The RTC++ compiler which translates a RTC++ source program into C++ and C programs are currently implemented. [6] described the implementation hint of a RTC++ compiler and runtime routine. A technical report which describes the language features and implementation will be published soon.

Acknowledgements

One of the authors would like to express his gratitude to Dr. Akio Tojo and Dr. Kokichi Futatsugi, members of ETL, who support his research environment.

References

[1] G.A. Agha, "ACTORS," MIT Press, 1986.

[2] Dijkstra, E.W., "Guarded commands, nondeterminacy, and formal derivation of programs," Communication of ACM 18, August 1975, pp.435-457.

[3] Grimshaw, A.S, Silberman, A., Liu, J.W.S, "Real-Time Mentat, A Data-Driven, Object-Oriented System," Proceedings of IEEE Globecom, Dallas, Texas, November 1989, pp. 141-147.

[4] Ishikawa, Y., Tokoro, M., "A Concurrent Object-Oriented Knowledge Representation Language Orient84/K: Its Features and Implementation," Proceedings of OOPSLA-86, Portland, Sept. 1986, pp. 232-241.

[5] Ishikawa, Y., "A Study on Object-Oriented Concurrent Programming Languages for Describing Knowledge-Based System," Ph.D. Dissertation, Keio Univ., 1986.

[6] "Object-Oriented Real-Time Language Design: Constructs for Timing Constraints", CMU Technical Report, 1990.

[7] Kligerman, E., Stoyenko, A.D., "Real-Time Euclid: A Language for Reliable Real-Time Systems," IEEE Transactions on Software Engineering, 12(9), September 1986, pp.941-949.

[8] Sha, L., Rajkumar, R. and Lehoczky, J.P., "Priority Inheritance Protocols: An Approach to Real-Time Synchronization," Technical Report CMU-CS-87-181, Computer Science Department, Carnegie Meollon University, November, 1987.

[9] Tokuda, H., "Compensatable Atomic Objects in Object-oriented Operating Systems," Proceedings of Pacific Computer Communication Symposium, 1985.

[10] Tokuda, H., Kotera, M., "A Real-Time Tool Set for the ARTS Kernel," Proceedings of the 9th IEEE Real-Time Systems Symposium, December, 1988.

[11] Tokuda, H., Mercer, C.W. "ARTS: A Distributed Real-Time Kernel," Operating Systems Review, Vol.23, No.3, July, 1989, pp.29-53.

[12] Tokuda, H., Mercer, C.W., Ishikawa, Y., Marchok, T.E., "Priority Inversions in Real-Time Communication," 10th IEEE Real-Time Systems Symposium, December 1989, pp.348-359.

[13] Yokote, Y., Tokoro, M., "Experience and Evolution of ConcurrentSmalltalk," Proceedings of OOPSLA-87, Orland, Oct. 1987, pp.406-415.

[14] Yonezawa, A., Briot, J.-P., Shibayama, E., "Object-Oriented Concurrent Programming in ABCL/1," Proceedings of OOPSLA-86, Orland, Oct. 1986, pp.258-268.

Building Flexible Real-Time Systems Using the Flex Language

Kevin B. Kenny and Kwei-Jay Lin

University of Illinois at Urbana-Champaign

A real-time computation must be completed by a deadline and, unlike nonreal-time computation, must simultaneously satisfy both functional and temporal correctness criteria. Failure to satisfy either criteria makes the result unacceptable.

Real-time systems usually consist of many real-time computations with different but related deadlines. These computations must be scheduled so all deadlines are met. To ensure that a real-time program meets its specification, a real-time programming language must

- have the capacity to express different types of timing requirements,
- provide mechanisms for runtime systems to enforce timing constraints, and
- be based on a model that makes it easier to ensure the program's temporal correctness.

If either the complexity of a computation or the available resources can vary, meeting deadlines becomes especially difficult. The complexity of many common computational operations, such as searching, sorting, and matrix-inversion, is data-dependent. In addition, the resources available for a computation can differ in systems with a variable amount of resources

Programs in real-time systems have stringent timing requirements. The Flex programming language makes it possible to program real-time systems that can respond to dynamic environments to make sure critical deadlines are met.

as in many fault-tolerant systems. For these types of applications, the language used for system implementation must provide powerful and flexible primitives to ensure that deadlines will be met, even in a worst-case scenario.

Our approach to implementing flexible real-time systems is to design computations whose execution times can be adjusted so all important deadlines are guaranteed to be met under all circumstances. One way to do this is to allow computations to return imprecise results.

In many hard real-time applications, obtaining an approximate result before the deadline is much more desirable than obtaining an exact result after the deadline. We have identified several classes of computations that can flexibly adapt themselves to produce faster but less precise results.

Another approach is to provide multiple implementation versions for a computation, each with a different performance capacity. As soon as the timing constraint can be determined for the computation, one of the versions is selected to produce a result before the deadline.

This article presents the design and im-

Reprinted from *IEEE Computer*, Vol. 24, No. 5, May 1991, pp. 70-78. Copyright © 1991 by The Institute of Electrical and Electronic Engineers, Inc. All rights reserved.

300

plementation of a real-time programming language called Flex,[1] which is a derivative of C++. We describe how different types of timing requirements might be expressed and enforced in Flex, how they might be fulfilled in a flexible way using different program models, and how the programming environment can help in making binding and scheduling decisions. The article also presents a real-time programming environment.

In designing Flex, our goal was not to implement yet another programming language. Rather, we were interested in the general real-time programming primitives that can be added to most existing nonreal-time languages.

Issues in programming real-time systems

To date, four approaches to programming real-time systems have been identified. The first approach is to program in assembler or other low-level languages. These programs are not only difficult to write but are also difficult to modify, reuse, or port. Exhaustive trial-and-error testing is needed to establish that they meet timing requirements.

Another approach is to use languages such as Ada and Modula-2, which are primarily general-purpose programming languages. The programmer writes a logically correct program, using mechanisms such as coroutines, processes, priorities, interrupts, and exception handling to control the execution behavior. Knowledge of the runtime environment is required to tailor the program to meet timing specifications, but this makes the program sensitive to hardware characteristics and system configuration.

A third approach, as in Real-Time Euclid,[2] restricts the constructs provided in the language to those that are time-bounded. The programmer cannot use recursion, dynamic memory allocation, or dynamic process instantiation because their execution time is unpredictable. These restrictions make it easier to estimate the execution time of the program, and this information facilitates scheduling to meet deadlines. However, writing programs becomes more difficult with a restricted set of constructs.

The fourth approach, adopted in programming languages such as Esterel,[3] permits direct expression of timing requirements. The program specifies the deadlines for procedures and largely leaves ensuring that the requirements are met to the runtime system. Rather than requiring that all timing behavior be known at compile time, they permit the programmer to specify not only the timing requirements but also exception handlers to be executed if the timing requirements are not met. The lack of compile-time analysis, however, means that predictability, in the strong sense of completing without exception, is lost.

Each of the approaches described above has its merits, but none is totally satisfactory. In this section, we review some of the issues involved in programming real-time systems. For each issue, we also identify our proposed solution.

Scheduling real-time systems. Many traditional real-time systems have been programmed to be as fast as possible, without formal assurance that performance will be equal to the requirements. In early real-time systems, this haphazard method was workable, since the tasks were so simple that the performance of the computer system was not taxed.

Today, more severe timing requirements are placed on real-time systems, demanding more effort on the part of the system designer to ensure that all deadlines are met.

The issue of scheduling computations so all deadlines are met is central to this problem. Frequently, this scheduling problem is resource constrained. In addition to meeting deadlines, the schedule has to be organized so tasks will fit within the scarce computational resources available.

Resource-constrained scheduling is usually a computationally intractable problem. Even in the simple case of a number of tasks with deadlines that must fit in a limited amount of memory, the problem is *NP*-complete.

Our solution is to accept the computational intractability and provide for flexible trade-offs among time, precision, and resources. Instead of carrying out tasks that require a fixed amount of space and time, we do each task as (a set of) computations that can be executed using a flexible amount of time. This produces results with various degrees of precision or consumes different amounts of resources.

What makes this approach feasible is that, generally, a basic schedule in which all computations meet deadlines can be easily found if each task only needs a minimum degree of precision or consumes a minimum amount of resources. In this basic schedule, however, extra time and resources are usually available in the system for the computations. We can then use the extra time and resources and find a better schedule with more precise results.

Timing constraint systems. To carry out our proposed scheduling approach, there must be a way to define the constraints on time and resources to the computations. Some notion of a "constraint" must therefore be part of the system. Allen presented a consistent theory of timing constraints in his study of how to maintain knowledge about the temporal ordering of a set of actions using temporal logic.[4] He represents each action as taking place in an interval of time and defines seven relations between intervals that describe the synchronization of one event with respect to another. These relations correspond to intuitive notions, such as "A takes place before B," "A and B begin and end at the same time," and "A takes place during the time that B does."

Dasarathy was one of the first researchers to describe timing constraints in a manner consistent with the logic used in the Flex language.[5] He constructed a language called the Real-Time Requirements Language. In his scheme, timing constraints could express the minimum or maximum time allowed between the occurrence of stimuli S, actions in the outside world, and responses R, the completion of the actions that a system takes. All four combinations $S - S$, $S - R$, $R - S$, and $R - R$ could be specified.

Constraints on the time before a stimulus were constraints on the behavior of the outside world. Constraints on the time before a response were interpreted as constraints on the amount of time that the system could use to process the corresponding stimuli. Dasarathy's RTRL was a specification language and was not intended for automatic processing.

The Real-Time Logic scheme by Jahanian and Mok[6] was similar. In it, events and actions corresponding more or less to Dasarathy's stimuli and responses were identified. To describe periodic events, Jahanian and Mok used an occurrence function to specify the *i*th occurrence of a repeated event. A mechanized inference procedure, the first of its kind, was presented to perform automatic reasoning about timing properties, and the events and responses could be associated by annotation with program constructs.

Flex includes a constraint mechanism as a basic programming primitive. User-defined constraints, including timing constraints, can be associated with a block of statements. Although not as powerful as RTL, Flex timing primitives are able to carry out most of the relationships that can be defined by RTRL. We discuss our constraint block structure in the Flex timing mechanism section.

Predicting program performance. To verify if timing constraints can be satisfied, we must be able to predict a program's performance. The time-honored method of determining the performance behavior of a program is to run it, either on the target hardware or on a simulator that models the hardware. The simulation or test run must be presented with data and/or stimuli representative of those that will be seen in actual service of the system.

The problem with this approach is that the testing is limited and generally cannot include the entire set of possible inputs. The worst case for the consumption of time or some other resource might not be uncovered in testing. Moreover, if a simulator is used, an uncertainty might exist that the simulator actually reflects the performance of the underlying hardware.

For this reason, designers of real-time languages have generally preferred to conduct analyses that examine a form of the program code and try to prove assertions about the program's performance behavior. Leinbaugh conducted one of the first attempts to characterize the performance of high-level programs.[7] For such an early project, his work was remarkably thorough. The work characterized the time required by a higher level construct in terms of its CPU time, time spent waiting to enter a critical section, time spent ready and waiting for a processor, time spent performing I/O, and time spent waiting at a synchronization point. Conservative bounds for all of these quantities were estimated.

Leinbaugh's work, and all similar systems using code analysis, cannot solve the general problem of determining execution time for all programs. The problem is undecidable, being equivalent to the halting problem. Real-Time Euclid[2] made the analysis easier by forbidding many programming constructs, including While loops (only counted loops were allowed), recursion, and recursive data structures such as linked lists. The timing tools built at the University of Texas at Austin[8] allow While loops, but the programmer must supply the worst-case number of iterations of each unbounded loop using a separate timing analysis language.

We took an alternative approach based on program measurements. Our approach

alleviates some of the objections to program measurements by showing how statistical confidence in the program's performance behavior can be achieved. It also allows actual behavior — not just worst-case performance — of programs to be estimated by letting a performance model contain dependencies on the input data. More information on our performance analyzer can be found in the "Language support" section.

Flexible performance models. The concepts of constraining performance characteristics on the one hand and deriving expected performance characteristics on the other hand provide us with enough tools to implement basic real-time systems. However, they naturally give rise to the problem of how to deal with the situation where constraints cannot be met.

One possibility is to use an exception mechanism that takes actions such as aborting low-priority tasks to provide more resources for high-priority ones. However, using the exception mechanism alone might not be appropriate for real-time software. Bihari[9] identifies some of the issues:

• Real embedded systems have inertial properties that can smooth over temporary failures and overloads. Even deadlines that are asserted to be hard can occasionally be missed provided the system has the opportunity to correct itself within a specified time period.

• Time constraints themselves can be changed by the system. For instance, in a vehicle control system an appropriate action to overload is not "dump low-priority tasks" but rather "slow down and increase the distance to the vehicle in front." A process control system might similarly relax its deadlines by decreasing gain in feedback-control loops.

• Changes in the environment of a system might not only change the quantities with which the system works but require rapid, major changes in the control software, on the level of substituting entire algorithms.

All of these issues suggest that software in real-time systems should have flexible structures. For example, computations in real-time systems can provide multiple algorithms and data structures, all of which perform the same function. Having a runtime system that can select from among these versions, based on the performance constraints, should be a major aid in performing these complex functions effec-

tively. Flex has adopted such a model, called *performance polymorphism*, to address the use of different versions of an action in response to different performance criteria. This and the *imprecise computation* model are discussed in the section entitled "Models of flexible real-time programs."

The Flex timing mechanism

The Concord project at the University of Illinois involves building a programming environment for large real-time systems, supporting explicit timing constraints, imprecise computations, and multiple implementations of a single computation. The goal is to support different configuration and timing constraints. This environment is built around the programming language Flex.

Constraint blocks. The Flex programmer describes time and resource requirements by specifying constraints and propagating information among them. Rather than doing a general propagation scheme in which new information might be propagated through long chains of constraints, Flex uses a disciplined scheme where any change in execution state causes only those constraints immediately dependent on the change to be checked. No propagation of constraints is done. This discipline, which puts restrictions on the form of constraints, must be adopted to ensure that the execution time of the constraint mechanism will be predictable.

In Flex, constraints on time and resources are described by a new language construct, the *constraint block*. A constraint block identifies a constraint that must apply while a section of code is in execution and takes the form

```
[label : ] (constraint; constraint; ...)
[ → {...}] {
    ... statements ...
}
```

This block specifies that the sequence of statements is to be executed and asserts that all of the constraints will be satisfied during the execution of the block. The optional label is provided so one constraint block can refer to another. The block of statements following the → is optional and represents an exception procedure to be executed if any of the constraints fails. A constraint might be either a Boolean expression that is treated as an assertion to be kept throughout the block's lifetime or a timing constraint that describes a constraint on the time when the block might begin or end its execution.

An interval of time representing the lifetime of the block is associated with each constraint block. Another block might refer to the *start* and *finish* times of a given block by using the block's label. Thus, *A.start* represents the start time of block *A*, and *A.finish* represents the finish time of the block. As a convenience for the support of periodic and sporadic tasks, the boundaries of a constraint block might also be designated in terms of the relative time from the start of the block. *B.duration* represents the difference between the start and finish times of block *B*, and *B.interval* represents the difference between the start time of one execution and the start time of the next execution of the same block. Figure 1 shows all four of these timing attributes.

A timing constraint can take any of the forms shown in Table 1. The headings are

Start or Finish time: Constraints can refer either to the time the computations represented by a constraint block begin or to the time that they complete.

Absolute or Relative time: Absolute time is just what the name suggests and represents the actual time of the start or finish event. Relative time represents the elapsed time from the start event to the event described.

Earliest or Latest time: Constraints can refer either to the earliest time when an event might occur or to the latest time when it is permitted to occur. If a constraint refers to the earliest time and the flow of control reaches the beginning or end of the constraint block before the specified time, execution is delayed until the constraint is satisfied. If a constraint refers to the latest time and the flow of control reaches the beginning or end of the constraint block after the specified time, a *timing fault* occurs and execution is diverted to the recovery procedure (specified by the → operator) or to a system fault handler.

The left-hand side of a timing constraint is always a timing attribute of the block. The relational operator (≥ or ≤) can specify either the earliest or the latest time for the block. The right-hand side of a constraint can be a constant or an expression involving the program variables and/or the timing attributes of another constraint block.

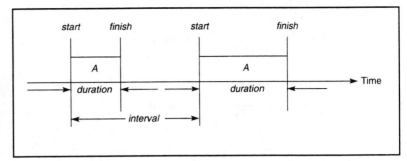

Figure 1. Timing attributes of constraint blocks.

Table 1. Timing constraints in Flex.

Type of Constraint	Absolute Time		Relative Time	
	Start	Finish	Start	Finish
Earliest	$start \geq t$	$finish \geq t$	$interval \geq t$	$duration \geq t$
Latest	$start \leq t$	$finish \leq t$	$interval \leq t$	$duration \leq t$

We can define a timing constraint relative to the execution of another block. When one block refers to the attributes of another block that might be executed many times, the values always refer to the most recent activation of the block.

The following are two examples that should help clarify the notation.

Example 1: ($start \geq t_1$; $finish \leq t_2$; *temperature* < 110)

This constraint specifies that the computations must start at a time no earlier than t_1 and end at a time no later than t_2. During the computations, the contents of the variable *temperature* must be less than 110 at all times.

Example 2: A: ($start \geq B.finish$)

This constraint specifies that the computation, identified as block *A*, cannot begin until another computation, identified as block *B*, has completed.

Representing time. In Flex, we assume that time is represented as a sequence of discrete, quantized instants t_0, t_1, ... An "event" is anything that can be identified with a specific instant. For Flex, the most significant events are the start and end of a computation. Instants are well ordered; for any two instants a and b, we assume that we

know that a is earlier than, at the same time as, or later than b. In situations such as those that can arise in distributed systems, where events might actually occur simultaneously, we require that the systems have an unambiguous way to determine an "earlier" or "later" relationship between events. On a single-processor system, two events might occur simultaneously if and only if they are the same event. While Flex does not specifically require that simultaneity be impossible — since many parallel systems can easily support it — neither does it require that the underlying system support it.

If an event has occurred in the past, we assume we know the precise time of its occurrence. Future events, however, are not known to the same degree of accuracy. We might know that an event is not allowed to occur until a certain time, or that it is not allowed to occur after a given time. We also always know that an event that has not occurred cannot occur before the current time *now*.

Flex represents the interval of time within which an event is known to take place as a *time interval*. A time interval comprises two times, the earliest and latest time when the event might occur. Thus, time intervals have the same structure as the familiar intervals of numerical analysis. A time interval represents the range of uncertainty about when an event occurs. It does not represent the duration of a continued process.

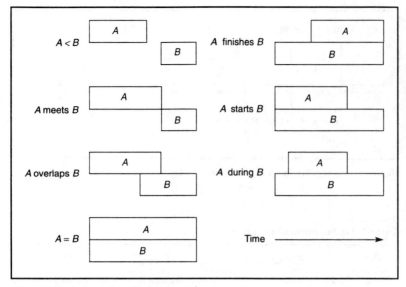

Figure 2. Relations that Allen defined.[4]

Table 2. Samples of timing relations in Flex.

Relation	Implementation in Flex

$A = B$	$A : (finish \geq B'.finish)$ {
	    $A' : (start \geq B.start)$ { ... }
	}
	
	$B : (finish \geq A'.finish)$ {
	    $B' : (start \geq A.start)$ { ... }
	}

A meets B	$A : (finish \geq B.start)$ {
	    $A' : (1)$ { ... }
	}
	
	$B : (start \geq A'.finish)$ { ... }

A starts B	$A : (1)$ {
	    $A' : (start \geq B.start)$ { ... }
	}
	
	$B : (finish \geq A.finish)$ {
	    $B' : (start \geq A.start)$ { ... }
	}

Implementing and enforcing timing constraints. With the timing mechanisms provided in Flex, we can easily carry out many temporal relations. Allen presents a temporal logic based on intervals and defines 13 relations operating on pairs of intervals.[4] Figure 2 shows seven of the relations, and Table 2 shows the Flex code for three of them. The rest can also be easily carried out. In all cases, the "wait" and "synchronization point" (see the two sidebars) semantics are used, and no extraneous deadlines are introduced. The changes needed to define deadline semantics are straightforward.

Next, we describe the complete structure of a constraint block. The flow of control through the block is as follows:

(1) A context for exception handling is established so the handler, if invoked, has the correct state to process.

(2) The constraints that must be checked throughout the block's execution are established. These are the nontemporal constraints and the constraints on earliest finish time ($finish \leq t$ and $duration \leq t$).

(3) Execution is delayed until the earliest start time is reached, fulfilling the $start \geq t$ and $interval \geq t$ constraints. This delay is performed under the control of additional timing constraints describing the latest start time ($start \leq t$ and $interval \leq t$). If these latter constraints are violated, the block's exception handler is invoked. The structures describing the constraints on the latest start time are then deleted, being deemed satisfied.

(4) The block's actual start time is recorded. Its finish time is set to an unknown time. As a side effect of setting the start time, the interval (that is, the interarrival time of the block) is also set.

(5) The user code for the body of the constraint block is executed. The nontemporal constraints and the constraints on latest finish time are still in effect.

(6) The appropriate delays are made to satisfy constraints on the earliest possible finish time ($finish \geq t$ and $duration \geq t$).

(7) The constraints on finish time and the nontemporal constraints are revoked.

(8) Finally, the finish time of the block is recorded. As a side effect, the duration of the block is also set.

Our current implementation on a Sun 3/50 workstation takes roughly 9.5 milliseconds to enter a constraint block, establish a nontemporal constraint involving two variables, revert the constraint, and exit the block. Nearly half of this time is spent on calls to the memory management routines. Specialized memory management for the constraint data structures is expected to reduce this time substantially.

Temporal constraints do not perform as well, needing about 15 milliseconds to enter a constraint block, establish a two-variable temporal constraint, revert the constraint, and leave the block. Virtually all the additional time is spent in Unix signal management routines. An implementation of our scheme using lightweight processes could no doubt do much better.

'Fault' versus 'wait' semantics

The timing constraints in Flex come in two varieties: the "earliest time" and "latest time" constraints. If these are applied with dependencies among different blocks, there are two fundamental ways of carrying out relations among the events.

The first is what we call the "wait" semantics. Let us say that block A might not start until block B has finished. We might view this as a requirement to delay the execution of block A:

$A : (start \geq B.finish) \{ \dots \}$
.
.
$B : (1) \{ \dots \}$

Alternatively, we can adopt the "fault" semantics: We might view the constraint as a deadline on block B and require that B be completed before A starts, causing a timing fault if this constraint is violated:

$A : (1) \{ \dots \}$
.
.
$B : (finish \leq A.start) \{ \dots \}$

Clearly these two constraints are synonymous in terms of the blocks' temporal relationship, but there is a world of difference in their behavior at runtime.

As a matter of programming style, we prefer to impose as few arbitrary deadlines as possible on tasks. The former usage of causing a delay is preferred over the latter usage of imposing an additional deadline whenever possible. The range of applications where this will be possible will be extended when a timing analyzer is added to Flex.

The analyzer will make it possible to determine implicit deadlines on tasks for which the programmer has supplied no explicit deadline by determining the time required for the computations of succeeding tasks that are deadline driven.

Equality between times

Flex does not depend on the possibility of simultaneous events. Our interpretation of an equality constraint is that it represents a synchronization point. When events A and B are constrained to occur "at the same time," the first to arrive must be delayed until the second arrives.

The programmer describes such a constraint in Flex by the use of nested constraint blocks. Assume that operations A and B must begin at the same time. The Flex notation to express this relationship is

```
A: (1) {
      A': (start ≥ B.start) {
          .
          .
          .
      }
}

B: (1) {
      B': (start ≥ A.start) {
          .
          .
          .
      }
}
```

Note that the constraints here are symmetrical; A bears the same relationship to B as B does to A. Let us examine what happens when we try to satisfy these constraints. Assume without loss of generality that the flow of control reaches A first. The constraint on block A is always satisfied, and so we try to enter block A'. The system finds that the current time is less than $B.start$ (a future event is always known to occur after the current time), and therefore must delay execution until the flow of control reaches B.

When control reaches B, the execution proceeds into block B, since B's constraint is always satisfied. Now, however, $B.start$ is known. This information propagates to the process waiting at block A', and this process is allowed to proceed, finding that the current time is now at least $B.start$. Meanwhile, the process in block B tries to enter block B' and finds that the current time is at least $A.start$. The entry to block B' therefore can proceed immediately.

The naive implementation of synchronization points

```
A: (start ≥ B.start) {
       .
       .
       .
}

B: (start ≥ A.start) {
       .
       .
       .
}
```

might be erroneous. This implementation results in deadlock on any system incapable of supporting simultaneous actions. Each block will be waiting for the other to begin, and neither will begin until the wait is complete.

Models of flexible real-time programs

The timing constraint block structure described above lets users define totally dynamic timing constraints. In addition, the runtime mechanism ensures that the timing constraints will always be followed, or else the block is aborted and the exception handler is invoked.

However, the constraint has solved only half of the problem for real-time computations. It has attempted to ensure only the *temporal* correctness but not the *functional* correctness. It is still up to the programmer to carry out real-time programs that can provide an acceptable degree of functional correctness whenever the system must abort the computation to satisfy its temporal correctness.

We have identified two program models that can provide some functional correctness when the temporal correctness is enforced under different system conditions. In this section, we describe the rationale behind these two models and their implementations.

Imprecise computations. In a real-time system, if a computation in progress has not completed when its deadline is reached, we have two alternatives: either we can discard the partial results from the computation, or we can try to use them in some fashion. If the partial results could constitute a useful approximation to the desired output, it is preferable not to discard them.

We call this model of allowing incomplete computations to produce approximate results *imprecise computation*. The notion of an imprecise result is a simple one, and adopting it for practical systems is easy. For example, many image processing systems can produce fuzzy pictures even before their operations are completely finished. Many real-time applications use iterative numerical methods that can produce early approximate results after enough, but not all, iterations are completed.

To meet timing constraints in real-time programs, a computation must be able to behave gracefully whenever it is aborted prematurely. Whenever possible, we suggest that real-time programs be carried out as imprecise computations so they can produce acceptable results given any reasonable amount of time.

Programs can be carried out as iterative processes that produce more refined results as more time is permitted, or they can use the divide-and-conquer strategy that provides partial results along the way. Other approaches are also possible to return partial, early, or imprecise results.

To invoke an imprecise computation, a program might call the computation using the *impcall* command instead of the normal procedure call. There are two timing models of *impcall* commands. In the synchronous model, the timing constraint for the computation is defined at the time of the invocation; in the asynchronous model, the timing constraint is not known until after the computation is started. In either case, the imprecise computation then starts its computation using the parameter values passed from the caller program.

From time to time, the computation will make imprecise results available by using the *impreturn* command. The computation is terminated when the deadline is reached or the computation has completed.

Once the program for an imprecise computation is constructed, we can define its performance capacity in a *reward* function by running test data and monitoring the resultant qualities along the time line. Given the reward function, we can decide how much time should be given to a computation to receive a result of acceptable quality for a given application. Much research has been done on the various issues on imprecise computation. We refer interested readers to another article, by Liu et al.,[10] in this issue (pp. 58-68).

Performance polymorphism. Another approach to addressing the need for multiple program performances is to carry out multiple versions of a function that carries out a given computation. These versions all perform the same task and differ only in the amount of time and resources they consume, the system configuration to which they are adapted, the precision of the results that they return, and similar performance criteria.

The versions might be specialized for a particular machine architecture, a particular problem size, a particular optimization strategy, and so on. The multiple versions might be supplied by the programmer, as when different algorithms adapted to problems of different sizes are supplied. They might also be generated automatically, as when a program rewriting tool adapts a sequential program to a vector or parallel machine.

For real-time programs, we present a model for specifying these multiple versions. We call this model *performance polymorphism* because of its similarities to the conventional polymorphism where different functions carry out the same operation on different types of data.[11]

The example we use is that of sorting on a parallel computer system. We have (at least) three different sorting techniques available: a fast insertion sort *isort*, a heap sort *hsort*, and a parallel merge sort *bsort*. The amount of time that these sorts take is $An^2 + Bn + C$, $Dn \log n + E$, and $F(n \log n)/p + G \log p + H$, respectively, where n is the number of elements to sort and p is the number of processing elements given to the parallel sort. We expect H, the overhead of starting the parallel sort, to be quite large. Therefore, it might be more effective to sort a short list of numbers on the local processor. We also expect the constant factor in the time required for heap sort to be greater than that for insertion sort. Therefore, choosing the $O(n^2)$ insertion sort for extremely short lists might be more effective.

Language support. To carry out the model of performance polymorphism, we augment Flex with a means to describe the candidates, their performance, and the goals. In this section, we use simple examples to show the various primitives.

We begin by providing a means to declare a performance polymorphic function, by letting the keyword "perf_poly" replace the function body in a function declaration.

Example 3: void sort (int n, int* list) perf_poly;

This example declares *sort* to be a performance polymorphic function accepting an integer n and a "pointer to integer" *list*. Presumably, *sort* is a function that sorts a list of integers.

Next, we provide a way to give a candidate for a performance polymorphic function. We do this by adding an external definition to the language:

Example 4: provide hsort for void sort (int, int*);

This example supplies the function *hsort* as a candidate for the *sort* function defined above. The description of the types accepted and returned by the *sort* function must be supplied because sort might be polymorphic in the conventional sense as well. There might, for instance, be another *sort* function that sorts a list of floating-point numbers.

Finally, we need to add a description of the goal. We do this by extending the definition of a compound statement:

Example 5: #pragma objective minimize duration

The directive shown in this example requests that the system minimize the real time taken to perform the computations enclosed in the braces, subject to all constraints.

The only other data needed to perform the binding step are the claims that describe the resource requirements for the candidates. We have carried out a program timing tool[12] that can measure the time required for a computation under various conditions and integrate these measured times into a parametric model supplied by the programmer. Novel features in our tool include the capacity to

- analyze program structures that are difficult for other systems, such as unbounded loops and recursive control structures;
- provide accurate timing information even on hardware whose timing behavior is difficult to model and analyze; and
- provide confidence in the timing model, by validating it statistically for goodness of fit.

To support timing measurement and modeling, Flex is augmented with a measurement directive, "#pragma measure." This directive both instructs the compiler to generate code to measure the time or resources consumed by a block of code and provides the parametric model for analyzing the measurement. Next, we show an example of the pragma directive.

Example 6: #pragma measure mean duration defining A, B, C in $(A * n + B) * n + C$ safety 2

The pragma informs the timing tool that the mean duration (average time) taken by the computation is expected to be a quadratic function of the input variable n. Once the program has been compiled and run, possibly a number of times to collect the measurement data, the analysis tool is run.

This tool determines the best fit of the parameters to the observed runtime. It produces the values of the parameters A, B, and C, and also reports the confidence level (using the χ^2 statistic) for the analysis. In this example, the programmer has also specified that a safety factor of two is to be provided. This safety factor reflects the programmer's knowledge that the algorithm used, in the worst case, requires twice the amount of time that it does on average.

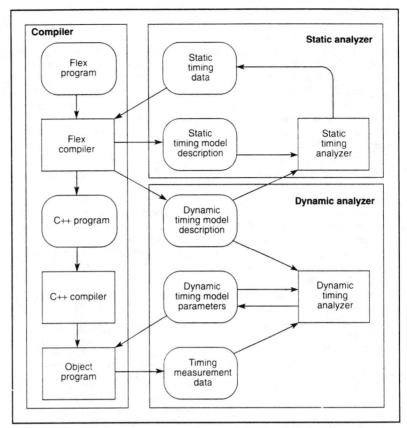

Figure 3. A programming environment for performance polymorphism.

Binding issues. Given all the information described above, late binding at runtime is easy to describe. This algorithm simply loops through all the candidates, looking for feasibility, and selects the candidate with the greatest figure of merit. This is obviously somewhat expensive (the computation of the resource claims is a loop that is nested within the loop through the candidates). However, assuming that a few configurations of the parameters account for most of the invocations, we can improve the binding overhead by caching the resource claims and feasibility information.

The caching records the configuration of the parameters for the last few calls to the function and, as the first part of the binding step, checks whether the parameters supplied match a recent invocation. If so, the binding need not be recomputed; the system can simply reuse the binding that was used on the earlier invocation.

The advantage of runtime binding is its flexibility. It is required for cases where the relevant parameters cannot be determined at compile time. Such cases include data-dependent performance, where input data obtained at runtime can affect the binding decision; fault-tolerant systems, where runtime binding might be needed to reconfigure around a system failure; and runtime allocation of time and resources.

The disadvantage of runtime binding is the overhead involved in making the binding decision; therefore, we prefer early binding in the cases that do not require late binding. We also recommend appropriate choice of granularity for performance polymorphic functions that will require late binding. Short functions that complete in only a few instruction times are not appropriate candidates because the cost of choosing an inappropriate function is small compared to the cost of binding.

A programming environment. A programming environment that supports performance polymorphism is being implemented. It provides the programmer the tools to specify and conduct the performance measurements and to decide the binding time. Figure 3 shows the overall structure of our system.

In the figure, boxes are tools implemented, and rounded boxes are program and data files used as inputs or produced as outputs by the tools. The left subsystem has all the compilers. Flex programs are processed by the Flex compiler.

The output of the Flex compiler is a C++ program that is, in turn, processed by a C++ compiler to produce an object program. The object program contains the guarded commands needed to invoke performance polymorphic functions. It also contains the codes to measure the execution time and resource commitment required for the various versions of the performance polymorphic functions.

The lower right subsystem in the figure is the dynamic timing analyzer. It starts with the dynamic timing model that is produced by the Flex compiler from "#pragma measure" directives supplied by the programmer. The model describes a parametric function whose parameters are to be determined by the actual timing data obtained by running the program.

Determining these parameters is the role of the dynamic timing analyzer. It reads the model description and the actual time and resource measurement data obtained by running the program. It writes a file containing the parameters of the model. Subsequent runs of the Flex program might use these parameter values to estimate the running times of performance polymorphic function versions in making binding decisions.

The static timing analyzer at the upper right in Figure 3 is a planned future subsystem. Its role is to determine the times and resource commitments required for high-level constructs. It can determine these times based on the measured times, examination of the object code, the constraint structure of the program, or any combination of these. The static analyzer will be capable of generating a description of the performance of the versions of a function. The description can be used in a subsequent compilation to optimize for early binding.

Many real-time-system environments are dynamic. They are subject to different work loads, unexpected failures, and dynamic time constraints. Real-time systems that are to perform in such environments need to be able to handle such variations. Currently, the environmental problems are handled by using low-level operating system primitives that are neither flexible nor portable.

The timing constraint primitives in the Flex programming language are easy to use yet powerful enough to define both independent and relative timing constraints. Program models like imprecise computation and performance polymorphism can carry out flexible real-time programs. In addition, programmers can use a performance measurement tool that produces statistically correct timing models to predict the expected execution time of a program and to help make binding decisions.

Using our approach, the burden of meeting all deadlines is partly shifted from the programmer to the runtime system. Of course, the programmer still has to carry out programs that can produce results with adequate precision, given a reasonable amount of time. In this way, the flexibility needed for dynamic real-time systems can be achieved. ∎

Acknowledgments

This research was sponsored by the Office of Naval Research under Grant N00014-89-J-1181, by the National Science Foundation under Grant CCR-89-11773, and by the National Aeronautics and Space Administration under Grant NASA-NAG-1-613.

References

1. K.-J. Lin and S. Natarajan, "Expressing and Maintaining Timing Constraints in Flex," *Proc. Ninth Real-Time Systems Symp.*, IEEE CS Press, Los Alamitos, Calif., Order No. 894, 1988, pp. 96-105.

2. A.D. Stoyenko, "A Schedulability Analyzer for Real-Time Euclid," *Proc. Eighth Real-Time Systems Symp.*, IEEE CS Press, Los Alamitos, Calif., Order No. 815, 1987, pp. 218-227.

3. G. Berry and L. Cosserat, "The Esterel Synchronous Programming Language and Its Mathematical Semantics," *Lecture Notes in Computer Science*, Vol. 197, Springer-Verlag, Feb. 1985, pp. 389-448.

4. J.F. Allen, "Maintaining Knowledge About Temporal Intervals," *Comm. ACM*, Vol. 26, No. 11, Nov. 1983, pp. 832-843.

5. B. Dasarathy. "Timing Constraints of Real-Time Systems: Constructs for Expressing Them, Methods for Validating Them." *IEEE Trans. Software Eng.*, Vol. SE-11, No. 1, Jan. 1985, pp. 80-86.

6. F. Jahanian and A. K.-L. Mok, "Safety Analysis of Timing Properties in Real-Time Systems," *IEEE Trans. Software Eng.*, Vol. SE-12, No. 9, Sept. 1986, pp. 890-904.

7. D.W. Leinbaugh, "Guaranteed Response Times in a Hard Real-Time Environment." *IEEE Trans. Software Eng.*, Vol. SE-6, No. 1, Jan. 1980, pp. 85-91.

8. A.K. Mok et al., "Evaluating Tight Execution Time Bounds of Programs by Annotations," *Sixth IEEE Workshop on Real-Time Operating Systems and Software*, May 1989, pp. 272-279.

9. T.E. Bihari, "Current Issues in the Development of Real-Time Control Software," *Real-Time Systems Newsletter*, Vol. 5, No. 1, Winter 1989, pp. 1-5.

10. J.W.-S. Liu et al., "Algorithms for Scheduling Imprecise Computation," *Computer*, Vol. 24, No. 5, May 1991.

11. L. Cardelli and P. Wegner, "Understanding Types, Data Abstractions, and Polymorphism," *ACM Computing Surveys*, Vol. 17, No. 4, Dec. 1985, pp. 471-522.

12. K.B. Kenny and K.-J. Lin, "A Measurement-Based Performance Analyzer for Real-Time Programs," *Proc. Int'l Phoenix Conf. Computers and Comm.*, IEEE CS Press, Los Alamitos, Calif., Order No. 2133, 1991, pp. 93-99.

Kevin B. Kenny is a member of the research technical staff at the Northrop Research and Technology Center in Rancho Palos Verdes, California. His research interests are in software engineering and programming environments for embedded systems.

Kenny received the AB degree from Dartmouth College, the MS from Arizona State University, and the PhD from the University of Illinois at Urbana-Champaign. He is a member of the IEEE Computer Society and the ACM.

Kwei-Jay Lin is an assistant professor in the Department of Computer Science at the University of Illinois at Urbana-Champaign. His research interests include real-time systems, distributed systems, programming languages, and fault-tolerant systems. He was program chair for the Seventh IEEE Workshop on Real-Time Operating Systems and Software in May 1990.

Lin received his BS in electrical engineering from the National Taiwan University in 1976, and his MS and PhD in computer science from the University of Maryland in 1980 and 1985. He is a member of the IEEE Computer Society.

Readers can contact Kenny at Northrop Research and Technology Center, Mail Zone 0331-T20, 1 Research Park, Palos Verdes, CA 90274, e-mail kkenny@nrtc.northrop.com; and Lin at the Department of Computer Science, University of Illinois at Urbana-Champaign, Urbana, IL 61801.

Chapter 5:   Design and Analysis Techniques

There are several ways to verify whether a real-time system meets its requirements. One popular approach is to test real-time systems by simulating numerous scenarios in which the system is expected to function. As is well known, testing only reveals a system's bugs, and it is fraught with many problems. First, we can only be confident about the areas covered by the test scenarios. Second, even a small change to the system can affect the results of the simulations, and hence the tests have to be repeated. This is especially true with regard to timing requirements, because changing even one instruction may impact many of a system's timing characteristics. In large systems this approach has delayed missions and increased project costs. Clearly, we need alternatives.

Another approach is to directly measure a system's performance by introducing probes to monitor system behavior. The concomitant changes to system performance are unavoidable. However, finding problems at this stage of system development may imply expensive and time-consuming redesign and reimplementation efforts. Furthermore, recreating worst case behavior (when a real-time system must meet its requirements) may be difficult, since it may be impossible to deploy the system to conduct the measurements.

Both simulation-based and experimentation-based approaches provide a developer with some confidence that, in a *probabilistic* or stochastic sense, the system works. Analytical or queueing-theoretic approaches work towards this goal as well. However, they can be employed much earlier in the development process and therein lies their attraction. Furthermore, if the analysis indicates that the probabilities of system failure are smaller than, say the system being hit by a meteor, then for all practical purposes the system meets its requirements — unless of course, it it supposed to withstand meteor hits.

Contrasting probabilistic approaches are those that show via constructive means or by system verification that the system, even under worst case scenarios, will function correctly. These techniques obviously need information about worst case arrival patterns, worst case execution times, and worst case fault hypotheses. Such worst case based approaches are especially essential to verify the correctness of the *safety-critical* parts of a real-time system. When applied to other parts of a real-time system, they are most likely to produce over-designed and over-configured systems. Thus, the predictability requirements (see Chapter 1 and the paper by Stankovic and Ramamritham) imposed on a system and its components governs the technique used to evaluate the system's performance and verify its correctness.

Timeliness is a particularly crucial property. As discussed earlier, (see Scheduling) real-time systems use time-constraint-driven scheduling algorithms to ensure timely behavior of real-time activities. Most of these use task execution time information in making scheduling decisions. Here again, we see the differences arising from using stochastic versus worst case execution times. If we use the former, we have to provide for the exceptional situation in which there is a time overrun. In the latter case, resource utilization is likely to be very small if resources are allocated with respect to worst case execution times. However, as we have noted before, there may be no choice but to use worst case times when designing safety-critical components.

Worst case execution times of programs depend on the system hardware, the operating system, the compiler, and the programming language. Many hardware features introduced to speed-up the average behavior of programs pose problems when information about worst case behat-vior is sought. For instance, the ubiquitous caches, pipelining, dynamic RAMs, and virtual (secondary) memory lead to highly nondeterministic hardware behavior. (See Chapter on Architecture and fault tolerance). Similarly, compiler optimizations tailored to better use these architectural enhancements as well as techniques such as constant folding contribute to poor predictability of code execution times. System interferences due to interrupt handling, shared memory references, and preemptions further complicate matters. In summary, any approach to the determination of execution times of real-time programs must address many complexities.

In general, predicting execution times is easier if compiled code follows the parsing structure. However, the complexities in the implementation of machine instructions on the one hand and complex program construction on the other exacerbate the problem. For instance, most implementations of the simple multiplication operator are optimized for different types of operands. Hence, seemingly straight-line code can involve branches. The use of go-to's, pointers (to functions), recursion, and loops are problematic not only from the viewpoint of determining the execution times, but also from predetermining resource (such as memory) requirements of programs.

The first two papers in this chapter deal with computing worst case execution times of tasks and hence contend with the above issues. Both papers work with the source code for a program, in contrast with [Mok 89], which uses compiled code. The advantage of using source code is that, once we determine the computation times of the straight line code segments (by, perhaps, examining the corresponding compiled code) we can use higher-level techniques (like Park and Shaw's *timing schemes*) to derive the overall execution times. The disadvantage is that compiler optimizations are not factored in. Because of this, the execution time estimates produced are likely to be larger than when they are computed using compiled code.

In "Experiments with a Program-Timing Tool Based on Source-Level Timing Schema," Park and Shaw discuss a method based on the use of timing schemas, formulas that describe the timing behavior of different control structures used in high-level programming languages. One of the key ingredients of their approach is that they compute not only the worst case (that is, upper bound) execution times of programs but also the best case (lower bound). The former is useful in ensuring that a time-constrained activity is completed *before* a deadline, while the latter is essential to make sure that it will complete only *after* a given time. The timing schema works in conjunction with assertional techniques to produce a technique that combines the execution times of the building bocks of a program to produce the execution times for the whole program. Essentially, Park and Shaw's method involves breaking up a program into *atomic blocks*, determining the execution time (of the compiled code) of each atomic block, and using the timing schemas, deriving the execution time of the program. They have experimented with this approach by examining programs written in a subset of C compiled by a Gnu C compiler and running on an MC 68010 processor. They carefully study the uncertainties introduced, for example, by dynamic memory refreshes though measurements carried out via an oscilloscope. They even take into account the effect of clock interrupt handling times on program execution times. They also compare the predictions of their approach with actual execution times of programs, and the correlations are very encouraging. Their experiments suggest that with careful study of the language, the operating system and the hardware, one can either avoid or at least reduce the pessimism introduced by the use of worst case execution times.

There are several similarities between this paper and the next one, "Calculating the Maximum Execution Time of Real-Time Programs," by Puschner and Koza. Both papers work at the source language level, both expect loops to be bounded (specifically, they expect the user to specify loop bounds), and both use parameterized formulas that describe the execution times of code segments. In addition, Puschner and Koza follow through on the recognition that better (less pessimistic) bounds can be derived if further information is available. Two sources of additional information are exploited:

- a user can declare a *scope* of execution within a program and specify upper bounds on the number of times points (called *markers*) within that scope will be encountered (a program can contain multiple scopes), and
- a bound can be placed on the total number of times *a sequence of loops* will be executed.

The authors propose new language constructs to embed this information into a program. They demonstrate through a fairly elaborate example that these additions can indeed lower the worst case execution time of a program. A timing tool that is based on this approach is currently being implemented.

Whereas the first two papers in this section deal with a program-theoretic analysis of real-time programs to determine their computation times, "Real-time Systems Performance in the Presence of Failures" by Muppala, Woolet, and Trivedi is devoted to a queuing-theoretic analysis for determining the performance of real-time systems when system components fail. The paper uses the notion of *performability* introduced by Meyer [Meyer 82], which combines the seemingly orthogonal concerns of performance and reliability. It also extends the performance measures, defined by Shin and Krishna [Shin and Krishna 86], that account for the effects of processor failures on a system's ability to meet deadlines. Specifically, it provides a methodology that combines Meyer's approach with that of Shin and Krishna for modeling soft and hard real-time systems. Their approach is based on the addition of transitions to the

Markov model of a system's behavior for modeling a system failure due to the missing of a hard deadline. They perform a transient analysis of the Markov *reward* models to understand the failure behavior. The system's response time and throughput distributions are used to denote the reward rates. The models are solved numerically using an extension of stochastic Petri nets called stochastic reward nets. The approach is quite general in that it is applicable to multiple resource models, multiple task types, and complex failure-handling scenarios. The paper discusses the application of the technique to an on-line transaction processing system to demonstrate its usefulness. One of the key issues in using techniques like the one in this paper is whether the assumptions of Poisson task arrival rates, exponentially distributed failure rates, and so on, hold in practice.

Experiments with a Program Timing Tool Based on Source-Level Timing Schema

Chang Yun Park and Alan C. Shaw

University of Washington

Our goal is to develop tools and techniques for predicting the deterministic timing behavior of programs coded in contemporary higher level languages. Achieving this goal would permit performance guarantees before programs are run and, more generally, would allow a priori analysis of software timing properties. This is important for many real time systems, where failure to meet timing deadlines can result in unacceptable human and property losses and where stochastic data is not sufficient. (Stochastic measures deal with statistical behaviors, such as average program performance. We are concerned with deterministic timing, by which we mean either an exact time or a tightly bounded time.)

We believe that software timing properties should be specified and verified at the source-program level rather than at the assembly or machine levels, since the former is the notation where programs are written, analyzed, debugged, and maintained. The arguments for treating time at the source level are similar to those made for programming in a higher level language rather than an assembly language.

An earlier version of this article appeared in *Proc. 11th IEEE Real-Time Systems Symposium*, Dec. 1990, pp. 72-81.

> **This timing tool, developed for a subset of C, predicts the deterministic execution times of programs.**

Preliminary and related work

A reasoning methodology for deterministic timing was introduced by Shaw.[1] This method is based both on timing schema for source-program constructs, which are essentially formulae for computing the lower and upper bounds for the execution times of these constructs, and on an assertional program logic extended with a real-time clock. The timing schema idea can be used in principle to predict deterministic execution times of programs in best- and worst-case bounds; however, it was evident that much experimental work was necessary to validate and refine the concept.

Surprisingly, little research has been published on deterministic timing prediction. A standard method in practice is to actually run a program on representative test data and measure the execution times. While this approach is clearly useful, it has some of the same flaws as debugging: The test data may not cover the domain of interest, and measurements may not be feasible (or realistic) without setting up an actual production environment.

Another common and useful technique is to simulate the target system using some specification or modeling language.[2] The problem here is that the results may not accurately reflect the target, since the simulation model is only an approximation of the real system.

The only efforts we know of that directly relate to ours are the time tool development of Mok and his students,[3] the Maxt approach (maximum execution time) to computing the maximum execution time of a program,[4] and Stoyenko's schedulability analyzer of real-time Euclid.[5]

Mok's time tool graphically analyzes an assembly language stream to produce a worst-case path and computes execution times by simulating the machine. The tool was also expanded to analyze a higher level language program directly through annotations that are carried down into the assembly language level. However, it still relies on target hardware simulation and extensive analysis of assembly language streams.

Maxt also involves the analysis of a source program through time formula for high-level language statements; however, control costs are not handled explicitly. It introduced a few new language constructs, such as "scope" and "marker," to help the analysis of larger statement blocks.

In the schedulability analyzer, a program is decomposed into a tree of segments. Then the time of each segment is computed, and the worst-case program execution time is determined from the segment tree. The analyzer also works in some processor-sharing and distributed environments with interprocess communication and resource sharing. Blocking times of processes are predicted by simulating all possible paths and resource contentions.

Current approach

All of the above studies attempt to bound the worst-case execution time. Our work differs in several ways: We employ analytic methods at the source-language level using formal timing schema that include control costs, handle interferences such as interrupts, and produce guaranteed best- and worst-case bounds. (Often, doing something too quickly is as unacceptable as doing it too slowly; hence, best-case performance is also a useful measure.)

Our timing tool computes the deterministic execution times for programs that are written in a subset of C and run on a bare machine. We wrote two versions of the tool using two granularity extremes for the atomic elements of the timing schema.

We found several interesting results from our first experiments in building and using this kind of tool. First, for the relatively small programs tested, predicted times were close to actual measured times, indicating that deterministic predictions are indeed potentially practical. We also demonstrated that in a practical setting — that is, using a popular language, compiler, and computer — the timing schema approach leads to a natural implementation partition into an abstract, system-independent portion and a lower level system-dependent part. The independent part can be viewed as defining the timing semantics of the programming language. The system-dependent part in our experiments illustrates some of the complexities of predicting code generation in a modern compiler. Third, the work points out some of the problems and features of many modern machine architec-

tures that make deterministic predictable performance difficult.

Overview

Timing tool. Our timing tool predicts deterministic bounds of execution times for elementary expressions, control structures, statements, and procedures. Given a program P and bounds for each loop, the tool computes estimates of the best- and worst-case execution times of P.

The factors that affect a program's execution time are program logic, data values, and implementations by a compiler, run-time system, operating system, and machine. Some information on program logic and data values must be provided by users because they are unpredictable in general. In the tool, we require the input of *loop bounds* only, specified as a minimum and maximum number of iterations. (There is an implicit assumption that the user gives correct input. Loop bounds could be the result of a formal proof or an informal specification.) The details of the compiler are analyzed to predict the possible code generated for each basic program element. The tool predicts the execution times of the possible code using the characteristics of the target machine. The effects of some nondeterministic features of the machine are included by translating them into determinate bounds. We also handle the interference due to unavoidable clock interrupts. Experiments were done on a bare machine without an operating system.

Timing schema approach. Shaw's method of predicting the execution time of a high-level language statement[1] implies the following steps:

(1) Decompose a statement into its primitive or basic components, as defined by the timing schema for the statement. These basic components are called *atomic blocks*. The schema is language dependent, but system (compiler/machine) independent.

(2) Predict the implementation (for example, the object code generated by the compiler) of each atomic block. We call this step *code prediction*.

(3) Determine the execution times of the atomic blocks from the times of the machine instructions produced by the implementation.

(4) Compute the execution time of the statement, using the times of the atomic blocks and timing schema for the statement.

The time T of a statement or a block S is represented by a pair of best/worst-case bounds. That is, $T(S) = [\ t_{min}(S), t_{max}(S)\ ]$, where $t_{min}(S)$ and $t_{max}(S)$ are the best- and worst-case execution times of S, respectively. (We will use uppercase T for a pair of time bounds and lowercase t for a scalar time.)

For example, the execution time of statement $S1: a = b + c$; could be computed in the following way (corresponding to the previous steps):

(1) A timing schema corresponding to $S1$ could be

$$T(S1) = T(b) + T(+) + T(c) + T(a) + T(=)$$

The statement is decomposed into five atomic blocks, corresponding to b, $+$, c, a, and $=$. Here, addition over intervals is defined as follows: $[\ w, x\ ] + [\ y, z\ ] \equiv [\ w + y, x + z\ ]$

(2) Object code for each atomic block could be predicted as follows:

b :   mov M,R /* mov b,d0 */
$+$:   add M,R /* add c,d0 */
c :   none
a :   none
$=$:   mov R,M /* mov d0, a */

where M and R are generic memory locations and registers, respectively.

(3, 4) According to the timing schema, the execution time of $S1$ becomes the sum of the times of three predicted instructions.

The execution times for control statements can be computed similarly. For instance, the timing schema for S: if (exp) then $S1$ else $S2$ is

$$T(S) = [\ \min(t1_{low}, t2_{low}), \max(t1_{up}, t2_{up})\ ]$$

where $[t1_{low}, t1_{up}] = T(exp) + T(S1) + T(then)$, $[t2_{low}, t2_{up}] = T(exp) + T(S2) + T(else)$, and $T(then)$ and $T(else)$ denote control flow times (times to transfer to and from $S1$ and $S2$).

Target language and system. We tested whether our timing schema approach could produce useful best- and worst-case execution time bounds for modern high-level languages and their underlying systems. We chose a subset of C, the Gnu C compiler (nonoptimizing option), and the MC68010-based Sun 2/100U as the target language, compiler, and machine, respectively.

The subset of C is small enough to be

tractable and large enough to write some interesting programs. In the second version, it includes expressions with simple arithmetic and relational operators; assignment statements; if and while statements; and procedure calls, where a simple operator means an operator whose implementation is not a library call. Any simple data type including array, pointer, and structure is allowed, but float and long (which require library calls) are not. The criteria for deciding the subset was its ease for constructing a simple prototype of the tool. The excluded features such as logical operators and complex operators could be added, but it would require some care; for example, library calls and system calls would be treated like special kinds of procedure calls with predetermined execution time bounds (assuming these bounds are available or computable).

The Gnu C-1.34 compiler from Free Software Foundation was selected mainly because its source programs are available for public scrutiny and modification. These programs clearly show how each high-level construct is compiled. Moreover, we can directly use the parser to analyze a program and produce atomic blocks for each timing schema.

The CPU has a 10-megahertz clock and a 2-megabyte main memory (with no cache). There is also an AM9513 timer chip, which provides five user-programmable timers. Although the MC68010 has instruction prefetch and instruction execution overlap features, it executes most instructions deterministically. Except for instructions with variable execution time and the occurrence of exceptions, each instruction nominally executes exactly according to its predefined time.

Timing schema and code prediction

A basic decision in defining timing schema and predicting code is the granularity of an atomic block. We investigated small atomic block (SAB) and large atomic block (LAB) granularities. The SAB system permitted an extreme test through all elements of the language, while LAB lent itself to tighter timing predictions.

Small atomic block. In the SAB approach, atomic blocks correspond to the terminal symbols of the source language. Since each atomic block has some basic semantic meaning, the timing schema can be defined in a straightforward way, as in

the example in "Timing schema approach." Conceptually, code prediction can be easy if code generation follows the parsing structure. For many modern compilers, this assumption is true for compiling control constructs but may not be true for expressions.

Many compilers generate efficient code through default optimizations, such as constant folding and register allocation. The generated code is tuned to the target machine. As a result, the compilers use the information of related atomic blocks to generate the code for one atomic block and sometimes consolidate several atomic blocks into one. (Some eminent compiler writers emphasize a simpler, less optimized approach for clarity and maintainability.[6])

For example, in the compiler we used, the sequence of statements $a = b + c$; $d = d + a$ can be compiled as follows:

$$a = b + c; ==> \text{mov } @b, d0$$
$$\text{add } @c, d0$$
$$\text{mov } d0, @a$$
$$d = d + a; ==> \text{add } d0, @d$$

where $@a$ means the memory address of variable a, and $d0$ means data register 0.

The first statement is compiled to three instructions without optimizations. However, the second statement (which has the same structure as the first) is compiled to just one assembly instruction, because a is already in the register and d is both the destination and one of the operands.

These kinds of optimizations cause two problems in applying the timing schema approach in its pure form. First, it becomes hard to precisely predict the actual compiled code of an atomic block because the code can vary widely, depending on the context. Second, sometimes two or more atomic blocks are merged into one machine instruction, also depending on the context. In the above example, two atomic blocks, add (+) and assignment (=), are implemented by one instruction, add $d0, @d$. In this case, it is not clear what corresponds to the implementation of add and what corresponds to assignment. These two related problems complicate code prediction for an atomic block.

One solution to the above problems, which yields tighter code predictions, involves *parameterized* timing schema. Contextual information is generated in statement analysis and passed to code prediction through parameters in the timing schema. As an example, a parameterized timing schema for an assignment statement S: <var> = <exp>; may be $T(S) = T(\text{var}, \text{var\_type}) + T(=, \text{var\_type}, \text{exp\_type}) +$

$T(\text{exp}, \text{exp\_type})$, where the parameters var_type and exp_type are determined in statement analysis.

Large atomic block. This approach defines atomic blocks as large as possible. When a block such as an assignment statement generates straight-line code (no branches), further decomposition into smaller elements is not necessary because the time of the block is simply the sum of the times of each instruction in the code. The LAB idea considers such a straight-line block as an atomic block; for example, an assignment statement $a = b + c$; is considered one atomic block. Several assignment statements could be combined into one atomic block, but a control statement such as an If should be decomposed into multiple blocks.

LAB can eliminate the problems caused by some compiler optimizations. By matching atomic blocks to code generation units of a compiler, we can predict the code of an atomic block in the same way a compiler generates and optimizes its code. If the compiled code of a program is available, code can be predicted simply by lookup; code generation and optimization inside a block are transparent to code prediction.

A block can be atomic as long as it consists of straight-line code. However, there are some subtleties that require further study. For example, an apparently straight-line block may be implemented with branching code: A simple multiplication may be implemented by a sequence of shifts, adds, and branches.

Timing schema and code prediction for the C subset. We have applied two approaches to the C subset, SAB in the first version and LAB in the second. A partially parameterized timing schema with SABs was tested in the first version. Park[7] describes the details of the timing schema and code prediction in the SAB version. Below, we explain the simpler LAB method.

First, an atomic block for our C subset and tool is defined as follows:

(1) Every expression statement is an atomic block.
(2) Every control construct has one or more atomic blocks corresponding to possible transfer of control.

This definition provides a straightforward correspondence between the atomic blocks of the timing schema and the code generation rules of the compiler. In Figure

1, the schema for a While statement is the sum of its constituent expression, statement, and control, essentially as suggested by Shaw.[1] For an expression statement S: exp; , the schema is simply $T(S) = T(exp_{code})$, where exp_{code} is the predicted sequence of codes for exp.

Code prediction for an atomic block is achieved by looking up the compiled assembly code and extracting the corresponding part. An extended compiler generates markers between the codes of atomic blocks; code prediction is then the result of an easy matching operation. The remaining constructs of the C subset are handled in a similar manner, with a schema for the construct and system-dependent code prediction.

Machine analysis

Instructions with variable execution times. On the MC68010, some instructions have variable execution times that depend on operand values and machine status. These include shift and multiple data move instructions, whose execution times are variable but predictable from their operand value; multiply,[*] whose time is unpredictable; and conditional jump, where the time depends on whether the branch is taken or not. In the tool, these execution times are described by time bounds (such as shift), or only a worst-case time (such as multiply), or by treating the best and the worst case as different instructions (such as conditional jump).

System interferences. For a program to execute without interruption, we eliminate the sources of some interferences and prevent others by disabling the interfering process. However, some interferences cannot be eliminated or should not be prevented. In this subsection, we describe two such interferences: a clock interrupt and memory refresh.

Time or clock services are important in computer systems, especially in hard real-time systems where timing behavior must be monitored. We also need a time service in our experiments to measure real execution times for comparison with predicted times. Time services are often provided through a clock interrupt that comes from a hardware or a timer chip, as in our target system. (We could directly read/write times in the Am9513 timer chip and avoid using an interrupt. However, the times that can be represented in the chip are too short to measure a long execution because of the limited size of the internal registers.) We use our home-built clock utility whose interrupt handling time, a source of interference, is 70 microseconds.

Another interference comes from machine hardware. The main memory of our target system, composed of dynamic RAMs, must be restored periodically to maintain its content. The memory refresh process has higher priority in accessing the memory than the CPU does. Thus, it impedes the execution of a normal program running on the CPU.

Because we could not find any detailed quantitative data on the effects of memory refresh on program execution times, we made our own hardware measurements with an oscilloscope. The results were surprising to us in at least two ways. First, memory refresh is the main source of nondeterminism in the target machine. Second, the amount of nondeterminism and the effects of memory refresh are much larger than expected (based on data published by the manufacturer for a similar Sun 68000 board), mainly due to bus arbitration costs. Our measurements showed that memory refresh is accomplished by performing 128 memory cycles (each taking four clock cycles) in sequence, one per row address, at a rate of one cycle every 13 microseconds; an additional one or two clock cycles are required for the bus arbitration before and after each refresh cycle. From this, we computed that a worst-case (but unlikely) processor slowdown was 6.7 percent and that a minimum slowdown was 0 percent (also very unlikely); we observed that a frequent slowdown appeared to be 5 percent with considerable variation above and below.

Effects of system interferences. System interferences complicate timing analysis. However, their effects can be estimated if they have determinate characteristics, such

---

[*]The execution times of multiply is decided by an internal micro-instruction algorithm that is unpredictable at the machine-instruction level. The MC68010 processor manual gives only the upper time bound (that is, the worst case); the lower bound is undefined. Experiments show that the execution times for very simple cases (possibly the best cases) are only slightly smaller than the worst time. Thus, we assume that the best time is the same as the worst time.

```
Statement:
    S : while (exp) stmt;

Timing schema:

    T(S) = (N+1) · T(exp) + N · T(stmt) + T(while,N)
    where N is a pair of loop bounds (i.e., N = [n_min , n_max]).

Gnu C's code generation rules:

                    start_loop          L1:
                    exp                     exp
    S ==>           exit_if_false ==>       JRF L2
                    stmt                    stmt
                    end_loop                JRA L1
                                        L2:

    where JRF means "jump_relative if false,"
    and JRA means "jump_relative always."

Code prediction:

    T(exp)      : T( exp_code )
    T(stmt)     : T( stmt_code )
    T(while,N)  : N · T(JRF,fail) + T(JRF,succ) + N · T(JRA)

    where exp_code and stmt_code are predicted codes for
    exp and stmt , and JRF,fail is a jump instruction whose branch is not taken.
```

Figure 1. Timing schema and code prediction for While statement.

as bounded frequency and duration. In this section, we introduce two complementary techniques to handle the effects of some system interferences. One approach involves adjusting the measured data; the other adjusts the time prediction.

Measured data can be adjusted simply by removing interference times from measured times. We consider the effect of a clock interrupt as an example.

Suppose that clock interrupt period (p_{clock}) and interrupt handling time (t_{clock}) are given. Let a measured execution time of program P be t_P^m, which is a multiple of p_{clock}. Then, clock interrupts occur t_P^m / p_{clock} times during the execution of P,

and its total interference time is $\left(t_P^m / p_{clock}\right) \cdot t_{clock}$. Thus, adjusted time t'_P, the pure execution time of program P, is

$$t'_P = t_P^m - \frac{t_P^m}{p_{clock}} \cdot t_{clock}$$

This is the technique used in our timing tool.

The second method, adjusting the time prediction, includes interference effects directly in program execution times. Shaw[1] presented such a timing analysis for processor sharing between a user process and one or more interrupt handlers. Not sur-

prisingly, it gives the same formula as shown above. In this approach, the granularity of adjustment is significant. At one extreme, we can apply the adjustment whenever the time of an atomic block is predicted; at the other extreme, we can adjust the time of a whole program after it has been predicted. The result in the first case potentially produces looser bounds because of the possibility of dealing with more fractional interrupts.

Timing tool design

The timing tool consists of the preprocessor, the language analyzer, and the architecture analyzer. The preprocessor has two major functions. First, it interprets user commands and prepares the working environment for the tool, including the compiled assembly code with atomic block markers of a source program. Second, it converts the internal time scale (clock cycles) into a real time scale (microseconds). The language analyzer, the heart of our timing tool, is decomposed into the five functional blocks shown in Figure 2. The time schema block is system independent but language dependent, while code prediction is a function of the compiler and architecture. The architecture analyzer maintains instruction execution times for access by the language analyzer.

We built the parser of our tool by modifying the parser of the Gnu C compiler. Adding some lines to several compiler source files is sufficient to extend the compiler with atomic block markers. Figure 3 shows a binary search example using the LAB version of our timing tool. Time bounds as a pair of clock cycles are output at the end of each statement. In the middle of the figure, "1 4" is the user's loop bounds input, which can be derived from the knowledge that the number of data items is less than 15. The tool gives two predictions, one for the whole procedure time including control transfer and register savings and the other for the procedure body only. The latter is used to validate a prediction with the measured time.

Experiments and validation

Measurement techniques. Our basic measurement technique is the *control/test loop* method, similar to that described by Clapp.[8] A control loop contains time mea-

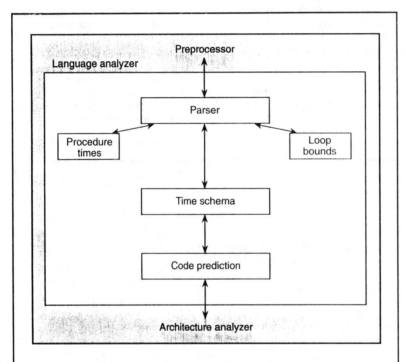

Parser: analyzes the input C program, statement by statement.

Procedure times: manages the table of procedure names and their execution times.

Loop bounds: interacts with a user to obtain loop bounds.

Time schema: analyzes a statement into atomic blocks and computes the execution time of the statement using the times of the atomic blocks computed in code prediction. The timing schema are applied here.

Code prediction: predicts the exact code for a given atomic block by looking up the assembly code prepared by the preprocessor and computes the time of the block using instruction execution times provided by the architecture analyzer.

Figure 2. Organization of language analyzer.

surements and loop control for iterations, and a test loop is a modified control loop that includes the program to be measured. The execution time of a program is computed by taking the difference between the measured times of the control loop and the test loop. With a 5-millisecond tick period and 1,500,000 iterations, the maximum measurement error is 0.01 microseconds.[7] This error is so small that it can be ignored, because the shortest instruction execution time is 0.4 microseconds. (To increase our confidence in this kind of data, we confirmed the clock frequencies of the machine and the timer chip using an oscilloscope.)

Validation approach. To validate the tool's predictions, we experimented with different sample programs and compared their measured times to the time bounds predicted by the timing tool. Test data for the best/worst cases of a sample program were generated by tracing the program's shortest and longest execution paths. Ideally, we can say that the tool gives a safe prediction if every measured time is within the predicted time bounds. However, system interferences (see "Machine analysis") will increase measured times. To handle this problem, we introduce the notion of a *pure execution time*, the execution time if there were no interferences. (Pure execution time of a program is computed by hand, tracing paths and counting cycles from the assembly program generated by the compiler.) Safe prediction is then defined as follows: Pure execution times must be within the predicted time bounds.

It is often the case that pure execution times are not available. Then, measured times will determine safety. We adjusted the measured times by removing the effect of a clock interrupt. (All "measured time" data in the table refer to this adjusted measured time.) Even after this adjustment, we still get a maximum 7 percent longer measured time (see Table 1) than the pure execution time, which we can attribute to dynamic RAM refresh interference (see "System interferences"). Thus, we use the following simple sufficient condition for safe prediction: The measured time of the worst case is smaller than the upper bound of the prediction, and that of the best case decreased by 7 percent is greater than the lower bound. A necessary condition is that the worst measured time decreased by 7 percent may not be greater than the upper bound, and the best measured time may not be smaller than the lower bound.

However, when a measured time is very close to the prediction, the above simple conditions do not always determine safety. For example, the sufficient condition may fail even though a prediction is safe. If a prediction is extended to include interferences as well as a pure execution time, a prediction corresponds directly to a measured time; we can then validate the safety

```
struct {
  int key;
  int value;
}   data[15];

binary_search(x)
{
  int fvalue, mid, up, low ;

  low = 0;
                                          [ 16 , 16 ]
  up = 14;
                                          [ 20 , 20 ]
  fvalue = −1 /* all data are positive */ ;
                                          [ 20 , 20 ]
  while (low <= up)
                    *** WHILE statement ***
                    Input LOOP-BOUNDS   [ low up ]: 1 4
  {
    mid = (low + up) >> 1;
                                          [ 52 , 52 ]
    if ( data[mid].key == x )  { /* found */
    up = low − 1;
                                          [ 40 , 40 ]
     fvalue = data[mid].value;
                                          [ 72 , 72 ]
    }
                                          [ 112 , 112 ]
    else /* not found */
     if ( data[mid].key > x ) up = mid − 1;
                                          [ 40 , 40 ]
    else              low = mid + 1;
                                          [ 40 , 40 ]
                                          [ 128 , 134 ]
                                          [ 206 , 222 ]
  }
                                          [ 258 , 274 ]
                                          [ 352 , 1340 ]
  return fvalue;
                                          [ 26 , 26 ]
}
                                          [ 434 , 1422 ]

*** Target procedure( binary_sea )
    Cycles = [ 478 , 1466 ]
    Times = [ 48.62 , 149.13 ] (microseconds)

*** Target procedure( binary_sea ) body time
    Cycles = [ 434 , 1422 ]
    Times = [ 44.15 , 144.65 ] (microseconds)
```

Figure 3. An example using the timing tool.

Table 1. Times of language constructs.

Language construct[*]	Predicted time bounds (SAB)	Predicted time bounds (LAB)	Measured time (μsec)	Pure execution time
Expression:				
a + b;	[1.42 , 3.46]	[3.46 , 3.46]	3.66	3.46
a * b;	[5.29 , 7.32]	[6.31 , 6.31]	6.43	6.31
a > b;	[2.44 , 4.07]	[3.86 , 3.86]	3.97	3.86
a[b];	[3.86 , 5.09]	[4.27 , 4.27]	4.42	4.27
Assignment:				
a = b;	[1.22 , 2.03]	[2.03 , 2.03]	2.15	2.03
a = b + c;	[1.63 , 4.07]	[3.66 , 3.66]	3.91	3.66
If:				
simple_if:	[3.46 , 4.48]	[3.86 , 4.48]	[3.98 , 4.71]	[3.86 , 4.48]
While:				
simple_while:	[1.83 , 6.71]	[2.24 , 6.31]	[2.34 , 6.62]	[2.24 , 6.31]
Procedure call:				
null_proc_call:	[6.72 , 26.44]	[6.72 , 6.72]	6.97	6.72

simple_if:	if(a)b = 1;	**best time when a is zero	
	else c = 1;	worst time when a is nonzero	
simple_while:	while(a) a = 0;	**best time when a is zero	
		worst time when a is nonzero	
null_proc_call:	prcd();		
	where prcd() { ; }		

[*]All variables are short type.

of a prediction with respect to a measured time. We say that the measurements and predictions are *consistent* if the predicted bounds adjusted for all possible interferences cover the measurements. On the one hand, prediction and validation, including such unavoidable interferences as interrupts and memory refresh, may be more practical than using pure execution times only, because these adjusted times are eventually part of any real execution. On the other hand, they are less rigorous in testing the correctness of a prediction because some errors in the prediction may be covered by the adjustment.

Experiments were conducted in three stages. First, we predicted, measured, and validated each language construct of our subset C. Next, we tested simple procedures whose execution paths are completely known. Finally, more complex procedures were tested and analyzed.

Experiments. Table 1 presents the timing data for most of the basic C constructs used. First, we can say that time prediction with SAB for each language construct is safe because every pure execution time (and most measured times) is included in the corresponding predicted time bounds. (Measured execution times for code generated by sequences of a = b + c; were checked electronically by an oscilloscope to give us more confidence that our measured results were correct.)

In most cases, the tool gives very tight upper bounds but looser lower bounds, except in a procedure call, where the number of saved registers can vary widely. The LAB predictions are identical to the pure execution times for every construct, as expected, because we defined the atomic blocks to be compatible with the target compiler.

The results of experiments on five simple procedures are shown in Table 2, where the adjusted bounds are added. Since arrsum has only one execution path, its data illustrates how precisely the tool predicts the execution time of a specific path. Other procedures have multiple execution paths based mainly on the number of loop iterations and input data. The tool predicts the best and worst of those variable data-de-

pendent execution times. To validate the predictions, we generated the best- and worst-case data and measured the time of each.

The tool gives very tight predictions for all the procedures — too tight to be validated by our simple sufficient condition (see "Validation approach"). All predictions satisfy the necessary condition for safety. When interference due to memory refresh is taken into account, as in the second column (the same lower bound for the best case with no interference and about 7 percent higher upper bound for the worst case with maximum interference), the predictions and measurements are consistent. The only unusual result is that the lower bound of sqrt seems too close to the best execution time. However, it could be explained by the observation that multiplication is dominant in sqrt; the worst-time data for the multiply instruction yields a higher prediction, and less interference from memory refresh during multiplication results in a smaller measurement. Finally, it is worth noting that these tight bounds are possible because loop bounds are sufficient to describe the execution paths of the procedures.

We tested an insertion sort program and a modified version of a multiprocessor scheduler algorithm as more complex examples (see Table 3); the scheduler program, for example, consists of 160 lines of C code. The tool produces safe but loose bounds for both of them. The lower bound of the complete scheduler is six times less than the measured time, although the prediction for each phase (P1, P2, P3) is much tighter.

Execution time is heavily dependent on the program execution path, and the logic of most programs severely limits the set of possible execution paths. For example, the scheduler program has an interesting relation between the phases, P1 and P2. The best case of P2 (that is, ready_process = false) occurs only when the worst case of P1 (that is, no ready processes in the processlist) happens. This is the main reason for the looseness of the scheduler's lower bound.

Both the insertion sort and the scheduler have a nested loop where the maximum number of iterations in the inner loop is a function of the outer loop index value. In such a nested loop, the time of the inner loop is changed with every outer loop iteration. The pure timing schema approach cannot handle such interrelations among program statements. We also assume here that the execution time of a loop body is constant. As a result. the tool produces loose bounds for these procedures. (Similar results were obtained with SAB on both simple and complex procedures, but with looser bounds.[7])

One lesson we learned from the complex program experiments is that the use of loop bounds as the only program execution information may not be sufficient, because many impossible (infeasible) paths may be added. In recent experiments. we have tested more complicated user input where a user can pick a path (then or else) in an alternative (if) statement (even inside a simple loop). This user input can specify one execution path, and the tool then can predict a very tight time for that path, for example, as in the procedure arrsum. If the best and worst execution paths of a program can be specified by a user's input, the tool can predict the time bounds of the best- and worst-case execution, respectively. Then, the guaranteed time bounds of the program are the result of merging two bounds, the lower bound of the best path and the upper bound of the worst. For the scheduler in Table 3, we could achieve the very tight prediction [256.55, 3356.34]. We are going to develop this idea further. Some related issues will be mentioned in the next section.

The results of our experiments can be summarized as follows. All the predicted times are consistent, and most are safe. Some predictions are fairly tight, while others are a little loose. There are clear technical reasons that explain the differences between measured and predicted times, and we see technical solutions that should minimize these differences within the timing schema framework.

Issues and future work

Our timing schema approach produced a convenient division between the more abstract programming language timing units and the lower level compiler/machine-oriented units, with a parameterized interface to the latter. Further programming and paper experiments with other language/compiler/machine combinations are needed to determine whether such a clean partition always exists, whether language timing semantics are independent of the lower levels, and whether parameterized schema and/or LABs are a tractable framework for organizing the lower level code rules.

One attractive refinement of the timing tool is using more detailed execution path information. The recent experiments discussed in the previous section showed that

Table 2. Times of simple procedures.

Procedure	Predicted time bounds (LAB)	Time bounds adjusted for memory refresh	Measured times
arrsum	[155.64 , 155.64]	[155.64 , 166.17]	160.39
bi _search	[44.15 , 144.65]	[44.15 , 154.76]	[47.0 , 147.57]
max l	[7.73 , 60.22]	[7.73 , 64.27]	[8.56 , 63.81]
sqrt	[10.78 , 113.32]	[10.78 , 121.42]	[11.00 , 115.79]
fib	[7.93 , 121.46]	[7.93 , 129.56]	[8.37 , 127.95]

```
arrsum() :                    ** For 10 array elements,
i = 0;                              best :    # loop = 10
sum = 0;                            worst :   # loop = 10
while (i < 10) {
  sum = sum + data[i] ;
  i++;
}
return sum ;

max1(a,b) :                   ** For a,b <= 10,
  x = a;                            best  : a = 10, b = 1      ==> # loop = 0
  if ( x < 1 ) x = 1;               worst : a = 0,  b = 10    ==> # loop = 9
  while ( x < b ) x = x + 1;

sqrt(x) :                     ** For 1 <= x <= 100
  a = 1;                            best  : x = 0      ==> # loop = 0
  while ( a * a < x )               worst : x = 100    ==> # loop = 9
    a = a + 1;

fib(n) :                      ** For 1 <= n <= 10
  Fnew = 1; Fold = 0;               best  : n = 1     ==> # loop = 0
  i = 2;                            worst : n = 10    ==> # loop = 9
  while( i <= n ) {
    temp = Fnew;
    Fnew = Fnew + Fold;
    Fold = temp;
    i++;
  }
```

Table 3. Times of complex procedures.

Procedure	Predicted time bounds	Measured times[1]
Insertion sort[2]	[187.17 , 3450.10]	[197.2 , 2071.1]
Scheduler[3]	[51.88 , 4253.31]	[280.68 , 3242.6]
- search_processlist	[25.84 , 838.21]	[37.14 , 826.6]
- allocate_idle	[25.02 , 129.29]	[52.26 , 127.2]
- preempt	[105.38 , 225.02]	[113.72 , 230.7]

```
Scheduler:
  repeat
      search_processlist /* P1 */
      if ready_process then allocate_idle /* P2 */
      if ready_process and no_idle_processor then preempt /* P3 */
  until no_ready_process  or  not_preemptable
```

[1] All data are obtained with 150,000 iterations.
[2] The number of data elements sorted is 10.
[3] The scheduler allocates five processors.

very tight bounds could be predicted with such interactions and that path data could be easily introduced into the existing tool without spoiling the timing schema framework. However, more fundamental studies are required. We need a better understanding of what kind of execution path information is valuable for prediction. It is then necessary to investigate verifiable ways in which the information should be gathered from specifications, program contexts, and users. Methods for merging this information into the timing schema framework should also be developed.

Some refinements of the schema idea could yield tighter timing bounds on programs, but these should not sacrifice the essential simplicity of the concept. In particular, we are considering the combination of assertional program logic with the schema so that context can be taken into account when deriving bounds for specific programs. Similar improvements may be obtained using symbolic execution techniques; an interesting combination of path tracing and symbolic computation, not involving time. is described for concurrent programs by Young.[9]

Instruction times in contemporary computers seem notoriously nondeterministic (unpredictable), not only because machines contain a myriad of complex performance-enhancing features, such as caches and pipelining, but also because they have a number of architectural elements that are hidden from the programmer, including virtual memory implementations, dynamic memory refresh, interrupts, and hardware monitors. Careful analysis of a relatively simple processor such as the MC68010 can account for many of the causes of nondeterministic timing and lead to satisfactory, if not perfect, predictions. More machines need to be studied in a similar way. It is possible that features such as caches can be handled by incorporating their effects at a large enough granularity or by hardware modifications that allow data and instructions to be locked in. A long-term solution to this problem could very well be RISC-like machines with instructions that have equally simple timing properties, at some possible sacrifice in performance.

Because of some of the above problems and measurement difficulties, it has proven surprisingly difficult to precisely validate our deterministic timing predictions. (It took much longer than we care to admit before we realized that it was necessary to also obtain more precise data on hardware, through oscilloscope measurement.)

Clearly, a necessary condition for correctness is that measured results be close to predicted ones. But how close is good enough? More work is required to get a better understanding of these issues. Certain classes and structures for programs are more amenable to timing analysis than others, for example those without dynamic elements (dynamic data structures, processes, types, object instantiations, etc.). Also, it would be useful to characterize these classes precisely and understand their timing behaviors. Our present ideas are to analyze with dynamic elements using execution paths.

This first experimental test of our ideas has been confined to a subset of a sequential programming language. The addition of more control and data structures would permit experiments with more realistic programs and with software systems. The timing schema approach can also be applied to concurrent programs running on shared-memory multiprocessors and distributed systems. We have been devising schema for parallel languages and defining the timing properties of standard process interactions, such as critical section locking, message passing, and remote procedure calls.[10] Some initial experiments for parallel systems are reported by Kim.[11] A particular model for programming-in-the-large, based on unadorned processes and abstract data types, has recently been defined by us for real-time software[12]; this model appears to offer a convenient framework for performing deterministic timing analysis with our timing schema, and we plan to develop this combination further.

O ur first experiments in building and using a software tool to predict the deterministic execution times of programs have been successful and promising. While many interesting and challenging problems must still be solved before such predictions are practical for realistic systems, our research has demonstrated that the timing schema approach can lead to a clean implementation and accurate predictions, and the remaining problems appear manageable with some effort.

We are particularly pleased that we could construct a source-language-level tool and that many of the compiler and machine nondeterminisms became determinate after careful study. We view this work not only as research in performance prediction, but also as the initial steps toward developing and validating a general methodology for reasoning about timing properties of programs. ∎

References

1. A. Shaw, "Reasoning About Time in Higher Level Language Software," *IEEE Trans. Software Eng.*, Vol. 15, No. 7, July 1989, pp. 875-889.

2. R. Lauber, "Forecasting Real-Time Behavior During Software Design Using a CASE Environment," *J. Real-Time Systems*, Vol. 1, No. 1, June 1989, pp. 61-76.

3. A. Mok et al., "Evaluating Tight Execution Time Bounds of Programs by Annotations," *Proc. Sixth IEEE Workshop Real-Time Operating Systems and Software*, May 1989, pp. 74-80.

4. P. Puschner and C. Koza, "Calculating the Maximum Execution Time of Real-Time Programs," *J. Real-Time Systems*, Vol. 1, No. 2, Sept. 1989, pp. 159-176.

5. A. Stoyenko, "A Real-Time Language with a Schedulability Analyzer," doctoral dissertation, Univ. of Toronto, Computer Systems Research Institute, Tech. Report CSRI-206, Toronto, Dec. 1987.

6. N. Wirth, "A Fast and Compact Compiler for Modula-2," Tech. Report No. 64, 9, Institut Fur Informatik, ETH, Zurich, July 1986.

7. C. Park and A. Shaw, "A Source-Level Tool for Predicting Deterministic Execution Times of Programs," Tech. Report 89-09-12, Dept. of Computer Science and Engineering, Univ. of Washington, Seattle, Sept. 1989.

8. R. Clapp et al., "Toward Real-Time Performance Benchmarks for Ada," *Comm. ACM.* Vol. 29, No. 8, Aug. 1986, pp. 760-778.

9. M. Young and R. Taylor, "Combining Static Concurrency Analysis with Symbolic Execution," *IEEE Trans. Software Eng.*, Vol. 14, No. 10, Oct. 1988, pp. 1,499-1,511.

10. A. Shaw, "Deterministic Timing Schema for Parallel Programs," Tech. Report 90-05-06, Dept. of Computer Science and Engineering, Univ. of Washington, Seattle, May, 1990. (To appear in *Proc. Fifth Int'l Parallel Processing Symp.*, CS Press, Order No. 2167, Los Alamitos, Calif., Apr. 1991.)

11. J. Kim and A. Shaw, "An Experiment on Predicting and Measuring the Deterministic Execution Times of Parallel Programs on a Multiprocessor," Tech. Report 90-09-01, Dept. of Computer Science and Engineering, Univ. of Washington, Seattle, Sept. 1990.

12. H. Callison and A. Shaw, "Building a Real-Time Kernel: First Steps in Validating a Pure Process/Adt Model," to be published in *Software — Practice & Experience*, 1991.

Acknowledgments

This research was supported in part by the Office of Naval Research under Grant Number N00014-89-J-1040.

Chang Yun Park is a PhD student in the Department of Computer Science and Engineering at the University of Washington, Seattle. His research interests include real-time systems, software engineering, and operating systems.

He received the BS and MS degrees in computer engineering from Seoul National University, Seoul, Korea, in 1984 and 1986, respectively.

Alan C. Shaw is a professor of computer science and engineering at the University of Washington. In the past, he has worked as a systems engineer at IBM, research associate at the Stanford Linear Accelerator Center, visiting professor at ETH Zurich and at the University of Paris, and computer science faculty member at Cornell University. His current research interests are in real-time systems, software engineering, operating systems, and software specification methods.

He obtained the BA degree in engineering physics from the University of Toronto, the MS degree in mathematics from Stanford University, and the PhD in computer science from Stanford University in 1968. Shaw is a member of the IEEE Computer Society.

The authors can be contacted by mail at the Department of Computer Science and Engineering, FR-35, University of Washington, Seattle, WA 98195 or by e-mail at cypark@ cs.washington.edu or shaw@cs.washington.edu.

Calculating the Maximum Execution Time of Real-Time Programs

P. PUSCHNER,
CH. KOZA
Institut für Technische Informatik, Technische Universität Wien
A-1040 Vienna, Austria

Abstract. In real-time systems, the timing behavior is an important property of each task. It has to be guaranteed that the execution of a task does not take longer than the specified amount of time. Thus, a knowledge about the maximum execution time of programs is of utmost importance.

This paper discusses the problems for the calculation of the maximum execution time (MAXT ...MAximum eXecution Time). It shows the preconditions which have to be met before the MAXT of a task can be calculated. Rules for the MAXT calculation are described. Triggered by the observation that in most cases the calculated MAXT far exceeds the actual execution time, new language constructs are introduced. These constructs allow programmers to put into their programs more information about the behavior of the algorithms implemented and help to improve the self checking property of programs. As a consequence, the quality of MAXT calculations is improved significantly. In a realistic example, an improvement factor of 11 has been achieved.

1. Introduction

The significant difference between real-time systems and other computer systems is the importance of correct timing behavior. Each hard real-time task has a deadline that has to be met, otherwise the real-time system fails. As a consequence, in a real-time system it has to be guaranteed that each task finishes before its deadline, even in the worst case, that is when the task's execution takes a maximum amount of time.

Obviously, the worst case execution time of a task—we call it maximum execution time—is of significant importance for the construction and verification of real-time systems.

In many articles about scheduling in real-time systems, the maximum execution times of tasks are assumed to be known. One example is the classic article about scheduling in hard real-time systems by Liu and Layland (1973). They assume that the run time for each task is constant, that is, that it does not exceed a known amount of time. In (Mok 1984) the properties and impacts of the use of semaphores, rendezvous constructs, and monitors on real-time systems are discussed. Mok's work is also based on the assumption that the maximum execution time of program blocks is known.

Kligerman (1986) and Stoyenko (1981) address the problem of a worst case analysis of tasks' run-time properties. They discuss the real-time programming language *Real-Time Euclid*. Real-Time Euclid is defined in a way that allows the calculation of the maximum execution time for every program. We will come back to some of the language's concepts later.

In Leinbaugh's papers (Leinbaugh 1980; Leinbaugh and Yamini 1982; Leinbaugh and Yamini 1986) one can find discussions on guaranteeing response times in hard real-time systems. Leinbaugh takes into account task priorities, mutual exclusion, resource conflicts, task communications, and interrupt handling. The MAXT of tasks is expected to be known.

It is the main focus of the MARS (MAintainable Real-time System) research group at the Technical University in Vienna to build a distributed real-time system with a deterministic, guaranteed timing behavior (Kopetz et. al. 1989). The design system of MARS (Senft and Zainlinger 1989) integrates all steps from system design to programming in the small. Tasks are scheduled statically by a pre run-time scheduler. The scheduler takes into account the precedence constraints describing synchronization needs and dependencies among tasks, the maximum execution time of tasks, and the activation frequencies of the tasks and produces a dispatch table which is interpreted at run time (Fohler and Koza 1989). The maximum execution time is provided by a special tool based on an analysis of task source codes.

In this paper, the different aspects of the maximum execution time calculation of real-time programs are discussed.

First we will show that the maximum execution time cannot be calculated for an arbitrary program. Problems for the MAXT calculation are described. This leads to some restrictions for analyzable programs and to the introduction of bounded loops.

The following section gives a description of some simple rules for the calculation of the maximum execution time of programs which obey the restrictions. When looking at the quality of the results of the MAXT calculation, you will see that it is necessary to introduce new programming language constructs which provide a means to state more information about the application context of programs. These constructs enable a program to compute a bound for the maximum execution time which is much closer to the real maximum execution time. Language constructs called markers, scopes, and loop sequences are described.

2. Preconditions for the maximum execution time calculation

In this article we analyze the software aspects of the calculation of the maximum execution time of programs. We make the assumption that the behavior of the underlying hardware and operating system is deterministic and known (this framework is provided by our MARS system (Kopetz et. al. 1989)). This implies that the timing behavior of all hardware components and the effects of caching, pipelining, and DMA performance on task performance are predictable. On the other hand, the operating system must provide static memory management (no paging with statistical behavior), system calls with a calculable timing behavior, and the absence of asynchronous interrupts. Task synchronization is provided by the pre run-time scheduler and thus does not produce any overhead at run time.

We define the technical terms application specific maximum execution time and calculated maximum execution time as follows:

Definition 1 (Application Specific Maximum Execution Time ... MAXT$_A$) *The Application Specific Maximum Execution Time of a program is the time it maximally takes to execute this program in the given application context provided that all needed resources are available, the program is not interrupted, and the performance of the hardware is known.*

Note that the application-specific maximum execution time of a task is the maximum CPU time that the task can actually consume. When trying to get a value for the timing behavior of a task by an analysis of its source code—this is what can be done by a software tool—one can often derive only a high upper bound for the maximal time consumption of a task. This is due to the fact that the program code does not contain the full information about the application context of a task (for more details see Section 4). Hence, we define the term of the calculated maximum execution time.

Definition 2 (Calculated Maximum Execution Time ...MAXT$_C$) *The Calculated Maximum Execution Time of a task is the least upper bound for the MAXT$_A$ of this task that can be derived from the task's program code.*

In order to calculate the maximum execution time of a task, the MAXT (for better readability we will use this abbreviation instead of MAXT$_C$ in the rest of the paper) for all parts of that task—sequences, loops, and so forth—must be computable. This suggests that full information about the control flow and constraints for the control flow in the worst case, that is, when every program part executes as long as possible, have to be known for all language constructs of the programming language used.

The main problem is that the control flow of a program at run-time depends on the input data and the current variable settings. The values of variables used in conditions (loop conditions or conditions of alternatives) and the values of pointers to functions determine the control flow and, as a consequence, the timing properties of each task. Since it is impossible to simulate the execution of a task for all its possible variable settings and to determine if the task terminates, or how long it takes to execute (termination problem), some restrictions have to be made in order to get analyzable programs.

The problems in detail are:

- In most current programming languages the programmer does not have to declare the maximum number of iterations or a time limit for the *loops* he programs. This imposes a problem on the MAXT calculation because the maximum iteration number or a time limit for the loop execution generally cannot—or only with great effort—be extracted from the loop condition. Thus the time maximally spent in a loop cannot be calculated in most cases.

- The usage of recursions leads to a similar problem. The maximal depth of recursive procedure calls, and consequently the MAXT for recursions, cannot be determined statically, since these attributes depend on the variable state at program execution time.

  A related problem of using recursions in a real-time applications is that the demand of stack space cannot be determined before run time. Therefore, the maximal amount of stack space needed at run time cannot be allocated statically as is done in many real-time sytems.

- *Parameters and pointers to functions* can reference functions of distinct timing properties. Because of the dependence of the MAXT on the different functions, it does not make sense to assign the maximum time it takes to evaluate a function to the MAXT for a function referenced.

  Furthermore, the use of pointers to functions provides a means for the implementation of recursions (see above for more details).

- The danger of GOTO usage is that one can write programs which lack any structure in the sense of structured programming. These programs cannot be analyzed by an automated software analysis tool.

We make the following restrictions in order to eliminate the problems listed above (some are mentioned in (Kligerman and Stoyenko 1986):

- Programs must not contain any (direct or indirect) recursions. Recursive algorithms have to be either replaced by iterative ones or transformed into non-recursive schemes by applying program transformation rules (Darlington and Burstall 1978).
- The absence of function variables and parameters is enforced in programs for which the MAXT has to be calculated. Calls of subroutines via variables or parameters have to be substituted by explicit subroutine calls.
- In third generation programming languages every semantic that can be programmed with GOTOS can also be achieved with the standard language constructs—sequences, loops, and iterations. As a consequence, the elimination of GOTOS does not result in any restrictions on programming.
- Since loops are fundamental for the implementation of almost every algorithm, one cannot eliminate loop constructs from programming languages. Nevertheless it has to be guaranteed that every loop terminates within a specified amount of time. As a consequence, loop constructs which force the programmer to give some information about the time spent in a loop have to be introduced. Loops of this kind are called *bounded loops*.
  We differentiate two kinds of bounded loops:

  - Loops with a specified limit for the number of iterations
  - Loops which are bounded by a time limit that must not be overrun at run-time.

The bound of each loop depends on its particular application context. It is specified using the appropriate language construct. Limits for both the maximal number of iterations and for time have to be known at compile time to make the computation of the maximum execution time possible.

2.1. Bounded loops

The constructs for bounded loops look very similar to conventional loop constructs. They differ from the usual loop constructs in two ways:

- All loop constructs ensure that a loop bound is specified—this has first been demanded in (Ehrenberger 1983) and (Halang 1984). A loop bound can either be a limit for the maximum number of iterations or a time limit for the termination of the loop. Loop bounds have to be known at compile time.
- If a loop bound is overrun a specified action is started. The default for this action is the activation of the operating system's exception handler (see Exceptions). However the programmer may override this default and specify a different treatment for this case[1].

The benefit of using bounded loops is twofold. On the one hand they are necessary for MAXT calculation; on the other hand they serve as a control mechanism for checking iteration limitations at run time.

Examples for bounded loop constructs are demonstrated below. The constructs are presented in the C-like syntax as used in a prototype implementation of MARS. In contrast to the original C loop constructs, the keywords of bounded loops are written in capital letters. We provide FOR, WHILE and DO-WHILE loops which are derivatives of the respective C loops.

```
FOR(exprl;expr2;expr3 ) MAX_COUNT(const_expr)
    stmtl
[ON_OVERRUN stmt2]


FOR(exprl; expr2; expr3 ) MAX_TIME(const_texpr)
    stmtl
[ON_TIMEOUT stmt2]
```

The statements of the loop body are executed as long as the evaluation of the running condition (expr2) returns true and the loop bound—defined with MAX_COUNT or MAX_TIME—is not exceeded. If the running condition returns false, the loop terminates and the program execution continues after the loop statement. If the running condition is true and the loop bound is found violated then either the statement in the ON-OVERRUN or ON_TIMEOUT clause or—if such statements do not exist—an operating system exception will be executed.

In our implementation the bounds of loops with an iteration limit are checked by a counter. In order to guarantee that the limits of time-bounded loops are met, we determine the maximal amount of time it takes to perform exactly one iteration. Every time a new iteration is to be started it is tested whether another iteration of maximal duration can be finished within the time limit or not.

We prefer this approach to the solution described in (Kligerman and Stoyenko 1986). In (Kligerman and Stoyenko 1986) the time limit is transformed into an iteration bound at compile time. If the time needed for the single iterations is short compared to the maximal duration, the loop executes only a fraction of the specified time. We consider this a disadvantage, because in many cases the actual timing behavior of loops will substantially differ from the behavior specified in the program.

2.2. Exceptions

An exception is an abnormal situation during the execution of a program. We distinguish two kinds of exceptions—recoverable and non-recoverable exceptions.

Exceptions which are recoverable, that is, those for which an exception handler is provided, are considered part of the program. Their timing behavior has to be taken into account in the timing analysis the same way as in the timing behavior of all program parts (Halang 1989).

Non-recoverable exceptions are those for which the system is not prepared, that is, if a non-recoverable exception is raised, the specified behavior of the system cannot be guaranteed. Thus the occurrence of a non-recoverable exception leads to a system failure. All that can be done in this case is to try to minimize the resulting damage. The system has to be transferred into a save state and then shut down.

3. Calculating an upper bound for the maximum execution time

Programs which do not violate the conditions of Section 2 and contain only simple constructs can be analyzed by an automated MAXT analysis tool. The maximum execution time can be calculated recursively using a small set of formulas for the simple language constructs. The simple language constructs for which formulas have to be provided are simple statements, statement sequences, alternatives, bounded loops, and subroutines.

The maximum execution time of a simple language construct (for example, simple construct or simple expression) is the time required for the sequential execution of the corresponding machine instructions on the given processor. It can be obtained from the hardware specifications of the processor.

In order to calculate the $MAXT_C$ for sequences ($construct_1$; $construct_2$; ...; $construct_n$;), we only have to sum up the maximum execution times of the single constructs. If we have to determine the maximal amount of time consumed by an alternative (IF *condition* THEN $construct_1$; ELSE $construct_2$;), we have to add the maximal time for the evaluation of the condition and the time maximally spent in one of the branches. The same rule can be used to calculate the maximum execution time for multiple branch instructions (switch in C, case in Pascal).

When calculating the maximum execution time for loop constructs, we have to distinguish between loops with a limited iteration number and loops which are bounded by a time limit. For the former, the number of iterations has to be multiplied with the execution times of loop condition and body[2]. For loops with the running condition at the heading (FOR, WHILE) we have to add the time for one more evaluation of the condition. In the case of a FOR loop, the time for initializations also has to be taken into account.

The maximum execution time of a time-bounded loop is simply the timing constraint of the loop.

For both kinds of loops we have to consider the case that the loop bound is exceeded, which means that the loop has consumed its maximum time and the overrun or timeout statement is activated. Hence we have to add the maximum execution time for this statement.

The maximal time used up by a subroutine is the sum of the time for organization (copying parameters, jumping, returning from a subroutine) plus the maximal amount of time for executing the subroutine body.

Table 1 summarizes the rules for the MAXT calculation for all constructs.

The function τ takes a simple action—simple statement, simple expression, or subroutine organization whose MAXT is directly derived from the number of machine instruction cycles—as an argument and returns the amount of time it takes to execute this action in accordance to the prerequisites of definition 1. The *maxt* function is defined to calculate an upper bound for the execution time of its argument.

Table 1. Formulas for the calculation of the maximum execution time.

Construct	MAXT	
primitive	*maxt(primitive)*	$= \tau(primitive)$
sequence	*maxt(sequence)*	$= \displaystyle\sum_i maxt(construct_i)$
alternative	*maxt(alternative)*	$= maxt(condition) + \max(maxt(construct_1), maxt(construct_2))$
$loop_{number}$	*maxt(loop$_{head}$)*	$= maxt(init) + maxt(condition) + count * (maxt(body) + maxt(condition))$ $+ maxt(overrun\_statement)$
	maxt(loop$_{tail}$)	$= count * (maxt(body) + maxt(condition)) + maxt(overrun\_statement)$
$loop_{time}$	*maxt(loop$_{time}$)*	$= time + maxt(timeout\_statement)$
subroutine	*maxt(subroutine)*	$= \tau(organization) + maxt(body)$

4. Adding knowledge to programs in order to improve the MAXT computation

Using the rules introduced so far we are able to compute an upper bound for the $MAXT_C$ of programs. We will demonstrate this in the following example. The example shows that our results can be improved if we add some more information about constraints on the control flow to the program. This will encourage us to introduce new language constructs.

4.1. An example

An enterprise specializes in the production of goods that are filled into tin cans. The fabrication is automated and robots are involved in the job. In the last production step the cans are packed into boxes. We observe the following scenario: The tin cans are transported on a conveyor belt. A robot arm seizes the cans and puts them into the boxes. The computer controlling the robot arm is connected to a video camera in order to determine the position of the can on the belt.

The program for the localization of the can has to regard the specifications listed below:

- The image read by the camera is presented in an array of $640 * 200$ pixels.
- The colors of the tin cans and the conveyor belt are contrasting. Due to shape and size, cans produce an image that covers a maximum of 2200 pixels.
- There may be some noise in the image data. The maximal noise ratio which is tolerated is specified with one percent (that is, 1280 pixels) of the array.
- In order to steer the robot arm to the right location, the program has to calculate the center of the marked area. The influence of noisy data on the result has to be minimized.

The program which performs as described is given by the Nassi-Schneidermann diagram shown in Figure 1.

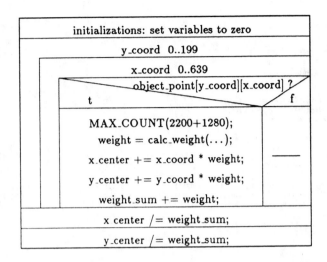

Figure 1. Nassi-Schneidermann diagram for the camera example.

A listing for the camera application is shown in Figure 2 (the keyword SCOPE and the statement MAX__COUNT(MAX__AREA); should be ignored at this time. They will be described later in this paper). The execution times for all parts of the program calculated from the machine instructions generated by a UNIX C compiler are provided in comments[3]. They are given in number of CPU cycles.

We can calculate an upper bound for the maximum execution time for the *calc__center*-subroutine by applying the introduced rules (see Figure 3).

Looking at the program specifications we realize that the number of pixels that may be set is limited to 3,480(= 2,200 + 1,280). This knowledge is not contained in the program because currently we have no means to state that the respective program part can be executed a maximum of 3,480 times. Hence, the above calculation does not make use of this knowledge but assumes that each of the 128,000 pixels might be set, which results in a $MAXT_C$ much higher than a realistic execution time for this subroutine.

4.2. New constructs: markers and scopes

This example demonstrates that we can only determine an extremely high upper bound for the $MAXT_A$ if we are content with the language constructs introduced so far. The unsatisfactory results are due to the fact that we cannot express our full knowledge about the control flow of a program by means of the existing constructs. Thus we define new language constructs—markers and scopes—in order to reduce the difference $MAXT_C$–$MAXT_A$.

Definition 3 (Scope) *A Scope is a part of a program's instruction code, limited by a special scope language construct, that is embedded into the syntax of a programming language.*

Definition 4 (Marker) *A Marker is a special mark located within a scope. It specifies the maximal number of times the marked position in the program may be passed by the program flow between entering and leaving the scope.*

```
#define MAX_ROWS    200                                                              /* CPU cyles */
#define MAX_COLS    640
#define MAX_AREA    3480


int calc_weight(image, x_coord, y_coord)                                             /*  44 */
char    image[MAX_ROWS][MAX_COLS];
int     x_coord, y_coord;
{
    int x_lim, y_lim, i, j, count=0;                                                 /*  72 */

    x_lim = x_coord + 1;
    y_lim = y_coord + 1;

    FOR(i=y_coord-1;i<=y_lim;i++) MAX_COUNT(3)          /* loop1 */                   /* (54+26;84;32) */
        FOR(j=x_coord-1;j<=x_lim;j++) MAX_COUNT(3)      /* loop2 */                   /* (54+26;84;32) */
            if (image[i][j]) count++;                   /* alt1 */                    /* (146) 16 */

    count--;    /* Number of neighbours */                                           /* 122 */
    return count * count >> 2;
}


int calc_center(image, x_center, y_center)                                           /*  44 */
char    image[MAX_ROWS][MAX_COLS];
int     *x_center, *y_center;
{
    int pixel_count, x_coord, y_coord, x_sum, y_sum;                                 /*  48 */

    pixel_count = x_sum = y_sum = 0;

    FOR(y_coord = 0; y_coord < MAX_ROWS; y_coord++) SCOPE MAX_COUNT(MAX_ROWS)        /* (42+26;76;32) */
    {                                                   /* loop3 */
        FOR(x_coord = 0; x_coord < MAX_COLS; x_coord++) MAX_COUNT(MAX_COLS)          /* (42+26;76;32) */
        {                                               /* loop4 */
            if (image[x_coord][y_coord])                /* alt2 */                    /* 146 */
            {
                int weight;

                MAX_COUNT(MAX_AREA);                                    /* marker */  /*  40 */
                weight = calc_weight(image, x_coord, y_coord);                        /* 310 + */
                x_sum += x_coord * weight;
                y_sum += y_coord * weight;
                pixel_count += weight;
            }
        }
    }

    if (pixel_count)                                    /* alt3 */                    /*  22 */
    {
        *x_center = x_sum / pixel_count;                                             /* 424 */
        *y_center = y_sum / pixel_count;
    }
    else
        *x_center = *y_center = 0;                                                    /*  56 */

    return 1;                                                                        /*  14 */
}
```

Figure 2. Program listing of the camera example.

$$maxt(calc\_center) \quad = \quad 44 + 48 + maxt(loop_3) + maxt(alt_3) + 14 =$$
$$= \underline{551\ 475\ 096}$$

$$maxt(loop_3) \quad = \quad 42 + 76 + 200 * ((maxt(loop_4) + 32) + 76) + 26 =$$
$$= 551\ 474\ 544$$

$$maxt(loop_4) \quad = \quad 42 + 76 + 640 * ((maxt(alt_2) + 32) + 76) + 26 =$$
$$= 2\ 757\ 264$$

$$maxt(alt_2) \quad = \quad 146 + \max(310 + maxt(calc\_weight), 0) = 4\ 200$$

$$maxt(alt_3) \quad = \quad 22 + \max(424, 56) = 446$$

$$maxt(calc\_weight) \quad = \quad 44 + 72 + maxt(loop_1) + 122 = 3\ 744$$

$$maxt(loop_1) \quad = \quad 54 + 84 + 3 * ((maxt(loop_2) + 32) + 84) + 26 = 3\ 506$$

$$maxt(loop_2) \quad = \quad 54 + 84 + 3 * ((maxt(alt_1) + 32) + 84) + 26 = 998$$

$$maxt(alt_1) \quad = \quad 146 + \max(16, 0) = 162$$

Figure 3. MAXT calculation for the camera example.

Using markers, we can state the maximal number of times the control flow can pass through a specified position within a special part of a program designated by the scope construct. An arbitrary number of markers may be set in each scope.

Markers are mainly used to state that the number of executions of one or more paths through a loop can be bounded. It does not make sense to locate a marker in a sequence or a branch of an alternative which does not lie in a loop, because these program parts could be passed, at most, once within the scope. Hence, we design our scope language constructs to coincide with loop constructs.

We have to make a restriction for the use of markers inside scopes in order to avoid a complexity explosion, as might happen if all language constructs could be used arbitrarily within a scope. In loops in which the maximal number of iterations is limited, markers (1) must not lie inside a piece of code which is contained by a loop (2) that is part of an alternative (3) (see Figure 4). They can only be used in statement sequences or randomly nested alternatives which are only embedded in arbitrarily nested loops (limited by an iteration-bound) inside the scope (4).

In time bounded loops, markers may only be used at the highest level. This means that it is not allowed to set a marker inside nested loops which are bound by a time limit. An implementation of this feature would necessitate complex tests and thus evoke a substantial overhead at run time.

Scopes are embedded in MARS-C, our programming language, which is a descendant of the C programming language, as an extension of the syntax of bounded loop constructs. The programmer defines a scope containing a bounded loop writing the SCOPE keyword into the loop's head. The extended syntax of FOR loops is shown below (the extensions for WHILE and DO-WHILE loops are equivalent). As the syntax suggests, scopes can be nested arbitrarily. In the case of nested scopes, a marker always refers to the innermost scope in which it is contained.

```
FOR(exprl;expr2;expr3 ) [SCOPE] MAX__COUNT(const__expr)
    stmtl
[ON__OVERRUN stmt2]
```

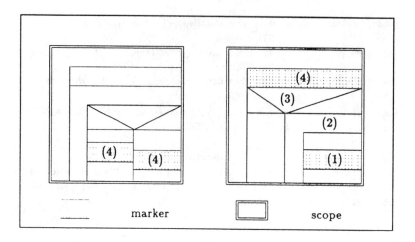

Figure 4. Example for validly (4) and invalidly (1) set markers (each of the diagrams represents a scope).

```
FOR(exprl;expr2;expr3 ) [SCOPE] MAX_TIME(const_texpr)
     stmtl
[ON_TIMEOUT stmt2]
```

If a marker is to be set, there must always be an explicitly defined scope that it is contained in. We prefer this approach to the solution of a global, implicitly defined scope which contains all markers that are not inside any explicitly defined scope, since it leads to a more transparent behavior and helps to detect errors. Furthermore, we favor the homogenous concept that every scope has to be defined explicitly with its contained loop.

To set a marker we simply have to write

```
MAX_COUNT(const_expr);
```

The constant expression *const_expr* can be evaluated at compile time. It is the maximal number of times the marker may be passed inside its scope. Markers are checked at run time in order to verify that the calculated timing behavior can be met. If the bound of a marker is violated an exception is raised.

Let us have another look at our example. We can improve the result of the code analysis by the use of markers and scopes. Now we need the code fragments which we ignored when we first looked at the listing in Figure 2. We define a scope which contains the loop in the *calc_center*-subroutine with the keyword SCOPE. Furthermore we set a marker MAX_COUNT(MAX_AREA);. The MAXT calculation for the new program is sketched in Figure 5 (for MAXT calculation rules for markers and scopes see Section 5).

4.3. Loop sequences

Many programs use sequences of loops whose maximal iteration numbers complement each other, that is, the sum of the iterations of the loops does not exceed a constant value at execution time. This kind of behavior becomes interesting if the bound for the iteration sum is smaller than the sum of the maximal iteration numbers of the single loops. We can reach a better result for the MAXT calculation in such cases if we are able to inform the MAXT analysis tool about loops that belong together.

Definition 5 (Loop Sequence) *A Loop Sequence is a series of loops (limited by an iteration limit) which has the property that the sum of the iterations of the single loops does not exceed a given constant value at run-time.*

Loop sequences are marked by an additional construct which is embedded into the extended C syntax.

> LOOP-SEQUENCE ITERATION__SUM(*const__expr*)
>   *stmtl*
> [ON__OVERRUN *stmt2*]

The body of the loop sequence (*stmtl*) contains the loops that are part of the sequence and arbitrary other constructs—even loops—that may be programmed between the single loops. Loops which are members of a loop sequence are identified by the keyword IN__SEQUENCE. These loops must not be scoped since this would raise the complexity of programs immensely both for programmers and the MAXT analysis tool as well. The syntax definition for bounded loops, occurring in loop sequences, is a modification of the known constructs (see below).

> FOR(*exprl;expr2;expr3*) {IN__SEQUENCE | SCOPE}
> MAX__COUNT(*const__expr*)
>   *stmtl*

A bounded loop inside a loop sequence must not contain an ON__OVERRUN clause, since a violation of a loop bound inside the sequence is treated as an exception of the whole loop sequence. Loop sequences may provide an ON__OVERRUN statement.

5. Calculating the MAXT of programs using the language constructs introduced

The gain of markers, scopes, and loop sequences is obvious by intuition. Here we want to give definite formulas for the calculation of the maximum execution time of these constructs.

5.1. MAXT calculation for scopes containing markers

In this section we provide some formulas for the calculation of the $MAXT_C$ of a scope containing n nested loops $loop_1, \ldots, loop_n$ with the innermost loop containing an arbitrary set of markers[4]. Each loop $loop_i$ contains all $loop_j$ with $i < j \leq n$. The maximal number of iterations of the loops are specified by $bound_1, \ldots, bound_n$. $loop_j'$ specifies the whole loop $loop_j$ except for the loops $loop_{j+1}, \ldots, loop_n$ in it.

The maximum execution time calculation for scopes with markers can be performed in two steps:

1. First we calculate the maximum execution time of the loop parts ($loop_j'$) that do not contain markers, that is, the time for the evaluation of loop conditions, loop organization, and statement sequences between nested loops[5].
2. Next we treat the constructs of the innermost loop's body, which may contain paths that are restricted by markers.

For both steps, the maximum number the innermost loop body can actually be entered—*gmax*—is needed. This figure can be calculated out of the bounds ($count_i$) of the n single loops and the restriction that markers place on the number of iterations (*mmax*).

$$gmax = \min(\prod_{i=1}^{n} count_i, mmax)$$

1. The loops have to be passed in a way that makes the execution time of the loops maximal. Hence, in our calculation we have to assume that the outer loops are passed as often as possible. All inner loops are executed in each iteration of a loop surrounding them.

   Deriving the contribution of the j-th loop to the MAXT of a scope we have to distinguish between three situations[6]:

• $\prod_{i=1}^{j} count_i \leq gmax$

   This means that the loop is an *outer loop*. In the worst case it will be entered $\prod_{i=1}^{j-1} count_i$ times, every time performing $count_j$ iterations. The maximal time consumption for this loop is

$$\prod_{i=1}^{j-1} count_i * maxt(loop_j'(count_j)).$$

• $\prod_{i=1}^{j-1} count_i < gmax \land \prod_{i=1}^{j} count_i > gmax$

   If this condition holds for a loop, the loop will iterate both more than once and less than a maximal number of times at least once in the worst case. The MAXT of this loop—obviously only one such loop can occur in each scope—can be calculated with the formula

$$\sum_{1 \leq k \leq \prod_{i=1}^{j-1} count_i; \ \Sigma_k \ count_{j_k} = gmax; count_{j_k} \leq count_j} maxt(loop_j'(count_{j_k}))$$

We consider it essential to mention that the maximal time for the overhead of $loop_j$ cannot be simply calculated as $maxt(loop_j'(gmax))$. This is due to the fact that it makes a difference whether a loop is entered $\Pi_{i=1}^{j-1} count_i$ times or only once. A FOR–loop, for example, has to be initialized every time it is entered.

Also note that we do not have to care about the number of iterations of the single instances of the loop—$count_{j_k}$. For a constant number of loop instances, the $MAXT_C$ is all the same if the sum total of the iterations ($\Sigma_k count_{j_k}$) is constant ($gmax$). It should be mentioned that the condition $count_{j_k} \leq count_j$ can be omitted. It has been introduced in order to establish a parallel to the loop's execution model.

- $\Pi_{i=1}^{j-1} count_i \geq gmax$

In this case the surrounding loops reach the maximal possible number of iterations. This means that in the worst case $loop_j$ can iterate maximally once each time it is executed. Consequently the contribution of $loop_j'$ to the MAXT is

$$gmax * maxt(loop_j'(1)).$$

2. In order to calculate the MAXT of a loop body with markers, we build a graph which reflects its timing behavior. When constructing the graph, we reduce program constructs that do not contain a marker—the MAXT for these constructs is calculated applying the known rules.

   The resulting graph consists of nodes representing branches or joins of program paths and edges which are marked with the MAXT of the appropriate program parts and execution restrictions imposed by markers.

   The MAXT for the graph is calculated in a repeated execution of the two steps outlined below:

   - The graph is searched for the longest path that has not yet been marked by the algorithm.
   - The path which has been found in the first step is marked and the MAXT of the path is added to the MAXT of the whole graph.

5.2. Calculating the MAXT for loop sequences

In order to compute the maximum execution time for loop sequences we have to distribute the global maximal iteration number among the single loops, maximizing the sum of the MAXTs of the loops. We can apply the formula

$$maxt(loop\_sequence) = \max_{count_j \leq bound_j,\ \Sigma_j count_j\ \leq bound_{seq}} \left(\sum maxt(loop_j(count_j)) \right)$$

where $bound_{seq}$ is the global maximal number of iterations in the loop sequence, $bound_j$ are the upper iteration bounds of the single loops, and $count_j$ are the actual bounds. $loop_j(count_j)$ stands for the time it maximally takes to execute $count_j$ iterations of loop $loop_j$.

6. Benefits and costs of the new constructs

In section 4.3, we introduced some changes to the example given in Section 4.1. We put a scope around the main loop and introduced two markers in the program listing. Based on the rules for the MAXT calculation of these constructs that have been described, we want to give a demonstration of their benefits. Figure 5 shows the steps in the calculation of the maximum execution time for the modified program fragment.

The main gain is due to the marker. With the marker we express that the time consuming procedure $calc\_weight(\ldots)$ is not called in every iteration (128,000 times) but at most 3,480 times (this is the maximal number of pixels which may be set according to the specifications). Thus the portion of the $MAXT_C$ which is contributed by the statement sequence containing the procedure call is immensely reduced in comparison to the first version of $calc\_center(\ldots)$.

$$
\begin{aligned}
maxt(calc\_center) &= 44 + 48 + maxt(scope) + maxt(alt_3) + 14 = \\
&= 46\ 810\ 232 \\
maxt(scope) &= maxt(loop'_3) + maxt(body') = 46\ 809\ 680 \\
maxt(loop'_3) &= 16 + 42 + 76 + 200 * ((maxt(loop'_4 + 32) + \\
&+\ 76) + 26 = 13\ 874\ 560 \\
maxt(loop'_4) &= 42 + 76 + 640 * ((0 + 32) + 76) + 26 = 69\ 264 \\
maxt(body') &= 200 * 640 * 146 + 3480 * (40 + 310 + maxt(calc\_weight)) = \\
&= 32\ 935\ 120 \\
maxt(calc\_weight) &= 3\ 744 \\
maxt(alt_3) &= 22 + \max(424, 56) = 446
\end{aligned}
$$

Figure 5. MAXT calculation for the enhanced camera example.

The upper bound value calculated for the maximum execution time of the original example was about 551 million CPU cycles. When analyzing the new version we derive a bound of only 47 million cycles for the program execution. So the calculated MAXT is reduced by a factor of more than 10 by the use of a scope and a marker. Although this result is remarkable we cannot generalize it. This is due to the fact that the reduction depends on the complexity of the program parts involved (the complexity of $calc\_weight(\ldots)$ has a significant impact on the improvement factor in our example).

It is also interesting to remember that markers are a means not only for an improvement of the calculation of the MAXT but also for the supervision of the correct program behavior. As the example shows, plausibility checks which are based on application-specific knowledge can be built into programs. In this way, failures in the program logic may be detected at run time so that the self checking property of programs can be improved.

Every marker is a kind of cheap investment that pays for itself. Checking a marker costs 40 CPU cycles every time the marker is passed. These 40 cycles have to be invested only as often as the marker is passed, not for the other iterations of the loop. The time for a marker's evaluation will be outweighed by the benefits its information brings for MAXT calculation. The gain will be greater the more a marker restricts the number of iterations through a program part and the longer this program part takes to execute.

$MAXT_C$ of the two versions of the example:

bounded loops only	551 475 096
bounded loops and markers	46 810 232

Overhead for bounded loops and markers:

bounded loops (calc weight)	2 115 840
bounded loops (calc_center)	4 879 238
marker	139 216
bounded loops and markers	7 134 294 cycles

Figure 6. CPU cycles and overhead for the camera example.

When calculating the time overhead for the markers of our example we got a number of less than 140,000 cycles, which is only about 2% of the total overhead in the example. The gain of introducing these constructs can be extracted from Figures 3 and 5 and is summarized in Table 6—504 million CPU cycles could be saved and a processor idle time of 91% could be prevented by reducing the calculated maximum execution time to a realistic value. So the investment has proved worthwhile.

7. A concept for a MAXT analysis tool

In the previous sections we introduced some new language constructs for real-time programming languages. The constructs were defined in a C-like syntax as we use them in MARS-C, which is an extension of the C programming language (Kernighan and Ritchie 1986). Besides the constructs mentioned in this paper MARS-C also provides statements for sending and receiving messages in the MARS distributed real-time system (Pflügl, Damm, and Schwabl 1989).

The calculation of the maximum execution time of a MARS-C program is done in two steps, a compilation and an analysis step. In the first phase, the program is compiled with the MARS-C precompiler. The result of the precompilation is a program in C source code with some additional information about loop bounds, markers, and loop sequences. The C program is then compiled into assembler code.

In the analysis step (the tool for the calculation of the MAXT is in development), the real calculation of the upper bound for the application-specific maximum execution time of the program takes place. This calculation also consists of two parts.

- In a first run, information about program structure and timing behavior has to be combined. In this step the result of the precompiled MARS-C source code and the assembler source are parsed. As an intermediate result, a file is created that includes full information about the program structure (alternatives, loops, loop limits, markers, scopes, and loop sequences) and the execution time for all parts, derived from the execution times of the single assembler instructions.
- In the second step of the analysis, the intermediate file is read and the MAXT of the program is calculated. The calculation is based on the formulas described in this paper.

Representing the intermediate results of the analysis step in a file has two advantages: In the development phase of the tool the file can easily be read so that results can be verified. When the tool is used, the file gives the programmer detailed information about the timing properties of all parts of his program.

8. Conclusions

In this paper we discussed the aspects of a source code based calculation of the maximum execution time of tasks. We introduced restrictions for analyzable programs and presented formulas for the MAXT calculation of the fundamental language constructs of third generation programming languages.

Comparing the calculated maximum execution time of tasks to the actual maximum execution time, we observed large differences in some cases. The calculated upper bound for the maximum execution time of programs was much higher than the actual maximum execution time. We managed to reduce this gap by the introduction of new programming language constructs—markers, scopes, and loop sequences—that allow programmers to utilize knowledge about the execution of their algorithms.

It has also been pointed out that markers can be used as a means of flow monitoring. Application-specific knowledge can be expressed in the program code directly so that the self checking property of programs can be improved.

A simple example demonstrated the gains of the new programming means. The MAXT value for the example program was decreased by a factor of 11. Considering that the example is relatively simple, we expect that the new constructs can yield even greater gains when the complexity of the application increases.

Acknowledgements

This work has been supported by Digital Equipment Corporation under contract EERP/AU-011.

Notes

1. It is a conceptual decision whether the action provided for an overrun of a loop is treated as an exception handler or as a feature for expressing a special timing behavior of a program. The timing behavior of the overrun action is only of interest in the latter case—when the action is part of the regular program (this is our interpretation). In the case of an exception, the timing behavior cannot be guaranteed (see Exceptions).
2. Note that for bounded loops the overhead for testing the bounds also has to be regarded in the calculation of the maximum execution time.
3. The program has been compiled with the portable C compiler on a 68000 machine.
4. Note that this is a special case. More generally the single loops may contain an arbitrary number of loops with markers, and markers may be set at any level. However, the calculation model for this generalization varies only slightly from the model provided.
5. For simplicity, the time consumed by OVERRUN-statements has been neglected.
6. If $mmax \geq gmax$ all loops belong to the first group.

References

Darlington J., and R.M. Burstall. 1978. A system which automatically improves programs. In David Gries *Programming Methodology*. Springer, New York.

Ehrenberger W. 1983. Softwarezuverlässigkeit und Programmiersprache. *Regelungstechnische Praxis*, 25. Jhrg., Nr. 1:24–29.

Fohler G., and Ch. Koza. 1989. Heuristic scheduling for distributed real-time systems. *Research Report No. 6/89* (Apr.). Institut für Technische Informatik, Technical University of Vienna.

Halang W.A. 1984. A proposal for extensions of PEARL to facilitate the formulation of hard real-time applications. Proceedings "Fachtagung Prozessrechner 1984," Karlsruhe, Sept. 1984. Informatik-Fachberichte 86, Springer, Berlin-Heidelberg-New York-Tokyo, 1984, pp. 573–582.

Halang W.A., 1989. A priori execution time analysis for parallel processes. *Proceedings of the Euromicro Workshop on Real-Time*. (Como, June), Washington, IEEE Computer Society Press.

Kernighan B.W., and D.M. Ritchie. 1986. The C Programming Language. Prentice Hall, New Jersey.

Kligerman E., and A.D. Stoyenko. Real-time Euclid: A language for reliable real-time systems. *IEEE Transactions on Software Engineering*, SE-12, 9 (Sept), 941–949.

Kopetz, H., A. Damm, Ch. Koza, M. Mulazzani, W. Schwabl, Ch. Senft, and R. Zainlinger. 1989. Distributed fault-tolerant real-time systems: The MARS approach. *IEEE Micro* (Feb.).

Leinbaugh, D.W. 1980. Guaranteed Response times in a hard-real-time environment. *IEEE Transactions on Software Engineering*, SE-6, 1 (Jan.), 85–91.

Leinbaugh, D.W. and M.-R. Yamini. 1982. Guaranteed response times in a distributed hard-real-time environment. *Proceedings of Real Time Systems Symposium* (Dec.), IEEE Press, 157–169.

Leinbaugh, D.W., and M.-R. Yamini. Guaranteed response times in a distributed hard-real-time environment. 1986. *IEEE Transactions on Software Engineering*, SE-12, 12 (Dec.), 1139–1144.

Liu, C.L. and J.W. Layland. 1973. Scheduling algorithms for multiprogramming in a hard-real-time environment. *Journal of the ACM*, 20, 1 (Jan.), 46–61.

Mok, A.K. 1984. The design of real-time programming systems based on process models. *Proceedings of Real Time Systems Symposium* (Dec.), IEEE Press, 5–16.

Pflügl, M., A. Damm, and W. Schwabl. 1989. Interprocess communication in MARS. *Proc. of the ITG/GI Conference on Communication in Distributed Systems* (Stuttgart, Feb.).

Senft, Ch., and R. Zainlinger. 1989. A graphical design environment for distributed real-time systems. *Proceedings of the 22nd IEEE Conference on System Science* (Kailua-Kona, Jan.), Washington, IEEE Computer Society Press, 871–880.

Stoyenko, A.D. 1987. A real-time language with a schedulability analyzer. Technical Report CSRI-206 (Dec.), Computer Systems Research Institute, University of Toronto.

Real-Time Systems Performance in the Presence of Failures

Jogesh K. Muppala, Duke University

Steven P. Woolet, IBM

Kishor S. Trivedi, Duke University

The growing use of real-time systems in such diverse areas as transaction processing, air-traffic control, process control, and mission-critical control has created a need for effective analysis techniques to model these systems. Real-time systems are characterized by stringent deadlines and high-throughput and high-reliability requirements. Traditional analysis techniques, which rely mostly on mean values of the measures, cannot capture all the nuances of these systems.

When analyzing a transaction processing system, we often wish to compute the response time for a transaction. A typical performance requirement for transaction processing systems is a 1-second response for at least 95 percent of the transactions (usually referred to as the 95th percentile). Because failure to meet the deadline results in losses but may not be catastrophic, such systems are called *soft* real-time systems.

A mission-critical system is best characterized by how fast it can respond to a change in input stimuli or the environment. Typically we would require a guaranteed response within a short period of time commonly referred to as a *hard deadline*. Thus, such systems are called *hard* real-time systems, since the consequences of failing

This unified methodology for modeling real-time systems uses techniques that combine the effects of performance, reliability/availability, and deadline violation into a single model.

to meet the deadline could be catastrophic. Here, it is important to know the probability that the response time will be less than the deadline; this implies that the response-time distribution must be computed.

Queueing networks[1] have been used traditionally to study the performance of computer systems. They are useful in representing contention for resources, as occurs in transaction processing systems. Computing the response-time distribution for queueing networks using closed-form expressions is extremely difficult even for networks with a simple structure.[2] Numerical evaluation of the response-time distribution, however, is not difficult, as we will show.

Failures and repairs of components in a real-time system can noticeably affect performance. Thus, any realistic system model must also incorporate the effect of failures and repairs. Meyer[3] introduced a useful framework called *performability* for combining performance and reliability. In this case, the performance levels can be incorporated into the failure-repair model to study overall system behavior. When the failure-repair behavior is Markovian in nature, the approach results in a Markov reward model.[4]

Shin and Krishna[5] defined some interesting performance measures for hard real-time multiprocessor systems. Failure to meet a hard deadline is assumed to be catastrophic, leading to system failure. They compute the dynamic failure probability, taking into account hard-deadline failures. A cost function associated with the tasks in the model is used as an optimization criterion for designing real-time systems. Al-

0-8186-3792-7/93 $03.00 © 1991 IEEE

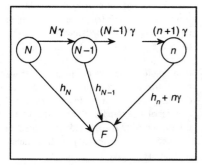

Figure 1. Markov chain model used by Shin and Krishna.

though Shin and Krishna's performance measures are general, their example is restricted to a single-resource model. Their approach complements Meyer's.

In this article we present a unified methodology for modeling both soft and hard real-time systems, combining Meyer's approach with that of Shin and Krishna. We use an on-line transaction processing system as an example to illustrate our modeling techniques. We consider dynamic failures due to a transaction's violating a hard deadline by incorporating additional transitions in the Markov chain model of the failure-repair behavior, as described by Shin and Krishna. We also take into account system performance in the various configurations by using throughput and response-time distribution as reward rates. Since the Markov chains used in computing the distribution of response time are often very large and complex, we use a higher level interface based on a variation of stochastic Petri nets called stochastic reward nets.[6]

A motivating example

Shin and Krishna present an interesting model for a real-time multiprocessor system incorporating hard-deadline failures. The performance of a multiprocessor system with m processors is modeled using an $M/M/m$ queue with Poisson arrival of tasks at the rate λ. The system's initial configuration has N processors. The processors are allowed to fail, and the time to failure of

---

Markov chains and Markov reward models

A Markov chain is a state-space-based method for modeling systems. It is composed of states, and transitions between states. The states of a Markov chain can be used to represent various entities associated with a system — for example, the number of functioning resources of each type, the number of tasks of each type waiting at a resource, the number of concurrently executing tasks of a job, the allocation of resources to tasks, and states of recovery for each failed resource. A transition represents the change of the system's state due to the occurrence of a simple or a compound event, such as the failure of one or more resources, the completion of executing tasks, or the arrival of jobs. A transition thus connects one state to another.

A Markov chain is a special case of a discrete-state stochastic process in which the current state completely captures the past history pertaining to the system's evolution. Markov chains can be classified into discrete-time Markov chains and continuous-time Markov chains, depending on whether the events can occur at fixed intervals or at any time — that is, whether the time variable associated with the system's evolution is discrete or continuous. This article is restricted to continuous-time Markov chains. Further information on Markov chains is available in the literature.[1]

In a graphical representation of a Markov chain, states are denoted by circles with meaningful labels attached. Transitions between states are represented by directed arcs drawn from the originating state to the destination state. Depending on whether the Markov chain is a discrete-time or a continuous-time Markov chain, either a probability or a rate is associated with a transition.

To illustrate these concepts further, let's consider an example based on a multiprocessor system comprising two dissimilar processors, P1 and P2. When both processors are functioning, the time to occurrence of a failure in processors P1 and P2 is assumed to be a random variable with the corresponding distribution being exponential with rates γ_1 and γ_2, respectively. We also consider a common-mode failure whereby both processors can fail simultaneously. The time to occurrence of this event is also assumed to be exponentially distributed with rate

γ_C. When only one processor is functioning, the rate of failure could be correspondingly altered to reflect the fact that a single processor carries the load of both processors. When only P1 is functioning, we assume its failure rate is γ_1', and when only P2 is functioning, its failure rate is γ_2'. We could consider repair of the processors where the time to repair the processors is also exponentially distributed with rates δ_1 and δ_2, respectively. We also assume that when both processors are waiting for repair, P1 has priority over P2.

The behavior of this system can be represented by a continuous-time Markov chain, shown in the figure in this sidebar. In this figure the label (i, j) of each state is determined as follows: $i = 1$ if P1 is up, and $i = 0$ if P1 is failed; similarly, $j = 0$ or 1, depending on whether P2 is failed or up. Solving this Markov chain involves computing either $P_{i,j}(t)$, the probability of being in state (i, j) at time t, or $\pi_{i,j}$, the steady-state probability of being in state (i, j).

Now let's consider the formal notation for a Markov chain. Let $\{Z(t), t \geq 0\}$ represent a homogeneous finite-state continuous-time Markov chain with state space Ω. Typically, we are interested in computing $P_i(t)$, the unconditional probability that the continuous-time Markov chain will be in state i at time t. The corresponding row vector $\mathbf{P}(t) = [P_i(t)]$ represents the *transient state probability vector* of the continuous-time Markov chain. Let π_i be the steady-state probability of state i of the continuous-time Markov chain. Then $\pi = [\pi_i]$ is the corresponding steady-state probability vector.

A Markov reward model is obtained by associating a *reward rate* r_i with each state i of the continuous-time Markov chain. Let $X(t) = r_{Z(t)}$ be the random variable corresponding to the reward rate at time t. Then the expected reward rate $E[X(t)]$ can be computed as follows:

$$E[X(t)] = \sum r_i P_i(t)$$

The expected reward rate in steady state can be computed as

$$E[X] = E[X(\infty)] = \sum r_i \pi_i$$

each processor is exponentially distributed with rate γ. The system is assumed to be nonrepairable, and at least n processors are required for the system to be stable. Figure 1 shows the corresponding Markov model. The hard deadline is assumed to be a random variable. To model hard-deadline failures, Shin and Krishna use additional transitions from each up state to the failure state. In this figure, h_i ($n \leq i \leq N$) is the product of the task arrival rate and the probability that a task violates the hard deadline; that is, $h_i = \lambda \int_0^\infty [1 - F_{MMi}(t)]dF_d(t)$, where $F_{MMi}(t)$ is the response-time distribution of an $M/M/i$ queue, and $F_d(t)$ is the cumulative distribution function of the random variable corresponding to the hard deadline. It is assumed that the queue is stable in state i, that is, $\lambda < i\mu$, where μ is the service rate of a single processor.

For this example Shin and Krishna compute the dynamic failure probability, given by the instantaneous probability $P_F(t)$, of state F. The dynamic failure probability is computed as a function of the number of processors as well as the number-power product (number of processors times the service rate of each processor). By defining a cost function for this model, the mean cost over the mission's lifetime was also computed.

For the same example, we might want to compute the amount of work processed until hard-deadline failure. This can be done using Markov reward models. The probability that a job will violate the dead- line in state i has already been specified as $\int_0^\infty [1 - F_{MMi}(t)]dF_d(t)$. Thus, the rate of the arriving jobs that will meet the deadline in state i is given by $\lambda(1 - \int_0^\infty [1 - F_{MMi}(t)]dF_d(t))$. This is the effective throughput of the system in state i. If we assign this as the reward rate in state i and compute $E[Y(t)]$, it yields the expected number of jobs completed successfully until time t, while $E[Y(\infty)]$ yields the expected number of jobs processed until hard-deadline failure.

Thus we see that combining Meyer's work with that of Shin and Krishna makes possible the analysis of real-time fault-tolerant systems, so that we can consider different types of failures in a single model. We can consider soft deadlines by

where X is the random variable corresponding to the steady-state reward rate. For a detailed discussion of using Markov reward models for evaluating computer systems, see Smith, Trivedi, and Ramesh.[2] As an example, by assigning a reward rate of 1 to *up* states and 0 to *failure* states, $E[X(t)]$ yields the instantaneous system availability and $E[X]$ the steady-state system availability. Alternatively, we might wish to compute the accumulated reward $Y(t)$ over the interval $[0,t)$, where $Y(t)$ is given by

$$Y(t) = \int_0^t X(\tau)d\tau = \int_0^t r_{z(\tau)}d\tau$$

It is possible to compute the expected accumulated reward $E[Y(t)]$ by using the following expression:

$$E[Y(t)] = \sum_i r_i \int_0^t P_i(\tau)d\tau$$

This lets us determine how much total work has been done by time t. We can also consider the time-averaged measure $E[Y(t)/t]$.

Computing the distribution of $Y(t)$ is comparatively difficult.[2] On the other hand, if we consider a system with absorbing failure states, we could compute the distribution of accumulated reward until absorption, $P[Y(\infty)<y]$, using a technique proposed by Beaudry.[3] In this technique we divide each transition rate emanating from a state by the reward rate associated with that state. The distribution of time to absorption for this transformed Markov chain yields the distribution of $Y(\infty)$ for the original Markov chain.

The question remaining is, what constitutes an appropriate reward assignment? We saw earlier that binary reward assignment (0 and 1) yields traditional reliability/availability measures. We could assign the performance levels as reward rates. In the above example let's assume that the service rate of the two processors P1 and P2 is μ_1 and μ_2, respectively. A capacity-based reward rate assignment so that $r_{i,j} = i\mu_1 + j\mu_2$ yields the computational availability.[3] Alternatively, if we assume a more general structure for the performance model, we can compute the throughput in each system state. If we set $r_{i,j}$ to be the sys- tem's throughput in state i, j, then we can obtain the through- put-oriented availability.[4]

References

1. K.S. Trivedi, *Probability and Statistics with Reliability, Queueing, and Computer Science Applications*, Prentice Hall, Englewood Cliffs, N.J., 1982.

2. R.M. Smith, K.S. Trivedi, and A.V. Ramesh, "Performability Analysis: Measures, an Algorithm, and a Case Study," *IEEE Trans. Computers*, Vol. C-37, No. 4, Apr. 1988, pp. 406-417.

3. M.D. Beaudry, "Performance-Related Reliability Measures for Computing Systems," *IEEE Trans. Computers*, Vol. C-27, No. 6, June 1978, pp. 540-547.

4. J.F. Meyer, "Closed-Form Solutions of Performability," *IEEE Trans. Computers*, Vol. C-31, No. 7, July 1982, pp. 648-657.

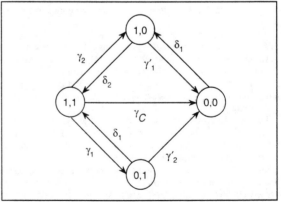

Continuous-time Markov chain for the two-processor system.

combining throughput and response-time distributions into the reward rates, and we can consider dynamic failures due to deadline violations. Failure due to imperfect coverage can also be modeled. The method applies to multiple-resource models as well. Nevertheless, for successful analysis, we must be able to generate and solve large, complex Markov chains. In the next section we describe our method, using an example.

We realize that we must compute the response-time distributions for tasks in a system with multiple resources. Computing the response-time distribution in general is difficult. Closed-form expressions are available only for simple queueing systems. For networks of queues, numerical solution using Markov chains appears to be the only possible method. To automatically generate and solve the Markov model for computing response-time distribution, we use stochastic Petri nets. Finally, the assignment of rewards to the failure-repair Markov model is essential to our approach. Thus, we must automatically generate reward rates for the Markov chain that is generated automatically from a stochastic Petri net. We use an extension of stochastic Petri nets, called stochastic reward nets, for this purpose.

Modeling an on-line transaction processing system

On-line transaction processing systems have become a major application area for computers. They are needed when many users require instant access to information such as records in large databases. Examples include airline reservation systems and automated bank-teller systems. These systems are characterized by high-throughput and high-availability requirements.

Figure 2 shows a typical architecture for

Stochastic reward nets

A stochastic reward net is an extension of a stochastic Petri net. The latter, in turn, is an extension of a Petri net. We will briefly introduce Petri nets and stochastic Petri nets and then describe some structural and stochastic extensions.

Basic terminology. A Petri net is a bipartite diagraph whose nodes are divided into two disjoint sets called places and transitions. Directed arcs in the graph connect places to transitions (input arcs) and transitions to places (output arcs). A *multiplicity* may be associated with these arcs. A marked Petri net is obtained by associating tokens with places. Marking a Petri net means distributing tokens in its places. In a graphical representation of a Petri net, circles represent places, bars represent transitions, and dots or integers in the places represent tokens. Input places of a transition are the set of places that are connected to the transition through input arcs. Similarly, output places of a transition are those places connected to the transition by output arcs.

A transition is considered *enabled* in the current marking if the number of tokens in each input place is at least equal to the multiplicity of the input arc from that place. The firing of a transition is an atomic action in which one or more tokens are removed from each input place of the transition and one or more tokens are added to each output place of the transition, possibly resulting in a new marking of the Petri net. When the transition is fired, the number of tokens deposited in each of its output places is equal to the multiplicity of the output arc. Each distinct Petri net marking constitutes a separate state of the Petri net. A marking is reachable from another marking if there is a sequence of transition firings starting from the original marking that results in the new marking. The reachability set (graph) of a Petri net is the set (graph) of markings reachable from the other markings. In any Petri net marking, a number of transitions may be simultaneously enabled.

Another type of arc in a Petri net is the *inhibitor* arc. An inhibitor arc drawn from a place to a transition means that the transition cannot fire if the place contains at least as many tokens as the multiplicity of the inhibitor arc.

Extensions to Petri nets have been considered by associating firing times with the transitions. By assuming the firing times of the transitions to be exponentially distributed, we get the stochastic Petri net. The underlying reachability graph of a stochastic Petri net is isomorphic to a continuous-time Markov chain. Further generalization of stochastic Petri nets has been introduced by Marsan et al.,[1] allowing transitions to have either zero firing times (immediate transitions) or exponentially distributed firing times (timed transitions), in turn giving rise to the generalized stochastic Petri net. In the figures accompanying this article, hollow rectangles represent timed transitions, while thin bars represent immediate transitions. The markings of a generalized stochastic Petri net are of two types: A marking is *vanishing* if only immediate transitions are enabled in the marking and *tangible* if only timed transitions or no transitions are enabled in the marking. Conflicts among immediate transitions in a vanishing marking are resolved using a random switch.[1]

Structural extensions. Ciardo et al.[2] introduced several structural extensions to Petri nets that increased their modeling power. These include enabling functions, general marking dependency, and variable cardinality arcs.

Enabling function. A Boolean enabling function $E(.)$ is associated with each transition. Whenever a transition satisfies all the input and inhibitor conditions in a marking M (that is, when the input places contain enough tokens to enable the transition, and the number of tokens in the inhibitor places is less than the multiplicity of the corresponding inhibitor arc), the enabling function is evaluated. The transition is considered enabled only if the enabling function $E(M)$ = true. Enabling functions are very useful in expressing complex interdependencies, simplifying the model structure, and implementing state truncation.

Variable cardinality arc. The multiplicity of an arc in a Petri net can be defined as a function of the Petri net marking. This facility is useful in simplifying the Petri net's structure. It is especially useful if an input place needs to be flushed. This facility can be used with input arcs, output arcs, and inhibitor arcs.

Marking dependency. The rates and probabilities of transi-

---

an on-line transaction processing system. The system's front end comprises a transaction generator — a terminal or a bar code reader — and transaction processors that analyze the submitted transaction to determine the information needed from the databases and to provide error recovery capabilities. The system's back end consists of a set of database processors that read and update the records in the databases according to the requests submitted by the transaction processors. The transactions visit the transaction processors and database processors in succession until the necessary processing is completed. Thus, a good measure of performance for an on-line

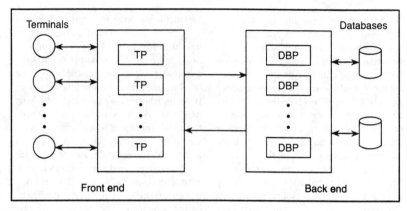

Figure 2. Architecture of an on-line transaction processing system.

tions can also be defined as general functions of the marking of a stochastic Petri net. This would be very useful in modeling a multiple-server queue, for example.

Stochastic extensions. We are interested in automatically generating Markov reward models. For this purpose stochastic Petri nets have been extended by associating reward rates with the markings to obtain stochastic reward nets.[2] The reward rate definitions are specified at the net level as a function of net primitives, such as the number of tokens in a place or the rate of a transition. For each marking of the net, the reward rate function is evaluated and the result is assigned as the reward rate for that marking. The underlying Markov model is then transformed into a Markov reward model, thus permitting evaluation of performance and availability both separately and in combination. We associate a reward rate r_i with every tangible marking i. Since the probability of being in a vanishing marking is zero, there is no need to assign reward rates to vanishing markings. We can then compute $E[X]$, the expected steady-state reward rate; $E[X(t)]$, the expected instantaneous reward rate; $E[Y(t)]$, the expected value of the accumulated reward; $E[Y(\infty)]$, the mean of the accumulated reward until absorption; and $P[Y(\infty) \leq y]$, the distribution of the accumulated reward until absorption.

Note that the definition of reward rates is orthogonal to the analysis type used. Thus, with the same reward definition we can compute the steady-state expected reward rate as well as the instantaneous reward rate at time t, the expected accumulated reward, and the expected time-averaged reward over the interval $[0,t)$.

The figure in this sidebar shows the stochastic reward net model corresponding to the two-processor example considered earlier. In this figure timed transitions t1fl, t2fl, and tcfl represent the failure of processors P1 and P2, and the common-mode failure, respectively. Transitions t1rp and t2rp represent the repair of the two processors. The inhibitor arc from place p1dn to transition t2rp implements the repair priority of P1 over P2. The firing rates of transitions t1fl and t2fl are marking dependent, as shown in the figure. We see that when processor P2 is up, that is, when place p2up contains a token, the firing rate of t1fl is γ_1. However, when P2 has failed, that is, when place p2up is empty, the firing rate is γ_1'. The rate function for transition t2fl is similarly defined.

References

1. M.A. Marsan, G. Conte, and G. Balbo, "A Class of Generalized Stochastic Petri Nets for the Performance Evaluation of Multiprocessor Systems," *ACM Trans. Computing Systems*, Vol. 2, No. 2, May 1984, pp. 93-122.
2. G. Ciardo, J. Muppala, and K. Trivedi, "SPNP: Stochastic Petri Net Package," *Proc. Third Int'l Workshop Petri Nets and Performance Models*, CS Press, Los Alamitos, Calif., Order No. 2001, 1989, pp. 142-151.

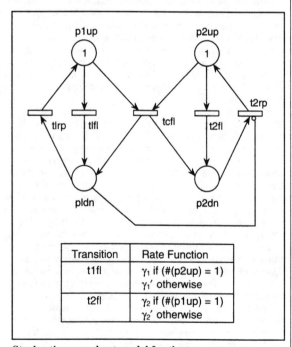

Transition	Rate Function
t1fl	γ_1 if (#(p2up) = 1) γ_1' otherwise
t2fl	γ_2 if (#(p1up) = 1) γ_2' otherwise

Stochastic reward net model for the two-processor system.

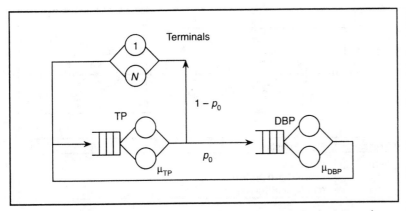

Figure 3. Closed queueing network model of the on-line transaction processing system.

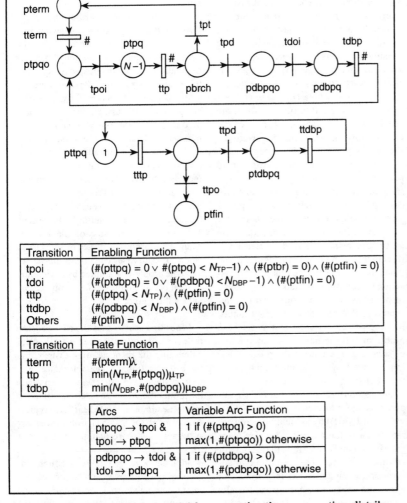

Transition	Enabling Function
tpoi	$(\#(\text{pttpq}) = 0 \lor \#(\text{ptpq}) < N_{TP}{-}1) \land (\#(\text{ptbr}) = 0) \land (\#(\text{ptfin}) = 0)$
tdoi	$(\#(\text{ptdbpq}) = 0 \lor \#(\text{pdbpq}) < N_{DBP}{-}1) \land (\#(\text{ptfin}) = 0)$
tttp	$(\#(\text{ptpq}) < N_{TP}) \land (\#(\text{ptfin}) = 0)$
ttdbp	$(\#(\text{pdbpq}) < N_{DBP}) \land (\#(\text{ptfin}) = 0)$
Others	$\#(\text{ptfin}) = 0$

Transition	Rate Function
tterm	$\#(\text{pterm})\lambda$
ttp	$\min(N_{TP},\#(\text{ptpq}))\mu_{TP}$
tdbp	$\min(N_{DBP},\#(\text{pdbpq}))\mu_{DBP}$

Arcs	Variable Arc Function
ptpqo → tpoi & tpoi → ptpq	1 if ($\#(\text{pttpq}) > 0$) $\max(1,\#(\text{ptpqo}))$ otherwise
pdbpqo → tdoi & tdoi → pdbpq	1 if ($\#(\text{ptdbpq}) > 0$) $\max(1,\#(\text{pdbpqo}))$ otherwise

Figure 4. Stochastic reward net model for computing the response-time distribution.

transaction processing system is the response time of a transaction.

Next we model various aspects of the on-line transaction processing system, including the response-time distribution for a transaction and the effects of soft-deadline and hard-deadline failures.

Response-time distributions. The performance of the on-line transaction processing system can be studied using the queueing network model shown in Figure 3, since the system involves contention for resources. In this model it is assumed that the transaction processors share a single queue from which transactions are selected for processing using a scheduling discipline that satisfies product-form assumptions.[1]

The transaction processors are modeled using a multiserver queue with the number of servers equal to the number of transaction processors. The database processors are similarly configured. The service times of the transaction processors are exponentially distributed with mean $1/\mu_{TP}$; the service times of the database processors are also exponentially distributed with mean $1/\mu_{DBP}$. The average time between completion of a transaction and submission of the next transaction at a terminal (equivalent to the "think time" at the terminal) is also exponentially distributed with mean $1/\lambda$.

The number of terminals available in the system is assumed to be N. A transaction completing execution at the transaction processor may visit the database processor with probability p_0 or complete execution and return to the terminals with probability $1-p_0$. Since this queueing network obeys product-form assumptions, we could use efficient algorithms such as mean value analysis[1] to compute such steady-state performance measures as average throughput, average queue length at each queue, and average response time for a transaction. Given that there are i transaction processors and j database processors in the system, we can compute the average system throughput T_{ij}. This measure gives the average number of transactions completing in a unit time.

Although computing the averages of various performance measures is easy, this does not present the complete picture, especially with respect to on-line transaction processing systems. It then becomes necessary to evaluate the response-time distributions to obtain the percentiles. Computing response-time distributions for a queueing network with arbitrary structure is very difficult. Closed-form solutions are available for only a small subset of queueing networks.[2] However, it is possible to numerically evaluate the response-time distributions using the *tagged-customer* approach.[7] In this method a target customer is chosen whose movement through the network is observed to compute the response-time distribution. We also adopt the tagged-customer approach to numerically evaluate the response-time distribution for the on-line transaction processing system. We will assume a first come, first served service discipline at the transaction processor queue and database processor queue. The method can be easily extended to other service disciplines.

The stochastic reward net shown in Figure 4 is used to implement the tagged-customer approach. In the figure, #(p) represents the number of tokens in place p, and # associated with a transition means that its service rate is marking dependent.

Let's look at how the position of the tagged customer is tracked through the network. In the figure the places ptpqo, ptpq, and pttpq and the transitions tpoi, ttp, and tttp together implement the multiserver first come, first served queue corresponding to the transaction processors. When the tagged customer is in the queue, all customers ahead of it are represented by the tokens in place ptpq (for convenience we can call this place the inner queue), and customers behind the tagged customer are in place ptpqo (we can refer to this place as the catchment area). The tagged customer will be scheduled for service only when the number of customers ahead becomes less than the number of transaction processors. This procedure is implemented by the enabling function controlling the firing of transition tttp. All customers arriving after the tagged customer are deposited in place ptpqo. Whenever a transaction processor becomes available and the tagged customer is already in service, another customer can be admitted to the inner queue from the catchment area and scheduled for service. This is implemented by allowing the transition tpoi to fire, taking one token out of ptpqo and depositing a token in ptpq. If the tagged customer is not in the queue, an arriving customer can proceed directly from the catchment area to the inner queue. This complex structure is implemented using the variable arc function defined in Figure 4. A similar structure is used for the database processor queue.

Since this is a closed product-form network, by applying the Sevcik-Mitrani (Lavenberg-Reiser) arrival theorem,[1,8] we know that an arriving customer sees the network in equilibrium with one less cus-

tomer; that is, if we are evaluating the system with N customers, the tagged customer sees the network in equilibrium with $N - 1$ customers. When the tagged customer arrives at the transaction processor queue, it sees the network in equilibrium with i customers in the transaction processor queue, j customers in the database processor queue, and the remaining $N - (i + j + 1)$ customers at the terminals. Thus, the steady-state probabilities for all the states ($i, j, N - (i + j + 1)$), where $0 \leq i, j \leq N - 1$, are needed. These probabilities can be calculated by solving the stochastic reward net shown in Figure 5 with $N - 1$ customers.

Figure 5 represents a stochastic reward net model of the queueing network corresponding to the on-line transaction processing system. In this network, places ptpq and pdbpq represent the queues for the transaction processors and database processors, respectively. Place pterm represents the terminals. Transitions ttp and tdbp represent the service time at the transaction processors and database processors, respectively, and transition tterm corresponds to the think time at the terminals. Routing of the customer to the database processor or the terminal upon completion of service at the transaction processor is implemented by place pbrch and transitions tpd and tpt, respectively.

The response-time distribution is computed as the expected instantaneous reward rate $E[X(t)]$ by associating a reward rate of 1 with those markings where place ptfin is nonempty and a reward rate of 0 for all other markings. The mean time to absorption (token appearing in place ptfin) gives the mean response time for the queueing network. This has been used to validate the stochastic reward net model,

since the mean response time can be computed using other product-form solution methods like mean value analysis or convolution.[1]

The response-time distribution $P[R \leq t]$ for various configurations is shown in Figure 6 (the label $[T, D]$ represents the number of transaction processors and the number of database processors, respectively). For this example we set $\lambda = 1.0$ per second, $\mu_{TP} = 50.0$ per second, $\mu_{DBP} = 20.0$ per second, and $p_0 = 0.8$. We assume that the number of transaction processors is equal to the number of database processors. We also assume that with every additional transaction processor, the number of terminals increases by five. Note that the response time decreases with an increase in the number of processors even if the number of terminals is correspondingly increased. Table 1 shows the size of the Markov chains and the number of arcs in the Markov chain for each case. The maximum size of solvable problems is limited by the amount of memory available on the computer and not by the method.

Modeling soft- and hard-deadline failures. Earlier we showed a method for computing the response-time distribution for a transaction. In characterizing real-time systems, we often wish to compute the probability that a transaction will fail to meet a deadline. As stated earlier, a typical requirement for a transaction processing system is for 95 percent of the transactions to complete within a second. This is often characterized by the deadline violation probabilities, which in turn can be easily computed from the response-time distribution. Failure to meet a deadline can be due to several reasons. Resources avail-

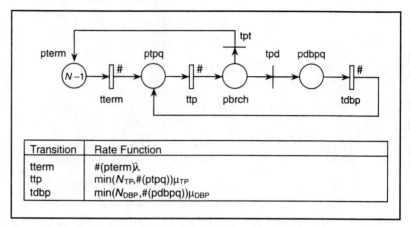

Transition	Rate Function
tterm	#(pterm)λ
ttp	min(N_{TP},#(ptpq))μ_{TP}
tdbp	min(N_{DBP},#(pdbpq))μ_{DBP}

Figure 5. Stochastic reward net model of the closed queueing network.

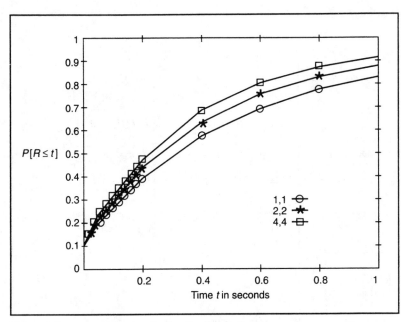

Figure 6. Response-time distribution for the on-line transaction processing system.

Table 1. Sizes of the Markov chains for different configurations.

No. of TPs/DBPs	No. of Terminals	No. of States	No. of Arcs
1	5	85	205
2	10	405	1,305
3	15	1,088	3,722
4	20	2,262	7,998
8	40	14,428	53,932

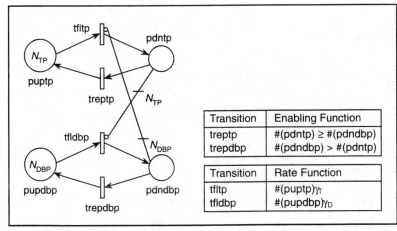

Transition	Enabling Function
treptp	#(pdntp) ≥ #(pdndbp)
trepdbp	#(pdndbp) > #(pdntp)

Transition	Rate Function
tfltp	#(puptp)γ_T
tfldbp	#(pupdbp)γ_D

Figure 7. Failure-repair behavior of the transaction processors and the database processors.

able in a system are subject to failure and repair. Transactions may face inordinate delays, or, in the worst case, be rejected if the system is unavailable when they arrive. Even if a fault-free system provides satisfactory service, a degraded configuration may not. Depending on the nature of the system, soft or hard deadlines may best describe its behavior.

Now let's consider the performance of the on-line transaction processing system in the presence of resource failures and repairs. We will assume that only the processors are subject to faults and the remaining system, including the interconnection networks and the communication medium, is fault free. This is a reasonable assumption, since failure rates for the rest of the components are much lower than those of the processors. We consider both soft- and hard-deadline violations with the implicit assumption that a hard-deadline violation is catastrophic.

The failure-repair behavior of the transaction processors and the database processors is modeled by the stochastic reward net model shown in Figure 7. In this model we assume that the failed transaction processors and database processors share a single repair facility. When both types of processors fail, priority for repair is given to whichever type has the most failures. When an equal number of transaction processors and database processors fail, transaction processors get a higher priority. This is reflected by the enabling functions shown in the figure. The times to failure for the transaction processors and database processors are exponentially distributed with rates γ_T and γ_D, respectively. The corresponding repair times are also exponentially distributed with rates β_T and β_D, respectively.

We assume that transactions in the system must meet a fixed deadline τ. First the soft-deadline case is considered. We assume that violation of the soft deadline results in the transaction's being aborted. The system continues to function, however. We will assign a reward rate of $T_{ij}P[R_{ij} \leq \tau]$ to the stochastic reward net marking having i tokens in place puptp and j tokens in place pupdbp. Here, T_{ij} is the throughput of the on-line transaction processing system with i transaction processors and j database processors, and $P[R_{ij} \leq \tau]$ is the probability that the response time is less than τ. The reward rate assigned corresponds to the average number of transactions completing in a unit time that meet the deadline.

We assume implicitly that whenever a

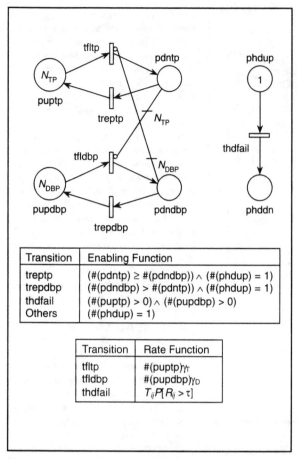

Transition	Enabling Function
treptp	$(\#(pdntp) \geq \#(pdndbp)) \wedge (\#(phdup) = 1)$
trepdbp	$(\#(pdndbp) > \#(pdntp)) \wedge (\#(phdup) = 1)$
thdfail	$(\#(puptp) > 0) \wedge (\#(pupdbp) > 0)$
Others	$(\#(phdup) = 1)$

Transition	Rate Function
tfltp	$\#(puptp)\gamma_T$
tfldbp	$\#(pupdbp)\gamma_D$
thdfail	$T_{ij}P[R_{ij} > \tau]$

Figure 8. Failure-repair behavior with hard-deadline failures.

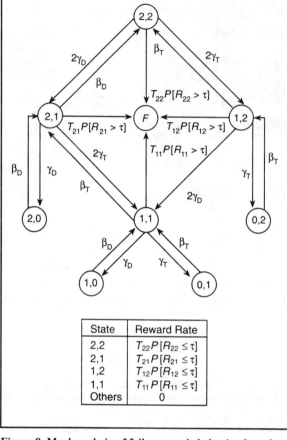

State	Reward Rate
2,2	$T_{22}P[R_{22} \leq \tau]$
2,1	$T_{21}P[R_{21} \leq \tau]$
1,2	$T_{12}P[R_{12} \leq \tau]$
1,1	$T_{11}P[R_{11} \leq \tau]$
Others	0

Figure 9. Markov chain of failure-repair behavior for a 2 × 2 system.

transaction arrives while the system is in a particular configuration with i transaction processors and j database processors, it will complete in the same configuration. This is a reasonable assumption, since failure rates for the processors are very small. Thus, from the viewpoint of a transaction, the system is assumed to be in a quasi-stable state. Shin and Krishna used a similar assumption.[5]

If we consider the deadline to be hard, then we assume that the system will fail if this deadline is violated. In this case the system's failure-repair behavior is modified, as shown in Figure 8. In this figure the failure rate of the transition thdfail is set to $T_{ij}P[R_{ij} > \tau]$ — the rate at which transactions fail to meet the deadline. This is analogous to the failure rate for the hard-deadline violation considered by Shin and Krishna. Note, however, that we have considered a fixed deadline. This procedure can be extended easily to a case in which the deadline itself is a random variable, as

with Shin and Krishna. They considered an open queueing system, so the throughput was configuration independent (equal to λ). The response-time distribution was available as a closed-form expression for the simple queue they considered, whereas the response-time distribution had to be computed numerically for our queueing system. In Figure 9 we show the failure-repair Markov chain (structure-state process) corresponding to a system with two transaction processors and two database processors. This Markov chain corresponds to a case in which hard-deadline failures are considered. States (2,0), (1,0), (0,1), and (0,2) are considered system down states. The reward rates assigned to the Markov chain states are also shown explicitly.

We consider various measures to characterize the on-line transaction processing system in the presence of failures and repairs. In our numerical example, we consider a system with four transaction processors and four database processors. The

failure rate for the processors is assumed to be 0.01 per hour; the repair rate is 2 per hour. Figure 10 shows a plot of the expected time-averaged system throughput $E\ [Y(t)/t]$ as a function of time for both the soft- and hard-deadline cases, where we plot the cases when the deadline τ is 1 and 2 seconds. As a comparison, we also plot the expected time-averaged throughput for the system with no deadlines. This represents the upper bound on the overall system throughput that can be achieved. From the figure, we notice that as the deadline is relaxed, the throughputs for the systems with deadlines move closer to this upper bound. As expected, the system with soft deadlines outperforms the system with hard deadlines, since a hard-deadline violation is catastrophic.

Figure 11 plots the probability of system failure, $P_{SF}(t)$, as a function of time for both soft- and hard-deadline cases for a system with four transaction processors and four database processors. In this exam-

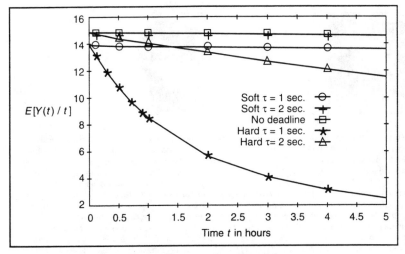

Figure 10. Throughput with deadlines as a function of time.

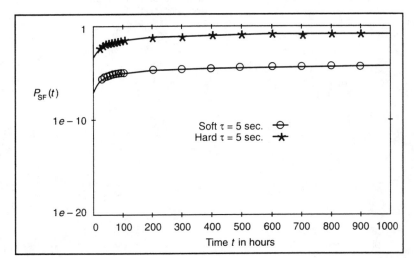

Figure 11. Unreliability as a function of time.

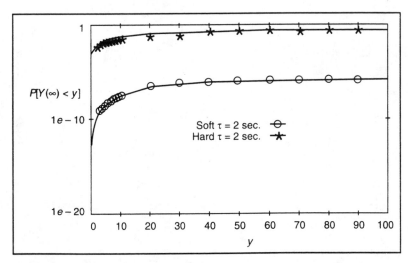

Figure 12. Distribution of number of tasks successfully completed until absorption.

ple we consider as absorbing states those (static failure) states in which all the transaction processors or all the database processors have failed. The figure shows that hard-deadline failure (dynamic failure) is the leading cause of system failure.

In Figure 12 we plot the distribution of number of tasks successfully completed until absorption for both the soft- and hard-deadline cases for a system with four transaction processors and four database processors. The figure shows that the probability of failing to accumulate reward *y* for the hard-deadline case is much higher than for the soft-deadline case. This is to be expected, since hard-deadline failures are catastrophic.

We have presented some interesting techniques for evaluating real-time systems. These techniques combine the effects of performance, reliability/availability, and deadline violation into a single model. We use a numerical method for computing the response-time distribution for a queueing network. Using throughputs and response-time distributions as reward rates, we have been able to handle systems with multiple resources as well as soft- and hard-deadline constraints. Transient analysis of Markov reward models is the basis of our analysis. Stochastic reward nets are used to generate and solve these models.

Our technique can be extended to cases with multiple types of tasks and mixed hard and soft deadlines. Processing power and cost-based trade-off studies, along with other such design optimizations, can be carried out much as Shin and Krishna demonstrated. Imperfect coverage, failure dependencies, and complex fault-handling behavior can also be taken into account.■

References

1. S.S. Lavenberg, *Computer Performance Modeling Handbook*, Academic Press, New York, 1983.

2. O.J. Boxma and H. Daduna, "Sojourn Times in Queueing Networks," in *Stochastic Analysis of Computer and Communication Systems*, H. Takagi, ed., Elsevier Science Publishers (North-Holland), Amsterdam, 1990, pp. 401-450.

3. J.F. Meyer, "Closed-Form Solutions of Performability," *IEEE Trans. Computers*, Vol. C-31, No. 7, July 1982, pp. 648-657.

4. R.M. Smith, K.S. Trivedi, and A.V. Ramesh, "Performability Analysis: Measures, an Algorithm, and a Case Study," *IEEE Trans. Computers*, Vol. C-37, No. 4, Apr. 1988, pp. 406-417.

5. K.G. Shin and C.M. Krishna, "New Performance Measures for Design and Evaluation of Real-Time Multiprocessors," *Computer Systems Science and Eng.*, Vol. 1, No. 4, Oct. 1986, pp. 179-192.

6. G. Ciardo, J. Muppala, and K. Trivedi, "SPNP: Stochastic Petri Net Package," *Proc. Third Int'l Workshop Petri Nets and Performance Models*, CS Press, Los Alamitos, Calif., Order No. 2001, 1989, pp. 142-151.

7. B. Melamed and M. Yadin, "Randomization Procedures in the Computation of Cumulative-Time Distributions over Discrete-State Markov Processes," *Operations Research*, Vol. 32, No. 4, July-Aug. 1984, pp. 926-944.

8. K.C. Sevcik and I. Mitrani, "The Distribution of Queueing Network States at Input and Output Instants," *J. ACM*, Vol. 28, No. 2, Apr. 1981, pp. 358-371.

Steven P. Woolet is working on system performance analysis for IBM at Research Triangle Park in North Carolina. He is also working toward a PhD in electrical engineering at Duke University. His research interests include reliability, and performance and performability modeling of networks and multiprocessor systems. Woolet received bachelors' degrees in mathematics and electrical engineering from Bethel College, Indiana, and the University of Notre Dame, respectively, and an MS in electrical engineering from the University of Minnesota. He is a member of the IEEE, the IEEE Computer Society, and the ACM.

Kishor S. Trivedi is a professor of electrical engineering and computer science at Duke University. He has served as a principal investigator on various projects and as a consultant to industry and to research laboratories. He is the author of *Probability and Statistics with Reliability, Queueing, and Computer Science Applications* (Prentice Hall). Both the text and his related research activities focus on computing-system reliability and performance evaluation. Trivedi has a B.Tech degree from the Indian Institute of Technology, Bombay, and MS and PhD degrees in computer science from the University of Illinois at Urbana-Champaign. He is a member of the IEEE Computer Society and a senior member of IEEE.

Jogesh K. Muppala is a student in the Department of Electrical Engineering at Duke University, where he is completing requirements toward a PhD. His research interests include stochastic Petri nets, performance and dependability modeling, and multiprocessor systems. He received a BE in electronics and communication engineering from Osmania University, Hyderabad, India, in 1985 and an MS in computer engineering from the Center for Advanced Computer Studies, University of Southwestern Louisiana, Lafayette, Louisiana, in 1987. He is a student member of the IEEE, the IEEE Computer Society, and the ACM.

Readers can contact Muppala and Trivedi at Duke University, Dept. of Electrical Engineering, Durham, NC 27706; e-mail jkm@egr.duke.edu or kst@cs.duke.edu. Woolet is with IBM at Research Triangle Park, NC 27709

Chapter 6: Communication

The design of distributed real-time systems must include communication protocols with various properties. For example, some applications require deterministic behavior of the communicating components. To achieve this determinism, protocols must have bounded channel access delays and bounded communication delays. Note that the bounds have different semantics depending on the protocols used. For example, it may be known a priori that a message can be delivered in bounded time X. Consequently, scheduling message transmission so as to meet deadlines can take this time into account. However, this time can be long since all worst case situations must be accounted for. Alternatively, a specific message may be given a bound which is determined upon arrival to the communication system. This guaranteed bound might be computed based on the current communication load rather than a worst case scenario. This generally provides a much lower bound but at the cost of some form of dynamic reservation scheme for the message. Another aspect of computing the bound involves the maximum degree of failure and retry that must be accounted for in determining the guaranteed delivery time. Subsequently, the guarantee is subject to these failure and retry assumptions. In some recent literature, deterministic real-time communication is referred to as real-time virtual circuits.

Another class of applications, called *real-time datagrams,* may have timing constraints for messages, but a best effort delivery policy is sufficient if it meets average performance requirements for meeting deadlines. Real-time datagrams are suitable for certain soft real-time applications or for some traffic in hard real-time systems.

Timing constraints for messages become necessary for many reasons. For example, if two communicating hard, real-time tasks are on different nodes, and one task must precede the other, a message between them must be delivered on time. Scheduling decisions include

- determining when to execute the first task,
- identifying when the message is ready for delivery, and
- guaranteeing that once ready it can be delivered by a deadline, which is the start time of the second task.

Finally, this second task must also be scheduled to complete by its deadline. This entire process is called the *end-to-end* scheduling problem and requires an integrated scheduling approach.

Deadlines are also necessary in situations where nodes monitor each other for failure through periodic transmission of status messages. Typically, if a node does not receive a message from another node before a certain time, it initiates recovery. The time chosen depends on the preiodicity of message exchanges and the maximum communication delay. Consequently, a status message may be given a deadline equal to the period used to detect failures, and the communication protocol must guarantee that it will be delivered in time.

We believe that distributed real-time systems require specialized network architectures that incorporate various classes of services and protocols. "A Local Area Network Architecture for Communication in Distributed Real-Time Systems" by Arvind, Ramamritham, and Stankovic itemizes a four-layer architecture that provides both connection-oriented and connectionless services that account for timing constraints. In particular, various protocols are described for the medium access control (MAC) layer to support *guarantee-seeking messages* and *best effort messages.* The paper also describes a homogeneous set of MAC protocols that may be used to support both classes of services using a uniform window-splitting paradigm. This window-based protocol is a variation of the protocol presented in the next paper by Zhao, Stankovic, and Ramamritham. However, this first paper changes the original time-constrained window protocol to guarantee bounded delivery time. This serves as a basis for its suitability to support both classes of services.

The second paper, "A Window Protocol for Transmission of Time Constrained Messages," is by Zhao, Stankovic, and Ramamritham. This paper assumes a multi-access shared bus network. The protocol extends the traditional window-based protocol by explicitly taking time constraints into account in such a way as to implement a minimum-laxity-first policy. A major advantage of the new protocol is that new messages are immediately considered for transmission based on their laxity, rather than the more traditional approach where all previously colliding messages are transmitted first, before any new arrivals are permitted to contend for the bus. This protocol is an example of a best effort time-constrained communication protocol and no worst case bounds are guaranteed. The paper includes a performance evaluation done via simulation that shows the good performance of this protocol over a wide range of environments (compared to various baselines and other real-time communication protocols) and identifies an interesting performance anomaly.

The third paper, "Responsive, Deterministic IEEE 802.5 Token Ring Scheduling" by Strosnider and Marchok, discusses an analyzable scheduling technique applicable to the 802.5 token bus. The goal of the scheduling technique is to improve the performance of three classes of traffic: alarm messages (called alert messages in the paper), synchronous traffic, and asynchronous traffic. Deadlines for alarms and synchronous traffic must be guaranteed, and fast response time is necessary for asynchronous traffic. The paper presents an idealized LAN model for supporting the needed scheduling environment and then presents the scheduling approach itself. Further, they show how to implement their approach on the IEEE 802.5 token ring. Their algorithm is called a deferrable server, which is an extension to the well-known rate monotonic scheduling algorithm. However, the deferrable server algorithm has the nice property that it not only guarantees that the alarms and synchronous traffic will make their deadlines but also provides good response time to the asynchronous traffic. Finally, they present a simulation study that validates their performance claims.

Real-time communication is the backbone of a distributed real-time system. It is also one basic mechanism used to support several availability and fault tolerance aspects of real-time systems. In the paper entitled "Synchronous Atomic Broadcast for Redundant Broadcast Channels," Cristian describes one of these higher-level uses of real-time communication. The idea is to implement a reliable service by a group of processes executing on different nodes so that even in the presence of failures the service is provided. Real-time communication is needed to transmit state updates so that replica consistency is maintained. A synchronous atomic broadcast ensures the existence of a time constant Δ such that, even if up to f failures occur, several properties are still guaranteed. These properties include atomicity, order, and termination. This paper presents a protocol to achieve a synchronous atomic broadcast based on redundant broadcast channels (for example, redundant token rings). It can handle processor crashes, channel adaptor performance failures, and channel omission failures. Two main advantages of the protocol are that it achieves a significant message overhead reduction compared to earlier work and it provides a bound.

A Local Area Network Architecture for Communication in Distributed Real-Time Systems

K. ARVIND, KRITHI RAMAMRITHAM AND JOHN A. STANKOVIC
Department of Computer and Information Science, University of Massachusetts at Amherst, Amherst, MA 01003

Abstract. Distributed real-time systems of the future will require specialized network architectures that incorporate new classes of services and protocols in order to support time-constrained communication. In this paper, we propose a new local area network architecture for such systems. This four-layered architecture is characterized by new classes of connection-oriented and connectionless services that take into account the timing constraints of messages. We describe various aspects of the logical link control layer of the architecture and various real-time protocols that may be employed at the medium access control layer in order to support the new classes of services. We also describe a homogeneous approach to the implementation of medium access control protocols to support both connection-oriented and connectionless services, based on a uniform window splitting paradigm.

1. Introduction

A real-time system is defined as a system whose correctness depends not only on the logical results of computation, but also on the time at which the results are produced (Stankovic and Ramamritham 1988). This is a general definition that encompasses a wide variety of systems including digital filters, multimedia communication systems, on-line transaction processing systems, message switching systems, manufacturing control systems and process control systems. In this paper, we restrict the scope of our attention to the last category of real-time systems. A real-time process control system (Figure 1), which constitutes the context for this paper, may be abstractly modeled as a feedback loop consisting of four components, viz., a controlled process, a controller, sensors and actuators. The sensors provide the controller with information about the current state of the controlled process. The controller is an information processing system that makes use of the information provided by the sensors to compute the actions required to reduce the disparity between the current state and the specified desired state of the system. The actuators realize the actions computed by the controller.

A simple illustrative example of a real-time control system is a servomechanism used to control the position of a motor shaft (the motor may in turn control the rotation of a robot arm joint). The controller in this system could be a microprocessor that performs a simple numerical computation such as determining the difference between the current position and the desired final position of the shaft and multiplying it by a constant. However, in many real-time systems such as nuclear power plant control systems (Alger and Lala 1986), air traffic control systems (Christian, Dancey and Dehn 1990), space mission control systems (Muratore et al. 1990, Strosnider 1988) and industrial process control systems

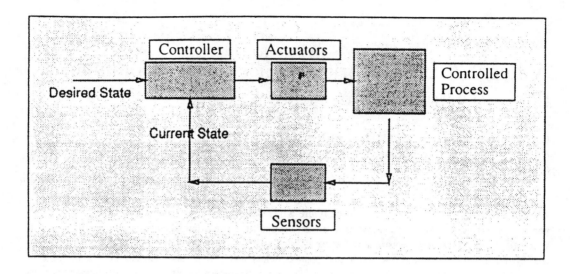

Figure 1. Model of a real-time control system.

(Martin 1967), the computations performed by the controller are more involved; the controller in the feedback control loop typically includes human components (in the form of one or more human controllers), in addition to computers (for this reason, such systems are also known as *open loop* systems (Martin 1967)). These human controllers make decisions on the basis of raw or processed sensor data with the help of computers. The space shuttle mission control scenario depicted in Figure 2 (adapted from (Strosnider 1988)) is an example of such a system. In this system, network data drivers transmit raw telemetry data received from space to a real-time host computer for processing. Mission controllers responsible for various aspects of the mission, with the help of the host and the processed telemetry data, monitor and control the operation of the mission.

While systems such as the mission control system depicted in Figure 2 are typically large and distributed, they are not autonomous since many of the high-level activities are performed by cooperating human experts. A lot of work has already been done in the context of these open loop systems (Stankovic and Ramamritham 1988). The next logical step in the evolution of real-time systems is the introduction of autonomy. Real-time systems are steadily evolving towards the next generation of *closed loop* autonomous real-time systems (Iyengar and Kashyap 1989) in which human experts in the feedback loop are replaced by software. Figure 3 depicts an abstract model of such an autonomous control system. In this system, cooperating human experts are replaced by communicating problem-solving software tasks. In Japan (Whittaker and Kanade 1990), the Space Robot Forum, a prestigious group from Government, industry and academia, funded by the National Space Development Agency, recently outlined an ambitious schedule for *third-generation* space robotics, where machines work without much, if any, human intervention. This trend towards autonomy is driven both by techno-economic objectives such as enhanced productivity, profitability and quality, and by a desire to relieve humans from dangerous, difficult and dull tasks (Iyengar and Kashyap 1989). The culmination of this trend towards autonomy would be the fully autonomous closed loop real-time control system. These real-time systems

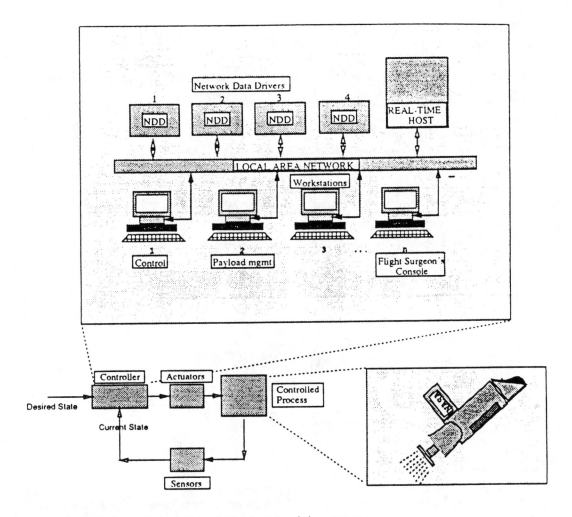

Figure 2. A mission control scenario: A distributed real-time system.

of the next generation will be distributed, complex, exhibit highly dynamic, adaptive and intelligent behavior and possess several types of timing constraints and operate in a highly nondeterministic environment (Stankovic 1988, Stankovic and Ramamritham 1990). Examples of harbingers of this trend towards autonomy are the NASA mission control system (Muratore et al. 1990), the Lockheed Pilot Associate system (Lark et al. 1990, Rouse, Geddes and Hammer 1990) and various ongoing projects in Robotics (Whittaker and Kanade 1990, Bares et al. 1989, Bihari, Walliser and Patterson 1989, Iyengar and Kashyap 1989, Weisbin et al. 1989).

In this paper, we address the communication requirements that arise in these complex closed loop real-time systems. The rest of the paper is organized as follows. In Section 2, we describe the distributed real-time system model that we assume as a basis in this paper. In Section 3, we discuss the approach to real-time communication in today's systems and illustrate the limitations of this approach and the requirements for future systems. In Section 4, we give a brief description of existing local area network architectures, and in Section 5, we propose RTLAN, a new local area network architecture for communication in distributed real-time systems. In Section 6, we describe the logical link control layer of

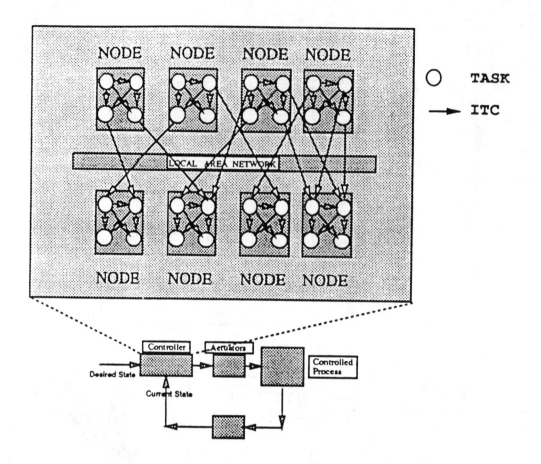

Figure 3. An autonomous real-time controller.

this architecture. In Section 7, we describe the medium access control layer of RTLAN, and look at several MAC protocols that may be used at this layer to support the requirements of the LLC layer. In Section 8, we describe a uniform approach to implementing a homogeneous set of MAC protocols based on a window-splitting paradigm. In Section 9, we conclude the paper with a brief summary.

2. System model

The field of next generation real-time control systems is still evolving and we do not have sufficient experience to generate a precise set of requirements for such systems. We have adopted a general model that incorporates well-accepted requirements for these systems. We describe our model below:

1. *Distributed System.* The system is distributed and is based on a local area newtwork. The need for distribution will arise to satisfy performance, reliability and functional requirements. This trend towards distribution is evident even in today's real-time systems (Nielsen 1990, Muratore et al. 1990). Local area networks are typically used with distributed real-time systems because of the limited geographical span[1] of the system.

2. *Timing Constraints.* Activities in the system may have various types of timing constraints such as periodicity and deadlines associated with them.
3. *Dynamic Nature.* In addition to static periodic activities, the system will also be required to handle dynamically spawned activities.
4. *Predictability.* Predictability (Stankovic and Ramamritham 1990, Stankovic 1988) is considered an important requirement in real-time systems. For certain activities that are critical or essential, it is important to be able to determine whether the timing constraints of the activities will be met prior to actually accepting the activity for execution.
5. *Intertask Communication.* The functional requirements of the system will be realized through a set of tasks. Tasks will cooperate in order to achieve desired objectives. Cooperation will induce intertask communication requirements. Like all other activities in the system, intertask communication activities have timing constraints which will translate to individual message deadlines. We address this aspect in more detail in the next section.

3. Real-time communication

The term *real-time communication* may be used to describe any kind of communication activity in which the messages involved have timing constraints associated with them. For example, packet-switched voice communication, in which the individual voice packets have maximum delay constraints associated with them, is often termed real-time communication. However, in the rest of this paper we restrict this term to mean *communication in distributed real-time systems*. While some of the protocols developed here may be applicable to voice communication, we do not consider that application any further in this paper.

Communication requirements in a distributed real-time system are induced by the need for interaction between various entities in the distributed system. Messages that arise in a distributed real-time system may be classified into two categories:

1. *Guarantee Seeking Messages.* These are messages typically critical or essential for the proper operation of the system. The requirements of these messages include a *guarantee* from the system that, if the actvitity that gives rise to them is accepted for execution, their timing constraints will be met with certainty.
2. *Best Effort Messages.* These are messages, typically with soft timing constraints, that do not require a *guarantee* from the system that their timing constraints will be met. However, the system will try its best to satisfy the timing constraints of these messages, since minimizing the number of such messages whose timing constraints are violated will result in increased value (in some sense) for the system.

In the current generation of open loop distributed real-time systems (Strosnider 1988), the guarantee seeking messages are of two types, viz., *periodic* messages and *alarm* (alert) messages. Periodic messages, as the name implies, are messages that are transmitted periodically. They typically carry sensor information about the current state of the controlled process. For example, in an industrial process control system, computers at various sites in the plant *periodically* collect information about the state of the process such as flow rates, pressures and temperatures, with the help of sensors, and transmit this state information to a central control room, where human controllers make decisions on the basis of this information. Periodic messages require guarantees that their delivery deadlines will be met in order to ensure that the actual state of the controlled process and the controller's view of the state obtained through these messages are close to each other. *Alarm* messages are used to disseminate information in an emergency situation. For example, in an emergency, the controller may have to shut down certain devices within a predetermined amount of time. Even though alert messages arise very rarely, due to their critical nature the system has to guarantee that alert messages will be delivered within their deadlines.

Examples of best effort messages in today's systems include some classes of commands from human controllers, and some classes of advisories and responses. For example, certain status and control messages, and trajectory advisory and response messages in the space shuttle mission control system (Strosnider 1988) may be classified as best effort messages. These messages occur asynchronously and are usually treated as soft real-time messages. The system is designed to minimize the response time for these messages.

Most current work in real-time communication (Lehoczky and Sha 1986, Le Lann 1987, Strosnider 1988, Strosnider and Marchok 1989) is based on the above model of communication in distributed real-time systems, i.e., they assume that the guarantee seeking messages are either *periodic* or occur *rarely*. They also assume that the characteristics of these messages are *statically* specifiable. However, this conventional model of communication requirements is likely to prove inadequate for the autonomous real-time systems of the future. These systems will be characterized by *dynamic* activities with *several* types of timing constraints (Stankovic and Ramamritham 1990). *Cooperation requirements* of distributed problem solving software that will replace cooperating human controllers, and distributed real-time operating system software (e.g., distributed scheduling (Ramamritham and Stankovic 1989, Ramamritham, Stankovic and Zhao 1989) will necessarily induce *richer communication patterns* than periodic state message communication. The system will have to provide mechanisms to predictability handle, in addition to the traditional communication requirements, *dynamically* spawned activities with communication requirements that will include *general* kinds of timing constraints. For example, each message in the set of messages involved in a distributed activity may have its own individual timing constraints that are independent of other messages. Consider the scenario depicted in Figure 4. A team of telerobots on a planet is coordinated by an autonomous mission controller. The object of the mission is to explore the planet. If the controller detects a crater near the current location of the robots that appears to be worth exploring, then it might decide to command the robots to explore the crater, if this (dynamically arising) activity can be accommodated into the system's schedule without violating the deadlines of other scheduled critical activities. In order to ensure predictability, the controller will first try to seek a *guarantee* that the timing requirements of this cooperative activity (including the timing requirements of all the messages that arise because of cooperation) can be met before actually committing itself to exploring the crater. Many of the messages exchanged in this high level cooperative activity will be aperiodic, since this is not a low level sensing activity. Depending on how essential they are to the progress of the exploration, some of the messages exchanged will require guarantees, while others will be best effort messages. The exact details of the communication involved in the activity, including the number of messages

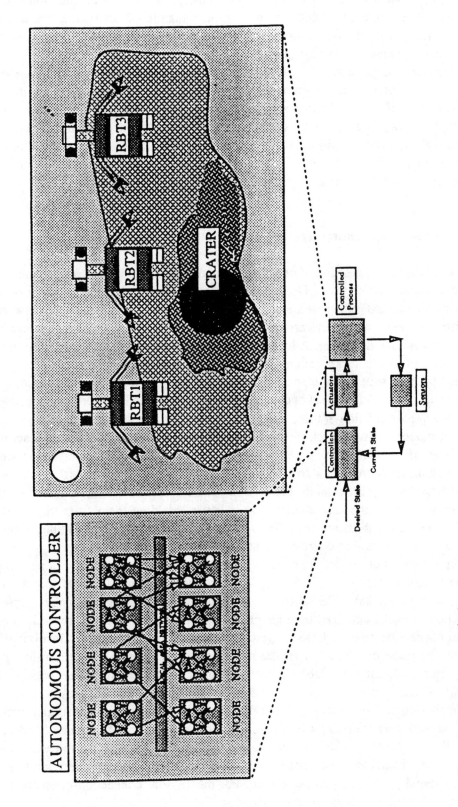

Figure 4. Cooperating team of robots.

exchanged, their contents and individual timing constraints such as arrival times and deadlines will depend on both the activity and various dynamic factors such as the nature of the terrain near the crater, the number of robots assigned to this task and the desired degree to which the crater is to be explored.

While the above example may sound futuristic[2], it serves well to illustrate an important requirement of the evolving generation of autonomous real-time systems, viz., support for dynamic guarantees of communication activities with general types of timing constraints. The challenge in designing operating systems and communication mechanisms for the autonomous real-time systems of the future is to develop mechanisms that support these more complex requirements. The rest of this paper addresses network support for the *communication requirements* that arise in these systems.

4. Local area network architectures

A computer network is a collection of geographically dispersed computers interconnected through a communication network. Depending on the geographic span of the network, a network may be classified[3] either as a local area network (LAN) or a wide area network (WAN). Distributed real-time systems are typically based on a LAN, and therefore we restrict our attention to LANs in this paper. A local area network is a network that spans a limited geographical area (0.1 km–10 km) such as a building or a campus. A LAN is typically characterized by high speed, low error rates and ownership by a single organization.

A *network architecture* defines a set of communication services, and protocols and message formats for the implementation of these services. In order to modularize and simplify implementation, modern network architectures are typically structured in terms of a set of functional *layers*. For example, the Open Systems Interconnection (OSI) reference model proposed by the International Standards Organization consists of 7 layers, viz., physical, data link, network, transport, session, presentation and the application layers. Each layer offers certain services to the immediately higher layers shielding them from the details of the implementation of these services. The services offered by a layer are implemented through a set of protocols that operate at that layer.

Two different classes of services that can be offered by the various layers of a network are *connection-oriented service* (COS) and *connectionless service* (CLS) (Knightson, Knowles and Larmouth 1988). COS is based on the establishment of a logical channel known as a connection. It is characterized by three phases, viz., *connection establishment, data transfer* and *connection release*. COS is typically suited for communication involving a long data transfer phase or a logically related sequence of messages, e.g., file transfer applications. Since a context is available (namely the logical connection) within which individual units of data passed between the communicating entities can be logically related, COS has smaller control overheads and can provide sequencing, flow control and error recovery. A network may use either a connectionless or connection-oriented mode of operation *internally* in order to provide communication services to its users. An *internal* connection in a wide area network that uses the connection-oriented mode of operation (e.g., TYMNET) internally is called a *virtual circuit*. For this reason, connection-oriented service is sometimes referred to as *virtual circuit service*.

The second category of communication services, connectionless service (CLS), as the name implies, is characterized by the absence of a logical connection between sender and receiver. There are no distinct phases since there is no connection to be established or released. Each unit of data is entirely self-contained and since there is no context in the form of a logical connection, the overhead information necessary to deliver the data to the receiver is duplicated in each unit of data. CLS is simpler and typically suited for short communications. However, CLS does not provide sequencing, flow control or error recovery. In networks (e.g., ARPANET) that use the connectionless mode of operation *internally*, the independent packets involved in this operation are referred to as *datagrams*. Hence connectionless service is sometimes referred to as *datagram service*.

The architecture proposed by the IEEE Project 802 committee for local area networks (Figure 5) may be used to illustrate these concepts. This is a simple architecture that addresses only the lowest two layers in the OSI reference model, viz., the physical and data link layers. However the data link layer provides transport layer functionality in the case of an isolated (i.e., not internetworked) LAN and provides both connectionless (or Type 1) service and connection-oriented (or Type 2) service. These two classes of service are sufficient for many applications. If an application requires higher level functionality, it must implement it itself.

The data link layer in the IEEE 802 architecture is divided into two sublayers, viz., *logical link control* (LLC) sublayer and *medium access control* (MAC) sublayer. The *LLC sublayer*, specified in the IEEE 802.2 Standard (IEEE 1985), is responsible for implementing medium-independent data link functions, such as connection management, error handling and flow control, and has the overall responsibility for the exchange of data between nodes. The main function of the *MAC sublayer* is the management of access to the shared physical channel. It is responsible for transmitting data units received from the LLC layer over the physical channel after adding the required framing, addressing and checksum information. The 802 Architecture specifies three protocol standards for medium access control, viz., the CSMA/CD (802.3 standard), the token bus (802.4 standard) and the token ring (802.5 standard). The *physical layer* is responsible for the management of physical connections and for the transmission of bits over the transmission medium.

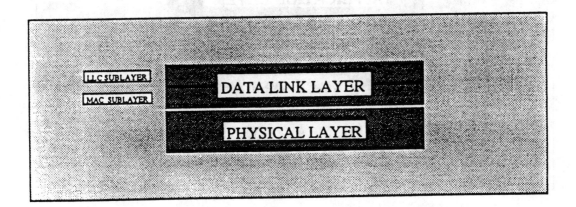

Figure 5. IEEE 802 LAN architecture.

The services and protocols defined by the IEEE 802 architecture and other network architectures, although sufficient for many applications today, have an important limitation. Comer and Yavatakar (1989) point out that existing protocols do not make provisions for applications to specify their performance needs such as maximum delay, minimum throughput, maximum error rate etc., and existing network architectures do not have mechanisms to meet and guarantee these performance requirements. While they make this observation in the context of research in voice and video communication in future wide area networks, a similar observation may be made in the context of distributed real-time systems. It is important for tasks executing in a distributed real-time system to be able to specify their performance requirements including timing constraints of individual messages to the operating system, and for the operating system and the underlying network to provide support for meeting and guaranteeing these requirements. However, existing operating systems and networks provide little support for this. For example, the Type 1 LLC service in the IEEE 802 architecture does not take timing constraints of messages into account explicitly, and the Type 2 service does not try to guarantee timing requirements of connections. Below, we propose the elements of RTLAN, a new local area network architecture for communication in distributed real-time systems, that alleviates this deficiency.

5. RTLAN

The RTLAN (real-time local area network) architecture is a local network architecture for communication in distributed real-time systems, that permits applications to dynamically specify their communication timing requirements and provides mechanisms to guarantee these requirments, if needed and if at all possible. RTLAN is targeted for complex embedded control applications and so we do not consider internetworking aspects. We therefore propose a simple four layer structure for RTLAN (Figure 6), along the lines of the IEEE 802

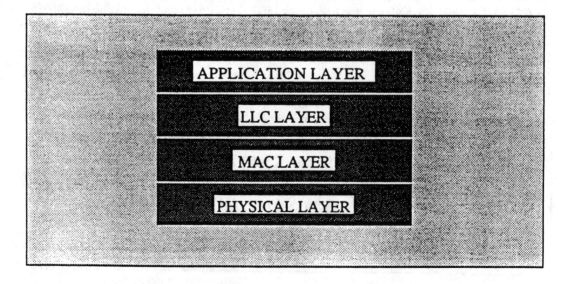

Figure 6. RTLAN architecture.

architecture. The four layers are the physical layer, the medium access control (MAC) layer, the logical link control (LLC) layer and the application layer. Some of the salient features of the RTLAN architecture are listed below:

1. *Real-Time Applications*. RTLAN is targeted for complex real-time applications which have time-constrained communication requirements that range from simple best effort delivery requirements to dynamic guarantees of general timing requirements.
2. *Time-Constrained Services*. RTLAN provides both connection-oriented and connectionless services, both of which consider the timing requirements of applications.
3. *LLC Layer Supports Guarantee*. Connection establishment at the LLC level is more complicated than in conventional architectures. The LLC layer incorporates *scheduling* algorithms that take a set of message timing requirements and try to guarantee that the requirements will be met.
4. *Real-Time MAC Protocols*. The MAC layer employs specialized real-time protocols to help the LLC layer provide its real-time services. Some of the protocols are geared to supporting the connectionless class of service, while others are geared to supporting the connection-oriented class of service.
5. *Multiple Physical Channels*. The physical layer consists of multiple physical channels and interfaces for fault-tolerance and for meeting performance and functional requirements.

We describe the various aspects of the RTLAN architecture in more detail below, focusing mainly on the LLC and MAC layers. In order to maintain readability, wherever possible we stick to natural language in preference to OSI terminology. We also discuss only those elements of the architecture that are either novel or relevant to real-time communication. Thus we have omitted certain routine aspects such as protocol data unit structures and the details of link control rules of procedure.

6. RTLAN LLC Layer

The logical link control layer provides communication services to the layer above it by implementing functions that are responsible for medium-independent data link functions such as connection management, error handling, flow control and fragmentation. The RTLAN architecture distinguishes itself from a conventional LAN architecture by providing new classes of connection-oriented and connectionless services, that provide support for meeting the timing requirements of application messages. In order to meet the timing requirements of messages, it also takes an unconventional approach to error handling and flow control. We describe these aspects of the LLC layer in the following sections.

6.1. Services

The LLC layer in RTLAN offers a connection-oriented service known as RTCOS (real-time connection-oriented service) and a connectionless service known as RTCLS (real-time connectionless service). These services are accessible to applications through LLC service access points.

6.1.1. Real-time connection-oriented service. RTCOS is a connection-oriented service that permits the sender to specify its timing requirements at the time of connection establishment. RTCOS is meant for supporting the requirements of the class of guarantee-seeking messages. The service is characterized by the establishment of a logial connection known as a *real-time connection*. A real-time connection (Figure 7) represents a simplex end-to-end communication channel between two communicating application level entities, a *sender* and a *receiver*. In order to set up a real-time connection, the sender specifies the timing requirements of the messages that it plans to send over the connection to the LLC layer at the time of connection establishment (connection establishment is done at the time of scheduling a task; the connection request is typically made by the operating system, which is also part of the application layer, on behalf of the sender). The timing constraints may be fairly general and may include periodicity, arrival time, laxity, deadline, etc. Figure 8 depicts an example of the requirements that may be specified by an application task to the LLC layer. In this example, the application task requires guarantees that the timing constraints of a session involving four messages will be satisfied. The first message is periodic and a guarantee is requested for M consecutive instances of the message. The remaining three messages are aperiodic with various arrival time and deadline requirements. As in a typical connection-oriented service, the service provider tries to set up the requested connection through a process of negotiation that may involve the sender and the receiver in addition to itself (Knightson, Knowles and Larmouth 1988). The connection is set up only if the specified requirements can be guaranteed; otherwise the sender is informed that the connection cannot be established. In order to set up the connection, the RTCOS service provider employs the services provided by the MAC layer and suitable scheduling algorithms, which we discuss later. The following operations that comprise real-time connection-oriented service summarize the above descriptions:

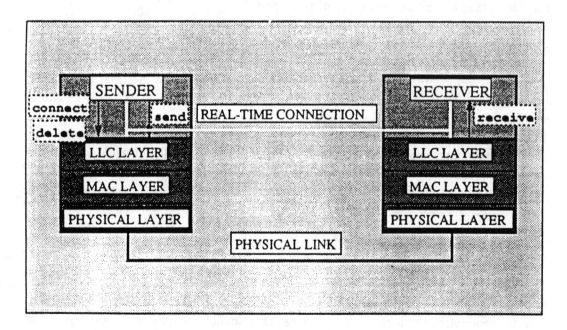

Figure 7. Real-time connection.

```
┌─────────────────────────────────────┐
│                                      │
│          RTC  REQUIREMENTS           │
│                                      │
│   MESSAGE #1                         │
│       Periodic  Period: P1           │
│       Maximum Number of Cycles:  N1  │
│                                      │
│   MESSAGE #2                         │
│       Aperiodic                      │
│       Latest Arrival Time  T2        │
│       Deadline  D2                   │
│                                      │
│   MESSAGE #3                         │
│       Aperiodic                      │
│       Latest Arrival Time  T3        │
│       Deadline  D3                   │
│                                      │
│   MESSAGE #4                         │
│       Aperiodic                      │
│       Latest Arrival Time  A4        │
│       Earliest Delivery Time  E4     │
│       Deadline  D4                   │
│                                      │
└─────────────────────────────────────┘
```

Figure 8. Real-time connection requirements.

- rtcid ← connect(receiverid, requirements)
  The communication service provider checks to see if it can set up a connection that satisfies the specified real-time requirements. If so, it returns a real-time connection identifier; otherwise it returns an error code.
- send(rtcid, message)
  Sender requests delivery of a message to the receiving end of the specified real-time connection.
- message ← receive(rtcid)
  Receiver requests receipt of a message sent over the specified real-time connection.
- delete(rtcid)
  Sender or receiver requests termination of specified real-time connection.

6.1.2. Real-time connectionless service. RTCLS is an unreliable *connectionless* service for transmitting time-constrained messages. It is unreliable in the sense that the timing constraints of messages transmitted using this service may not be satisfied. However, RTCLS tries to deliver messages within their timing constraints on a *best effort* basis. Thus this service is suitable for the class of best effort messages. By best effort, we mean that at each decision making point within the service, decisions are made on the basis of timing constraints of the pending packets. For example, if there are several packets waiting to be transmitted, then the system would try to transmit them in an order that minimizes the number of messages whose deadlines are not met. Since real-time connectionless service does not involve setting up a connection, it is defined by a simpler set of operations:

- send(receiver, message, requirements)

  Sender requests delivery of a message to the specified receiver; sender also specifies timing requirements (e.g., a deadline for the message) that it would like to be met if possible.
- (message, sender) ← receive()

  Receiver requests receipt of a message.

In order to support RTCLS, the LLC layer makes use of the services provided by suitable protocols at the MAC layer that explicitly consider timing constraints of packets in arbitrating access to the medium.

6.2. Fragmentation

One of the functions implemented by the logical link control layer is the transformation of messages provided to it by the application layer to a form suitable for the medium access control layer. One step involved in this function is known as *fragmentation* or *packetization*. This refers to the division of a long message into smaller packets or *frames* that satisfy the maximum packet length requirements of the medium access control layer. Since messages have timing requirements associated with them, the LLC layer propagates these requirements to the individual packets, by propagating the requirements of a message to each of its fragments. For example, the deadline of a message could be copied to all its fragments, or the deadlines of the fragments can be staggered such that the last fragment is assigned the deadline of the message and the leading fragments are assigned earlier deadlines. We refer to a fragment that is derived from a RTCLS message as a *real-time datagram*, in analogy with datagrams in a wide area network.

6.3. Guaranteeing real-time connections

One of the distinguishing characteristics of the RTLAN architecture is its connection-oriented communication service, RTCOS, that permits the sender to specify its timing requirements at the time of setting up a connection and seek a guarantee from the system that these timing requirements will be met. In this section, we examine mechanisms that the LLC layer may use in order to provide such a guarantee.

6.3.1. Priority assignment approach. The first approach that we discuss assumes that all the messages are periodic and statically specified. By dedicating a separate physical channel for these messages, this approach may be used to handle the static periodic message components of systems that involve both static and dynamic communication requirements.

This approach is based on the *rate monotonic* priority assignment scheme (Liu and Layland 1973). The rate monotonic priority assignment scheme, originally developed in the context of scheduling periodic tasks on a uniprocessor, is a fixed priority assignment scheme in which tasks with a smaller period (i.e., higher rate) are assigned higher priorities. Scheduling then consists of merely allocating the processor to the pending task with the highest priority, preempting the currently running task if necessary. Liu and Layland (1973) have shown that the rate monotonic priority assignment scheme is optimal in the following sense—if some priority assignment scheme can assign suitable priorities to tasks such that every task will complete within its period, then the rate monotonic priority assignment scheme can do so. They also show that a sufficient condition for such a priority assignment to exist is that the sum of the utilizations of the individual tasks must satisfy

$$\sum_{i=1}^{n} U_i \leq n\,(2^{1/n} - 1), \tag{1}$$

where n is the number of tasks and U_i is the utilization of task i defined as

$$U_i = \frac{C_i}{T_i},$$

where C_i and T_i are respectively the computation time and period of the task. Lehoczky and Sha (1986) have extended this result to the problem of scheduling n periodic messages on a shared bus. Strosnider (1988) has further extended this result to the *deferrable server* and priority exchange algorithms that make use of a periodic server to service aperiodic messages. He has used these algorithms to provide guarantees for both periodic messages and a limited class of alert messages that are assumed to occur rarely.

Guaranteeing an application's message timing requirements, in the priority assignment approach, consists of merely assigning fixed priorities to each of the periodic messages (and the periodic server that services aperiodic messages) involved (on the basis of their periods), and ensuring that the sum of the utilizations of the messages is appropriately bounded. Actual implementation of priority arbitration is left to suitable MAC protocols.

6.3.2. Real-time virtual circuit approach.

An alternative approach, that may be used to guarantee the timing requirements of both statically known and dynamically arising messages, is to use the notion of *real-time virtual circuits* (RTVCs). An RTVC is a *logical channel* that has the property that the *service time* of a packet queued on this channel, the length of the interval between the instant at which the packet enters service and the instant at which transmission of the packet completes successfully, is bounded for a fixed packet length. Thus the LLC layer can assume that once a packet queued onto a RTVC has been accepted for service, it will be transmitted within a bounded amount of time. This bound is determined by the MAC protocols used to implement RTVCs.

The LLC layer makes use of RTVCs as follows. Each RTVC has a transmission queue associated with it. When an application entity requests a real-time connection from the LLC layer, the LLC layer firsts *fragments* messages in the request that are longer than the maximum packet length into multiple packets and propagates the timing constraints of messages to their fragments. The set of fragments are then passed on to a LLC layer entity known as the *scheduler*. The scheduler takes a set of message fragments with timing requirements, and applies a *scheduling algorithm* (Cheng, Stankovic and Ramamritham 1988) to determine if the set of fragments can be inserted (according to some insertion discipline, such as the first-in first-out (FIFO) or the minimum laxity first (MLF) discipline[4]) into the queue associated with some RTVC, without violating the timing constraints of the packets that have already been admitted into the queue and that are awaiting transmission. In order to make this determination the scheduler makes use of a worst case assumption, since the scheduler cannot predict the service time exactly. The assumption made is that each packet in the queue will have a service time equal to the worst case service time. Such a worst case service time is guaranteed to exist, since an RTVC by definition has a bounded packet service time. The example shown in Figure 9 illustrates these ideas. In this example, there is one RTVC (with a worst case service time of 10) which already has three guaranteed packets waiting to be transmitted. Packet M1 has a laxity (time until deadline for start of transmission) of 10, M2 has a laxity of 30 and M3 has a laxity of 40. If a packet M4 of laxity 10 arrives, then it cannot be admitted into the system, if the MLF discipline is used, since the deadlines of both M1 and M4 cannot be simultaneously met. However a packet M5 with a laxity of 20 can be admitted, since it is possible to meet its laxity requirements without violating the requirements of any of the messages already in the queue. It should be pointed out that, for the real-time virtual circuit approach to guarantee a reasonable fraction of the connection requests that are made, the worst-case packet service time must be of the same magnitude or smaller than the average laxity of the packets involved.

Note that RTVCs are abstractions provided by the MAC layer to the LLC layer, Figure 10 illustrates how each layer in the architecture provides an abstraction that is used by the layer at the immediately higher level to implement its services. The physical layer receives a bitstream from the MAC layer and converts the bits into *electrical signals* that are transmitted over the physical link. The physical layer hides the physical details of the link and thus provides the abstraction of a virtual *bit pipe* (Bertsekas and Gallager 1987) to the MAC layer entities. Protocols in the MAC layer make use of this raw *multiple access* bit pipe with *potentially unbounded packet service times* to provide the abstraction of logical channels with bounded packet service times, viz., RTVCs. The LLC layer employs these channels to provide the abstraction of a real-time connection to the application layer.

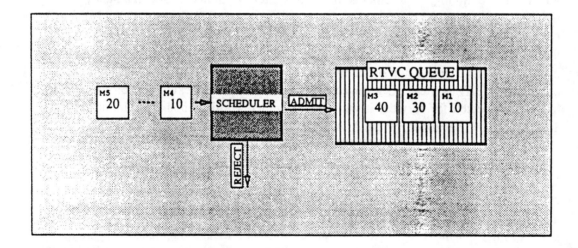

Figure 9 Real-time virtual circuit scheduling.

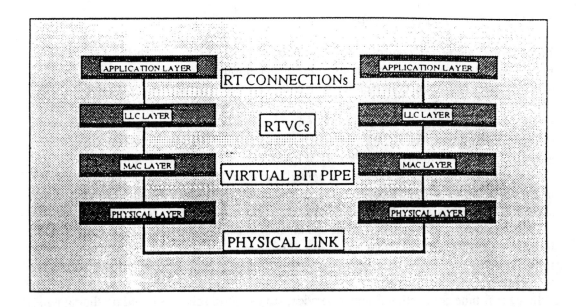

Figure 10. Abstractions provided by RTLAN layers.

Note that the MAC layer has to employ suitable protocols in order to provide such an abstraction. For instance, an Ethernet based system is unsuitable, since a message that has entered service may *never* get transmitted because of the randomized collision *resolution* strategy used in the Ethernet MAC protocol. In Section 7.1.2, we will look at several medium access control protocols that may be used to realize the RTVC abstraction.

6.3.3. Reservation approach. The real-time virtual circuit approach that we described in the previous section distributes the available channel bandwidth into RTVCs and tries to guarantee connections on individual RTVCs based only on local knowledge of connection requests. This forces each node to *pessimistically* assume a *worst case* packet service time for each packet. This can result in connection requests that can actually be guaranteed to be unnecessarily rejected. The reservation approach tries to make use of *global knowledge* of all the connection requests in the system, thereby increasing the chances of guaranteeing connections.

The reservation approach treats the entire channel as a single schedulable entity on which the LLC layers at the various nodes try to schedule their connection requests. Such an approach requires that the LLC layers have a *system-wide* view of all the accepted reservation requests made at *any* node in the system. With such a global view, the LLC layer at a node can apply a scheduling algorithm based on an appropriate insertion discipline (as in Section 6.3.2) to determine whether a connection request can be accepted or not. However, since the scheduling algorithm has global knowledge of all the packets (in all the nodes) in the system that are awaiting transmission, it does not have to make worst case assumptions about the service time of a packet. Thus the chances of guaranteeing connections can be expected to be better under this approach.

Implementation of such a system-wide view requires special support from the MAC layer in the form of suitable MAC protocols. We discuss approaches to implementing such a queue in Section 7.1.3.

6.4. Flow control and error control

Flow control and error control are two important functions for which the LLC layer is responsible. Flow control is a synchronization technique to ensure that a sending entity does not overwhelm a receiving entity with data, causing its buffers to overflow. Flow control is typically implemented through acknowledgment based sliding window protocols. Error control mechanisms are responsible for detecting and correcting errors that occur in the transmission of packets. These mechanisms are required because it is possible for a transmitted packet to be *lost* or *damaged* because of noise on the communication channel. Error control is typically implemented through ARQ (automatic-repeat request) mechanisms. In an ARQ mechanism, the receiver sends a positive acknowledgment to the sender, if it receives an undamaged packet (damage is typically detected through the use of an error-detecting code such as cyclic redundancy check); if it receives a damaged packet, it sends a negative acknowledgment. If the sender receives no acknowledgment within a time-out period or receives a negative acknowledgment, then it retransmits the packet to the receiver.

In the real-time connection oriented service, flow control schemes based on sliding window protocols where the receiver may block the sender by withholding acknowledgments, are inappropriate. If a receiver can block the sender for an arbitrary amount of time (because of an insufficient number of buffers), then the timing constraints of guaranteed packets may be violated. In order to guarantee the timing constraints of packets, the required number of buffers will have to be *reserved* at the destination node. This will permit the sender to transmit its packets whenever they are ready, rather than wait for permission from the receiver. This *buffer reservation* is part of the three way negotiation involved in setting up a real-time connection. When a connection is requested under any of the approaches described in Section 6.3, the LLC layer makes sure that sufficient buffer space is reserved at the destination nodes for the packets involved in the request. In a real-time connectionless service, flow control can be exercised by merely dropping packets that arrive when the receiver's buffers are full. This is acceptable, since RTCLS does not offer any guarantee on the delivery of packets.

Two kinds of error control schemes may be used for RTCOS. The first scheme is an ARQ scheme based on *temporal redundancy* that is appropriate when the deadlines of the packets involved in a connection are large enough to permit the use of timeouts. At the time of connection establishment, the maximum number of retransmissions possible for each packet is computed based on the packet's deadline and the retransmission timeout (alternatively, this number may be included in the specification of the requirements for the connection). The scheduler takes into account all the potential retransmissions in determining whether the requested connection can be guaranteed or not. When the packet is actually transmitted, the receiver returns an acknowledgment (transmitted as a real-time datagram) to the sender. If the acknowledgment is received within the retransmission timeout period, then all the remaining duplicates are dequeued; otherwise, the next duplicate is transmitted, when its turn comes. A variation on this scheme is to use temporal redundancy and avoid acknowledgments all together (Kopetz 1983). In this variation all the duplicates are transmitted, irrespective of whether or not the earlier duplicates suffer transmission errors, leaving it to the receiver to select an error-free duplicate and discard the others.

The second scheme is based on *spatial redundancy* and is appropriate when the deadlines of the packets involved in a connection are too small to permit retransmissions based on timeouts. In this scheme, the LLC layer tries to schedule a connection request on multiple physical channels. A request for a real-time connection is guaranteed only if it is possible to redundantly schedule the request on the specified number of physical channels. Thus multiple copies of each message involved in an accepted connection are transmitted on multiple channels, thereby improving the probability of error-free receipt. The receiver is then responsible for discarding duplicates.

Note that neither of the above schemes can guarantee reliability with certainty; they can only provide a conditional guarantee that if the number of faults (errors) does not exceed a certain number, then a packet will be transmitted successfully because of the redundancy in the system. However, this is true of *any* mechanism for fault-tolerance. RTCLS does not require any error control mechanism, since it does not guarantee reliability.

7. RTLAN MAC layer

A local area network is typically based on a shared physical channel such as a bus or a ring, commonly referred to as a multiple access channel. Since multiple nodes may simultaneously contend for access to this shared channel, a mechanism is needed to manage access to it. The main function of the medium access control layer is to arbitrate access to the channel. The MAC layer implements this arbitration mechanism through a suitable *multiple access protocol*. Kurose, Schwartz and Yemini (1984) provide a good survey of multiple access protocols. Multiple access protocols can be classified into *real-time* and *non-real-time* protocols on the basis of whether or not they provide support for real-time communication. Many protocols that have been proposed in the literature, such as the Aloha protocol (Abramson 1970) the CSMA protocols in (Kleinrock and Tobagi 1975) and the Ethernet protocol (Metcalfe and Boggs 1976) are non-real-time protocols since they do not incorporate any notion of packet timing constraints. In this section, we look at examples of real-time protocols that have been proposed in the literature that may be used to provide support for RTCOS and RTCLS.

7.1. RTCOS/MAC protocols

In Section 6.1.1, we defined RTCOS as a connection-oriented service that permits an application layer entity to specify its communication timing requirements to the LLC layer and seek a guarantee that these requirements will be satisfied. We also described three different approaches to providing such guarantees, viz., *priority assignment* approach, *real-time virtual circuit* approach and *reservation* approach. The LLC layer invokes the services of the MAC layer in order to provide such guarantees. In this section, we look at several MAC protocols that may be used to support the services required by the LLC layer, for each of these approaches. The priority assignment approach requires priority resolution protocols at the MAC layer; the real-time virtual circuit approach requires MAC protocols that can guarantee bounded packet service times and the reservation approach requires reservation protocols.

7.1.1 Priority resolution protocols. In Section 6.3.1, we described a priority-based scheduling approach based on the rate monotonic algorithm and the extensions to this algorithm proposed by Lehoczky and Sha (1986), and Strosnider (1988). This approach may be used to guarantee certain classes of statically specifiable messages. In order to ensure that packets are actually transmitted according to the priorities assigned to them by the LLC layers, the MAC layers will have to employ an appropriate *priority resolution protocol*. A priority resolution MAC protocol always selects for transmission, the packet with the highest priority among all the contending packets in the system.

The IEEE 802.5 standard for token ring local area networks includes a priority resolution scheme. In a token-passing ring network, access to the ring is arbitrated through a short control packet known as a token. At any moment, only the node that is in possession of the token is permitted to transmit. A node that has completed transmission or that has no packets to transmit passes on the token to the next node. This simple token-passing scheme may be augmented to support priority resolution by including additional fields in the token. In the IEEE 802.5 standard, priority resolution is supported using two 3 bit fields in the token known as the *priority* field and the *reservation* field. The priority resolution scheme works as follows. When a station captures the token, it sets a one bit field in the token known as the *token bit* to indicate that the token has been *claimed*. It then transmits the claimed token followed by the data packet. Each node examines the claimed token as it passes by. It overwrites the reservation field in the token with the priority of its pending packet, if this priority is greater than the value in the reservation field. Thus the reservation field contains the priority of the packet with the highest priority among all the packets at the heads of MAC transmission queues at the various nodes in the system. After the transmitting station has received the token and the data packet back, it removes the data packet from the ring and clears the token bit in the token. It also copies the reservation field of the token to the priority field before releasing the free token. Any node with a pending packet with priority greater than or equal to the priority field of the free token may now capture the token. Strosnider and Marchok discuss the use of the token ring priority resolution scheme for scheduling statically specified message sets in more detail in (Strosnider and Marchok, 1989).

Priority resolution protocols for bus-based systems are classified by Valadier and Powell (1984) into three categories, on the basis of the underlying scheme involved:

1. *Deference delays*. In this scheme at the end of a packet transmission, each node defers transmission of its packet (if any) by a period of time whose length in round trip propagation delay units is equal to $p_{max} - p$. Here p is the priority associated with a node and p_{max} is the largest priority value possible. At the end of its deference period, each node senses the channel. If the channel is sensed to be idle, it means that no other node has a value of p greater than that of the node that sensed the channel. So this node is allowed to transmit its packet. Thus this scheme selects the node with the largest value of p (highest priority) that has a packet to transmit. Note that the length of the deference delay, the worst case overhead (in the form of wasted channel time) per packet that arises because of priority resolution, lies in the range $[0, p_{max} - p_{min}]$. The average overhead, assuming all possible values of the overhead are equally likely, is given by

$1/2$ $(p_{max} - p_{min})$, i.e., it is a linearly increasing function of the number of priority levels. The protocols proposed by Franta and Bilodeau (1980) and Tobagi (1982) are examples of this class.

2. *Preamble lengths*. In this scheme, at the end of a packet transmission, each node transmits a preamble signal for a period of time whose length in round trip propagation delay units is equal to $p - p_{min}$, where p_{min} is the smallest priority value possible. Thus a node with a higher priority will transmit a longer preamble signal. Collision detection is suppressed at a node during the period that its preamble is being transmitted. If a node detects a collision at the end of the transmission of its preamble, it means that there is another node with a larger value of p that is still transmitting its preamble. Only the node which does not detect a collision at the end of its preamble, i.e., the node with the longest preamble length or the largest value of p, is allowed to transmit its packet. The per packet overhead that arises because of priority resolution again lies in the range $[0, p_{max} - p_{min}]$ units of time. Thus the average overhead is again a linearly increasing function of the number of priority levels. The protocol proposed by Iida et al. (1980) is an example of a protocol that employs this scheme.

3. *Forcing Headers*. The forcing header scheme makes use of the inherent wired-OR property of a broadcast bus, namely the property that the value of the bit received by a node from the bus is equal to the logical OR of the bits transmitted by all the nodes. In this scheme, each packet transmission is preceded by a header epoch, during which all the nodes with packets to transmit, simultaneously transmit their priorities from the most significant to the least significant bit in successive slots (of length equal to a round trip propagation delay). The nodes sense the medium as they transmit their priority bits. If a node has transmitted a 0 bit in a slot and receives a 1 bit, it means that some node with a higher priority value is contending for access to the channel. In this case the node that transmitted the 0 bit drops out of contention. At the end of the header epoch, only the node with the highest priority value remains and this node transmits its packet to completion. The length of the header epoch is equal to the number of bits required to represent the range of values $[p_{min}, p_{max}]$, i.e., $\lceil \log_2(p_{max} - p_{min} + 1) \rceil$ time units. This represents the priority resolution overhead and is constant for all packets and hence also represents the average overhead. Thus the average overhead for this scheme increases *logarithmically* with the number of priority levels. The MLMA or multilevel multiaccess protocol (Rothauser and Wild, 1977) employs such a scheme.

It is clear that, among the above schemes for bus-based systems, the scheme based on forcing headers incurs the least overhead, because of the logarithmic relationship between the overhead and the number of priority levels in this scheme. In fact, such a scheme is used in the Distributed Systems Data Bus (DSDB) developed by IBM, which forms the hub of a large distributed real-time system (Strosnider 1988). In Section 8.1, we describe a priority resolution protocol based on a window splitting paradigm whose overheads are about the same as the forcing headers scheme.

7.1.2. Real-time virtual circuit protocols. A real-time virtual circuit is a logical channel that has the property that the service time of a packet queued on the channel is bounded. The packet service time consists of two components, the physical *channel access time* and the packet *transmission time* (Figure 11). The channel access time arises because the underlying physical channel in a local area network is typically a multiple access channel that is shared by all the nodes on the network; a node may therefore have to wait for the channel arbitration mechanism to permit it to transmit. The packet transmission time is the time required to transmit a packet. Note that the packet transmission time may be bounded by restricting the maximum size of a packet. However, unless a suitable medium access control (MAC) protocol is used, the channel access time can be unbounded. For example, in a CSMA/CD (Ethernet) based system, a message that has entered service may *never* get transmitted because of the randomized collision *resolution* strategy used in the MAC protocol. In this section, we look at several MAC protocols, each of which can guarantee a bounded channel access time.

In Time Division Multiple Access (TDMA), time is divided into fixed length intervals known as *frames*. Each frame is further subdivided into slots with at least one slot per node. If there are S slots in a frame, then the maximum separation between two instances of the same slot is given by the frame length $S\,P$, where P is the packet transmission time (assuming that only one packet is permitted per slot). Real-time virtual circuits may be implemented by dedicating one slot per real-time virtual circuit. In this case the worst case channel access time for a packet queued on a real-time virtual circuit is given by $S\,P$.

In token-passing protocols, the nodes are organized in a logical (e.g., token bus (IEEE 1982)) or physical ring (e.g., token ring (IEEE 1986)). A real (e.g., token ring, token bus) or virtual (e.g., BRAM (Chlamtac, Franta and Levin 1979), MSAP (Kleinrock and Scholl 1980) token that circulates around this ring is used to arbitrate access to the channel. The token confers upon its holder the privilege to transmit on the channel for a bounded amount of time (the token holding time). If there are no packets to transmit, or if the token holding time has been exceeded, the token is passed onto the next node in the ring. If the token holding time per node is P time units (i.e., a node is permitted to transmit only one packet in each cycle), then the maximum length of the interval between successive channel accesses by a node is given by $N(P + \tau)$, where N is the number of nodes in the system and τ is the token passing overhead.

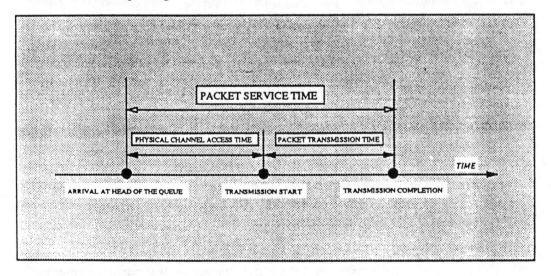

Figure 11. Packet service time.

The 802.3D protocol proposed by Le Lann (1987) is another MAC protocol that may be used to guarantee a bounded channel access time. The '802.3' in the name refers to the IEEE 802.3 MAC layer standard (IEEE 1985) for CSMA/CD (the access control method used in Ethernet) which, owing to the collision resolution strategy (binary exponential backoff) used, cannot guarantee an upper bound on the channel access time. The 'D' refers to the fact that the 802.3D protocol is deterministic, i.e., it can guarantee an upper bound on the channel access time. This protocol is essentially an adaptive tree walk protocol. Normally, the nodes are in the *random access* mode in which they access the channel randomly without any coordination. Thus under low load conditions, channel access is immediate. However, the moment a collision occurs, the nodes switch to the *epoch* mode in which a tree search process is used to resolve the collision within a bounded amount of time. The worst case channel access time for the 802.3D protocol is the worst case time required to resolve a collision involving all the nodes and is equal to $N(P + \tau)$, where τ is the round trip propagation delay.

The notion of waiting room priorities (Valadier and Powell 1984, Ramamritham 1987) has been used to implement the *waiting room protocol* which is characterized by bounded channel access times. The waiting room protocol is based on a logical waiting room which a packet has to enter before it can be transmitted. A packet can enter a waiting room only when the waiting room is empty. However, since packets belonging to different nodes can simultaneously find the waiting room to be empty, more than one packet can enter it simultaneously. The packets in the waiting room are then transmitted in some prespecified order (e.g., descending order of node addresses). If there are N nodes in the system and the transmission order is the descending order of node addresses, then the worst case channel access time occurs for a packet belonging to the node with the smallest address and is equal to $2(N - 1)P$ units of time (Valadier and Powell 1984).

Thus a variety of paradigms may be used to realize the abstraction of a real-time virtual circuit, all with approximately the same worst case channel access time (except the waiting room protocol that has a larger worst case channel access time). In Section 8.2, we describe another protocol, this time based on a window splitting paradigm, that has approximately the same bound on the channel access time as most of the protocols above, but which also provides structural homogeneity.

7.1.3. Reservation protocols.

In Section 6.3.3, we described the reservation approach to implementing RTCOS, in which LLC layers make use of global knowledge of all the connection requests in the system in deciding whether a connection request can be accepted or not. We also pointed out that such an approach requires that the LLC layers have a global view of all the accepted reservation requests made at *any* node in the system. In a distributed system, such a global view may be realized through a replicated, globally consistent queue of reservation requests.

One approach to maintaining such a global queue is to broadcast each arriving connection request to all the nodes, during specific time slots (reservation slots) dedicated for this purpose. Schedulers at the LLC layer of each node execute identical scheduling algorithms to determine if a connection request is to be accepted or rejected, and update the local copy of the global queue accordingly. In a broadcast channel, in the absence of transmission errors or component failures, since all the nodes receive the same request messages at the same time, and all the schedulers apply the same scheduling algorithm, the local copies of the queue at each node remain consistent.

The Priority Oriented Demand Assignment (PODA) reservation protocol proposed by Jacobs et al. (1978) in the context of satellite-based communication is an example of a MAC protocol that uses this approach. In this protocol, channel time is divided into frames each of which consists of an *information subframe* and a *control subframe* (Figure 12). The information subframe is used for scheduled packet transmissions. These transmissions may contain additional reservation requests in their headers. The control subframe is used to broadcast reservations that cannot be sent as part of the data transmissions in a timely manner (e.g., when a station wants to make a reservation for a high priority message or when a station wants to join the system). In the PODA protocol, all stations maintain a local copy of a scheduling queue ordered by reservation urgency, which is a function of the delay class and priority of a message. Reservations with the same urgency are ordered further to ensure fairness to all the stations involved. Channel time in the information subframe is allocated to the stations according to this queue. Whenever a reservation request for a message is broadcast, all the nodes that successfully receive the message enter the request in their respective local scheduling queues (on the basis of its reservation urgency).

The main problem with a reservation protocol such as PODA is the lack of robustness. In the presence of transmission errors and failures, the local copies of the global queue at each node may become mutually inconsistent resulting in possible simultaneous channel access by more than one node. This would cause collisions and a violation of the guarantees offered. In order to ensure proper operation despite failures and errors, additional mechanisms for fault-tolerance are required.

One approach to improving the system's tolerance of errors and failures is the standard approach based on redundancy. The shared bus is replicated *n* times with the same MAC protocol being employed on all the buses. There are *n* copies of the global queue at each node, one associated with each bus. The queue associated with a bus is constructed entirely using the reservation requests that are received on the bus. This ensures that as long as there is at least one copy of the queue that is consistent across all the nodes, the system will function correctly.

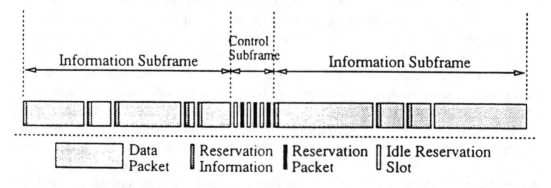

Figure 12. Priority-oriented demand assignment.

376

An alternative approach is to employ a synchronoous atomic broadcast protocol (Cristian 1990), again based on redundancy. Such a protocol guarantees the following three properties:

1. *Atomicity*. Every message whose broadcast is initiated by a sender is either delivered to all receivers or to none.
2. *Order*. All delivered messages are received in the same order at all receiving nodes.
3. *Termination*. Every message broadcast by a sender and delivered to some correct receiver, is delivered to all correct receivers after some known time interval.

These properties and the fact that the scheduling algorithms executed at each node are identical ensure that the local copies of the global queue are mutually consistent in spite of errors.

The reservation approach is a good way of avoiding the pessimism inherent in the real-time virtual circuit approach that makes use of worst case assumptions. However, as we saw above, it incurs high implementation complexity in the form of special mechanisms for fault-tolerance.

7.2. RTCLS/MAC protocols

In Section 6.1.2, we defined RTCLS as an unreliable connectionless service that tries to deliver messages within their timing constraints on a best effort basis. In order to provide such a service to the application layer, the LLC layer invokes suitable MAC layer services that are implemented through a class of MAC protocols which we refer to as *best effort* protocols. Best effort protocols take into account the timing constraints of the individual contending packets in arbitrating access to the shared channel. Even though these protocols do not provide the ability to guarantee that the timing constraints of messages will be satisfied, they try to minimize the number of messages that are *lost*, i.e., that do not meet their deadlines.

The window protocol proposed by Kurose, Schwartz and Yemini (1983) is an example of a protocol that considers timing constraints of messages in arbitrating channel access. The protocol assumes that all packets have identical laxities, as would be the case in a voice communication application. The protocol effectively implements a global first-in first-out (FIFO) policy of message transmission augmented with an additional policy element that dictates the discarding of messages that have missed their deadlines before transmission.

The FIFO policy is appropriate when all the packets have identical laxities. This policy chooses the packet that arrived first, i.e., the packet that has waited longest and hence is likely to miss its deadline first (the most *urgent* packet). However other policies have also been proposed in the literature. For example, Kallmes, Towsley and Cassandras (1989) have considered the LIFO (Last In First Out) policy, and shown that under certain conditions (when the deadlines are i.i.d. with concave CDFs) this policy is optimal. In (Panwar, Towsley and Wolf 1988) the minimum laxity first policy (also known as the shortest time to extinction policy) or its variations have been shown to maximize the fraction of the number of customers in a queueing system that meet their deadline under fairly general conditions. The virtual time CSMA protocol (Zhao and Ramamritham 1987) and the MLF window protocol (Zhao, Stankovic and Ramamritham 1990) try to implement a global minimum laxity first policy for message transmission on a bus-based system, i.e., they select the message with the smallest laxity in the *entire* system for transmission.

In the virtual time CSMA protocol (Zhao and Ramamritham 1987), each node maintains two clocks, a real-time clock and a virtual time clock that runs at a higher rate than the real-time clock. Whenever a node senses the channel to be idle, it resets and restarts its virtual-time clock. When the reading on the virtual clock is equal to some parameter value of a message waiting to be transmitted, the node transmits the message. Collisions are resolved through a random backoff procedure. Different transmission policies are implemented by using different message parameters to control the operation of the virtual clock. For example, choice of message arrival time as the parameter used by the protocol corresponds to the first-in first-out transmission policy (Molle and Kleinrock 1985), while use of message laxity corresponds to the minimum laxity first policy.

The MLF window protocol belongs to the class of inference-seeking protocols (Zhao, Stankovic and Ramamritham 1990). In the window protocol, a window that slides along the real-time axis is used to identify the node that has the message with the most urgent transmission requirements (the message whose 'latest time to send' is smallest) and this node is granted transmission rights on the channel. The protocol effectively tries to implement a global minimum laxity first policy. In this protocol, each node maintains a window that spans a segment of the real-time axis. When a node has a message to transmit, it waits for the channel to become idle and then transmits the message, if the latest time to send the message falls within the current window. If there is a collision (which can occur if another node also had a message that fell within the window), then all the nodes split the window into two halves and examine the left window first. If there is only one node with a message in the left window, then that node transmits its message successfully. If there are two or more nodes in the window, then a collision occurs again and the splitting process is repeated until a message is successfully transmitted. If there are no nodes with a message whose latest time to send falls within the left window, the window is expanded to include the left half of the right window and the window examination process is repeated again. This process is continued until a message is transmitted, or the whole of the initial window has been examined. The window protocol has been shown to very closely approximate an ideal protocol that implements, without incurring any arbitration overheads, the minimum laxity first policy for message transmission (Zhao, Stankovic and Ramamritham 1990). An important advantage of this protocol over traditional window protocols is that a newly arriving message need not wait for all the messages currently involved in contention resolution to be transmitted, before being considered for transmission.

8. A uniform approach to MAC protocols

In the previous section, we looked at several kinds of MAC protocols that may be used to support RTCLS and RTCOS, including forcing header protocols, token-passing protocols, tree walk protocols, virtual time protocols and window protocols. Each of these protocols is based on a particular distinct medium access control paradigm and is suitable for a particular kind of communication service. In (Arvind, Ramamritham and Stankovic 1991), we have proposed homogeneous MAC protocols, all based on a uniform window-splitting medium access control paradigm, to support RTCOS and RTCLS.

The starting point for this work was provided by the MLF window protocol proposed by Zhao, Stankovic and Ramamritham (1990). This protocol can be used to closely approximate the system-wide minimum laxity first policy for message transmission over a shared bus. Thus it is well-suited to supporting RTCLS. However this protocol cannot guarantee bounded channel access times for nodes. Therefore this protocol, as it is, is not suitable for implementing RTCOS. In (Arvind, Ramamritham and Stankovic 1991) we have generalized and extended this protocol and developed uniform window protocols to support both RTCLS and RTCOS. The unifying thread that is common to all the new window protocols is a contention resolution technique known as *parameter-based contention resolution* (PBCR). The term PBCR describes the following channel arbitration problem. Consider a set of N nodes sharing a multiple access channel. Each node is associated with a parameter $p \in [p_{min}, p_{sup})$ that can vary with time. The problem is to allocate the channel to the node that has the smallest value of p, whenever there is contention for the channel. PBCR may be implemented using a window splitting paradigm as follows. Each node maintains a data structure known as a window that is characterized by the current position π of its left edge and its current size δ. The window at any moment spans the range of values $[\pi, \pi + \delta)$. If the parameter p associated with a node lies in the range of values spanned by the window, the node is said to be in the window. At the end of a packet transmission epoch, each node that lies within the initial window $[p_{min}, p_{min} + \delta_{max})$, where δ_{max} is the maximum size the window is allowed to assume, starts transmitting its packet. If there is only one node in the window, then that node continues to transmit its packet to completion; if two or more nodes lie within the window, then the window is split into two and the protocol is recursively repeated with the left half of the window, and if necessary again with the right half of the window, until a packet is transmitted successfully. In the example shown in Figure 13, the initial window spans the range $[0, 128)$ and there are three nodes with p values 75, 99 and 120 respectively, that are in the window. All of them start transmitting, and consequently there is a collision on the channel. The nodes sense the collision and split the window into two, making the left half of the window the current window. Since none of the nodes lie within this half, the nodes sense the channel to be idle. The right half is then made the current window. All the nodes lie within the current window once again, resulting in a collision. The window is therefore split into two and the left half considered first. Only one node, the node with the smallest value of p, lies within this half and it transmits to completion. This window splitting paradigm may be used to implement MAC protocols that can support RTCOS and RTCLS as described below.

8.1. RTCOS/MAC: Priority resolution protocol

Implementation of priority resolution using the above contention resolution approach is straightforward. Note that priority resolution is an instance of PBCR, where the parameter p associated with each node is the priority associated with the packet with the highest priority (assuming that higher priorities correspond to smaller p values) at the node.[5] It can be shown that the contention resolution overhead per packet for the priority resolution window protocol

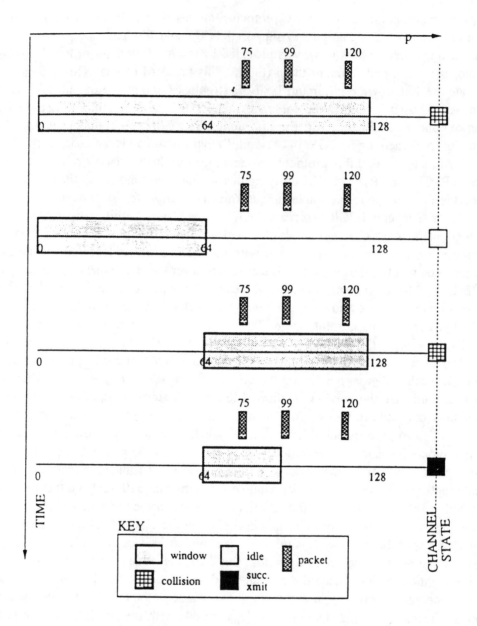

Figure 13. An example of the window protocol in operation.

lies in the range $[0, 2\lceil \log_2 K\rceil - 1]$, where K is the number of priority levels. Note that the average overhead, given by $\lceil \log_2 K\rceil - 0.5$, increases logarithmically with K and is about the same as that for the forcing headers scheme.

8.2. RTCOS/MAC: Real-time virtual circuit protocol

We have proposed a protocol known as the RTVC window protocol, based on the same window splitting approach, that can guarantee bounded channel access times and hence can be used to support the abstraction of real-time virtual circuits. This protocol assumes that the system consists of a fixed number (N_{rtvc}) of real-time virtual circuits, chosen a priori. Each real-time virtual circuit is characterized by a unique identifying integer known as its capability value. The packets at the heads of real-time virtual circuit transmission queues contend for channel access using the window protocol described above. The parameter p in the window protocol that is associated with a node is equal to the capability value of the enabled real-time virtual circuit with the smallest capability value (a real-time virtual circuit is said to be enabled, if it is permitted to contend for access to the channel; otherwise it is said to be disabled). A real-time virtual circuit is disabled, whenever a packet belonging to a real-time virtual circuit with a higher capability value is transmitted. It remains disabled until all real-time virtual circuits, with a capability value that is higher than that of the real-time virtual circuit that just transmitted a packet, have had a chance to transmit. These actions of enabling and disabling real-time virtual circuits ensure that the channel access time for each real-time virtual circuit is bounded. The reader is referred to (Arvind, Ramamritham and Stankovic 1991) for more details. The RTVC window protocol has a worst case channel access time given by $N_{rtvc} (P + \xi)$, where the overhead $\xi = (2 \lceil \log_2 N_{rtvc} \rceil - 1) \tau$ and τ is the round trip propagation delay. This is slightly larger than the worst case channel access time of $N_{rtvc}(P + \tau)$ for some of the other protocols that we saw in Section 7.1.2. The fractional increase in the worst case channel access time because of using the RTVC window protocol is given by

$$\frac{2\alpha(\lceil \log_2 N_{rtvc} \rceil - 1)}{1 + \alpha},$$

where α is the ratio of the round trip propagation delay to the packet size. Thus the fractional increase in the worst case channel access time for a system with 32 real-time virtual circuits and $\alpha = 0.01$ is about 8 percent; for a system with 1024 real-time virtual circuits the increase is about 18 percent (note the logarithmic relationship between the number of real-time virtual circuits and the worst case contention resolution overhead). However, results of a simulation study in (Arvind, Ramamritham and Stankovic 1991) indicate that the performance of the RTVC window protocol (measured in terms of the guarantee ratio, the fraction of the number of packets that arrive that get guaranteed) is close to that of an idealized protocol that can guarantee a bounded channel access time of $N_{rtvc}P$ with zero overhead. This is to be expected since the guarantee ratio is mainly dependent on the worst case channel access time. It is not significantly affected unless the worst case channel access time increases by an amount that is of a magnitude similar to that of packet laxities. But packet laxities have to be greater than the worst case channel access time in order for packets to be accepted for transmission. Therefore, fractional increases in the worst case channel access time do not significantly affect the performance.

8.3. RTCLS/MAC protocol

Implementation of real-time datagram arbitration based on the minimum laxity first policy using the above window splitting paradigm is again a simple matter. The parameter p

associated with each node is made equal to the laxity of the packet with the smallest laxity awaiting transmission at the node. However, since laxity values need not be bounded, a maximum window size is chosen so that the window protocol will have a starting point. Packets whose laxities are greater than the maximum window size do not participate in the contention resolution process. Thus only the most *urgent* packets are considered for transmission at any instant of time. However, since the laxity of a waiting packet continuously decreases with time, the laxity of every packet will eventually fall within the window. We have incorporated these ideas into a new window protocol for real-time datagram arbitration known as the RTDG window protocol. The results of simulation experiments indicate that the performance of the RTDG protocol is close to that of an idealized protocol that implements the minimum laxity first policy for channel arbitration with zero overhead, and is superior to the performance of protocols that have no notion of packet timing constraints.

The RTDG protocol and the RTVC protocol have further been combined to implement two integrated window protocols known as INTPVC and INTPDG, that can be used to support both RTCLS and RTCOS on a common channel. In addition to the usual advantages of integrated protocols, including reduced costs resulting from common interfaces and cabling, and efficient bandwidth utilization, these protocols also display an improvement in the quality of support for RTCLS and/or RTCOS over a range of system parameters. The protocol INTPVC accords greater importance to servicing real-time virtual circuit packets; real-time datagrams are considered for transmission, only if there are no real-time virtual circuits with packets pending for transmission. The protocol INTPDG accords greater importance to real-time datagram services; real-time datagrams are considered for transmission even if there are real-time virtual circuit packets pending for transmission (but in a manner that does not violate the bounded channel access time property of real-time virtual circuits). The reader is referred to (Arvind, Ramamritham and Stankovic 1991) for more details on these protocols.

In this section, we described a suite of window protocols that represents an attempt to support both RTCOS and RTCLS in a uniform manner. In addition to providing the advantage of homogeneity (enabling the use of a uniform medium access control logic and LAN controller hardware to support both RTCOS and RTCLS), these protocols also have performance characteristics that are close to the best available (or ideal) protocols that can be used to provide the same functionality.

9. Conclusions

Most current work in real-time communication deals with static systems in which messages with timing constraints are mainly periodic, or occur only rarely. However, the dynamic closed loop distributed real-time systems of the future will be characterized by richer communication patterns. Specialized network services and protocols will be required to support the communication requirements of these systems. In this paper, we proposed RTLAN, a new local area network architecture for communication in such systems. RTLAN provides new classes of connection-oriented and connectionless services known as RTCOS and RTCLS respectively, that take the timing constraints of messages explicitly into account.

In order to provide these services, RTLAN employs specialized real-time medium access control protocols. We presented several medium access control protocols that can be used at the MAC layer of RTLAN. Finally, we also described a homogeneous set of MAC protocols that may be used to support both RTCOS and RTCLS using a uniform window splitting paradigm.

Notes

1. Even applications with a wider geographic span may be based on local area networks. For example, in air traffic control the entire air space is divided into smaller units (sectors) and the traffic within each unit is controlled by a distributed real-time system based on a local area network (Christian, Dancey and Dehn 1990).
2. In fact, considerable effort is currently being invested to realize such autonomous systems (Bares et al. 1989, Iyengar and Kashyap 1989, Whittaker and Kanade 1990).
3. A finer classification, though not relevant to this paper, would include metropolitan area networks (MAN) that span distances of the order of 50 km and thus fall in between LANs and WANs in terms of geographical extent.
4. A commonly used discipline in the scheduling of real-time tasks is the minimum *laxity first* (MLF) discipline, which is known to be optimal in the following sense—*if some discipline can schedule a set of independent tasks so that all the tasks meet their deadlines, then the minimum laxity first policy can do so.*
5. A similar protocol is specified in the IEEE 802.4 token bus standard for station addition. However, this protocol uses recursive quarternary partitioning, while our protocol uses recursive binary partitioning.

Acknowledgments

We would like to thank Erich Nahum, Douglas Niehaus, David Yates and Goran Zlokapa for their constructive comments and criticisms on an earlier version of this paper.

References

Abramson, N., 1970. The Aloha System—Another Alternative for Computer Communications. *Proceedings of the AFIPS Fall Joint Computer Conference*, 37: 281–285.

Alger, L.S. Lala, J.H. 1986. A Real-Time Operating System for a Nuclear Power Plant Computer. *Proc. Real-Time Systems Symposium*, pp. 244–248.

Arvind, K., Ramamritham, K., Stankovic, J.A. 1991. Window Protocols for Real-Time Communication Services. (Submitted to IEEE Transactions on Communications).

Bares, J., Hebert, M., Kanade, T., Krotkov, E., Mitchell, T., Simmons, R., Whittaker, W. 1989. Ambler, An Autonomous Rover for Planetary Exploration. *Computer*, vol. 22, pp. 18–26.

Bertsekas, D., Gallager, R. 1987. *Data Networks*. Englewood Cliffs, NJ: Prentice-Hall.

Bihari, T.E., Walliser, T.M., Patterson, M.R. 1989. Controlling the Adaptive Suspension Vehicle. *Computer*, vol. 22, pp. 59–65.

Cheng, S., Stankovic, J.A. Ramamritham, K. Scheduling Algorithms for Hard Real-Time Systems—A Brief Survey. 1988. *Tutorial Hard Real-Time Systems*, IEEE Computer Society Press, pp. 150–173.

Chlamtac, I., Franta, W.R., Levin, D., 1979. BRAM: The Broadcast Recognizing Access Method. *IEEE Transactions on Communications*, vol. COM-27: 1183–1190.

Comer, D., Yavatkar, R. FLOWS: Performance Guarantees in Best Effort Delivery Systems. *IEEE INFOCOM '89*, pp. 100–109.

Cristian, F. 1990. Synchronous Atomic Broadcast for Redundant Broadcast Channels. *Real-Time Systems*, vol. 2, pp. 195–212.

Cristian, F., Dancey, R.D., Dehn, J. 1990. Fault-Tolerance in the Advanced Automation System. *IBM Research Report* RJ 7424 (69595).

Franta, W.R., Bilodeau, M.B. 1980. Analysis of a Prioritized CSMA Protocol Based on Staggered Delays. *Acta Informatica*, vol. 13, pp. 299–324.

IEEE Standards for Local Area Networks. Token-Passing Bus Access Method, IEEE, New York, 1982.

IEEE Standards for Local Area Networks: Logical Link Control, IEEE, New York, 1984.

IEEE Standards for Local Area Networks: Carrier Sense Multiple Access with Collision Detection, IEEE, New York, 1985.

IEEE Standards for Local Area Networks. Token Ring Access Method, IEEE, 1986.

Iida, I., Ishizuka, M., Yasuda, Y., and Onoe, M. 1980. Random Access Packet Switched Local Computer Network with Priority Function. *Proceedings National Telecommunications Conference*, pp. 37.4.1–37.4.6.

Iyengar, S.S., Kashyap, R.L. 1989. Autonomous Intelligent Machines. *Computer*, vol. 22, 1989.

Jacobs, I.M., Binder, R., Hoversten, E.V. 1978. General Purpose Packet Satellite Networks. *Proceedings of the IEEE*, pp. 1448–1468.

Kallmes, M.H., Towsley, D., Cassandras, C.G. 1989. Optimality of the Last-In-First-Out (LIFO) Service Discipline in Queueing Systems with Real-Time Constraints. *Proceedings of the 28th Conference on Decision and Control (CDC)*, Tampa, Florida, pp. 1073–1074.

Kleinrock, L., Scholl, M.O. 1980. Packet Switching in Radio Channels: New Conflict-Free Multiple Access Schemes. *IEEE Transactions on Communications*, COM-28, 7, pp. 1015–1029.

Kleinrock, L., Tobagi, F. 1975. Packet Switching in Radio Channels: Part I-Carrier Sense Multiple Access Modes and their Throughput-Delay Characteristics, *IEEE Transactions on Communications*, COM-23, 12, pp. 1015–1029.

Knightson, K.G., Knowles, T., Larmouth, J. 1988. *Standards for Open Systems Interconnection*, New York: McGraw-Hill.

Kopetz, H. 1983. Real-Time in Distributed Real-Time Systems. *Proc. IFAC Distributed Computer Control Systems*, pp. 11–15.

Kurose, J.F., Schwartz, M., Yemini, Y. 1984. Multiple-Access Protocols and Time-Constrained Communication. *Computing Surveys* 16(1):43–70.

Kurose, J.F., Schwartz, M., Yemini, Y. 1983. Controlling Window Protocols for Time-Constrained Communication in a Multiple Access Environment. *Proc. Eighth IEEE International Data Communications Symposium*, pp. 75–84.

Lark, J.S., Erman, L.D., Forrest, S. Gostelow, K.P., Hayes-Roth, F., Smith, D.M. 1990. Concepts, Methods, and Languages for Building Timely Intelligent Systems. *The Journal of Real-Time Systems*, vol. 2, pp. 127–148.

LeBlanc, T.J., Markatos, E.P. 1990. Operating System Support for Adaptable Real-Time Systems. *Proc. Seventh IEEE Workshop on Real-Time Operating Systems and Software*, pp. 1–10.

Lehoczky, J.P., Sha, L. 1986. Performance of Real-Time Bus Scheduling Algorithms. *ACM Performance Evaluation Review*, Special Issue 14(1).

Le Lann, G. 1987. The 802.3D Protocol: A Variation on the IEEE 802.3 Standard for Real-Time LANs, *INRIA-BP 105, F-78153 Le Chesnay Cedex, France*.

Le Lann, G. 1983. Real-Time Protocols, *Local Area Networks, An Advanced Course* (Hutchison, D., et al., eds.), Springer-Verlag, 1983.

Liu, C.L., Layland, J.W. 1973. Scheduling Algorithms for Multiprogramming in a Hard Real-Time Environment. *Journal of the Association for Computing Machinery*, vol. 20, pp. 46–61.

Martin, J. 1967. *Design of Real-Time Computer Systems*, Englewood Cliffs, NJ: Prentice-Hall.

Metcalfe, R.M. Boggs, D.R. 1976. Ethernet: Distributed Packet Switching for Local Computer Networks. *Communications of the ACM*, vol. 19, pp. 395–404.

Molle, M.L., Kleinrock, L. 1985. Virtual Time CSMA: Why Two Clocks are Better than One. *IEEE Transactions on Communications*, vol. COM-33: 919–933.

Muratore, J.F., Heindel, T.A., Murphy, T.B., Rasmussen, A.N., McFraland, R.Z. 1990. Real-Time Data Acquisition at Mission Control. *Communications of the ACM*, vol. 33, pp. 18–31.

Nielsen, K. 1990. *Ada in Distributed Real-Time Systems*. New York: McGraw-Hill.

Panwar, S.S., Towsley, D., Wolf, J.K. 1988. Optimal Scheduling Policies for a Class of Queues with Customer Deadlines to the Beginning of Service. *Journal of the Association for Computing Machinery*, vol. 35: 832–844.

Ramamritham, K. 1987. Channel Characteristics in Local-Area Hard Real-Time Systems. *Computer Networks and ISDN Systems*, vol. 13, pp. 3–13.

Ramamritham, K., Stankovic, J.A., Zhao, W. 1989. Distributed Scheduling of Tasks with Deadlines and Resource Requirements. *IEEE Transactions on Computers*, vol. 38, pp. 1110–1123.

Ramamritham, K. Stankovic, J.A. 1989. Time-Constrained Communication Protocols for Hard Real-Time Systems. *Sixth IEEE Workshop on Real-Time Operating Systems and Software*. Pittsburgh, PA.

Rothauser, E.H., Wild, D. 1977. MLMA-A Collision-Free Multi-Access Method. *Proceedings IFIP Congress 77*, pp. 431–436.

Rouse, W.B., Geddes, N.D., Hammer, J.M. 1990. Computer-Aided Fighter Pilots. *IEEE Spectrum*, vol. 27, pp. 38–41.

Stankovic, J.A. 1988. Misconceptions about Real-Time Computing: A Serious Problem for Next-Generation Systems. *Computer*, pp. 10–19.

Stankovic, J.A., Ramamritham, K. 1990. What is Predictability for Real-Time Systems?, vol. 2: 247–254.

Stankovic, J.A., Ramamritham, K. 1988. *Tutorial Hard Real-Time Systems*. IEEE Computer Society Press.

Strosnider, J.K. 1988. Highly Responsive Real-Time Token Rings. Ph.D. Thesis, Carnegie-Mellon University, Pittsburgh, PA.

Strosnider, J.K., Marchok, T. 1988. Responsive, Deterministic IEEE 802.5 Token Ring Scheduling. *The Journal of Real-Time Systems*. vol. 1, pp. 133–158.

Tanenbaum, A.S. 1989. *Computer Networks*, Englewood Cliffs, NJ: Prentice-Hall.

Tobagi, F.A. 1982. Carrier Sense Multiple Access with Message-Based Priority Functions. *IEEE Transactions on Communications*, vol. COM-30, pp. 185–200.

Valadier, J.C., Powell, D.R. 1984. On CSMA Protocols Allowing Bounded Channel Access Times. *Fourth International Conference on Distributed Computing Systems*, San Francisco.

Weisbin, C.R., de Saussure, G., Einsten, J.R., Pin, F.G. Heer, E. 1989. Autonomous Mobile Robot Navigation and Learning. *Computer*, vol. 22, pp. 29–35.

Whittaker, W.L., Kanade, T. 1990. Japan Robotics Aim for Unmanned Space Exploration. *IEEE Spectrum*, vol. 27, pp. 64–67.

Zhao, W., Ramamritham, K. 1987. Virtual Time CSMA Protocols for Hard Real-Time Communication, *IEEE Transactions on Software Engineering*, vol. SE-13.

Zhao, W., Stankovic, J.A., Ramamritham, K. 1990. A Window Protocol for Transmission of Time Constrained Messages. *IEEE Transactions on Computers*.

A Window Protocol for Transmission of Time-Constrained Messages

WEI ZHAO, MEMBER, IEEE, JOHN A. STANKOVIC, SENIOR MEMBER, IEEE, AND KRITHI RAMAMRITHAM, MEMBER, IEEE

Abstract—In this paper, we propose and study a new window protocol suitable for transmitting time-constrained messages in a multiaccess network. Our protocol differs from traditional window protocols in that it explicitly takes time constraints into account. In our protocol, the window is formed based on the *latest time to send a message* (LS). A major advantage of our window protocol is that a newly arriving message is immediately considered for transmission if its LS is less than that of all pending messages in the system. As a result, our new protocol closely approximates the optimal *minimum-laxity-first* policy. A performance evaluation through simulation shows that the new window protocol performs well in a wide range of environments, even under overloaded conditions.

Index Terms—Minimum-laxity-first scheduling, multiaccess networks, time-constrained communication, window protocols.

I. Introduction

IN this paper, we propose and analyze a communication protocol for distributed real-time systems [28], [29]. A *real-time system* is one in which the correctness of the system depends not only on the logical results, but also upon the time at which those results appear. Messages transmitted in such systems are referred to as *time constrained,* meaning that a message must be received by a deadline or it is lost. The protocol which we propose in this paper specifically takes messages' time constraints into account, and hence is suitable for the control of communication in distributed real-time systems.

The most common communication network used in distributed real-time systems is the multiple access network. In this type of network, stations transmit messages via a shared channel. Only one message can be successfully transmitted over the channel at any time. A *collision* occurs if, at any time, two or more messages are transmitted on the channel. No message can be received correctly in the event of a collision.

Based on how the collisions are handled, multiple access communication protocols can be broadly divided into three categories [20], [21]:

1) *Inference avoiding* protocols: These protocols operate without taking past history of the channel into account. This category includes ALOHA [1] and various CSMA and CSMS/CD protocols [10].

2) *Inference seeking* protocols: These protocols make inference on the collision history, and usually solve collisions by partitioning some parameter space of the messages. Various tree, window, stack, and urn protocols [2], [4], [5], [7], [8], [11], [13], [31]–[33] belong to this category.

3) *Deterministic* or *Collision-free* protocols: These protocols work in such a way that collisions do not occur at all. The time division multiple-access protocols (TDMA), the bit-map protocol [12], the broadcast recognition with alternative priorities protocol [26], [3], [6], and the multilevel multiaccess protocol [25] are examples of protocols in this category.

The majority of communication protocols found in these three above categories do not directly address timing constraints. Each of the categories serves different application areas, and hence are valuable in different parts of the requirement space. Recently, protocols for real-time communication belonging to the first category have been developed and reported in [34]. In this paper, we show that our new window protocol, which incidently belongs to the second category, is better than the real-time communication protocols of the first category.

Let us now briefly consider the state of the art in time-constrained message communication. We begin with an analogy. The design objectives of multiple access protocols and uniprocessor scheduling algorithms are quite similar. Both are used for allocation of a serially-used resource to a set of processes [14]. It is known from the theory of real-time scheduling that, in the static case, i.e., when all the task characteristics are known *a priori,* minimum-deadline-first and the minimum-laxity-first scheduling policies are optimal in the sense that they can schedule a set of tasks if there is some policy which can do so [17]. In the dynamic case, these policies also usually offer better performance than others [9]. Due to this fact, in our window protocol we will adopt a network-wide transmission policy in which the message with the minimum laxity is transmitted first.

Kurose *et al.* suggest a window protocol for real-time communication [13], [14], implementing the minimum-laxity-first policy. However, they assume that the laxities of all the messages are constant. This is a restrictive assumption. Under this assumption, the minimum-laxity-first policy is identical to the first-come-first-served policy. Panwar *et al.* [22], [23] have also studied the problem of optimal transmission policy for real-time communication. In their work, it is assumed that

Manuscript received December 1, 1987; revised January 6, 1989. This work is part of the Spring Project at the University of Massachusetts funded in part by the Office of Naval Research under Contract N00014-85-K-0389 and by the National Science Foundation under Grant DCR-8500332.

W. Zhao is with the Department of Computer Science, University of Adelaide, South Australia, Australia.

J. A. Stankovic and K. Ramamritham are with the Department of Computer and Information Science, University of Massachusetts, Amherst, MA 01003.

IEEE Log Number 9037195.

Reprinted from *IEEE Transactions on Computers*, Vol. 39, No. 9, September 1990, pp. 1186-1203. Copyright © 1990 by The Institute of Electrical and Electronic Engineers, Inc. All rights reserved.

0-8186-3792-7/93 $03.00 © 1990 IEEE

the length of the ith message being transmitted on the channel is *independent of what the ith message is*. In other words, the lengths of messages vary with the order in which they are transmitted. They prove that if the channel is not allowed to remain idle when there is a message waiting to be sent, the minimum-laxity-first policy is the best. Their assumptions are restrictive. In our protocol, all of above assumptions are removed. We allow messages to have arbitrary laxities, and allow message lengths to be determined at the instant they arrive, and hence to be invariant with the order in which they are transmitted.

The literature sometimes associates message priority with real-time communication [37]. That is, deadline information is mapped onto a priority. Using priorities is limited because of the fixed number of priority levels available, and because it can be quite difficult to dynamically assign priorities to accurately reflect deadlines of currently active messages.

Our protocol is a window based protocol. We have developed several extensions to the traditional window based protocols including basing the window on a message's latest time to send (LS), and managing the window such that a newly arriving message is immediately considered for transmission if its LS is less than that of *all* pending messages in the system. As a result, our protocol closely approximates the optimal minimum-laxity-first policy (a real-time scheduling policy). The protocol is also not constrained by arbitrary limits on the number of priority levels, nor is it necessary to perform any dynamic analysis of the relative deadlines (or equivalently laxities or latest time to send) of active messages. Our performance evaluation through simulation shows that the time-constrained window protocol performs well in a wide range of environments.

The remainder of this paper is organized as follows. Section II defines the system model. Section III describes the new time-constrained window protocol when no two messages have the same laxity. It is shown that under these circumstances, the protocol accurately implements the minimum-laxity-first transmission policy. Section IV extends the protocol to the case where two or more messages may have the same laxity. Section V presents the results of simulation studies comparing the performance of our protocol to that of two baseline protocols—one ideal protocol, and another known as the VTCSMA/CD protocol [34]. The results show that the new window protocol performs very close to the ideal protocol and it performs better than the virtual time CSMA/CD protocol most of the time. Section VI summarizes the conclusions of the paper.

II. MODEL

In a multiple access network, a set of nodes is connected to one communication channel. At any given time, only one message can be successfully transmitted over the channel. The maximum end-to-end delay for a bit is τ. We assume that the time axis is *slotted*. The length of a slot is defined to be one time unit. Given that the maximum end-to-end delay is τ, we let the length of a slot be equal to τ. A node can start transmitting a message only at the beginning of a slot. The length of a message is a multiple of the length of a slot. *The*

normalized end-to-end delay α is defined as

$$\alpha = \tau / \text{Mean of Message Length}.$$

Each message M is characterized as follows:

- Identification number of the message I_M is a positive integer. At a given instant of time, each message waiting at a node should have a unique identification number.
- Length L_M, which is the total number of time units needed to transmit message M;
- Deadline D_M is the time by which message M must be received by its destination;
- Latest time to Send the message M, LS_M, is equal to $D_M - L_M$;
- Laxity at time t for message M, $\text{LA}_M(t)$, is the maximum amount of time the transmission of message M can be delayed given current time t. Therefore,

$$\text{LA}_M(t) = D_M - L_M - t = \text{LS}_M - t.$$

When it is clear from the context, we may omit argument t as well as subscript M in the above expressions. Note that each node maintains a queue of its messages in the order of increasing LS.

From these definitions, it is clear that if we transmit messages in order of their latest time to send, it is equivalent to the maximum-laxity-first transmission policy.

III. THE TIME-CONSTRAINED WINDOW PROTOCOL

A. Problems with Traditional Window Protocols

In traditional window protocols [2], [4], [5], [7], [13], [31], which were not designed for time-constrained communication, each node maintains a data structure called a *window*. The window simply is a pair of numbers, denoted by $[a, b]$, defining an interval on the axis of some message parameter. Different window protocols use different message parameters, such as message arrival time, node id, etc. Each node continually monitors the channel state, maintaining a current window. If a node senses that the channel is idle and it has a message in the current window, i.e., the message parameter is greater than or equal to a and less than b, it transmits the message. There are three possible outcomes for the transmission. 1) This transmission is successful if only one node transmits. In this case, the node transmitting the message continues the transmission until completion. 2) A collision results if more than one node transmits its message. In this case, all nodes sending the messages abort transmission. Then the window is *partitioned* or *split* into two or more smaller windows and the protocol deals with each of these smaller windows separately and recursively. 3) It is also possible that no message is in the current window; hence, no message is transmitted. At this point, every node notices that the channel is idle. In this case, if the wndow resulted from a previous split, the protocol uses the other window. Otherwise, a new larger window is examined. We also note that after there is a collision, most of the traditional window protocols have a policy that a newly arriving message is not allowed to join the competition. That is, a newly arriving message must wait until all the old messages in the (split) windows have been transmitted. With this policy, the number of collisions and the variation in response time may be reduced, and hence it is reasonable when the communication is not time constrained. However, as we will show, this policy is not adequate for time-constrained communication.

Let us now consider using the window approach to implement the minimum-laxity-first transmission policy for time-constrained communication. One may think that it is very simple: set the window along the axis of messages' LS and use the above approach to manage the window. Will this trivial method work? Let us consider the following scenario.

Example 1: Assume that at time $t = 0$, there are two messages $M1$ and $M2$ on different nodes in the system. $LS_{M1} = 4$ and $LS_{M2} = 16$. The length of $M1$ is one time unit and $M2$ is two time units. Also assume that the initial window size is 20, and hence the initial window is $[0, 20)$.

Because both messages are in the window, they are sent out at the same time, causing a collision. Assume that the collision is detected at time $t = 1$; the nodes abort the transmission. At $t = 2$, the channel is idle again. Now, with the traditional window technique, the window should be *split* into two small windows $[2, 11)$ and $[11, 20)$, and then be processed separately. Assume that the protocol deals with the window $[2, 11)$ first. Because only $M1$ is in this window, its transmission is now successful.

The transmission of $M1$ completes at $t = 3$ and the channel is idle at $t = 4$. Assume that while transmitting message $M1$, a new message, $M3$, arrives which has an LS of 4 and length 1. According to the traditional window protocol, this message would not take part in the protocol at this time. Hence, the window $[11, 20)$ is used next, and $M2$ is transmitted.

The transmission of $M2$ finishes at $t = 6$ and the channel becomes idle at $t = 7$. At this time, the current time t is larger than $M3$'s LS, and hence $M3$ is lost.

The loss of $M3$ occurs because the traditional window approach cannot *accurately* implement the minimum-laxity-first policy if the window is set along the axis of the messages' LS. With the minimum-laxity-first policy, $M3$ should be transmitted before $M2$. In the design of our new protocol, this problem is solved. We do this by letting the lower bound of the window equal the current real time t. After a collision, we *modify* the window size rather than *split* the window. The method we use to modify the window implements the minimum-laxity-first policy by allowing a newly arriving message to take part in the protocol immediately after an ongoing message transmission completes, if the new message has its LS in the current window. In this way, the newly arriving messages with small laxities can always be considered early, rather than waiting until all the old messages in the window have been transmitted. This is a major advantage of our protocol.

B. The Time-Constrained Window Protocol Without Laxity Ties

We now present our new protocol in detail. In our protocol, the window has the form $[t, up)$ where t is the current real time, and up is the upper bound of the current window. We say that a *message M is in a window* $[t, up)$ if

$t \leq LS_M < up$. Messages are queued at each node according to their LS, which is the deadline of the message minus the length of the message. On each node, in addition to the message queue, there is a stack that saves the information needed to resolve contentions, making recursive execution of the protocol possible. Each item of the stack is an integer number u which is the upper bound of a (previous) window. Throughout this section, we assume that at any time t, different messages in the system have different laxities. That is, there is no tie among them. The extension to the case where two or more messages may have the same laxity is discussed in Section IV.

The pseudocode of our window protocol is presented in Fig. 1. At the time of initialization, the upper bound of the window is set to be $t + \delta$ where t is the current time, and δ is the protocol parameter for the initial window size. Any node having a message in the window attempts to transmit the message.

At the beginning of each time unit, every node first drops any message from the message queue if its LS is less than the current time t. In addition, the stack on each node is *cleared*—any item in the stack whose value is less than or equal to the current time t is discarded. Then, each node calls a subroutine *get_state* to obtain the information on the state of the channel. We define five channel states:

1) channel_collision: Two or more messages are being transmitted over the channel.

2) channel_idle_after_a_collision: The channel is idle now, and there was a collision over the channel one time unit ago.

3) channel_busy: One message is being transmitted over the channel.

4) channel_idle_after_a_successful_transmission: The channel is idle now, and a message transmission occurred one time unit ago.

5) channel_continuing_idle: The channel is idle now, and was also idle one time unit ago.

Depending on the channel state, each node takes the following actions.

1) channel_collision: The nodes which are transmitting messages immediately abort transmission. Then, in the next time unit, each node should observe that the channel is in the state of *channel_idle_after_a_collision*.

2) channel_idle_after_a_collision: Procedure Contract_Window_and_Send is called. See Fig. 2 for the pseudocode. Each node realizes that two or more messages are in the current window so that the window size should be reduced to resolve the collision. Hence, the upper bound of the window, up, is reduced to $t + \lceil (up - t)/2 \rceil$, i.e., the middle point of the old window. Then, a node sends out the collided message again if its LS is in the reduced window.

It is possible for the old value of up to be equal to or less than the current time t.[1] In this case, Procedure Pop_and_Send is called. For the pseudocode, see Fig. 3. In this procedure, if the stack is not empty, the upper bound of the window, up, is set to be the value of up which is on the top of the stack. If the stack is empty, a new window with enlarged size δ, where δ

---

[1] This happens if the size of the old window is 2.

```
Initialization:

    up := t + δ
    empty(stack); (* make the stack empty *)
    send out the first message if its LS is between [t, up);

At the beginning of each time unit:

    drop any message M if D_M - L_M < t;
    clean(stack); (* pop out and discard any item u if u < t
    *)
    get_state(state);
    CASE state OF
    channel_busy_due_to_a_collision:

        Abort the message transmission if any;

    channel_idle_after_a_collision:

        Contract_Window_and_Send(up, t);

    channel_busy_due_to_a_message_transmission:

        Continue the transmission if any;

    channel_idle_after_a_successful_transmission:

        Pop_and_Send(up, t);

    channel_continuing_idle:

        Expand_Window_and_Send(up, t);

    END (* CASE *)
```

Fig. 1.   The time-constrained window protocol.

```
Procedure Contract_Window_and_Send(up, t);
BEGIN
        IF up > t
        THEN
        BEGIN
          push(stack, up);
          up = t + ⌈ (up - t)/2 ⌉; (* reduce up *)
          send out the message if its LS is in [t, up)
        END
        ELSE (* up ≤ t *)
          Pop_and_Send(up, t); (* See Figure 3 *)
END;
```

Fig. 2.   Procedure Contract_Window_and_Send.

```
Procedure Pop_and_Send(up, t);
BEGIN
    IF not empty(stack)
    THEN
        up = pop(stack)
    ELSE
        up = max(up, t) + δ;
    send out the first message in the queue if its LS is in
    [t, up);
END;
```

Fig. 3.   Procedure Pop_and_Send.

is the parameter for the initial window size, is used. In either
case, a message can be sent if its LS is in the new window.

3) *channel_busy:* The node transmitting the message
continues the transmission. The other nodes wait until the transmission completes. After the transmission
completes, each node notices that the channel state is
channel_idle_after_a_successful_transmission.

4) *channel_idle_after_a_successful_transmission:* Procedure Pop_and_Send is called (see Fig. 3). At this point, the
message in the current window has been processed.[2] That is,

---

[2] This would not be true if a newly arrived message has its LS in the current
window. However, because the lower bound of the window is always set to
the current time, the new message has a chance to be considered.

```
Procedure Expand_Window_and_Send(up, t);

BEGIN
    IF empty(stack)
    THEN
    BEGIN
        up = t + δ;
    END
    ELSE
        IF up < top(stack) - 1
        THEN
        BEGIN
            up = ⌈ (up + top(stack))/2 ⌉;
        END
        ELSE    (* the old up = top(stack) - 1 *)
        BEGIN
            up = pop(stack);
        END
        send out the first message if its LS is in [t, up)
END;
```

Fig. 4.   Procedure Expand_Window_and_Send.

if the current window resulted from a previous collision, then the protocol extends the window to its original upper bound before the collision. Otherwise, a new window is created with the additional size δ.

5) *channel_continuing_idle:* Procedure Expand_Window_and_Send is called. The pseudocode for the procedure is in Fig. 4. When the channel is in this state, there is no message in the current window. If the stack is empty, each node simply expands the window to increase its size by δ. However, by keeping additional information, we can improve the performance of the protocol. That is, a nontrivial inference can be made if the previous window information is retained. Specifically, if we know that the current window was created from a previous window because a collision occurred, and there is no message in the current window (otherwise the channel cannot be continuously idle), then there should be at least two messages in the interval [up, top(stack)) where top(stack) indicates the upper bound of the previous window. Thus, if the window is expanded to top(stack), we are guaranteed to have a collision. Knowing this, the new value ot up is set to the middle point of the current up and top(stack), i.e., $\lceil(\text{up}+\text{top(stack)})/2\rceil$, rather than expanding it to the old window's upper bound which is on the top of the stack.

Note that because of the roundup effect, if the old value of up is equal to top(stack)-1, the new value of up will be the same as top(stack). In this case, the top of stack is popped out and that value is used as the new value of up.

Once the new window is determined, if a node has a message with LS in the new window, the node transmits the message.

The next example helps us better understand the general behavior of the time-constrained protocol just presented.

Example 2: Let us take the same scenario as in Example 1. Messages $M1$ and $M2$ are in the system at $t = 0$. $M1$ has its LS equal to 4 and length 1, and $M2$ has its LS equal to 16 and length 2. We also assume that the initial window size has been chosen to be 20, i.e., $\delta = 20$. At $t = 0$, $M1$ and $M2$

both are transmitted over the channel, causing a collision. See Fig. 5(a).

At $t = 1$, the collision is detected. The transmissions of $M1$ and $M2$ abort. At $t = 2$, the channel is idle after the collision. Now, the window size is reduced. The new window is [2, 11). The old value of up is pushed onto the stack at each node. Top(stack) = 20. Because $M1$ is in the new window, it is transmitted. See Fig. 5(b).

At $t = 3$, $M3$ arrives in the system. Transmission of $M1$ completes. At $t = 4$, the channel is idle. The protocol now goes back to the previous window [4, 20). The stack is empty. Because both $M3$ and $M2$ are in the window, they start to be transmitted, causing a collision. See Fig. 5(c).

At $t = 5$, the collision is detected. The transmissions of $M3$ and $M2$ abort. At $t = 6$, the channel becomes idle. The window size is reduced. The new window is [6, 13). $M3$ is transmitted. See Fig. 5(d). Only after the transmission of $M3$, will $M2$ be transmitted.

C. Property of the Time-Constrained Protocol Without Laxity Ties

We now show that with the protocol discussed above, the minimum-laxity-first policy is preserved.

Lemma 1: At any time t, with the time-constrained window protocol without laxity ties, for any two messages M and M', $\text{LA}_M(t) < \text{LA}_{M'}(t)$ if and only if $\text{LS}_M < \text{LS}_{M'}$.

Proof: This lemma follows from the definitions of LA(t) and LS.

We say that *a message M is in the system at time t* if at time t, M has arrived at the system, and M has neither started its successful transmission, nor has it been lost, i.e., M's arrival time $\leq t \leq \text{LS}_M = D_M - L_M$ where D_M is the message deadline, and L_M is the length.

Lemma 2: With the time-constrained window protocol without laxity ties, at any time t, if a message M starts a successful transmission, LS_M is the minimum among all the LS values of messages which are in the system at time t.

```
t = 0: The channel is idle. The initial window = [0, 20).
       Both M1 and M2 both are transmitted, causing a collision.
```

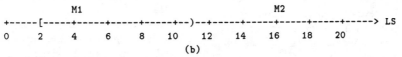

```
          M1                          M2
[-----+-----+-----+-----+-----+-----+-----+-----+-----+-----+-----)----> LS
0     2     4     6     8     10    12    14    16    18    20
                              (a)
```

```
t = 2: The channel is idle after the collision. The window is reduced. The
       new window = [2, 11). top(stack) = 20. M1 is to be transmitted.
```

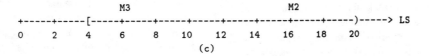

```
          M1                          M2
+-----[-----+-----+-----+-----+--)--+-----+-----+-----+-----+-----> LS
0     2     4     6     8     10    12    14    16    18    20
                         (b)
```

```
t = 3: M3 arrives. Transmission of M1 completes.
t = 4: The channel is idle. Protocol goes back to the previous window
       [4, 20). Both M3 and M2 are to be transmitted, causing a collision.
```

```
                M3                          M2
+-----+-----[-----+-----+-----+-----+-----+-----+-----+-----)----> LS
0     2     4     6     8     10    12    14    16    18    20
                              (c)
```

```
t = 5: The collision is detected. The transmissions of M3 and M2 abort.
t = 6: The channel becomes idle. The window size is reduced.
       The new window = [6, 13). M3 is to be transmitted.
```

```
                      M3                          M2
+-----+-----+-----[-----+-----+-----+--)--+-----+-----+-----+-----> LS
0     2     4     6     8     10    12    14    16    18    20
                              (d)
```

```
After the transmission of M3, M2 will have a chance to be transmitted.
```

Fig. 5. Example 2—Using the new window protocol.

Proof: Assume at time t, message M starts a successful transmission in a window $[t, \text{up})$. From the protocol, $t \leq \text{LS}_M < \text{up}$. If M does not have the minimum LS among all the messages in the system at t, then, there must be another message M' with $t \leq \text{LS}_{M'} < \text{LS}_M$. Hence, $t \leq \text{LS}_{M'} < \text{LS}_M < \text{up}$. This means that both M and M' are in the window $[t, \text{up})$. Consequently, the transmission of M cannot be successful. This is a contradiction. ∎

Theorem 1: The window protocol described in this section preserves the minimum-laxity-first policy. That is, with this protocol, at any time t, if a message M starts its successful transmission, M has the minimum laxity among all the messages which are in the system at time t.

Proof: According to Lemma 2, any message successfully transmitted by the protocol has the minimum LS in the system at the time when the transmission starts. Then, following Lemma 1, this message must also have the minimum laxity at the time when its transmission starts. ∎

In summary, our new window protocol differs from the traditional ones not only in the semantics given to the time axis of the window, but also in the way we manage the window. As a result, in the case where there is no tie on message laxity, the optimal minimum-laxity-first transmission policy is accurately implemented with our protocol.

IV. THE TIME-CONSTRAINED WINDOW PROTOCOL WITH MESSAGE LAXITY TIES

In Section III, we presented a version of our new window protocol for the case when there is no tie on message laxity. In reality, it is possible that multiple messages (on different nodes) have the same laxity, and hence have the same LS value. Hence, such messages will always cause a collision when they are in a window whose axis is based on messages' LS. Splitting the window, as in a traditional window protocol, or reducing the window size, as we do in our new protocol, cannot break the tie. A practical window protocol must be able to recognize message ties and resolve them. In this section, we extend the time-constrained protocol to handle message laxity ties.

The idea to handle message laxity ties is as follows. At first, all the nodes should be able to recognize the tie at some point in time. Once a tie is recognized, every node involved in the tie randomly modifies its message's LS value between the earliest next channel available time, $t + 2$, and $D_M - L_M$, to try and resolve the tie. In other words, the messages have their LS value reduced in time in a random fashion in order to resolve the tie. Later we discuss the impact of this policy on accurately emulating the minimum-laxity-first algorithm.

TABLE I
PROCEDURES AND FUNCTIONS FOR STACK USED IN THE EXTENDED PROTOCOL

Name	Operation
Reset(stack)	Make the stack empty.
Clean(stack)	Pop out and discard any item (u, i) if u < t.
Empty(stack)	Return true if the stack is empty.
Top_u(stack)	Return the u value of the top item in the stack if any.
Top_i(stack)	Return the i value of the top item in the stack if any.
Push(stack, (u, i))	Push (u, i) onto the stack.
Pop_u(stack)	Pop the top item of the stack and return the value of u.
Pop_i(stack)	Pop the top item of the stack and return the value of i.

Clearly, the messages that have collided in a window are the messages with possible laxity ties. The stack used to maintain the window history now needs to keep information of not only the upper bounds of the windows in which collision occurred, but also the identification numbers of messages which caused the collision. In this way, once a tie is recognized by all the nodes, a node is able to know which of its messages is involved in the tie if any.[3] That is, a stack item now is a tuple (u, i) where u is the upper bound of a window which had a collision and i is the identification number of the message which caused the collision. Note that on different nodes, the values of i represent different messages. In the case that a node has no message involved in a collision, the value of i is zero. The functions and procedures used for the operations on the stack are listed in Table I.

A. Recognition and Resolution of Message Laxity Ties

In a traditional window protocol, a tie is recognized when the window size is reduced to one and there is still a collision. As we will see, in our protocol, due to the style of window management, a tie can be recognized both during window contraction and during window expansion.

1) Recognition and Resolution of Message Laxity Ties During Window Expansion: In our protocol, a tie can be recognized when a window expands to its upper limit. To help understand this, let us consider the following example.

Example 3: At $t = 0$, there are two messages, $M1$ and $M2$, (on different nodes) in the system. Each message has a unit length. $M1$ and $M2$ have LS of 10 (a tie!). Assume that the initial window size is 20, so the initial window is [0, 20]. $M1$ and $M2$ both start transmitting, causing a collision. See Fig. 6(a).

At $t = 1$, the collision is detected. Transmission of $M1$ and $M2$ aborts. At $t = 2$, the channel is *idle_after_the_collision*. Each node pushes the old value of up onto stack. Top_u(stack) = 20. The window is reduced. The new window is [2, 11]. Because both $M1$ and $M2$ are in the window, they start transmitting, again causing a collision. See Fig. 6(b).

At $t = 3$, the collision is detected. The transmission of $M1$ and $M2$ aborts. At $t = 4$, the channel becomes *idle_after_the_collision*. The old value of up is pushed onto the stacks at each of the nodes. The window is reduced to [4, 8]. Top_u(stack) = 11. No message is in the current window. See Fig. 6(c).

[3] The details of how this can be done will be explained in the later part of this section. Here, we concentrate on the changes to the stack.

At $t = 5$, all the nodes notice that the channel is *continuing_idle*. The window expands. The new window is [5, 10]. Top_u(stack) still is 11. Again, no message is in the current window.

At $t = 6$, the channel is *continuing_idle*. If we were using the version of the protocol for the case of no laxity tie, described in the last section, the window would be expanded to [6, 11]. Because both messages are in the window, they are sent, causing the collision. Then the window would be reduced and expanded as above, until time 10 passes after which both messages, $M1$ and $M2$, are lost.

From this example, we see that when the channel is in the state of *continuing_idle* and the current window $[t, up)$ is to be expanded to its upper limit, i.e., the old value of up = top_u(stack) -1, two or more messages may have the same laxity which is equal to top_u(stack)-1. The reason is that two or more messages were in an old window with upper bound of top_u(stack), causing a collision and forcing the upper bound of the old window to be pushed onto the stack. Now that no message is in the window $[t,$ up) $= [t,$ top_u(stack) $-1)$, we conclude that the two or more collided messages may have their LS equal to top_u(stack) -1. Contraction or expansion of the window cannot resolve this kind of tie. We propose the following extension to Procedure Expand_Window_and_Send to resolve this kind of tie.

The pseudocode of the extended procedure *Expand_Window_and_Send* is shown in Fig. 7. In the extended Procedure Expand_Window_and_Send, if the value of up is equal to top_u(stack) -1, the expansion of the window stops. A probabilistic scheme is invoked. The messages, which collided in the window with the upper bound of top_u(stack), have their ids equal to top_i(stack) (on different nodes). If such a message exists in a node, the node draws a random real number in the interval of $(0, 1)$. In the case that the random number drawn is larger than P, a protocol parameter, the message is sent. Otherwise, the message's LS is modified for a future consideration of transmission. This is done by assigning LS a random value between the earliest next channel available time, $t + 2$, and $D_M - L_M$, which is the latest time this message could be sent. It is clear that in this version of the protocol, message parameter—LS—is used for the purpose of controlling the transmission. It is initialized to $D_M - L_M$.

With the above extension, let us consider the situation in Example 3 again.

Example 3 (continued): See Fig. 8. Assume the same scenario as described in the original Example 3 until $t = 6$.

At $t = 6$, the channel is in the state of *continuing_idle*. The old value of up is 10 and top_u(stack) = 11. Because top_u(stack) $-1 = 10 =$ up, the probabilistic scheme is invoked. The nodes which have $M1$ and $M2$ draw the random number independently. Assume that based on the random numbers drawn, the node with $M1$ decides to transmit again and the node with $M2$ decides to modify $M2$'s LS to 9. $M1$ is successfully transmitted over the channel. The top of stack is popped as the new value of up. Note that although $M2$ is still in the window, the protocol explicitly prohibits the transmission of $M2$ at this time. See Fig. 8(d).

At $t = 7$, the transmission of $M1$ completes. And at $t = 8$,

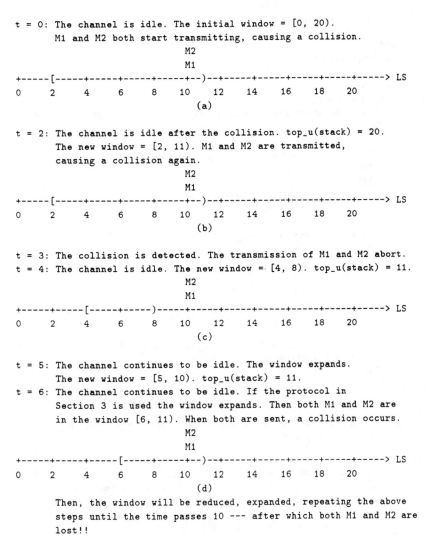

```
t = 0: The channel is idle. The initial window = [0, 20).
       M1 and M2 both start transmitting, causing a collision.
                              M2
                              M1
+-----[-----+-----+-----+-----+--)--+-----+-----+-----+-----+-----> LS
0     2     4     6     8     10    12    14    16    18    20
                              (a)


t = 2: The channel is idle after the collision. top_u(stack) = 20.
       The new window = [2, 11). M1 and M2 are transmitted,
       causing a collision again.
                              M2
                              M1
+-----[-----+-----+-----+--)--+-----+-----+-----+-----+-----> LS
0     2     4     6     8     10    12    14    16    18    20
                        (b)


t = 3: The collision is detected. The transmission of M1 and M2 abort.
t = 4: The channel is idle. The new window = [4, 8). top_u(stack) = 11.
                        M2
                        M1
+-----+-----[-----+-----)-----+-----+-----+-----+-----+-----> LS
0     2     4     6     8     10    12    14    16    18    20
                  (c)


t = 5: The channel continues to be idle. The window expands.
       The new window = [5, 10). top_u(stack) = 11.
t = 6: The channel continues to be idle. If the protocol in
       Section 3 is used the window expands. Then both M1 and M2 are
       in the window [6, 11). When both are sent, a collision occurs.
                              M2
                              M1
+-----+-----+-----[-----+-----+--)--+-----+-----+-----+-----> LS
0     2     4     6     8     10    12    14    16    18    20
                        (d)
```

Then, the window will be reduced, expanded, repeating the above
steps until the time passes 10 --- after which both M1 and M2 are
lost!!

Fig. 6. Example 3—A message laxity tie.

the channel state is *channel_idle_after_a_transmission*. The top of the stack is popped as the new value of up. Hence, the new window is [8, 20). Now, *M2* can be transmitted. See Fig. 8(e).

Note that if at $t = 6$, it is decided that both *M1* and *M2* are to be retransmitted, then a collision would occur. Then, the protocol would recognize the situation and use the same random scheme to try to break the tie again. This process repeats until the tie is actually broken or the messages are lost.

2) Recognition and Resolution of Message Laxity Ties During Window Contraction: In our protocol, as in traditional window protocols, a tie can be recognized when the window size is reduced to one and there is still a collision.

When the channel is in the state of *channel_idle_after_collision*, Procedure Contract_Window_and_Send (for which, the original pseudocode is in Fig. 2) is called. In this procedure, the window size is reduced by letting up $= t + \lceil (up - t)/2 \rceil$. If two or more messages have the same laxity, the window will (eventually) be reduced to a point where up $= t + 1$. At this point, if up is further reduced by the

formula up $= t + \lceil (up - t/2 \rceil$, the new value of up is equal to the old one. This means that the window has been reduced to its minimum and the messages in window [t, up) have LS equal to the current time t. Hence, a collision would occur again if the new window, which is the same as the old one, is just simply used. To resolve the tie, we extend Procedure Contract_Window_and_Send as follows (for the pseudocode, see Fig. 9): if up $= t + 1$, the protocol does not reduce the window size, but invokes the probabilistic scheme. Each node which has a message in the current window draws a random real number in the interval of $(0, 1)$ and if the number drawn is larger than a predefined probability P (which is a parameter of the protocol), the node transmits the message. In the case that the random number is not larger than P, if the message's laxity is zero, the message is discarded because there is no chance to transmit it before its time constraint. Otherwise, if the message's LS was previously (and artificially) moved forward due to some previous execution of the protocol, then it is possible to again modify the message's LS for possible future transmission as long as the current (modified) LS is less than or equal to the original LS.

```
Procedure Expand_Window_and_Send(up, t);

BEGIN
   IF empty(stack)
   THEN
   BEGIN
      up = t + δ;
      send out the first message if its LS is in [t, up);
   END
   ELSE
      IF up < top_u(stack) - 1
      THEN
      BEGIN
         up = ⌈ (up + top_u(stack))/2 ⌉;
         send out the first message if its LS is in [t, up)
      END
      ELSE  (* a tie on message's LS *)
      BEGIN (* use a random scheme to make a decision *)
         IF message M with I_M = top_i(stack) is in the queue
         THEN
            IF Random(0, 1) > P
               THEN
                  send out message M again
               ELSE
                  LS_M = Random(t+2, D_M - L_M) (* Not to be sent !  *)
         up = pop_u(stack);
      END;
END;
```

Fig. 7.   Extended procedure Expand_Window_and_Send.

```
Assume the extended protocol is used. Example 3 continues
from Figure 8.d --- t = 6.
```

```
t = 6: The channel is continuing_idle. Because the old value of up
       is equal to 10 = top_u(stack) - 1, the probabilistic scheme is used.
       Assume randomly it is decided that M1 is to be sent and M2's LS is
       modified to 9. The top value of the stack is popped, the new window
       is [6, 11). Protocol explicitly prohibits the transmission
       of M2 at this time although it is in the window.
```

```
                            M2
                                 M1
+-----+-----+-----[-----+-----+--)--+-----+-----+-----+-----+-----> LS
0     2     4     6     8     10    12    14    16    18    20
                            (d)
```

```
t = 8: The transmission of M1 has completed. The old window = [8, 11).
       top_u(stack) = 20. After popping the stack, the new window is
       [8, 20). M2 is considered for transmission.
```

```
                       M2
+-----+-----+-----+-----[-----+-----+-----+-----+-----+-----)-----> LS
0     2     4     6     8     10    12    14    16    18    20
                            (e)
```

Fig. 8.   Example 3—Using the extended protocol.

B. Property of the Extended Protocol

For the extended protocol, the tied message's LS values are modified, and hence the maximum-laxity-first policy is not always preserved as in the case when there is no tie. However, the following theorem shows that in the extended protocol, an individual message M will still be sent according to the minimum-laxity-first policy if the tie among messages with larger laxity is resolved after message M's arrival, or if the tied messages have a smaller laxity than M.

Lemma 3: For the extended protocol, at time t, consider any two messages M and M' which do not have a tie. If

a) M' has no laxity tie with any other messages, or

b) M' does have a laxity tie with one or more other messages but the tie has not been resolved at time t then,

$$LS_M < LS_{M'} \text{ if and only if } LA_M(t) < LA_{M'}(t).$$

Proof: When the first condition is true, this lemma holds from Lemma 1. When the second condition is true, this lemma

```
Procedure Contract_Window_and_Send(up, t);

BEGIN
01      IF up > t
02      THEN
03          IF up > t + 1
04          THEN
05          BEGIN
06              IF this node is involved in the collision
07              THEN
08                  i = I_M (* M is the collided message *)
09              ELSE
10                  i = 0;
11              push(stack, (up, i));
12              up = t + ⌈ (up - t)/2 ⌉; (* reduce up *)
13              send out the message if its LS is in [t, up)
14          END
15          ELSE  (* up = t + 1 *)
16          BEGIN (* use the random scheme to make a decision*)
17              IF message M with I_M = top_i(stack) is in the queue
18              THEN
19                  IF Random(0, 1) > P
20                  THEN
21                      Send message M again
22                  ELSE
23                      IF LA_M = 0
24                      THEN
25                          discard message M
26                      ELSE
27                          LS_M = Random(t+2, D_M - L_M)
28          END
29      ELSE (* up ≤ t *)
30          Pop_and_Send(up, t); (* See Figure 3 *)
END;
```

Fig. 9. Extended procedure Contract_Window_and_Send.

holds because only *after* a tie resolution, can an involved message's LS be reduced. ∎

Lemma 4: With the extended protocol, if at any time t, the protocol is not performing the tie resolution (i.e., not using the probabilistic scheme), and at the same time t, a message M starts its successful transmission, then M has the minimum LS value among all the messages which are in the system at time t.

Lemma 4 simply says that if the extended protocol is not resolving ties, then Lemma 2 is still true. The proofs of both Lemmas 2 and 4 are similar. The proof for Lemma 4 is hence omitted.

Theorem 2: Assume that a message M arrives at the system at time t_1. Let t_2 ($> t_1$) be the earliest time at which the channel is idle, and t_3 be the time at which message M leaves the system (either transmitted or lost). Then for any message M' transmitted in the time interval $[t_2, t_3)$, $LA_{M'} \leq LA_M$, unless M' has a laxity tie with other messages and the tie is resolved at $t_0 < t_2$.

The theorem states that with the extended protocol, the minimum-laxity-first cannot always be guaranteed because of tie resolutions which modify the LS values. However, under certain conditions for an individual message M, the minimum-laxity-first policy can still be preserved. The conditions are that messages with larger laxities 1) have no laxity ties, or 2) have not resolved their ties by the time M is transmitted. The probability of our protocol deviating from the minimum-laxity-first policy is related to the probability of the occurrence of messages with equal laxity.

Proof: For any message M' without a laxity tie with other messages, according to Lemma 1 and Lemma 4, M' may be transmitted in the time interval of $[t_2, t_3)$ only if $LA_{M'} < LA_M$. Hence, the theorem holds for this kind of message.

Now, consider the messages with laxity tie. Let $\{M_1, M_2, \cdots, M_n\}$, $n \geq 2$, be a set of messages which have a tie on their laxity, i.e., $LA_{M_1} = LA_{M_2} = \cdots = LA_{M_n}$. Also, their laxity is larger than that of message M, i.e., $LA_{M_1} > LA_M$. We need to show that if the tie is not broken at t_2, then no message in $\{M_1, M_2, \cdots, M_n\}$ could be transmitted in the interval of $[t_2, t_3)$.

First, we show that it is impossible for the tie resolution for $\{M_1, M_2, \cdots, M_n\}$ to occur in the time interval of $[t_2, t_3)$. If this is not true, i.e., the tie is resolved at t_0 and $t_2 \leq t_0 < t_3$, then the extended protocol, at t_0, uses either the extended Procedure Expand_Window_and_Send (Fig. 7) or the extended Procedure Contract_Window_and_Send (Fig. 9). If at t_0, the extended Procedure Expand_Window_and_Send is used, then the old window has the form of $[t_0, \mathrm{LS}_{M_1})$. And there should be no message in that window. However, because $t_2 \leq t_0$ and $\mathrm{LS}_M < \mathrm{LS}_{M_1}$, message M is indeed in window $[t_0, \mathrm{LS}_{M_1})$. Hence, it is impossible that at t_0 the extended procedure Expand_Window_and_Send is used. It is also not possible that at t_0 the extended Procedure Contract_Window_and_Send is used. If the extended Procedure Contract_Window_and_Send is used, the window size must be one and the lower bound of the window, i.e., the current time t_0, is equal to the original LS value of tied messages. This certainly cannot be true for $M_1, M_2, \cdots,$ and M_n because before the tie resolution, $\mathrm{LS}_{M_1} = \mathrm{LS}_{M_2} = \cdots = \mathrm{LS}_{M_n} > \mathrm{LS}_M \geq t_3 - 1 \geq t_0$. Hence, in any case, the tie resolution for $\{M_1, M_2, \cdots, M_n\}$ cannot happen in the time interval of $[t_2, t_3)$.

Therefore, if the laxity tie among $M_1, M_2, \cdots,$ and M_n is not resolved before t_2, the resolution will not happen before t_3. Consequently, by Lemma 3, since $\mathrm{LA}_{M_1} = \mathrm{LA}_{M_2} = \cdots = \mathrm{LA}_{M_n} > \mathrm{LA}_M$, in the time interval of $[t_2, t_3)$, $\mathrm{LS}_{M_1} = \mathrm{LS}_{M_2} = \cdots = \mathrm{LS}_{M_n} > \mathrm{LS}_M$ holds. Then by Lemma 4, no message in the set of $\{M_1, M_2, \cdots, M_n\}$ can be successfully transmitted in the time interval of $[t_2, t_3)$. ∎

V. PERFORMANCE EVALUATION BY SIMULATION

In this section, we evaluate the performance of the new window protocol with its extensions. We first introduce two baseline protocols to be used for comparison purposes. Then, we present the simulation model and discuss the simulation results.

A. Baseline Protocols

The first baseline protocol is called *Centralized Minimum Laxity message transmitted first,* abbreviated as CML. In this protocol, transmission of all messages is assumed to be scheduled by a centralized controller. This controller contains perfect knowledge about the nodes and the channel and experiences no communication overhead. It schedules the transmissions of messages such that the message with the minimum laxity is transmitted first. This protocol is used to provide an upper bound on performance.

The second baseline protocol is called *Virtual Time CSMA-L* [34]. It has been previously shown that in terms of various performance metrics and stability, in a wide range of real-time communication environments, the virtual time CSMA-L protocol[4] performs well and is better than a traditional CSMA/CD protocol. We use it here to serve as a baseline and show that the new time-constrained window protocol is even better.

In the virtual time CSMA-L protocol, each node maintains two clocks: a real-time clock and a virtual time clock. Messages waiting to be transmitted are queued in the order of their LS values. Whenever a node finds the channel to be idle, it resets its virtual clock to equal the real clock. The virtual clock then runs at a higher rate, $\eta \geq 1$, than the real clock. A node transmits its first message waiting in the queue when the time

---

[4] Note that all the virtual time CSMA protocols also include collision detect (CD), but these initials are not used in describing these protocols in the original paper.

on the virtual clock is equal to the LS value of that message. If there is a collision, a probabilistic scheme is invoked for resolution. It is clear that if there are no collisions, this protocol also implements the minimum-laxity-first transmission policy.

One may actually think of the virtual time protocol as a simplified form of the window protocol in which the "window" keeps expanding at a constant rate until either a message transmission starts, or a collision happens. In the latter case, the probabilistic resolution scheme is used immediately, rather than modifying the window.

B. Simulation Model

A simulation model is developed and used to evaluate the performance of the above protocols. The simulation program is written in Simscript II.5, and runs in an ULTRIX environment on MicroVAX-II. The simulation model is parameterized by the distributions of message arrivals, transmission times, and laxities. In these simulations, we did not model the execution time of our protocol.

In the simulations reported in this paper, messages arrive as a Poisson process. Message lengths are exponentially distributed with mean $= 100$ (corresponding to $\alpha = 0.01$), or mean $= 10$ (corresponding to $\alpha = 0.1$). Message laxities are uniformly distributed in the interval $[0, 2^*\mathrm{AL}]$ where AL is the average laxity.

In each simulation run, statistics are reset after the transient phase. Statistics used to determine the performance are then collected after an additional (5000^* mean of message interarrival time) simulation time units. We observed that with this setting for the simulation length, the collected data are within a 90% confidence interval.

We consider the case of an *infinite* population of nodes in the system [14], [30]. That is, in the simulation model, it is assumed that a message always arrives at a node where no message is waiting. Note that the infinite population presents the worst case for a multiaccess network. It maximizes the number of messages in a window, and hence causes maximum number of collisions.

The system load L is defined as

$$L = \text{Message Arrival Rate} * \text{Mean of Message Length.}$$

In our simulations, when the system load and the mean of message length are defined, the message arrival rate is decided by the above formula.

For simplicity, in all the simulations, parameter P, the probability of immediate retransmission in the resolution of message laxity tie, takes a value of 0.5.

For each run of the simulation, the following performance measures are collected:

1) *Ratio of Message Lost,* ML, which is defined as

$$\mathrm{ML} = \frac{\mathrm{TNML}}{\mathrm{TNMT} + \mathrm{TNML}}$$

where TNML is the total number of messages lost, and TNMT is the total number of messages transmitted.

2) *Effective Channel Utilization,* ECU, defined as

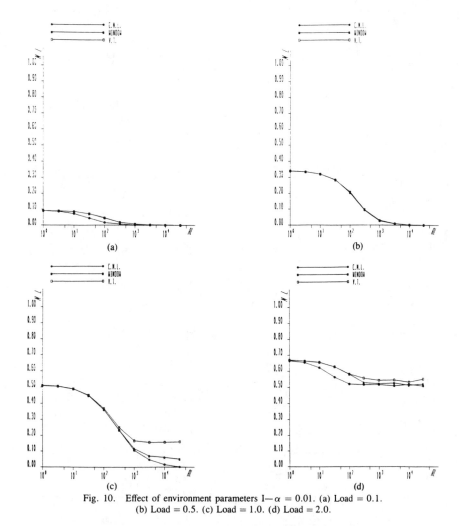

Fig. 10. Effect of environment parameters I—$\alpha = 0.01$. (a) Load = 0.1.
(b) Load = 0.5. (c) Load = 1.0. (d) Load = 2.0.

$$\text{ECU} = \frac{\text{Total Time Units Channel is Used for Transmitting Messages}}{\text{Total Time Units Simulated}}.$$

3) *Collision Channel Utilization,* CCU, which is

$$\text{CCU} = \frac{\text{Total Time Units Channel is Wasted due to Collisions}}{\text{Total Time Units Simulated}}.$$

4) *Normalized Average Transmitted Message Length,* NTL, which is defined as

$$\text{NTL} = \frac{\text{Average Length of Transmitted Messages}}{\text{Average Length of Received Messages}}.$$

A good protocol should minimize the message loss, ML, and the collision channel utilization, CCU, and maximize the effective channel utilization, ECU. A protocol which does not have a bias toward short or long messages should have its NTL close to 1. As shown in [34] and also confirmed in this simulation study, using the minimum-laxity-first policy results in NTL very close to 1. That is, the minimum-laxity-first policy has no bias based on the message length. Consequently, when using the minimum-laxity-first policy, ECU directly depends on ML and is given by $(1 - \text{ML})*L$. We also find that CCU for the window protocol is very small when the ML is close to the optimal (minimum) point. Based on these facts, to save space and time, in this paper, we concentrate only on the performance metric ML. We would like to refer our enthu-

siastic reader to [35] for the complete set of data from the simulations.

C. Simulation Study Results

We discuss the simulation results in two parts. The first part shows the effect of the environmental parameters on the performance of the protocols, and the second shows the parameter sensitivity of the protocol.

1) Environmental Parameters' Effect on Performance: In this part of the simulation, we study how the application environment parameters such as the average message laxity (AL), system load (L), and the normalized end-to-end delays (α) affect the performance of the baseline and the new window protocol.

Two cases of simulation studies are conducted. In the first case, α is 0.01, and in the second case, $\alpha = 0.10$. In both cases, the system load changes from 0.1, to 0.5, to 1.0, and to 2.0, and the mean of message laxity changes from 1 to $10^{4.5}$ in a logarithmic scale. Figs. 10 and 11 present the results,

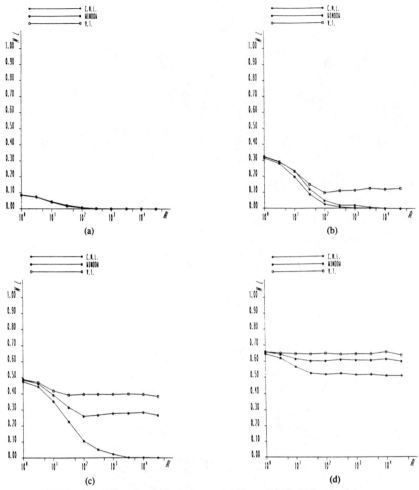

Fig. 11.　Effect of environment parameters II—$\alpha = 0.10$. (a) Load = 0.1.
(b) Load = 0.5. (c) Load = 1.0. (d) Load = 2.0.

plotting the percentage of message loss (ML) versus the mean of message laxities (AL) for the CML, window, and virtual time protocols.

From Figs. 10 and 11, we see that, when the laxity increases or the system load decreases, the performance of each protocol improves as expected. However, after a certain increase in laxity, the improvement is saturated, i.e., the message loss does not decrease even though the laxity is further increased. We note that when the load is light ($L = 0.1$), the laxity is tight (up to 10^2), and α is small ($\alpha = 0.01$), the performance of three protocols is very close. On the other hand, when the system load is heavy, the message laxity is large, or α is large, the performance is different. Our new window protocol is usually better and never worse than the virtual time protocol.

A careful reader may further notice that the differences between CML and the window protocol, and CML and the virtual time protocol do not always decrease as the laxity increases. Actually, in many instances [see Figs. 10(c), 11(b), 11(c), and 11(d)], it increases. Although this sounds contradictory to one's intuition, the explanation is quite simple: this phenomenon is due to the fact that when the laxity increases,

the number of active messages in the system increases. The reason why increasing laxity increases the number of active messages is as follows. When the messages which have long laxities arrive, they typically wait longer in the system because the protocol favors the short laxity messages and the long laxity messages have a lot of time to still meet their time constraints. The increased number of active messages in the system causes more collisions and hence the performance of protocols such as the window and virtual time, which always takes certain time (cost) to resolve a collision, does not improve with increase in laxity as much as the ideal baseline protocol CML. We call this phenomenon the *laxity abnormality in real-time scheduling.* We will observe a similar phenomenon again in the next subsection.

2) Sensitivity of Protocol Parameters: In the simulations reported above, the protocol parameters—δ for the window protocol and η for the virtual time protocol—are selected in such a way that the best performance of the system is achieved. The sensitivity of the system performance to the selection of the protocol parameters is the subject of this subsection.

We conduct two cases of simulation studies of the window protocol to test its sensitivity to the protocol parameters. The

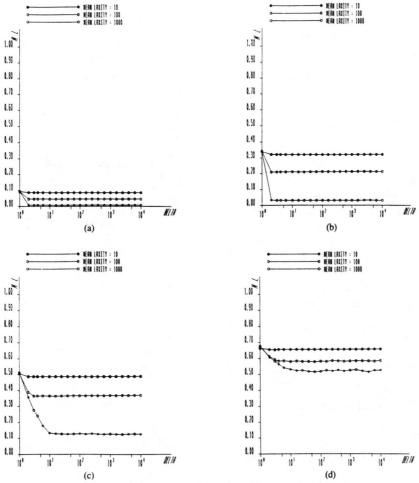

Fig. 12. Sensitivity of δ for window protocol I—$\alpha = 0.01$. (a) Load $= 0.1$.
(b) Load $= 0.5$. (c) Load $= 1.0$. (d) Load $= 2.0$.

first case is for $\alpha = 0.01$, and the second case is for $\alpha = 0.10$. In each case, the average laxity (AL) takes values of 10, 100, and 1000, and the system loads (L) are 0.1, 0.5, 1.0, and 2.0, respectively. The value of δ, the parameter for the initial window size, changes from 10^0 to 10^4 in a logarithmic scale. Figs. 12 and 13 show the results.

For the purpose of comparison, we also show the simulation results for the virtual time protocol in Figs. 14 and 15, where the simulation parameters are set the same as for window protocol except that instead of varying δ, we vary η, the rate at which virtual clock runs; η changes from 10^0 to 10^4.

From Fig. 12, we notice that in the case when the normalized end-to-end delay is small, i.e., $\alpha = 0.01$, the performance of our window protocol is very stable in terms of the selection of the value δ. As the δ increases from 10^0, the message loss decreases and reaches its minimum no later than when $\delta = 10^2$. Then the message loss stabilizes at the minimum value up to $\delta = 10^4$.

Now consider the case where α is large, i.e., equal to 0.1 (Fig. 13). When the system load is light ($L = 0.1$) or medium ($L = 0.5$), the sensitivity of the window protocol with respect to the choice of δ is almost the same as in the case where

$\alpha = 0.01$. When the load is high ($L = 1.0$), we see that the performance is stable for the values of $\delta = 10$ to 100. Even when the system is extremely overloaded ($L = 2.0$), there are still certain ranges of δ values in which the system is stable.

The virtual time protocol has been reported to be insensitive in terms of the protocol parameter η [20], [21], [34]. However, if we compare each of corresponding cases of the two protocols, i.e., Figs. 12 and 14, and Figs. 13 and 15, we find that the new window protocol does much better. With the window protocol, the range in which the system is stable is always much greater than with the virtual time protocol.

In these sensitivity tests, we can observe another kind of the laxity abnormality. In Figs. 13(d), 14, and 15, we see that when the laxity increases, message loss may even increase. The situation becomes worse when the system is highly loaded ($L = 1$) or overloaded ($L = 2$). We believe that the same explanation as stated in Section V-C1 still applies. As the laxity increases, the number of active messages in the system increases. Hence, the chance of collision increases which increases the overhead of these algorithms. Hence, the performance degrades with respect to the ideal baseline where it is assumed that it takes zero time to resolve a collision. A

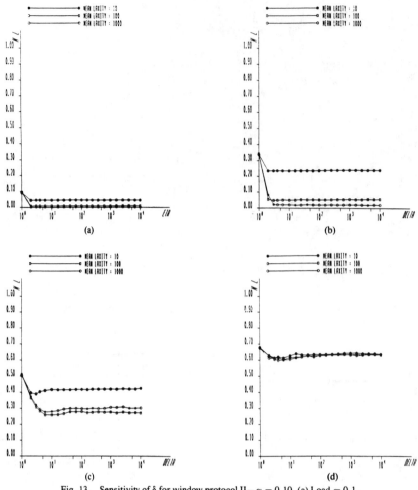

Fig. 13.   Sensitivity of δ for window protocol II—$\alpha = 0.10$. (a) Load = 0.1.
(b) Load = 0.5. (c) Load = 1.0. (d) Load = 2.0.

further observation is that when the protocol parameter is far from the optimal value, the system is more likely to be in an abnormal state. However, if we compare the corresponding cases of the window and the virtual time protocols, we see that at least in these simulations, the laxity abnormality is observed much less often for the window protocol than for the virtual time protocol. Indeed, in Figs. 12–15, the laxity abnormality appears only once [Fig. 13(c)] for the window protocol, but seven times [Figs. 14(b), 14(c), 14(d), 15(a), 15(b), 15(c), and 15(d)] for the virtual time protocol—giving us another reason to favor the new window protocol.

From the data in Figs. 12 and 13, we also notice that for a given α, one can always easily choose a δ value independently from the system load and message laxities such that the performance is at or very close to the minimum value. For example, when $\alpha = 0.01$, any value for δ between 10^2 and 10^4 is very good. And when $\alpha = 0.10$, a δ value around 10 may keep the system in an optimal performance stage. Because in practice, α is often a fixed parameter of the network working environment, the above fact indicates that the implementation and maintenance of the protocol would not be difficult in terms of the parameter setting.

D. Summary of the Performance Observations

We now summarize the performance observations as determined by the simulation studies.

1) Most of the time, the new window protocol performs very close to that of CML which is an unrealizable protocol that provides the upper bound on the performance.

2) The window protocol often performs better and never worse than the virtual time protocol which in turn has previously been shown to work well and be better than a general CSMA/CD protocol [34].

3) The window protocol is extremely insensitive to the choice of parameter δ. For a given α, one may identify good values of δ independently of the system load and message laxity. Moreover, the window protocol is often much more stable than the virtual time protocol though the latter has been shown to be stable most of the time [20], [21], [34].

4) The laxity abnormality, i.e., the phenomenon that when the laxity is relaxed, the system performance may not be improved, or may even become worse, is observed for both the window and virtual time protocols. However, with the window protocol, the abnormality occurs less frequently, or to

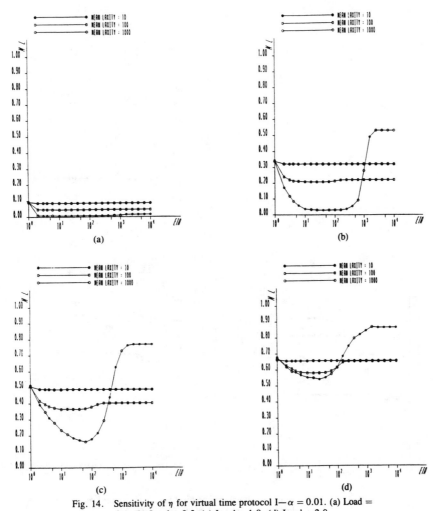

Fig. 14.   Sensitivity of η for virtual time protocol I— $\alpha = 0.01$. (a) Load = 0.1. (b) Load = 0.5. (c) Load = 1.0. (d) Load = 2.0.

a lesser degree if it does occur, than with the virtual time protocol.

VI. Final Remarks

We have proposed and studied a new window protocol suited for time-constrained communication. The new protocol differs from the traditional window protocol approach in the sense that it explicitly takes messages' time constraints into account, in particular, the message deadlines. The management of the window is done in such a way that a newly arriving message always has a chance to be considered for transmission if its latest time to send (so that it reaches its destination before the deadline) is less than that of the active messages in the system. As a result, our new protocol accurately implements the optimal minimum-laxity-first policy if there is no tie among message laxities. In case there is a laxity tie among some messages, the minimum-laxity-first policy can still be preserved for an individual message M if the tied messages have a smaller laxity or if the tie has not been resolved at the time message M arrives. Simulation studies show that it performs well in a wide range of environments, even under overloaded conditions.

Turning our attention to implementation support for our protocol, an exact implementation requires the synchronization of the clocks at all nodes. In a distributed system, clock synchronization is an interesting and challenging problem. However, our protocol is robust in the sense that it will continue functioning even if clocks are not perfectly synchronized. Of course, in this situation, the performance of the protocol may deteriorate because message transmission will not be exactly according to the minimum-laxity-first transmission policy. (In fact, as the protocol stands, laxity ties distort the message transmission policy.) Further studies are needed to evaluate the effect of a given maximum skew of the clocks on the desired performance metrics.

In this paper and in our previous studies [34], we have used virtual time and window protocols to implement specific transmission policies suitable for real-time communication. This method can be generalized to many other network applications. For example, in [8], a special window protocol is introduced for load balancing, and in [36], a virtual time protocol is used to implement a transmission policy suitable for distributed simulation. Currently, we are working on generalized virtual time and window protocols in which the trans-

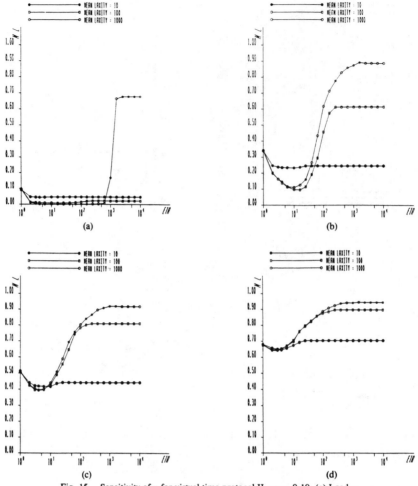

Fig. 15. Sensitivity of η for virtual time protocol II—$\alpha = 0.10$. (a) Load = 0.1. (b) Load = 0.5. (c) Load = 1.0. (d) Load = 2.0.

mission policy is parameterized and hence can be adjusted to suit a given network application.

REFERENCES

[1] N. Abramson, "The ALOHA System—Another alternative for computer communications," in *AFIPS Proc. Fall Joint Comput.*, vol. 37, 1970.

[2] J. I. Capetanakis, "Tree algorithm for packet broadcast channels," *IEEE Trans. Commun.*, vol. COM-27, no. 10, Oct. 1979.

[3] I. Chlamtac, W. R. Franta, and D. Levin, "BRAM: The broadcast recognizing access method," *IEEE Trans. Commun.*, vol. COM-27, no. 8, Aug. 1979.

[4] G. Fayolle, P. Flajolet, M. Hofri, and P. Jacquet, "Analysis of a stack algorithm for random multiaccess communication," *IEEE Trans. Inform. Theory*, vol. IT-31, no. 2, Mar. 1985.

[5] A. Grami, K. Sochraby, and J. Hayes, "Further results on probing," in *Proc. IEEE Int. Commun. Conf.*, 1982.

[6] L. W. Hansen and M. Schwartz, "An assigned-slot listen-before-transmission protocol for a multiaccess data channel," *IEEE Trans. Commun.*, vol. COM-27, no. 6, June 1979.

[7] J. F. Hayes, "An adaptive technique for local distribution," *IEEE Trans. Commun.*, vol. COM-26, no. 8, Aug. 1978.

[8] J. Y. Juang and B. W. Wah, "Unifies window protocols for contention resolution in local multi-access networks," in *Proc. Third Annu. Joint Conf. IEEE Comput. Commun. Soc.*, Apr. 1984.

[9] E. D. Jensen, C. D., Locke, and H. Tokuda, "A time-driven scheduling model for real-time operating systems," in *Proc. IEEE Real-Time Syst. Symp.*, Dec. 1985.

[10] L. Kleinrock, "Packet switching in radio channels: Part 1—Carrier sense multiple-access modes and their throughput-delay characteristics," *IEEE Trans. Commun.*, vol. COM-23, no. 12, Dec. 1975.

[11] L. Kleinrock and Y. Yemini, "An optimal adaptive scheme for multiple access broadcast communication," in *Proc. ICC*, 1978.

[12] L. Kleinrock and M. O. Scholl, "Packet switching in radio channels: New conflict-free multiple access schemes," *IEEE Trans. Commun.*, vol. COM-28, no. 7, July 1980.

[13] J. F. Kurose, M. Schwartz, and T. Yemini, "Controlling window protocols for time-constrained communication in a multiple access environment," in *Proc. 8th IEEE Int. Data Commun. Symp.*, 1983.

[14] J. F. Kurose, "Time-constrained communication in multiple accesses networks," Ph.D. dissertation, Columbia Univ., 1984.

[15] J. S. Meditch and D. H. Yin, "Performance analysis of virtual time CSMA," in *Proc. IEEE Infocom'86*, Apr. 1986.

[16] J. Misra, "Distributed discrete-event simulation," *Comput. Surveys*, vol. 18, no. 1, Mar. 1986.

[17] A. K. Mok and M. L. Dertouzos, "Multiprocessor scheduling in a hard real-time environment," in *Proc. Seventh Texas Conf. Comput. Syst.*, Nov. 1978.

[18] A. K. Mok and S. A. Ward, "Distributed broadcast channel access," *Comput. Network*, vol. 3, Nov. 1979.

[19] A. K. Mok, "Fundamental design problems of distributed systems for the hard real-time environment," Ph.D. dissertation, Massachusetts Inst. Technol., Cambridge, MA, May 1983.

[20] M. L. Molle, "Unifications and extensions of the multiple access communications problem," Ph.D. dissertation, Univ. of California at Los Angeles, July 1981.

[21] M. L. Molle and L. Kleinrock, "Virtual time CSMA: Why two clocks

are better than one," *IEEE Trans. Commun.*, vol. COM-33, no. 9, Sept. 1985.

[22] S. Panwar, D. Towsley, and J. Wolf, "Optimal scheduling policies for a class of queues with customer deadlines to the beginning of service," *J. ACM*, vol. 35, no. 4, Oct. 1988.

[23] S. Panwar, "Time constrained and multiaccess communications," Ph.D. dissertation, Univ. of Massachusetts at Amherst, Feb. 1986.

[24] K. Ramamritham, "Channel characteristics in local area hard real-time systems," *Comput. Networks ISDN Syst.*, vol. 3, no. 13, 1987.

[25] E. H. Rothauser and D. Wild, "MLMA—A collision-free multi-access method," in *Proc. IFIP Congr. 77*, 1977.

[26] M. Scholl, "Multiplexing techniques for data transmission over packet switched radio systems," Ph.D. dissertation, Univ. of California at Los Angeles, 1976.

[27] K. Sevcik and M. Johnson, "Cycle time properties of the FDDI token ring protocol," *IEEE Trans. Software Eng.*, vol. SE-13, no. 3, Mar. 1987.

[28] J. A. Stankovic, "A perspective on distributed computer systems," *IEEE Trans. Comput.*, vol. C-33, no. 12, Dec. 1984.

[29] J. A. Stankovic, "Misconceptions about real-time computing," *IEEE Comput. Mag.*, Oct. 1988.

[30] A. S. Tanenbaum, *Computer Networks.* Englewood Cliffs, NJ: Prentice-Hall, 1981.

[31] D. Towsley and G. Venkatesh, "Window random access protocols for local computer networks," *IEEE Trans. Comput.*, vol. C-31, no. 8, Aug. 1982.

[32] B. W. Wah and J. Y. Juang, "An efficient protocol for load balancing on CSMA/CD networks," in *Proc. Eighth Conf. Local Comput. Networks*, Oct. 1983.

[33] Y. Yemini, "On the channel sharing in discrete-time packet switched, multiaccess broadcast communication," Ph.D. dissertation, Univ. of California at Los Angeles, 1978.

[34] W. Zhao and K. Ramamritham, "Virtual time CSMA protocols for hard real-time communication," *IEEE Trans. Software Eng.*, vol. SE-13, no. 8, Aug. 1987.

[35] W. Zhao *et al.*, "Performance evaluation of a window protocol for hard real-time communication," Tech. Rep., Dep. Comput. Inform. Sci., Univ. of Massachusetts, Aug. 1987.

[36] W. Zhao, "Using the continuous simulation clock to control the discrete distributed simulation," in *Proc. 21st Simulation Conf.*, Mar. 1988.

[37] T. Znati and L. Ni, "A prioritized multiaccess protocol for distributed real-time applications," in *Proc. IEEE 7th Int. Conf. Distributed Comput. Syst.*, Sept. 1987.

Wei Zhao (S'85–M'86) received the Diploma in Physics from Shaanxi Normal University, Xian, China, in 1977, and the M.S. and Ph.D. degrees in computer science from the University of Massachusetts, Amherst, in 1983 and 1986, respectively.

His current research interests include scheduling algorithms, communication protocols, performance analysis and simulation studies of distributed real-time systems, concurrency control for database systems, resource management in operating systems, and knowledge-based systems.

Dr. Zhao was a Guest Editor for a special issue of *Operating System Review* on real-time operating systems. He is a member of the Association for Computing Machinery and the IEEE Computer Society.

John A. Stankovic (S'77–M'79–SM'86) received the B.S. degree in electrical engineering, and the M.S. and Ph.D. degrees in computer science, all from Brown University, Providence, RI, in 1970, 1976, and 1979, respectively.

He is a Professor in the Computer and Information Science Department at the University of Massachusetts at Amherst. His current research interests include investigating various approaches to scheduling on local area networks and multiprocessors, and developing flexible, distributed, hard real-time systems. He is currently building a hard real-time kernel, called Spring, which is based on a new scheduling paradigm and on ensuring predictability. He is also performing research on a distributed database testbed called CARAT. The CARAT testbed has been operational for several years and includes protocols for real-time transactions. He has held visiting positions in the Computer Science Department at Carnegie-Mellon University and at INRIA in France. He received an Outstanding Scholar Award from the School of Engineering, University of Massachusetts.

Dr. Stankovic is an editor-in-chief for *Real-Time Systems* and an editor for IEEE TRANSACTIONS ON COMPUTERS. He also served as a Guest Editor for a special issue of IEEE TRANSACTIONS ON COMPUTERS on parallel and distributed computing. He is a member of the Association for Computing Machinery and Sigma Xi.

Krithi Ramamritham (M'89) received the Ph.D. degree in computer science from the University of Utah in 1981.

Since then he has been with the Department of Computer and Information Science at the University of Massachusetts at Amherst where he is currently an Associate Professor. During 1987–1988, he was a Science and Engineering Research Council (U.K.) Visiting Fellow at the University of Newcastle-upon-Tyne, U.K. and a Visiting Professor at the Technical University of Vienna, Austria. His primary research interests lie in the areas of real-time systems, and distributed computing. He co-directs the Spring project whose goal is to develop scheduling algorithms, operating system support, architectural support, and design strategies for real-time applications. In addition, he directs the Gutenberg project which deals with structuring distributed computations through the control of interprocess communication and with enhancing concurrency in distributed applications through the use of semantic information.

Dr. Ramamritham is an editor for the new journal on *Real-Time Systems*, and is the co-author of an IEEE tutorial text on hard real-time systems. He is a member of the Association for Computing Machinery.

Responsive, Deterministic IEEE 802.5 Token Ring Scheduling

JAY K. STROSNIDER,
THOMAS E. MARCHOK
Department of Electrical and Computer Engineering, Carnegie Mellon University, Pittsburgh, Pennsylvania 15213

Abstract. This paper presents a novel approach for scheduling the IEEE 802.5 token ring. This approach not only guarantees deadlines for synchronous class messages, but also dramatically reduces asynchronous class response times. Further, highly responsive guaranteed service is introduced for alert class asynchronous messages. Conventional use of the IEEE 802.5 token ring standard guarantees synchronous communication services using Time Domain Multiplexing (TDM) techniques while relegating asynchronous class message services to background status. The result is poor responsiveness. Further, the TDM schedules tend to be fragile and difficult to modify and extend. This paper presents an algorithmic-based scheduling approach that supports *a priori* schedulability determination for arbitrary synchronous message sets without the costly development, testing, and tuning of TDM schedules. This capability allows the IEEE 802.5 standard to support dynamic, adaptive, and reconfigurable run-time environments where the inflexibility of TDM would be prohibitive. Advanced real-time scheduling theory is applied to the IEEE 802.5 token ring standard and dramatically enhances asynchronous class messages' responsiveness while still maintaining guaranteed service for the synchronous class. The result is a highly responsive real-time ring that can form the backbone of predictable, stable, and extendible real-time systems.

1. Introduction

Real-time networking solutions require deterministic message-level response time performance. In contrast, some notion of aggregate throughput and/or average delay is sufficient for non real-time networking solutions. The current state of the art and predominant practice is to use Time Domain Multiplexing (TDM) techniques manifesting themselves as time-lines on buses and round-robin schedulers on rings (Kopetz, Herman et. al. 1989). The current practice for the IEEE 802.5 scheduling is to use round-robin scheduling with each station's token timer set proportional to the bandwidth required to support its synchronous message set.

Networks for distributed real-time systems will be required to form the backbone upon which predictable, stable, and extendible system solutions will be built. To be successful, the real-time communication subsystem must be able to predictably satisfy individual message level timing requirements in the presence of contention. The timing requirements are driven not only by applications' inter-process communication, but also by time-constrained operating system functions invoked on behalf of application processes. The current state of the art and practice is to use handcrafted TDM techniques to assure timing correctness. The limitations and weaknesses of the TDM approach for processor scheduling have been well documented by Hood and Grover (1986), and are summarized below:

• *Design problems* from the high cost handling multiple modes and hand tuning time-lines.

- *Run time problems* from the lack of flexibility making it difficult for the system to respond to changing needs.
- *Maintenance problems* from the lack of formalized documentation of the tuning process and *ad hoc*, handcrafted time-lines making the systems "delicate beasts" (Hood and Grover 1986).

This and other experiences with using TDM for real-time processor scheduling have found that as the task periods grow in number and become relatively prime, the TDM schedule tends to be *ad hoc* in nature, painful to generate, very inflexible, and difficult to modify. The real-time communications scheduling problem for distributed systems shares the same problems as the uniprocessor scheduling problem with additional levels of difficulties arising from the following factors:

- The communications problem will be inherently distributed for the next generation systems where reliability demands that the nodes be highly independent to support fault tolerance. Distributed scheduling is almost always more difficult than centralized scheduling.
- The communications media will generally be required to handle a larger number of independent and unique tasks/messages than the processor environment. This increases the magnitude of the scheduling problem.
- The communications media will typically be subject to a more highly dynamic environment than the processor environment. Changes in the communications requirements for any of the attached processor nodes requires the network to adapt.

To further exacerbate the problem, distributed real-time systems are projected to be more complex than todays systems, exhibiting intelligent, adaptive, and highly dynamic behavior (Stankovic 1988). Not only will the inflexibility of TDM be prohibitive for such systems, but the implied reconfigurability of such systems results in a combinatorial explosion in the number of unique TDM schedules to be designed, integrated, and tested. For these highly dynamic, adaptive systems, TDM techniques will be inadequate.

Other efforts address providing alternatives for TDM scheduling on networks. IBM (Dailey 1983) extended the Multi-Level Mutli-Access (MLMA) protocol originally developed by Rothauser and Wild (1977) to support priority-based media arbitration on buses. Zhao, Stankovic, and Ramaritham (1988) developed a sliding window protocol which provides an alternative non-TDM strategy for scheduling time constrained messages in networks. LeLann (1988) has developed a variant of the CSMA/CD protocol which uses an adaptive tree walk strategy for back-offs and which provides another non-TDM alternative for real-time communications. The SAE-9B High Speed Ring Bus (SA5-9B 1986) committee has recognized the limitations of TDM scheduling for real-time applications and has adopted a priority-based media arbitration approach which supports algorithmic scheduling.

This paper develops a scheduling model for the IEEE 802.5 that supports algorithmic scheduling. The algorithmic approach directly implies a set of algorithms that accurately model a particular behavior, in this case system timing behavior. Algorithmic scheduling provides a set of rules that determine which job is to be executed at any given moment. These algorithms provide the disciplined timing environment that allows prediction of system timing behavior. Application of these algorithms requires *preemption* and *message level priority*. Algorithmic scheduling determines resource allocation dynamically via prioritized, message-level contention resolution. *Priorities* are required to dynamically resolve the relative ordering of task access to the resource. *Preemption* is required to allow the higher priority task/message access to the resource.

Section 2 first defines an ideal scheduling model for local area networks and then develops models/methodologies for realizing this scheduling model using the IEEE 802.5. Section 3 selects scheduling algorithms and develops an application example. Section 4 summarizes the experimental results from the application example demonstrating guaranteed synchronous class deadlines (without time-lines) and dramatically enhanced asynchronous class responsiveness. Section 5 provides implementation guidelines for developing IEEE 802.5 based LAN boards that cleanly support the technology reported here. Section 6 summarizes the results of the research and outlines future directions of this work.

2. 802.5 Scheduling model development

In this section, we develop the models and methodologies necessary to realize the preemptive, priority-driven scheduling using the IEEE 802.5 standard. First, we develop the communication media requirements along with an idealized LAN model for supporting the desired scheduling environment. Then we develop the scheduling model/methodology for the IEEE 802.5.

2.1. Media requirements

To realize algorithmic scheduling in LANs, the communications media must support the following fundamental features:

- Message priority assignment via an appropriate scheduling algorithm.
- Prioritized contention resolution to determine which message has the highest priority. It is also necessary to have sufficient priority resolution granularity to successfully resolve different periods to unique priority levels. An insufficient number of priority levels degrades schedulability performance (Lehoczky and Sha 1986).
- Resource preemption to assure that the highest priority task ready for execution is allocated the processor/communication medium. Failure to do so results in priority inversions and degrades schedulable performance as reported (Rajkumar 1986).

In the processor domain, all tasks and associated priorities are centralized with the scheduler dispatching them in priority order. The problem is more complex in the communication domain, with the messages and associated priorities residing at physically disbursed nodes. This paper develops the models/methodologies that support global, decentralized contention resolution using the 802.5 token ring. The preemption requirement is addressed by quantizing all messages into packets. The appropriate quantization size is an engineering tradeoff between the desired high preemptability and the high control overhead inherent in fine grain control.

An idealized LAN subsystem model needed to directly support preemptive priority-driven scheduling is illustrated in Figure 1. In the following discussions, we examine its requirements relative to the ISO standards model (Tannenbaum 1981). The Data Link Layer includes the Logical Link Control (LLC) and Media Access Control (MAC). The LLC is required to packetize outgoing logical link messages and priority queue them with the priority assigned algorithmically. Similarly, the LLC must reassemble the incoming packets into properly ordered messages. The MAC layer is required to:

• Priority queue all pending logical link packets into a single common queue per node.
• Provide global contention resolution between the nodes to grant media access to the node with the highest priority packet pending.

It is not necessary that separate priority queues be maintained for the LLC and MAC. There could have been one priority queue at the MAC level. The LLC queueing abstraction was introduced to illustrate the concurrency requirements needed to support multiple logical links per node and to emphasize that packets within the same logical link need to be priority queued. Depending on buffering requirements driven by device memory/media speed differences, queues may be implemented as linked list pointers. Where device memory access is slow relative to the media signalling rate, rate matching data buffers are required. These data buffers must be managed as priority queues to support the scheduling models. The physical layer and the medium are as required to support the MAC layer. Typical 802.5 operation does not use frame-level global contention resolution but rather uses token timers to partition the media's bandwidth between the nodes.

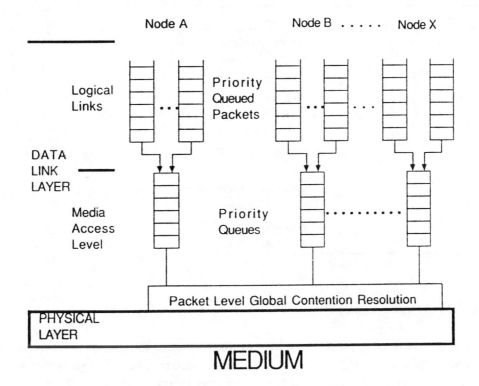

Figure 1. Generalized real-time communications model.

The operation of this model can be explained briefly as follows. Messages enter the system at each node, are broken into packets, and then queued in priority fashion. They then globally contend for media access with the highest priority message at each node. The node with the highest priority message gains media access and transmits the packet. For real-time systems, the notion of fairness is restricted to messages within the same priority level. When higher priority packets are pending, the lower priority packets can, and should, be subject to starvation until the higher priority packets have been serviced.

The essential features of this idealized LAN model may be summarized as follows:

- Individual message priorities are assigned by algorithmic discipline and not by message class.
- All pending packets within a node are priority queued.
- Global contention resolution is performed on the LAN for each packet, with the packet having the highest priority gaining access.
- Individual nodes can contend and capture back-to-back frames when they have multiple high priority packets queued.

In developing media models that support global contention resolution, the notational shorthand outlined in Table 1 will be used.

Table 1. Notational shorthand summary.

Real-Time Communication Parameters	
Notational Shorthand	Parameter
N_S	Number of Stations
N_{PB}	Number of Priority Bits
B_R	Bit Signalling Rate
W_T	Ring Walk Time
D_{SB}	Station Bit Delay
D_{ST}	Station Time Delay
D_{Prop}	Media Propagation Delay
$Media_L$	Media Length
$Media_{PS}$	Media Propagation Speed
$Packet_{BL}$	Packet Bit Length
Msg_{BL}	Message Frame (Bits)
$Token_{BL}$	Token Bit Length

2.2. IEEE 802.5 ring model

In this section, we develop the methodology for implementing the desired real-time scheduling model using the IEEE 802.5 token ring. Recommended operational ranges of the scheduling model are provided to guide real-time communications developers. The applicability of the model is limited by the IEEE 802.5's restricted priority range of eight levels of which only four are typically available to the user. The model is thus limited to application sets which require little priority discrimination. Real-time applications with response time requirements that are harmonically related fall into this category. Although, we would recommend that the priority and reservation fields within the IEEE 802.5 protocol be extended to eight bits, this is unrealistic with the chip sets already commercially available.

The format and protocol data units for the IEEE 802.5 token frame and message frame are provided in Figures 2 and 3[1]. A preemptive priority-driven scheduling environment is implemented on the IEEE 802.5 ring by operating the ring in the following fashion:

1. Single packet-per-token mode with all token timers set to a common value corresponding to the desired schedulable packet size. This packet size will be the globally schedulable message quanta. The actual packet size is chosen by making an engineering trade-off between the high preemptability and responsiveness afforded by small packet sizes against the high overhead associated with fine grain control.
2. Set packet priorities using the algorithms selected in Section 3.1.

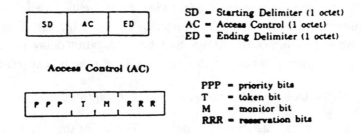

Figure 2. 802.5 token frame format and protocol data units.

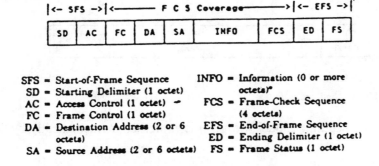

Figure 3. 802.5 message frame format.

Global frame-level contention resolution then comes automatically using the priority and reservation fields within the tokens as follows:

1. Each station examines the reservation field of claimed tokens as the token passes and inserts the priority of its pending packet (if any) if and only if it is greater than the priority currently in the reservation field. This allows the reservation field to reflect the highest priority pending packet in the network.

2. The transmitting station waits until it receives back the claimed token with the reservation field before releasing the next free token with the priority field set to the returned reservation field.
3. Subsequent stations do not capture the free tokens unless the priority of their pending packet (if any) is greater than or equal to the priority field in the free token.
4. Upon capturing the token, transmitting stations append their pending packet behind the token and set the reservation field appropriately. It would have been sufficient to simply reset the reservation field to the lowest priority but the IEEE 802.5 uses a more complex stacking station technique which also provides the desired arbitration environment.

The cycle then repeats providing global priority arbitration for each packet.

The resulting IEEE 802.5 schedulable unit model is illustrated in Figure 4. The frame has the following components:

- FREE TOKEN is the IEEE 802.5 free token frame format illustrated in Figure 2.
- W_T is the ring walk time defined as the time it takes a single bit to propagate around the ring. The walk time shows up in the model twice; once for the free token and once for the message frame. It has two basic components; the bit delay associated with the station's relay delays and latency buffer delays, and the propagation delay associated with propagation down the physical media. The ring walk time may be expressed as

$$W_T = ((N_S-1) \times D_{SB} + Lat\_Buff_{BL})/B_R + Media_L/Media_{PS}.$$

The 802.5 ring has a nominal latency buffer delay of 27 bits for the active monitor and a 2-bit relay delay for all other stations. The latency buffer is required to assure minimum latency and compensate for phase jitter.

- MESSAGE FRAME is the IEEE 802.5 message frame illustrated in Figure 3.

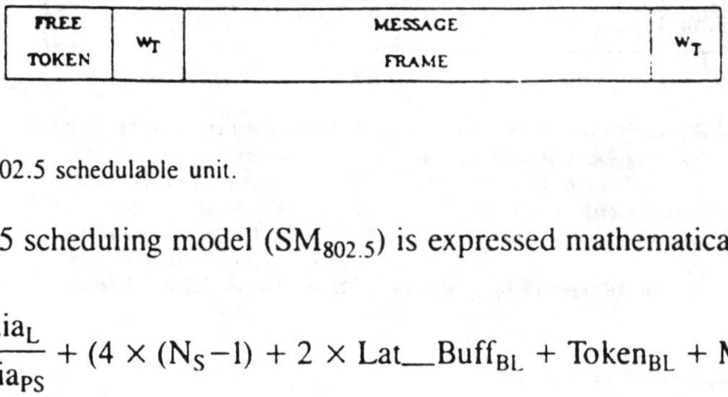

FREE TOKEN	W_T	MESSAGE FRAME	W_T

Figure 4. Model of 802.5 schedulable unit.

The IEEE 802.5 scheduling model ($SM_{802.5}$) is expressed mathematically by the following equation

$$SM_{802.5} = 2\frac{Media_L}{Media_{PS}} + (4 \times (N_S-1) + 2 \times Lat\_Buff_{BL} + Token_{BL} + Msg_{BL})/B_R. \quad [1]$$

The Msg_{BL} will vary depending upon address length and the length of the INFO field. Assuming full addresses and a nominal latency buffer length of 27 bits, equation (1) may be rewritten as

$$SM_{802.5} = 2\frac{Media_L}{Media_{PS}} + (4 \times (N_S-1) + 246 + Packet_{BL})/B_R,$$

where the $Packet_{BL}$ is the bit length of the application packet.

The model assumes the free token makes a full rotation before being claimed. This allows the establishment of a constant schedulable frame rate which greatly simplifies *a priori* timing analysis. For real-time systems covering relatively short distances and small numbers of stations, this assumption imposes a minimal performance penalty. Most real-time systems are in this category. As an example, consider a network of 20 stations each separated by 100 meters transmitting 512 byte packets. Equation (1) yields a schedulable frame time of 1.13 milliseconds. With a ring walk time of 29.59 microseconds, the range of frame times is restricted between 1.10 milliseconds and 1.13 milliseconds resulting in an average loss of less than 2% associated with the worst-case assumption.

Tables 2 and 3 summarize the recommended operational ranges for the IEEE 802.5 scheduling model for 1 Kbyte and 2 Kbyte packet sizes, respectively. The table entries indicate the globally-schedulable, packetized bandwidth (measured in 1 Kbyte packets) available as a function of media length and the number of stations on the network. The tables illustrate the broad operational range of the IEEE 802.5 scheduling model supporting real-time operations in the kilometer range with up to 256 stations. Entries in the tables with asterisks indicate where ring overhead accounts for more than 15% of the schedulable ring utilization. This 15% point is an arbitrary operational threshold chosen as a reasonable rule of thumb. Operation beyond this point further increases the contention overhead, thereby further reducing the model's efficiency. Depending on the particular application, differing packet sizes will be appropriate. Equation (1) may be used to generate other tables with differing packet sizes.

Table 2. Operational range: 1 Kbyte

Stations	Schedulable Packetized Bandwidth			
	50 m.	500 m.	5000 m.	50000 m.
256	423	422	411	330*
128	447	446	434	345
64	460	459	447	352
32	467	466	453	356
16	471	469	456	358
8	472	471	458	359
4	473	472	459	360

*15% contention overhead bound.

Table 3. IEEE 802.5 real-time operational range.

Stations	Schedulable Packetized Bandwidth			
	50 m.	500 m.	5000 m.	50000 m.
256	227	226	223	197
128	233	233	230	202
64	237	237	233	205
32	239	238	235	206
16	240	239	236	207
8	240	240	236	207
4	240	240	237	207

3. 802.5 algorithmic scheduling

Advances in real-time scheduling theory may now be applied to the IEEE 802.5 based LANs using the schedulable frame model provided in Figure 4 along with its associated frame equation, equation (1). In this section, we select algorithms that provide the desired timing behavior, then develop an application example.

3.1. Algorithm selection

The metrics used for algorithm selection for real-time communication are schedulable utilization (schedulability) and responsiveness. Schedulability addresses synchronous message deadline requirements and is defined as the utilization limit for which synchronous message deadlines are guaranteed. Responsiveness addresses the asynchronous message class and is defined to be the timeliness of asynchronous service. Specifically, we define responsiveness in this context to be the end-to-end response time of a single packet including input/output interrupt and transfer overheads.

Liu and Layland (1923) studied the problem of scheduling periodic tasks in the uniprocessor context and determined the optimal fixed and dynamic scheduling algorithms to be the rate monotonic and dynamic deadline algorithms respectively. Liu and Layland derived a worst-case schedulability bound of 69.3% utilization for the rate monotonic algorithm and 100% utilization for the dynamic deadline algorithm. Lehoczky and Sha (1986) later determined the average schedulability bound for rate monotonic scheduling to be 88% utilization.

Although offering higher schedulability performance, dynamic scheduling algorithms require the representation of continuous time which with the limited priority levels available with the IEEE 802.5 standard is impossible. Consequently, the rate monotonic algorithm, as the optimal fixed priority algorithm, is chosen for scheduling synchronous messages. Although the rate monotonic algorithm appears to be the default selection, it offers a very strong combination of high schedulability performance and very low implementation complexity, an attractive feature for real-time systems.

The above algorithms address periodic task/message scheduling assuming that any aperiodic tasks/messages are serviced in a noninterfering, background fashion. This often results in sluggish responsiveness, particularly under high periodic loading conditions. Strosnider (1988) developed the Deferrable Server (DS) algorithm to enhance the responsiveness of asynchronous requests while still guaranteeing periodic class deadlines. Noting that there is no value to the system for the synchronous class messages completing early, the DS algorithm assigns higher priority to asynchronous messages up until the point where the synchronous messages would start to miss their deadlines. High priority asynchronous service is limited by a Deferrable Server which has a fixed capacity. When the server's capacity is exhausted by aperiodic arrivals, additional arrivals are assigned background priority until the Deferrable Server's capacity is replenished at the start of the next period. The priorities of the synchronous class messages are still assigned as in the rate monotonic fashion, but the schedulability bounds are changed (Strosnider 1988).

The DS algorithm creates a periodic server τ_1 with C_1 message capacity with priority defined by the server's period T_1. This server has its entire period to use its C_1 message capacity at P_1 priority. If at the end of the period, any portion of the C_1 is not used, it is discarded. The server's capacity, C_1, is renewed at the beginning of each server period. Assigning the server the highest priority allows us to introduce guaranteed alert class service as well as enhance the responsiveness of soft deadline asynchronous messages. Each node on the LAN that requires either guaranteed alert class service or enhanced asynchronous service establishes a Deferrable Server to manage priority assignment of its incoming asynchronous messages. It is important to note that the available DS capacity, C_1, is not unlimited, but is bounded by the network capacity required to guarantee synchronous messages' deadlines. If the synchronous load component is high, the high priority DS capacity is low, and the number of asynchronous messages which can be assigned high priority service is low. In the following application example, we perform the required schedulability analysis necessary to jointly guarantee the timing correctness of each message class.

3.2. Application example

The preceding section selected the Deferrable Server algorithm as the appropriate preemptive priority scheduling algorithm. In this section we apply the combination of the IEEE 802.5 scheduling models and the Deferrable Server algorithm to an application example. A methodology is presented that demonstrates how to translate the application messages' timing requirements into LAN control parameters. Section 3.2.1 briefly describes the target application. Section 3.2.2 outlines a methodology for selecting the maximum LAN packet size based upon the application's most stringent timing requirements. Section 3.2.3 takes the resulting maximum packet size and evaluates the packetized loading components to determine if all messages will meet their timing requirements.

3.2.1. Application requirements.
Tables 4, 5, and 6 summarize the configuration, asynchronous message, and synchronous message requirements for the example developed here. The example is patterned after a distributed acoustic system made up of 20 processors configured around a LAN. The synchronous message set reflects the requirements for two concurrent modes operating at 12 Hz and 13 Hz. The synchronous load component is driven by periodic sensor data in various stages of processing. The asynchronous load component was selected to reflect the requirements of three classes of asynchronous traffic: high urgency (alert) messages, medium urgency (soft real-time) messages, and low urgency messages. For this work, we characterize and limit alert class messages to occur rarely. Table 5 contains two such high urgency messages (messages 21 and 22) with their associated hard deadline requirements. We included three medium urgency messages of varying lengths to reflect requirements of soft real-time messages. Three low urgency messages that mirror the medium urgency messages were included to provide a direct responsiveness comparison between the two classes.

Table 4. Application configuration data.

LAN Configuration Requirements	
Requirement	Value
Number of Stations	20
Media Length	100 meters
Latency Buffer Length	27 bits
Input Overhead ($Input_{OVH}$)	50 μsec
Output Overhead ($Output_{OVH}$)	50 μsec
Input Transfer Rate ($Input_{rate}$)	48 megabits/sec
Output Transfer Rate ($Output_{rate}$)	48 megabits/sec

Table 5. Application's asynchronous message requirements.

Asynchronous MSG Requirements				
MSG	Length	Mean Interval	Urgency	Hard/Soft Deadline
21	1024 bits	rare	high	1.5 msecond
22	1024 bits	rare	high	1.5 msecond
23	8192 bits	83.3 msec	medium	10 msecond
24	4096 bits	83.3 msec	medium	10 msecond
25	2048 bits	83.3 msec	medium	10 msecond
26	8192 bits	83.3 msec	low	
27	4096 bits	83.3 msec	low	
28	2048 bits	83.3 msec	low	

3.2.2. Maximum packet length selection. Selecting a common maximum packet size for the LAN along with the configuration requirements (length and number of nodes) determines the schedulable frame size and level of preemptability for the network. The choice of a maximum packet size is a trade-off between the conflicting goals of high responsiveness and low overhead. The smaller the packet size, the more highly responsive the system but the higher the control overhead. In general, the maximum packet size that supports the application's response time requirements should be used. For this example, alert message response time requirements from Table 5 dictate a single packet responsiveness of 1.5 milliseconds. The most stringent medium urgency, soft deadline requirements is for message number 23 in Table 5. This message requires four packets to be transferred in 10 milliseconds.

We now determine the maximum packet size needed to guarantee alert class traffic and to provide the desired soft deadline performance for the medium urgency messages. Worst case analysis is used to insure hard deadline alert class service. For this example, the worst case occurs when both alert class messages arrive simultaneously, immediately after another message has captured the token. Both alerts must then wait a single frame time before global arbitration allows them to capture the next token. One of the alerts must then wait another

414

Table 6. Synchronous message requirements.

Synchronous MSG Requirements		
Message	Period	Length
0	76.9 msec	23104 bits
1	76.9 msec	22112 bits
2	76.9 msec	21269 bits
3	76.9 msec	16784 bits
4	76.9 msec	15936 bits
5	76.9 msec	13312 bits
6	76.9 msec	10880 bits
7	76.9 msec	3296 bits
8	76.9 msec	3040 bits
9	76.9 msec	1536 bits
10	76.9 msec	768 bits
11	83.3 msec	4096 bits
12	83.3 msec	21408 bits
13	83.3 msec	19232 bits
14	83.3 msec	608 bits
15	83.3 msec	8448 bits
16	83.3 msec	8192 bits
17	83.3 msec	6656 bits
18	83.3 msec	6544 bits
19	83.3 msec	6400 bits
20	83.3 msec	4672 bits

frame for the other alert to finish before it gains media access. Assuming that the maximum packet size is sufficiently large such that the 1024 bit alerts can be sent in a single packet, the end-to-end worst case response time may be expressed as

$$\text{Resp} = \text{Input}_{OVH} + \text{Alert}_{BL}/\text{Input}_{rate} + F_{802.5}(\text{Max.}) + 2 * F_{802.5}(\text{Alert}_{BL}) \\ + \text{Output}_{OVH} + \text{Alert}_{BL}/\text{Output}_{rate}. \tag{2}$$

where: Input_{OVH} and Output_{OVH} reflect the input and output overheads respectively. Input_{rate} and Output_{rate} reflect the interface data rate to and from device memory, and $F_{802.5}$ is the schedulable frame time obtained from equation (1). Substitution of the application's configuration parameters into equation (1) yields a schedulable frame time equation given by

$$F_{802.5} = 81.83 \ \mu\text{sec} + \text{Packet}_{BL}/4e6. \tag{3}$$

Substituting in: 50 microseconds input/output overhead, input/output bit rate of 48 megabits/second (PC rate), and 1024 bits for the alerts packet length into equation (2) and reducing yields

$$\text{Alerts\_Resp} = 900.2 \ \mu\text{sec} + \text{Maximum Packet}_{BL} \left(\frac{1}{4e6} \right) .$$

The guaranteed alert response times (as a function of maximum packet size) along with the resulting schedulable frame times and media efficiencies are provided in Table 7. From Table 7 we see that the maximum packet size that meets the 1.5 millisecond alert response time requirement is 256 byte packets (1.41 milliseconds guaranteed response time). This packet size yields 1684 globally schedulable packets per second at 86% media efficiency. Media efficiency is defined as the percentage of the schedulable frame time defined in equation (3) spent signalling the information packet onto the media. The total frame time includes the time for control overhead (both token and message frame) plus all propagation and relay delay components as well as the actual packet signalling time.

Table 7. Packet size vs. guaranteed alert response times.

Packets (bytes)	Guaranteed Response	Frame Time	Packets per second	Media Efficiency
128	1.16 msec	0.338 msec	2960	76%
256	1.41 msec	0.594 msec	1684	86%
512	1.92 msec	1.106 msec	904	93%
1024	2.95 msec	2.130 msec	470	96%
2048	5.00 msec	4.178 msec	239	98%
4096	9.09 msec	8.274 msec	121	99%

We now evaluate the soft real-time requirements for the medium urgency messages. In the following, we determine the expected single packet response time for medium urgency class messages as a function of packet size, and then we calculate the expected response times for each of the medium urgency messages. Assuming an "N" frame delay across the LAN, the single packet response time may be expressed as

$$\text{Resp} = \text{Input}_{OVH} + \text{Packet}_{BL}/\text{Input}_{rate} + \text{N}x\text{F}_{802.5} + \text{Output}_{OVH} + \text{Packet}_{BL}/\text{Output}_{rate}. \qquad [4]$$

Substituting and reducing equation (4) yields

$$\text{Resp} = \text{N} \times (81.83\ \mu\text{sec}) + 100\ \mu\text{sec} + \text{Packet}_{BL} \left(\frac{N}{4e6} + \frac{2}{48e6} \right),$$

assuming 50 microseconds input/output overhead plus an input/output bit rate of 48 megabits/second (PC rate). The Deferrable Server algorithm, properly used, will grant nearly instantaneous media access for the asynchronous class as long as it is not overloaded. Assuming two frames transfer time, one frame for access contention and one frame for transfer, we have

$$\text{Resp} = 263.7\ \mu\text{sec} + \text{Packet}_{BL}/(1.85\ e6\ \text{bits/sec}). \qquad [5]$$

Equation (5) represents the expected end-to-end response time per packet. Table 8 provides the expected single packet response times along with the expected response times for the packetized medium urgency messages. Note that this is the expected end-to-end message responsiveness. Overloading the Deferrable Server will degrade the expected performance. In Table 8 we see the response time requirements for all the medium urgency messages are met for the packet sizes evaluated.

Table 8. Expected response times vs. packet size

Packets (bytes)	Single Packet	Message 23	Message 24	Message 25
128	0.82 msec	6.56 msec	3.28 msec	1.64 msec
256	1.37 msec	5.48 msec	2.74 msec	1.37 msec
512	2.48 msec	4.96 msec	2.48 msec	2.48 msec**
1024	4.70 msec	4.70 msec	4.70 msec**	4.70 msec**

**Pessimistic, partial packets not considered.

The alert class response time requirements for this example are the most stringent, limiting the maximum packet size to 256 bytes. The 256 byte packet size yields a guaranteed end-to-end alert deadline of 1.41 milliseconds (1.5 milliseconds is the requirement) and delivers expected response times for the medium urgency messages well under their 10 millisecond requirement. This packet size results in a media efficiency of 86%. The maximum packet size for all the terminals on the network is then set to 256 bytes. The token timers are also set corresponding to the time required to send a single packet so as to prohibit multiple packet-per-token operation. The multiple packet-per-token mode violates the desired scheduling model, and is therefore not allowed. The preceding analysis assumed there was sufficient Deferrable Server capacity available to provide the desired responsiveness. The following section provides the necessary timing and scheduling analysis to verify this assumption.

3.2.3. Timing and scheduling analysis. With a maximum packet size of 256 bytes established, the application messages are now packetized and their utilization components tabulated as shown in Tables 9 and 10. The subtotals for each mode are provided along with the total utilizations. Periodic class priority assignment and Deferrable Server capacity determination and allocation are now addressed.

Table 9. Packetized synchronous utilizations.

MSG	Length (bits)	Packets	Time (ms)	Utilization	MSG	Length (bits)	Packets	Time (ms)	Utilization
0	23104	11.28	6.76	8.8%	11	4096	2.00	1.27	1.5%
1	22112	10.80	6.43	8.4%	12	21408	10.45	6.25	7.5%
2	21269	10.40	6.23	8.1%	13	19232	9.39	5.63	6.8%
3	16784	8.20	4.94	6.4%	14	608	0.30	0.23	0.3%
4	15936	7.78	4.64	6.0%	15	8448	4.13	2.52	3.0%
5	13312	6.50	3.90	5.1%	16	8192	4.00	2.46	2.9%
6	10880	5.31	3.21	4.2%	17	6656	3.25	1.99	2.4%
7	3296	1.61	0.99	1.3%	18	6544	3.20	1.96	2.4%
8	3040	1.48	0.93	1.2%	19	6400	3.13	1.93	2.3%
9	1536	0.75	0.47	0.6%	20	4672	2.25	1.40	1.7%
10	768	0.38	0.28	0.4%					
Subtotal	132,037	64.49	38.5	50.1%	Subtotal	86,256	42.10	25.92	31.2%
Total									81.3%

Message times are calculated according to equation (4). Messages are divided into whole packets and transmitted. Partial packet frame times are also computed with equation (4) using the number of bits they contain.

The IEEE 802.5 has eight levels of priority of which the network reserves the highest for its own use. The application is thus restricted to seven priority levels. Of these, the highest and the lowest are required for the Deferrable Server (preferably the two highest and the lowest) to provide responsive asynchronous service. This leaves four or five levels for synchronous class message scheduling. Fortunately, many real-time systems tend to have harmonically-related task/message sets and/or a small number of unique task/message sets.

Table 10. Packetized asynchronous utilizations.

MSG	Length (bits)	Packets	Time (ms)	Utilization	Urgency
21	1024	0.5	0.34	Low	High
22	1024	0.5	0.34	Low	High
Total				Low	
23	8192	4	2.13	2.6%	Medium
24	4096	2	1.11	1.3%	Medium
25	2048	1	0.59	0.7%	Medium
Total				4.6%	
26	8192	4	2.13	2.6%	Low
27	4096	2	1.11	1.3%	Low
28	2048	1	0.59	0.7%	Low
Total				4.6%	

For this example, synchronous class messages are limited to two periods, 83.3 msec (12 Hz) and 76.9 msec (13 Hz). Applying the rate monotonic algorithm, we assign the 13 Hz messages to priority level 3 and the 12 Hz messages to priority level 2. With the Deferrable Server using levels 0, 5 and 6, this leaves levels 1 and 4 available to support future synchronous messages with differing message periods.

Using subtotals from Table 6, we determine the maximum Deferrable Server capacity that still maintains synchronous class guarantees. The maximum Deferrable Server utilization is determined using straightforward critical zone techniques. Setting the Deferrable Server's period equal to the shortest period synchronous message results in the following utilization for the Deferrable Server

$$U_{DS} = \frac{1}{2} \left(\frac{76.9 - T_{13\,Hz} - T_{12\,Hz}}{76.9} \right), \qquad [6]$$

where $T_{13\,Hz}$ and $T_{12\,Hz}$ are the total media access time (milliseconds) required in each period to service the 13 Hz and 12 Hz messages respectively. Substituting in the values from Table 6, we solve equation (6) to obtain a $U_{DS} = 8.1\%$. With a server period of 76.9 milliseconds, the available access time per period is 6.26 milliseconds or 10.5 packets. The next step is to assign server capacity to the asynchronous messages.

With three priority levels allocated for the Deferrable Server, the asynchronous class messages are assigned to one of three classes:

- Guaranteed high responsive asynchronous messages (alerts)
- Responsive asynchronous messages
- Background asynchronous messages

The guaranteed highly responsive asynchronous class is intended to address the very limited class of fairly rare, high urgency aperiodic messages (alerts). For this example, we have two messages in this class, each 128 bytes long. Guaranteeing deadlines for these two messages requires that 10.7% of the server capacity be allocated for the alerts. These two messages will be assigned the highest priority Deferrable Server, level 6.

With 0.67 milliseconds of the available server capacity assigned to class one, 5.58 milliseconds (9.4 packets) are available every 76.9 milliseconds to service the asynchronous messages in class two. To assure highly responsive service, the Deferrable Server's loading should be limited to less than 70%. For higher loading levels, the value of "N" used in equation (4) needs to be increased. For this example, the mean aperiodic load is 7 packets per 76.9 ms resulting in 74.5% server loading. Although over 70%, high responsiveness will be demonstrated.

The background class messages are not allocated server capacity and will contend for media access at priority level 0. The more messages that the applications designer puts into the background category, the less loaded the Deferrable Servers will be and the higher the responsiveness for the class two messages.

Using the above procedures, we have:

- Established the LANs maximum packet size needed to support the application's most stringent response time requirements.
- Performed scheduling analysis that:
  - Guarantees asynchronous, alert class messages' timing requirements.
  - Guarantees synchronous messages' timing requirements.
  - Predicts asynchronous medium urgency messages' timing requirements.

Note that the above procedures can be automated using standard spreadsheet analysis techniques. This not only provides the disciplined timing environment that support *a priori* verification of timing correctness, but also provides a means of documenting and managing message timing requirements. Further, these procedures can potentially be automated to support dynamic online analysis. In the next section, we conduct simulation experiments to validate the ability of our models and methodologies to accurately predict and guarantee the applications' timing requirements.

4. IEEE 802.5 simulation studies

Network simulation studies for the IEEE 802.5 focus on demonstrating that the algorithms, models, and methodologies developed in this research result in a highly responsive real-time ring that provides *a priori* determination of timing correctness. We use an acoustic-based application example to show how the technology developed in this thesis can be used to:

- Introduce highly responsive, guaranteed alert class message service while still maintaining guaranteed synchronous message class service.
- Introduce highly responsive soft-deadline service for medium urgency asynchronous messages while still maintaining guaranteed synchronous class service.
- Demonstrate how application timing requirements can be translated into LAN control parameters.
- Demonstrate that the technologies developed in this research support *a priori* determination of timing correctness.

We use a LAN simulation package developed by Synetics Corporation as the testbed for these experiments. This paper presents the results of four experiments:

- Experiment 1: IEEE 802.5 Scheduling Model Validation
- Experiment 2: Guaranteed Synchronous Service
- Experiment 3: Enhanced Asynchronous Service
- Experiment 4: TDM Scheduling Comparison

4.1. Experiment 1: 802.5 scheduling model validation

It is first necessary to validate that the IEEE 802.5 LAN can be configured to operate as modeled by equation (1). We set up the Synetics simulator for the example LAN configuration defined earlier in Table 4; 20 nodes, 100 meters media length, and so forth. The maximum packet size and token timers were set to restrict the network to a single packet-per-token operation with values corresponding to 256 byte packets. To eliminate the variability associated with the worst case assumption that the free token makes a full rotation before being claimed, we use a single 100 packet message for testing. The input/output overheads and transfer times are set to zero, and the message is sent. The simulation time needed to send the message is 59.39 milliseconds (0.5939 milliseconds/frame). Equation (1) predicts a frame time of 0.594 milliseconds per frame for this configuration, which is less than 1% error.

4.2. Experiment 2: guaranteed synchronous service

For the next test, we validate that the rate monotonic scheduling algorithm applied to the 802.5 scheduling model developed in this research provides guaranteed synchronous class service. The experiment assigns the 13 Hz message priorities to level 4 and the 12 Hz message priorities to level 3. The asynchronous messages are assigned priorities as follows: alerts to level 2, medium urgency to level 1, and low urgency to level 0. Although there is priority discrimination between the asynchronous message classes, all the asynchronous messages run in the background relative to the synchronous class messages. The average response times and maximum response times for the synchronous and asynchronous messages are shown in Tables 11 and 12 respectively. In Table 11 we see that the response times for the

420

Table 11. Synchronous response times.

MSG	Period	Priority	Updates	Ave. Delay (ms)	Max. Delay (ms)	MSG	Period	Priority	Updates	Ave. Delay (ms)	Max. Delay (ms)
0	76.9	4	650	30.6	31.7	11	83.3	3	600	24.3	48.7
1	76.9	4	650	29.2	30.3	12	83.3	3	600	42.7	60.7
2	76.9	4	650	39.8	41.5	13	83.3	3	600	48.8	65.0
3	76.9	4	650	36.6	37.6	14	83.3	3	600	8.1	37.6
4	76.9	4	650	32.4	33.4	15	83.3	3	600	37.3	57.6
5	76.9	4	650	30.1	31.1	16	83.3	3	600	35.7	56.4
6	76.9	4	650	32.8	33.8	17	83.3	3	600	25.4	49.6
7	76.9	4	650	5.9	7.3	18	83.3	3	600	25.6	49.8
8	76.9	4	650	6.3	7.3	19	83.3	3	600	33.4	54.5
9	76.9	4	650	3.0	4.1	20	83.3	3	600	21.7	46.0
10	76.9	4	650	1.6	4.2						

13 Hz and 12 Hz synchronous messages were always less than 76.9 and 83.3 milliseconds, respectively, thus always making their respective deadlines. Earlier in Table 9 we projected that the 13 Hz and 12 Hz messages would require 38.5 milliseconds and 25.92 milliseconds, respectively, each period. From these numbers we project a worst-case response time of 65.5 milliseconds (38.5 + 25.9 + 1.1). The 1.1 millisecond quantity represents input/output overheads and transfer times. The LAN simulation experiment yields a maximum response 65.0 milliseconds (message 13 in Table 11). Table 12 summarizes the response times for the asynchronous messages running in the background. The average response time for the alerts is almost 20 milliseconds with the maximum response times nearly 60 milliseconds, far greater than the required 1.5 millisecond response times. The average response times for medium urgency asynchronous messages run between 20 and 30 milliseconds with their maximums running up to 85 milliseconds, again exceeding the 10 millisecond requirement. The low urgency messages run at the lowest priority and have long response times due to the heavy loading of this scenario.

Table 12. Background asynchronous responsiveness.

MSG	Urgency	Priority	Updates	Ave. Delay (ms)	Max. Delay (ms)
21	High	2	46	17.9	59.9
22	High	2	46	19.7	58.1
23	Medium	1	613	29.5	85.5
24	Medium	1	649	24.4	65.7
25	Medium	1	1191	21.8	62.8
26	Low	0	648	35.5	198.5
27	Low	0	617	29.8	159.7
28	Low	0	1251	24.6	67.5

This experiment verified that synchronous class deadlines can be guaranteed using the rate monotonic algorithm scheduling algorithm running on the IEEE 802.5 scheduling model developed in this research. Additionally, the experiment provides a point of reference for the following experiment which uses the Deferrable Server scheduling algorithm.

4.3. Experiment 3: enhanced asynchronous responsiveness service

For this experiment, we again use the IEEE 802.5 scheduling model but run the Deferrable Server scheduling algorithm to validate that guaranteed alert class service and enhanced medium urgency asynchronous service can be realized on 802.5 LANs while still maintaining guaranteed synchronous class service. We applied a priority level 6 Deferrable Server to the alert messages and a priority level 5 Deferrable Server to the medium urgency messages. The low urgency messages are left to run in the background. Table 13 shows the simulation response time results for the synchronous messages. Again, all synchronous message deadlines are met, but their slack time has been reduced. Slack time is defined as the difference between the message's deadline and its completion time. In Experiment 2, the minimum slack time was 18.3 milliseconds for message 13 (83.3–65.0). For this experiment, the Deferrable Server algorithm defers synchronous class service allowing the alerts and medium urgency message to run at the high priority level, thus reducing the slack time to 5.8 milliseconds (83.3–77.5). The difference of 12.5 milliseconds works out to be the amount of time required to send 21 packets. Thus 21 asynchronous message packets in one 83.3 millisecond period ran at a priority higher than the synchronous messages supporting enhanced response times while still maintaining synchronous class deadlines.

Table 13. Synchronous response times.

MSG	Period	Priority	Updates	Ave. Delay (ms)	Max. Delay (ms)	MSG	Period	Priority	Updates	Ave. Delay (ms)	Max. Delay (ms)
0	76.9	4	650	32.6	43.3	11	83.3	3	600	26.6	57.4
1	76.9	4	650	31.1	40.2	12	83.3	3	600	45.6	73.2
2	76.9	4	650	41.8	54.7	13	83.3	3	600	51.8	77.5
3	76.9	4	650	39.1	49.8	14	83.3	3	600	7.1	44.3
4	76.9	4	650	34.5	44.5	15	83.3	3	600	40.7	69.9
5	76.9	4	650	32.0	41.0	16	83.3	3	600	39.6	67.9
6	76.9	4	650	34.9	44.8	17	83.3	3	600	27.6	57.1
7	76.9	4	650	6.3	12.0	18	83.3	3	600	28.0	57.9
8	76.9	4	650	6.7	12.4	19	83.3	3	600	35.9	63.8
9	76.9	4	650	3.2	9.1	20	83.3	3	600	23.0	53.4
10	76.9	4	650	1.6	9.2						

Table 14 shows the asynchronous response time results for this experiment. The maximum response time for the guaranteed alert messages is 1.04 milliseconds, thus meeting the 1.5 millisecond requirement. The soft deadline requirements for the medium urgency messages are also well under the 10 millisecond requirement. Earlier in Table 8, we predicted mean response times of 5.48, 2.74, and 1.37 milliseconds respectively for messages 23, 24, and

25 using a 256 byte packet size. The experiment yielded average response times for messages 23, 24, and 25 of 4.5, 2.2, and 1.0 milliseconds, respectively. We have thus demonstrated the ability to *a priori* guarantee timing correctness.

Table 14. Enhanced asynchronous responsiveness.

MSG	Urgency	Priority	Updates	Ave. Delay (ms)	Max. Delay (ms)
21	High	6	56	0.74	1.04
22	High	6	54	0.69	1.03
23	Medium	5	571	4.47	8.81
24	Medium	5	605	2.17	3.80
25	Medium	5	1137	1.03	1.88
26	Low	0	647	32.6	121.8
27	Low	0	597	29.5	72.4
28	Low	0	1199	23.8	71.1

Not only was the timing correctness predicted, but, while maintaining synchronous class guarantees, a highly responsive guaranteed alert class and a greatly enhanced, medium urgency, asynchronous class service was provided.

Table 15 summarizes the performance gains using the Deferrable Server algorithm over the background approach used in Experiment 2. The alert messages not only made their deadlines, but their responsiveness improved 98%. The medium urgency messages typically gain nearly two orders of magnitude (over 90%) improvement in responsiveness. The results show the performance advantage offered by the Deferrable Server algorithm to improve (84.8% to 91.1% to 95.3%) as messages get shorter (4 packets to 2 packets to 1 packet). The responsiveness of background messages would be expected to remain essentially unchanged since they still run at the lowest priority, but some improvement in responsiveness is evident from the experiments. This improvement is an artifact of a simulation model that assigns medium urgency messages to priroity level 0 when the Deferrable Server's capacity is exhausted. This allows the low urgency messages to go sooner than would be expected. Ideally, when the server's capacity is exhausted the medium urgency messages should be assigned priority level 1.

Table 15. DS responsiveness enhancement.

MSG	Urgency	Ave. Delay Enhancement	Max. Delay Enhancement
21	High	95.8%	98.3%
22	High	96.5%	98.2%
23	Medium	84.8%	89.7%
24	Medium	91.1%	94.2%
25	Medium	95.3%	97.0%
26	Low	8.2%	38.6%
27	Low	1.0%	54.7%
28	Low	3.2%	-5.3%

4.4. Experiment 4: TDM scheduling comparison

TDM scheduling on token rings/buses takes the form of high priority round-robin scheduling for the synchronous messages with the asynchronous messages assigned background priority. The size of each slot in the round-robin is set with the token timers and is proportional to the bandwidth needed for each node to support its synchronous message set. For asynchronous class messages (alerts) where background service is inadequate, a slot in the round-robin schedule is reserved for their use, and the message's priority is elevated to the same level as the synchronous class messages. This results in polling type service for alert class asynchronous messages with the polling period equal to the token rotation time. We ran the same application scenario using TDM techniques assigning all the synchronous messages to a common priority level and elevating the two alert class messages to the same priority as the synchronous class messages, thus allocating alerts a slot in the round-robin. We ran the medium urgency messages at priority level 1 and the low urgency passages at priority level 0. Table 16 summarizes the response time results for the synchronous class messages. Again all synchronous message deadlines were met.

Table 16. TDM synchronous response times.

MSG	Period	Priority	Updates	Ave. Delay (ms)	Max. Delay (ms)	MSG	Period	Priority	Updates	Ave. Delay (ms)	Max. Delay (ms)
0	76.9	3	650	39.4	53.7	11	83.3	3	600	14.3	20.7
1	76.9	3	650	37.3	51.7	12	83.3	3	600	34.4	50.7
2	76.9	3	650	52.1	63.6	13	83.3	3	600	41.2	57.2
3	76.9	3	650	49.2	61.0	14	83.3	3	600	1.1	4.1
4	76.9	3	650	41.7	56.0	15	83.3	3	600	28.3	40.8
5	76.9	3	650	38.1	52.6	16	83.3	3	600	27.9	39.8
6	76.9	3	650	42.5	56.8	17	83.3	3	600	15.3	21.5
7	76.9	3	650	7.5	15.1	18	83.3	3	600	15.5	21.7
8	76.9	3	650	7.8	15.5	19	83.3	3	600	23.3	33.2
9	76.9	3	650	3.3	5.9	20	83.3	3	600	10.6	15.6
10	76.9	4	650	1.8	5.4						

Table 17 shows the asynchronous response time results using TDM. The maximum response time for the alert messages is 6.4 milliseconds. This time arises from an alert message having to wait its turn within the round-robin with the synchronous messages. The performance of the medium urgency messages is only marginally better than the low urgency messages with average response time ranging from 22.1 to 29.8 milliseconds and maximum response times ranging from 61.5 to 95.0 milliseconds. Neither the alerts nor the medium urgency asynchronous messages met their response time requirements.

Table 17. TDM asynchronous responsiveness.

MSG	Urgency	Priority	Updates	Ave. Delay (ms)	Max. Delay (ms)
21	High	3	48	1.22	3.78
22	High	3	57	1.21	6.40
23	Medium	1	636	29.8	95.0
24	Medium	1	610	26.2	65.0
25	Medium	1	1190	22.1	61.6
26	Low	0	566	34.1	143.9
27	Low	0	570	28.3	92.5
28	Low	0	1166	24.7	69.5

Table 18 summarizes the performance advantage using the Deferrable Server algorithm (Experiment 2) over the TDM techniques used in this experiment. TDM alerts took two to three times longer to complete than it took using the Deferrable Server algorithm. The big difference was with the response times for the medium urgency asynchronous messages. For this case, the Deferrable Server had a response time advantage of nearly two orders of magnitude. Overall, the TDM approach provides a level of service comparable to the 802.5 scheduling model running the asynchronous messages at background priority (Experiment 2). This experiment demonstrates the performance gains possible when using the technology developed in this research over conventional TDM techniques.

Table 18. DS enhancement over TDM

MSG	Urgency	Ave. Delay Enhancement	Max. Delay Enhancement
21	High	39.3%	72.5%
22	High	43.0%	83.9%
23	Medium	85.0%	90.7%
24	Medium	91.7%	94.1%
25	Medium	95.3%	96.9%
26	Low	4.4%	15.4%
27	Low	-4.2%	21.7%
28	Low	3.6%	-2.3%

5. Implementation notes

When implementing a Token Ring Chipset or a Network Adapter Card, system designers must incorporate a number of requirements in order to realize the performance potential of this technology. These requirements fall under the area of concurrency control and buffer management. In general, when there is concurrency, preemptive priority-based arbitration should be used. Where there is queueing, priority queues, as opposed to FIFO queues, should be used. Failure to adhere to these basic guidelines can result in the loss of predictability and serious degradation in the response time performance. In the following paragraphs, we provide general implementation guidelines for IEEE 802.5 implementations along with specific recommendations for implementations using Texas Instruments' TMS380 Adapter Chipset.

5.1. Concurrency control and buffer management

In real-time systems, it is important that consistent priority-based concurrency management be used between and within each layer of the protocol stack. Ideally the priority granularity, resource sharing, and the degree of preemptability should be uniform up and down the protocol stack. In reality, there are significant variations up and down the protocol stack with the higher layers in the protocol stack typically having a greater degree of priority discrimination than the lower levels. Further, the degree of preemptability can vary radically. As an implementor, it is important to minimize these differences so as not to introduce undesirable artifacts into the communications subsystem.

When a process accesses a queue of pending messages, the pending message with the highest priority should be serviced first. Otherwise system schedulability and responsiveness are compromised by priority inversions. Priority inversion is said to occur when a higher priority message is blocked behind a lower priority message. This can occur at any level within the protocol stack. Queues in the higher layers of the protocol stack are typically software queues, which are flexible and easy to implement. Thus existing FIFO queues at these layers are easily modified to true Priority Queues[2]. Queues at lower layers require higher operating speeds. Thus lower layers, including the ISO Reference Model's Data Link Layer[3], often use less-flexible but faster hardware queues. Here we are concerned with priority inversion caused by the hardware implementations using FIFO queueing. If FIFO queues must be used, there are methods to minimize the performance degradations. Available methods are based on the concept of priority inheritance (Sha, Rajkumar, and Lehoczky 1988), in which lower priority tasks contend for media access using the priority of the higher priority tasks which they are blocking. These methods reduce the blocking time and expedite the service of the high priority task.

Concurrency management guidelines are summarized as follows:

- When concurrency is supported within a protocol layer, priority-based arbitration should be used to insure threads are serviced in priority order. At least three bits of priority are required, and eight bits of priority should be provided wherever possible. Ties between equal priorities can be broken arbitrarily. However, a user-programmable, tie-breaking facility is desirable.
- Priority granularity should be consistent from the bottom to the top of the protocol stack. When not possible, resources should be provided to support mapping priorities between protocol layers. These mapping functions should be programmable by the network management function.
- At all times, peer-to-peer priority consistency and visibility should be maintained. For example, the priority at the User Agent on the transmit side should be visible on the receive side at the User Agent protocol level.

- When there are queues within and between the protocol layers, they should be priority queues wherever possible. An eight deep queue is sufficient for all but the most rigorous applications. If a FIFO queue must be used, it should not be more than two deep and should support priority inheritance.
- To bound blocking durations and maintain responsiveness, the maximum length of block transfers and frames should be programmable under the control of higher level network management functions.

5.2. TMS380 limitations

The Texas Instruments TMS380 Adapter Chipset is a commercially available implementation of IEEE 802.5 standard. Unfortunately, the TMS380 Chipset has a number of features which artificially limit the performance potential of this realization of the IEEE 802.5 standard. We have already mentioned that the IEEE 802.5 standard specifies only eight priority levels. However, the TMS380 Adapter Chipset is even more restrictive and provides only four priority levels.

The greatest problem, with regard to ring scheduling, is that the Transmit Buffers in the Adapter Chipset RAM are managed as a FIFO Queue. Frames are DMA'ed into the Transmit Buffers before being signalled onto the ring. Nodes contend for ring access using the priority of the frame at the head of their Transmit FIFO Queue. When a higher priority frame enters the Transmit FIFO and finds itself behind a lower priority frame, it is desirable to be able to suspend transmission of the lower priority frame(s) in favor of the higher priority frames. Unfortunately the TMS380 Chipset does not feature a Frame Suspend capability. Instead, a more expensive TRANSMIT HALT command is provided. When invoked, this command destroys the contents of the Transmit FIFO Queue and terminates the Transmit Process. That station must re-issue the transmit command before it can transmit subsequent frames. Alternatively, the signalling station could use the priority of the higher priority frame when contending for media access for the lower priority frames[4]. This would bound the blocking time of high priority messages. Unfortunately, the TMS380 Chipset does not support a Priority Inheritance mechanism either. The absence of these capabilities degrades both performance and analyzability.

6. Conclusions

In this paper, we outlined the problems encountered using TDM-based scheduling; in particular, that the inflexibility of TDM-based scheduling in LANs will limit their applicability in highly dynamic, adaptive real-time environments. We noted that the IEEE 802.5 is generally scheduled using TDM techniques by setting the stations' token timers proportional to their synchronous bandwidth requirements. Scheduling models/methodologies were developed that support algorithmic media access scheduling as opposed to conventional TDM-based scheduling. We selected real-time scheduling algorithms that:

- Guarantee synchronous class message deadlines.
- Guarantee asynchronous alert class message deadlines.
- Dramatically reduce (nearly two orders of magnitude) asynchronous class response times.

An application example was developed to illustrate how application timing requirements can be translated into operational LAN parameters, maximum packet size, priority assignment, and so forth. We then transported the application example to a LAN simulator testbed for experimentation. The IEEE 802.5 scheduling model, equation (1), was validated. We demonstrated that the *a priori* timing predictions were met providing guaranteed alert class service and greatly enhanced asynchronous responsiveness while still maintaining synchronous class guarantees. The procedures and algorithms may be readily automated allowing the IEEE 802.5 to support dynamic, adaptive, and reconfigurable run-time environments where the inflexibility of TDM would be prohibitive. Further, we demonstrated asynchronous message response time improvements of nearly two orders of magnitude using the technology developed in this research over the conventional TDM approach.

In the final section, we provided implementation guidelines that need to be followed to realize the full potential of this technology using the IEEE 802.5 standard. Proper implementations will result in a highly responsive real-time LAN that can form the backbone of predictable, stable, extensible real-time systems.

Acknowledgement

The authors wish to thank Harry Gold of the FCDSSASD Navy Command in San Diego for his time and effort in extending the Synetics Corporation LAN simulator to support our research.

Notes

1. Repeated from ANSI/IEEE Std. 802.5 — 1985 pages 27 and 28.
2. Priority Queues offer the task with the highest priority for execution, regardless of the arrival time of other pending tasks.
3. The Data Link Layer is usually implemented on the network adapter card.
4. Here the frame of lower priority *inherits* the higher priority for media contention purposes only. The receiving node uses the original frame priority when processing the frame.

References

Dailey, G.E. 1983. Distributed systems data bus, external audit — PDR, 03J/04273/03. Tech. report (May). IBM FSD. Manassas, Virginia.

Hood, P., and V. Grover. 1986. Designing real time systems in Ada. Tech. report 1123-1 (8 Jan.). SofTech, Inc. 460 Totten Pond Road, Waltham, Massachusetts.

Kopetz, Hermann, et. al. 1989. Distributed fault-tolerant real-time systems: The MARS approach. *IEEE Micro*, 9, 1 (Feb.), 25–40.

Lehoczky, J.P., and L. Sha. 1986. Performance of real-time bus scheduling algorithms. *ACM Performance Evaluation Review*, *Special Issue*, 14, 1 (May).

Le Lann, G. 1988. Real-time communications systems. Tech. report, *Real-Time Communications Workshop* (NASA-JSC, Houston, Texas, January 21-22).

Liu, C.L. and J.W. Layland. 1973. Scheduling algorithms for multiprogramming in a hard real-time environment. *JACM*, 20, 1:40–61.

Rajkumar, R. 1986. Scheduling periodic tasks with hard deadlines and data input/output. Master's thesis (Oct.), Department of Electrical and Computer Engineering, Carnegie-Mellon University.

Rothauser, E.H., and D. Wild. 1977. MLMA-A collision-free multi-access method. *Proc. JFIP Congress 77.*

SAE-9B. 1986. SAE AE9-B high speed data bus standard. Tech. report Issue 1, Draft 2 (Jan. 21). Society of Automotive Engineers, Subcommittee 9-B.

Sha, L., R. Rajkumar, and J.P. Lehoczky. 1988. Priority inheritance protocols: an approach to real-time synchronization. Accepted for publication in *IEEE Transactions on Computers.*

Stankovic, John A. 1989. A serious problem for the next-generation systems. *Computer* (Oct.), 10–19.

Strosnider, Jay K. 1988. Highly Responsive Real-Time Token Rings (Aug.). PhD dissertation, Carnegie Mellon University.

Tannenbaum, Andrew S. 1981. *Computer Networks.* Prentice-Hall.

Zhao, W., and K. Ramamitham. 1986. A virtual time CSMA protocol for hard real time communications. *IEEE Real-Time Systems Symposium.*

Zhao, W., J. Stankovic, and K. Ramamitham. 1988. A window protocol for transmission of time contrained messages. *Proceedings of the 8th International Conference on Distributed Computing Systems.*

Synchronous Atomic Broadcast for Redundant Broadcast Channels

FLAVIU CRISTIAN

IBM Almaden Research Center, 650 Harry Road, San Jose, California 95120-6099

Abstract. We propose a synchronous atomic broadcast protocol for distributed real-time systems based on redundant broadcast channels. The protocol can tolerate a finite number f of concurrent processor crash failures, channel adapter performance failures and channel omission failures. Its message cost is optimal: when no failures occur only $f + 1$ messages are sent per broadcast. The cost implications of providing tolerance to other failure classes are also investigated.

1. Introduction

To achieve high-availability of a computing service despite failures, a key idea is to implement the service by a group of processes running on distinct processors. Replication of service state information among group members enables the group to provide the service even when some of its members fail since the remaining members know enough about the service state to be able to continue to provide it. Replication creates a need for a *communication service* which can be used by processes to disseminate state updates so that replica consistency is maintained despite random message delays and component failures. This communication service is variously termed reliable (Chang and Maxemchuck 1984) or atomic (Cristian, Aghili, Strong and Dolev 1985) broadcast. We will refer to it as *atomic broadcast*. Two classes of protocols for atomic broadcast have been proposed to date: *synchronous* protocols, such as (Babaoglu and Drummond 1985) and (Cristian, Aghili, Strong and Dolev 1985), which rely on synchronized clocks and the passage of clock time to achieve replica consistency, and *asynchronous* protocols, such as (Birman and Joseph 1987; Carr 1985; Chang and Maxemchuck 1984; Garcia-Molina and Spauster 1989; Lamport 1989; Melliar-Smith and Moser 1989; Verissimo, Rodrigues and Marques 1987), which use message acknowledgments.

A synchronous atomic broadcast protocol ensures the existence of a time constant Δ such that, even if up to f failures occur during a broadcast, the following properties are satisfied. *Atomicity*: if any correct processor delivers an update at time U on its clock, then that update was initiated by some processor and is delivered by all correct processors at time U on their clocks; *Order*: all updates delivered by correct processors are delivered in the same order by each correct processor; and *Termination*: every update whose broadcast is initiated by a correct processor at time T on its clock is delivered by all correct processors at time $T + \Delta$ on their clocks. The atomicity and order properties ensure that the same updates are applied to all correct replicas in the same order. Therefore, if replicas are initially consistent, they stay consistent. The termination property ensures that updates broadcast by correct processors are applied to each correct replica Δ time units later. In this way, all correct replicas display identical contents at identical clock times.

Synchronous atomic broadcast protocols are needed for critical real-time applications which must enforce bounds on response times even when component failures occur. This bounds are achieved by assuming that message delays among correct processors are bounded and there exist enough redundant communication paths between processors so that, if all paths are used in parallel for a broadcast, the probability that all fail during the broadcast is negligible. The bounded message delays assumption requires that the processors which implement a synchronous protocol be controlled by real-time operating systems capable of guaranteeing bounds on task scheduling delays. When message delays are not bounded, that is, communication performance failures causing partitions can occur, broadcast termination within a bounded time cannot be guaranteed. Asynchronous atomic broadcast protocols sacrifice termination for the sake of providing tolerance to communication performance failures, including partition failures. Because they do not guarantee a bound on the time it takes to broadcast an information in the presence of failures, asynchronous atomic broadcast protocols cannot be used in critical applications which must ensure that deadlines are always met (even in the presence of component failure occurrences). However, since asynchronous protocols do not require that communication delays be bounded, they can be implemented by processors controlled by conventional time-sharing (non real-time) operating systems, for applications where the cost of missing some deadlines is not too high.

This paper proposes a synchronous atomic broadcast protocol for distributed real-time systems based on redundant broadcast channels. Examples of popular broadcast channels are Ethernet, Token Bus, Token Ring, and fiber optic FDDI. To broadcast an update in the absence of failures (that is, the vast majority of times), the protocol sends $f + 1$ messages, independently of the number n of processors participating in broadcast. We show that this is the minimum failure-free message overhead that must be spent to achieve both atomicity and termination despite up to f failures, so our protocol is optimal in this respect. The very low message overhead makes the protocol scalable to systems with large numbers of processors.

The failure classes considered are processor crashes, channel adapter performance failures, and channel omission failures. The paper uses the nested failure classification of (Cristian, Aghili, Strong and Dolev 1985), which we briefly recall. An *omission* failure occurs when a component omits to respond to an input event; we talk of a *crash* failure when after a first omission the component systematically omits to respond to subsequent input events until restart. A *timing* failure occurs when a component either omits to respond or responds too early or too late. Most of the timing failures observed in practice are late timing failures, or *performance* failures. Crash failures are a subclass of omission failures, omission failures are a subclass of timing failures, and timing failures are a subclass of the class of all (or *arbitrary*) failures.

We begin by stating our assumptions. We then describe the basic idea behind our protocol. A detailed protocol description follows. The cost implications of providing tolerance to other failure classes are then briefly investigated. A comparison with previous work concludes the paper.

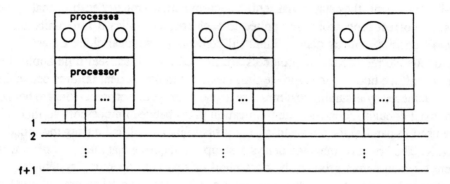

Figure 1. System model.

2. System model and assumptions

We consider a system of *processes* which maintain replicated state information. Updates to replicas are disseminated by using the atomic broadcast service implemented by n distributed *processors* with different, totally ordered, names. Each processor is connected via $f + 1$ independent channel *adapters* to $f + 1$ independent broadcast *channels* (see Figure 1).

A process can ask a processor to broadcast an update σ by invoking a *SEND* command. To receive broadcasts from its underlying processor a process invokes a *RECEIVE* command. Each adapter contains buffer memory, logic to control access to its channel, as well as logic for sending messages to and receiving messages from the channel. It is convenient to understand each adapter as being composed of two unidirectional halves: an *out-adapter*, which accepts messages from its attached processor and transmits them on the channel, and an *in-adapter* which accepts messages from the channel and delivers them to its attached processor. To transmit a message on a channel c, a processor invokes a *send* command on the out-adapter for c. To receive a broadcast message from its attached in-adapters, a processor invokes a *receive* command. After a message is entrusted to an out-adapter for transmission, it waits in the out-adapter buffer memory until its transmission on the channel becomes possible. Whenever an out-adapter gets control of its attached channel c, it inserts a message on c. The broadcast channel c then delivers the message to all in-adapters connected to it. As in-adapters receive messages, they deliver them to their attached processors, which in turn deliver updates to their processes.

We make the following assumptions.

1. *Bounded broadcast rate.* The rate at which updates are generated is bounded. This bound is smaller than the rate at which processors can *receive* the messages which carry the updates as well as the rate at which processes can *RECEIVE* these updates.
2. *Broadcast channels suffer only omission failures.* The error detecting codes used by the physical channel transmission protocol detect any message corruption due to transmission errors, so that corrupted messages can be discarded by in-adapters. Thus, a channel c can behave in only the following two ways. When no channel failure occurs a message m transmitted on c is delivered to all correct in-adapters attached to c within a short

432

constant time C, as measured on any correct processor clock. When a channel failure occurs only a (possibly empty) subset of the in-adapters attached to c get m within C clock time units from its insertion on c. In all cases, the message m disappears from the channel C clock time units after its transmission began.

3. *Out-adapters suffer only performance failures.* Under normal circumstances, the delay between the moment a processor enqueues a message m on an out-adapter by invoking a *send* command and the moment the out-adapter begins to successfully transmit m on its attached channel is bounded in time by a constant O, as measured on any correct processor clock. Temporarily, this delay can become greater than O. For example, in a Token Ring, the loss of a token can delay all messages enqueued in out-adapters until a new token is regenerated. Similarly, the occurrence of too many collisions on an Ethernet can result in excessive delays between the moment an out-adapter attempts to transmit a message and the moment the adapter successfully transmits the message without detecting further collisions. Thus, in response to a *send(m)* event, an out-adapter o can behave in only the following two ways: either o successfully sends m on its attached channel c within O clock time units, or o suffers a performance failure. When o fails to insert m on c within O clock time units, it might either send m on c later or it might never send m on c.

4. *In-adapters suffer only omission failures.* The delay between the moment a channel delivers a message to an in-adapter and the moment the message is *received* by the attached processor is bounded in time by a constant I, as measured on any correct processor clock. Thus, an in-adapter can only behave in one of the following two ways: when it receives a message m from its attached channel, it either delivers m to its processor within I clock time units from the receipt of m or it never delivers m.

5. *Processors suffer only crash failures.* The delay between the moment a processor initiates processing a $SEND(\sigma)$ command invoked by a process and the moment the processor finishes enqueueing messages containing σ on all its $f + 1$ attached out-adapters is bounded by a time constant P, as measured on any correct processor clock. We also assume that P is a bound on the delay which can elapse between the moment an adapter is ready to deliver a message m to a processor p and the moment p *receives* and processes m. To ensure that this assumption holds at run-time, it is necessary that the operating system(s) controlling the processors be real-time executive(s), capable of enforcing bounded delays for processing atomic broadcast messages under worst case load conditions. Under this assumption, a processor p which interprets a $SEND(\sigma)$ command issued by a process can behave only in the following two ways. Either p correctly enqueues messages m containing σ on all its attached out-adapters within P time units, or p crashes after enqueueing m only on a (possibly empty) subset of adapters within P time units. In the latter case, m is never enqueued on the remaining out-adapters.

6. *Processors have access to correct clocks that are approximately synchronized.* A correct clock drifts from real time at a rate whose absolute value is bound by a small, manufacturer specified, constant ρ. A correct clock also yields different, monotonically increasing time values each time it is read. We assume that processor clocks are approximately synchronized within a known, constant, maximum deviation ϵ. (A clock synchronization algorithm that works under the above assumptions on processors, adapters and channels can be found in (Cristian 1989).)

7. *Tasks can be scheduled for certain deadlines.* The real-time executive controlling the execution of processors provides a *schedule A(B) at T* command that allows a task (or process) *A* to be scheduled for execution at local time *T* with input parameters *B*. An invocation of *schedule A(B) at T* at a local time $U > T$ has no effect, and multiple invocations of *schedule A(B) at T* have the same effect as a single invocation.

8. *At most $f \leq n - 2$ components can be faulty during a broadcast.* By a component, we mean a processor, an adapter, or a channel. This assumption ensures that if a correct processor *s* successfully completes executing *send(m)* commands on all its $f + 1$ out-adapters, then *m* will be received by each correct processor *r*. Indeed, there exist $f + 1$ independent *paths*, which we denote $1, 2, \ldots, f + 1$, between *s* and *r*, where path *c* consists of the out-adapter interfacing *s* to channel *c*, the channel *c*, and the in-adapter interfacing *c* to *r*. At most *f* faulty components leave all components on at least one path between *s* and *r* correct, thus, *r* receives a copy of *m* on at least this path. (Algorithms that detect at run-time a violation of this assumption and recover from such events are described in (Strong, Skeen, Cristian and Aghili 1987).)

3. Basic idea: lazy forwarding

Assumptions 2-6, ensure that, in the absence of failures, any update σ accepted for broadcast by a processor *s* at time *T* on its clock, is received and processed by any processor *q* by time $T + \delta + \epsilon$ on *q*'s clock, were $\delta = P + O + C + I + P$ denotes the processor-to-processor message delay bound. The term ϵ has to be added because *q*'s clock can be as far as ϵ time units ahead of the clock of *s*.

In the presence of failures, the situation is more complicated. If at least two failures can occur during a broadcast ($f > 1$), then a correct processor *q* may not receive by time $T + \delta + \epsilon$ on its clock a message *m* sent by a processor *s* at time *T* on its clock, while another correct processor *r* may receive *m* by $T + \delta + \epsilon$ on its clock. To see how this is possible, consider the following scenario: the sender *s* crashes after enqueuing *m* only on the out-adapter for channel 1, and a transmission error on channel 1 corrupts *m* after it is delivered to the in-adapter for *r* and before it arrives at the in-adapter for *q* (Figure 2). The first adapter will deliver *m* to *r* while the second adapter will discard the corrupted

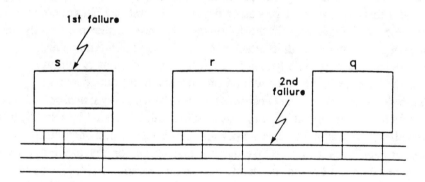

Figure 2. Failure scenario showing the need for message forwarding.

message it receives. Thus, when $f > 1$, it is sometimes necessary that a processor which receives a new message m forward it, to ensure m is received by all correct processors.

One possible rule for message forwarding is that described in (Cristian, Aghili, Strong and Dolev 1985): a processor forwards any new message it receives from a channel on all other channels as soon as it receives the message. With this *prompt forwarding* rule, $(f + 1) + (n - 1)f = nf + 1$ messages are sent per broadcast. The main drawback is that message forwarding always takes place, even when no failures occur (the vast majority of cases). The protocol we present is based on a new, lazy forwarding rule. The goal is to not forward when there is no need to, for example when no failures occur. A simple version of the rule follows. The complete rule is given later.

Simple lazy forwarding rule. A sending processor s enqueues any message m to be broadcast on the out-adapters to channels $1, 2, \ldots, f + 1$ in this (increasing) order. Let p be an arbitrary processor different from s that receives m and let c be the highest channel number on which p receives a copy of m. If $c \geq f$ then p does not need to forward m, else, p forwards m on channels $c + 1, \ldots, f$.

The above forwarding rule ensures the following *unanimity* property: if a processor s initiates the broadcast of a message m and some correct processor p receives m, then any correct processor q receives m. (When m does not reach any correct processor—this can only happen if s is faulty—there is no need to worry about forwarding m, since the atomic broadcast specification allows for the case that no correct processor delivers a message when its initiator fails.) We prove the above property as follows. Consider the two possible cases (a) $c \geq f$ and (b) $c < f$. If $c = f + 1$ then s enqueued m on all its $f + 1$ out-adapters, so the at most f components which can fail during the broadcast of m cannot prevent an arbitrary correct processors q from receiving at least a copy of m (remember there are $f + 1$ independent communication paths between s and q). If $c = f$ then (a1) either s correctly sent m on all its out-adapters and a failure on the path $f + 1$ between s and r prevented r from receiving m from its $f + 1$ in-adapter or, (a2) m was only sent by s on channels $1, 2, \ldots, f$ (because s crashed). We have already mentioned that when s sends m correctly on all channels, all correct processors get at least one copy of it, thus, if (a1) is true, any correct processor q gets m. If (a2) is true, the crash of s counts as one failure. Since by assumption 8 we assume that at most f components can fail during the broadcast of m, it follows that besides the faulty sender s there exist at most $f - 1$ other faulty components. These cannot prevent a correct processor q from getting at least a copy of the message m broadcast on the f independent paths numbered $1 \ldots f$. Consider now case (b): $c < f$. This can only happen when at least one failure has occurred before the correct processor r received m: either s crashed or a channel with number higher than c failed, or an adapter attached to such a channel failed. Since processor r forwards m on channels $c + 1, \ldots, f$, and the at most $f - 1$ additional faulty components which, by assumption 8, may exist cannot affect all of the f disjoint communication paths $1, 2, \ldots, f$ on which copies of m were sent (by s and r), it follows that any correct processor q must receive at least one copy of m on one of these paths.

The key advantage of lazy forwarding is that, in the absence of failures, only $f + 1$ messages are sent per broadcast. Since in a general system, no processor p knows in advance the time at which another processor s chooses to broadcast, $f + 1$ is the *minimum* number of messages that must be sent if both atomicity and termination must be provided despite up to f component failures. The minimality of the $f + 1$ message overhead can be proven by contradiction as follows. Assume there exists a synchronous atomic broadcast protocol P, tolerant of up to f component failures and having termination time Δ, which, in the absence of failures, uses only $k \leq f$ messages to atomically broadcast an update. Consider now a broadcast scenario S in which a sender s broadcasts an update σ at time T on its clock and no failures occur during the broadcast of σ, so that all processors deliver σ at time $T + \Delta$ on their clocks. Since by assumption 8: $k \leq n - 2$, it follows that at least two correct processors p and q do not send messages in S. Consider now another broadcast scenario S' in which s broadcasts the update σ as in S and all k in-adapters interfacing the correct processor q to the k channels on which σ was transmitted fail. Scenarios S and S' are indistinguishable to correct processor p by construction. Since p delivers σ at $T + \Delta$ in S, p also delivers σ in S'. On the other hand, scenario S' was constructed so that q will not know by $T + \Delta$ that s has initiated a broadcast at time T, so q will not deliver σ at $T + \Delta$ in S', thereby violating the atomicity property that P is supposed to achieve. Thus, the hypothesized protocol P does not exist.

4. Detailed protocol description

We begin our detailed description by first considering the simpler case of providing tolerance to a single failure ($f = 1$). In this particular case no forwarding is necessary, since a single failure cannot cause both independent communication paths between two correct processors to fail. By first studying this simple—but practically important—case, we hope to make it easier to follow the description of the more complex protocol for $f > 1$.

4.1. The single-fault tolerant protocol

Each message broadcast by a processor carries its initiation time (or *timestamp*) T, the name of the source processor s, and an update σ. Since all processor names are distinct, and by assumption 6 each clock reading yields a different value, the T and s values uniquely identify each broadcast. As messages are received by a processor p, these are processed and stored in a *history* log H, local to p, until p delivers them to its local processes. The order property required of atomic broadcasts is achieved by letting each processor deliver the updates it receives in timestamp order, by ordering the delivery of updates with identical timestamps in increasing order of their initiator's name, and by ensuring that no correct processor p begins the delivery of updates timestamped T before time $T + \delta + \epsilon$ on its clock, at which point p is certain that it has received all updates with timestamp at most T that it may ever have to deliver. We call the time $\Delta = \delta + \epsilon$ the protocol *termination time*, and $T + \Delta$ the *delivery time* for updates with timestamp T.

To keep the local history H finite, messages are purged from H when the updates contained in them are delivered. However, a simple-minded application of the above garbage-collection rule would not be sufficient for ensuring that local histories remain bounded, since it is possible that copies of a message (T, s, σ) continue to be reeived by a correct processor p after the delivery time $T + \Delta$ has passed on p's clock (for example because an out-adapter attached to the sending processor suffers a performance failure). To prevent such late residual messages from accumulating in local histories, we use a *late message acceptance test*. This test discards a message (T, s, σ) if it arrives at a local time U past the delivery time $T + \Delta$, that is, if $U \geq T + \Delta$. The late message acceptance test and assumption 1 ensure that local histories stay bounded.

A detailed description of the single-fault tolerant atomic broadcast protocol is given in Figures 3, 4, and 5. Each processor runs three concurrent tasks: a Start task (Figure 3)

```
1  task Start;
2     const Δ = δ + ε;
3     var T: Time; σ: Update; s: Processor;
4     cycle SEND(σ); T←clock;
5        for c = 1 to 2 do send(T,myid,σ) on c;
6        H←H⊕(T,myid,σ);
7        schedule Deliver(T) at T + Δ;
8     endcycle;
```

Figure 3. Start Task of the single-fault tolerant protocol.

```
1  task Receive;
2     const Δ = δ + ε;
3     var U,T: Time; σ: Update; s: Processor;
4     cycle receive(T,s,σ) from c; U←clock;
5        if U≥T + Δ then "late message" iterate fi;
6        if T∈dom(H)&s∈dom(H(T)) then "deja vu" iterate fi;
7        H←H⊕(T,s,σ);
8        schedule Deliver(T) at T + Δ;
9     endcycle;
```

Figure 4. Receive Task of the single-fault tolerant protocol.

```
1  task Deliver(T:Time);
2     var p: Processor; val: Processor → Update;
3     val←H(T);
4     while dom(val)≠{}
5     do p←min(dom(val));
6        RECEIVE(val(p));
7        val←val\p;
8     od;
9     H←H\T;
```

Figure 5. Deliver Task of the single-fault tolerant protocol.

that initiates atomic broadcasts, a Receive task (Figure 4) that receives atomic broadcast messages and a Deliver task (Figure 5) that delivers broadcast updates to processes which invoke *RECEIVE* commands. In what follows we refer to line j of figure i as $(i.j)$.

A process triggers the broadcast of an update σ by invoking the $SEND(\sigma)$ command exported by its local processor. This will activate the Start task at the matching $\overline{SEND}$ entry point with σ as input (3.4). The broadcast of σ is identified by the local time T at which σ is received (3.4) and the identity of the sending processor, obtained by invoking the function *myid* (3.5). This function returns different processor identifiers when invoked by distinct processors. The broadcast of σ then proceeds by invoking the *send* command exported by the out-adapters to channels 1, 2 (3.5). We do not assume that the FOR loop command is atomic with respect to crashes: a processor crash can prevent messages from being sent on some out-adapters. The fact that the broadcast of σ has been initiated is then recorded in the history variable H shared by all broadcast tasks:

$$var\ H\text{: Time} \rightarrow \text{(Processor} \rightarrow \text{Update)}.$$

We assume H is initialized to the empty function at processor start. The variable H keeps track of ongoing broadcasts by associating with instants T in Time a function $H(T)$ (of type Processor $\rightarrow$ Update). The domain of $H(T)$, denoted dom($H(T)$), consists of names of processors that have initiated atomic broadcasts at time T on their clock. For each such processor p, $H(T)(p)$ is the update broadcast by p at T. We use the following operators on histories. The update "$\oplus$" of a history H by a message (T, s, σ) yields a (longer) history, denoted $H \oplus (T, s, \sigma)$, that contains all the facts in H, plus the fact that s has broadcast σ at local time T. The deletion "\" of some instant T from a history H yields a (shorter) history, denoted $H \backslash T$, which does not contain T in its domain, that is, everything about the broadcasts that were initiated at time T is deleted. Once the history H is updated (3.6), the Deliver task is scheduled to deliver σ at local clock time $T + \Delta$ (3.7).

The Receive task uses the *receive* command to receive messages formatted as (T, s, σ) from in-adapters. The identity c of the channel on which a message is received is a return parameter of this command (4.4). In describing this task, we use double quotes to delimit comments and the command *iterate* to mean *terminate the current iteration and begin the next cycle*, (4.5, 4.6). If a received message is a duplicate of a message that was already received (4.6) or delivered (4.5) it is discarded. A message is inserted in the history variable (4.7) only if it passes both the *late message* and *deja vu* acceptance tests (4.5, 4.6). When a message (T, s, σ) is inserted in the history variable, we say that it is *accepted* (for delivery). Once a message originated at clock time T is accepted, the Deliver task is scheduled to start at local time $T + \Delta$ (4.8). The Deliver task (Figure 5) starts at clock time $T + \Delta$ to deliver to processes which have invoked *RECEIVE* commands (5.6) updates timestamped T in increasing order of their sender's identifier ((5.5)–(5.8)) and to delete from the local history H everything about broadcasts initiated at time T (5.9).

4.2. The multiple-fault tolerant protocol

To guarantee order, the broadcast termination time Δ must be chosen to be at least equal to the worst case delay which can elapse between the time a broadcast is initiated and the time by which all correct processors have received the broadcast. This ensures that, when any correct processors p and q begin to deliver a broadcast initiated at time T, p and q know the set B of *all* broadcasts with timestamp at most T that a correct processor will ever have to deliver. Processors p and q can then order the delivery of the updates in B identically to achieve order. The above worst case delay depends on how many times a message can be forwarded before it reaches a correct processor for the first time. Below we simultaneously derive Δ and generalize the simple lazy forwarding rule introduced earlier. We also make the rule sufficiently precise so that it becomes implementable, for example, we give phrases such as: let c be the highest channel on which a processor r receives m the more precise meaning: let c be the highest channel on which a processor r receives m *by a certain local time*. (Without a point in time by which r must decide, r might wait forever in the hope of receiving m on a higher channel.)

To enable processors to determine how many times a message was forwarded, we add to each message a hop count h. A sender s initiating the broadcast of a message m sets h to 1. Each time a processor forwards m, h is incremented by 1. Since a combination of processor crash and out-adapter performance failures can cause a message originated by a processor to be delayed more than δ time units before it is received by another processor, we use the timeliness test of the second protocol of (Cristian, Aghili, Strong and Dolev 1985) to detect and discard late messages. A message timestamped T with hop count h received at local time U will be called *timely* if

$$U < T + h(\delta + \epsilon).$$

A message is *accepted*, that is, is inserted in the local history variable, only if it passes the *late message* and *deja vu* tests mentioned earlier and *is* timely. The above timeliness test ensures that if a correct processor p accepts a broadcast (T, s, σ, h) that needs to be forwarded, then the messages $(T, s, \sigma, h + 1)$ that p will forward will also be timely for all correct processors.

In a system based on redundant broadcast channels governed by the failure assumptions 2–6, the failure scenarios which can delay most the reception of a message by a first correct processor are of the type examined in Figure 2, where a processor crash—after a message is output just on one out-adapter—is followed by a performance failure of the out-adapter or an omission failure of the attached channel. For example if f is even, that is, $f = 2k$ for some integer $k \geq 1$, the following scenario containing $2k$ failures can lengthen the route which a message $(T, s, \sigma, 1)$ must travel before being accepted by a first correct processor to k hops: the sender $s = p_0$ crashes after sending $(T, s, \sigma, 1)$ on channel 1 and channel 1 suffers an omission failure after delivering $(T, s, \sigma, 1)$ to a single correct in-adapter attached to processor p_1 which accepts the message, p_1 crashes after forwarding $(T, s, \sigma, 2)$ on channel 2 and channel 2 suffers an omission failure after delivering $(T, s, \sigma, 2)$ to a single correct in-adapter attached to processor p_2 which accepts the message, $\dots p_{k-1}$ crashes after sending (T, s, σ, k) on channel k and channel k suffers an omission failure after having delivered (T, s, σ, k) to a single correct in-adapter attached to a first correct processor p_k which accepts the message. If f is odd, that is, $f = 2k + 1$ for some integer $k \geq 1$, then the first correct processor to receive a message (T, s, σ, h) sent by a faulty processor s can be as far as $k + 1$ hops away from s. Indeed, an initial scenario containing $f - 1 = 2k$

failures identical to the one above can lead to the acceptance of (T, s, σ, k) by a processor p_k which is k hops away from $s = p_0$. Another failure (the last possible according to assumption 8) can crash p_k after forwarding $(T, s, \sigma, k + 1)$ on channel $k + 1$, so the first correct processor to receive a message $(T, s, \sigma, *)$ is $k + 1$ hops away from s_0.

The above worst-case-delay-to-first-correct-processor scenarios suggest that, if $f = 2k$, $k \geq 1$, then $\Delta = (k + 1)(\delta + \epsilon)$ is an acceptable broadcast termination time, since if p is a correct processor that accepts as timely a message (T, s, σ, h) arriving on highest channel $c < f + 1 - h$ which needs forwarding, $h \leq k$, then p has enough time (that is, has at least $\delta + \epsilon$ time units) to forward $(T, s, \sigma, h + 1)$ to all correct processors before the delivery time $T + \Delta$ occurs on their clock. If $f = 2k + 1$, $k \geq 1$, the time $(k + 2)(\delta + \epsilon)$ would be an acceptable termination time since we have seen that the latest clock time by which a correct processor can accept a broadcast is $(k + 1)(\delta + \epsilon)$. This termination time can be improved by observing that, if ever a correct processor p accepts by local time $T + k(\delta + \epsilon)$ a message (T, s, σ, k) which, because of a failure scenario equivalent to the $2k$ failures scenario described previously could be missed by some other correct processor by local time $T + k(\delta + \epsilon)$, then if p forwards $(T, s, \sigma, k + 1)$ on the channels $k + 1$, $k + 2 = f + 1 - k$, the last $(2k + 1)$th failure allowed by assumption 8 will not prevent the other correct processors from receiving at least a copy of $(T, s, \sigma, k + 1)$ by time $T + (k + 1)(\delta + \epsilon)$. Thus, it is safe to reduce the termination time to $\Delta = (k + 1)(\delta + \epsilon)$ when $f = 2k + 1$, $k \geq 1$.

Knowledge of the hop count h allows us not only to detect late messages, but also to minimize the set of channels on which a processor has to forward messages. To this end, we now give the complete rule for lazy forwarding.

Lazy forwarding rule. To initiate a broadcast, a sender s enqueues messages $(T, s, \sigma, 1)$ on its out-adapters to channels $1, 2, \ldots, f + 1$ in this order. Let (T, s, σ, h), $h \leq k$, be a message accepted by a processor $p \neq s$, and let c be the highest channel on which p receives a copy of the message by local time $T + h(\delta + \epsilon)$. If at $T + h(\delta + \epsilon)$ on p's clock $c < f + 1 - h$, then p forwards $(T, s, \sigma, h + 1)$ on channels $c + 1, \ldots, f + 1 - h$, else, p does not forward.

This forwarding rule, like the original simple lazy forwarding rule, ensures the *unanimity* property mentioned earlier: if a correct processor p accepts a broadcast by time $T + \Delta$ on q's clock, then each correct processor q accepts the broadcast by time $T + \Delta$ on q's clock. A proof that a broadcast protocol satisfying the unanimity property satisfies the atomicity, order, and termination properties required for atomic broadcast is given in (Cristian, Aghili, Strong and Dolev 1984). The proof of the unanimity property is based on the following lemma (proven in the Appendix):

LEMMA. Let (T, s, σ, h), $h \leq k$, be a message accepted by a processor p and let c be the highest channel on which p receives a copy of the message by local time $T + h(\delta + \epsilon)$. If at time $T + h(\delta + \epsilon)$ on p's clock $c \leq f + 1 - h$, then at least h component failures have occurred since the broadcast was initiated, else, at least $h - 1$ failures have occurred.

The proof of the unanimity property is by case analysis. If the highest channel c on which p receives a timely message (T, s, σ, h) by time $T + h(\delta + \epsilon)$ on its clock is such that $c < f + 1 - h$, $h \leq k$, then, by the lazy forwarding rule, p forwards $(T, s, \sigma, h + 1)$

at local time $T + h(\delta + \epsilon)$ on channels $c + 1, \ldots, f + 1 - h$. Thus, the at most $f - h$ components which, by assumption 8 and the above lemma, can fail after p forwards $(T, s, \sigma, h + 1)$ will not prevent at least one of the messages $(T, s, \sigma, *)$ sent on channels 1, 2, $\ldots, f + 1 - h$ by s, the processors which have forwarded $(T, s, \delta, *)$ before p, and p, to reach all correct processors. If $c = f + 1 - h$, $f + 1 - h$ messages have already been sent on channels 1, 2, $\ldots, f + 1 - h$, so the at most $f - h$ component failures which can occur after p's clock displays time $T + h(\delta + \epsilon)$ will not prevent at least one of these messages from reaching all correct processors. If at local time $T + h(\delta + \epsilon)$ $c > f + 1 - h$, at least $f + 2 - h$ messages have already been sent, so the at most $f - (h - 1) = f + 1 - h$ components which, by the above lemma, can still fail cannot prevent at least one of these messages from reaching all correct processors.

The lazy forwarding rule, like the simple rule given previously, ensures that in the absence of failures only $f + 1$ messages are sent for each broadcast. The worst case message cost in the presence of failures is $(f + 1) + (f - 1)(n - 1) = (f - 1)n + 2$.

The Start, Receive, and Forward tasks of the multiple-fault tolerant protocol are given in Figures 6, 7, and 8. In expressing the protocol termination time (6.2), we denote "/" the integer division operator and $[x]$ the floor function, that is, if x is a rational number, $[x]$ denotes the greatest integer i such that $i \le x$. In addition to the history variable H, the tasks of the multiple-fault tolerant protocol also share a variable C of type

$$var\ C:\ \text{Time} \to (\text{Processor} \to \{1, \ldots, f + 1\}).$$

For each broadcast (T, s) in the history, C records the highest channel on which a message $(T, s, *, *)$ was received. As for H, we assume that the C shared variable is initialized to the empty function. A broadcast initiation time T is purged from the domain of C at the same time it is purged from the domain of H (5.9). Because the Deliver task for the multiple-fault tolerant protocol is so similar to that described in Figure 5, we do not describe it in detail for brevity reasons.

We conclude our description by mentioning an optimization to the lazy forwarding rule which lowers the average number of messages forwarded when failures occur. When ϵ is large compared to δ, it is possible that a processor p among the processors which have to forward a message $(T, s, \sigma, h + 1)$, $h < k$, forwards the message so early that other

Figure 6. Start Task of the multiple-fault tolerant protocol.

```
1  task Receive;
2    const Δ = [f/2](δ + ε) + (δ + ε);
3    var U,T: Time; σ: Update; s: Processor; h: Integer;
4    cycle receive(T,s,σ,h) from c; U←clock;
5        if U≥T + Δ then "late message" iterate fi;
6        if U≥T + h(δ + ε) then "too late to forward" iterate fi;
7        if T∈dom(H)&s∈dom(H(T))
8        then "deja vu" C(T)(s)←max{c,C(T)(s)};
9        else H←H⊕(T,s,σ);
10           if h≤[f/2] & c < f + 1-h
11           then C←C⊕(T,s,c);
12               schedule Forward (T,s,h) at T + h(δ + ε)
13           fi;
14           schedule Deliver(T) at T + Δ;
15       fi;
16   endcycle;
```

Figure 7. Receive Task of the multiple-fault tolerant protocol.

```
1  task Forward(T: Time; s: Processor; h: Integer);
2    if C(T)(s) < f + 1-h
3    then for i = C(T)(s) + 1 to f + 1-h do send(T,s,H(T)(s),h + 1) on i fi;
```

Figure 8. Forward Task of the multiple-fault tolerant protocol.

processors which had to forward the same message receive it before the forwarding deadline $T + h(\delta + \epsilon)$ occurs on their clocks. If q is such a processor, then q can omit to forward $(T, s, \sigma, h + 1)$ when the deadline for forwarding occurs on its clock. What q needs to do, however, is to check at local time $T + (h + 1)(\delta + \epsilon)$ whether a crash has prevented p from successfully completing the forwarding. Processor q has to forward $(T, s, \sigma, h + 2)$ at local time $T + (h + 1)(\delta + \epsilon)$ if the highest channel c' on which q has received a copy of $(T, s, \sigma, h + 1)$ is smaller than $f - h$ and, of course, q has not received other (early) copies of $(T, s, \sigma, h + 2)$ forwarded by some other fast processor.

5. What does it cost to tolerate other failure classes?

Because of the timeliness tests (4.5, 7.6, 7.7) in-adapter or channel performance failures can be tolerated at no additional cost. An increase in cost is observed when processors (instead of adapters) can suffer performance failures, for example because standard time-sharing (not real-time) operating systems are used to control them. Indeed, if the delay between the time T at which a processor s accepts to broadcast an update σ and the moment the processor s finishes to enqueue messages $(T, s, \sigma, 1)$ on all its $f + 1$ out-adapters can be greater than P, the previous protocols no longer achieve atomicity despite the timeliness tests mentioned earlier. This can be demonstrated by the following counter-example for the two-fault tolerant protocol.

Let s, p, e, and g be four processors with correct clocks running at the speed of real-time, such that s and p are faulty and e and g are correct, but e's clock is earlier than (or in advance of) g's clock. To fix ideas, let $\delta = 8$ and $\epsilon = 6$, and assume that at real-time 0, the clocks were showing the times: $C_s(0) = 0$, $C_p(0) = 1$, $C_g(0) = 3$, $C_e(0) = 5$. Assume that, at real time 0, s accepts to broadcast an update σ but, because of a performance failure, s invokes the $send(0, s, \sigma, 1)$ command on channels 1, 2, and 3 at real-times 5, 6, and 7, respectively. Assume also that all messages take exactly 7 real-time units (note: $7 < \delta$) to be delivered to processors p, g, and e. Processor p will accept the message $(0, s, \sigma, 1)$ coming on channel 1 at real-time 12 (because it arrives at local time $C_p(12) = 13$ before the deadline 14 for accepting messages with timestamp 0 and hop count 1 occurs at p) but will reject the copies coming on 2 and 3. Processors g and e will reject all copies of $(0, s, \sigma, 1)$ because they will receive them at local times past the deadline for accepting messages with timestamp 0 and hop count 1. Assume now that, because of a performance failure, p forwards $(0, s, \sigma, 2)$ on channels 1, 2, and 3 at real-time 17 instead of 14, and that all messages are delivered to g and e after exactly 7 real-time units, at real-time 24. Processor g will accept all copies of $(0, s, \sigma, 2)$ coming on channels 1, 2, 3 because the delivery time 28 has not yet passed on its clock $C_g(24) = 27$, but processor e will reject all copies of the message on all channels as being late, because the delivery time 28 has passed on its clock $C_e(24) = 29$. This violates atomicity.

The reasons why the previous protocol based on lazy forwarding does not work if processors can suffer performance failures are as follows:

1. because of clock differences between correct processors, a message sent by a slow processor s on all channels can be accepted only by a subset of correct processors even if no failures other than the failure of s occur,
2. the hop count of a message received for the first time by a first correct processor can now be as high as f (as opposed to a maximum of $[f/2]$ for the previous protocol).

Since, a correct processor g which accepts a message m on a high channel c can no longer infer that any correct processor e also accepts m from channel c when no failures affect the components on the c path between g and e, to tolerate processor performance failures one has to use *prompt* forwarding. Moreover, because the termination time $([f/2] + 1)(\delta + \epsilon)$ does no longer ensure that if a correct processor p accepts a timely message m that needs forwarding, then all correct processsors which receive the messages forwarded by p accept them as timely, we have to increase the termination time to $(f + 1)(\delta + \epsilon)$. This will ensure that if a correct processor p ever accepts a message m timestamped T as timely by $T + h(\delta + \epsilon)$ on its clock, where $h \leq f$, then p has enough time (that is, at least $\delta + \epsilon$ time units) to forward m to all correct processors so that these accept the message as timely too.

The second protocol of (Christian, Aghili, Strong and Dolev 1985) is based on prompt forwarding and has a termination time of $(f + 1)(\delta + \epsilon)$. If appropriately adapted to forward messages on all channels other than the incoming channel instead of on all links other than the incoming link, this protocol can be used to achieve atomic broadcast in systems based on redundant broadcast channels in the presence of processor timing failures and *locally consistent* clock failures (Dolev, Strong and Cristian 1989). Roughly speaking, a clock failure is locally consistent if it cannot be detected by detection mechanisms local to a processor only; knowledge of the values of other clocks in the system or of external time might be necessary for that. A stopped clock or a clock that runs backward are examples of locally detectable faulty clocks (to detect such failures it is sufficient to compare successive clock readings). A monotonically increasing clock that drifts from real time at an actual rate inferior to $-\rho$ or greater than ρ is an example of a locally consistent faulty clock. The cost increase for tolerating locally consistent clock failures and timing processor failures is $nf + 1$ messages, instead of $f + 1$ messages for processor crash failures, and a termination time of $(f + 1)(\delta + \epsilon)$, instead of $([f/2] + 1)(\delta + \epsilon)$. If tolerance of arbitrary clock failures and arbitrary processor and communication failures detectable by using message authentication methods is desired, then the third protocol of (Cristian, Aghili, Strong and Dolev 1985) can be used at the following cost: $nf + 1$ messages per broadcast and a termination time of $(f + 1)(\delta' + \epsilon')$, where δ' is the upper bound on message transmission and processing delays that includes the time needed for message authentication, and ϵ' is the worst case deviation among clocks when components can suffer authentication detectable failures.

While tolerance of timing, clock or authentication detectable arbitrary failures costs more, one might ask what cost savings are possible by strengthening our failure assumption 3, for example by assuming that out-adapters can suffer only omission—instead of performance—failures (this can be achieved by using out-adapters based on Time Division Multiple Access or Tree Collision Resolution methods (Gallager 1985) which ensure upper bounds on the time needed to insert atomic broadcast messages on non-faulty channels). If adapters can only suffer omission failures, then it is possible to achieve a termination time of $([f/2] + 1)\delta + \epsilon$ by eliminating the (now) unnecessary timeliness checks (7.6, 7.7), and by using the following (slightly changed) lazy forwarding rule. Let c be the highest channel on which a processor p receives a message (T, s, σ, h) with hop count $h \leq k$. If at time $T + h\delta + \epsilon$ on p's clock $c < f + 1 - h$ then p must forward $(T, s, \sigma, h + 1)$ on channels $c + 1, \ldots, f + 1 - h$ else, p does not have to forward. Since the resulting protocol is so similar to the one described in Figures 5–8, we do not give its detailed description for brevity reasons.

6. Comparison with previous work

The synchronous atomic broadcast protocol proposed in this paper achieves a significant message overhead reduction over the synchronous atomic broadcast protocols proposed for point-to-point networks earlier (Cristian, Aghili, Strong and Dolev 1985): when no failures occur only $f + 1$ messages are sent per broadcast, instead of between n and n^2 messages. The termination time is at least halved: $([f/2] + 1)\delta + \epsilon$ instead of $(f + d)\delta + \epsilon$ when only omission component failures can occur, and $[f/2](\delta + \epsilon) + \delta + \epsilon$ instead of $f(\delta + \epsilon) + d\delta + \epsilon$ when adapter performance failures but no timing processor failures can occur, where $d \geq 1$. When processors can suffer timing or authentication detectable arbitrary failures and processor clocks can be faulty, the use of broadcast channels does not help much: the termination time stays the same as in (Cristian, Aghili, Strong and Dolev 1985) and the number of messages becomes $nf + 1$ instead of between n and n^2.

The comparison between our protocols and the synchronous atomic broadcast protocols proposed by Babaoglu and Drumond (Babaoglu and Drumond 1985) is made difficult by the use of different system models and assumptions. For example, while Babaoglu and Drumond assume a model based on message rounds and exactly synchronized clocks in which all receiving processors know the time at which a sending processor broadcasts, we do not assume exact synchronization or the existence of any (pre)agreement on the times when messages can be broadcast. Because of the exact clock synchronization assumption of (Babaoglu and Drumond 1985) for example, some of the issues that we had to address explicitly, like the possibility that a message broadcast by a faulty slow processor is accepted by only a subset of correct processors even if no adapters or channels fail, just because of differences between correct processor clocks, did not have to be considered in (Babaoglu and Drumond 1985).

Another important difference is that we do not assume that channels are *atomic*[1]. The atomic channel assumption of (Babaoglu and Drumond 1985) states that: for any message m inserted on a channel c either all (in case the channel is non-faulty) or none (in case the channel is faulty) of the processors connected to c through non-faulty adapters receive m. Instead of this assumption on faulty channel behavior we use a strictly weaker assumption: if a channel c fails while it carries a message m any subset (not only the total subset) of correct processors attached through correct adapters to c can miss m. This weaker assumption was needed to model run-time situations observed in common local area networks, such as Ethernet and Token Ring, in which the bits of a message are corrupted while the message transits on the channel. For example, undetected collisions or an improper functioning at run-time of a repeater between two Ethernet transceivers can cause a degradation of the signal on the Ether so that only a subset of the correct adapters receive a message while the remaining ones discard it because of check-sum errors (Metcalfe and Boggs 1976). Similarly, in a Token Ring context, the malfunctioning of any (active) adapter p when it re-transmits a sequence of received bits to a downstream adapter q can cause q and all the following down-stream adapters to receive (and discard) a corrupted sequence of bits (Tusch, Meyr and Zurfluh 1988).

These differing system models and assumptions lead to differing termination times. While the stronger assumptions of (Babaoglu and Drumond 1985) enable the protocols tolerant of omission and authentication detectable arbitrary failures proposed by Babaoglu and Drumond to terminate in a constant number of two rounds (in our model this would probably correspond to a termination time of $2(\delta + \epsilon)$ with $\epsilon = 0$), our weaker assumptions cause our protocols to only achieve termination times proportional to the maximum number of failures to be tolerated. The number of messages per broadcast is also different: while the protocols tolerant of adapter omission and performance failures need $f + 1$ messages in the absence of failures, the omission tolerant protocol of (Babaoglu and Drumond 1985) sends $n(f + 1)$ messages per broadcast. For timing, authentication detectable arbitrary and clock failures the message overheads are similar: while our protocols send $nf + 1$ messages, the protocol of (Babaoglu and Drumond 1985) sends $n(f + 1)$ messages.

Acknowledgments

The research presented was partially sponsored by IBM's Systems Integration Division group located in Rockville, Maryland, as part of a FAA sponsored project to build a new, highly available air traffic control system. A prototype of the system, including one of the protocols presented in this paper, was successfully demonstrated in June 1988. We would like to thank Paul Ezhilchelvan, Ray Strong, and the referees for their criticisms and suggestions on earlier versions of this paper.

Notes

1. Although Babaoglu and Drumond examine later in their paper the consequences of relaxing the *atomic channel* failure assumption and derive $n \geq \lambda' + \pi$ as being a sufficient condition for correctness in the presence of omission failures, where λ' is the worst case number of in-adapters attached to all channels that might miss a message broadcast on all channels because of channel failures and π is the worst case number of processor failures, their condition is generally false under failure assumptions 2 and 8, which allow λ' and π to be as high as $f(n - 1)$ and f, respectively.

References

Babaoglu, O., Drumond, R. 1985. Streets of Byzantium: Network architectures for fast reliable broadcast. *IEEE Tr. on Software Engineering*, SE-11, (6).

Birman, K., Joseph, T. 1987. Reliable communication in the presence of failures. *ACM Tr. on Computer Systems*, 5, (1) (Feb.).

Carr, R. 1985. The tandem global update protocol. *Tandem Systems Review*, 1 (2) (June).

Cristian, F., Aghili, H., Strong, R., Dolev., D. 1985. Atomic Broadcast; From Simple Diffusion to Byzantine Agreement, *FTCS15*, Ann Arbor, Michigan. (also IBM Research report RJ 4540, October 1984).

Chang, J.M., Maxemchuck, N. 1984. Reliable Broadcast Protocols, *ACM Tr. on Computer Systems*, 2, (3) (Aug.).

Cristian, F. 1989. Probabilistic Clock Synchronization. *Distributed Computing*, 3:146–158.

Dolev, D., Strong, R., Cristian, F. 1989. Distinguishing Timing Failures from Clock Failures. IBM Research Report RJ 7150, (Nov.)

Gallager, R. 1985. A Perspective on Multiaccess Channels. *IEEE Trans. on Information Theory*, IT-31, 2, (March).

Garcia-Molina, H., Spauster, A. 1989. Message Ordering in a Multicast Environment. *9th Int. Conf. on Distributed Systems*. Newport Beach, California.

Lamport, L. 1989. The Part-time Parliament. DEC-SRC Research Report. 49.

Metcalfe, R., Boggs, D. 1976. Ethernet: Distributed Packet Switching for Local Computer Networks, *CACM*, 19, (7): 395–404.

Melliar-Smith, M., Moser, L. 1989. Fault-Tolerant Distributed Systems Based on Broadcast Communication. *9th Int Conf. on Distributed Systems*. Newport Beach, California.

Strong, R., Skeen, D., Cristian, F., Aghili, H. 1987. Handshake Protocols. *7th Int. Conf. on Distributed Computing Systems*. Berlin.

Tusch, J., Meyr, H., Zurfluh, E. 1988. Error Handling Performance of a Token Ring Local Area Network. *13th IEEE Int. Conf. on Local Area Networks*. Minneapolis, Minnesota.

Verissimo, P., Rodriques, L., Marques, J. 1987. Atomic Multicast Extensions for 802.4 Token Bus. *11th Int. Fiber Optic Communications and Local Area Networks Exposition*. Anaheim, California.

Appendix

We prove below a stronger version of the lemma used to justify the correctness of the general lazy forwarding rule.

LEMMA. Let c_h be the highest channel number on which a correct processor p_h receives a message (T, s, σ, h) with hop count $h \leq k$. Let p_i and c_i, $i = 1, \ldots, h - 1$, be sequences of processors and channels defined recursively as follows: p_{h-1} forwarded the message (T, s, σ, h) received by p_h after receiving $(T, s, \sigma, h - 1)$ on highest channel $c_{h-1}, \ldots,$ processor p_1 forwarded the message $(T, s, \sigma, 2)$ received by p_2 after receiving from $s = p_0$ the message $(T, s, \sigma, 1)$ on highest channel c_1. Let A_i be the set of components $\{p_{i-1}$, channel $c_i + 1$, p_{i-1}'s out-adapter to $c_i + 1$, p_i's in-adapter to $c_i + 1\}$, and denote C_h the union of the sets A_i, $i = 1, \ldots, h - 1$. If at time $T_h = T + h(\delta + \epsilon)$ on the clock of processor p_h, $c_h \leq f + 1 - h$, then at least h components in the set C_h are faulty.

The proof of the lemma is by induction on h.

Consider the reception of a timely message (T, s, σ, h) with $h = 1$ by p_1 on highest channel c_1. If at time $T_1 = T + (\delta + \epsilon)$ on p_1's clock $c_1 \leq f + 1 - h = f$, then the sender $s = p_0$ did not enqueue a message $(T, s, \sigma, 1)$ on the out-adapter to channel $c_1 + 1 = f + 1$ because of a crash, or this out-adapter suffered a performance failure, or the channel $c_1 + 1$ suffered an omission failure, or the in-adapter between channel $c_1 + 1$ and p_1 suffered an omission failure. Thus, at least one component in the set C_1 is faulty.

Assume now that the lemma is true for $h = i$, $i \geq 1$, and consider the case $h = i + 1$. By induction hypothesis, some processor p_i forwarded the message $(T, s, \sigma, i + 1)$ after it received (T, s, σ, i) on highest channel c_i. By the lazy forwarding rule, processor p_i had to forward the message $(T, s, \sigma, i + 1)$ on channels $c_i + 1, \ldots, f + 1 - i$. If at time $T_{i+1} = T + (i + 1)(\delta + \epsilon)$ on p_{i+1}'s clock, the highest channel c_{i+1} on which p_{i+1} received a message $(T, s, \sigma, i + 1)$ is such that $c_{i+1} \leq f + 1 - (i + 1) = f - i$, it follows that p_{i+1} did not receive in time the message $(T, s, \sigma, i + 1)$ that p_i should have sent on channel $f + 1 - i$. This could only happen if at least a component in the set $A_{i+1} = \{p_i$, p_i's out-adapter to channel $f + 1 - i$, channel $f + 1 - i$, p_{i+1}'s in-adapter from channel $f + 1 - i\}$ is faulty. Since $c_i < c_{i+1}$, the intersection between the component sets C_i and A_{i+1} is empty. Since by induction hypothesis, the set C_i contains at least i faulty components, it follows that the set $C_{i+1} = C_i \cup A_{i+1}$ contains at least $i + 1$ faulty components. The lemma is thus true for any integer h.

Chapter 7: Architecture and Fault Tolerance

Given the applications of real-time systems, they must function in spite of failures, that is, they must tolerate faults. Fault tolerance requires error processing followed by fault treatment. Error processing, typically takes one of two forms: error recovery or error compensation [Laprie88]. Error recovery replaces an erroneous state with an error-free state in one of two ways. In backward error recovery [Randell 75], recovery points are maintained and when a failure occurs, the system state is restored to that reflected by an appropriate recovery point. In forward error recovery, the system is moved to a new state which may or may not have been occupied prior to the failure. Implicit in the use of error recovery is the capability to detect errors.

Error compensation, on the other hand, involves providing enough redundancy in the system such that the system is able to provide acceptable level of services in spite of the failure of one or more of its components. Thus this technique *masks* the faults in a system from its environment.

Let us analyze the applicability of these techniques for time-critical systems. Backward error recovery involves maintaining recovery points, which introduces overhead during normal system functioning. Also, on the occurrence of a failure, typically, certain actions may have to be *undone* before the system state is restored to an earlier error-free state. Thus, in this case, recovery entails time and resource overheads. In addition, the recovery activity competes for resources with ongoing time-constrained activities thus affecting the performance of the system. Furthermore, to *guarantee* that a real-time task will meet its timing requirements, the estimated worst case processing time of the task should consider the time needed for recovery [Klingerman and Stoyenko 86]. Such an estimation is bound to be quite pessimistic, thus resulting in poor system performance.

Backward error recovery has another drawback when tasks interact with the environment. Since the system is restored to a previous state and some tasks are undone, this implies that the undone tasks' interactions with the environment should be reversible. Of course, many interactions, especially in real-time systems, fail this requirement.

The opposite problem occurs with forward error recovery. Forward error recovery may cause the system to move to a new set of states. States that would normally have occurred will not occur; they will be *skipped*. Again, this implies that certain expected interactions with the environment may not occur. Other problems with forward error recovery relate to the effect on data and resources when some processing is skipped. First, shared resources like files and data structures may be left in an inconsistent state. Second, if some or all of the processing by a task is skipped, subsequent tasks that depend on its output may be jeopardized. Forward error recovery also incurs overheads: In some situations, upon failure, the system is forced to take the most recent correct state before proceeding forward. To facilitate this, recovery points are maintained during normal system execution. In general, determining the state to which the system should be moved incurs time overheads.

The primary advantage of error compensation or fault masking is that faults do not affect guaranteed timing constraints since the fault is masked. But redundancy incurs overheads whether or not failures occur. The nature and amount of the overheads incurred depends on the type of faults that need to be masked and the number of faults of a specified type that must be tolerated. For example, in real-time systems where tasks share (writable) resources, overheads are incurred to ensure that redundant copies of a task execute on the same inputs and in an order that ensures the consistency of the resources.

Based on this discussion, we can state that faults should be masked if the task has tight timing constraints, if the resources accessed by the task have to remain consistent, and if the interactions of the task with the environment are not reversible. Since all of these are true for real-time systems, most real-time systems mask faults via redundancy-based architectures.

The number of replicates needed depends on the types of failures that a system is designed to handle. Types of failures span a spectrum from *fail-stop/fail-silent* components [Schlichting and Schneider 83] to components that can experience *Byzantine* failures [Lamport et al. 82]. A classification of other faults along this spectrum is found in [Ezhilselvan and Shrivastava 86]. Tolerating up to t fail-stop failures requires maintenance of at least $t + 1$ replicates while tolerating up to t Byzantine failures requires maintenance of at least $3t + 1$ replicates. Different ways of realizing nodes with specific failure semantics are discussed in [Cristian90].

Constructing fail-stop nodes involves considerable overheads. For example, one way is to build self-correcting processors that use error-correcting and detecting codes. The other way, which is supposed to be more advantageous [Cristian90], is to build fail-stop processors from dual processors. Each dual processor executes in lock step with outputs compared at each step. If the processors' outputs do not match, no output is produced.

These overheads, however, make it straightforward to achieve agreement: A task has been processed completely and correctly when one of its replicates produces an output. Since this output is known to be correct, additional overheads have to be incurred only for ensuring ordering. If nodes can fail arbitrarily, the results of executions of task replicates have to be voted before being used by succeeding tasks.

All four papers in this section describe real-time system architectures specifically designed for fault tolerance through redundancy. In the first paper, Cristian, Dancey, and Dehn show how many of the proposed approaches to realize fault tolerance have been brought to bear for achieving "Fault-Tolerance in the Advanced Automation System." This system is being designed to replace the en-route and terminal approach air-traffic control systems in the United States. Its primary goals are providing high availability while meeting complex responsiveness requirements. Not surprisingly, high availability is achieved though redundancy of processing elements, communication channels, and I/O devices. The paper starts by presenting the basic fault-tolerant system structuring concepts, introducing the notions of service, servers, and the dependence of one server on another. The authors identify different failure semantics and offer the notion of a server group — a set of redundant servers — as a generic solution for realizing a given fault tolerance requirement. In some sense, this provides a unified view of different approaches to redundancy. The paper presents the redundancy management techniques adopted in the advanced automation system via a series of questions and answers that relate to redundancy management. Since air traffic control has very stringent availability requirements and demands that air traffic controllers should be shielded from hardware and software faults, redundancy is provided at the application level where lower-level faults are masked from these servers by appropriate exception-handling techniques. The authors worry about the costs of providing redundancy and its management and so, where such costs are likely to be very high, they have taken decisions that imply inferior quality of performance. For instance, for some types of arbitrary failures, the system will rely on the air traffic controllers' knowledge of the physical laws governing the airspace being controlled.

In some ways, the approaches taken in this paper contrast with those based purely on hardware redundancy. For instance, in building a fail-safe processor, the authors reject the approach of using a pair of processors working in lock-step and comparing results They consider it too expensive and redundant since the processors use failure detection features like runtime checking, error detecting, and correcting codes. Further, processors are just one aspect of a complex application; a designer would also have to consider busses, memories, input/output devices, and — in this particular application — radars, and controller consoles.

The authors employ active redundancy (where all group members execute service requests) and passive redundancy (one member serves requests, another takes over when it fails), depending on a server's characteristics and the service specifications. Clock synchronization is achieved via a new probabilistic clock synchronization algorithm (see Cristian's paper in the chapter on "Clock Synchronization"). The Advanced Automation System is now being implemented, and the authors hope to gain a better understanding of their initial design and its adequacies as the implementation progresses.

In their paper "A Design Approach for Ultrareliable Real-Time Systems," Lala, Harper, and Alger correctly point out that while providing redundancy is easy, managing redundancy is not. In fact, without appropriate redundancy management techniques the failure probability of systems increases rather than decreases, given an increase in the hardware components. Complexity of redundancy management arises from fault and error propagation, synchronizing redundant components, and achieving consensus. The paper focuses on systems that provably possess extremely low failure probabilities. For instance, the fly-by-wire Airbus A-320 requires a 10^{-10} probability of failure per hour of flight. They also have very tight timing constraints, in the tens of milliseconds. Given the impossibility of *testing* these systems, analytical methods and proofs are the primary means to evaluate their correctness. The paper discusses the philosophy underlying the building of ultrareliable systems at Draper Laboratory. The building block of such systems is the Fault Containment Region (FCR), which functions correctly independent of faults external to the FCR. Failure within an FCR is hence assumed to be an independent uncorrelated event. However, since this does not preclude erroneous inputs to FCRs, the notion of *voting planes* is used to mask errors at different stages of a system. In addition to voting that occurs on sensor values and on values sent to actuators, computing devices vote to isolate the results produced by faulty components. The voting is based on an exact bit-by-bit consensus among redundant FCRs. Draper's approach employs a fault-tolerant clock, and the redundant hardware executes a given instruction in the same number of cycles. (See the section on "Clock Synchronization" on ways to build such clocks.) The approach has been applied in the design of an advanced information processing system and a fault-tolerant parallel processor. The paper provides details of the former.

In "HARTS: A Distributed Real-Time Architecture" Shin describes a wrapped hexagonal mesh-based hardware architecture to meet the performance, fault tolerance, and I/O requirements of real-time systems. The paper discusses how the architecture meets these needs. The HARTS project is based on the premise that the architecture should provide the facilities that an operating system can then use to build predictable real-time systems. The wrapped hexagonal mesh was chosen since it is a planar architecture with fixed connectivity, and it scales well. Fault tolerance is provided by the mesh's robustness with respect to link and node failures, given the multiplicity of processing elements and by the many redundant paths between a pair of nodes. The authors have implemented the communication and routing algorithms via customized hardware that also monitors the network load, looks for link failures, and time stamps messages. Different time-constrained communication protocols can be realized using the support provided. The routing algorithms are based on virtual cut-through and wormhole routing. Thus, messages that are en-route are not buffered at intermediate nodes if the communication resources are available. Facilities are provided for microprogramming different routing algorithms. Clock synchronization in HARTS is basically via software with some hardware support (HARTS uses the interactive convergence algorithm of Lamport and Melliar-Smith; see chapter on clock synchronization.) HARTS has been evaluated via a combination of analytical and simulation methods using parameters derived from the system components that have been implemented.

In "Distributed Fault-Tolerant Real-Time Systems: The MARS Approach" Kopetz, Damm, Koza, and Mulozzani describe MARS, a comprehensive effort exploring interrelated aspects of safety-critical real-time system development, starting from specification of requirements and ending with system implementation. The work's goals are designing for fault tolerance, meeting timeliness constraints, and being maintainable. MARS achieves predictability by using deterministic communication protocols and static scheduling approaches. In MARS, communication occurs via the time division multiple-access (TDMA) protocol. This deterministic communication contributes to the determinancy of the system. Fault tolerance is achieved through active redundancy. Replicates are assigned to system components that are designed to be fail-silent through the use of self-checking hardware. MARS provides a global time base by synchronizing the clocks on each component using a VLSI clock synchronization unit that exists on each component. All information maintained by MARS components has an associated validity time. A piece of information becomes useless once its validity-time expires. Components communicate by exchanging *state messages,* which contain information maintained by the sending component and needed by the receiving component. The MARS approach calls for the information about the peak loads to be made available: Complete specification about the tasks that will execute, including the computation time and precedence relationships among the various components of a task, the maximum frequency with which data will arrive and the expected response time from the system, that is, the acceptable delay in processing the data. Given this information, the tasks are assigned to various components of the clusters such that the system will meet the specifications of the safety-critical parts of the application. This task assignment and the scheduling of activities (keeping in mind that the TDMA protocol is used) then forms a crucial aspect of an application development using the MARS approach. Since MARS application development is based on worst case requirements, any small change in the requirements specification may cause a complete overhaul of the system.

FAULT-TOLERANCE IN THE ADVANCED AUTOMATION SYSTEM

Flaviu Cristian
IBM Almaden
Research Center

Bob Dancey
IBM SID
Rockville

Jon Dehn
IBM SID
Rockville

The Advanced Automation System is a distributed real-time system under development by IBM's Systems Integration Division for the US Federal Aviation Administration. The system is intended to replace the present en-route and terminal approach US air traffic control computer systems over the next decade. High availability of air traffic control services is an essential requirement of the system. This paper discusses the general approach to fault-tolerance adopted in AAS, by reviewing some of the questions which were asked during the system design, various alternative solutions considered, and the reasons for the design choices made.

1. Introduction

The goal of the Advanced Automation System (AAS) is to provide Air Traffic Control (ATC) services to its end users: the US air traffic controllers. Some of these services, such as radar data reception and display, are critical, in that if they are not available, the controllers cannot carry out their duty normally. The requirement is that critical services should not be unavailable more than 3 seconds per year. The requirements allow for some other services a limited unavailability of up to 156 seconds per year. Since the unavailability of existing commercial single-fault tolerant systems is measured in tens of minutes or hours per year, the above very stringent availability requirements make AAS a system beyond the current state of the art. To achieve these requirements, new design techniques, which enable the system to automatically mask *multiple* concurrent component failures, had to be used.

2. Air traffic control services and subsystems

The U.S. airspace is administratively divided into 23 areas, each area being in its turn divided into sectors. There are approximately 650 sectors in total. In each area, an Area Control Computer Complex (ACCC) provides support to controllers in performing ATC functions. The ACCCs receive aircraft surveillance and weather data from radars, communicate with Tower Control Computing Complexes (TCCC) installed in airport towers to coordinate arrival and departure at airports in the area controlled, and communicate with other ACCCs to keep aircraft moving smoothly from one area to another area. All ACCCs adhere to the standard time broadcast by the WWV radio station of the National Bureau of Standards. The ACCCs also communicate with a central FAA Technical Center in New Jersey and provide testing and training service for new software and personnel, but in what follows, issues related to the Technical center, test, and personnel training are ignored for reasons of simplicity. Since the set of hardware and software components that form a TCCC is a subset of the components that form an ACCC, we further simplify our presentation by focusing on the ACCC approach to fault-tolerance.

From a functional point of view, an ACCC system (see Figure 1) consists of radar gateway processors, which receive surveillance data for the monitored air sectors from radars, a number of up to 288 common console processors, which are the workstations assisting air traffic controllers to perform their function, several larger central processors capable of hosting computationally and storage intensive ATC appli-

cations, communication gateway processors, which control communications with other systems, such as TCCCs, ACCCs, the FAA Technical Center, weather systems, flight data systems, and WWV, and monitor and control processors which interface the ACCC system to operators and administrators. Processors of the same type are grouped into subsystems, for example radar gateway processors form the radar gateway subsystem and the central processors form the central processing subsystem. A local communications network (LCN) enables processors to communicate by exchanging messages. The physical network and the associated communication software forms the communication subsystem. An ACCC system is distributed: no volatile or stable storage is shared among processors.

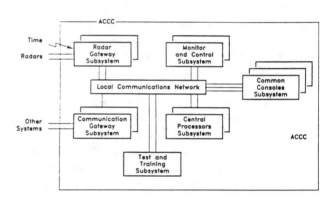

Figure 1

Air traffic control services are geographically partitioned among the various subsystems mentioned above. For example, the Surveillance Processing and Correlation service (which receives radar data and correlates it with individual aircraft tracks) is hosted by radar gateway processors with direct physical access to radar input. CPU and storage-demanding ATC services, such as Flight Plan Processing and Conflict Alert are hosted by central processors with access to high speed CPUs and high capacity magnetic storage devices. The Controller Interface Processing service (which inputs and interprets commands entered by air traffic controllers) and the Logical Display Management service (which manages all data characterizing the state of an air traffic sector and displays portions of it as directed) are hosted by common console processors directly connected to the physical displays and keyboards used by controllers.

Redundancy of components is used inside each subsystem to ensure that it provides its specified services despite failures or changes affecting individual subsystem components. The goal is to mask such events from subsystem users. The remainder of the paper discusses the issues that had to be addressed in managing the above mentioned redundancy. Since presently there is no agreement on terms when it comes to system structuring and fault-tolerance concepts, we first define the basic architectural building blocks of AAS, classify the failures that these building blocks can experience, and in-

Reprinted from *Proc. 20th Int'l Symp. Fault Tolerant Computing,*
June 1990, pp. 6-17. Copyright © 1990 by The Institute of
Electrical and Electronic Engineers, Inc. All rights reserved.

troduce the general approach to fault-tolerance adopted. We then investigate the issues that had to be addressed to provide high availability at the various abstraction levels of AAS, from hardware to the software applications.

3. Basic system structuring concepts

An ACCC system is structured hierarchically by using a small number of primitive concepts such as service, server, and the "depends" relation.

3.1 Services, servers, and the "depends" hierarchy

A computing *service* specifies a collection of operations whose execution can be triggered by inputs from service users, changes in the environment monitored by the service, or the passage of time. Operation executions may result in outputs to users and in service state changes. For example, an IBM4381 raw processor service consists of all the operations defined in a 4381 processor manual, and a DB2 database service consists of all the relational query and update operations that clients can make on a database.

The operations defined by a service specification can be performed only by a *server* for that service. A server implements a service without exposing to users the internal service state representation and operation implementation details. Such details are hidden from users, who need know only the externally specified service behavior. Servers can be hardware or software implemented. For example, a 4381 raw processor service is typically implemented by a hardware server; however, sometimes one can see this service 'emulated' by software. A DB2 service is typically implemented by a software server, although it is conceivable to implement this service by a hardware database machine.

Servers implement their service by using other services implemented by other servers. A server *u* implementing service U *depends* on a server *r* implementing service R if the correctness of *u*'s behavior depends on the correctness of *r*'s behavior. This definition naturally extends to services: service U depends on service R if a server *u* implementing U depends on the correct implementation of R. The server *u* is called a *user* (or client) of *r*, while *r* is called a *resource* for *u*. Resources in turn might depend on other resources to provide their service, and so on, down to the atomic resources of a system, which one does not wish to analyze any further. Thus, the user/client and resource/server names are relative to the "depends" relation: what is a resource or server at a certain level of abstraction can be a client or a user at another level of abstraction. The ACCC "depends" graph, which represents servers by nodes and the "depends" relation by arrows, is *acyclic* (see Figure 6). In drawing this graph, we follow the convention of representing a user *u* of a resource *r* above *r*, and we say of *u* that it is at a level of abstraction "higher" than *r* [D71], [P79], [R75].

A distributed system, such as ACCC, consists of software servers which depend on processor services and communication services. Processor service is provided concurrently to several software servers by multi-user operating systems. These operating systems in turn depend on raw processor service provided by physical processors, which in turn depend on lower level hardware resources such as CPUs, random access memories, busses, I/O controllers, disks, and displays. Communication services are implemented by distributed communication servers which depend on lower level hardware networking services. It is customary to designate the union of processor and communication services provided for application processes as a *distributed operating system* service [TR85].

This paper focuses on redundancy management at the ACCC distributed operating system level, and addresses the issues pertinent to ensuring application fault-tolerance mostly by discussing the support that the distributed operating system provides for making the ATC applications highly available. We intend to address the subject of redundancy management in the ATC applications in a forthcoming paper.

3.2. Server failure classification

For completeness, we briefly review in this section the nested failure classification of [CASD85] which will be used in what follows. A server is *correct* if, in response to inputs, it behaves in a manner consistent with its specification. We assume a service specification prescribes both the server's response for any sequence of inputs and the real-time interval within which this response should occur. The response includes any outputs to be delivered to users and any state transitions that should take place.

A server *failure* occurs when the server does not behave in the manner specified. Thus, failure means discrepancy between actual and specified behavior. An *omission* failure occurs when a server omits to respond to a sequence of inputs. A *timing* failure occurs when a server either omits to respond or responds too early or too late. The vast majority of timing failures observed in practice are *late* timing, or *performance*, failures: no response occurs before the end of the specified real time interval. An *arbitrary* failure occurs when a component does not behave in the manner specified: it either does not respond, or it responds too early or too late, or some response different from the one specified occurs. If, after a first omission to respond, a server omits to respond to all subsequent inputs until its restart, the server suffers a *crash* failure. Crash failures are a proper subclass of omission failures, omission failures are a proper subclass of timing failures, and timing failures are a proper subclass of the class of arbitrary (or all) failures.

An operating system crash and a communication service that occasionally loses messages are examples of omission failures. An excessive message transmission or processing delay due to an overload affecting a set of communication servers is an example of a performance failure. When some action is taken by a processor too soon, perhaps because of a timer that runs too fast, we speak of an early timing failure. A search procedure that "finds" a key that was never inserted in a table and the alteration of the contents of a message by a communication link affected by random noise are examples of arbitrary failures.

3.3. Server failure semantics

Since the recovery actions invoked upon detection of a server failure depend upon what possible failure behaviors the server can exhibit, in a fault-tolerant system such as ACCC one has to *extend* the standard specification of servers to include, in addition to their familiar failure-free semantics, their possible failure behaviors, or *failure semantics* [C85]. If the specification of a server *s* prescribes that all the failures observable by *s* users should be in class F, we say that "*s* has F failure semantics". For example, if a communication link is allowed to lose messages, but cannot delay or corrupt messages, we say that it has omission failure semantics, and if it is allowed to lose or delay (but not corrupt) messages, we say that it has performance failure semantics. Similarly, if a processor can only crash or a disk can only omit to read certain sectors in response to read requests (for example, because of parity errors) we say that they have crash and read omission failure semantics, respectively.

It is the responsibility of the designer of a server *s* to ensure that the failure semantics specified for *s* is properly implemented, so that *s* users can correctly program the recovery actions to be invoked when *s* fails. For example, to ensure that a network has performance failure semantics, it is standard practice for network designers to use error detecting codes. Similarly, to ensure that a processor has crash failure semantics, one can use error detecting codes or a pair of processors which execute the same instruction stream and continuously compare their results, so that a crash occurs when a disagreement between processor outputs is detected [TW89]. In general, the stronger the failure semantics specified, the more expensive it is to build a server that implements that semantics. For example, a memory that uses error detecting codes to implement read omission failure semantics is more expensive to build and will have a slower access time than a memory that does not use error detecting codes and hence, can behave in arbitrary ways when physical faults affect it.

3.4. Fault-tolerant services through server groups

To ensure that a service remains available to clients despite server failures, one can implement the service by a *group* of redundant, physically independent, servers, so that if some of these fail, the remaining ones provide the service. We say that a group *masks* the failure of a member *m* whenever the group (as a whole) responds as specified to users despite the failure of m. The *group output* is a function of the outputs of individual group members. For example, the group output can be the output generated by the fastest member of the group, the output generated by some distinguished member of the group, or the result of a majority vote on group member outputs. We use the phrase "group g has F failure semantics" as a shorthand for "the failures observable by users of g are in class F".

A server group able to mask from its clients any k concurrent member failures will be termed k-fault tolerant; when k is 1, the group will be called *single*-fault tolerant, and when k is greater than 1, the group will be called *multiple*-fault tolerant. For example, if the k members of a server group have performance failure semantics and the group output is defined to be the output of the fastest member, the group can mask up to k-1 concurrent member failures and provide performance failure semantics to its clients. Similarly, a primary/standby group of k servers with performance failure semantics, with members ranked as primary, first back-up, second back-up, ... , (k-1)th back-up, can mask up to k-1 concurrent member failures and provide performance failure semantics. A group of 2k + 1 members with arbitrary failure semantics whose output is the result of a majority vote among outputs computed in parallel by all members can mask a minority, that is, up to k member failures. The failure semantics of the group is the same as that of its components: when a majority of members fail in an arbitrary way, the entire group can fail in an arbitrary way. Although the failure semantics of a group is never stronger than the weakest member failure semantics, the reason for using groups is to reduce the likelihood that service failures are ever observed by service users.

The specific mechanisms needed for managing redundant server groups in a way that makes their input/output behavior functionally indistinguishable from that of single servers depend critically on the failure semantics specified for group members. The stronger these semantics, the simpler and more efficient the group management, or fault-tolerance mechanisms, can be. Conversely, the weaker these semantics, the more complex and expensive the fault-tolerance mechanisms become. Since the design of servers with stronger failure semantics has a cost higher than that of servers with weaker - possibly arbitrary - failure semantics, a key issue in designing multi-layered fault-tolerant systems is how to *balance* the amounts of failure detection, recovery, and masking redundancy mechanisms used at the various abstraction levels of the system, so as to obtain the best possible *overall* cost/performance/dependability results.

4. How should failures be handled in AAS?

This global question can be broken down into two orthogonal questions. First, at what abstraction level should replication be used to automatically mask ACCC component failures to human users? And second, what class of component failures should the system be able to mask automatically?

4.1. At what level of abstraction should automatic failure masking occur?

It is possible to mask component failures at the hardware level, at the operating system level, or at the application level. For example the FTMP system [H78] implemented redundancy management mechanisms which mask hardware server failures directly *in hardware*, by triplexing physical hardware servers with arbitrary failure semantics and using voting. The Stratus system [TW89] also masks most hardware server failures at the hardware level by duplexing hardware servers with crash failure semantics (which in their turn are implemented by pairs of hardware servers with arbitrary failure semantics which execute in lock-step). This allows single hardware server failures to be masked from higher software levels of abstraction and increases the mean time between failures for raw processor service. Note however that hardware implemented triplexing or quadruplexing does not in general eliminate the need for handling at application software level processor service failures in the same way as if this service was implemented by using a non-redundant processor (although such failures will occur more rarely, they will occur and presumably must be handled). For example if the operations implemented at a higher software level server, such as a database server, must be atomic with respect to processor service crashes, the code for implementing this semantics will have to be written anyway, possibly by relying on logging and recovery facilities provided by the underlying operating system, whether the processor service is implemented by using a simple CPU or a quadruplex CPU arrangement. Note also that hardware triplexing or quadruplexing is of no help in masking to end users application server failures caused by residual design faults in either server or operating system programs.

Several commercial systems attempt to mask hardware server failures at the *operating system* level, so that the application software servers running above can continue to provide their service without interruption when a lower level hardware server fails. For example the MVS operating system can mask single CPU failures to application servers by restarting a server which was running on a failed CPU from a previously saved check-point in a manner transparent to that server. Failures of hardware servers such as processors, buses and disk controllers are also masked at the operating system level by systems such as Tandem [BGH86], Sequoia [B88] and VAX cluster [KLS86]. Although the choice of masking hardware server failures at the operating system level will provide a more reliable processor service to application servers, this will not help mask to end users application server failures caused either by application design faults or lower level processor service failures.

To mask all software as well as hardware server failures in a uniform way to end users, one has to use redundancy at the highest level of abstraction: the application level. The idea is to implement any service that must be available to its users despite hardware or software failures by a redundant software *server group* whose members run on distinct hardware processor hosts and maintain redundant information about the service state. When a group member fails (either because of a lower level hardware or software service failure or because of a residual design fault in its program) the surviving group members have enough service state information to continue to provide the service without interruption. This complicates somewhat the development of applications, especially when they make use of persistent data, but since the specification for AAS required that the system be able to automatically mask both hardware *and* software failures [AB87] and the very stringent availability requirements practically forbid users from observing situations in which there exist no operational servers for a critical ATC service, the decision was taken to use application server groups, and rely on systematic hierarchical methods for exception handling [Cri89] to mask lower level failures to application servers whenever economically appropriate.

4.2. What failure classes should be automatically masked?

As mentioned before, the redundancy management mechanisms designed for managing server groups with arbitrary failure semantics are not only more costly and complex than those designed for managing groups with stronger failure semantics, such as omission or performance, but also lead to higher run-time overheads and slower response times. For example, experience indicates that mechanism designed for managing groups of application servers with arbitrary failure semantics [Wa78] can consume up to 80% of the total throughput of a system [PB85].

Experience also indicates that commercially available, fault-tolerant systems, such as Tandem , which use group redundancy mechanisms based on stronger, yet realistic, failure hypotheses, such as omission hardware failures and performance software failures, can have acceptable overhead levels. Considerable expertise exists in building hardware whose vast majority of failures are omission failures and production quality software which occasionally crashes or is slow, but does not output bad results. Thus, the vast majority of failures likely to be observed in practice in production quality systems are performance failures.

Recent statistical evidence [G86] indicates that group masking mechanisms designed for software servers with performance failure semantics can be effective in providing tolerance to server failures caused either by hardware server failures or by residual design faults left in production quality software after extensive reviews and testing. The study reported in [G86] is based on a sample set of 2000 Tandem Nonstop distributed operating systems representing over 10 million system hours. The systems studied use hardware processors based on error detecting/correcting codes and groups of two primary/back-up software servers to mask hardware as well as software failures. The statistics indicate that for the primary/back-up spooling server group used in Tandem's distributed operating system, only 0.7% of the failures affecting the group were double server failures, that is, group failures. The remaining 99.3% of the failures detected in the group were single member failures which left the other member, and hence, the group, running correctly. A plausible explanation for this phenomenon is that most transient faults affecting physically independent processors occur independently, and hence cause any affected software servers to crash independently. Similarly, most residual software design faults manifest themselves intermittently in rare limit (or exceptional) conditions which result in time-dependent synchronization errors or in a slow accumulation of resources acquired for temporary use and never released. Such errors and residues seem to accumulate at different rates in operating system tables and group members running independently on different processors and eventually lead individual group members to fail at different times.

Faced with the choice of adopting either redundancy management mechanisms for servers with arbitrary failure semantics or mechanisms for servers with performance failure semantics, in view of the accumulated experience described above, the decision was taken to go with the latter alternative. With this choice, we expect to provide automatic masking at a reasonable cost for the vast majority of component failures likely to be observable: performance failures resulting either from crash or omission hardware failures or from performance operating system, communication, and application server failures. As highlighted by the study of [G86], such mechanisms can also be effective in providing tolerance to a significant portion of, although not all, arbitrary failures which are likely to occur because of imperfect coverage by the hardware error detecting codes and the software checking used. The, hopefully rare, arbitrary application failures not detected and masked automatically by these mechanisms will ultimately be detected by the human users, the air traffic controllers who know the physical laws of the airspace environment they are controlling and can diagnose abnormal system behavior. In such a case, a controller can unilaterally decide to switch to an alternate service provided by a *back-up system* of a different, very simple, design. This alternate system is capable of providing *emergency* service until the faulty components of the *main* ACCC system that caused the user visible failure behavior are repaired. More about this back-up system will be given in section 10. Although no attempt is presently planned for automatically masking arbitrary application server failures to users, a plan is in place for detecting and diagnosing automatically as many as possible of these failures, and shutting down application servers which display an errant behavior. This decision is consistent with a growth-oriented system design philosophy, of implementing efficient automatic means for detecting design defects and offering system maintainers help for diagnosing and correcting problems without causing service interruption to the end users.

Our decision to base the automatic redundancy management mechanisms on the hypothesis that software servers will suffer performance failures, results in two subsidiary system-wide objectives: ensure that 1) the hardware which will be used has, with high probability, omission failure semantics and 2) the programs which implement software servers are partially correct [Cri89], that is, in the absence of failures of the servers they depend upon, these programs can only crash or be slow, but cannot output erroneous answers. To prevent arbitrary failures of software servers, extensive use is made of modern software engineering ideas, such as pursuance of simplicity in design, hierarchical decomposition of the software by using information hiding and abstract data types, disciplined detection and handling of all exceptions, and extensive design and code inspections. A modern programming language (Ada) was selected by IBM and the FAA to enforce as much error checking as possible at compilation and execution time.

4.3. What mechanisms are needed for implementing redundant application software server groups?

First, one needs to decide what *processor services* should be provided to application servers, so as to satisfy both their response time requirements under the specified maximum system load and the requirement that processor services have performance failure semantics. To make the behavior of server groups indistinguishable from that of non-redundant servers one has to provide group members with *communication* primitives enabling them to communicate with other groups and reach agreement on the state of the service they implement despite random communication delays and failures. The semantics of the ATC applications requires that group communication be of two kinds: either group to group request/reply or one group to many groups multicast (Figure 2). An important issue is that of how to decide on the *availability policy* to be inforced for each software server group, that is, *how closely synchronized* should the local states of members be and *how many members* should each group have. A related issue is to design *group availability manage-*

ment mechanisms that will automatically enforce the availability policies defined for application groups.

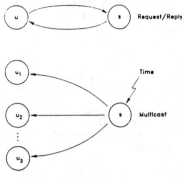

Figure 2

We list below some of the key questions that were asked when deciding what automatic fault-tolerance mechanisms should be employed at the various abstraction levels of an ACCC system. For most of these questions we examine the alternatives envisaged and the initial design choices made. Many of these decisions are still subject to debate, and implementation activity accompanied by testing and measurements is going on to help evaluate the consequences of some of these decisions before the system is deployed. Alternative solutions to some of these questions are being pursued in parallel with the main development activity.

5. How should processor service be provided to applications?

In view of the load and response time requirements specified for ACCC and the requirement by the customer -the Federal Aviation Administration- that off-the-shelf basic hardware and software components be used extensively to run all specified ATC applications, one of the earliest decisions taken was to use 308X or 937x class main frame processors for running computationally and storage intensive ATC applications, and RS6000 processors embedded in a specially engineered display system as workstations for air traffic controllers. These processors are interconnected by a local communication network (LCN) based on IEEE 802.5 token rings. Since an ACCC system is required to accommodate more processors than a single token ring can support, classes of similar processors are clustered by attaching them to distinct horizontal *access* token rings (Figure 3). The set of processors attached to the same access ring forms a *cluster*. Clusters are connected among themselves by a vertical *backbone* ring structure (Figure 3). Specialized hardware servers, called bridges, are used for relaying messages between access and back-bone rings. The chosen hardware can not only handle the specified peak ATC load, but can also interface with a variety of specialized I/O servers required for the ATC applications, such as large workstation displays especially manufactured for this application, radars, and foreign communication networks. The hardware, which in the past has been characterized by significant mean times between failures and observed omission failure behavior, was considered to provide an acceptable cost/performance ratio. The adoption of MVS and a real-time version of AIX as the operating systems that will be used for providing high end and workstation processor service to communication servers and applications allows the FAA to take advantage of the growth in reliability that comes from many users and the software tools already existing for these systems.

5.1. What are the hardware replaceable units?

By a *replaceable hardware unit* we understand a physical unit of failure, replacement and growth, that is, a unit which fails independently of other units, can be removed without affect-

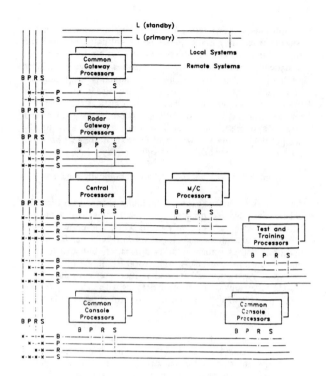

Figure 3

ing physically the behavior of other units, and can be added to a system to augment its performance, capacity, or availability. The small and large ACCC processors have a considerable variety of physical resources attached to them such as disks, tapes, printers, common console displays, keyboards, radar adaptors, external WWV time radio receivers, and specialized I/O adapters. For a small processor, a failure of the physical access path to such a resource or the failure of the resource itself results in an entire processor failure. For example the failure of the display attached to a common console processor results in a failure of the entire common console processor. Thus, an entire small processor with all its computing, storage, user interface, and communication resources is a replaceable unit. For large main frame processors, concurrent maintenance of certain attached resources is possible while the processor continues to function perhaps with degraded capacity. In this case the hardware unit of failure/replacement is finer than an entire processor. For example a failed spindle of disks attached to a main frame processor can be replaced without stopping the entire main frame complex, so the spindle, rather than the entire complex, is an atomic hardware unit of failure/replacement. For the LCN component, the atomic units of failure/replacement are the cables, the bridges between token rings, and the ring adaptors used to attach large and small processors to access rings.

5.2 What mechanisms are used to ensure that the hardware replaceable units have omission failure semantics?

The extensive error detecting/correcting mechanisms embodied in the chosen main frame and workstation processors, in the IBM 802.5 token ring and bridges, justify to a high degree -although not entirely- our goal of providing hardware with crash or omission failure semantics to applications. An implementation of raw processor services with crash failure semantics by using pairs of main frame and RS6000 processors which execute in lock-step and systematically compare their results, as described in [TW89], was rejected as being too expensive and redundant with the run-time checking that the error detecting/correcting codes used in these processors do anyway. The use of processors from

456

other vendors which implement crash failure semantics by lock-step duplication and comparison was also considered and rejected because of problems related to lack of sufficient computational capacity, lack of real-time executives designed for such processors, and cost reasons. Moreover, it was felt that processors were just one link of a larger hardware chain that contains a variety of hardware servers, some of which use error detecting codes (e.g. memories, busses, disks) and some of which do not (e.g. electronic displays, radars), and that using duplexing in just one link of the larger chain was not economically justifiable.

5.3 How much hardware redundancy is needed for achieving the required availability goals?

Assuming independence of the ACCC hardware replaceable units and the failure data accumulated from past field experience for the chosen hardware, extensive stochastic modelling and simulation studies were used to determine the number of hardware servers needed in the various ACCC subsystems to ensure that there exist enough working host processors for each ATC service at any time and that timely communication is possible among these hosts with very high probability. Figure 3 illustrates the redundant LCN topology chosen following these studies: a set of four physical backbone token rings, represented vertically, are used to interconnect several horizontal access rings, consisting themselves of up to four physical rings.

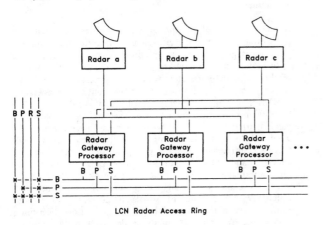

Figure 4

Figure 4 illustrates the hardware redundancy employed in the radar gateway subsystem: each radar can be connected to three different radar gateway processors forming a radar gateway processor group. In this way the group can mask the failure of any two of its members and still provide the hardware resources necessary for running the Surveillance Processing and Correlation application which processes radar input. Redundancy is employed in a similar way in the Communication Gateway, Monitor and Control, and Central Processor subsystems, by grouping the processors in these subsystems into *redundant processor groups*.

Figure 5 illustrates how hardware redundancy is used to ensure the availability of processor services needed for running the ATC services responsible for monitoring a sector of airspace: from one to four common console processors (with their attached displays and keyboards) can be grouped together into a *sector suite* processor group. The configuration choice is made by the user based on human factor considerations for the management of the air sector and a plan for redundancy. When a console is lost, the display real estate, and the associated processing workload is redistributed among the surviving common console processors. If the number of working common console processors in a sector

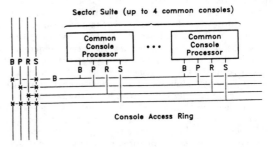

Figure 5

suite group drops below a user specified threshold, the sector suite can be reconfigured to add a nearby idle console, or the set of ATC services controlling that air sector can be *moved* to a spare sector suite processor group. This *mobility* of air sector monitor/control services contrasts with the immobility of all the other ATC services, which are bound to their original host processor groups, the only ones with physical access to the resources needed for providing these services. For example the Surveillance Processing and Correlation service responsible for receiving radar data from a given radar and associating tracks with that data is *bound* to the processor group (of maximum size three) whose members are physically attached to the monitored radar.

6. What availability policies should be defined for the various application services?

The availability policy for a certain server group prescribes how closely should the local states of group members be synchronized and how many members should the group have, so as to meet the specified response time and service availability requirements.

6.1 How should the local states of application servers be synchronized to achieve the required response times?

For any service, the *server group synchronization* policy prescribes the degree of local state synchronization that must exist between the servers implementing the service. There are two extreme synchronization policies with a continuum of mixed policies in between.

Close synchronization (also called masking redundancy [A76] or active redundancy [Pa88]) prescribes that local member states be closely synchronized to each other by letting all members execute all service requests in parallel and go through the same sequence of state transitions. Since we assume that software servers have performance failure semantics, the group output can be the output computed by any member. If all members send their outputs in parallel, the group output can be understood as being the output computed by the set of fastest members. The advantage of this output sending technique is that group clients do not see performance failures as long as the group has at least a correct member. The drawback is a high communication overhead. To reduce this overhead, group members can be ranked with respect to communication, or *c-ranked*, and output sending can be restricted to the highest c-ranked member. The cost is an increased output delay when the highest c-ranked member fails, due to the need to detect its failure and agree on a new c-ranking among surviving members.

In contrast to close synchronization, *loose synchronization* (also called dynamic redundancy [A76], standby or passive redundancy [Pa88]) ranks group members with respect to how closely their internal state is synchronized to the service state, which can be understood as being the application of all operations requested by clients since the service initialization to the initial service state. To distinguish the ranking with respect to state synchronization from the c-ranking introduced before we call it s-ranking. Standby redundancy requires only the highest s-ranking group member, usually called the *primary* server, to process service requests and store locally the service state. This is also the member who usually sends the answers (since it is the first to know them) so for standby redundancy the c- and s-rankings coincide. One or more *back-up* servers with lower s-ranks can log service requests and can periodically receive state checkpoints from the primary. In such an arrangement, the local state of a back-up is behind the state of the primary, since it does not reflect the execution of some recent service requests by the primary server. Were the primary to fail, the highest s-ranking back-up can recover a service state existing before the primary failure by re-executing the service requests logged since the last state check-point obtained from the primary.

The main advantage of loose synchronization over close synchronization is that only primary servers make full use of their share of the replicated service resources while back-ups make only a reduced use. This allows more servers to coexist for a given amount of computing power. The main drawback is that the delays seen by clients are longer when failures occur. If we call the maximum sequence of service requests processed by a primary between successive state check-points the primary/back-up *processing lag*, then the worst case delay in answering a client request after a primary failure will not only be composed of the time needed to detect and reach agreement about the primary failure, but also of the time needed by the new primary to absorb the primary/back-up processing lag.

Some ATC services are implemented by closely synchronized server groups, while others are implemented by loosely synchronized groups. For example, the Surveillance Processing and Correlation (SPC) service for a certain radar is implemented by three closely synchronized servers which all receive input in parallel from the radar and associate aircraft tracks with the radar data. To minimize multicast traffic, the servers are c-ranked, so that only the highest ranking server multicasts the current position of tracks to common console processors. The Flight Planning service hosted by the central processors subsystem is an example of a loosely synchronized service, implemented by a group of three s-ranked servers: a primary server, a back-up server, and a ready server. The primary maintains the current service state and checkpoints any state change to the back-up. The ready server is just an address space loaded with its program, ready to become back-up when the back-up is promoted to the role of primary. The s-ranked arrangement reflects the fact that response time requirements for this service are less stringent than for the SPC service.

6.2 How many redundant servers should an application server group have?

For any given service, the *replication policy* prescribes how many redundant servers should ideally be used to implement the service. For example if a service S can be hosted by a processor group g of three processors (which all possess all the physical resources needed by servers for S), then a replication policy of 2 for S means that two servers for S should run on the g processors for as long as at least two of them are up, and one server for S should run when only one processor of g is up. The synchronization and replication policies selected for a service constitute the *availability policy* for that service. The determination of the availability policy for the various ATC services was done by taking into account the response time requirements specified by the FAA as well as initial performance and reliability data from a stochastic modelling study. For example the Surveillance and Correlation service is implemented by a group of three

closely synchronized redundant servers; in this way the service of periodic aircraft track data broadcasting remains available to ATC services running in common console processors despite any two concurrent server failures. Most other ATC services are implemented by s-ranked groups (e.g. Flight Plan Processing, Conflict Alert). Some services are required to have servers on any correctly functioning host in a processor group. For example the Logical Display Management service is required to have c-ranked closely synchronized servers on all working common console processors of a sector suite group.

7. How are highly available communication services provided to application server groups?

First, one needs to find out the current *topology* of correctly working LCN components. Once the topology of active components is known, one is able to compute point-to-point and multicast *routes* that avoid failed LCN components. Second, if servers for a service can move from one processor to another, another important issue is that of *naming*: how do users address their service requests to server groups? Third, assuming the users are able to address service requests to server groups, one also needs protocols for controlling the *sequencing and delivery* of messages between client groups and server groups.

7.1 How is knowledge of the communication network topology maintained?

A *network topology management* service depends on LCN-wide connectionless as well as connectionless point-to-point message communication and multicast services (Figure 6) to maintain up-to-date knowledge of the physical topology of the LCN network at any point in time. The topology consists of the following basic elements: processors, processor-to-ring adapters, rings, and bridges. The LCN-wide point-to-point and multicast message services depend in their turn on the Media Access Layer services defined for each individual ring. The topology management service is implemented by a group of up to four servers, which maintain redundantly four copies of the LCN topology image. The group members are s-ranked, the highest ranking member being the leader. A simple protocol which requires a topology management server to acquire control over a majority of LCN bridges before becoming leader ensures the unicity of the leader even in the presence of partition failures (low level bridge primitives guarantee that a bridge is owned by at most one topology server at any time). Leader existence is achieved by periodic mutual surveillance of group members: if a member detects a leader failure it attempts to become leader by acquiring a majority of bridges. The topology database consists of two mappings, the ring/adaptor table and the processor/adaptor table, which change dynamically as processor, adapters, bridges, and rings join or leave the active LCN topology (because of failures or maintenance actions). Events which affect the LCN topology are detected either by servers outside the topology manager group (e.g. bridges detect adaptor insert/deinsert events on the rings to which they are attached) or by the leader of the topology management group, which periodically tests via special "circuit test" messages components such as bridges and rings. Topology updates detected by the leader are reliably check-pointed to all its active peers.

7.2 How should the availability of communication routes be ensured?

To enable quick masking of a message loss due to the failure of a route between two processors, the decision was taken that two independent routes should be maintained between any two processors that need to communicate by a *route management service*. In this way, if the failure of a route to

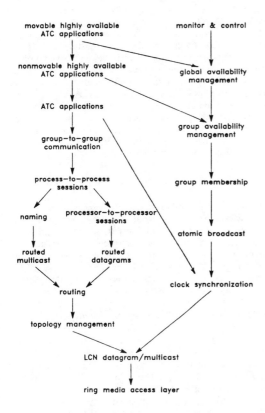

Figure 6

a target processor is detected by a sender processor (by the absence of timely acknowledgements for messages sent along that route), the sender processor can use the alternate route to re-send the unacknowledged messages to the target processor. If the route failure is diagnosed as being permanent by the topology management service, the route management service computes and sends an alternate route to the sender processor so as to maintain two routes between any two processors which need to communicate. The redundancy inherent in the LCN topology allows the routes (i.e. sequences of adapter and bridge addresses) between any two processors to be physically disjoint, so that no single hardware failure affects both routes simultaneously. The route management service is implemented by a group of up to four s-ranked route servers. Communication costs between topology management servers and route management servers are minimized by letting the latter run in the same address spaces as the former. The route managers depend on the topology service to compute a pair of routes whenever they are requested by a processor which wants to establish a session with another processor (Figure 6). Such sessions are used to multiplex several higher level sessions between processes running on the two processors. To avoid sending unnecessary requests to the route management servers whenever new process-to-process sessions must be open, processors cache such routing information locally. The topology service informs the route management service about any topology changes, so that new routes which avoid failed components or take advantage of repaired components can be computed and sent via connectionless messages to all processors affected while these use alternate routes. Inconsistencies between the locally cached routing information and the route servers are resolved in the usual way: when a processor detects that its cached information is out-of-date, either because it has missed a route update message from the

route servers or because it detects a route failure, it requests the route server group for a new route.

Dual routes are not only maintained for point to point communication, but also for multicast communication. Although the token rings allow all-rings-multicast in addition to routed multicast, the former form of multicast is not used for bandwidth reasons. To ensure that the periodic multicast communication pattern of Figure 2 (implemented by using the token ring functionally addressed multicast service and the dual multicast routing service provided by the route managers) is available despite component failures, a reliable periodic multicast protocol based on the use of negative acknowledgments was designed [Cr90]. This protocol does not have any message overhead in the absence of failures. It uses a new technique for batching the negative acknowledgements that broadcast targets send to broadcast sources when they detect LCN failures in order to reduce the LCN message traffic to a minimum after LCN component failures are detected. This allows the LCN bandwidth to remain available for the topology/routing server groups and the other normal ATC traffic in the critical moments which follow LCN component failures.

7.3 What communication services should be provided for application server groups?

In addition to the one-to-many multicast services mentioned in the previous section, another important class of communication services is provided to enable client groups to request services to server groups and match replies with requests. These request/reply services among process groups depend on lower level process-to-process session services, which in their turn depend on location transparent naming and processor-to-processor session management services (Figure 6).

A *processor-to-processor session* management service uses dual routes as mentioned before to guarantee sequenced and reliable delivery of messages. A server for the distributed processor-to-processor session management service exists on each processor. A *naming service* makes use of the routed multicast service (Figure 6) to record the current host processor for the highest c-ranking server of each ATC server group into a table which maps service names to processors. Fragments of this names mapping are cached in each processor, so that these need to access the name service only at initialization or when detecting cache inconsistencies. The naming service is implemented by up to four replicated *name servers*, co-located in the same address spaces as the topology and routing manager servers mentioned previously. Like the topology and routing servers, the naming servers are c-ranked.

The *process-to-process session managers* depend on the naming (Figure 6) and the processor to processor session services to provide *location transparent sessions* for ATC application in the following way. When a server s for an ATC service S on processor p becomes the highest c-ranking member of the group which implements S, it informs the name service of the fact that service requests for S must now be addressed to p. To any subsequent request that a server t running on a processor q makes for opening a session with S, the name server leader responds by giving the process-to-process session manager on q two low level routes (i.e. sequence of adaptor and bridge addresses) between p and q. All service S requests are routed by this session manager to p without t knowing anything about where s resides. If s fails, and a new server s′ for S on another processor p′ becomes the highest c-ranking S member, s′ will inform the name manager leader that it now services requests for service S. The name manager uses an unacknowledged inexpensive multicast to inform all session managers which had sessions with s that now they should use two new routes for sending service S requests to s'. If each session manager that maintains sessions with S stores all S requests sent and not yet acknowledged, these can be resent by using the new route. In this way, the crash of the primary server s for S and the fact that service S requests are subsequently being processed by an alternate server s' for S remains transparent to all S users, who experience the failure as a mere delay in getting their answers. To minimize the time between the detection of the failure of s and the moment communication is re-established with an alternate server s', the decision was taken to implement all ATC services by groups of at least two active servers. This avoids a start of s' after the failure of s, which would delay the replies to service S users.

The point-to-point location transparent process-to-process sessions services are in their turn used to implement application specific request/reply protocols among ATC application groups. Some of these protocols provide an "at least once" semantics (when the operations exported by servers are idempotent) and some an "at most once" semantics (when the operations exported by servers are not idempotent). Some send messages in parallel to all members of a group, some only to the highest c-ranking members. We plan to report in detail about these protocols in a forthcoming paper focusing on the ATC applications.

8. How should the specified availability policies be enforced automatically for application services?

The set of all ATC services hosted by a processor group, such as a sector suite group or a radar gateway group, forms a *service group*. The processor group contains all the physical resources needed by the servers which implement the services in the group. For example, the service group hosted by a radar gateway processor group consists of the Surveillance Processing and Correlation (SPC) services for the radars connected to the group processors, while an air sector surveillance service group consists of the Aircraft/Track Management (ATM), Logical Display Management (LDM), Controller Interface Processing (CIP), and Weather Data Management (WXDM) services for the air sector monitored by a sector suite processor group. The synchronization and replication policies for each service in a service group constitute the *availability* policy for that service.

The mechanisms which ensure internal synchronization of the local member states in a server group depend on the synchronization policy prescribed for the service implemented by the group. For example if group members are required to be closely synchronized, it is sufficient that they receive the same sequence of inputs to stay synchronized, and a member need communicate with other members only when joining to get the group state [C88]. If group members are s-ranked, the check-pointing which goes on among members at join as well as periodically is very much application dependent and, in ACCC, is left to the service implementors. A forthcoming paper will deal with the issue of how internal synchronization and join are achieved in the ATC applications. In this paper we focus on the complementary issue of how to ensure that, for all services of a service group, there are enough members with the right rankings (if applicable) despite failures and joins.

One possible approach would be to implement for each ATC service S mechanisms for reaching agreement on the c- and s-rankings (if applicable) in the group which implements S, as well as mechanisms for detecting group member failures and procedures for handling new member joins and promotions to higher ranks. This would result in substantial code duplication and lack of modularity, since the mechanisms for enforcing the various availability policies defined for ATC services are basically the same. To avoid such duplication and achieve a clear separation between the notion of service availability policy and the mechanism used for au-

tomatic policy enforcement, the decision was taken to implement a unique *group service availability management* service (gSAM) for all ATC service groups hosted by the various ACCC processor groups. This requires ATC servers to implement only the application specific get-state and check-point procedures needed for local state synchronization at join and check-point time. Once an ACCC administrator inputs to a gSAM service (via a monitor and control console) the availability policies intended for all the ATC services in the service group hosted by a processor group, the gSAM service handles the tasks of detecting server failures, coordinating promotions, and enforcing replication policies automatically, without need for human intervention.

8.1 How to build a group service availability manager?

A group service availability management service must ensure that for each service in the group, the prescribed availability policy is enforced automatically despite processor and server departures (due to failures and scheduled shut-downs) and processor and server joins (due to recovery from failures, changes or growth). To achieve this objective, the gSAM servers must agree on a global processor group state despite random communication delays and failures. The global group state consists of the set of group processors that are correctly working, called the *processor group membership* [C88], as well as of several mappings (or tables) recording what availability policies have been defined for the various services hosted by the group, what servers run on what processors and what s-and c-rankings exists among the members of the running server groups. The problem of building a generic gSAM service for any ACCC processor group was broken down into three sub-problems: first, build a *processor group membership* service which ensures agreement on processor group membership, second, build an *atomic broadcast* service which ensures that all updates to the state of the mappings mentioned above are applied by all gSAM servers in the same order, and third, *synchronize* the states of the gSAM servers to as to ensure that they react as promptly as possible to operator commands and failures.

8.1.1 How to reach agreement on processor group membership?

A processor group membership protocol needs to ensure a number of *safety* properties, such as "at any time, all members of a group agree on the group membership", and *timeliness* properties, such as "there is an upper bound on the time it takes to detect group member failures or joins" [C88]. The design of a processor group membership protocol satisfying such safety and timeliness requirements depends critically on whether communication partition failures, which prevent group members from communicating in a timely manner, can occur or not. If partition failures can be a priori avoided, for example by using real-time operating systems capable of guaranteeing bounds on message delays under worst case system load conditions and by sending messages along multiple physically independent paths - so as to mask individual path failures, then it is possible to build a *synchronous* protocol for solving the membership problem. Such a protocol relies on the fact that processor clocks are synchronized. It is called synchronous because it provides all correct processors of a group with the same membership information at the same local times. Three such protocols are described in [C88]. All guarantee *bounded* processor failure detection and join delays despite any number of concurrent join and failure events. The upper bounds on join and failure detection delays are proportional to the bounds on message delays and to the maximum deviations among clocks. To make the system reaction to failures and joins prompt, the message delay bound and maximum clock deviation constants must be estimated as tightly as possible. However, if they are estimated too tightly, communication performance failures leading to transient partition occurrences among group members can follow. These can lead to violations of the basic safety property that group processors should always agree on the group membership. Such temporary disagreements can in their turn lead to temporary group instabilities such as temporary existence of two primaries for an s-ranked ATC server group when the processor running the second s-ranking server is partitioned from the processor which hosts the highest s-ranking server.

We have also investigated *asynchronous* protocols which can be used to reach agreement on processor group membership in the presence of network partitions [C90]. Such protocols are called asynchronous because they do not guarantee any upper bound on the amount of time which can elapse between the moment one processor detects an event (such as a failure or join) and another processor detects the same event. The main advantage of an asynchronous approach is that the safety property requiring all members of a group to agree on group membership is never violated, even when communication partitions occur because of excessive traffic load or because the bounds of message delays are estimated erroneously. Moreover, asynchronous membership protocols do not rely on clock synchronization, so the dependence on the correct functioning of this lower level service is removed. A main drawback of an asynchronous approach is weak timeliness properties: no upper bound exists on the amount of time needed for detecting group membership changes. Indeed, if failures and joins continue to occur during the execution of an asynchronous membership protocol, the surviving members will not be able to reach agreement on a new membership. Agreement can be reached only when no new failures and joins occur during a protocol execution. Thus, if an asynchronous membership protocol is used for agreeing on the membership of gSAM server groups, there is no a priori guarantee that a surviving ATC service group member becomes primary within some known bound of time after the failure of the highest s-ranking member of the group. Another drawback is the following: to prevent simultaneous activity in several partitions (which might result in conflicting actions taken by processors which are unable to communicate) asynchronous protocols require a *majority* (or more generally a quorum) of processors to be present in a group before the group can do any work. This is particularly annoying for groups of size two, where a majority approach would not enable the "minority" member to automatically differentiate between a communication partition and a failure of the other group member. The solution that most systems based on an asynchronous membership service adopt in such situations is to involve the human operator in the failure handling loop: if a surviving group could be a minority group, it has to asks the human operator for permission to continue [KLS86].

Although the base-line AAS design (Figure 6) is based on the use of a synchronous processor group membership protocol (built on top of a lower level "control" atomic broadcast protocol, which differs from group atomic broadcast because it can reach also processors outside a group, see for more details [C88]), we are continuing to investigate alternative asynchronous membership protocols. Our choice of a synchronous approach was motivated by the AAS requirement of providing bounded failure detection delays and by the availability of a real-time version of the AIX operating system that promises to bound message transmission delays on correctly functioning processors and token rings.

8.1.2 How to reach agreement on a processor group state?

Since the operations that affect the global state of a gSAM group are in general not commutative, gSAM servers use a *group atomic broadcast* communication service to broadcast global group state updates among themselves. As for mem-

bership, depending on whether communication partitions can occur or not, there are two approaches to implementing a group atomic broadcast service.

If partitions can be avoided, one can use a synchronous group atomic broadcast protocol which ensures that 1) each message whose broadcast is attempted by a group member is either accepted by all correct members of by none of them (atomicity), 2) all broadcasts accepted are accepted in the same order by all correct group members (order), and 3) there is an upper bound on the time necessary for a correct group member to broadcast a message to all other correct group members (termination). Reference [C89] describes a family of synchronous atomic broadcast protocols designed for the AAS system. The protocols are optimal in their failure-free message cost: to tolerate up to f concurrent component failures, they use $f + 1$ messages to broadcast a global state update atomically, independently of the size of the group participating in broadcast.

An asynchronous atomic broadcast ensures only the atomicity and order properties. Reference [C90] describes the asynchronous group atomic broadcast designed for AAS. If failures continue to occur in a group or group members continue to join, it does not guarantee any bound on the time it takes to broadcast an information. Despite this apparent drawback, asynchronous atomic broadcast has an important advantage over synchronous atomic broadcast: it guarantees the atomicity and order safety properties even in the presence of network partition occurrences, while a synchronous atomic broadcast protocol can violate the above properties in the presence of network partitions. Methods are known [SSCA] for detecting *a posteriori* the inconsistencies which can result from partition occurrences among availability servers that use synchronous membership and atomic broadcast protocols. Since the consequences of such temporary state inconsistencies among gSAM servers are just a decrease in ATC service performance, the decision was taken to adopt a synchronous atomic broadcast approach in the AAS baseline system and keep the asynchronous approach of [C90] as a fall-back.

A clock synchronization service (Figure 6), which synchronizes clocks to external time signals received by radio, is used by both the synchronous atomic broadcast service and some ATC applications. This service is implemented by following a new probabilistic approach to synchronizing clocks [Cr89]. The new approach does not assume bounded processor to processor message delays and can achieve maximum deviations superior to those achievable by previously published (deterministic) clock synchronization algorithms.

8.1.3. How to synchronize the local states of group service availability managers?

To ensure that the specified availability policies are enforced for all services hosted by a processor group for all possible group memberships, gSAM servers are replicated on *all* group members. Following [C85], the gSAM service is viewed as being an interpreter for two classes of concurrent events: human commands input by ACCC operators and component failure occurrences caused by the adverse group environment. The service is fault-tolerant because it undergoes specified state transitions not only in response to human operator commands, such as join processor or join server, but also in response to any number of server and processor performance failures. The failure of a server running on a processor is detected either by the operating system running on that processor or by the local gSAM server via periodic tests. In all cases the local gSAM server notifies the other gSAM servers about the failure (which changes the global group state) via a group atomic broadcast. The failure of a processor is detected by the processor group membership service. The failure notification sent by this service to the surviving gSAM servers looks to them just the same as a group atomic broadcast [C88]. In this way all events affecting the global group state are seen in the same order by all correct group members.

Previous experience with the design of a service availability management service within the Highly Available Systems project at the Almaden Research Center indicated that close synchronization among the servers implementing the service yields a simpler overall design than loose synchronization, with no loss of performance. The reasons for this are that in a closely synchronized group there is no need to program the (often complicated) promotion protocols that must be executed when a server becomes the highest s-ranking member or the s-leader of its group after the previous s-leader fails. Moreover, since in a loosely synchronized approach it is the leader's role to synchronize all concurrent events affecting the group, special point-to-point communication mechanisms are needed to enable ordinary group members to inform the leader about all events that they detect. This not only leads to more complicated code, but also to longer delays in reconfiguring the group after component failures.

In view of the above experience, the decision was taken to use close synchronization in the server groups that implement the gSAM service for all AAS processor groups. To give an idea of how a service availability management server group works, we illustrate below how a sector suite gSAM server group reacts to a server or processor failure. Consider a sector suite group composed of three common console processors p, q, r, with servers for the Aircraft Track Management (ATM) service running on all three processors. These servers are s-ranked: the highest s-ranked is on processor p, the next is on q, and the last is on r. If the group service availability manager on p detects the failure of the local ATM (primary) server, it atomically broadcasts the news about the crash to all gSAM group members. The algorithm executed by an arbitrary group member x when it receives the broadcast is the following: if there is a local ATM server and its s-rank is lower than the s-rank of the failed server, x promotes its local ATM server to the next higher s-rank; otherwise, if there is no local ATM server, then x starts one with the lowest possible s-ranking. In this way the ATM server on q becomes the highest s-ranking server in the ATM group, the one on r becomes the next, the server on p becomes the last in the s-ranking group, and the handling of the original server failure on p is considered terminated. A processor failure is handled in a similar manner by being interpreted at each surviving processor as being the failure of all ATC servers that were running on that processor.

9. How should the failure of a movable service group be masked?

For non-movable service groups (such as those bound to radar, communication or central processor groups) the failure of all servers in the group implementing the service results in a service failure. This can in its turn result in a service group failure or at least a degradation of the level of service provided by that group. This need not be the case if an air sector surveillance service group hosted by a common console processor group fails. Indeed, as mentioned earlier, this service group is movable from one common console processor group to another one, since each common console processor group has all the physical resources needed for running the surveillance services for *any* air sector. In AAS there is a special service responsible for ensuring the availability of movable ATC service groups: the *Global Availability Management Service* (GSAM). Besides this role, the GSAM service also plays the important role of *interface* between an ACCC system and its human operators and administrators. To this end it must collect status data about the various

hardware and software system components on a periodic basis to be able to display it to operators on demand. The GSAM service also transmits operator commands to processor groups. For example a command such as "enable the SPC service for a certain radar R to be provided" is entered by an ACCC operator from a keyboard attached to a GSAM server, and it is the GSAM server which monitors whether the command is successfully executed by the gSAM servers in the radar gateway processor group with access to radar R.

9.1 How to structure the global availability management service?

Like the gSAM service, the GSAM service is implemented by a closely synchronized group of up to four servers. The group keeps track of the status of all ATC service groups as well as of a pool of spare sector suite processor groups defined for each ACCC. The highest c-ranking gSAM servers for all processor groups of an ACCC report periodically to all GSAM servers the status of the processor group to which they belong by using a routed multicast communication service. The periodicity of status reporting makes the GSAM group *self-stabilizing*: the group state (which should reflect the current ACCC state, including load) is completely defined when the "last" broadcasts from all ACCC processor groups are received in a timely manner. If d is the upper bound on the time needed by a group status report multicast to reach all GSAM group members in the absence of failures, and the multicasts occur every p time units, then, in the absence of failures the local state of a GSAM server is up-to-date $p + d$ time units after it starts. A processor group failure can be detected if a GSAM server does not receive a status report multicast from that group within $p + d$ time units from the last broadcast. Given the massive redundancy used in the LCN such events should be very rare. If the group has crashed and is movable, it will be moved by the GSAM servers to a spare sector suite. If the group is not movable but the clients of the group can continue to function in a degraded service mode without the group's services, the GSAM servers will wait until the group comes back again. If the service group is essential for its clients then a switch to an alternate communication mechanism described below can occur.

10. What if component failures outside the considered failure hypotheses occur?

The radar gateway processors are connected to common console processors not only by the LCN network described previously, but also by a back-up Ethernet local area network, with enough capacity to transport essential, periodically generated radar data to all common consoles. If an air traffic controller detects that the main ACCC system experiences what to him looks like a failure, he can unilaterally switch to receive radar data about the aircraft in his sector from the back-up network. The back-up data is rather low level and only enables a controller to continue his job under an "emergency" work mode, until the normal, higher level service through the main ACCC system is restored. Very few hardware and software components are shared between the primary ACCC radar data path and the back-up Ethernet radar data path, to ensure a high degree of physical independence and design diversity between the two paths. The expectation is that a high degree of physical independence and design diversity will cause the ACCC primary radar distribution path and the Ethernet back-up radar distribution path to fail independently.

11. Other questions and issues

Although the work described in this paper was done in connection with the design of a particular fault-tolerant distributed system, the Advanced Automation System for the

Federal Aviation Administration, we believe that many of the system structuring concepts used are quite general. For example, the notions of service, server, and "uses" relation, the nested failure classification and the notion of server failure semantics, the methods of masking server failures through server groups and the associated redundancy management and group communication mechanisms, provide powerful conceptual tools which can be used in other fault-tolerant system designs as well. We believe in particular that any team which designs a distributed system with high availability objectives has to provide answers to questions similar to the ones mentioned in this paper. Thus, these questions can be useful as a guide through the labyrinth of fault-tolerant system design.

A number of important questions, not discussed in this paper for brevity reasons, will have to be addressed in future publications about the AAS system. We mention some of them below. What is the failure semantics specified for the various ATC application services and what methods are used to implement this semantics? How have the ATC applications been structured hierarchically and how is exception handling and crash recovery performed in this hierarchy? How is check-pointing being implemented in s-ranked groups and what specific communication protocols are used for communication among ATC application groups? How will changes to hardware and software be managed without causing any disruption to the availability of ATC application services? How will a very quick recovery after a total system failure be possible? How will we accurately predict and measure the availability of ATC services? A set of other important questions which need to be answered concern the cost of fault-tolerance in terms of software and hardware complexity and run-time overhead and the methods used to test and validate the system. As implementation proceeds, we hope to clarify our understanding of the issues mentioned and of the adequacy of our overall approach to fault-tolerance and report on our findings.

REFERENCES

[A76] A. Avizienis: Fault-Tolerant Systems, IEEE Transactions on Computers, Vol. C-25, No. 12, December 1976.

[AB87] A. Avizienis, D. Ball: On the Achievement of a Highly Dependable and Fault-tolerant Air Traffic Control System, IEEE Computer, February 1987.

[B88] P. Bernstein: Sequoia: a Fault-tolerant Tightly Coupled Multiprocessor for Transaction Processing, IEEE Computer, February 1988.

[BGH86] J. Bartlett, J. Gray, B. Host: Fault-tolerance in Tandem Computer Systems, in Symp. on the Evolution of Fault-Tolerant Computing, Baden, Austria, June, 1986.

[C85] F. Cristian: A Rigorous Approach to Fault-tolerant Programming, IEEE Tr. on Softw. Eng., Vol. SE-11, No. 1, Jan. 1985.

[C88] F. Cristian: Reaching agreement on processor group membership in synchronous distributed systems, 18th Int. Conf. on Fault-tolerant Computing, Tokyo, June 1988

[C89] F. Cristian: Atomic broadcast for redundant broadcast channels. IBM Research Report RJ7203, 1989.

[C90] F. Cristian: Atomic broadcast in the presence of network partitions, IBM Research Report, in preparation, 1990.

[CASD85] F. Cristian, H. Aghili, R. Strong, D. Dolev: Atomic Broadcast: From Simple Message Diffusion to Byzantine Agreement, Proc. 15th Int. Symp. on Fault-tolerant Computing, June 1985.

[Cr89] F. Cristian: Probabilistic clock Synchronization, Distributed Computing, Vol. 3, No. 3, pp. 146-158, Springer Verlag, 1989.

[Cr90] F. Cristian: Reliable periodic broadcast based on batched negative acknowledgements, IBM Research Report, in preparation, 1990.

[Cri89] F. Cristian: Exception Handling, in "Dependability of Resilient Computers", T. Anderson Ed., BSP Professional Books, Blackwell Scientific Publications, 1989.

[D71] E. Dijkstra: Hierarchical Ordering of Sequential Processes, Acta Informatica, Vol 1, pp. 115-138, 1971.

[G86] J. Gray: Why do computers stop and what can be done about it? Invited paper, 5th Symp. on Reliability in distributed software and database systems, Los Angeles, January 1986.

[H78] A. L. Hopkins et al, FTMP-A highly reliable fault-tolerant multi-processor for aircraft, Prc. IEEE, Vol. 66, Oct 1978.

[KLS86] N. Kronenberg, H. Levy, W. Strecker: VAXclusters, a closely coupled distributed system, ACM Tr. on Computer Systems, Vol. 4, No. 2, 1986.

[Pa88] D. Powell et al: The Delta-4 Approach to Dependability in Open Distributed Computing Systems, 18th Int Conf. on Fault-tolerant Computing, Tokyo, June 1988.

[P79] D. Parnas: Designing Software for Ease of Extension and Contraction, IEEE Tr. on Software Engineering, Vol. SE-5, No. 2, March 1979.

[PB85] D. L. Palumbo, R. W. Butler: Measurement of SIFT operating system overhead, NASA Tecn. Memo. 86322, 1985.

[R75] B. Randell: System Structure for Software Fault-Tolerance, IEEE Trans. on Software Eng., Vol. SE-1, No. 2, 1975.

[SSCA87] R. Strong, D. Skeen, F. Cristian, H. Aghili: Handshake Protocols, 7th Int. Conf. on Distributed Computing Systems, Berlin, September 1987.

[TR85] A. S. Tanenbaum, R. V. Renesse: Distributed Operating Systems, ACM Comp. Surveys, Vol. 17, No. 4, Dec 1985.

[TW89] D. Taylor and G. Wilson: The Stratus System Architecture, in "Dependability of Resilient Computers", T. Anderson, Ed., Blackwell Scientific Publications, Oxford, 1989.

[Wa78] J. Wensley, et al: SIFT: Design and Analysis of a Fault tolerant Computer for Aircraft Control, Proc IEEE Vol. 66, Oct 1978.

A Design Approach for Ultrareliable Real-Time Systems

Jaynarayan H. Lala, Richard E. Harper, and Linda S. Alger

Charles Stark Draper Laboratory

Managing redundancy is vital to the correct operation of critical systems. We present several approaches to masking errors and achieving congruency in the presence of a fault.

Ultrareliable real-time computing became an important issue at the Charles Stark Draper Laboratory when designers began to incorporate digital computers into guidance, navigation, and control systems. Although we had been designing these systems for missiles and spacecraft for 30 years, we began to focus on a class of applications characterized by an unusually stringent set of reliability and real-time performance requirements. Hence, we coined the term ultrareliable real-time systems for these applications.

Real-time information processing is intrinsic to the operation of all these systems. Early systems emphasized fault avoidance through rigorous quality control and component engineering to enhance reliability. This approach proved quite satisfactory for the US Navy's fleet ballistic missile series of Polaris, Poseidon, Trident I, and Trident II, and for the guidance and navigation computer on board the Apollo expeditions to the moon.

There was a cost penalty, however, for engineering high reliability into devices through a reduced component failure rate.

With the advent of the microprocessor, the weight, volume, and power associated with redundant hardware decreased. (These physical resources, of course, are always at a premium in aerospace vehicles.) The mi-

croprocessor made it possible to trade off fault-tolerance and fault-avoidance techniques to minimize the overall cost.

Redundancy-based architectures designed in the early 1970s included duplex and triplex systems. Reconfigurable architectures evolved later, culminating in the late 1970s in Draper's Fault-Tolerant Multiprocessor (FTMP), which uses parallel-hybrid redundancy. Hopkins, Lala, and Smith summarize a selected set of Draper-developed ultrareliable computers from the Apollo Guidance Computer to the FTMP.[1]

Experience with these early systems showed that redundancy can provide a cost-effective alternative to fault avoidance. However, redundancy also substantially complicated the task of validation. In fact, it was all too easy to end up with a redundant system that was more failure prone than a simplex system.

Correct management of redundancy is essential to making a redundant system fault tolerant. The complexity of the validation of fault-tolerant systems relates directly to the approach taken to manage their redundancy. Fault propagation, error

Reprinted from *IEEE Computer*, Vol. 24, No. 5, May 1991, pp. 12-22. Copyright © 1991 by The Institute of Electrical and Electronic Engineers, Inc. All rights reserved.

0-8186-3792-7/93 $03.00 © 1991 IEEE

propagation, synchronization of and consensus between redundant elements, and other redundancy management issues had to be based on a solid theoretical foundation if designers had any hope of formally validating these systems.

In this article, we describe the design approach evolved at Draper over the past few years to formalize redundancy management and validation. We developed several architectures with this approach. We discuss the Advanced Information Processing System (AIPS), which is a fault-tolerant distributed architecture, and conclude with a brief overview of recent applications of these systems and our current research.

Requirements and design approach

Fault-tolerant computers are now used in a diverse set of applications, and the techniques for achieving fault tolerance vary as much as the application requirements. We focus here on achieving fault tolerance for ultrareliable real-time systems.

One way to define reliability requirements for these systems and to distinguish them from other fault-tolerant applications is to measure them in terms of a maximum acceptable probability of failure. Because of the total dependence of the application on the correct operation of the system, the acceptable probability of failure of the computer is very small, typically in the range of 10^{-5} to 10^{-10}, depending on the consequences of the failure. Safety-critical applications are the most demanding. Commercial transport fly-by-wire, such as the Airbus A-320, require a 10^{-10} probability of failure per flight hour. (In this type of flight control, a computer processes all pilot commands. There is no direct mechanical link between the pilot control wheel and the control-surface actuators.)

Similar applications in military aircraft are several orders of magnitude less demanding, typically around 10^{-7} per hour (presumably because the crew can bail out). Vehicle-critical applications in which the cost of failure is a huge economic penalty rather than loss of life (such as unmanned launch vehicles, autonomous underwater vehicles, and full-authority engine controls) require 10^{-6} to 10^{-7} probabilities of failure per hour.

Mission-critical applications in which a computer failure would cause an incomplete or aborted mission occupy the low end of the ultrareliable spectrum. Typical reliability requirements are 10^{-4} to 10^{-6} probabilities of mission failure.

The real-time response requirements for the applications under consideration are also very demanding. For example, statically unstable fighter aircraft can develop divergent flight modes if correct control inputs are not applied every 40 to 100 milliseconds. Similarly, advanced variable-cycle jet engines can blow up if correct control inputs are not applied every 20 to 50 milliseconds. Mission-critical functions do not have such stringent response-time requirements but typically need higher throughput.

A third requirement, although no one ever states it explicitly, is system capability for validation. Commercial fly-by-wire systems cannot be placed into service in the US until the Federal Aviation Administration is satisfied with their safety. Similarly, the Nuclear Regulatory Commission must certify nuclear power-plant trip monitors and controls, the National Aeronautics and Space Administration must certify the avionics used on board spacecraft, and so on.

Because of the extremely low failure rate required of these systems, life-time testing for the purposes of certification is out of the question. Although empirical data collected on test articles in the laboratory and/or flight systems can be used as part of the validation process, the primary means is a hierarchy of analytical models, simulations, and proofs that would satisfy any determined inquisitor that a system can perform its intended function correctly under all expected conditions.

Draper design philosophy. We have evolved a philosophy to address the unique requirements of ultrareliable real-time systems based on a number of major precepts.

Hardware redundancy protects against random hardware faults (also known as operational faults). Due to the stringent real-time requirements discussed earlier, application functions cannot be suspended for more than a few milliseconds when a component fails. Fault effects must be masked until recovery measures can be taken. A majority voting architecture with a triplex-or-higher level of redundancy masks errors and provides spares to restore error masking after a failure. Use of redundancy, of course, is quite common in critical systems. However, managing that redundancy is supremely important.

Redundancy alone does not guarantee fault tolerance. The only thing it does guarantee is a higher fault arrival rate compared to a nonredundant system of the same functionality. For a redundant system to continue correct operation in the presence of a fault, the redundancy must be managed properly. Redundancy management issues are deeply interrelated and determine not only the ultimate system reliability but also the performance penalty paid for fault tolerance. Some fault-tolerant computers end up spending as much as 50 percent of their throughput managing redundancy.[2]

As a first step in addressing this issue, we partitioned the redundant elements into individual fault containment regions. An FCR is a collection of components that operates correctly regardless of any arbitrary logical or electrical fault outside the region. Conversely, a fault in an FCR cannot cause hardware outside the region to fail.

To form a fault containment boundary around a collection of hardware components, one must provide that hardware with independent power and clocking sources. Additionally, interfaces between FCRs must be electrically isolated. The isolation should be robust enough to tolerate a short to the maximum voltage available in the FCR. Depending on the application, this may be 5V or 28V DC, 115V AC — or even higher in a HERF/EMI (high-energy radio frequency/electromagnetic interference) environment.

Some applications also require tolerance to such physical damage as a weapons hit or flooding. In those cases, FCRs must also be physically separated, typically done by locating redundant elements in different avionics bays on aircraft or in compartments separated by bulkheads in underwater vehicles.

Due to all these requirements, it is impractical to make each semiconductor chip, or even a board, an FCR. A realistic FCR size is that of a whole computer, also called a channel in the avionics parlance. A typical channel contains a processor, memory, I/O interfaces, and data and control interfaces to other channels. If the FCR requirements are enforced rigorously, one can argue that random hardware component failures in FCRs constitute independent and uncorrelated events. This is an important underpinning of the analytical models used to predict the probability of failure of these systems.

Although an FCR can keep a fault from propagating to other FCRs, fault effects manifested as erroneous data can propagate across FCR boundaries. Therefore, the system must provide error containment. The basic principle is fairly straightforward: "Voting planes" mask errors at different stages in a fault-tolerant system. For example, a typical embedded control application involves three steps: read redundant sensors, perform control law computation, and output actuator commands.

In this embedded application, an input voting plane masks failed sensor values to keep them from propagating to the control law. Internal computer voting masks erroneous data from a failed channel to prevent propagation to other channels. Output voting and an interlock mechanism prevent outputs of failed channels from propagating outside the computational core.

The interlock is a hardware device in each channel that can enable or disable the outputs of that channel. Only a majority of the channels can change the interlock state. Therefore, in triplex or higher redundancy level computers, the majority of channels can disable the outputs of a failed channel.

Finally, a voting plane at the actuator masks errors in the transmission medium that connects the computer to the actuators. The typical actuator is driven by multiple electrical or hydraulic inputs so that a majority of inputs can drive it to the correct position even when one of the inputs fails to its maximum value, or a "hardover failure."

Masking faults and errors obviates the need for immediate diagnostics, isolation, and reconfiguration. The application functions need not be suspended. The majority of channels can continue to execute these functions correctly and provide correct outputs. This approach meets the stringent real-time response requirements.

Exact versus approximate consensus. To mask errors, outputs of redundant channels must be compared and voted. Two distinct voter approaches have evolved to provide these functions. These methods affect everything from efficiency of fault tolerance to coverage of faults to validation of hardware and software.

The two approaches seem to affect only the voter at first glance, but they actually go to the heart of the architecture. Draper favors an architectural approach that requires the outputs of all channels to agree bit-for-bit under no-fault conditions. This *exact bit-wise consensus* is used in most fault-tolerant computers (such as the Space Shuttle; Software-Implemented Fault Tolerance, or SIFT; Tandem; Stratus; X-29 Flight Control System; and Biin).

In contrast, a few others (such as AFTI/F-16 Flight Control System and Sperry/B-737 Yaw Damper) use the *approximate consensus* approach in which the outputs of redundant channels agree within some threshold (also called a window of agreement) under no-fault conditions.

The use of the exact consensus approach can best be motivated and discussed by addressing the limitations of approximate consensus. Fault-detection coverage in the latter approach is a function of how precisely one defines the thresholds.

For most dynamic systems, thresholds are a function of the process and its inputs and outputs. Thresholds may also change with the operating mode. For example, the outputs of a redundant flight-control computer can be expected to be very close in a level, cruising flight with control-law inputs relatively constant. However, in a high-speed maneuver in which aircraft altitude, velocity, and other inputs change very rapidly, the outputs of redundant channels can be much farther apart.

Since there is no mathematically precise way to define these thresholds, most designers use heuristics guided by two opposing requirements. Making the threshold or window of agreement too small generates nuisance false alarms. Making the window too wide to avoid false alarms will miss some real faults and lower fault-detection coverage. Due to this dilemma, fault-detection coverage in approximate consensus systems cannot approach 100 percent. In fact, there is no formal methodology for accurately calculating the coverage achieved for a given threshold size. This makes analytical modeling and validation extremely tedious, if not impossible. Furthermore, the use of application-process-derived thresholds for fault detection and isolation puts a serious and uncalled-for burden on the applications programmer to assure fault tolerance in the host machine.

Consider another limitation of the approximate consensus approach. A distributed network of redundant computers could only exchange and vote interprocessor messages that consisted of physical quantities. Most of the communication traffic in a distributed system typically has no physical semantics. The notion of approximate equality between redundant copies of such abstract messages is meaningless. The concepts of approximately near or far apart, in fact, are meaningless for most variables in a computer.

The exact consensus approach, in contrast, rests on a foundation of clearly de-

fined requirements and is amenable to formal methods and analytical validation. It begins with the realization that digital computers are finite-state machines. Under the following well-defined conditions, redundant digital computers produce bit-for-bit identical results.

Identical initial states. The redundant copies of the hardware must be initialized to the same state. For a typical channel, this implies that at some initial time t_0 all volatile memory, processor cache and registers, control registers, and clock and counter values (including the states of intermediate stages, discretes, etc.) are identical in all copies.

Identical inputs. Each hardware copy must then be provided with an identical sequence of inputs. In real-time systems, typical inputs include data (such as sensor values) and events (such as interrupts generated within a channel or asserted by an external device). The interfacing of sensors (simplex and redundant) to redundant channels and correct distribution of sensor values to all channels is a very important aspect of ultrareliable real-time architectures. Interrupts must be asserted in each channel at identical points in the instruction stream.

Identical operations. Each channel must execute the same sequence of operations on the same inputs.

Bounded time skew. An upper bound on the time skew Δt_{skew} must be defined so that the time of completion for a given sequence of instructions for the slowest channel, t_s, is no larger than the time for the fastest channel, t_f, by more than Δt_{skew}. The time skew is bounded by synchronizing the operations of redundant channels.

If all these requirements are satisfied, then each nonfaulty channel will produce bit-for-bit identical outputs by a well-defined point in time.

Synchronization, input agreement, and input validity conditions. Two or more identically initiated processes that receive identical inputs and operate on them the same way are called congruent processes. Congruence, unlike threshold-based approaches, allows a mathematically precise and concise means for detecting and isolating faults:

• *Fault detection.* Two congruent processes that do not agree bit-wise produce an error condition, which indicates the presence of a fault.

• *Fault isolation.* A congruent process that does not agree bit-wise with the majority of congruent processes is faulty. Note that the majority vote for congruent systems is a simple truth table.

Synchronization. Synchronizing redundant channels places an upper bound on the time skew. Since the workload typically consists of iterative execution of various application programs at different frequencies, a commonly used technique synchronizes the start of the next frame by having the redundant processes exchange semaphores at the end of an iteration.

Two major problems with this approach are the high software overhead for synchronization and the additional burden on the applications programmer to perform the synchronization task. Because of multiple frame rates and passing of I/O data between various frames, the high cognitive overhead of maintaining synchronism falls to the applications programmer. This worsens in the presence of faults, complicating the task of validating applications software.

An alternative approach developed at Draper uses a hardware-implemented synchronization scheme transparent to applications software. This approach relies on identical redundant hardware clocked by a fault-tolerant clock. The copies of hardware execute a given instruction in an identical number of CPU clock cycles. The fault-tolerant clock source provides exactly the same number of CPU clock ticks in a given time period to each redundant copy of the hardware.

The fault-tolerant clock, as the name implies, is not a single clocking source but is independently derived in each channel by a majority vote of a redundant set of clocks. We used this hardware synchronization scheme in the Advanced Information Processing System (AIPS) fault-tolerant processor by making all hardware clock-deterministic. The clock determinism attribute can be imparted to digital hardware through appropriate design rules and makes the execution time of each instruction, as measured in the number of CPU clock cycles, a fixed and deterministic number.

Input agreement. Correct distribution of inputs (in general) and sensors (in particular) is a very important aspect of ultrareliable real-time architectures. Incorrect distribution has caused at least one in-flight failure of a redundant computer.[3]

There are two conditions attached to inputs: congruency (or agreement) and validity. Input congruency occurs when each channel has an identical copy of that input, that is, all channels agree on the input value. Input validity occurs when all channels have a valid or correct value of that input.

Note that congruency does not imply validity. All channels may have the same wrong value, for example, and still be in agreement. Input congruency is the only necessary condition for bit-wise output consensus. Validity is necessary for correct channel outputs.

A recent theory, sometimes referred to as the Byzantine Generals' Problem, identifies the necessary conditions for input congruency in the presence of an arbitrary fault (see sidebar). According to this theory,[4-7] to achieve input source congruency in the presence of f arbitrary, or Byzantine, faults

(1) the system must consist of $3f + 1$ FCRs,
(2) the FCRs must be interconnected through $2f + 1$ disjoint paths,
(3) the inputs must be exchanged $f + 1$ times between the participants, and
(4) the FCRs must be synchronized to provide a bounded skew.

The $3f + 1$ rule was actually discovered at Draper in 1973 — but only in the limited context of designing fault-tolerant clocks.[8] We had observed malicious clock failures and concluded that $3f + 1$ — rather than the simple majority voting scheme that uses $2f + 1$ clocks — is required to design a fault-tolerant clock. We did not, however, realize that data communication can also display Byzantine behavior.

A redundant system that can achieve exact consensus in the presence of one arbitrary fault must have at least four fully cross-strapped FCRs that execute a two-round exchange algorithm to distribute inputs. Note that the most commonly found triple-redundant majority-voting architectures do not meet these requirements.

A number of single-point failures can be postulated that would cause the inputs to be noncongruent in the three channels, leading to a total system failure. Can such failures occur? A commonly observed Byzantine failure occurs when a marginal bus transmitter causes two receivers to perceive different values for a transmission. The question is not whether such failures can occur but how probable they are.

To design ultrareliable systems that can be validated, one must either demonstrate that these probabilities are very low (10^{-5} to 10^{-10}, depending on the application) or meet the aforementioned requirements of Byzantine tolerance. We believe that systems that meet these very precise requirements are considerably easier to validate analytically. Based on our own experience with digital systems, as well as that of others,[3] we also believe that such failures are not rare.

Even though four FCRs are required to tolerate one arbitrary fault, it is not necessary to use four processors in a system. We built triply redundant versions of the AIPS

The Byzantine Generals' Problem

The analogy between fault-tolerant systems and Byzantine generals originates in the famous paper by Lamport, Shostak, and Pease[4]:

Reliable computer systems must handle malfunctioning components that give conflicting information to different parts of the system. The situation can be expressed abstractly in terms of a group of generals of the Byzantine army camped with their troops around an enemy city. Communicating only by messenger, the generals must agree upon a common battle plan. However, one or more of them may be traitors who will try to confuse the others. The problem is to find an algorithm to ensure that the loyal generals will reach an agreement.

The generals in this analogy correspond to processors in a redundant computing system, the traitors correspond to faulty processors, and the messengers correspond to interprocessor communications links. It is typically assumed that faulty-link (traitorous messenger) behavior is subsumed by faulty-source processor (traitorous general) behavior.

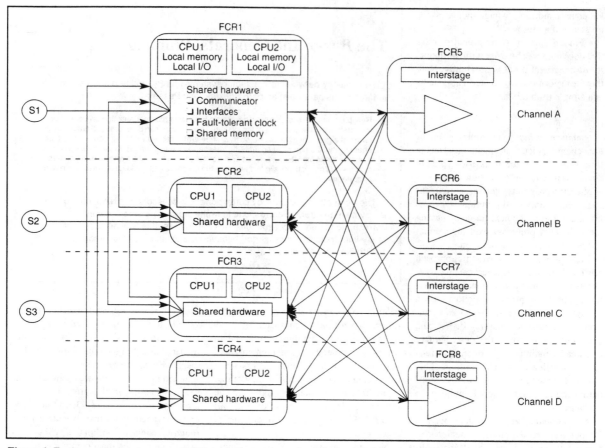

Figure 1. Fault containment regions (FCRs) and interconnections in the AIPS quad-redundant fault-tolerant processor.

Fault-Tolerant Processor (FTP) to comply with all requirements by providing extra FCRs. The FCRs took the form of independent data-replicating devices, also called interstages. We also built a quadruply redundant version with four interstages (for a total of eight FCRs) that can tolerate any two sequential arbitrary FCR failures.[9] Because it performs only a two-round exchange, this system can tolerate some (but not all) double simultaneous faults (see Figure 1).

We also built a fault-tolerant parallel processor in which only three processors can mask an arbitrary failure.[7] We achieved this by placing the minimum four FCRs into the network elements that interconnect the processors and execute the source congruency algorithm.

Input validity. A redundant input source satisfies the condition of validity for external inputs. Typically, critical sensors are replicated and interface with different channels of the redundant computer. Fig-

ure 1 shows the quad-redundant FTP with a triplicated sensor. The three redundant sensors (S1, S2, and S3) physically interface with channels A, B, and C, respectively. The design provides a valid and congruent sensor value to all four channels.

Channel A reads sensor S1, and all four channels execute the two-round exchange algorithm that culminates in their receiving a congruent value of S1, say, V1. The process repeats for sensors S2 and S3. Now all four channels have the same three sensor values, say, V1, V2, and V3.

To obtain a valid sensor value *V*, the system must compare and vote the three sensor values. However, a bit-for-bit voting of redundant sensors is usually not possible since sensors measure such realworld parameters as pressure, temperature, angle, and acceleration. which are all analog quantities. Even under no-fault conditions, digital representations of redundant sensor values differ. However, since the sensor values do represent realworld physical quantities, one can use a

number of reasonableness checks (such as rate of change and minimum-maximum range of values) to filter out a grossly misbehaving sensor. Midvalue select, average, or mean value of the remaining sensors can then be used to arrive at a valid sensor value in all channels. Note that the value will also be congruent since all channels execute an identical sensor-redundancy management algorithm with congruent sensor inputs.

We have designed two systems — AIPS, described in the next section, and the Fault Tolerant Parallel Processor[7] — to meet the requirements discussed above.

AIPS

Requirements. Digital computers with centralized architectures have significantly enhanced the performance of aerospace vehicles. Although these centralized systems have served their applications well, many advanced aerospace vehicles could

Table 1. AIPS design requirements.

Requirement	Specification
Short-term reliability	10^{-9} failure probability* at 10 hours with no repair
Long-term reliability	0.95 failure probability* at 5 years with no repair
Fault tolerance	*N*-fail operation* (hardware only)
Throughput	100 MIPS*† (expandable)
Memory	500 Mbytes*† (expandable)
I/O	100 Mbits/sec.*† (expandable)
Transport lag	5 ms*
Cycle rate	100 Hz*
System real-time clock accuracy/quantization	Variable*

*Varies with technology, mission
†Increases by one order of magnitude every few years

benefit significantly from distributed computer systems. These applications include the Space Station, the Aeroassisted Orbital Transfer Vehicle, the Advanced Launch System, the National Aerospace Plane, and advanced fighter aircraft for the US Air Force and Navy.

Fault-tolerant distributed systems are superior in some ways to centralized systems and are better suited to the highly integrated electronic information systems of future vehicles. These attributes include

- function integration,
- parallel computation,
- graceful performance growth,
- selective technology upgrade,
- appropriate levels of function reliability,
- graceful degradation of system capabilities in the presence of faults or damage, and
- efficient use of hardware resources.

Furthermore, the architectural concept should be validated so that the physical realization of these attributes in hardware and software meet such quantitative mission requirements as throughput performance, transport lag, and mission success probability. The implementations must also be well within such mission constraints as cost, weight, volume, and power.

The overall program objective of AIPS, developed under the sponsorship of NASA, is to produce a knowledge base that allows designers to achieve validated fault-tolerant, distributed, computer-system architectures for a broad range of aerospace vehicles. Table 1 summarizes the overall AIPS design requirements for seven aerospace applications, obtained by an extensive survey of NASA centers and published as Draper Report AIPS-83-50. The architecture conceived to meet these requirements is based on the notion of prevalidated building blocks.

The AIPS multicomputer architecture consists of hardware and software building blocks that can be configured according to certain design rules and guidelines to meet the specific requirements of a given application.

Building blocks. The hardware building blocks consist of FTPs, networks, and interfaces (see Figure 2). FTPs are general-purpose computers that can be built in redundancy levels that vary from simplex to quadraplex, using up to four identical channels to meet different levels of reliability requirements. The communication-media networks are circuit-switched nodes joined by full-duplex links. The networks can be configured in ring, braided mesh, and irregular mesh topologies. Networks can also be made redundant. They connect FTPs to I/O devices (called I/O networks) and to other FTPs (called intercomputer or IC networks).

I/O and IC networks consist of identical nodes and links. The interface building blocks connect an FTP channel to an I/O network, which is then called the I/O sequencer or IOS, and to the IC network, which is then called the IC interface sequencer or ICIS.

The software building blocks furnish local, I/O, and intercomputer system services, and the system manager. These building blocks provide the services necessary in a traditional real-time computer, such as task scheduling and dispatching, and communication with sensors and actuators. The software also supplies the redundancy-management services necessary in a redundant computer or a distributed system, such as interfunction communication across processing sites, management of distributed redundancy, network management, and function migration between processing sites.

Virtual architecture. A unique attribute of AIPS (and other Draper-designed fault-tolerant computers) is that redundancy and its management are transparent to the application software. They are also transparent to all system software except for those services that manage the redundancy. This attribute allows programmers to develop and validate most software on a simplex processor in a familiar development environment that uses mature tools. We call the architecture that appears to the programmer the virtual architecture.

The AIPS virtual architecture is a conventional multicomputer that consists of a

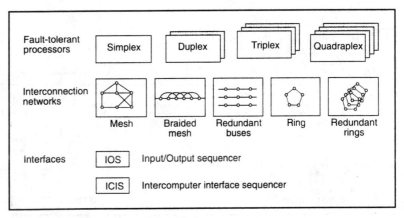

Figure 2. AIPS hardware building blocks.

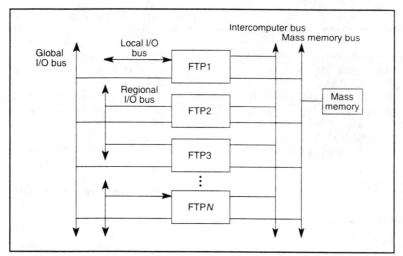

Figure 3. AIPS overall virtual architecture.

number of FTP processing sites and external interfaces (see Figure 3). An IC bus links the processing sites. An FTP at any processing site can also access varying numbers and types of I/O buses, which are separate from the IC bus. Separate buses carry sensor and intercomputer data because the bandwidth and reliability requirements for these two classes of data in most real-time systems vary widely. The I/O buses may be global, regional, or local in nature. I/O devices on the global I/O bus are available to all, or at least a majority of, the FTPs. Regional buses connect I/O devices in a given region to the processing sites located in their vicinity. Local buses connect an FTP to the I/O devices dedicated to that computer. Additionally, I/O devices may connect directly to the internal

bus of a processor and be accessed as though they reside in computer memory (like memory-mapped I/O).

The regional and global buses allow sharing of raw sensor data among functions that reside on different processing sites, thus reducing the overall system cost. These buses also allow functions to migrate between FTPs in real time in the event of faults, damage, or change in mission phase and work load. The memory-mapped I/O accesses time-critical sensors to meet stringent transport lag requirements for real-time control applications.

Figure 4 shows the virtual architecture of a processing site. It consists of three sections: computational, I/O, and the resources shared between them. The computational and I/O sections are identical, con-

ventional processor architectures. Each consists of a processor, memory, interval timers, and memory-mapped I/O unique to each processor. Although identical in hardware design, the computational processor, or CP, is typically devoted to application functions (such as executing a vehicle control law) while the I/O processor, or the IOP, is devoted to such I/O functions as reading and validating sensors and sending out actuator commands. The CP and IOP communicate with each other via shared memory. Other shared resources include a data-exchange mechanism that votes data with other redundant channels in this FTP, a real-time clock, and interfaces to several I/O buses and the IC bus.

Physical architecture. The parameters that define the physical architecture include

- redundancy levels of FTPs;
- interconnections of redundant channels in an FTP;
- redundancy levels of sensors, actuators, and other I/O devices;
- cross-strapping of I/O devices to channels of FTPs and the redundancy levels of their interfaces; and
- redundancy levels of IC and I/O networks and their physical topologies.

Figure 1 showed the physical architecture of the quad-redundant AIPS FTP. It is designed strictly according to the theory we discussed and complies with all requirements for tolerating two sequential Byzantine failures of FCRs. In addition to redundancy, other features that provide fault tolerance include watchdog timers, processor interlocks, a privileged operating mode, hardware and software excep-

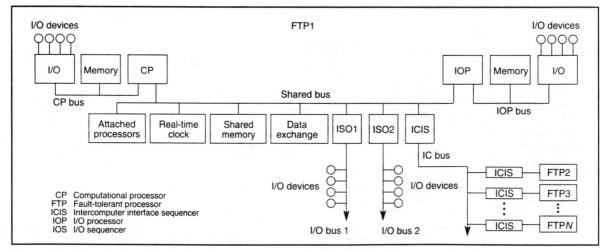

Figure 4. AIPS processing-site virtual architecture.

tion handlers, and self-testing. A majority of correctly operating channels can disable all outputs of a failed channel using the processor interlock mechanism. A channel that is "failed active" cannot transmit erroneous data or commands on I/O and IC networks or to local I/O devices.

The physical realizations of the virtual I/O and IC buses are the fault- and damage-tolerant circuit-switched networks. A network consists of a number of full-duplex links interconnected by circuit-switched nodes. In steady state, the circuit-switched nodes route information along a fixed communication path, or virtual bus, within the network, without the delays associated with packet-switched networks. Once the virtual bus is set up within the network, its protocols and operation are similar to those of typical multiplex buses.

Although the network performs exactly as a bus does, it is far more reliable and damage tolerant than a linear bus. A single fault or limited damage can disable only a small fraction of the virtual bus, typically a node or a link connecting two nodes. Reconfiguring the network around the faulty element constructs a new virtual bus. The nodes are sufficiently intelligent to recognize reconfiguration commands from the network manager (explained in the system services section), which resides in one of the FTPs. Adding more nodes linked to spare ports in existing nodes easily expands the network.

To maintain fault-tolerance requirements, each FTP channel receives data from all three IC network layers but can physically transmit on only one layer (see Figure 5). For example, simplex 1 can only transmit on layer L, as shown by an outgoing arrow on the left, but receives on all three layers, as shown by three incoming arrows. Similarly, channels A, B, and C of FTP4 can transmit only on layers L, M, and N, respectively (again, as shown by a single outgoing arrow from each channel to one IC network layer). All three layers of the IC network operate together to transmit and receive data. Since all channels of a triplex site are executing the same code synchronously, the three channels (each channel transmitting on a different layer) transmit identical messages. Thus, within some skew, the redundant layers of the network contain the same message. This allows the receiving site to vote the three layers, masking any failure. Although they always receive on three layers, duplex sites can transmit on only two of the three layers of the network, and simplex sites can transmit on only one of the them. Thus, mali-

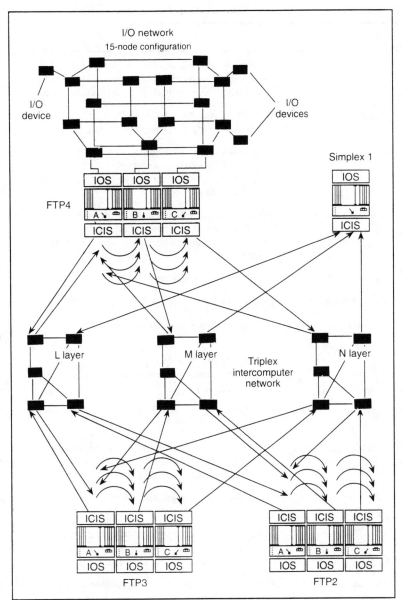

Figure 5. AIPS engineering model configuration.

cious failure of a channel can disrupt only one layer.

For access arbitration purposes, the triplex network is treated as a single entity. FTPs, regardless of their redundancy level, contend for all three layers of the network. At the end of the contention sequence one — and only one — FTP can access three layers of the network.

The IC networks, the FTP interfaces to the networks (ICISs), and the arbitration logic are designed in strict accordance with the theory we advanced in the Requirements and design approach section.[10] The

system provides error-masking capability for intercomputer communication between triplex (or higher redundancy level) FTPs. An arbitrary hardware fault (including Byzantine faults) within the system cannot disrupt communication between FTPs of triplex or higher redundancy level.

System services. Each processing site can operate autonomously, particularly to perform critical functions. However, the system services software allows a coordinated information processing system to provide attributes superior to the more fed-

Table 2. Relationships between requirements and attributes.

Requirement	Attributes
100-Hz cycle rate	Concurrent I/O, computation, implementation technology, low fault-tolerance overhead, low system services overhead, transient fault tolerance
Adaptability	Layered system services, prevalidated building blocks, reconfigurability, simplex programming model
Availability	Diagnosability, function migration, low component failure rate, non-Byzantine-resilient fault tolerance, real-time operation, reconfigurability, repairability, software fault avoidance
Cost-effectiveness	Copies in only $2f + 1$ fault containment regions, flexible function allocation, graded redundancy, low fault-tolerance overhead, software development environment
Environment	Implementation technology
Expandable I/O	Implementation technology, variable local I/O
Expandable memory	On-line memory, shared mass memory
Expandable throughput	Low fault-tolerance overhead, low I/O network transport delay, low intercomputer network delay, low system services overhead, variable number of processing sites
Function distribution	Function migration, variable number of processing sites
Graceful degradation	Byzantine resilience, function prioritization, variable number of processing sites, variable number of processors per channel
Hardware N-fail operation	Ada programming language, diagnosability, reconfigurability
Low life-cycle cost	Diagnosability, low component failure rate, portability of software tools, prevalidated building blocks, reconfigurability, simplex programming model
Low transport lag	Implementation technology, low component failure rate, low I/O network transport delay, low system services overhead, memory-mapped I/O
Maintainability	Diagnosability, low fault-tolerance overhead, reconfigurability, repairability, testability
Mission reliability	Byzantine resilience, damage tolerance, function migration, graded redundancy, intercomputer network, latent fault detection, low competence failure rate, real-time operation, reconfigurability, software fault tolerance, transient fault tolerance
Modularity	Common-mode fault tolerance, graded redundancy, heterogeneous load modules, identical fault tolerant processor design, intercomputer network, layered system services, prevalidated building blocks, symmetric computational processor or I/O processor
System real-time clock	Timer-based interrupt

erated systems typical for current aerospace vehicles.

The local system services in each FTP include initialization; a real-time operating system; local resource allocation; fault detection, isolation, and reconfiguration (FDIR); and local time management. The real-time operating system supports task execution management, including priority scheduling, and time and event occurrence. It is also responsible for task dispatching, suspension, and termination. It uses the vendor-supplied Ada Run Time System (RTS) and includes additional features for the AIPS real-time distributed operating system.

FDIR detects and isolates hardware faults in the CPs, IOPs, and shared hardware. It synchronizes both groups of processors in the redundant channels of the FTP and disables outputs of failed channel(s) through interlock hardware. FDIR also performs CPU hardware exception handling and down-modes and up-modes hardware in response to configuration commands from the system manager. It also detects transient hardware faults and runs low-priority self-tests to detect latent faults. The local time manager works in cooperation with the system time manager to keep the local real time initialized and consistent with the universal time.

I/O system services provide communication between the user and external devices (sensors and actuators). They also detect faults, and isolate and reconfigure the I/O network hardware and the IOS.

The IC user communication service is designed along the seven-layer Open Systems Interconnect model. It provides local and distributed interfunction communication (point-to-point or broadcast mode) transparent to the user. It also provides synchronous and asynchronous communication, performs error detection and source congruency on inputs, and records and reports IC network errors to the network layer managers. The IC network manager is responsible for the fault detection, isolation, and reconfiguration of that network.

The system manager is a collection of system-level services. The system resource manager allocates migratable functions to FTPs. This involves monitoring various triggers for function migration such as failure or repair of hardware components, mission phase or work-load change, operator or crew requests, and timed events. The system FDIR collects status from the IC network managers, the I/O network managers, and the local FTP redundancy managers. It resolves conflicting local fault-isolation decisions, isolates unresolved faults, correlates transient faults, and handles processing site failures. The system time manager, in conjunction with the local time manager on each FTP, maintains a consistent time across all FTPs.

Engineering model. We developed an AIPS engineering model to demonstrate and validate the major architectural concepts and attributes. The model includes all hardware and software building blocks described earlier and consists of four processing sites connected by a three-layer IC network. Three processing sites are triply redundant FTPs, and the fourth is a simplex processor. One processing site also accesses a 15-node I/O network. Each channel of each FTP contains two Motorola 68010 microprocessors with 4 Mbytes of memory each, data exchange and voting hardware, monitor-interlock, an IOS, and an ICIS. FTPs using Motorola 68020 microprocessors in quadruply redundant versions have also been fabricated. The I/O and IC networks use 2-MHz HDLC protocol. The laboratory model does not contain a mass memory.

We wrote the system software in Ada. The basic operating system incorporates vendor-supplied Ada RTS, which we enhanced with certain real-time capabilities. Over 100,000 lines of Ada source code comprise system services. All AIPS hardware and software has been integrated and operated under fault-free conditions as well as in the presence of various faults. However, we have not yet implemented the function migration concept. Extensive measurements of performance- and reliability-related parameters have been obtained on the engineering model.[11]

Architecture and performability knowledge base. The AIPS program goal is to produce a knowledge base that allows achievement of validated fault-tolerant distributed computer architectures at reduced cost. We have compiled a very extensive knowledge base to this end.

The knowledge base involves many relationships among entities called requirements, attributes, rules, specifications, and guidelines. A requirement is a quantitative or qualitative statement of an AIPS mission objective, such as availability. An attribute is an unambiguous statement of an AIPS characteristic, such as Byzantine resilience. A rule is a principle that must be followed to assure that a higher-level AIPS attribute holds, and a specification is an aggregate of rules that describe the rele-

Table 3. AIPS/ALS performance projections.

Attribute	Specification
Raw CPU throughput	15 MIPS (Digital Avionics Instruction Set mix) per processor
Total overhead	Computational processor: 11% of throughput I/O processor: 16% of throughput
Useful throughput	Computational processor: 13.35 MIPS I/O processor: 11.85 MIPS Fault-tolerant processor: 25.2 MIPS
Fault-tolerant clock	2 MHz
Data-exchange bandwidth	64 Mbits/sec.
I/O and intercomputer network bandwidth	100 Mbits/sec.
Interfunction communication (fault-tolerant processor to fault-tolerant processor)	1.28 ms

vant characteristics of an AIPS building block. The specification should be sufficiently detailed to allow one "unskilled in the art" to construct the component. Finally, a guideline is a statement of policy or philosophy based on our laboratory's experience, along with a statement of the effects of deviating from the guideline.

The interentity relationships may be intuitive, quantitative, or formally defined. Our methodology depicts the entities and relationships in a directed graph format. The set of requirements, attributes, rules, specifications, guidelines, and their relationships provides a framework for structuring and interconnecting AIPS building blocks into a computational system that satisfies the mission requirements.

Table 2 depicts the top two tiers of the directed graph. The mission requirements appear in the left column. One or more directed arcs (not shown) emanate from each requirement to one or more AIPS attributes, shown in the right column. We assert that a system that possesses the set of attributes corresponding to a requirement meets that requirement. At successive layers of the graphical structure, each attribute implies, in turn, an additional set of attributes, architectural rules, or architectural guidelines. At the lowest level of the graph reside the AIPS architectural rules and guidelines, which provide sufficiently detailed design guidance to ensure that the mission requirements are achieved by the implementation.

Under a recent contract with the NASA Langley Research Center, we synthesized

an AIPS-based fault-tolerant avionics architecture for the Advanced Launch System (ALS).[12] NASA and the US Department of Defense are jointly developing the ALS vehicle to launch heavy payloads into low earth orbit at one tenth the cost (per pound of payload) of the current generation of launch vehicles.

To illustrate the AIPS performability knowledge base, we summarize some AIPS characteristics for the ALS avionics architecture.

The ALS processor will be a 40-MHz, R3000 from MIPS Inc. (or a similar 32-bit reduced instruction-set computing architecture). The CPU module will have both RAM and ROM for a total of 1 to 4 Mbytes with a local bus interface for memory expansion. A 2-MHz fault-tolerant clock will synchronize interchannel operations and provide a data-exchange bandwidth of 64 Mbits/sec. The I/O and IC network protocol will be based on the Fiber Distributed Data Interface (FDDI) standard with a bit rate of 100 Mbits/sec. A modified Laning Poll will be used to access the network of virtual buses rather than the FDDI token. Table 3 summarizes the AIPS/ALS performance projections.

All nonpropulsion ALS functions such as guidance, navigation, and control require a total of 8.8 million instructions per second, executable by one FTP. Because the ALS design guidelines require that the engine controller be colocated with the engine, each ALS engine has a dedicated FTP to perform propulsion control functions. Using the projected hardware-failure and recovery rates, we solved the analytical models to predict the ALS avionics reliability. The probability of failure of a quadruply redundant FTP was projected to be 8.9×10^{-9} for the 10-minute boost phase, and 5.3×10^{-7} for the 48-hour on-orbit phase, assuming class B components. The launch availability — that is, the probability that the FTP will be in a fault-masking configuration — was estimated to be 0.9988 after a week on the launch pad.

The applications of the fault-tolerant computers described here have included a jet engine controller, a nuclear power plant trip monitor, research test beds, and undersea vehicle controls. A US Department of Defense Advanced Research Projects Agency-sponsored Unmanned Underwater Vehicle, about 36 feet long and 44 inches in diameter, is controlled by a triplex FTP and has successfully undergone sea trials. A quadruply redundant version of the FTP, programmed in Ada, was delivered in July 1990 to the US Army Strategic Defense Command in Huntsville, Alabama, for use in Strategic Defense Initiative Organization Battle Management/Command Control and Communications functions. Another quad FTP under fabrication will be used to control the Navy's latest nuclear attack submarine, the SSN-21 Seawolf.

Significant research at Draper has laid a firm theoretical foundation for the design of virtually perfect mechanisms for tolerating random hardware faults. We are extending it to common-mode faults, which affect more than one FCR simultaneously. We are investigating a number of approaches in this regard, including formal methods and design diversity. We are also researching use of authenticated protocols to provide Byzantine resilience at a lower hardware cost. Redundant architectures that use encoded rather than triplicated memory, yet can still provide 100 percent fault coverage, are also under design. Reduced instruction-set microprocessors, fiber optic buses, and multichip modules are some of the technologies being investigated to reduce the overall hardware failure rates and simplify designs for validation. ∎

Acknowledgment

The NASA Langley Research Center under Contract NAS1-18565 sponsored this work. We gratefully acknowledge its support.

References

1. A.L. Hopkins, Jr., J.H. Lala, and T.B. Smith III, "The Evolution of Fault-Tolerant Computing at the Charles Stark Draper Laboratory, 1955-85," *Dependable Computing and Fault-Tolerant Systems, Vol. I: The Evolution of Fault-Tolerant Computing,* Springer-Verlag, Wien, Austria, 1987, pp. 121-140.

2. D.L. Palumbo and R.W. Butler, "A Performance Evaluation of the Software-Implemented Fault-Tolerance Computer," *AIAA J. Guidance, Control, and Dynamics,* Vol. 9, No. 2, Mar.-Apr. 1986, pp. 175-180.

3. D.L. Martin and D. Gangsaas, "Testing of the YC-14 Flight Control System Software," *AIAA J. Guidance, Control, and Dynamics,* Vol. 1, No. 4, July-Aug. 1978, pp. 242-247.

4. L. Lamport, R. Shostak, and M. Pease, "The Byzantine Generals' Problem," *ACM Trans. Programming Languages and Systems,* Vol. 4, No. 3, July 1982, pp. 382-401.

5. D. Dolev, "The Byzantine Generals Strike Again," *J. Algorithms,* Vol. 3, No. 1, 1982, pp. 14-30.

6. M.J. Fischer and N.A. Lynch, "A Lower Bound for the Time to Assure Interactive Consistency," *Information Processing Letters,* Vol. 14, No. 4, June 13, 1982, pp. 183-186.

7. R.E. Harper, "Critical Issues in Ultrareliable Parallel Processing," PhD thesis, Massachusetts Institute of Technology, Cambridge, Mass., 1987.

8. W.M. Daly, A.L. Hopkins, Jr., and J.F. McKenna, "A Fault-Tolerant Digital Clocking System," *Proc. Third Int'l Symp. Fault-Tolerant Computing,* IEEE CS Press (out of print), 1973.

9. J.H. Lala et al., "A Fault-Tolerant Processor Architecture to Meet Rigorous Failure Requirements," *Proc. Seventh AIAA-IEEE Digital Avionics Systems Conf.,* IEEE Press, Piscataway, N.J., CSDL-P-2705, Oct. 1986, pp. 555-562.

10. J.H. Lala and S.J. Adams, "Inter-Computer Communication Architecture for a Mixed Redundancy Distributed System," *J. Guidance, Control, and Dynamics,* Vol. 12, No. 4, July-Aug. 1989, pp. 539-547.

11. L.S. Alger and J.H. Lala, "Performance Evaluation of a Real-Time Fault-Tolerant Distributed System," *Proc. 23rd Hawaii Int'l Conf. System Sciences,* Vol. 1, HICSS-23, IEEE CS Press, Los Alamitos, Calif., 1990, pp. 278-287.

12. J.H. Lala et al., "Advanced Information Processing System (AIPS)-Based Fault-Tolerant Avionics Architecture for Launch Vehicles," *Proc. Ninth AIAA/IEEE Digital Avionics Systems Conf.,* IEEE Press, Piscataway, N.J., 1990, pp. 125-132.

Jaynarayan H. Lala has been the division leader of the fault-tolerant systems division at the Charles Stark Draper Laboratory in Cambridge, Massachusetts, since 1985. His research interests include the design, evaluation, and validation of fault-tolerant architectures for high-integrity systems.

Lala received the BS degree in aeronautical engineering from the Indian Institute of Technology, Bombay, India, in 1971. He received the MS degree in aeronautics and astronautics and the PhD degree in instrumentation from the Massachusetts Institute of Technology in 1973 and 1976. He is a senior member of the IEEE and a member of the Computer Society.

Richard E. Harper has worked in the fault-tolerant systems division of the Charles Stark Draper Laboratory since 1983. His technical interests lie in the areas of reliable computing and communication systems.

Harper received the BA degree in physics and the MA degree in aeronautics and astronautics from Mississippi State University in 1976 and 1977. He received his PhD degree from MIT in 1987. He is a member of the IEEE.

Linda S. Alger joined the Charles Stark Draper Laboratory in 1978, where her interests focus on fault-tolerant systems along with real-time distributed computing. She has been a section chief in the fault-tolerant systems division since 1985.

Alger received the BA degree in mathematics from Wellesley College in 1960. She is a senior member of the IEEE.

Readers may contact the authors at the Charles Stark Draper Laboratory, Fault-Tolerant Systems Division, MS: 6F, 555 Technology Square, Cambridge, MA 02139.

HARTS:
A Distributed
Real-Time Architecture

Kang G. Shin, University of Michigan

The growing importance of real-time computing in numerous applications, such as aerospace and defense systems and industrial automation and control, poses problems for computer architectures, operating systems, fault tolerance, and evaluation tools. The interplay of three major components characterizes real-time systems. First, time is the most precious resource to manage. Tasks must be assigned and scheduled to be completed before their deadlines. Messages must be sent and received in a timely manner between the interacting real-time tasks. Second, reliability is crucial, since failure of a real-time system could cause an economic disaster or the loss of human lives. Third, the environment in which a computer operates is an active component of any real-time system. For example, in a "drive by wire" transportation system, in which important functions such as emission control and braking are automated with computers, it would be meaningless to consider the on-board computers without considering the automobile itself.

Because their multiplicity of processors and internode routes gives them the potential for high performance and high reliability, distributed systems with point-to-point interconnection networks are natural candidate architectures for time-critical applications. This article focuses on the

Consisting of shared-memory multiprocessor nodes interconnected by a wrapped hexagonal mesh, HARTS is designed to meet the special communications and I/O needs of time-critical applications.

design, implementation, and evaluation of a distributed real-time architecture called HARTS (hexagonal architecture for real-time systems), with emphasis on its support of time-constrained, fault-tolerant communications and I/O requirements. Currently under development at the University of Michigan's Real-Time Computing Laboratory (RTCL), HARTS consists of shared-memory multiprocessor nodes, interconnected via a wrapped hex-

agonal mesh. This architecture is intended to meet three main requirements of real-time computing: high performance, high reliability, and extensive I/O.*

High-level architecture

The primary goal of HARTS is the study of low-level architectural issues, such as message buffering, instruction set design, scheduling, and routing, in a setting that gives designers internal access to many system parameters. To meet this goal, my colleagues at RTCL and I used a hybrid system of commercially available processors and custom-designed interfaces. Several processor cards are grouped to form a cluster of application processors (APs). Each cluster serves as a multiprocessor node and is interconnected by custom interfaces to form a distributed system. The presence of both multiprocessor and distributed aspects permits investigating the behavior of real-time tasks under either architectures. In parallel with the hardware

---

*Although predictability of task execution behavior is essential for any real-time system design to guarantee on-time completion of tasks, it is not an architectural issue but an operating system issue. Real-time systems architects must provide hardware facilities on which one can readily build an operating system that guarantees deadlines.

0-8186-3792-7/93 $03.00 © 1991 IEEE

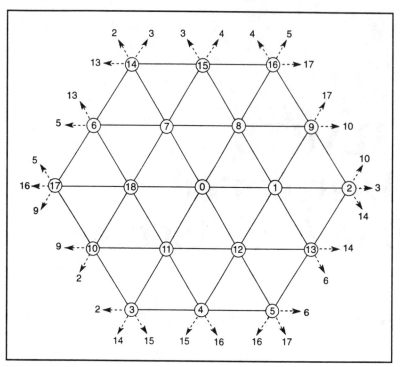

Figure 1. Hexagonal mesh of size 3.

development, our work on a real-time operating system called HARTOS[1] influences the specification, architecture, and implementation of the custom-designed HARTS components.

Node architecture. Each node in the testbed consists of up to three APs, a system controller, a shared memory segment, an Ethernet processor, and the network processor (NP), a custom-designed interface to the interconnection network.

The APs are commercially available VME bus multiprocessing engines based on Motorola's MC68020. Each processor card has four major sections: a CPU core, a VME bus interface, a memory system, and a VMX bus interface. The CPU core consists of a 32-bit 16-MHz MC68020 CPU, an MC68881 floating-point processor, and an MC68851 paged memory management unit. The memory subsystem provides four megabytes of high-performance dual-ported dynamic RAM, with an additional 256 bytes of special mailbox hardware. This mailbox feature facilitates efficient interprocessor communication by allowing a remote processor to write a semaphore that automatically interrupts the local processor.

The Ethernet processor card supports several functions for the nodes, although it is not a permanent HARTS component. First, it provides a secondary means of distributing code and data. This is especially important during the early stages of development of the network interfaces. Second, the high-level protocols that manage reliable packet handling and provide internode communication can be experimentally tested on the Ethernet processor. Third, the Ethernet processor is used to collect experimental data by monitoring the APs and network interfaces with minimal interference.

Interconnection network. A distributed system's interconnection network often connects thousands of homogeneously replicated processor-memory pairs, which are called processing nodes (PNs). All synchronization and communication between PNs for program execution are via message passing. The homogeneity of PNs and the interconnection network is very important because it allows cost and performance benefits from the inexpensive replication of multiprocessor components.[2] It is preferable that each PN in the multiprocessor have fixed connectivity so that

standard VLSI chips and communication software can be used. Also, the interconnection network should contain a reasonably high degree of connectivity so that alternative routes can be made available to detour faulty nodes and links. More important, the interconnection network must facilitate efficient routing and broadcasting to achieve high performance in task execution. For structural flexibility, a system must also possess fine scalability, measured in terms of the number of PNs necessary to increase the network's dimension by one.

To meet these requirements, we considered several topologies, including hypercubes, square meshes, 3D tori, hexagonal meshes, and octal meshes. Of these, the hexagonal (H) mesh best meets the requirements of fixed connectivity and planar architecture for easy VLSI and communications implementation, fine scalability, reasonably high fault tolerance, and ease of construction. (Detailed comparisons of the H-mesh to other topologies are given by Stevens[2] and by Chen, Shin, and Kandlur.[3] The robustness of an H-mesh to link and node failures is shown by Olson and Shin.[4]) Hence, we chose a C-wrapped ("C" stands for continuous) H-mesh topology to interconnect HARTS nodes.

H-mesh size (the term "dimension" was used in an earlier article[3]) is defined as the number of nodes on its peripheral edge. One can visualize what is happening in the C-wrapping by first partitioning the nodes of a nonwrapped H-mesh of size e, denoted by H_e, into rows in three different directions. The mesh can be viewed as composed of $2e-1$ horizontal rows (called the d_0 direction), $2e-1$ rows in the 60-degree clockwise direction (called the d_1 direction), or $2e-1$ rows in the 120-degree clockwise direction (called the d_2 direction). In each of these partitions we label from the top the rows R_0 through R_{2e-2}. The C-wrapping is then performed by connecting the last node in R_i to the first node in $R_{[i+e+1]2e-1}$ for each i in each of the three partitions, where $[a]_b$ denotes a mod b. Figure 1 illustrates an example of a C-wrapped H_3 in which the links on the periphery (represented by dashed-line arrows) are connected to the nodes as indicated by their labels.

The C-wrapped H-mesh is isomorphic to the interconnection topology presented by Stevens.[2] However, the formalism just described allows uniform treatment of message routing between all pairs of nodes and does not require any special treatment of the wrap lines, as was necessary in

Stevens' topology when the axial offset was between e and $2(e-1)$.

A C-type wrapping has several salient properties, as shown by Chen, Shin, and Kandlur.[3] First, this wrapping results in a homogeneous network. Consequently, any node can view itself as the center of the mesh (labeled as node 0 in Figure 1). Second, the diameter of an H_e is $e-1$. Third, there is a simple, transparent addressing scheme that uses only one coordinate — instead of three as in Stevens' topology — to uniquely identify any node in an H-mesh. An example of this addressing for an H_4 is shown in Figure 2a, where all edges are omitted for clarity. On the basis of this addressing scheme, one can determine the shortest paths between any two nodes with a $\Theta(1)$ algorithm; that is, the complexity is constant and independent of system size. Note that at each node on a shortest path there are at most two different neighbors of the node to which the shortest path runs. Fourth, with this addressing scheme one can devise a simple routing algorithm that can be efficiently implemented in hardware, as shown by Dolter, Ramanathan, and Shin.[5]

To send a message, the source calculates the shortest paths to the destination and encodes this routing information into three integers denoted by m_0, m_1, and m_2, which represent the number of hops from the source to the destination along the d_0, d_1, and d_2 directions, respectively. Before sending the packet to an appropriate neighbor, intermediate nodes update these values to indicate the remaining hops in each direction to the destination. Hence, $m_0 = m_1 = m_2 = 0$ indicates that the packet has reached its destination.

Suppose node 11 sends a message to node 5 in the H_4 of Figure 2. The original H_4 is given in Figure 2a and $H_4(11)$ — node 11 is placed at the center of the H_4 — is in Figure 2b. From the Chen-Shin-Kandlur routing algorithm, we get $m_0 = 0$, $m_1 = -2$, and $m_2 = -1$. Note that the route from node 11 to node 5 in Figure 2b is isomorphic to that from node 0 to node 31 in Figure 2a. This is not a coincidence but rather a consequence of the homogeneity of H_4.

Applications in various domains require an efficient method for a node to broadcast a message to all the other nodes in an H-mesh. Due to interconnection costs, it is very common to use point-to-point communications for broadcasting. Without loss of generality, one can assume the center node is the broadcast source. The set of nodes that has the same distance from the source node is called a ring. The main idea of this algorithm is to broadcast a message, ring by ring, toward the periphery of an H-mesh. The algorithm consists of two phases. In the first phase, which takes three steps, the message is transmitted to the origin's six nearest neighbors. Note that there are six corner nodes in each ring. In the second phase, which takes $e-1$ steps, the six corner nodes of each ring send the message to two neighboring nodes, while all other nodes propagate the message to the next node in the same direction as the previous transmission. Figure 3 is an example of H_4 broadcasting. The numeric labels denote the communication step numbers.

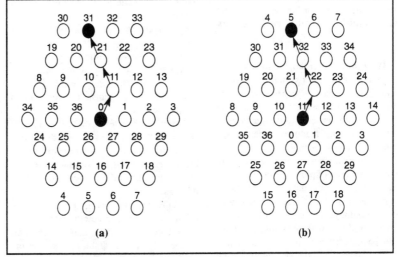

Figure 2. Example of routing in an H_4: (a) original H_4; (b) H_4 with node 11 placed at the center, H_4 (11).

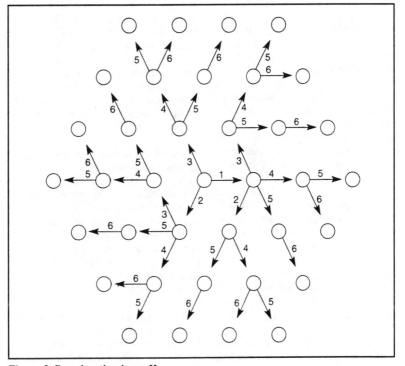

Figure 3. Broadcasting in an H_4.

Low-level architecture

We have developed special hardware support for time-constrained, fault-tolerant communications in HARTS, based on the addressing, routing, and broadcasting methods just described. Below, we discuss the need for extra hardware for communication processing, the main functional requirements of the NP, and a system-level architecture that realizes these functions.

Why communication hardware? Each node in a distributed system must be responsible for packet processing, routing, and error and flow control. Real-time applications impose additional functions related to meeting deadlines, time management, and housekeeping.

Packet processing can consume a substantial number of processor cycles and, in the absence of communication hardware, can deprive the host (node) of much needed computation power. In particular, the host is saddled with breaking a message into packets for transmission, constructing packet headers and trailers, framing packets, and calculating checksums. On reception of packets, the receiving host has to depacketize the message, strip headers and trailers, and compute the checksum for error checking. Each time a packet is transmitted or received, the host must be interrupted and context-switched to routines that perform these chores. This introduces substantial overhead because contemporary off-the-shelf processors are optimized to compute with register and cache data, which are lost in a context switch. For time-constrained, fault-tolerant communications, the host AP also has to handle several other functions that introduce significant computational overhead. These include message scheduling, route selection for reliable and timely delivery of messages, and clock synchronization.

All these functions divert significant computing power from time-critical applications. It is therefore necessary to offload such processing from the AP to special communication-processing hardware — that is, the NP.

Requirements of the network processor. Before designing and building the NP, we identified required functions, which must include efficient support for message processing, low-latency message transmission, and support for time-constrained, fault-tolerant communications. The oper-

ating system must establish deadline guarantees based on these functions.

Communication protocol processing. The NP's main function is to offload communication processing from the APs. When an AP needs to transmit a message, it provides the NP with information about the intended message recipient and the location of the message data. The NP's function is then to execute the operations necessary to pass the message data through the various layers of protocol down to the physical layer where it can be transmitted. In terms of the OSI (Open Systems Interconnection) reference model, the NP is responsible for functions from the transport layer down to the physical layer.

At the transport level, the NP establishes connections dependent only on the source and destination nodes, without concern for the route to be used. It also handles end-to-end error detection and message retransmission.

At the network level, the NP selects primary and alternate routes for establishing virtual circuits, forms data blocks and segments, and reassembles packets at the destination node. There are various switching methods, such as virtual cut-through switching, wormhole routing, store-and-forward packet switching, and circuit switching. Depending on traffic conditions in the network and the message type, the NP chooses an appropriate switching method for the message. The NP also detects and corrects errors at this level.

At the data link level, the NP provides access to the network for the messages. It performs framing and synchronization and packet sequencing. In addition to error checking at the network level, the NP performs checksum error detection and correction at this level.

Low-latency message transmission. Low communication latency is a key goal for NP design, and it influences task migration, task distribution, and load sharing. Latency impacts the system from application tasks down to hardware components. Because a significant portion of latency occurs in communication processing, achieving low-latency communications is intimately related to the implementation of communication protocols.

Support for time-constrained communications. The timely delivery of messages requires a global time base across the different nodes in HARTS. The NP is equipped with special hardware for clock synchroni-

zation and message time-stamping, providing the basis for the implementation of various real-time communication algorithms.

The NP also must support multiple interrupt levels to manage messages with different priority levels. The hardware must provide sufficient interrupt levels to give urgent messages priority over less urgent ones. Urgent messages must also have priority in the use of scarce resources such as message buffers and bandwidths. The NP must implement buffer management policies that maximize buffer space utilization while guaranteeing buffer availability to the highest priority messages. Similarly, if noncritical messages hold other resources needed by more critical messages, the NP must provide for resource preemption by the critical messages.

Another important NP function is monitoring the network's state in terms of traffic load and link failures. The traffic load affects the NP's ability to send real-time messages to other processors, while link failures affect system reliability. It is also possible for the NP to track its host's (or hosts') processing load and use the information for load balancing, load sharing, and task migration.

NP architecture. The NP architecture must support the functions just discussed. Although the HARTS NP architecture is similar to other communication architectures,[6] it has new features to facilitate real-time fault-tolerant communication. At the same time, it attempts to cost-effectively minimize message latency by intelligent management of messages and buffer memory.

The NP has five major components: the interface manager unit (IMU), the packet controller (PC), the routing controller (RC), the buffer memory, and the application processor interface (API), interconnected as shown in Figure 4. (The bus management unit and page management unit are auxiliary components.)

The API moves data between the NP and the host-node APs, while the RC moves data between the NP and the network. Within the NP, the IMU is the main processor that controls the movement and processing of message data. The buffer memory acts as a staging area for data to be transmitted to, or received from, the network, and for message data that must be temporarily stored at the node due to unavailability of outgoing links to the next node on the route to its destination. The RC implements the physical layer protocols for accessing the network and routing data to the node's neigh-

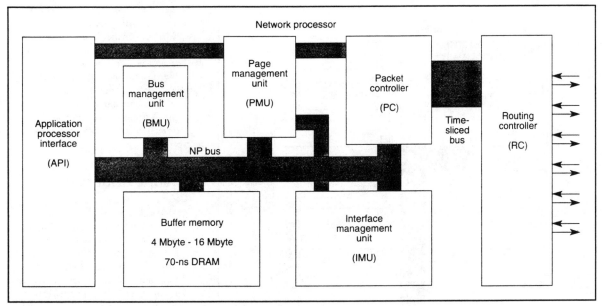

Figure 4. Block diagram of the network processor.

bors. It also supports virtual cut-through and wormhole routing by moving a message from an incoming to an outgoing link without buffering the message at the NP. Finally, the PC performs such functions as checksumming, packet framing, and deframing.

Interface manager unit. The IMU packetizes and depacketizes messages, schedules messages with different levels of priority, decides on switching methods based on message priority levels and network state, monitors the network state, performs error correction and message acknowledgment, and implements various real-time communication algorithms. Ease of software and hardware development and support, and availability, make a general-purpose RISC processor a reasonable choice for the IMU.

The IMU must provide multiple levels of interrupts and a short context switching time. To minimize message latency, the IMU must respond quickly to host requests for message transmission or reception services. The register window schemes in a typical RISC processor allow fast context switches, thus meeting this requirement.

The IMU has memory that can be used to store code and data. It also has access to the buffer memory, the staging area for messages being moved between the host and the network. To avoid excessive copying, the buffer memory usually serves as the

IMU's data memory. Hence, the buffer memory is part of the IMU's address space.

Buffer memory. The buffer memory consists of RAM for the buffers and a buffer management unit. It stores messages waiting to be transmitted to or from the current node, and it acts as a temporary storage area for messages being routed through the current node. The amount of memory needed, usually only a few megabytes, is determined by the usage patterns of the application tasks.

The word size is 32 bits. With current DRAM access speeds of 70 nanoseconds, this gives a memory bandwidth as high as 457 megabits per second. This bandwidth is sufficient for access by the RC, the API, and the IMU, and for refresh cycles. Therefore, expensive static RAM or multiport memories are unnecessary.

The buffer manager arbitrates between the IMU, the API, and the PC for access to the buffer. It also handles buffer memory refresh by periodically accessing rows in the DRAM. The access priorities given to these different sources can be static, dynamic, or random, depending on the buffer management policy adopted.

Another function of the buffer manager is to provide addresses of free buffers for storing incoming packet data and to determine the location of packets ready for forwarding to an outgoing link. In other words, the buffer manager keeps the list of

free buffer pages and tracks the location of various messages stored in the buffer. In instances where a message or packet spans more than a single page, the buffer manager keeps track of linked pages. The buffer management policy for the free list and the buffer allocation policy can be implemented with a separate microcontroller or the IMU.

Packet controller. The PC functions as a DMA (direct memory access) interface between the RC and the buffer memory, providing the IMU with inbound and outbound channels on which to transmit messages from or receive messages into the buffer. It accesses the buffer memory through the arbitration block of the buffer manager and transmits and receives messages without the IMU's intervention.

In transmitting and receiving packets, the PC performs the function of transparently framing and deframing packets. It does this by adding start-of-packet and end-of-packet bytes to the data bytes and computing the checksum as a packet is being sent. On reception of packets at the destination NP, the PC removes the packet header and trailer and computes the checksum to detect transmission errors. The detection of errors is signaled to the IMU via an interrupt, to trigger an appropriate recovery procedure.

Another function of the PC is to time-stamp messages as they are received and

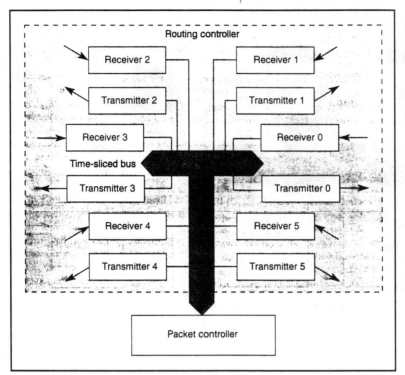

Figure 5. Block diagram of the routing controller.

Inside the figure:
Routing controller
Receiver 2
Receiver 1
Transmitter 2
Transmitter 1
Receiver 3
Receiver 0
Time-sliced bus
Transmitter 3
Transmitter 0
Receiver 4
Receiver 5
Transmitter 4
Transmitter 5
Packet controller

transmitted. As will be discussed later, hardware time-stamping support is crucial to clock synchronization. The time stamp is appended to the message before the checksum bytes.

Routing controller. The RC is the interface between the NP and the network. It implements the physical layer and part of the data link layer. As Figure 5 shows, the RC consists of six receiver-transmitter pairs connected to the buffer manager and IMU through a time-sliced bus. The transmitters convert outgoing data into serial form for transmission on the outgoing serial line. Correspondingly, the receivers convert incoming serial data into parallel form and forward the data to a transmitter for onward transmission, in the case of virtual cut-through or wormhole routing, or to the buffer manager, if the data is to be stored in the current node. A single half-duplex serial line connects each receiver to a transmitter in a neighboring node.

A distinct feature of the RC is that the receivers can be microprogrammed to implement various routing algorithms used in HARTS. Various switching methods can also be programmed simultaneously into the RC and used selectively, on the basis of

the type of messages being sent through the node and the network traffic at any particular time. This allows giving the highest switching and routing priority to critical messages, while optimizing the overall latency of other types of messages.

AP interface. The interface between the NP and the host APs is a VME bus. Data copying between a host AP and the NP is done by the API, which is a DMA interface to the VME bus. There are two ways of designing this interface for data transfer: mapping the NP's data memory into the host address space or copying data from the host's data memory to the NP's data memory. Mapping the NP into the address space of the host is may appear efficient, since it avoids the overhead of a system call. However, this mapping requires dedicated memory management hardware and kernel support for mapped address spaces, and it also incurs the overhead of data access over the VME bus. Depending on the typical size of the messages, burst-mode DMA transfer from the host memory to the NP memory may be more efficient.

In the burst-mode DMA transfer, the host initiates data transfer to the NP by writing to an API control register a pointer

to the data in the host, as in a typical DMA sequence. The API then contends for the host VME bus and the NP buffer memory. When both resources are acquired, it copies the message data in burst mode directly from the host to the NP buffers. Upon completion of the transfer, the IMU is notified, and communication processing can begin. A similar sequence of operations is performed in reverse order for message receipt.

System evaluation

We have evaluated HARTS, using modeling and simulation with actual parameters derived from our implementation. Specifically, we examined how different switching methods can be combined to yield low latency. First, we evaluated the performance of virtual cut-through switching by developing analytic models and a low-level, event-driven simulator. Then, we compared virtual cut-through switching and wormhole routing.

Modeling and simulation of virtual cut-through. Since real-time applications normally require short response times, simple store-and-forward switching schemes are not suitable for HARTS. Hence, it supports fast switching methods such as virtual cut-through[7] and wormhole routing.[8] In virtual cut-through, packets arriving at an intermediate node are forwarded to the next node in the route without buffering if a circuit can be established to the next node.

Kermani and Kleinrock did a mean-value analysis of virtual cut-through performance for a general interconnection network.[7] However, a mean-value analysis is inadequate for real-time applications because worst-case communication delays often play an important role in real-time system design. A mean-value analysis cannot, for example, answer these questions: What is the probability of a successful delivery given a delay? What is the delay bound such that the probability of a successful delivery is greater than a specified threshold?

Kermani and Kleinrock wanted to avoid any dependence on the interconnection topology in their analysis. As a result, they assumed that the probability of packet buffering at an intermediate node is a given parameter. Since a reasonable estimate of virtual cut-through performance cannot be obtained without an accurate estimate of buffering probability, their approach becomes useful only if one can accurately

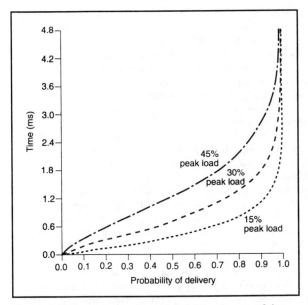

Figure 6. Delivery time versus probability of successful delivery.

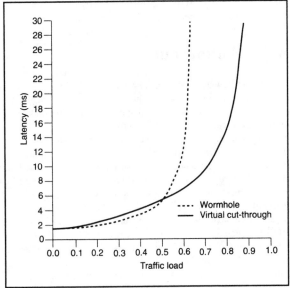

Figure 7. Latencies of wormhole routing and virtual cut-through switching for an H_5.

determine buffering probability for a given interconnection topology. This determination is not a simple matter, because each node in a distributed system handles not only all packets generated at the node, but also all packets passing through the node (transit packets). Consequently, to evaluate the probability of buffering, we have to account for the fraction of packets generated at other nodes that pass through each given node.

In contrast to Kermani and Kleinrock, we first derive the probability that a packet is destined for a particular node by characterizing the H-mesh topology. We use this probability of branching as a parameter in a queueing network to determine the throughput rate at each node in the mesh. Once the throughput rates are found, we can derive the probability that a packet can establish a cut-through at an intermediate node. From these parameters, we finally derive the probability distribution function of delivery times for a packet traversing a specified number of hops.

Figure 6 plots the inverse of the probability distribution function for a message traveling five hops. The three curves show the variation in the inverse of the probability distribution function for different message-generation rates or network traffic. These curves are useful in determining design parameters such as delay bounds. For example, one can select a delay bound such that the probability of message delivery

within that bound is greater than a specified threshold. This would provide a probabilistic measure on the guarantees provided for real-time system operation.

In contrast to the analytic model, a simulator makes very few simplifying assumptions in modeling the behavior of virtual cut-through in HARTS. The simulator accurately models the delivery of each message by emulating the timing of the routing hardware along the packet route at the microcode level. It also captures the internal bus access overheads that the packets experience if they are unable to cut through an intermediate node. The simulator's detailed timing and tracking of messages allows investigation of various message scheduling strategies, access protocols, and memory management strategies. The simulator can also use any discrete distribution of packet lengths for which the user specifies the number, length, and probability of the different types of message. The simulator has been used to check the validity of analytic models by evaluating the HARTS communication subsystem under various realistic settings.

Evaluation of hybrid routing schemes. The basic idea of wormhole routing is that if a channel is not available, a message waits for it. Because the message is not removed from the network, it retains all resources from its source to the node at which it is waiting. Wormhole routing can be thought

of as incrementally establishing a route because it does not surrender the resources it has acquired along the path from source to destination. One benefit is that the message need not reacquire resources once it has acquired them. Deadlock-free algorithms based on wormhole routing have been proposed by Dally and Seitz.[8]

Virtual cut-through differs from wormhole routing in that it stores the message at the node where it is blocked and releases the resources acquired on the path from the source to the blocking node once the message has been stored.

The advantage of both wormhole routing and circuit switching is that they guarantee delivery once a source-to-destination connection has been established. Virtual cut-through, however, can lower latency when the hogging of links due to wormhole routing and circuit switching worsens the congestion in the network.

To show the difference in performance of wormhole routing and virtual cut-through switching, we plotted their message latencies in Figure 7. For low traffic loads, wormhole routing takes less time on average to deliver messages; the opposite is true for high loads. The traffic load break-even point decreases as mesh size increases, because the average message distance increases with mesh size. Which routing method is more advantageous depends on the traffic load and average message distance. The routing controller described earlier has the flexibility to dynamically select the better of the two methods.

Fault-tolerant routing

One attractive feature of point-to-point networks is their ability to withstand link and node failures. Exploiting this feature requires developing algorithms and providing mechanisms that preserve network communication in the presence of component failures. In this context, one must address correct routing of messages when one or more mesh components fail. This is of particular importance when the mesh is large and component failures thus are more likely, and when the system is expected to operate for long periods without maintenance. The ideal fault-tolerant routing algorithm would route messages by the shortest fault-free path, would require no extra hardware, would not cause unnecessary delays at intermediate nodes, and would quickly determine whether a destination was unreachable. The algorithm presented by Olson and Shin[4] comes close to meeting these criteria and requires each node to know only the condition (faulty or nonfaulty) of its own links.

Each node of an H-mesh can be seen as the convergence point of three axes, and the shortest path between two nodes can be expressed as offsets along no more than two of the three axes. Since each of the six links represents movement along one of these three axes, either in the positive or negative direction, fault-free routing can be accomplished by forwarding messages along links that will bring them toward zero. Our idea is to not interfere with this process until the message finds its path blocked. A message is routed by the fault-free algorithm until it reaches a node where all the links through which the message would ordinarily be forwarded (called the optimal links) are faulty. At that point the fault-tolerant algorithm intervenes.

At the point of message detouring, routing control is split between the fault-free algorithm and the fault-tolerant algorithm. A single bit in the message header determines which algorithm is currently making routing decisions. If this bit is clear, the message is in free mode, and the fault-free algorithm does the routing. Otherwise, the message is in detour mode, and the fault-tolerant algorithm does the routing. The fault-tolerant algorithm remains in control until it believes it has bypassed the faults that blocked the message path.

The fault-tolerant algorithm can be viewed as a simple wall-following algorithm. The message travels around the edge of a cluster of faults until it reaches the other side. Implementation is simple. When the optimal links are found to be faulty, the message is placed in detour mode, and the NP looks for nonfaulty links, starting with the link immediately counterclockwise of the optimal links and proceeding counterclockwise. The message is sent out on the first nonfaulty link found. If a message arrives at a node already in detour mode, it is sent out on the first nonfaulty link counterclockwise of the link by which it arrived. While in detour mode, the offsets to the destination are continually recalculated, and the message leaves detour mode when the distance to the destination is less than it was when the message entered detour mode.

As an example, consider the situation in Figure 8. A message has arrived at node 18, with node 1 as its eventual destination. At 18 the only optimal link is the one to node 0, which has failed; the message is placed in detour mode and sent to node 7. At 7 the fault-tolerant algorithm first tries to send the message to node 0, then to node 8, but finally must send it to node 15. At 15 the message is immediately forwarded to node 8. At 8 the message returns to free mode as node 8 is closer to node 1 than node 18 is. The message then completes routing normally.

An unreachable destination is revealed by the presence of a cycle. If the fault-tolerant algorithm cannot get the message to the destination, the message will cycle. Unfortunately, for certain classes of fault configurations, called incisions, the message will cycle even though the destination is reachable. Simulation results show that this type of fault is rare, occurring only with large numbers of faults. It can be dealt with at a cost of increased complexity in the routing algorithm. Strategies for detecting and routing in the presence of incisions are outlined by Olson and Shin.[4] They show that the H-mesh is extremely robust: If 50 percent of the links in an H_3 are faulty, a randomly chosen destination is reachable with probability greater than 0.95.

Clock synchronization

Widely recognized as one of the important requirements of a distributed real-time system, a global time base simplifies the solutions to design problems such as checkpointing, interprocess communication, and resource allocation.[9]

Central to the establishment of a global time base is the synchronization of the local clocks on different nodes in the system. Both hardware and software solutions to this problem have been proposed. The software solutions are flexible and economical but require the exchange of additional messages solely for synchronization.[10] The overhead imposed by these additional messages could be substantial, especially if a tight synchronization between processes is desired. Hardware solutions, on the other hand, require additional hardware at each node of the distributed system. They can achieve very tight synchronization between processes, with very little time overhead, but they require a separate network of clocks that is usually different from the network between the nodes.

For HARTS, we use a software solution that requires minimal hardware support at each node.[11] It is based on the interactive convergence algorithm given by Lamport and Melliar-Smith.[10] (Note, however, that any other software clock synchronization algorithm can be used for our scheme.) The algorithm assumes that the clocks drift apart only by a bounded amount during each resynchronization interval, R, during which each process reads the value of every process's clock. If the value of a clock read differs from its own clock by an amount greater than a threshold, the process replaces that value with its own clock value. The process then computes the average of all such values and sets its own clock to this average. Lamport and Melliar-Smith show that this algorithm can achieve synchronization and requires $3m+1$ processors to tolerate m faults.

Three major problems arise when this algorithm is used in a distributed system with a point-to-point interconnection network. First, it is difficult for a process to read the clock of a process to which it is not directly connected. Second, the message received by a process may be corrupted by a faulty intermediate process. Third, a queueing delay for the clock messages may cause a substantial difference between the real times at which a clock value is sent and received. Therefore, subtracting the clock value in the received message from the current clock value will not reflect the actual skew between the clocks of the sending and receiving processes. This problem is aggravated when the clock message must pass through multiple intermediate nodes.

Ramanathan, Kandlur, and Shin[11] solve the first problem by letting each process broadcast its clock to all processes at a specified time, with respect to its own local

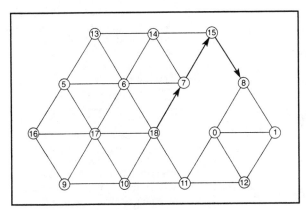

Figure 8. Example of fault-tolerant routing.

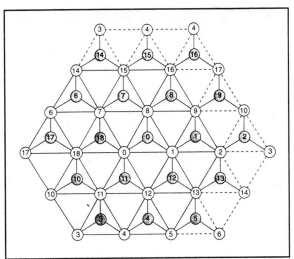

Figure 9. I/O controller placement.

clock, in the resynchronization interval. The second problem is eliminated by a broadcast algorithm that delivers multiple copies of the message to all processes through node-disjoint paths. For the third problem, it is not the size of the delay, but the fact that it is not known, that affects the clock skew. The message delivery time for clock messages is obtained by requiring each intermediate process to append to the message the delay incurred at that process.

The accurate computation of this delay needs some hardware support. There is some uncertainty in determining time of receipt because of a variable delay between the processor's receiving notification of arrival and actually "seeing" the message. Also, to compute the time delay within the node, the processor must have control on the exact time at which a message is transmitted on a link. These potential errors in estimating the time delay limit the accuracy with which we can compute the clock skew. This in turn affects the clock skew achievable with the synchronization.

To alleviate this problem, we use a hardware time-stamping mechanism at the link level for clock messages (see earlier section on the packet controller). When a link receiver detects a clock message, it appends a receive time stamp to the message. Similarly, when a clock message is transmitted, the link transmitter appends a transmit time stamp. At an intermediate node, the receive and transmit time stamps use the same local clock, so their difference gives a very accurate estimate of message time in that node. By computing the difference at intermediate nodes, we can keep the total number of time stamps down

to five and prevent message length from growing as network size increases.

For any synchronization algorithm, R is a function of the maximum clock skew desired. R decreases with the desired maximum skew and becomes negative for small values. From a practical viewpoint, overheads for the synchronization algorithm increase as R decreases, so it is desirable to have R as large as possible. This function effectively determines the type of skew that can be achieved for the system with a particular synchronization algorithm. The derivation of this function for the synchronization algorithm described here is given by Ramanathan, Kandlur, and Shin.[11] This algorithm can achieve moderately tight synchronization. For example, in an H_3, a maximum clock skew of 100 microseconds can be achieved using $R=6.23$ seconds.

I/O architecture

Most work on distributed computing systems has centered on interconnection networks, programming and communications paradigms, and algorithms. However, little has been done specifically about the I/O subsystem in a real-time environment, despite its obvious importance. Clearly, a real-time computer can process data no faster than it can acquire the data from sensors and operators. Note that I/O devices in a real-time environment are sensors, actuators, and displays, whereas they are magnetic disks and tapes for general-purpose systems. Due to the distinct timing and reliability requirements of real-time applications, solutions suited to general-

purpose systems are not usually applicable to the real-time environment.

To avoid the accessibility problems of nondistributed I/O, I/O devices need to be distributed and managed by relatively simple, and reliable, controllers. Moreover, to improve both accessibility (and thus reliability) and performance, there must be multiple access paths (called multiaccessibility or multiownership) to these I/O devices.

I/O interconnection architecture. I/O devices are clustered, and a controller manages access to the devices of each cluster. The I/O controller (IOC) can be simple since HARTS uses simple data links to the computation nodes. The IOC need only handle sending and receiving simple messages via a set of full-duplex links, not providing virtual cut-through capabilities and other features of a full-blown NP. To keep the IOCs and the I/O links down to a reasonable number, the number of IOCs is restricted to no greater than the total number (p) of computation nodes in the mesh. This has certain benefits for one of the management protocols explained later.

Having established the potential number of I/O nodes, we need to decide how many nodes each IOC will be connected to. If the maximum number (p) of IOCs are assumed to exist in an H_3, for example, then Figure 9 shows a logical connection scheme.[12] Each IOC can be thought of as being in the center of one of the upward-pointing triangles in this figure; the IOC is connected to each of the nodes that make up the triangle, called its left, right, and upper partners. This gives three possible avenues of access to each IOC. Note that if the maximum

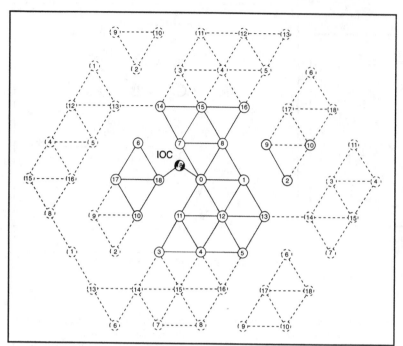

Figure 10. Unreachable static owner.

All the high-level architectural issues of HARTS have been resolved, and the lower-level components are being designed or implemented. The routing controller, a key component for fast switching, has been fabricated, and its testing is almost complete. The packet controller, the second generation of the routing controller, and other NP components are currently being designed and simulated. In parallel with the architectural work, we are also designing and implementing a software communication subsystem for HARTS. The primary objectives of this subsystem are to deliver messages within certain deadline constraints, support mechanisms for group communication and reliable broadcasting, offer services such as maintenance of a global time base, and monitor system behavior. ■

Acknowledgments

The work reported in this article was supported in part by the Office of Naval Research under contract N00014-85-K-00122. The author would like to thank all current and former members of the RTCL for their contributions to the HARTS project. Specifically, Ming-Syan Chen developed wrapping, labeling, and routing techniques, James Dolter and Parameswaran Ramanathan designed and implemented the routing controller chip, Stuart Daniel and Teng-Kean Siew are currently working on the design and implementation of the network processor, Dilip Kandlur and Daniel Kiskis developed HARTOS, Alan Olson developed a fault-tolerant routing algorithm, and Greg Dykema played a key role in developing the I/O architecture. The author is also indebted to Andre van Tilborg, Gary Koob, and James Smith at the Office of Naval Research for their encouragement.

number of IOCs are used, the number of I/O links required is equal to the number of standard communication links, or $9e2-9e+3$ for an H_e. One could similarly place IOCs at the (logical) center of the downward-pointing triangles as well, allowing for up to $2p$ IOCs, but this would double the maximum possible number of I/O links required and disturb certain homogeneous effects of limiting the number of IOCs to the number of nodes.

Management protocols. The desire for simple I/O controllers presents a problem in HARTS, because the natural tendency would be to assign sensors and actuators, both relatively complex and expensive devices, to individual nodes or NPs and use the given interprocess communication (IPC) channels in HARTS to handle the I/O traffic. We can still use the given IPC channels, but instead of permanently tying down a given I/O device to one node, we allow several nodes to communicate with each I/O device. There are two fundamentally different protocols for managing this communication.

The first management protocol, the static protocol, assigns one node to each IOC as its owner, but with the important provision that the owner can be changed if the original owner becomes faulty. In this protocol, one of the IOC links is defined as the active link, and the rest remain inactive as spares. The second, dynamic protocol, allows the IOC owner to be defined dynamically, providing greater accessibility and requiring fewer hops on average to reach the IOC owner. In this protocol, the IOC decides which link will be active at any given time.

Figure 10 is an example in which a process in node 13 wants service from IOC 18, but since node 18 is the owner under the static protocol and is not reachable from 13, it cannot obtain service. If node 0 were the owner instead of 18 — which is possible under the dynamic protocol — it could be serviced.

In addition to making IOCs accessible where static ownership would make them inaccessible, the dynamic protocol takes into account the fact that one partner may be closer to a node requesting service than the other partner. Since this protocol chooses the closest of the partners that respond, the I/O traffic may have fewer hops to travel. However, its disadvantages are that it is more difficult to implement and involves arbitration overhead after servicing each I/O request. It may also be undesirable because there is no single node through which all I/O requests will travel and which could perform some I/O management tasks. Shin and Dykema give a comparative analysis of these two protocols.[12]

References

1. D.D. Kandlur, D.L. Kiskis, and K.G. Shin, "HARTOS: A Distributed Real-Time Operating System," *ACM SIGOPS Operating Systems Review*, Vol. 23, No. 3, July 1989, pp. 72-89.

2. K.S. Stevens, "The Communication Framework for a Distributed Ensemble Architecture," AI Tech. Report 47, Schlumberger Research Laboratory, Palo Alto, Calif., Feb. 1986.

3. M.-S. Chen, K.G. Shin, and D.D. Kandlur, "Addressing, Routing and Broadcasting in Hexagonal Mesh Multiprocessors," *IEEE Trans. Computers*, Vol. C-39, No. 1, Jan. 1990, pp. 10-18.

4. A. Olson and K.G. Shin, "Message Routing in HARTS with Faulty Components," *FTCS-19, Digest of Papers,* Computer Society Press, Order No. 1959, June 1989, pp. 331-338.

5. J.W. Dolter, P. Ramanathan, and K.G. Shin, "A Microprogrammable VLSI Routing Controller for HARTS," *Proc. Int'l Conf. Computer Design: VLSI in Computers,* Computer Society Press, Order No. 1971, Oct. 1989, pp. 160-163.

6. E.A. Arnould et al., "The Design of Nectar: A Network Backplane for Heterogeneous Multicomputers," *Proc. Third Int'l Conf. Architectural Support for Programming Languages and Operating Systems,* ACM, New York, 1989, pp. 205-216.

7. P. Kermani and L. Kleinrock, "Virtual Cut-Through: A New Computer Communication Switching Technique," *Computer Networks,* Vol. 3, 1979, pp. 267-286.

8. W.J. Dally and C.L. Seitz, "Deadlock-Free Message Routing in Multiprocessor Interconnection Networks," *IEEE Trans. Computers,* Vol. C-36, No. 5, May 1987, pp. 547-553.

9. L. Lamport, "Using Time Instead of Timeout for Fault-Tolerant Distributed Systems," *ACM Trans. Programming Languages and Systems,* Vol. 6, No. 2, Apr. 1984, pp. 254-280.

10. L. Lamport and P.M. Melliar-Smith, "Synchronizing Clocks in the Presence of Faults," *J. ACM,* Vol. 32, No. 1, Jan. 1985, pp. 52-78.

11. P. Ramanathan, D.D. Kandlur, and K.G. Shin, "Hardware-Assisted Software Clock Synchronization for Homogeneous Distributed Systems," *IEEE Trans. Computers,* Vol. C-39, No. 4, Apr. 1990, pp. 514-524.

12. K.G. Shin and G.L. Dykema, "Distributed I/O Architecture for HARTS," *Proc. 17th Int'l Symp. Computer Architecture,* Computer Society Press, Order No. 2047, June 1990, pp. 332-342.

Kang G. Shin is a professor and associate chair of electrical engineering and computer science at the University of Michigan, Ann Arbor. From 1978 to 1982 he was on the faculty of Rensselaer Polytechnic Institute. He has authored or coauthored more than 180 technical papers on fault-tolerant computing, distributed real-time computing, computer architecture, and robotics and automation. In 1987 he received the Outstanding Paper Award from the *IEEE Transactions on Automatic Control* for a paper on robot trajectory planning. In 1989 he received the Research Excellence Award from the University of Michigan.

Shin received the BS degree in electronics engineering from Seoul National University, South Korea, in 1970, and the MS and PhD degrees in electrical engineering from Cornell University in 1976 and 1978, respectively. He is a distinguished visitor of the IEEE Computer Society.

Readers may write Shin at the University of Michigan, Real-Time Computing Laboratory, Dept. of Electrical Engineering and Computer Science, Ann Arbor, MI 48109-2122.

Distributed Fault-Tolerant Real-Time Systems:
The Mars Approach

Most computer systems for real-time process control must meet high standards of reliability, availability, and safety. In many of these real-time applications, the costs of a catastrophic system failure can exceed the initial investment in the computer and the controlled object. To prevent such failures, system design must guarantee performance as specified in the domains of both value and time during all anticipated operational situations. The computer system must also be designed to tolerate faults caused by environmental disturbances or a physical degradation of the hardware.

Distributed computer-system architectures have gained general acceptance in the area of real-time process control. These architectures offer a significant potential for fault tolerance and functional degradation as well as for testability and extensibility. However, many of the distributed computer-system architectures presently on the market[1] or proposed by the research community as academic prototypes (the V-Kernel,[2] Accent,[3] or Chorus[4]) do not support some key points that are essential to reliable control of real-time applications. These points are

- limited time validity of real-time data,
- predictable performance under peak load,
- fault tolerance, and
- maintainability and extensibility.

Consequently, we developed the Maintainable Real-Time System, a fault-tolerant distributed system for process control. The Mars project started in 1980 at the Technische Universitat Berlin. The first prototype appeared in 1984 and demonstrated the fundamental concepts of Mars. The second academic prototype developed at the Technische Universitat Wien in Vienna has been functional since the beginning of 1988. Its main feature is predictable performance under a specified peak load. Its industrial applications include rolling mills and railway-control systems in which the controlled system imposes hard deadlines.

This article presents the Mars approach to real-time process control, its architectural design and implementation, and one of its applications. But first, let's explore the characteristics of distributed real-time systems as background to this discussion.

Real-time process control has to be timely and has to be right. Here's how one system promotes these features through a number of key functions.

Hermann Kopetz
Andreas Damm
Christian Koza
Marco Mulazzani
Wolfgang Schwabl
Christoph Senft
Ralph Zainlinger

Technische Universitat Wien

Reprinted from *IEEE Micro*, Vol. 9, No. 1, February 1989, pp. 25-40.

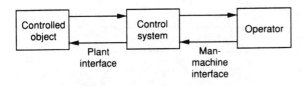

Figure 1. Real-time system.

Distributed real-time systems

In a real-time system, a controlled object (the controlled environment) and a control system (the computer) are connected via sensor- and actuator-based interfaces. The control system either accepts data from the sensors at regular intervals or is driven by events. It processes the data and outputs the results to the controlled object via the actuators. The output data influence the controlled object, and the sensors observe the effects, thus closing the loop as shown in Figure 1.

It is extremely important to avoid inconsistencies between the internal states of the control system, the control object, and the operator. The control system must respond to a stimulus from the control object within an interval dictated by the environment, called *response time*.

The system must guarantee this response time under extreme load and anticipated fault conditions. Typical systems respond in 1 millisecond to 1 second or more.

If a serious failure—either in the control system or the controlled object—closes down the plant, the system must shut down in a controlled, predetermined manner (fail-safe operation).

We considered the following characteristics to achieve the requirements of timeliness and high availability.

Correct versus valid information. In a real-time environment, one must access information in two domains: value and time. Information is *correct* if it corresponds with the intentions of the user. Information is *timely* if it is available within the intended interval of real time. Information qualifies as *valid* if it is both correct and timely.

In the nonreal-time world, we concern ourselves only with the value domain, that is, with correctness. The inclusion of the time domain in real-time systems adds a new dimension to the problem of providing valid information. The speed of processing in a given interval of real time (system performance) becomes an essential property.

Real-time versus archival data. A real-time control system performs real-time control functions and also collects data for archival purposes. We therefore distinguish between the two databases required for these purposes.

A *real-time database* consists of the set of data elements essential to instantaneous real-time control, operator display, alarm monitoring, and other real-time functions. An *archival database* includes the set of data elements required for archival purposes.

Major differences exist between these two databases from the point of view of time and fault tolerance.

The real-time database changes as time progresses, that is, the passage of real time invalidates the information in the database. Losing the real-time database suspends control of the environment.

After an element has been stored in the archival database, one cannot modify it again. It does not change as time progresses (it is not allowed to modify "history"). Losing the archival database does not immediately affect real-time control of the environment.

To correctly respond to an external or internal stimulus, the real-time database inside the control system must contain a valid (correct and timely) image of the external state of the environment.

Event-driven versus periodic systems. An event (state change) or a time signal initiates action in a real-time system. In *event-driven systems*, a state change in the environment or an external event (such as an interrupt) usually initiates activities spontaneously. In *periodic systems*, an equidistant time signal initiates all system activities at predefined points in time. The time period between related sequences of actions that are initiated by equidistant time signals is called a *duty cycle*.

If a system is driven by events, shielding it from faults in the environment can be very difficult. Spurious events can cause the initiation of more activity than the system was designed to handle. Any good design must contain mechanisms to protect the system from such conditions. One common hardware technique for the suppression of unwanted signals provides a low-pass filter.

In a periodic system, the response-time requirements of the given application under worst-case conditions determines the duty cycle (sample rate). System design guarantees that only a single event of a given type will be active within a given duty cycle. A periodic system has the advantage of implicit flow control and the protection of the system from (erroneous) overload conditions caused by a fault in the environment.

A maintainable system

This section outlines the architectural principles we followed in the design of Mars based on the principal considerations just described.

Design for peak load. In many real-time applications, one most urgently needs the services of the control system under peak-load conditions in which all stimuli (events) occur with maximum (but specified) frequencies. Consider the case of an air-traffic control system or a nuclear-reactor shutdown system. The systems must handle a peak-load condition without missing any hard real-time deadlines. If a system can do this, it can accommodate all low-load conditions automatically. Consequently, we designed hard real-time systems for peak loads.

Transaction orientation. Mars uses a transaction model to describe the activities of a real-time system. A *transaction* is the single execution of a specified set of tasks (generally in different nodes) between the stimulus and the corresponding response. We structured a transaction as an acyclic-directed graph with tasks that appear as nodes and messages that appear as arcs. If the corresponding response has to be produced within a given time interval after a stimulus, we have a *real-time* transaction.

A transaction transfers the system from one consistent state into another. In a distributed system, a transaction can decompose into a sequence of subtransactions consisting of executing tasks and communication phases between these subtransactions. An external event (generated by an external state transition) or an internal event (generated inside the computer system like a clock tick) can serve as the stimulus that initiates a transaction.

Network structure with clustering. The operational structure of a distributed, real-time control application consists of a set of *components* that form a network. These components include self-contained computers and the application *tasks*[5] that consume, process, produce, and interchange messages between components. The concept of *clustering* helps to manage the complexity of a large network of components. A Mars cluster is a subset of the network with a high functional connectivity. Clusters are the basic elements of our system architecture (Figure 2). Each cluster consists of several components interconnected by a synchronous, real-time Mars bus.

Global time. Distributed real-time systems require a common time base (called global time) of known synchronistic accuracy to measure the

• absolute time of an event occurrence,
• causal ordering of events,
• calculation of time intervals, and
• establishment of information consistency between the real-time database and the environment.

In Mars, the underlying architecture (operating system and hardware) provides a fault-tolerant, global time base called *system time*.[6]

Interprocessor communication. Mars introduces a new type of message for interprocessor communica-

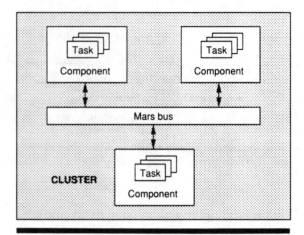

Figure 2. Mars cluster.

tions called the *state message*. The semantics of a state message is similar to that of a global variable. A new version of a state message updates the previous version. State messages are not consumed when read. An arbitrary number of tasks can read a state message an arbitrary number of times. State messages exchange information about the state of the environment that has been observed at a given point in time and is assumed to hold for a certain interval of time. Since every change of state is an event, in principle, a set of (periodic) state messages can realize any information exchange.

In real-time systems, the validity of information does not exclusively depend on its correctness in the value domain. This validity also depends on the timeliness of the information.[7] Each message has an attached *validity time*. As soon as the validity of a message expires, the operating system discards the message.

End-to-end protocols. Reliable communication can only occur with the knowledge and help of the application software residing at the endpoints of the communication system.[8] Dynamic time redundancy in the lower levels of the communication protocols increases communication reliability. However, this redundancy also leads to an uncontrolled increase in communication traffic under error and heavy-load conditions (for example, implementing Positive Acknowledge or Retransmission protocols). Real-time systems do not allow for a gain in communication reliability at the expense of unpredictability in communication delays. We feel that strict control over the communication traffic by the application software is necessary in real-time systems to meet the timing requirements. Mars provides merely an unacknowledged datagram[9] with a "no wait send" semantic as the communication service. That is, the sender does not wait until the receiver accepts the message. The (periodic) state messages realize implicit flow control between sender and receiver(s). One can derive the timing properties of the application from an analysis of the end-to-end protocols in the application software.

Dependability Analysis

Dependability[1] is the property of a system that allows reliance to be justifiably placed on the service it delivers. Dependability analysis concentrates on estimation and analysis of failures and their impact. Examples of quantitative measures are reliability and availability. Other measures depend on the type of application.

In Mars applications, two aspects are of special interest for dependability analysis. First, an *early dependability analysis* is preferable because of its cost-effectiveness. The later a design change becomes necessary, the more it costs. The dependability analysis requires close examination of the system, including failures and mutual dependencies of sensors, actuators, man-machine interface, operator, plant, and other subsystems.

The architecture shown in Figure A helps to structure the concepts, unify the methods and tools, and provide an easy framework for development. Expected long-term benefits include reusability, variability, and possible standardization of methods, interfaces, and tools. A layered architecture forms the underlying principle for the design and implementation of the Mars Reliability Predictor and Low-Cost Estimator (Marple).[2]

Marple fits perfectly into the concept of the contractual approach used in the Mars design-system environment. Figure B shows the interaction of the different programs and their layering according to the reference architecture.

One major difference exists between Marple and other tools for dependability analysis. Most tools require a model as their input. In contrast, Marple *generates* dependability models. It is a compiler, translating a general-purpose design language for

Figure A. Architectural layers and their abstractions.

Layer	Abstraction
	Project
7. Application	Architectural variants
6. Optimization	Refined architecture
5. Model-generation	Dependability model
4. Model	(Sub)models
3. Transformation	Algorithms
2. Algorithmic	Numbers
1. Physical	

Figure B. Interaction of Marple with the design system and SHARPE.

TDMA media-access strategy. Since we designed Mars to master peak-load situations, its performance must not degrade because of variations in external-stimuli frequencies or message congestion on the real-time bus. The media access-delay time to the bus should be independent of bus activity. In Mars, a time-division, multiple-access strategy (TDMA) provides a deterministic, load-independent, and collision-free method for media access. The duty cycles of all tasks are synchronized in advance with the TDMA slots to optimize the system-response behavior.

Fault tolerance by active redundancy. The fault hypothesis in the Mars design covers permanent and transient physical faults in the components and on the real-time bus. Examples include transient faults caused by alpha particles or permanent faults caused by physical degradation of hardware components. Errors in the design and implementation of the software are not currently included in the present Mars fault hypothesis.

We assume that components possess self-checking properties[10] and fail silently, that is, that they either operate as intended or do not produce any results. The various inner-failure modes of a component thus reduce to a single-failure mode of the component from the standpoint of its environment: The component doesn't operate.

In Mars, fault tolerance relies on self-checking components that run with active redundancy. Fault tolerance also relies on multiple transmissions of messages on the real-time bus. Active redundancy better enhances reliability in hard real-time systems than passive redundancy because it has superior timing properties. As long as any one of a set of redundant, synchronized, self-checking components can operate, the required service can be maintained. Every message is transmitted n times, either in parallel over n buses or sequentially over a single bus (or a combination thereof). Therefore, the loss of $n - 1$ messages is tolerable. We have developed a special tool to assess the reliabili-

distributed systems into corresponding reliability models. Marple concentrates on application-layer and model generation. The generated dependability models are then analyzed by the Symbolic Hierarchical Automated Reliability and Performance Evaluator (SHARPE),[3] which covers layers 4 to 1 of the reference architecture. Currently, the design is translated into SHARPE processor-memory-switch (PMS) models. The generation of models based on Markov chains (MCs) is under way. Future extensions may include generation of various other models, approximation methods, and/or usage of other tools for dependability analysis.

The application layer of Marple analyzes system designs. Marple receives a detailed description of the designed system in the form of a structured, text-oriented, specification language. The basic elements of this language are objects (such as clusters, sensors, operators, and tasks), information items (notions for the abstract entities of information exchange), and transactions (describing the functionality of objects) in a system-wide context. The power of the input language stems from the ability to combine these elements hierarchically in a flexible way.

The general description of the design is augmented with dependability data including

- redundancy,
- failure and repair distributions,
- failure modes of the elements,
- coverage values,
- cost functions of failures (in preparation), and
- repair dependencies (in preparation).

For more complicated subsystems, one can define submodels (reliability block diagrams, MCs, series-parallel graphs, and combined performance and reliability models). On the other hand, one can also

use default values for the different types of elements of the system. Due to this general design language, Marple is independent of the Mars design-system environment in terms of such features as a specific database or user interface.

Our first experience in using Marple produced an interesting effect. Although Marple was intended as a reliability predictor, the term "unreliability predictor" proved more appropriate. Systems without massive redundancy of sensors, actuators, and computers expose poor reliability behavior due to their wide-spread dependencies. Feedback occurs immediately (not after two months of reliability analysis) that the actual design is unreliable. This information forces the designer to

- think about failures,
- decide which functions are important,
- analyze which parts are important, and
- determine where and to what extent redundancy should be applied.

Thus consideration of faults and their impact becomes an integral part of each design step.

References

1. A. Avizienis and J.C. Laprie, "Dependable Computing: From Concepts to Design Diversity," *Proc. IEEE*, Vol. 74, No. 5, May 1986, pp. 629-638.

2. M. Mulazzani, "An Open Layered Architecture for Dependability Analysis and Its Application," *Proc. 18th Fault-Tolerant Computing Symp.*, IEEE CS Press, Los Alamitos, Calif., June 1988, pp. 96-101.

3. R.A. Sahner and K.S. Trivedi, "Reliability Modeling Using SHARPE," *IEEE Trans. Reliability*, Vol. 36, No. 2, June 1987, pp. 186-193.

ty of a given Mars application. For more details, refer to the box entitled Dependability Analysis.

Maintainability and extensibility. In Mars, maintainability and extensibility result from the clustering of components. One can remove redundant components from a running cluster (for repair) and reintegrate them later. A Mars cluster can be configured with spare capacity in TDMA-bus access, messages, and CPU utilization. One can add new components without modification of the running components until the configuration limit is reached. If more extension is needed, existing components can expand into a cluster. This process converts one component in the original cluster to an interface component showing the same I/O behavior as the old component. This interface component forwards all messages to the added cluster (Figure 3). The additional cluster can be designed independently from the rest of the system as long as the I/O characteristics of the interface component remain unchanged.

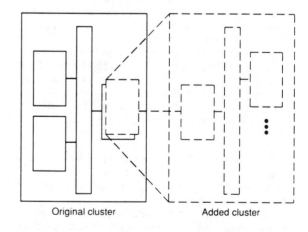

Original cluster   Added cluster

Figure 3. Expansion of a component into a cluster.

Mars operating system

We developed a new operating system to implement the Mars architecture and to guarantee a deterministic system behavior. An identical copy of the operating system runs locally and autonomously in each Mars component, which is a hardware/software unit as shown in Figure 4. The operating system consists of a small kernel and a set of system tasks.

The kernel consists of the entire code running in supervisor mode on the CPU. The kernel's primary goals are

- administering resources (CPU, memory, bus), and
- hiding all hardware details from the tasks.

The kernel provides its functionality via a set of defined system calls. The interfaces of the system calls—as well as major parts of the kernel—are written in the C programming language. Adapting the kernel alone lets Mars port to a new hardware environment. The kernel is responsible for the periodic execution of hard real-time (Hrt)—or time-critical—tasks according to a schedule calculated off line. (The section on timing analysis describes the off-line task and message scheduler.) The kernel also maintains global time and oversees the efficiency of message passing.

Real-time tasks. Hrt tasks are periodically scheduled and must terminate before a given deadline. Thus their reaction time and latency must be deterministic and known in advance. An off-line scheduler calculates the activation periods (duty cycle) based on the transaction specification during the system-design phase. The kernel executes these tasks according to the results of the off-line scheduler.

Most Hrt tasks are *application tasks*, but some of them are *system tasks*. System tasks perform specific, hardware-independent functions of the operating system. These functions include time synchronization and protocol conversions to and from RS-232 strings and Mars messages, for example. Privileged system calls are restricted to system tasks.

All tasks that are not subjected to strict deadlines are called *soft real-time tasks*. Normally an Srt is non-periodic and utilizes the CPU idle time in low-load situations.

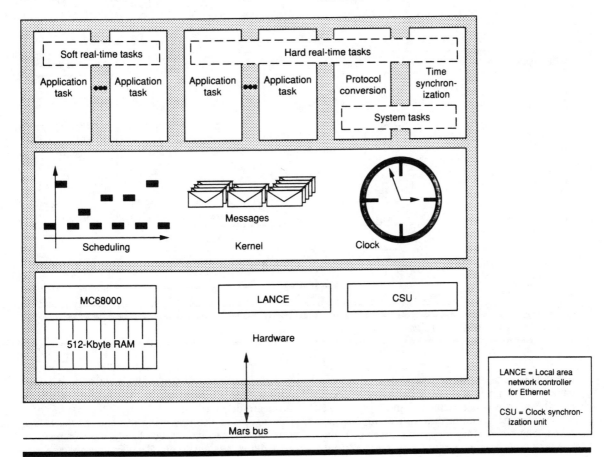

Figure 4. Structure of the current Mars component.

Clock Synchronization in Mars

Each Mars component has its own real-time clock with a resolution of 1 μs. Clock synchronization consists of two parts. *Internal synchronization* keeps all clocks within a cluster synchronized within a known constant, the internal synchronistic accuracy ΔD^{int}. *External synchronization* adjusts the clocks of a cluster to international atomic time. IAT is a physical time measure. It does not suffer from switching seconds due to irregularities in the rotation of the earth.

We based internal synchronization on normal message passing to avoid special hardware links for time-signal propagation. Each message contains the time stamp of the sender's clock. The receiving component attaches the time stamp of the receiver's clock to each incoming message. Each component records the time differences to the other components periodically. Based on this information, a correction term for the local clock is calculated with the *Fault-Tolerant Average Algorithm* (Fta). In the Fta,

an ensemble of n clocks may contain up to k faulty clocks. The local clock differences d from clock i to clock j are sorted by value. The k lowest and the k highest values are discarded. The arithmetic average of the remaining values is the new correction for the local clock j. According to theory,[1] an upper bound for the internal synchronization Δ^{int} is given by

$$\frac{\Delta^{int}}{\epsilon + \xi} = \frac{n - 2k}{n - 3k}$$

where ξ is the maximal tolerable drift of the clocks during a resynchronization interval. The *reading error* ϵ is the measurement error in reading the time of one component by another component. Due to the cooperation between the clock synchronization unit (CSU) and the Mars bus-controller chip LANCE (see Figure 4), the reading error in Mars is bounded (with 4 μs) as explained later.

Figure C schematically shows the time-stamp mechanism for messages in Mars. The CPU places

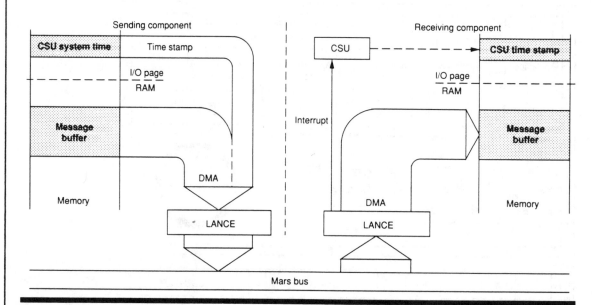

Figure C. Time-stamp mechanism in Mars.

Global time. The operating system maintains synchronized global time. The synchronization of local clocks is based on message exchange[6] and is supported in hardware by the clock synchronization unit (see the accompanying box on that topic). We developed this special very large scale integration unit especially for this project. Using global time helps to implement the following Mars features.

Validity. The system provides tasks with messages only if their validity time has not expired when the tasks are delivered. A task initiates the reading of a message, and the operating system checks to see whether the message is valid. The sender of a message must define a validity time. The operating system internally and automatically discards outdated messages. Thus, every task observes only valid messages.

waiting messages in a buffer, and LANCE starts. LANCE transmits the data to the Mars bus by direct memory access (DMA) after this access to the bus has been granted. LANCE can package several memory fragments continuously into one message. The last fragment of each message is a memory-mapped, real-time register of the CSU that is accessed at the moment of sending. At the receiver LANCE issues an interrupt immediately after a message arrives. This interrupt is directed to the CSU, which generates a time stamp. Afterwards, the CPU stores the CSU time stamp into the received message.

We use external synchronization to calibrate to IAT. Long-wave radio signals provide an economical access to world time, or universal time coordinated. Since UTC and IAT differ an integral number of seconds (in 1988, IAT − UTC = + 24.0 seconds) and the Bureau International de l'Heure publishes the time differences between UTC and IAT in advance, any UTC receiver provides a source for IAT.

Each Mars cluster contains a component with access to a time standard that measures the deviation between the cluster's time and the world time. The external clock-synchronization task broadcasts an appropriate rate correction that affects the speed of all internal clocks independently of corrections due to internal-clock synchronization.

An instantaneous change of the local clock(s) would lead to errors in running measurements and disturb the periodic schedules. So the CSU supports continuous time adjustment in hardware in multiples of 1 μs/s. Currently, we can achieve a typical clock synchronistic accuracy of better than 10 μs within a cluster consisting of eight components and 100 μs between two clusters.

References

1. H. Kopetz and W. Oshsenreiter, "Clock Synchronization in Distributed Real-time Systems," *IEEE Trans. Computers*, Vol. 36, No. 8, Aug. 1987, pp. 933-940.

Schedules. Task and message schedules are calculated off line and interpreted at runtime. The schedules are a periodic function of global time, and thus all tasks within a cluster are synchronized according to the communication and transaction description specified within the Mars design system.

Consistency. A real-time database consisting of valid messages naturally changes with time. The real-time database of a component is stored in message lists in the kernel. Any new message—regardless of origin—alters the database. However, the message lists in the kernel are updated solely during the clock-interrupt routine. Thus the changes of message states occur simultaneously in all running components. After such updates, the real-time database remains constant until the next occurrence of a clock-interrupt routine. Therefore, tasks operating in different components receive the same input if they read a message with the same name at the same time.

Self-checking features. As stated, self-checking components produce either correct results or no results at all. Ideally, all messages sent by a self-checking component are correct. The processor itself detects errors within a Mars component at the level of the operating system. The kernel must perform numerous checks to prevent erroneous messages from being sent to other components.

The mechanisms within the Mars operating system check both the correctness of information in the value domain and its validity in the time domain. Checks in the value domain include plausibility tests and time-redundant execution of tasks. In the time domain, these mechanisms check runtime limits, global time limits, and the timing behavior of the tasks with respect to the timing requirements of the controlled system.

When the operating system detects an error, it attempts to logically turn off the component regardless of whether the fault is transient or permanent or has occurred in hardware or software. The operating system fails silently to prevent error propagation within the cluster and to provide fault isolation. We conducted numerous experiments with specially designed, fault-insertion hardware to evaluate the self-checking features of Mars components

Message passing. Mars messages are sent as periodic real-time datagrams that each contain a validity time. These messages carry status information only. State-message semantics provide the following advantages for operating-system design.

Flow control. A periodic state message implicitly controls flow in the duty cycles of involved senders and receivers. The off-line scheduler synchronizes sending and receiving rates. Even in case of a fault (a sender is too fast or a receiver too slow), a buffer overflow in the operating system is impossible due to the overwriting of previous state messages by more recent instances.

Message redundancy. Backward-error-recovery protocols usually delay communication unpredictably. Thus these protocols can implement massive redundancy at the message level. Each message on the Mars bus is sent twice or more, depending on the fault hypothesis and the transient-failure probability of the bus.

The Mars bus is a Cheapernet version in which we measured an experimental message-loss probability of $1:10^5$. Sending each message twice decreases the message-loss probability to $1:10^{10}$ (in case of statistically independent failures), which is comparable to the failure rates of the component hardware.

Support of component redundancy and recovery. Two or more components running in active redundancy produce logically equivalent messages. Due to the state semantics of messages, only the most recent of two or more valid messages must be stored at the operating-system level. The filtering of redundant messages occurs within the kernel.

The operating system does not note the actual number of receivers or senders of a Mars message. Thus, one can insert redundant components into an operational system without any reconfiguration, modification, or notification of the running components.

As explained, every message contains a validity time to limit its lifetime. If a new component is added to a running system, it needs to fetch the real-time database. Since the message lifetime has a global upper bound, a new component collects messages only for this maximum period. After that, the recovery of the real-time database completes, and the new component can start its activity.

Efficiency issues. Any real-time system must guarantee reaction or transaction times. Therefore, it is reasonable (but not sufficient) to optimize certain operating-system procedures. This process requires the efficient handling of peak loads even at the expense of degrading the performance under average loads.

Interrupts. Only the real-time clock can interrupt the CPU. Other interrupt routines are disabled or used for time-stamping mechanisms by the CSU chip. The clock-interrupt routine periodically polls all peripherals—even the serial input-output chip for an RS-232 line. Thus the operating system is time rigid and deterministic in its kernel.

Path length. The application-independent overhead involved in message passing, measured in number of executed assembler instructions, is known as *path length*. The total path length for sending and receiving a message can be 20,000 to 50,000 in an Open Systems Interconnection protocol.[11] In Mars we keep the total path length as short as possible. When a task sends or receives a message, only a pointer to the message exchanges with the operating system. Any physical message copying is avoided. Otherwise the CPU would totally occupy itself with copying messages.

Message buffers. We kept constant the number of buffers needed within a component to overcome the buffer-allocation problem. We used the following method. All tasks must have preallocated message buffers before they can send or receive a message. A task must return one of its message buffers to the kernel when it receives a message. Similarly, it receives a new buffer when it sends a message.

Schedule switch. Process-control systems exhibit mutually exclusive phases of operation and control. For example, the start-up of an industrial plant can consist of a complicated procedure that is quite different from the control of a production line or an emergency stop of a machine. The overhead for control changes must be kept low, while the reaction time in emergency situations must be short.

In Mars, introducing a set of schedules solves this problem. All tasks for all schedules must reside within a component, but only one schedule activates at a given point in time. In case of a phase change or an emergency, a Mars message can trigger a simultaneous switch to another schedule in involved components. The reaction time to switch to a new schedule equals the time until the next clock-interrupt routine.

Timing analysis

One can guarantee the predictability of the time behavior of real-time systems only if the peak-load conditions of the system are known before runtime. This requirement necessitates using a static set of tasks for a component. From the aspect of timing analysis, such a static set of communicating periodic tasks are described by their duty cycle, their *maximal execution time* (Maxt), and the component in which they are executed. The designer specifies all these attributes through the Mars design system (see the box on the next page). This system provides all relevant data for timing analysis.

The TDMA slots of the Mars bus are assigned to the components in round-robin fashion. If a receiving task of a message resides on a component different from that of the sending task, that message must be broadcast (or exported) on the Mars bus. Each exported message requires a TDMA slot of the component running the sender task.

The tasks of a transaction in their entirety represent the implementation of a required stimulus-response action. The timing requirement of such a transaction is expressed by its *maximal response time* (Mart). A Mart includes

• the latency between the stimulus to the first task that uses this stimulus,
• a Maxt of the tasks involved,
• the communication times between these tasks, and

The Mars Design System

To control the design of Mars objects—such as transactions, clusters, components, tasks, and messages—we developed a special design methodology supporting both the creation of a Mars application and its evaluation. This computer-aided, real-time design methodology allows cost reduction and fault minimization in the development of critical and complex real-time applications.

The Mars design system does not view design activities and the support of a special design methodology as isolated problems. Respectively, the system does not provide isolated tools but rather integrates them into a *coherent design environment*. Our approach covers management aspects and life-cycle support of system development right from the beginning. These environments are termed *method-based* environments in the classification system developed by Dart et al.[1]

Figure D gives an overview of the entire tool system.[2] Its structure contains two dimensions:

• programming in the large and programming in the small, and
• design creation and evaluation.

The term *programming in the large* covers the phases from the specification of requirements and overall system design to the specification of the component level characterized by tasks and messages. Programming-in-the-large design steps manage design creation and its evaluation before coding takes place. *Programming in the small* is concerned with the inner construction of tasks, their implementation, and programming issues.

The second dimension distinguishes between *design-creation* tools and *design-evaluation* tools. Design-creation tools support the system analyst in the creation of a distributed real-time application. The activities in each step are detailed in Senft.[3] Evaluation tools analyze a given design and verify the proposed requirements. The dependability-analysis tool analyzes the system structure and possible failures. It computes measures for reliability, safety, and availability of the entire system (or system parts). The timing-analysis tool concentrates on the pre-runtime, static scheduling of the designed tasks and messages. If a schedule exists, the programmer has to code the tasks to meet specified execution times and interfaces. A key concept of the design environment is that the design-verification phases precede the coding activities.

Each tool maintains its own local information base. The highly interactive design-creation tools must provide the engineers with efficient storing and retrieval mechanisms of the designed information as well as with consistency and integrity checks. Relational database systems offer these services. Actually, we used an extended relational database approach to manage large objects of variable length. For the first prototype, we employed the relational database management system DB + + ,[4] in connection with the Unix file system. (The current version comprises 103 relations, each containing an average of 5.2 domains.)

Strictly defined interfaces control data exchange between tools. The management structure of a contract[5] handles these interfaces, more explicitly the inputs, outputs, environmental data of a tool, and the management of the project members. The fundamental prerequisites for reasonable design consist of well-defined activities and clear assignment of responsibilities to members at all times. A tool and its local information are based on the principle of an information-hiding module; the contract is based on the principle of an abstract interface.[6]

In principle, each tool can execute on a different machine, thus supporting project members in various organizational or geographical entities. Tools (and project members) exchange information via contracts. The entire setup is Unix-based. Hence, contract passing is embedded in standard Unix mail and is transparent to the user.

We developed the highly interactive, design-creation tools under the X Window System. Their user interface is uniformly organized. Tiled windows allow engineers to concentrate on their design activities without having to waste time on window management and hidden-window searches.

Figure E illustrates the user interface of the sys-

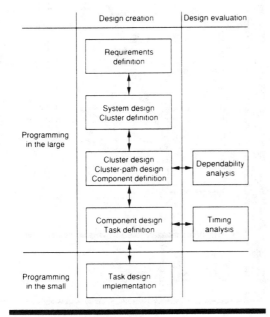

Figure D. The tool system.

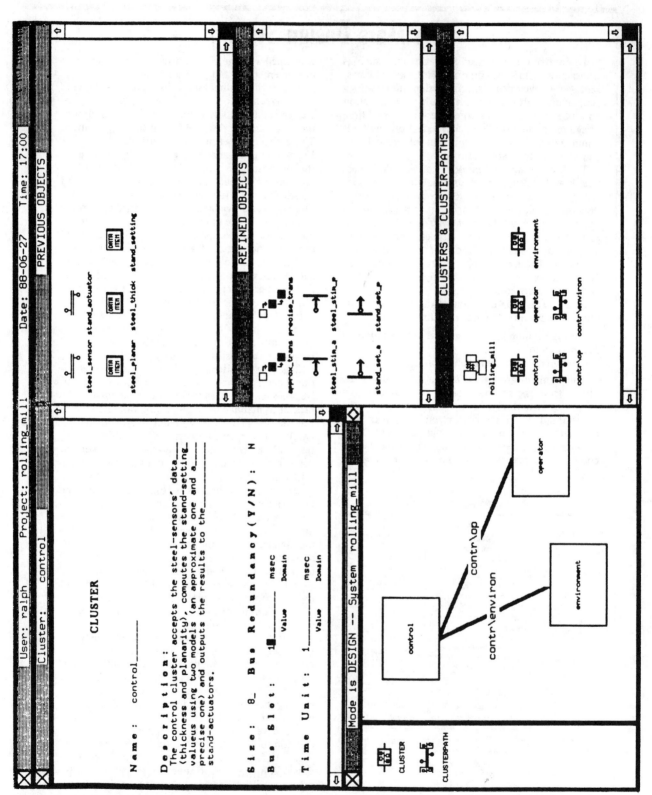

Figure E. User interface of a Mars system-design tool.

496

tem design for a rolling mill controlled by Mars (discussed elsewhere in this article). The right side of the screen shows objects in an iconic representation. The upper right window contains objects—that is, transactions, spots, and data items resulting from a previous design step (in this case from the requirements-definition phase). We refined some of them to further subobjects (transactions to subtransactions), which are displayed in the middle right window. The lower right window displays new objects such as cluster and cluster paths that have been designed at the current design level. The left side of the screen is reserved for design and development in a textual and graphical manner. The window in the upper left half shows a textual representation of the currently treated object, while the window in the lower left part offers the following functions:

- definition and refinement of objects with a built-in graphics editor,
- display of several decomposition and relationship diagrams,
- graphical support for establishing relations between objects, and
- document preparation.

The interaction between designer and tool is mainly managed by dragging icons to the different windows. This process of combining an icon with a window invokes a predefined action. For example, moving a cluster icon into the text window displays an editable template for gathering the information relevant to a cluster.

References

1. S. Dart et al., "Software Development Environments," *Computer*, Vol. 20, No. 11, Nov. 1987, pp. 18-28.

2. C. Senft, "A Computer-Aided Design Environment for Distributed Realtime Systems," *Proc. IEEE Compeuro 88, System Design: Concepts, Methods and Tools*, IEEE CS Press, Los Alamitos, Calif., Apr. 1988, pp. 288-297.

3. C. Senft, "Remodel—a Realtime System Methodology on Design and Early Evaluation," *Proc. IFIP Conf. Distributed Processing*, Oct. 1987, pp. 305-321.

4. M. Agnew and R. Ward, "The DB++ Relational Database Management System," *Proc. European Unix Users Group (EUUG) Conf.*, Apr. 1986, pp. 1-15.

5. M. Dowson, "Integrated Project Support with Istar," *IEEE Software*, Vol. 4, No. 6, Nov. 1987, pp. 6-15.

6. D. Parnas, "On the Criteria to be Used in Decomposing Systems into Modules," *Comm. ACM*, Vol. 15, No. 12, Dec. 1972, pp. 1,053-1,058.

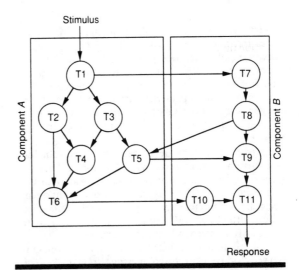

Figure 5. Communication structure of tasks T1 through T11 in a transaction.

- the time from the end of the last task until the response.

Here we assume that all tasks in a transaction are allocated to components within a single cluster.

As soon as the designer has refined the transactions to a task-message system and has estimated the Maxts of the tasks, the off-line task and bus scheduler calculates a preliminary schedule for the designed tasks. As the task implementation proceeds, a value derived from the actual source code using a source-level, execution-time analysis tool replaces the estimated Maxts. If no schedule for the task set can be found to guarantee the specified transaction times, the design needs revision.

Off-line task and bus scheduling. The schedules for tasks and messages are calculated by the off-line task and bus scheduler before runtime and stored in a run-time scheduling table. Figure 5 shows task transactions executed on components A and B and their internal and external communication. Figure 6 outlines a possible schedule for this example of a transaction. Because all tasks of components A and B have the same time period, both component cycles equal the period of the tasks.

For the bus schedule of the entire cluster, we assume a system with eight components. Only the TDMA slots assigned to components A and B are marked explicitly. The TDMA slots not available for components A and B are marked with the letter X. The schedule of the tasks within a component satisfies the precedence constraints according to internal message exchange. Figure 6 shows only the exported messages that are of interest for the bus schedule. The CPU schedule must be synchronized to the bus schedule to minimize the communication time between tasks of different components.

Because only one message can be sent per TDMA slot, exported messages have to be scheduled appropriately. For example, if TDMA-slot B_2 where task T8 sends its message were already used by a T7 message, the T8 message would have to be scheduled for another bus slot available for component B (B_3 in our example).

In a first attempt, we developed a two-pass scheduling algorithm. The first pass tries to minimize the communication times between the tasks allocated to the same component. Tasks executed on one component have a higher interconnectivity. We used a modified version of the CP/MISF (critical path/most immediate successor first) strategy[12] for this purpose.

In the second pass, a TDMA slot of its component is reserved for each exported message of a task. The schedules of all components shift to minimize the communication times between tasks of different components. Koza provides a detailed description of this two-pass sceduling algorithm.[13] This algorithm attempts to reduce the communication times in a cluster. Totalling the execution and communication times of the tasks involved in the transaction verifies whether the Mart of the transactions can be met.

To improve schedule generation, we developed an off-line algorithm that better accounts for the Mart of a transaction. This algorithm is based on a heuristic search strategy.[14] A heuristic function that calculates task urgency according to estimates of the time necessary to complete the transaction controls the inspected part of the search tree. Zhao, Ramamritham, and Stankovic describe an algorithm that works similarly on a problem that is quite different because it does not take precedence relationships between tasks into account.[15]

Source-level, execution-time analysis. Because the Maxt estimation of real-time tasks is critical, a special tool that derives the Maxt of a task from its source code supports designers. The estimation of the execution time of tasks requires bounded loops and prohibits recursions.[16] Maxt estimates must be very close to real Maxts. If the estimate is too high, excess time reserved for task execution unfavorably reduces CPU activity. Good Maxt estimations require program constructs that allow programmers to exploit knowledge about the execution of their algorithms.

Processor performance also affects the execution time of application tasks, and designers must consider this during timing analysis. On each clock tick a known amount of time is used to dispatch tasks and administer incoming and outgoing messages. The percentage of CPU time that is not available for application tasks is expressed as the CPU availability factor. This factor can vary according to hardware devices connected to the component and their generated DMA load. This factor also makes it possible for the scheduler to adapt the theoretical Maxt of each task in a component to an effective Maxt.

A typical Mars application

This section discusses the control of a rolling mill, which produces metal plates and bars.

Production control proceeds as follows. A sheet of steel passes through three pairs of rolls with a speed of about 10 meters/second (see Figure 7 on the next page). A sophisticated sensor system periodically measures the thickness and planarity of the surface of the steel. The raw sensor data are processed in node D (processing time, 2 milliseconds) to generate a periodic message

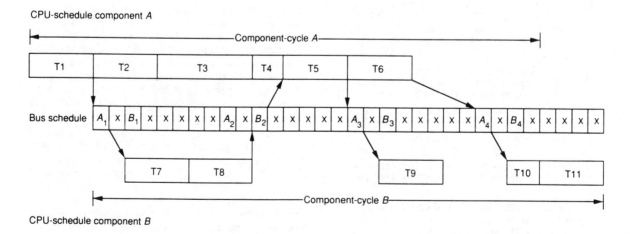

CPU-schedule component A

CPU-schedule component B

Figure 6. Bus and CPU schedule of a simple cluster.

M_1 describing the quality parameters of the product. This message is broadcast on the Mars bus. Nodes G and H accept M_1 from the bus and calculate the set-point vectors for the stands. Node G contains a simple model that always produces an approximate result message M_2 ahead of the deadline (say 10 ms). Node H contains a sophisticated model that produces a better result M_3 than node F but sometimes misses the deadline.

The results of both model calculations are broadcast on the bus. If the "better" result, M_3, has not arrived until the specified deadline (or does not arrive due to a failure of node G), nodes A, B, and C take the approximate result, M_2, from node G and position the stands accordingly. Furthermore, nodes A, B, and C collect operating data from each stand and distribute them on the Mars bus. The operator station E can access any real-time data from the Mars bus without interfering with the operation of the other components. It can also output the data in an appropriate format on a man-machine interface. Node F collects relevant information about the operation of the process and transmits it to other computers.

In this application, the real-time clock in node D triggers the most important time-critical transaction. It visits nodes G and H in parallel before delivering the results to nodes A, B, and C in parallel. The response time of this transaction has an important influence on the quality of rolling-mill control. Since this transaction is scheduled without any unnecessary delay, it takes 2 ms of processing in D, 1 ms for transport on the Mars bus to F and G, 10 ms of processing in F and G, and, finally, 1 ms for transport to A, B, and C—for a total of 14 ms. This time is about an order-of-magnitude faster than the response time achieved with a standard, central real-time computer. (A single computer has to perform all the parallel tasks in a timesharing mode that are assigned to eight nodes in the Mars distributed solution.) Exploiting the parallelism inherent in Mars' distributed architecture achieves a significant degree of its acceleration.

We configured the message formats, the CPU slots, and the TDMA protocol with spare capacity in the original design. As long as any change can be accommodated within this spare capacity, no modification of the schedules is required. If, however, a more powerful model is developed that cannot be processed on node G within the allocated time of 10 ms, that node can expand into a new cluster. This cluster increases the processing power manyfold without changing the interface (value and timing) to the original cluster. If the incorporation of fault tolerance is envisaged, additional slots on the TDMA bus for the redundant components must exist. As long as any of the redundant components is operating, the system provides the intended service on time.

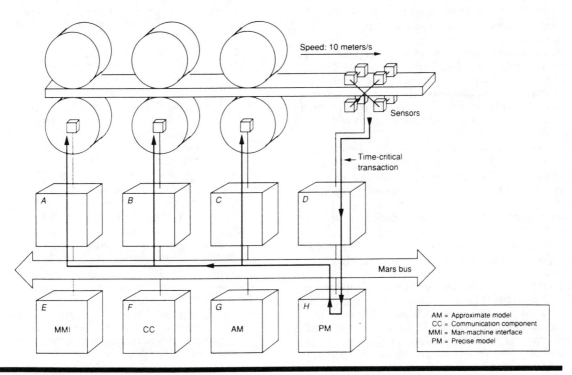

Figure 7. A rolling mill controlled by Mars.

The Mars project presents a solution to the problems of distributed, fault-tolerant, real-time systems. Mars copes with the needs of hard real-time systems in a number of ways. Each application for Mars is evaluated during its design and implementation phase with respect to runtime behavior to guarantee its transaction times. Users must know the frequency of all control procedures and involved reaction times in advance and realize them with an appropriate off-line schedule for the CPU and bus access. Each schedule is a periodic function in time, and the entire operating system is consequently driven only by time and not by events. Thus unexpected events cannot disturb the system behavior, which guarantees a time-rigid determinism.

The granularity of the system time is 1 μs. The system time is synchronized with an accuracy of 10 μs among the components of a Mars cluster. Scheduling decisions with a granularity of 8 ms achieve synchronism in the distributed system.

Mars messages have a fixed length and header format for standard interfacing to application tasks and intelligent process-control peripherals. Mars messages are state messages, that is, a more recent instance of a message updates the older one (comparable to global variables) to overcome flow-control and buffer-allocation problems. Mars messages have a validity time attached, after which the operating system automatically discards the message. Thus only valid messages arrive at the application, which guarantees short-term data integrity. The bus can transport a data volume of up to 1,000 messages per second.

Mars achieves fault tolerance by means of active redundancy (logically by sending each message twice and physically by having two or more components execute the same tasks). The Mars dependability analysis determines the degree of redundancy required. Each component has intrinsic self-checking mechanisms that safeguard the component's fail-stop behavior for fault isolation. Thus a component either sends correct information, or it is silent.

The cluster concept allows extensibility of the whole system. A logically equivalent interface to a new cluster can substitute for each component without modification of the rest of the system. One can add components for such passive observations as process monitoring or data logging to the bus without modification of other components.

Mars' current implementation serves experimental purposes. Presently, we have 16 available Mars hardware components that can be split into one-to-four Mars clusters. The purpose of this experimental system is to help evaluate the Mars architecture and to provide a testbed for future research in distributed fault-tolerant, real-time systems. Exploratory areas include self-checking methods, reliable broadcast, real-time databases, recovery strategies, time-synchronization algorithms, and consensus algorithms.

Acknowledgments

Grants from the Osterreichische Fond zur Forderung Wissenschaftlicher Forschung (the Austrian Fund for Support of Scientific Research) under contract number P6251 and in part by the Osterreichische Bundesministerium fur Wissenschaft und Forschung (the Austrian Federal Ministry for Science and Research) under contract number GZ 605.504/3-26/87 supported this project.

Many students contributed to the implementation of the details of the experimental Mars system. We thank Thomas Brustbauer, Thomas Fahringer, Gerhard Fohler, Ewald Halbedl, Heinz Kantz, Thomas Keil, Franz Lackinger, Manfred Pflugl, Peter Puschner, Johannes Reisinger, and Alexander Vrchoticky. We also thank Gunther Grunsteidl, Krithi Ramamritham, Johannes Reisinger, Karin Schneider, and Werner Schutz for their useful comments and criticisms on the early versions of this article. █

References

1. "Product Guide for SCADA (Supervisory Control and Data Acquisition) Systems," *J. Modern Power Systems*, Jan. 1987, pp. 56-67.

2. D.R. Cheriton, "The V Kernel: A Software Base for Distributed Systems," *IEEE Software*, Vol. 1, No. 2, Apr. 1984, pp. 19-42.

3. R. Fitzgerald and R.F. Rashid, "The Integration of Virtual Memory Management and Interprocess Communication in Accent," *J. ACM Trans. Computer Systems*, May 1986, pp. 147-177.

4. H. Zimmermann et al., "Basic Concepts for the Support of Distributed Systems: The Chorus Approach," *Proc. 2nd Conf. Distributed Computing Systems*, Apr. 1981, pp. 60-66.

5. A.H. Kopetz and W. Merker, "The Architecture of MARS," *Proc. 15th Fault-Tolerant Computing Symp.*, June 1985, pp. 274-279.

6. H. Kopetz and W. Ochsenreiter, "Clock Synchronization in Distributed Real-Time Systems," *IEEE Trans. Computers*, Vol. 36, No. 8, Aug. 1987, pp. 933-940.

7. H. Kopetz, "Design Principles for Fault-Tolerant Real-Time Systems," *Proc. 19th Hawaii Conf.*, Vol. II, IEEE CS Press, Los Alamitos, Calif., 1986, pp. 53-62.

8. J.H. Saltzer, D.P. Reed, and D.D. Clark, "End-to-End Arguments in System Design," *ACM Trans. Computer Systems*, Vol. 2, No. 4, Nov. 1984, pp. 277-288.

9. M. Sloman and J. Kramer, "Distributed Systems and Computer Networks," Prentice-Hall Series in Computer Science, Englewood Cliffs, N.J., p. 140.

10. R.D. Schlichting and F.B. Schneider, "Fail Stop Processors: An Approach to Designing Fault-Tolerant Computing Systems," *ACM Trans. Computing Systems*, Vol. 1, No. 3, Aug. 1983, pp. 222-238.

11. L.C. Mitchell, "A Methodology for Predicting End-to-

End Responsiveness in a Local Area Network," *Tutorial Local Network Technology*, 2nd ed., W. Stallings, ed., IEEE CS Press, Washington D.C., 1985, pp. 320-328.

12. H. Kasahara and S. Narita, "Parallel Processing of Robot-Arm Control Computation on a Multimicroprocessor System," *IEEE J. Robotics and Automation* Vol. 1, No. 2, June 1985, pp. 104-113.

13. C. Koza, "Scheduling of Hard Real-Time Tasks in the Fault-Tolerant Distributed Real-Time System MARS," *Proc. 4th IEEE Workshop Real-Time Operating Systems*, July 1987, pp. 31-36.

14. R.E. Korf, "Depth-First Iterative-Deepening: An Optimal Admissible Tree Search," *Artificial Intelligence*, Vol. 27, 1985, pp. 97-109.

15. W. Zhao, K. Ramamritham, and J.A. Stankovic, "Preemptive Scheduling Under Time and Resource Constraints," *IEEE Trans. Computers*, Vol. 36, No. 8, Aug. 1987, pp. 949-960.

16. E. Kligerman and A.D. Stoyenko, "Real-Time Euclid: A Language for Reliable Real-Time Systems," *IEEE Trans. Software Eng.*, Vol. 12, No. 9, Sept. 1986, pp. 941-949.

H. Kopetz   **A. Damm**   **C. Koza**   **M. Mulazzani**   **W. Schwabl**   **C. Senft**   **R. Zainlinger**

Hermann Kopetz is professor of computer science at the Institut fur Technische Informatik, Technical University of Vienna (TU Wien), where he directs research on the Mars project. He previously was a department manager in industrial process control and a professor for process-control computers at the Technical University of Berlin.

Kopetz received the Dr. Phil. degree in physics from the University of Vienna. He is a charter member of the Austrian Computer Society (OCG) and the Int'l Federation for Information Processing working group 10.4 on reliable computing. He is a senior member of the IEEE and the IEEE Computer Society, and a member of the ACM. He has served on the program committees of many international conferences and was the general chairman of the Fault-Tolerant Computing Symposium held in Vienna in 1986.

Andreas Damm is an assistant of computer science at the TU Wien. His main field of interest is the design of fault-tolerant, distributed, real-time operating systems and the experimental evaluation of error-detection mechanisms at the operating-system level. He received the Dipl. Ing. degree in computer science and the Dr. Techn. degree from the TU Wien. He is a member of the IEEE Computer Society, the ACM, and the OCG.

Christian Koza is an assistant of computer science at the TU Wien. His interests focus on real-time scheduling and execution-time analysis of programs. He received the Dipl. Ing. degree in computer science from the TU Wien. Koza is a member of the IEEE Computer Society and the ACM.

Marco Mulazzani was an assistant of computer science at the TU Wien until he recently joined the Alcatel-Elin Research Center in Vienna. His research interests concentrate on dependable computing and fault-tolerant systems. He received the Dipl. Ing. degree in mathematics and the Dr. Techn. degree from the TU Wien. He is a member of the IEEE Computer Society, the ACM, the OCG, and a charter member of the Unix User Group Austria.

Wolfgang Schwabl, an assistant of computer science at the TU Wien, previously worked on electronic-mail communication. His current interests are distributed real-time operating systems and clock synchronization. He received the Dipl. Ing. degree in computer science and the Dr. Techn. degree from the TU Wien. He is a member of the IEEE Computer Society, the ACM, the European Unix Users Group, the /usr/group, and a charter member and former president of the Unix User Group Austria.

Christoph Senft currently works as an assistant of computer science at the TU Wien. His research interests include software design concepts, methodologies, and their computer-aided support. He received the Dipl. Ing. degree in computer science and the Dr. Techn. degree from the TU Wien, and the Magister degree in economics from the University of Vienna. He is a member of the IEEE Computer Society, the ACM, the OCG, the EUUG, and a charter member of the Unix User Group Austria.

Ralph Zainlinger is employed as an assistant of computer science at the TU Wien. His current interests are software design methodologies and computer graphics. He received the Dipl. Ing. degree in computer science from the TU Wien and is a member of the OCG.

Questions concerning this article can be directed to Christian Koza, Institut fur Technische Informatik, Technische Universitat Wien, Treitistrasse 3/182, A-1040 Wien, Austria; Email: koza@vmars.uucp.

Chapter 8:   Clock Synchronization

Clocks are used for a variety of reasons, including monitoring the current time and setting timer interrupts, so a system needs efficient mechanisms for maintaining and reading time. For instance, if a distributed system maintains a central clock, access to the current time will involve (possibly large and perhaps even unbounded) delays, and parts of the system will not be able to read the clock accurately. Communication overheads arising from clock-related messages will be overwhelming. This is also true, perhaps to a lesser extent, within a multiprocessor system. Hence, in a distributed system or even a multiprocessor system, each node in the system or each processor on a node may maintain its own clock.

Even if clocks are initialized with the same time, physical clocks drift (due to, for example, temperature changes). Eventually the individual clocks will indicate different times. The *drift rate* of a clock is typically about 1 μsec/sec; thus, an initially synchronized fault-free clock could drift away from the reference by a few seconds every few days, in the worst case.

This introduces the problem of *clock synchronization*. Systems with many processing elements require clock synchronization for several reasons. For example, if a real-time system executes tasks with a real-time (that is, wall clock time) deadline, then the clocks must be accurate with respect to real time. Also, as noted in the previous chapter on fault tolerance, algorithms that maintain consistency among replicas rely on the replicas' clocks for synchronization.

Clock synchronization poses two problems. One is *external synchronization*, wherein each clock in a system must be synchronized with the real-world clock. The other problem is *internal synchronization*, which relates to the synchronization among multiple clocks in a system, so as to keep the relative deviation between individual clock values small. If each clock in a system is externally synchronized, internal synchronization follows. Several sources (for example, the National Institute of Standards and Technology's WWV) provide clock signals, that can be used to know the real-world time. A clock maintains external synchronization by receiving these signals and correcting its own time accordingly. However, this implies that you must provide each clock with a signal receiver, which costs money and space. Hence, the solution is for one or more clocks to maintain external synchronization while other clocks maintain internal synchronization among themselves as well as with these clocks.

Synchronization involves the periodic resetting of clocks, in other words, periodic changes to the clock values. But if clocks are reset at arbitrary points, discontinuous clock values will result and some clock ticks may be lost (if clock values are moved forward) or be repeated (if clock values are moved back). We prefer to change them gradually. This is done by *spreading* the change gradually over a finite interval. In practice, this is achieved by using *logical* clocks whose values are derived as a function of the physical clock and the amount the physical clock must be compensated to maintain synchronization.

Clearly, to achieve internal synchronization, clocks must be in a position to read each other's values so that they can determine the amount by which they are out of synchrony. This reading involves communication delays, which limit the synchronization achieveable. The last paper in this chapter examines this limit.

The first two papers discuss algorithms that show how clocks synchronize by reading each other's clocks in the presence of communication delays, clock drifts, and failures. The first paper assumes maximum communication delay and uses it to provide *deterministic clock synchronization*. The second discusses a *probabilistic clock synchronization* algorithm that capitalizes on the observation that most messages incur communication delays shorter than the maximum end-to-end delay of clock synchronization messages.

The paper by Lamport and Melliar-Smith titled "Synchronizing Clocks in the Presence of Faults" describes three algorithms that maintain synchronized clocks despite arbitrary clock and process failures, even when malicious or Byzantine failures occur. Using the *interactive convergence algorithm,* correctly functioning clocks converge as long as at least two thirds of the clocks are correct. The degree to which synchronization can be reestablished depends on how far apart the clocks are before synchronization is attempted. The second algorithm is an *interactive consistency algorithm* where the synchronization among the clocks depends on the accuracy with which they can read each other's clocks and how far they drift while synchronization is attempted. This algorithm also requires at least two thirds of the clocks to be nonfaulty. This requirement is minimal in that algorithms that do not use digital signatures, such as these two, require that at least $3m + 1$ processes be present if m faults are required to be tolerated. The third algorithm in the paper, which is also an interactive consistency algorithm, uses unforgeable digital signatures to read clocks and requires $2m + 1$ processes to handle m faults. In addition to a detailed description of these algorithms, the paper derives the synchronization error among clocks and discusses the message overheads for the algorithms.

The algorithm in the above paper is a *deterministic* clock synchronization algorithm, which means the algorithm guarantees a certain worst case clock deviation with *certainty*. If we relax the requirement of certainty and permit an algorithm to provide a probabilistic guarantee (the guarantee provided by the algorithm may fail sometimes, but with a *failure probability* that is known or that has a known bound), then we can find algorithms that can guarantee a clock deviation smaller than the one suggested by the Lundelius and Lynch bound (see next paper). However, for a probabilistic guarantee to be useful, it must be possible to reduce the failure probability to any desired level by choosing the parameters of the algorithm suitably. We call algorithms that can provide such a guarantee *probabilistic* clock synchronization algorithms.

In "Probabilistic Clock Synchronization," Cristian presents one (probably the first) such probabilistic clock synchronization algorithm capable of guaranteeing much lower clock synchronization errors than deterministic algorithms. The algorithm is based on sending a *clock read* request to a remote node, measuring the round trip delay and estimating the remote clock value based on the measured round trip delay. The algorithm trades off the maximum clock synchronization error, the probability of not achieving synchronization, and the maximum number of attempts one clock makes at reading another clock (denoted by k). It guarantees a clock reading error of $D - d_{min}$, where D denotes half of the round trip delay. If the specified maximum clock synchronization error is $U - d_{min}$, then the process repeats its remote clock read every W units of time until $D \leq U$. Since the method limits the maximum number of retries, D may never be $\leq U$. The probability of such a failure can be reduced, for a specified probability of losing synchronization, by increasing the maximum number of attempts permitted. This clock reading approach is used to implement a master-slave scheme that guarantees a specified maximum clock synchronization error. The master ensures external clock synchronization and the slaves ensure internal clock synchronization by reading the master's clock using the method outlined above. The maximum deviation between the master and the slave clocks is approximately $U - d_{min} + \rho k W$ where ρ is the worst case clock drift rate. Remember that this deviation is not guaranteed with certainty, however, since there is a nonzero probability that even after k attempts, a slave is unable to successfully read the master's clock such that $D \leq U$. The paper discusses the exact relationship between the desired maximum synchronization error, the probability of not achieving synchronization, and k.

Recently, Arvind has proposed another probabilistic clock synchronization algorithm based on averaging end-to-end delays of synchronization messages [Arvind 89]. It uses a new probabilistic protocol that can be used to transmit the time on one clock to another with a desired accuracy. The protocol involves the transmission of multiple synchronization messages and works by filtering out the random variations in the end-to-end delays of the synchronization messages through an averaging process. One node in the system is designated as the master. It sends its local clock value to the other nodes periodically by executing the above protocol. This implies that in a broadcast network, such as an Ethernet, only one set of clock synchronization messages needs to be transmitted by the master per period. This is unlike Christian's protocol where, since the slaves are responsible for synchronizing themselves with the master, each slave must perform a set of remote reads per period.

In "An Upper and Lower Bound for Clock Synchronization," Lundelius and Lynch consider the following problem: Suppose clocks do not drift, they run at the same rate, and no failures occur. Given these assumptions, once the clocks are synchronized, they will remain synchronized. Thus, the remaining problem is to synchronize them initially. The authors show that n clocks cannot be synchronized closer than $(d_{max} - d_{min})(1 - 1/n)$, where d_{max} denotes the maximum end-to-end delay of clock synchronization messages and d_{min} denotes the minimum delay. The authors assume a fully connected network where all the links have the same d_{max} and d_{min} values. The bound mentioned above implies that the clocks cannot be initialized to the same value in a system where d_{max} and d_{min} are different. The end-to-end delay represents the time taken to prepare the message, to transmit the message, and for the receiver to process the message. It can depend on the current computations at the sending and receiving nodes, the distance the message must travel, and other messages contending for transmission. This delay can hence be affected by random events, such as errors in transmission, page faults, and context switches. However, once such a bound on the delay can be found, the worst case clock synchronization error can be known with certainty. This implies that if d_{max} is much larger than d_{min} — which is likely, given the various components of the end-to-end delay — the error is also likely to be large.

Synchronizing Clocks in the Presence of Faults

LESLIE LAMPORT AND P. M. MELLIAR-SMITH

SRI International, Menlo Park, California

Abstract. Algorithms are described for maintaining clock synchrony in a distributed multiprocess system where each process has its own clock. These algorithms work in the presence of arbitrary clock or process failures, including "two-faced clocks" that present different values to different processes. Two of the algorithms require that fewer than one-third of the processes be faulty. A third algorithm works if fewer than half the processes are faulty, but requires digital signatures.

Categories and Subject Descriptors: D.4.5 [**Operating Systems**]: Reliability—*fault tolerance*; D.4.7 [**Operating Systems**]: Organization and Design—*real-time systems*

General Terms: Theory

Additional Key Words and Phrases: Byzantine failures, synchronization

1. Introduction

In a fault-tolerant multiprocess system, it is often necessary for the individual processes to maintain clocks that are synchronized with one another [4, 5, 9]. Since physical clocks do not keep perfect time, but can drift with respect to one another, the clocks must periodically be resynchronized. Such a fault-tolerant system needs a clock synchronization algorithm that works despite faulty behavior by some processes and clocks. This paper describes three such algorithms.

It is easy to construct fault-tolerant synchronization algorithms if one restricts the type of failures that are permitted. However, it is difficult to find algorithms that can handle arbitrary failures—in particular, failures that can result in "two-faced" clocks. As an example, consider a network of three processes. We would like an algorithm in which a fault in one of the processes or in its clock does not prevent the other two processes from synchronizing their clocks. However, suppose that

—Process 1's clock reads 1:00.
—Process 2's clock reads 2:00.
—Process 3's clock is faulty in such a way that when read by Process 1 it gives the value 0:00 and when read by Process 2 it gives the value 3:00.

Processes 1 and 2 are in similar positions; each sees one clock reading an hour earlier and one clock reading an hour later than its own clock. There is no reason

This work was supported in part by NASA under contract number NAS1-15428 and the National Science Foundation under Grant MCS-8104459.

Authors' address: SRI International, Computer Science Laboratory, 333 Ravenswood Ave., Menlo Park, CA 94025.

why Processes 1 and 2 should change their clocks in such a way that would bring their values closer together.

The algorithms described in this paper work in the presence of any kind of fault, including such malicious, two-faced clocks. The first one is called an *interactive convergence algorithm*. In a network of at least $3m + 1$ processes it will handle up to m faults. Its name is derived from the fact that the algorithm causes correctly working clocks to converge, but the closeness with which they can be synchronized depends upon how far apart they are allowed to drift before being resynchronized.

The final two algorithms are called *interactive consistency algorithms*, so named because the nonfaulty processes obtain mutually consistent views of all the clocks. The closeness with which clocks can be synchronized depends only upon the accuracy with which processes can read each other's clocks and how far they can drift during the synchronization procedure. They are derived from two basic interactive consistency algorithms presented in [6]. The first one requires at least $3m + 1$ processes to handle up to m faults. The second algorithm assumes a special method of reading clocks, requiring the use of unforgeable digital signatures, to handle up to m faults with as few as $2m + 1$ processes. The latter algorithm seems to be of little practical value, since Halpern, Simons, and Strong [3] have recently developed a more efficient algorithm based upon the same method of clock reading. However, we feel that the way our algorithm is derived from the Byzantine Generals algorithm is interesting enough to warrant its description.

Strong and Halpern [9] have recently proved that $3m + 1$ processes are required to allow clock synchronization in the presence of m faults if digital signatures are not used. Hence, our first two algorithms use the minimal number of processes.

2. An Informal Discussion

Before stating and analyzing our algorithms in detail, we give an informal description of how they work. We make no attempt at rigor here; the purpose of this section is to provide the intuition needed to understand the more rigorous exposition of the succeeding sections. The assumptions, conditions, and algorithms stated here are restated more precisely later. The reader who is not interested in all the details may wish to read only this section and skip the rigorous treatment, going directly from the end of this section to the conclusion.

2.1. THE PROBLEM. Implementing reliable clock synchronization presents many problems—from building accurate hardware clocks to designing programming language primitives for reading the clocks. The purpose of this paper is to present algorithms to solve one of these problems: maintaining clock synchronization once the clocks are initially synchronized. As discussed briefly in [5], the type of message passing used by our clock-synchronization algorithms seems to require that the sender and receiver have clocks that are already synchronized. Achieving initial synchrony is a separate problem, whose solution will depend strongly upon the details of how clock reading and interprocess communication are implemented. We do not address that problem, and instead make the following assumption.

*A*0. All clocks are initially synchronized to approximately the same value.

We assume that processes are provided with reasonably accurate clocks—an assumption that we state as

*A*1. A nonfaulty process's clock runs at approximately the correct rate.

Of course, the "correct rate" for a clock is one second of clock time per second of real time. We make no assumptions about faulty processes' clocks.

Assumptions A0 and A1 leave us with the problem of correcting for the slow drifting apart of the clock values caused by slightly differing clock rates. The easiest way to do this is for processes periodically to reset their clocks. A process will have a physical clock that "ticks" continually and a logical clock whose value equals the value of the physical clock plus some offset. It is the logical clocks that are maintained in synchrony by periodically resetting them, a logical clock being reset by simply changing its offset.

Instead of discontinuously changing clock values in this way, it might be desirable to change the clocks gradually. This can be done by making the logical clock value a more complicated function of the physical clock value, effectively spreading the change over a finite interval. Given an algorithm for discontinuously resynchronizing the clocks and a bound on how closely synchronized it keeps them, it is easy to devise an algorithm that spreads out the change and to deduce how well it keeps the clocks synchronized. We therefore consider only resynchronization algorithms that periodically increment the clocks.

Having accurate clocks does no good unless those clocks can be read. Synchronizing the clocks requires that each process be able to read not just its own clock, but other processes' clocks as well. Clock values are different from most other values in a computer system because they are continually changing. This poses a problem for a clock-synchronization algorithm unless the algorithm is so fast that clocks do not change significantly during the resynchronization period. The solution to this problem requires that a process read not another process's clock, but rather the difference between that clock and its own. We therefore make the following assumption:

A2. A nonfaulty process p can read the difference Δ_{qp} between another nonfaulty process q's clock and its own with at most a small error ϵ.

Exactly how A2 is satisfied is of no concern for our first two algorithms. However, our third algorithm is based upon a special method of reading clocks, which will be described below. Assumption A2 asserts that a process can read every other process's clock. In the conclusion, we mention how our algorithms can be extended to work when a process can read the clocks of only some other processes.

Before describing any clock-synchronization algorithms, we should specify what conditions such an algorithm should satisfy. The first and most obvious requirement is

S1. At any time, the values of all the nonfaulty processes' clocks must be approximately equal.

While it is obviously necessary, S1 is not a sufficient condition. For example, it is satisfied if all clocks are simply set to zero and stopped. The additional requirement we need must intuitively say that the logical clocks keep a reasonable approximation to real time.

By assuming that clocks are periodically resynchronized, and that a process's logical clock runs at the same rate as its physical clock except for this periodic resynchronization, we have ruled out such trivial "solutions" as stopping the clocks. However, we still have the possibility that each resynchronization causes the clocks to jump arbitrarily far. Our second condition places a bound on the amount that a clock can be incremented.

S2. There is a small bound Σ on the amount by which a nonfaulty process's clock is changed during each resynchronization.

Condition S2 has two important consequences:

—If Σ is much smaller than the resynchronization period, then resynchronization introduces a small error in the average running rate of the clocks. This implies that the processes' clocks maintain a good approximation to absolute real time.

—Resynchronization can cause a process to change its clock's value by some amount A. If $A > 0$, then A seconds of clock time have disappeared. Anything that the process should have done during those vanished A seconds cannot be done at the proper time. If $A < 0$, then A seconds of clock time occur twice, which could also cause problems. The easy way out of this difficulty is to let each synchronization interval begin (or end) with an interval of length Σ during which nothing is scheduled to happen, so the process is idle for Σ seconds during each resynchronization period. This is an acceptable solution if Σ is small. (If it is not acceptable, then incrementation by A can be spread across a finite interval of time, as mentioned above.)

2.2. The Interactive Convergence Algorithm. Our first solution is the interactive convergence algorithm CNV. It relies heavily upon the assumption that the clocks are initially synchronized, and that they are resynchronized often enough so two nonfaulty processes' clocks never differ by more than δ. How closely clocks can be synchronized depends upon how far apart they are allowed to drift before being resynchronized. At least $3m + 1$ processes are needed to handle up to m faults. The algorithm works essentially as follows.

Algorithm CNV. *Each process reads the value of every process's clock and sets its own clock to the average of these values—except that if it reads a clock value differing from its own by more than δ, then it replaces that value by its own clock's value when forming the average.*

To see why this works, let us consider by how much two nonfaulty processes' clocks can differ after they are resynchronized. For simplicity, we ignore the error in reading another process's clock and assume that all processes execute the algorithm instantaneously at exactly the same time.

Let p and q be nonfaulty processes, let r be any process, and let c_{pr} and c_{qr} be the values used by p and q, respectively, as process r's clock value when forming the average. If r is nonfaulty, then c_{pr} and c_{qr} will be equal. If r is faulty, then c_{pr} and c_{qr} will differ by at most 3δ, since c_{pr} lies within δ of p's clock value, c_{qr} lies within δ of q's clock value, and the clock values of p and q lie within δ of one another.

Let n be the total number of processes and m the number of faulty ones, and assume that $n > 3m$. Processes p and q set their clocks to the average of the n values c_{qr} and c_{pr}, respectively. We have $c_{qr} = c_{pr}$ for the $n - m$ nonfaulty processes r, and $|c_{qr} - c_{pr}| \leq 3\delta$ for the m faulty processes r. It follows from this that the averages computed by p and q differ by at most $(3m/n)\delta$. The assumption $n > 3m$ implies $(3m/n)\delta < \delta$, so the algorithm succeeds in bringing the clocks closer together. Therefore, we can keep the nonfaulty processes' clocks synchronized to within δ of one other by resynchronizing often enough so that clocks which are initially within $(3m/n)\delta$ seconds of each other never drift further than δ seconds apart.

It appears that by repeated resynchronizations, each one bringing the clocks closer by a factor of $3m/n$, this algorithm can achieve any desired degree of synchronization. However, we have ignored two factors:

(1) The time taken to execute the algorithm.
(2) The error in reading another process's clock.

The fact that a process p does not read all other clocks at exactly the same time means that it must average not clock values, but the differences Δ_{qp} defined in A2. It then increments its clock by the average of the values Δ_{qp}, except with values that are too large replaced by zero.

The clock-reading error ϵ in Assumption A2 means that if δ is the maximum true difference between the two clocks, then the difference read by process p could be as great as $\delta + \epsilon$. Therefore, a value of Δ_{qp} read by process p is regarded as too large, and replaced by zero, if it is greater than $\delta + \epsilon$.

2.3. THE INTERACTIVE CONSISTENCY ALGORITHMS. In the interactive convergence algorithm, a process sets its clock to the average of all clock values. Since a single bad value can skew an average, bad clock values must be thrown away. Another approach is to take a median instead of an average, since a median provides a good value so long as only a minority of values are bad. However, because of the possibility of two-faced clocks, the processes cannot simply read each other's clocks and take a median; they must use a more sophisticated method of obtaining the values of other processes' clocks. We now investigate what properties such a method must have.

The median computed by two different processes will be approximately the same if the sets of clock values they obtain are approximately the same. Therefore, the Clock Synchronization Condition S1 will hold (for some suitably small δ) if the following condition holds for every process r.

CC1. Any two nonfaulty processes obtain approximately the same value for r's clock—even if r is faulty.

While CC1 guarantees that all processes will compute approximately the same clock values, it does not ensure that the values they compute will be reasonable. For example, CC1 is satisfied if every process always obtains the value zero for any process's clock—a procedure yielding an algorithm that violates the Clock Synchronization Condition S2. To ensure that S2 is satisfied, we make the following additional requirement.

CC2. If r is nonfaulty, then every nonfaulty process obtains approximately the correct value of r's clock.

If a majority of processes are nonfaulty, then this implies that the median clock value computed by any process is approximately equal to the value of a good clock.[1] Since good clocks do not drift apart very fast, resetting a clock to the value of another good clock ensures that Clock Condition S2 is satisfied for a small value of Σ.

Conditions CC1 and CC2 are very similar to the requirements for a solution to the interactive consistency or "Byzantine Generals" problem [6, 7]. In this problem, some process r must send a value to all processes in such a way that the following

[1] More precisely, it is either approximately equal to a good clock's value or else lies between the values of two good clocks.

two conditions are satisfied:

*IC*1. All nonfaulty processes obtain the same value.

*IC*2. If process r is nonfaulty, then all processes obtain the value that it sends.

Our two interactive consistency algorithms are modifications of two Byzantine Generals solutions from [6] to achieve conditions CC1 and CC2. The reasons for using these Byzantine Generals solutions, and the possibility of using other solutions, is discussed in the conclusion.

2.3.1. *Algorithm COM.* Our first interactive consistency algorithm, denoted COM(m), works in the presence of up to m faulty processes when the total number n of processes is greater than $3m$. It is based upon Algorithm OM(m) of [6].

We first consider the case $n = 4$, $m = 1$, and describe a special case of Algorithm OM(1) in which the value being sent is a number. In this algorithm, process r sends its value to every other process, which in turn relays the value to the two remaining processes. Process r uses its own value. Every other process i has received three "copies" of this value: one directly from process r and the other two from the other two processes.[2] The value obtained by process i is defined to be the median of these three copies.

To show that this works, we consider separately what happens when process r is faulty and when it is nonfaulty. First, suppose r is nonfaulty. In this case, at least two of the copies received by any other process p must equal the value sent by r—the one received directly from r and the one relayed by another nonfaulty process. (Since there is at most one faulty process, at least one of the two processes that relay the value to p must be nonfaulty.) The median of a set of three numbers, two of which equal v, is v, so condition IC1 is satisfied. When process r is nonfaulty, IC1 implies IC2, which finishes the proof for this case.

Next, suppose that process r is faulty. Condition IC1 is then vacuous, so we need only verify IC2. Since there is at most one faulty process, the three processes other than r must be nonfaulty. Each one therefore correctly transmits the value it receives from r to the other processes. All of the other processes thus receive the same set of copies, so they choose the same median, showing that the IC2 is satisfied.

To modify Algorithm OM(1) for clock synchronization, let us suppose that instead of sending a number, a process can send a copy of a clock. (Imagine clocks being sent from process to process, continuing to tick while in transit.) Let us further suppose that sending a clock from one nonfaulty process to another can perturb its value by at most ϵ, but leaves it otherwise unaffected. However, a faulty process can arbitrarily change a clock's value before sending it.

In Algorithm COM(1), we apply Algorithm OM(1) four times, once for each process r. However, instead of sending values, the processes send clocks. Exactly the same argument used above to prove IC1 and IC2 proves CC1 and CC2, where "approximately" means to within $O(\epsilon)$.

The more general Byzantine Generals solution OM(m), which handles m faulty processes, $n > 3m$, involves more rounds of message passing and additional median taking. This algorithm can be found in [6]. Algorithm COM(m) is obtained from OM(m) in the same way we obtained COM(1) and OM(1)—namely, by sending clocks instead of messages.

---

[2] In case a process fails to receive a message, presumably because the sender is faulty, it can pretend to have received any arbitrary message from that process. See [6] for more details.

This completes our description of Algorithm COM(m), except for one question: how do processes send clocks to one another? The answer is that the processes don't send clocks, they send the clock differences. Process p sends a "copy" of q's clock to another process r by sending a message with the value Δ_{qp}—a message that means "q's clock differs from mine by Δ_{qp}."

Now, suppose r receives a copy of q's clock from p in the form of a message (from p) saying "q's clock differs from mine by x." How does r relay a copy of this clock to another process? Process r reasons as follows:

—p tells me that q's clock differs from his by x.
—I know that p's clock differs from mine by Δ_{qr}.
—Therefore, p has told me that q's clock differs from mine by $x + \Delta_{pr}$.

In other words, then r relays a clock difference sent to him by p, he just adds Δ_{pr} to that difference.

2.3.2. *Algorithm CSM.* It is shown in [7] that, with no assumptions about the behavior of failed processes, the Byzantine Generals problem is solvable only if $n > 3m$. However, we can do better than this by allowing the use of digital signatures. We assume that a process can generate a message that can be copied but cannot be undetectably altered. Thus, if r generates a signed message, and copies of that message are relayed from process to process, then the ultimate recipient can tell if the copy he receives is identical to the original signed message generated by r. With digital signatures, we are assuming that a faulty process cannot affix the signature of another process to any message not actually signed by that process. See [6] for a brief discussion of how digital signatures can be generated in practice.

Algorithm SM(m) of [6] solves the Byzantine Generals problem in the presence of up to m faults for any value of n. (The problem is vacuous if there are more than $n - 2$ faults.) We first consider the case $n = 3$, $m = 1$. In Algorithm SM(1), process r sends a signed message containing its value to the other two processes, each of which relays a copy of this signed message to the other. Each process p other than r winds up with a pile containing up to two properly-signed messages: one received directly from process r and another relayed by the third process. Process p may receive fewer than two messages because a faulty process could fail to send a message. The value process p obtains is defined to be the largest of the values contained in this pile of properly signed messages. (If no message is received, then some arbitrary fixed value is chosen.)

For notational convenience, we pretend that r sends a signed message to itself, which it does not relay. It is easy to see that the piles of messages received by the three processes satisfy the following two properties.

SM1. For any two nonfaulty processes p and q, every value in p's pile is also in q's.

SM2. If process r is nonfaulty, then every process's pile has at least one properly signed message, and every properly signed message has the same value.

Note that SM1 holds for p or q equal to r because of our assumption that r sends a properly signed message to itself. Condition IC1 follows immediately from property SM1, and condition IC2 follows immediately from property SM2, proving that SM(1) is a Byzantine Generals solution.

In the general Algorithm SM(m), messages are copied and relayed up to m times, with each relaying process adding its signature. When a process p receives a message with fewer than m signatures, p signs the message, copies it, and relays it to every process that has not already signed the message. The reader can either verify for himself or find the proof in [6] that the stacks of messages received by the processes satisfy conditions SM1 and SM2. (Again, we assume that r sends a signed message to itself, so SM1 is satisfied when p or q equals r.) Hence, defining the value obtained by a process to be the largest value in its pile gives an algorithm that solves the Byzantine Generals problem.

To turn the Byzantine Generals solution $SM(m)$ into the clock-synchronization Algorithm $CSM(m)$, we again send clocks instead of messages. Moreover, we allow processes to sign the clocks that they send. As before, we assume that a clock's value is perturbed by at most ϵ when sent by a nonfaulty process. However, instead of allowing a faulty process to set a clock to any value when relaying it, we assume that the process can turn the clock back but not ahead. More precisely, we assume that, when relaying a clock, a faulty process can set it back arbitrarily far, but can set it ahead by at most ϵ.

We now use the same relaying procedure as in Algorithm $SM(m)$ to send copies of r's clock to all processes. For this intuitive discussion, we assume that all clocks run at exactly the same rate, except for the perturbations they receive when being relayed. Each process keeps a copy of every properly signed clock, so after all the relaying has ended, it has a pile of copies of r's clock. (We assume that r keeps a signed copy of its own clock.) Since a nonfaulty process perturbs a clock's value by at most ϵ when relaying it, the same reasoning used to prove SM1 and SM2 shows that the following properties are true of these piles of copies of r's clock.

CSM1. For any two nonfaulty processes p and q, if p has a properly signed clock with value c, then q has a properly signed clock whose value is within $m\epsilon$ of c.

CSM2. If process r is nonfaulty and its clock has the value c, then every other process has at least one properly signed clock whose value is within ϵ of c, and every properly signed clock that it has reads no later than $c + m\epsilon$.

The value that a process obtains for r's clock is defined to be the fastest clock in its pile. Conditions CC1 and CC2 then follow immediately from CSM1 and CSM2, where "approximately" means to within $O(m\epsilon)$. Hence, this provides a fault-tolerant clock-synchronization algorithm.

To finish the description of Algorithm $CSM(m)$, we must describe how clocks can be signed and relayed in such a way that they are disturbed by at most ϵ when relayed by a nonfaulty clock and can be set forward at most ϵ by a faulty one. As in Algorithm $SM(m)$, we require a method for generating unforgeable signed messages.

Let us first assume that processes and transmission lines are infinitely fast, so a message can be relayed from process to process in zero time. We use this assumption to construct a method of relaying clocks for which ϵ equals zero. The message that r sends, and that all the processes relay, is r's clock value c_r. The message c_r acts like a clock whose value is now c_r. A nonfaulty process relays this value in zero time, so the clock is sent with no perturbation. A faulty process cannot change the value of the clock, since the value is contained in a signed message; all it can do is delay sending the value. This is equivalent to stopping the clock while holding it, which is tantamount to turning the clock back. Hence, the assumption about sending clocks is satisfied, with zero perturbation.

In practice, processes and transmission lines are not infinitely fast. Instead, we assume that the delay in processing and transmitting a message can be determined to within some small ϵ. If we include the time needed to generate a message as part of the transmission delay, this can be expressed as:

A2'. (a) A message from a nonfaulty process is received at its destination $\gamma \pm \epsilon$ seconds after it is sent, for some constant γ.

(b) A message from a faulty process is received at its destination at least $\gamma - \epsilon$ seconds after it is sent.

Assumption A2' permits the implementation of a clock-reading scheme satisfying A2: process p reads process q's clock by having it send a message with the current time. To compute Δ_{qp}, process p adds γ to the value in the message and subtracts its own clock value. However, A2' provides more than a way of implementing A2; combined with digital signatures, it allows a clock value to be relayed from process to process, each process in the chain adding its signature to the message. By counting the number of signatures in the message, a process knows how many times the message has been relayed, so it can correct the clock value in the message by adding the appropriate multiple of γ. The net effect is to introduce an error of at most ϵ each time the message is relayed by a nonfaulty process, and to allow a faulty process to set the clock ahead by at most ϵ, as required. Of course, this uses the additional assumption:

A3.   A process can generate an unforgeable digital signature for any message.

3. *The Problem*

We now begin our formal exposition. This section gives the precise statement of the Assumptions A0–A2 and the correctness conditions.

3.1. CLOCKS.   Any discussion of clocks involves two kinds of time:

Real Time.   An assumed Newtonian time frame that is not directly observable.
Clock Time.   The time that is observed on some clock.

We adopt the convention of using lowercase letters to denote quantities that represent real time and uppercase letters to denote quantities that represent clock time. Thus, we will let the "second" denote the unit of real time and the "SECOND" denote the unit of clock time. Within this convention, we use Roman letters to denote large values and Greek letters to denote small values. In most applications, "large" times may be on the order of milliseconds or more and "small" times on the order of microseconds.

It is customary to define a clock to be a mapping C from real time to clock time, where $C(t) = T$ means that at real time t the clock reads T. This is appropriate when clocks are used to measure the time at which some event occurred—for example, when a runner crossed the finish line. Thus, if t is the real time at which the runner finished, then $|C(t) - C'(t)|$ represents the difference in the finishing times recorded by two such clocks C and C'.

In the process-control systems for which our clock-synchronization algorithms were devised, systems such as the SIFT avionics computer [10], clocks are used to determine when events are generated—for example, when a valve should be shut. In this case, it is more appropriate to define a clock to be the inverse of the usual function, so it is a mapping c from clock time to real time, with $c(T)$ denoting the real time at which the clock c has the value T. Thus, if T is the clock time at which the valve is to be shut, then $|c(T) - c'(T)|$ represents the difference in the real times at which two processors with clocks c and c' issue the command to shut it. We thus consider this kind of clock.

Two clocks c and c' are said to be synchronized to within δ at a clock time T if $|c(T) - c'(T)| < \delta$, so they reach the value T within δ seconds of one another. This is the way that we will measure clock synchronization, since it is the appropriate one for the class of applications that immediately concern us. If two processes' clocks are synchronized to within δ at time T, then actions generated by the two processes at that time occur within δ seconds of one another.

If the clocks are used to measure when events occur, rather than to generate events, then one is concerned with the difference between the inverse clocks—the mappings from real time to clock time. Below, we formally state a result whose intuitive meaning is that if c and c' are good clocks that are synchronized to within δ seconds on some interval, then their inverse clocks are synchronized to within approximately δ SECONDS on the inverse interval. Hence, our synchronization algorithms can be used in this situation too.

It is most convenient to pretend that clocks run continuously, so a clock c is a continuous function on some interval. (Otherwise, c would be defined only for a discrete set of clock values.) Of course, real processor clocks advance in discrete steps. We can model the discreteness of a real clock as an error in reading the clock. Thus, discreteness adds a clock-reading error at most equal to the interval between "ticks."

Although we have been calling our clocks "functions," only a monotonically increasing clock can be represented by a single-valued function. This is not a problem, since nonfaulty clocks are assumed to be monotonic. However, some care must be taken when formalizing our concepts. We assume that the inverse of a clock c is a single-valued function, so for any real time t there is a unique T such that $c^{-1}(t) = T$.

Definition 1. A clock c is a *good clock* during the real-time interval $[t_1, t_2]$ if it is a monotonic, differentiable function on $[T_1, T_2]$, where $T_i = c^{-1}(t_i)$, $i = 1, 2$, and for all T in $[T_1, T_2]$:

$$\left| \frac{dc}{dT}(T) - 1 \right| < \frac{\rho}{2}.$$

This definition involves an arbitrary fixed value ρ, which represents twice the maximum error in a clock's running rate. (A perfect clock has dc/dT equal to one second per SECOND.) Rather than fixing ρ, we could define a ρ-good clock. However, this would require that all our results include an explicit mention of the parameter ρ, which would needlessly complicate their statements. We will introduce several similar quantities; they are all listed in a glossary at the end of the paper, which contains a brief reminder of what they mean.

In terms of Definition 1, we can state the precise relation between the synchronization of clocks and of inverse clocks as the following remark. Its proof is an exercise in elementary calculus.

Remark. Let c and c' be good clocks on an interval $[T_1, T_2]$, such that $|c(T) - c'(T)| < \delta$ for all times T in that interval. If $\rho \ll 1$, then the inverse functions C and C' of these clocks exist and are differentiable on the interval $[c(T_1) + \delta, c(T_2) - \delta]$, and $|C(t) - C'(t)| \lesssim \delta$ for all t in that interval.

We consider a network of n processes, where each process p contains a clock c_p. We assume that the clocks are initially synchronized to within δ_0 of one another at the "starting time" $T^{(0)}$, so we have

A0. For all processes p and q: $|c_p(T^{(0)}) - c_q(T^{(0)})| < \delta_0$.

Our algorithms have the property that if enough processes are nonfaulty, then the clocks of nonfaulty processes remain synchronized. To give a formal proof of such a property, we would need a formal definition of a nonfaulty process. More precisely, we would have to define what it means for a process to be nonfaulty during a certain interval. There are two assumptions that must be made about a nonfaulty process: that it correctly executes the algorithm and that its clock is good. A rigorous statement of the first assumption would be tedious and unrewarding, so we do not make a formal definition of "nonfaulty during an interval." Instead, we informally assume that a nonfaulty process does what it is supposed to during the interval in question. However, we do rigorously analyze the degree of synchronization achieved by our algorithms, and this requires us to state the second assumption precisely. This is done as follows.

A1. If process p is nonfaulty during the real time interval $[t_1, t_2]$, then c_p is a good clock during that interval.

3.2. SYNCHRONIZATION. As mentioned in our informal description of the algorithms, clock synchrony is maintained by having processes periodically increment their clocks. Incrementing a clock c by A SECONDS means adding A to the value read from the clock. This is described formally as defining a new clock c' by

$$c'(T) = c(T - A).$$

For simplicity, we assume that clocks are resynchronized every R SECONDS. Let $T^{(i)} = T^{(0)} + iR$, and let $R^{(i)}$ be the interval $[T^{(i)}, T^{(i+1)}]$. The clock c_p represents process p's physical clock. Resynchronizing the clocks every R SECONDS means having process p use a logical clock $c_p^{(i)}$ on the time interval $R^{(i)}$, where

$$c_p^{(i)}(T) = c_p(T + C_p^{(i)}) \tag{1}$$

for some constant $C_p^{(i)}$. For convenience, we assume that $C_p^{(0)} = 0$, so $c_p^{(0)} = c_p$.

No algorithm can maintain clock synchronization in the presence of too many faulty processes, so the condition to be satisfied by our algorithms must contain the hypothesis that there are enough nonfaulty ones. To help state this hypothesis, we introduce the following terminology.

Definition 2. A process p is said to be nonfaulty up to time $T^{(i+1)}$ if it is nonfaulty during the real-time interval $[c_p^{(0)}(T^{(0)}), c_p^{(i)}(T^{(i+1)})]$.

Note that this interval runs from the time process p is started until the time its clock reaches the end of the ith synchronization interval $R^{(i)}$.

Our informal requirements for clock synchronization were that processes' clocks are synchronized to within a small bound, which we shall call δ, and that resynchronization increments a clock by at most Σ. These conditions depend upon the parameters δ and Σ, so we should talk about a "δ–Σ synchronization algorithm." For notational simplicity, we leave implicit the dependence on δ and Σ, as well as the dependence on m, the number of faulty processes tolerated. The following condition defines correct synchronization on the interval $R^{(i)}$, again leaving i an implicit parameter.

Clock Synchronization Condition.   For all p and q, if all but at most m processes are nonfaulty up to time $T^{(i+1)}$, then

S1.   If Processes p and q are nonfaulty up to time $T^{(i+1)}$, then for all T in $R^{(i)}$

$$|c_p^{(i)}(T) - c_q^{(i)}(T)| < \delta.$$

S2.   If Process p is nonfaulty up to time $T^{(i+1)}$, then

$$|C_p^{(i+1)} - C_p^{(i)}| < \Sigma.$$

Our problem is to find an algorithm for choosing the values $C_p^{(i+1)}$ such that if the Clock Synchronization Condition holds for i, then it will hold for $i + 1$.

We place no restriction on the clock of a process that has failed. Thus, we are not considering the problem of restarting a failed process and bringing it into synchrony with the other processes. This is a nontrivial problem whose solution depends upon the details of how a process reads other processes' clocks, and is beyond the scope of this paper.

3.3.   READING CLOCKS.   We now formalize our Assumption A2 about clock reading. All the reading of clocks and transmitting of information in the computation of $C_p^{(i+1)}$ is assumed to take place in the final S seconds of the interval $R^{(i)}$— that is, during the interval $S^{(i)} \equiv [T^{(i+1)} - S, T^{(i+1)}]$. Assumption A2, required by Algorithms CNV and OM, is then stated as follows.

A2.   If the Clock Synchronization Condition holds for i, and process p is nonfaulty up to time $T^{(i+1)}$, then for each other process q: p obtains a value Δ_{qp} during the interval $S^{(i)}$. If q is also nonfaulty up to time $T^{(i+1)}$, then

$$|c_p^{(i)}(T_0 + \Delta_{qp}) - c_q^{(i)}(T_0)| < \epsilon \qquad (2)$$

for some time T_0 in $S^{(i)}$.

For $p = q$, we take $\Delta_{pq} = 0$, so 2 holds in this case too. Remember that ϵ is an implicit parameter of A2.

The actual method by which p reads q's clock might involve cooperative action by both processes. In this case, determining Δ_{qp} may require the synchrony of the two processes' clocks, which is why we assume in A2 that the Clock Synchronization Condition holds for i.

3.4.   APPROXIMATIONS.   For real clocks, the maximum rate ρ by which they may drift apart can be reduced to the order of 10^{-6} or less. We will simplify our calculations by making approximations based upon the assumption that $n\rho \ll 1$, where n is the number of processes. This means that we will neglect quantities of order $n\rho\epsilon$ and $n\rho^2$ in our calculations. The reader will be able to check the validity of these calculations by showing that for an approximate inequality of the form $x \lesssim y$, the neglected terms are at most of order $n\rho y$. (The inequality $x \lesssim y$ means $x < y'$ for some $y' \approx y$.) We also assume $R \gg \epsilon$, which is the only case of practical interest.

4. *The Interactive Convergence Algorithm*

Recall that the interactive convergence algorithm CNV is based upon the following observation: the Clock Synchronization Condition for i implies that if p and q are nonfaulty, then the true difference in their clocks is less than δ, and the observed difference is less than $\delta + \epsilon$. Process p increments its clock by the average of all the Δ_{qp}, with values greater than $\delta + \epsilon$ set to zero. This is expressed precisely as follows, where we assume that the processes are numbered from 1 through n.

ALGORITHM CNV.   *For all p:*

$$C_p^{(i+1)} = C_p^{(i)} + \Delta_p$$

$$\text{where } \Delta_p \equiv \left(\frac{1}{n}\right) \sum_{r=1}^{n} \overline{\Delta}_{rp}$$

$$\overline{\Delta}_{rp} \equiv \text{ if } r \neq p \text{ and } |\Delta_{rp}| < \Delta \text{ then } \Delta_{rp}$$
$$\text{else } 0$$

$$\Delta \approx \delta + \epsilon$$

Note that Algorithm CNV depends explicitly upon δ and ϵ. We now prove its correctness.

LEMMA 1.   *If Clock Synchronization Condition S1 holds for i, and processes p and q are nonfaulty up to time $T^{(i+1)}$, then*

$$|\Delta_{qp}| \lesssim \delta + \epsilon.$$

PROOF.   Let T_0 and Δ_{qp} be as in A2. Writing

$$c_p^{(i)}(T_0) - c_p^{(i)}(T_0 + \Delta_{qp}) = c_p^{(i)}(T_0) - c_q^{(i)}(T_0) + c_q^{(i)}(T_0) - c_p^{(i)}(T_0 + \Delta_{qp}),$$

it follows easily from S1 and A2 that

$$|c_p^{(i)}(T_0) - c_p^{(i)}(T_0 + \Delta_{qp})| < \delta + \epsilon.$$

The desired result then follows from A1 and the assumption that $\rho \ll 1$. □

THEOREM 1.   *If*

$$-3m < n$$
$$-\delta \geq max(n'(2\epsilon + \rho(R + 2S')), \delta_0 + \rho R),$$
$$\text{where } n' \equiv n/(n - 3m)$$
$$S' \equiv (n - m)S/n$$
$$-\delta \ll min(R, \epsilon/\rho)$$

then Algorithm CNV satisfies the Clock Synchronization Condition with $\Sigma = \Delta$.

PROOF.   Condition S2 is easy, since Δ_p is the average of n terms, each less than Δ. We prove Condition S1 by induction on i. For $i = 0$, A1 implies that two nonfaulty clocks that are synchronized to within δ_0 up to time $T^{(0)}$ will remain synchronized to within $\delta_0 + \rho R$ at time $T^{(1)} = T^{(0)} + R$. Condition S1 then follows immediately from A0 and the second hypothesis.

We therefore assume that S1 holds for i and prove it for $i + 1$. We begin with the following lemmas.

LEMMA 2.   *If Clock Synchronization Condition S1 holds for i and process p is nonfaulty up to time $T^{(i+2)}$, then for any Π such that $|\Pi| < R$ and any T in $S^{(i)}$:*

$$|c_p^{(i)}(T + \Pi) - [c_p^{(i)}(T) + \Pi]| < \left(\frac{\rho}{2}\right) \Pi.$$

Hence, if $\rho\Pi$ is negligible, then

$$c_p^{(i)}(T + \Pi) \approx c_p^{(i)}(T) + \Pi.$$

PROOF.   This follows easily from A1. □

LEMMA 3.   *If Clock Synchronization Condition S1 holds for i, and p and q are nonfaulty up to time $T^{(i+2)}$, then for any T in $S^{(i)}$ and any Π such that $|\Pi| < R$ and*

518

$\rho\Pi \ll \epsilon$:

$$|c_p^{(i)}(T + \Pi + \Delta_{qp}) - c_q^{(i)}(T + \Pi)| \lesssim \epsilon + \rho S.$$

PROOF.   Letting T_0 be as in A2, we have

$$|c_p^{(i)}(T + \Pi + \Delta_{qp}) - c_q^{(i)}(T + \Pi)|$$
$$= |c_p^{(i)}(T_0 + \Delta_{qp} + T - T_0 + \Pi) - c_q^{(i)}(T_0 + T - T_0 + \Pi)|$$
$$\leq |c_p^{(i)}(T_0 + \Delta_{qp}) - c_q^{(i)}(T_0)| + \rho|T - T_0 + \Pi|$$

[by two applications of Lemma 2]

$$\lesssim \epsilon + \rho|T - T_0| \quad \text{[by A2 and the hypothesis that } \rho\Pi \text{ is negligible]}.$$

The result now follows from the hypothesis that T is in $S^{(i)}$.   □

LEMMA 4.   *If Clock Synchronization Condition S1 holds for i, and processes p, q, and r are nonfaulty up to time $T^{(i+2)}$, then for any T in $S^{(i)}$:*

$$|c_p^{(i)}(T) + \overline{\Delta}_{rp} - [c_q^{(i)}(T) - \overline{\Delta}_{rq}]| \lesssim 2(\epsilon + \rho S).$$

PROOF.   It follows from Lemma 1 that $|\Delta_{rp}|$ and $|\Delta_{qp}|$ are both less than Δ, so $\overline{\Delta}_{rp} = \Delta_{rp}$, $\overline{\Delta}_{rq} = \Delta_{rq}$, and $\rho\Delta_{rp}$ and $\rho\Delta_{rq}$ are both negligible. We therefore have

$$|c_p^{(i)}(T) + \overline{\Delta}_{rp} - [c_q^{(i)}(T) + \overline{\Delta}_{rq}]|$$
$$= |c_p^{(i)}(T) + \Delta_{rp} - [c_q^{(i)}(T) + \Delta_{rq}]|$$
$$\approx |c_p^{(i)}(T + \Delta_{rp}) - c_q^{(i)}(T + \Delta_{rq})| \qquad \text{[by Lemma 2]}$$
$$\leq |c_p^{(i)}(T + \Delta_{rp}) - c_r^{(i)}(T)| + |c_r^{(i)}(T) - c_q^{(i)}(T + \Delta_{rq})|$$
$$\lesssim 2(\epsilon + \rho S) \qquad \text{[by Lemma 3]}$$

proving the result.   □

LEMMA 5.   *If Clock Synchronization Condition S1 holds for i, and Processes p and q are nonfaulty up to time $T^{(i+2)}$, then for any r and any T in $S^{(i)}$*

$$|c_p^{(i)}(T) + \overline{\Delta}_{rp} - [c_q^{(i)}(T) + \overline{\Delta}_{rq}]| < \delta + 2\Delta.$$

PROOF.   By the assumption that S1 holds for i, we have

$$|c_p^{(i)}(T) - c_q^{(i)}(T)| < \delta.$$

Since $|\overline{\Delta}_{rp}|$ and $|\overline{\Delta}_{rq}|$ are by definition no larger than Δ, the result follows immediately.   □

We now complete the proof of the theorem. Assume that processes p and q are both nonfaulty until time $T^{(i+2)}$. For notational convenience, let T denote $T^{(i+1)}$. For any T' in $R^{(i+1)}$ we have

$$|c_p^{(i+1)}(T') - c_q^{(i+1)}(T')| < |c_p^{(i+1)}(T) - c_q^{(i+1)}(T)| + \rho R \qquad \text{[by A1]}$$
$$= |c_p^{(i)}(T + \Delta_p) - c_q^{(i)}(T + \Delta_q)| + \rho R \qquad \text{[from the algorithm]}$$
$$\approx |c_p^i(T) + \Delta_p - [c_q^{(i)}(T) + \Delta_q]| + \rho R \qquad \text{[by Lemma 2, since } |\Delta_p|, |\Delta_q| < \Delta]$$
$$= \left|\left(\frac{1}{n}\right) \sum_{r=1}^{n} (c_p^{(i)}(T) + \overline{\Delta}_{rp} - [c_q^{(i)}(T) + \overline{\Delta}_{rq}])\right| + \rho R$$

[by definition of Δ_p and Δ_q]

$$\leq \left(\frac{1}{n}\right) \sum_{r=1}^{n} |c_p^{(i)}(T) + \overline{\Delta}_{rp} - [c_q^{(i)}(T) + \overline{\Delta}_{rq}]| + \rho R$$
$$\lesssim \left(\frac{1}{n}\right) [2(n - m)(\epsilon + \rho S) + m(\delta + 2\Delta)] + \rho R,$$

where the last inequality is obtained by applying Lemma 4 to the $n - m$ nonfaulty processes r and Lemma 5 to the remaining m processes. Since $\Delta \approx \delta + \epsilon$, a little algebraic manipulation shows that if

$$\delta \gtrsim n'(2\epsilon + \rho(R + 2S')),$$

then

$$\frac{1}{n} [2(n - m)(\epsilon + \rho S) + m(\delta + 2\Delta)] + \rho R \lesssim \delta.$$

Combining this with the above string of inequalities, we see that for any T' in $R^{(i+1)}$

$$|c_p^{(i+1)}(T') - c_q^{(i+1)}(T')| \lesssim \delta,$$

so S1 holds for $i + 1$. This completes the proof of Theorem 1. $\square$

For any clock synchronization algorithm, we will have $\delta \geq \delta_1 + \rho R$, where δ_1 is the closeness with which the clocks can be resynchronized and ρR is how far they can drift apart during an R-SECOND interval. In the interactive convergence algorithm CNV, there is a term $(n' - 1)\rho R$ in δ_1, so how close the clocks can be resynchronized depends upon how far apart they are allowed to drift.

5. *Interactive Consistency Algorithms*

We begin our rigorous discussion of the interactive consistency algorithms by formalizing conditions CC1 and CC2, given in Section 2.3. When p "obtains the value" of r's clock, what it actually finds is a constant $\overline{\Delta}_{rp}$ such that

$$c_r^{(i)}(T) \approx c_p^{(i)}(T + \overline{\Delta}_{rp}).$$

(The values $\overline{\Delta}_{rp}$ are not the same ones defined in the interactive convergence algorithm.) We also allow the possibility that if r is faulty, then p may not be able to read r's clock. This is denoted by letting $\overline{\Delta}_{rp}$ have the special value NULL. Recalling the definition of Δ_{qp} given by A2, and letting a NULL clock be approximately equal only to another NULL clock, we see that conditions CC1 and CC2 can be restated as follows:

CC. For some constant $\Omega \ll R$ and all i: if the Clock Synchronization Condition holds for i, then for any processes p and q that are nonfaulty up to time $T^{(i+2)}$:

(1) For all $r \neq p, q$: either

    (a) $|\overline{\Delta}_{rp} - [\Delta_{qp} + \overline{\Delta}_{rq}]| < \Omega$, or
    (b) $\overline{\Delta}_{rp} = \overline{\Delta}_{rq} = $ NULL.

(2) $\overline{\Delta}_{qp} \neq$ NULL, and $|\overline{\Delta}_{qp} - \Delta_{qp}| < \Omega$.

For convenience, we let $\overline{\Delta}_{pp} \equiv 0$ for all p. Condition CC2 is then equivalent to CC1(a) for $r = q$.

Before stating our next result, we introduce some notation. We let **n** denote the set $\{1, \ldots, n\}$. A *multiset* is a set in which the same element can appear more than once. We use ordinary set notation for describing multisets, so the multiset $\{1, 1, 2\}$ contains three elements, two of which are equal. The multiset $\{a_i : i \in \mathbf{n}\}$ contains n elements, not all of which need be distinct. If **M** is a multiset, then "median **M**" denotes the median of **M**, defined by

$$\text{median } \mathbf{M} \equiv a_{\lfloor n/2 \rfloor},$$

where $\mathbf{M} = \{a_1, \ldots, a_n\}$ with $a_1 \le a_2 \le \cdots \le a_n$.

Our two interactive consistency algorithms are based upon the following result.

THEOREM 2.   *If $m \le \lfloor n/2 \rfloor$, $\delta_0 < \Omega + \epsilon + \rho S$, and CC holds for all i, then letting*

$$c_p^{(i+1)}(T) \equiv c_p^{(i)}(T + \Delta_p)$$

where

$$\Delta_p \equiv median\{\overline{\Delta}_{rp} : r \in \mathbf{n} \text{ and } \overline{\Delta}_{rp} \ne NULL\},$$

satisfies the Clock Synchronization Condition for all i, with

$$\delta \approx \Omega + \epsilon + \rho(R + S),$$
$$\Sigma \approx 2(\Omega + \epsilon) + \rho(R + S).$$

The proof of Theorem 2 requires the following two results about medians.

LEMMA 6.   *If $|a_r - b_r| < \pi$ for all $r \in \mathbf{n}$, then*

$$|median\{a_r : r \in \mathbf{n}\} - median\{b_r : r \in \mathbf{n}\}| < \pi.$$

PROOF.   We prove the stronger result that for any k: the kth highest values of the multisets $\{a_r\}$ and $\{b_r\}$ lie within π of one another. Let the permutations α and β be chosen such that:

$$a_{\alpha(1)} \le a_{\alpha(2)} \le \cdots \le a_{\alpha(n)},$$
$$b_{\beta(1)} \le b_{\beta(2)} \le \cdots \le b_{\beta(n)}.$$

We prove that, for all k, $|a_{\alpha(k)} - b_{\beta(k)}| < \pi$.

There are at least k values of i such that $a_i \le a_{\alpha(k)}$. However, the hypothesis implies that, if $a_i \le a_{\alpha(k)}$, then $b_i < a_{\alpha(k)} + \pi$. Hence there are at least k values of i such that $b_i < a_{\alpha(k)} + \pi$, which implies that $b_{\alpha(k)} < a_{\alpha(k)} + \pi$. A symmetric argument shows that $a_{\alpha(k)} < b_{\alpha(k)} + \pi$, and combining these two inequalities gives the desired result.   □

LEMMA 7.   *If $|a_r - a| < \pi$ for a majority of values r in $\mathbf{n}$, then*

$$|median\{a_r : r \in \mathbf{n}\} - a| < \pi.$$

PROOF.   It is easy to see that if A is any submultiset containing a majority of the elements of $\{a_r\}$, then

$$\min(A) \le median\{a_r : r \in n\} \le \max(A).$$

Letting A be the multiset $\{a_r : |a_r - a| < \pi\}$, this implies that

$$a - \pi \le median\{a_r : r \in \mathbf{n}\} \le a + \pi,$$

which proves the lemma.   □

PROOF OF THEOREM 2.   The proof is by induction on i. For $i = 0$, the result is trivial. (Note that S2 is vacuous for $i = 0$.) Assume that the theorem is true for i. By CC2 and Lemma 1, we see that

$$|\overline{\Delta}_{qp}| < \Omega + \delta + \epsilon$$

for all nonfaulty p and q, so S2 follows easily from Lemma 7.

Since Δ_p is the median of the $\overline{\Delta}_{rp}$, and a majority of the processes r are nonfaulty, the above inequality shows that we can neglect terms of order $\rho \Delta_p$, and likewise terms of order $\rho\Delta_q$. Lemma 1 implies that we can neglect terms of order $\rho\Delta_{qp}$. Letting $T = T^{(i+1)}$, we then have

$$|c_p^{(i+1)}(T) - c_q^{(i+1)}(T)|$$
$$= |c_p^{(i)}(T + \Delta_p) - c_q^{(i)}(T + \Delta_q)| \qquad \text{[by hypothesis]}$$
$$= |c_p^{(i)}(T + \Delta_{qp} + \Delta_p - \Delta_{qp}) - c_q^{(i)}(T + \Delta_q)|$$
$$\approx |c_p^{(i)}(T + \Delta_{qp}) + \Delta_p - \Delta_{qp} - [c_q^{(i)}(T) + \Delta_q]| \qquad \text{[by Lemma 2]}$$
$$\leq |\Delta_p - \Delta_{qp} - \Delta_q| + \epsilon + \rho S \qquad \text{[by Lemma 3]}$$
$$= |\text{median}\{\overline{\Delta}_{rp} - \Delta_{qp} : r \in \mathbf{n} \text{ and } \overline{\Delta}_{rp} \neq \text{NULL}\}$$
$$\quad - \text{median}\{\overline{\Delta}_{rq} : r \in \mathbf{n} \text{ and } \overline{\Delta}_{rq} \neq \text{NULL}\}| + \epsilon + \rho S$$
$$\lesssim \Omega + \epsilon + \rho S \qquad \text{[by CC and Lemma 6]}.$$

Condition S1 follows easily from this inequality and A1. □

5.1. THE ALGORITHM COM. Achieving Condition CC requires that the processes not only read each other's clocks, but also send values to one another. If x_p is a value that process p sends to the other processes, then we let x_{pq} denote the value that q receives from p. The manner in which the value is transmitted is irrelevant—it might be sent as a message from p to q, or p might leave it in some register where q can read it. We assume that if p and q are both nonfaulty, then $x_{pq} = x_p$. If p or q is faulty, then x_{pq} may have any value.

We specify Algorithm COM as a recursive algorithm by which a process q obtains a value $\text{COM}(m, \mathbf{P}, x_p, p)_q$ from process p, where x_p is the value that p is sending and $\mathbf{P}$ is some set of processes. The value x_p being sent by p represents the difference between some clock and p's clock. If $x_p = 0$, then p is sending its own clock value. The actual clock-synchronization algorithm consists of each process q letting $\text{COM}(m, \mathbf{n}, 0, q)_p$ be the $\overline{\Delta}_{qp}$ of Theorem 2. We write $\mathbf{P} - p$ to denote $\mathbf{P} - \{p\}$, for any set $\mathbf{P}$.

ALGORITHM COM. *For any integer $m \geq 0$, any subset $\mathbf{P}$ of $\mathbf{n}$, any value x_p and any $p, q \in \mathbf{P}$:*

$$\text{COM}(0, \mathbf{P}, x_p, p)_q \equiv x_{pq} + \Delta_{pq}$$
$$\text{COM}(m, \mathbf{P}, x_p, p)_q \equiv \text{median}\{\text{COM}(m - 1, \mathbf{P} - p, x_{pr} + \Delta_{pr}, r)_q : r \in \mathbf{P} - p\}$$

To prove the required properties of Algorithm COM, we need the following result.

LEMMA 8. *If Clock Synchronization Condition S1 holds for i, and processes p, q, and r are nonfaulty up to time $T^{(i+2)}$, then*

$$|\Delta_{pr} + \Delta_{rq} - \Delta_{pq}| \lesssim 3\epsilon + 2\rho S.$$

PROOF. Let T be the time, obtained from A2, such that

$$|c_p^{(i)}(T) - c_q^{(i)}(T + \Delta_{pq})| < \epsilon.$$

We then have

$$|\Delta_{pr} + \Delta_{rq} - \Delta_{pq}|$$
$$\approx |c_q^{(i)}(T + \Delta_{pr} + \Delta_{rq}) - c_q^{(i)}(T + \Delta_{pq})| \qquad \text{[by Lemma 2]}$$
$$\leq |c_q^{(i)}(T + \Delta_{pr} + \Delta_{rq}) - c_r^{(i)}(T + \Delta_{pr})|$$
$$\quad + |c_r^{(i)}(T + \Delta_{pr}) - c_p^{(i)}(T)| + |c_p^{(i)}(T) - c_q^{(i)}(T + \Delta_{pq})|$$
$$\lesssim 3\epsilon + 2\rho S \qquad \text{[by A2 and Lemma 3]}$$

which is the required result. □

522

The following result is the analogue of Lemma 1 of [6].

LEMMA 9. *For all m and k, if $n > 2k + m$, Clock Synchronization Condition S1 holds for i, and all but at most k processes in $\mathbf{P}$ are nonfaulty up to time $T^{(i+2)}$, then for any of those nonfaulty processes p and q, and any x_p:*

$$|COM(m, \mathbf{P}, x_p, p)_q - [x_p + \Delta_{pq}]| \lesssim m(3\epsilon + 2\rho S).$$

PROOF. The proof is by induction on m. The result is trivial for $m = 0$. Assume it for $m - 1$. For any processor r in $\mathbf{P} - p$ that is nonfaulty up to time $T^{(i+2)}$, we have

$$|COM(m - 1, \mathbf{P} - p, x_{pr} + \Delta_{pr}, r)_q - [x_p + \Delta_{pq}]|$$
$$= |COM(m - 1, \mathbf{P} - p, x_{pr} + \Delta_{pr}, r)_q - [x_{pr} + \Delta_{pr} + \Delta_{rq}]$$
$$+ [\Delta_{pr} + \Delta_{rq} - \Delta_{pq}]| \quad \text{[since } p \text{ and } r \text{ nonfaulty implies } x_{pr} = x_p]$$
$$\lesssim (m - 1)(3\epsilon + 2\rho S) + (3\epsilon + 2\rho S),$$

where the last inequality comes from Lemma 8 and the induction hypothesis, which can be applied because $\mathbf{P} - p$ has $n - 1$ elements and $n - 1 > 2k + (m - 1)$. Therefore, for every nonfaulty process r, we have

$$|COM(m - 1, \mathbf{P} - p, x_{pr} + \Delta_{pr}, r)_q - [x_p + \Delta_{pq}]| \lesssim m(3\epsilon + 2\rho S).$$

The lemma now follows from Lemma 7, since $n > 2k + m \geq 2k + 1$. □

Our next lemma is the analogue of Theorem 1 of [6].

LEMMA 10. *If Clock Synchronization Condition S1 holds for i, and $\mathbf{P}$ is a set containing more than 3m processes, all but at most m of which are nonfaulty up to time $T^{(i+2)}$, then for any of the nonfaulty processes p and q:*

(1) *For all r in $\mathbf{P}$,*

$$|COM(m, \mathbf{P}, x_r, r)_p - [\Delta_{qp} + COM(m, \mathbf{P}, x_r, r)_q]| \lesssim (2m + 1)(3\epsilon + 2\rho S),$$

(2) $|COM(m, \mathbf{P}, x_q, q)_p - x_q - \Delta_{qp}| \lesssim m(3\epsilon + 2\rho S).$

PROOF. Part 2 follows immediately from Lemma 9 by letting $k = m$. Part 1 is proved by induction. For $m = 0$, it follows easily from the definition of COM and Lemma 8. Let $m > 0$ and assume it holds for $m - 1$. We consider two cases: (i) r faulty and (ii) r nonfaulty.

If r is faulty, then there are at most $m - 1$ faulty processes in $\mathbf{P} - r$, and we can apply the induction hypothesis to obtain

$$|COM(m - 1, \mathbf{P} - r, x_{rs}, s)_p - \Delta_{qp} - COM(m - 1, \mathbf{P} - r, x_{rs}, s)_q|$$
$$\lesssim (2(m - 1) + 1)(3\epsilon + 2\rho S)$$

for any s in $\mathbf{P} - r$. The result now follows easily from Lemma 6.

If r is nonfaulty, then we can apply the inequality from part 2 to obtain

$$|COM(m, \mathbf{P}, x_r, r)_p - [x_r + \Delta_{rp}]| \lesssim m(3\epsilon + 2\rho S),$$
$$|COM(m, \mathbf{P}, x_r, r)_q - [x_r + \Delta_{rq}]| \lesssim m(3\epsilon + 2\rho S). \tag{3}$$

We then have

$$|COM(m, \mathbf{P}, x_r, r)_p - \Delta_{qp} - COM(m, \mathbf{P}, x_r, r)_q|$$
$$= |COM(m, \mathbf{P}, x_r, r)_p - [x_r + \Delta_{rp}]$$
$$- (COM(m, \mathbf{P}, x_r, r)_q - [x_r + \Delta_{rq}]) + \Delta_{rp} - \Delta_{rq} - \Delta_{qp}|$$
$$\lesssim 2m(3\epsilon + 2\rho S) + (3\epsilon + 2\rho S),$$

where the last inequality follows from the triangle inequality (3) and Lemma 8. This finishes the proof of part 1 for m. $\quad\square$

Taking $x_r = 0$, Lemma 10 yields the following result.

THEOREM 3. *If all but at most m processes are nonfaulty up to time $T^{(i+2)}$, and $n > 3m$, then Condition CC is satisfied by*

$$\overline{\Delta}_{qp} = COM(m, \mathbf{n}, 0, q)_p,$$

with $\Omega \approx (2m + 1)(3\epsilon + 2\rho S)$.

Combining this with Theorem 2 yields our first interactive consistency clock synchronization algorithm, with

$$\delta \approx (6m + 4)\epsilon + (4m + 3)\rho S + \rho R,$$
$$\Sigma \approx (12m + 8)\epsilon + (8m + 5)\rho S + \rho R.$$

This algorithm requires that n be greater than $3m$—that is, that more than two-thirds of the processes be nonfaulty. As shown in [9], this is the best one can do.

5.2. THE ALGORITHM CSM. We begin our formal development of Algorithm CSM with a precise statement of Assumption A2′.

$A2'$. If an event in a process q occurring at (real) time t_0 causes q to send a message to a process p, then that message arrives at a time t_1 such that

(a) if p and q are nonfaulty, then $|t_1 - t_0 - \gamma| < \epsilon$,
(b) $t_1 - t_0 > \gamma - \epsilon$,

for some constant γ such that $n\rho\gamma \ll \epsilon$.

In practice, the value of γ may depend upon p and q and on the type of event generating the message. To avoid having to cope with all these different values, we assume a single γ for all messages. The only restriction we place on the size of γ is that $n\rho\gamma \ll \epsilon$, which means that γ may be "medium-sized." It will typically be larger than ϵ but much smaller than R.

We next restate our assumption of unforgeable digital signatures. Formally, a digital signature mechanism consists of a function S_p for each process p, satisfying the following condition:

$A3$. For any process p and any data item D:

(a) No faulty process other than p can generate $S_p[D]$.
(b) For any X, any process can determine if X equals $S_p[D]$.

Note that the first assumption is stronger than the one made in [6], since it does not permit one faulty process to forge the signatures of another faulty process.

Assumption A3(a) means that a faulty process cannot generate any arbitrary value, so it restricts the class of faults that may occur. Hence, we can hope to find a clock synchronization algorithm to handle m faults with fewer than $3m + 1$ processes, and, indeed, our second interactive consistency algorithm requires that only a majority of the processes be nonfaulty.

We define the message $M(T, p_0 \cdots p_s)$, for any sequence $p_0, \ldots, p_s$ of processes—including the null sequence λ—as follows:

$$M(T, \lambda) \equiv (T, p_0, S_{p_0}(T)),$$
$$M(T, p_0 \cdots p_s) \equiv (M(T, p_0 \cdots p_{s-1}), p_s, S_{p_s}[M(T, p_0 \cdots p_{s-1})]).$$

By A3(a), the value $M(T, p_0 \cdots p_s)$ can be generated only as the result of process p_0 sending the message $M(T, p_0)$ to process p_1, which sends the message $M(T, p_0p_1)$ to process $p_2 \cdots$ which sends the message $M(T, p_0 \cdots p_{s-1})$ to process p_s, which generates $M(T, p_0 \cdots p_s)$. Moreover, A3(b) implies that any process can determine whether a given data item X equals $M(T, p_0 \cdots p_s)$ for some T and $p_0 \cdots p_s$.

In Algorithm CSM, for some time T_p in $S^{(i)}$, process p sends the message $M(T_p, p)$ to all other processes when its clock reaches T_p. Immediately upon receiving this message, each other process p_1 sends the message $M(T_p, pp_1)$ to all processes other than itself and p, and so forth. Any process q will therefore receive messages $M(T_p, pp_1 \cdots p_s)$ for many different sequences $p_1 \cdots p_s$. Each such message tells q that p's clock read T_p approximately $(s + 1)\gamma$ SECONDS ago. If p and all the p_i are nonfaulty, then this message is correct. If one or more of the p_i are faulty, then they can either fail to relay the message, so q never receives it, or they can delay it. However, they cannot alter the value of T_p or cause the message to arrive too early. Hence, process q believes the message indicating the earliest time at which p's clock reached T_p.

There is a practical problem in implementing this approach. In order to perform the appropriate message relaying, a process must be prepared to receive the incoming message. This may require that the process not do anything else while waiting, so it should know when the message will arrive and be able to ignore the message if it does not arrive when it should. Since the uncertainty in message transmission time is ϵ, and the difference between p's clock and q's clock is δ, q can expect to receive the message $M(T_p, p)$ within about $\epsilon + \delta$ seconds of when its clock reads $T_p + \gamma$. If q relays this message only if it arrives when it should, then another process r can expect to receive the message $M(T_p, pq)$ within about $2(\epsilon + \delta)$ of when its clock reads $T_p + 2\gamma$. Continuing, this leads us to the following definition:

Definition 3.　The message $M(T, p_0 \cdots p_s)$ is said to arrive *on time* at process q if either

(1) $s \geq 0$ and the message arrives at (real) time $c_q^{(i)}(T')$, or
(2) $s = -1$ (so $p_0 \cdots p_s$ is the null sequence) and $T' = T$

and $|T' - T - (s + 1)\gamma| \leq (s + 1)(\delta + \epsilon)$.

The δ in this definition is the same one as in the Clock Synchronization Condition. Its value will be given later.

The following algorithm describes how each process q determines the value $\overline{\Delta}_{pq}$ for every $p \neq q$.

ALGORITHM CSM(m).　*For each process p, and for some clock time T_p in $S^{(i)}$:*

(1) *When its clock $c_p^{(i)}$ reaches T_p, process p sends the message $M(T_p, p)$ to every other process.*
(2) *For each process $q \neq p$:*
　　(A) Process q initializes $\overline{\Delta}_{pq}$ to ∞.
　　(B) If the message $M(T_p, pp_1 \cdots p_s)$ arrives on time at q, at time $c_q^{(i)}(T)$, and $T - T_p - (s + 1)\gamma < \overline{\Delta}_{pq}$, then
　　　　(a) Process q sets $\overline{\Delta}_{pq}$ equal to $T - T_p - (s + 1)\gamma$.
　　　　(b) If $s < m$, then immediately upon receiving this message, q sends the message $M(T_p, pp_1 \cdots p_s q)$ to every other process q' not contained among the processes $pp_1 \cdots p_s$.

(C) *At time $T_p + (m + 1)(\gamma + \delta + \epsilon)$, if $\overline{\Delta}_{pq} = \infty$, then q sets $\overline{\Delta}_{pq}$ equal to NULL.*

We have assumed A2′ instead of A2, so the values Δ_{qp} are not yet defined. In order to apply Theorem 2, we must define the Δ_{qp} and prove A2.

LEMMA 11. *Assumption A2 is satisfied, except with the strict inequality replaced by approximate inequality, if Δ_{qp} is defined to equal $T - T_q - \gamma$, where T is the value such that p receives the message $M(T_q, q)$ at time $c_p^{(i)}(T)$, and to have any value if p receives no such message.*

PROOF. If p and q are nonfaulty, then the message $M(T_q, q)$ is sent by q and received by p. Taking $T_0 = T_q$, we find

$$| c_p^{(i)}(T_0 + \Delta_{qp}) - c_q^{(i)}(T_0) |$$
$$= | c_p^{(i)}(T - \gamma) - c_q^{(i)}(T_q) |$$
$$\approx | c_p^{(i)}(T) - \gamma - c_q^{(i)}(T_q) | \qquad \text{[by Lemma 2]}$$
$$< \epsilon \qquad \text{[by A2′(a)]}$$

which proves the lemma. □

Lemma 11 allows us to use the earlier results that assumed A2. (Since these results all involve approximate inequalities, they are not invalidated when the exact inequality in A2 is replaced by an approximate inequality.) We now prove the main result for Algorithm CSM.

THEOREM 4. *If all but at most m processes are nonfaulty up to time $T^{(i+2)}$, then the values $\overline{\Delta}_{pq}$ found by Algorithm CSM(m) satisfy condition CC with $\Omega \approx (m + 5)\epsilon + 2\rho S$.*

The proof uses the following lemmas.

LEMMA 12. *Let Clock Synchronization Condition S1 hold for i, and let p and q be nonfaulty up to time $T^{(i+2)}$. If the message $M(T, p_0 \cdots p_s)$ arrives on time at p, and $s < m$, then the message $M(T, p_0 \cdots p_s p)$ arrives on time at q.*

PROOF. Let $c_p^{(i)}(T')$ be the time at which $M(T, p_0 \cdots p_s)$ arrives at p, letting $T' = T$ if $p_0 \cdots p_s$ is the null sequence, and let $c_q^{(i)}(T'')$ be the time at which $M(T, p_0 \cdots p_s p)$ arrives at q. Then

$$| c_p^{(i)}(T'') - c_p^{(i)}(T' + \gamma) |$$
$$\approx | c_p^{(i)}(T'') - c_p^{(i)}(T') - \gamma |$$
$$\leq | c_q^{(i)}(T'') - c_p^{(i)}(T') - \gamma | + \delta \qquad \text{[by S1]}$$
$$\lesssim \epsilon + \delta \qquad \text{[by A2]}.$$

It follows from A1, and the assumption that $\rho\gamma$ is negligible, that

$$| T'' - T' - \gamma | \lesssim \delta + \epsilon. \qquad (4)$$

We then have

$$| T'' - T - (s + 2)\gamma |$$
$$\leq | T'' - T' - \gamma | + | T' - T - (s + 1)\gamma |$$
$$\lesssim \delta + \epsilon + (s + 1)(\delta + \epsilon) \qquad \text{[by 4 and the on-time arrival of } M(T, p_0 \cdots p_s)]$$

which implies that $M(T, p_0 \cdots p_s p)$ arrives on time at q. □

LEMMA 13. *If Clock Synchronization Condition S1 holds for i, all but at most m processes are nonfaulty up to $T^{(i+2)}$, and p and q are among the nonfaulty ones, then for any process r: if $\bar{\Delta}_{rp} \neq$ NULL then $\bar{\Delta}_{rq} \neq$ NULL and*

$$\bar{\Delta}_{rq} + \Delta_{qp} \lesssim \bar{\Delta}_{rp} + (m + 3)\epsilon + \rho S.$$

(For r = q or p, $\bar{\Delta}_{rr}$ is defined to be 0.)

PROOF. Let $r_0 = r$, and let T be the time such that

$$\bar{\Delta}_{rp} = T - T_r - (s + 1)\gamma \tag{5}$$

and the message $M(T_r, r_0 \cdots r_s)$ arrived at p (on time) at time $c_p^{(i)}(T)$. (If $r = p$, so $s = -1$, then $T = T_r$.) We consider two cases:

(1) $q = r_j$
(2) q not in the sequence $r_0 \cdots r_s$.

In case 1, it follows from A3(a) that the message $M(T_r, r_0 \cdots r_{j-1})$ must have arrived on time at q at some time $c_q^{(i)}(T')$, so $\bar{\Delta}_{rq} \neq$ NULL, and

$$\bar{\Delta}_{rq} \leq T' - T_r - j\gamma. \tag{6}$$

A simple induction argument using A2′(b) shows that

$$c_p^{(i)}(T) - c_q^{(i)}(T') - (s - j + 1)\gamma > -(s - j + 1)\epsilon. \tag{7}$$

We then have

$$c_p^{(i)}(T) - c_p^{(i)}(T' + (s - j + 1)\gamma)$$
$$\geq c_p^{(i)}(T) - c_q^{(i)}(T' + (s - j + 1)\gamma - \Delta_{qp}) - \epsilon - \rho S \quad \text{[by Lemma 3]}$$
$$\approx c_p^{(i)}(T) - c_q^{(i)}(T') - (s - j + 1)\gamma + \Delta_{qp} - \epsilon - \rho S \quad \text{[by Lemma 2]}$$
$$> -(s - j + 2)\epsilon - \rho S + \Delta_{qp} \quad \text{[by (7)]}.$$

By A1, this yields

$$T - (T' + (s - j + 1)\gamma) \geq -(s - j + 2)\epsilon - \rho S + \Delta_{qp},$$

so

$$T' - j\gamma + \Delta_{qp} \lesssim T - (s + 1)\gamma + (s - j + 2)\epsilon + \rho S.$$

Subtracting T_r from both sides of this inequality, we see that (5) and (6) imply

$$\bar{\Delta}_{rq} + \Delta_{qp} \lesssim \bar{\Delta}_{rp} + (s - j + 2)\epsilon + \rho S,$$

which yields the desired result, since $s \leq m$.

For case 2, q not equal to any of the r_j, we consider two subcases: $s < m$ and $s = m$. If $s < m$, then p sends q the message $M(T_r, r_0 \cdots r_s p)$, which, by Lemma 12, arrives on time at q. Hence, $\bar{\Delta}_{rq} \neq$ NULL and

$$\bar{\Delta}_{rq} \leq T' - T_r - (s + 2)\gamma, \tag{8}$$

where $c_q^{(i)}(T')$ is the time at which the message arrives. We then have

$$c_p^{(i)}(T' + \Delta_{qp} - \gamma) - c_p^{(i)}(T)$$
$$\approx c_p^{(i)}(T' + \Delta_{qp}) - c_p^{(i)}(T) - \gamma \quad \text{[by A1]}$$
$$\lesssim c_q^{(i)}(T') - c_p^{(i)}(T) - \gamma + \epsilon + \rho S \quad \text{[by Lemma 3]}$$
$$< 2\epsilon + \rho S \quad \text{[by A2′(a)]}.$$

This implies that

$$T' + \Delta_{qp} - \gamma - T \lesssim 2\epsilon + \rho S,$$

which can be rewritten as

$$T' - (s + 2)\gamma + \Delta_{qp} \lesssim T - (s + 1)\gamma + 2\epsilon + \rho S.$$

Subtracting T_r from both sides of this inequality shows that the desired result follows immediately from (5) and (8).

Finally, we consider the case $s = m$, where q is not one of the r_j. Since there are at most m faulty processes, there is at least one process r_j that is nonfaulty up to time $T^{(i+2)}$. Let $c_q^{(i)}(T')$ be the time at which r_j received the message $M(T_r, r_0 \cdots r_{j-1})$—or at which it sent the message $M(T_r, r)$, if $j = 0$. The same argument as before shows that (7) again holds.

By Lemma 12, the message $M(T_r, r_0 \cdots r_j)$ arrives on time at q, so $\overline{\Delta}_{rq} \neq$ NULL, and

$$\overline{\Delta}_{rq} \leq T'' - T_r - (j + 1)\gamma, \tag{9}$$

where $c_q^{(i)}(T'')$ is the time at which the message arrives. By A2'(a) we have

$$c_q^{(i)}(T'') - c_q^{(i)}(T') - \gamma < \epsilon,$$

and combining this with (7) yields

$$c_p^{(i)}(T) - c_q^{(i)}(T'') - (s - j)\gamma > -(s - j + 2)\epsilon.$$

Using Lemma 3, we can deduce from this that

$$c_p^{(i)}(T) - c_p^{(i)}(T'' + \Delta_{qp}) - (s - j)\gamma \gtrsim -(s - j + 3)\epsilon - \rho S.$$

Since $\rho(s - j)\gamma$ is negligible, this implies by A1 that

$$T - T'' - \Delta_{qp} - (s - j)\gamma \gtrsim -(s - j + 3)\epsilon - \rho S,$$

which can be rewritten as

$$T'' - (j + 1)\gamma + \Delta_{qp} \lesssim T - (s + 1)\gamma + (s - j + 3)\epsilon + \rho S.$$

Subtracting T_r from both sides, we obtain the desired result from (9) and (5). $\square$

PROOF OF THEOREM 4. Let p, q be as in Condition CC. It follows easily from Lemma 12 that $\overline{\Delta}_{qp} \neq$ NULL. Condition CC2 then follows from CC1(a) for $r = q$. It therefore suffices to prove CC1 for all r. This requires proving that if $\overline{\Delta}_{rp} \neq$ NULL, then $\overline{\Delta}_{rq} \neq$ NULL and

$$\overline{\Delta}_{rp} - \Delta_{qp} - \overline{\Delta}_{rq} \lesssim (m + 5)\epsilon + 2\rho S,$$
$$\overline{\Delta}_{rq} + \Delta_{qp} - \overline{\Delta}_{rp} \lesssim (m + 5)\epsilon + 2\rho S.$$

The fact that $\overline{\Delta}_{rq} \neq$ NULL and the second inequality follow from Lemma 13. Reversing p and q in Lemma 13, we obtain

$$\overline{\Delta}_{rp} + \Delta_{pq} - \overline{\Delta}_{rq} \lesssim (m + 3)\epsilon + \rho S.$$

To prove the theorem, we therefore need only show that

$$|\Delta_{pq} + \Delta_{qp}| \lesssim 2\epsilon + \rho S.$$

We write

$$|c_p^{(i)}(T_0 + \Delta_{qp}) - c_p^{(i)}(T_0 - \Delta_{pq})|$$
$$\leq |c_p^{(i)}(T_0 + \Delta_{qp}) - c_q^{(i)}(T_0)| + |c_q^{(i)}(T_0) - c_p^{(i)}(T_0 - \Delta_{pq})|$$
$$\lesssim \epsilon + \epsilon + \rho S \quad \text{[by A2 and Lemma 3]}$$

where T_0 is as in A2, and the result follows from A1. $\square$

Combining Theorem 4 with Theorem 2 gives an interactive consistency algorithm with

$$\delta \approx (m + 6)\epsilon + 3\rho S + \rho R,$$
$$\Sigma \approx (2m + 12)\epsilon + 5\rho S + \rho R.$$

This is the value of δ that should be used in the definition of on-time arrival.

6. Conclusion

We have described three clock synchronization algorithms. The interactive convergence Algorithm CNV is the simplest, requiring only that every process read every other process' clock. The interactive consistency algorithms are more complex, requiring a great deal of message passing. These algorithms are based upon two Byzantine Generals solutions from [6]. A number of different Byzantine Generals solutions have been proposed; a survey of them can be found in [8]. The solutions we have used as the basis for our clock-synchronization algorithms are optimal in the sense that they require the fewest "rounds" of message passing—$m + 1$ rounds being required to handle m faults. Since each round adds an $O(\epsilon)$ term to the synchronization error, minimizing the number of rounds is a reasonable criterion for choosing an algorithm.

In addition to minimizing the number of rounds, one also wants to reduce the number of messages generated. Algorithm COM generates approximately n^{m+1} messages. All Byzantine Generals solutions we know of that generate fewer messages either use more rounds or require digital signatures. Fortunately, in process-control applications, n and m tend to be small enough so that n^{m+1} is not an unreasonable number of messages. However, there may be other applications in which one would be willing to use more rounds in order to generate fewer messages. While there are Byzantine Generals solutions that do this, it is not clear how they can be converted to clock-synchronization algorithms. Our method of deriving Algorithm COM depended upon the specific details of Algorithm OM. We have not tried to derive clock-synchronization algorithms from the other Byzantine Generals solutions.

The situation is different if we allow digital signatures. Algorithm CSM generates almost as many messages as Algorithm COM. However, it is possible to reduce the number of messages. In [2], Dolev and Strong reduced the number of messages generated by Algorithm SM to $2n^2$ by simply eliminating redundant messages—for example, a process never sends the same value twice to the same process. In our intuitive description of Algorithm CSM, we can reduce the number of "clocks" sent by having each process p obey the following two rules:

(1) p never sends a clock if it has already sent a faster clock.
(2) p never sends a clock that is approximately the same as one it has already sent.

In view of the improved algorithm of [3], which is not based upon a Byzantine Generals solution, there seems little point in investigating these improvements to Algorithm CSM.

To compare the closeness of synchronization achieved by these algorithms, we assume that $\rho S \ll \epsilon$. This is a reasonable assumption, since, for most practical applications, ϵ will be on the order of microseconds, S at most a few milliseconds, and $\rho \lesssim 10^{-6}$. To simplify comparisons with the interactive convergence algorithm, in which δ depends upon n, we assume that $n = 3m + 1$. This will be the case if the only reason for having multiple processes is to achieve fault-tolerance through redundancy. We then get the following values of δ:

$$\text{Algorithm CNV: } (6m + 2)\epsilon + (3m + 1)\rho R,$$
$$\text{Algorithm COM: } (6m + 4)\epsilon + \rho R,$$
$$\text{Algorithm SCM: } (m + 6)\epsilon + \rho R.$$

We have proved only that the synchronization errors of the algorithms are less than these quantities; we do not know if the errors can really become this large. However, for want of an alternative, we use these bounds in comparing the algorithms.

From these numbers, Algorithm CSM appears to be superior. However, this is misleading because the ϵ for Algorithm CSM is not necessarily the same as the ϵ of the other two algorithms, since it may come from a very different way of reading the clocks. The Algorithms CNV and COM can use any method of reading clocks, but clock reading in Algorithm CSM requires measuring the arrival times of messages and knowing the delay in processing and sending a message. For the tightly-coupled multiprocessors typical of process-control applications, we believe that ϵ is likely to be much larger for CSM than for COM. In this case, Algorithm CSM is to be preferred only because it requires fewer processes to achieve the same degree of fault-tolerance.

The algorithm of [3] reduces the term $(m + 6)\epsilon$ of Algorithm CSM to ϵ. However, that algorithm involves the same form of clock reading as Algorithm CSM, so its ϵ may be larger than that of our other two algorithms. For process-control applications, Algorithms CNV and COM may provide closer synchronization than any algorithm requiring digital signatures.

Since Algorithms CNV and COM can use the same method of clock reading, the above error bounds provide a meaningful comparison for them. If R is small enough—that is, if the clocks are resynchronized often enough—then Algorithm CNV can achieve slightly better synchronization than Algorithm COM. However, one usually wants to resynchronize only as often as is necessary to achieve a desired value of δ. If this value of δ is much larger than $6m\epsilon$, then it is necessary to synchronize $3m + 1$ times as often with Algorithm CNV than with the interactive consistency algorithms. For example, if $m = 2$, $\epsilon = 2$ microseconds, $\rho = 10^{-6}$, and $\delta = 50$ microseconds—values that are reasonable for process-control systems in which one process can directly read another's clock—we obtain the following resynchronization intervals R:

$$\text{Algorithm CNV: } 3.1 \text{ seconds,}$$
$$\text{Algorithm COM: } 18 \quad \text{seconds.}$$

We suspect that in most applications, Algorithm CNV will provide sufficiently short resynchronization times.

We have assumed a system in which each process can communicate with all the others, and have considered only process failure, not communication failure. Our interactive consistency algorithms can be generalized to incompletely connected networks of processes. In the same way that Algorithm COM was derived from Algorithm OM(m), Algorithm OM(m, p) of [6] and the algorithm of [1] can be used to obtain clock synchronization algorithms for incompletely connected networks. Algorithm CSM also works, with obvious modifications, in the more general case. It can be shown that for a network of diameter d, Algorithm CSM(m) satisfies Theorem 4 except with the maximum number of faulty processes reduced to $m - d + 1$.

530

In algorithms not using digital signatures, the failure of a communication line joining two processes must be considered a failure of one of the two processes. Indeed, a two-faced clock is perhaps more likely to be caused by communication failure than by failure of the clock itself. For Algorithm CSM, assuming that a faulty communication line cannot "forge" properly signed messages, a faulty communication line is equivalent to a missing one. Hence, Algorithm $CSM(m + d - 1)$ can handle up to m process faults plus any number of communication line failures, so long as the remaining network of nonfaulty processes and communication lines has diameter at most d.

Glossary

δ The maximum error in clock synchronization—Clock Synchronization Condition S1.

δ_0 The maximum initial difference between the values of different processes' clocks—A0.

ϵ The maximum error in reading clocks—A2.

γ The "normal" message-transmission time—A2'.

ρ The rate at which nonfaulty clocks can drift apart—Definition 1.

Δ_{qp} The difference between process q's clock and process p's clock, as read by p.

Σ The maximum amount by which a clock is advanced during resynchronization—Clock Synchronization Condition S2.

Ω Defined in Condition CC.

m The maximum number of faulty processes.

n The total number of processes.

R The length of a synchronization interval—that is, the time between successive clock resynchronizations.

$R^{(i)}$ The ith synchronization interval.

$S^{(i)}$ The period at the end of the ith synchronization interval during which the resynchronization algorithm is executed.

$T^{(i)}$ Ending time of the ith synchronization period.

ACKNOWLEDGMENTS. We wish to thank our fellow members of the SRI Computer Science Laboratory, especially Robert Shostak, for their assistance and encouragement, and Nancy Lynch for simplifying the proof of Lemma 6 and pointing out many flaws in an earlier version.

REFERENCES

1. DOLEV, D. The Byzantine Generals strike again. *J. Algor. 3*, 1 (1982), 14–30.
2. DOLEV, D., AND STRONG, R. Authenticated algorithms for Byzantine Agreement. *SIAM. J. 12*, 4 (Nov. 1983), 656–666.
3. HALPERN, J., SIMONS, B., AND STRONG, R. An efficient fault-tolerant algorithm for clock synchronization. IBM Tech. Rep. RJ-4094, IBM Thomas J. Watson Research Center, Yorktown Heights, N.Y., 1983.
4. LAMPORT, L. The implementation of reliable distributed multiprocess systems. *Comput. Netw. 2* (1978), 95–114.
5. LAMPORT, L. Using time instead of timeout for fault-tolerant distributed systems. *ACM Trans. Prog. Lang. Syst.*, to appear.
6. LAMPORT, L., SHOSTAK, R., AND PEASE, M. The Byzantine Generals problem. *ACM Trans. Prog. Lang. Syst. 4*, 3 (July 1982), 382–401.
7. PEASE, M., SHOSTAK, R., AND LAMPORT, L. Reaching agreement in the presence of faults. *J. ACM 27*, 2 (Apr. 1980), 228–234.
8. STRONG, H. R., AND DOLEV, D. Byzantine Agreement. In *Intellectual Leverage for the Information Society (Compcon)*. New York: IEEE Computer Society Press, pp. 77–82.

9. DOLEV, D., HALPERN, J. Y., AND STRONG, H. R. On the possibility and impossibility of achieving clock synchronization. In *Proceedings of 16th Annual ACM Symposium on Theory of Computing* (Washington, D.C., Apr. 30–May 2). ACM, New York, 1984, pp. 504–511.
10. WENSLEY, J., ET AL. SIFT: Design and analysis of a fault-tolerant computer for aircraft control. *Proceedings of the IEEE 66,* 10 (Oct. 1978).

RECEIVED JULY 1981; REVISED MARCH 1982, FEBRUARY 1984, AND JULY 1984; ACCEPTED AUGUST 1984

Probabilistic clock synchronization

Flaviu Cristian
IBM Almaden Research Center, 650 Harry Road, San Jose, CA 95120, USA

Flaviu Cristian is a computer scientist at the IBM Almaden Research Center in San Jose, California. He received his PhD from the University of Grenoble, France, in 1979. After carrying out research in operating systems and programming methodology in France, and working on the specification, design, and verification of fault-tolerant programs in England, he joined IBM in 1982. Since then he has worked in the area of fault-tolerant distributed protocols and systems. He has participated in the design and implementation of a highly available system prototype at the Almaden Research Center and has reviewed and consulted for several fault-tolerant distributed system designs, both in Europe and in the American divisions of IBM. He is now a technical leader in the design of a new U.S. Air Traffic Control System which must satisfy very stringent availability requirements.

Abstract. A probabilistic method is proposed for reading remote clocks in distributed systems subject to unbounded random communication delays. The method can achieve clock synchronization precisions superior to those attainable by previously published clock synchronization algorithms. Its use is illustrated by presenting a time service which maintains externally (and hence, internally) synchronized clocks in the presence of process, communication and clock failures.

Key words: Communication – Distributed system – Fault-tolerance – Time service – Clock synchronization

Introduction

In a distributed system, *external* clock synchronization consists of maintaining processor clocks within some given maximum derivation from a time reference external to the system. *Internal* clock synchronization keeps processor clocks within some maximum relative deviation of each other. Externally synchronized clocks are also internally synchronized. The converse is not true: as time passes internally synchronized clocks can drift arbitrarily far from external time.

Clock synchronization is needed in many distributed systems. Internal clock synchronization enables one to measure the duration of distributed activities that start on one processor and terminate on another processor and to totally order distributed events in a manner that closely approximates their real time precedence. To allow exchange of information about the timing of events with other systems and users, many systems require external clock synchronization. For example external time can be used to record the occurrence of events for later analysis by humans, to instruct a system to take certain actions when certain specified (external) time deadlines occur, and to order the occurrence of related events observed by distinct systems.

This paper proposes a new approach for reading remote clocks in networks subject to unbounded random message delays. The method can be used to improve the precision of both internal and external synchronization algorithms. Our approach is *probabilistic* because it does not guarantee that a processor can always read a remote clock with an a priori specified precision (such a guarantee cannot be provided when there is no bound on message delays). However, by retrying a sufficient number of times, a process can read the clock of another process with a given precision with a probability as close to one a desired. An important characteristic of our method is that when a process succeeds in reading a remote clock, it *knows* the actual reading precision achieved.

The use of the remote clock reading method is illustrated by describing a distributed time service which maintains externally synchronized clocks despite process, communication and clock failures. The service is implemented by a group of time servers which execute a simple probabilistic clock synchronization protocol. After presenting the protocol and its performance, we conclude by comparing it with other published clock synchronization protocols.

Message delays

To synchronize the clocks of their host processors, time server processes communicate among themselves by sending messages via a communication network. Since there is a one to one correspondence between time server processes and processors, we do not distinguish between processes and processors. For example, when we say "the clock of process P" we mean "the clock of the processor on which P runs".

In distributed systems the task of synchronizing clocks is made difficult (among other things) by the existence of unpredictable communication delays. Between the moment a process P sends a message to a process Q and the moment Q receives the message, there is an arbitrary, *random* real time delay. A minimum min for this delay exists. It can be computed by counting the time needed to prepare, transmit, and receive an empty message in the absence of transmission errors and any other system load. In general, one does not know an upper bound on message transmission delays. These depend on the amount of communication and computation going on in parallel in the system, on the possibility that transmission errors will cause messages to be retransmitted several times, and on other random events, such as page faults, process switches, the establishment of new communication routes, or a freeze of the activity of a process caused by a human operator who pushes the 'halt' button on the panel of the processor hosting that process.

Measurements of process to process message delays in existing systems indicate that typically their distribution has a shape resembling that illustrated in Fig. 1. This distribution has a maximum density at a mode point between the minimum delay min and the median delay, usually close to min, with a long thin tail to the right. For instance, a sample measurement of 5000 message round trip delays between two light-weight MVS processes (running on two IBM 4381 processors connected via a channel-to-channel local area network) performed at the Almaden Research Center (Dong, private communication, June 1988), indicates a median round trip delay of 4.48 ms situated between a minimum delay of 4.22 ms and an average observed delay of 4.91 ms. While the maximum observed delay in this experiment (during which no route changes or 'halt' button pushes occurred) was very far at the right: 93.17 ms, 95% of all observed delays were shorter than 5.2 ms.

Previous work

Most published clock synchronization algorithms (e.g., Cristian et al. 1985; Dolev et al. 1984; Lamport 1987; Lamport and Melliar-Smith 1985; Lundelius-Welch and Lynch 1988; Schneider 1987; Srikanth and Toneg 1987) assume the existence of an upper bound max on real time message transmission delays. If the delays experienced by delivered messages are smaller than max with probability 1, these algorithms keep clocks within a maximum relative deviation greater than max-min with probability one. It is known (Lundelius and Lynch 1984) that the closeness with which clocks can be synchronized with certainty (i.e., with probability one) is limited: n clocks cannot be synchronized with certainty closer than $(\text{max}-\text{min})(1 - 1/n)$, even when no failures occur and clocks do not drift.

Other authors (e.g., Gusella and Zatti 1987; Marzullo 1984) adopt the premise that message delays are unbounded, and use as upper bounds on synchronization message delays the timeout delays employed for detecting communication failures between processes. Such timeouts are introduced by system designers to prevent situations in which some process P waits forever for a message from another process Q that will never arrive (for example because of a failure of Q). Since message delays are unbounded, it is understood that a small percentage of messages may need more than a given timeout delay to travel between processes, i.e., there is a chance that "false" communication failures are detected. This is the price paid for letting systems

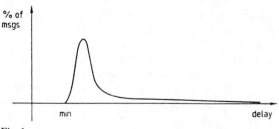

Fig. 1

subject to unbounded message transmission delays continue to work despite process failures and message losses. To reduce the likelihood of "false" alarms, a timeout delay is conservatively estimated from network delay statistics to ensure that message delays are smaller than the chosen timeout with a very high probability p (typically $p > 0.99$). If such a timeout delay is denoted by "maxp", the best synchronization precision achievable by the algorithms proposed in Gusella and Zatti (1987) and Marzullo (1984) can be characterized as being 4(maxp-min).

Assumptions on clocks, processes, and communication

Each time server process has access to the hardware clock H of its host processor. To simplify our presentation, we assume these clocks have a much higher resolution than the time intervals (e.g., process to process communication delays) which must be measured. For example, if the delays observable are of the order of milliseconds, we assume the hardware clocks have a microsecond resolution. A clock H is *correct* if it measures the length $t - t'$ of any real time interval $[t', t]$ with an error of *at most* $\rho(t - t')$, where ρ is the maximum clock drift rate from external (or real) time specified by the clock manufacturer:

$$(1 - \rho)(t - t') \leq H(t) - H(t') \leq (1 + \rho)(t - t'). \quad (C)$$

In the above formula, it is implicit that the delay $t - t'$ is long enough so that the worst case error in measuring its length caused by the discrete clock granularity is negligible compared to that due to drift. For most types of quartz clocks, the constant ρ is of the order of 10^{-6}. For example the worst actual drift rate measured for the microsecond resolution clocks existing on the IBM 4381 processors in our laboratory is $6 * 10^{-6}$ (Dong, private communication, June 1988). Since ρ is such a small quantity, we ignore in this paper terms of the order of ρ^2 or smaller (e.g., we equate $(1 + \rho)^{-1}$ with $(1 - \rho)$ and $(1 - \rho)^{-1}$ with $(1 + \rho)$). A clock *failure* occurs if the clock correctness condition (C) is violated. Examples of clock failure types are: crash failures (i.e., the clock stops), timing failures (e.g., a change in the frequency of the quartz oscillator driving the clock counter causes the clock value to be incremented too fast or too slowly), and arbitrary, or Byzantine, failures (e.g., the clock counter displays a nonmonotonic time because some of its bits are stuck at 0 or at 1). To simplify our presenta-

tion, we assume initially that processor clocks are correct. We relax this assumption later, by showing how one can detect and handle arbitrary clock failures.

We assume that message delays between processes are *unbounded*. As we will see later, the closer the distribution of such delays resembles that illustrated in Fig. 1 (i.e., the closer the median delay is to min), the better our probabilistic clock synchronization algorithms perform. What is remarkable, however, is that their correctness *does not* depend on any assumption about the particular shape of the message delay density function. We also assume that, to let processes continue to work despite process failures or message losses, a timeout delay maxp is chosen. The adoption of such a timeout delay divides observable network behaviors into two classes. A communication path (P, Q) between processes P and Q is said to function *correctly* if any message sent by P is delivered uncorrupted to Q within maxp time units. If a message accepted at one path end is never delivered at the other end or is delivered after more than maxp time units, the path suffers a late timing or *performance failure* (Cristian et al. 1985). We assume that communication channels between processes can only be affected by performance failures.

Processes undergo state transitions in response to message arrivals and timeout events generated by timers. To simplify our presentation we assume that between the occurrence of a timeout and the invocation of the associated timeout handler there is a null (process scheduling) delay and that process timers advance at the same rate as the clocks of the underlying processors. Thus, a correct process which at real time t sets a timer to measure W time units, is awakened in the real time interval $[t + (1 - \rho)W, t + (1 + \rho)W]$. We say that a process behaves *correctly* if in response to trigger events (such as message arrivals or timeout occurrences) it behaves in the manner specified. The specification prescribes the state transitions which should occur as well as the time intervals within which these transitions should occur. If, in response to some trigger event, a process never performs its specified state transition or undergoes it too early or too late (i.e., outside the time interval specified), the process is said to suffer a *timing failure* (Cristian et al. 1985). Processes which crash, omit to send certain messages, respond too slowly to trigger events (because of excessive load or slow timers), or time out too early (because of timers running at speeds greater than $1 + \rho$) are examples of timing failures. We assume that processes can suffer only *timing* failures.

Attempting to read a remote clock

To read the clock of a process Q, a process P sends a message ("time = ?") to Q. When Q receives the message it replies with a message ("time = ", T) where T is the time on Q's clock. If P does not receive a reply because of a failure, its attempt at reading Q's clock fails. Assume that P receives a reply and let D be half of the round trip delay measured on P' clock between the sending of the ("time = ?") message and the reception of the ("time = ", T) message.

Theorem. *If the clocks of processes P and Q are correct, the value displayed by Q's clock when P receives the ("time = ", T) message is in the interval $[T + \min(1-\rho), T + 2D(1+2\rho) - \min(1+\rho)]$.*

Proof. Let t be the real-time when P receives the ("time = ", T) message from Q and $C_Q(t)$ be the value displayed by Q's clock at that time. Let $\min + \alpha, \min + \beta, \alpha \geq 0, \beta \geq 0$, be the real time delays experienced by the ("time = ?") and ("time = ", T) messages, respectively, and let $2d$ be the real time round trip delay:

$$2d = 2\min + \alpha + \beta. \tag{1}$$

Since α and β are positive, (1) implies:

$$0 \leq \beta \leq 2d - 2\min. \tag{2}$$

From the definition of β, and the fact that Q's clock can run at any speed in the interval $[1-\rho, 1+\rho]$, we can infer that, at real time t, Q's clock satisfies the condition:

$$C_Q(t)\{[T + (\min + \beta)(1-\rho), T + (\min + \beta)(1+\rho)]. \tag{3}$$

By combining (2) and (3) we obtain:

$$C_Q(t) \in [T + \min(1-\rho), T + (2d - \min)(1+\rho)]. \tag{4}$$

Since the clock that P uses to measure the round trip delay can drift at a rate of at most ρ from real time, it follows that

$$d \leq D(1+\rho). \tag{5}$$

By substituting (5) into (4) we get (after some simplifications):

$$C_Q(t) \in [T + \min(1-\rho), \\ T + 2D(1+2\rho) - \min(1+\rho)]. \quad \square \tag{6}$$

The above theorem indicates that P can determine an interval which contains Q's clock value if *it measures* the round trip delay $2D$. Since possible scenarios such as $\alpha = 2(d - \min), \beta = 0$ and $\alpha = 0, \beta = 2(d - \min)$ are indistinguishable to P, and we

assume that P does not know the drift rate of Q's clock or its own clock, the value $C_Q(t)$ can be *any* point in this interval. In other words: $[T + \min(1-\rho), T + 2D(1+2\rho) - \min(1+\rho)]$ is the *smallest* interval which P can determine in terms of T and D that covers Q's clock value.

Since P has no means of knowing exactly where Q's clock is in the interval (6), the best it can do is to *estimate* $C_Q(t)$ by a function $C_Q^P(T, D)$ of what *it knows*, that is, T and D. In doing so, the actual error that P makes is:

$$|C_Q^P(T, D) = C_Q(t)|.$$

P minimizes the maximum error it can make in estimating $C_Q(t)$ by choosing $C_Q^P(T, D)$ to be the *midpoint* of the interval (6):

$$C_Q^P(T, D) \equiv T + D(1+2\rho) - \min \rho. \tag{7}$$

For this choice of $C_Q^P(T, D)$, the maximum error e that P can make when reading Q's clock is half the length of the interval (6):

$$e = D(1+2\rho) - \min. \tag{8}$$

Any other estimate choice leads to a bigger maximum error. We refer to the expression (7) as "P's reading of Q's clock" and to (8) as "P's reading error" or "P's reading precision".

Reading a remote clock with a specified precision

Formula (8) can be interpreted as follows: the shorter the round trip delay is, the smaller P's error in reading Q's clock is. Thus, if P wants to achieve a reading error smaller than a certain specified maximum error (or precision) ε, it must *discard* any reading attempt for which it measures an actual round trip delay greater than $2U$, where

$$U = (1 - 2\rho)(\varepsilon + \min). \tag{9}$$

Indeed, by (8), such clock readings can lead to actual reading errors greater than ε. For this reason, we call a round trip delay smaller than $2U$ *successful*, and refer to $2U$ as the *timeout delay* necessary for achieving the reading precision ε. When the process P observes a successful round trip, we say that it *reaches rapport* with Q.

The closer U is to min, the better P's reading precision is. However, since in the worst case P's timer can run at a rate as fast as $1 + \rho$, P must chose a timeout delay greater than

$$U_{\min} = \min(1+\rho), \tag{10}$$

to ensure that between the sending of a message and its reception there is a real time delay of at least min. To achieve the best possible precision for which there exists a positive probability of rapport, P must chose a timeout delay as close to U_{min} as possible. For such a limit timeout delay, formula (8) implies that the best reading precision achievable by a clock reading experiment is

$$e_{min} = 3\rho \text{ min.} \tag{11}$$

The first two ρs correspond to the relative drift between Q's clock and P's clock while the ("time = ", T) message travels between Q and P, and the third ρ corresponds to P's error in setting its timeout delay so that it measures at least min real time units.

Let p be the probability that P observes a round trip delay greater than $2U$. The larger U is, the smaller p will be. Conversely, the smaller U is, the larger p will be. Thus, there exists a *fundamental trade-off* between the precision achievable when attempting to read a remote clock and the probability $1 - p$ of success. The better the desired precision is, the smaller is the probability of success. Conversely, the worse the precision is, the greater is the probability of success. In the limiting case, if a maximum real time message delay max is known, by settling for a remote clock reading precision of $\max(1 + 3\rho) - \min$ (corresponding to a timeout delay of $\max(1 + \rho)$), one obtains a *deterministic* remote clock reading algorithm (similar to the ones used by the synchronization algorithms presented in Cristian et al. (1986), Dolev et al. (1984), Lamport (1987), Lamport and Melliar-Smith (1985), Lundelius-Welch and Lynch (1988), and Srikanth and Toueg (1987)) which *always* achieves rapport. The price for such a choice is poor precision.

Consider now a certain specified precision ε and the associated probability p that a reading attempt fails. For this precision, the probability that process P reaches rapport with process Q can be increased if *several* clock reading attempts are allowed before P gives up. To achieve a certain degree of independence between successive attempts, these should be separated by a minimum waiting delay W. This delay must be chosen so as to ensure that if P and Q stay connected and correct, then any transient network traffic bursts that may effect their communication disappear within W clock time units with high probability. (A solution to the problem of how to adapt to slower, nonbursty, network load changes is sketched later.) To avoid P attempting, ad infinitum, to read Q's clock when Q is permanently partitioned from P or has crashed, one must decide on a maximum value k for the number of successive attempts that P is allowed

to make. For a given choice of k, allowing for up to k reading attempts increases the probability of success to $1 - p^k$. Since $p < 1$, this probability can be made arbitrarily close to 1 by choosing a sufficiently large k.

For large values of k and a choice of W that ensures independence between successive reading attempts, Bernoulli's law yields that the average number of reading attempts needed for achieving rapport is $(1 - \rho)^{-1}$. Since each attempt costs two messages, it follows that the average number of messages $\bar{n}$ for achieving rapport is

$$\bar{n} = \frac{2}{(1-p)}. \tag{12}$$

Formulae (8) and (12) indicate the existence of a *continuum* of different clock reading algorithms indexed by different timeout delays U: from aggressive but risky algorithms indexed by U's close to min which are capable of achieving high precisions by possibly using a very large number of messages, to low risk "deterministic" algorithms indexed by U's close to max which achieve poor precisions by using a small number of messages.

A distributed time service

The probabilistic clock reading method described above can be used to improve the precision achievable by most of the internal clock synchronization algorithms surveyed in Schneider (1987) by letting time servers read probabilistically the remote clock values used as inputs to the convergence functions mentioned there. Instead of exploring this avenue, we devote the rest of the paper to describing a simple distributed time service which provides external clock synchronization.

The goal is to keep clocks synchronized to an official source of external time signals, such as the Universal Time Coordinated (UTC) signals broadcast by the WWV radio station of the National Bureau of Standards. Commercially available receivers (e.g., Kinemetrics/Truetime 1987) can receive such signals. The receivers can be attached to processors via dedicated busses. To guard against a physical receiver failure, it is possible to pair physically independent receivers into a *self-checking* receiver unit, by continuously comparing their results, and interpreting any disagreement among them as a failure of the pair (Kinemetrics/Truetime 1987). If no multiple failures occur, a self-checking receiver either displays correctly the external time or signals an error. We assume that all radio receivers used by the time service are self-checking. We also assume that, for reasons of economy, only certain processors, called *masters*, have time receivers attached to them. The other processors are referred to as *slaves*. To simplify our presentation we initially assume the existence of a unique, continuously available, master time source. Issues related to the implementation of this master time source by a group of redundant physical masters are discussed later. To further simplify the presentation, we do not distinguish between real (or atomic) time and astronomical UTC time, that is, we ignore problems related to the existence of yearly UTC time discontinuities known as "leap seconds". (For a discussion of the differences between these two time references, see Kopetz and Ochsenreiter (1987)). We furthermore assume that the official source of external time is reliable and that its signals are always available for reception by the radio receivers attached to master processors. The investigation of the issues related to maintaining synchronization in the presence of erroneous external time signals or in the absence of such signals constitutes a research topic in its own right.

Continuously adjustable clocks

Some processor architectures enable the speed of a hardware clock to be changed by software while others do not. Since the former make clock management dependent on the particular commands available for changing clock speeds, in this paper we chose to discuss the latter alternative. To compensate for the fact that the speed of a hardware clock H is not adjustable, a logical clock C with adjustable speed is implemented in software. The value of C is defined as the sum of the local hardware clock H and a periodically computed adjustment function A:

$$C(t) \equiv H(t) + A(t).$$

To avoid logical clock discontinuities (i.e., jumps) A must be a continuous function of time. For simplicity we consider only linear adjustment functions

$$A(t) = m * H(t) + N,$$

where the m and N parameters are computed periodically as described below. If, at local rapport time L, a slave estimates that the master clock displays time M, $M \neq L$, the goal is to increase (if $M > L$) or decrease (if $M < L$) the speed of the slave clock C so that it will show time $M + \alpha$ (instead of $L + \alpha$) α clock time units after rapport, where α is a positive clock *amortization* parameter. Since at the beginning and end of the amortization peri-

od the slave clock displays the values $L = H(1 + m) + N$ and $M + \alpha = (H + \alpha)(1 + m) + N$, respectively, where H is the hardware clock value at rapport, by solving the above system of equations we conclude that the parameters m, N must be set to

$$m = (M - L)/\alpha, \qquad N = L - (1 + m) * H \qquad \text{(A)}$$

for the α clock time units following rapport. After the α amortization period elapses, at local time $L' = M + \alpha$, the slave clock C can be allowed to run again at the speed of the local hardware clock until the next rapport by setting m to 0 and (to ensure continuity of C) N to $L' - H'$, where H' is the value displayed by the hardware clock at the end of the amortization period.

The master-slave synchronization protocol

The time service is implemented by a group of distributed time server processes, one per correctly functioning processor in the system. The master server running on the master processor M keeps the master logical clock C_M within a maximum deviation em (external-master) of external (or real) time. A slave server S keeps its logical clock C within a maximum deviation ms (master-slave) from the master clock. In this way the maximum deviation es of a slave from external time will be $em + ms$ and the maximum relative deviation of two slaves will be $ss = 2ms$.

Since the protocol used for synchronizing a master clock to the clock of an attached self-checking receiver is similar to that used for synchronizing a slave clock to a master clock, we only describe the latter in detail. The main difference between the two protocols lies in the variability of observed round trip delays. While a variability of the order of milliseconds is reasonable for master slave communications, variabilities much smaller can be achieved for the communication between a master time server and the self-checking receiver attached via a dedicated bus (for instance by ensuring that the master server does not relinquish control of the master CPU during a receiver clock reading attempt). By formula (8) this yields a very high receiver clock reading precision. If this high reading precision is supplemented by the adoption of a high master clock resynchronization frequency, the em constant can be kept so small that it is reasonable to assume in what follows that a master clock runs at the same speed as the external time.

The absence of master drift, the fact that for current local area network technology round trip delays smaller than 10 s are the rule, and that a drift rate ρ of the order of 10^{-6} or less makes terms of the form $d\rho$-where d is a round trip delay-insignificant, allows us to simplify the formulae (6)–(9) as follows. When a slave S receives a successful round trip of length $2D$ from the master M, the master clock C_M is in the interval $[T+\min, T+2D-\min]$:

$$C_M(t) \in [T+\min, T+2D-\min]. \qquad (6')$$

By estimating the value of the master clock as being the midpoint of this interval

$$C_M^S(T, D) \equiv T + D \qquad (7')$$

the maximum reading error that S can make is

$$e = D - \min. \qquad (8')$$

The protocol followed by a slave S relies upon the above simplified formulae. The remainder of this section presents this protocol informally and analyzes its behavior. A detailed description is given in the Appendix.

To keep synchronized with a master, a slave S attempts periodically to reach rapport. Each attempt at rapport consists of at most k attempts at reading the master clock, where successive reading attempts are separated by W clock time units. We assume $W > 2U$, i.e., a slave knows whether its previous reading attempt has succeeded when it is time to try again reading. If during an attempt to reach rapport all k reading attempts fail, S must leave the group of synchronized slaves (such a departure can be followed by a later rejoin). Consider now that one of the reading attempts results in a round trip delay $2D < 2U$ allowing S to reach rapport with M. At rapport, the speed of the slave logical clock C is set according to the equations (A) for the next t_α real time units, $(1-\rho)\alpha \le t_\alpha \le (1+\rho)\alpha$, so that during amortization, say t real time units after rapport, $0 \le t \le t_\alpha$, the worst case distance d between the slave clock C and the master clock is

$$d = (1 - t/t_\alpha) ms + t/t_\alpha e + \rho t, \qquad (9')$$

where e is the reading error and ms is the worst case distance between C and C_M at rapport. The term ρt in (9') reflects the fact after rapport the slave clock C continues to drift from C_M. During amortization d is required to stay smaller than ms, i.e.,

$$(1 - t/t_\alpha) ms + te/t_\alpha + \rho t \le ms. \qquad (10')$$

By rewriting (10') we get

$$e + \rho t_\alpha \le ms. \qquad (11')$$

We show later that if amortization ends before a next attempt at rapport, (11') is satisfied.

Since the slave clock continues to drift from the master clock after amortization ends, it follows that for any $t \ge t_\alpha$, the distance between C and C_M can be as large as $e + \rho t$. To keep C and C_M within ms of each other, i.e.,

$$e + \rho t \le ms, \qquad (12')$$

it is sufficient to ensure that after each rapport (with error e) the real time delay to the next rapport dnr is smaller than

$$dnr = \rho^{-1}(ms - e). \qquad (13')$$

If at most k reading attempts are allowed (during which the slave S can drift from the master by as much as $\rho k w$, where $w = (1+\rho)W$ is the maximum real time which can elapse between successive reading attempts), it follows that the maximum real time delay dna between a rapport and the next *attempt* at rapport must be

$$dna = \rho^{-1}(ms - e) - (1 + \rho)kW. \qquad (14')$$

Since S must measure this delay with its own timer (which can run as fast as $1 + \rho$), S must set the timer measuring the delay to the next attempt at rapport conservatively to

$$DNA = (1 - \rho)dna = \rho^{-1}(1 - \rho)(ms - e) - kW. \qquad (15')$$

Note that the time interval which elapses between a rapport and the beginning of the next attempt at rapport is *variable*, since it is a function of the round trip delay $2D$ observed at the last rapport. If D is close to min, the tight synchronization precision achieved allows the delay to the next attempt at rapport to be as long as:

$$DNA_{\max} = \rho^{-1}(1 - \rho)ms - kW. \qquad (16')$$

When rapport is achieved with a round trip delay that is barely acceptable (i.e., the reading error is close to $U - \min$) the delay to the next attempt can be as short as

$$DNA_{\min} = \rho^{-1}(1 - \rho)(ms + \min - U) - kW. \qquad (17')$$

We constrain amortization to end before a next attempt at rapport, i.e.,

$$\alpha \le DNA_{\min}. \qquad (18')$$

Condition (18') implies (11'), that is, if amortization ends before a next attempt at rapport then C and C_M stay within ms during amortization. To keep logical clocks monotonic, the amortization period must also be chosen so that the speed change parameter m of (A) satisfies the relation $m > -1$. For this, it is sufficient to chose α greater than $ms + U$

−min (see (23′) for more details). Since the amortization parameter α is positive

$$0 \leq \alpha. \tag{19′}$$

we infer from (17′) and (19′) that

$$ms \geq U - \min + \rho k (1 + \rho) W. \tag{20′}$$

Thus, for a given choice of the U, k, and W constants, the smallest master slave maximum deviation that can be achieved is

$$ms_{\min} = U - \min + \rho k (1 + \rho) W. \tag{21′}$$

For aggressive risky algorithms for which U is close to min, maximum deviations as small as $\rho k (1 + \rho) W$ can be achieved at the expense of many synchronization messages (recall ρ is of the order of 10^{-6}). For sure "deterministic" algorithms for which U is close to an assumed maximum delay max, we get synchronization precisions slightly worse than max − min with only two messages per synchronization, a result comparable to the precisions achievable by previously published deterministic synchronization algorithms (Cristian et al. 1986; Dolev et al. 1984; Lamport 1987; Lundelius and Lynch 1984; Lamport and Melliar-Smith 1985; Schneider 1987; Srikanth and Toueg 1987).

The clock reading method described naturally tolerates communication failures: up to $k - 1$ successive performance failures can be masked if they are followed by a successful rapport. The existence of variable delays between successive slave synchronizations is a useful property, since it will tend to uniformly spread the synchronization traffic generated by independent slaves in time.

Performance: two numerical examples

To illustrate the synchronization precisions achievable by our time service, we analyze in this section its performance in the context of a simple system of two 4381 processors (Dong, private communication, June 1988), assuming one plays the role of master and the other one the role of slave.

If we chose $2U$ to be the median round trip delay $2U = 4.48$ milliseconds, the probability p of an unsuccessful round trip is 0.5. By (12) this yields an average number $\bar{n}$ of messages per successful rapport of $\bar{n} = 4$. Assuming that a probability of losing synchronization of 10^{-9} is acceptable, we find that at least $k = 30$ successive attempts at rapport should be allowed $((0.5)^{30} < 10^{-9})$. Assuming a worst case drift rate of $\rho = 6 * 10^{-6}$, a waiting time constant between successive reading attempts W of 2 seconds, formulae (16′) and (17′) indicate that it is possible to achieve a maximum master

slave deviation ms of 1 millisecond. The minimum, average, and maximum delays between successive synchronization are 63, 67, and 108 seconds, respectively. Thus, for this choice of U, ρ, k, and W, a slave stays within a maximum deviation of $ms = 1$ millisecond from a master with probability greater than $1 - 10^{-9}$ by sending on the average $\bar{n} = 4$ messages every 1.11 minutes.

A more conservative choice of $2U' = 5.2$ milliseconds, yields a probability p' of an unsuccessful round trip of 0.05 and an average number $\bar{n}'$ of messages per successful rapport of 2.1. For this p', to achieve a probability of successful rapport greater than $1 - 10^{-9}$, k must be chosen to be at least 7 (i.e., $((0.05)^7 < 10^{-9})$). Since for this choice of U', the reading error is 0.98 milliseconds, we settle for the goal of achieving a maximum master slave deviation of $ms' = 2$ milliseconds. Assuming as in the previous example $\rho = 6 * 10^{-6}$, and $W = 2$ seconds, we find that to achieve the 2 milliseconds maximum deviation, a slave must on the average spend 2.1 messages to reach rapport with a master every 231 seconds (3.85 minutes). The minimum and maximum delays between successive resynchronizations are 230 and 273 seconds, respectively.

The above example precisions compare favorably with the best precision of at most 44.47 milliseconds achievable by the deterministic synchronization algorithms described in Cristian et al. (1986), Dolev et al. (1984), Lamport and Melliar-Smith (1985), Lundelius and Lynch (1984), Marzullo (1984), Schneider (1987), Srikanth and Toueg (1987).

Extensions

In this section we relax two of the assumptions made earlier: the existence of a continuously available master processor and the existence of reliable clocks that never fail. We also mention how to handle slave failures, how one can improve synchronization accuracy by taking advantage of past local clock drift statistics and how to adapt to a variable system load.

Dealing with master server failures

With a unique master server, the master time service fails when the unique process implementing it fails. The probability of a master service failure can be reduced if the service is implemented by a group of *redundant* master servers, all synchronized within em of external time. There are several ways in which such a group can be structured. We mention three alternatives.

Active Master Set. In this arrangement each slave multicasts ("time = ?") requests to all masters, each master answers each time request, and slaves pick up the first answer that arrives. With such a strategy, synchronized slaves will stay within $es = em + ms$ of external time, but since some slaves might be synchronized to one master, and some others to another, the relative deviation among slaves ss becomes $2es$, instead of $2ms$ as before. This solution leads to an increase in message cost: $2m$ messages per attempt at rapport, where m is the number of members in the master group. Note, however, that if all processors are on a broadcast local area network, this number can be reduced to $m + 1$.

Ranked Master Group. To reduce the message cost, one can use a synchronous membership protocol (Cristian 1988) to rank the group of active masters into a primary synchronizer, back-up, and so on. With such an arrangement slaves would send their requests only to the primary. This results in a message cost per attempt at rapport of 2. Let C be the upper bound on the failure detection time guaranteed by the synchronous master membership protocol (C is a function of the timeout delay maxp chosen for detecting communication failures (Cristian 1988)) and let A be the time needed to inform the slaves that all subsequent time requests should be sent to a new master. If W is chosen greater than $C + A$, a slave cannot distinguish between a master failure and an excessive synchronization message delay, so the maximum deviations es and ss stay as before, i.e., $es = em + ms$, $ss = 2es$. If W is chosen smaller than $C + A$, then one has to adopt a higher upper bound on the maximum number of successive attempts at rapport and the analysis of the probability of achieving rapport becomes slightly more complex.

Active Master Ring. A third solution would use a master membership protocol to order all active masters on a virtual ring. To send a time request a slave chooses an active master at random. If no answer arrives within $2U$, the slave asks the next active master on the ring, and so on. The message cost of each attempt at rapport is 2 as in the *Ranked Master Group* case, but the maximum deviations es and ss stay the same as in the *Active Master Set* architecture, irrespective of the relation between W and $C + A$, where A corresponds in this case to the worst case time needed to inform all slaves of a master group membership change.

Detecting clock failures

Let U_M, $\min_M$ be the parameters of the probabilistic algorithm run by a master M to synchronize its clock C_M to the clock C_R of its attached receiver R. The maximum difference which can exist between C_M and M's estimate of C_R at rapport is

$$maxadj_M = e_M + em. \tag{22'}$$

The first term $e_M = U_M - \min_M$ represents the maximum error in reading C_R while the second term accounts for the maximum distance which might exist between C_R and C_M at rapport. If a previously synchronized master M detects at rapport that the distance between C_M and its estimate of C_R is greater than $maxadj_M$, a master clock failure has occurred (recall our assumption that the source of external time signals is reliable and that receivers are self-checking). Upon detecting the failure of its local clock, a master server leaves the active master group after reporting the failure to an operator.

Similarly, if a master M and a slave S are correct and synchronized within ms, the maximum difference at rapport between the clock C of the slave and the slave's estimate of C_M is

$$maxadj_S = (U - \min) + ms + 2em. \tag{23'}$$

The last term is added because S can successively synchronize to different masters that are $2em$ apart from each other. A slave which at rapport detects that its clock is more than $maxadj_S$ apart from a master, detects either a master or a local clock failure. Assuming that masters synchronize more frequently than slaves, if a master clock failure has occurred, the master will detect the failure before the next rapport with the slave. Thus, a slave detects a local clock failure if it observes twice in a row that its distance to the same master clock is greater than $maxadj_S$. Upon detecting the failure of its clock, a slave leaves the group of synchronized time servers after reporting the failure to an operator.

Better bounds on the actual drift rate of a slave

The delay between successive resynchronizations of a slave (see (15')) can be increased by using better lower and upper bounds on the actual drift rate ρ_A of a slave's hardware clock than the manufacturer specified lower and upper bounds $-\rho, \rho$. This will have the desirable consequence of decreasing the number of messages which must be sent per slave per time unit for synchronization purposes.

It is possible to compute estimates of the actual drift rate ρ_A as well as upper and lower bounds for ρ_A under a variety of different assumptions. For example one might assume that ρ_A is a constant, or the ρ_A is a time varying function possessing a first derivative that is bounded by constant from above and below, etc. In what follows we limit ourselves to discussing the problem of approximating ρ_A and determining lower and upper bounds for it under the assumption that it is a constant.

By definition

$$\rho_A = \frac{H_i - H_0}{t_i - t_0} - 1$$

where t_i denotes the real time at which the i'th rapport is achieved, $i = 1, \ldots,$ and $H_i = H(t_i)$ denotes the value of the slave hardware clock at the i'th rapport. A slave can read H_i but cannot read t_i. It is however possible to estimate t_i as being the value displayed by the master clock at rapport: $M_i = T_i + D_i$, where T_i is the clock value sent by the master and D_i is half the round trip delay observed at the i'th rapport. In estimating t_i by M_i, a slave makes an error of at most $e_i = D_i - \min$, that is:

$$M_i - e_i \le t_i \le M_i + e_i.$$

The above set of inequalities ($i = 0, 1, \ldots$) implies

$$\frac{H_i - H_0}{M_i - M_0 + e_i + e_0} - 1 \le \frac{H_i - H_0}{t_i - t_0} - 1$$
$$\le \frac{H_i - H_0}{M_i - M_0 - e_i - e_0} - 1.$$

This leads us to define the i'th upper and lower bound drift estimates ρ_i^{max} and ρ_i^{min} as:

$$\rho_i^{max} = \min \left\{ \rho_{i-1}^{max}, \frac{H_i - H_0}{M_i - M_0 - e_i - e_0} - 1 \right\},$$

$$\rho_i^{min} = \max \left\{ \rho_{i-1}^{min}, \frac{H_i - H_0}{M_i - M_0 + e_i + e_0} - 1 \right\}$$

where $\rho_0^{max} = \rho$ and $\rho_0^{min} = -\rho$. These bounds on ρ_A can be used to compute a longer delay to the next attempt at achieving the $i + 1$'th rapport by using the formula (15'') below instead of (15'):

$$DNA_i' = \bar{\rho}_i^{-1} (1 - \bar{\rho}_i)(ms - e_i) - kW,$$
where $\bar{\rho}_i = \max \{ |\rho_i^{min}|, |\rho_i^{max}| \}.$ (15'')

Self-adjusting logical clocks

Since for each i, we know upper and lower bounds ρ_i^{max}, ρ_i^{min} on the actual drift rate ρ_A, it is natural to define the i'th estimate ρ_i of ρ_A as the midpoint of the interval $[\rho_i^{max}, \rho_i^{min}]$:

$$\rho_i \equiv \tfrac{1}{2}(\rho_i^{min} + \rho_i^{max}).$$

One can easily verify that

$$\lim_{i \to \infty} (\rho_i^{min} - \rho_i^{max}) = 0 \quad \text{and hence:} \lim_{i \to \infty} (\rho_A - \rho_i) = 0.$$

The successive estimates ρ_i of the actual drift rate ρ_A can be used to define a sequence of "virtual" hardware clocks $VH_i \equiv (1 - \rho_i)H$, such that when i increases to ∞ the speed of VH_i converges towards 1. Indeed, the drift rate $v\rho_i$ of VH_i is $v\rho_i = (\rho_A - \rho_i)$, and since ρ_i converges towards ρ_A, it follows that $v\rho_i$ converges towards 0. For this reason, we call the sequence of clocks VH_i self-adjusting.

Self-adjusting clocks not only improve the accuracy with which delays can be measured, but can also cause drastic reductions in the clock synchronization related message traffic. Define the i'th self-adjusting logical slave clock C_i as being $(1 + m)VH_i + N$ during the amortization period following the i'th rapport, and as VH_i between the end of the amortization and the $i + 1$'th rapport. To compute the delay between successive resynchronizations of C_i we need to know an upper bound $\overline{v\rho_i}$ for $|v\rho_i|$. This can be computed as follows. Since $\rho_i^{min} \le \rho_A \le \rho_i^{max}$, it follows that

$$\rho_i^{min} - \rho_i \le \rho_A - \rho_i \le \rho_i^{max} - \rho_i.$$

Thus,

$$|\rho_A - \rho_i| \le \max \{ |\rho_i^{min} - \rho_i|, |\rho_i^{max} - \rho_i| \}$$
$$= \tfrac{1}{2}(\rho_i^{max} - \rho_i^{min}) \equiv \overline{v\rho_i}.$$

By substituting $\overline{v\rho_i}$ for ρ in (15'), we get:

$$DNA_i'' = 2(\rho_i^{max} - \rho_i^{min})^{-1}$$
$$(1 - \tfrac{1}{2}(\rho_i^{max} - \rho_i^{min}))(ms - e_i) - kW. \quad (16'')$$

Note that since $\rho_i^{min} - \rho_i^{max}$ converges towards 0 as better estimates of the actual drift rates become known, the delays between successive resynchronizations can increase apparently without bound. In practice these delays have to stay bounded if one wants to ensure upper bounds on clock failure detection times by tests such as (23'). To determine the new resynchronization delays corresponding to the use of self-adjusting clocks, one might also want to take into account terms of the order of ρ^2 or smaller, ignored (for simplicity reasons) in this paper.

Dealing with slave server failures

A slow slave, which takes too long to read its messages or to time out, eventually discovers that the distance between its clock and a master clock has become unacceptable when it evaluates the test (23'). Early slave timing failures (e.g., caused by fast slave timers) lead to an increase in network synchronization traffic. The occurrence of such failures can be detected by the master group, if the masters keep track of the last time each slave has asked for the time. If a slave asks too often, the masters could simply ignore it. The faulty slave will then fail to synchronize and will eventually leave the group of synchronized servers.

Adapting to changing system load

Another extension consists in making the choice of the acutal U-indexed slave synchronization algorithm used in a system at a given moment dependent on the system load. We sketch here a possible way to take into consideration system load when deciding on a round trip acceptability threshold U. The intention is that U should increase when load increases and should decrease when load decreases. This can be achieved in the following way. If *at least one* slave experiences $k' < k$ successive unsuccessful attempts at reaching rapport with a master, it should announce to the master group that all slaves have to adopt a higher timeout delay $U'(U' > U)$ known in advance. The masters could then agree on this and diffuse a decision that beginning with some time in the future everybody has to switch to the new round trip acceptability threshold U' and, hence, to bigger master-slave maximum deviations. The effect will be to increase the maximum master slave clock deviation when the system load increases.

To decrease the maximum clock deviation when load is light, a slave processor could communicate to the master group the fact that it measures round trip delays that are consistently smaller than U'', for some $U'' < U$ known in advance. If the masters receive such messages from *all* slave processors, they could diffuse the information that beginning with some time in the future, everybody should decrease their round trip acceptability threshold to U''. The effect will be to decrease the master slave clock deviation when the system load decreases.

Conclusions

A new probabilistic approach for reading remote clocks was proposed and illustrated by presenting a synchronization algorithm that achieves external clock synchronization. The new approach allows one to achieve precisions better than the best precision bound $(max - min)(1 - 1/n)$ guaranteeable by previously published deterministic algorithms (Cristian et al. 1986; Dolev et al. 1984; Lamport 1987; Lundelius and Lynch 1984; Lamport and Melliar-Smith 1985; Lundelius-Welch and Lynch 1988; Schneider 1987; Srikanth and Toueg 1987). (Specialized hardware can be used to reduce the difference between max and min (Kopetz and Ochsenreiter 1987), but the inherent limitation of deterministic protocols remains unchanged.) When indexed by a conservative parameter U, such as a communication failure detection timeout delay maxp, our external clock synchronization algorithm also achieves a relative deviation at rapport $2(maxp - min)$ smaller than the best precision $4(maxp - min)$ achievable by previously published algorithms based on communication failure detection timeouts (Gusella and Zatti 1987; Marzullo 1984). One of the key observations of this paper is that no relation needs to exist between clock synchronization and communication detection timeout delays. Synchronization algorithms indexed by timeout parameters U close to min can in theory achieve synchronization precisions close to $3\rho min$, where ρ and min are of order of 10^{-6} and 10^{-3} seconds, respectively, for commercially available clocks and local area networks. One can envisage that by estimating actual clock drift rates and using self-adjusting clocks one could achieve precisions even better than the above bound.

Besides improving synchronization precision, the new approach has other properties worth mentioning. Since a probabilistic approach does not assume an upper bound on message transmission delays, it can be used to synchronize clocks in all systems, not only those which guarantee an upper bound on message delays. A probabilistic time service such as the one sketched previously distributes uniformly the clock synchronization traffic in time, avoiding the periodic synchronization traffic bursts produced by the existence of synchronization points in previously known synchronization algorithms. The service is simple to implement (see Appendix) and robust. Likely process and communication failures are tolerated. Clock failures are detected and processes with faulty clocks are shut down. Finally the time service described is efficient: it uses a number of messages that is linear in the number of processes to be synchronized.

While deterministic synchronization protocols *always* succeed in synchronizing clocks, the probabilistic approach proposed in this paper carries with it a certain *risk* of not achieving synchronization. In view of the impossibility result of Lundelius and Lynch (1984) that deterministic clock synchronization algorithms cannot synchronize the clocks of n processes closer than $(max - min)(1 - 1/n)$, this seems to be an unavoidable price for wanting to achieve a higher precision. As the desired precision becomes higher, more messages are sent and the risk of not achieving synchronization becomes higher. Conversely, as the desired precision becomes lower, the risk of not achieving synchronization becomes lower and fewer messages need to be sent. Actually, the U-indexed family of master-slave synchronization algorithms presented achieves a *continuum* between, at one end, sure "deterministic" protocols (indexed by large Us close to maxp or max) that achieve poor precision with a high probability and a small number of messages, and "aggressive" protocols (indexed by small Us close to min) capable of achieving very high precision but which carry with them a significant risk of not achieving synchronization even when substantial numbers of messages are exchanged. In practice, one needs to choose a parameter U that achieves the right balance between precision and message overhead, and reduces the risk of losing synchronization to a level that is acceptably small.

The new view cast on clock synchronization in this paper prompts a number of questions which can lead to further research. We mention here several. How is it possible to improve the accuracy of some of the internal clock synchronization algorithms surveyed in Schneider (1987) by using probabilistic remote clock reading methods? What lower bounds exist for probabilistic synchronization algorithms? How can the accuracy of clock synchronization be improved if one knows the distribution obeyed by message delays? How can one estimate bounds on the actual drift rate of hardware clocks if this rate is a function of time? And finally, how can one design algorithms which adapt to variable system load?

Acknowledgements. The idea that the randomness inherent in message transmission delays can be used to improve clock synchronization precision originated while the author was working with John Rankin and Mike Swanson on problems related to synchronizing the clocks of high end IBM processors in Poughkeepsie, NY, during February 1986. In the summer of 1987, John Palmer independently proposed a similar clock synchronization protocol for the high end Amoeba system prototype under development at the Almaden Research Center. The round trip delay measurements used in this paper were performed by Margaret Dong in the Amoeba system. Discussions with Danny Dolev, Frank Schmuck, Larry Stockmeyer, and Ray Strong helped improve the contents and the form of this exposition. The research presented was partially sponsored by IBM's Systems Integration Division group located in Rockville, Maryland, as part of a FAA sponsored project to build a new air traffic control system for the US.

References

Cristian F (1988) Reaching agreement on processor group membership in synchronous distributed systems. 18th Int Conf on Fault-Tolerant Computing, Tokyo, Japan (June 1988)

Cristian F, Aghili H, Strong R (1986) Approximate clock synchronization despite omission and performance failures and processor joins. 16th Int Symp on Fault Tolerant Computing, Vienna, Austria (June 1986)

Cristian F, Aghili H, Strong R, Dolev D (1985) Atomic broadcast: from simple message diffusion to Byzantine agreement. 15th Int Symp on Fault-Tolerant Computing, Ann Arbor, Michigan (June 1985)

Dolev D, Halpern J, Simons B, Strong R (1984) Fault-tolerant clock synchronization. Proc 3rd ACM Symp on Principles of Distributed Computing

Gusella R, Zatti S (1987) The accuracy of the clock synchronization achieved by tempo in Berkeley Unix 4.3 BSD. Rep UCB/CSD 87/337

Kinemetrics/Truetime (1986) Time and Frequency Receivers, Santa Rosa, California

Kopetz H, Ochsenreiter W (1987) Clock synchronization in distributed real-time systems. IEEE Trans Comput 36:933–940

Lamport L (1987) Synchronizing time servers, TR 18. DEC Systems Research Center, Palo Alto, California (June 1987)

Lundelius J, Lynch N (1984) An upper and lower bound for clock synchronization. Inf Control 62:190–204

Lamport L, Melliar-Smith M (1985) Synchronizing clocks in the presence of faults. J Assoc Comput Mach 32:52–78

Lundelius-Welch J, Lynch N (1988) A new fault-tolerant algorithm for clock synchronization. Inf Comput 77:1–36

Marzullo K (1984) Maintaining the time in a distributed system. Xerox Rep OSD-T 8401 (March 1984)

Schneider F (1987) Understanding protocols for Byzantine clock synchronization. TR 87-859, Cornell University (August 1987)

Srikanth TK, Toueg S (1987) Optimal clock synchronization. JACM 34:626–645

Appendix

Detailed description of the master slave protocol

A detailed description of a slave time server under the simplifying unique master assumption is given in Figs. 2 and 3. To simplify this presentation, we do not give a detailed description of the master time server, since it is similar to a slave server and we do not use self-adjusting logical slave clocks. In what follows, we refer to line j of Fig. i as $(i.j)$.

The round trip acceptability threshold U, the maximum number of successive reading attempts k, waiting time between reading attempts W, the amortization delay α, and the maximum deviation ms are parameters of the protocol (2.1). Once U is chosen, the probability p that, under worst case load conditions, a round trip delay is greater than $2U$ is also determined. The constant k must be chosen to ensure that the probability p^k of observing k successive round trip delays greater than $2U$ is acceptably small (typically two or more orders of magnitude smaller then the instantaneous crash rate of the underlying processor). We assume that the constant W is chosen greater than the acceptable round trip delay $2U$.

The slave protocol uses three timers (2.5): a "Synch" timer for measuring delays between successive synchronization attempts, an "Attempt" timer for measuring delays between successive master clock reading attempts, and an "Amort" timer

```
1    task Slave(U:Time, k:Int, W,α,ms:Time);
2    const min: Time;
3       master: processor;
4    var T,T',T'',D,N: Time; try: Integer; m: Real;
5       Synch,Attempt,Amort: Timer;
6       synchronized: Boolean; H: hardware-clock;

7    synchronized←false; Synch.set(0);
8    cycle
9       when lreceive("time?") do send-local-time;
10      when Synch.timeout
11      do try←1; T'←H;
12         send("time = ?",T') to master; Attempt.set(W);
13      when receive("time = ",ET,T'')
14      do if T' ≠ T'' then iterate fi;
15         T←H; D←(T−T')/2;
16         if D>U then iterate fi;
17         Attempt.reset; compute-adjustment;
18         Synch.set(ρ⁻¹(1−ρ)(ms + min − D)−kW);
19      when Attempt.timeout
20      do if try ≥ k then synchronized←false; "leave" fi;
21         try←try+1; T'←H;
22         send("time = ?",T') to master; Attempt.set(W);
23      when Amort.timeout do m←0; N←N−H;
24   endcycle
```

Fig. 2

for measuring amortization periods. There are two kinds of operations that are defined on a timer T: set and reset. The meaning of a

```
1    procedure send-local-time;
2       if synchronized
3       then lsend("time = ",H + N + m ∗ H)
4       else lsend("undefined")
5    fi;

6    procedure compute-adjustment;
7       if synchronized
8       then if ¬okadj then synchronized←false; "leave" fi;
9          m←((ET + D)−(T + N + m ∗ T))/α;
10         N←N − m ∗ T; Amort.set(α);
11      else m←0; N←(ET + D)−T;
12         synchronized←true;
13   fi;
```

Fig. 3

$T.set(\delta)$ invocation is "ignore all previous T.set invocations and signal a T.timeout event δ clock time units from now". The meaning of a T.reset invocation is "ignore all previous T.set invocations". Thus, if after invoking T.set(100) at local time 200, a new T.set(100) invocation is made a local time 250, there is no T.timeout event at time 300. If no other T.set or T.reset invocation is made before time 350, a T.timeout event occurs at local time 350.

A local Boolean variable "synchronized" (2.6) is true when the local clock is synchronized to the master clock and is false when the local clock can be out of synchrony with respect to the master clock. The local logical time is undefined when "syn-

chronized" is false (3.4). To prevent any confusion between messages pertaining to old and current clock reading attempts in the presence of performance failures each message is identified by the value of the local hardware clock H when the message is sent. This ensures that the identifiers of messages are unique with extremely high probability. For example, if we assume a typical hardware clock of 64 bits, the probability that some "old" message – still existing undelivered in the communication network because of a performance failure – is confused with a recently sent message by the test (2.14) is smaller than 5×10^{-18}, even if we make the unrealistic assumption that messages can stay undelivered in the network for all the time needed to wrap around a clock: approximately 58 centuries for a clock whose low level bit is incremented every micro-second. Another variable "try" counts the number of unsuccessful master clock reading attempts (2.4).

After initializing the "synchronized" local variable, an attempt to synchronize with the master is immediately scheduled (2.7). When the Synch.timeout event occurs (2.10), the counter for unsuccessful attempts "try" is initialized and a message identified by the local hardware clock value T' is sent to the master (2.12). The master responds to this message by sending its logical clock value (4.3). To simplify our presentation, we assume that a master clock is always synchronized to external time (the absence of synchrony with external time at the master can be handled in a manner similar to the absence of synchrony with the master at a slave). When a master response

```
1    task Master;
4       var N: Time; m: Real; H: Hardware-clock;

2    cycle
3       when receive ("time = ?", T) from s
4       do send("time = ",H + N + m ∗ H,T) to s
5    endcycle;
```

Fig. 4

arrives (2.13), if the received and locally saved message identifiers match (2.14) the message is accepted, otherwise it is discarded (the *iterate* command terminates the current iteration of the loop (2.8–2.24) and begins a new iteration). Unacceptably long round trips are discarded (2.16). Unsuccessful reading attempts cause Attempt.timeout events (2.19). Indeed, the "Attempt" timer is set by each new attempt at reaching rapport (2.12, 2.22) and is reset only when rapport is reached (2.17). If k successive unsuccessful attempts occur (2.20), a slave can no longer be sure that its clock is within ms from the master clock and must leave the group of synchronized slaves. Such a departure can be followed by a later rejoin.

Consider now that a matching answer which arrives in less than $2U$ time units leads to a successful rapport and causes the "Attempt" timer to be reset (2.17). If the slave logical clock was not previously synchronized, it is bumped to the estimate (7') of the master time (3.11). If the slave was previously synchronized, and the adjustment to be made passes the resonableness test "okadj" (3.8) defined in (23'), the speed of the local logical clock C is set so as to reach the slave's estimate of the master clock within α clock time units (3.9–3.10) following equation (A). After amortization ends (2.23) the logical slave clock is let again to run at the speed of the hardware clock until the next rapport (2.17).

An Upper and Lower Bound for Clock Synchronization*

JENNIFER LUNDELIUS AND NANCY LYNCH

*Laboratory for Computer Science, Massachusetts Institute of Technology,
Cambridge, Massachusetts 02139*

The problem of synchronizing clocks of processes in a fully connected network is considered. It is proved that, even if the clocks all run at the same rate as real time and there are no failures, an uncertainty of ε in the message delivery time makes it impossible to synchronize the clocks of n processes any more closely than $\varepsilon(1 - 1/n)$. A simple algorithm is given that achieves this bound.   ©1984 Academic Press, Inc.

1. INTRODUCTION

Keeping the local clocks of processes synchronized in a distributed system is important in many applications and is an interesting problem in its own right. In order to be practical, algorithms to synchronize clocks should be able to tolerate process failures, clock drift, and varying message delivery times. However, these conditions complicate the design and analysis of algorithms.

In this paper, we consider a simple special case of the general clock synchronization problem. Namely, we assume that clocks run at a perfect rate and that there are no failures. However, clocks initially have arbitrary values, and there is an uncertainty of ε in the message delivery time. For this case, once the clocks are synchronized, they will remain synchronized, so the only problem is to synchronize them in the first place.

We show that, even under these simplifying assumptions, no algorithm can synchronize clocks exactly. More precisely, we show that $\varepsilon(1 - 1/n)$ is a lower bound on how closely the clocks of n processes can be synchronized in this case. Since these are strong assumptions, this lower bound also holds for the more realistic case in which clocks drift and arbitrary faults occur. We show that the bound of $\varepsilon(1 - 1/n)$ is tight for the simplified case, by describing a simple algorithm that achieves this bound.

The problem of synchronizing clocks in a distributed system has been a topic of considerable research interest recently. Several algorithms have appeared in the literature (Halpern, Simons, and Strong, 1983; Halpern, Simons, Stong, and Dolev, 1984; Lamport, 1978; Lamport and Melliar-Smith, 1984; Lundelius and Lunch, 1984; Marzullo, 1983), each working under different assumptions. Dolev, Halpern, and Strong (1984) show that it is impossible to synchronize clocks if one third or more of the processes are subject to Byzantine failures. They also demonstrate a lower bound similar to ours (proved independently), but characterizing the closeness of synchronization obtainable along the real time axis. That is, they prove a lower bound on how close the real times can be when two processes' clocks have the same values whereas our result is a lower bound on how close the clock values can be at the same real time.

The remainder of the paper is organized as follows. Section 2 contains a description of the properties we require of our system model, and a statement of the clock synchronization problem of this paper. Section 3 contains the lower bound result, and Section 4 contains the corresponding upper bound. We conclude with an open question in Section 5.

* This work was supported in part by the NSF under Grant MCS83-06854, US Army Research Office Contracts DAAG29-79-C-0155 and DAAG29-84-K-0058, and Advanced Research Projects Agency of the Department of Defense Contract N00014-83-K-0125.

2. The Clock Synchronization Problem

2.1 *Systems of Processes with Clocks*

One way of presenting our results would be by using a specific formal model for systems of processes with clocks. However, the results of this paper are not dependent on the precise details of a particular model. Therefore, we do not give a complete description of a formal model in this paper; rather, we just state the properties which we require of such a model. We refer the interested reader to Lundelius and Lynch (1984) for a detailed development of a particular model for systems of processes with clocks; also, preliminary versions of the results of the present paper are given in terms of such a model in Lundelius (1984).

The system is assumed to consist of *n processes,* located at the vertices of a complete communication graph. All processes are assumed to know the size and topology of the network. Each process has a local "physical clock," whose value it can read. Processes communicate by sending and receiving messages.

We do not make many explicit assumptions about the form of a process. We presume that a process can be modelled as some kind of automaton, having state set, including initial and final states, and a transition relation, which defines the algorithm to be executed. However, processes might be deterministic or nondeterministic. They might be assumed to have significant or insignificant local processing time. They might buffer incoming messages until they are ready to process them, or they mighrt process incoming messages immediately. They might take steps only upon receipt of a message, or also upon discovering that their physical clocks have reached certain values, or at arbitrary times. Many other variations are possible, and our results will hold equally well for all of these cases.

We introduce some notation and definitions. Let P be a set of n processes. A *clock* is a monotone increasing function from $\mathbf{R}$ (real time) to $\mathbf{R}$ (clock time). In this paper, we assume that clocks do not drift; thus, we assume that all clock functions have derivative exactly 1 everywhere. A *system of processes with clocks* (or simply a *system*), denoted by $(P, \mathscr{C})$, is a set of processes P together with a set of clocks $\mathscr{C} = \{C_p\}$, one for each p in P. Clock C_p is called p's *physical clock.*

Each process' physical clock is assumed to be a fixed function, i.e., it cannot be modified by the process. We assume that processes do not have access to the real time; each process obtains its only information about time from its physical clock. Thus, a process' physical clock value might be used in its transition relation, but the real time cannot be so used. By modelling the clocks separately from the processes, we can study the effect of using different clock functions with the same set of processes.

2.2 *Executions*

In this subsection, we define the "executions" of a system of processes with clocks. We begin by defining executions for individual processes. The *events* which can occur at a process include the arrival of messages from other processes, as well as any significant events internal to the process. These events may cause the process to send messages to other processes. An *action* describes the changes made by a particular event to the processes' state. An *execution* of process p with clock C is a partial mapping from $\mathbf{R}$ (real time) to actions; the action for a given time describes the changes to p which occur at that time. Process executions are assumed to satisfy certain constrains, as given by the process model and the particular process definition.

An *execution* for a system $(P, \mathscr{C})$ of processes with clocks is a set of process executions, one for each process p in P, with clock C_p in $\mathscr{C}$, together with a one-to-one correspondence between the messages sent by p to q and the messages received by q from p, for any processe p and q. We use the message correspondence to define the *delay* of any message in a system execution, in the obvious way. For each system execution e, define *last-step* (e) to be the earliest time in e at which all processes are in final states. If there is no such time, then last-step (e) is undefined.

2.3 *Views and Equivalence*

As we have already stated, we are assuming that the processes do not have access to the real time, but only to their physical clock time. In the lower bound proof, we will consider different system executions that are indistinguishable to the processes because the events occur at the same physical clock times, although they might occur at different real times.

Thus, we define the *view* of any process p in any process execution e (for p with clock C), to be the actions in e, together with their physical clock times of occurrence. The real times of occurrence are not represented in the view. The notion of a view allows us to define a natural notion of equivalence for process executions. Define two process executions, one of process p with clock C and the other of process p with clock C', to be *equivalent* provided that the view of p is the same in both executions. We extend this definition to a definition of equivalence for system executions. Define two system executions, execution e of system $(P, \mathcal{C})$ and execution e' of $(P, \mathcal{C}')$, to be *equivalent* provided that for each prcess p, the component process executions for p in e and e' are equivalent. Thus, the executions are indistinguishable to the processes. Only an outside observer who has access to the real time can tell them apart.

2.4 *Shifting*

We introduce the notion of "shifting," both for a system execution and for a set of clocks. Shifting a system execution by some amount, relative to p, means modifying p's process execution so that every action for p occurs that amount earlier in real time. Shifting a set of clocks by some amount, relative to a process p, means adding that amount to the function that defines p's clock. We make assumptions which insure that, if an execution and a set of physical clocks are both shifted by the same amount relative to the same process, the resulting execution is equivalent to the original one. No process can tell the difference, because the change in the time of occurence of actions in the execution is compensated for by the chance in the physical clock.

We begin by defining a shift of a process execution and of a single clock. Given execution e of process p with clock C, and real number ζ, a new execution $e' = shift(e, \zeta)$ is defined by $e'(t) = e(t + \zeta)$ for all t. All actions are shifted earlier in e' by ζ if ζ is positive, and later by $-\zeta$ if ζ is negative. Given a clock C and real number ζ, a new clock $C' = shift(C, \zeta)$ is defined by $C'(t) = C(t) + \zeta$ for all t. The clock is shifted forward by ζ if ζ is positive, and backward by $-\zeta$ if ζ is negative.

We make the following important assumption.

AXIOM 1. *Let e be an execution of process p with clock C, and let ζ be a real number. Let $C' = shift(C, \zeta)$. Then $shift(e, \zeta)$ is an execution of p with clock C'.*

That is, if a process execution and physical clock are modified in corresponding ways, the result is also an execution. It is easy to see that this resulting execution must be equivalent to the original execution.

Now we define a shift of a system execution and of a set of clocks. Given execution e of system $(P, \mathcal{C})$ and real number ζ, a new execution $e' = shift(e, p, \zeta)$ is defined by replacing p's process execution in e, e_p, by $shift(e_p, \zeta)$, and by retaining the same correspondence between sends and receives of messages. (Technically, the correspondence is redefined so that a pairing in e that involves the event for p at time t, in e' involves the event for p at time $t - \zeta$). All actions for process p are shifted by ζ, but no other actions are altered. Given a set of clocks $\mathcal{C} = \{C_q\}_{q \in P}$ and real number ζ, a new set of clocks $\mathcal{C}' = shift(\mathcal{C}, p, \zeta)$, is defined by replacing clock C_p by clock $shift(C_p, \zeta)$. Process p's clock is shifted forward by ζ, but no other clocks are altered.

LEMMA 1. *Let e be an execution of system $(P, \mathcal{C})$, p a process and ζ a real number. Let $\mathcal{C}' = shift(\mathcal{C}, p, \zeta)$ and $e' = shift(e, p, \zeta)$. Then e' is an execution of $(P, \mathcal{C}')$, and e' is equivalent to e.*

Proof. The result follows immediately from the definition of a system execution, together with Axiom 1 and the immediately following remarks. ∎

The following lemma quantifies how message delays change when a system execution is shifted.

LEMMA 2. *Let e be an execution of system $(P, \mathcal{C})$, p a process, ζ real number. Let $\mathcal{C}' = shift(\mathcal{C}, p, \zeta)$ and $e' = shift(e, p, \zeta)$. Then when the obvious correspondence is made between messages in e and in e', all messages have the same delay in e' as in e, with the following two exceptions. If q is any process other than p, then*

(a) *the delay of any message from q to p is* ζ *less in e' than in e, and*

(b) *the delay of any message from p to q is* ζ *greater in e' than in e.*

Proof. Without loss of generality, asume ζ is nonnegative. Since all events for p happen ζ earlier in e' than in e, and since the correspondence between sends and receives is updated appropriately, messages are received ζ earlier (causing ζ less delay), and are sent ζ earlier (causing ζ greater delay). ∎

2.5 *Admissible Executions*

For the remainder of the paper, fix nonnegative values, ε, μ, and v such that $v - \mu = \varepsilon$. We say that a system execution e is *admissible* provided that for every p and q, every message in e from p to q has its delay in the range $[\mu, v]$. Thus μ is the smallest message delay, v is the largest delay, and the difference between them, ε, is the *message uncertainty*.

We note that our results would hold with almost identical proofs in the case where μ and v differ from link to link, as long as ε is the same. The restriction to uniform μ and v is made only for notational simplicity.

2.6 *Problem Statement*

Now we describe the particular clock synchronization problem which is considered in this paper. Assume that the system model is as described so far in this section. We consider only admissible executions, and we assume further that the processes have knowledge of the message delay bounds μ and v.

The processes are supposed to establish synchronization of their "local times." These local times are not the values of the physical clocks, since we assume that the physical clocks cannot be reset by the processes. Rather, each process obtains its notion of the local time by adding the value in a particular local variable CORR to the physical clock time. The process is able to modify the value in its CORR variable, so that during an execution, p's local variable CORR can take on different values. We assume that the value of CORR is 0 in any initial state, and cannot be changed after a process enters a final state. For a particular execution, we define a function $\text{CORR}_p(t)$, giving the value of p's variable CORR at time t. Then, for a particular execution, we define the *local time* for p to be the function L_p, which is given by $C_p + \text{CORR}_p$.

Since the processes have physical clocks which are progressing at the same rate as real time, the only part of the clock synchronization problem which is of interest is the problem of bringing the clocks into synchronization—once this has been done, synchronization is maintained automatically.

Since an algorithm is coded into the transaction function for a process, P is all that is needed to specify an algorithm. A clock synchronization algorithm P is said to *synchronize to within* γ if the algorithm terminates (i.e., all processes eventually enter final states), and after it terminates, the processes' local times differ by no more than γ. More precisely, we require that every admissible execution e for $(P, \mathcal{C}')$, for any set of clocks $\mathcal{C}'$, satisfies the following conditions:

(a) Termination. All processes eventually enter final states. Thus, last-step (e) is defined.

(b) Agreement. $|L_p(t) - L_q(t)| \leq \gamma$ for any processes p and q and time $t \geq$ last-step (e).

3. LOWER BOUND

In this section we show that no algorithm can synchronize n processes' clocks any more closely than $\varepsilon(1 - 1/n)$. The main idea of the proof is that different execution can be constructed that look the same to the processes but that result in different local times. We consider an arbitrary algorithm P that synchronizes clocks to within γ. We begin with an admissible execution of P that has a particular pattern of message delays, and then alter this execution by judicious shifting so that the resulting message delays are still within the allowable range (i.e., the result is another admissible execution), and so that no process can tell the difference (i.e., the old and new executions are equivalent). The equivalence implies an inequality concerning γ. By constructing n equivalent executions in this manner, n inequalities concerning γ are obtained. Solving the inequalities for γ produces the claimed lower bound.

THEOREM 3. *No clock synchronization algorithm can synchronize a system of n processes to within γ, for any* γ < ε(1 − 1/n).

Proof. Fix a set of processes P that synchronizes to within γ. We will show that $γ \geq ε(1 − 1/n)$.

Let P consist of processes 1 through n. We construct a sequence of systems $\mathscr{L}^i = (P, \mathscr{C}^i)$, for $1 \leq i \leq n$, and a corresponding sequence of executions e^i for those systems. All of the executions e^i will be equivalent to each other, and all will be admissible. Furthermore, in e^i, all messages sent by process i will have delay μ and all messages received by i will have delay v. The construction is carried out inductively on i.

Let $\mathscr{L}^1 = (P, \mathscr{C}^1)$, where $\mathscr{C}^1$ is an arbitrary set of clocks. Let e^1 be any execution of $\mathscr{L}^1$ in which all messages from process j to process k have delay exactly μ if $j < k$, and have delay exactly v if $j > k$. That is, messages from processes to higher-numbered processes take the minimum delivery time, while messages from processes to lower-numbered processes take the maximum delivery time. Clearly, e^1 is admissible, all messages sent by process 1 have delay μ, and all messages received by process 1 have delay v. (For the special case where $n = 4$, we represent the execution e^1 as in Fig. 1. There is a vertical line for each of the four processes. All the messages from j to k have the delay that labels the arrow from j to k.)

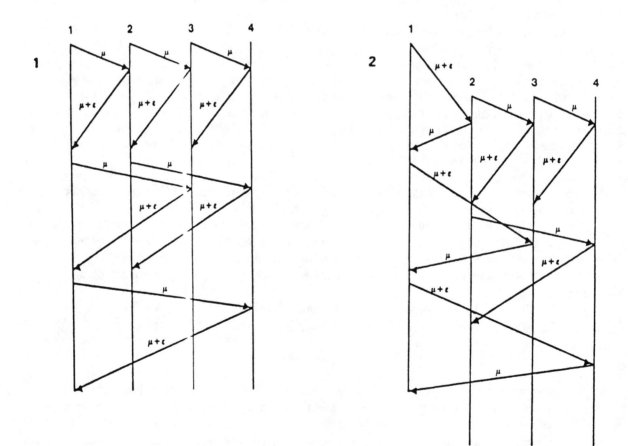

FIG. 1. Message delays for execution e^1 in the case $n = 4$.

FIG. 2. Message delays for execution e^2 in the case $n = 4$

550

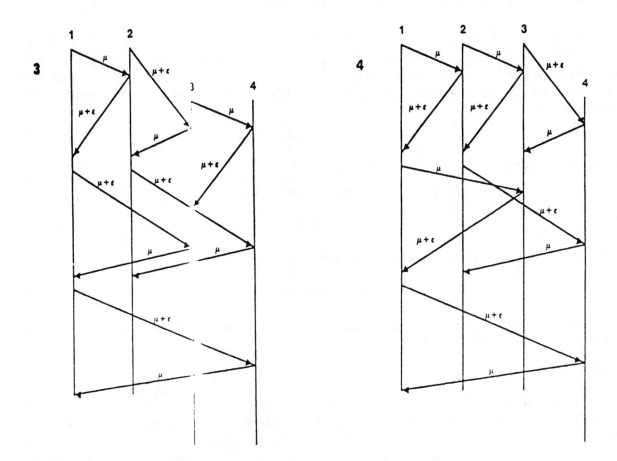

FIG. 3. Message delays for execution e^3 in the case $n = 4$.

FIG. 4. Message delays for execution e^4 in the case $n = 4$.

Now assume that $\mathscr{L}^{i-1}$ and e^{i-1} have been constructed for $2 \le i \le n$, and, furthermore, that e^{i-1} is admissible, and that, in e^{i-1}, all messages sent by process $i - 1$ have delay μ and all messages received by $i - 1$ have delay v. We construct $\mathscr{L}^i$ and e^i. Let $\mathscr{C}^i = \text{shift}(\mathscr{C}^{i-1}, i - 1, \varepsilon)$ and $\mathscr{L}^i = (P, \mathscr{C}^i)$. Let $e^i = \text{shift}(e^{i-1}, i - 1, \varepsilon)$. Thus, the ith execution is obtained from the $(i - 1)$th execution by shifting the execution and set of clocks by ε relative to process $i - 1$. (For the case of $n = 4$, the three executions e^2, e^3, and e^4 are depicted in Figures 2, 3, and 4.)

By Lemma 1 and the inductive hypothesis, e^i is an execution of $(P, \mathscr{C}^i)$, and is equivalent to e^{i-1}. We now argue that e^i is admissible. By Lemma 2, the only changes between e^{i-1} and e^i, are for messages involving process $i - 1$. Messages received by $i - 1$ take ε less time, so they have delay $v + \varepsilon = \mu$; messages sent by $i - 1$ take ε more time, so they have delay $\mu + \varepsilon = v$. These delays are in the specified range.

The last part of the induction is showing that in e^i all messages received by process i have delay v and all messages sent by process i have delay μ. Messages to and from a higher-numbered process have delays as in e^1, i.e., μ and v, respectively. All lower-numbered processes have been shifted by ε, so the delays, which were originally μ (for receiving) and v (for sending) have become $\mu + \varepsilon = v$ and $v - \varepsilon = \mu$, respectively.

Since e^1 is an admissible execution, it must terminate; let $t_f = \text{last-step}(e^1)$. By equivalence, all the e^i terminate, and the direction of the shifts implies that they all terminate by time t_f.

Let $V_1, ..., V_n$ by the values for the respoctive processes' local times at real time t_f, in execution e^1. Since the algorithm is assumed to synchronize to within γ, all of these values are within γ of each other. In particular,

$$V_n \leq V_1 + \gamma.$$

Now consider e^i, $1 < i \leq n$. Since e^i is equivalent to e^1, the correction variable for any process p is the same in both executions at real time t_f. This fact, together with the definition of $\mathcal{C}^i$, implies that in e^i, process $i - 1$'s local time at real time t_f is $V_{i-1} + \varepsilon$ and process i's local time at real time t_f is V_i. Since these values must be within γ of each other, we have

$$V_{i-1} \leq V_i + \gamma - \varepsilon.$$

Adding the n inequalities together and collecting terms, we have

$$\sum_{i=1\cdots n} V_i \leq \sum_{i=1\cdots n} V_i + n\gamma - (n-1)\,\varepsilon,$$

or

$$(n-1) \leq n\gamma.$$

In order for this inequality to hold, it must be the case that $i \geq \varepsilon\,(1 - 1/n)$. ∎

4. Upper Bound

In this section we show that the $\varepsilon(1 - 1/n)$ lower bound is tight, by exhibiting a simple algorithm which synchronizes the clocks within this amount.

4.1 Algorithm

There is an extremely simple algorithm that achieves the closest possible synchronization. Define δ to be $(\mu + v)/2$, the media message delay. As soon as each process p awakens, it sends its local time in a mesage to the remaining processes and waits to receive a similar message from every other process. Immediately upon receiving such a message, say from q, p estimates q's current local time by adding δ to the value received. Then p computes the difference between its estimate of q's local time and its own current local time. After receiving local times from all the other processes, p sets its correction variable to the average of the estimated differences (including 0 for the difference between p and itself).

We describe this algorithm below in pseudo-code. The particular language used can be translated unambiguously into the formal model of Lundelius and Lynch (1984); we refer the reader to that paper for more details. For this paper, we do not require the complete generality; thus, we just describe the meaning of the single program below.

The algorithm is interrupt-driven, where an interrupt can be either the arrival of a message or the arrival of a special START signal from the outside world. A *beginstep* (u) statement indicates the beginning of a step of the process, triggered by interrupt u. The step of the process continues (indivisibly), executing statements of the code just until the next *endstep* statement is reached. Then the process suspends execution until another interrupt arrives.

We assume that the state of a process consists of values for all the local variables, DIFF, SUM, RESPONSES, and CORR, together with a location counter which indicates the next beginstep statement (if any) to be executed. The initial state of a process consists of the value 0 for all the local variables, and the location counter positioned at the first beginstep statement of the program. Final states are those in which the location counter is at the end of the code. A step of the process involves receiving an interrupt, reading the local physical clock, carrying out some local computation (which can read and modify the variables and location counter in the process state), and perhaps sending some messages. NOW indicates the current local time.

Code For Process p:

```
beginstep (u)
send (NOW) to all q ≠ p
```

```
do forever
      if u = message V from process q then
              DIFF : = V + δ – NOW
              SUM : = SUM + DIFF
              RESPONSES : = RESPONSES + 1
              endif
      if RESPONSES = n – 1 then exit endif
      endstep
      beginstep(u)
      enddo

CORR : = CORR + SUM/n
endstep
```

For the remainder of the paper, fix P to be a set of n processes, each running the proceeding code.

4.2 *Correctness*

We will show that any admissible execution e of the algorithm synchronizes to within γ, where γ is fixed for this section as $\varepsilon(1 - 1/n)$. The upper bound is not quite as strange as it might look at first glance. It can be rewritten as $(2(\varepsilon/2) + (n - 2)\varepsilon)/n$, which is the average of the possible discrepancies between the estimates two particular process p and q can make, for the values of the physical clocks of all the processes. Processes p and q can agree on a clock value for p (or for q) to within accuracy at most $\varepsilon/2$ (giving the $2(\varepsilon/2)$ term, and can agree on a clock value for any other process r to within accuracy at most ε (giving the $(n - 2)\varepsilon$ term). Then the possible discrepancies are averaged, so the sum is divided by n.

We now give a careful analysis . Fix $\mathscr{C}$ to be an arbitrary set of physical clocks; we must show that $\mathscr{P} = (P, \mathscr{C})$ synchronizes to within γ. First, we define Δ_{pq}, the actual difference between the physical clocks of p and q, to be $C_p - C_q$. Since there is no drift in the clock rates, this difference is a well defined constant. Moreover, note the following.

LEMMA 4. *For any processes p, q, and r,*

    (a) $\Delta_{pp} = 0,$

    (b) $\Delta_{pq} = - \Delta_{qp},$

    (c) $\Delta_{pq} = \Delta_{pr} + \Delta_{rq}.$

Proof.   Immediate from the definition of Δ. ∎

Next, we define D_{pq}, the estimated difference between the physical clocks of p and q, as estimated by q. For $p \neq q$, let D_{pq} be the value of process q's local variable DIFF immediately after process p's message is handled by process q. It is easy to see that $D_{pq} = C_p(t) + \delta - C_q (t')$, where local time $L_p(t) + C_p(t)$ is sent by p at real time t and received by q at real time t'. Let $D_{pp} = 0$. We relate the estimates D to the actual differences Δ.

LEMMA 5. *Let p and q be processes. Then $\left| D_{pq} - \Delta_{pq} \right| \leq \varepsilon/2.$*

Proof. Suppose at real time t, p sends the value $C_p(t)$, which is received by q at real time t'. Then

$$
\begin{aligned}
|D_{pq} - \Delta_{pq}| &= | C_p(t) + \delta - C_q(t') - \Delta_{pq}| \\
&= | C_q(t) + \Delta_{pq} + \delta - C_q(t') - \Delta_{pq}|, \qquad \text{by definition of } \Delta_{pq}, \\
&= |C_q(t) + \delta - C_q(t')| \\
&= | \delta - (C_q(t') - C_q(t))| \\
&= | \delta - (t' - t)|, \text{ since the rate of clock } C_q \text{ is } 1, \\
&\leq \varepsilon 2, \qquad \text{ since } \delta - \varepsilon/2 \leq t' - t \leq \delta + \varepsilon/2. \qquad ∎
\end{aligned}
$$

The next lemma concerns the relationships between two processes' estimated differences and the actual differences.

LEMMA 6. *Let p, q, and r be processes. Then*

(a) $| (D_{pq} - D_{pr}) - \Delta_{rq}| \le \varepsilon$,

(b) $| (D_{pp} - D_{pr}) - \Delta_{rp}| \le \varepsilon/2$,

(c) $| (D_{pq} - D_{pp}) - \Delta_{pq}| \le \varepsilon/2$.

Proof.

(a)

$$|(D_{pq} - D_{pr}) - \Delta_{rq}| = | (D_{pq} - D_{pr}) - (\Delta_{pq} - \Delta_{pr}) |, \qquad \text{by Lemma 4,}$$
$$= | D_{pq} - \Delta_{pq}) - (D_{pr} - \Delta_{pr}) |$$
$$\le | D_{pq} - \Delta_{pq}| + | D_{pr} - \Delta_{pr}|$$
$$\le \varepsilon, \qquad \text{by two applications of Lemma 5.}$$

(b)

$$| (D_{pp} - D_{pr}) - \Delta_{rp}| \le | D_{pp} - \Delta_{pp}| + | D_{pr} - \Delta_{pr}|, \qquad \text{as in part (a),}$$
$$= 0 + | D_{pr} - \Delta_{pr}|,$$
$$\le \varepsilon/2, \qquad \text{by Lemma 5.}$$

(c) is similar to (b), and is left to the reader. $\blacksquare$

Here is the main result.

THEOREM 7 (Agreement). *Algorithm P guarantees clock synchronization to within* $\varepsilon(1 - 1/n)$.

Proof. Fix a set of clocks $\mathcal{C}$, and let $\mathcal{P} = (P, \mathcal{C})$. We must show that for any admissible execution e of $\mathcal{P}$, any two processes p and q, and any time t after last-step (e),

$$| L_p(t) - L_q(t) | \le \varepsilon(1 - 1/n).$$

Now

$$| L_p(t) - L_q(t) | = | (C_p(t) + \text{CORR}_p(t)) - (C_q(t) + \text{CORR}_q(t)) |$$
$$= | \Delta_{pq} - (\text{CORR}_q(t) - \text{CORR}_p(t))|$$
$$= | \Delta_{pq} - ((1/n) \sum_{r \in P} D_{rq} - (1/n) \sum_{r \in P} D_{rp})|,$$

by the way the algorithm works,

$$= (1/n) \left| n\Delta_{pq} - \sum_{r \in P} (D_{rq} - D_{rp}) \right|$$

$$= (1/n) \left| \sum_{r \in P} (\Delta_{pq} - (D_{rq} - D_{rp})) \right|$$

$$= (1/n) \left| \sum_{r \in P} ((\Delta_{rq} - \Delta_{rp}) - (D_{rq} - D_{rp})) \right|, \qquad \text{by Lemma 4,}$$

$$\le (1/n) \sum_{r \in P} | (\Delta_{rq} - \Delta_{rp}) - (D_{rq} - D_{rp}) |.$$

Now, the summation consists of n terms, each of which can be bounded using Lemma 6. The two terms for $r = p$ and $r = q$ are each bounded by $\varepsilon/2$, while the other $n - 2$ terms are each bounded by ε. Thus, the entire expression is

$$| L_p(t) - L_q(t) | \leq (1/n) (2\varepsilon/2 + (n - 2)\varepsilon)$$
$$= \varepsilon(1 - 1/n). \quad \blacksquare$$

4.3 *Validity*

There is one other property of the algorithm which is worth noting. Namely, it produces local times which are not very far from the values of the physical clocks of the processes. We make this condition more precise by defining a clock synchronization algorithm P to be α - *valid* provided that for every $\mathscr{C}$ and every admissible execution e for $(P, \mathscr{C})$, the following is true. For any process p, there exist processes q and r such that $C_q(t) - \alpha \leq L_p(t) \leq C_r(t) + \alpha$ for all times t after last-step(e).

THEOREM 8. *Algorithm P is ε /2-valid.*

Proof. Let e be an admissible execution for $(P, \mathscr{C})$, where $\mathscr{C}$ is any set of physical clocks. Let p be any process, and let t be any time after last-step (e). By definition, the value of $CORR_p$ at time t is equal to the average, $(1/n)$ $\Sigma_{q \in P} D_{qp}$. Then there exist processes q and r such that

$$D_{qp} \leq CORR_p(t) \leq D_{rp}.$$

By applying Lemma 5 to each end of this inequality, we get

$$\Delta_{qp} - \varepsilon/2 \leq D_{qp} \leq CORR_p(t) \leq D_{rp} \Delta_{rp} + \varepsilon/2.$$

Thus, $C_p(t) + \Delta_{qp} - \varepsilon/2 \leq C_p(t) + CORR_p(t) \leq C_p(t) + \Delta_{rp} + \varepsilon/2$, which together with the definition of Δ implies that

$$C_q(t) - \varepsilon/2 \leq L_p(t) \leq C_r(t) + \varepsilon/2. \quad \blacksquare$$

5. OPEN QUESTION

It would be interesting to know how the results of this paper generalize to arbitrary communication graphs rather than just complete graphs. Also, it would be interesting to consider what happens when there are different uncertainties for the message delays on the different links.

ACKNOWLEDGMENTS

We thank Brain Coan, Cynthia Dwork, Joe Halpern, and Michael Merritt for their suggestions concerning earlier versions of this paper. Michael, in particular, gave us many excellent suggestions for improving the presentation.

REFERENCES

DOLEV, D, HALPERN, J, AND STRONG, R. (1984), On the possibility and impossibility of achieving clock synchronization, in "Proc. 16th Annual ACM Symp. on Theory of Computation," ACM SIGACT, Washington, D.C., pp. 504-511.

HALPERN, J, SIMONS, B, AND STRONG, R. (1983), "An Efficient Fault-tolerant Algorithm for Clock Synchronization," IBM Computer Science Research Report RJ 4094 (45492).

HALPERN, J., SIMONS, B., STRONG, R., AND DOLEV, D. (1984), Fault -tolerant clock synchronization, in "Proc. 3rd Annual ACM Symposium on Principles of Distributed Computing," ACM SIGACT and SIGOPS, Vancouver, pp. 89-102.

LAMPORT, L. (1987) Time, clocks, and the ordering of events in a distributed system, Comm. ACM 21, No. 7, 558-565.

LAMPORT, L., AND MELLIAR-SMITH, P.M. (1984), Byzantine clock synchronization, in "Proc. 3rd Annual ACM Symposium on Principles of Distributed Computing," ACM SIGACT and SIGOPS, Vancouver, pp. 68-74.

LUNDELIUS, J. (1984), "Synchronizing Clocks in a Distributed System," S.M. thesis, Massachusetts Institute of Technology.

LUNDELIUS, J. AND LYNCH, N. (1984), A new fault-tolerant algorithm for clock synchronization, in "Proc. 3rd Annual ACM Symposium on Principles of Distributed Computing," ACM SIGACT and SIGOPS, Vancouver, pp. 75-88.

MARZULLO, K. (1983), "Loosely-coupled Distributed Services: A Distributed Time Service," Ph.D. dissertation, Stanford University.

Chapter 9: Databases

A real-time database system is one in which (at least some) transactions have explicit timing constraints, such as deadlines. In these systems, transaction processing must satisfy not only consistency constraints, but also timing constraints. Real-time database systems are becoming increasingly important in a wide range of applications. One example is computer-integrated manufacturing systems, where the database tracks the state of physical machines, manages production line processes, collects statistical information from manufacturing operations, and responds to operators' control messages. For instance, the information describing the current state of an object may need to be updated before a team of robots can work on the object. The update transaction is considered successful only if the data is changed consistently (in the view of all the robots) and the update is accomplished within a specified time period. Other applications of real-time databases are program trading in the stock market, radar-tracking systems, command and control systems, airline reservation systems, and air traffic control systems.

Most research on databases focuses on query processing and database consistency and recovery, but not on meeting time constraints. Conventional real-time systems research has focused on guaranteeing deadlines, but has largely ignored the problem of guaranteeing consistency of shared data. The papers in this chapter represent some of the new research being conducted to extend database research into the real-time arena. Almost all the work in this section represents the view that transactions have deadlines associated with them. Some work on temporal databases assumes that data's value is associated with time. However, to date the work on temporal databases has not been integrated with real-time transactions, so we have no papers on this topic. Future research will probably address this issue. Note that these papers deal with single site real-time databases; distributed real-time databases are the subject of future research.

The first paper in this section, "Real-Time Databases," explores the issues in real-time database systems and presents an overview of the state of the art. It introduces the idea that data in real-time databases has to be logically consistent as well as temporally consistent. The latter arises from the need to preserve the temporal validity of data items that reflect the state of the environment being controlled by the system. Some of the timing constraints on the transactions that process real-time data come from this need. Others arise from responsiveness requirements imposed on the system. These constraints, in turn, necessitate time-cognizant transaction processing so transactions can be processed to meet their deadlines. After introducing the characteristics of data and transactions in real-time databases, the paper discusses issues that relate to the processing of time-constrained transactions. Specifically, it examines different approaches to resolving contention over data and processing resources. The paper also reviews the problems of recovery, managing I/O, and handling overloads. Real-time databases have the potential to trade off the quality of the result of a query or a transaction for its timely processing. Quality can be measured in terms of the completeness, accuracy, currency, and consistency of the results. Several aspects of this tradeoff are also discussed.

The second paper, "Real-Time Transaction Processing: Design, Implementation and Performance Evaluation" by Huang, Stankovic, Towsley, and Ramamritham, describes a fairly comprehensive and integrated approach to real-time databases. They discuss a suite of algorithms for CPU scheduling, conflict resolution, deadlock resolution, transaction wake-up, and transaction restart — all tailored to real-time constraints. The algorithms are implemented on a real-time database testbed (called RT-CARAT) and performance results are presented. The performance results show that CPU scheduling is the most important factor in good performance; conflict resolution is also very important. The special real-time features of the other protocols are shown *not* to affect overall performance. This paper does not address the issue of real-time I/O, because the physical limitations of the testbed prevented implementing a real-time I/O protocol. However, the next paper addresses real-time I/O protocols.

In "Performance Evaluation of Two New Disk Scheduling Algorithms for Real-Time Systems," Chen, Stankovic, Kurose, and Towsley present algorithms that combine seek-time and deadline information to improve disk access time. The work is presented in terms of a database application so that the important metric is minimizing transaction loss ratio (minimizing the number of transactions that miss their deadlines) rather than average disk access time. The basic idea behind the new algorithms is to give the disk I/O request with the earliest deadline a high priority, but if another request with a larger deadline is very close to the disk head, then it may be serviced first. The two new algorithms trade off deadline and seek time in different ways. The authors present a performance evaluation based on simulation, in which the two new algorithms are compared to three other real-time disk scheduling algorithms and four conventional non-real-time algorithms. The simulation is validated using the RT-CARAT testbed (see also the first paper in this chapter). The new algorithms show significant and impressive performance gains over all the other disk access algorithms.

Abbott and Garcia-Molina in "Scheduling Real-Time Transactions: A Performance Evaluation" present a group of algorithms for scheduling real-time transactions, which produce serializable schedules. In their paper, they work with a main-memory database, in contrast to the first two papers which deal with disk resident databases. The scheduling algorithms evaluated are FCFS, earliest deadline, and least slack. Concurrency control is based on locking (as is true for the first two papers also). They develop conflict resolution policies based on high priority and conditional restart. The evaluations are done via simulation and they focus on high conflict rate situations. They conclude that for their environment earliest deadline and conditional restart work the best. Both the first paper in this section and this one find similar results, even though the configurations, assumptions, and method of evaluation are significantly different.

For real-time databases it might be better to use an approach based on optimistic concurrency control rather than two-phase locking. In "Dynamic Real-Time Optimistic Concurrency Control," Haritsa, Carey, and Livny develop and evaluate a new optimistic concurrency control (OCC) algorithm, called WAIT-50, for real-time databases. Their study shows that OCC always outperforms locking-based approaches. Their system model includes an open system with respect to the number of users, many disks, priorities assigned based on earliest deadline, and serializability as the correctness criteria. While not included in this tutorial text, readers might be interested in another paper on real-time optimistic concurrency control [Huang et al. 91] where the environment and assumptions are very different and the evaluation is done on a testbed rather than by simulation. In this other paper (again, based on another set of assumptions) OCC is shown to outperform locking only under certain conditions (for example, when the conflict rate is low).

The last paper in this chapter, "Triggered Real-Time Databases with Consistency Constraints" by Korth, Soparkar, and Silberschatz, discusses a very novel and interesting approach that focuses on how a real-time database interacts with the environment. In their model, deadlines are associated with database consistency constraints rather than with transactions per se. When a consistency constraint is violated (say due to inputs from the environment) transactions are invoked to correct the problem. For each consistency constraint there are predetermined transactions waiting to be triggered. Timing constraints determine how long a consistency violation is permitted to exist. Another strength of the paper is that the authors provide a formal model for reasoning about transactions and constraints. On the other hand, the model is quite complicated, and several open questions need answering before this approach is practical.

Real-Time Databases

KRITHI RAMAMRITHAM
Department of Computer Science, University of Massachusetts, Amherst, MA 01003

Received May 18, 1992, Revised August 18, 1992

Abstract. Data in real-time databases has to be logically consistent as well as temporally consistent. The latter arises from the need to preserve the temporal validity of data items that reflect the state of the environment that is being controlled by the system. Some of the timing constraints on the transactions that process real-time data come from this need. These constraints, in turn, necessitate time-cognizant transaction processing so that transactions can be processed to meet their deadlines.

This paper explores the issues in real-time database systems and presents an overview of the state of the art. After introducing the characteristics of data and transactions in real-time databases, we discuss issues that relate to the processing of time-constrained transactions. Specifically, we examine different approaches to resolving contention over data and processing resources. We also explore the problems of recovery, managing I/O, and handling overloads. Real-time databases have the potential to trade off the quality of the result of a query or a transaction for its timely processing. Quality can be measured in terms of the completeness, accuracy, currency, and consistency of the results. Several aspects of this trade-off are also considered.

Keywords: Real-time, transaction processing, databases, concurrency control, databases, consistency

1. Introduction

Many real-world applications involve time-constrained access to data as well as access to data that has temporal validity. For example, consider telephone switching systems, network management, program stock trading, managing auto-mated factories, and command and control systems. More specifically, consider the following activities within these applications: looking up the "800 directory", radar tracking and recognition of objects and determining appropriate response, as well as automatic tracking and directing of objects on a factory floor. All of these involve gathering data from the environment, processing of gathered information in the context of information acquired in the past, and providing *timely* response. Another aspect of these examples is that they involve processing both temporal data, which loses its validity after a certain interval, as well as archival data.

For instance, consider recognizing and directing objects moving along a set of conveyor belts on a factory floor. An object's features are captured by a camera to determine its type and to recognize whether it has any abnormalities. Depending on the observed features, the object is directed to the appropriate workcell. In addition, the system updates its database with information about the object. The following aspects of this example are noteworthy. First of all, features of an object must be collected while the object is still in front of the camera. The collected features apply just to the object in front of the camera, i.e., they lose their validity once a different object enters the system. Then the object must be recognized by matching the features against models for different objects stored in a database. This matching has to be completed in time so that the command to direct the object to the appropriate destination can be given before the object reaches the point where it must be directed onto a different conveyor belt that will carry it to its next workcell. The database update must also be completed in time so that the system's attention can move to the next object to be recognized. If, for any reason, a time-constrained action is not completed within the time limits, alternatives may be possible. In this example, if feature extraction is not completed in time, the object could be discarded for now to be brought back in front of the camera at a later point in time. Applications such as these introduce the need for *real-time database systems.*

During the last few years, the area of real-time databases has attracted the attention of researchers in both real-time systems and database systems. The motivation of the database researchers has been to bring to bear many of the benefits of database technology to solve problems in managing the data in real-time systems. Real-time system researchers have been attracted by the opportunity real-time database systems provide to apply time-driven scheduling and resource allocation algorithms. However, as we shall see, a simple integration of concepts, mechanisms, and tools from database systems with those from real-time systems is not feasible. Even a cursory examination of the characteristics of database systems and the requirements of real-time systems will point out the various forms of "impedance mismatch" that exist between them. Our goal in this paper is to point out the special characteristics, in particular the temporal consistency requirements, of data in real-time databases, and show how these lead to the imposition of time constraints on transaction execution. Meeting these timing constraints demands new approaches to data and transaction management some of which can be derived by tailoring, adapting, and extending solutions proposed for real-time systems and database systems. Hence, as we present the issues in real-time database systems, we review recent attempts at developing possible approaches to addressing these issues.

This paper is divided into roughly three parts. The first part, corresponding to Sections 2, 3, and 4, introduces real-time database systems. Section 2 discusses the characteristics of *data* in real-time database systems, while Section 3 presents the characteristics of *transactions* in real-time database systems. Many of these remind us of active databases. Hence Section 4 is devoted to an examination of the relationship between active databases and real-time databases to point out the additional features we need in active databases in order to make them suitable for use in a real-time database context.

The second part of the paper, contained in Section 5, discusses transaction processing in real-time database systems. We review recent research in this area and show the need to capitalize on, but *adapt,* current techniques from both real-time systems and database systems.

The third part of the paper, contained in Section 6, discusses a number of issues in real-time databases some of which have seen little or no research. These include techniques to trade off timeliness for quality, recovery of real-time transactions, and managing resources other than CPU and data. Section 7 summarizes the paper.

In the rest of this introduction, we examine those characteristics of databases and real-time systems that are relevant to real-time database systems. We also point out the advantages of using databases to deal with data in real-time systems.

1.1. Databases and real-time systems

Traditional databases, hereafter referred to simply as databases, deal with persistent data. Transactions access this data while maintaining its consistency. Serializability is the usual correctness criterion associated with transactions. The goal of transaction and query processing approaches adopted in databases is to achieve a good throughput or response time.

In contrast, *real-time systems,* for the most part, deal with temporal data, i.e., data that becomes outdated after a certain time. Due to the temporal nature of the data and the response time requirements imposed by the environment, tasks in real-time systems possess time constraints, e.g., periods or deadlines. The resulting important difference is that the goal of real-time systems is to meet the time constraints of the activities.

One of the key points to remember here is that real-time does not just imply fast. Recall the story of the tortoise and the hare. The hare was fast but was "busy" doing the *wrong activity at the wrong time.* Even though we would like real-time systems to be faster than the tortoise, we do require them to posses its *predictability.* Also, real-time does not imply timing constraints that are in *nano*seconds or μseconds. For our purposes, real-time implies the need to handle *explicit* time constraints, that is, to use time-cognizant protocols to deal with deadlines or periodicity constraints associated with activities.

1.2. Why real-time databases?

Databases combine several features that facilitate (1) the description of data, (2) the maintenance of correctness and integrity of the data, (3) efficient access to the data, and (4) the correct executions of query and transaction executions in spite of concurrency and failures. Specifically,

- Database schemas help avoid redundancy of data as well as of its description;
- Data management support, such as indexing, assists in efficient access to the data; and
- Transaction support, where transactions have ACID (atomicity, consistency, isolation, and durability) properties, ensures correctness of concurrent transaction executions and ensure data integrity maintenance even in the presence of failures.

However, support for real-time database systems must take into account the following. Firstly, not all data in a real-time database are permanent; some are temporal. Secondly, *temporally correct* serializable schedules are a subset of the serializable schedules. Thirdly, since timeliness is more important than correctness, in many situations, (approximate) correctness can be traded for timeliness. Similarly, atomicity may be relaxed. For instance, this happens with *monotonic* queries and transactions, which are the counterparts of monotonic tasks [34] in real-time systems. Furthermore, many of the extensions to serializability that have been proposed in databases are also applicable to real-time databases (see [38] for a review of these proposals). Some of these assume that isolation of transactions may not always be needed.

In spite of these differences, given the many advantages of database technology, it will be beneficial if we can use of them for managing data found in real-time systems. In a similar vein, the advances made in real-time systems to process activities in time could be exploited to deal with time-constrained transactions in real-time database systems.

As illustrated by the examples cited at the beginning of this section, many real-time applications function in environments that are inherently distributed. Furthermore, many real-time systems employ parallel processing elements for enhanced performance. Hence, parallel and distributed architectures are ubiquitous in real-time applications and hence real-time database must be able to function in the context of such architectures.

The above discussion indicates that while many of techniques used in real-time systems on the one hand, and databases systems on the other hand, may be applicable to real-time database systems, many crucial differences exist which either necessitate fresh approaches to some of the problems or require adaptations of approaches used in the two areas. In the rest of the paper we will be substantiating this claim.

2. Characteristics of data in real-time database systems

Typically, a real-time system consists of *controlling system* and a *controlled system*. For example, in an automated factory, the controlled system is the factory floor with its robots, assembling stations, and the assembled parts, while the controlling system is the computer and human interfaces that manage and coordinate the activities on the factory floor. Thus, the controlled system can be viewed as the *environment* with which the computer interacts.

The controlling system interacts with its environment based on the data available about the environment, say from various sensors, e.g., temperature and pressure sensors. It is imperative that the state of the environment, as perceived by the controlling system, be consistent with the actual state of the environment. Otherwise, the effects of the controlling system's activities may be disastrous. Hence, timely monitoring of the environment as well as timely processing of the sensed information is necessary. The sensed data is processed further to derive new data. For example, the temperature and pressure information pertaining to a reaction may be used to derive the rate at which the reaction appears to be progressing. This derivation typically would depend on past temperature and pressure trends and so some of the needed information may have to be fetched from archival storage (a temporal database [45]). Based on the derived data, where the derivation may involve multiple steps, actuator commands are set. For instance, in our example, the derived reaction rate is used to determine the amount of chemicals or coolant to be added to the reaction. In general, the history of (interactions with) the environment are also logged in archival storage.

In addition to the timing constraints that arise from the need to continuously track the environment, timing correctness requirements in a real-time (database) system also arise because of the need to make data available to the controlling system for its decision-making activities. For example, if the computer controlling a robot does not command it to stop or turn on time, the robot might collide with another object on the factory floor. Needless to say, such a mishap can result in a major catastrophe.

The need to maintain consistency between the actual state of the environment and the state as reflected by the contents of the database leads to the notion of temporal consistency. Temporal consistency has two components [47, 4]:

- *Absolute consistency* — between the state of the environment and its reflection in the database. As mentioned earlier, this arises from the need to keep the controlling system's view of the state of the environment consistent with the actual state of the environment.
- *Relative consistency* — among the data used to derive other data. This arises from the need to produce the sources of derived data close to each other.

Let us define these formally. Let us denote a data item in the real-time database by

$$d : (value, avi, timestamp)$$

where d_{value} denotes the current state of d, and $d_{timestamp}$ denotes the time when the observation relating to d was made. d_{avi} denotes d's *absolute validity interval*, i.e., the length of the time interval following $d_{timestamp}$ during which d is considered to have absolute validity.

A set of data items used to derive a new data item form a *relative consistency set*. Each such set R is associated with a *relative validity interval* denoted by R_{rvi}. Assume that $d \in R$; d has a correct state iff

1. d_{value} is logically consistent — satisfies all integrity constraints.
2. d is temporally consistent:
   - Absolute consistency: $(current\_time - d_{timestamp}) \leq d_{avi}$.
   - Relative consistency: $\forall d' \in R, |\, d_{timestamp} - d'_{timestamp}\,| \leq R_{rvi}$.

Consider the following example: Suppose $temperature_{avi} = 5$, $pressure_{avi} = 10$, $R = \{temperature, pressure\}$, and $R_{rvi} = 2$. If $current\_time = 100$, then (a) $temperature = (347, 5, 95)$ and $pressure = (50, 10, 97)$ are temporally consistent, but (b) $temperature = (347, 5, 95)$ and $pressure = (50, 10, 92)$ are not. In (b), even though the absolute consistency requirements are met, R's relative consistency is violated.

Whereas a given *avi* can be realized by sampling the corresponding real-world parameter often enough, realizing an *rvi* may not be that straightforward. This is because, achieving a given *rvi* implies that the data items that belong to a relative consistency set have to be observed at times close to each other.

Also, achieving an *rvi* along with the *avi*'s will mean that smallest of the *avi*'s of the data items belonging to the relative consistency set will prevail. Consider the *temperature* and *pressure* example, where both of them belong to R. The transactions writing *temperature* and *pressure*, respectively, must always write them within 2 time units of each other. This will implicitly lower the *avi* of *pressure* to 5.

One way out of this predicament is to realize that relative consistency requirements result from the need to derive data from data produced within close proximity of each other. Thus meeting relative consistency requirements is necessary only when data is *used* to derive other data. So rather than reducing the *avi*'s, we need to ensure that an *rvi* is satisfied just when a transaction is executed to derive new data.

If two data items belong to multiple relative consistency sets, the smallest of the *rvi*'s will prevail. Suppose *temperature* and *pressure* also belong to relative consistency sets R' where $R'_{rvi} = 1$. Clearly, the timestamps of *temperature* and *pressure* must be within 1 time unit of each other to satisfy the relative consistency requirements of R and R'.

Another issue in this context relates to the manner in which *timestamps* of derived data are set. Clearly, there will be some correlation between these timestamps and those of the data from which new data is derived. One possibility is to assign the timestamp of d' derived from data items in R to be equal to $min_{d \in R}(d_{timestamp})$ [47]. That is, derived data is only as recent as the oldest data from which the derivation occurs. In general, however, temporal validity criteria are likely to be application dependent and so the timestamp of derived data can be stated as some function of those of the data in the corresponding R [4].

Let us pursue the relationships between avi's and rvi's further. Suppose data items u and v are used to derive data items x and y which in turn are used to derive z. As we saw earlier, z_{avi} is derived from x_{avi} and y_{avi}, which in turn are derived from u_{avi} and v_{avi}. Thus (z derived_from* x) where derived_from* is the transitive closure of the relation derived_from. Given the avi and the rvi of the derived data, the derived_from* relationship, and the function used to assign the timestamps of the derived data we can determine the rvi and avi of the data items they are derived from.

This discussion shows the interrelationships between the derived_from relationship, the manner in which timestamps are set for derived data, and the composition of the relative consistency sets. Furthermore, the observation that relative consistency is significant only when data is being derived is an additional consideration. Methodical approaches must be developed to address this problem such that the system is not overconstrained, i.e., temporal consistency requirements are not stricter than necessary. This is important since, as we will see in the next section, temporal consistency requirements translate into timing constraints on transactions, and the more restrictive the temporal consistency requirements, the tighter the time constraints, and the harder it is to satisfy them.

Before we conclude this section, it should be noted that avi and rvi may change with system dynamics, e.g., mode changes. For instance, while it is necessary to monitor temperature and pressure closely, i.e., have a small avi, during the early stages of a reaction, it might be appropriate to increase the avi once the reaction reaches a steady state.

Given that integrity constraints are typically expressed via predicates and temporal constraints can also expressed via predicates, we have a set of predicates to be satisfied by data. Why not use standard integrity maintenance techniques? The answer lies in observing that while not executing a transaction will maintain logical consistency, temporal consistency can still be violated. For instance, take case (b) in the example discussed earlier. Here, time has progressed to a point where temperature and pressure become temporally invalid even if they are logically consistent.

Thus, to satisfy logical consistency we use concurrency control techniques such as two phase locking [7] and to satisfy temporal consistency requirements we use time-cognizant transaction processing by tailoring the traditional concurrency control and transaction management techniques to explicitly deal with time. To prepare the stage for discussing how this is done (in Section 5), we present the characteristics of transactions next.

3. Characteristics of transactions in real-time database systems

In the first part of this section, transactions are characterized along three dimensions based on the nature of transactions in real-time database systems: the manner in which data is used by transactions, the nature of time constraints, and the significance of executing a transaction by its deadline, or more precisely, the consequence of missing specified time constraints. Subsequently, we show how the temporal consistency requirements of the data lead to some of the time constraints of transactions.

Real-time database systems employ all three types of transactions discussed in the database literature. For instance:

- *Write-only transactions* obtain state of the environment and write into the database.
- *Update transactions* derive new data and store in the database.
- *Read-only transactions* read data from the database and send them to actuators.

The above classification can be used to tailor the appropriate concurrency control schemes.

Some transaction time constraints come from temporal consistency requirements and some come from requirements imposed on system reaction time. The former typically take the form of periodicity requirements: For example,

> *Every 10 s* Sample wind velocity.
> *Every 20 s* Update robot position.

We show later in this section how the periodicity requirements can be derived from the *avi* of the data.

System reaction requirements typically take the form of deadline constraints imposed on aperiodic transactions: For example,

> If *temperature* > 1000
> *within 10 s* add coolant to reactor.

In this case, the system's action in response to the high temperature must be completed by 10 s.

Transactions can also be distinguished based on the effect of missing a transaction's deadline. In this paper, we use the terms *hard*, *soft*, and *firm* to categorize the transactions. Viewed differently, this categorization tells us the *value* imparted to the system when a transaction meets its deadline. Whereas arbitrary types of value functions can be associated with activities [28], we confine ourselves to simple functions as described below.

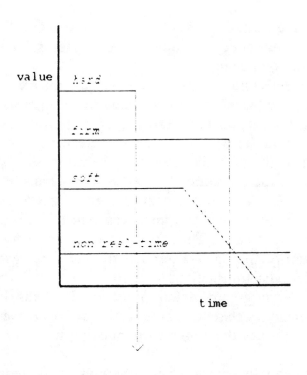

Figure 1. Types of real-time transactions.

- *Hard* deadline transaction are those which may result in a catastrophe if the deadline is missed. One can say that a large negative *value* is imparted to the system if a hard deadline is missed. These are typically safety-critical activities, such as those that respond to life or environment-threatening emergency situations.
- *Soft* deadline transactions have some value even after their deadlines. Typically, the value drops to zero at a certain point past the deadline. If this point is the same as the deadline, we get *firm* deadline transactions, which impart no value to the system once their deadlines expire [21]. For example, if components of a transaction are assigned deadlines derived from the deadline of the transaction, then even if a component misses its deadline, the overall transaction might still be able to make its deadline. Hence these deadlines are soft. Another example is that of a transaction that is attempting to recognize a moving object. It must complete acquiring the necessary information before the object goes outside its view and hence has a firm deadline.

Figure 1 plots the value versus time behavior of different types of transactions.

The processing of transactions must take their different characteristics into account. Since meeting time constraints is the goal, it is important to understand how transactions are scheduled and how their scheduling relates to time constraints. So in the rest of this section, we discuss how absolute validity requirements on the data induce periodicity requirements. As we shall see, it is not as straightforward as it seems.

Suppose the *avi* of *temperature* is 10, i.e., *temperature* must be no more than 10 s old. Consider one of the many possible semantics of transactions with period P: One instance of the transaction must execute every period, as long as the start time and completion time lie within a period, the execution is considered to be correct with respect to the periodicity semantics. Suppose a simple transaction takes at most e units of time to complete ($0 \leq e \leq P$). Thus, if an instance starts at time t and ends at $(t + e)$ and the next instance starts at $(t + 2 * P - e)$ and ends at $(t + 2 * P)$, then we have two instances, which are separated by $(2 * P)$ units of time in the worst case. This, for example, will be the case if the rate monotonic static priority approach, extended to deal with resources [41, 42], is used to schedule periodic transactions executing on a main memory database. (Scheduling is discussed in greater detail in Section 5.) Thus, it follows from the above periodicity semantics that to maintain the *avi* of *temperature*, the period of the transaction that reads the *temperature* must be no more than half the *avi*, that is 5.

Let us assume instead that periodic transactions are scheduled so that each instance of a transaction is guaranteed to start at the same time, relative to the beginning of a period. Then, the worst case separation between the start time of one instance and the finish time of the subsequent instance will be $(P + (2 * e))$. Since a transaction could write the relevant data item any time during its execution, the interval $(P + (2 * e))$ must be less than the given *avi*. Thus, $P = (avi - (2 * e))$.

The above discussion illustrates the dependence of transaction timing constraints not only on the temporal consistency requirements of the data but also on the execution times of the transaction and the scheduling approach adopted. The overall issue is one of *predictability* and we return to this in Section 5.

Now we consider deriving transactions' timing constraints from relative consistency specifications. Recall that they must hold when a transaction uses the data in a relative consistency set to derive other data. So we must ensure that in an interval where such a transaction executes, from the point where relative consistency holds until the end of the interval, there is sufficient time for the transaction to complete execution. Handling *rvi*'s is clearly more involved [4]. Also, when we have a series of data derivations, each derivation being handled by a transaction, an alternative to using the *rvi*'s is to impose precedence constraints on the transactions to conform with the derived-from relationship. Much work remains to be done for methodically deriving transaction characteristics from the properties of the data.

4. Relationship to active databases

Many of the characteristics of data and transactions discussed in the last two sections may remind a reader of active databases. Hence this section is devoted to a discussion of the specific distinctions between active databases and real-time databases.

The basic building block in active databases is the following:

ON *event*
   IF *condition*
      DO *action*.

Upon the occurrence of the specified *event*, if the *condition* holds, then the specified *action* can be taken. This construct provides a good mechanism by which integrity constraints can be maintained among related or overlapping data or by which views can be constructed [13]. The *event* can be arbitrary, including external events (as in the case of real-time events generated by environment), timer events, or transaction related events (such as the begin and commit of transactions). The *condition* can correspond to conditions on the state of the data or the environment. The *action* is said to be *triggered* [32, 12] and it can be an arbitrary transaction.

Given this, it is not difficult to see that active databases provide a good model for the *arrival* (i.e., triggering) of periodic/aperiodic activities based on events and conditions. Even though the above construct implies that an active database can be made to react to timeouts, time constraints are not *explicitly* considered by the underlying transaction processing mechanism.

However, as we have discussed before, the primary goal of real-time database systems is to *complete* the transactions on time. One can thus state the main deficiency in active databases in relation to what is required for them to deal with time constraints on the completion of transactions: time constraints must be *actively* taken into consideration.

Consider a system that controls the landing of an aircraft. Ideally, we would like to ensure that once the decision is made to prepare for landing, necessary steps, for example, to lower the wheels, to begin deceleration, and to reduce altitude, are completed within a given duration, say 10 s. Here the steps may depend on the landing path, the constraints specific to the airport, and the type of aircraft, and hence may involve access to a database containing the relevant information. In those situations where the necessary steps have not been completed in time, we would like to abort the landing within a given deadline, say within 5 s; the abort must be *completed* within the deadline, presumably because that is the "cushion" available to the system to take alternative actions. This requirement can be expressed as follows:

ON (*10 s after* "initiating landing preparations")
   IF (steps not completed)

DO (*within 5 s* "Abort landing").

In summary, while active databases possess the necessary features to deal with many aspects of real-time database systems, the crucial missing ingredient is the active pursuit of the timely processing of actions.

5. Transaction processing in real-time database systems

In this section, we discuss various aspects of transaction and query processing where the transactions and queries have characteristics discussed in Section 3; i.e., they have time constraints attached to them and there are different consequences of not satisfying those constraints.

A key issue in transaction processing is *predictability*. It the context of an individual transaction, this relates to the question: "will the transaction meet its time-constraint"? We discuss the sources of unpredictability in Section 5.1 and present ways by which the resulting problems can be addressed. Section 5.2 deals with the processing of transactions that have hard deadlines, while Section 5.3 deals with transactions that have soft deadlines.

5.1. The need for predictability

If a hard real-time transaction misses its deadline, it has catastrophic consequences. We can also say that missing the deadline has a large negative value to the system. Thus, we would like to *predict* beforehand that such transactions will complete before their deadlines. This prediction will be possible only if we know the worst-case execution time of a transaction and the data and resource needs of the transaction. In addition, it is desirable to have small variance between the worst-case predictions and the actual needs. Predictability is also important for soft deadline transactions, albeit to a lesser extent. In these cases, knowing before a transaction begins that the transaction may not complete within its deadline allows the system to discard the transaction, so that no time is spent on the transaction and no recovery overheads are incurred.

In a database system, a number of sources of unpredictability exist:

- Dependence of the transaction's execution sequence on data values
- Data and resource conflicts
- Dynamic paging and I/O
- Transactions aborts and the resulting rollbacks and restarts

Distributed databases have additional problems due to communication delays and site failures. Below we elaborate upon these and point out ways by which individual problems can be alleviated. Finally, we outline a technique that is being developed to address these problems in the context of soft real-time transactions.

Since a transaction's execution path can depend on the values of the data items it accessed, it may not be possible to predict the worst-case execution time of the transaction. A similar problem arises for tasks in real-time systems. A similar solution applies: it is advisable to avoid use of unbounded loops and recursive or dynamically constructed data structures in real-time transactions. Since a real-time database is used in closed loop situations where the environment being controlled closes the loop, the data items accessed by a transaction are likely to be known once it functionality is known.

Since a typical transaction accesses data as it is needed in the execution sequence, it may be forced to wait until the data becomes available. Similarly, a transaction may be forced to wait for resources, such as CPU and I/O devices, to become available. While both these problems have their counterparts in real-time systems, the problems are exacerbated in real-time database systems due to data consistency requirements. Specifically, consider a database that employs strict two-phase locking for concurrency control. In this case, a transaction may wait, in the worst case for an unbounded amount of time, when it attempts to acquire a data item. The cumulative delays can be very long; with deadlocks and restarts it could even be unbounded. Conflict avoiding data access protocols and the preallocation of resources have been developed to reduce this problem in real-time systems, but they do not apply directly to real-time database systems. We review some of these in Section 5.3 and show how it may be possible to adapt them in our context.

If disk-resident databases use demand-paged memory management, delays can occur while accessing disks both for fetching both data and program pages. These can lead to pessimistic worst-case scenarios since worst-case assumptions must be made about the need to fetch data or program page from disk whenever the need arises. This will depend on the disk scheduling and buffer management algorithms used. Main memory databases [1] eliminate these problems.

Transaction rollbacks also reduce predictability. Assume that a transaction is aborted and restarted a number of times before it commits. This has two negative consequences. The total execution time for the transaction increases and, if the number of aborts cannot be controlled, it may be unbounded. Second, the resources and time needed to handle the rollbacks will be denied to other transactions. Recovery time can be reduced by using semantics-based recovery discussed in Section 6. Real-time database systems may introduce transaction aborts due to deadline misses. One way to avoid these aborts is to begin a transaction only if we know that it will complete by its deadline. We give an overview of this approach below. Details can be found in [36].

Preanalysis of a transaction is desirable because it provides an estimate of its computation time and data and resource requirements. But, for complex transactions this may not be feasible. In this case, to get the necessary information about a transaction the following approach can prove useful. It has the potential to deal with the four sources of unpredictability mentioned above. Transactions go through two phases. In the first phase, called the prefetch phase, a transaction is run once, bringing in the necessary data into main memory if they are not in memory already. No writes are performed in this phase and conflicts with other transactions are not considered. The computational demands of the transactions are also determined during this phase. Assume that the data-dependent portions of the transactions are such that a transaction's execution path does not change due to possible concurrent changes done to the data by other transactions while a transaction is going through its prefetch phase [15]. That is to say, at the end of the prefetch phase, all the necessary data is in memory. We now attempt to guarantee that the transaction will complete by its deadline. This is done by planning the execution of the transaction—respecting conflicts with the transactions already guaranteed—such that the transaction meets its deadline. This plan takes into account both the computational and resource requirements of the transaction and ensures that the necessary data and processing resources are available at the appropriate times for the transactions to complete within their time constraints. If such a plan cannot be constructed, the transaction is aborted without even starting it. The notion of guarantee and the planning algorithm are based on the resource constrained scheduling approach proposed for real-time systems and described in [40].

Let us see how this approach tackles the four major sources of unpredictability mentioned above. By using the prefetch phase to bring in the pages, the actual execution sequence is determined during this phase. Data and resource conflicts during execution are avoided by the use of explicit planning of the execution phase of transactions. Since necessary pages are brought into memory during the prefetch phase, dynamic I/O is avoided during the execution phase. Finally, transaction aborts and rollbacks are avoided because all changes are done during the execution phase and this phase is not begun unless it is known that it will complete in time.

If the state of the data changes during the prefetch phase, which can be detected by detecting the writes to the data brought into memory by the transaction, then the prefetch phase can be reexecuted. In any case, this approach provides a way by which if access invariance holds, once guaranteed, a transaction will complete by its deadline and no recovery actions are necessary if a transaction is unable to execute. The price paid in the latter situation is the overheads of the prefetch phase. Several optimizations are possible. For example, in some situations, there may not even be a need to go to the execution phase. As in optimistic concurrency control this will happen if the data items used by the transaction were not used by any other concurrent transaction. Details can be found in [36].

5.2. Dealing with hard deadlines

All transactions with hard deadlines must meet their time constraints. Since dynamically managed transactions cannot provide such a guarantee, the data and processing resources as well as time needed by such transactions have to be guaranteed to be made available when necessary. There are several implications of this.

Firstly, we have to know when the transactions are likely to be invoked. This information is readily available for periodic transaction, but for aperiodic transactions, by definition, it is not. The smallest separation time between two incarnations of an aperiodic transaction can be viewed as its period. Thus, we can cast all hard real-time transactions as *periodic* transactions.

Secondly, in order to ensure a priori that their deadlines will be met, we have to determine their resource requirements and worst-case transaction execution times. As outlined in Section 5.1, this requires that many restrictions be placed on the structure and characteristics of real-time transactions.

Once we have achieved the above, we can treat the transactions in a manner similar to the way real-time systems treat periodic tasks that require guarantees, i.e., by using *static table-driven* schedulers or preemptive *priority-driven* approaches. Static *table-driven* schedulers reserve specific time slots for each transaction. If a transaction does not use all of the time reserved for it, the time may be reclaimed [43] to start other hard real-time transactions earlier than planned. Otherwise, it can be used for soft real-time transactions or left idle. The table-driven approach is obviously very inflexible. A priority-driven approach is the rate-monotonic priority assignment policy. One can apply the schedulability analysis tools associated with it to check if a set of transactions are schedulable given their periods and data requirements. This is the approach discussed in [42] where periodic transactions that read and write main memory resident data are scheduled using rate-monotonic priority assignment.

We mentioned earlier that the variance between the worst-case computational needs and actual needs must not be very large. We can see why. Since the schedulability analysis is done with respect to worst-case needs, if the variance is large, many transactions that may be doable in the average case will be considered infeasible in the worstcase. Also, if the table-driven approach is used, a large variance will lead to large idle times.

In summary, while it is possible to deal with hard real-time transactions using approaches similar to those used in real-time systems, many restrictions have to be placed on these transactions so that their characteristics are known a priori. Even if one is willing to deal with these restrictions, poor resource utilization may result given the worst-case assumptions made about the activities.

5.3. Dealing with soft deadlines

With soft real-time transactions, we have more leeway to process transactions since we are not required to meet the deadlines all the time. Of course, the larger the number of transactions that meet their deadlines the better. When transactions have different values, the value of transactions that finish by their deadlines should be maximized. The complexity involved in processing real-time transaction comes from these goals. That is to say, we cannot simply let a transaction run, as we would in a traditional database system, and abort it should its deadline expire before it commits. As we discussed in Section 4, we must *actively* pursue the goal of meeting transaction deadlines by adopting priority-assignment policies and conflict resolution mechanisms that explicitly take time into account. Note that priority assignment governs CPU scheduling and conflict resolution determines which of the many transactions contending for a data item will obtain access. As we will see, conflict resolution protocols make use of transaction priorities and because of this, the priority assignment policy plays a crucial role [27]. We discuss these two issues in Section 5.3.1. We also discuss the performance implications of different deadline semantics. Additional aspects of transaction management, such as, distribution, transaction commitment, and deadlock detection are discussed in Section 5.3.2.

5.3.1. Priority assignment and conflict resolution
Rather than assigning priorities based on whether the transactions are CPU or I/O (or data) bound, real-time database systems must assign priorities based on transaction time constraints and the value they impart to the system. Possible policies include

- *Earliest-deadline-first,*
- *Highest-value-first,*
- *Highest-value-per-unit-computation-time-first,* and
- *Longest-executed-transaction-first.*

It has been shown that the priority assignment policy has significant impact on performance and that when different transactions have different values, both deadline *and* value must be considered [27].

For the purpose of conflict resolution in real-time database systems, various *time-cognizant* extensions of two phase locking, optimistic, and timestamp based protocols have been proposed in the literature [1, 2, 9, 20, 25–27, 33, 46, 48]. These are discussed below.

In the context of two-phase locking, when a transaction requests a lock that is currently held by another transaction we must take into account the characteristics of the transactions involved in the conflict. Considerations involved in conflict resolution are the deadline and value (in general, the priority) of transactions, how long the transactions have executed, and how close they are to completion. Consider the following set of protocols investigated in [26].

- If a transaction with a higher priority is forced to wait for a lower priority transaction to release the lock, a situation known as *priority inversion* arises. This is because a lower-priority transaction makes a higher-priority transaction to wait. In one approach to resolving this problem, the lock holder *inherits* the lock requester's priority whereby it completes execution sooner than with its own priority.
- If the lock-holding transaction has lower priority, abort it. Otherwise let the lock requester wait.
- If the lock-holding transaction is closer to its deadline, lock requester waits, independent of its priority.

Priority inheritance is shown to reduce transaction blocking times [26]. This is because the lock holder executes at a higher priority (than that of the waiting transaction) and hence finishes early, thereby blocking the waiting higher priority transaction for a shorter duration. However, even with this policy, the higher priority transaction is blocked, in the worst case, for the duration of a transaction under strict two-phase locking. As a result, the priority inheritance protocol typically performs even worse than a protocol that makes a lock a requester wait independent of its priority.

If a higher-priority transaction always aborts a low-priority transaction, the resulting performance is sensitive to data contention. On the other hand, if a lower-priority transaction that is closer to completion inherits priority rather than aborting, then a better performance results even when data contention is high. Such a protocol is a combination of the abort-based protocol proposed for traditional databases [49] and the priority-inheritance protocol proposed for real-time systems [41]. Said differently, the superior performance of this protocol [26] shows that even though techniques that work in real-time systems, on the one hand, and database systems, on the other hand, may not be applicable directly, they can often be tailored and adapted to suit the needs of real-time database systems. It should be noted that abort-based protocols (as opposed to wait-based) are especially appropriate for real-time database systems because of the time constraints associated with transactions.

Let us now consider optimistic protocols. In protocols that perform backward validation, the validating transaction either commits or aborts depending on whether it has conflicts with transactions that have already committed. The disadvantage of backward validation is that it does not allow us to take transaction characteristics into account. This disadvantage does not apply to forward validation. In forward validation, a committing transaction usually aborts ongoing transactions in case they conflict with the validating transaction. However, depending on the characteristics of the validating transaction and those with which it conflicts, we may prefer not to commit the validating transaction. Several policies have been studied in the literature [20, 21, 25]. In one, termed *wait-50*, a validating transaction is made to wait as long as more than half the transactions that conflict with it have earlier deadlines. This is shown to have superior performance.

Time-cognizant extensions to timestamp-based protocols have also been proposed. In these, when data accesses are out of timestamp order, the conflicts are resolved based on their priorities. In addition, several combinations of locking-based, optimistic and timestampbased protocols have been proposed but require quantitative evaluation [33].

Exploiting multiple versions of data for enhanced performance has been addressed in [29]. Multiple versions can reduce conflicts over data. However, if data must have temporal validity, old versions which are outdated must be discarded. Also, when choosing versions of related data, their relative consistency requirements must be taken into account: consider a transaction that uses multiversioned data to display aircraft positions on an air-traffic controller's screen. The data displayed must have both absolute validity as well as relative validity.

Different transaction semantics are possible with respect to discarding a transaction once its deadline is past. For example, with firm deadlines, a late transaction is aborted once its deadline expires [21]. In general, with soft deadlines, once a transaction's value drops to zero, it is aborted [27]. On the other hand, in the transaction model assumed in [1], all transactions have to complete execution even if their deadlines have expired. In this model, delayed transactions may cause other transactions also to miss their deadlines and this can have a cascading effect. Needless to say, it is important to exploit transaction semantics so as to abort them as soon as it is clear that there is little benefit to continuing the execution of a transaction. Of course, aborting a transaction also has performance implications given the costs of recovery. We discuss this in Section 6.3.

Before we end this section, it should be pointed out that special time-cognizant deadlock detection, transaction wake-up, and restart policies appear to have little impact [27]. For example, breaking a deadlock cycle by aborting a transaction based on transaction timing characteristics does not seem to produce significantly better results. Similarly, which of many rolled-back transactions to restart next or which of many waiting transactions to wake-up next can be determined by taking transaction's timing characteristics into account. However, in many situations tested to date, the differences between the possible choices do not seem to warrant special handling of restarts or wake-ups.

5.3.2. Commitment, distribution, and nested transactions

Let us now consider the transaction commitment process. Once a transaction reaches its commit point, it is better to let it commit quickly so that its locks can be released soon. If commit delays are not high, which will be the case in a centralized database, the committing transaction can be given a high enough priority so that it can complete quickly. The solution is not so easy in a distributed system because of the distribution of the commitment process. Furthermore, since a deadline typically refers to the deadline until the end of the two-phase commit, but since the decision on whether or not to commit is taken in the first phase, we can enter the second phase only if we know that it will complete before the deadline. This requires special handling of the commit process. An alternative is to associate the deadline with the beginning of the second phase, but this may delay subsequent transactions since locks are not released until the second phase.

A distributed real-time database system introduces other complications as well, especially when we go beyond flat transactions. Let us consider nested transactions [35]. Even though transaction models that are more complex than flat transactions introduce additional unpredictability, some activities with soft time constraints may find them more suitable since, for instance, nested transactions allow the independent recovery of subtransactions.

So far we assumed that each transaction has a value and a deadline. These can be used in several ways in the nested transaction model.

- Suppose we assign a deadline and value only to the top-level transaction. Some scheme will have to be designed to propagate these to the nested child transactions, to their children, and so on, so that conflicts between the components of a nested transaction and other transactions can be dealt with as though they were separate transactions.

  Knowledge of computation times of (child) transactions will prove useful in appropriately assigning the intermediate deadlines of the child transactions. The deadline for a child transaction should depend on the deadline of the top-level transaction, the computation time of the transaction and its children, as well as the system load.

- Suppose individual deadlines and values are assigned to each component of a nested transaction. Then the system will have to "reassign" the value and the deadline so that they are consistent with each other, for example, to make sure that the deadline of a parent is no earlier than that of its children.

The former is more applicable to multilevel transactions where nesting is implicit and is hidden from the user and the latter more applicable to nested transactions where the nesting structure is visible to the user. In either case, deadlines associated with children have implications when a deadline is missed. Since it is the top-level transaction that must meet its deadline, it may be possible for children to miss deadlines and yet the top-level transaction may meet its deadline. That is, the deadlines for the children are soft deadlines. In certain situations, it may be possible to abort a delayed child and run an alternative child transaction instead.

In a flat transaction model, transactions are competing against each other for data as well as computational and I/O resources, but components of a nested transaction, even if they have individual deadlines, are executing on behalf of that transaction. Hence scheduling and conflict resolution strategies have to be tailored to handle the case of components of the same nested transaction competing with each other. Further problems arise when components of a nested transaction execute on different sites. Specifically, transaction priorities must be set in a *consistent* fashion at all the sites visited by a transaction (or its components).

A related topic is the replication of data. Its potential for fault tolerance is an especially important one for distributed real-time database systems. However, very little work has been done to date on this and other issues raised above for distributed real-time databases or for transaction models beyond flat transactions.

6. Other issues in real-time database systems

In this section, we would like to bring together a number of issues that have not been adequately addressed in the real-time database literature. These include managing resources other than CPU and data, trading off timeliness for quality, managing recovery, and handling overloads. The subsections in this section deal with these topics individually. Since little work has been done in these areas, the discussion is, by necessity, speculative.

6.1. Managing I/O and buffers

Whereas the scheduling of CPU and data resources has been studied fairly extensively in the real-time database literature, studies of scheduling approaches for dealing with other resources, such as disk I/O, and buffers has begun only recently. In this section we review some recent work in this area and discuss some of the problems that remain.

I/O scheduling is an important area for real-time systems given the large difference in speeds between CPU and disks and the resultant impact of I/O devices' responsiveness on performance. However, real-time systems research has essentially ignored this problem because of the perception that disk access introduces high degree of unpredictability and so disks are seldom accessed when time constraints exist. However, in real-time database systems the reading and writing of (archival) data is essential and so disk scheduling when transactions have time constraints becomes a significant problem. Since the traditional disk scheduling algorithms attempt to minimize average I/O delays, just like traditional CPU scheduling algorithms aim to minimize average processing delays, time-cognizant I/O scheduling approaches are needed.

It must be recognized that what is important is the meeting of transaction deadlines and not the individual deadlines that may be attached to I/O requests. Assume that we model a transaction execution as a sequence of (disk I/O, computation) pairs culminating in a set of disk I/O's, the latter arising from writes to log and to the changed pages. Suppose we assign (intermediate) deadlines to the I/O requests of a transaction given the transaction's deadline.

One of the interesting questions with regard to disk I/O scheduling is: How does one derive the deadline for an I/O request from that of the requesting transaction? First of all, it must be recognized that depending on how these I/O deadlines are set, deadlines associated with I/O requests may be *soft* since even if a particular I/O deadline is missed, the transaction may still complete by a deadline. This is the case if I/O deadlines are set such that the overall laxity (i.e., the difference between the time available before the deadline and the total computation time) of a transaction is uniformly divided among the computations and the I/O. On the other hand, assume that an intermediate deadline is equal to the latest completion time (i.e., the time an I/O must complete assuming that subsequent computations and I/O are executed without delay). This is the less preferred method since we now have a firm deadline associated with I/O requests – if an I/O deadline is missed, there is no way for the transaction to complete by its deadline and so the requesting transaction must be aborted.

Recent work on I/O scheduling includes [3, 10, 11]. The priority driven algorithm described in [10] is a variant of the traditional SCAN algorithm which works on the elevator principle to minimize disk arm movement. Without specifying how priorities are assigned to individual I/O requests, [10] proposes a variant in which the SCAN algorithm is applied to each priority level. Requests at lower priority are serviced only after those at higher priority are served. Thus, if after servicing a request, one or more higher-priority requests are found waiting, the disk arm moves toward the highest-priority request that is closest to the current disk arm position. In the case of requests arising from transactions with deadlines, priority assignment could be based on the deadline assigned to the I/O request.

Another variant of SCAN, one which directly takes I/O deadlines into account is FDSCAN [3]. In this algorithm, given the current position of the disk arm, the disk arm moves toward the request with the earliest deadline that can be serviced in time. Requests that lie in that direction are serviced and after each service it is checked whether (1) a request with an even earlier deadline has arrived and (2) the deadline of the original result cannot be met. In either case, the direction of disk arm movement may change.

Clearly, both these protocols involve checks after each request is served and so incur substantial run-time overheads. The protocols described in [11] are aimed at avoiding the impact of these checks on I/O performance. Specifically, the protocols perform the necessary computations while I/O is being performed. In the SSEDO algorithm (shortest-seek and earliest deadline by ordering), the need to give higher priority to requests with earlier deadlines is met while reducing the overall seek times. The latter is accomplished by giving a high priority to requests which may have large deadlines but are very close to the current position of the disk arm. A variant of SSEDO is SSEDV which works with specific deadline values, rather than deadline orderings. Reference [11] shows how both the algorithms can be implemented so as to perform disk scheduling while service is in progress and shows that the algorithms have better performance that the other variants of the SCAN algorithms.

Another resource for which contention can arise is the database buffer. What we have here is a conflict over buffer slots—akin to conflicts that occur over a time slot, in the case of a CPU. Thus, similar issues arise here also. Specifically, how to allocate buffer slots to transactions and which slots to replace when a need arises are some of the issues. Consider buffer replacement: in case there is a need to replace an existing buffer slot to make room for a new entry, the replacement policy may have an impact on performance, especially if the slot being replaced is used by an uncommitted transaction. Work done in this area includes [10, 24]. Whereas [24] reports of no significant performance improvements when time-cognizant buffer management policies are used, studies discussed in [10] show that transaction priorities must be considered in buffer management. Clearly, the jury is still out on the issue and further work is needed.

6.2. Performance enhancement: trading off quality for timeliness

Before we examine the specific performance enhancement possibilities unique to real-time database systems, it is important to point out that several proposals made for performance enhancement in traditional databases are also applicable to real-time databases. For instance, given that the data objects in real-time database systems will be abstract data type objects, as opposed to read/write objects, the semantics of the operations on these objects can be exploited to improve concurrent access to these objects (see, for example, [5]). Generalizing this, the parallelism and distribution inherent in real-time systems, which by their very nature function in physically distributed environments with multiple active processing elements, can be put to use to improve performance. Of course, as we discussed earlier, distribution brings with it some special problems in the real-time context. With regard to predictability many advantages can be gained by the use of main memory databases. Also, the benefits afforded by database machines for real-time database systems are worth exploring.

Now let us consider approaches that are in some sense unique to real-time database systems. In the context of activities having timing constraints, the statement, "it is better to produce a partial result before the deadline instead of the complete result after the deadline" has become a cliche. However, it is not always clear what an acceptable partial result is or how a computation can be structured to provide acceptable partial results. Recent work in the real-time area can lead us to some partial answers [34]. In general, *timeliness*, a key performance measure, could be achieved by trading it off with completeness, accuracy, consistency, and currency [19, 39]. Below we consider each of these in turn.

Let us first consider *completeness*. Suppose a transaction updates the screen of an operator in a chemical plant periodically. If during a certain time interval, during overloads, it is unable to update all the valve positions, but has the time to update those that are crucial to the safety of the plant, then such a transaction should be allowed to execute even if not all its actions may be performed.

When query processing involves computing aggregates, especially in a time-constrained environment, then one can achieve different degrees of *accuracy* by resorting to approximate query processing by sampling data [23]. Here, depending on time availability, results with different accuracies can be provided. Another example is that of a transaction that does not have all the necessary data for its processing but can recover from this situation by extrapolating based on previous data values. Here again, if previous data values of different data items are used, their relative consistency must be considered.

Turning to *consistency*, in the context of traditional databases, it has often been mentioned that correctness notions that relax serializability are appropriate (see [38] for a review of such relaxed notions.) For instance, epsilon serializability [37] allows a query to execute in spite of concurrent updates wherein the deviation of the query's results, from that of a serializable result, can be bounded. Such relaxations allow more transactions to execute concurrently thereby improving performance.

In the context of *currency* of a transaction's results it may not always be necessary for a transaction to use the latest version of a data item. This is true, for example, when a transaction is attempting to derive trends in the changes to some data. Clearly, old versions of the data are required here and the transaction can complete even if the latest version is unavailable.

The examples mentioned above make it clear that there are situations where imprecision can be tolerated, and in fact must be exploited, to improve performance. However, how to achieve this systematically is yet to be studied. What we need are notions similar to the degrees of consistency adopted in traditional database systems [17]. In this context, scheduling approaches that have been developed for the imprecise computation model in real-time systems could be tailored to apply to real-time database systems. Preliminary work in this area is reported in [44].

6.3. Recovery issues

Recovery is a complex issue even in traditional databases and is more so in real-time database systems for two reasons. (The approach discussed at the end of Section 5.1 was motivated in part by these complexities.) Firstly, the process of recovery can interfere with the processing of ongoing transactions. Specifically, suppose we are recovering from a transaction aborted due to a deadline miss. If locks are used for concurrency control, it is important to release them as soon as possible so that waiting transactions can proceed without delay so as to meet their deadlines. However, it is also necessary to undo the changes done by the transaction to the data if in-place updates are done. But this consumes processing time that can affect the processing of transactions that are not waiting for locks to be released. Whereas optimistic concurrency control techniques or a shadow-pages based recovery strategy can be used to minimize this time, they have several disadvantages [18]. Secondly, unlike traditional databases where permanent data should always reflect a consistent state, in real-time databases, the presence of temporal data, while providing some opportunities for quicker recovery [50], adds to the complexities of the recovery of transactions. Specifically, if a transaction's deadline expires before it completes the derivation of a data item, then rather than restoring the state of the data to its previous value, it could declare the data to be invalid thereby disallowing other transactions from using the value. The next instance of the transaction, in case the data is updated by a periodic transaction, may produce a valid state.

In general, real-time database recovery must consider time and resource availability to determine the most opportune time to do recovery without jeopardizing ongoing transactions, whether they are waiting for locks or not. Available transaction as well as data semantics (or state) must be exploited to minimize recovery overheads. Contingency or compensating transactions [31] are applicable here: Contingency transactions can take the form of multiple versions of a transaction each with different values and different computational and data requirements. If we know that one with the highest quality will be unable to complete in time, the system can recover by trying an alternative with acceptable quality. This is a situation where quality is traded off to minimize recovery costs and to achieve timeliness. Revisiting the factory floor example from the introduction, we saw that if there is insufficient time to complete object recognition, the system discards the object for now and directs the object to appear once again in front of the camera (at perhaps a later point in time). In case a real-time transaction has interacted with the environment, a compensating transaction may have to be invoked to recover from its failure [31]. The nature and the state of the environment can be used to determine recovery strategies. In some situations, in the absence of new data that was to have been produced by an aborted transaction, extrapolation of new values from old values may be possible. In other cases, more up-to-date may be available soon.

The following highly simplified example may help in illustrating some of the considerations in recovery. Suppose two robots on a factory floor have to rendezvous at point x by time t: t is a firm deadline by which either both should be at x or both should know that they cannot make it. The controller of the robot, i.e., the real-time system, first obtains their current position and those of the pertinent objects on the factory floor. It determines the type of moves the robots are capable of by retrieving their characteristics from archival storage. It then creates a path for each robot to follow to reach x by time t and sends this path to each robot. The controller also reserves this path for the duration for these two robots. As the robots follow this path, the controller monitors their movement, looks out for obstacles in their slated path and continually checks if there is a delay in reaching specific points along the path due to incorrect estimations made during path construction or unanticipated other delays. If it detects such a situation, the controller recovers from it by determining an alternative path given the robots' current position. Should there be no time to follow the new path, recovery involves instructing the robots to halt, informing each of them that their rendezvous is not possible. In either case, path reservation information is modified appropriately. Note that all of this involves reading information from the environment, retrieving information from the database, and updating other information.

It also shows some aspects of recovery: Recovery here comprises two contingency actions, one of which involves termination of the transaction after informing the robots.

6.4. Managing overloads

Perhaps the most critical of the outstanding issues is one of managing overloads. How should real-time transaction processing be done when more transactions arrive than can meet their deadlines? In traditional systems, if an overload does not remain for too long, in most cases, the result is a slow response for the duration of the overload. However, in real-time databases that interact with the environment, catastrophic consequences can arise. These can be minimized by ensuring that transactions that are critical to the performance of the system are declared to possess hard deadlines and are guaranteed to meet deadlines even under overloads. In addition, if we make sure that transaction values are considered for priority assignment and during conflict resolution, then the transaction that misses its deadline will typically have a low value. However, missing too many low-valued transactions with soft deadlines may eventually lead to situations where many transactions with high values arrive, thus stressing the system: For example, if periodic maintenance is postponed due to the arrival of more important activities, it may eventually be necessary to shut down the system. Hence dealing with overleads is complex and solutions are still in their infancy [6, 8, 30]. An approach to this problem, based on discarding transactions immediately upon their arrival, given current system load and arriving, transaction characteristics, is described in [22]. In managing overloads, some of the trade-offs that we discussed earlier, involving timeliness versus quality are also very pertinent.

7. Conclusions

In this paper, we presented the characteristics of data and transactions in real-time database systems and discussed the differences between real-time database systems and traditional databases. Many of the differences arise because temporal consistency requirements are imposed on the data in addition to the usual integrity constraints. Maintaining temporal consistency imposes time constraints on the database transactions. In addition, the reaction requirements demanded by the environment can also place time constraints. The performance of real-time database systems is measured by how well the time constraints associated with transactions are met. The system must meet all hard deadlines and minimize the number of transactions whose soft deadlines are missed. This is a crucial difference from traditional databases and necessitates *time-cognizant* transaction processing.

We examined various aspects of transaction processing in real-time database systems including concurrency control and recovery and showed that recovery becomes an even more complex problem when transactions have time constraints. In many situations, one can trade off timeliness for quality of the transaction's results where the quality depends on the completeness, accuracy, currency, and consistency of the results. Furthermore, many recent advances in databases, for exploiting parallelism, distribution, object semantics, and transaction semantics should be very useful in real-time database systems also.

Whereas recently there has been a spurt of research activity in the area, many open questions remain. These include the derivation of transaction timing properties from the temporal consistency requirements of the data, developing suitable hardware and software architectures for real-time database systems, seamless management of transactions with hard and soft deadlines, real-time transaction recovery, and the trade-offs between timeliness and quality.

Acknowledgments

I am indebted to real-time database researchers for many of the ideas discussed in this paper. Particular thanks to A. Buchmann, K. Dittrich, C. Mohan, and S. Son, who participated in the panel on real-time database systems at VLDB in Barcelona. Thanks also to A. Bestavros, P. Chrysanthis, J. Haritsa, L. Molesky, P. O'Neil, B. Purimetla, D. Shasha, C. Shen, C.-S. Shih, N. Soparkar, J. A. Stankovic, Z. Wei, and the anonymous reviewers for their comments on previous versions of this paper. This work was supported in part by NSF under grants CDA-8922572, IRI-9109210, and IRI-9114197.

References

1. R. Abbott and H. Garcia-Molina, "Scheduling real-time transactions: a performance evaluation," in *Proc. 14th VLDB Conf.*, 1988.
2. R. Abbott and H. Garcia-Molina, "Scheduling real-time Transactions with disk resident data," in *Proc. 15th VLDB Conf.*, 1989.

3. R. Abbott and H. Garcia-Molina, "Scheduling I/O requests with deadlines: a performance evaluation," in *Proc. Real-time Systems Symp.* 1990.

4. N. Audsley, A. Burns, M. Richardson, and A. Wellings, "A database model for hard real-time systems," Technical Report, Real-Time Systems Group, University of York, U.K., 1991.

5. B.R. Badrinath and K. Ramamritham, "Semantics-based concurrency control: beyond commutativity," *ACM Trans. Database Systems*, vol. 17, no. 1, pp. 163–199, March 1992.

6. S. Baruah, G. Koren, D. Mao, B. Mishra, A. Raghunathan, L. Rosier, D. Shasha, and F. Wang, "On the competitiveness of on-line real-time scheduling," in *Proc. Real-Time Systems Symp.*, 1991.

7. P.A. Bernstein, V. Hadzilacos, and N. Goodman, *Conncurrency Control and Recovery in Database Systems*, Addison-Wesley: Reading, MA, 1987.

8. S. Biyabani, J.A. Stankovic, and K. Ramamritham, "The integration of deadline and criticalness in hard real-time scheduling," in *Proc. Real-Time Systems Symp.*, 1988.

9. A.P. Buchmann, D.R. McCarthy, M. Chu, and U. Dayal, "Time-critical database scheduling: a framework for integrating real-time scheduling and concurrency control," in *Proc. Conf. Data Engineering*, 1989.

10. M.J. Carey, R. Jauhari, and M. Livny, "Priority in DBMS resource scheduling," in *Proc. 15th VLDB Conf.*, 1990, pp. 397–410.

11. S. Chen, J. Stankovic, J. Kurose, and D. Towsley, "Performance evaluation of two new disk scheduling algorithms for real-time systems," *Real-Time Systems*, vol. 3, no. 3, pp. 307–336, Sept. 1991.

12. U. Dayal et. al, "The HiPAC project: combining active databases and timing constraints," *SIGMOD Record*, vol. 17, pp. 51–70, 1988.

13. K.R. Dittrich and U. Dayal, "Active database systems" (tutorial notes), in *seventeenth Int. Conf. Very Large Databases*, 1991.

14. K.P. Eswaran, J.N. Gray, R.A. Lorie, and I.L. Traiger, "The notion of consistency, and predicate locks in a database system," *Comm. ACM*, vol. 19(11), pp. 624–633, 1976.

15. Peter A. Franaszek, John T. Robinson, and Alexander Thomasian, "Access invariance and its use in high contention environments", in *Proc. Sixth Int. Conf. Database Engineerinng*, 1990, pp. 47–55.

16. M.C. Graham, "Issues in real-time data management," *Real-Time Systems*, vol. 4, no. 3, pp. 185–202, Sept. 1992.

17. J.N. Gray, R.A. Lorie, G.R. Putzulo, and I.L. Traiger, "Granularity of locks and degress of consistency in a shared database," in *Proc. First Int. Conf. Very Large Databases*, Framingham, MA, 1975, pp. 25–33.

18. J.N. Gray and A. Reuter, *Transaction processing: techniques and concepts*, Morgan Kaufman, 1992.

19. N. Griffeth and A. Weinrib, "Scalability of a real-time distributed resource counter", in *Proc. Real-Time Systems Symp.*, Orlando, 1990.

20. J.R. Haritsa, M.J. Carey and M. Livny, "On being optimistic about real-time constraints," in *Proc. ACM PODS*, 1990.

21. J.R. Haritsa, M.J. Carey, and M. Livny, "Dynamic real-time optimistic concurrency control," in *Proc. Real-Time Systems Symp.*, 1990.

22. J.R. Haritsa, M.J. Carey, and M. Livny, "Earliest deadline scheduling for real-time database systems," in *Proc. Real-Time Systems Symp.*, 1991.

23. W. Hou, G. Ozsoyoglu, and B.K. Taneja, "Processing aggregate relational queries with hard time constraints," in *Proc. ACM SIGMOD Int. Conf. Management of Data*, 1989.

24. J. Huang and J. Stankovic, "Real-time buffer management," in COINS TR 90–65, 1990.

25. J. Huang, J.A. Stankovic, K. Ramamritham, and D. Towsley, "Experimental evaluation of real-time optimistic concurrency control schemes," in *Proc. Conf. Very Large Data Bases*, 1991.

26. J. Huang, J.A. Stankovic, K. Ramamritham, and D. Towsley, "On using priority inheritance in real-time databases," in *Proc. Real-Time Systems Symp.*, 1991.

27. J. Huang, J.A. Stankovic, D. Towsley, and K.Ramamritham, "Experimental evaluation of real-time transaction processing," in *Proc. Real-Time Systems Symp.*, 1989.

28. E.D. Jensen, C.D. Locke, and H. Tokuda, "A time-driven scheduling model for real-time operating systems," in *Proc. 1985 IEEE Real-Time Systems Symp.*, pp. 112–122.

29. W. Kim and J. Srivastava, "Enhancing real-time DBMS performance with multiversion data and priority-based disk scheduling," in *Proc. Real-Time Systems Symp.*, 1991, pp. 222–231.

30. G. Koren and D. Shasha, "D-Over: an optimal on-line scheduling algorithm for overloaded real-time systems," in *Real-Time Systems Symp.*, 1992.

31. H.F. Korth, E. Levy, and A. Silberschatz, "Compensating transactions: a new recovery paradigm," in *Proc. Sixteenth Int. Conf. Very Large Databases*, Brisbane, Australia, 1990, pp. 95–106.

32. H.F. Korth, N. Soparkar, A. Silberschatz, "Triggered real-time databases with consistency constraints," in *Proc. Conf. Very Large Data Bases*, 1990.

33. Y. Lin and S.H. Son, "Concurrenncy control in real-time databases by dynamic adjustment of serialization order," in *Proc. Real-Time Systems Symp.*, 1990.

34. J. Liu, K. Lin, W. Shih, A. Yu, J. Chung, and W. Zhao, "Algorithms for scheduling imprecise computation," *IEEE Comput.*, vol. 24, no. 5, 1991.

35. J.E.B. Moss, "Nested transactions: an approach to reliable distributed computing," Ph.D. thesis, Massachusetts Institute of Technology, Cambridge, MA, 1981.

36. P. O'Neil, K. Ramamritham, and C. Pu, "Towards predictable transaction executions in real-time database systems," Technical Report 92–35, University of Massachusetts, 1992.

37. C. Pu and A. Leff, "Replica control in distributed systems: an asynchronous approach," in *Proc. ACM SIGMOD Int. Conf. Management of Data*, 1991, pp. 377–386.

38. K. Ramamritham and P. Chrysanthis, "In search of acceptability criteria: database consistency requirements and transaction correctness properties," in *Distributed Object Management*, T. Ozsu, Dayal, and P. Valduriez (Eds.), Morgan Kaufmann, 1992.

39. K. Ramamritham, S. Son, A. Buchmann, K. Dittrich, and C. Mohan, "Real-time databases," panel statement, *Proc. Conf. Very-Large Databases*, 1991.

40. K. Ramamritham, J. Stankovic, and P. Shiah, "Efficient scheduling algorithms for real-time multiprocessor systems," *IEEE Trans. Parallel Distrib Systems*, vol. 1, no. 2, pp. 184–194, 1990.

41. L. Sha, R. Rajkumar, and J. Lehoczky, "Priority inheritance protocols: an approach to real-time synchronization," *IEEE Trans. Comput.*, 39, pp. 1175–1185, 1990.

42. L. Sha, R. Rajkumar, and J.P. Lehoczky, "Concurrency control for distributed real-time databases," *ACM SIGMOD Record*, vol. 17, no. 1, pp. 82–98, March 1988.

43. C. Shen, K. Ramamritham, and J. Stankovic, "Resource reclaiming in real-time," in *Proc. Real-Time System Symp.* 1990. (To appear in) *IEEE Trans. parallel Distrib. Systems*, March 1993.

44. K.P. Smith and J.W.S. Liu, "Monotonically improving approximate answers to relational algebra queries," *Proc. Compsac*, 1989.

45. R. Snodgrass and I. Ahn, "Temporal databases," *IEEE Comput.*, vol. 19, no. 9, pp. 35–42, 1986.

46. S. H. Son, Y. Lin, and R.P. Cook "Concurrency control in real-time databases systems," in *Foundationns of Real-time Computing: Scheduling and Resource Management*, Andre van Tilborg and Gary Koob, (eds.), Kluwer 1991, pp. 185–202.

47. X. Song and J.W.S. Liu, "How well can data temporal consistency be maintained?" in *Proc. IEEE Symp. Computer-Aided Control Systems Design*, pp. 275–284, March 1992.

48. J.A. Stankovic, K. Ramamritham, and D. Towsley, "Scheduling in real-time transaction systems," in Andre van Tilborg and Gray Koob, (eds.), *Foundations of Real-Time Computing: Scheduling and Resource Management*, 1991, pp. 157–184.

49. Y.C. Tay, Nathan Goodman, and Rajan Suri, "Locking performance in centralized databases," *ACM Trans. Database Systems*, vol.10, 4, pp. 415–462. 1985.

50. S. V. Vrbsky and K.J. Lin, "Recovering imprecise computations with real-time constraints," in *Proc. Seventh Symp. Reliable Distributed Systems*, 1988, pp. 185–193.

Real-Time Transaction Processing:
Design, Implementation and Performance Evaluation *

Jiandong Huang
Department of Electrical and Computer Engineering

John A. Stankovic
Don Towsley
Krithi Ramamritham
Department of Computer and Information Science
University of Massachusetts
Amherst, MA 01003

May, 1990

Abstract

In addition to satisfying database consistency requirements, as in traditional database systems, real-time transaction processing systems must also satisfy timing constraints. To support real-time transaction processing, some new criteria and issues should be considered in design and implementation of real-time database systems. In this paper, we design algorithms for handling CPU scheduling, data conflict resolution, deadlock resolution, transaction wakeup, and transaction restart, based on a locking scheme for concurrency control. We implement a real-time database testbed containing these algorithms and evaluate their performance. The performance data indicates that (1) for a CPU-bound system, the CPU scheduling algorithm is the most significant of all the algorithms in improving the performance of real-time transactions, (2) conflict resolution protocols which directly address deadlines and criticalness can have a substantial impact on performance compared to protocols that ignore such information, and regardless of whether the system bottleneck is the CPU or the I/O, the protocols always improve performance for the most critical transactions, (3) both criticalness and deadline distributions strongly affect transaction performance, and (4) overheads such as locking and message communication are non-negligible and can not be ignored in real-time transaction analysis. We believe that these empirical results represent the first experimental results for real-time transactions on a testbed system.

Index terms - concurrency control, operating systems, performance evaluation, real-time databases, real-time systems, system design and implementation.

---

*This work was supported, in part, by the U.S. Office of Naval Research under Grant N00014-85-K0398, by the National Science Foundation under Grant IRI-8908693, and by Digital Equipment Corporation.

1 Introduction

A real-time database is a database system where (at least some) transactions have explicit timing constraints such as deadlines. In such a system, transaction processing must satisfy not only the database consistency constraints but also the timing constraints. Real-time database systems are becoming increasingly important in a wide range of applications. One example of real-time database systems is a computer integrated manufacturing system where a database keeps track of the state of physical machines, manages various processes in the production line, and collects statistical data from manufacturing operations. Transactions executing in the database may have deadlines in order to reflect, in a timely manner, the state of manufacturing operations or to respond to the control messages from operators. For instance, the information describing the current state of an object may need to be updated before a team of robots can work on the object. The update transaction is considered successful only if the data (the information) is changed consistently (in the view of all the robots) and the update operation is done within the specified time period. Other applications of real-time database systems can be found in program trading in the stock market, radar tracking systems, command and control systems, and air traffic control systems.

Most research work on databases focuses on query processing and database consistency, but not on meeting any time-constraints associated with transactions. On the other hand, real-time systems research deals with task scheduling to guarantee responses within deadlines, but has largely ignored the problem of guaranteeing the consistency of shared data, especially for data that resides on a disk. These traditional mechanisms for consistency enforcement and for timing constraint enforcement are not suited for real-time transaction processing. Rather, algorithms from the two areas have to be extended and combined or entirely new algorithms are needed in order to handle the requirements of real-time transactions in a unified manner. To study real-time database systems, new techniques are required to specify the properties of transactions, to define correctness, and to specify proper metrics.

Some papers have recently been published in the area of time-critical database systems. The topics covered in these papers include the identification of the characteristics of real-time transactions as well as a model of the underlying real-time operating system primitives [17,1,5], consistency issues[15,17,12], access control and conflict resolution [17,2], transaction scheduling [2,5], I/O scheduling [3,6], deadlock prevention [14], knowledge modelling [7,8,10] and data buffering [6]. These previous studies provide insight into many of the issues encountered in the design of real-time transaction systems, and present some basic ideas for solving some of the problems.

Because research on real-time transactions is still in its infancy, the results reported in the literatures are incomplete. For example, timing constraints and criticalness are two important factors in describing real-time transactions. The relation between the two factors and their combined effect with respect to system performance has not been addressed. In addition, some of the previous work concentrates on only one or two specific issues, thus lacking an integrated systemwide approach. Furthermore, none of the ideas or proposed algorithms in the previous studies, though well thought out, have been evaluated in real systems. Indeed, only [2,6] present any experimental results. However, these results are based on simulation and the effect of many important overheads, such as locking and process communication, are ignored.

The work reported here uses an integrated approach to study real-time transaction processing on a testbed system. We consider a real-time database system where data consistency based on the notion of serializability is preserved while the timing constraints are soft real-time.[1] Using a basic locking scheme for concurrency control, we investigate several algorithms for handling CPU scheduling, data conflict resolution, deadlock resolution, transaction wakeup, and transaction restart. The focus of this study is to understand the effect of these processing components on real-time databases and to identify the dominant components in real-time transaction processing. Another aspect of this work is to study the relationship between transaction timing constraints and criticalness and their combined effects on system performance. To provide deeper insight into our performance studies, we built a real-time database testbed, called RT-CARAT. The testbed captures the system overheads, which are largely ignored in simulation studies, and provides an improved understanding of the functional requirements and operational behavior of real-time database systems.

The rest of this paper is organized as follows. In section 2, we describe our real-time database model and a model for real-time transactions. The protocols and policies for real-time transaction processing are described in section 3, where we focus on CPU scheduling, data conflict resolution, transaction wakeup policies, deadlock resolution, and transaction restart. In section 4, we present our real-time database testbed, briefly showing how the proposed protocols and policies are implemented and integrated as a whole. The performance results are demonstrated and discussed in section 5. We make concluding remarks in Section 6.

2 A Real-Time Database Model

In this study we investigate a centralized, secondary storage real-time database. As is usually required in traditional database systems, we also require that all the real-time transaction operations should maintain data consistency as defined by serializability. The property of data consistency may be relaxed in some real-time database systems, depending on the application environment and data properties [15,17,12]. Relaxation of consistency is not considered in this paper. In our system, serializability is enforced by using the two-phase locking protocol.

Figure 1 depicts our system model from the perspective of transaction flow. This model is an extended version of the model used in [4]. The system is a closed queueing network, where a fixed number of users submit transaction requests one after another. Any new or re-submitted transaction will enter a scheduling queue first. The *scheduling* component performs dynamic CPU scheduling according to a certain policy. Before a transaction performs operation on a data object, it must go through the *concurrency control* component (CC) to obtain a lock on that object. If the request for the lock is denied, the transaction

---

[1]Soft real-time transactions are those that should meet their deadlines, but there may still be some (but diminishing) value for completing the transactions after their deadlines.

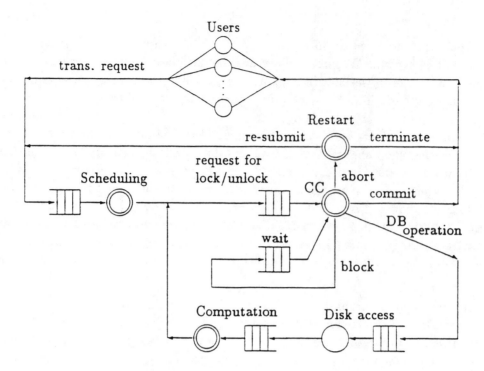

Figure 1: The system model

will be placed into a wait queue. The waiting transaction will be awakened when the requested lock is released. If the requested lock is granted, the transaction will perform the operation which consists of *disk access* and *computation*. A transaction may continue this "lock request − operation cycle" many times until it commits. At its commit stage, the transaction releases (unlocks) all the locks it has been holding. The concurrency control algorithm may abort a transaction for any number of reasons (to be discussed later). In that case, the *restart* component will decide, according to its current policy, whether the aborted transaction should be re-submitted or terminated. Note that this model only reflects the logical operations involved in transaction processing and it does not show the interaction of the processing components with physical resources. In practice, all of the processing components depicted by a double circle in Figure 1 compete for the CPU. Access to the CPU resource is determined by the *scheduling* component.

A real-time transaction is characterized by its length and a value function. [2] The transaction length is dependent on the number of data objects to be accessed and the amount of computation to be performed, which may not be always known. In this study, some of the protocols assume that the transaction length is known when the transaction is submitted to the system. This assumption is justified by the fact that in many application environments like banking and inventory management, the transaction length, i.e. the number of records to be accessed and the number of computation steps, is likely be known in advance.

---

[2]Note that there are no standard workloads for real-time transactions, but a value function has been used in other real-time system work [13,1].

In a real-time database, each transaction imparts a value to the system, which is related to its criticalness and to when it completes execution (relative to its deadline). In general, the selection of a value function depends on the application [1]. In this work, we model the value of a transaction as a function of its criticalness, start time, deadline, and the current system time. Here criticalness represents the importance of transactions, while deadlines constitute the time constraints of real-time transactions. Criticalness and deadline are two characteristics of real-time transactions and they are not necessarily related. A transaction which has a short deadline does not imply that it has high criticalness. Transactions with the same criticalness may have different deadlines and transactions with the same deadline may have different criticalness values. Basically, the higher the criticalness of a transaction, the larger its value to the system. On the other hand, the value of a transaction is time-variant. A transaction which has missed its deadline will not be as valuable to the system as if it completed before its deadline. We use the following formula to express the value of transaction T:

$$V_T(t) = \begin{cases} c_T, & s_T \leq t < d_T \\ c_T \times (z_T - t)/(z_T - d_T), & d_T \leq t < z_T \\ 0, & \text{otherwise} \end{cases} \qquad (1)$$

where t - current time;

s_T - start time of transaction T;

d_T - deadline of transaction T;

c_T - criticalness of transaction T, $1 \leq c_T \leq c_{Tmax}$;

c_{Tmax} - the maximum value of criticalness.

In this model, a transaction has a constant value, i.e. its criticalness value, before its deadline. The value decays when the transaction passes its deadline and decreases to zero at time z_T. We call z_T the *zero-value point*. As an example, Figure 2 shows the value functions of two transactions T_1 and T_2.

The decay rate, i.e. the rate at which the value of a transaction drops after its deadline, is dependent on the characteristics of the real-time transaction. To simplify the performance study, we model the decay rate as a linear function of deadline and criticalness. Here we study two models with z_T expressed by the following two formulas.

$$z_T = d_T + (d_T - s_T)/c_T \qquad (2)$$

$$z_T = d_T + (d_T - s_T)/(c_{Tmax} - c_T + 1) \qquad (3)$$

For a given c_{Tmax}, when c_T increases, under Eq. (2), z_T decreases, whereas under Eq. (3), z_T increases. With Eq. (2), if a transaction is extremely critical ($c_T \to \infty$), its value drops to zero immediately after its deadline. This is the case that we can see in many hard real-time systems. In this work, we use Eq. (1) and Eq. (2) as the base model, and we consider Eq. (3) as an alternative for Eq. (2) as a sensitivity study.

The transactions considered here are solely soft real-time. Given the value function, real-time transactions should be processed in such a way that the total value of completed

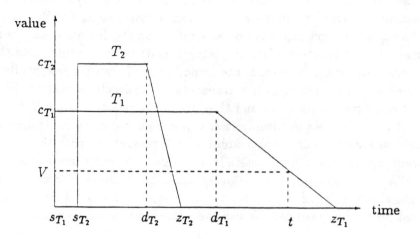

Figure 2: Value functions for transaction T_1 and T_2

transactions is maximized. In particular, a transaction should abort if it does not complete before time z_T (see Figure 2), since its execution after z_T does not contribute any value to the system at all. On the other hand, a transaction aborted because of deadlock or data conflict may be restarted if it may still impart some value to the system. [3]

Finally, at times, the estimated execution time of a transaction, r_T, may be known. This information might be helpful in making more informed decisions regarding which transactions are to wait, abort, or restart. This hypothesis is tested in our experiments by using algorithms that make use of r_T.

3   Real-Time Transaction Processing

Given the above system model and the characteristics of real-time transactions, the objective of our work is to develop and evaluate policies that provide the necessary support for real-time transactions. In this section, we explicitly address the problems of CPU scheduling, conflict resolution, transaction wakeup, deadlock resolution and transaction restart.

3.1   CPU Scheduling

There is a wide variety of algorithms for scheduling the CPU in traditional database systems. Such algorithms usually emphasize fairness and attempt to balance CPU and I/O bound transactions. These scheduling algorithms are not adequate for real-time transactions. In real-time environments, transactions should get access to the CPU based on criticalness and deadline, not fairness. If the complete semantics of transactions, e.g., the data access requirements and timing constraints, are known in advance, then scheduling can be done

---

[3] In some situations, a transaction may have to be completed even if time is past z_T. We do not consider such transactions here.

through transaction preanalysis [5]. On the other hand, in many cases complete knowledge may not be available. Then a priority based scheduling algorithm may be used, where the priority is set based on deadline, criticalness, length of the transaction, or some combination of these factors.

We consider three simple CPU scheduling algorithms. The first two algorithms are commonly found in real-time systems, and the third is an attempt to combine the first two so as to achieve the benefits of both.

- **Scheduling the most critical transaction first** (MCF)

- **Scheduling by earliest deadline first** (EDF)

- **Scheduling by criticalness and deadline** (CDF): In this algorithm, when a transaction arrives, it is assigned a priority based on the formula $(d_T - s_T)/c_T$. The smaller the calculated value, the higher the priority.

Under all of these three algorithms, when a transaction begin its commit phase, its priority is raised to the highest value among all the active transactions. This enables a transaction in its final stage of processing to complete as quickly as possible so that it will not be blocked by other transactions. This policy also reduces the chance for the committing transaction to block other transactions. In all three algorithms, the transactions are preemptable, i.e., an executing transaction (not in its commit phase) can be preempted by a transaction with higher priority.

3.2   Conflict Resolution Protocols (CRP)

Two or more transactions have a data conflict when they require the same data in non-compatible lock modes (i.e. *write-write* and *write-read*). The conflict should be resolved according to the characteristics of the conflicting transactions. Here we present five protocols for conflict resolution.

In the following descriptions, T_R denotes the transaction which is requesting a data item D, and T_H is another transaction that is holding a lock on D. The five protocols have the same algorithmic structure as follows:

```
T_R requests a lock on the data item D
if no conflict with T_H
    then T_R accesses D
    else  call CRPi    (i = 1,2,3,4,5)
end if
```

We start with the simple protocols in terms of complexity and the amount of information required.

3.2.1   Protocol 1 (CRP1): Based on criticalness only

This simple protocol only takes criticalness into account.

```
if c_{T_R} < c_{T_H} for any T_H
    then T_R waits
    else T_R aborts all T_H
end if
```

Note that protocol 1 is a deadlock-free protocol, since waiting transactions are always considered in criticalness order. In addition, this protocol implements an *always-abort* policy in a system where all the transactions have the same criticalness.

3.2.2   Protocol 2 (CRP2): Based on deadline-first-then-criticalness

We anticipate that criticalness and deadlines are the most important factors for real-time transactions. Protocol 2 only takes these two factors into account. Here we separate deadline and criticalness by checking the two parameters sequentially. The algorithm for this protocol is:

```
if d_{T_R} > d_{T_H} for any T_H
    then T_R waits
    else
            if c_{T_R} ≤ c_{T_H} for any T_H
                then T_R waits
                else T_R aborts all T_H
            end if
end if
```

3.2.3   Protocol 3 (CRP3): Based on deadline, criticalness and estimation of remaining execution time

CRP3 is an extension of CRP2. Besides deadline and criticalness, we further examine the remaining execution time of the conflicting transactions. Here we assume that the computation time and I/O operations of a transaction are known and they are proportional. Then the remaining execution time of transaction T can be estimated by the following formula:

$$time\_needed_T(t) = (t - s_T) \times (R\_total_T - R\_accessed_T(t))/R\_accessed_T(t)$$

where R_total_T is the total number of records to be accessed by T; $R\_accessed_T(t)$ is the number of records that have been accessed as of time t. The protocol is as follows:

```
if dT_R > dT_H for any T_H
    then T_R waits
    else
            if cT_R < cT_H for any T_H
                then T_R waits
                else
                        if cT_R = cT_H for any T_H
                            then
                                    if (time_needed_T_R(t) + t) > dT_R
                                        then T_R waits
                                        else T_R aborts all T_H
                                    end if
                            else  T_R aborts all T_H
                        end if
            end if
end if
```

3.2.4 Protocol 4 (CRP4): Based on a virtual clock

Each transaction, T, has a virtual clock associated with it. The virtual clock value, $VT_T(t)$, for transaction T is calculated by the following formula.

$$VT_T(t) = s_T + \beta_T * (t - s_T), \quad t \geq s_T$$

where β_T is the clock running rate which is proportional to transaction T's criticalness. The higher the c_T, the larger the value β_T. The protocol controls the setting and running of the virtual clocks. When transaction T starts, $VT_T(t)$ is set to the current real time s_T. Then, the virtual clock runs at rate β_T. That is, the more critical a transaction is, the faster its virtual clock runs. In this work, $\beta_T = c_T$. The protocol is given by the following pseudo code.

```
if dT_R > dT_H for any T_H
    then T_R waits
    else
            if any VT_T_H(t) ≥ dT_H
                then T_R waits
                else T_R aborts all T_H
            end if
end if
```

In this protocol, transaction T_R may abort T_H based on their relative deadlines, and on the criticalness and elapsed time of transaction T_H. When the virtual clock of an executing transaction has surpassed its deadline, it cannot be aborted. Intuitively, this means that for the transaction T_H to make its deadline, we are predicting that it should not be aborted. For further details about this protocol, the reader is referred to [17].

3.2.5 Protocol 5 (CRP5): Based on combining transaction parameters

This protocol takes into account a variety of different information about the involved transactions. It uses a function $CP_T(t)$ to make decisions.

$$CP_T(t) = c_T * (w_1 * (t - s_T) - w_2 * d_T + w_3 * p_T(t) + w_4 * io_T(t) - w_5 * l_T(t))$$

where $p_T(t)$ and $io_T(t)$ are the CPU time and I/O time consumed by the transaction, $l_T(t)$ is the approximate laxity[4] (if known), and the w_k's are non-negative weights. The protocol is described by the following pseudo code.

> if $CP_{T_R}(t) \leq CP_{T_H}(t)$ for any T_H
>   **then** T_R waits
>   **else** T_R aborts all T_H
> **end if**

By appropriately setting weights to zero it is easy to create various outcomes, e.g., where a smaller deadline transaction always aborts a larger deadline transaction. The reader is referred to [17] for further discussion of this protocol.

In a disk resident database system, it is difficult to determine the computation time and I/O time of a transaction. In our experiments, we simplify the above formula for CP calculation as follows:

$$CP_T(t) = c_T * [w1 * (t - s_T) - w2 * d_T + w3 * (R\_accessed_T(t)/R\_total_T)]$$

where R_total_T and $R\_accessed_T(t)$ are the same as defined in CRP3.

In summary, the five protocols resolve data conflict by either letting the lock-requesting transaction wait or aborting the lock holder(s), depending on various parameters of the conflicting transactions.

3.3 Policies for Transaction Wakeup

When a lock holder releases the lock, it is possible that more than one transaction is waiting for the lock. At this point, it is necessary to decide which waiting transaction should be granted the lock. The decision should be based on transaction parameters, such as deadline and criticalness, and also should be consistent with the conflict resolution protocols (CRP) discussed in the previous section. Here we give the policies for transaction wake-up operation which correspond to each CRP.

- For CRP1, wake up the waiting transaction with the highest criticalness.

---

[4]Laxity is the maximum amount of time that a transaction can afford to wait but still make its deadline.

- For CRP2 and CRP3, wake up the waiting transaction with the minimum deadline.

- For CRP4, wake up the waiting transaction with maximum $VT_T(t)$ - the value of virtual clock.

- For CRP5, wake up the waiting transaction with maximum $CP_T(t)$ - the value of combined transaction parameters.

3.4 Deadlock Resolution

The use of a locking scheme may cause deadlock. This problem can be resolved by using deadlock detection, deadlock prevention, or deadlock avoidance. For example, CRP1 presented in the previous section is a kind of scheme for deadlock prevention. In this study, we focus on the problem of deadlock detection as it is required by the remaining concurrency control algorithms.

With the deadlock detection approach, a deadlock detection routine is invoked when a transaction is to be queued for a locked data object. If a deadlock cycle is detected, one of the transactions involved in the cycle must be aborted in order to break the cycle. Choosing a transaction for abort is a policy decision. For real-time transactions, we want to choose a victim so that the timing constraints of the remaining transactions can be met as much as possible, and at the same time the abort operation will incur the minimum cost. Here we present five deadlock resolution policies which take into account the timing properties of the transactions, the cost of abort operations, and the complexity of the protocols.

Deadlock resolution policy 1 (DRP1): *Always abort the transaction which invokes the deadlock detection.* This policy is simple and efficient since it does not need any information from the transactions in the deadlock cycle.

Deadlock resolution policy 2 (DRP2): *Trace the deadlock cycle. Abort the first transaction T with $t > z_T$; otherwise abort the transaction with the longest deadline.*

Recall that a transaction which has passed its zero-value point, z_T, may not have been aborted yet because it may not have executed since passing z_T, and because preempting another transaction execution to perform the abort may not be advantageous. Consequently, in this and the following protocols we first abort any waiting transaction that has passed its zero-value point.

Deadlock resolution policy 3 (DRP3): *Trace the deadlock cycle. Abort the first transaction T with $t > z_T$; otherwise abort the transaction with the earliest deadline.*

Deadlock resolution policy 4 (DRP4): *Trace the deadlock cycle. Abort the first transaction T with $t > z_T$; otherwise abort the transaction with the least criticalness.*

Deadlock resolution policy 5 (DRP5): Here we use $time\_needed_T(t)$ as defined in CRP3. A transaction T is *feasible* if $(time\_needed_T(t) + t) < d_T$ and *tardy* otherwise. This policy aborts a tardy transaction with the least criticalness if one exists, otherwise it aborts a feasible transaction with the least criticalness. The following algorithm describes this policy.

Step 1: set tardy_set to empty
       set feasible_set to empty

Step 2: trace deadlock cycle
       for each T in the cycle do
       if $t > z_T$
         then abort T
            return
         else
            if T is tardy
              then add T to tardy_set
              else add T to feasible_set
            end if
       end if

Step 3: **if** tardy_set is not empty
           then search tardy_set for T with the least criticalness
           else search feasible_set for T with the least criticalness
       end if
       abort T
       return

3.5 Transaction Restart

A transaction may abort for any number of reasons. Basically, there are two types of aborts.

- *termination abort:* This type of abort is used to terminate a transaction. For example, a transaction may abort itself due to some execution exception. Also, a transaction could be aborted by the system if it has a zero value. Such aborts always lead to transaction termination.

- *concurrency abort:* This type of abort results from concurrency control. For instance, a transaction may be aborted in order to resolve a deadlock, or, a transaction may be aborted by another transaction because of a data access conflict. These aborted transactions should be restarted as long as they may still contribute a positive value to the system.

Based on our transaction model, we propose three policies for transaction restart from *concurrency abort*.

Transaction restart policy 1 (TRP1): *Restart an aborted transaction T if $t < z_T$.* In other words, an aborted transaction will be restarted as long as it may still have some value to the system. Note that the transaction may have already passed its deadline at this point. This policy is intended to maximize the value that the transaction may contribute to the system.

Transaction restart policy 2 (TRP2): *Restart an aborted transaction T if $r_T + t <$* z_T. Here we assume that the runtime estimate r_T of transaction T is known. The decision on transaction restart is based on the estimate of whether the transaction can complete by time z_T, if it is restarted.

Transaction restart policy 3 (TRP3): TRP3 is an extension of TRP2 and is given by the following algorithm.

```
if zT − t < rT
    then terminate T
    else
            if dT − t > rT
                then restart T
                else increase cT by one
                        restart T
            end if
    end if
end if
```

Here if it is estimated that T can not complete by d_T, then T's criticalness is increased by one. This restarted transaction has a higher priority than it did in its previous incarnation. Thus the transaction will have a greater chance to meet its timing constraint after its restart. Note that the performance of other concurrent transactions may be affected by this dynamic change of transaction criticalness. The impact of this strategy on system performance is examined through the performance tests.

4   The Testbed System

We implemented and used a real-time database testbed named RT-CARAT. It is an extension of a previously built testbed, called CARAT (Concurrency and Recovery Algorithm Testbed) [11]. RT-CARAT was designed to be a flexible tool for the testing and performance evaluation of real-time database protocols. Currently, RT-CARAT testbed is a centralized, secondary storage real-time database system. The testbed is complete. It contains all the major functional components of a transaction processing system, such as transaction management, data management, log management, and communication management. The testbed is build on top of the VAX/VMS operating system. By appropriate settings of various VMS system parameters, non-essential overheads of VMS, such as memory paging and process swapping, are eliminated.

The testbed is implemented as a set of cooperating server processes which communicate via efficient message passing mechanisms. Figure 3 illustrates the process and message structure of RT-CARAT. A pool of transaction processes (TR's) simulate the users of the real-time database. Accordingly, there is a pool of data managers (DM's) which service transaction requests from the user processes (the TR's). There is one transaction manager, called the TM server, acting as the inter-process communication agent between TR and DM processes. The communications between TR, TM and DM processes are carried out

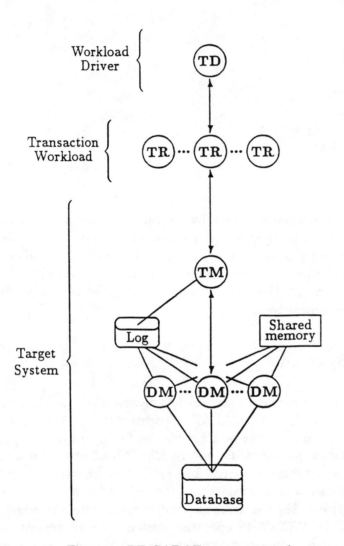

Figure 3: RT-CARAT processes and message structure

through the mailbox, a facility provided by VAX/VMS. In order to speed up the processing of real-time transactions, the communication among DM processes is implemented using a shared memory space, called a global section in VAX/VMS.

For concurrency control and recovery, RT-CARAT has adopted the two-phase locking protocol (2PL) and after-image (AI) journaling mechanism from the CARAT implementation. These operations, plus deadlock detection and conflict resolution, are carried out in the DM processes.

In RT-CARAT, the CPU is scheduled based on transaction priority with preemption using the underlying VAX/VMS operating system real-time priorities. The CPU scheduler is embedded in the TM. Upon receiving a transaction execution request from a TR, the scheduler assigns a priority to the transaction according to the CPU scheduling policy (see Section 3.1). The scheduling operation is done by mapping the assigned transaction priority to the real-time priority of the DM process which carries out the transaction execution. At this point, an executing DM will be preempted if it is not the highest priority DM process at the moment, otherwise it will continue to run. Note that an executing transaction with high priority can be blocked by a low priority transaction because of data conflict. The blocking is resolved by the conflict resolution protocols (see Section 3.2) embedded in the DM.

In a secondary storage database system, disk I/O is an important operation. From the point of view of real-time, especially for I/O bound real-time database systems, these I/O operations should be scheduled according to the characteristics of real-time transactions [3,6]. In our testbed, unfortunately, disk access is under the control of disk controllers instead of the operating system, i.e. there is no way to directly manipulate disk access through the system utilities. Thus, in the current implementation, there is no component dealing with real-time I/O scheduling. However, through careful design of the experiments, we are able to determine the impact of not doing real-time I/O scheduling on system performance.

5 Experimental Results

5.1 The Test Environment

In our experiments, the database consists of 3000 physical blocks (512 bytes each) with each block containing 6 records for a total of 18,000 records. Two separate disks are used, one for the database and the other for the log. In all the experiments, the multi-programming level in the system is 8.

A transaction generator in each TR process generates transactions according to a configuration file where transaction type (write or read only), length (the number of records to be accessed and the amount of computation time), criticalness, and deadline are specified. A transaction performs a certain number of predefined operations, called *steps*, and each operation may access a certain number of records and do a certain amount of computation. A transaction terminates upon completion or a termination abort. In the tests described here, the transaction generator submits a new transaction immediately after the previous transaction has terminated, i.e. there is no external think time between consecutive transactions.

In the experiments presented in this paper, each transaction is either a *read only* transaction or *a write* transaction. To achieve a mix of read and write operations in the system, we specify the number of *read* transactions and *write* transactions, which is represented by w/r - the ratio of *write* transactions to *read* transactions.

We express the length of a transaction by the form $T(x, y, u)$, where x is the number of steps, y the number of records accessed in each step, and u the amount of computation units per step with 1 unit = 50 ms. The transaction deadline is randomly generated from a uniform distribution within a deadline window, $[d\_base, \alpha \times d\_base]$, where d_base is the window baseline and α is a variable determining the upper bound of the deadline window. For each workload in the experiments, d_base is specified first by the formula:

$$d\_base = avg\_rsp - stnd\_dvi$$

where avg_rsp is the average response time of the same real-time transactions when executed in a non real-time database environment, and $stnd\_dvi$ is the standard deviation of the response time. Besides the deadline, each transaction, when initiated, is randomly assigned a criticalness from a uniform distribution. In the experiments, there are up to 8 levels of criticalness and accordingly, the transactions are classified into 8 classes. We specify the criticalness of transaction T as a function of its class, i.e.

$$c_T(class) = 8 - class + 1, \quad class = 1, 2, ..., 8$$

The smaller the class number, the higher the corresponding criticalness, or vice versa. Once the deadline and criticalness are specified, the value function of the transaction is fixed and the transaction value can be computed at any time (see Section 2).

5.2 Baseline and Metrics

For these tests, the performance baseline is a non real-time transaction processing system (NRT), which is defined by the following baseline algorithms:

- CPU scheduling policy: *schedule transactions by a multi-level feedback queue* (MFQ);

- conflict resolution: *place the lock-requesting transaction into a FIFO wait queue* (CRP0);

- deadlock resolution: DRP1;

- transaction restart: TRP1.

We use the following metrics to evaluate the proposed algorithms and protocols.

- Deadline guarantee ratio (DGR_{class}) - the percentage of transactions in a class that complete by their deadline.

- Average deadline guarantee ratio (ADGR) - the percentage of transactions in all classes that complete by their deadline, i.e.

$$ADGR = \frac{1}{8} \sum_{class=1}^{8} DGR_{class}$$

- Weighted value (WV_{class})- the total value of all transactions in a class that complete by their zero-value points (z_T) divided by the total maximum value of the invoked transactions in all classes.

- Total weighted value (TWV) - the sum of weighted values in all classes, i.e.

$$TWV = \sum_{class=1}^{8} WV_{class}$$

- Abort ratio (AR_{class})- the percentage of aborted transactions in a class.

- Total abort ratio (TAR) - the percentage of aborted transactions in all classes, i.e.

$$TAR = \sum_{class=1}^{8} AR_{class}$$

Our data collection is based on the method of *replication*. In the experiments each test consists of two to six runs where each run was two hours long. The data was collected and averaged over the total number of runs. The number of runs for each test depends on the stability of the data. Our requirement on the statistical data is to generate 95% confidence intervals for the deadline guarantee ratio whose width is less than 10% of the point estimate of the deadline guarantee ratio.

5.3 Experiments

We present results from the following six *sets* of experiments:

- **System performance measurements:** The purpose of this experiment is to study the supporting system software performance and to identify the dominant overheads and their magnitudes.

- **CPU scheduling:** The effect of CPU scheduling on the performance of real-time transactions was studied by varying transaction length, deadline setting, write/read ratio, and mixing transactions with different lengths.

- **Conflict resolution:** In these experiments we compared the performance of all the conflict resolution policies by varying transaction length, deadline setting, and write/read ratio.

- **CPU scheduling vs. conflict resolution**: In these experiments we studied the impact of CPU scheduling versus conflict resolution on the performance of real-time transactions.

- **CPU bound vs. I/O bound systems**: This experiment was intended to identify the degree of the system performance degradation due to the lack of real-time based I/O scheduling.

- **Sensitivity study for value functions**: Based on the value function model proposed in Section 2, we investigated the impact of two different value functions on the experimental results.

Besides the above studies, we also investigated the proposed *deadlock resolution policies*. The results show that for the wide range of workloads we tested, the performance of all the policies are similar because the deadlock cycle involved only two transactions most of the time. We also did experiments for the three *transaction restart policies*, and found no significant differences between them. This is because the runtime estimate (r_T) used in the algorithms was based on the transaction average response time. Due to the large deviation of the response time, r_T was not accurate enough to support algorithms TRP2 and TRP3. Thus, to save space, we do not show these experimental results here. For all the experiments discussed below, DRP1 and TRP1 were used for deadlock resolution and transaction restart, respectively.

Table 1 summarizes the parameter settings and protocol selections in the experiments.

5.3.1 System Performance Measurements

To study various system overheads, several experiments are conducted with different workloads and different combinations of the protocols. To focus on the overheads, the user computation time u is set to zero. This has the effect of maximizing number of data requests and the subsequent overheads. Table 2 shows the measurement results with respect to (average) CPU utilization over all the runs. In the table, the data for RT-CARAT is the overall system CPU utilization which is the sum of the CPU utilizations of the TR, TM and DM processes. *Locking* is a processing component of DM, which in addition includes *deadlock detection* and *conflict resolution*. *CPU scheduling* is part of the TM process. The item *communication* includes all the overhead involved in message communication through mailboxes in the system.

It can be seen that locking and message communication are the main overheads of the system, while the overhead from CPU scheduling, deadlock detection and conflict resolution is negligible. These measures indicate that in the analysis of real-time transaction processing, some overheads such as locking and process communication cannot be simply ignored, while some overheads such as conflict resolution should not be over-emphasized.

Table 1: Experimental Settings

Parameter	Setting
Disks	disk1: database; disk2: log.
Database size	3000 blocks (18000 records)
Multiprogramming level	8
Transaction class	8 levels of criticalness
α (deadline window factor)	2.0 - 5.0
w/r (ratio of write/read trans.)	2/6, 4/4, 6/2, 8/0
x (steps per transaction)	4 - 20 steps
y (records accessed per step)	4 records
u (computation time per step)	0 or 10 units
Protocol	Selection
CPU scheduling	MFQ, MCF, EDF, CDF
Conflict resolution	CRPi, $i = 0, 1, 2, 3, 4, 5$
Deadlock resolution	DRP1
Transaction restart	TRP1
Wakeup policy	A function of conflict resolution policy (see 3.3)

Table 2: System Performance Measurements

Process/Component	Avg. CPU util.	Standard. devi.
RT-CARAT	0.944	0.012
TRs	0.080	0.001
TM	0.167	0.017
DMs	0.697	0.019
Locking (lock/unlock)	0.438	0.021
Deadlock detection	0.003	0.002
Conflict resolution	0.001	0.000
CPU scheduling	0.006	0.003
Communication	0.213	0.017

5.3.2 CPU Scheduling

In this experiment, in order to observe the effects that different CPU scheduling policies have on performance, we used CRP0 for conflict resolution, i.e. in case of data access conflict, it is always the lock-requesting transaction that is queued.

Figures 4-6 compare three scheduling schemes with respect to deadline guarantee ratio, weighted value, and total abort ratio, respectively. In this experiment, all the transactions were of equal length, $T(12, 4, 10)$, with $w/r=2/6$ and $\alpha=3$. Figure 4 plots the deadline guarantee ratio versus the transaction class. Our first observation is that CPU scheduling algorithms that make use of transaction information perform better than the baseline NRT, except for the transactions in classes 7 and 8 when executed under the scheduling algorithms MCF and CDF. As compared with the baseline and the scheduling algorithms EDF, both MCF and CDF result in a higher deadline guarantee ratio for the transactions with high criticalness, but a lower deadline guarantee ratio for the transactions with low criticalness. This is because the two algorithms take the criticalness of transactions into account and hence the high critical transactions perform better when they compete with low critical transactions. Of the two algorithms, CDF performs better than MCF, since CDF considers not only the criticalness but also the relative deadline of a transaction. Note that for transaction class 1, CDF improves the deadline guarantee ratio from 60% for the baseline to 97% for CDF. With the scheduling algorithm EDF, the performance was basically the same over all classes of transactions. This is understandable since the algorithm totally ignores criticalness.

Figure 5 depicts the weighted value that each class of transactions contributed to the system using a linear weighting scheme where each of the 8 criticalness levels differs in value by 1 unit. The performance results indicate that the system gains more value through CPU scheduling compared with the baseline. Overall, the higher the criticalness of a transaction, the larger the value it imparts to the system. Since the current value weighting scheme is linear, other weighting schemes, such as exponential, would result in even higher gains by the real-time CPU scheduling algorithm.

The transaction total abort ratio is shown in Figure 6. These plots are basically the inverse of plots for deadline guarantee ratio, i.e. the higher the deadline guarantee ratio, the lower the abort ratio. For MCF and CDF, the low abort ratio for high criticalness transactions is achieved by aborting more low critical transactions. The abort ratio with EDF is low over all classes of transactions.

The low transaction abort ratio under EDF scheduling policy results from the fact that under EDF most of the time transactions execute in a kind of sequential order. This interesting result can be explained as follows. First, transaction deadline and transaction arrival time are highly correlated in the experiments. Later arriving transactions usually have farther deadlines. Figure 7 shows the transaction deadline distributions under scheduling policy EDF. [5] Here the horizontal axis represents the deadline order of arriving transactions. Upon arrival of every transaction, we compare its deadline value with the deadlines

---

[5] Note that we also measured the transaction deadline distributions under NRT, MCF and CDF. The results are similar to what we show in Figure 7.

606

of those transactions executing in the system. As a result, the smaller its deadline value, the smaller its deadline order. For instance, an arriving transaction will be in order 1 if its deadline value is the smallest compared to the transactions already in the system, and will be in order 8 if its deadline value is the largest. The vertical axis represents the probability of the occurrence of each order. Clearly, the large percentage of arriving transactions have the longer deadline values, compared to the transactions executing in the system. Thus, under EDF most of the later arriving transactions have lower priority than the transactions already in their execution. Therefore, transaction preemption due to transaction arrivals seldom occurs. Second, the system is highly CPU-bound and the computation time in each transaction step is very long (500ms for $u=10$), compared to I/O time (about 80ms for $y=4$). Under such a system, with the given deadline distribution as just discussed, EDF actually reduces the concurrency of transaction execution. This is corroborated by the measures of the average number of granted locks at any instant in the system. Figure 8 plots the average number of granted locks as a function of transaction length x, under NRT, MCF, EDF and CDF, respectively. The measures indicate that EDF results in the lowest concurrency among the four scheduling policies. The degree of concurrency under the baseline NRT is the highest, since NRT uses a multi-level feedback queue scheduling policy which emphasizes equality for concurrent transactions. After examining these performance results in detail, it is clear now that under EDF, transaction execution is almost sequential.

The scheduling algorithms were also tested for transactions of different lengths and the performance results were basically the same as in the figures presented above [9].

We next study the sensitivity of the scheduling algorithms to transaction deadline settings. α is varied from 2.0 to 4.0 in steps of 0.5 with $w/r = 2/6$ and $T(12, 4, 10)$. Figure 9 shows the average deadline guarantee ratio over 8 classes of transactions. Among the scheduling algorithms EDF is most sensitive to deadline setting. This is because EDF uses only the information about deadline for scheduling. Also note that EDF performs best when the deadline is loose, and worst when the deadline is tight. As we mentioned above, under EDF, transactions execute almost in sequential order most of the time. Thus, when the deadline is tight, it performs worse than the baseline which is scheduled using a multi-level feedback queue. Both MCF and CDF are not sensitive to the deadline distributions. This is obvious for MCF, since it does not use deadline information. For CDF, criticalness is a dominant factor even though it uses deadline information.

We further examine the overall effects of the scheduling algorithms by varying the transaction length. Figure 10 presents the total weighted value versus the transaction length x, with $w/r = 2/6$ and $\alpha = 3$. The reader can see that the total value that the system gains under CPU scheduling is far more than the value gained by the baseline. However, when transactions become longer, the performance degrades as much as 20% because of higher data conflict rate, higher deadlock rate, and relatively tighter deadline windows (due to the larger *stnd_dvi* value).

All the above results are for workloads with $w/r = 2/6$. The CPU scheduling algorithms are also studied by varying the ratio of write/read transactions. Figure 11 and 12 depicts the performance results for different w/r ratio. Under the baseline NRT and the scheduling algorithms MCF and CDF, the data access conflict increases as w/r ratio increases, thus increasing the transaction abort ratio (due to deadlock) and lowering the deadline guarantee ratio. Owing to its sequential execution nature discussed above, EDF is not sensitive to the change of w/r ratio.

These observations and discussions lead to the following points:

- CPU scheduling by MCF and CDF significantly improves the overall performance of real-time transactions for the tested workloads. Further, MCF and CDF achieve good performance for more critical transactions at the cost of losing some transactions that are less critical. This trade-off reflects the nature of real-time transaction processing that is based on criticalness as well as timing constraints. Moreover, in order to get the best performance, both criticalness and deadline of a transaction are needed for CPU scheduling.

- EDF is most sensitive to deadline distributions and relatively independent of data access conflict. It performs well only when deadlines are not tight.

5.3.3 Conflict resolution

In this experiment, we study the performance of conflict resolution protocols by varying transaction length, deadline settings, and w/r ratio. The CPU scheduling algorithm used in the experiment is CDF, since it was shown to be the best in the previous section. Unlike the other experiments, the baseline compared in this experiment was chosen to be NRT_CDF - non real-time, applying CPU scheduling (CDF) only. This baseline enables us to isolate the performance differences due to the use of conflict resolution protocols. To create a high conflict rate, we first exercised the workloads with all write transactions (Figures 13-15) and then the workloads with the mix of read and write transactions (Figure 16).

Figure 13 presents the performance results with respect to total weighted value versus x, with w/r=8/0 and $\alpha = 3$. With short transactions ($x = 4, 8$), all the protocols perform basically the same, and there is no significant performance improvement as compared with NRT_CDF. This is not surprising since with short transactions, the data access conflict is low, and thus, none of the conflict resolution protocols play an important role. The performance difference can be seen as the conflict rate becomes high with long transactions ($x = 12, 16, 20$), where all the protocols outperform NRT_CDF.

Figure 14 provides a detailed examination of the performance results of long transactions with w/r=8/0, $x = 16$ and $\alpha = 3$. Among the five protocols, CRP1, the simplest one, performs best. This is largely due to the fact that CRP1 is a deadlock-free protocol by which all transaction aborts result from conflict resolution but not from deadlock resolution. Here the point is that if a transaction will be aborted, then it should be aborted as early as possible in order to reduce the waste in using the resources (e.g. CPU, I/O, critical section and data). Since the conflict resolution is applied before deadlock resolution in the course of transaction execution, an early abort from conflict resolution decreases the amount of resources that would be wasted if the transaction is aborted later from deadlock resolution.

The performance of CRP2 and CRP3 is almost identical, since CRP3 checks only one more condition than CRP2, namely the amount of time that the transaction needs to finish before its deadline. It is clear now that this additional estimated information does not substantially improve the performance.

CRP4 only outperforms NRT_CDF for transactions with high criticalness, but it performs slightly better than CRP2 and CRP3, as well as CRP1, for low critical transactions. This is because CRP4 does not take into account the criticalness of the lock-requesting transactions. When the deadline of lock-requesting transaction is earlier than that of lock-holding transaction, CRP4 allows the lock requester with high criticalness to wait for the lock holder with low criticalness, thus lowering the performance for higher criticalness transactions. This situation never occurs with the other conflict resolution protocols.

The performance of CRP5 is not as good as CRP1 but is better than that of other protocols. [6] This is because the dominant factor in CRP5 is criticalness (c_T is a multiplicand in calculation of $CP_T(t)$), which results in transaction aborts similar to those due to CRP1, i.e. the large percentage of transaction aborts come from conflict resolution. But because CRP5 is not a deadlock-free protocol, there are still some aborts due to deadlock.

The conflict resolution protocols were also studied with respect to transaction deadline distribution. The performance results illustrated in Figure 15 show that the protocols CRP2, CRP3 and CRP4, which explicitly use deadline information, are sensitive to deadline settings. Note that the three protocols do not provide better performance than the baseline when the deadline is tight, and as the deadline window increases, the total weighted value becomes "saturated" (no relative gain occurs as compared with the baseline). This indicates that the conflict resolution plays an important role only for a certain range of deadline distributions.

Thus far, we have shown the performance of conflict resolution protocols under the situation where only write-write conflicts exist. Now we consider the workloads which lead to write-read as well as write-write conflicts. Figure 16 presents the performance results in terms of total weighted value versus the ratio of write/read transactions. As we can see, the performance difference among the proposed protocols and the baseline is small when the w/r ratio is equal to 2/6. This is because the majority of concurrent transactions are executing *read* operations, and therefore the conflict rate is low. As the w/r ratio increases, the transaction performance degrades sharply under all the conflict resolution protocols, except CRP1. There are two reasons for the good performance of CRP1. First, under our value weighting scheme, CRP1 maximizes the total value that transactions impart to the system. Second, as we mentioned previously, the implementation makes CRP1 most efficient in using the system resources.

We also studied the conflict resolution protocols with the mix of write/read transactions by varying the deadline window factor α. The results are similar to what we have shown in Figure 15, where only write transactions were considered.

The overall results from this set of experiments show that

- the conflict resolution protocols which directly address deadlines and criticalness produce better performance than protocols that ignore such information;

---

[6] Different sets of weights $w1$, $w2$ and $w3$ were exercised in testing of CRP5. There was very little difference in terms of CRP5's performance.

- the relative performance among the proposed conflict resolution protocols is consistent, under different deadline distributions, transaction lengths and the ratio of write/read transactions;

- among the five protocols, CRP1 provides the best performance. This is due to two factors: 1) it is a simple protocol which maximizes the value and 2) its implementation leads to the efficient use of system resources.

5.3.4 CPU scheduling vs. conflict resolution

To explicitly distinguish between the effects of CPU scheduling and conflict resolution on system performance, we conducted an experiment which tested four different schemes for real-time transaction processing: (1) NRT - the baseline; (2) CRP1 - applying conflict resolution protocol CRP1 with MFQ (the baseline of the CPU scheduling algorithm); (3) CDF - applying CPU scheduling CDF with CRP0 (the baseline of conflict resolution protocol); and (4) CDF_CRP1 - applying both CPU scheduling CDF and conflict resolution protocol CRP1. The workload for the test presented here is $T(12, 4, 10)$ with deadline setting $\alpha = 3$.

It is observed in Figure 17 that CRP1 improves the performance only for the transactions with very high criticalness (class 1), but severely degrades the performance, much worse than NRT, as transactions become less critical. CDF, on the other hand, greatly improves the performance of transactions in most classes. CDF_CRP1, the combination of CDF and CRP1, provides the best performance. The observations that can be made from this experiment indicate that real-time CPU scheduling improves the deadline guarantee ratio of real-time transactions as much as 80% and that there is a need to combine the CPU scheduling scheme with the conflict resolution so as to achieve up to an additional 12% performance improvement.

5.3.5 CPU bound vs. I/O bound systems

In the previous experiments all the transactions examined had the same computation time - 10 units in each transaction step. Under such workloads, the system is highly CPU bound with the (database) disk utilization being around 15% and the CPU utilization reaching as high as 97%. In this experiment we examine the behavior of workloads which yield systems which are not CPU bound. We created an I/O bound system by reducing the computation time to zero and further increasing the number of I/O operations in each transaction step. Figure 18 illustrates a performance result from the I/O bound system where the disk utilization was about 94% and the CPU utilization was approximately 50%. As compared with the baseline NRT, the CPU scheduling scheme (CDF), which performs very well in the CPU bound system (see Figure 17), does not improve the performance at all. This is understandable, since now the system bottleneck is at I/O, not at CPU. Here the interesting observation is that in the I/O bound system, the conflict resolution protocols, combined with CPU scheduling, still improve performance in terms of meeting deadlines for high critical transactions.

Clearly, I/O scheduling sensitive to the real-time nature of transactions is needed for I/O bound systems. We hypothesize that by applying real-time based I/O scheduling algorithms, together with the conflict resolution protocols, the system performance will be improved. For Figure 18, in particular, we expect that the deadline guarantee ratio of transactions with higher criticalness will increase through I/O scheduling, similar to what we have achieved from CPU scheduling for a CPU bound system (see Figure 17).

5.3.6 Sensitivity of different value functions

As we discussed in Section 2, for all of the above experiments, we used Eq. (1) and Eq. (2) as the basic value function. To study the sensitivity of our value function model, we now use Eq. (3) as an alternative to Eq. (2) and hence combine Eq. (1) and Eq. (3) to produce value function VF2.

Figure 19 illustrates the performance comparisons between the two different value functions used for CPU scheduling. Here we plot the total weighted value with respect to the deadline window factor α. For the baseline NRT, the total weighted value gained under VF2 is larger than that under VF1. This is what one can expect, since under VF2, the transaction's zero-value point (z_T) is proportional to its criticalness value, and thus, in the case of missing deadline, transactions with high criticalness, modeled by VF2, may impart a larger value to the system than the transactions modeled by VF1. For the same reason, we see the performance difference between VF1 and VF2 for the CPU scheduling scheme EDF. Because the deadline guarantee ratio of EDF is lower than that of NRT when deadlines are tight, and higher when deadlines are loose (see Figure 9), the change of the performance difference between VF1 and VF2 is greater with EDF than with NRT. For the CPU scheduling schemes MCF and CDF, there is no large performance difference between VF1 and VF2. This is because both algorithms consider transaction criticalness for scheduling. According to our value weighting scheme, the large percentage of the total weighted value results from the committed transactions with high criticalness. Since for the tested workloads, the deadline guarantee ratio of the transactions with high criticalness is very high (above 95%, see Figure 4), the difference on modeling the decay value will not affect the overall performance results.

VF2 was also exercised with the proposed conflict resolution policies. The observations from these experiments were basically the same as what we just discussed for the results from CPU scheduling.

In general, our experimental results show that the two value functions may result in some performance difference for each protocol. In any case, however, the relative performance among the different protocols is the same.

6 Conclusions

Real-time transaction processing is complex. Many issues arise as data consistency has to be maintained and timing constraints for the transactions have to be met. In this paper, we have presented a real-time database model where the general notion of value function is used to characterize real-time transactions. Based on a basic locking scheme for concurrency control, we have developed several algorithms with regard to the issues of CPU scheduling, data conflict resolution, transaction wakeup, deadlock resolution, and transaction restart. In addition, we have briefly presented the RT-CARAT testbed where the proposed algorithms are integrated and implemented.

In general, our experimental results from the testbed indicate the following:

- In a CPU-bound system, the CPU scheduling algorithm has a significant impact on the performance of real-time transactions, and dominates all the other types of protocols. In order to obtain good performance, both criticalness and deadline of a transaction are needed for CPU scheduling;

- Various conflict resolution protocols which directly address deadlines and criticalness produce better performance than protocols that ignore such information. In terms of transaction's criticalness, regardless of whether the system bottleneck is the CPU or the I/O, criticalness-based conflict resolution protocols always improve performance;

- Both criticalness and deadline distributions strongly affect transaction performance. Under our value weighting scheme, criticalness is a more important factor than the deadline with respect to the performance goal of maximizing the deadline guarantee ratio for high critical transactions and maximizing the value imparted by real-time transactions;

- Overheads such as locking and message communication are non-negligible and can not be ignored in real-time transaction analysis.

An important issue we have not yet addressed is I/O scheduling. Unfortunately, most of today's disk controllers have built-in scan algorithms that do not take deadlines and criticalness into account and are not easily modified.

Our work presented in this paper can be extended in many directions. For example, optimistic concurrency control (OCC) is another scheme for enforcing data consistency in traditional database systems. If, and under which conditions, OCC is suitable for real-time databases remains to be answered. Another issue is the buffer management. Buffer management plays an important role in traditional database systems. We would like to know how important the buffer management is in real-time databases and how to improve performance through buffer management. Finally, with our developed soft real-time database system, we plan to study how to interface the system with hard real-time systems and how to integrate them as a whole.

References

[1] Abbott, R. and H. Garcia-Molina, "Scheduling Real-Time Transactions," *ACM SIG-MOD Record*, March 1988.

[2] Abbott, R. and H. Garcia-Molina, "Scheduling Real-Time Transactions: A Performance Evaluation," *Proceedings of the 14th VLDB Conference*, Aug. 1988.

[3] Abbott, R. and H. Garcia-Molina, "Scheduling Real-Time Transactions with Disk Resident Data," *A Technical Report, CS-TR-207-89, Princeton University*, Feb. 1989.

[4] Agrawal, R., M.J. Carey and M. Livny, "Concurrency Control Performance Modeling: Alternatives and Implications," *ACM Transaction on Database Systems, Vol.12, No.4*, Dec. 1987.

[5] Buchmann, A.P., D.R. McCarthy, M. Hsu, and U. Dayal, "Time-Critical Database Scheduling: A Framework For Integrating Real-Time Scheduling and Concurrency Control," *Data Engineering Conference*, Feb. 1989.

[6] Carey, M.J., R. Jauhari and M. Livny, "Priority in DBMS Resource Scheduling," *Proceedings of the 15th VLDB Conference*, 1989.

[7] Dayal, U. et. al., "The HiPAC Project: Combining Active Database and Timing Constraints," *ACM SIGMOD Record*, March 1988.

[8] Dayal, U., "Active Database Management Systems," *Proceedings of the 3rd International Conference on Data and Knowledge Management*, June 1988.

[9] Huang, J., J.A. Stankovic, D. Towsley and K. Ramamritham, "Experimental Evaluation of Real-Time Transaction Processing," *A Technical Report, COINS 89-48, University of Massachusetts*, April 1989.

[10] Hsu, M., R. Ladin and D.R. McCarthy, "An Execution Model for Active Database Management Systems," *Proceedings of the 3rd International Conference on Data and Knowledge Management*, June 1988.

[11] Kohler, W. and B.P. Jenq, "CARAT: A Testbed for the Performance Evaluation of Distributed Database Systems," *Proceedings of the Fall Joint Computer Conference*, Nov. 1986.

[12] Lin, K.J., "Consistency issues in real-time database systems," *Proceedings of the 22nd Hawaii International Conference on System Sciences*, Jan. 1989.

[13] Locke, C.D., "Best-Effort Decision Making for Real-Time Scheduling," *Ph.D. Dissertation*, Canegie-Mellon University, 1986.

[14] Sha, L., R. Rajkumar and J.P. Lehoczky, "Concurrency Control for Distributed Real-Time Databases," *ACM SIGMOD Record*, March 1988.

[15] Son, S.H., "Using Replication for High Performance Database Support in Distributed Real-Time Systems," *Proceedings of the 8th Real-Time Systems Symposium*, Dec. 1987.

[16] Son, S.H. and C.H. Chang, "Priority-Based Scheduling in Real-Time Database Systems," *Proceedings of the 15th VLDB Conference*, 1989.

[17] Stankovic, J.A. and W. Zhao, "On Real-Time Transactions," *ACM SIGMOD Record*, March 1988.

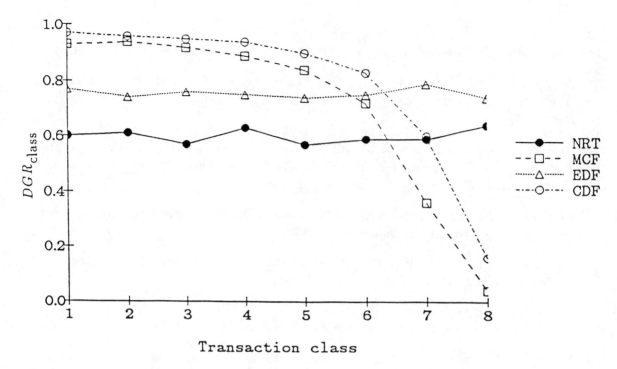

Fig. 4: CPU scheduling with w/r=2/6, T(12,4,10), a=3

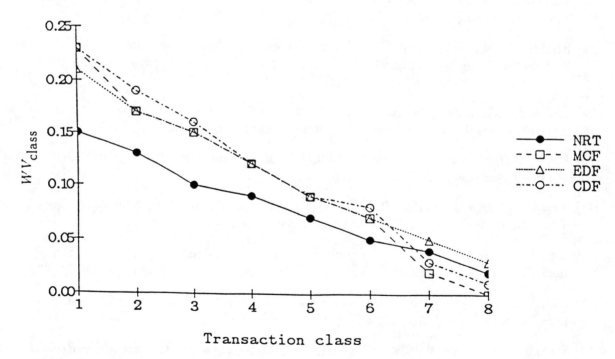

Fig. 5: CPU scheduling with w/r=2/6, T(12,4,10), a=3

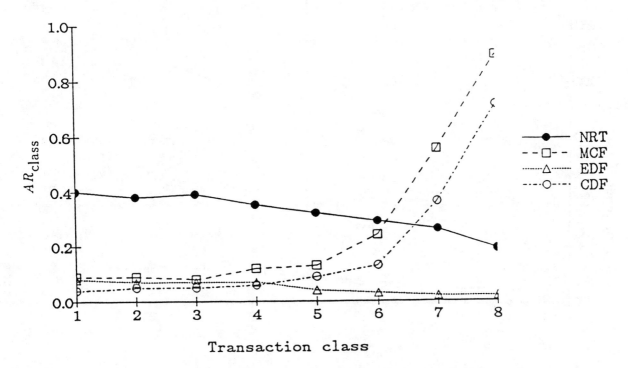

Fig. 6: CPU scheduling with w/r=2/6, T(12,4,10), a=3

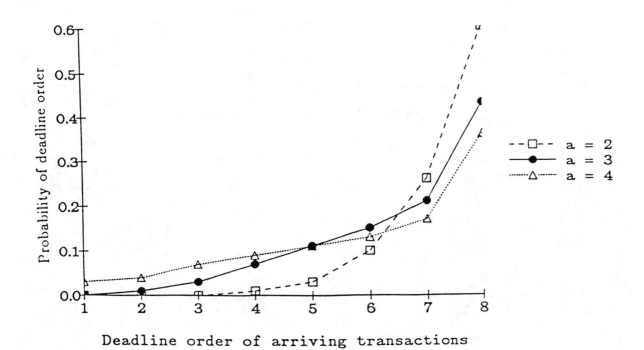

Fig. 7: Deadline distribution under EDF

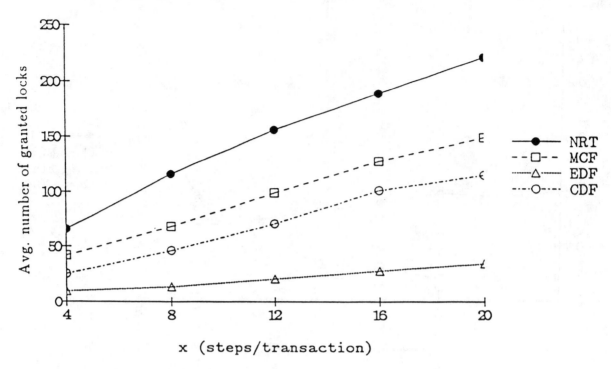

x (steps/transaction)

Fig. 8: Concurrency measurement with w/r=2/6, T(x,10,4), a=3

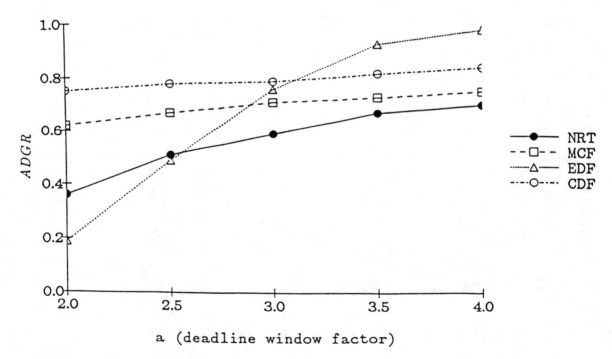

a (deadline window factor)

Fig. 9: CPU scheduling with w/r=2/6, T(12,4,10)

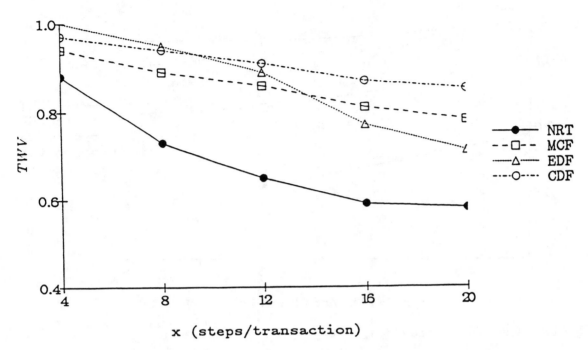

x (steps/transaction)

Fig. 10: CPU scheduling with w/r=2/6, T(x,4,10), a=3

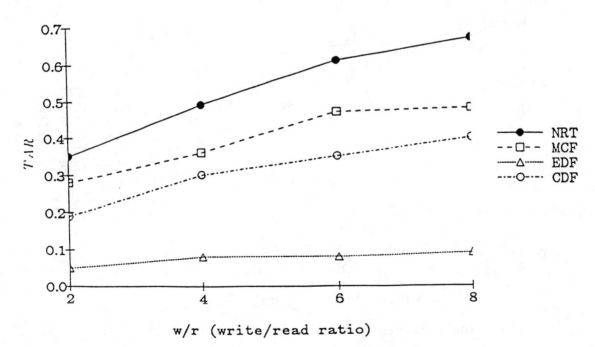

w/r (write/read ratio)

Fig. 11: CPU scheduling with T(12,4,10), a=3

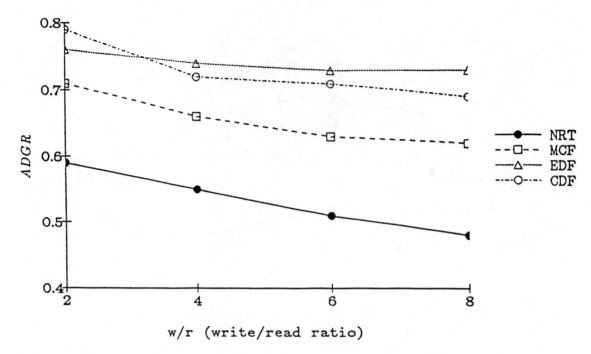

Fig. 12: CPU scheduling with T(12,4,10), a=3

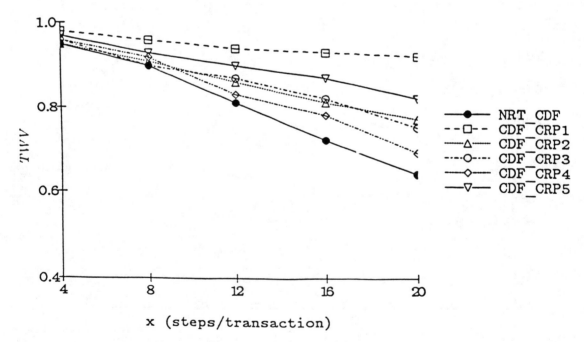

Fig. 13: Conflict resolution with w/r=8/0, T(x,4,10), a=3

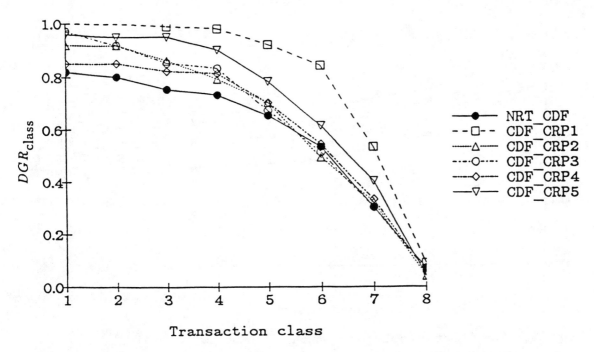

Fig. 14: Conflict resolution, with w/r=8/0, T(16,4,10), a=3

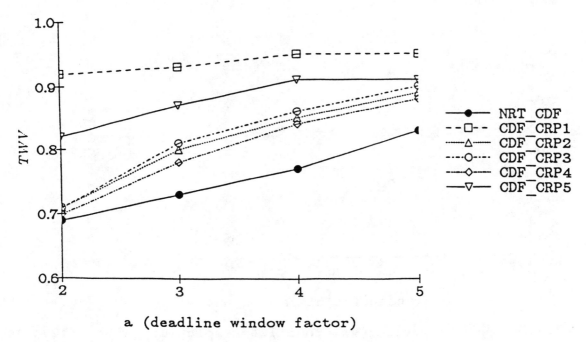

Fig. 15: Conflict resolution with w/r=8/0, T(16,4,10)

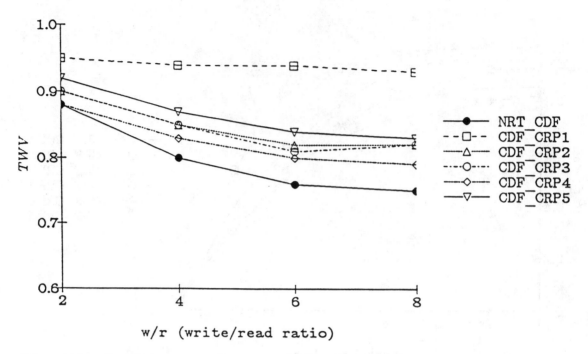

w/r (write/read ratio)

Fig. 16: Conflict resolution with T(16,4,10), a=3

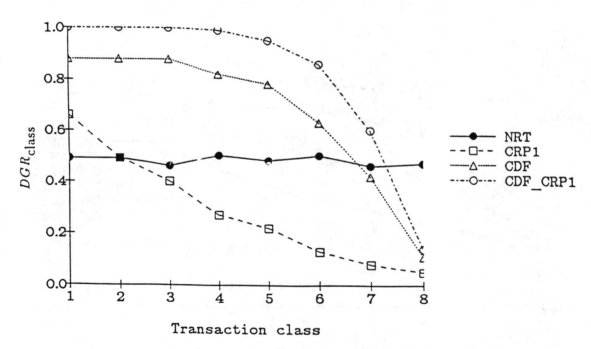

Transaction class

Fig. 17: CPU scheduling vs. conflict resolution, with T(12,4,10),
w/r = 8/0

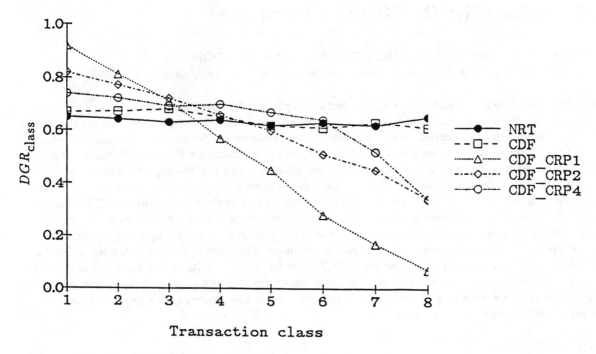

Fig. 18: An I/O bound system, with w/r=8/0, T(12,4,0), a=4

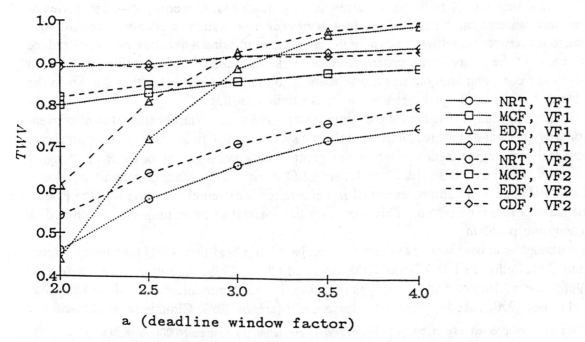

Fig. 19: Value functions with w/r=2/6, T(12,4,10)

Performance Evaluation of Two New Disk Scheduling Algorithms for Real-Time Systems*

SHENZE CHEN, JOHN A. STANKOVIC, JAMES F. KUROSE, AND DON TOWSLEY
Department of Computer & Information Science, University of Massachusetts, Amherst, MA 01003

Abstract. In this paper, we present two new disk scheduling algorithms for real-time systems. The two algorithms, called SSEDO (*Shortest Seek and Earliest Deadline by Ordering*) and SSEDV (*Shortest Seek and Earliest Deadline by Value*), combine *deadline* information and *disk service time* information in different ways. The basic idea behind these new algorithms is to give the disk I/O request with the earliest deadline a high priority, but if a request with a larger deadline is *very* close to the current disk arm position, then it may be assigned the highest priority. The performance of the SSEDO and SSEDV algorithms is compared with three other proposed real-time disk scheduling algorithms ED, P-SCAN, and FD-SCAN, as well as four conventional algorithms SSTF, SCAN, C-SCAN, and FCFS. An important aspect of the performance study is that the evaluation is not done in isolation with respect to the disk, but as part of an integrated collection of protocols necessary to support a real-time transaction system. The transaction system model is validated on an actual real-time transaction system testbed, called RT-CARAT. The performance results show that SSEDV outperforms SSEDO; that both of these new algorithms can improve performance of up to 38% over previously-known real-time disk scheduling algorithms; and that all of these real-time scheduling algorithms are significantly better than nonreal-time algorithms in the sense of minimizing the transaction loss ratio.

1. Introduction

Recently, interest in real-time systems research has been growing. In a real-time system, each computational entity (e.g., a task, a process, a thread, or a transaction) has a deadline when submitted to the system. These entities must be scheduled and processed in such a way that they complete by their corresponding deadlines. Generally, two categories of real-time systems can be identified. In a *hard real-time* system, missing a deadline may lead to a catastrophe, while in a *soft real-time* system, missing a deadline may only reduce the *value* of the entity to the system. In this work we focus on soft real-time systems, in which the computational entities are scheduled to maximize the *value* they impart to the system, but they are not guaranteed to make their deadlines.

Since performance criteria for real-time systems are quite different from that of conventional systems, and since research on real-time systems is still in its infancy, there are many new and challenging issues raised in designing such a system. One of these challenging issues is real-time I/O scheduling. Because I/O devices are orders of magnitude slower than CPU speeds, the improvement of I/O efficiency is extremely important to the performance of a real-time system. This motivates our interest in examining the real-time disk scheduling problem.

Although extensive work has been done on issues like real-time CPU scheduling (Buchmann, McCathy, Hsu and Dayal 1989; Son and Chang 1989; Abbott and Garcia-Molina 1988; Locke, Tokuda and Jensen 1985) and real-time communications (Malcolm, Zhao and Barter 1990; Tokuda, Mercer, Ishikawa, and Marchok 1989; Cimimiera, Montuschi and

*This work is supported, in part, by the Office of Naval Research under contract N00014-87-K-796, by NSF under contract IRI-8908693, and by an NSF equipment grant CERDCR 8500332.

Valenzano 1989; Kopetz and Ochsenreiter 1987), interestingly enough, very few papers have dealt with I/O disk scheduling problem in a real-time environment. This is, in part, because the problem is difficult, and because in many real-time systems disks are not accessed under time constraints. However, many real-time systems are becoming large and complex, and it is becoming necessary to incorporate time constrained disk access. Previous work on the disk I/O scheduling for real-time systems can be found in (Abbott and Garcia-Molina 1990) and (Carey, Jauhari, and Livny 1989). Abbott (1990) suggested a real-time disk scheduling algorithm called FD-SCAN (*Feasible Deadline SCAN*), which is a variant of the SCAN algorithm. Specifically, FD-SCAN differs from SCAN in the way that it dynamically adapts the scan direction towards the request with the earliest feasible deadline, where a deadline is said to be *feasible* if it is estimated that it can be met. In (Carey, Jauhari, and Livny 1989), Carey gives a priority disk scheduling algorithm which is also based on the SCAN algorithm. In this work they only looked at a conventional database system. Therefore, the performance criteria are quite different from ours. However, in order to examine the performance of the priority SCAN algorithm in a real-time environment, we implemented such an algorithm, P-SCAN, and tested it in our experiments. In addition, from CPU scheduling results, it is obvious that the *earliest deadline* (ED) algorithm is valuable in many situations. While it is unlikely to be a good algorithm for disk scheduling, we evaluate its performance as a baseline. Details concerning these three algorithms are further described and examined in later sections of this paper. Because of the difficulty in developing analytical model for disk scheduling when real-time constraints are involved, to our knowledge, there has been no analytic work in this area.

In this paper, we present two new real-time disk scheduling algorithms, SSEDO and SSEDV, and compare their performance with previously known real-time disk scheduling algorithms, ED, P-SCAN, and FD-SCAN, as well as with four conventional algorithms, SSTF, SCAN, C-SCAN, and FCFS. The performance measures of interest are the transaction loss probability and the average response time for committed transactions under different disk I/O scheduling algorithms. The performance results show that the SSEDV algorithm outperforms the SSEDO algorithm; that both of these new algorithms can improve performance up to 38% over the three previously suggested real-time disk scheduling algorithms, or up to 53% over the four conventional algorithms; and that all of these real-time scheduling algorithms are significantly better than nonreal-time algorithms in the sense of minimizing the transaction loss ratio. An important observation is that our two new real-time algorithms are not based on scanning, and they outperform P-SCAN and FD-SCAN which both rely on scanning, modified to suit real-time constraints. Reasons for this are presented later in this paper. Another important aspect of the performance study is that the evaluation is not done in isolation with respect to the disk itself, but rather as part of an integrated collection of protocols necessary to support a real-time transaction system. The transaction system model is validated on an actual real-time transaction system testbed, called RT-CARAT.

The remainder of this paper is organized as follows: Section 2 describes the real-time transaction system model and its validation. Section 3 introduces the two new real-time disk scheduling algorithms SSEDO and SSEDV, and then discusses the other algorithms examined in this paper. The performance results are presented in Section 4. Section 5 summarizes this paper.

2. The Real-Time Transaction System Model

2.1. The Model Description

Our system model takes an integrated view of real-time transaction performance. While it is our intent to specifically study real-time disk I/O scheduling algorithms, we do so in a complete system setting. The overall metric of interest is to minimize the transaction loss probability, i.e., the probability that a transaction does not meet its deadline; note that this is only partially affected by the disk I/O policy. Consequently, we study 9 disk I/O scheduling algorithms in a system with fixed algorithms for concurrency control, lock conflict resolution, commit processing, CPU scheduling, deadlock detection, deadlock resolution, transaction restart, and transaction wakeup. We now describe the system model in detail.

Since we are interested in the disk I/O scheduling problem for real-time transaction systems, the database is assumed to be very large and disk resident. Specifically, the transaction system is modeled as a closed system which consists of multiple users, a CPU, and a disk for storing the database (Figure 1). All log information is placed on a separate log disk. The log disk does not show up in the figure because its cost is accounted for and subsumed as part of the CPU operation.

In this system model, each user spends a random amount of time in a *think* state before generating a transaction. Each transaction is considered to have the same importance and is assigned a deadline when submitted to the system. If a transaction cannot commit before its deadline, it is said to be lost and is removed from the system immediately. The user who submitted the lost transaction returns to the *think* state. A transaction consists of a random number of operational steps. Each step performs an access to the database, (only

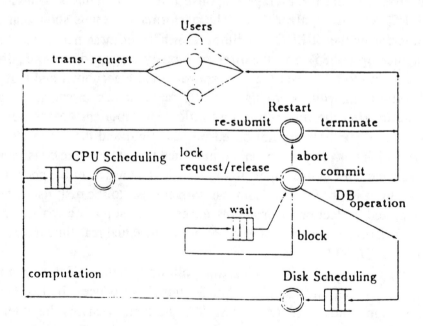

Figure 1. The system model.

624

if the desired page is not in the main memory buffer), and manipulates the data items retrieved. In some of our experiments, we assume that the number of steps for a transaction is known to the system as soon as the transaction arrives. This assumption is often reasonable since the knowledge of a transaction's length can sometimes be obtained from the compiler or some other transaction preprocessor by counting the transaction's I/O requests.

Generally, we assume that transactions randomly access records and that multiple records are stored on each page of data. We also assume that the size of a page is the same as the size of a disk block. The random access assumption is removed when we examine the locality effect of transactions' accesses. In case of transactions randomly accessing the database, since the database is assumed large, the memory buffer hit ratio is low and therefore a disk I/O is required most of the time. This better enables us to investigate the impact of I/O scheduling algorithms when the system is I/O bound.

To maintain the consistency of the database, serializability is enforced by using the *two-phase locking* protocol. Specifically, each page is associated with a lock. Each transaction step needs to request and hold a lock before being allowed to access the database. For any transaction, all locks obtained at each step will be held until it commits or aborts. Two types of locks are identified, shared locks and exclusive locks. A shared lock can be granted to multiple users for inquiry (read) operations, and an exclusive lock is granted to only one user for update (write) operations. A lock conflict may occur when a requested lock has been granted to other transactions, and either the requesting or the holding transaction is to perform an update operation. In order to handle this situation, a lock conflict resolution policy must be defined. The policy we use is as follows:

Lock Conflict Resolution. When there is a lock conflict, we always let the requesting transaction suspend, i.e., join a queue waiting for the lock. There is no preemption. This is based on the assumption that all transactions are of the same importance so preemption is not warranted. When each transaction carries, in addition to a deadline, a different importance value, preemption has been shown to be a good strategy (Huang, Stankovic, Towsley and Ramamritham 1989).

The locking scheme used may cause deadlocks. A simple cycle detection deadlock detection algorithm is employed in our model.

When a deadlock is detected, a victim is selected to be aborted according to some rule. Our resolution strategy follows a simple rule:

Deadlock Resolution. If a deadlock is detected, then the requesting transaction is aborted. In this case, the transaction releases all resources held and proceeds according to the restart strategy.

Restart Policy. A transaction aborted from a deadlock is restarted as long as its deadline has not yet expired. Transactions aborted for other reasons, such as user termination, arithmetic overflow, and execution exceptions, are removed from the system and return to the *think* state. In the former case, a smarter policy might be to restart a transaction only if its estimated minimum processing time is less than the remaining time before missing its deadline. For the latter case, a more sophisticated strategy might restart a transaction if it aborted due to arithmetic overflow and/or execution exception, after doing some exception handling.

The transaction wakeup and commit strategies are as follows:

Wakeup Strategy. When a transaction commits, aborts, or misses its deadline, it releases all of its resources. If some of these resources (pages) are needed by more than one other transaction, then we select the one with earliest deadline among all waiting transactions to wakeup, and grant it the associated lock.

Transaction Commit. When a transaction commits, it releases all its resources after completion of logging and goes back to the *think* state. If there are any dirty pages in the memory buffer, they are flushed to the disk. Obviously, these flushing operations do not deserve a high priority since the transaction issuing these operations has already committed. On the other hand, from the buffer manager's standpoint, flushing operations should complete as soon as possible to free up buffer space. This means that they should not have a low priority. In a transaction system, since committing is more important than the buffer, it seems that flushing writes should get a low priority. However, in the simulations we do not degrade the priority of flushing writes because such a strategy would only be applicable to transaction systems, and our new disk I/O algorithms are more general and apply also to nontransaction real-time systems.

Buffer Manager. The buffer manager is not explicitly modeled in order to simplify the simulation programs. Instead, a *buffer hit probability*, which is assumed to be 0.1, is used to determine whether a disk access is required.

CPU scheduling is an important issue when dealing with real-time transaction systems. We chose the following algorithm.

CPU Scheduling. The *earliest deadline* (ED) algorithm is used for CPU scheduling. As mentioned in the literature (Abbott and Garcia-Molina 1989), a major drawback of this algorithm is that it may assign the highest priority to a transaction that has already missed or is about to miss its deadline. To partially overcome this weakness, we propose a modified ED algorithm which, instead of scheduling according to a transaction's deadline, schedules by the *step deadline* of a transaction given the number of steps of a transaction is known to the system at the time of submission. Specifically, let L, a, and n be a transaction's (absolute) deadline, arrival time, and the number of operational steps. A simple way to assign a step deadline for step i is to set

$$step\text{-}deadline(i) = a + \frac{i}{n}(L - a) \tag{1}$$

Note that under this policy, the earlier the step, the smaller the step deadline, and therefore, the higher the priority for the transaction when executing its earlier steps. Also note that the deadline for the last step is always equal to the transaction's deadline. One consideration for using the step deadline is that if two transactions have the same deadline, but one has more steps than the other, then the longer transaction will have higher priority for its earlier steps. We tested the effect of using step deadline on both CPU and I/O scheduling. The results show that this strategy does indeed improve the system performance (see Section 4.2.4).

In summary, in order to achieve good performance in the sense of minimizing the transaction loss ratio, there is a collection of algorithms that must be developed including CPU scheduling, commit processing, I/O disk scheduling, concurrency control, lock conflict resolution, deadlock resolution, restart, and wakeup. Since our main goal is to examine the impact I/O scheduling in a real-time transaction system, many of the algorithms used in our study are typical or sometimes simple, but suitable for a real-time system.

2.2. Model Validation

In order to validate our basic model of an integrated set of protocols required to perform real-time transaction processing, we conducted a series of experiments on an actual real-time database testbed, called RT-CARAT (Huang, Stankovic, Towsley and Ramamritham 1989; Kohler and Jeng 1986). Given the same workloads and algorithm settings (including CPU scheduling, lock conflict resolution, deadlock resolution, restart strategy, and commit processing), our simulation results concerning the basic simulation model (which uses the FCFS disk service strategy) match quite well with that of the testbed. On the other hand, it was not possible for us to validate the simulation results comparing all the nine I/O disk scheduling algorithms because the disk controller in the testbed could not be modified.

RT-CARAT is currently running on a VAX Station II/GPX under the VMS operating system. The database consists of 3000 pages, with each page containing 6 records. The number of users is fixed at 8. Each user continuously generates transactions with a fixed number of operational steps. When a previous transaction commits or aborts, a user submits his next transaction immediately. In the validation runs there was no *thinking time* between transaction submissions. On RT-CARAT, each operational step accesses 4 records, which are randomly located in the database, and therefore up to 4 I/O requests may be generated for each step. In our model, since we assume each operational step only needs to access the database once, we set the total number of steps for each transaction to four times of that in RT-CARAT so that a transaction will generate the same number of I/O requests. Although RT-CARAT implements various real-time CPU scheduling algorithms, conflict resolution protocols, deadlock resolutions, and wakeup strategies, the I/O disk scheduling algorithm used is the basic strategy employed by the underlying VMS operating system and its disk controller. In fact, since the VAX Station II/GPX uses an RQDX3 controller and the RD54 disk drive (Warchol and Shirron 1986), both of which are very early models, I/O requests are simply served in an approximate first come first serve fashion.

In setting deadlines for transactions we follow two steps: first, a selected workload is placed on RT-CARAT in a nonreal-time database setting and the mean transaction response time and its standard deviation are measured. In other words we make a preliminary run to determine the transactions' mean response time (*avg_resp*) and its standard deviation (*std_devi*). assuming the transactions have no deadlines. This is done with a basic set of protocols that do not use deadlines to make decisions. Then a base deadline value (*base_line*) is calculated by

$$base\_line = avg\_resp - std\_devi$$

and each transaction's deadline is randomly selected from the range [*base_line*, *f* * base_line]. where *f* is a factor that enables us to test a wide range of deadlines. We set *f* to 3 in the validation experiments.

In order to compare the performance of the simulation model and the testbed, the database configuration and the collection of algorithms supporting a real-time transaction system are configured to be the same on both. The system overhead, such as context switching, interprocess communication, locking mechanism, and logging, are considered and assimilated into the computation time for each step in our model. In order to compare their performance. the step computation time in our model is tuned to that both systems have approximately the same disk utilization in the nonreal-time cases. The statistics on RT-CARAT show that the average CPU time for each step is approximately 41ms and that is the value we used in our simulation experiments.

The comparison of the performance of RT-CARAT and our simulation model is shown in Figure 2. The X-axis gives the number of steps for each transaction in our simulation model. In Figure 2a we see that transaction loss ratio in our simulation model is slightly less than that in RT-CARAT when the system is lightly loaded, and slightly higher than that of RT-CARAT when the workload increases. One reason for this is that the variance of transaction response time in our model is less than that in RT-CARAT when the load is low, and it increases faster than its counterpart in RT-CARAT as the load increases. In Figure 2b, we see that average transaction response time in both models is the same. In Figure 2c, we see that the average disk utilizations are nearly the same on both systems. On the other hand. CPU utilization drops faster in our simulation model than in the testbed.

3. Description of Various Disk Scheduling Algorithms

In this section we describe all nine disk scheduling algorithms examined in this paper. We first introduce the two new real-time disk scheduling algorithms, SSEDO and SSEDV. We then describe three other real-time disk scheduling algorithms, ED, P-SCAN and FD-SCAN. It should be noted that the *earliest deadline strategy* (ED) is a special case of each of the two new real-time algorithms. Finally, we very briefly describe four traditional disk algorithms.

3.1. Two New Real-Time Disk Scheduling Algorithms

3.1.1. Motivation. In a real-time system, timing constraints are important to consider when making scheduling decisions. For real-time task scheduling, Towsley and Panwar (1990)

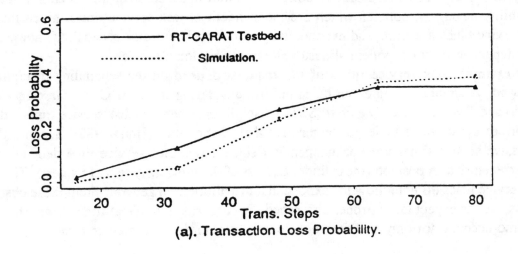

(a). Transaction Loss Probability.

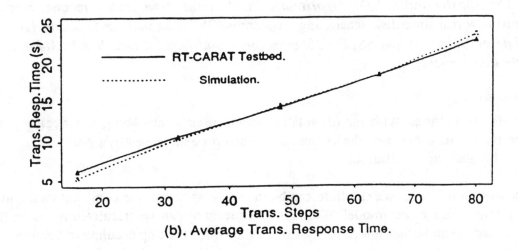

(b). Average Trans. Response Time.

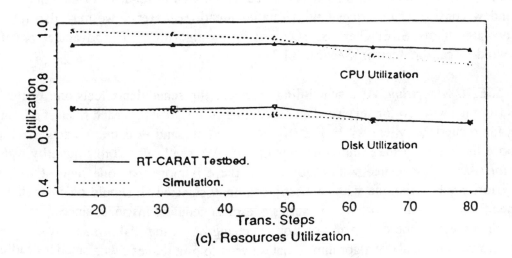

(c). Resources Utilization.

Figure 2. Results compared with RT-CARAT testbed. (*Users* = 8, p_r = 0.8, p_s = 0).

have proved that the *earliest deadline* policy is optimal in the sense of minimizing the loss probability among all policies which are independent of task service times, given these task service times are *i.i.d.* and exponentially distributed. For disk scheduling, however, the independence and exponential assumptions are no longer valid.

For example, disk service times of I/O requests depend on the scheduling discipline employed. A simple example can be found in considering the *First Come First Service* (FCFS) and *Shortest Seek Time First* (SSTF) disciplines, where the disk service time under the former discipline is believed longer than that of the latter (Hofri 1980). Second, the successive service times are not independent since a request's service time depends on the current disk arm position (the cylinder address of the previously served request). Third, disk service times do not follow the exponential distribution, in general. From these observations, we can expect that a proper disk scheduling algorithm for a real-time system should take into account not only the time constraint but also the disk service time.

3.1.2. The SSEDO and SSEDV Algorithms.

Based on the above considerations, we propose two new real-time disk scheduling algorithms, SSEDO (*Shortest Seek and Earliest Deadline by Ordering*) and SSEDV (*Shortest Seek and Earliest Deadline by Value*), for a single disk device.

Let

r_i : be the I/O request with the ith smallest deadline at a scheduling instance;
d_i : be the distance between the current arm position and request r_i's position;
L_i : be the absolute deadline of r_i.

Note that an I/O request's deadline can be the same as that of the computational entity (e.g., a transaction in our model) issuing the request, or can be calculated by using the entity's deadline and other information, as was shown for the step deadline in Section 2.1. The two algorithms maintain a queue sorted according to the (absolute) deadline, L_i, of each request. A window of size m is defined as the first m requests in the queue, i.e., the window consists of m requests with smallest deadlines. Hence we may also refer to these two algorithms, SSEDO and SSEDV, as window algorithms. The advantage of defining a window can be seen in Section 3.1.3.

The SSEDO Algorithm. At a scheduling instance, the scheduler selects one of the requests from the window for service. The scheduling rule is to assign each request a weight, say w_i for request r_i, where $w_1 = 1 \leq w_2 \leq \ldots \leq w_m$ and m is the window size, and to choose the one with the minimum value of $w_i d_i$. We shall refer to this quantity $w_i d_i$ as the *priority value* associated with request r_i. If there is more than one request with the same priority value, the one with earliest deadline is selected. It should be clear that for any specific request, its priority value varies at each scheduling instance, since d_i, r_i's position with respect to the disk arm position, is changing as the disk arm moves.

The idea behind the above algorithm is that we want to give requests with smaller deadlines higher priorities so that they can receive service earlier. This can be accomplished by assigning smaller values to their weights. On the other hand, when a request with large deadline is *very* close to the current arm position (which means less service time), it should get higher priority. This is especially true when a request is to access the cylinder where the arm is currently positioned. Since there is no seek time in this case and we are assuming the seek time dominates the service time, the service time can be ignored. Therefore these requests should be given the highest priority. There are various ways to assign these weights w_i. In our experiments, the weights are simply set to

$$w_i = \beta^{i-1} \quad (\beta \geq 1) \quad i = 1, 2, \ldots, m.$$

where β is an adjustable scheduling parameter. Note that w_i assigns priority only on the basis of the *ordering* of deadlines, not on their absolute or relative *values*. In addition, when all weights are equal ($\beta = 1$), we obtain an approximate SSTF algorithm which converges to pure SSTF as the window size becomes large. When the window size is equal to one, the algorithm is the same as the ED algorithm. In the following section, we will see that the performance of the system is improved dramatically when a window size of three or four is chosen.

The SSEDV Algorithm. In the SSEDO algorithm described above, the scheduler uses only the ordering information of request's deadline and does not use the differences between deadlines of successive requests in the window. For example, suppose there are two requests in the window, and r_1's deadline is very close but r_2's deadline is far away. If r_2's position is *very* close to the current arm position, then the SSEDO algorithm might schedule r_2 first, which may result in the loss of r_1. However, if r_1 is scheduled first, then both of r_1 and r_2 might get served. On the other extreme, if r_2's deadline is almost the same as r_1's, and the distance d_2 is less than d_1 but greater than d_1/β, then SSEDO will schedule r_1 for service and r_2 will be lost. In this case, since there could be a loss anyway, it seems reasonable to serve the closer one (r_2) for its service time is smaller. Based on these considerations, we expect that a more intelligent scheduler might use not only the deadline *ordering* information but also the deadline *value* information for decision making. This leads to the following algorithm: associate a priority value of $\alpha d_i + (1 - \alpha)l_i$ to request r_i and choose the request with the minimum value for service, where l_i is the *remaining life time* of request r_i, defined as the length of time between the current time and r_i's deadline L_i and $\alpha(0 \leq \alpha \leq 1)$ is a scheduling parameter.

Again when $\alpha = 1$, this approximates the SSTF algorithm, and when $\alpha = 0$, we obtain the ED algorithm.

A common characteristic of the SSEDV and SSEDO algorithms is that both consider *time constraints* and *disk service times*. Which part plays a greater role in decision making can be adjusted by tuning the scheduling parameters α or β, depending on the algorithm.

3.1.3. Scheduling Costs of the SSEDO and SSEDV Algorithms. For the two algorithms defined above, since the priority value of each request in the window needs to be evaluated at every scheduling point, we might hope to estimate their scheduling cost. The overhead involved in scheduling should be *small* since we don't want the disk to be idle for a long time waiting for the scheduling algorithm to finish, as this might dramatically increase I/O response time and therefore the transaction loss ratio.

From an implementation point of view, the ED queue required for the SSEDO and SSEDV algorithms can be maintained by the operating system or the device controller when requests arrive at a cost $O(\log n)$, where n is the number of requests in the queue. For a fixed window size m (usually $m = 3$ is enough as shown in the next section), the priority value calculation cost is $O(1)$. That is why we define a window, rather than compute all the requests in the queue which will result in a cost of $O(n)$, and this is motivated by the approximate calculations used in (Hong, Tan and Towsley 1989). Since the $O(\log n)$ queue maintenance cost at arrival instances can be performed in parallel with disk operations, and since there is only an $O(1)$ cost at scheduling instances, scheduling cost can be kept low. In addition, the $O(1)$ priority value computation cost can be further reduced by scheduling the request while performing a disk service. This is feasible since the cylinder address (and, therefore, the service time) of the request under service is known. Hence, the seek distance and remaining lifetime of all the requests waiting in the window can be calculated in advance. The only exception is when the transaction in service misses its deadline while the service is proceeding. In this case, the resulting arm position is unpredictable. This will invalidate the pre-calculated distance and the remaining lifetime calculations, and necessitate a rescheduling. A more intelligent scheduler might test if a request will miss its deadline before providing the service, since disk service time is predictable. In this way, only those requests which can successfully complete their service will be selected to use the disk. This can avoid the above drawbacks and allow full parallelism of disk scheduling and disk service.

3.2. Other Real-Time Disk Scheduling Algorithms

Three other real-time disk scheduling algorithms, ED, P-SCAN and FD-SCAN, have been suggested in the literature.

3.2.1. The ED Algorithm. In the ED algorithm, I/O requests are served based on their deadlines. The request with an earliest deadline has the highest priority.

3.2.2. The P-SCAN Algorithm. The priority SCAN (P-SCAN) strategy is based on the idea suggested by (Carey, Jauhari and Livny 1989). Specifically, all requests in the I/O queue are divided into multiple priority levels. The SCAN algorithm is used within each level, which means that the disk serves any requests that it passes in the current served priority level until there are no more requests in that direction. On the completion of each disk service, the scheduler checks to see whether a disk request of a higher priority is waiting for service. If found, the scheduler switches to that higher level. In this case, the request with the shortest seek distance from the current arm position is used to determine the scan direction. It is observed in (Carey, Jauhari and Livny 1989) that a small number of priority levels is preferred in order to provide reasonable I/O performance. How to assign priority to a I O request is an interesting question and which is not explained in (Carey, Jauhari and Livny 1989). In our experiments, all I/O requests are mapped into three priority levels according to their deadline information. Specifically, we assume transactions' relative deadlines are uniformly distributed between *LOW-DL* and *UP-DL*, where *LOW-DL* and

UP-DL are lower and upper bounds for transaction deadline settings. If a transaction's relative deadline is greater than (*LOW-DL* + *UP-DL*)/2, then it is assigned the lowest priority. If the (relative) deadline is less than (*LOW-DL* + *UP-DL*)/4, then the transaction receives the highest priority. Otherwise the transaction is assigned a middle priority. This strategy is shown to be better than the *one-third* strategy which evenly divides the deadline range into 3 intervals and maps each interval into a priority level.

3.2.3. The FD-SCAN Algorithm.

Recently, Abbott (Abbott and Garcia-Molina 1990) proposed another variant of the SCAN algorithm, called FD-SCAN. In FD-SCAN, the track location of the request with earliest feasible deadline is used to determine the scan direction. A deadline is *feasible* if we estimate that it can be met. Determining the feasibility of a request's deadline is simple since once the current arm position and the request's track location are known, its service time can be determined. A request's deadline is feasible if it is greater than the current time plus the request's service time. At each scheduling point, all requests are examined to determine which has the earliest feasible deadline. After selecting the scan direction, the arm moves toward that direction and serves all requests along the way.

3.2.4. Scheduling Costs of P-SCAN and FD-SCAN Algorithms.

As stated before, scheduling cost is an important factor for on-line scheduling algorithms in a real-time environment. Unfortunately, real-time variants of the SCAN algorithm may suffer from the cost standpoint, since at each scheduling point, they need to check all requests to determine the scan direction. For P-SCAN, this problem can be alleviated by maintaining a separate queue for each priority level at the cost of a higher maintenance overhead. At each scheduling point, the scheduler just checks whether there is any request waiting in some queue with a higher priority. For FD-SCAN, however, overhead seems to be a problem, since the scheduler must check whether there were any new arrivals carrying the earliest feasible deadline while serving the last request. Even if there are no such new arrivals, it still needs to check whether the previous target request is still feasible, and if not, a new direction must be determined.

3.3. The Four Classical Disk Scheduling Algorithms

The four classical scheduling algorithms described below are well-known. They have been discussed extensively in the literature. Here we simply list them for ease of reference.

FCFS. This is the simplest strategy in which each request is served in a first-come-first-served fashion.

SCAN. This is also known as the *elevator* algorithm in which the arm moves in one direction and serves all the requests in that direction until there are no further requests in that direction. The arm then changes its scan direction and repeats the operations.

C-SCAN. The circular SCAN algorithm works in the same way as SCAN except that it always scans in one direction. After serving the last request in the scan direction, the arm returns to the start position (typically an edge of the disk) without servicing requests and then begins scanning again.

SSTF. The SSTF, *shortest seek time first*, algorithm simply selects the request closest to the current arm position for service.

A common feature of all these classical scheduling algorithms is that none of them takes the time constraint of requests into account. As we shall see this results in poor performance of these classical algorithms in real-time systems.

4. Performance Comparisons of Various I/O Scheduling Algorithms

In order to compare the performance of various disk scheduling algorithms in an integrated real-time transaction system as described in Section 2, we conducted a series of simulation experiments on the nine algorithms. In Section 4.1, we first describe the system parameter settings for our experiments, including: system configuration, transaction characteristics, deadline settings, and the parameters for the two new algorithms, SSEDO and SSEDV. The experimental results are given in Section 4.2. In particular, we study the performance over a wide range of workloads, assess the two new algorithms' sensitivity to window size and algorithm parameters, determine the impact of scheduling via step deadlines, examine the system behavior by varying transaction deadline settings and read probability, investigate the locality of transaction accesses, and report the importance of real-time scheduling by comparing real-time and nonreal-time scheduling.

4.1. System Parameter Settings

4.1.1. System Configuration. In our model, the disk has 1000 tracks. The database consists of 6000 pages, which are uniformly distributed on the disk with each page corresponding to a disk block. Disk service time is defined by

$$S = X_s + X_r + X_t \tag{2}$$

where X_r is the rotational latency which is uniformly distributed among [0, 16.7] milliseconds, X_t is the transfer time which is considered constant and equal to 0.8 ms, and X_s is the seek time defined by.

$$X_s = \begin{cases} a + b\sqrt{i} & i > 0; \\ 0 & i = 0; \end{cases} \tag{3}$$

where a is the arm moving acceleration time (8 ms), b is the seek factor (0.5 ms), and i is the number of tracks for the arm to move (Seltzer, Chen and Ousterhout 1990; Bitton and Gray 1988). The average disk service time is 25 ms.

4.1.2. Transaction Characteristics. Transaction characteristics and load to the system are defined as follows: the number of users, which limits the maximum number of transactions in the closed system, ranges from 4 to 20. Each user may think a random of time, which comes from an exponential distribution with mean 1 second, before generating a transaction. A transaction consists of a random number of operational steps which is uniformly distributed between 1 and 20. Each step needs to access the database once and is followed by a manipulation of those data items fetched. The computation time of each step is assumed to be 15 ms, and the time needed to abort a transaction is 5 ms. With these parameter settings, the workloads we use show a I/O bound characteristic, which can satisfy our goal of examining the disk scheduling algorithms.

Further, each transaction step may perform a read or an update operation to the database. While a transaction is progressing, it brings those pages desired into a main memory buffer and does a corresponding inquiry or update there. In the case of update operations, the updated pages are also written on a separate log disk. When a transaction commits, all of its dirty pages are flushed to disk. In our model, the main memory buffer is assumed large enough to accommodate all of the pages desired by currently active transactions. In most of our experiments, the read probability, p_r, is set to 0.8, since most of time users are inquiring the database. We also investigate the effect of varying the read probability from 0 to 1. To examine the effect of locality of a transaction's accesses, we define the *probability of sequential access*, p_s, to be the probability that a transaction step is to access the same cylinder as that of its previous step. There is no locality assumed among different transactions. The p_s is usually set to 0 except when we study the locality effect in Section 4.2.7, where the p_s is varied from 0 to 0.8.

4.1.3. Deadline Settings. The deadline setting for each transaction in our model depends on the system load and a transaction's length. The system load can be characterized by the number of users in the closed system (with the mean thinking time fixed), and the transaction length corresponds to the number of steps. Specifically, we roughly estimate a transaction's minimum system time by

$$T_{min} = (CPU\_TIME + I/O\_Time) * Num\_Steps$$

where *CPU_Time* and *I/O_Time* are the estimated average CPU and disk service time for each step under FCFS strategy. Then the transaction deadline is set by

$$Trans\_Deadline = T_{min} * \eta$$

where η is a *r.v.* drawn from a uniform distribution on [*DL_Factor*, $f * DL\_Factor$]. The *DL_Factor* is a *deadline factor* selected proportional to the number of users in the system. *DL_Factor* = $k * Num\_Users$. In most of our experiments, k is equal to 0.25 and f is 4. However, we also examine the case where transactions' deadlines are very tight and/or very loose by varying *DL_Factor*.

The deadline setting for each I/O request is inherited from that of the transaction issuing the request in most of experiments. However, several experiments are performed by using a step deadline for each I/O request as will be discussed in Section 4.2.4.

4.1.4. Parameters for SSEDO and SSEDV. The scheduling parameters, β and α, for SSEDO and SSEDV algorithms are set to 2 and 0.8 in most cases. One of our experiments shows the sensitivity of changing α and β under two different workloads. Another experiment gives the results for varying the window size while other parameters are the same. The results show that a window size of 3 or 4 is satisfactory, and therefore usually the window size m is set to 3.

4.2. Simulation Results

In this section, we report our experimental results. The five real-time disk scheduling algorithms, SSEDO, SSEDV, ED, P-SCAN, FD-SCAN, and the four conventional algorithms, SSTF, SCAN, C-SCAN, and FCFS, are examined in these experiments. Results of each experiment is averaged over 20 runs. In each run 1050 transactions are executed. 95% *confidence intervals* are obtained by using the method of independent replications. Confidence interval widths are less than 11% of the point estimates of the loss probability in all cases (these intervals are not shown in our figures in order to clearly show the results). For each run, the execution of the first 50 transactions are considered the transient phase and is excluded from our statistics. In order to avoid congested plots, the nine curves are divided into two groups, classical algorithms and real-time algorithms, and plotted separately. The curve for the FD-SCAN algorithm is shown in both plots to provide the basis of comparison. In the following, all transactions and I/O requests are scheduled according to the transaction deadline except where explicitly indicated.

4.2.1. Resource Utilizations and I/O Queue Length. By using those parameter settings specified in Section 4.1, the CPU and disk utilizations for some workloads under several scheduling algorithms are provided in Tables 1 and 2 respectively, and the mean I/O queue length is provided in Table 3. Other algorithms fall between those shown in these tables. From these results, we can see there are only slight differences in CPU, disk utilizations and I/O queue lengths due to the different algorithms, except for the high load case where differences in CPU utilization begin to show up. However, we will show later that if we increase the step computation time, the I/O queue length may differ depending on the CPU and disk scheduling algorithms.

Table 1. CPU utilization.

Users	FCFS	SCAN	SSTF	FD-SCAN	ED	SSEDV
4	0.3661	0.3721	0.3729	0.3746	0.3685	0.3736
8	0.5004	0.5592	0.5600	0.5284	0.4914	0.5261
20	0.5176	0.6539	0.6557	0.6097	0.4997	0.5462

Table 2. Disk utilization.

Users	FCFS	SCAN	SSTF	FD-SCAN	ED	SSEDV
4	0.7419	0.7316	0.7292	0.7449	0.7484	0.7395
8	0.9906	0.9878	0.9849	0.9932	0.9955	0.9955
20	0.9997	0.9996	0.9996	0.9997	0.9997	0.9997

Table 3. Average I/O queue length.

Users	FCFS	SCAN	SSTF	FD-SCAN	ED	SSEDV
4	0.735	0.706	0.699	0.728	0.738	0.701
8	3.70	3.41	3.366	3.658	3.587	3.472
20	16.22	15.79	15.62	15.63	15.11	15.02

4.2.2. *Performance of Various Disk Scheduling Algorithms.* In this experiment, we explore the transaction loss probability of these nine algorithms under different system workloads. The read probability is set to 0.8. For SSEDO and SSEDV, the window size is 3. The scheduling parameters α and β are set to 0.8 and 2, respectively. The results are shown in Figure 3, from which we can see the SSEDO and SSEDV algorithms significantly reduce the transaction loss ratio compared to other SCAN-based real-time algorithms (up to a 38% improvement) or conventional algorithms (up to a 53% improvement). Between these two, SSEDV is better than SSEDO since SSEDV uses more timing

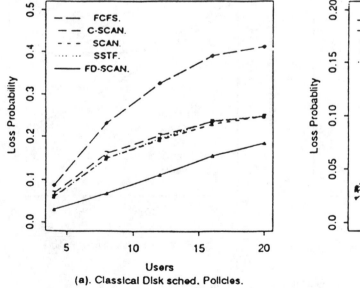
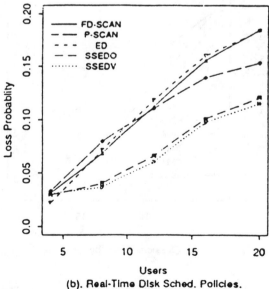

(a). Classical Disk sched. Policies.   (b). Real-Time Disk Sched. Policies.

Figure 3. Performance of various disk scheduling algorithms. ($p_r = 0.8$, $p_s = 0$).

information than SSEDO for decision making. All of the real-time algorithms perform better than nonreal-time ones. P-SCAN and FD-SCAN perform essentially at the same level, with one better at high load cases, but worse for low load cases. The ED algorithm is good when the system is lightly loaded, but it degenerates as soon as load increases. The conventional algorithms SSTF, SCAN and C-SCAN basically perform the same, and FCFS is the worst, by far.

The mean disk service time for this experiment is plotted in Figure 4. As expected, FCFS and ED both give the highest mean disk service time which is independent of the system load, since the request which first joined the I/O queue or with the earliest deadline is randomly located on the disk, regardless of the system workload. The smallest mean disk service time belongs to SSTF, as its name suggests. SCAN algorithm shows almost the same performance as SSTF, and C-SCAN is a little bit higher (Teorey and Pinkerton 1972). Disk service times of the two variants of SCAN algorithm, P-SCAN and FD-SCAN, are basically the same. The reason for why they are higher than that of SCAN is clear. A common characteristic for SSTF and various SCAN algorithms is that their disk access time drops as the system load increases, since the increase of density of waiting I/O requests results in a decrease of the seek time under these algorithms. For the SSEDO and SSEDV algorithms, their disk access times decrease as the load increases, but after a point they become constants. This turning point depends on the window size, where the candidate for next service can only be selected from the window. From Table 3 we can see when the number of users exceeds 8, the mean queue length will be over 3. As mentioned above, the window size is set to 3 in this experiment. Consequently, further increasing system workload will have no influence on the mean disk access time.

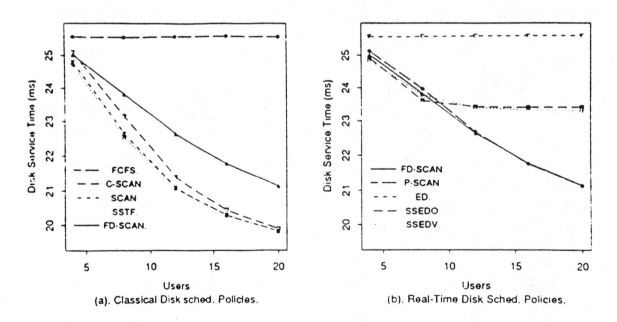

(a). Classical Disk sched. Policies.

(b). Real-Time Disk Sched. Policies.

Figure 4 Mean disk service time for different algorihthms. ($p_r = 0.8$, $p_s = 0$)

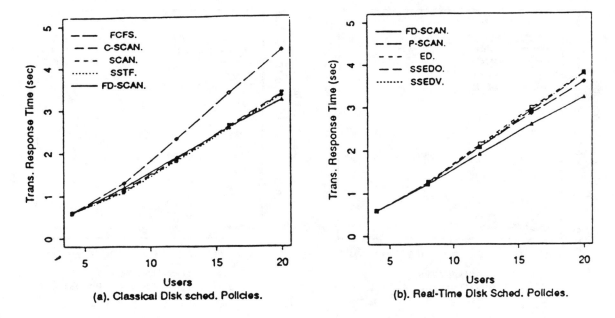

Figure 5. Mean transaction response time for different algorithms. ($p_r = 0.8$, $p_s = 0$)

Figure 5 shows the average response time for committed transactions. From mean disk service times shown in Figure 4, it is not hard to understand why transactions under SSEDO and SSEDV take more time to finish than that of SSTF and various SCANs but less than FCFS and ED. FD-SCAN has the same mean response time as the SSTF, SCAN, and C-SCAN. This is because although the FD-SCAN has longer disk access time, its transaction loss ratio is less than that of SSTF and SCAN. Since lost transactions miss their deadlines while in progress, the already completed steps may be blocking other transactions, and therefore increase the response time of transactions which do commit.

From Table 1, we see that for a fixed workload, there is no significant difference in disk utilizations under the different disk scheduling algorithms. Figure 6 depicts the performance of all the nine algorithms as a function of the disk utilization. The advantage of real-time algorithms over nonreal-time ones is obvious. For real-time algorithms, the window algorithms SSEDO and SSEDV begin to show better performance than P-SCAN and FD-SCAN when the disk utilization is over 55%. Their advantage becomes more explicit when the disk is kept busy over 90% of the time. For example, at 95% disk utilization, SSEDV outperforms FCFS by 71% and FD-SCAN by 36%.

4.2.3. Sensitivity of Changing Window Size and Scheduling Parameters in SSEDO and SSEDV.
With this experiment, we are interested in how the system performs when the window size and/or scheduling parameters α and β are changed in the two window algorithms SSEDO and SSEDV. Note that the leftmost points in Figure 7 correspond to the window size of 1, which is equivalent to the earliest deadline (ED) algorithm. By increasing the window size, we observe an improvement of the performance, especially in the case of high load. If the system is extremely lightly loaded, e.g., the average CPU and I/O queue length is less than one, we expect all algorithms to perform the same. As the load increases, the benefit of window sizes larger than one becomes more pronounced. This is because

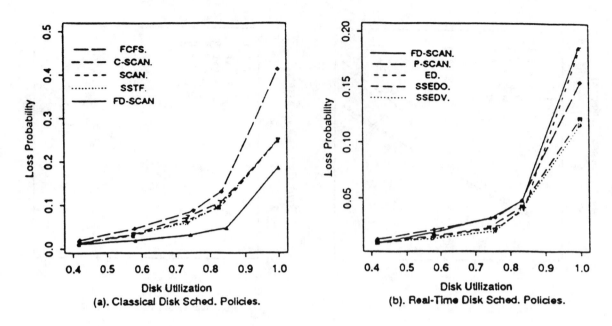

Figure 6. Performance with fixed disk utilizations. ($p_r = 0.8$, $p_s = 0$).

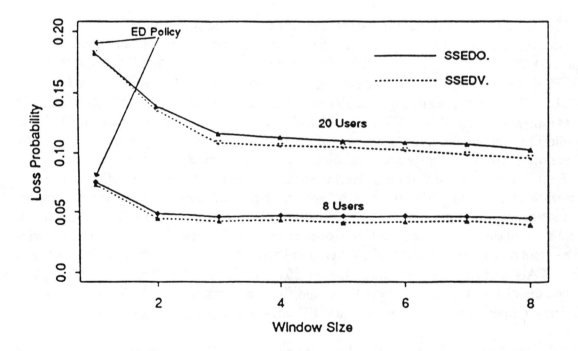

Figure 7. Performance of SSEDV and SSEDO with different window size. ($p_r = 0.8$, $p_s = 0$).

at a higher load, the improvement caused by the *shortest seek time* component of these two window algorithms increases. On the other hand, we also observe that a window size of three or four is good enough in most cases. Increasing the window size further contributes very little to the system performance, but increases the scheduling cost. We also performed experiments for the case of tight deadline settings, and similar results were observed. They are not shown in this paper because of space limitations.

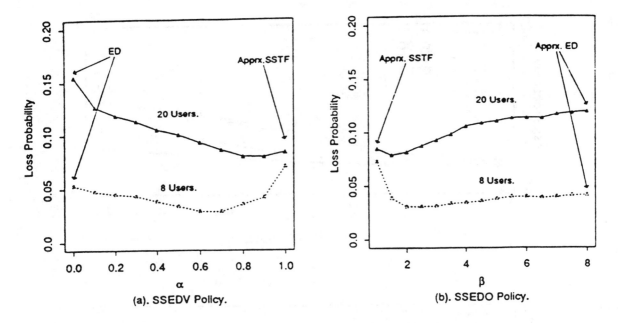

Figure 8. Sensitivity of scheduling parameters of SSEDV and SSEDO. ($p_r = 0.8$, $p_s = 0$).

Figure 8 shows the sensitivity of scheduling parameters α and β for the SSEDV and SSEDO algorithms, respectively. Intuitively, larger (smaller) value of α (β) implies greater bias towards the *shortest seek time* component, and smaller α (β) implies greater bias towards the *earliest deadline* component of the SSEDV (SSEDO) algorithms. From Figure 8a, we can see a large α is preferred in a highly loaded system, and a moderate value of α is proper for a lightly loaded system. In either case, a range of 0.7 to 0.8 for α is acceptable. This observation is consistent to the conclusions drawn from the results of Figure 7. A similar observation can be made from Figure 8b, where $\beta = 2$ is found appropriate in either high or low workload cases.

4.2.4. Impact of Scheduling by Step Deadlines.

As mentioned in Section 2.1, if the system has knowledge of the number of steps required by each transaction, it can use this knowledge for CPU and/or I/O scheduling. That is, instead of using transaction deadlines, the scheduler can make its decision by using step deadlines. Recall that the step deadlines are only used to provide priority information for scheduling and that missing a step deadline, except for the last step, does not abort a transaction. Two experiments were conducted to show the effect of scheduling by step deadlines under the SSEDV, SSDO, and ED algorithms.

In the first experiment, in which step deadlines were incremented evenly, i.e., calculated by Equation (1), we show results for four combinations of scheduling by step deadlines. From Figure 9 we observed that the strategy of scheduling both CPU and I/O scheduling by step deadline (CSDS) performs consistently the best under all the three disk scheduling algorithms, and the worst case is when both CPU and disk are scheduled by transaction deadlines (CTDT). The other two alternatives, i.e., CPU scheduled by transaction deadline and disk by step deadline (CTDS), and vice versa (CSDT), fall in between. For instance, in high load cases, scheduling by step deadline can achieve up to 53% improvement over scheduling by transaction deadline under SSEDV. Also, we observed that applying step

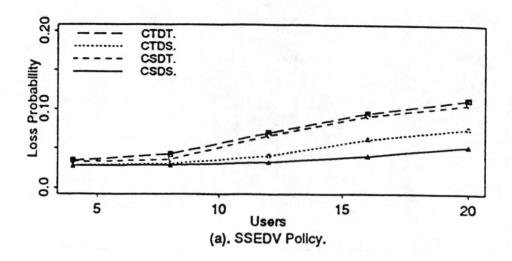

(a). SSEDV Policy.

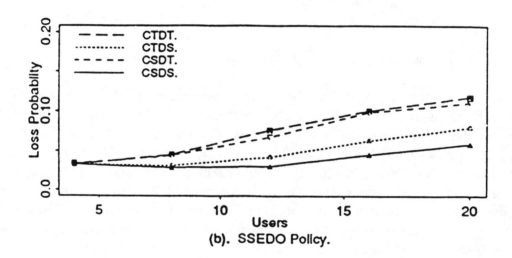

(b). SSEDO Policy.

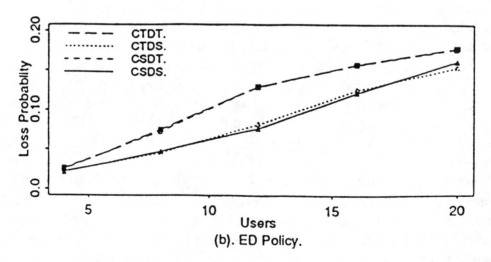

(b). ED Policy.

Figure 9. Scheduling by step deadlines under SSEDV and SSEDO. (*Users* = 20, p_r = 0.8, p_s = 0).

deadline on I/O scheduling results in proportionately more improvement than using it with CPU scheduling and that generally, the larger the workload, the greater the improvement.

In the second experiment, we fix CPU scheduling by transaction deadline, but perform I/O scheduling by step deadline (CTDS). The objective is to determine how to assign step deadlines. One way, as defined in Equation (1), is to evenly divide transaction's deadline among the steps so that each step has the same relative deadline (EVEN). Another way is to let early steps have loose and later steps have tight relative step deadlines (ELLT). The motivation for this is that we may expect an almost finished transaction to have a relatively higher priority. A third alternative is to allow early steps to have tight and later steps to have loose step deadlines (ETLL). In this experiment, we use the following methods to assign step deadlines with ELLT and ETLL: let L, a, and n be a transaction's (absolute) deadline, arrival time, and the number of operational steps, as before. In addition, denote b as the *base step length*, and Δ as the step increment; then for ETLL, we set the deadline for step i by

$$step\_deadline(i) = step\_deadline(i - 1) + b + i\Delta \qquad i = 1, 2, \ldots, n. \qquad (4)$$

where $step\_deadline(0) = a$, or in other words,

$$step\_deadline(i) = a + ib + \frac{i(i + 1)}{2}\Delta \qquad i = 1, 2, \ldots, n. \qquad (5)$$

Since the last step's deadline is the same as transaction's deadline, we have

$$step\_deadline(n) = a + nb + \frac{n(n + 1)}{2}\Delta \qquad (6)$$

$$= L \qquad (7)$$

or

$$\frac{L - a}{n} = b + \frac{n + 1}{2}\Delta \qquad (8)$$

When $\Delta = 0$, substituting Equation (8) into Equation (5) reproduces Equation (1). By changing the value of b and Δ (while maintaining the constraint from Equation (8)), we can adjust the looseness of step increment. In this experiment, b is equal to $2(L - a)/3n$, and Δ can be obtained from (5). For ELLT, in a similar manner, we have

$$step\_deadline(i) = step\_deadline(i - 1) + b + (n - i + 1)\Delta \qquad (9)$$

$$= a + ib + \frac{(n + n - i + 1)i}{2}\Delta \qquad i = 1, 2, \ldots, n. \qquad (10)$$

The results are illustrated in Figure 10, and we can see that ELLT performs slightly better than the other two under both SSEDV and SSEDO under a variety of workloads. However,

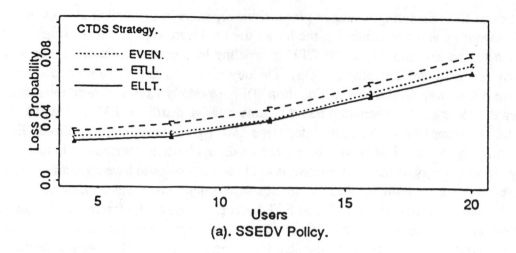

(a). SSEDV Policy.

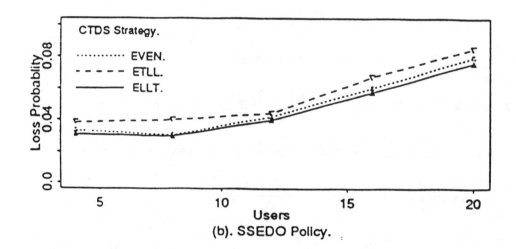

(b). SSEDO Policy.

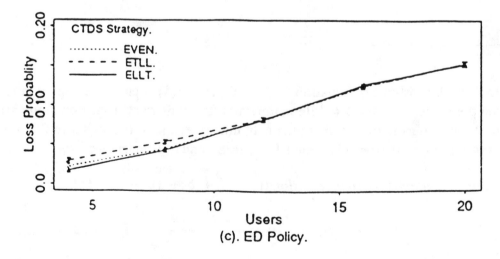

(c). ED Policy.

Figure 10. Step deadline assignment with SSEDV and SSEDO. (*Users* = 20, p_r = 0.8, p_s = 0).

in either case, step deadlines should not be too *loose*, otherwise the policies will degenerate to the case of scheduling by transaction deadlines which was shown to be the worst in Figure 9. For the ED algorithm, there is no significant difference between various ways of assigning the step deadlines, especially when the I/O load is high.

4.2.5. Varying Transaction's Deadline Settings.

This experiment examines all the nine disk scheduling algorithms under various deadline settings, from very loose to extremely tight. At one extreme, every transaction is successfully served and none are lost. At the other end of the spectrum, almost every transaction misses its deadline. From the results shown in Figure 11, we observe that SSEDV and SSEDO perform the best over the entire range of deadline settings, and FCFS remains the worst. As also shown in the figure, when deadlines are tight (e.g. approximately 60% of transactions being lost), SSEDV still outperforms FD-SCAN by 6% and SCAN by 16%. The SSTF, SCAN, and C-SCAN algorithms are shown to perform almost the same. Once again, FD-SCAN outperforms P-SCAN when the deadline is tight and is outperformed by P-SCAN when the deadline becomes loose. The average transaction response time for committed transactions is depicted in Figure 12. For the case of loose deadline settings, when nearly all the transactions can make their deadline, the mean transaction response time is proportional to the mean disk service time of various disk scheduling algorithms. On the other hand, when the deadline is tight, SSEDV and SSEDO have a lower loss ratio than others, which helps to achieve the lower mean response time for committed transactions.

4.2.6. Varying Read Probability.

The purpose of this experiment is to study how the various disk scheduling algorithms perform when the read probability, p_r, is changed. In our database model, an increase in update probability (i.e., a decrease in read probability) implies more lock conflicts since update requests require exclusive locks. This also increases

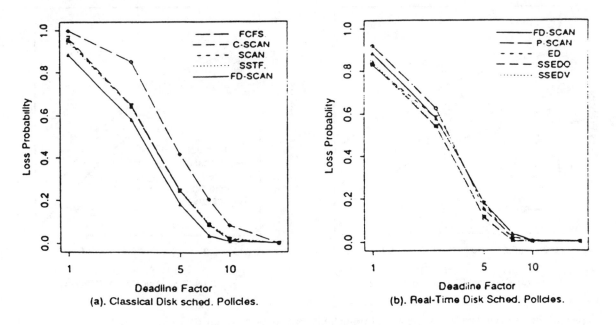

(a). Classical Disk sched. Policies.

(b). Real-Time Disk Sched. Policies.

Figure 11. Performance with various deadline settings. (*Users* = 20. p_r = 0.8. p_s = 0).

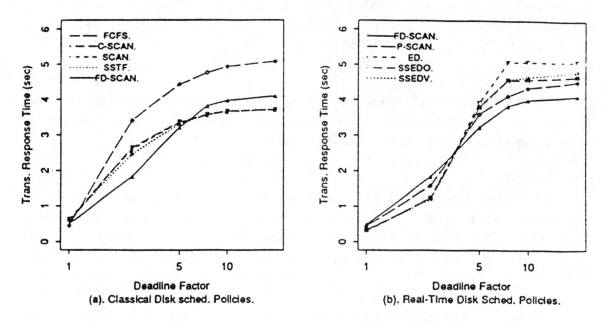

Figure 12. Mean transaction response time with various deadline settings. (*Users* = 20, p_r = 0.8. p_s = 0).

I/O load because more flushing work of dirty pages is required. The experimental results are shown in Figure 13. As expected, when read probability increases, the transaction loss probability decreases for all the nine I/O scheduling algorithms. However, the performance order of these algorithms remains the same as in previous discussions except for the ED algorithm which has a proportionately greater improvement as the read probability approaches one.

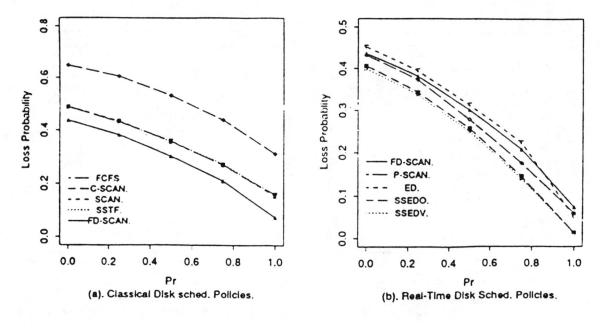

Figure 13. Performance under different read probability. (*Users* = 20, p_s = 0).

646

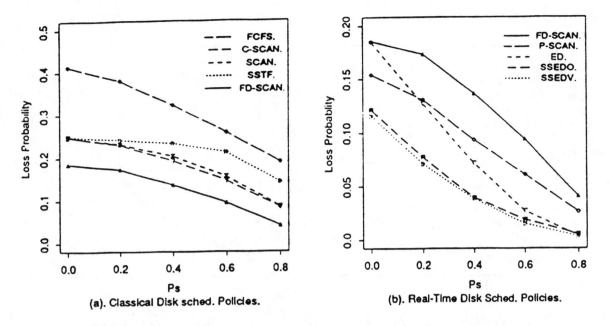

Figure 14. Performance under different sequential access probability. (*Users* = 20, p_r = 0.8).

4.2.7. *Locality of Transaction Accesses*. In this subsection, we examine the locality impact of transactions' accesses. We first investigate the system behavior when the transaction sequential access probability, p_s, varies from 0 to 0.8. In this experiment, we choose a high workload case (20 Users), and a read probability of 0.8. From Figure 14, we again see that the performance of all algorithms improves when p_s increases, and that SSEDV and SSEDO are consistently better than the others. Interestingly, the increased benefit for SSTF (42% improvement) is not as large as the benefit for SCAN and C-SCAN (66% improvement) when the *sequential access probability* increases. Whereas for the ED algorithm the gain is quite large (90% improvement) when sequential accesses occur. A partial reason for this is that the main benefit gained by increasing p_s is the reduction in seek time, which the SSTF algorithm has already taken advantage of, but ED hasn't.

Viewing the locality effect from another perspective, we rearrange the layout of the database on the disk so that the database only occupies a portion of the disk (this situation is found in the RT-CARAT testbed), say the center 100 tracks, rather than randomly scattered on 1000 tracks. The results are shown in Figure 15. If we compare these results with Figure 3, we can see that the SSEDV, SSEDO, and ED algorithms gain more than the others by this arrangement. Among these, the ED algorithm received tremendous improvement. The reason for this is that both the SSEDV, SSEDO and ED are *time-constraint-oriented* algorithms, which means they put more weight on the *time constraint* component rather than on the *disk service time* component like the various SCANs do. For example, the SSEDV and SSEDO algorithms might choose the request with earliest deadline for next service over 80% of the time, whereas the ED algorithm would choose that request 100% of the time. The new layout reduces the disk service time. This will help the SSEDV, SSEDO and ED algorithms to make up their deficiency with respect to the *disk service time* component, and therefore improves their relative performance.

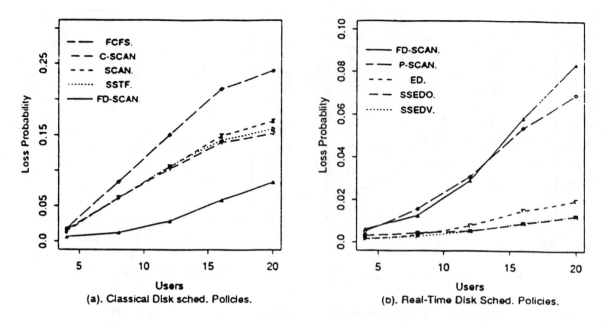

Figure 15. Performance under different database layout. ($p_r = 0.8$, $p_s = 0$).

4.2.8. Importance of Real-Time Scheduling. This final experiment is designed to see how the performance varies when the system employs real-time or nonreal-time scheduling algorithms in CPU and/or disk scheduling. To examine the effect of CPU scheduling, we increase the computation time for each step to 25 msec (which is approximately the same as the mean disk service time). Four combinations, CPU scheduled by FCFS and I/O by SCAN, CPU by FCFS and I/O by SSEDO, CPU by ED and I/O by SCAN, and CPU by ED and I/O by SSEDO, are investigated. Figure 16a gives the transaction loss ratio in each case. Obviously, when both CPU and I/O are scheduled by real-time strategies, the performance is much better than when no real-time algorithms are used for CPU and disk scheduling (with up to an 84% performance improvement in high load cases). We also observe that the use of a real-time disk scheduling algorithm is more beneficial than the use of a real-time CPU scheduling algorithm. The transaction response times for the cases of I/O scheduled by real-time algorithms are shown to be higher than that of I/O scheduled by nonreal-time algorithms in Figure 16b. This is because the disk service times for real-time algorithms (SSEDO) are higher than nonreal-time algorithms (SCAN). Therefore, we conclude that real-time disk scheduling algorithms do reduce the transaction loss ratio at the cost of higher mean transaction response time than some nonreal-time algorithms do.

Interestingly, under the parameter settings above, for the two cases of I/O scheduled by nonreal-time algorithms, the CPU tends to be a bottleneck as the system load increases (Figure 17). In contrast, most transactions will be queued up at the I/O device if SSEDO is employed as the I/O scheduling algorithm. The shorter seek time of SCAN algorithm partially explains why this could happen.

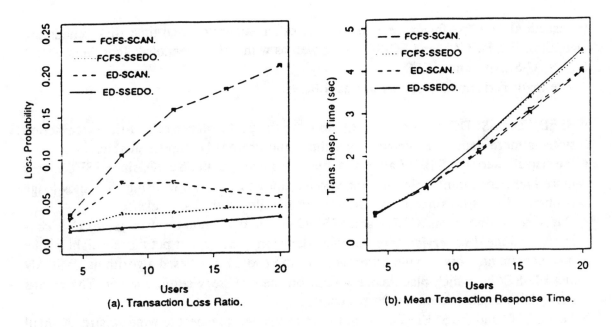

Figure 16. Importance of real-time scheduling. (p_r = 0.8, p_s = 0, *Comp_Time* = 25ms).

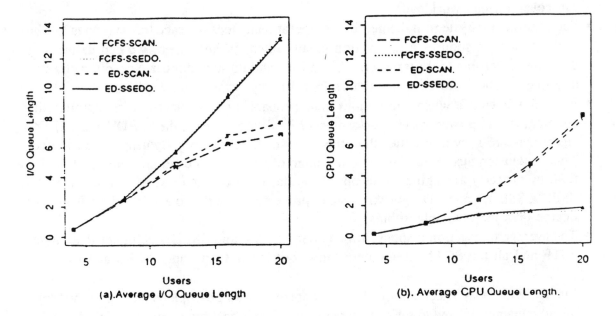

Figure 17. Average CPU and I/O Queue Length. (p_r = 0.8, p_s = 0, *Comp_Time* = 25ms).

5. Conclusions

In this paper we examined the performance of various disk scheduling algorithms in an integrated real-time transaction system. Specifically, we first proposed two new real-time disk scheduling algorithms SSEDV and SSEDO, and then compared their impact on system (transaction) level performance with that of other suggested real-time disk scheduling algorithms ED, P-SCAN and FD-SCAN, as well as with the conventional algorithms, SSTF, SCAN, C-SCAN, and FCFS.

The main performance results are as follows:

- SSEDV and SSEDO can significantly improve the performance of real-time transaction systems more than other known algorithms and are easily implementable.
- We also showed that SSEDV algorithm performs better than SSEDO, since SSEDV uses more knowledge concerning the time constraint and the cost of using that knowledge is obtained for free since it can be used in parallel with disk seeks.
- Our window algorithms SSEDV and SSEDO take into account two factors, *the time constraint* and *the disk service time*, for their decision making, but put more weight on the time constraint. This is quite different from the two SCAN based algorithms, P-SCAN and FD-SCAN, which place more weight on the disk service time factor. The results show that our algorithms perform better.
- The SSEDV and the SSEDO algorithms are robust with respect to window size. A small window works well under a wide variety of workloads. Careful adjustment of algorithm parameters α and β may improve system performance, but small range of these parameters can cover various workloads.
- For a transaction system, if the number of operational steps for each transaction is known to the system as soon as a transaction is submitted to the system, we can define step deadlines according to the transaction's deadline and its step number. Scheduling by step deadlines is shown to be better than scheduling by transaction deadlines.
- It is well known that when transactions' read probability or sequential access probability are high, this improves system performance. In all these cases, the SSEDV and SSEDO algorithms are shown to better than the other disk scheduling algorithms considered. This conclusion also holds over a wide range of transaction deadline settings. In addition, by properly arranging the layout of the database on the disk, it is shown that the SSEDV, SSEDO, and ED algorithms can improve performance to a *proportionally* greater degree than the other algorithms.
- The average transaction response time under SSEDV and SSEDO is higher than under SSTF and all the SCAN based algorithms, but lower than under FCFS and ED.

Finally, with today's technology, the disk controller can be implemented to monitor the I/O load dynamically, and to select a proper scheduling algorithm accordingly (Bates 1989). This technique can be used here with our SSEDV and SSEDO algorithms in a soft real-time environment. For example, when the I/O queue length is less than a threshold, the ED algorithm (window size 1 in SSEDV or SSEDO) might be used for scheduling, otherwise the window size would be set to 3 or 4. Alternatively, we might dynamically update the scheduling parameter α or β according to a queue length threshold.

Acknowledgments

The authors wish to thank K. Ramamritham for his constructive comments on a draft of this paper. Thanks are also due to J. Huang for his invaluable help with the experiments on the RT-CARAT testbed.

References

Abbott, R. and Garcia-Molina, H. 1988. Scheduling Real-Time Transactions. A Performance Evaluation. *Proc. of the 14th VLDB Conf.*, pp. 1-12.

Abbott, R. and Garcia-Molina, H. 1989. Scheduling Real-Time Transactions with Disk Resident Data. *A Technical Proc. of the 15th VLDB Conf.*, pp. 385-396.

Abbott, R. and Garcia-Molina, H. 1990. Scheduling I/O Requests with Deadlines: A Performance Evaluation. *Proc. of Real-Time Systems Symposium*, pp. 113-124.

Bates, K.H. 1989. Performance Aspects of the HSC Controller. *Digital Technical Journal* 8:25-37.

Bitton, D. and Gray, J. 1988. Disk Shadowing. *Proc. of the 14th VLDB Conf.* pp. 331-338.

Buchmann, A.P. et al. 1989. Time-Critical Database Scheduling: A Framework for Integrating Real-Time Scheduling and Concurrency Control. *Data Engineering Conference*, pp. 470-480.

Carey, M.J., Jauhari, R. and Livny, M. 1989. Priority in DBMS Resource Scheduling. *Proc. of the 15th VLDB Conf.*, pp. 397-410

Cimimiera, L., Montuschi, P. and Valenzano, A. 1989. Some Properties of Double-Ring Networks with Real-Time Constraints. *Proc. of Real-Time Systems Symposium*, pp. 360-368.

Hofri, M. 1980. Disk Scheduling: FCFS vs. SSTF Revisited. *ACM Communications*, (11), pp. 645-653.

Hong, J., Tan, X. and Towsley, D. 1989. A Performance Analysis of Minimum Laxity and Earliest Deadline Scheduling in a Real-Time System. *IEEE Trans. on Computer*, 38, (12): 1736-1744.

Huang, J., Stankovic, J.A., Towsley, D. and Ramamritham, K. 1989. Experimental Evaluation of Real-Time Transaction Processing. *Proc. Real-Time System Symposium*, pp. 144-153.

Kohler, W. and Jenq, B.P. 1986. CARAT: A Testbed for the Performance Evaluation of Distributed Database Systems. *Proc. of the Fall Joint Computer Conference*, pp. 1169-1117.

Kopetz, H. and Ochsenreiter, W. 1987. Clock Synchronization in Distributed Real-Time Systems. *IEEE Trans. on Computers*, 36(8):933-940.

Locke, C.D., Tokuda, H. and Jensen, E.D. 1985. A Time-Driven Scheduling Model for Real-Time Operating System. *Technical Report, CMU*.

Malcolm, N., Zhao, W. and Barter, C. 1990. Guarantee Protocols for Communication in Distributed Hard Real-Time Systems. *Proc. of IEEE INFORCOM '90*, pp. 1078-1086.

Seltzer, M., Chen, P. and Ousterhout, J. 1990. Disk Scheduling Revisited. *Proc. of USENIX, Winter '90*, pp. 313-323.

Tokuda, H., Mercer, C.W., Ishikawa, Y. and Marchok, T.E. 1989. Priority Inversions in Real-Time Communication. *Proc. of Real-Time Systems Symposium*, pp. 348-359.

Teorey, T.J. and Pinkerton, T.B. 1972. A Comparative Analysis of Disk Scheduling Policies. *ACM Communications*, 5 (3): 177-184.

Towsley, D. and Panwar, S.S. 1990. On the Optimality of Minimum Laxity and Earliest Deadline Scheduling for Real-Time Multiprocessors. *Proc. Euromicro'90 Workshop on Real-Time*, pp. 17-24.

Warchol, N.A. and Shirron, S.F. 1986. The RQDX3 Design Project. *Digital Technical Journal*, 2:66-75.

Scheduling Real-time Transactions: a Performance Evaluation

Robert Abbott and Hector Garcia-Molina

Department of Computer Science
Princeton University
Princeton, NJ 08544

Abstract

Managing transactions with real-time requirements presents many new problems. In this paper we focus on two: How can we schedule transactions with deadlines? How do the real-time constraints affect concurrency control? We describe a new group of algorithms for scheduling real-time transactions which produce serializable schedules. We present a model for scheduling transactions with deadlines on a single processor memory resident database system, and evaluate the scheduling through detailed simulation experiments.

1. Introduction

Transactions in a database system can have real-time constrains. Consider for example program trading, or the use of computer programs to initiate trades in a financial market with little or no human intervention [8]. A financial market (e.g. a stack market) is a complex process whose state is partially captured be variables such a current stock prices, changes in stock prices, volume of trading, trends, and composite indexes. These variables and others can be stored and organized in a database to model a financial market.

One type of process in this system is a sensor/input process which monitors the state of the physical system (i.e.) the stock market) and updates the database with new information. If the database is to contain an accurate representation of the current market then this monitoring process must meet certain real-time constraints.

A second type of process is an analysis/output process. In general terms this process reads and analyzes database information in order to respond to a user query and to initiate a trade in the stock market. An example of this is a query to discover the current bid and ask prices

of a particular stock. This query may have a real-time response requirement of say 3 seconds. Another example is a program that searches the database for arbitrage opportunities. Arbitrage trading involves finding discrepancies in prices for objects, often on different markets. For example, an ounce of silver might sell for $10 in London and fetch $10.50 in Chicago. Price discrepancies are normally very short-lived and to exploit them one must trade large volumes on a moments notice. Thus the detection and exploitation of these arbitrage opportunities is certainly a real-time task.

Another kind of real-time database system involves threat analysis. For example, a system may consist of a radar to track objects and a computer to perform some image processing and control. A radar signature is collected and compared against a database of signatures of known objects. The data collection and signature look up must be done in real-time.

A *real-time database system* (RTDBS) has many similarities with conventional database management systems and with so called real-time systems. however, a RTDBS lies at the interface and is not quite the same as either type of conventional system. Like a database system, a RTDBS must process *transactions* and guarantee that the database consistency is not violated. However, conventional database systems do not emphasize the notion of time constraints or deadlines for transactions. The performance goal of a system is usually expressed in terms of desired *average* response times rather than constrains for individual transactions. Thus, when the system makes scheduling decision (e.g., which transaction gets a lock, which transaction is aborted), individual real-time constrains are ignored.

Conventional real-time systems do take into account individual transaction constrains but ignore date consistency problems. Furthermore, real-time systems typically deal with simple transactions (called processes) that have simple and predictable data (or resource) requirements. For a RTDBS we assume that transactions make unpredictable data accesses (by far the more common situation in a database system). This makes the scheduling problem much harder, and this leads to another difference between a conventional real-time system and a RTDBS. The former usually attempts to

"Scheduling Real-Time Transactions: A Performance Evaluation" by R. Abbott and H. Garcia-Molina from *Proceedings of the 14th VLDB Conference,* 1988, pp. 1-12. Copyright © 1988 Morgan Kaufmann.

ensure that no time constraints are violated, i.e., constraints are viewed as "hard." [7] In a RTDBS, on the other hand, it is very difficult to guarantee all time constraints, so we strive to minimize the ones that are violated.

In the previous paragraphs we have "defined" what we mean by a RTDBS (our definition will be made more precise in Section 2). However, note that other definitions and assumptions are possible. For instance, one could decide to have hard time constrains and instead minimize the number of data consistency violations. However, we believe that the type of RTDBS that we have sketched better matches the needs of applications like the ones mentioned earlier. For instance, in the financial market example, it is probably best to miss a few good trading opportunities rather than permanently compromise the correctness of the database, or restrict the types of transactions that can be run.

We should at this point make two comments about RTDBS applications. It may be argued that real-time applications do not access databases because they are "too slow." This is a version of the chicken and the egg problem. Current database systems have few real-time facilities, and hence cannot provide the service needed for real-time applications. The way to break the cycle is by studying a RTDBS, designing the proper facilities, and evaluating the performance (e.g., what is the price to be paid for serializability?).

It is also important to note that with good real-time facilities, even applications one does not typically consider "real-time" may benefit. For example, consider a banking transaction processing system. In addition to meeting average response time requirements, it may be advantageous to tell the system the urgency of each transaction so it can be processed with the corresponding priority. As a matter of fact, a "real" banking system may already have some of these facilities, but not provided in a coherent fashion by the database management system.

The design and evaluation of a RTDBS presents many new and challenging problems: What is the best data model? What languages can we use to specify real-time constraints? What mechanisms are needed for describing and evaluating triggers (a trigger is an event or a condition in the database that causes some action to occur)? How are transactions scheduled? How do the real-time constraints affect concurrency control?

In this paper we focus on the last two questions. In particular, if several transactions are ready to execute at a given time, which one runs first? If a transaction requests a lock held by another transaction, so we abort the holder if the requester has greater urgency? If transactions can provide an estimate of their running time, can we use it to tell which transaction is closest to

missing a deadline and hence should be give higher priority. If we do use run time estimates, what happens if they are incorrect? How are the various strategies affected by the load, the number of database conflicts, and the tightness of the deadlines?

In the next section we summarize our transaction model and basic assumptions. In Section 3 we develop a group of new scheduling/concurrency control algorithms for RTDBS. The performance of the various algorithms has been studied via detailed event driven simulations. Section 4 contains the results as well as some answers to the questions posed in the previous paragraph.

2. Model and Assumptions

In this section we describe our basic assumption and real-time transaction model. We assume that transactions are scheduled dynamically on a single processor machine with enough main memory to accommodate the entire database. Our main justification for studying a single processor and a memory resident database is that this reduces the number of parameters (no multiple processors, buses, or disks to model) and makes it easier to understand the scheduling options and their impact on performance. However, we believe that these are reasonable restrictions for a first study of real-time database scheduling. Most existing real-time systems currently hold all their data in memory. Furthermore, since memory prices are steadily dropping, memory sizes are growing and memory residence becomes less of a restriction. Along similar lines, multiple processor real-time systems do exist, but it is important to understand the single processor case first.

A transaction is characterized by its timing constraints and its data and computation requirements. The timing constraints are a release time r and a deadline d. A computation requirement is represented by a run time estimation E which approximates the amount of computation required by the transaction. These characteristics, release time, deadline and run time estimate are known to the scheduler when a task enters the system. The last characteristic, data requirements, is not known beforehand but is discovered dynamically as the transaction executes. Our decision to assume knowledge of computation requirements but no knowledge of data requirements is justified because it is easier to estimate the execution time of a transaction than to predict its data access pattern. And in any case, E is simply an estimate that could be wrong or not given at all.

Our goal is to minimize the number of transactions that miss their deadlines, i.e., that finish after time d. If transactions can miss their deadlines, one must address the question of what happens to transaction that have already missed their deadlines but have not finished yet.

There are two alternatives. One is to assume that a transaction that has missed its deadline, i.e., is tardy, is worthless and can be aborted. This may be reasonable in our arbitrage example. Suppose that a transaction is submitted to buy and sell silver by 11:00 am. If the deadline is missed, it may be best not to perform the operation at all; after all the conditions that triggered the decision to go ahead may have changed. The user who submitted the transaction may wish to reconsider the operation.

A second option is to assume that all transactions must be completed eventually, regardless of whether they are tardy or not. This may be the correct mode of operation in, say, a banking system where customers would rather do the transaction late than not at all. (Of course, the user may on his own decide to abort his transaction, but this is another matter.) If tardy transactions must be executed, there is still the question of their priority. Tardy transactions could receive higher and higher urgency as their tardiness increases. On the other hand, since they already missed the deadline anyway, they may simple be postponed to a later, more convenient time (e.g., execute at night).

In this paper we will study both cases, when tardy transactions must be completed and when they can be aborted. If they must complete, we will assume that their priority increases as the tardiness increases (they are not put off). (Incidentally, [1] discusses a more detailed deadline model where users can specify how the "value" of a transaction changes over time, both as the deadline approaches and passes.)

We assume that transaction executions must be serializable [2]. For most applications we believe that it is desirable to maintain database consistency. It is possible to maintain consistency without serializable schedules but this requires more specific information about the kinds of transactions being executed [3]. Since we have assumed very little knowledge about transactions, serializability is the best way to achieve consistency.

Finally, we assume that serializability is enforced by using a locking protocol. Our purpose is not to do a comparative study of concurrency mechanisms. Instead we have chosen a well-understood and widely-used mechanism and explored the different ways that transactions can be scheduled using this mechanism. Of course, it is conceivable that some other algorithms, like an optimistic protocol, may be better for a RTDBS, but this will have to be addressed by further research.

3. Some Scheduling Algorithms

Our scheduling algorithms have three components: a policy to determine which tasks are eligible for service, a policy for assigning priorities to tasks and a concurrency control mechanism. The concurrency control mechanism can be thought of as a policy for resolving conflicts between two (or more) transactions that want to lock the same data object. Some concurrency control mechanisms permit deadlocks to occur. For these a deadlock detection and resolution mechanism is needed.

Each component may use only some of the available information about a transaction. In particular we distinguish between policies which do not make use of E, the run time estimate, and those that do. A goal of our research is to understand how the accuracy of the run time estimate affects the algorithms that use it.

3.1. Determining Eligibility

The scheduler is invoked whenever a transaction terminates and, for preemptive scheduling, whenever a new transaction arrives. The concurrency control mechanism is invoked to resolve lock conflicts whenever one occurs. The first action of the scheduler is to divide the set of ready transactions into two lists, those that are eligible for scheduling and those that are not. All ineligible transactions are aborted and their locks released. Eligible transactions remain in the system and are eligible for service. If a transaction never becomes ineligible than it is eventually executed. Finally, an eligible transaction may become ineligible but an ineligible transaction can not become eligible. We consider three different policies for determining eligibility.

All Eligible. All jobs are eligible for service. This means that no job is unilaterally aborted.

Not Tardy. All jobs which currently are not tardy are eligible for service. Jobs that have already missed their deadlines are aborted.

Feasibility Deadlines. All jobs with feasible deadlines are eligible for service. A transaction T has a feasible deadline if $t + E - P \leq d$ where P is the amount of service time that T has received. In other words, based on the run time estimate there is enough time to complete the transaction before its deadline. Jobs with infeasible deadlines are aborted. Note that this policy uses E, the run time estimate.

3.2. Assigning Priorities

There are many ways to assign priorities to real-time tasks [5,6]. We have studied three.

First Come First Serve. This policy assigns the highest priority to the transaction with the earliest release time. If release times equal arrival times then we have the traditional version of FCFS.

The primary weakness of FCFS is that it does not make use of deadline information. FCFS will discriminate against a newly arrived task with an urgent deadline in favor of an older task which may not have such an urgent deadline. This is not desirable for real-time systems.

Earliest Deadline. The transaction with the earliest deadline has the highest priority. A major weakness of this policy is that it can assign the highest priority to a task that has already missed or is about to miss its deadline. One way to solve this problem is to use the eligibility policy Not Tardy or Feasible Deadlines to screen out transactions that have missed or are about to miss their deadlines.

Least Slack. For a transaction T we define a slack time $S = d - (t + E - P)$. The slack time is an estimate of how long we can delay the execution of T and still meet its deadline. If $S \geq 0$ then we expect that if T is executed without interruption then it will finish at or before its deadline. A negative slack time is an estimate that it is impossible to make the deadline. A negative slack time results either when a transaction has already missed its deadline or when we estimate that it cannot meet its deadline.

Least Slack is similar to Earliest Deadline in that it can assign high priorities to tasks which have missed or are about to miss their deadlines. Again we can use the eligibility policies Not Tardy and Feasible Deadlines to ameliorate this problem. Using Not Tardy disallows jobs with negative slack times that result from missed deadlines. Feasible Deadlines disallows all jobs with negative slack times. Least Slack is very different from Earliest Deadline in that the priority of a task depends on how much service time it has received. Thus restarting a transaction changes its priority. We return to this issue in the next section.

3.3 Concurrency Control

If transactions are executed concurrently then we need a concurrency control mechanism to order the updates to the database so that the final schedule is a serializable one. We now discuss three possible solutions. Once again we distinguish between policies which make use of the runtime estimate E and those that do not.

Serial Execution. The simplest way to resolve conflicts is not to let them happen in the first place. The way to achieve this and maintain database consistency is to execute transactions serially and without preemption. Once the highest priority transaction gains the processor it runs to completion. This method is efficient only if not transactions are forced to wait for data transfers from disk to memory and back. If the entire database is memory resident then this may be a good method for maintaining serializability at low cost. A drawback of this method is that an arriving task with an urgent deadline must wait until the current task (possibly one with a less urgent

deadline and a large remaining computation) completes.

It may be possible to improve performance by executing transactions concurrently. If this is done then we can expect conflicts to occur. In the following discussions let T_H denote a transaction which holds a code on data object X. Let T_R be a transaction which is requesting a lock on X. We now present two methods to resolve conflicting transactions.

High Priority. The idea of this policy is to resolve a conflict in favor of the transaction with the higher priority. The favored transaction, the winner of the conflict, gets the resources, both data locks and the processor, that it needs to proceed. The loser of the conflict relinquishes control of any resources that are needed by the winner. We implement this policy by comparing transaction priorities at the time of the conflict. If the priority of T_R is greater than the priority of T_H then we abort T_H thereby freeing the lock for T_R. T_R can resume processing: T_H is rolled back and scheduled for restart. If the priority of T_R is less than or equal to the priority of T_H then we let T_H keep its lock and T_R blocks to wait for T_H to finish and release its locks.

Consider the following set of transactions with release time r, deadline d, runtime estimate E and data requirements.

Transaction	r	E	d	updates
A	0	2.6	5	X
B	1	2	4	X
C	2	2.4	8	Y

Example 1.

Note that transactions A and B both update item X. Therefore these transactions must be serialized. If we use Earliest Deadline to assign priority and High Priority to resolve conflicts then the following schedule is produced. (It assumes that estimates are perfect and ignores the time required to make scheduling decisions or rollback transactions.)

lock X; conflict; A aborted

A	B	A	C
0	1	3	5.6	8

In this schedule, A runs in the first time unit during which it acquires a lock on item X. Transaction B gains the processor at time 1 (it has an earlier deadline) and requests a lock on item X. Thus a conflict is created which is resolved by rolling back A thereby freeing the lock on X. Transaction B continues processing and completes before its deadline. After B completes at time 3, A is restarted. Transactions B and C meet their deadlines but A is tardy.

An interesting problem arises when we use Least Slack to prioritize transactions. Recall that under this policy, a transaction's priority depends on the amount of service time that it has received. Rolling back a transaction to its beginning reduces its effective service time to 0 and raises its priority under the Least Slack policy. Thus a transaction T_H, which loses a conflict and is aborted to allow a higher priority transaction T_R to proceed, can have a higher priority than T_R immediately after the abort. The next time the scheduler is invoked, T_R will be preempted by T_H. T_H may again conflict with T_R initiating another abort and rollback.

Our solution to this problem is to compare the priority of T_R against that of T_H assuming that T_H were aborted. We can write this new conflict resolution policy as follows:

High Priority Conflict Resolution Policy.

if $p(T_H) < p(T_R)$ and $p(T_H^A) < p(T_R)$
then
> Abort T_H
> Run T_R

else
> T_R blocks
> Run T_H

The function $p(T_H)$ is the priority of T_H and $p(T_H^A)$ is the priority of T_H were it to be aborted. Using this revised policy, the schedule produced by Least Slack is as follows:

lock X; conflict; B waits

	A	B	A	B	C	
0		1	1.5	3.1	4.6	7

Now when the conflict occurs at time 1.5, B has a slack of 1 but A were it aborted has a slack of .9. So A is not aborted but is assigned to the processor while B waits for A to finish. Transaction B is unblocked when A finishes at time 3.1. Transactions A and C meet their deadlines but B is tardy.

For FCFS and Earliest Deadline policies, $p(T_H) = p(T_H^A)$, so it does not matter if we use the original High Priority resolution rule or the modified one above. Since the modified rule is clearly superior for Least Slack priority assignment, we will use it for our performance evaluations.

We make two final observations about High Priority. First, if T_R waits for T_H it is possible that T_H is not a ready transaction. That is, T_H may be blocked waiting for a lock held by another transaction T_J. In this case the conflict resolving mechanism is applied again

except that T_H is now the lock requesting transaction and T_J is the lock holder. And second, because transactions wait for lock, deadlock is a possibility. Deadlock detection can be cone using one of the standard algorithms [4]. Victim selection, however, should be done with consideration of the time constraints of the tasks involved in the deadlock.

Conditional Restart

Sometimes High Priority may be too conservative. Let us assume that we have chosen the first branch of the algorithm, i.e., T_R has a greater priority than T_H and T_H^A. We would like to avoid aborting T_H because we lose all the service time that it has already consumed. We can be a little cleverer by using a conditional restart policy to resolve conflicts. The idea here is to estimate if T_H, the transaction holding the lock, can be finished within the amount of time that T_R the lock requester, can afford to wait. Let S_R be the slack time of T_R and let $E_H - P_H$ be the estimated remaining time of T_H. If $S_R \geq E_H - P_H$ then we estimate that T_H can finish within the slack of T_R. If so then we let T_H proceed to completion, release its locks and then let T_R execute. This saves us from restarting T_H. If T_H cannot be finisher in the slack time of T_R then we restart T_H and run T_R (as in the previous algorithm). This modification yields the following algorithm:

Conditional Restart Conflict Resolution Policy

if $p(T_H) < p(T_R)$ and $p(T_H^A) < p(T_R)$
then
> if $E_H - P_H \leq S_R$
> then
> > T_R blocks
> > Run T_H
> else
> > Abort T_H
> > Run T_R

else
> T_R blocks
> Run T_H

The following example illustrates the idea for this policy. Again we use Earliest Deadline to assign priority. (We continue to assume that estimates are exact and scheduling decisions and rollbacks are done instantly.)

Transaction	r	E	d	updates
A	0	2	5	X
B	1	2	4	X
C	2	3	8	Y

Example 2.

lock X; conflict; B waits

A	B	A	B	C	
0	1	1.5	2.5	4	7

A conflict occurs when B requests a lock on X at time 1.5. the algorithm calculates the slack time of B as $S = 4 - 1.5 - 1.5 = 1$. This equals exactly the remaining run time for A. Therefore B waits for A to finish and release its locks. A finishes at time 2.5 and B, with 1.5 time units left to compute, regains the processor and completes at time 4. All transactions meet their deadlines.

In this example the runtime estimate was an excellent approximation of the actual computation time of A. If the actual computation time for A was a little longer than the runtime estimate then B would miss its deadline. Thus the ability of this algorithm to successfully exploit slack time information in order to avoid aborting and restarting transactions is dependent on the accuracy of the runtime estimates. Note that Conditional Restart allows transactions to wait for locks, thus deadlock is a possibility.

As described the Conditional Restart policy has two problems. First, we assume that only one job T_H has to run before T_R. In fact T_H may be waiting for a lock held by another transaction T_j and we must decide how to resolve the conflict between T_H and T_j. More generally, let $D = T_1, T_2, ..., T_n$ be a chain of tasks such that T_1 is waiting for a lock held by T_2 which is waiting for a lock held by T_3,..., which is waiting for a lock held by T_n (We assume that this chain is deadlock free but we make no assumptions about the relative priorities of the tasks in the chain.) Let T_0 with slack time S be the currently executing task and say it requests a lock held by T_1. The idea of the conditional restart algorithm is to compute the maximum number of tasks in the chain which can be completed in the slack of T_0. Because of the serializability constraint we assume the T_i must be either completed or aborted before T_{i-1} can continue.

Let j be the greatest integer such that $\sum_{i=1} (E_i - P_i) \leq S$.

We execute in order the tasks $T_j, T_{j-1}, ..., T_1$. If $j < n$ then we must first abort T_{j+1} in order to free the lock for T_j. When T_1 completes the lock is released for T_0.

The second problem with conditional abort is illustrated by the following set of tasks and the schedule produced by using Earliest Deadline and Conditional Restart.

Transaction	r	E	d	updates
H	0	3	12	X
R	1	2	6	X
T	2	2	7	Y

Example 3.

lock X; conflict; R waits

H	R	H	T	H	R
0	1	1.5	2	4	5.5

At time 1.5 the scheduler decides to run H because it can be completed within the slack time of R. Transaction H only runs for a short time before it is preempted by arriving transaction T with an earlier deadline and therefore a higher priority than H. (R is not considered in the priority assignment because it is not a ready task.) Scheduling T and H before R causes R to miss its deadline. The problem lies in the assumption that H would not be preempted while it was executing during the slack time of R. The way we correct this problem is by letting R remain in the ready queue and be considered for scheduling. Since T has a later deadline than R then R will be scheduled. When R begins execution it requests the lock that is still held by H. If H can still be completed within the slack of R then it is executed while R waits. Thus H ultimately regains the processor and is not preempted by T. This revised algorithm is illustrated by the following schedule.

lock X; conflict; R waits

H	R	H	R	T	
0	1	1.5	3.5	5	7

The examples we have used to illustrate the different algorithms are greatly simplified. They were presented to motivate the algorithms, not to prove that one algorithm is better than another. For instance, in reality transaction may update several items or none at all. (i.e. read-only), and this will obviously affect the performance of the algorithms. In the next section we discuss detailed simulation model that can help us to compare the various scheduling and concurrency control options.

4. Simulation Results

To study the algorithms we have built a program to simulate a RTDBS. To focus on the issues of concurrency control and scheduling we have simulated a single processor, memory resident database system.

Three parameters control the configuration of the database system. The first Arr_rate is the average arrival rate of new transaction entering the system, The second

DB_size controls the number of objects in the database. The third, Rebort, controls the amount of time needed to abort or restart a transaction. Aborting a transaction consists of rolling it back and removing it from the system. The transaction is not executed. When a transaction is restarted it is rolled back and placed again in the ready queue. Aborts are generated by eligibility screening, restarts result from lock conflicts. The program does not explicitly account for time needed to execute the lock manager, conflict manager and deadlock detection manager. These routines are executed on a per data object basis and we assume that the costs of these calls are included in the variable that states how much CPU time is needed per object that a transaction accesses. Context switching and the time to execute the scheduler is also ignored.

Transactions enter the system with exponentially distributed inter-arrival times and they are ready to execute when they enter the system (i.e., release time equals arrival time). The number of objects updated by a transaction (at least one, i.e., there are no read-only transactions) is chosen from a normal distribution and the actual database items are chosen uniformly from the database. A transaction has an execution profile which alternates lock requests with equal size chunks of computation, one for each object accessed. Thus the total computation time is directly related to the number of items accessed. The accuracy of a transaction's runtime estimate E with respect to the actual computation time C is controlled by the parameter *Run_err* and is computed as follows:

$E = C * (1 + Run\_err)$. Note $E = 0$ when $Run\_err = -1$, $E = C$ when $Run\_err = 0$, and $E > C$ when $Run\_err > 0$. The assignment of a deadline is controlled by two parameters *Min_slack* and *Max_slack* which set a lower and upper bound respectively on a transaction's slack time. A deadline is assigned by choosing a slack time uniformly from the range specified by the bounds.

In the following section we discuss some of the results of four different experiments that we performed. Due to space considerations we cannot present all our results but have selected the graphs which best illustrate the differences and performance of the algorithms. For example, we have omitted the results of an experiment that varied the size of the database, and thus the number of conflicts, because they only confirm and not increase the knowledge yielded by other experiments. Each experiment exercises a different parameter: *Arr_rate*, *Run_err*, *Max_slack*, and *Rebort*. For each experiment we ran the simulation with the same parameters for 20 different random number seeds. Each run continued until at least 500 transactions were executed. For each algorithm tested, numerous performance statistics were collected and averaged over the 20 runs. In particular we measured the percentage of transactions which missed

their deadlines, the number of restarts caused by lock conflicts and the overall throughput. The percentage of missed deadlines is calculated with the following

equation: $\%missed = 100 * \frac{tardy.\,jobs + aborts}{jobs.\,processed}$. A job is processed if either it executes completely or it is aborted. It is these averages and 95% confidence intervals that are plotted in the following figures.

In this study we have included tardy jobs and aborted jobs together in the *%missed* metric. For some application it may be useful to describe a separate metric for aborted jobs as they represent tasks which were never completed and as such may be more serious than simply tardy jobs. Another interesting metric is mean tardy time for transactions. For reasons of space we do not study these other metrics here. Note that we are not particularly interested in transaction response time as conventional performance evaluations of concurrency control mechanisms are. The reason is that response time is not critical as long as a transaction meets its deadline. We are interested in learning how the various strategies are affected by load, the number of database conflicts and the tightness of deadlines. Also, for the algorithms which use E, we are interested in learning how the accuracy of the run time estimate affects performance.

For many of the experiments the base values for parameters determining system configuration and transaction characteristics are shown in Table 1.

Arrival rate (job/sec)	18
Database size	200
Restart/abort cost (ms)	0
Updates per transaction (mean)	15
Computation/update (ms)	3
Runtime estimate error	0
Min slack as fraction of total runtime	0.5
Max slack as fraction of total runtime	5.0

Table 1. Base parameter values.

These values are not meant to model a specific real-time application but were chosen as reasonable values within a wide range of possible values. In particular we wanted transactions to access a relatively large fraction of the database (7.5% on average) so that conflicts would occur frequently. The high conflict rate allows the concurrency control mechanism to play a significant role in scheduling performance. We chose the arrival rate so that the corresponding computation load (an average 0.81 seconds of computation arrival per second) is high enough to test the algorithms. It is more interesting to test the algorithms in a heavily loaded rather than lightly loaded system. (We return to this issue in the conclusions section.

Section 3 proposed three different method each for determining eligibility, assigning priority and managing concurrency. Taking the cross product yields 27 different algorithms. however, in our model, using FCFS scheduling with High Priority or Conditional Restart is equivalent to FCFS with Serial Execution. This eliminates six algorithms, leaving 21. Table 2 summarizes the methods of Section 3 and provides the abbreviations that we will use when referring to them.

Eligibility	AE - All Eligible
	NT - Not Tardy
	FD - Feasible Deadlines
Priority	FCFS - First Come First Serve
	ED - Earliest Deadline
	LS - Least Slack
Concurrency	SE - Serial Execution
	HP - High Priority
	CR - Conditional Restart

Table 2. Summary of scheduling policies.

Arrival rate experiment

In this experiment we varied the arrival rate from 4 jobs/sec to 22 jobs/sec in increments of 2. This corresponds to a range in load of 0.18 to 0.99 seconds of computation arriving per second.

Our simulation experiments show that the eligibility tests NT and FD substantially reduce the number of deadlines missed compared with the AE policy. Aborting a few late transcripts helps all other jobs meet their deadlines. This is illustrated in Figure 1 which shows the three eligibility policies for FCFS scheduling. All three algorithms perform equally well when the arrival rate is low but when the load is higher, NT and FD yield a 40-50% decrease in % missed deadlines over AE. The improvement is due entirely to the eligibility policy since the concurrently control used is SE. this same behavior holds true for the other priority assignment policies as well.

Scheduling transactions concurrently is better than serial execution because it allows transactions with more urgent deadlines to preempt transactions with less urgent deadlines. This is true for the ED scheduling policy. Figure 2 shows that CR and HP are both better than SE and CR is better than HP.

The situation is somewhat different when LS is used to assign priority. Figure 3 shows that at low arrival rates, the concurrent versions perform better than SE. However, at higher arrival rates SE is comparable to HP and CR, the concurrent versions. Under high loads the time lost to restarts that result from lock conflicts causes the concurrent versions to lose their performance edge over SE.

The relative performance of the priority policies is affected by the type of concurrency allowed. Under SE, ED and LS perform comparably, Figure 4. When the load is small they both perform better than FCFS but when the load is high all three algorithms perform the same. The reason for this is that under high load all algorithms start to fall behind. It does not pay to make smart scheduling decisions (ED, LS), since transactions with the earliest deadlines (or lease slack) are likely to miss their deadlines anyway.

When non-serial execution is allowed the results are different, Figure 5. Under CR, ED is clearly the superior policy for priority assignment. It performs better than LS at both low and high load level. At the highest load LS and FCFS are comparable and ED is better than both.

Figure 6 plots restarts against arrival rate for ED, HP. The number of restarts climbs steeply and is similar for all policies up to an arrival rate of 12. After this point the number of restarts declines sharply for AE, declines slightly for NT and flattens out for FD. The reason for the sharp decline for AE is that when the arrival rate is high many deadlines are being missed and the system falls behind.. It is less likely that an arriving transaction will have an earlier deadline than the currently executing job. Thus fewer jobs are preempted and there are fewer opportunities for restarts.

Figure 7 shows that throughputs is highest for AE, it declines with NT and FD. Since we are using serial execution no job is aborted once it has started, so the decreases in throughput are not due to wasted computation time. The throughput declines because the algorithms choose not to execute jobs that have missed or are about to miss their deadlines. This is true even if there is only one job (say a tardy one) in the ready queue. Ignoring this job empties the ready queue and idles the CPU until the next arrival. With increased idle time, the throughput drops.

Run time estimate experiment

In this experiment we varied *Run_err* from -1 to 0.8 by increments of 0.2. Recall that when *Run_err* = -1, $E = 0$ and when *Run_err* = 0.8, $E = 1.8 * C$. The other parameters had the values in Table 1. The run time estimate can affect each component of a scheduling algorithm: of the eligibility policies, FD, of the priority assignment, LS, and of the concurrency control policies, CR. We would expect the accuracy of the estimate to have a large effect on the policy FD. The eligibility policy is responsible for aborting transactions and since aborted transactions are counted as having missed their deadlines, the policy directly affects the performance.

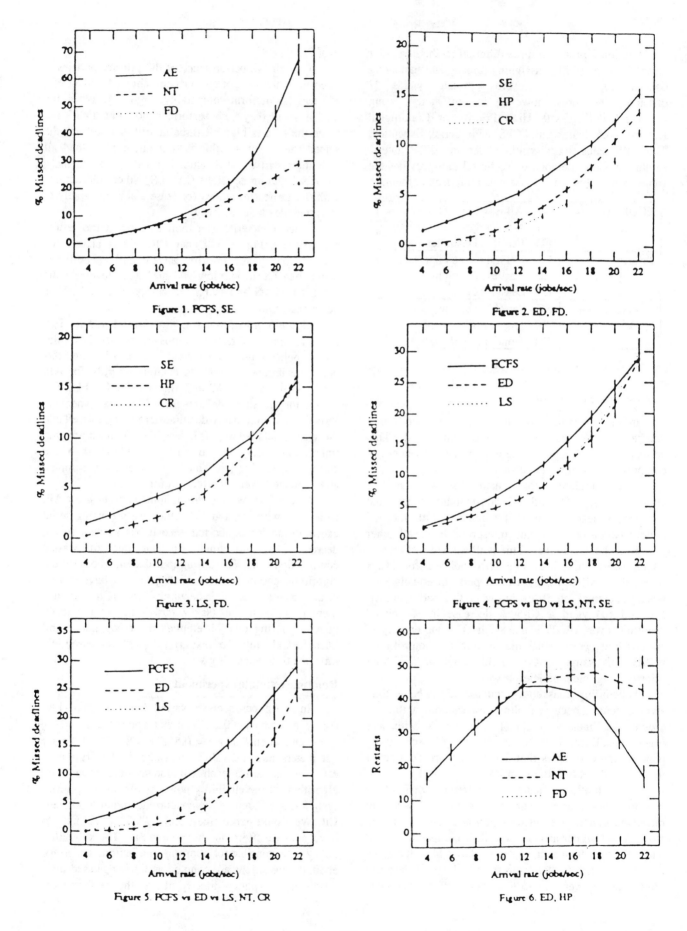

Figure 1. PCFS, SE.

Figure 2. ED, FD.

Figure 3. LS, FD.

Figure 4. FCFS vs ED vs LS, NT, SE.

Figure 5. PCFS vs ED vs LS, NT, CR

Figure 6. ED, HP

660

When the run time estimates for jobs is zero, FD behaves like NT, aborting jobs only if they have missed their deadlines. When the estimate is high, FD thinks that jobs are much longer than they are and will judge incorrectly, that they have infeasible deadlines. Thus jobs with feasible deadlines are unnecessarily aborted. This behavior is confirmed in Figure 8 which shows the results of the three forms of ED which use Feasible deadlines. The algorithms perform best when the estimate is perfect and less well when the estimate is too small or too large. The relative performance of the three concurrency control policies remains the same. This is despite the fact that CR also uses the run time estimate.

We would expect the effect of the accuracy of the run time estimate on the CR policy to be less pronounced than the effect on FD because the estimate is used only when transactions conflict, not every time a scheduling decision is made. To better observe the effect on the concurrency control policy CR we reduced the size of the database from 200 to 40 in order to increase the number of conflicts. Figure 9 shows the performance of ED, HP which does not use the estimate against ED, CR. The eligibility policy is NT, and does not use the estimate.

When the estimate is perfect CR performs better than HP. When the estimate is high, CR will rarely (in the limit, never) judge that the transaction holding the lock can finish in the slack of the lock requester. Thus conflicts are always resolved by restarting the lock holder and CR behaves exactly like HP. When the estimate is low, CR nearly always decides that the lock holder can finish within the slack time of the requester. In this case our experiment shows the CR perfumes slightly better then HP. We conclude that the performance penalty paid for always waiting for locks is comparable to the penalty paid in lost computation time that results from using HP.

Slack time experiment

The average amount of slack in job deadlines affects all scheduling algorithms. If all deadlines are extremely tight then most algorithms will perform poorly. Similarly, if all deadlines are very loose then most algorithms will perform well. Figure 10 shows the performance of the three priority assignment policies combined with FD and CR as the upper bound for slack time increases. When the slack is 0.5 (and deadlines are tight) the three algorithms perform comparably. As the slack increases, the performance of all three betters but ED is clearly the superior priority assignment policy. If the slack is very much greater (not shown) then the three curves would converge to zero because no deadlines would be missed.

Restart/abort cost experiment

In this experiment the cost of restarting or aborting a transaction ranges from 0 ms (i.e. no cost) to 27 ms in increments of 3. For reference, when the cost is 15 it is equal to one-third the average transaction computation time.

The cost of restarting or aborting a transaction affects the eligibility policies NT and FD, and the concurrency control policies HP and CR. It follows that as the cost of restarting or aborting increases, the performance of algorithms which use any of the above policies will deteriorate. This is indeed the case as shown by Figure 11 which plots the results for the three different concurrency policies of ED using FD. When the restart/abort cost is zero, CR and HP are both better than SE, and CR is best. The performance of SE decreases slowly because it only performs aborts and not restarts. The concurrent algorithms perform both aborts and restarts. As the cost increases SE outperforms HP and eventually equals CR.

Cost of serializability

In a final experiment we modified the simulation program so that serializability was not enforced. Thus a transaction was never denied a lock request and no transaction was restarted due to a lock conflict. Figure 12 shows the performance of the serialized and unserialized versions of the best algorithm, FD, ED, CR. The unserialized version performs somewhat better than the serialized. Thus serializability does cause the algorithms to miss more deadlines. However, missed deadlines is only one cost metric. Database inconsistency occurs as a result of unserialized schedules. For some applications the cost of database inconsistency may far outweigh the performance benefit in terms of missed deadlines gained by ignoring concurrency control.

5. Conclusions

In this paper we have presented various transaction scheduling options for a real-time database system. Our simulation results have illustrated the tradeoffs involved, at least under one representative database and transaction model. Before reaching some general conclusions, we would like to make two observations.

The first observation is that our base parameters represent a high load scenario (relatively high number of conflicts, relatively tight deadlines). One could argue that such a scenario is "unrealistic." However, we believe that for designing real-time schedulers, one must look at precisely these high load situations. Even though they may not arise frequently, one would like to have a system that misses as few deadlines as possible when these peaks occur. In other words, when a "crisis" hits and the database system is under pressure is precisely

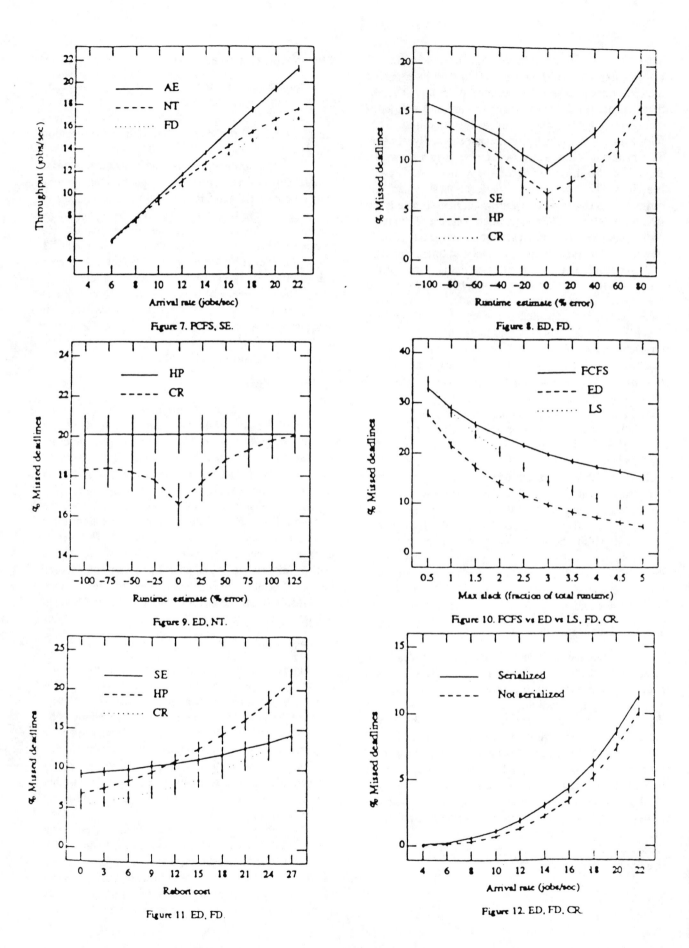

Figure 7. PCFS, SE.

Figure 8. ED, FD.

Figure 9. ED, NT.

Figure 10. PCFS vs ED vs LS, FD, CR

Figure 11 ED, FD.

Figure 12. ED, FD, CR

when making a few extra deadlines could be most important.

It could also be argued that some of the differences between the various scheduling options is not striking. In many cases, the difference between one option and another one is a few percentage points. If we were discussing transaction response times, then a say 10 percent improvement would not be considered impressive by some. However, our graphs show missed deadlines (in most cases) and we believe that this is a very different situation. Again, the difference between missing even one deadline and not missing it could be significant. (In our introductory trading example, we did state that it was permissible to miss a few deadlines. But we would still like to miss the very fewest trading opportunities.) Thus, if we do know that some scheduling options reduce the number of missed deadlines, why not go with the best one?

And which are the best options? It is difficult to make any absolute statements, but we believe the following statements hold under most of the parameter ranges we tested. (All our additional results not shown in this paper also substantiate these statements.)

(a) Of the tested priority policies for real-time database systems, Earliest Deadline (ED) is the best overall. It always performed better than or at least the same as the other policies. Least Slack (LS) is the second choice for assigning priorities. It performs better than simple First Come First Served (FCFS) under all but the highest load conditions.

(b) Of the concurrency control policies we tested, Conditional Restart (CR) is the best overall. Its success depends on the accuracy of the run time estimate, but even when the estimate is totally incorrect, CR will not perfume worse than the two other concurrency control policies (HP, SE). It has very stable performance.

(c) There is one case where Serial Execution (SE) may be superior to Conditional Restart (CR). This occurs when there is a high cost for restarting transactions. However, SE does not become a better method until the cost of restarting is more than half of the computation time of average transactions. We believe that this will usually not be the case. (Note that if the database is on disk, not our assumption here, then SE may be even less desirable than what our results show.)

(d) Using an eligibility test to screen out transactions that have missed (NT) or are about to miss their deadlines (FD) greatly improves system performance. FD performs better than or the same as NT, unless the execution estimates for transactions are more than 60 percent greater than the actual computation time. Of course, in some applications we may be forced to use the less efficient All Eligible (AE) test because transactions must be executed even if they miss their deadlines.

Acknowledgments

The authors would like to thank Alex Buchmann, Umesh Dayal, and the referees for their valuable comments.

This research was supported by the Defense Advanced Research Projects Agency of the Department of Defense and by the Office of Naval Research under Contracts Nos. N00014-85-C-0456 and N00014-85-K-0465, and by the National Science Foundation under Cooperative Agreement No. DCR 8420948. The views and conclusions contained in this document are those of the authors and should not be interpreted as necessarily representing the official policies, either expressed or implied, of the Defense Advanced Research Projects Agency or the U.S. Government.

References

1. Abbot, Robert and Hector Garcia-Molina "Scheduling Real-Time Transactions," *SIGMOD Record,* ACM, March 1988.

2. Eswaran, K.P., J.N. Gray, R.A. Lorie, and I.L. Traiger, "The Notions of Consistency and Predicate Locks in a Database System," *CACM,* vol 19, no. 11, pp. 624-633, November 1979.

3. Garcia-Molina, Hector, "Using sematic knowledge for transaction processing in a distributed database," *ACM Transactions on Database Systems,* vol. 8, pp. 186-213, ACM, June 1983.

4. Isloor, Sreekaanth S. and T. Anthony Marsland, "The Deadlock Problem: An Overview," *IEEE Computer,* pp. 58-78, IEEE, September 1980.

5. Jensen, E. Douglas, C. Douglass Locke, and Hideyuki Tokuda, "A time-driven scheduler for real-time operating systems," *Proceedings IEEE Real-time Systems Symposium,* pp. 112-122, IEEE 1986.

6. Liu, C.L. and J.W. Wayland, "Scheduling algorithms for multiprogramming in hard real-time environment," *Journal of the ACM,* vol 20, pp. 46-61, ACM, January 1973.

7. Mok, Aloysius, "Fundamental Design Problems of Distributed Systems for the Hard Real-Time Environment," MIT Laboratory for Computer Science, MIT, May 1983.

8. Voelcker, John, "How Computers Helped Stampede the Stock Market," *IEEE Spectrum,* vol. 24, pp. 30-33, IEEE, December 1987.

Dynamic Real-Time Optimistic Concurrency Control

Jayant R. Haritsa   Michael J. Carey   Miron Livny

Computer Sciences Department
University of Wisconsin
Madison, WI 53706

ABSTRACT

In a recent study, we have shown that in real-time database systems that discard late transactions, optimistic concurrency control outperforms locking. Although the optimistic algorithm used in that study, OPT-BC, did not factor in transaction deadlines in making data conflict resolution decisions, it still outperformed a deadline-cognizant locking algorithm. In this paper, we discuss why adding deadline information to optimistic algorithms is a non-trivial problem, and describe some alternative methods of doing so. We present a new real-time optimistic concurrency control algorithm, WAIT-50, that monitors transaction conflict states and gives precedence to urgent transactions in a controlled manner. WAIT-50 is shown to provide significant performance gains over OPT-BC under a variety of operating conditions and workloads.

1. INTRODUCTION

A Real-Time Database System (RTDBS) is a transaction processing system that attempts to satisfy the timing constraints associated with each incoming transaction. Typically, a constraint is expressed in the form of a *deadline*, that is, the user submitting the transaction would like it to be completed before a certain time in the future. Accordingly, greater value is associated with processing transactions before their deadlines as compared to completing them late. Therefore, in contrast to a conventional DBMS where the goal usually is to minimize response times, the emphasis here is on satisfying the timing constraints of transactions.

The problem of scheduling transactions in an RTDBS with the objective of minimizing the percentage of late transactions was first addressed in [Abbo88, Abbo89]. Their work focused on evaluating the performance of various real-time scheduling policies. All these policies enforced data consistency by using a two-phase locking protocol as the underlying concurrency control mechanism. Performance studies of concurrency control methods for conventional DBMSs (e.g.[Agra87]) have concluded that locking protocols, due to their conservation of resources, perform better than optimistic techniques when resources are limited. In a recent study [Hari90a], we investigated the behavior of these concurrency control schemes in a real-time environment. The study showed that for *firm deadline* real-time database systems, where late transactions are

This research was partially supported by the National Science Foundation under grant IRI-8657323.

immediately discarded, optimistic concurrency control outperforms locking over a wide range of system loading and resource availability. The key reason for this surprising result is that the optimistic approach, due to its validation stage conflict resolution, ensures that eventually discarded transactions do not restart other transactions. The locking approach, on the other hand, allows these soon-to-be-discarded transactions to cause other transactions to be either blocked or restarted due to lock conflicts, thereby increasing the number of late transactions.

An important difference between the locking algorithm and the optimistic algorithm that were compared in the above study lies in their use of transaction deadline information. The locking algorithm used this information, which was encoded in the form of transaction priorities, to provide preferential treatment to urgent transactions. The optimistic algorithm, however, was just the conventional broadcast commit optimistic scheme [Mena82, Robi82], and ignored transaction priorities in resolving data contention. The study therefore concluded that, in the firm real-time domain, a "vanilla" optimistic algorithm can perform better than a locking algorithm that is "tuned" to the real-time environment. The following question then naturally arises: How can we use priority information to improve the performance of the optimistic algorithm and thus further decrease the number of late transactions?

A simple answer to this question would be to use priority information in the resolution of data conflicts, that is, to resolve data conflicts always in favor of the higher priority transaction. This solution, however, has two problems: First, giving preferential treatment to high priority transactions may result in an increase in the number of missed deadlines. This can happen, for example, if helping a high priority transaction to make its deadline causes several lesser priority transactions to miss their deadlines. Second, if fluctuations can occur in transaction priorities, repeated conflicts between a pair of transactions may be resolved in some cases in favor of one transaction and in other cases in favor of the other transaction. This would hinder the progress of both transactions and hence degrade performance. Therefore, a priority-cognizant optimistic algorithm must address these two problems in order to perform better than a simple optimistic scheme.

In this paper, we report on our efforts to develop such an algorithm, and present a new optimistic concurrency control algorithm, called **WAIT-50**. The algorithm incorporates a *priority wait* mechanism that makes low priority transactions wait for conflicting high priority transactions to complete, thus enforcing preferential treatment for high priority transactions.

To address the first problem raised above, WAIT-50 features a *wait control* mechanism. This mechanism monitors transaction conflict states and, with a simple "50 percent" rule, dynamically controls when and for how long a transaction is made to wait. The second problem is handled by having the priority wait mechanism resolve conflicts in a manner that results in the commit of at least one of the conflicting transactions. Simulation results show that WAIT-50 performs significantly better than OPT-BC, the optimistic algorithm used in our earlier study.

The remainder of this paper is organized in the following fashion: Section 2 reviews our earlier study. In Section 3, we discuss deficiencies of OPT-BC. The new optimistic algorithm, WAIT-50, is presented in Section 4. Then, in Section 5, we describe our RTDBS model and its parameters, while Section 6 highlights the results of the simulation experiments. Finally, Section 7 summarizes the main conclusions of the study.

2. BACKGROUND

Our earlier study [Hari90a] investigated the relative performance of locking protocols and optimistic techniques in an RTDBS environment. In particular, the performance of a locking protocol, 2PL-HP, was compared with that of an optimistic technique, OPT-BC. These particular instances were chosen because they are of comparable complexity and are general in their applicability since they make no assumptions about knowledge of transaction semantics or resource demands. The details of these algorithms are explained below.

In 2PL-HP, classical two phase locking [Eswa76] is augmented with a *High Priority* [Abbo88] conflict resolution scheme to ensure that high priority transactions are not delayed by low priority transactions. This scheme resolves all data conflicts in favor of the transaction with the higher priority. When a transaction requests a lock on an object held by other transactions in a conflicting lock mode, if the requester's priority is higher than that of all the holders, the holders are restarted and the requester is granted the lock; otherwise, the requester waits for the lock holders to release the object. The High Priority scheme also serves as a deadlock prevention mechanism.[1]

In OPT-BC, classical optimistic concurrency control [Kung81] is modified to implement the notion of a *Broadcast Commit* [Mena82, Robi82]. Here, when a transaction commits, it notifies other running transactions that conflict with it and these transactions are immediately restarted. Since there is no need to check for conflicts with already committed transactions, a transaction which has reached the validation stage is guaranteed to commit. The broadcast commit method detects conflicts earlier than the basic optimistic algorithm, resulting in less wasted resources and earlier restarts; this increases the chances of meeting transaction deadlines. An important point to note is that transaction priorities are *not* used in resolving data conflicts.

---

[1] This is true only for priority assignment schemes that do not change a transaction's priority during the course of its execution.

The results of our study showed that both the policy for dealing with late transactions and the availability of resources have a significant impact on the relative behavior of the algorithms. In particular, for a *firm deadline* system, where late transactions are discarded without being run to completion, OPT-BC outperformed 2PL-HP over a wide range of system loading and resource availability. Figures 1 and 2 present sample graphs of how the percentage of late transactions varies as a function of the transaction arrival rate. These graphs were derived for the baseline model of the study, which characterized an RTDBS system with high data contention, under conditions of limited resources and plentiful resources, respectively.

In the above scenario, 2PL-HP suffered from two major problems: *wasted restarts* and *mutual restarts*. A "wasted restart" occurs when an executing transaction is restarted by another transaction that later misses its deadline. Such restarts are useless and cause performance degradation. In OPT-BC, however, we are guaranteed the commit of any transaction that

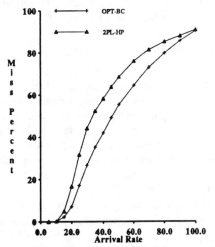

Figure 1: Baseline Model (Limited Resources)

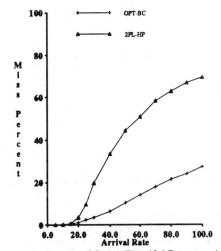

Figure 2: Baseline Model (Plentiful Resources)

reaches the validation stage. Since only validating transactions can cause restarts of other transactions, *all* restarts generated by the OPT-BC algorithm are useful.

The problem of "mutual restarts" arises when fluctuations occur in transaction priority profiles. For certain types of dynamic transaction priority assignment schemes (e.g. Least Slack [Jens86]), it is possible for a pair of concurrently running transactions to have opposite priorities relative to each other at different points in time during their execution. We will refer to this phenomenon as "priority reversal".[2] For algorithms like 2PL-HP, which use transaction priorities to resolve data conflicts, priority reversals may lead to "mutual restarts" – a pair of transactions restart each other, thus hindering the progress of both transactions. Since OPT-BC does not use transaction priorities in resolving data contention, such problems simply *do not arise*.

3. PROBLEMS WITH OPT-BC

In this section, we will motivate why there is room for improvement on the OPT-BC algorithm. The validation algorithm of OPT-BC can be succinctly written as:

> restart all conflicting transactions;
> commit the validating transaction;

Although this algorithm provides immunity from priority dynamics due to its unilateral commit, it does not allow for using transaction priorities to further decrease the number of missed deadlines. To illustrate this problem, consider the scenario in Figure 3, where the execution profile of two concurrently executing transactions, X and Y, is shown. X has an arrival time A_X and deadline D_X, and Y has an arrival time A_Y and deadline D_Y. Also, assume that transaction X, by virtue of its earlier deadline, has a higher priority than transaction Y. Now, consider the situation where at time $t = V_Y$, when transaction X is close to completion, transaction Y reaches its validation point and detects a conflict with X. Under the OPT-BC algorithm, Y would immediately commit and in the process restart X. Restarting X at this late stage guarantees that it has no chance of meeting its deadline.

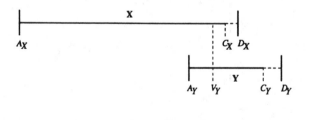

Figure 3: Poor OPT-BC data conflict decision

---

[2] This is different from *priority inversion* [Sha87], which refers to the situation where a transaction is blocked (due to data or resource conflict) by another transaction with a lower priority.

If a priority-cognizant algorithm had been used instead, it would have recognized that X's priority was higher than that of Y. Then, in some fashion, it would have *prevented Y from committing* until X had completed. With this decision, we could possibly gain the completion of both transactions X and Y before their deadlines, as shown in Figure 3 where X completes at time $t = C_X$ and Y completes later at time $t = C_Y$.

The above example shows how OPT-BC's indifference to transaction priorities can degrade performance. Another drawback of OPT-BC is that it has an inherent bias against long transactions, just like the classical optimistic algorithm. The use of priority information in resolving conflicts can help counter this bias.

4. PRIORITY-COGNIZANT ALGORITHMS

As explained in the previous sections, although the OPT-BC algorithm highlights some major strengths of optimistic concurrency control in real-time database systems, there remains potential for improving its performance. We therefore tried to develop new optimistic algorithms that address the problems of OPT-BC without sacrificing the performance-beneficial aspects of the broadcast commit scheme. These algorithms are described in this section. In the subsequent discussion, we will use the term *conflict set* to denote the set of currently running transactions that conflict with a validating transaction. The acronym *CHP (Conflicting Higher Priority)* will be used to refer to transactions that are in the conflict set and have a higher priority than the validating transaction. Similarly, the acronym *CLP (Conflicting Lower Priority)* will be used to refer to transactions that are in the conflict set and have a lower priority than the validating transaction. In this section, our aim is to motivate the development of the algorithms and discuss, at an intuitive level, their potential strengths and weaknesses.

The example in Section 3, illustrating poor conflict decisions by OPT-BC, showed that we need a scheme to prevent low priority transactions that conflict with higher priority transactions from unilaterally committing. The following two options are available:

(1) *Restart:* The low priority transaction is restarted.

(2) *Block:* The low priority transaction is blocked.

Two algorithms, OPT-SACRIFICE and OPT-WAIT, were developed based on these options. WAIT-50 was then developed as an extension of the OPT-WAIT algorithm. These three algorithms are presented below.

4.1. OPT-SACRIFICE

In this algorithm, when a transaction reaches its validation stage, it checks for conflicts with currently executing transactions. If conflicts are detected and at least one of the transactions in the conflict set is a CHP transaction, then the validating transaction is restarted – that is, it is *sacrificed* in an effort to help the higher priority transactions make their deadlines. The validation algorithm of OPT-SACRIFICE can therefore be written as:

```
if CHP transactions in conflict set then
    restart the validating transaction;
else
    restart transactions in conflict set;
    commit the validating transaction;
```

Referring back to Figure 3, if we were using OPT-SACRIFICE, then at time $t = V_Y$, transaction Y would restart itself due to the conflict with the higher priority transaction X.

OPT-SACRIFICE is priority-cognizant and satisfies the goal of giving preferential treatment to high priority transactions. It suffers, however, from two potential problems. First, there is the problem of *wasted sacrifices*, where a transaction is sacrificed on behalf of another transaction that is later discarded. Such sacrifices are useless and cause performance degradation. Second, the algorithm does not have immunity to priority dynamics. For example, the situation may arise where transaction A is sacrificed for transaction B because B's priority is currently greater than that of A, and transaction B at a later time is sacrificed for transaction A because A's priority is now greater than that of B. Therefore, priority reversals may lead to *mutual sacrifices*. These two drawbacks are analogous to the "wasted restarts" and "mutual restarts" problems of 2PL-HP.

4.2. OPT-WAIT

This algorithm incorporates a *priority wait* mechanism: a transaction that reaches validation and finds CHP transactions in its conflict set is "put on the shelf", that is, it is made to wait and not allowed to commit immediately. This gives the higher priority transactions a chance to make their deadlines first. While a transaction is waiting, it is possible that it will be restarted due to the commit of one of the CHP transactions. The validation algorithm of OPT-WAIT can therefore be written as:

```
while CHP transactions in conflict set do
    wait;
restart transactions in conflict set;
commit the validating transaction;
```

Referring back to Figure 3, if we were using OPT-WAIT, then at time $t = V_Y$, transaction Y would wait, without committing, for transaction X to complete first. Of course, X's completion may cause Y to be restarted.

There are several reasons that suggest that the priority wait mechanism may have a positive impact on performance, and these are outlined below:

(1) In keeping with the original goal, precedence is given to high-priority transactions.

(2) The problem of "wasted sacrifices" does not exist because if a CHP transaction is discarded due to missing its deadline, or is restarted by some other transaction, then the waiter is immediately "taken off the shelf" and committed if no other CHP transactions remain.

(3) Priority reversals are not a problem because, if a CHP transaction being waited for were to become a CLP transaction, the waiting transaction will no longer wait for it, and will immediately commit if no other CHP transactions remain.

(4) Since transactions wait instead of immediately restarting, a blocking effect is derived – this results in conservation of resources, which can be beneficial to performance [Agra87].

(5) The fact that a CHP transaction commits does not necessarily imply that the waiting transaction has to be restarted (!).

The last point requires further explanation: The key observation here is that if transaction A conflicts with transaction B, it does not necessarily mean that the converse is true [Robi82]. This is explained as follows: Under the broadcast commit scheme, a validating transaction A is said to conflict with another transaction B if and only if

$$WriteSet_A \cap ReadSet_B \neq \phi \qquad (1)$$

We will denote such a conflict from transaction A to B by $A \rightarrow B$. For transaction B to also conflict with transaction A, i.e. for $B \rightarrow A$, it is necessary that

$$WriteSet_B \cap ReadSet_A \neq \phi \qquad (2)$$

As is obvious from Equations (1) and (2), $A \rightarrow B$ does not imply $B \rightarrow A$. Therefore, if in fact $B \rightarrow A$ is not true, then by committing the transactions in the order (B, A) instead of the order (A, B), both transactions can be committed without restarting either one.

As per the explanation given above, it is possible with our waiting scheme for the CHP transaction and the waiting transaction to commit in that order without either transaction being restarted. Therefore, the priority wait mechanism has a potential to actually *eliminate* some data conflicts. (A simple probabilistic analysis of the extent to which waiting can reduce data conflicts is presented in [Hari90b]).

Although the waiting scheme has many positive features, it is not an unmixed blessing. One potential drawback is that if a transaction finally commits after waiting for some time, it causes all of its CLP transactions to be restarted at a later point in time. This decreases the chances of these transactions meeting their deadlines, and also wastes resources. A second drawback is that the validating transaction may develop new conflicts during its waiting period, thus causing an increase in conflict set sizes and leading to more restarts. Another way to view this is to realize that waiting causes objects to be, in a sense, "locked" for longer periods of time. Therefore, while waiting has the capability to reduce the probability of a restart-causing conflict between a given pair of transactions, it can simultaneously increase the probability of having a larger *number* of conflicts per transaction. This increase may be substantial when there are many concurrently executing transactions in the system.

4.3. WAIT-50

The WAIT-50 algorithm is an extension of OPT-WAIT – in addition to the priority wait mechanism, it incorporates a *wait control* mechanism. This mechanism monitors transaction conflict states and dynamically decides when, and for how long, a low priority transaction should be made to wait for its CHP transactions. A transaction's conflict state is assumed to be characterized by the index *HPpercent*, which is the percentage of the transaction's total conflict set size that is formed by CHP transactions. The operation of the wait mechanism is conditioned on the value of this index. In WAIT-50, a simple "50 percent" rule is used – a validating transaction is made to wait only while HPpercent $\geq$ 50, that is, while half or more of its conflict set is composed of higher priority transactions. The validation algorithm of WAIT-50 can therefore be written as:

>**while** CHP transactions in conflict set **and**
>   HPpercent $\geq$ 50 **do**
> wait;
>restart transactions in conflict set;
>commit the validating transaction;

The aim of the wait control mechanism is to detect when the beneficial effects of waiting, in terms of giving preference to high priority transactions and decreasing pairwise conflicts, are outweighed by its drawbacks, in terms of later restarts and an increased number of conflicts. Therefore, while OPT-WAIT and OPT-BC represent the extremes with regard to waiting – OPT-WAIT always waits for a CHP transaction, and OPT-BC never waits – WAIT-50 is a *hybrid* algorithm that controls the amount of waiting based on transaction conflict states. In fact, we can view OPT-WAIT, WAIT-50, and OPT-BC as all being special cases of a general algorithm **WAIT-X**, where X is the cutoff HPpercent level, with X taking on the values 0, 50, and ∞, respectively, for these algorithms.

We conducted experiments to evaluate the performance of the various optimistic algorithms, and the following sections describe our experimental framework and results.

5. REAL-TIME DBMS MODEL

The real-time database system model employed here is the same as that of our earlier study – in this model, the system consists of a shared-memory multiprocessor DBMS operating on disk resident data.[3] The database itself is modeled as a collection of pages. Transactions arrive in a Poisson stream and each transaction has an associated deadline. Each transaction consists of a sequence of page read and write accesses. A read access involves a concurrency control request to get access permission, followed by a disk I/O to read the page, followed by a period of CPU usage for processing the page. Write requests are handled similarly except for their disk I/O – their disk activity is deferred until the transaction has committed. The following two subsections describe the workload generation process and the hardware resource configuration.

5.1. Workload Model

The workload model characterizes transactions in terms of the pages that they access and the number of pages that they update. Table 1 summarizes the key workload parameters. *ArrivalRate* specifies the rate of transaction arrivals.

---

[3] It is assumed, for simplicity, that all data is accessed from disk and buffer pool considerations are therefore ignored.

DatabaseSize gives the number of pages in the database. The number of pages accessed by a transaction varies uniformly between half and one-and-a-half times the value of *PageCount*. Page requests are generated from a uniform distribution spanning the entire database. *WriteProb* gives the probability that a page that is read will also be updated.

We use two transaction deadline assignment formulas in this study. The first formula, which is the same as the one used in our previous study, is:

$$D_T = A_T + SF * R_T \qquad \text{(DF1)}$$

where D_T, A_T, and R_T are the deadline, arrival time and resource time, respectively, of transaction T, while SF is a slack factor. The *resource time* is the total service time at the resources that the transaction requires for its data processing. The *slack factor* is a constant that provides control over the tightness/slackness of deadlines. The formula ensures that all transactions, independent of their service requirement, have the same *slack ratio* – this is defined to be the ratio $(D_T - A_T) / R_T$. Therefore, all transactions have SF as their slack ratio.

In order to evaluate the effects of variability in transaction slack ratios, a second deadline assignment formula is used in the present study. This formula is:

$$D_T = \begin{cases} A_T + LSF * R_T \\ A_T + HSF * R_T \end{cases} \qquad \text{(DF2)}$$

With this formula, transactions will have a slack factor of either *LSF* or *HSF*, with both choices being equally likely. Therefore, the slack ratio for a transaction will be either *LSF* or *HSF*. The *LSF* and *HSF* workload parameters set the slack factors to be used in the deadline formulas. (For DF1, these two parameters have the same value).

The transaction priority assignment scheme used in all the experiments reported here is *Earliest Deadline* – transactions with earlier deadlines have higher priority than transactions with later deadlines. The system operates under firm deadlines, and therefore discards late transactions. It is important to note that while the workload generator uses transaction resource requirements in assigning deadlines, we assume that the system itself lacks any knowledge of these requirements. This implies that a transaction is detected as being late only when it actually misses its deadline.

Table 1: Workload Model Parameters

Parameter	Meaning
ArrivalRate	Transaction arrival rate
DatabaseSize	Number of pages in database
PageCount	Avg. # pages accessed/transaction
WriteProb	Write probability/accessed page
DeadlineFormula	DF1 or DF2
LSF	Low Slack Factor
HSF	High Slack Factor

5.2. Resource Model

The physical resources in our model consist of multiple CPUs and multiple disks. There is a single queue for the CPUs and the service discipline is preemptive-resume, with preemption being based on transaction priorities. Each of the disks has its own queue and is scheduled according to a priority-based variant of the elevator disk scheduling algorithm [Care89]. Requests at each disk are grouped into priority levels and the elevator algorithm is applied within each priority level; requests at a priority level are served only when there are no pending requests at higher priority levels. The details of our implementation of this algorithm are described in [Hari90b]. The data pages are modeled as being uniformly distributed across all the disks and across all tracks within a disk.

6. EXPERIMENTS and RESULTS

In this section, we present performance results for our simulation experiments comparing the various optimistic algorithms in a real-time database system environment. Our experiments evaluated the algorithms under a variety of operating conditions, workloads, and data access patterns [Hari90b]. We present only a subset of the results here due to space limitations. The performance metric is *MissPercent*, which is the percentage of transactions that do not complete before their deadline. MissPercent values in the range of 0 to 20 percent are taken to represent system performance under "normal" loadings, while MissPercent values in the range of 20 to 100 percent represent system performance under "heavy" loading.[4] The simulations also generated a host of other statistical information, such as the number of data conflicts, the time spent in priority waiting, etc. These secondary measures help explain the behavior of the algorithms under various loading levels. The resource parameter settings are such that the CPU time to process a page is 10 milliseconds while disk access times are between 15 and 30 milliseconds, depending on the level of disk utilization. Disk access times depend on disk utilization due to the elevator scheduling policy.

For experiments that were intended to factor in the effect of resource contention on the performance of the algorithms, the number of processors and number of disks were set to 10 and 20, respectively. For experiments intended to isolate the effect of data contention, we approximately simulated an "infinite" resource situation [Agra87], that is, where there is no queueing for resources. This was done by increasing twenty-fold the number of processors and the number of disks, from their baseline values of 10 and 20 to 200 and 400, respectively. A point to note here is that while abundant resources are usually not to be expected in conventional database systems, they may be more common in RTDBS environments since many real-time systems are sized to handle transient heavy loading. This directly relates to the application domain of RTDBSs, where functionality,

---

[4] Any long-term operating region where the miss percent is large is obviously unrealistic for a viable RTDBS. Exercising the system to high miss levels, however, provides valuable information on the response of the algorithms to brief periods of stress loading.

rather than cost, is usually the driving consideration.

We began our experiments by evaluating the various optimistic algorithms for the baseline model of our earlier study. This was done to provide continuity from that study to the present work. Subsequently, for reasons explained in the following discussion, we moved to a new baseline model. After initial experiments with this model, further experiments were constructed around it by varying a few parameters at a time. These experiments evaluated the impact of data contention, resource contention, deadline slack variation, transaction write probabilities, and the wait control mechanism parameter. We will hereafter refer to the old baseline model as FIX-SR (Fixed Slack Ratio), and the new baseline model as VAR-SR (Variable Slack Ratio).

6.1. FIX-SR Baseline Model

The settings of the workload parameters and resource parameters for the FIX-SR baseline model are listed in Tables 2 and 3. These settings generate an appreciable level of both data contention and resource contention. For this model, Figures 4a and 4b show MissPercent behavior under normal load and heavy load, respectively. When the same experiment is carried out under infinite resources, Figures 5a and 5b are obtained. From this set of graphs, we can make the following observations:

(1) OPT-SACRIFICE performs significantly worse than the wait-based algorithms over the entire operating region, and for the most part, also performs worse than OPT-BC. The poor performance of this algorithm is primarily due to the problem of "wasted sacrifices", discussed in Section 4. Also, in the infinite resource case, the sacrifice policy generates a steep rise in the number of data conflicts by causing a significant increase in the average number of transactions in the system. This is brought out quantitatively in Figure 5c, which plots the average number of conflicts per input transaction.

(2) OPT-WAIT, due to its priority cognizance, performs very well at low levels of data contention (Figs.4a, 5a). As data contention increases, however, its performance

Table 2: FIX-SR Baseline Model Workload Settings

Parameter	Value
DatabaseSize	1000 pages
PageCount	16 pages
WriteProb	0.25
DeadlineFormula	DF1
SlackFactor$_l$	4.0
SlackFactor$_h$	4.0

Table 3: FIX-SR Baseline Model Resource Settings

Parameter	Value
NumCPUs	10
NumDisks	20

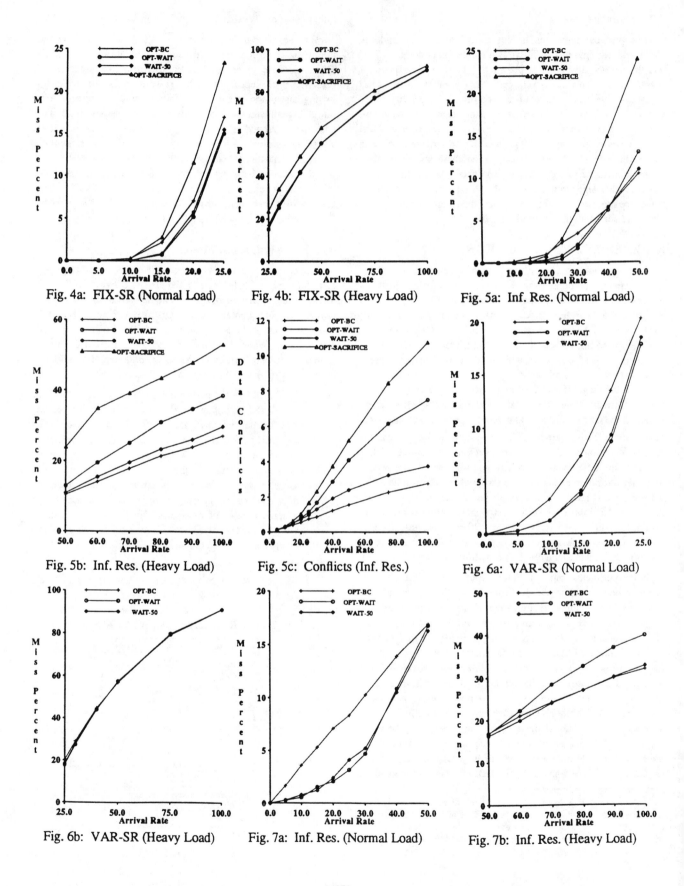

Fig. 4a: FIX-SR (Normal Load)

Fig. 4b: FIX-SR (Heavy Load)

Fig. 5a: Inf. Res. (Normal Load)

Fig. 5b: Inf. Res. (Heavy Load)

Fig. 5c: Conflicts (Inf. Res.)

Fig. 6a: VAR-SR (Normal Load)

Fig. 6b: VAR-SR (Heavy Load)

Fig. 7a: Inf. Res. (Normal Load)

Fig. 7b: Inf. Res. (Heavy Load)

steadily degrades. Finally, at high contention levels under infinite resources (Fig.5b), it performs significantly worse than OPT-BC. The reason for OPT-WAIT's poor performance in this region is that its priority wait mechanism, just like the sacrifice policy, causes an increase in the average number of transactions in the system. This population increase generates a corresponding rise in the number of data conflicts (see Fig. 5c), resulting in higher miss percentages.

(3) WAIT-50 provides the *best overall* performance. At low data contention levels, it behaves like OPT-WAIT, and at high contention levels it behaves like OPT-BC. The explanation for this behavior is given in the next section.

(4) Under high resource contention (Fig.4b), WAIT-50 and OPT-WAIT behave identically to OPT-BC. This is because, with heavy resource contention, it is uncommon for a low priority transaction to reach its validation stage much before its deadline, and therefore the wait-times of transactions are mostly small. Accordingly, the priority wait mechanism has very limited impact, and WAIT-50, OPT-WAIT, and OPT-BC become essentially the same algorithm.

The above results are encouraging because they show that there are performance benefits to be gained by using priority-cognizant algorithms. It is all the more encouraging that these performance improvements are obtained despite all transactions having the same slack ratio (from using deadline formula DF1). A fixed transaction slack ratio reduces the likelihood of a validating transaction finding a higher priority transaction in its set of conflicting transactions. This creates favorable circumstances for OPT-BC since the detrimental effects of its priority insensitivity are reduced.

6.2. VAR-SR Baseline Model

In order to generate a workload with variation in transaction slack ratios, the VAR-SR baseline model was developed for the current study. This model uses deadline assignment formula DF2 to generate variation in transaction slack ratios. The workload parameters *LSF* and *HSF* are set at 2.0 and 6.0, respectively.[5] The remaining workload parameter settings and resource parameter settings are the same as those for the FIX-SR baseline model (see Tables 2 and 3). In the subsequent discussions, we will compare the performance of only the OPT-BC, OPT-WAIT and WAIT-50 algorithms since OPT-SACRIFICE invariably performed worse than the wait-based algorithms.

For the VAR-SR baseline model, Figures 6a and 6b show the behavior of the algorithms under normal load and heavy load, respectively. When the same experiment was carried out under infinite resources, Figures 7a and 7b were obtained. From this set of graphs we can make the following observations:

---
[5] These parameter selections ensure that the *mean* slack ratio is the same as that of the FIX-SR baseline model, namely 4.0.

(1) The priority-cognizant algorithms, WAIT-50 and OPT-WAIT, now perform *significantly better* than OPT-BC under normal loads.

(2) WAIT-50 again turns in the best overall performance by behaving like OPT-WAIT at low data contention levels and like OPT-BC at high data contention levels.

As can be seen from this experiment, and will be further confirmed in subsequent experiments, WAIT-50 provides performance close to either OPT-BC or OPT-WAIT in operating regions where they behave well, and provides the same or slightly better performance at intermediate points. Therefore, in an overall sense, *WAIT-50 effectively integrates priority and waiting* into the optimistic concurrency control framework. The control mechanism is clearly quite competent at deciding when the benefits of waiting, in terms of helping high priority transactions to make their deadlines, are outweighed by the drawbacks of causing an increased number of conflicts. In Figure 7c, we plot the "wait factor" of OPT-WAIT and WAIT-50, which measures the total time spent in priority-waiting due to each algorithm, normalized by the waiting time of OPT-WAIT. As can be seen from this figure, WAIT-50's wait factor is close to that of OPT-WAIT at low contention levels but decreases steadily as the data contention level is increased. Therefore, while OPT-WAIT and OPT-BC represent the extremes with regard to waiting, WAIT-50 gracefully controls the waiting to match the data contention level in the system.

6.3. Write Probability

All the previously described experiments were carried out for a write probability of 0.25. The next set of experiments look into the performance effects of varying transaction write probabilities. In the first experiment, the write probability was increased to 1.0, keeping the other parameters the same as those of the baseline model. This experiment was conducted for both finite resource and infinite resource scenarios, and the results are shown in Figures 8 and 9a. From this set of figures, we can make the following observations:

(1) OPT-WAIT suffers a substantial performance degradation and does worse than OPT-BC over almost the entire operating region. There are two reasons for this: First, the increased write probability generates higher levels of data contention which, in combination with the population increase effect of the priority wait mechanism, results in a steep increase in the number of conflicts. Second, the conflict-elimination capability of OPT-WAIT vanishes since *all* conflicts are now *bi-directional*. These effects are captured dramatically in Figure 9b, which profiles the average number of conflicts per input transaction under infinite resources.

(2) Although WAIT-50 also employs the priority wait mechanism, it does not suffer OPT-WAIT's performance degradation. This is due to its control mechanism, which ensures OPT-BC-like behavior when high data contention levels are reached by sharply reducing its wait factor. Figure 9c, which plots the wait factor of the algorithms for the infinite resources case, shows this

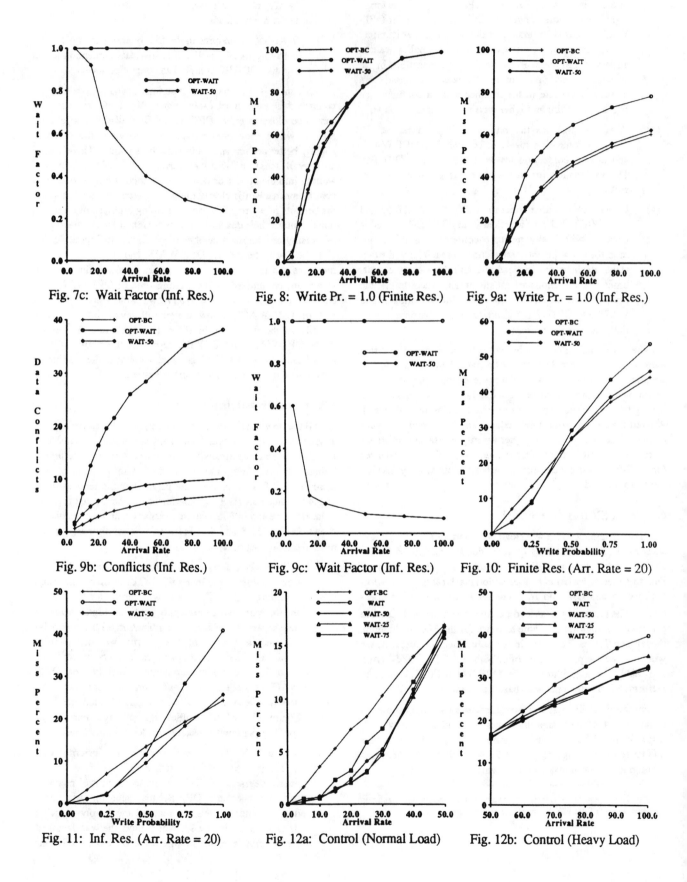

Fig. 7c: Wait Factor (Inf. Res.)

Fig. 8: Write Pr. = 1.0 (Finite Res.)

Fig. 9a: Write Pr. = 1.0 (Inf. Res.)

Fig. 9b: Conflicts (Inf. Res.)

Fig. 9c: Wait Factor (Inf. Res.)

Fig. 10: Finite Res. (Arr. Rate = 20)

Fig. 11: Inf. Res. (Arr. Rate = 20)

Fig. 12a: Control (Normal Load)

Fig. 12b: Control (Heavy Load)

effect quantitatively.

In the second experiment, the write probability was varied from 0.0 to 1.0, keeping the arrival rate constant at 20 transactions/sec. Figures 10 and 11 show how the algorithms behave under conditions of finite and infinite resources, respectively. These graphs clearly show that while OPT-WAIT performs well at low conflict levels, OPT-BC does much better at high conflict levels. We also observe that WAIT-50 again provides good performance over the entire range.

6.4. Wait Control Mechanism

The final experiment presented here examines the effect of the choice of 50 as the cutoff value for the HPpercent control index. Keeping all parameters the same as those of the baseline model, we measured the performance of WAIT-25 and WAIT-75 under conditions of infinite resources. Figures 12a and 12b give the results of this experiment under normal load and heavy load, respectively. From these graphs, we can make the following observations:

(1) Lowering the cutoff value to 25 percent results in a slight improvement of normal load performance, but worsens the heavy load performance. This behavior is due to the increased wait factor that is delivered by the lowered cutoff value.

(2) Raising the cutoff value to 75 percent has the opposite effect: the normal load performance becomes worse, while there is a slight improvement in heavy load performance. This behavior is due to the decreased priority cognizance that is delivered by the increased cutoff value.

A 50 percent cutoff, therefore, appears to establish a reasonable tradeoff between these opposing forces, providing good performance across the entire range of loading. The basic philosophy is that at light loads, when data contention levels are low, waiting is always beneficial. At heavy loads, however, when data contention levels are high, waiting is the wrong thing to do. WAIT-50 is effective in dynamically making this transition.

7. CONCLUSIONS

In this paper, we have addressed the problem of incorporating transaction deadline information into optimistic concurrency control algorithms. We presented a new real-time optimistic concurrency control algorithm, called WAIT-50, that uses transaction deadline information to improve data conflict resolution decisions. The algorithm features a *priority wait* mechanism that gives precedence to urgent transactions. This mechanism forces low priority transactions to wait for conflicting high priority transactions to complete, thus enforcing preferential treatment for high priority transactions. We showed that the mechanism has a capacity to eliminate some data conflicts due to its wait component, which causes changes to be made to the commit order of transactions. The priority-wait mechanism provides immunity to priority fluctuations by resolving conflicts in a manner that results in the commit of at least one of the conflicting transactions.

While the priority wait mechanism works well at low system contention levels, it can cause significant performance degradation at high contention levels by generating a steep increase in the number of data conflicts. A simple *wait control* mechanism consisting of a "50 percent" rule is used in the WAIT-50 algorithm to address this problem. The "50 percent" rule is the following: If half or more of the transactions conflicting with a transaction are of higher priority, the transaction is made to wait; otherwise, it is allowed to commit.

Using a simulation model of a RTDBS, we studied the performance of the WAIT-50 algorithm over a range of workloads and operating conditions. WAIT-50 was shown to provide significant performance gains over OPT-BC, a priority-insensitive optimistic algorithm. The wait control mechanism of WAIT-50 was found to be effective in maintaining good performance, even at high data contention levels. In summary, we conclude that the WAIT-50 algorithm utilizes transaction priority information to stably provide improved performance.

REFERENCES

[Abbo88] Abbott, R., and Garcia-Molina, H., "Scheduling Real-Time Transactions: a Performance Evaluation," *Proc. of the 14th VLDB Conference*, Aug. 1988.

[Abbo89] Abbott, R., and Garcia-Molina, H., "Scheduling Real-Time Transactions with Disk Resident Data," *Proc. of the 15th VLDB Conference*, Aug. 1989.

[Agra87] Agrawal, R., Carey, M., and Livny,M., "Concurrency Control Performance Modeling: Alternatives and Implications," *ACM Trans. on Database Systems*, Dec. 1987.

[Care89] Carey, M., Jauhari, R., and Livny, M., "Priority in DBMS Resource Scheduling," *Proc. of the 15th VLDB Conference*, Aug. 1989.

[Eswa76] Eswaran, K., Gray, J., Lorie, R., and Traiger, I., "The Notions of Consistency and Predicate Locks in a Database System," *Communications of the ACM*, Nov. 1976.

[Hari90a] Haritsa, J., Carey, M., and Livny, M., "On Being Optimistic about Real-Time Constraints," *Proc. of the 1990 ACM PODS Symposium*, April 1990.

[Hari90b] Haritsa, J., Carey, M., and Livny, M., "Dynamic Real-Time Optimistic Concurrency Control," *Tech. Report*, University of Wisconsin-Madison, October 1990.

[Jens86] Jensen, E., Locke, C., and Tokuda, H., "A Time-Driven Scheduling Model for Real-Time Operating Systems," *Proc. 7th IEEE Real-Time System Symposium*, IEEE 1986.

[Kung81] Kung, H., and Robinson, J., "On Optimistic Methods for Concurrency Control," *ACM Trans. on Database Systems*, June 1981.

[Mena82] Menasce, D., and Nakanishi, T., "Optimistic versus Pessimistic Concurrency Control Mechanisms in Database Management Systems," *Information Systems*, vol. 7-1, 1982.

[Robi82] Robinson, J., "Design of Concurrency Controls for Transaction Processing Systems," *Ph.D. Thesis*, Carnegie Mellon University, 1982.

[Sha87] Sha, L., Rajkumar, R., and Lehoczky, J., "Priority Inheritance Protocols: An Approach to Real-Time Synchronization," *Tech. Report* Carnegie Mellon University, Dec. 1987.

Triggered Real-Time Databases with Consistency Constraints *

Henry F. Korth
Nandit Soparkar
Abraham Silberschatz

Department of Computer Sciences
University of Texas at Austin
Austin, TX 78712-1188

Abstract

Real-time database systems incorporate the notion of a *deadline* into the database system model. Usually, deadlines are associated with transactions, and the system attempts to execute a given set of transactions so as to both meet the deadlines and ensure the database consistency. This paper presents an alternative model of real-time database processing in which deadlines are associated with consistency constraints rather than directly with transactions. This model leads to a predicate-based approach to transaction management that allows greater concurrency and more flexibility in modeling real-world systems.

1 Introduction

Real-time database systems (RTDBs) incorporate timing considerations into a database system. Not only must the transactions execute correctly, but also, they must complete execution within some time limit called a *deadline*. Systems that incorporate strict deadlines are called *hard* real-time systems while those that do not are called *soft* real-time systems.

Real-time systems are usually applied for process-control which often require a large database of information. Hence, recent efforts have aimed at integrating the real-time systems with database systems to facilitate the efficient and correct management of the resulting *real-time database* systems [Son88]. There are several difficulties in accomplishing such an integration. A database operation (read or write) takes a highly variable amount of time depending on whether disk I/O, logging, etc. are required. Furthermore, if concurrent transactions are allowed, the concurrency control may cause aborts or delays of indeterminate length.

Most previous work on real-time transactions assumes a set of transactions and associated deadlines. It is the responsibility of the transaction manager to find a correct schedule for the transactions that will ensure that the deadlines are met.

---

*Research partially supported by TARP grant 4355, NSF grant IRI-8805215, and a grant from the IBM Corporation.

There has been extensive study of real-time systems [Sta88]. Formal aspects of such systems have been examined from the standpoints of scheduling (e.g., [HMR$^+$89]) and verification [JM86]. In the context of real-time databases, [AGM88a, AGM88b] consider alternative queuing disciplines with lock-based concurrency control of real-time transactions, and use simulation results to compare these techniques. [SRL88] proposes concurrency control techniques for distributed real-time systems based on a partitioning of data. [PR88] discusses the specific time-dependent application of stock-market trading.

The RTDB models outlined above apply time-constraints directly to transactions, but they do not model situations where the time-constraints apply directly to states of the systems. Time-constraints on the states of the system enforce similar time-constraints on transactions that are triggered by those states. As an example, consider an RTDB application in a manufacturing environment. We consider the automated control of a complex set of machines, materials, and resources — perhaps under the supervision of a rule-based system. Given that a large number of diverse activities require monitoring, the controlling processes would need to use database techniques to function efficiently. Suppose that the state of the information maintained in the database indicates that the temperature in a furnace has fallen below a particular threshold value. This state of the system may necessitate the triggering of some actions that restore the temperature to a value above the threshold. The application may enforce a maximum period of time that the temperature is permitted to remain below the threshold — and that enforces a deadline on the actions that are triggered by the low value. Furthermore, it may be the case that several actions may be candidates for the restoration of the temperature. For instance, there may be actions that initiate more fuel getting pumped-in, or actions that increase the oxygen supply etc. Thus, a choice may be available, and depending on the time constraints (and other factors such as the cost of the actions), one particular action may be initiated to restore the temperature value. These actions are reflected as triggered transactions within the database. Previous research does not examine this approach to triggered RTDBs where several choices are available. Notice that a triggered transaction may trigger further transactions as result of its execution, and this imposes not only a logical relationship between the transactions, but also a temporal one. As will become clear, such relationships are captured in a natural manner by the formalisms of nested transactions and the one introduced in this paper. Again, this facet has not been dealt with in earlier research on RTDBs.

In this paper, we propose a new approach to the modeling of an RTDB. Our approach is based on a set of explicitly defined consistency constraints for the database. Each transaction ensures that upon completion, the database remains in a state that satisfies these consistency constraints. However, in addition to such transactions that maintain correct database states, transactions may be invoked to record the effects of some external event that is generated outside the system. The ensuing change in the database state may render a consistency constraint invalid, and that constraint may need to be restored within a specific deadline. The system restores constraints by choosing one or more transactions from a pre-defined library of transactions. These transactions restore certain constraints but may invalidate other constraints. In the absence of further external events, the system must eventually return the entire database to a consistent state. In a dynamic real-time system, external events may occur with sufficient frequency to prevent global consistency, but the system must seek to ensure that no constraint remains invalid for an interval longer than a specified limit, the *deadline* of the constraint. Note that our approach incorporates the notions of active data and "triggers" in the form of the consistency constraints. The model also facilitates the algorithmic analysis of the functioning of the system.

Let us return to our earlier example of an RTDB in a manufacturing environment. Assume that the temperature in the furnace is detected by a transducer to have dropped below the required threshold. This may require corrective actions to be performed within a very short period of time by the control processes. In such a situation, a transaction is invoked to record the inadequate temperature in the database. This fact is reflected as a violation of a constraint on the temperature readings in the database. The prompt execution of the transaction would allow the new value of the data to trigger other transactions that, perhaps, increase the fuel supply to the furnace. These actions, in turn, may deplete the fuel reservoir — detected as another violation of the consistency constraints on the safe levels of the fuel reservoir — and hence trigger further corrective actions, and so on.

The example provides several points of note. Since delays could be incurred in the case that serializability (see, e.g., [BHG87]) is imposed, and thereby jeopardize timely corrective actions, it may be appropriate to sacrifice serializability during such occasional instances. Also, this may result in the violation of certain constraints on the database that govern the safe functioning of the system. In turn, this may lead to further corrective actions. Thus, constraints in our model are used to enforce correctness aspects of transaction management during the normal system operation, and during occasional crisis situations, they function as active data triggers.

2 Transaction Model

Consider the occurrence of an "error" condition in the real world. An error condition is one that may need correction by the control-system, and the actions that make the corrections may be triggered by some consistency constraint that is violated. Thus, a transaction that reports the error condition must necessarily leave the database in an inconsistent state which is reflected in the violated consistency constraint.

The database consistency may thus be viewed in a *weak* sense and a *strong* sense. The weak sense of consistency may be regarded as maintaining the structural integrity of the data, and all transactions must preserve this consistency. However, the strong view of consistency may be regarded as the case where the database faithfully reflects the outside world, and hence, the transactions recording changes in the external environment may violate this notion of consistency. Thus, the standard transaction model, where transactions are mappings from consistent states to consistent states, is not of sufficient semantic richness to capture real-time transactions. Below, we give an informal characterization of real-time transactions and relate this to other work on extended transaction models. In Section 3, we present a formal model for reasoning about transactions and constraints.

A real-time transaction system interacts with the external world in several ways. Events in the external world are recorded in the database. Transactions in the transaction system initiate external actions. This leads us to partition the set of transactions in a real-time system into three categories:

1. **External-input Transactions.** Such a transaction records in the database some event that has occurred in the external world. Often, such a transaction is a write-only transaction, and is usually of short-duration. An example of this type of transaction is the transaction that is invoked to record the inadequate temperature in the example above.

2. **Internal Transactions.** Such a transaction accesses the database in a similar manner as any standard database transaction except that it may be of long-duration. The purpose of this type of transaction is the restoration of "consistency" that may have been violated as a result of some external-input transaction. By consistency we mean the strong notion of consistency discussed above. Transactions of this type may be viewed as system monitors that maintain "normal" system operation.

3. **External-output Transactions.** Such a transaction causes some event to occur in the world external to the system. These transactions are of short-duration from a system perspective, although the external actions they trigger may take a longer time to complete. We do not permit external-input transactions to wait for the acknowledgement of completion of the external activity. Instead, we treat transactions of this type as performing only the initiation. If further action is to be taken as a result of completion of the external activity, another transaction (an external-input transaction) must record in the database the completion of the external activity, which then triggers the execution of further internal or external output transactions. In our earlier example, a transaction that initiates an increase of the fuel supply to the furnace is an example of an external-output transaction.

These three types of transactions differ in their atomicity and concurrency requirements. A write-only external-input transaction should never wait. Its writes should succeed immediately unless a "newer" value has already been recorded in the database. For example, consider the setting of a new value for the value of a stock option in a stock market situation — delaying this may cause substantial financial losses. These requirements are justified since the external-input transactions are used to record the outside world within the system. In a real-time application, such events need to be recorded in the database as soon as possible so that any resulting inconsistency may be corrected. A consequence of this is that it may not be desirable to ensure serializable executions even if multiple versions of data are retained.

The notion of transactions violating the database consistency and other transactions reading possibly inconsistent database states is a major deviation from the standard transaction model. We represent such actions using the NT/PV model of [KS88] by defining input and output conditions for each transaction. These conditions are predicates on the database state. The input condition is a pre-condition of transaction execution and must hold on the state that the transaction "observes". The output condition is a post-condition which the transaction guarantees on the database state at the end of the transaction provided that there is no concurrency and the database state seen by the transaction satisfies the input condition. Thus, in the NT/PV model, as in the standard model, transactions are assumed to be correct programs, and responsibility for correct concurrent execution lies with the transaction manager.

The actions required to restore consistency may involve more than direct database access. Internal transactions spawn external-output transactions as *subtransactions* to modify the outside world as part of a process of restoring consistency. Other subtransactions may be required to test the results of external-output transactions. The potential long-duration of internal transactions make a requirement of serializability impractical (as argued in [KS88, KKB88] based on results of [Yan82]). Furthermore, the nested nature of these transactions requires an extension of the transaction model to support *nested transactions* [Mos87]. A serializability-based approach to nested transactions is discussed in [Mos87] while correctness of nested transactions without the requirement of serializability is presented in [KS88, BBG89, HH88].

Use of multiple versions of data is often indicated in real-time database applications. An obvious utility is in situations which require the monitoring of data as it assumes different values in time; that is, the "trends" exhibited by the values of the data are used to trigger actions. Examples include rising temperature of a furnace in a nuclear application, falling market values in stock-market trading, and the change in the distance of an approaching aircraft in radar tracking systems. Version-mapping functions could be used to provide the necessary historical information to transactions that require the information. Given that the formal model that we propose to use supports versions, the use of these methods is easily incorporated.

The above considerations lead us to suggest that our real-time transaction model may include (1) nesting, (2) versions, and (3) correct concurrent execution without the requirement of traditional serializability. We use the NT/PV model of [KS88] as the basis for our work since this model supports the above features.

Transactions in real-time systems may be submitted either by users, or by external devices. In addition, transactions may also be triggered by the state of the system. If an external-input transaction changes the database state to an inconsistent state, an internal transaction must be run to restore consistency. These transactions are not necessarily triggered by an external-input transaction. Rather they may depend on both the external-input transaction and the database state. For a given inconsistent state, there may be several transactions that are enabled for triggering. The transaction system is free to choose a subset of those transactions that are enabled provided that subset is sufficient to restore consistency. This choice is, in its most general form, computationally complex. We explore this idea further in Section 4. Our model of triggered transactions is related to that used in *active* database [MD89]. However, for the purposes of this paper, the manner in which transactions are selected for execution differs from active databases in that we base selection on the goal of consistency restoration.

The concept of triggered transactions, along with our characterization of real-time transactions above, provides five types of transactions: (1) external-input transactions (non-triggered by definition), (2) triggered internal transactions, (3) non-triggered internal transactions, (4) triggered external-output transactions, and (5) non-triggered external-output transactions.

The system model we consider in this paper may be regarded as comprising of a set $T = \{t_1, t_2, \ldots, t_n\}$ of predefined *transaction-types*, and a finite set $C = \{c_1, c_2, \ldots, c_m\}$ of predefined consistency constraints in the form of *conjuncts*. Conjuncts are formulae consisting of a disjunction of possibly negated terms. The consistency constraint for the entire database may be represented by $P \equiv \bigwedge_{i=1}^{m} c_i$. For the purposes of this paper, we restrict our attention to predicate calculus rather than first-order logic since all quantifiers will be over a finite set (the database). Some instances of the transaction-types are triggered by the falsehood of a conjunct, and may function to restore the truth of the conjunct. Certain instances of the transaction-types, upon execution, may render inconsistent some conjuncts. Thus, the system may be regarded as consisting of transaction-types and conjuncts that interact with each other.

3 The Predicate-Priority Graph

To facilitate the description of our model, and to make the algorithmic analyses easier, we define a *predicate-priority graph* (PPG). The PPG captures the relationships between the transaction-types and the conjuncts, and its annotations are used to incorporate various timing constraints. A PPG is a directed bipartite graph with a set of vertices $V = T \cup C$, where T denotes the set of transaction-types, and C denotes the set of conjuncts.

The edges in a PPG represent the triggering of transaction-types by the falsehoods of the conjuncts, and the invalidation of conjuncts by the transaction-types. If an instance of a transaction-type t_i may invalidate a conjunct c_j, then the directed edge (t_i, c_j) appears in the graph. If a transaction-type t_k ensures the truth of a conjunct c_l upon completion, then the directed edge (c_l, t_k) appears in the graph. Thus, the PPG represents the transaction-types available to the system for restoring consistency.

We exclude non-triggered transactions in order that the PPG may be a static structure. The only dynamic aspect to this graph will be the *markings* introduced below. The term *transaction-type* was used above to emphasize that we are creating a vertex for each type of triggered transaction, not a vertex for each execution of a specific transaction. If we had a vertex for each actual execution, then the PPG would become a dynamic structure. In this paper, we restrict attention to only static PPGs. The reason is that the static situation is a subcase of the dynamic one, and hence, it indicates some problems that may be encountered in the analyses of the more general situation. As we shall see, the analysis of the static PPG itself reveals several computationally intractable problems that indicate the need for heuristic approaches — and these results also apply to the dynamic PPG.

An example of a PPG is shown in Figure 1. Transaction-types are represented by square vertices, and the round vertices correspond to conjunct vertices. In the example, an inconsistency in conjunct c_1 may be resolved by executing an instance of either one of the transaction-types t_1 or t_2. Furthermore, the execution of a transaction of type t_1 may result in the invalidation of the conjuncts c_5, c_6 and c_7.

Let us now examine how the PPG is used. If the database is inconsistent, the vertices corresponding to the false conjuncts are *marked*. To restore consistency, it is necessary to run an instance of the transaction-type associated with the head of at least one out-edge of each marked vertex. However, running these transactions may lead to side-effects beyond restoring the truth of certain previously-false conjuncts. Possibly, these side effects will result in other conjuncts becoming false. This results in further marked vertices. It is important to note that, given a graph and a set of marked vertices, there may exist many ways to resolve the inconsistencies. For each marked vertex, the out-degree indicates the number of potential options for restoring the truth of the corresponding conjunct. A few observations should be made at this point:

- If a vertex corresponding to a conjunct is a sink (has no out-edges). then there is no way to restore the truth of this conjunct within the system. A non-triggered transaction (either an external-input of a non-triggered internal transaction) is required to restore the truth of this conjunct. Such a situation requires either human intervention or a "lucky" turn of events external to the system. Thus, we require that all sinks correspond to transaction-types.

- A cycle in the PPG represents a potentially unstable situation. The situation is only *potentially* unstable, since an edge from a transaction-type vertex to a conjunct vertex means only that an instance of the transaction-type *may* make the conjunct false. Also, if in restoring the truth of a conjunct, a transaction-type vertex that is not within the cycle is chosen, the situation may not be unstable.

- A safe strategy (i.e., one that is not potentially unstable) for resolving an inconsistent database state can be represented by an acyclic subgraph of the PPG such that the subgraph contains all the marked conjunct vertices of the PPG, retains all outedges in the PPG of transaction-type vertices in the subgraph, and retains at least one outedge of each conjunct vertex in the subgraph. We shall restrict attention to strategies that are not potentially unstable.

  As an example, consider the PPG of Figure 1 again. The subgraph shown within the dotted outline in the figure provides a strategy to resolve the inconsistencies if c_1 and c_2 (and possibly any or all of c_5, c_6, and c_7) are the only marked vertices.

- We consider sub-DAGs of the PPG that resolve an inconsistent database to have roots at all marked vertices and sinks that are transaction-types. As before, all outedges in the PPG from transaction-types in such a DAG must be included in the DAG. The partial order on transaction-types induced by the DAG must be observed if the execution will, in fact, restore consistency (without requiring the execution of multiple instances of a transaction-type).

As described above, a DAG subgraph may be identified in a marked PPG so as to resolve the inconsistencies. The subgraph should include all the marked vertices, and all the sinks should correspond to transaction-types with no outgoing edges. We call such a subgraph an *inconsistency-resolution subgraph* (IRS) for a given marked PPG. An IRS provides a strategy by which the inconsistencies in the PPG may be resolved: Executions of the transactions within an IRS that obey the partial order imposed by the IRS will resolve the inconsistencies.

Notice that although we describe a system in which the PPG is used only to restore the consistency of the system, the approach may be used more generally. The consistency constraints may be replaced by states of the system that trigger certain transaction-types. Hence, triggered systems that have a pre-defined library of transaction-types and states that trigger them, may be represented in our formalism. The markings of the vertices would correspond, in that case, to the states by which the triggers are activated.

The PPG is constructed from a given set of transaction-types and conjuncts. As the system evolves over time, it may be desirable to have the flexibility of adding or deleting certain transaction-types and conjuncts. However, this is not likely to occur in a dynamic manner, and hence, the pre-analysis of a PPG to identify IRSs that resolve inconsistencies efficiently may be useful. From the viewpoint of the flexibility just mentioned, it may be desirable to study the PPG in an incremental manner which, however, is beyond the scope of this paper.

A more formal definition a PPG and an IRS is now provided.

Definition 1. *A predicate-priority graph is a 3-tuple (C, T, E) representing a bipartite graph with vertex set $C \cup T$ and edge set $E \subseteq ((C \times T) \cup (T \times C))$. A marked PPG is a PPG in which a nonempty set of vertices $X \subseteq C$ is identified as being "marked".* □

The inconsistency-resolution subgraph (IRS) defined below represents a strategy for restoring consistency to the database given that the marked set of conjuncts are false.

Definition 2. *Let $G = (C, T, E)$ be a PPG in which the vertices in $X \subseteq C$ are marked. An inconsistency-resolution subgraph of G is a 3-tuple $G' = (C', T', E')$ such that,*
(1) $X \subseteq C' \subseteq C$, $T' \subseteq T$, and $E' \subseteq E$,
(2) For all edges $(t_j, c_i) \in E$ such that $t_j \in T'$, we have $c_i \in C'$ and $(t_j, c_i) \in E'$,
(3) For all $c_i \in C'$, there exists a path in G' from c_i to t_k, where t_k is a sink in G, and
(4) G' is acyclic. □

A natural question arises as to whether an IRS exists for a particular marked PPG. The following result implies that the question is easily settled.

Theorem 1. *Let G be a marked PPG. The problem of deciding whether there is an IRS G' for G is solvable in polynomial-time.*

Proof Sketch. We provide a sketch of a requisite polynomial-time algorithm that manipulates the PPG, G. For the ease of presentation, introduce a (pseudo) transaction-type vertex, $t' \in T$, with out-edges (t', c_i) for every $c_i \in X$, and a (pseudo) conjunct vertex, $c' \in C$, with an out-edge (c', t').

1. **while** $c' \in C$ **do**

    (a) Choose a sink transaction-type vertex, t_j. If none exists, **print** "No IRS exists", and **stop.**

    (b) For each conjunct vertex c_i such that $(c_i, t_j) \in E$, delete all edges that involve c_i. Hence, delete c_i.

(c) Delete t_j.

endwhile

2. **print** "IRS exists", and stop.

With appropriate data structures, the algorithm takes $O(|C| + |T| + |E|)$ time, and since it finds a way to resolve every vertex in X, it places the EP problem in P-time. $\square$

4   Incorporating Timing Considerations

Timing constraints are represented in the PPG by associating a *time interval* with each conjunct and a *time cost* with each transaction-type. The value associated with each conjunct represents the maximum duration of a time interval during which the corresponding conjunct may be false. The time cost represents an estimate of the execution time of the transaction-type. Typically, real-time analysis is based upon worst-case assumptions about execution time so as to ensure the correctness of a schedule. If we took that approach to real-time database management, we would be forced to make drastic assumptions about page-fault frequency, delays due to concurrency control requirements, and other resource-contention factors. For example, unless detailed information about the physical-level schema is made available to the real-time system, it is necessary to assume that every data item reference incurs a page fault, consisting of the write of a page frame back to disk, the reading of the data page, plus requisite disk access to support write-ahead logging and index page access. The difference between the worst case and the expected case is so large that a worst-case analysis for real-time database transactions would find a solution only for systems that have an economically unjustifiable amount of redundant computing power. Therefore, for the purposes of this paper, we consider the expected-case estimates of the transaction-type execution times which we assume may be made. Indeed, if the database is entirely memory-resident (see, e.g., [Sin88]), the differences between the worst-case and expected time estimates are likely to be negligible.

The incorporation of time into our model is achieved by the use the functions W_κ and W_τ which denote mappings from the conjuncts C and the transaction-types T, respectively, to the set of non-negative integers. This requires the redefinition of the PPG to incorporate the timing constraints. We term this new PPG as a *weighted* PPG, while the original PPG is termed an *unweighted* PPG. These terms will be used in case of ambiguity in referring to the different types of the PPGs.

Definition 3. *A (weighted) predicate-priority graph (PPG) is a 5-tuple $(C, T, E, W_\kappa, W_\tau)$ representing a bipartite graph with vertex set $C \cup T$ and edge set $E \subseteq ((C \times T) \cup (T \times C))$. W_κ and W_τ are the time interval and time cost functions, respectively.* □

Notice that an unweighted PPG can be represented by a PPG in which W_τ maps all elements of T to 1, and W_κ maps all elements of C to l (where l is suitably chosen). Also, we can extend the notion of a marked unweighted PPG to a marked weighted PPG in a natural manner. Note that the case where $W_\kappa(c_i) < W_\tau(t_j)$ for a conjunct c_i and a transaction-type t_j, it is not worthwhile to include an edge (c_i, t_j) in the PPG. Hence, we shall always assume that for an edge (c_i, t_j) in a PPG, it is always the case that $W_\kappa(c_i) \geq W_\tau(t_j)$.

We also need to redefine the inconsistency-resolution subgraph for a weighted PPG. Again, the IRS represents a strategy for restoring consistency to the database given that the marked set of conjuncts are false.

Definition 4. *Let $G = (C, T, E, W_\kappa, W_\tau)$ be a weighted PPG in which the vertices $X \subseteq C$ are marked. An inconsistency-resolution subgraph of G is a 5-tuple $G' = (C', T', E', W'_\kappa, W_t au')$ such that,*

(1) $X \subseteq C' \subseteq C$, $T' \subseteq T$, and $E' \subseteq E$,

(2) For all edges $(t_j, c_i) \in E$ such that $t_j \in T'$, we have $c_i \in C'$ and $(t_j, c_i) \in E'$,

(3) For all $c_i \in C'$, there exists a path in G' from c_i to t_k, where t_k is a sink in G,

(4) G' is acyclic,

(5) W'_κ is the restriction of W_κ to C', and W'_τ is the restriction of W_τ to T', and

(6) For all $c_i \in C'$, there is an edge $(c_i, t_j) \in E'$ such that $W_\tau(t_j) \leq W_\kappa(c_i)$. □

An IRS can be used to decide how to resolve the inconsistencies, and it must ensure that each conjunct is false for a period no longer than its time interval, on the assumption that time costs for transaction-types are accurate. There may exist several DAGs that may be used for a particular marked PPG and each represents an IRS as defined above. In this case, a decision needs to be made as to which particular one is to be chosen. Intuitively, the IRS that represents the best strategy to resolve the inconsistencies should be the one that is selected. Although the precise definition of a good IRS is dependent on the application, it is possible to identify certain important traits that the IRS should possess. For example, an IRS that provides a method to restore consistency promptly should be regarded as being better than one that implies a slower method. Concurrency aspects for running the restoring transaction-types need to be considered to achieve this. Another measure of goodness could be the choice of an IRS that renders the least number of consistency constraints false. A third measure of goodness arises from the potential inaccuracy in time costs for transaction-types. This measure is related to the scheduling of transactions with regard to the available *slack time* which, in the case of a transaction-type t_j that is chosen to resolve the inconsistency in a conjunct c_i, is $W_\kappa(c_i) - W_\tau(t_j)$. Sufficiently large slack times "absorb" the inaccuracies of the time estimates for transactions that are scheduled sufficiently early, and this is further discussed in Section 5. Therefore, we suggest that the goodness of an IRS be measured as a function of the amount of slack time left for the restoration of the truth of conjuncts. The nature of this function is application-dependent. Example functions include the total slack time, the geometric mean of slack times, and the minimum of the slack times for each conjunct.

The conjunct-based model of real-time transactions represented by the PPG provides the system with additional degrees of freedom in managing a real-time database. Not only can the concurrency and recovery managers take into account the conjunct deadlines and time costs associated with the transaction-types, but also the system has some choice among the set of transaction-types to use in response to a particular collection of violated conjuncts that arise due to external events. Below, we consider the computational complexity of taking optimal advantage of these degrees of freedom.

5 Selecting the Inconsistency-Resolution Subgraph

The PPG and the IRS defined above allow us to pose several important questions regarding the algorithms that will use them. The issues related to a PPG and an IRS are two-fold. First, an efficient selection procedure is needed to identify a good IRS, where goodness is related to how profitably the IRS can be used to resolve the inconsistencies within the deadlines imposed. Second, once the IRS has been identified, efficient approaches are needed to execute the actions of the transaction-types specified by the IRS. For the time being, let us disregard the effects of concurrency control and partial ordering among the transaction-types.

5.1 IRS Selection Based on Vertex Weights

Consider an unweighted, acyclic PPG, G. We may assume that the selection criterion for an IRS is obtaining one that includes the fewest number of transaction-type vertices.

Problem 1. *(TUAP) The Transaction-weight Problem for a marked, unweighted, acyclic PPG is: Given a marked, unweighted, acyclic PPG, G, and an integer K, is there an IRS, G', such that the number of elements in T' is at most K?* □

Theorem 2. *The TUAP problem is NP-complete.*

Proof Sketch. The proof of NP easiness is as follows. We demonstrate how to verify in polynomial-time that a non-deterministically selected graph G' is an IRS with $|T'| \leq K$. Verifying that G represents an IRS is accomplished by checking that $X \subseteq C'$, and that for every $c_i \in C'$, there exists an edge $(c_i, t_j) \in E'$. Checking that $|T'| \leq K$ completes the verification.

We now prove NP-hardness. An instance of the NP-complete Satisfiability problem (L01 in [GJ79]) is reduced to the TUAP problem. Let P represent the conjunction of m clauses in L01, i.e., $P \equiv \bigwedge_{i=1}^{m} C_i$ where the clauses are formed over n boolean variables $x_1, x_2, \ldots, x_n$. As shown in Figure 2, form an instance of a PPG, G, with $C = \{p, c, c_1, c_2, \ldots, c_m, x_1, x_2, \ldots, x_n\}$, $T = \{p', c', Fx_1, Fx_2, \ldots, Fx_n, Tx_1, Tx_2, \ldots, Tx_n\}$, and $X = \{p\}$. Besides the edges explicitly shown in Figure 2, G includes an out-edge from a vertex c_i to either Tx_j or to Fx_j for every positive or negative literal, respectively, formed using an x_j occurring in the clause C_i of the Satisfiability problem instance. We prove that P is a satisfiable instance of L01 if and only if G contains an IRS, G', with $|T'| \leq (n+2)$. Note that the construction guarantees the existence of an IRS.

Assume that a requisite IRS, G', exists. $|T'| \geq (n+2)$ since included in G' are p', c', and at least one of Tx_i or Fx_i for every x_i. Since G' is a requisite IRS, we have $|T'| = (n+2)$. This implies that exactly one of the vertices reachable from a vertex x_i is included in T'. Assign a boolean value of **T** or **F** to the corresponding variable x_i in L01 according as Tx_i or Fx_i is included, respectively, in T'. It is clear that every clause of L01 will have one satisfied literal by this assignment.

If there is a truth assignment for every x_i in the problem instance of L01 that satisfies P, consider a subgraph G' as described next. The set T' consists of p', c', and Tx_i or Fx_i according as x_i is assigned **T** or **F**, and the set $C' = C$. The subgraph G' contains all possible edges of G. It is easy to see that G' is an IRS with $|T'| \leq (n+2)$. $\square$

If we introduce the timing constraints in terms of the functions W_κ and W_τ, a selection criterion for an IRS could be the minimization of the sum of the time costs of the transaction type vertices included in the IRS. This criterion is suggested by the need for the "fastest" inconsistency-resolution strategy.

Problem 2. *(TWP) The Transaction-weight Problem for a marked, weighted, acyclic PPG is: Given a marked, weighted PPG, G, and an integer K, is there an IRS, G', such that the sum of the weights of the elements in T' is at most K?* $\square$

Theorem 3. *The TWP problem is NP-complete.*

Proof Sketch. The TUAP problem is the TWP problem with unit weight assignments to the elements of T. $\square$

We consider now a different selection criterion that is based on the number of conjuncts that may be rendered false. In the case of an marked, unweighted, acyclic PPG, a related measure of goodness would be to find an IRS which minimizes the number of consistency conjuncts that it renders false.

Problem 3. *(PUAP) The Predicate-weight Problem for a marked, unweighted, acyclic PPG is: Given a marked, unweighted, acyclic PPG, G, and an integer K, is there an IRS, G', such that the number of elements in C' is at most K?* □

Theorem 4. *The PUAP problem is NP-complete.*

Proof Sketch. The proof of NP-easiness is the same as that for the TUAP problem with a verification of $|C'| \leq K$ replacing $|T'| \leq K$.

To prove NP-hardness, we exhibit a similar reduction from the problem L01 as we did for the TUAP problem. The instance of the PPG constructed is modified to have the additional subgraphs at the nodes Tx_i and Fx_i as shown in Figure 3. Set $K = (2n + m + 2)$. The proof is now clearly similar to the NP-hardness proof of the TUAP problem. □

The above theorems indicate that the selection procedures to find optimal IRS graphs for the PPG graphs is difficult. We conjecture that there exist interesting cases of the PPG problems that are both of practical interest and of polynomial complexity. Furthermore, we begin to anticipate the need for heuristic approaches to find good IRS graphs in place of the "best" IRS graph.

5.2 IRS Selection Based on Slack Times

Large slack times allow a greater flexibility in scheduling transactions, and in time-constrained systems, this flexibility is valuable. To analyze the PPG in terms of slack times and scheduling, we first formalize some of these notions.

Definition 5. *The* potential slack time *for a conjunct vertex c_i in a PPG, $G = (C, T, E, W_\kappa, W_\tau)$, is given by $S_\kappa(c_i) = W_\kappa(c_i) - \min_{(c_i, t_j) \in E}(W_\tau(t_j))$.* □

The slack time $S_\kappa(c_i)$ does not provide a precise value for a conjunct c_i since there is an inherent inaccuracy associated with the W_τ values. Furthermore, unless the transaction-type vertex t_j that corresponds to the minimum weight is chosen to resolve the inconsistency, the potential slack time may not be realized. However, S_κ does serve the purposes of approximation, especially if the transaction-types can be assumed to take unit time — in which case the potential slack time is always realized subject to accurate estimates for the transaction-type time costs.

5.2.1 Total Slack Time

The sum of the slack times associated with the conjunct vertices of an IRS, G', is called the total slack time of the IRS, and is denoted by $slack(G')$. As mentioned earlier, assume that some application indicates that a selection criterion may be based on the maximization of the the total slack time. With the S_κ values as provided, the IRS chosen directly would be the PPG itself — clearly an unacceptable choice. Hence, we use the method described below to limit the number of vertices chosen while retaining the criterion of total slack time maximization.

Definition 6. *The* inverse slack time *associated with a conjunct vertex c_i is given by $S'_\kappa(c_i) = \eta - S_\kappa(c_i)$ where $\eta \geq (1 + \max_{c_j \in C}(S_\kappa(c_j)))$.* □

The constraint on the value of η is to ensure that $S'_\kappa(c_i) \geq 1$ for all $c_i \in C$. The reason why η is left unspecified in the definition is explained below.

Suppose that an IRS, G'_{min}, is chosen such that the sum of the S'_κ values associated with its conjunct vertices is the smallest among all the IRSs, G', that are possible. Using the above definition, we have $\eta|C'_{min}| - slack(G'_{min}) \leq \eta|C'| - slack(G')$. Notice that $|C'_{min}| = |C'|$ implies that $slack(G'_{min}) \geq slack(G')$, and that $slack(G'_{min}) = slack(G')$ implies that $|C'_{min}| \leq |C'|$. Thus, for two IRSs, if the number of conjunct vertices in each is the same, the one with a larger total slack time is preferred by this minimization criterion. If the total slack times of the two IRSs are equal, then this criterion chooses the one with fewer conjunct vertices.

As mentioned above, attempting to maximize the total slack time *without* using a notion such as the inverse slack time leads to the selection of an unnecessarily large IRS with too many conjunct vertices. This is undesirable since the inclusion of a conjunct vertex in an IRS implies that the inconsistency-resolution process may cause that conjunct to become inconsistent. Thus, there exists a trade-off between increasing the total slack time, $slack(G')$, and decreasing the number of conjunct vertices, $|C'|$, in the IRS. It is the value of η that determines the importance attached to each. A small value of η gives more importance to maximizing $slack(G')$, whereas a large value of η gives more importance to minimizing $|C'|$. This is clear by examining the expression $\eta|C'| - slack(G')$ which is the sum of the inverse slack times of the vertices in C'.

Consider a modified PPG, G, in which for all $c_i \in C$ and $t_j \in T$, we set $W_\kappa(c_i) = S'_\kappa(c_i)$ and $W_\tau(t_j) = 1$. By introducing inverse slack times in this manner, and choosing a desired value for η, the question of maximizing the total slack time for an IRS reduces to the following problem.

Problem 4. *(PWP) The Predicate-weight Problem for a marked, weighted PPG is: Given a marked,* *weighted, acyclic PPG, G, and an integer K, is there an IRS, G', such that the sum of the weights of the elements in C' is at most K?* □

Theorem 5. *The PWP Problem is NP-complete.*

Proof Sketch. The PUAP problem is the PWP problem with unit weight assignments to the elements in C. □

5.2.2 Large Individual Slack Times

It may be argued that it is more germane to use a selection criterion for an IRS based on the largeness of the slack times associated with the conjuncts. That is, the cost of an IRS $G' = (C', T', E', W_\kappa', W_\tau')$ is $\max_{c_i \in C'}(S_\kappa'(c_i))$. Large slack times provide the flexibility in scheduling the inconsistency-resolving instances of transaction-types which may be necessitated by concurrency control considerations. As mentioned earlier, if a transaction is scheduled early, the inaccuracies in the transaction execution time estimates are less likely to affect the deadline requirements on the conjunct inconsistencies. We examine slack times in more detail in Section 6. In the discussion to follow, we assume for simplicity that an IRS exists.

Problem 5. *(IST) The Individual Slack Time Problem for a PPG is: For a given marked, weighted, acyclic PPG, G, and an integer K, is there an IRS, G', such that $\max_{c_i \in C'}(S_\kappa'(c_i))$ is at most K?* □

Theorem 6. *The IST problem is in polynomial-time.*

Proof Sketch. Add a (pseudo) transaction-type vertex t' to T with outedges (t', c_i) to every $c_i \in X$. With each vertex $v \in C \cup T$, associate two values, $V(v)$ and $tag(v)$. Set $tag(t_j) = 1$ for each sink transaction-type vertex t_j, and set all the remaining V and tag values to 0.

1. while $tag(t') = 0$ do

   (a) Choose vertex v with $tag(v) = 0$ and all successor vertices u with $tag(u) = 1$.

   (b) if $v \in T$ then set $V(v) = \max_{(v,u) \in E}(V(u))$.

   if $v \in C$ then set $V(v) = \max(S_\kappa'(v), \min_{(v,u) \in E}(V(u)))$.

   (c) Set $tag(v) = 1$.

2. if $V(t') \leq K$ then print "Yes" else print "No", and stop.

At the end of loop statement, a tagged vertex, v, has the value $V(v)$ that provides the cost of the subgraph of the best IRS (in the IST sense) that is rooted at that vertex. With the use of suitable data structures, the algorithm runs in $O(|C| + |T| + |E|)$ time — thereby placing IST in P-time. □

5.3 Interpreting the Complexity Results

The significance of the intractable results is only that the optimal solutions are computationally very costly to obtain. However, as in many other situations, near optimal solutions would serve almost as well. By sacrificing optimality, we can make use of several approximation methods available in the literature (e.g., from [GJ79]). Such heuristic methods are well-studied and provide computationally inexpensive means to obtain near-optimal solutions. The fact that formal analysis of this nature is possible in our formulation is a very encouraging indication.

The PPG that we have dealt with so far may be regarded as "static", since the only "dynamic" aspect of the PPG are the markings. It is possible to consider a more complex "dynamic" version of a PPG where the weights may change dynamically, or the transaction-types are replaced by transaction instances. However, the intractability of the problems encountered in the static case indicate that the dynamic version would definitely pose problems that are at least as difficult. Thus, the study of a simpler model provides a basis for directly seeking heuristics in the more complicated models.

6 Using the Inconsistency-Resolution Subgraph

Once an IRS is chosen, the question arises as to how the actions that it implies should be scheduled. It may be argued that since the transactions are likely to interact, concurrency control requirements may render the selection criteria for the IRS untenable. However, note that the intractability of the problems encountered indicate that additional criteria will not make the problems any easier, and heuristic methods must be used. Therefore, we separate the two issues of selection and scheduling for an IRS. The detailed analysis of the use of an IRS is beyond the scope of this paper, and we restrict ourselves to indicating the important issues involved in such analyses.

6.1 Scheduling, Slack Times, and Nested Transactions

Consider a subgraph of an IRS in Figure 4. The parenthesized numbers give the values of W_κ and W_τ for the conjunct vertices and the transaction-type vertices, respectively. Assume that c_2 and c_3 become inconsistent immediately after the completion of t_1. The IRS chosen does not allow any slack time for the resolution of the inconsistency in either of these conjuncts, and hence, t_2 and t_3 are scheduled immediately. The conjuncts c_4 and c_5 may become inconsistent immediately after t_2 and t_3 complete, respectively. Notice that since neither c_4 nor c_5 have any slack time, and hence, as soon as either of them becomes inconsistent, t_4 must be scheduled. However, in this example, c_4 and c_5 become inconsistent within $W_\tau(t_4) = 3$ time units of each other — but not simultaneously. Thus, if the same transaction from the transaction-type t_4 is used to resolve the inconsistencies, irrespective of when it is scheduled, one of the two conjuncts will remain inconsistent for a period greater than its deadline. Furthermore, assuming that c_4 and c_5 do not become inconsistent within $W_\tau(t_4)$ time units of each other, it is the case that a single execution of t_4 will not suffice to resolve *both* the inconsistencies.

In a similar situation, the example in Figure 5 shows a conjunct vertex, c_1, that may become inconsistent due to the execution of either t_1 or t_2. Suppose that t_1 makes c_1 inconsistent, and t_2 does the same within the next $W_\kappa(c_1) = 3$ units of time. In this situation, no matter when t_3 is scheduled, the time period for which c_1 will remain inconsistent will exceed $W_\kappa(c_1)$.

The occurrence of problems such as those illustrated in the two examples above is not peculiar to our particular formulation. They will occur in general in systems with timing constraints, and the problems must be addressed if real-time databases are to be realized. Our model serves to exhibit these problems as well as to serve as a tool by which they may be analyzed.

In the examples just discussed, notice that if the conjuncts have larger slack times due to larger deadlines, the problems may be alleviated. For example, if we changed Figure 4 to have $W_\kappa(c_5) = 4$, and changed Figure 5 to have $W_\kappa(c_1) >> 3$, then the scheduling of the inconsistency-resolution transactions may be successfully accomplished. These examples show how large slack times permit the transaction-types to exceed their inherently inaccurate estimates of execution-times so long as their instances are scheduled sufficiently early.

Large slack times are useful in other contexts as well. Before transactions begin executing, it is often the case that the resources they need must be obtained — and this could be time-consuming. Furthermore, the duration of this resource-gathering phase is indeterminate and it depends on the other transactions that are executing concurrently in the system. If the transactions are triggered by conjuncts with large slack times, the initial phase of the transactions could be safely accommodated by scheduling the transactions early. One way to accomplish this to a certain extent is to identify the conjuncts with large slack times, and to use the notion of nested transactions as follows. The conjuncts with small slack times that occur in the IRS are embodied within the nested transaction-types. The conjuncts that have been identified with large slack times serve as triggering conjuncts for the nested transactions. Thus, the IRS is regarded as a collection of partially ordered nested transaction-types — most of which are triggered by conjuncts with large slack times. Details regarding nested transactions are available in [Mos87, KS88].

As an example, consider the PPG shown in Figure 6. We represent conjuncts that have been identified to have large slack times by triangular vertices. In the manner explained above, some vertices of the PPG are shown to be grouped together by the dotted outlines to form nested transaction-types that are denoted by nt_1, nt_2, nt_3, and nt_4. The conjunct vertex c_1 may trigger instances of either one of the nested transaction-types nt_1 or nt_2. In nt_1, the parent transaction of type t_1 may spawn the child transactions of type t_5, t_6, and t_7 by making the conjuncts c_5, c_6, and c_7 inconsistent. Similarly, nt_2 has a parent transaction-type t_2, an instance of which may spawn child transactions of type t_6 and t_7. Notice that an instance of nt_2 could make c_8 inconsistent, and this would trigger an instance of nt_4 which consists of the single transaction-type t_8. The nested transaction-type nt_3 has a parent transaction-type t_4, an instance of which may spawn just a single child transaction of type t_8.

6.2 Concurrency Control Issues

In the execution of the transactions indicated by an IRS, besides correctness, the issue of the timing constraints is also of importance. We have noted above that an inconsistency-resolution subgraph induces a partial order on the set T' of transaction-types. Given that we seek the prompt restoration of consistency in a real-time system, the need for a significant amount of concurrency among instances of the transaction-types in T' is required. In this section, we briefly examine aspects of concurrency control protocols germane to our model. While we do not advocate or require any one specific concurrency control protocol, the desirable traits in these are highlighted. The extensive number of methods available in the literature should provide a sufficiently large choice.

From the model of transactions described earlier, the use of methods that deal with nested transactions is indicated clearly. The subgraphs of an IRS are best described as nested transaction-types with added timing constraints. Existing work on nested transactions should be modified to handle the timing considerations to be used in this context.

Obviously, the presence of timing constraints will affect the concurrency control. The increased needs for concurrency may be achieved using less restrictive correctness criteria as compared to the traditional serializability — for example, the correct concurrent execution criteria of [KS88]. Our model allows for external-output transactions and transactions with stringent timing requirements. Both of these suggest that the facility for undoing the effects of a transaction may be unavailable. Also, situations that may result in cascading aborts must be avoided — which does not necessarily preclude other transactions from "observing" data produced by uncommitted transactions since our model is not the traditional one. These factors suggest that it may be necessary to introduce the notion of compensating transactions [Gra81, KL89].

Transactions that run concurrently in our system interact due to the shared data that they may access. The timing constraints imply that the delays arising as a result of these interactions should be minimized. For example, deadlock or livelock situations should be avoided. The use of versions of data in this context also helps to alleviate the problem. Clearly, it is important to identify where the transactions may interact so as to reduce the interactions to limit the delays. Thus, our model plays the dual role of describing the transactions as well as prescribing their design to control the contention. We highlight some of the immediate facets of transaction interaction next.

Let S be an IRS of a PPG G. Let $c_{k_1}, t_{j_1}, c_{k_2}, t_{j_2}, \ldots, c_{k_m}, t_{j_m}$ be a path in S. We assume the NT/PV model of [KS88] with input and output conditions (pre- and post-conditions) for each transaction-type. Then, we expect the following to hold in many cases. For an edge $e = (c_{k_i}, t_{j_i})$ in S, since t_{j_i} is triggered by the falsehood of c_{k_i}, the input condition of t_{j_i} mentions all the data items occurring in c_{k_i}. Also, since t_{j_i} makes c_{k_i} true, the output condition of t_{j_i} mentions potentially all the data items occurring in c_{k_i}. For an edge $e = (t_{j_i}, c_{k_{i+1}})$ in S, since t_{j_i} may invalidate $c_{k_{i+1}}$, the output condition of t_{j_i} mentions potentially all the data items occurring in $c_{k_{i+1}}$. It is unlikely that all the data items of a conjunct will be affected by one transaction-type. These observations can be used to identify bounds on the read and write sets of transaction-types. Such information can be used to advantage in concurrency control. Concurrency along paths in S could be managed by the preemptive protocol described in [KS88], perhaps simplified to its single-version variant.

It is valuable to identify the potential for concurrency among the transaction-types that do not lie on the same path in the IRS. Although two transaction-types may not have any common conjuncts in their pre- and post-condition sets, it may happen that they access common data items. This is because different conjuncts may mention common data items. Also, consider an example of a PPG in which there are two out-edges (c_1, t_1) and (c_1, t_2) from the same conjunct vertex c_1. It may happen that the IRS for the PPG contains both the transaction-types t_1 and t_2, but only one of the two edges, say (c_1, t_1). This could happen if t_2 is chosen to resolve the inconsistency for some conjunct other than c_1. In such a situation, the analysis to find common data items should include consideration for both the edges (c_1, t_1) and (c_1, t_2). After this analysis is done, it becomes necessary to ensure that the instances of the transaction-types that access the common data are correctly controlled by the concurrency protocol.

Even after reducing the extent to which the transaction-types interact, any reasonable real-time database system will have transactions competing for the resources. In such situations, the study of pre-emptive protocols to manage the timing and priority constraints is important. Thus, the satisfaction of transaction-type timing constraints may result in the sacrifice of the best overall throughput of the system. Research along these lines is desirable for our model, and in this context, work such as [AGM88a] may be extendible.

7 Conclusions

We have proposed a model of real-time transaction processing based upon deadlines associated with consistency constraints. We have demonstrated that, in general, finding a strategy for restoring database consistency is computationally intractable. This negative result does not preclude the practical use of our model. Rather, it indicates that heuristics or suitable "protocols" are required for transaction processing. An analogous situation exists for standard transaction processing, where the set of two-phase locked schedules is usually accepted as a suitable subset of the set of serializable schedules whose recognition problem is NP-complete.

We have suggested some approaches toward the development of practical transaction management algorithms for our real-time model, but many issues remain to be addressed. For example, heuristics for the selection of an acceptable inconsistency-resolution subgraph are needed as is the development of a complete concurrency protocol that exploits the semantics of the inconsistency-resolution subgraph. The introduction of dynamic violations of consistency constraints in real-time database systems requires the system to modify its consistency restoration strategy as external events occur. Rather than recomputing a complete strategy, an incremental algorithm is desirable. Techniques of this nature are already in use in expert database systems [For82].

Acknowledgements

The authors wish to thank Robert Abbott, Hector Garcia-Molina, and Eliezer Levy for helpful discussions.

References

[AGM88a] R. Abbott and H. Garcia-Molina. Scheduling real-time transactions. *SIGMOD Record*, 17(1):71–81, March 1988.

[AGM88b] R. Abbott and H. Garcia-Molina. Scheduling real time transactions: A performance evaluation. In *Proceedings of the Fourteenth International Conference on Very Large Databases, Los Angeles*, pages 1–12, 1988.

[BBG89] C. Beeri, P. A. Bernstein, and N. Goodman. A model for concurrency in nested transaction systems. *Journal of the ACM*, 36(2):230–269, April 1989.

[BHG87] P. A. Bernstein, V. Hadzilacos, and N. Goodman. *Concurrency Control and Recovery in Database Systems*. Addison-Wesley, Reading, MA, 1987.

[For82] C. Forgy. RETE: A fast match algorithm for the many pattern/ many object pattern match problem. *Artificial Intelligence*, (19):17–37, 1982.

[GJ79] M. R. Garey and D. S. Johnson. *Computers and Intractability*. W. H. Freeman and Company, New York, 1979.

[Gra81] J. N. Gray. The transaction concept: Virtues and limitations. In *Proceedings of the Seventh International Conference on Very Large Databases, Cannes*, pages 144–154, 1981.

[HH88]   T. Hadzilacos and V. Hadzilacos. Transaction synchronisation in object bases. In *Proceedings of the Seventh ACM SIGACT-SIGMOD-SIGART Symposium on Principles of Database Systems, Austin*, pages 193–200, March 1988.

[HMR$^+$89] R. Holte, A. K.-L. Mok, L. Rosier, I. Tulchinsky, and D. Varvel. The pinwheel: A real-time scheduling problem. In *Proceedings of the 22nd Hawaii International Conference on System Sciences, Kailua-Kona*, pages 693–702, January 1989.

[JM86]   F. Jahanian and A. K.-L. Mok. Safety anaylsis of timing properties in real-time systems. *IEEE Transactions on Software Engineering*, SE-12(9):890–904, September 1986.

[KKB88]   H. F. Korth, W. Kim, and F. Bancilhon. On long duration CAD transactions. *Information Sciences*, 46:73–107, October 1988.

[KL89]   H. F. Korth and E. Levy. Formal approach to recovery by compensating transactions. Submitted for Publication, December 1989.

[KS88]   H. F. Korth and G. Speegle. Formal model of correctness without serializability. In *Proceedings of ACM-SIGMOD 1988 Annual Conference, Chicago*, pages 379–388, June 1988.

[MD89]   D. R. McCarthy and U. Dayal. The architecture of an active data base management system. In *Proceedings of ACM-SIGMOD 1989 Annual Conference, Portland, Oregon*, pages 215–224, June 1989.

[Mos87]   J. E. B. Moss. Nested transactions: An introduction. In B. Bhargava, editor, *Concurrency Control and Reliability in Distributed Systems*, pages 395–425. Van Nostrand Reinhold, 1987.

[PR88]   P. Peinl and A. Reuter. High contention in a stock trading database: A case study. In *Proceedings of ACM-SIGMOD 1988 Annual Conference, Chicago*, pages 260–268, June 1988.

[Sin88]   M. Singhal. Issues and approaches to design of real-time database systems. *SIGMOD Record*, 17(1):19–33, March 1988.

[Son88]   S. H. Son, editor. *SIGMOD Record: Special Issue on Real-Time Databases*. ACM, March 1988.

[SRL88]   L. Sha, R. Rajkumar, and J. P. Lehoczky. Concurrency control for distributed real-time databases. *SIGMOD Record*, 17(1):82–98, March 1988.

[Sta88]   J. A. Stankovic. Misconceptions about real-time computing. *IEEE Computer*, pages 10–19, October 1988.

[Yan82]   M. Yannakakis. Issues of correctness in database concurrency control by locking. *Journal of the ACM*, 29(3):718–740, July 1982.

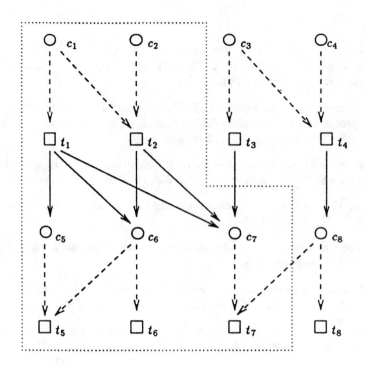

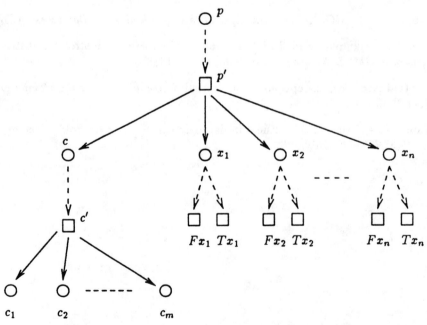

Figure 1: An example PPG

□ Transaction Vertices

○ Conjunct Vertices

The dotted outline shows a DAG subgraph

Figure 2: Construction of the PPG for the TUAP problem

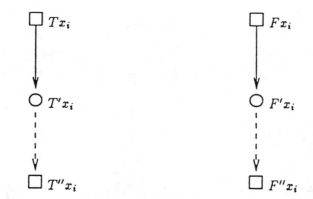

Figure 3: Construction of the PPG for the PUAP problem

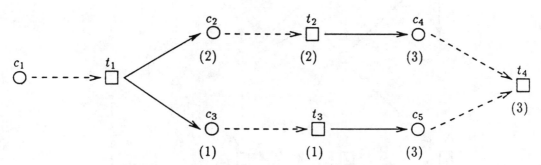

Figure 4: First Example of Scheduling Problems

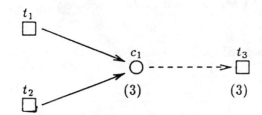

Figure 5: Second Example of Scheduling Problems

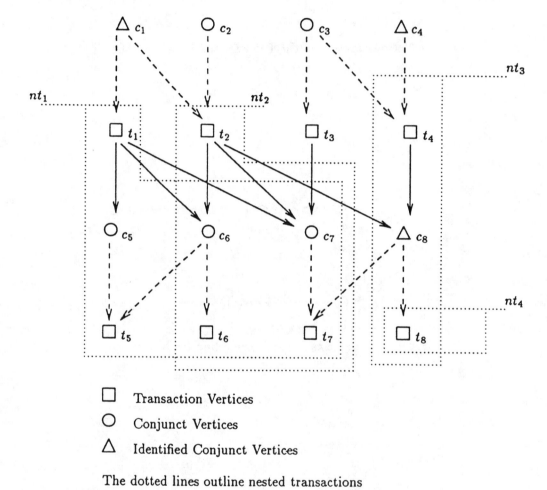

Transaction Vertices
Conjunct Vertices
Identified Conjunct Vertices

The dotted lines outline nested transactions

Figure 6: Large Slack Times and Nested Transaction-types

Chapter 10: Artificial Intelligence

Many complex applications require knowledge-based on-line assistance operating in real-time, including the Pilot's Associate Program, intelligent manufacturing, intelligent process control, and autonomous robot control. This requires a major change to some of the paradigms and implementations previously used by AI researchers. For example, AI systems must be made to

- run much faster (a necessary but not sufficient condition),
- allow preemption to reduce latency for responding to new stimuli,
- attain predictable memory management via incremental garbage collection or by explicit management of memory,
- include deadlines and other timing constraints in search techniques,
- develop anytime algorithms (algorithms where an albeit non-optimal solution is available at any point in time),
- develop time-driven inferencing, and
- develop time-driven planning and scheduling.

Rules and constraints may also have to be imposed on AI design, models, and languages to facilitate predictability; for example, recursion and backtracking should be limited to a fixed bound. It is important to come to grips with what predictability means in such applications. Review the article on predictability in the first chapter, and try to reconcile definitions and discussions there with the papers in this chapter.

In addition to these changes in AI, real-time AI (RTAI) techniques must be integrated with lower-level real-time systems technology to produce a functioning, reliable, and carefully analyzable system. Should the higher-level RTAI techniques ignore the system level, or treat it as a black box, or be developed in an integrated fashion with it so as to best build these complex systems? What is the correct interface between these two systems? Integrating RTAI and low-level real-time systems software is quite a challenge for several reasons:

- these RTAI applications are operating in non-deterministic environments,
- there is missing or noisy information,
- some of the control laws are heuristic at best,
- objectives may change dynamically,
- partial solutions are sometimes acceptable so that a trade-off between the quality of the solution and the time needed to derive it can be made,
- the amount of processing is significant and highly data dependent, and
- the execution time of tasks may be difficult to determine.

What must change at the low levels to provide adequate support for the higher-level, more application-oriented tasks?

The Pilot's Associate is one type of complex RTAI application. "Concepts, Methods, and Languages for Building Timely Intelligent Systems" by Lark et al. uses this application to illustrate the overall problems and proposed solutions for dealing with multiple, interacting real-time expert systems. The authors discuss a toolkit for building real-time intelligent systems, where the system architect must guarantee the timeliness of the system at design time. The toolkit stresses the need for a methodological approach, an integrated set of languages and tools used throughout the life cycle, and the need for good analysis techniques. Advanced features of the current toolkit are being developed.

Another interesting application domain for RTAI is robotics. In "Intelligent Real-Time Control of Robotic Vehicles," Payton and Bihari discuss how to combine two approaches: taking immediate actions based on monitoring the environment and formulating longer-term plans and actions based on data accumulated over time. Advantages and disadvantages of both approaches are detailed. The authors also describe two robotic applications: the adaptive suspension vehicle (a six-legged vehicle) where centralized control is appropriate, and the autonomous land vehicle where decentralized control is appropriate. The paper contains a good description of the breakdown of functions into sensor processing, servo-level control, terrain modeling, and motion planning. They discuss the need for predictability, guarantees (some of which are renegotiable), and stability.

Paul et al.'s paper, "Reducing Problem Solving Variance To Improve Predictability," addresses some significant issues confronting RTAI systems. The paper provides an architecture that integrates low-level control functions (the more classical real-time system aspects) with the higher-level knowledge-based problem solving tasks (encapsulated within an AI server task). Using this approach the authors then demonstrate what is predictable and what isn't, and how this interface facilitates evaluations and guarantees for both the conventional real-time tasks as well as the AI server. A key ingredient in achieving predictability is determining the worst case execution time for tasks. The authors argue that worst case time may not be meaningful for many RTAI tasks; rather what is required are techniques to reduce the variance in execution time. They present several such techniques. The authors also identify several problems with OPS5 for real-time systems and describe CROPS5, an implementation that removes these deficiencies. CROPS5 allows concurrent prioritized streams, predictable preemption points, and predictable context switch costs.

Concepts, Methods, and Languages for Building Timely Intelligent Systems

JAY S. LARK, LEE D. ERMAN, STEPHANIE FORREST,[1] KIM P. GOSTELOW,[2]
FREDERICK HAYES-ROTH, DAVID M. SMITH[3]
Cimflex Teknowledge Corporation, 1810 Embarcadero Road, P.O. Box 10119, Palo Alto, CA 94303

Abstract. We describe the ABE/RT toolkit—a set of design, development, and experimentation tools for building time-stressed intelligent systems—and its use for the Lockheed Pilot's Associate application. We use the term *timely systems* to refer to systems with hard real-time requirements for interacting with a human operator or other agents with similar time-scales. The ABE/RT methodology is based on a philosophy of rigorous engineering design in which the application developer works to guarantee the system's timeliness by identifying the various events which require timely responses, determining the worst-case frequencies of these events and the deadlines and durations of the tasks that respond to the events, and then verifying that the run-time system has enough processing resources to complete all mandatory tasks by their deadlines. We believe this is the only way in the near-term to build complex real-time intelligent systems that will be reliable enough for critical applications with demanding users. The ABE/RT Toolkit contains a set of languages for specifying the structure and behavior of timely systems, together with tools to simulate those models, log and analyze data collected during simulation runs, predict an application's performance on a specified target hardware architecture, and deploy the application on the target architecture.

1. Introduction

We address the problem of building real-time intelligent systems. Our driving example is the DARPA Pilot's Associate, a multicomputer system comprising several cooperating expert systems that together act as a back-seater for a fighter pilot. (Smith and Broadwell 1988). The Pilot's Associate comprises six major functional areas: mission planning, system status, situation assessment, tactics planning, pilot-vehicle interface, and plan integration and mission management. The component expert subsystems integrate information from the aircraft's internal and external sensors, produce plans in response to that information, present the pilot with high-level decision-oriented information, and interact with the pilot

[1]Current address: Los Alamos National Laboratory, NM.
[2]Current address: Jet Propulsion Laboratory, Pasadena, CA.
[3]Lockheed Aeronautical Systems Co, Marietta, GA.

This research was partially funded by the Defense Advanced Research Projects Agency, 1400 Wilson Blvd., Arlington, VA 22209, under contracts F30602-85-C-0135 and F33615-85-C-3804, administered by the Air Force Systems Command, Rome Air Development Center and the Air Force Cockpit Technology Directorate, Wright Research and Development Center, respectively. Use of this material, including copying, by the U.S. government is permitted in accordance with the terms of those contracts.

in the successful execution of those plans. Each of the subsystems is organized differently, utilizing structures such as conventional functional organizations (implemented in C++ or Common Lisp code), blackboards, and production-rule shells. Each subsystem has its own rules and goals and a controller that responds to requests for information and suggestions from the other systems.

1.1. Application characteristics

The Pilot's Associate is an example of a broad class of applications characterized by several key roles and requirements: mission-critical operation; timeliness and reliability of operator interaction; multiple interacting functional requirements; scarce computing resources; rapid prototyping and evolutionary development; distributed development; and timeliness as a fundamental requirement. The following paragraphs expand these key characteristics.

Mission-critical operation. The application forms an integral part of a larger system, and the success of the whole depends on the individual successes of its critical components. For example, the effectiveness of a Pilot's Associate-equipped aircraft, measured in terms of survivability or exchange ratios, would be greatly degraded by the loss or malfunction of its Pilot's Associate component. This mission-critical nature stresses requirements such as verification and validation, robustness, and fault tolerance.

Timeliness and reliability of operator interaction. The class of applications we are addressing has strong timeliness requirements, but not in the same sense as conventional real-time systems such as flight control systems, inertial navigation systems, machine-tool controllers, or other systems which interact with fast hardware devices. Applications like the Pilot's Associate have event-response requirements on the order of seconds, with a response generated by a sequence of tasks each running on the order of tens of milliseconds. An application like the Pilot's Associate can afford to miss a pilot-interaction deadline by 50 milliseconds without significantly degrading system performance. However, these longer and less precise deadlines do not give the application permission to spend an arbitrary amount of time computing a response. We use the term *timely systems* to refer to systems with hard real-time requirements for interacting with a human operator or other agents with similar time-scales.

We are also concerned with applications in which the human operator requires the system to function reliably, with no surprises. That is, we seek *predictability* in our timely systems. For example, pilots will use an automated aid only if they can acquire an accurate model of how it will perform and if, in day-to-day use, the aid does not violate their expectations.

Multiple interacting functional requirements. Complex applications must perform many distinct functions simultaneously and must extract results from each function in accordance with its specific timeliness requirement. An application architect must have a way to specify each of these functions individually. The architect also must be able to specify how multiple functions interact, particularly in terms of contention for shared resources.

Scarce computing resources. We assume that the available computing resources are inadequate to perform all the functions the application would want to perform at every point in time. During high-stress periods the computing load on the application invariably will exceed the computing power available. Thus, significant compromises have to be made by the constituent processes in order to make the system as a whole complete the most vital work on time. The application architect must have ways of characterizing and detecting such high-load periods and reallocating resources appropriately.

Rapid prototyping and evolutionary development. Large-scale intelligent systems are typically developed in an evolutionary fashion using rapid prototyping techniques. This approach is necessitated by several common properties:

- The functional requirements of the application change, either by request from the customer or because the developer's understanding of the problem changes.
- The target environment (the hardware systems upon which the finished application will operate) is under-specified.
- The ways the application will interact with other systems in its environment are poorly specified.
- The application requires high-risk components. We define a high-risk software component as one which cannot be scoped and budgeted using conventional software engineering techniques. Knowledge-based software currently fits in this category.
- The developer does not have a proven application architecture that assures the key performance objectives for the application.

Distributed development. Large-scale software development projects today are frequently composed of multiple development teams, and these teams often are geographically distributed and use different prototyping languages and methodologies. The prime contractor must employ some integrating methodology which allows the individual teams to develop their own pieces independently, but which supports the efficient integration of those pieces into the complete application.

Timeliness, a fundamental requirement. A comprehensive model and design system is needed to apportion limited time, and focus-of-attention is an important aspect of that allocation. By focus-of-attention we mean the following problem: Given that there are several things the system can do at any one time, which is to be done, and for how long? This problem is difficult because the answer depends upon what is happening at the time. For a given set of tasks waiting to be done, an allocation appropriate at one point may be inappropriate at another. These concerns for timely behavior cannot be addressed after building the application's functionality, but must be considered at all stages of the development.

1.2. The development process

Real-time systems for embedded applications such as the Pilot's Associate are often built in a multi-step process.

1. System architects perform requirements analysis and architecture design in a modeling environment, using Computer-Aided Software Engineering (CASE) tools. These tools

incorporate graphical or textual editors to build structure charts, data flow diagrams, function-call diagrams, and data item descriptions, and run on a variety of computing platforms. The output of this stage is a comprehensive set of design documents. We refer to this stage as *modeling*, and the software and hardware components used as the *modeling environment*.

2. Software engineers produce working prototypes of the application from the design documents. They typically build these prototypes in high-productivity software-development environments, such as UNIX workstations. The result of this stage is a working prototype of the application running in a laboratory. We refer to this stage as *prototyping*, which occurs in the *host* environment.

3. Embedded system coders convert the prototype to software that will run on the application's target hardware. This stage may involve cross-compilation from the host environment, or recoding in a language suitable for embedded systems such as Ada or JOVIAL. The result of this stage is the completed application system. We refer to this stage as *fielding* the application on the *target* environment.

The ideal process as described above has many drawbacks in practice:

- The models produced in the modeling stage are incomplete and inaccurate because there are no tools or methods to verify and validate the models.
- There is little or no feedback from the prototyping stage to the modeling stage to maintain and update the models as the structure of the prototype evolves.
- The design documents produced in the prototyping stage are often ignored by later stages because they are too complex, too difficult to use, or do not correspond to the implementors' version of reality, and are therefore irrelevant.
- The cost of fixing design problems increases in later stages. In the worst-case, architectural problems detected during fielding may invalidate all work to date and require a redesign from scratch, such as determining that the target hardware is not adequate to support the application's mandated functionality.

We can summarize these and many other similar problems as having one of two root causes: (1) an inability to test models before finalizing a design; and (2) poor linkages between the development stages, which increase the cost of making changes.

1.3. The ABE/RT approach

We are developing an integrated set of software tools to support the development of timely intelligent systems as we have described. The *ABE/RT Toolkit* includes the following: Facilities to specify the structure, timeliness, and resource utilization of an application operating within its run-time environment; aids for simulating, instrumenting, studying, and modifying the system during evolutionary development; and tools to help deploy the system on a target hardware architecture that may differ substantially from the host or modeling hardware architecture. We aim to automate much of the model-prototype-field process by addressing both of the deficiencies identified above. In this paper we will focus primarily on the former, and on our efforts to build experimental models to test and verify that the application's design will satisfy its functional and timeliness requirements. The ABE/RT Toolkit is an extension to the ABE facilities for developing complex, distributed, intelligent systems. (Erman, Lark and Hayes-Roth 1988; Hayes-Roth, Erman, Fouse, Lark and Davidson 1989)

In this paper we describe the ABE/RT design, development, and experimentation tools that we have built and are using for the Lockheed Pilot's Associate. The Pilot's Associate was originally developed without specific structural concerns for real-time operation; it is currently a laboratory demonstration, capable of performing a significant portion of its required functions, some in considerable depth, but not yet in real-time. We are now helping the Lockheed team reformulate and reconstruct the application for timely performance, using the ABE/RT toolkit.[1]

We have adopted a philosophy of *rigorous engineering design*, a strong engineering approach which requires the system architect to guarantee the system's timeliness at design time. The ABE/RT methodology specifies that the system architect must identify the various events which require timely responses, determine the worst-case frequencies of these events and the deadlines and durations of the tasks that respond to the events, and then verify that the run-time system has enough processing resources to complete all mandatory tasks by their deadlines. As much as possible, we believe schedules should be determined at system definition and compilation time.

We believe the approach described here is both simple and comprehensive. In our opinion, timely intelligent systems must address many of the same real-time problems that arise in conventional real-time applications. Introducing AI techniques within the application aggravates an already difficult problem because of the lack of experience building intelligent systems to work with guaranteed timeliness in embedded system environments such as avionics. Our efforts focus on two key concerns: (1) helping the programmer insure that an application system designed to run in real-time will assuredly run in real-time in its target environment; and (2) assigning the processing resources to the functions that need them. Other concerns, such as producing efficient schedules, though important to overall performance, are not results of this work. Nevertheless, as advances are made in these areas our methods should be capable of exploiting them.

In order to simplify the process of analyzing and verifying performance, we have challenged the wisdom of run-time control reasoning being pursued by AI researchers and developers working in similar time-stressed areas—for example, see (Decker, Lesser and Whitehair 1990; Hayes-Roth 1990; Howe, Hart and Cohen 1990). We take this strong stand in the belief that, although it is a promising area, run-time control reasoning will not be reliable, predictable, nor fast enough in the near-term for critical applications with demanding users.[2]

We can also contrast our approach to commercial real-time CASE tools [CASE 1989]. These tools provide an extensive library of functions which allow an architect to specify numerous aspects of an application's architecture. However, these tools do not provide support for specifying the timeliness of an application's functions or the allocation of available resources to those functions. Also, these tools deal with static models suitable for producing design documents, with limited facilities for simulating the models, analyzing the results of such simulations, running what-if experiments, or translating the paper models to prototype code. We have designed and implemented the ABE/RT Toolkit to address directly these deficiencies.

2. Languages and tools

The ABE/RT Toolkit contains a set of languages for building models of the structure and behavior of timely systems, together with tools to simulate those models, log and analyze data collected during simulation runs, predict an application's performance on a specified target hardware architecture, and deploy the application on the target architecture.

An application model built with ABE/RT contains three distinct kinds of information, each with its own language. The languages describe

1. the application's structure, as collections of processes, shared data objects, events, and the interconnections and embeddings of processes and data;
2. the application's timeliness characteristics, as the response time requirements for each of the input-output functions performed by the application; and
3. policies for allocating scarce processing resources to the application's activities during periods of high-time stress to maximize the application's value.

An application built according to the ABE/RT model requires all three sets of information to completely specify its behavior. However, the supporting methodology and tools allow an application architect to build models incrementally, progressing from structure through timeliness to resource allocation, while retaining the ability to execute and experiment with the application at any stage of development.

The ABE/RT languages are integrated into ABE's complete graphical development environment. Each language has its own graphical editor, built on ABE's common window and graphics substrate. The ABE/RT interpreter executes the application model in the development environment, allowing the application architect to observe the execution via graphical animation of the model. The development environment also has hooks to the other analysis and experimentation tools.

We now describe each of the three ABE/RT languages in turn: for structures, event processing plans, and resource allocation. Following that, we will discuss a methodology for using these languages. We will then close with a brief description of some of the development and experimentation tools we have built.

2.1. The structure view

The ABE/RT structural description language defines three major building-blocks—processes, shared data, and events—and the means for connecting them to build structural models. The processes and data objects in an application may themselves be described as other structural objects. The ability to embed the objects hierarchically allows developers to deal with multi-level abstractions of the application's structure. The general embedding also allows for clear modularities that support multi-team development. For example, the top-level of Pilot's Associate's structural model includes processes corresponding to the six major functional subsystems enumerated earlier; each of the subsystems is further decomposed into major functional modules.

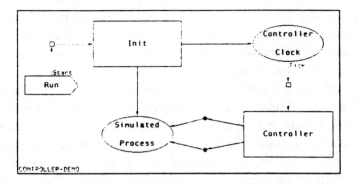

Figure 1. An ABE/RT structural model. This is the top-level of a structure model of a process controller application, such as an automobile cruise control. The controller starts by accepting an input event from the user via the event port Run. That event triggers (along the dashed event links) the Init process, which starts up Simulated_Process and Controller_Clock as concurrent activities. Simulated_Process runs continuously, updating a state variable by integrating a rate variable. Controller_Clock will periodicially produce an output event named Tick, which will trigger Controller. When Controller runs it will check if Simulated_Process is within preset bounds (by sending a message over the solid data links) and if so exit. If the simulated process is out of bounds, Controller will attempt to bring the process state variable back into bounds by modifying the rate variable in Simulated_Process. Note that from Controller's perspective, Simulated_Process appears as just a data structure which can return its current state and accept a new rate, and Controller_Clock functions as a source of periodic events; Controller does not have to know the internal structure of these components, only that they have certain external behaviors it can depend upon.

The graphical editor, in addition to displaying the ABE/RT objects as shown here and in subsequent figures, also allows for editing. With the editor, the developer can add, delete, rename, and rearrange components.

Figure 1 shows the top-level structural model of a simple process controller application we built to illustrate some of the features of ABE/RT. We will use other pieces from this application throughout the rest of this article. We will start with a detailed description of the primitive components that make up a structural model and the ways of interconnecting them. Subsequently, we will describe how to assemble structural models into higher-order structures.

Processes are the main functional components of the application. A process is a persistent object which has a single thread of control, a procedure or set of procedures it can execute, and private persistent data. A process is triggered by the occurrence of one of a specific set of events. Once triggered, the process starts executing one of its procedures.[3] A process can access and modify the application's state through the shared data objects. When a process completes the execution of one of its procedures, it suspends itself and waits for the next occurrence of one of its triggering events.

Processes are time-aware; when invoked, a process has a specific deadline (the absolute point in time when it must complete) and a duration (the maximum computing time budget). A process can provide alternate procedures that each perform the process's task with varying cost and quality; the process can select among alternatives based on its deadline and duration. For example, the Situation Assessment (SA) subsystem in the Pilot's Associate uses alternate methods to answer certain queries regarding the status of external objects, such as enemy fighters and missiles. Given a very short deadline, SA just looks up the value most recently stored in its database, even though that value may not accurately represent the current situation. With more time, SA executes algorithms that quickly extrapolate previous state data to estimate the current state. With still more time, SA uses a rule-based system to take into account heuristic models of threat behavior to produce various estimates qualified by relative degrees of certainty.

The ABE/RT toolkit depicts processes as rectangular boxes. The graphical language does not distinguish between primitive and composite processes when viewed from the outside. Whether primitive or composite, a process is triggered by events and accesses data objects. Using the graphical editor to look into a process reveals its internal structure: composite processes contain yet another structural model, while primitive processes contain a special set of structures for defining the procedures, persistent data, and connections to shared data objects (see Figure 2).

The shared data in a structural model is described in the form of *State-Transition Objects* (STOs), modeled after the State Transition Events of Faulk and Parnas (Faulk and Parnas 1988). STOs have two major functions: they store and maintain shared state data, and they signal events when they detect significant state transitions in their data. As a data repository, an STO is similar to an object in an object-oriented programming system. Each STO contains private persistent data, organized into a number of named *slots*, and a number of *access methods*. Each slot can hold an arbitrary data structure, as defined by the STO. The access methods define the formal interface to the data contained in the slots. A process accesses the state within an STO by sending it a *message*. The method corresponding to that message can read or modify the value of any of the STO's slots. A process can supply additional arguments in a message, which are bound to formal parameters in the methods, and the method can return a value to the process that sent the message.

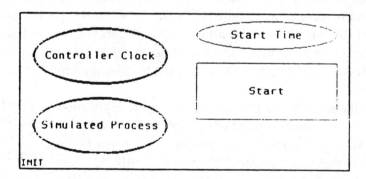

Figure 2. Example of a primitive process. This is a view of the internal structure of the primitive process labeled Init from Figure 1. The Start procedure will be invoked when the Start event at the top-level is passed into Init. The code in the Start procedure can send messages out through its STO connections (ports) Controller_Clock and Simulated_Process to start the controller clock and simulated process; these messages are directed to the appropriate place by the data connections between Init and the STOs of the same names at the top-level. The Start procedure will also store the time at which the application was started in its persistent data area Start_Time.

Unlike processes, a STO's methods do not have their own control threads. When a process sends a message to a STO, the invoked method executes in the control thread of the sending process. Therefore, sending a message is like making a function call. However, special care must be taken to handle concurrency. In general, multiple processes will be executing simultaneously, either with multiple processors or with multiprogramming on a single processor, and more than one process may send a message to the same STO at the same time. To handle this case correctly, each method must use locking or some other synchronization mechanism to insure coherent access to data contained in slots.

The second major function of STOs is to detect significant state transitions in the data they contain and signal the appropriate event (which then will trigger processes). The definition of a significant state transition is application specific, and the responsibility for detecting such a transition lies with the methods which update a STO's slots. This mechanism of event detection insures a strong degree of modularity; the responsibility for signaling an event resides within the object which implements the state transitions defining that event. In the Pilot's Associate the SA subsystem continuously updates a threat database which contains the state of all enemy objects (for example, missiles and aircraft). When the threat database detects a significant change in a threat, such as an enemy fighter closing to within 100 nautical miles, the threat database signals a Fighter_Of_Concern event.

Graphically, the ABE/RT structural language displays STOs as ellipses. Solid arrows from processes to STOs depict messages. By convention, these arrows always point from the process to the STO, although data can travel in both directions in a message transaction. As with processes, STOs may be primitive or composite; Figure 3 shows the internal structure of a primitive STO.

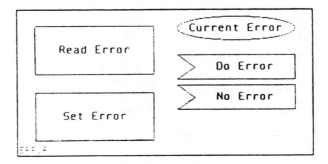

Figure 3. Example of a primitive STO. This is the internal view of the primitive STO in the inside of the Controller process, labeled Error in Figure 4. This STO has one slot, Current_Error, which it uses to store the current process error (deviation of the process from its setpoint). The Read_Error method can be invoked to return the value of Error to a requesting process. The Set_Error method will change the value of Error, but will also signal an event if it detects a significant state change. In this case, significant means the process has gone out of bounds or has come back within bounds. The Set_Error method will signal a Do_Error event in the former case or a No_Error event in the latter. These events will trigger downstream processes shown in Figure 4.

The final components of an ABE/RT structural model are the *event objects*, which connect STOs and processes. In the simplest case an event object provides a global name for an event signaled by a STO to trigger a process. In the general case event objects allow for disjunction of events and the distribution of events to multiple processes. Graphically, event objects are small hollow squares, with multiple event arcs (dashed arrows) entering from STOs and leaving the event object to processes. An event object acts as an or-gate, passing events signaled from any of its inputs to all its outputs. Event objects provide additional modularity between the signaling of events and the triggering of processes based on those events.

The structural description language allows the application architect to define a network of processes, STOs, and event objects. Processes send messages to STOs, which signal events, which trigger other processes. Given a structural model, the language provides a means to embed that model as a unitary process or STO within another model. Such embedding requires adding interface components to the basic structural network. For a composite process, these components include event input ports to allow events to enter the composite from the outside, and STO ports to forward messages from processes in the composite to STOs outside the composite. For a composite STO, event output ports allow events to pass out from the composite STO, and STO ports allow messages to enter the composite STO. Event objects are primitive and cannot be decomposed. See Figure 4 for an example of a composite process and Figure 5 for a composite STO.

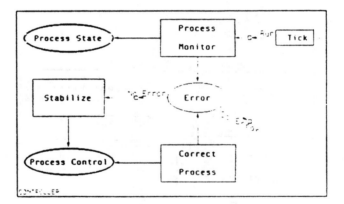

Figure 4. Example of a composite process. This is a view of the inside of the Controller process from Figure 1. We refer to Controller as a composite process because it is composed of more processes and STOs. When Controller receives a clock event through its event input Tick, the Process_Monitor process sends a message through the STO port Process_State to return the current value of the process state, which it then writes into the STO Error (whose internals are shown in Figure 3). If Error signals the Do_Error event, the process Correct_Process will send a message through the Process_Control STO port to change the simulated process' rate. If Error signals a No_Error event the process Stabilize will be triggered to reset the simulated process' rate to a reasonable value.

710

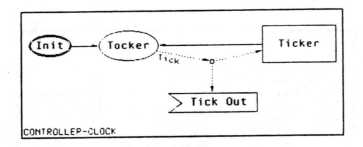

Figure 5. Example of a composite STO. CONTROLLER_CLOCK is a simple composite STO which periodically produces an output event; this is a view of the STO labeled Controller_Clock in Figure 1. A start message received in the Init STO port is forwarded to the Tocker STO, which immediately signals the Tick event. This event both triggers the process Ticker and exits the composite STO via the event output Tick_Out, where it will trigger Process_Monitor in the controller (as shown in Figure 4). Meanwhile, Ticker waits for a predetermined period of time and then sends a message to Tocker, which signals Tick again, and the cycle repeats.

The composition operators provide means to build abstractions which can control the model's level of apparent complexity. However, the use of hierarchical models does not imply any particular subroutine-call or function-nesting form of the code which implements the model, nor does it imply additional communication overheads in traversing levels. The semantics (that is, the interpretation) of the structural language is unaffected by the use of composite processes or data objects. We guarantee this by providing compilers which collapse a hierarchical model into an equivalent flat model before execution.

To summarize, here are some of the important points about our structural model.

- State persists over time; however, an event is instantaneous and does not persist. If the programmer wants other behavior, such as a queue of events, it must be programmed explicitly. Not all state changes are of interest, so not all transitions indicate an event, and any number of transitions may entail the same event. Finally, any number of processes may write to an object and any number may wait on an event's occurrence, but no process is explicitly aware of any other.
- Structurally, the modeling approach is extremely flexible. Both objects and processes may be nested arbitrarily with each other. We place no restrictions on the language used to write a primitive process' procedures or an STO's methods.
- Processes do not signal one another; instead they share access to objects through defined interface functions, as in object-oriented programming. This means that processes do not wait for signals from other specific processes or necessarily even know their names. Rather, each process waits for state changes induced on objects of interest to it by any processes that affect those objects. This provides a high degree of abstraction.

2.2. Event processing plans

The ABE/RT timeliness specification language centers on a concept called an *Event Processing Plan* (EPP). An EPP consists of a triggering event (the *trigger*), a directed acyclic graph of processes rooted at the trigger which must execute in response to that event, and the timeliness requirements for that response. Figure 6 illustrates the EPP concept with an

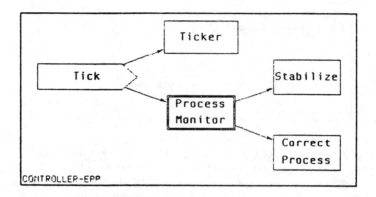

Figure 6 Example of an EPP (Event Processing Plan). This EPP specifies the thread of processes which make up the controller. The trigger Tick corresponds to the like-named event in Figure 5. When that event is signaled two parallel branches start executing. The upper branch (Ticker) runs the controller clock again, causing another clock event one clock period later. The lower branch starts the controller proper. Process_Monitor is an embedded EPP which runs the composite process of the same name in Figure 4. After it completes, one of Stabilize or Correct_Process may execute, as described in Figure 3 and Figure 4.

example. An EPP is a plan for achieving a timely response to a critical event. Typically, one or more EPPs will be written for each of the application's functional requirements. In the Pilot's Associate, there are a number of EPPs which are triggered by significant changes in the external world, such as the detection of a missile launch. Each distinct external event has its own EPP; a typical EPP specifies that the Pilot's Associate first assess the external situation, generate a planned response to the situation, and finally propose that planned response to the pilot. Note also that EPPs often cross subsystem boundaries.

EPPs relate the structure of an application to its functional requirements (input-output behavior) by specifying the timely execution threads through the structure. The trigger and processes in an EPP must exist in the structural model of the application. Furthermore, the processes in an EPP must be logically linked in the structure chart: this is, each process-to-process link in an EPP must have a corresponding process-STO-event-process path in the structural model. In essence, an EPP is an abstraction of a path through the structural model, created for several reasons:

- The processes in an EPP can span multiple levels in the structure hierarchy, so it is difficult if not impossible to view the entire path at once.
- A single process can serve in multiple EPPs (that is, take part in many paths), with a different timeliness specification for each (see below).
- The intervening STOs do not contribute to the timeliness specification, as any time spent in an STO method is charged to the process that sent the corresponding message.

The timeliness specification in an EPP takes the form of a *process budget table*, which specifies the deadline, duration, and priority for executing each process in the EPP, as well as for the EPP as a whole (see Figure 7). The deadline specifies that point in time when the process or EPP must finish its execution, relative to the time the triggering event

```
;;; The :WHOLE entry refers to the EPP's target values.  The other
;;; entries refer to the actual values for (:RTO) processes, or the
;;; multipliers for nested epps (:EPP).   The formats are:
;;;
;;; (:whole <name> (<mode> <deadline> <duration> <priority>) ...)
;;; (:rt0 <name> (<mode> <deadline> <duration> <priority>) ...)
;;; (:epp <name> (<mode> <multiplier>) ...)
;;;
;;; <name>       symbol naming the component of the EPP
;;; <mode>       keyword naming a mode of the application
;;; <deadline>   number of milliseconds after the trigger event
;;; <duration>   absolute value in milliseconds
;;; <priority>   integer: 0 = required, >0 lower priority, <0 never run
;;; <multiplier> number


((:WHOLE CONTROLLER-EPP
    (:NORMAL 7000 4000 0)   (:EMERGENCY 5000 4000 0))
 (:RTO    TICKER
    (:NORMAL 3000 2800 0)   (:EMERGENCY 3000 2800 0))
 (:RTO    STABILIZE
    (:NORMAL 7000  500 0)   (:EMERGENCY 5000  200 0))
 (:RTO    CORRECT_PROCESS
    (:NORMAL 7000  500 0)   (:EMERGENCY 5000  200 0))
 (:EPP    PROCESS_MONITOR
    (:NORMAL 1.0)           (:EMERGENCY 0.75)))
```

Figure 7. Example of an EPP's process budget table. This is the process budget table for the EPP shown in Figure 6, showing the developer-supplied scheduling information. The comments in the figure describe the format of the annotations. Modes are described in Section 2.3; for now notice that the deadlines and durations specified are shorter for :EMERGENCY mode than for :NORMAL mode. The last entry in the table for the embedded EPP PROCESS_MONITOR specifies a multiplier for modulating the allocations specified in the embedded EPP in this particular context. The (:EMERGENCY 0.75) entry specifies that in the named mode all deadlines and durations specified in the embedded EPP should be scaled by the given factor; this capability allows one to reuse a common EPP in many contexts with different timeliness requirements.

occurred. The duration specifies an upper bound on the processor time a process may use, or for an EPP. the upper bound on the time consumed by all processes which constitute the EPP. The priority specifies whether the process or EPP is mandatory or optional, and if optional, its priority relative to other optional processes. These quantities are used by the scheduler to determine when to execute a process relative to all other processes which have been triggered. and are also supplied to the process when it is scheduled to run to allow it to select among its alternative methods.

The ABE/RT EPP language provides a graphical editor for building the EPP process graphs, a tabular editor for entering the process budget table, and a composition operator for building hierarchical EPP structures. This last capability has proven particularly useful in the Pilot's Associate domain as a way of reusing common execution subthreads. For example. all Pilot's Associate subsystems must present plans they generate to the pilot for approval. and the Pilot Vehicle Interface mediates each interaction with the pilot. By defining a single Propose_Plan_To_Pilot EPP, the system architect avoids the work of recreating an equivalent thread in every EPP that needs to propose plans. As with the structural language. we supply a compiler to convert a hierarchical EPP structure into an equivalent flat structure.

The scheduler does not schedule an entire EPP as a whole. Instead, it accepts processes to schedule as they are triggered by events. When a process is triggered the scheduler looks in the process budget table of the EPP which contains the process and uses the deadline and duration allocation it finds there to determine when to execute the process. This scheme allows some variability in an EPP's execution; the execution of any branch in an EPP can end at any point if the corresponding event is not signaled. In the general case, however, the application architect will still have to verify timeliness assuming the entire set of processes in an EPP execute.

Allowing reusable EPPs can cause a complication when a single process is triggered by different EPPs. This causes a problem when the different EPPs specify different deadlines and durations. We avoid possible confusion by associating each process instance in the scheduler's queue with the EPP that triggered that process; this allows the scheduler to determine the correct budget for each instance in the queue.

The EPP language does place some restrictions on the kinds of behavior the application can exhibit. It is not permissible to jump into an EPP, as the scheduler will have no way of determining a deadline because there was no triggering event. The execution along a branch cannot skip a process; this follows from the correspondence between the structural model and the EPP. An EPP may not contain loops, as there is not way to guarantee that the loop will execute in finite time; deterministic looping can be expressed by unfolding and replicating the loop in the EPP. Finally, no process may execute unless it is contained in an active EPP; otherwise the scheduler has no way to determine the process' deadline and duration. The ABE/RT development environment relaxes some of these restrictions, allowing the model to execute by providing default deadline and durations where necessary, while logging information that will help the architect to later detect and resolve these problems.

In summary, an application's EPPs define the timely threads of activity (connected executions of processes) through the structural model. An EPP defines the budget for each of its constituent processes, and the budget is used by the scheduler to determine when to schedule a process for execution.

2.3. Resource allocation

The third form of information required by the ABE/RT model is the way the application allocates its scarce processing resources. We have identified three aspects to this resource allocation problem:

1. How are the resources available to the application partitioned among the application's various functions in a coherent manner?
2. How are resources reallocated when the current allocation is inadequate to maintain acceptable performance in the application's current operational context?
3. How are processes and STOs assigned to processors?

We will consider each question in order.

The ABE/RT model requires the application architect to allocate processing resources to various groups of application activities. These groups, called *areas*, form an exhaustive partition of the application's EPPs. The resource allocation takes the form of a pie chart, with each area allocated a different slice of the pie. The size of the slice determines the amount of processing resources available to all the EPPs in an area; these resources are then subdivided into the deadlines and durations for individual EPPs, and finally to the processes within the EPPs. The ABE/RT resource allocation language allows an application architect to create areas, assign EPPs to areas, and partition the resource pie among those areas.

The application's workload varies in response to events generated by both the application itself and the environment within which the application operates. This changing workload puts various time stresses on the application. For example, in certain circumstances the instantaneous processing power required by all the Pilot's Associate functions can jump from ~20 MIPS (million instructions per second) to ~60 MIPS in a four-second period (Smith and Barnette 1989). Clearly, the application must have a means for changing its process budgets dynamically to insure that it is doing the most valuable set of tasks at any point in time.

The ABE/RT model defines a *mode* as a particular allocation of resources to all the possible activities within an application, expressed as a particular division of the resource pie among the applications areas and, in turn, the allocation of deadlines, durations, and priorities in all of its EPPs. Based on analysis and experimentation, the application architect can define alternate modes, each with its own unique resource allocation. Each mode is tuned to maximize the application's value in some set of circumstances. When the application detects a change in the system's state that necessitates a mode change, the application refocuses its attention by redirecting resources to the current highest-value activities. The process of changing a mode can be quite fast, as it requires only the replacement of the current process allocation tables with those associated with the new mode, which ABE/RT implements by index manipulation. All newly-triggered processes will use the new mode's allocation tables without further intervention.

The preceding paragraph described a mechanism for specifying and changing modes, but left many open design questions:

How does the application detect mode changes?
We have not prescribed any particular means for detecting when the state of the application and its environment necessitate a mode change. A likely candidate is StateCharts (Harel 1987), a powerful and novel approach to hierarchical state machines. Note that detecting mode changes is the only runtime control reasoning in the ABE/RT model.

What happens to the processes already scheduled when a mode change occurs?
We have considered three approaches to this question: (1) not doing anything, which lets the currently scheduled processes run under the old mode's budget (the ABE/RT default); (2) recalculating the budgets for all processes according to the new mode; and (3) allowing the application to specify an arbitrary function which cleans up the agenda in an application-specific way. Each alternative has its advantages and disadvantages, and we expect that characteristics of the particular application will dictate the best solution.

How many modes does an application need?

Underlying this question is the fact that creating a new mode is an expensive task for the application architects and engineers, because deadlines, durations, and other scheduling information needs to be specified for each process in each mode. This is a methodological question, and one for which we do not yet have a good answer.

Is this approach to resource allocation non-modular, making maintenance difficult?

The problem of resource allocation is inherently non-modular, as any resources allocated to one activity are not available for any other activities. This problem is made more difficult if the allocation of processes to processors is static (see below). The use of areas helps to reduce the complexity by breaking the problem into smaller pieces. One possible solution suggested by Lesser[4] is to reason about the differential utility of various EPPs in different operational contexts, and thereby automatically derive resource allocations. However, this approach will not work for mission-critical systems like the Pilot's Associate because of their verification and validation requirements.

Finally, the ABE/RT resource allocation language includes a tabular editor to specify the allocation of processes and STOs to processors. While this seems like a straightforward task, it is complicated by the dynamic reallocation caused by mode changes. Assuming a fixed allocation of processes to processors, with no duplication or process migration, the task becomes one of balancing processor load for all possible modes. Again, we have not fully addressed this problem and do not have a good solution at this time.

2.4. Methodology

The preceding sections described the structure, timeliness, and resource allocation languages within which an application architect can build models. However, the utility of these tools requires a good methodology for applying the tools to produce results. We have been developing a methodology incrementally, based on our own intuitions and experiences gained working with the Pilot's Associate. This section describes some elements of our evolving methodology.

Simulate early and often. The ability to run simulations on models has been an invaluable aid in understanding the operation of an application. The simulation tools allow an architect to start from scratch and build an executable model in less than an hour. In this nascent model the processes will contain stub code which sends empty messages to stub STOs. Even with this level of detail, however, the architect can begin to understand the dynamics of the application. As the fidelity of the stub code improves incrementally, the model evolves. Adding calls to wait functions which represent the operation of actual code is the first type of enhancement we typically make.[5]

Order the development. The order in which we introduced language concepts in this section corresponds to an ideal order for building models. Addressing issues of structure, timeliness, and resource allocation in that order maximizes the value of the model as a communication device and minimizes feedback which can cause extensive redesign. The software tools also support this approach by providing a simulation environment which operates on structural models alone, on structural models with EPPs, or on complete models with structure, EPPs, and modes.

Guarantee timeliness through experimentation and analysis. Our approach to specifying timeliness places the responsibility on the application developer to determine valid upper bounds on process duration. The only way to produce these bounds is by extensive experimentation. The penalty for providing safe but overly pessimistic bounds is a loss of scheduling efficiency. One particular tactic is to look for a process with a bimodal distribution of durations, which suggests that the process may be executing two different paths through its procedure. After identifying these paths a developer can split the process into two distinct processes, each with a tighter upper bound.

Given good estimates on process duration, a combination of experimentation and analysis is required to verify that the application will meet its deadlines. We plan to extend the ABE/RT Toolkit with additional experimentation and analysis tools to support this task. Analytic tools such as Scheduler 1-2-3 (Tokuda and Kotera 1988) are also particularly appropriate.

Add modes on demand. Our approach in developing the Pilot's Associate is to avoid creating new modes wherever possible. See Figure 8 for a description of this methodology.

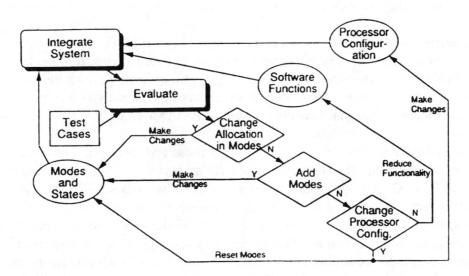

Figure 8. Methodology for adding modes. Starting with a complete model of an application and a description of the available target processors and modes, we run a simulation and evaluate the performance of the model. When the analysis shows that the application has a consistent resource deficit (that is, it misses deadlines), we characterize the external and internal situations which cause the problem. We first try to modify the mode running in that situation or find another existing mode which performs satisfactorily in the problem situation. If that does not work, we will have to create a new mode. If the number of modes becomes too large we will have to examine whether we are trying to squeeze too much functionality onto too little hardware. If so, we can either reduce the functionality or add more hardware; however, the latter choice will force us to discard all existing modes and start the mode definition process from scratch.

Allocate deadlines top-down, durations bottom-up. When assigning the deadlines in an EPP, work top-down from the EPP to its constituent processes. Conversely, when assigning durations start from the processes and aggregate up to the EPP. This sets up a reasonable strawman structure which seeds the experimentation process.

2.5. Development and experimentation tools

The ABE/RT Toolkit contains a number of development and experimentation facilities integrated with the language tools which support the task of model development and experimentation. It also supports translating a model to a target hardware environment. We will discuss these tools briefly here.

Simulation Harness. The Simulation Harness provides a what-if environment for simulating a variety of changes to an application model or its target environment. The Harness defines a virtual target hardware environment which supports multiple target processors, each with its own clock which can run at its own rate. By synchronizing the virtual clocks on each simulated processor, the Harness can simulate the effect of speeding up or slowing down an individual process or groups of processes. In the Pilot's Associate we are using the Harness to model the effects of a change of implementation language from Lisp to C, the change in performance due to increasing knowledge-base size, and changes in the power of the individual target processors. The Harness generates logs of simulation runs that can be examined using the Log Analyzer.

Log Analyzer. The Log Analyzer is a tool for graphically displaying the results of a simulation run, charting the activity of processes vs. time in a format similar to hardware logic analyzers. The Analyzer operates on logs collected automatically during the execution of a model, and it has proven invaluable in the debugging and analysis of time-dependent systems. Figure 9 shows an example of the Log Analyzer in use.

RT++ executive and model compiler. Given a tested and debugged application model, the next step in fielding the application is to translate that model to a prototyping environment, such as a C++ language environment on a UNIX workstation. The ABE/RT Toolkit includes a high-performance executive called RT++ which operates on a Sun Workstation and implements the runtime functions of the ABE/RT languages, such as processes and STO creation, event signaling, EPPs, modes, and scheduling. To simplify the port, the Toolkit also includes a compiler which translates a model into C++ code frames into which implementors can insert prototype code. The RT++ executive also supports logging hooks which can capture data for display on the Log Analyzer.

3. Results and status

We have implemented the ABE/RT Toolkit as described here in CommonLisp and as an extension to the basic ABE system, running on Symbolics computers. The RT++ executive has been implemented in C++ and runs on Sun Workstations under the SunOS 4.0 operating system.

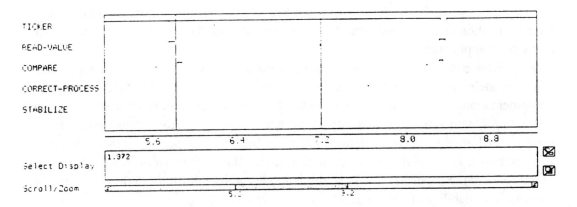

Figure 9. Example of the Log Analyzer. This shows a view of a run of an application, after the user has zoomed in to view a small section of the log; the scale near the bottom (5.6, 6.4, etc.) shows the time in seconds of that section. The left column names processes whose execution was logged. A solid horizontal line to the right of the process name indicates a period of time when that process was executing and a small dot indicates the declared deadline, relative to the start of the process.

The two vertical cursor lines on either side of 6.4 form an interactive measuring tool the user is manipulating. Here, the user marked the end of an execution of the READ-VALUE process with the left vertical cursor and the deadline of that process with the right cursor; the number in the Select Display line near the bottom reads off the distance between the two cursors, and shows that the process beat its deadline by 1.372 seconds. The Log Analyzer has a number of other kinds of interactive analysis tools.

The Toolkit was developed initially for the Real-Time Risk Reduction program of the Lockheed Pilot's Associate program, and our experience with the Pilot's Associate application has focused our development efforts and provided valuable feedback. We have completed a structural model for the entire breadth of the Pilot's Associate, going down several levels of detail. This model has approximately 110 processes, of which approximately 20 are composite; 85 STO's; and 80 events. We have constructed this model with about two person-months effort over the past twelve months. We have recently begun designing and testing EPPs and modes for that model.

Three other groups within the Lockheed Pilot's Associate effort, all at different sites, have started using the ABE/RT Toolkit to reimplement their respective subsystems, which they had originally implemented without concerns for time-critical response.

- One of these has, in a period of three months, modularized their original CommonLisp implementation and reorganized their pieces within the ABE/RT toolkit, so that it is now complete with its former functionality.
- A second group has built a complete model of their subsystem, with the code in the procedures stubbed out. They have begun performing experiments on this model, evaluating the performance impacts of various architectural decisions.
- Because their subsystem's design was fundamentally at odds with real-time concerns, the third group has been redesigning their subsystem from scratch. They are using ABE/RT to do that in a top-down manner. They have been at this for about three months, with much of the effort to date concentrated on conceptual design.

In addition, on another project we have worked with several developers and have modeled their application in a few days, including incorporating into the model some pieces of their preexisting application code.

In all these endeavors, the Toolkit has demonstrated its value in producing executable system models, which serve both to communicate designs and to guide further design and implementation. The structural language has been robust enough to express a variety of interesting system structures in highly perspicuous ways, especially when viewed through the animated graphical representation. Although we have just begun extensive use of the EPP language, our initial experience indicates that the EPP concept is sound. We have only just begun to experiment with multiple modes and do not have enough data to comment on the viability of that concept.

We have been using the Log Analyzer for more than a year; it has been extremely valuable both for debugging the applications as they are developed and for understanding the dynamics of their execution, especially relationships among concurrent processes. We expect it will prove very valuable also for tuning EPPs and resource allocations. We have just begun using the Harness and the RT++ facilities, and to develop other analysis tools in addition to the Log Analyzer.

Based on the experiences of our user-base, we plan to extend the language with two particular features. First, we will provide better support for periodic tasks. Models built to-date, including both Pilot's Associate and the process controller example shown in the figures here, have used an explicit clock to trigger periodic activities; while this idiom has proven adequate it complicates the model. Our proposed solution introduces a new event object type, a *periodic event*, which generates events at a user-specified frequency.

Another common model structure we have seen occurs when a process, triggered by an event, needs additional data from the STO that signaled the event. The process' first action is to read the data which caused the event (for example, a new threat written to a threat database) by sending a message back to the STO which signaled the event. As with periodic processes, this idiom complicates the structural models. The solution here is to introduce new event types which include mailbox and queue functionality. A STO will supply an argument when it signals an event of one of these types. A mailbox associated with the event has storage to hold a single datum, which it makes available to any processes it triggers, while a queue can store a user-specificable number of data items. Both of these changes, while not increasing the expressive power of the language, will reduce the complexity of structural models and possibly increase the efficiency of the interpreters as well.

Finally, we have noted several areas for improving the language editors. In particular, we plan to develop tools to help enforce consistency between EPPs and structural models, to help define exclusion relations (locking) in primitive STO messages, and tools for producing intelligent default deadlines and durations in EPPs and resource assignments for areas.

Overall, the Toolkit appears to be valuable for developing the Pilot's Associate application. As we are now moving into more advanced stages of that development, especially stressing the aspects of timely response and modeling the delivery hardware and software, we will continue to both test out the Toolkit and refine it.

4. Conclusion

We have identified a class of important problems called timely intelligent systems. These are characterized by a need for guaranteed timeliness in behaviors that are produced using, among other methods, one or more of the familiar AI paradigms such as blackboards and rule-based systems. Our paper has described contributions in three principal areas. First, we have formulated a set of three interlocking languages for describing key facets of timely systems: structures, timely functions, and resource allocation. Second, we have identified and addressed key methodological steps involved in using these languages in the evolutionary development of applications, from initial modeling and experimentation through prototyping to final fielding. Third, we have developed tools for supporting this evolutionary development process.

While there are many dimensions of AI and real-time systems, and many efforts outside the limits of our approach, we feel confident that we have selected an important class of problems and produced an excellent set of concepts and tools for handling it.

Acknowledgments

Many individuals have made important and substantial contributions to the development of ABE/RT and to its use on the Lockheed Pilot's Associate project. We gratefully acknowledge in particular the contributions of Terry Barnes, Wayne Caplinger, Keith Cooley, Alan Garvey, Russ Irving, and Bob Schulman.

(ABE is a trademark of Cimflex Teknowledge Corp. Ada is a registered trademark of the U.S. Government (Ada Joint Program Office). Sun Workstation is a registered trademark of Sun Microsystems Inc. Symbolics is a trademark of Symbolics, Inc. UNIX is a registered trademark of AT&T Bell Laboratories.)

Notes

1. The ABE RT technology was initially funded with the ABE development work under a DARPA/RADC contract to Teknowledge Federal Systems. The further development and application of the toolkit to Pilot's Associate is supported in the Real-Time Risk Reduction sub-project within the Lockheed Pilot's Associate effort, funded by DARPA/WRDC; Cimflex Teknowledge has a central role in that effort in determining the real-time architecture of the Pilot's Associate as it enters its Phase II in 1990.

2. This is especially true for the subset of the tasks within the application that are mandatory. We expect that run-time control reasoning will be useful sooner for allocating slack resources to optional tasks. But we are concentrating our efforts on the mandatory tasks.

3. In fact, the act of starting a process executing one of its procedures is controlled by a scheduler, which will be discussed later.

4. Personal communication.

5. The Simulation Harness (see Section 2.5) provides functions that simulate waiting for an arbitrary length of time, while not actually slowing the simulation.

References

CASE for Real-Time Systems Symposium, Digital Consulting, Andover, MA, Summer 1989.

Decker, K.S., V.R. Lesser, and R.C. Whitehair. 1990. Extending a Blackboard Architecture for Approximate Processing. *Real-Time Systems*, 2, 1, (Feb.).

Erman, L.D., Lark, J.S., and Hayes-Roth, F. 1988. ABE: An Environment for Engineering Intelligent Systems. *IEEE Trans. Software Eng.*, 14, 12, (Dec.).

Faulk, S.R. and D.L. Parnas. 1988. On Synchronization in Hard-Real-Time Systems. *Communications of the ACM*. 1989. 31, 3, (Mar.):274–287.

Harel, D. 1987. Statecharts: A Visual Formalism for Complex Systems. In *Science of Computer Programming*, 8.

Hayes-Roth, B. 1990. Architectural Foundations for Real-Time Performance in Intelligent Agents. *Real-Time Systems*, 2, 1, (Feb.).

Hayes-Roth, F., L.D. Erman, S. Fouse, J.S. Lark, and J. Davidson. 1989. ABE: A Cooperative Operating System and Development Environment. In *AI Tools and Techniques*, M. Richer, (ed.), Norwood, NJ: Ablex Publishing; 1989, 323–355. Reprinted in A. Bond and L. Gasser (eds.), *Readings in Distributed Artificial Intelligence*, Morgan-Kaufman, 1988, 457–488.

Howe, A.E., D.M. Hart, and P.R. Cohen. 1990. Addressing Real-Time Constraints in the Design of Autonomous Agents. *Real-Time Systems*, 2, 1, (Feb.).

Smith, D., and J.N. Barnette. 1989. Pilot's Associate Processing Requirements. *AIAA/AHS/ASEE Aircraft Design, Systems and Operations Conference*, Seattle, WA, July.

Smith, D., and Broadwell, M. 1988. The Pilot's Associate—An Overview. *SAE Aerotech Conference*, Los Angeles, CA, May.

Tokuda, H., and M. Kotera. 1988. Scheduler 1-2-3. Tech. report CMU-CS-88-179, Carnegie Mellon Univ., Computer Science Dept., June.

INTELLIGENT REAL-TIME CONTROL OF ROBOTIC VEHICLES

David W. Payton

Thomas E. Bihari

Driven by the need to control complex activities in unstructured domains, control software designers have recently been combining concepts from artificial intelligence (AI), real-time systems, and control theory to develop Intelligent Real-Time Controllers (IRTCs). This is a relatively new field, and alternative design philosophies are currently being examined. In our work on two large-scale intelligent vehicles, we have explored the relationship between system design and timing constraints and have arrived at different solutions to what appear, on the surface, to be similar problems. ✳ IRTCs are appropriate whenever time-critical decision-making functions are required within a control system. To understand the nature of these systems, it is helpful to understand the relevant attributes from the associated fields. ✳ *Control.* An IRTC usually controls some physical system or *plant* in the real world. Therefore, the IRTC is tightly coupled to the plant, and must react to events and states in the plant. The IRTC has the ability to sense part of the state of the plant, and to change part of the state of the plant. The plant is usually not a docile slave of the IRTC. Left alone, the plant could go out of control—possibly with dangerous results. ✳ *Real time.* In a real-time system, the specification of system correctness contains constraints related to time in the real world. These constraints may be expressed as explicit functions of time, or they may be implicit in other constraints (for example, in the allowable relative positions and velocities of two aircraft). Thus, in a real-time system, all constraints on resources and correct behavior are compounded by the addition of strict time constraints. This is a significant problem for real-time systems. In non-real-time systems, time is a resource that can be consumed to meet the other constraints. Constraints on computer memory or the required accuracy of a function may be rigid, but time can be used freely, within reason, to allow the system to meet these con-

straints. In many real-time systems there are no unconstrained resources. ✳ *Intelligent.* In the context of an IRTC, we suggest that the controller becomes more intelligent as it is given more capabilities to respond to its environment autonomously, without detailed external guidance. In a traditional real-time control system, the problem usually entails providing the most faithful transformation of externally provided control signals into physical actions. A real-time system is considered intelligent when, with minimal external guidance, it can perform complex actions in response to the sensed environment. Intelligence may include the ability to accept abstract task specifications in the form of general goals and constraints, and produce reasonable actions that are in accord with these specifications.

✳ In any real-time intelligent system, there is a fundamental trade-off between acting and reasoning. Time is a valuable resource that is lost if the system must reason about actions before performing them. This loss of time may limit the number of suitable action alternatives and thereby make the reasoning task even more difficult. In some cases, failure to act can be the worst possible action. Any action at all might be better than doing nothing. On the other hand, time spent reasoning can often avert future delays or disaster. Reasoning can become critical for safety and survival when actions entailing a great deal of commitment are involved. ✳ The effectiveness of an intelligent real-time system depends on its ability to partition reasoning efforts in accord with the demands of its environment and the available sensory inputs. This partitioning is usually difficult because of extreme information overload [10]. The visible state of the physical system is huge, and may contain incomplete or contradictory information. This information may change rapidly. It is impossible for the IRTC to fully digest the information and choose an optimal course of action within the given time constraints. Therefore,

"Intelligent Real-Time Control of Robotic Vehicles" by D.W. Payton and T.E. Bihari from *CACM*, Vol. 34, No. 8, August 1991, pp. 48-63. Copyright © 1991 by The Association for Computing Machinery, Inc., reprinted by permission.

the IRTC must choose to focus its attention on important subproblems, and allocate resources accordingly. However, determining the importance of a particular problem is difficult, and the importance may change rapidly.

System architects have explored numerous alternatives for partitioning an IRTC in order to gain the maximum benefit from limited computational resources. Approaches vary in how they deal with timing constraints and in how they allocate different responsibilities for decision making and control.

Timing Constraints: A Characterization

A variety of formalisms, including Petri nets [13], real-time logic [11], epistemic logic [27], and graph theory [9], have been used to specify and analyze timing constraints. All timing constraints eventually distill down to requirements on what actions to perform, and when to perform them. Given a correct set of timing constraints, it is necessary to allocate the available resources, including computers, sensors and actuators, over time.

Resource allocation requires a measure of the value of performing a particular action at a particular time. This is frequently represented as a value function:

VALUE = F(TIME). Given suitable value functions, scheduling algorithms can allocate resources effectively, even in overload conditions [29]. However, in the complex worlds inhabited by IRTCs, the development of value functions can be difficult. The value of an action at a particular time is closely linked to other constraints in the system, such as velocity, safety, and other timing constraints.

In practice, timing constraints are frequently characterized by two somewhat independent measures: *hardness* and *criticalness*. A timing constraint is hard if small violations of the constraint result in significant drops in a computation's value. Otherwise, the constraint is soft. Criticalness is a measure of the

range of the value. Highly critical constraints are frequently associated with essential system goals, while optional system goals result in less critical constraints.

Because real-time systems are usually constrained in all resources, and because the values of particular actions vary over time, IRTCs must be able to adjust the timeliness, reliability, and performance of the system to best meet the overall goals of the system [6,25]. A timing constraint is *negotiable* at a particular time if it can be relaxed, usually in exchange for constriction of some other constraint. This other constraint may be a timing constraint, or some quality constraint relating to system performance, reliability or cost.

Negotiability is tied to the concept of *guarantees* [28] made between producers and consumers of services. A producer and consumer may have a great deal of flexibility in negotiating a timing constraint on the delivery of a service. Once an agreement has been reached, however, the timing constraint may be both hard and critical. The abilities to negotiate timing constraints, and to guarantee their fulfillment, are keys to effective resource scheduling in an IRTC.

Sources of Timing Constraints

In principal, all timing constraints can be characterized within this uniform model. In practice, however, qualitative differences in hardness, criticalness, and negotiability arise from the different types of objects and relationships in the system. These qualitative differences, in turn, give rise to different ways of handling the constraints.

The timing constraints in many real-time systems are the result of the need for plant stability. These timing constraints are affected by

the plant's innate physical characteristics. For example, servo-control of a flexible robot arm depends on the mass and dimensions of the arm's links. Timing constraints for such a system can usually be described as a continuous range of acceptable timing values, with correspondingly continuous levels of physical accuracy. The constraints are negotiable within the acceptable range. Servo-control timing constraints are usually very critical, since failure to operate within the acceptable range can result in serious system instability.

In many systems, the subsystems form producer-consumer relationships. For example, a robot's motion planner may produce a motion plan which is consumed steadily by the robot's servo controller. In turn, the controller's timing constraints are driven by the robot's physical characteristics, as we discussed. The motion planner must therefore produce the plan at a steady rate. This is a synchronization constraint which imposes a hard timing constraint: the planner must generate new planned motions before the current motions are completed. Interposing a queue between the planner and controller allows more timing flexibility, at the cost of a lag in the performance of planned motions.

Humans have their own timing constraints. For example, a human pilot of a fly-by-wire vehicle requires consistent response time to joystick inputs. In such cases, consistent response time may be more important than fast best-case response time, since the pilot may plan joystick inputs based on an abstract model of the "personality" of the vehicle.

Immediacy vs. Assimilation

A number of timing constraints result directly from the manner in which the system resources are partitioned between providing immediate responses and performing time-consuming assimilation of data. Assimilation can be used for a variety of purposes, ranging from the construction of more accurate representations from inaccurate data sources to the production of plans. Assimilation may be performed on data gathered from a single sensor over a period of time, or from several sensors simultaneously. In either case, assimilation introduces some latency between sensing and action. When such latencies are unacceptable, the system must be designed to respond immediately using less refined information.

Nearly all IRTC architectures support decision-making tasks that range across the immediacy/assimilation spectrum. However, the nature of the decision-making tasks performed with different levels of immediacy and assimilation can vary significantly from one architecture to the next. Some architectures concentrate decision-making tasks at fairly high levels of assimilation, constructing accurate models of the world from sensor data, and using these models to plan robot actions [7,16,17]. Other architectures have emphasized the use of immediate data for decision-making [1,3,5,18,23]. These architectures take advantage of the fact that the ability to revise decisions at very high rates can often simplify their decision-making tasks.

Architectures that emphasize assimilation of data work from the perspective of obtaining relatively complete and accurate information about the current state of the system before deciding on future actions. Often, an internal world representation is constructed that anticipates environmental constraints along the system's projected state trajectory. If a course of action can be planned far enough into the future, then new data may be assimilated as the planned course of action is being executed. When the environment changes, however, the internal world model may become invalid. Such changes may force the current course of action to be interrupted. Therefore, special care must be taken to monitor immediate data for exceptions to the

planned actions.

Architectures that emphasize use of immediate data tend to make do with partial and inaccurate state information. These systems rely more on direct sensory-action control loops than on internal world models. Rather than performing lengthy computations to project and evaluate future state trajectories, these systems compute and execute actions one small step at a time. Consequently, each decision-making step can make use of the most recently acquired data. This allows these systems to respond very well to a constantly changing environment. In many cases, random errors and inconsistencies in data can be filtered through the dynamics of the plant itself rather than through computationally expensive statistical procedures. The weakness of immediate actions, however, is that some tasks require anticipation of future consequences. Anticipatory responses must either be compiled into immediate actions, or obtained from complementary methods involving higher degrees of assimilation.

Regardless of whether an architecture emphasizes immediacy or assimilation, there will always be many actions that an intelligent agent must perform before it has a chance to obtain a complete assessment of its current state. For example, it may be necessary to avoid a hazard before there is time to assess all possible paths for avoidance. Such actions may be suboptimal when considered in the absence of time constraints. However, when time is taken into account, these actions may be the best possible under the given circumstances. Taking the time to assess the alternatives may leave no time to execute the best alternative once it is found. To design a truly responsive

system, these time-critical responses should be identified. Highest priority should then be placed on computing whatever partial state information is needed to perform these actions.

The Locus of Control

In most control architectures, an understanding of how decision-making responsibilities are divided among components reveals a great deal about how the architecture will function. The responsibilities for different aspects of a control problem are usually divided among distinct modules. Each module usually is assigned a certain responsibility to achieve particular objectives. Modules often depend on one another in order to achieve their own objectives and the objectives of the system as a whole. These dependencies are usually established through clearly defined communication pathways between modules. The type of communication between modules and the type of responsibilities assigned to different modules have a significant impact on the way the system will interact with its environment.

The decision-making responsibility within a real-time system may be partitioned as a carefully ordered decomposition of specialized tasks at one extreme, or as a loosely ordered cooperation between shared tasks at the other. The first case is usually considered a form of centralized control, while the latter is considered to be decentralized control. While few systems lie entirely at one extreme or the other, most systems tend to lean toward one of these extremes. The differences between these extremes can be illustrated by a comparison between two possible approaches to mobile robot control.

Centralized Control

As an example of centralized control, we can consider a simple control hierarchy that consists of a motion planner and a motion controller. The motion planner might acquire data about the environment

from sensors, construct an internal model of the world from this data, and then project alternate paths for the robot within this model to find the best choice of action. Once a course of action is determined, this might be expressed to the motion controller as a trajectory of points in some fixed Cartesian coordinate frame. The job of the motion controller then would be to follow this trajectory as accurately as possible.

It is helpful to examine how real-time constraints and decision-making responsibilities are partitioned in this example. The motion controller has a critical real-time function to accurately steer the robot along a smooth path which passes over the specified points. Typically, this will require computation of the error between commanded positions and the actual position in the world. Appropriate steering corrections may then be determined in accord with these errors. All aspects of hard real-time constraints within the motion controller relate to its ability to provide smooth motion with minimal deviation from the specified path. The validity of this path is the responsibility of the motion planner.

The motion planner's job typically requires more detailed assimilation of sensor data. The trajectory-following capability of the motion controller gives the motion planner time to perform the necessary construction of a world model, and to search for paths within this model. Timing constraints for the motion planner are somewhat softer, less critical, and more negotiable than for the motion controller. New trajectories must be produced at a suitable rate, but if a trajectory is slightly late, the results will not be catastrophic. By producing longer trajectories, the motion planner can avail itself more time for future computations. However, a trajectory can become inappropriate if the environment should change during its execution. Therefore, the planner must either be fast enough to guarantee that no such change can occur while it is

working on the next trajectory segment, or the motion controller must incorporate special emergency procedures for dealing with such situations.

This example is sometimes called a *frequency hierarchy* because the low frequency assimilative processes supply commands to high frequency immediate processes. In this case, the data used within the immediate motion controller process is only position data. The motion controller uses no other information about the local environment. Consequently, the motion controller is entirely dependent upon the decision-making functions of the motion planner in order for its own actions to be of any value. More extensive hierarchies of this type have been developed for a variety of applications [2]. In these systems, each level works on a subproblem specified from the level above it. In this sense, control is centralized at the top of the hierarchy.

Decentralized Control

As more special-case procedures are added to the motion controller, the system begins to change from centralized to decentralized control. Eventually, enough decision-making capabilities may be placed in the controller itself for the relationship between motion planner and motion controller to take on an entirely different character. Consider, for example, that we allow the controller to compute its steering and speed commands directly from sensor data rather than from a specified trajectory. Certainly, it would not be difficult to implement simple routines such as "slow down when you get close to something," and "turn away from the closest object." Routines of this type require very little assimilation of sen-

sor data, and therefore can be made to satisfy the hard timing constraints of the motion controller. Because these routines are always looking at immediate sensory data, they can also be extremely responsive to changes in the sensed environment.

Brooks has coined the phrase "using the world as its own model" [5] to describe this kind of control because actions are based on immediate measurements of the real world rather than on projections performed within an assimilated world model. The error signal that the low-level controller is looking at is obtained at every instant from easily obtained measurements of objects in the environment. Position errors are no longer important at this level, because the controller is only concerned with its orientation relative to sensed objects. If data is unreliable, this is usually of little consequence as well. While spurious data errors may tend to lead to wildly varying control commands, it is possible to filter these commands in a way that will prevent wild changes in robot action.

The decentralized motion controller described here addresses certain fundamental system goals within the hard real-time control loops. The goals are essentially established at design time rather than at run time. Therefore, these goals must be broadly relevant throughout the robot's operation. In this case, the goal of moving about without hitting obstacles can be seen as a fairly broad goal. Any other objectives will most likely take this fundamental capacity for granted.

The simple control scheme used by the motion controller could easily get the robot caught in traps. Use of only immediate sensory data limits the robot's ability to avoid wandering in endless circles. If we have fairly specialized tasks for the robot, then problems like this may be circumvented by implementing specialized strategies for such circumstances. Wall-following strategies, for example, can usually get the robot out of many local traps. If

the goals for the system are known clearly in advance, these strategies can be incorporated within the motion controller at design time. Another alternative is to allow a more flexible motion planner to determine which strategies to use according to the current situation and goals.

The role of a motion planner in this system would now be quite different from what it would be in a centralized system. The motion planner may still use assimilated sensor data or an internal world model to anticipate possible undesirable outcomes, but it would not determine an explicit course of action. This is because the motion controller is expected to achieve certain goals already, so there is only a need to bias the controller's actions toward achieving other goals in the process. The basic controller can operate fairly well without any guidance at all; therefore the guidance provided by the motion planner should be designed to augment this performance rather than to mandate specific actions.

The partitioning of responsibilities is clearly different between the centralized and decentralized approaches. In the centralized approach, the responsibility of higher-level modules is to generate task specifications, and the responsibility of the lower-level modules is to execute these specifications as faithfully as possible. In a decentralized approach, even low-level modules can be responsible for achieving fairly high-level goals. In this case, the distinction between responsibilities of higher-level modules and lower-level modules may be based more on the variability of goals. Goals that can be designed into the lower levels need not be handled by the higher levels. Meanwhile, goals that may change considerably from one application to the next may best be handled by higher levels.

The Adaptive Suspension Vehicle Project and the Autonomous Land Vehicle Project are examples of recent vehicle control research.

In the following sections, we discuss these projects, with an emphasis on the underlying intelligence and timeliness characteristics of the vehicles and their missions, and how they affected our design of the vehicles' control software.

The Adaptive Suspension Vehicle

The Adaptive Suspension Vehicle (ASV) is a fully self-contained, six-legged vehicle, designed to explore the capabilities of walking vehicles of a useful scale [4,21]. The ASV Project, led by The Ohio State University and Adaptive Machine Technologies, ran from 1982 through 1989, funded by contracts with the Defense Advanced Research Projects Agency (DARPA).

The ASV, shown in Photo 1, weighs about 7,000 pounds, and is about 20 ft. long, 8 ft. wide, and 10 ft. tall. Power from an internal combustion engine drives 18 hydraulic actuators—three per leg. The ASV's sensor suite includes over 100 sensors, including leg position, velocity and pressure sensors, inertial sensors on the body, and an ERIM laser range scanner [24] which sweeps the area in front of the vehicle. The on-board multiprocessor contains seven Intel 80386-based computers and two special-purpose numeric processors. The human operator uses a joystick to drive the vehicle; the operator's simple commands are translated into complex leg motions by about 100,000 lines of Pascal code executing on the multiprocessor.

The ASV Control Architecture

The ASV's software performs many functions, including sensor data processing, servo-level control of the hydraulic actuators, terrain modeling, and motion planning.

The ASV's sensing and terrain modeling, while computationally intensive, are not conceptually difficult. The data from the sensors are combined to derive a description of the current positions and velocities of the vehicle's body and legs, and a Cartesian terrain elevation map. We do not analyze the terrain data to discriminate between types of features, such as trees or rocks.

Planning and control are more conceptually difficult. The ASV planning and control system can be envisioned as a hierarchy of subsystems, as shown in Figure 1. At each level in the hierarchy, the subsystems operate in a particular world which they can sense, reason about, and affect. Subsystems at higher levels generally have longer planning horizons or cycles than those at lower levels.

The human navigator views the Planned Vehicle as a six-degree-of-freedom vehicle whose movements mirror the navigator's joystick commands. The navigator "flies" the Planned Vehicle much as he would fly a helicopter. The Planned Vehicle accepts the navigator's commands and chooses leg movements that fulfill these commands, while avoiding local obstacles and other problems. Unlike the aforementioned helicopter, the Planned Vehicle will not carry out a command it thinks is dangerous. It will refuse to walk into a wall, for example. The Planned Vehicle views the Servoed Vehicle as a well-behaved system of interacting legs and body.

The Servoed Vehicle accepts plans from the Motion Planner and passes the appropriate commands to the individual Servoed Legs. A Servoed Leg knows about the corresponding Physical Leg's position, velocity, and acceleration and controls the Physical Leg's three hydraulic actuators.

For the most part, control of the ASV is hierarchical and centralized. Commands originate at the top level of the hierarchy, and all lower levels are designed to realize these control commands through successive refinement. This approach appears to be driven by the highly constrained nature of the vehicle's configuration. For example, a leg usually cannot make an appropriate movement without coordinating its actions with other legs. In the ASV architecture, such coordination is performed at the higher levels. Occasionally, the chain of command can be broken by reflex actions that may be carried out within the lower levels. For example, a leg may respond contrary to its commanded trajectory if it detects contact with an obstacle [31]. However, such local decision making is limited.

ASV Servo Control

The ASV's servo control levels include the six Servoed Legs and the Servoed Vehicle. The servo control subsystems operate in well-defined worlds of velocities, forces, inertias, and so on. The servo control algorithms compute the same mathematical functions, regardless of the current state of the underlying physical objects, and have fixed execution times. The Leg Servos run on 10ms periods, and the Vehicle Servo runs on a 25ms period. These periods are based on extensive analyses of the physical objects being controlled. Because physical attributes such as position and velocity are continuous characteristics, such timing constraints can be described as a continuous range of acceptable timing values, with correspondingly continuous levels of physical accuracy. The constraints are negotiable within this range. For example, the Leg Servo ideally runs at 5ms intervals, but processing power limitations force it to run only every 10ms, which provides slightly degraded, but acceptable smoothness. The Leg Servo can actually miss an occasional cycle, resulting in an isolated 20ms gap, without becoming unstable, but repeated misses can be dangerous.

The servo-control levels therefore allow limited timing constraint negotiability. However, servo-control timing constraints are very

critical, since the loss of servo control for any significant period of time can result in serious system instability. Furthermore, servo control operates at some of the highest frequencies present in the system. For these reasons, we choose safe fixed servo-control periods and give servo-control tasks a fixed, high criticality (priority).

We use rate-monotonic scheduling for the servo-control levels, and in fact, for all levels. In rate-monotonic scheduling, tasks with shorter periods are given priority over tasks with longer periods. The Leg Servos therefore run at the highest priority, above the Vehicle Servo. Rate-monotonic scheduling allows efficient use of resources, even under transient overload. Furthermore, the theory of rate-monotonic scheduling is well developed, allowing the timing correctness of control programs to be ensured [26].

ASV Motion Planning

Leg and body placement is chosen by the Motion Planner. Unlike the relatively unchanging worlds in which the servo subsystems operate, the Motion Planner operates in a world of constantly changing terrain. The Motion Planner executes an algorithm that is driven by body velocity requests from the navigator's joystick. The Motion Planner produces a continuous vehicle velocity plan which is consumed at a steady rate by the Servoed Vehicle. The plan is made up of plan segments, which the Motion Planner periodically computes and adds to the plan. A plan segment consists of two portions: a normal portion containing requested body acceleration to be used for a certain duration into the future, followed by a safety portion containing contingency deceleration to zero body velocity. The safety portion of a plan seg-

ment is overwritten by the following plan segment if the following plan segment is added before the deadline for beginning the safety segment. Since each validated plan ends with deceleration to zero velocity, the vehicle and its navigator will remain safe even if the Motion Planner fails to create a plan segment by its deadline. This is a form of forward recovery for Motion Planner failures.

When computing a plan segment, the Motion Planner uses a super-real-time dynamic simulation of the vehicle to verify the safety of all planned actions before they are executed by the actual vehicle. If the simulation reveals accelerations that render the vehicle unstable, the Motion Planner modifies the plan segment and tries again. Eventually, either the simulation is successful and the resulting sequence of body and leg states is appended to the previous plan, or the simulation fails and the previous plan remains in force.

Figure 2 shows a one-dimensional vehicle velocity plan (velocity is really a six-dimensional vector). The plan contains two plan segments, P1 and P2, each with a normal portion and a safety portion. If plan segment P2 is added to the plan before the real time reaches the end of P1n, the vehicle continues with P2n, and so on. If plan segment P2 has not been computed by its "deadline2," the plan follows P1s. Subsequent planning takes place based on the corresponding vehicle velocity.

The Motion Planner executes periodically. Generation of a new plan segment requires from 100ms to 500ms depending on the vehicle's state, the navigator's command, and the terrain. During each planning period, the Motion Planner generates one plan segment. The length of the normal portion of the plan segment may be fixed, or it may be allowed to vary. However, the Motion Planner must meet its deadline. That is, it must generate a plan segment and append it to the plan before the previ-

PHOTO 1.
The Adaptive Suspension Vehicle

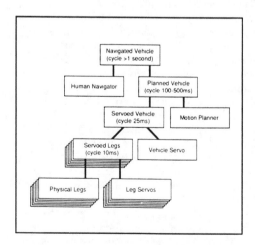

FIGURE 1.
The ASV Planning and Control Architecture

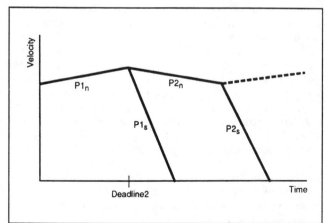

FIGURE 2.
ASV Plan Generation

ous plan segment's normal portion runs out. The scheduling problem for the Motion Planner is to determine an appropriate length of a plan segment, and corresponding planning period, given the available processing power.

For a given processor, the amount of time required to calculate a plan segment is approximately:

$$DTcp = \frac{Vmax/As}{SR - 1} + DTov$$

where

$DTcp$ = the time required to compute a plan segment;

$Vmax$ = the vehicle's maximum allowable velocity;

As = the acceleration during the safety portion of the plan segment;

SR = the rate at which the simulation runs, as a multiple of real time;

$DTov$ = a fixed amount of overhead time associated with computing a plan segment.

As this cost function shows, the cost of planning is related to $Vmax$. Since more can happen in a given planning period if the vehicle is moving rapidly, planning takes more time. However, the presence of $Vmax$ in the cost function could make it possible for scheduling algorithms to adapt performance to meet timing constraints. For example, the Motion Planner may be able to tell the vehicle: "Walk more slowly. I can't plan this fast," much the way humans presumably operate. Tests with an ASV simulation have shown this to be useful [12].

Furthermore, the cost of planning is inversely related to As. "Slamming on the brakes" in response to a missed planning deadline is easier to plan than coming to a slow, smooth stop. In fact, $Vmax/As$ is a measure of the time it takes to stop the vehicle. This fact could allow an adaptive scheduling algorithm to adjust the performance of the vehicle to available processing power.

When choosing the length of the plan segments, and therefore the planning period, we could choose to schedule the Motion Planner frequently, thereby generating many, shorter, plan segments. This would have a higher overall cost because of the repeated $DTov$ overhead. Furthermore, frequent, short executions of the Motion Planner are more likely to be affected by small scheduling disturbances. This may result in plan segments missing their deadlines and activating the previous plan segment's safety portion, resulting in a jerky ride.

Alternatively, we could choose to generate fewer, longer plan segments. However, because the time lag between a navigator's command and its enactment by the vehicle is related to the length of a plan segment, long plan segments imply slow response to the navigator's commands. This may not be acceptable when maneuvering in close quarters, and does not allow the Motion Planner to replan rapidly in response to changing environmental conditions, such as foot slippage.

The ASV currently uses an adaptive scheduling algorithm. It starts with short plan segments, computed frequently. It monitors the Motion Planner. If plan segments are completed uncomfortably close to their deadlines, it lengthens the normal portion of the plan segments and increases the planning period.

The centralized Motion Planner chooses the motions of all legs. The ASV's most common gait is a tripod gait in which the six legs are divided into two tripods, each of which contains the center leg on one side and the front and rear legs on the other side; each tripod moves as a single unit. It might seem that the ASV is a good candidate for distributed planning, in which each of the six

legs works independently to pursue some overall goal for the vehicle. In fact, we have experimented with free gaits in which a leg attempts to lift itself and move in an appropriate direction any time such an action would not cause vehicle instability. Our experiments have shown that free gaits are inefficient, unless strong constraints based on the other legs' states are added to each leg's motion-planning algorithm. Then the free gaits tend to converge to the standard tripod gait if the terrain allows [12]. This appears to be a result of the highly constrained nature of the vehicle and environment.

Discussion of the ASV

The ASV control architecture evolved over time, as we gained a better understanding of the vehicle. Design choices were arrived at after examining and—in some cases—implementing and testing alternatives. The choices seem to have been driven primarily by the nature of the ASV itself. The ASV is highly constrained: the allowable decisions for any ASV component depend heavily on the component's current state and the states of other components. The ASV is unstable: it must be controlled at all times, and at high servo rates. The ASV is potentially dangerous: the effects of mistakes cannot always be undone. The ASV is highly stressed: inefficient use of the mechanical components can severely affect the vehicle's performance. Our experiences with the ASV lead us to the following observations:

Architecture. The ASV is well suited to a centralized, hierarchical control architecture because the problem is tightly constrained and the basic interactions between components are well understood.

Resource Allocation. In the ASV, we choose fixed rates for the servo levels. We use adaptive schedulers for the planning levels, combined with provisions for forward recovery to safe states if timing constraints are missed. We cannot afford to lose a Leg Servo, because the vehicle would become unstable. If necessary, we would prefer to lose the Motion Planner, which would cause the vehicle to stop. For the ASV, the fully stopped state is a safe state. Defining safe states for winged aircraft, which must maintain forward velocity, is a different problem.

Simulation. The Motion Planner relies on a highly accurate dynamic simulation (model) of the vehicle and environment. The decision to simulate or not depends on two factors: (1) the ability to simulate the system in super-real-time accurately enough so actions of the simulation are very likely to be actions of the real system, and (2) the potential for damage or inefficiency if the real system commits to untested courses of action. Since the ASV cannot afford to make mistakes, it checks out all actions before it attempts them. In this case, the modeling of vehicle actions provides the assimilation needed to ensure stable coordination of the legs.

The Autonomous Land Vehicle

The Autonomous Land Vehicle (ALV) is a mobile computer laboratory, developed for use in autonomous road-following and cross-country navigation experiments [30]. The ALV project ran from 1984 through 1988. Started by DARPA, it supported a community of academic and industrial researchers. This community included Martin Marietta, Carnegie Mellon University (CMU), the University of Maryland, SRI International, Advanced Decision Systems (ADS), Hughes Aircraft Co. Research Labs, and Honeywell Corporation. The focus of this effort was to develop fully autonomous navigation capabilities.

The ALV built by Martin Marietta was a 20,000-pound, 8-wheeled vehicle as shown in Photo 2. Enclosed within its fiberglass upper body were two Sun 3 workstations, an Intel microprocessor, and a Vicom image processor. The vehicle also had a special-purpose radio

link that allowed these computers to communicate with two Symbolics Lisp Machines located in a remote lab. The vehicle's primary sensors were a video camera and an ERIM laser range scanner. The vehicle could also sense pitch and roll, and could estimate its location using a Bendix land navigation system. During autonomous navigation experiments, the vehicle would run entirely under computer control. It was successfully demonstrated to perform various road-following and cross-country navigation tasks without any human intervention.

The ALV Software Architecture

Several different software architectures were developed by the various ALV team members. This discussion will focus on the software architecture developed by Hughes for autonomous cross-country navigation [8]. When studying this system, it is important to recognize that the complete architecture, as originally conceived, was never fully implemented. Nevertheless, a working system was developed. In the process, a number of valuable insights were gained with respect to the original design notions. What originally might have been a fairly centralized control architecture, quickly evolved into a highly decentralized architecture.

The original architecture concept was intended to capture the advantages of both immediacy and assimilation. This was to be done through a hierarchical decomposition as shown in Figure 3. The major modules in this hierarchy were intended to be operated in parallel—with modules near the top performing tasks requiring a high degree of assimilation, and modules near the bottom performing tasks requiring a high degree of immediacy. In this way, the hierar-

chy covered the entire spectrum of immediacy/assimilation trade-offs, deriving unique benefits from each level.

In this decomposition of the real-time control problem, differing response time requirements and differing needs for programming flexibility form the basis for the segmentation of major modules. The layer of the hierarchy which interacts most directly with vehicle actuators was designed primarily for reflexive performance and was not required to employ any complex inference mechanisms. Each higher layer in the hierarchy was to be less specialized—making greater use of search and look-ahead in order to allow greater flexibility and provide extended capabilities for high-level reasoning.

Development of this architecture began at the bottom of the hierarchy. The goal was to treat perception and control as a unified problem. By doing this, the computational overhead between sensing and action could be minimized, thereby yielding a high degree of immediacy.

The lowest level of the architecture is composed of components called virtual sensors and reflexive behaviors [18]. Virtual sensors perform specialized sensor processing, and behaviors perform specialized control tasks. Each behavior makes control decisions appropriate for its particular task, using only selected features of the world provided by its associated virtual sensors. The final choice of action is obtained as a collective decision from multiple behaviors. Figure 4 shows a simplified example of behaviors for obstacle avoidance combined with behaviors for road following and navigation. As in other architectures that emphasize use of immediate data, fusion of all sensor data into a coherent world model is not required in order to generate actions. The fusion of behavior commands provides an alternative means of combining information from disparate sources.

Unlike a standard control hierar-

chy, the reflexive level alone can be designed to achieve high-level goals. Individual behaviors respond directly to perceived states of the environment that are relevant to their intended tasks. Behaviors respond to differences between desired and perceived states by issuing control commands likely to reduce these differences. If an obstacle is detected in front of the vehicle, a behavior might attempt to turn the vehicle until no obstacles are seen. By allowing behaviors to express their preferences for a range of commands, it is possible for the arbiter to select commands that can simultaneously satisfy multiple objectives [22].

The route and mission planners do not control the actions of behaviors. Rather, they serve to bias the actions of the behaviors [20]. If a behavior is weighing the choice between two alternative paths, the plans will influence this choice, but they will not dictate a choice absolutely. Rather than expressing an explicit course of action, plans are generated that express preferences and constraints as a function of the state of the vehicle. This allows more versatile and opportunistic responses from the behaviors. This reliance on developing behavior competences from the bottom up rather than on refining control commands from the top down results in a highly decentralized control approach.

Reflexive Behaviors

Behaviors for reflexive control are designed around the notion that their output commands should be simple and frequent. Behaviors do not project future motions or specify complex trajectories. Instead, using the most immediate virtual sensor data, behaviors constantly update vehicle turn-rate and speed commands. The time saved through the simplicity of these computations allows them to be run more frequently. Thus, the complex path that a vehicle follows is due only to the frequent revisions of these basic control parameters.

In developing behaviors and virtual sensors for cross-country navigation, the interfaces between perception and control functions could not be treated separately from the perception and control problems themselves. On the perception side, it was realized that there were no obvious structural features that could be used to characterize all obstacles. Many terrain features were only obstacles at certain vehicle orientations or speeds. On the control side, it was realized that detection of safe travel passages was as useful as detection of all obstacles. By closely integrating perception and control development efforts, a compromise was achieved in which the necessary control information was provided with minimal computational overhead.

The primary virtual sensor used in cross-country navigation merely indicates how far the vehicle can safely travel in seven different directions from its current heading. Using range images from a laser range scanner as input, the algorithm first converts the data into a planar Cartesian coordinate system, and then applies a 3D kinematic model of the vehicle over this high-resolution terrain model. In some ways, this is similar to the super-real-time simulation performed by the ASV planner. The vehicle model is tested at small increments over the sensed terrain model, detecting possible suspension, slope, or clearance problems at each location. The result is a simple representation of seven trajectories that extend until either an obstacle or uncertain data is encountered.

The behaviors that use this information do not merely choose a trajectory and then follow it. This aspect distinguishes the ALV control system from the ASV even though they both analyze the sensed data in a similar manner. While a preferred heading is selected from the data, it rarely coincides exactly with a tested trajectory. The vehicle has invariably moved between the time the trajectories are computed and the time a heading can be chosen. Rather than expend a great deal of effort attempting to realign the vehicle with one of these arbitrary trajectories, turn-rate behaviors merely try to steer the vehicle toward the largest area of most traversable space. This is found by locating clusters of long trajectories. Meanwhile, other behaviors look at the degree of free space found in the selected direction and adjust the speed accordingly.

Using a scanning resolution fine enough to detect paths that would meet the ALV's six-inch clearance constraint, a new set of trajectories could only be obtained every seven seconds. Meanwhile, the behaviors revised their speed and turn-rate commands every half second. Each incremental decision by the behaviors always used the most current set of trajectories available. The simple incremental updates of behaviors naturally provided smooth transitions between old and new sets of trajectories. If the vehicle got too close to the end of the current data, a behavior that tested the remaining distance would slow the vehicle to a stop. At vehicle speeds of three kilometers per hour, this behavior rarely needed to be invoked.

During development of these behaviors, it was realized they could perform much better if they knew the cause for termination of each trajectory. The interface was readily revised, allowing behaviors now to prefer trajectories that terminate in unknown data over those that terminate in obstacles. This information also allowed some behaviors to be designed to remember obstacle locations from previous scans. This considerably improved performance during sharp turns. The modular nature of behaviors and the flexibility of their interfaces made this change relatively easy to

PHOTO 2.
The Autonomous Land Vehicle in Cross-Country Terrain.

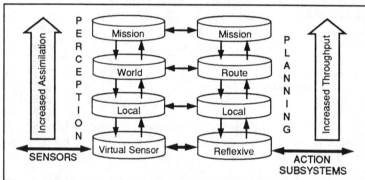

FIGURE 3.
A Hierarchical Architecture for Real-Time Autonomous Vehicle Control

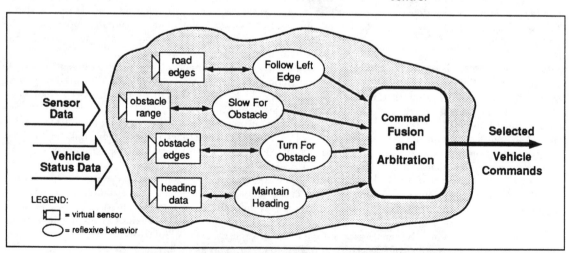

FIGURE 4.
Reflexive Behaviors and Virtual Sensors Provide the Basis for an Autonomous Agent's Fundamental Competences

accomplish.

If, at a later time, a faster means for detecting and avoiding obstacles is developed, this can easily be integrated into the existing control system. All behaviors are designed to represent their outputs in terms of simple commands such as speed and turn rate. This allows the outputs from different behaviors to be combined through command fusion. Conflicts may be resolved either through a fixed priority scheme [5], a dynamic priority scheme [18], a potential field scheme [3], or a voting scheme [22]. In any case, careful design and testing must be performed to ensure coherent behavior interaction.

By fusing behavior commands, reasonable responses can be generated from incomplete information. If an extremely fast, but inaccurate, means for detecting obstacles is developed, this can be used to immediately slow the vehicle until other behaviors can provide confirmation. In most cases, it would be very difficult to develop a smarter response based on complete information that could surpass the benefits obtained from this reduced reaction latency.

The use of behavior-based control architectures involves an important design time trade-off. Behaviors must be designed to provide reasonable responses to most situations with minimal assimilation of data. Rarely will it be possible to consider the detailed consequences of numerous alternative actions when generating these responses. However, a series of fast responses can often provide more overall benefit than a single carefully considered response. The range of acceptable responses to any situation diminishes rapidly as time passes. Thus, built-in responses that are invoked quickly can have a greater likelihood of performing acceptably than those that require more time for deliberation.

Mission and Route Planning

The ALV mission and route plan-

ning functions are responsible for long-range guidance of the vehicle. The mission-planning function translates user-specified objectives and constraints into numerical cost functions. The route planner applies these constraints and cost functions as it performs search in a digital map. The results of this search are then used to bias the actions of behaviors toward achieving mission goals.

The purpose of mission planning is to translate user requirements into appropriate numerical cost criteria. In the simplest of missions, the user specifies a goal location. In more complex missions, multiple goals may be established, and the vehicle may need either to choose one dynamically, or to achieve each one sequentially. A variety of mobility and visibility constraints may also be incorporated into a mission specification. For example, it may be important for the vehicle to stay within sight of a particular observation point. Alternatively, it may be important to stay hidden from various observers. In some scenarios, certain terrain features may play a complex role. For example, it may be desirable for the vehicle to travel near a road but remain hidden from the road at the same time. Mission-planning functions allow a variety of such requirements to be established.

Once mission objectives have been defined in terms of appropriate cost criteria, the route planner may then apply these costs while performing search in a digital map [14, 15]. The most straightforward way to use the results of the map-based search is to extract a route plan as shown in Figure 5. This optimal route is the path that will best meet all cost criteria, assuming the map has provided an accurate representation of the terrain. Of

course, if unknown obstacles are present, this path may be far from optimal, but there is no way this can be known until the path is traversed.

Because unknown obstacles will invariably be present, the optimal route cannot be used to direct vehicle actions. One alternative might be to use sensors to detect differences between the real world and the map, and to constantly update the optimal plan. Conceivably, this could then allow the optimal plan to be used to provide an explicit control trajectory. This, however, would mean the system could only respond to sensed differences after many complex steps of map updating and replanning have taken place. Invariably, the resulting response will be slower than necessary. In this sense, the resulting actions may be suboptimal even though each planned trajectory is optimal.

As stated earlier, a behavior-based architecture uses a quite different approach to the problem. With sufficiently competent behaviors, the plan only serves as general guidance toward the objective, and is not used for explicit control. Therefore, it does not matter that the plan may be partially incorrect or that it may fail to account for all obstacles. What does matter is that the plan be represented in such a way that it provides the best possible guidance to the behaviors.

In order to provide as much information as possible to the behaviors, an alternative plan representation has been developed [19]. As shown in Figure 6, the best guidance to behaviors can be provided if the notion of an explicit route plan is entirely abandoned. The gradient field representation serves the same purpose as a route plan, but in a much more effective manner. No matter where the vehicle may be, the gradient field can suggest a heading that will lead to the goal. Note that the guidance obtained from the gradient field makes no assumptions about how the behaviors will use that advice. Thus, if the

vehicle should stray from the optimal route, the gradient field will still provide meaningful information.

The ability to use a gradient field instead of a route plan highlights the notion that the behaviors are truly performing the majority of the decision-making tasks. In this context, the role of the higher assimilation layers is to enhance the quality of behavior decisions, rather than to control them. The plans produced are called internalized plans because they capture all the constraints of the mission problem in a way that can be used to influence action. In effect, internalized plans are used as supplementary sensory inputs to the behavior-based agent. The gradient field, for example, can be thought of as a phantom compass that always gives a general idea of the right way to go. The behaviors that use this information operate in the same way that sensor-based obstacle avoidance behaviors perform.

Discussion of the ALV

The ALV control architecture evolved in a bottom-up fashion. A great deal of attention was devoted to developing behaviors that could suitably avoid obstacles in cross-country terrain. As more behaviors were developed, and as these behaviors became more sophisticated, it became apparent that many of the functions intended for the higher levels were not essential.

A version of the Local planning module was implemented, but never used in cross-country experiments. While it was recognized that some mechanism would eventually be needed to allow switching between different groups of behaviors, it was clear that this would only be required for major changes in

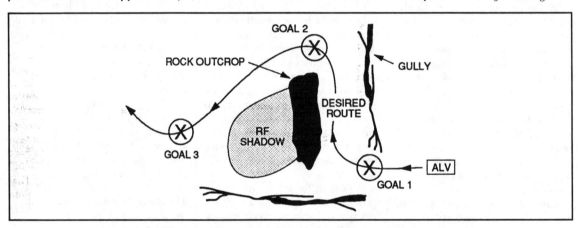

FIGURE 5.

An ALV Route Plan Expressed as a Sequence of Intermediate Waypoints

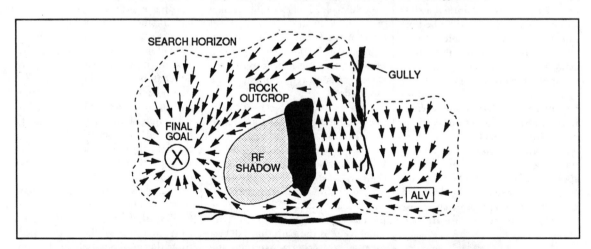

FIGURE 6.

A Gradient Field Representation Provides a More Useful Form of Advice to the Behaviors

vehicle tasks. Furthermore, by making each behavior sensitive to the context in which it should be used, much of the job of switching behaviors is distributed among the behaviors themselves. An obstacle avoidance behavior, for example, need not suggest any actions if no obstacles are present.

As more functionality was incorporated within the behaviors, this altered the role of the higher-level modules. The behaviors could perform quite well without any supervision. Therefore, the Mission and Route-planning modules were only needed to augment the existing performance. It was found that mission and route-planning functions can be used most effectively if the information they generate is treated as an alternate source of sensory input. Thus—whether the vehicle is approaching a visible obstacle or an invisible threat zone—the ultimate decision for action is left to the behaviors. Plans may suggest alternatives and project potential problems, but they do not dictate an explicit course of action. Consequently, the system is not a true control hierarchy. The lower levels are not subordinate to the higher levels.

Conclusion

An examination of the ASV and ALV architectures shows how different design concerns have resulted in different approaches to control. In one case, the need to enable a human to control a highly constrained and dynamic system has led to a centralized control approach. In the other, the need to create an unmanned system that must generate suitable responses to a variety of unanticipated circumstances has led to a decentralized control approach.

In the ASV, the primary concern is to achieve safe and reliable response to a driver's control commands. In order to provide such response, all of the legs must be carefully coordinated. Thus, in addition to the inherent centralization of control authority with the

driver, there is an underlying need for centralization to maintain coordination of the legs. While it is possible to further decentralize the control of the ASV's legs, such techniques do not appear to produce any significant benefits in efficiency, safety, or performance.

In the ALV, the primary goal is for the vehicle to achieve user-specified mission objectives without constant direction or supervision. Minimal coordination is required, but there are a variety of factors that may influence the choice of speed or heading at each instant in time. In this case, decentralized control permits the establishment of multiple pathways from sensing to action. Each independent pathway can provide the most immediate response possible for the associated sensory input. Aspects of mobility and navigation that are fundamental to all missions are compiled directly within the lowest-level control loops. The benefits of this approach are limited if it is restricted to follow only an explicit course of action. However, if sensory input is augmented by the rich information from internalized plans, the system can be extremely flexible and opportunistic.

The ASV and ALV illustrate two alternative approaches for dealing with critical timing constraints. In the ASV, the motion planner is isolated from immediate timing constraints, giving it time to generate a plan. If the plan is not ready when it is needed, the servo controllers fall back on a contingency plan. In the ALV, all functions that might normally be allocated to a motion planner are embedded within immediate control responses. Motion control is decomposed into elementary decisions that are made quickly and revised frequently. Each decision-making process is designed to

be simple enough that it can satisfy immediate timing constraints. If structured properly, the overall quality of performance may be better than can be obtained from more carefully deliberated decisions made at slower rates.

It would be interesting to combine the ASV and ALV approaches into a single system. For example, the ALV control system could replace the driver in the ASV, and provide speed and turn commands to the ASV control system. This would allow the centralized control system to maintain coordination of the legs while allowing the decentralized control system to guide the vehicle.

Acknowledgments
The authors owe many thanks to Marcel Schoppers for inspiring this article and for his many helpful insights along the way. Thanks to him, we both have had the opportunity to broaden our horizons. We would also like to express our appreciation to the other members of the ASV and ALV teams that have helped to make these systems work. In particular, Dennis Pugh, Tom Walliser, Eric Ribble, Vince Vohnout, and Mark Patterson were largely responsible for the ASV Control architecture, under the guidance of Bob McGhee and Ken Waldron. On the ALV project, Mike Daily, John Harris, David Keirsey, Karen Olin, Kurt Reiser, J. Kenneth Rosenblatt, Ram Nevatia, David Tseng, and Vincent Wong have all contributed immensely. ◨

References
1. Agre, P. and Chapman, D. Pengi: An implementation of a theory of activity. In *Sixth National Conference on Artificial Intelligence* (Seattle, Wash., July 1987), pp. 268–272.
2. Albus, J. A theory of intelligent systems. Fifth IEEE International Symposium on Intelligent Control (Philadelphia, Sept. 5–7 1990), pp. 866–875.
3. Arkin, R. Motor schema based navigation for a mobile robot: An approach to programming by behav-

ior. In *Proceedings of IEEE Conference on Robotics and Automation* (Mar. 1987), pp. 264–271.

4. Bihari, T.E., Walliser, T.M. and Patterson, M.R. Controlling the adaptive suspension vehicle. *IEEE Comput. 22*, 6 (June 1989), 59–65.

5. Brooks, R.A. A robust layered control system for a mobile robot. *IEEE J. Robo. Auto. RA-2*, 1 (1986).

6. Chung, J., and Liu, J. Algorithms for scheduling periodic jobs to minimize average error. In *Proceedings of the IEEE Real-Time Systems Symposium* (Dec. 1988), pp. 142–151.

7. Crowley, J.L. Navigation for an intelligent mobile robot. *IEEE J. Robo. Auto. RA-1* (1985), 31–41.

8. Daily, M. et al. Autonomous cross-country navigation with the ALV. In *Proceedings of IEEE Conference on Robotics and Automation* (Philadelphia, Apr. 1988).

9. Dasarathy, B. Timing constraints of real-time systems: Constructs for expressing them, methods of validating them. *IEEE Trans. Softw. Eng. 11*, 1 (Jan. 1985), 80–86.

10. Erman, L.D., Ed. Intelligent real-time problem solving. Air Force Office of Scientific Research, Workshop Rep. TTR-ISE-90-101, Jan. 1990.

11. Jahanian, F. and Mok, A. Safety Analysis of timing properties in real-time systems. *IEEE Trans. Softw. Eng. 12*, 9 (Sept. 1986), 890–904.

12. Kwak, S. and McGhee, R. Rule-based motion coordination for a hexapod walking machine. *Advanced Robo. 4*, 3 (1990), 263–282.

13. Leveson, N. and Stolzy, J. Safety analysis using petri nets. *IEEE Trans. Softw. Eng. 13*, 3 (Mar. 1987), 386–397.

14. Mitchell, J.S.B., Payton, D.W. and Keirsey, D.M. Planning and reasoning for autonomous vehicle control. *Int. J. Intell. Syst. 2* (1987), 129–198.

15. Mitchell, J.S.B. An algorithmic approach to some problems in terrain navigation. *Artif. Intell. 37* (1988), 171–201.

16. Moravec, H.P. The Stanford Cart and the CMU Rover. In *Proceedings of the IEEE 71* (1983), pp. 872–884.

17. Nilsson, N.J. Shakey the robot. SRI AI Center, Tech. Note 323, Apr., 1984.

18. Payton, D.W. An architecture for reflexive autonomous vehicle control. In *IEEE International Conference on Robotics and Automation* (San Francisco, Apr. 7–10, 1986), pp. 1838–1845.

19. Payton, D.W. Internalized plans: A representation for action resources. *Robo. Auto. Syst. 6*, 1 (1990), 89–103.

20. Payton, D.W., Rosenblatt, J.K. and Keirsey, D.M. Plan guided reaction. *IEEE Trans. Syst. Man and Cybern. 20*, 6 (1990), 1370–1382.

21. Pugh, D.R., et al. Technical description of the adaptive suspension vehicle. *Int. J. Robo. Res. 2*, 2 (1990), 24–42.

22. Rosenblatt, J.K. and Payton, D.W. A fine-grained alternative to the subsumption architecture for mobile robot control. In *Proceedings of International Joint Conference on Neural Networks* (Washington, D.C., June, 1989), pp. 317–324.

23. Rosenschein, S.J. and Kaelbling, L.P. The synthesis of digital machines with provable epistemic properties. In *Proceedings of Conference on Theoretical Aspects of Reasoning about Knowledge*, Morgan Kauffman Publishers, 1986, pp. 83–98.

24. Sampson, R.E. 3D range sensor phase-shift detection. *IEEE Comput. 20*, 8 (1987), 23–24.

25. Schwan, K., Gopinath, P. and Bo, W. CHAOS—Kernel support for objects in the real-time domain. *IEEE Trans. Comput. 36*, 8 (1987), 904–916.

26. Sha, L. and Goodenough, J.B. Real-time scheduling theory and Ada, *IEEE Comput. 23* (1990), 53–62.

27. Shoham, Y. Agent-oriented programming. *Tech. Rep.* STAN-CS-90-1335, Stanford University, 1990.

28. Stankovic, J. and Ramamritham, K. The design of the spring kernel. In *Proceedings of the IEEE Real-Time Systems Symposium* (Dec. 1987), pp. 146–157.

29. Tokuda, H., Wendorf, J. and Wang, H. Implementation of a time-driven scheduler for real-time operating systems. In *Proceedings of the IEEE Real-Time Systems Symposium* (Dec. 1–3, 1987), pp. 271–280.

30. Turk, M.A., et al. Video road-following for the autonomous land vehicle. In *IEEE International Conference on Robotics and Automation* (Raleigh, N.C., 1987).

31. Wong, H. and Orin, D. Reflex control of the prototype leg during contact and slippage. In *Proceedings of IEEE International Conference on Robotics and Automation* (Philadelphia, Apr. 1988), pp. 808–813.

Categories and Subject Descriptors: I.2.8 [**Artificial Intelligence**]: Problem Solving, Control Methods and Search—*plan execution, formation, generation;* I.2.9 [**Artificial Intelligence**]: Robotics—*Propelling mechanisms;* I.2.10 [**Artificial Intelligence**]: Vision and Scene Understanding—*architecture and control structures;* J.7 [**Computers in Other Systems**]: *real time;* C.3 [**Special-Purpose and Application-Based Systems**]: *real-time systems;* C.4 [**Performance of Systems**]: *Design studies*

General Terms: Design, Performance

Additional Key Words and Phrases: Autonomous vehicles, behavior-based control, hierarchical control, walking vehicles

About the Authors:

DAVID W. PAYTON is head of the Autonomous Systems Section in the Artificial Intelligence Department of the Hughes Research Labs. His research interests have included the development of knowledge representation and control strategies for context-based object recognition. His most recent work has been in the development of software architectures for autonomous vehicle control. **Author's Present Address:** Hughes Research Labs, 3011 Malibu Canyon Rd., Malibu, CA 90265.

THOMAS E. BIHARI is chief computer scientist at Adaptive Machine Technologies, Inc., in Columbus, Ohio. His research interests include real-time systems, robotics, artificial intelligence, and multimedia human interfaces. **Author's Present Address:** Adaptive Machine Technologies, Inc. 1218 Kinnear Road, Columbus, OH 43212.

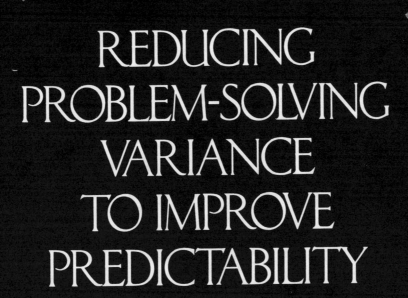

REDUCING PROBLEM-SOLVING VARIANCE TO IMPROVE PREDICTABILITY

C. J. Paul
Anurag Acharya
Bryan Black
Jay K. Strosnider

Real-time systems are playing an increasingly vital role in today's society. Such systems include manufacturing, control, transportation, aerospace, robotics and military systems. No longer are real-time systems limited to low-level control functions. They are now being asked to monitor and control complex, hierarchial systems in dynamic, sometimes hazardous, environments [7, 13]. Furthermore, some real-time systems such as the Mars Rover [2] are being asked to operate with little to no human interaction. Other large real-time systems are required to operate in environments that are not fully characterized [2]. The lack of information and the uncertainty of the environment requires the use of problem-solving techniques. To make things more difficult, real-time systems tend to be critical in nature where the impact of failures can have serious consequences. ✻ Current research in real-time artificial intelligence (AI) is driven by a need to make knowledge-based systems function in real time [12], and a need to integrate knowledge-based approaches to handle non-linearities and problem-solving behavior in control systems [3, 11, 17, 22]. Some of the early attempts to build such systems resulted in coincidentally real-time systems, which were difficult to analyze and predict [12]. At the other extreme, rule-based systems have been subject to exhaustive testing to guarantee they would be able to meet deadlines. Response time analysis is in general undecidable, and is PSPACE-hard in the case where all the variables have finite domains [18], making this technique infeasible for even moderate-sized systems. ✻ We believe execution time variance is the primary problem in providing performance guarantees for real-time problem-solving systems. Previous research in real-time scheduling has addressed some of the issues in integrating tasks with stochastic execution times into real-time systems [5]. However, the problem of taming the variance of problem-solving tasks has not been addressed. In typical real-time systems design, applications are created and worst-case times are calculated. Real-time scheduling is mostly based on worst-case execution times of the tasks in the system. The fundamental problem with problem-solving tasks for real-time applications is that the worst-case execution time is often unknown or orders of magnitude larger than the average case execution time. This results in systems which are either not schedulable or have very low utilization. Furthermore, if the execution time variance of the problem-solving tasks is not constrained, these tasks cannot be integrated into conventional real-time systems since the variance is likely to affect the predictability of the conventional real-time tasks. ✻ The execution time variance of problem-solving tasks manifests itself at two levels: the methodology level and the problem-solving architecture level. To improve predictability, it is necessary to tackle the variance at *both* these levels. We present an approach which integrates problem-solving methodology and architectural primitives to reduce the variance at both levels. We have designed and implemented an architecture, Concurrent Real-Time OPS5 (CROPS5) [20], illustrating these principles. Using this architecture, we demonstrate that problem-solving and real-time tasks can coexist within a readily analyzable framework, that hard deadlines can be guaranteed for critical problem-solving tasks, that soft deadlines for other problem-solving tasks can be provided so "best-effort" solutions are guaranteed within timing constraints. ✻ We begin by discussing the sources of execution time variance and methods to deal with them. We then develop the requirements of a real-time problem-solving architecture, providing not only the mechanisms to tackle the variance, but also the functionality required for integration into real-time environments. Later, we examine these issues in the context of CROPS5. An aircraft collision avoidance system is used as an example of how problem-solving tasks can coexist with conventional real-time tasks on a common computing platform while maintaining guaranteed response time performance for the conventional real-time tasks. We currently have implementations of CROPS5 running on two real-time operating systems, ARTS [30] and CHIMERA II [24], and are in the process of porting it to Real-Time Mach [29].

Execution-Time Variance: The Sources

We now examine the fundamental differences between conventional real-time tasks and problem-solving tasks, and discuss how these differences affect the execution time variance of these tasks.

First, let us consider the execution time variance of conventional real-time tasks. Typical real-time signal-processing algorithms have little to no variance associated with their execution times because, regardless of the complexity and size of most signal-processing algorithms (eg., FFTs, filters), there are generally no data dependencies which can cause the execution times to vary. The input data is simply processed in a uniform, deterministic fashion. On the other hand, control-oriented real-time tasks often have data dependencies. As the system to be controlled increases in complexity, the number of data dependencies will probably increase, resulting in an increased variance in the execution time of real-time tasks.

Next, let us consider the execution time variance of problem solving. According to the Problem-Space hypothesis advocated by Newell and Simon [19], all goal-oriented symbolic activity occurs in a problem space. Search in a problem space is posited to be a completely general model of intelligence. Search is thus fundamental to all problem-solving processes.

Figure 1 illustrates a continuum between tasks in a knowledge-poor domain and tasks in a knowledge-

rich domain. On the far right, knowledge-rich tasks are fully characterized, and there exists an explicit algorithm that transforms a given set of inputs to an appropriate output. There is no notion of search or backtracking at this end of the spectrum. Any variations in execution time are associated solely with data dependencies, as is the case for conventional real-time tasks.

As one moves to the left, either the task characteristics or their interactions with the environment are not completely known. Heuristics are now required to search the state space for an appropriate result. At the far left, there is no knowledge to direct the search; this results in a blind search. In this case, one would expect to have a large variance in execution time. To illustrate, let us consider a simple search tree of arity a, depth d. The total number of nodes in the tree is given by $(a^d - 1)(a - 1)$. In a simplistic sense, the worst-case and average-case execution times can be characterized by:

Worst-Case Execution Time =
$$K(a^d - 1)(a - 1)$$
Average-Case Execution Time =
$$KV(d)$$

where K is the average time to expand and evaluate a single node and $V(d)$ is the multiplier for the number of nodes examined in the average case. Assuming $d = 10$, $a = 3$, $V(d) = 30$, the ratio of the average case to the worst case is $30:29524$ ($\approx 1:1000$).

Given the large variance in the execution time of problem-solving tasks, and the fact that the worst-case execution time is either too large or unknown, traditional methods for the design of real-time systems cannot be directly applied

to problem-solving tasks. An attempt to blindly apply these techniques will result in systems which are either not schedulable or are grossly underutilized. For this simple example, the worst-case execution time is almost 1,000 times longer than the average case. A system designed with the worst-case estimate of execution time will have a schedulable utilization of <0.001

Most problem-solving falls midway between the two extremes shown in Figure 1. As one moves back to the right, increasing knowledge may be applied to reduce the variance due to search.

Search is manifested in the two levels of problem solving: the knowledge retrieval level and the knowledge application (problem space) level. Several methods exist for implementing both these levels. We will use the problem space approach mentioned earlier as a basis for developing our arguments. Even though the principles are illustrated in this context, they have wide applicability.

A problem space can be characterized by a set of states and a collection of operators that map states to states. A problem instance consists of a problem space, an initial state and a set of goal states. Problem solving can thus be viewed as finding the sequence of operations that map the initial state to the goal state. When more than one operator is applicable at a state, and there is insufficient information to select between the operators, search is required. A search in which exactly one operator is applicable to each state is often called an algorithm, corresponding to the far right of Figure 1.

At each state, selection of the next operator constitutes knowledge retrieval. Application of this knowledge controls the process of moving from state to state. The problem space search discussed here is at the knowledge application level. In addition, knowledge retrieval involves searching the available body of knowledge for knowledge that is applicable in the

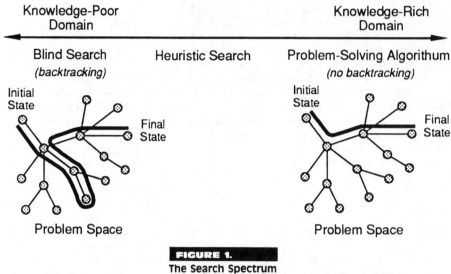

FIGURE 1.
The Search Spectrum

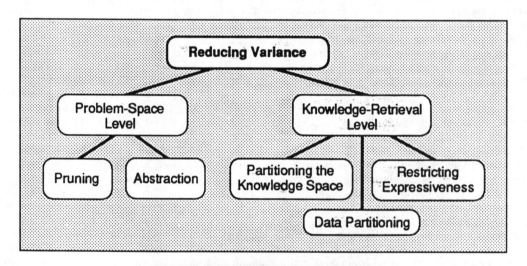

FIGURE 2.
Reducing Execution Time Variance of AI Tasks

THERE IS NO NOTION
OF SEARCH OR BACKTRACKING AT THIS
END OF THE SPECTRUM

current state. This is referred to as search in the *knowledge space* [27].

There is a fundamental difference between search in the problem space and search in the knowledge space. At the problem space level, the intent is to select the best possible operator applicable to the current state. On the other hand, at the knowledge retrieval level, the intent is to retrieve all knowledge that will influence the selection of the operator. Therefore, knowledge is available to prune and control the search in the problem space, but no comparable knowledge is available to restrict the search in the knowledge space.

Reducing Variance
The only way to reduce the variance at the problem space level is to reduce the number of states searched. There are two ways to achieve this goal as shown in the left half of Figure 2.

The first technique is to *prune* the search space. This involves looking earlier at the states that are more likely to lie along the solution path. This corresponds to the classical "best-first search" technique. The best-first search technique uses heuristics to achieve the pruning of the search space. The better the heuristic, the lower the variance.

The second technique is *abstraction*. This involves creating an abstract problem space whose states are less detailed than those in the original problem space. A single state in the abstract problem space corresponds to multiple states in the original problem space. Search in the abstract space provides guidance for search in the original problem space, thereby reducing the variance. For example, in planning a route from Pittsburgh to New York, one can work at the abstractions of interstate highways, major roads, or smaller roads. Determining the entry and exit points at the abstraction of interstate highways constrains the number of roads examined at the lower levels.

We will present a sample application illustrating these techniques later.

At the Knowledge Retrieval Level
The amount of processing required in the knowledge retrieval phase depends on the amount of knowledge in the system, the size of the state (data), and the amount of data each piece of knowledge is potentially applicable to. The variance of the knowledge retrieval phase can be reduced by the techniques illustrated in the right half of Figure 2:

Partitioning the Knowledge Space. This allows us to avoid searching sections of the knowledge space that contains knowledge which is *a priori* known to not be applicable to particular pieces of data.

Partitioning the data. Many pieces of knowledge express relations, desired or otherwise, between multiple pieces of data. Partitioning the data allows us to avoid considering sets of data which are *a priori* known not to belong to that relation.

Restricting expressiveness. Highly expressive knowledge representations allow a large number of relations to be represented. When a part of the state changes, a large number of potential relations with the rest of the state have to be checked. Representation formalisms which restrict expressiveness *a priori* restrict the number of relations that need to be checked during every state change.

Next, we will present a problem-solving architecture which not only controls execution time variance at the knowledge retrieval phase, but also provides architectural mechanisms to support a range of problem-solving methodologies to reduce the variance at the problem space level.

CROPS5: An Architecture for Real-Time Problem Solving
We contend that the function of an

integrated real-time problem solving architecture, as shown in Figure 2 is to provide *mechanisms* to partition, order and prune the search space; *predictable low-variance primitives* for problem solving; and *features* which facilitate easy integration into real-time operating environments. These three categories represent the mechanisms and features required for implementing the variance reduction methods.

We have designed a real-time problem-solving architecture, CROPS5, in accordance with the broad requirements we have outlined. It is based on the production system model [9], and borrows heavily from OPS5 for its syntax and semantics.

An OPS5 production system is composed of a set of *if-then* productions (rules) that constitute the *production memory* and a set of data items, called the *working memory*. The execution of an OPS5 program can be characterized by a cycle which has three phases: match, resolve, and act. Several efficient match algorithms have been designed for production systems. The best-known match algorithm is Rete [8]. The Rete algorithm performs matching using a special kind of data-flow network compiled from the left-hand side (the *if* part) of productions. This data-flow network passes items called *tokens* across the arcs between its nodes. Tokens are *partial instantiations* of productions. The basic computational step in the algorithm is to determine if the current set of partial instantiations (tokens) can be extended by matching more working memory elements against the productions involved. Checking whether a single token can be thus extended is the smallest logical unit of computation in the algorithm and is referred to as *token-processing* time. This time is typically on the order of 200–300 machine instructions.

There have been several efforts to use OPS5 or OPS5-like languages for real-time AI [6,23]. However, there are several characteristics of OPS5 that limit its utility for real-time applications. Some of these include the following:

- Current OPS5 systems can be interrupted only at rule-firing boundaries. The time period between successive rule-firings is, on the average, large and has a high variance. As a result, the responsiveness and predictability of these systems is severely impacted.

- OPS5 systems consist of a single problem-solving stream, whereas real-time applications typically require multiple streams to be active simultaneously. While it is possible to simulate multiple streams within OPS5 by using a special data item as context identifier, switching between these streams is extremely expensive and has unpredictable processing requirements.

In addition, OPS5 does not have an interface to the external environments. and its pattern-matching time is unpredictable due to the expressive power of the language and the incremental nature of the match algorithm.

CROPS5 Mechanisms

The design of CROPS5 attempts to remove these limitations by explicitly addressing each of these problems. CROPS5 is based on CParaOPS5 [1], a parallel implementation of OPS5 developed at Carnegie Mellon University. CROPS5 consists of an OPS5 to C compiler and a run-time library in C. It is significantly faster than Lisp-based versions of OPS5, and does not suffer from the unpredictability of the garbage collection mechanism in Lisp. The support of match parallelism in CParaOPS5 allows CROPS5 to be easily extended to run on parallel processors for enhanced performance.

Figure 4 shows the architecture of CROPS5 as a task in a real-time system. CROPS5 is shown to coexist on a common computing platform

with other hard real-time tasks like engine control and life support systems control. We address the issue of integration in greater detail later. First, we discuss the mechanisms provided by CROPS5 to efficiently partition, order and prune the search space. These mechanisms correspond to those in the leftmost branch of Figure 3.

Concurrent Prioritized Streams. As opposed to the single problem-solving stream in OPS5, CROPS5 [20] supports multiple problem-solving streams. Individual streams have disjoint sets of productions (and hence disjoint Rete nets). Each stream has a *private* working memory. The system uses a global working memory to communicate between streams. The mechanism of multiple streams facilitates knowledge base partitioning and data partitioning to reduce variance.

Associated with each stream is a stack of tokens that are yet to be matched and a buffer of working memory elements yet to be processed. A stream can therefore be characterized by a (Rete net, token-queue, working-memory-buffer) tuple. Fast and predictable switching between streams is achieved by switching between pointers to the corresponding tuples.

Knowledge-Based Scheduling and Context Switching. CROPS5 provides a dispatcher for the streams. The unit of time is the time to process a single token. Token counters keep track of the relative time spent in processing each stream, and can be used to implement a variety of user-defined scheduling policies.
Preemptability. While current OPS5 systems allow preemption only after all match processing is completed, CROPS5 allows preemption

of the match process at token-processing boundaries. This ability to interrupt the match at fine-grained intervals not only improves the responsiveness of CROPS5, but also provides a mechanism to guard against excessive data rates and runaway match processing.

These mechanisms allow the user to partition, order and prune the search space.

Predictable Primitives
CROPS5 also improves the predictability of some of the basic problem-solving primitives indicated in the middle branch of Figure 3.

Earlier, we identified context switching and the points of preemptability as having a large variance in OPS5. The CROPS5 primitives for context switching and preemption have much lower variance. Experiments were conducted with CROPS5 running under the CHIMERA II real-time operating system [25] on a VME-based Ironics IV3220 single-board computer with a 68020 CPU running at 20 MHz. Experimental results show that the variance decreases significantly. The rationale for this decrease involves the following factors:

Predictable Context Switching. CROPS5 reduces the variance of context switching by providing an architectural mechanism to switch streams. To perform a context switch in conventional OPS5, the old context element had to be deleted, and the new context element inserted into the working memory. This results in a flurry of match activity. The minimum time required for replacing the context element is a function of the sum of the number of productions in the two contexts. The context switch time is thus highly dependent on the partial state of the match and the uncertainty in the environment, and is on the order of the time required for a match-resolve-act cycle. The numbers presented next are an order of magnitude measure of the time required for a context switch. Notice that the variance in context-switching time is on the order of thousands of microseconds. In contrast, context switching in CROPS5 is two orders of magnitude faster and more predictable. Since each stream has its own Rete network, the new stream can immediately begin processing its data without having to spend significant time performing bookkeeping on the state of the match algorithm.

—Sample range in OPS5 context switch time: 1800 μseconds–4300 μseconds
—CROPS5 *Dispatcher Statistics:*
 * Context Switch to a different stream: 55 μseconds
 * Continue processing same stream: 9 μseconds

Predictable Preemption Points. Context switching can be done only at preemption points. Since preemption in conventional OPS5 systems is at the rule-firing boundary, there is a large variance in the points of preemption. CROPS5 reduces the variance in the points of preemption by reducing the granularity of preemption from the match-processing level to the token-processing level. Associated with the reduction in granularity is an order of magnitude decrease in variations and an equivalent increase in responsiveness.

—Sample range in OPS5 preemption points: 1800 μseconds–4300 μseconds
—CROPS5 *Granularity of preemption:*
 *Average token firing time: 134 μseconds

The predictability of the points of preemption, and the context switch time allows us to estimate *a priori* the time required to react to different events.
Predictable Match. Preemption points and context switching are not the only sources of variance. Match processing is another. Different techniques have been ex-

plored to bound the match processing to make it predictable [28]. These techniques have relied on restricting the expressive power of the language to eliminate match combinatorics. Of these techniques, the unique attribute formalism [28] appears promising. This formalism can be adopted in CROPS5 by restricting the types of productions written, and can be used to provide polynomially bounded match times for CROPS5 applications.

Integrating CROPS5 into Real-Time Systems

CROPS5 was designed for embedded real-time applications. Our approach allows CROPS5 to coexist with other real-time tasks on a common computing platform. Using operating system primitives, CROPS5 can run at any priority level while still guaranteeing deadlines of other tasks in the system. The integration features referred to in the rightmost branch of Figure 3 are addressed as follows:

Encapsulation within an AI Server. To guarantee temporal isolation between conventional real-time tasks and problem-solving tasks, we encapsulate all problem solving within an AI Server. We borrow the Server abstraction directly from the real-time scheduling community [24,26]. Servers have previously been developed to provide highly responsive aperiodic performance in periodic, hard deadline environments.

We utilize this approach to create an AI Server which is a bandwidth-limited task whose schedulability impact can be explicitly evaluated and guaranteed[1]. The AI Server differs from the Deferrable Server

---
[1]Schedulability of a system is the level of resource utilization attainable before a deadline is missed.

[26] and the Sporadic Server [24] in that it services both periodic and aperiodic tasks and has a different replenishment policy [20]. Given a set of conventional real-time tasks with deadlines, one can apply scheduling analytical techniques to determine the maximum possible capacity of the AI Server at any priority level. This technique is illustrated later, using an application example.
Responsiveness and Preemptability. The CROPS5 production system was specifically designed to be preemptive and priority driven. At the integrated-system level, the preemptability of the AI Server which encapsulates the CROPS5 system is identical to the preemptability of any other real-time task. Thus the schedulability analysis of the real-time task set, including the AI Server, can be performed in a uniform way. CROPS5 also provides a high degree of preemptability of problem solving, by allowing the problem-solving stream to be interrupted at the token-processing granularity. The fine granularity of preemption provides a high degree of responsiveness to the environment.
Environment Interface. The interface to the external world is through a Data Handler. The Data Handler accepts input from the other tasks in the system. This allows CROPS5 to run in embedded applications which process sensor data.
Integration with Conventional Systems: CROPS5 supports mechanisms to facilitate easy integration between the rule-based component and existing procedural software. A C-language interface is provided from the right-hand sides of productions, allowing external C functions to access and modify internal *working memory elements* of the production system.

CROPS5 is portable, and runs on most Unix and Mach machines. CROPS5 also runs on the ARTS [30] and CHIMERA II [25] real-time operating systems and is currently being ported to Real-Time Mach [29].

AI Architecture

Provide mechanisms to partition, prune and order the search space

- Prioritized Streams
- Knowledge-Based Scheduler
- Preemptability
- Context Swapping

Provide predictable primitives for problem-solving

- Predictable Preemption Points
- Predictable Context Switching
- Predictable Match
  - Restricting Expressiveness

Integrate into a real-time environment

- Sensor Interface
- Responsiveness
  - Fine Granularity Premption
  - Fast Context Switching
- Encapsulation

FIGURE 3.
Capabilities Required of Real-Time Problem-Solving Architectures

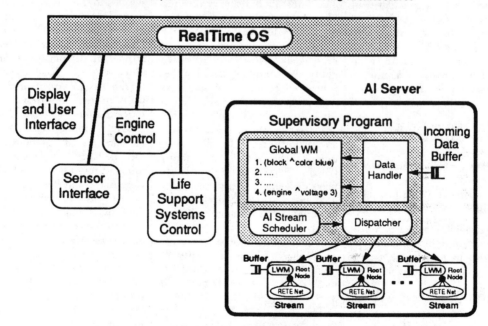

FIGURE 4.
CROPS5 in a Real-Time Environment

Application Example: The Collision Avoidance System

Two systems have been implemented using this architecture: an aircraft collision avoidance system and a dynamic factory-scheduling system [10]. We use the Collision Avoidance application as an illustration of how the techniques to reduce execution time variance improve the predictability of the system. The Collision Avoidance application has been in use as an experimental benchmark over the past few months. In this section, we describe how this system is implemented and substantiate our claims with experimental results.

Specifically, we will demonstrate the use of CROPS5 mechanisms to partition, order and prune the search space. We will compare the CROPS5-based implementation with an implementation using conventional OPS5, and show how the variance has been reduced. The application will be analyzed to determine the evolution of the system in response to changing data rates. We will demonstrate a best effort solution strategy with predictable breakdown points. We will also demonstrate that problem-solving processes can be successfully integrated with conventional hard real-time tasks on a common computing platform, while guaranteeing deadlines of all real-time tasks.

Application Background

The Collision Avoidance System (CAS) consists of an airplane receiver that listens to the signals emitted by radar transponders on other planes in response to interrogation signals from the host plane. By interpreting the transponder return, measuring the time delay of the response, and checking the angle the reply is coming from, the system can determine the altitude, distance and bearing of nearby transponder-equipped aircraft. While displaying the raw information is informative, it still must be processed to determine evasive action. Given the extremely limited

response time requirement (< 10 secs.), any decision aid in this situation would be extremely beneficial. The CAS provides decision support capability to the pilot by generating advice to climb, dive, or turn right or left to avoid potential threats.

We implemented this application using the problem space search technique discussed earlier. In this case, the problem space is defined by the dimensions along which advice needs to be generated, and the number and orientation of the target planes around the host plane. The solution space is the set of final advice recommendations to the pilot.

The nature of the application imposes specific real-time performance and resource requirements [20]. Due to limited footprint space on modern aircraft, it is desirable for the collision avoidance system to coexist with conventional real-time tasks on the same computing platform. The collision avoidance system must also share communication networks and system resources with other real-time tasks, without causing them to miss their deadlines.

Demonstration of Variance Reduction

As a first step to solving this problem, we partition the overall functionality among a number of real-time tasks at the system level. The basic tasks are the reading of radar sensors, the knowledge-based processing of the information, and the display of the advice generated. The knowledge-based processing of the information is done using both CROPS5 and OPS5.

We implemented the collision avoidance application in three different systems to illustrate the reduction in problem-solving variance—OPS5 without context elements; OPS5 with context ele-

ments; and CROPS5.

In the OPS5 implementation without context elements, a single program handled advice generation for all planes. This program had the following limitations:

- *No preemptability.* Once the program starts execution, it stops only after advice for all planes is generated.
- *Unpredictable match processing.* Since multiple data elements can match the condition elements of rules, data-dependent combinatorics result.

This approach and programming style are not suited to most real-time applications. A real-time system has to be aware of the possible limitations in time. It must order its computations so the most important ones are done first. The nonpreemptability and large execution time variance of the conventional OPS5 implementation makes it difficult to provide performance guarantees for the CAS. We used the variance-reduction techniques discussed previously and the mechanisms provided by CROPS5 to reduce the execution time variance of this application at both the problem space level and the knowledge retrieval level.

Problem Space Level

Pruning: In this application, partitioning is done so that each stream handles the processing for a single plane. Ordering of the search is done by prioritizing the streams based on the degree of the perceived threat. Figure 5 illustrates our problem-solving strategy. In our application, all streams calculate their own priorities at the beginning of every data cycle. This priority is passed to the dispatcher. Advice generation is ordered, starting with the highest-priority threat. Streams handling planes moving away from the host plane are set to the lowest priority. This solution strategy is a best effort strategy, in that if time runs out before all planes are processed, the system would have considered the highest priority threats and generated some partial advice [4].

Abstraction. For this problem, advice generation can occur at multiple levels of abstraction, each with varying amounts of detail [15]. The limiting cases of advice generation are characterized next, with other situations lying in between. On one hand, if a collision were imminent, advice is generated to immediately swerve to avoid the threat. On the other hand, if more time were available, factors such as weather, the range of available operating altitudes, and the expected intentions of the threat are taken into account

number of streams.

Restricting Expressiveness. Since we could make the match predictable by data partitioning only, we did not consider restricting the expressiveness of the language to bound the match time.

FIGURE 5.
Problem-Solving Strategy

input data, while the OPS5-based system is not similarly immune even though it uses context elements. In this experiment, we see that in generating advice for one plane, OPS5 takes 222 ms (545 tokens) when there is one plane, vs. 274 ms (789 tokens) when there are five. CROPS5, on the other hand, varies only between 148 ms and 154 ms (310 tokens–318 tokens). While both execution times and token numbers are presented, the token numbers are not affected by the limitations of the time measurement process. The net variation is 244 tokens in OPS5 vs. only 8 to-

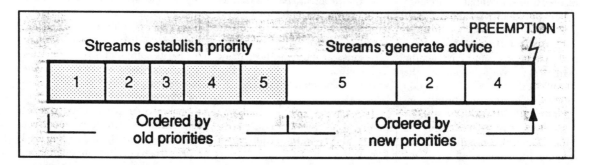

before advice is generated.

Knowledge Retrieval Level

Knowledge Base Partitioning. Since the knowledge base for this application is relatively small, we did not partition it.

Data Partitioning. The CAS uses data partitioning to ensure the predictability of the match process. In this application, we partition the data so that each stream looks only at the data associated with one plane. This ensures that at most, one working memory element matches any given condition element in the Rete net of the productions, thereby eliminating match combinatorics. The trade-off for limiting the match combinatorics is an increase in the number of streams (increased memory space). The relatively small size of the Rete net per stream allowed us to replicate streams without incurring too much memory cost. The maximum number of planes that can be considered is limited by the maximum

Our problem-solving strategy was to partition and order the computation to reduce the execution time variance of the application. A number of experiments were conducted to measure the performance of the application. We present some of these results to illustrate the reduction in variance.

In Table 1, we compare the performance of the OPS5 implementation using context elements, and the CROPS5 implementation using streams. To factor out dependencies due to programming style and implementation, all OPS5 problem solving was programmed using CROPS5—which is upward compatible with OPS5.

This experiment was conducted to determine the variation in the time taken to generate advice for one plane, as a function of the input data. We see that CROPS5 does better in two respects: predictability and efficiency.

The CROPS5-based system is relatively immune to changes in

kens in CROPS5. This demonstrates an order of magnitude improvement in CROPS5 predictability.

Table 2 isolates the context switch performance of OPS5 and CROPS5 at each of the data points. Notice that CROPS5 context/stream switching is constant in this application, unlike OPS5. The tokens processed for the OPS5 context switch increase in a regular fashion since the code to process a plane is the same across all contexts. The context switch processing is typically unpredictable in OPS5, while remaining constant in CROPS5.

Moreover, we find that CROPS5 primitives speeded up the application over that of OPS5 by a factor of about 2. This is due to the elimination of redundant processing.

We now discuss how the CROPS5 implementation can be analyzed and integrated into a hard real-time system so that performance guarantees can be provided.

TABLE 1.

Comparison of OPS5 and CROPS5 Performance

Number of Planes	Number Prioritized	Number Advice Gen.	Time Taken (msec.)		Tokens Processed	
			OPS5	CROPS5	OPS5	CROPS5
1	1	1	222	148	545	310
2	1	1	233	153	606	312
3	1	1	248	152	669	314
4	1	1	262	154	730	316
5	1	1	274	152	789	318

TABLE 2.

Context Switch Performance

Number of Planes	Number Prioritized	Number Advice Gen.	Tokens Processed	
			OPS5	CROPS5
1	1	1	77	2
2	1	1	87	2
3	1	1	97	2
4	1	1	107	2
5	1	1	117	2

TABLE 3.

Execution Characteristics of the Real-Time Task Set

Periodic Task	Run-Time msec.	Period msec.	Utilization	Rate Monotonic Priority
Engine Control	6.00	50.00	0.120%	1
Sensor Monitoring	36.00	250.00	0.144%	2
AI Task	C_{AI_S}	1000.00	U_{AI_S}	3
Display & User Int.	100.00	1200.00	0.083%	4
Life Support	120.00	1500.00	0.080%	5
Total			$0.427 + U_{AI_S}$%	

TABLE 4.

Comparison of Predicted vs. Measured Performance

Number of Planes	Number Prioritized	Number Advice Gen.	Predicted Time (msec.)	Measured Time (msec.)
5	5	1	421	380
5	5	2	498	445
5	5	3	574	517
5	5	4	650	583
5	5	5	726	660

Demonstration of System Analyzability

To demonstrate the ability of the problem-solving architecture to coexist with hard real-time tasks on a common computing platform, we consider the experimental task set shown in Table 3. This is the same task set illustrated in Figure 4. In addition to the radar sensor monitoring and display interface tasks required for the collision avoidance application, we have added two critical additional tasks with widely different responsiveness requirements—an engine control task with a very short period of 50 ms, and a Life Support Systems task with a relatively long period 1500 ms.

AI Server Capacity

Previously, we introduced our integrated, real-time problem-solving architecture and provided a qualitative discussion on how one can jointly schedule conventional real-time tasks and CROPS5 using an AI Server. Here, we will demonstrate, via the Collision Avoidance application example, how to assign priority to the AI Server and how to solve for its maximum capacity consistent with the RT tasks' scheduling requirements.

In general, the priority assigned to the AI server is a function of its response time requirements. In the Collision Avoidance application, the AI processing requirements are periodic with a period, T_{AI_S}, of 1000 ms. Since the conventional RT tasks are also periodic with periods summarized in Table 3, the Rate Monotonic scheduling algorithm [16] can readily be applied to evaluate the schedulability of the task set. The Rate Monotonic algorithm has been proven to the optimal fixed-priority scheduling algorithm for periodic tasks. Using this algorithm, the tasks are priority ordered by their rates—the shorter their period, the higher their priority. Note that assignment of priorities is based solely upon response time requirements and does not consider the relative semantic importance of the tasks. When the schedulability of the entire task set cannot be guaranteed, the relative semantic importance of the tasks comes into play. In such a case semantic-based load shedding is appropriate. Otherwise, the highest schedulable utilization is achieved by assigning priorities solely on response time requirements.

Given the maximum run time, C_i, and period, T_i of each of the conventional real-time tasks, we now solve for the maximum capacity of the AI Server task, C_{AI_s} which will not violate the response time requirements of the lower-priority Display and Life Support System tasks. A tight schedulability bound can be calculated by an exact-case analysis consistent with the rate-monotonic algorithm [14]. This bound expressed as:

$\forall i, 1 \leq i \leq n,$

$$\min \sum_{j=1}^{i} C_j \frac{1}{lT_k} \left[\frac{lT_k}{T_j} \right] \leq 1 \quad (1)$$

$$(k, l) \in R_i$$

$$R_i = \left\{ (k, l) | 1 \leq k \leq i, l = 1, \ldots, \left[\frac{T_i}{T_k} \right] \right\}$$

takes explicit account of the actual task sets' period ratios and run times. Equation 1 yields a maximum C_{AI_s} of 516 ms which corresponds to a maximum utilization of the AI Server of $U_{AI_s} = C_{AI_s}/T_{AI_s} = 0.516$ or 51.6%. Adding this to the utilization of the other real-time tasks, we get a total schedulable utilization of 94.3%. The following section provides an analytical treatment to answer whether the AI Server capacity is sufficient to meet the response time requirement of the Collision Avoidance application.

Application Analysis

To analyze the application, we use the following equation:

$$C_{AI} = n[t_{P_u}(s) + 2t_{sw}]$$
$$+ m[t_{lw}(d) + 2t_{sw}] + mt_{gw}(d, m)$$

where

n	maximum number of planes looked at and prioritized;
m	maximum number of planes for which advice is generated;
$t_{P_u}(s)$	worst-case priority calculation time for a stream, which is a function of the prioritization strategy s. In our example, we use an algorithmic evaluation strategy to calculate the priority of the plane;
t_{sw}	stream-switch overhead;
$t_{lw}(d)$	worst-case execution time in generating advice for each plane, and is a function of the number of dimensions d considered. In our example, we calculate advice along two dimensions, namely, altitude and turn;
$t_{gw}(d, n)$	worst-case execution time to resolve advice conflicts at a global level, and is a function of the number of dimensions d and planes n considered.

Given the number of planes (n-5), the worst-case computation requirement would be to generate advice for all planes ($n = 5$). From Table 4, the predicted value of C_{AI} is 726ms, using the fastest problem-solving strategy available. The server capacity C_{AI_s} is 516 ms. Thus this application cannot generate advice for all planes. The largest predicted time ($C_{AI} = 498$ ms), which is less than the server capacity is the level of guarantee. In this case, we can guarantee at least five planes will be looked at, and advice generated for the two highest-priority planes.

To verify the validity of our predictions, we ran experiments to determine the execution times. The results comparing our predicted performance and the actual performance are summarized in Table 4. The effectiveness of the techniques to reduce variance, and the relatively small size of the application have allowed us to make useful predictions about the performance of the system.

Predictable "Best Effort" Evolution

In real-world situations, the application can sometimes be subjected to overloads beyond the design limits. Even though the design requirements dictate that there will be less than five planes in the vicinity at any given time, the system must degrade gracefully in cases where this requirement is exceeded. If this happens, the application must continue to prioritize and generate advice starting from the highest-priority plane, until time runs out. We should note that regardless of the strategies available, a minimum amount of execution time is needed before a useful result can be generated. This minimum time is determined by using the fastest problem-solving strategies available. If the minimum time is greater than the server capacity, the system breaks. From an engineering perspective, it is useful to be able to predict the breakdown points of the system.

If the number of planes, n, crosses a threshold, the system spends all the time classifying the data that it has no time remaining to generate useful advice. In our example, the limiting case of the system is reached when it has just enough time to calculate advice for the highest-priority plane. Assuming the worst-case advice calculation time for a single plane, and a zero global-advice conflict resolution time (since advice is generated for only one plane), we estimate:

$$\overline{n}_{\text{breakdown}} = \frac{C_{AI_s} - [t_{lw}(d) + 2t_{sw}]}{[t_{P_u}(s) + 2t_{sw})} \quad (2)$$

Notice that the number of planes

processed in the limiting case is a function of the available computation bandwidth, C_{AI_s}. Substituting values of the variables in equation (2), the system breakdown point is computed to be $\bar{n}_{breakdown} = 7$ planes. With seven planes, we can now generate advice only for the highest-priority threat. If the number of planes goes beyond seven, the system will not have enough computation bandwidth to generate any advice. This provides a design margin of two planes over and above the design requirement of five planes. This analysis allows us to *a priori* predict the effect of changing the number of planes and computational bandwidth on the performance of the application.

Summary
In this article, we argued that large execution time variance is the primary problem in providing practical performance guarantees for integrated, real-time problem-solving systems. We showed that this variance is due to search which is inherent to problem-solving tasks. Search occurs at two levels in a problem-solving task—the problem space level and the knowledge retrieval level. To reduce the execution time variance, it is necessary to reduce the extent of search at both these levels. At the problem space level, the search can be reduced by the application of problem-specific knowledge, whereas at the knowledge retrieval level, no problem-specific knowledge is available. At this level, the search must be reduced by knowledge-lean methods like knowledge and data partitioning, and reducing the expressiveness of the knowledge representation formalism.

To evaluate the effectiveness of these techniques, we implemented CROPS5, a real-time problem-solving architecture. CROPS5 provides predictable primitives at the knowledge retrieval level and supports problem-specific strategies that reduce variance at the problem space level. In addition, CROPS5 has been designed to be easily integrable into conventional real-time systems. Implementations of CROPS5 currently run on two real-time operating systems. CROPS5 has been used to develop a prototype aircraft collision avoidance system and a dynamic factory-scheduling system.

We used the collision avoidance system as a benchmark to compare CROPS5 with OPS5. Results show that the variance of the real-time problem-solving primitives in CROPS5 is significantly lower. Specifically, the variance in context switching is reduced by two orders of magnitude, and the variance in preemption points is reduced by an order of magnitude. Furthermore, these primitives allowed us to eliminate redundant computation, resulting in a speedup of a factor of about 2. We achieved predictable match processing in this application by partitioning data across multiple streams. Overall, we were able to predict application execution times to within 10% of actual measured values in an integrated real-time environment. The AI server was successful in ensuring that conventional real-time tasks on the same computing platform continued to meet their deadlines even after the CAS application was introduced into the system.

Using these techniques, we were able to demonstrate that it is feasible to reduce problem-solving variance and thereby provide practical performance guarantees for time-constrained problem-solving tasks in integrated real-time environments, while maintaining all performance guarantees for the conventional real-time tasks.

Acknowledgments
We thank Herbert Simon for his valuable comments in organizing the arguments in this article. We thank Dorothy Setliff and the other reviewers for their suggestions on improving the clarity of this article. We also thank Hiroshi Arakawa, Dave Stewart, Gary Hildebrand, Stephen Chou and Hide Tokuda for their help at various stages in implementing the experimental testbed. ◨

References
1. Acharya, A. and Kalp, D. Release Notes on ParaOPS5 4.4 and CParaOPS5 5.4, 1989. Available with the CParaOPS5 distribution from the School of Computer Science, Carnegie Mellon University.
2. Bares, J., Hebert, M., Kanade, T., Krotkov, E., Mitchell, T., Simmons, R. and Whittaker, W. Ambler: An autonomous rover for planetary exploration. *IEEE Comput. 22*, 6 (June 1989).
3. Bastani, F.B. and Chen, I-R. The role of artificial intelligence in fault-tolerant process-control systems. In *Proceedings of the First International Conference on Industrial and Engineering Applications of Artificial Intelligence and Expert Systems*, Vol. 2, June 1988.
4. Boddy, M. and Dean, T. Solving time-dependent planning problems. In *Proceedings Eleventh International Joint Conference on Artificial Intelligence*, Aug. 1989.
5. Chung, Jen-Yao, Liu, J.W.S. and Lin, K.J. Scheduling periodic jobs that allow imprecise results. *IEEE Trans. Comput. 39*, 9 (Sept. 1990).
6. Dickey, F.J. and Toussaint, A.L. ECESIS: An application of expert systems on manned space stations. In *Proceedings of the First Conference on Artificial Intelligence Space Applications* (1984), pp. 483–89.
7. Fishetti, M.A. TMI Plus 5: Nuclear power on the Ropes. *IEEE Spectrum 21*, 4 (1984).
8. Forgy, C.L. Rete: A fast algorithm for the many pattern/many object pattern match problem. *Artif. Intell. 19*, 1 (1982), 17–37.
9. Hayes-Roth, F. and Waterman, D.A. Principles of pattern-directed inference systems. *Pattern-directed Inf. Syst.* (1978), 577–601.
10. Holloway, L., Paul, C.J., Strosnider, J. and Krogh, B. Integration of behavioral fault-detection models and an intelligent reactive scheduler. In *Proceedings of the 6th IEEE*

International Symposium on Intelligent Control (Aug. 1991).

11. Kohn, W. Declarative hierarchical controllers. In *Proceedings of the Workshop on Innovation Approaches to Planning, Scheduling and Control* (Nov. 1990).

12. Laffey, T.J., Cox, P.A., Schmidt, J.L., Kao, S.M. and Read, J.Y. Real-time knowledge-based systems. *AI Magazine 9*, 1 (1988), 27–45.

13. Laffey, T., Weitzenkamp, S., Read, J., Kao, S., and Schmidt, J. Intelligent real-time monitoring. In *Proceedings of the AAAI-88 Seventh National Conference on Artificial Intelligence* (Aug. 1988, Lockheed Artificial Intelligence Center), pp. 72–76.

14. Lehoczky, J.P., Sha, L. and Ding, Y. The rate monotonic scheduling algorithm—exact characterization and average case behaviour. In *Proceedings of the IEEE Systems Symposium* (1989).

15. Lesser, V.R., Pavlin, J., and Durfee, E. Approximate processing in real-time problem solving. *AI Mag.* (Spring 1988).

16. Liu, C.L. and Layland, J.W. Scheduling algorithms for multiprogramming in a hard real-time environment. *J. ACM 20*, 1 (1973), 46–61.

17. Meystel, A. Intelligent module for planning/control of master-dependent systems. In *Proceedings of the First International Conference on Industrial and Engineering Applications of Artificial Intelligence and Expert Systems*, Vol. 1, June 1988.

18. Mok, A.K. Formal analysis of real-time equational rule-based systems. In *Proceedings of the Real-Time Systems Symposium* (Dec. 1989).

19. Newell, A. and Simon, H. Human Problem Solving. Prentice-Hall, Englewood Cliffs, N.J., 1972.

20. Paul, C.J., Acharya, A. and Black, B., Strosnider, J.K. Concurrent real-time ops5: An architecture for real-time problem-solving. Tech. Rep., Carnegie Mellon University, May 1991.

21. Perry, T.S. and Wallich, P. A matter of margins. *IEEE Spectrum 23*, 11 (Nov. 1986).

22. Rao, M., Jiang, T.S. and Tsai, J.J.-P. Integrated environment for intelligent control. In *Proceedings of the First International Conference on Industrial and Engineering Applications of Artificial Intelligence and Expert Systems*, Vol. 1, June 1988.

23. Skapura, D.M. and Zoch, D.R. A real-time production system for telemetry analysis. In *Proceedings of the 1986 Expert Systems in Government*, (1986), pp. 203–209.

24. Sprunt, B., Sha, L. and Lehoczky, J. A periodic task scheduling for hard real-time systems. *J. Real-Time Syst. 1*, 1 (1989), 27–60.

25. Stewart, D., Schmitz, D.E. and Khosla, P. Implementing real-time robotic sytems using chimera ii. In *Proceedings of the 1990 IEEE International Conference on Robotics And Automation*, (May 1990), pp. 598–603.

26. Strosnider, J.K. Highly responsive real-time token rings. Ph.D. thesis, Carnegie Mellon University, Aug. 1988.

27. Tokuda, H. and Mercer, C. Arts: A distributed real-time kernel. *ACM Oper. Syst. Rev. 23*, 4 (July 1989).

28. Tokuda, H., Nakajima, T. and Rao, P. Real-time Mach: Towards a predictable real-time system. In *Proceedings of the USENIX Mach Workshop* (Oct. 1990).

29. Tambe, M. and Rosenbloom, P. Eliminating expensive chunks by restricting expressiveness. In *Proceedings of the Eleventh International Joint Conference on Artificial Intelligence* (Aug. 1989), pp. 731–737.

30. Tambe, M. and Rosenbloom, P. A framework for investigating production system formulations with polynomially bounded match. In *Proceedings of the AAAI-90 Eighth National Conference on Artificial Intelligence*, (Aug. 1990), pp. 693–700.

CR Categories and Subject Descriptors: D.4.7 [Operating Systems]: Organization and Design—*real-time and embedded systems;* I.2.8 [**Artificial Intelligence**]: Problem Solving, Control Methods and Search—*backtracking, graph and tree strategies, heuristic methods*

Additional Key Words and Phrases: Chimera, decision aids, expert systems, knowledge-based systems, predictability, production systems, real-time systems, search, variance

About the Authors:

C.J. PAUL is a Ph.D student in computer engineering at Carnegie Mellon University. Between 1987 and 1989, he designed and built networked real-time process-control systems at IBM, Research Triangle Park, N.C. His research interests include parallel computer architecture, real-time scheduling theory and artificial intelligence. **Author's Present Address:** Department of Electrical and Computer Engineering, Carnegie Mellon University, Pittsburgh, PA 15213, cjpaul@ece.cmu.edu.

ANURAG ACHARYA is a graduate student at the School of Computer Science at Carnegie Mellon. His research interests include theory and implementation of programming languages, parallel processing and production systems. **Author's Present Address:** School of Computer Science, Carnegie Mellon University, Pittsburg, PA 15213, acha@cs.cmu.edu.

BRYAN BLACK is currently working at Motorola Semiconductor Products Sector in Austin. His research interests include VLSI design, processor architectures, and real-time systems. **Author's Present Address:** Motorola Semiconductor Products Sector, 505 Barton Springs Road, Suite 400, Austin TX, black@ece.cmu.edu.

JAY K. STROSNIDER is currently an assistant professor of electrical and computer engineering at Carnegie Mellon. He has 10 years of industrial experience developing distributed, real-time systems with IBM. His current research focus is upon integrating technologies within a real-time, scheduling-theoretic framework. **Author's Present Address:** Department of Electrical and Computer Engineering, Carnegie Mellon University, Pittsburgh, PA 15213, strsnider@ece.cmu.edu.

This research is supported in part by a grant from Northrop Research and Technology Center, by the Office of Naval Research under contract N00014-84-K-0734, and by the Naval Ocean Systems Center under contract N66001-87-C-01155

Bibliography

R. Abbott and H. Garcia-Molina, "Scheduling Real-Time Transactions: A Performance Evaluation," *Proc. 14th VLDB Conf.*, Morgan Kaufmann, San Mateo, Calif., 1988.

R. Abbott and H. Garcia-Molina, "Scheduling I/O Requests with Deadlines: A Performance Evaluation," *Proc. 11th Real-Time Systems Symp.*, IEEE CS Press, Los Alamitos, Calif., Dec. 1990, pp. 113-124.

T. Ae and R. Aibara, "Programmable Real-Time Scheduler Using a Neurocomputer," *Real-Time Systems*, Vol. 1, No. 4, April 1990, pp. 351-364.

R. Agne, "Global Cyclic Scheduling: A Method to Guarantee the Timing Behavior of Distributed Real-Time Systems," *Real-Time Systems*, Vol. 3, No. 1, March 1991, pp. 45-66.

T. Anderson and J. Knight, "A Framework for Software Fault Tolerance in Real-Time Systems," *IEEE Trans. Software Engineering*, Vol. SE-9, No. 3, May 1983, pp. 355-364.

T. Anderson and P.A. Lee, *Fault Tolerance - Principles and Practice*, Prentice Hall, Englewood Cliffs, N.J., 1981.

R.G. Arnold, R.O. Berg, and J.W. Thomas "A Modular Approach to Real-Time Supersystems," *IEEE Trans. on Computers*, Vol. C-31, No. 5, May 1982, pp. 385-398.

K. Arvind, "A New Probabilistic Algorithm for Clock Synchronization," *Proc. Real-Time Systems Symp.*, Dec. 1989, pp. 330-339.

K. Arvind, K. Ramamritham, and J.A. Stankovic, "Window MAC Protocols for Real-Time Communication Services," COINS Tech. Report 90-127, Univ. Massachusetts, Amherst, Mass., 1990.

K. Arvind, K. Ramamritham, and J.A. Stankovic, "A Local Area Network Architecture for Communication in Distributed Real-Time Systems," *Real-Time Systems*, Vol. 3, No. 2, May 1991, pp. 115-148.

S. Ashour, Sequencing Theory, *Lecture Notes in Economics and Mathematical Systems*, Springer-Verlag, New York, 1972.

S.B. Auernheimer and R.A. Kemmerer, RT-ASLAN: A Specification Language for Real-Time Systems, *IEEE Trans. Software Engineering*, Vol. SE-12, No. 9, pp. Sept. 1986, pp. 879-889.

F. Baccelli, P. Boyer and G. Hebuterne, "Single-Server Queues With Impatient Customers," *Advanced Applied Probability*, Vol. 16, 1984.

R. Bagrodia and C.-C. Shen, "Integrated Design, Simulation, and Verification of Real-Time Systems," *Proc. Int'l. Conf. Distributed Computing Systems*, IEEE CS Press, Los Alamitos, Calif., May 1991, pp. 164-171.

K.R. Baker and Z.-S. Su, "Sequencing With Due-dates and Early Start Times to Minimize Maximum Tardiness," *Naval Research Logistics Q.* Vol. 21, 1974.

T. Baker, "The Use of Ada for Real-Time Systems," *Real-Time Systems Newsletter*, Vol. 6, No. 1, Jan. 1990, pp. 3-8.

T. Baker, "Stack-Based Scheduling of Real-Time Processes," *Real-Time Systems*, Vol. 3, No. 1, March 1991, pp. 67-100.

T.P. Baker and G.M. Scallon, "An Architecture for Real-Time Software Systems," *IEEE Software,* Vol. 2, No. 5, May 1986, pp. 50-58.

T.P. Baker and A. Shaw, "The Cyclic Executive Model and Ada," *Real-Time Systems*, Vol. 1, No. 1, June 1989, pp. 7-26.

J.A. Bannister and K.S. Trivedi, "Task Allocation in Fault-Tolerant Distributed Systems," *Acta Informatica*, Springer-Verlag, 1983, pp. 261-281.

A.B. Barsky, "Minimizing the Number of Computing Devices Needed to Realize a Computational Process within a Specified Time," *Engineering Cybernetics*, Vol. 6, 1968.

S. Baruah et al., "On-Line Scheduling in the Presence of Overload," *Proc. 1991 IEEE Symp. Foundations of Computer Science*, IEEE CS Press, Los Alamitos, Calif., Oct. 1991, pp. 100-110.

S. Baruah, A. Mok, and L. Rosier, "Preemptively Scheduling Hard, Real-Time Sporatic Tasks on One Processor," *Proc. 11th Real-Time Systems Symp.*, IEEE CS Press, Los Alamitos, Calif., 1990, pp. 182-190.

S.K. Baruah, L.E. Rosier, and R.R. Howell, "Algorithms and Complexity Concerning the Preemptive Scheduling of Periodic, Real-Time Tasks on One Processor," *Real-Time Systems*, Vol. 2, No. 4, Nov. 1990, pp. 301-324.

S.K. Baruah et al., "On the Competitiveness of On-Line Real-Time Task Scheduling," *Real-Time Systems*, Vol. 4, No. 2, June 1992.

R. Bettati and J. Liu, "Algorithms for Flow-Shop Scheduling to Meet Deadlines," *Proc. Eighth IEEE Workshop on Real-Time Operating Systems and Software*, May 1991.

T. Bially, A.J. McLaughlin, and C.J. Weinstein, "Voice Communications in Integrated Digital Voice and Data Networks," *IEEE Trans. Communication*, Vol. COM-28, Sept. 1980, pp. 1478-1490.

S. Biyabani, "The Integration of Deadline and Criticalness in Hard Real-Time Scheduling," master's thesis, Univ. Massachusetts, Amherst, Mass., Aug. 1987.

S. Biyabani, J.A. Stankovic, and K. Ramamritham, "The Integration of Deadline and Criticalness in Hard Real-Time Scheduling," *Proc. Real-Time Systems Symp.*, IEEE CS Press, Los Alamitos, Calif., Dec. 1988, pp. 152-160.

B.A. Blake and K. Schwan, "Experimental Evaluation of a Real-Time Scheduler for a Multiprocessor System," *IEEE Trans. Software Engineering*, Vol. 17, No. 1, Jan. 1991.

J. Blazewicz, "Scheduling Dependent Tasks with Different Arrival Times to Meet Deadlines," in *Modelling and Performance Evaluation of Computer Systems*, E. Gelenbe, ed., North-Holland, New York, 1976.

J. Blazewicz, "Simple Algorithms for Multiprocessor Scheduling to Meet Deadlines," *Information Processing Letters*, Vol. 6, No. 5, Oct. 1977.

J. Blazewicz, "Deadline Scheduling of Tasks with Ready Times and Resource Constraints," *Information Processing Letters*, Vol. 8, No. 2, Feb. 1979.

J. Blazewicz, "Solving the Resource Constrained Deadline Scheduling Problem via Reduction to the Network Flow Problem," *Euro. J. Operational Research*, Vol. 6, 1981.

J. Blazewicz et al., "Scheduling under Resource Constraints – Deterministic Models," *Annals of Operations Research*, AG Scientific Publishing, 1986.

J. Blazewicz, K. Drabowski, and J. Weglarz, "Scheduling Multiprocessor Tasks to Minimize Schedule Length," *IEEE Trans. Computers*, Vol. 35, No. 5, May 1986, pp. 389-393.

J. Blazewicz, J.K. Lenstra, and A.H.G.R. Kan, "Scheduling Subject to Resource Constraints: Classification and Complexity," *Discrete Applied Mathematics*, Vol. 5, No. 11, 1983.

J. Blazewicz and J. Weglarz, "Scheduling under Resource Constraints: Achievements and Prospects," *Performance of Computer Systems*, M. Arato, A. Butrimento, and E. Gelenbe, eds., North-Holland, New York, 1979.

S.H. Bokhari, "On the Mapping Problem," *IEEE Trans. Computers*, Vol. C-30, No. 3, March 1981, pp. 207-214.

P.P. Bonissone and P.C. Halverson, "Time-Constrained Reasoning Under Uncertainty," *Real-Time Systems*, Vol. 2, Nos. 1/2, May 1990, pp. 25-46.

M. Bonuccelli and D.P. Bovet, "Scheduling Unit Time Independent Tasks on Dedicated Resource Systems," Report S-6-21, Univ. degli studi di Pisa, Instituo di Scienze dell Informazione, Pisa, Italy, 1976.

M. Bottazzi and C. Salati, "A Hierarchical Approach to L Systems with Heterogeneous Real-Time Requirements," *Real-Time Systems*, Vol. 3, No. 2, May 1991, pp. 149-164.

P. Bratley, M. Florian, and P. Robillard, "Scheduling with Earliest Start and Due-Date Constraints," *Naval Research Logistics Q.*, Vol. 18, No. 4, Dec. 1971.

P. Bratley, M. Florian, and P. Robillard, "Scheduling with Earliest Start and Due-Date Constraints on Multiple Machines," *Naval Research Logistics Q.*, Vol. 22, 1975.

A.P. Buchmann et al., "Time-Critical Database Scheduling: A Framework For Integrating Real-Time Scheduling and Concurrency Control," *Proc. Data Engineering Conf.*, Feb. 1989.

A. Burns and A.J. Wellings, "Correspondence: Criticality and Utility in the Next Generation," *Real-Time Systems*, Vol. 3, No. 4, Dec. 1991, pp. 351-354.

A. Burns and A.J. Wellings, "Priority Inheritance and Message-Passing Communication: A Formal Treatment," *Real-Time Systems*, Vol. 3, No. 1, March 1991, pp. 19-44.

A. Burns and A.J. Wellings, *Real-Time Systems and Their Programming Languages*, Addison-Wesley, Reading, Mass., 1989.

M.J. Carey, R. Jauhari, and M. Livny, "Priority in DBMS Resource Scheduling," *Proc. 15th VLDB Conf.*, Morgan Kaufmann, San Mateo, Calif., 1989.

G.D. Carlow, "Architecture of the Space Shuttle Primary Avionics Software System," *CACM*, Vol. 27, No. 9, Sept. 1984, pp. 926-936.

M. Chandrasekharan, B. Dasarathy, and Z. Kishimoto, "Requirements-Based Testing of Real-Time Systems: Modeling for Testability," *IEEE Computer*, Vol 18, No. 4, April 1985, pp. 71-81.

H.Y. Chang and M. Livny, "Priority in Distributed Systems," *Proc. Real-Time System Symp.*, IEEE CS Press, Los Alamitos, Calif., 1985, pp. 123-130.

H.Y. Chang and M. Livny, "Distributed Scheduling Under Deadline Constraints: A Comparison of Sender-initiated and Receiver-initiated Approaches," *Proc. Real-Time Systems Symp.*, IEEE CS Press, Los Alamitos, Calif., 1986, pp. 175-180.

K. Chen, "A Study on the Timeliness Property in Real-Time Systems," *Real-Time Systems*, Vol. 3, No. 3, Sept. 1991, pp. 247-274.

M.-I. Chen and K.-J. Lin, "Dynamic Priority Ceilings: A Concurrency Control Protocol for Real-Time Systems," *Real-Time Systems*, Vol. 2, No. 4, Nov. 1990, pp. 325-346.

S. Chen et al., "Performance Evaluation of Two New Disk Scheduling Algorithms for Real-Time Systems," *Real-Time Systems*, Vol. 3, No. 3, Sept. 1991, pp. 307-336.

S. Chen and D. Towsley, "Performance of a Mirrored Disk in a Real-Time Transaction System," *Proc. ACM*, SIG Metrics, May 1991.

S. Cheng, "Dynamic Scheduling Algorithms for Distributed Hard Real-Time Systems, PhD thesis, Univ. Massachusetts, Amherst, Mass., May 1987.

S. Cheng, J. A. Stankovic, and K. Ramamritham, *Hard Real-Time Systems*, Chapter 5.1 on Scheduling, IEEE CS Press, Los Alamitos, Calif., 1988.

S. Cheng, J.A. Stankovic, and K. Ramamritham, "Dynamic Scheduling of Groups of Tasks with Precedence Constraints in Distributed Hard Real-Time Systems," *Proc. Real-Time Systems Symp.*, IEEE CS Press, Los Alamitos, Calif., 1986, pp. 166-174.

S. Cheng, J.A. Stankovic, and K. Ramamritham, "Scheduling Groups of Tasks in Distributed Hard Real-Time Systems," *IEEE Trans. Computers*, Nov. 1987.

T.C.E. Cheng, "Optimal Due-Date Determination and Sequencing of n Jobs on a Single Machine," *J. Operational Research Society*, Vol. 35, No. 5, May 1984.

H. Chetto and M. Chetto, "Some Results of the Earliest Deadline Scheduling Algorithm," *IEEE Trans. Software Engineering*, Vol. 15, No. 10, Oct. 1989.

H. Chetto, M. Silly, and T. Bouchentouf, "Dynamic Scheduling of Real-Time Tasks under Precedence Constraints," *Real-Time Systems*, Vol. 2, No. 3, Sept. 1990, pp. 181-194.

I. Chlamtac, W.R. Franta, and K.D. Levin, "BRAM: The Broadcast Recognizing Access Method," *IEEE Trans. Communication*, Vol. COM-27, Aug. 1979, pp. 1183-90.

W. Chu and L. Lan, "Task Allocation and Precedence Relations for Distributed Real-Time Systems," *IEEE Trans. Computers,* Vol. C-36, No. 6, June 1987, pp. 667-679.

V. Cingel and N. Fri, "A Temporal Logic-Based Model of Event-Driven Nets," *Real-Time Systems*, Vol. 3, No. 4, Dec. 1991, pp. 407-428.

E.M. Clarke, E.A. Emerson, and A.P. Sistla, "Automatic Verification of Finite-State Concurrent Systems Using Temporal Logic Specifications," *ACM TOPLAS*, Vol. 8, No. 2, April 1986.

E.G. Coffman (ed.), *Computer and Job/Shop Scheduling Theory*, John Wiley & Sons, New York, 1976.

E.G. Coffman and R.L. Graham, *Optimal Scheduling for Two-Processor Systems, Acta Informatica 1*, Springer-Verlag, New York, 1972.

J.E. Coolahan and N. Roussopoulus, "Timing Requirements for Time-Driven Systems Using Augmented Petri Nets," *IEEE Trans. Software Engineering*, Vol. SE-9, No. 5, Sept. 1983, pp. 603-616.

J. Corbett and G.S. Avrunin, "A Practical Method for Bounding the Time Between Events in Concurrent Real-Time Systems," *Proc. 1993 Int'l Symp. on Software Testing and Analysis (ISSTA)*, June 1993, pp. 110-116.

E. Corsetti, A. Montanari, and E. Ratto, "Dealing with Different Time Granularities in K-Formal Specifications of Real-Time Systems," *Real-Time Systems*, Vol. 3, No. 2, May 1991, pp. 191-216.

F. Cristian, "Synchronous Atomic Broadcase for Redundant Broadcast Channels," *Real-Time Systems*, Vol. 2, No. 3, Sept. 1990, pp. 195-212.

F. Cristian, "A Probabilistic Approach to Distributed Clock Synchronization," *Distributed Computing*, Vol. 3, 1989, pp. 146-158.

F. Cristian, "Understanding Fault-Tolerant Distributed Systems," *Comm. ACM*, Vol. 34, No. 2, Feb. 1991, pp. 56-78.

F. Cristian, B. Dancey, and J. Dehn, "Fault-Tolerance in the Advanced Automation System," *Proc. 20th Ann. Int'l Symp. Fault-Tolerant Computing*, IEEE CS Press, Los Alamitos, Calif., June 1990, pp. 6-17.

W.J. Dally and C.L. Seitz, "The Torus Routing Chip," *Distributed Computing*, Vol. 1, No. 3, 1986.

A. Damm et al., "The Real-Time Operating System of MARS," *Operating Systems Review*, July 1989, pp. 141-157.

B. Dasarathy, "Timing Constraints of Real-Time Systems: Constructs for Expressing Them, Methods of Validating Them," *IEEE Trans. Software Engineering*, Vol. SE-11, No. 1, Jan. 1985, pp. 80-86.

S. Davari and S. K. Dhall, "An On-Line Algorithm for Real-Time Tasks Allocation," *Proc. Real-Time Systems Symp.*, IEEE CS Press, Los Alamitos, Calif., Dec. 1986, pp. 194-200.

U. Dayal, "Active Database Management Systems," *Proc. Third Int'l Conf. Data and Knowledge Management*, June 1988.

U. Dayal et al., "The HiPAC Project: Combining Active Database and Timing Constraints," *ACM SIGMOD Record*, March 1988.

K.S. Decker, V.R. Lesser, and R.C. Whitehair, "Extending a Blackboard Architecture for Approximate Processing," *Real-Time Systems*, Vol. 2, Nos. 1/2, May 1990, pp. 47-80.

M. Dertouzos, "Control Robotics: The Procedural Control of Physical Processes," *Proc. IFIP Congress*, 1974, pp. 807-813.

M.L. Dertouzos and A.K.-L. Mok, "Multiprocessor On-Line Scheduling of Hard-Real-Time Tasks," *IEEE Trans. Software Engineering*, Vol. 15, No. 12, Dec. 1989.

A.A. Desrochers, ed., *Modeling and Control of Automated Manufacturing Systems,* IEEE CS Press, Los Alamitos, Calif., 1990.

S.K. Dhall and C. L. Liu, "On a Real-Time Scheduling Problem," *Operations Research*, Vol. 26, No. 1, 1978.

J. Du and J.Y.-T. Leung, "Scheduling Tree-Structured Tasks With Restricted Execution Times," *Information Processing Letter*, Vol. 28, July 1988.

J. Dunham, "Experiments in Software Reliability: Life Critical Applications," *IEEE Trans. Software Engineering*, Vol. SE-12, No. 1, Jan. 1986, pp. 110-123.

E.A. Elsayed, "Algorithms for Project Scheduling with Resource Constraints," *Int'l J. Production Research*, Vol. 20, No. 1, 1982.

J. Erschler et al., "A New Dominance Concept in Scheduling n Jobs on a Single Machine with Ready Times and Due Dates," *Operations Research*, Vol. 31, No. 1, 1983.

K.P. Eswaran et al., "The Notion of Consistency and Predicate Locks in a Database System," *Comm. ACM*, Vol. 19, No. 11, Nov. 1976, pp. 624-633.

P. Ezhilselvan and S.K. Shrivastava, "A Characterization of Faults in Systems," *Proc. Fifth Symp. on Reliability in Distributed Software and Database Systems*, Jan. 1986, pp. 215-222.

A.A. Faustini and E.B. Lewis, "Towards a Real-Time Dataflow Language," *IEEE Software*, Vol. 3, No. 1, Jan. 1986, pp. 29-35.

FDDI Token Ring, Media Access Control, draft proposed, American National Standards Institute, No. ANSIX3T9.5/83-16, March 1985.

E.B. Fernandez and B. Bussell "Bounds on the Number of Processors and Time for Multiprocessor Optimal Schedules," *IEEE Trans. Computers*, Vol. C-22, No. 8, Aug. 1973, pp. 745-751.

E. B. Fernandez and T. Lang, "Computation of Lower Bounds for Multiprocessor Schedules," *IBM J. Research and Development*, Vol. 19, No. 5, Sept. 1975.

G.N. Frederickson, "Scheduling Unit-Time Tasks with Integer Release Times and Deadlines," *Information Processing Letters*, Vol. 16, May 1983, pp. 171-173.

B. Furth et al., *Real-Time UNIX Systems Design and Application Guide*, Kluwer Academic Publishers, New York, 1991.

H.N. Gabow, "An Almost-Linear Algorithm for Two-Processor Scheduling," *J. ACM*, Vol. 29, No. 3, July 1982, pp. 766-780.

A. Gabrielian, "HMS Machines: A Unifying Framework for Specification, Verification, and Reasoning for Real-Time Systems," Tech. Report 90-24, Thomson-CSF Inc., Oct. 1990.

B.O. Gallmeister and C. Lanier, "Early Experience with POSIX 1003.4 and POSIX 1003.4A," *Proc. Real-Time Systems Symp.*, Dec. 1991, pp. 190-198.

M.R. Garey and R.L. Graham, "Bounds for Multiprocessor Scheduling with Resource Constraints," *SIAM J. Computing*, Vol. 4, No. 2, June 1975, pp. 187-200.

M.R. Garey and D.S. Johnson, "Complexity Results for Multiprocessor Scheduling Under Resource Constraints," *SIAM J. Computing*, Vol. 4, No. 4, Dec. 1975.

M.R. Garey and D.S. Johnson, "Scheduling Tasks with Nonuniform Deadlines on Two Processors," *J. ACM*, Vol. 23, No. 3, July 1976, pp. 397-411.

M.R. Garey and D.S. Johnson, "Two-Processor Scheduling with Start-Times and Deadlines," *SIAM J. Computing*, Vol. 6, No. 3, Sept. 1977.

M.R. Garey and D.S. Johnson, *Computers and Intractability: A Guide to the Theory of NP-Completeness*, W.H. Freeman and Co., 1979.

M.R. Garey et al., " Scheduling Unit-Time Tasks with Arbitrary Release Times and Deadlines," *SIAM J. Computing*, Vol. 10, No. 2, May 1981.

B. Gavish and P. Schweitzer, "The Markovian Queue with Bounded Waiting Time," *Management Science*, Vol. 23, No. 12, 1977.

N. Gehani and K. Ramamritham, "Real-Time Concurrent C: A Language for Programming Dynamic Real-Time Systems," *Real-Time Systems,* Vol. 4, No. 3, 1991, pp. 377-406.

R. Gerber and I. Lee, "A Proof System for Communicating Shared Resources," *Proc. Real-Time Systems Symp.*, IEEE CS Press, Los Alamitos, Calif., Dec. 1990, pp. 288-299.

C. Ghezzi, D. Mandriolli, and A. Morzenti, "Trio: A Language for Executable Specifications of Real-Time Systems," *J. Systems and Software*, Vol 12, No. 2, May 1990, pp. 107-123.

D.W. Gillies and J.W.-S. Liu, "Greed in Resource Scheduling," *Proc. 10th Real-Time Systems Symp.*, IEEE CS Press, Los Alamitos, Calif., 1989, pp. 285-294.

M.J. Gonzalez, "Deterministic Processor Scheduling," *Computing Surveys*, Vol. 9, No. 3, Sept. 1977, pp. 173-204.

T. Gonzalez and D.B. Johnson, "A New Algorithm for Preemptive Scheduling of Trees," Tech. Report 222, Computer Science Dept., Pennsylvania State Univ., 1977.

T. Gonzalez and S. Sahni, "Open Shop Scheduling to Minimize Finish Time," *J. ACM*, Vol. 23, No. 4, Oct. 1976, pp. 665-679.

R. Govindan and D.P. Anderson, "Scheduling and IPC Mechanisms for Continuous Media," *Proc. 13th ACM Symp. Operating Systems Principles*, Oct. 1991.

R.L. Graham, "Bounds for Certain Multiprocessing Anomalies," *Bell System Tech. J.*, Vol. 45, Nov. 1966, pp. 1653-1681.

R.L. Graham, "Bounds on Multiprocessing Timing Anomalies," *SIAM J. Appl. Math.*, Vol. 17, No. 2, March 1969.

R.L. Graham, "Bounds on Multiprocessing Anomalies and Related Packing Problems," *Proc. AFIPS Conf.*, Vol. 40, 1972.

R. Graham, "Bounds on the Performance of Scheduling Algorithms," E.G. Coffman, ed., *Computer and Job-Shop Scheduling Theory*, Wiley & Sons, New York, 1976.

R.L. Graham et al., "Optimization and Approximation in Deterministic Sequencing and Scheduling: A Survey," *Annals of Discrete Mathematics*, Vol. 5, 1979.

A.S. Grimshaw, A. Silberman, and J.W.S. Liu, "Real-Time Mentat Programming Language and Architecture," *Proc. Seventh Workshop on Real-Time Operating Systems and Software*, May 1990, pp. 82-87.

W.A. Halang and A.D. Stoyenko, *Constructing Predictable Real Time Systems*, Kluwer Academic Publishers, New York, 1991.

W.A. Halang and A.D. Stoyenko, "Comparative Evaluation of High-Level Real-Time Programming Languages," *Real-Time Systems*, Vol. 2, No. 3, Nov. 1990, pp. 365-382.

C.-C. Han and K.-J. Lin, "Scheduling Parallelizable Jobs on Multiprocessors," *Proc. Real-Time Systems Symp.*, Dec. 1989,

D. Harel et al., "Statecharts: A Visual Formalism for Complex Systems," *Science of Computer Programming*, Vol. 8, No. 3, June 1987, pp. 231-274.

J.R. Haritsa, M.J. Carey, and M. Livny, "On Being Optimistic about Real-Time Constraints," *ACM Symp. on Principles of Database Systems (PODS)*, 1990.

J.R. Haritsa, M.J. Carey, and M. Livny, "Dynamic Real-Time Optimistic Concurrency Control," *Proc. 11th Real-Time Systems Symp.*, IEEE CS Press, Los Alamitos, Calif., Dec. 1990, pp. 94-103.

V.H. Hasse, "Real-Time Behavior of Programs," *IEEE. Trans. Software Engineering*, Vol. SE-7, No. 5, Sept. 1981, pp. 494-501.

B. Hayes-Roth, "Architectural Foundations for Real-Time Performance in Intelligent Agents," *Real-Time Systems*, Vol. 2, Nos. 1/2, May 1990, pp. 99-126.

H. Hecht, "Fault-Tolerant Software for Real-Time Applications," *Computing Surveys*, Vol. 8, Dec. 1976, pp. 391-408.

R.K.J. Henn, "Feasible Processor Allocation in a Hard Real-Time Environment," *Real-Time Systems*, Vol. 1, No. 1, June 1989, pp. 77-94.

R.G. Herrtwich, "Time Capsules: An Abstraction for Access to Continuous-Media Data," *Real-Time Systems*, Vol. 3, No. 4, Dec. 1991, pp. 355-376.

R.F. Hodson and A. Kandel, *Real-Time Expert Systems Computer Architecture*, CRC Press, Boca Raton, Fla., 1991.

K.S. Hong and J.Y.-T. Leung, "Preemptive Scheduling with Release Times and Deadlines," *Real-Time Systems*, Vol. 1, No. 3, Dec. 1989, pp. 265-282.

J. Hong, X. Tan and D. Towsley, "A Performance Analysis of Minimum Laxity and Earliest Deadline Scheduling in a Real-Time System," *IEEE Trans. Computers*, Vol. 38, No. 12, Dec. 1989, pp. 1736-1744.

K.S. Hong and J.Y.-T. Leung, "On-Line Scheduling of Real-Time Tasks," *Proc. Real-Time Systems Symp.*, IEEE CS Press, Los Alamitos, Calif., Dec. 1988, pp. 244-250.

S. Honiden et al., "An Application of Structural Modeling and Automated Reasoning to Real-Time Systems Design," *Real-Time Systems,* Vol. 1, No. 4, Apr. 1990, pp. 313-332.

P. Hood and V. Grover, "Designing Real-Time Systems in Ada," Tech. Report 1123-1, SofTech, Inc., Waltham, Mass., Jan. 1986.

A.L. Hopkins et al., "FTMP: A Highly Reliable Fault-Tolerant Multiprocessor for Aircraft," *Proc. IEEE*, Vol. 66, No. 10, Oct. 1978, pp. 1221-1239.

W.A. Horn, "Some Simple Scheduling Algorithms," *Naval Research Logistics Quarterly*, Vol. 21, 1974.

W. Hou, G. Ozsoyoglu, and B.K. Taneja, "Processing Aggregate Relational Queries with Hard Time Constraints," *ACM SIGMOD Int'l Conf. Management of Data*, June 1989.

A.E. Howe, D.M. Hart, and P.R. Cohen, "Addressing Real-Time Constraints in the Design of Autonomous Agents," *Real-Time Systems,* Vol. 2, Nos. 1/2, May 1990, pp. 81-98.

HSRB, SAE AE9-B High Speed Data Bus Standard, Society of Automotive Engineers, Subcommittee 9-B, Issue 1, Draft 2, Jan. 1986,

M. Hsu, R. Ladin and D.R. McCarthy, "An Execution Model for Active Database Management Systems," *Proc. Third Int'l Conf. on Data and Knowledge Management*, June 1988.

T.C. Hu, "Parallel Sequencing and Assembly Line Problems," *Operations Research*, Vol. 9, 1961.

J. Huang et al., "Performance Evaluation of Real-Time Optimistic Concurrency Control Schemes," *Proc. Conf. on Very Large Databases*, Morgan Kaufmann, San Mateo, Calif., Sept. 1991.

J. Huang et al., "On Using Priority Inheritance in Real-Time Databases," *Real-Time Systems Symp.*, IEEE CS Press, Los Alamitos, Calif., Dec. 1991, pp. 210-221.

J. Huang et al., "Experimental Evaluation of Real-Time Transaction Processing," *Real-Time Systems Symp.*, IEEE CS Press, Los Alamitos, Calif., Dec. 1989, pp. 144-153.

M.C. McElvany Hugue and P.D. Stotts, "Guaranteed Task Deadlines for Fault-Tolerant Workloads with Conditional Branches," *Real-Time Systems*, Vol. 3, No. 3, Sept. 1991, pp. 275-306.

Y. Ishikawa, H. Tokuda, and C.W. Mercer, "Object-Oriented Real-Time Language Design: Constructs for Timing Constraints," *Proc. ACM OOPSLA/ECOOP 90*, ACM, New York, Oct. 1990, pp. 289-298.

J.R. Jackson, "Scheduling a Production Line to Minimize Maximum Tardiness," Research Report 43, Management Science Research Project, Univ. California, Los Angeles, 1955.

R. Jager, "Handling Real-Time Communication Constraints in a Mobile Station used for the Pan-European Digital Mobile Communication Network," *Real-Time Systems*, Vol. 4, No. 2, June 1992.

F. Jahanian and A.K. Mok, "Safety Analysis of Timing Properties in Real-Time Systems," *IEEE Trans. Software Engineering*, Vol. SE-12, No. 9, Sept. 1986, pp. 890-904.

K. Jeffay, D. L. Stone, and F. D. Smith, "Kernel Support for Live Digital Audio and Video," *Proc. Second Int'l Workshop on Network and Operating System Support for Digital Audio and Video*, Nov. 1991.

E.D. Jensen, C.D. Locke, and H. Tokuda, "A Time-Driven Scheduling Model for Real-Time Operating Systems," *Proc. Real-Time Systems Symp.*, IEEE CS Press, Los Alamitos, Calif., Dec. 1985, pp. 112-122.

H.H. Johnson and M.S. Madison, "Deadline Scheduling for a Real-Time Multiprocessor," NTIS (N76-15843), Springfield, Va., May 1974.

S.M. Johnson, "Optimal Two- and Three-Stage Production Schedules with Set-up Times Included," *Naval Research Logistics Q.*, Vol. 1, No. 1, 1954.

M. Joseph and A. Goswami, "Formal Description of Real-Time Systems: A Review," *Research Report 129*, Univ. of Warwick, Aug. 1988.

A.H.G.R. Kan and M.J. Magazine, Report of the Session on Scheduling, *Annals of Discrete Mathematics*, Vol. 5, 1979.

H. Kasahara and S. Narita, "Parallel Processing of Robot-Arm Control Computation on a Multimicroprocessor System," *IEEE J. Robotics and Automation*, Vol. RA-1, No. 2, June 1985, pp. 104-113.

H. Kasahara and S. Narita, "Practical Multiprocessor Scheduling Algorithms for Efficient Parallel Processing," *IEEE Trans. Computers*, Vol. C-33, No. 11, 1984, pp. 1023-1029.

T. Kawaguchi and S. Kyan, "Deterministic Scheduling in Computer Systems: A Survey," *J. Operations Research Society of Japan*, Vol. 31, No. 2, June 1988.

K.B. Kenny and K.J. Lin, "Building Flexible Real-Time Systems Using the FLEX Language," *Computer*, Vol. 24, No. 5, May 1991, pp. 70-78.

P. Kermani and L. Kleinrock, "Virtual Cut-Through: A New Computer Communication Switching Technique," *Computer Networks*, Vol. 3, 1979, pp. 267-286.

A. Kiran and M. Smith, "Simulation Studies in Job Shop Scheduling: I and II," *Computer and Industrial Engineering*, Vol. 8, No. 2, 1984.

H.D. Kirrmann and F. Kaufmann, "Poolpo: A Pool of Processors for Process Control Applications," *IEEE Trans. Computers*, Vol. C-33, No. 10, Oct. 1984, pp. 869-878.

H. Kise, "A Solvable Case of the One-Machine Scheduling Problem with Ready and Due Times, *Operations Research*, Vol. 26, No. 1, 1978.

L. Kleinrock and M.O. Scholl, "Packet Switching in Radio Channels: New Conflict-Free Multiple Access Schemes," *IEEE Trans. Communication*, Vol. COM-28, No. 7, July 1980, pp. 1015-1029.

E. Klingerman and A.D. Stoyenko, "Real-Time Euclid: A Language for Reliable Real-Time Systems," *IEEE Trans. Software Engineering*, Vol. SE-12, No. 9, Sept. 1986, pp. 941-949.

N. Komoda, K. Kera, and T. Kubo, "An Autonomous, Decentralized Control System for Factory Automation," *Computer*, Vol. 17, No. 12, Dec. 1984, pp. 73-83.

H. Kopetz, "Accuracy of Time Measurement in Distributed Real-Time Systems," *Proc. Fifth Symp. on Reliability in Distributed Software and Database Systems*, IEEE CS Press, Los Alamitos, Calif., 1986, pp. 35-41.

H. Kopetz et al., "Distributed Fault Tolerant Real-Time Systems: The Mars Approach," *IEEE Micro*, Vol. 9, No. 1, Feb. 1989, pp. 25-40.

H. Kopetz and W. Merker, "The Architecture of Mars," *Proc. 15th Ann. Int'l Symp. Fault-Tolerant Computing*, IEEE CS Press, Los Alamitos, Calif., June 1985, pp. 274-279.

H. Kopetz and W. Ochsenreiter, "Clock Synchronization in Distributed Real-Time Systems," *IEEE Trans. Computers*, Vol. C-36, No. 8, Aug. 1987, pp. 933-940.

R.E. Korf, "Depth-Limited Search for Real-Time Program Solving," *Real-Time Systems*, Vol. 2, Nos. 1/2, May 1990, pp. 7-24.

H. Korth, N. Soparkar, and A. Silberschatz, "Triggered Real-Time Databases with Consistency Constraints," *Proc. 16th VLDB Conf.*, Morgan Kaufmann, San Mateo, Calif., Aug. 1990.

R. Koymans, "Specifying Real-Time Properties with Metric Temporal Logic," *Real-Time Systems*, Vol. 2, No. 4, Nov. 1990, pp. 255-300.

R. Koymans et al., "Compositional Semantics for Real-Time Distributed Computing," Tech. Report 86.4, Eindhoven Univ. Technology, The Netherlands, June 1986.

C.M. Krishna and K.G. Shin, "On Scheduling Tasks with a Quick Recovery from Failure," *IEEE Trans. Computers*, Vol. C-35, No. 5, May 1986, pp. 448-455.

C.M. Krishna, K.G. Shin, and I.S. Bhandari, "Processor Trade-offs in Distributed Real-Time Systems," *IEEE. Trans. Computers*, Vol. C-36, No. 9, Sept. 1987, pp. 1030-1040.

J. F. Kurose and R. Chipalkatti, "Load Sharing in Soft Real-Time Distributed Computer Systems," *IEEE Trans. Computers*, Vol. C-36, No. 8, Aug 1987, pp. 993-1000.

J.F. Kurose, M. Schwartz, and Y. Yemini, "Multiple Access Protocols and Time-Constrained Communication," *Computing Surveys*, Vol. 16, No. 1, 1984, pp. 43-70.

J. F. Kurose, S. Singh, and R. Chipalkatti, "A Study of Quasi-Dynamic Load Sharing in Soft Real-Time Distributed Computer Systems," *Proc. Real-Time Systems Symp.*, IEEE CS Press, Los Alamitos, Calif., Dec. 1986, pp. 201-208.

J. Labetoulle, "Some Theorems on Real Time Scheduling," *Computer Architecture and Networks*, E. Gelenbe and R. Mahl, eds., North Holland, New York, 1974, pp. 285-298.

J. Lala, R. Harper, and L. Alger, "A Design Approach for Ultrareliable Real-Time Systems," *Computer*, Vol. 24, No. 5, May 1991, pp. 12-22.

L. Lamport, "What Good is Temporal Logic?" *Information Processing '81*, IFIP North-Holland, New York, Sept. 1983, pp. 657-668.

L. Lamport and P.M. Melliar-Smith, "Synchronizing Clocks in the Presence of Faults," *J. ACM*, Vol. 32, No. 1, Jan. 1978, pp. 52-78.

L. Lamport, R. Shostak, and M. Pease, "The Byzantine Generals Problem," *ACM TOPLAS*, Vol. 4, No. 3, July 1982, pp. 382-402.

T. Lang and E.B. Fernandez, "Scheduling of Unit-Length Independent Tasks with Execution Constraints," *Information Processing Letters*, Vol. 4, No. 4, Jan. 1976.

J.C. Laprie, "Dependability: A Unifying Concept for Reliable Computing and Fault Tolerance," *Resilient Computing Systems*, Vol. 2, T. Anderson, ed., Collins and Wiley, 1988.

J. Lark et al., "Concepts, Methods, and Languages for Building Timely Intelligent Systems," *Real-Time Systems*, Vol. 2, Nos. 1/2, May 1990, pp. 127-148.

R.J. Lauber, "Forecasting Real-Time Behavior During Software Design Using a CASE Environment," *Real-Time Systems*, Vol. 1, No. 1, June 1989, pp. 61-76.

P. S. Lavoie, "Tool to Analyze Timing on 68020 Processor," master's project, Univ. Massachusetts, Amherst, 1991.

E. Lawler, "Recent Results in the Theory of Machine Scheduling, in *Mathematical Programming: The State of the Art*, A. Bachem et al., eds., Springer-Verlag, New York, 1983.

E. Lawler, "Optimal Scheduling of a Single Machine Subject to Precedence Constraints," *Management Science*, Vol. 19, 1973.

E. Lawler and C.U. Martel, "Scheduling Periodically Occurring Tasks on Multiple Processors," *Information Processing Letters*, Vol. 12, No. 1, Feb. 1981.

H. Lawson, "Cy-Clone: An Approach to the Engineering of Resource Adequate Cyclic Real-Time Systems," *Real-Time Systems*, Vol. 4, No. 1, March 1992.

E.A. Lee and D.G. Messerschmitt, "Static Scheduling of Synchronous Data Flow Programs for Digital Signal Processing," *IEEE Trans. Computers*, Vol. C-36, No. 1, Jan. 1987, pp. 24-35.

I. Lee and S.B. Davidson, "Adding Time to Synchronous Process Communications," *IEEE. Trans. Computers*, Vol. C-36, No. 8, Aug. 1987, pp. 941-948.

I. Lee and V. Gehlot, "Language Constructs for Distributed Real-Time Programming," *Proc. Real-Time Systems Symp.*, IEEE CS Press, Los Alamitos, Calif., Dec. 1985, pp. 57-66.

J.P. Lehoczky and L. Sha, "Performance of Bus Scheduling Algorithms," *Performance Evaluation Review*, special issue, Vol. 14, No. 1, May 1986.

J.P. Lehoczky, L. Sha, and Y. Ding, "The Rate Monotone Scheduling Algorithm: Exact Characterization and Average Case Behavior," *Proc. 10th Real-Time Systems Symp.*, IEEE CS Press, Los Alamitos, Calif., Dec. 1989, pp. 166-171.

J.P. Lehoczky, L. Sha, and J. Strosnider, "Enhancing Aperiodic Responsiveness in a Hard Real-Time Environment," *Proc. Real-Time Systems Symp.,* IEEE CS Press, Los Alamitos, Calif., Dec. 1987.

D.W. Leinbaugh, "Guaranteed Response Time in a Hard Real-Time Environment," *IEEE Trans. Software Engineering*, Vol. SE-6, No. 1, Jan. 1980.

D.W. Leinbaugh, "High-Level Specification of Resource Sharing," *Proc. Int'l Conf. Parallel Processing*, IEEE CS Press, Los Alamitos, Calif., Aug. 1981.

D. W. Leinbaugh and M. R. Yamini, "Guaranteed Response Times in a Distributed Hard Real-Time Environment," *IEEE Trans. Software Engineering,* Vol. SE-12, No. 12, Dec. 1986, pp. 1139-1144.

G. LeLann, "A Deterministic Multiple CSMA-CD Protocol," INRIA-Project Score, Internal Report PRO-I-002, 1983.

G. LeLann, "Distributed Real-Time Processing," *Proc. 1985 BBC Int'l. Symp. on Process Control*, 1985.

J.K. Lenstra, A.H.G.R. Kan, and P. Bruchker, "Complexity of Machine Scheduling Problems," *Annals of Discrete Mathematics*, North-Holland, New York, 1977.

B. Lent and H. Kurmann, "The OR Dataflow Architecture for a Machine Embedded Control System," *Real-Time Systems*, Vol. 1, No. 2, Sept. 1989, pp. 107-132.

V. Lesser and D. Corkill, "Functionally Accurate, Cooperative Distributed Systems," *IEEE Trans. Systems, Man, and Cybernetics,* Vol. SMC-11, No. 1, Jan. 1981, pp. 81-96.

J. Y.-T. Leung, "Bounds on List Scheduling of UET Tasks with Restricted Resource Constraints," *Information Processing Letters*, Vol. 9, No. 4, Nov. 1979.

J.Y.-T. Leung and M.L. Merrill, "A Note on Preemptive Scheduling of Periodic, Real-Time Tasks," *Information Processing Letters*, Vol. 11, No. 3, Nov. 1980.

N.G. Leveson and J.L. Stolzy, "Safety Analysis Using Petri Nets," *IEEE Trans. Software Engineering,* Vol. SE-13, No. 3, March 1987, pp. 386-397.

A.L. Liestman and R.H. Campbell, "A Fault Tolerant Scheduling Problem," *IEEE Trans. Software Engineering*, Vol. SE-12, No. 11, Nov. 1986, pp. 1089-1095.

K.J. Lin, "Consistency Issues in Real-Time Database Systems," *Proc. 22nd Hawaii Int'l Conf. on System Sciences*, IEEE CS Press, Los Alamitos, Calif., Vol. II, Jan. 1989, pp. 654-661.

Y. Lin and S.H. Song, "Concurrency Control in Real-Time Databases by Dynamic Adjustment of Serialization Order," *Proc. 11th Real-Time Systems Symp.*, Dec. 1990.

C.L. Liu and J. Layland, "Scheduling Algorithms for Multiprogramming in a Hard Real-Time Environment," *J.ACM*, Vol. 20, No. 1, 1973, pp. 46-61.

C.L. Liu, "Deterministic Job Scheduling in Computing Systems," *Modeling and Performance Evaluation of Computer Systems*, E. Gelenbe, ed., North-Holland, New York, 1976.

J.W.S. Liu, K.-J. Lin and S. Natarajan, "Scheduling Real-Time, Periodic Jobs Using Imprecise Results," *Proc. Real-Time Systems Symp.*, IEEE CS Press, Los Alamitos, Calif., 1987, pp. 252-260.

J. Liu et al., "Algorithms for Scheduling Imprecise Calculations," *Computer*, Vol. 24, No. 5, May 1991, pp. 58-68.

V.M. Lo, "Heuristic Algorithms for Task Assignment in Distributed Systems," *Proc. Int'l Conf. Distributed Computing Systems*, IEEE CS Press, Los Alamitos, Calif., 1984, pp. 30-39.

V.M. Lo, "Task Assignment to Minimize Completion Time," *Proc. Int'l Conf. Distributed Computing Systems*, IEEE CS Press, Los Alamitos, Calif., May 1985, pp. 329-336.

C.D. Locke, "Best-Effort Decision Making for Real-Time Scheduling," Ph.D. thesis, Carnegie Mellon Univ., Pittsburgh, Penn., May 1985.

C.D. Locke, "Software Architecture for Hard Real-Time Applications: Cyclic Executives vs. Fixed Priority Executives," *Real-Time Systems*, Vol. 4, No. 1, March 1992.

C.D. Locke, H. Tokuda, and E.D. Jensen, "A Time-Driven Scheduling Model for Real-Time Operating Systems," Tech. Report, Carnegie Mellon Univ., 1985.

L. Lundelius and N. Lynch, "An Upper Bound for Clock Synchronization," *Information and Control*, Vol. 62, 1984, pp. 190-204.

N.A. Lynch, "Multi-level Atomicity: A New Correctness Criterion for Database Concurrency Control," *ACM Trans. Database Systems*, Vol. 8, No. 4, Dec. 1983.

R. P. Ma, "A Model to Solve Timing-Critical Application Problems in Distributed Computer Systems," *Computer*, Vol. 17, No. 1, Jan. 1984, pp. 62-68.

P.-Y.R. Ma, E. Y. S. Lee, and M. Tsuchiya, "A Task Allocation Model for Distributed Computing Systems," *IEEE Trans. Computers,* Vol. C-31, No. 1, 1982, pp. 41-47.

G. K. Manacher, Production and Stabilization of Real-Time Task Schedules," *J. ACM*, Vol. 14, No. 3, 1967.

C. Marlin et al., "GARTL: A Real-Time Programming Language Based on Multi-Version Computation," *Proc. Int'l Conf. Computer Languages*, 1990, pp. 107-115.

C. Martel, "Preemptive Scheduling with Release Times, Deadlines, and Due Times," *J. ACM*, Vol. 29, No. 3, 1982.

K. Marzulo and S. Owicki, "Maintaining Time in a Distributed System," *Proc. Second Symp. Principles of Distributed Computing*, ACM, New York, Aug. 1983.

M.C. McElvany, "Guaranteed Deadlines in MAFT," *Proc. Real-Time Systems Symp.,* IEEE CS Press, Los Alamitos, Calif., Dec. 1988.

R. McNaughton, "Scheduling with Deadlines and Loss Functions," *Management Science*, Vol. 6, No. 1, Oct. 1959.

R. Mehrotra and M.R. Varanasi, eds., *Multirobot Systems, Computer Society Robot Technology Series,* IEEE CS Press, Los Alamitos, Calif., 1990.

D. Mellichamp, *Real-Time Computing*, Van Nostrand Reinhold, New York, 1983.

G. Menga et al., "Modeling FMS by Closed Queuing Network Analysis Methods," *IEEE Trans. Components, Hybrids, and Manufacturing Technology*, Vol. CHMT-7, No. 3, Sept. 1984.

M. Merritt, F. Modugno, and M.R. Tuttle, "Time Constrained Automata," *CACM,* Vol. 19, July 1976, pp. 395-404.

J.F. Meyer, "Closed-Form Solutions of Performability," *IEEE Trans. Computers*, Vol. C-31, No. 7, July 1982, pp. 648-657.

A. Moitra and M. Joseph, "Implementing Real-Time Systems by Transformation," *Real-Time Systems, Theory and Applications*, H. Zedan (ed), *Elsevier Science Publications,* 1990.

A.K. Mok, "Fundamental Design Problems of Distributed Systems for the Hard Real-Time Environment," doctoral dissertation, Dept. Electrical Engineering and Computer Science, Massachusetts Inst. Technology, Cambridge, Mass., May 1983.

A. K. Mok, "The Decomposition of Real-Time System Requirements into Process Models," *Proc. Real-Time Systems Symp.,* IEEE CS Press, Los Alamitos, Calif., Dec. 1984, pp. 125-134.

A.K. Mok, "The Design of Real-Time Programming Systems Based on Process Models," *Proc. Real-Time Systems Symp.*, IEEE CS Press, Los Alamitos, Calif., Dec. 1984, pp. 5-17.

A.K. Mok, "A Graph-Based Computation Model for Real-Time Systems," *Proc. Int'l Conf. Parallel Processing,* IEEE CS Press, Los Alamitos, Calif., 1985, pp. 619-623.

A. Mok, "Evaluating Tight Execution Time Bounds of Programs by Annotations," *Proc. IEEE Workshop on Real-Time Operating Systems and Software*, IEEE CS Press, Los Alamitos, Calif., May 1989, pp. 74-80.

A. K. Mok and M. L. Dertouzos, "Multiprocessor Scheduling in a Hard Real-Time Environment," *Proc. Seventh Texas Conf. Computing Systems*, Nov. 1978.

A.K. Mok and S. Sutanthavibul, "Modeling and Scheduling of Dataflow Real-Time Systems," *Proc. Real-Time Systems Symp.,* IEEE CS Press, Los Alamitos, Calif., Dec. 1985, pp. 178-187.

L. Molesky et al., "Implementing a Predictable Real-Time Multiprocessor Kernel – The Spring Kernel," extended abstract, *Proc. Seventh IEEE Workshop on Real-Time Operating Systems and Software*, May 1990. Also in *Real-Time Systems Newsletter,* Vol. 6, No. 2, Spring 1990.

L. Molesky, C. Shen, and G. Zlokapa, "Predictable Synchronization Mechanisms for Multiprocessor Real-Time Systems," *Real-Time Systems*, Vol. 2, No. 3, Sept. 1990, pp. 163-180.

J. M. Moore, "An *n* Job, One Machine Sequencing Algorithm for Minimizing the Number of Late Jobs," *Management Science,* Vol. 15, No. 1, 1968.

S. Morasca, M. Pezze, and M. Trubian, "Timed High-Level Nets," *Real-Time Systems*, Vol. 3, No. 2, May 1991, pp. 165-190.

A. Moura and J. Field, "Collision Control Algorithms in CSMA-CD Networks," *Computer Communications*, Vol. 4, No. 1, Feb. 1981.

R.R. Muntz and E.G. Coffman, "Preemptive Scheduling of Real-Time Tasks on Multiprocessor Systems," *J. ACM,* Vol. 17, No. 2, April 1970, pp. 324-338.

J. Muppala, S. Woolet, and K. Trivedi, "Real-Time Systems Performance in the Presence of Failures," *Computer,* Vol. 24, No. 5, May 1991, pp. 37-47.

T. Murata and N. Komoda, "Real-Time Control Software for Transaction Processing Based on Colored Safe Petri Net Model," *Real-Time Systems*, Vol. 1, No. 4, April 1990, pp. 299-312.

P. Nain and D. Towsley, "Properties of the ML Policy for Scheduling Jobs with Real-Time Constraints," *Proc. 29th IEEE Control and Decision Conf.*, IEEE CS Press, Los Alamitos, Calif., Dec. 1990.

D. Niehaus, "Program Representation and Translation for Predictable Real-Time Systems," *Proc. Real-Time Systems Symp.,* IEEE CS Press, Los Alamitos, Calif., Dec. 1991, pp. 53-63.

D. Niehaus, E. Nahum, and J.A. Stankovic, "Predictable Real-Time Caching in the Spring System," *Proc. Joint IEEE Software and IFAC Workshop on Real-Time Programming*, IEEE CS Press, Los Alamitos, Calif., May 1991, pp. 80-87.

V. Nirkhe and W. Pugh, "A Partial Evaluator for the Maruti Hard Real-Time System," *Proc. Real-Time Systems Symp.,* IEEE CS Press, Los Alamitos, Calif., Dec. 1991, pp. 64-73.

V.M. Nirkhe, S.K. Tripathi, and A.K. Agrawala, "Language Support for the Maruti Real-Time System," *Proc. Real-Time Systems Symp.*, IEEE CS Press, Los Alamitos, Calif., Dec. 1990, pp. 257-266.

M. Norbis, "Heuristics for the Resource Constrained Scheduling Problem," PhD thesis, Univ. of Massachusetts, Amherst, 1987.

J.S. Ostroff and W.M. Wonham, "Modelling, Specifying, and Verifying Real-Time Embedded Computer Systems," *Proc. Real-Time Systems Symp.*, IEEE CS Press, Los Alamitos, Calif., Dec. 1987, pp. 124-132.

J.S. Ostroff, "A Verifier for Real-Time Properties," *Real-Time Systems*, Vol. 4, No. 1, March 1992.

S.S. Panwalkar and W. Iskander, "A Survey of Scheduling Rules," *Operations Research*, Vol. 25, No. 1, Jan. 1977.

C. Park and A. Shaw, "Experiments with a Program Timing Tool Based on Source-Level Timing Scheme," *Computer*, Vol. 24, No. 5, May 1991, pp. 48-57.

D. Parnas, A. van Schouwen, and S. Po Kwan, "Evaluation of Safety-Critical Software," *CACM*, June 1990.

C.J. Paul et al., "Reducing Problem-Solving Variance to Improve Predictability," *CACM*, Vol. 34, No. 8, Aug. 1991.

D. Payton and T. Bihari, "Intelligent Real-Time Control of Robotic Vehicles, *CACM*, Vol. 34, No. 8, Aug. 1991.

M. Pease, R. Shostak, and L. Lamport, "Reaching Agreement in the Presence of Faults," *J. ACM*, Vol. 27, No. 2, April 1980, pp. 228-234.

A. Pedar and V.V.S. Sarma, "Architecture Optimization of Aerospace Computing Systems," *IEEE Trans. Computers*, Vol. C-32, No. 10, Oct. 1983, pp. 911-922.

D. Peng and K. G. Shin, "Modeling of Concurrent Task Execution in a Distributed System for Real-Time Control," *IEEE Trans. Computer*, Vol. C-36, No. 4, 1987, pp. 500-516.

M. Pflugel, A. Damm, and W. Schwabl, "Interprocess Communication in MARS," *ITG/GI Conf. on Communication in Distributed Systems*, Feb. 1989.

P. Pleinevaux, "An Improved Hard Real-Time Scheduling for the IEEE 802.5," *Real-Time Systems*, Vol. 4, No. 2, June 1992.

A. Pnueli, "Applications of Temporal Logic to the Specification and Verification of Reactive Systems: A Survey of Current Trends," *Lecture Notes in Computer Science*, Vol. 224, J.W. de Bakker, ed., Springer-Verlag, New York, 1985.

POSIX, IEEE Working Group P1003.4, Real-Time Extension for Portable Operating Systems, Draft 9, 1989.

P. Puschner and C. Koza, "Calculating the Maximum Execution Time of Real-Time Programs," *Real-Time Systems*, Vol. 1, No. 2, Sept. 1989, pp. 159-176.

R. Rajkumar, *Synchronization in Real-Time Systems, A Priority Inheritance Approach,* Kluwer Academic Publishers, New York, 1991.

R. Rajkumar, L. Sha, and J. Lehoczky, "Real-Time Synchronization Protocols for Multiprocessors," *Proc. Real-Time Systems Symp.*, IEEE CS Press, Los Alamitos, Calif., 1988, pp. 259-269.

R. Rajkumar et al., "An Optimal Priority Inheritance Protocol for Real-Time Synchronization," (revised for second round of reviews) *ACM Trans. Programming Language and Systems*, April 1991.

K. Ramamritham, *Channel Characteristics in Local Area Hard Real-Time Systems, Computer Networks, and ISDN Systems*, North Holland, New York, Sept. 1987, pp. 3-13.

K. Ramamritham, "Allocation and Scheduling of Complex Periodic Tasks," *Proc. 10th Int'l Conf. on Distributed Computing Systems*, IEEE CS Press, Los Alamitos, Calif., June 1990, pp. 108-115.

K. Ramamritham, "Real-Time Databases," *Int'l J. Parallel and Distributed Databases*, Vol. 1, No. 2, 1993, pp. 199-226.

K. Ramamritham and J.M. Adan, "Load Balancing During the Static Allocation and Scheduling of Complex Periodic Tasks, COINS Tech. Report, Oct. 1990.

K. Ramamritham et al., "Toward Distributed Robot Control Systems," *Proc. Symp. on Robot Control*, Nov. 1985.

K. Ramamritham and J.A. Stankovic, "Scheduling Strategies Adopted in Spring: An Overview," *Foundations of Real-Time Computing: Scheduling and Resource Management*, Andre van Tilborg and Gary Koob, eds., Kluwer Academic Publishers, 1992, pp. 277-305.

K. Ramamritham and J. A. Stankovic, "Dynamic Task Scheduling in Distributed Hard Real-Time Systems," *IEEE Software*, Vol. 1, No. 3, July 1984, pp. 65-75.

K. Ramamritham, J.A. Stankovic, and P.-F. Shiah, "$O(n)$ Scheduling Algorithms for Real-Time Multiprocessor Systems," *Proc. Int'l Conf. Parallel Processing*, Penn. State University Press, University Park, Vol. III, Aug. 1989, pp. 143-152.

K. Ramamritham, J.A. Stankovic, and P. Shiah, "Efficient Scheduling Algorithms for Real-Time Multiprocessor Systems," *IEEE Trans. Parallel and Distributed Systems*, Vol. 1, No. 2, April 1990, pp. 184-194.

K. Ramamritham, J.A. Stankovic, and W. Zhao, "Distributed Scheduling of Tasks with Deadlines and Resource Requirements," *IEEE Trans. Computers*, Vol. 38, No. 8, Aug. 1989, pp. 1110-1123.

K. Ramamritham, J. A. Stankovic, and W. Zhao, "Meta-Level Control in Distributed Real-Time Systems," *Proc. Int'l Conf. Distributed Computing Systems*, IEEE CS Press, Los Alamitos, Calif., Sept. 1987, pp. 10-17.

B. Randell, "System Structure for Software Fault Tolerance," *IEEE Trans. Software Engineering*, Vol. SE-1, No. 2, June 1975, pp. 220-232.

P. V. Rangan and H. M. Vin, "Designing File Systems for Digital Video and Audio," *Proc. 13th ACM Symp. Operating Systems Principles*, ACM, New York, Oct. 1991.

R.R. Razouk, T. Stewart, and M. Wilson, "Measuring Operating System Performance on Modern Microprocessors," *Performance 86*, ACM, New York, 1986, pp. 193-202.

J.F. Ready, "VTRX: A Real-Time Operating System for Embedded Microprocessor Applications," *IEEE Micro*, Aug. 1986, pp. 8-17.

G.M. Reed and A.W. Roscoe, "A Timed Model for Communicating Sequential Processes," *Proc. ICALP '86*, Springer LNCS 226, New York, 1986, pp. 314-323.

M.G. Rodd, G.F. Zhao and I. Izikowitz, "RTMMS-An OSI-Based Real-Time Messaging System," *Real-Time Systems*, Vol. 2, No. 3, Sept. 1990, pp. 213-234.

H. Rzehak, A.E. Elnakhal, and R. Jaeger, "Analysis of Real-Time Properties and Rules for Setting Protocol Parameters of MAP Networks," *Real-Time Systems*, Vol. 1, No. 3, Dec. 1989, pp. 221-242.

S. Sahni and Y. Cho, "Nearly On-Line Scheduling of a Uniform Processor System with Release Times," *SIAM J. Computing*, Vol. 8, No. 2, May 1979, pp. 275-285.

S. Sahni and Y. Cho, "Scheduling Independent Tasks with Due Times on a Uniform Processor System," *J. ACM*, Vol. 27, No. 3, July 1980, pp. 550-563.

K. Sakamura, ed., *TRON Project 1990: Open-Architecture Computer Systems*, Springer-Verlag, Tokyo, 1990.

L. Salkind, "UNIX for Real-Time Control: Problems and Solutions," NYU Tech. Report, Sept. 1988.

S.C. Sarin, "Scheduling Independent Projects Against a Single Resource," *Int'l J. Prod. Res.*, Vol. 20, No. 2, 1982, pp. 135-146.

V. Sarkar, "Partitioning and Scheduling Parallel Programs for Multiprocessors," Ph.D. thesis, Stanford Univ., Stanford, Calif., 1989.

S. Savitzky, *Real-Time Microprocessor Systems*, Van Nostrand Reinhold, New York, 1985.

G. Scallon and D. Nast, "A Sample Problem in Real-Time Control," *Real-Time Systems Newsletter*, Vol. 3, No. 3, Fall 1987.

R.D. Schlichting and F.B. Schneider, "Fail-Stop Processors: An Approach to Designing Fault-Tolerant Computer Systems," *ACM TOCS*, Vol. 1, No. 3, Aug. 1983, pp. 222-238.

F.B. Schneider, "Abstractions for Fault Tolerance in Distributed Systems," *Proc. IFIP 86 Congress*, 1986, pp. 727-733.

F.B. Schneider, "The State Machine Approach: A Tutorial," *Proc. Workshop on Fault-Tolerant Distributed Computing, Lecture Notes in Computer Science,* Springer-Verlag, New York, 1988.

J.D. Schoeffler, "Distributed Computer Systems for Industrial Process Control," *Computer*, Vol. 17, No. 2, Feb. 1984, pp. 11-18.

L. Schrage, "Solving Resource-Constrained Network Problems by Implicit Enumeration: Preemptive Case," *Operations Research*, Vol. 20, No. 3, 1972.

K. Schwan et al., "High Performance Operating System Primitives for Robotics and Real-Time Control Systems," *ACM Trans. Computer Systems*, Vol. 5, No. 3, Aug. 1987, pp. 189-231.

K. Schwan, A. Gheith, and H. Zhou, "From CHAOS^{base} to CHAOS^{arc}: A Family of Real-Time Kernels," *Proc. Real-Time Systems Symp.,* IEEE CS Press, Los Alamitos, Calif., Dec. 1990, pp. 82-91.

M. Schwartz, "Telecommunication Networks: Protocols," in *Modeling and Analysis*, Addison-Wesley, Reading, Mass., 1987.

H. Schweinzer, "Fast Sensor Corrections of Robot Motion Paths Processed in Real-Time by Control Algorithms Running in Parallel," *Real-Time Systems*, Vol. 1, No. 3, Dec. 1989, pp. 207-220.

T. Sen and S.K. Gupta, "A State-of-Art Survey of Static Scheduling Research Involving Due Dates," *Omega, The Int'l J. Management Science*, Vol. 12, No. 1, 1984, pp. 63-67.

O. Serlin, "Scheduling of Time-Critical Processes," *Proc. AFIPS Spring Joint Computer Conf.*, AFIPS Press, Montvale, N.J., 1972, pp. 925-932.

R. Sethi, "Scheduling Graphs on Two Processors," *SIAM J. Computing*, Vol. 5, No. 1, 1976, pp. 73-82.

K.C. Sevcik and M.J. Johnson, "Cycle-Time Properties of the FDDI Token Ring Protocol," *IEEE Trans. Software Engineering*, Vol. SE-13, No. 3, March 1987, pp. 376-385.

L. Sha and J. Goodenough, "Real-Time Scheduling Theory and ADA," *Computer*, Vol. 23, No. 4, April 1990, pp. 53-62.

L. Sha, R. Rajkumar, and J. Lehoczky, "Priority Inheritance Protocols: An Approach to Real-Time Synchronization," *IEEE Trans.Computers*, Vol. 39, No. 3, 1990, pp. 1175-1185.

L. Sha, R. Rajkumar, and J.P. Lehoczky, "Concurrency Control for Distributed Real-Time Databases," *ACM SIGMOD Record*, March 1988.

L. Sha et al., "Mode Change Protocols for Priority-Driven Preemptive Scheduling," *Real-Time Systems*, Vol. 1, No. 3, Dec. 1989, pp. 243-264.

A. Shaw, "Deterministic Timing Schema for Parallel Programs," Tech. Report 90-05-06, Dept. Computer Science, Univ. of Washington, Seattle, Wash., May 1990.

A.C. Shaw, "Reasoning About Time in Higher-Level Language Software," *IEEE Trans. Software Engineering*, Vol. 15, No. 7, July 1989.

C. Shen, "An Integrated Approach to Real-Time Task and Resource Management in Multiprocessor Systems," Ph.D. thesis, Univ. of Massachusetts, Amherst, Mass., 1992.

C. Shen, K. Ramamritham, and J.A. Stankovic, "Resource Reclaiming in Real-Time," *Proc. Real-Time Systems Symp.*, IEEE CS Press, Los Alamitos, Calif., Dec. 1990, pp. 41-50.

P. Shiah, "Real-Time Multiprocessor Scheduling Algorithms," master's thesis, Univ. of Massachusetts, Amherst, Mass., Jan. 1989.

C. Shih and J. Stankovic, "Distributed Deadlock Detection in Ada Runtime Environments," *TRI-ADA 90*, Oct. 1990.

W-K. Shih, J.W.S. Liu, and J.-Y. Chung, "Fast Algorithms for Scheduling Imprecise Computation," *Proc. Real-Time Systems Symp.*, IEEE CS Press, Los Alamitos, Calif., 1989, pp. 12-19.

K.G. Shin, "Introduction to the Special Issue on Real-Time Systems," *IEEE Trans. Computers*, Vol. C-36, No. 8, Aug. 1987, pp. 901-902.

K.G. Shin, "HARTS: A Distributed Real-Time Architecture," *Computer,* Vol. 24, No. 5, May, 1991, pp. 25-35.

K.G. Shin and M.E. Epstein, "Intertask Communications in an Integrated Multirobot System," *IEEE J. Robotics and Automation*, Vol. RA-3, No. 2, April 1987.

K.G. Shin and C.M. Krishna, "New Performance Measures for Design and Evaluation of Real-Time Multiprocessors," *Computer Systems Science and Eng.*, Vol. 1, No. 4, Oct. 1986, pp. 179-192.

K.G. Shin, C.M. Krishna, and Y.-H. Lee, "A Unified Method for Evaluating Real-Time Computer Controllers and Its Application," *IEEE Trans. Automatic Control,* Vol. AC-30, No. 4, April 1985, pp. 357-366.

S.K. Shrivastava, "Replicated Distributed Processing," *Lecture Notes in Computer Science*, Vol. 248, 1987, pp. 325-337.

J.B. Sidney, "Extension of Moore's Due Date Algorithm," *Proc. Symp. on the Theory of Scheduling and its Applications*, May 1972.

B. Simons, "A Fast Algorithm for Single Processor Scheduling," *Proc. 19th Annual Symp. Foundation of Computer Science*, IEEE CS Press, Los Alamitos, Calif., Oct. 1978, pp. 246-252.

B. Simons, "A Fast Algorithm for Multiprocessor Scheduling," *Proc. 21st Annual Symp. Foundation of Computer Science*, IEEE CS Press, Los Alamitos, Calif., Oct. 1980.

B. Simons, "Multiprocessor Scheduling of Unit-Time Jobs with Arbitrary Release Times and Deadlines," *SIAM J. Computing*, Vol. 12, No. 2, 1983.

B. Simons and M. Sipser, "On Scheduling Unit-Length Jobs with Multiple Release Time/Deadline Intervals," *Operations Research*, Vol. 32, No. 1, 1984.

M. Solomon and S. Prince, "Local Network Architecture for Process Control," in *Local Networks for Computer Communications*, North-Holland, New York, 1981, pp. 407-427.

S.H. Son, "Using Replication for High Performance Database Support in Distributed Real-Time Systems," *Proc. Eighth Real-Time Systems Symp.*, IEEE CS Press, Los Alamitos, Calif., Dec. 1987, pp. 79-86.

S.H. Son and C.H. Chang, "Priority-Based Scheduling in Real-Time Database Systems," *Proc. 15th VLDB Conf.*, Morgan Kaufmann, San Mateo, Calif., 1989.

S.H. Son and C.-H. Chang, "Performance Evaluation of Real-Time Locking Protocols Using a Distributed Software Prototyping Environment," *Proc. 10th Int'l Conf. Distributed Computing Systems,* IEEE CS Press, Los Alamitos, Calif., May 1990, pp. 124-131.

J.M. Spivey, "Specifying a Real-Time Kernel," *IEEE Software*, Vol. 7, No. 5, Sept. 1990, pp. 21-28.

B. Sprunt, L. Sha, and J. Lehoczky, "Aperiodic Task Scheduling for Hard Real-Time Systems," *Real-Time Systems*, Vol. 1, No. 1, 1989, pp. 27-60.

J.A. Stankovic, "Decentralized Decision Making for Task Allocation in a Hard Real-Time System," *IEEE Trans. Computers*, March 1989.

J.A. Stankovic, "Misconceptions About Real-Time Computing," *Computer*, Vol. 21, No. 10, Oct. 1988, pp. 10-19.

J.A. Stankovic, "Stability and Distributed Scheduling Algorithms," *IEEE Trans. on Software Engineering,* Vol. SE-11, No. 10, 1985, pp. 1141-1152.

J.A. Stankovic, "The Spring Architecture," *Proc. EuroMicro Workshop on Real-Time*, IEEE CS Press, Los Alamitos, Calif., June 1990, pp. 104-113.

J.A. Stankovic, "On the Reflective Nature of the Spring Kernel," invited paper, *Proc. Process Control Systems '91*, Feb. 1991.

J.A. Stankovic and K. Ramamritham, "The Spring Kernel: A New Paradigm for Hard Real-Time Operating Systems," *IEEE Software*, Vol. 8, No. 3, May 1991, pp. 62-72.

J.A. Stankovic and K. Ramamritham, "The Spring Kernel: A New Paradigm for Hard Real-Time Operating Systems," in *Operating Systems for Mission Critical Computing,* Agrawala, Gordon, and Hwang, eds., IOS Press, Inc., 1992.

J.A. Stankovic and K. Ramamritham, "What is Predictability for Real-Time Systems?" *Real-Time Systems*, Dec. 1990, pp. 247-254.

J.A. Stankovic and K. Ramamritham, "Hard Real-Time Systems," tutorial text, IEEE CS Press, Los Alamitos, Calif., 1988.

J.A. Stankovic, K. Ramamritham, and S. Cheng, "Evaluation of a Flexible Task Scheduling Algorithm for Distributed Hard Real-Time Systems," *IEEE Trans. Computer*, Vol. C-34, No. 12, 1985, pp. 1130-1143.

J.A. Stankovic, K. Ramamritham, and E. Nahum, "Predictable Interprocess Communication for Hard Real-Time Systems," *Proc. 10th IFAC Workshop on Distributed Computer Control Systems*, Sept. 1991.

J.A. Stankovic and W. Zhao, "On Real-Time Transactions," *ACM SIGMOD Record*, March 1988.

D.B. Stewart and P.K. Khosla, "Real-Time Scheduling of Sensor-Based Control Systems," *Proc. Eighth IEEE Workshop on Real-Time Operating Systems and Software*, May 1991.

A. Stoyenko and T. Marlowe, "Schedulability, Program Transformations, and Real-Time Programming," *Proc. Eighth IEEE Workshop on Real-Time Operating Systems and Software*, May 1991, pp. 33-41.

J.K. Strosnider and T. Marchok, "Responsive, Deterministic IEEE 802.5 Token Ring Scheduling," *Real-Time Systems*, Vol. 1, No. 2, Sept. 1989, pp. 133-158.

I. Suzuki, "Formal Analysis of the Alternating Bit Protocol by Temporal Petri Nets," *IEEE Trans. Software Engineering*, Vol. 16, No. 11, Nov. 1990, pp. 1273-1281.

M. Takesue, "Dataflow Computer Extension Towards Real-Time Processing," *Real-Time Systems*, Vol. 1, No. 4, April 1990, pp. 333-350.

T. Teixeira, "Static Priority Interrupt Scheduling," *Proc. Seventh Texas Conf. on Computing Systems*, Nov. 1978.

K.W. Tindell, A. Burns, and A.J. Wellings, "Allocating Hard Real-Time Tasks: An NP-Hard Problem Made Easy," *Real-Time Systems*, Vol. 4, No. 2, June 1992.

H. Tokuda, T. Nakajima, and P. Rao, "Real-Time Mach: Towards a Predictable Real-Time System," *Proc. Usenix Mach Workshop*, USENIX Association, Berkeley, Calif., Oct. 1990, pp. 1-10.

H. Tokuda, J.W. Wendorf, and H.-Y. Wang, "Implementation of a Time-Driven Scheduler for Real-Time Operating Systems," *Proc. Real-Time Systems Symp.*, IEEE CS Press, Los Alamitos, Calif., Dec. 1987, pp. 271-280.

J.C. Valadier and D.R. Powell, "On CSMA Protocols Allowing Bounded Channel Access Times," *Proc. Fourth Int'l Conf. Distributed Computing Systems*, IEEE CS Press, Los Alamitos, Calif., May 1984, pp. 146-153.

A.M. van Tilborg and G.M. Koob, eds., *Foundations of Real-Time Computing: Scheduling and Resource Management*, Kluwer Academic Publishers, 1991.

A.M. van Tilborg and G.M. Koob, eds., *Foundations of Real-Time Computing: Formal Specifications and Methods*, Kluwer Academic Publishers, 1991.

J.P.C. Verhoosel et al., "A Static Scheduling Algorithm for Distributed Real-Time Systems," *Real-Time Systems*, Vol. 3, No. 3, Sept. 1991, pp. 227-246.

R.A.Volz and T.N. Mudge, "Timing Issues in the Distributed Execution of Ada Programs," *IEEE Trans. Computers*, Vol. C-36, No. 4, April 1987, pp. 449-459.

R.A. Volz, L. Sha, and D. Wilcox, "Maintaining Global Time in Futurebus+," *Real-Time Systems*, Vol. 3, No. 1, March 1991, pp. 5-18.

C.J. Walter, R.M. Kieckhafer, and A.M. Finn, "MAFT: A Multicomputer Architecture for Fault-Tolerance in Real-Time Control Systems," *Proc. Real-Time Systems Symp.,* IEEE CS Press, Los Alamitos, Calif., Dec. 1985.

F. Wang and D. Mao, "Worst Case Analysis for On-Line Scheduling in Real-Time Systems," COINS Tech. Report 91-54, Univ. of Massachusetts, Amherst, Mass., 1991.

F. Wang, K. Ramamritham, and J.A. Stankovic, "Bounds on the Performance of Heuristic Algorithms for Multiprocessor Scheduling of Hard Real-Time Tasks," *Proc. Real-Time Systems Symp.*, IEEE CS Press, Los Alamitos, Calif., 1992, pp. 136-145.

P. Ward and S. Mellor, *Structured Development for Real-Time Systems*, Vols. 1 and 2, Yourdan Press, 1985.

H.F. Wedde et al., "MELODY: A Completely Decentralized Adaptive File System for Handling Real-Time Tasks in Unpredictable Environments," *Real-Time Systems*, Vol. 2, No. 4, Nov. 1990, pp. 347-364.

J. Wensley et al., "SIFT: Design and Analysis of a Fault-Tolerant Computer for Aircraft Control," *Proc. IEEE,* Vol. 66, No. 11, Oct. 1978, pp. 1240-1255.

J. Winkowski, "Protocols of Accessing Overlapping Sets of Resources," *Information Processing Letters*, Vol. 12, No. 5, Oct. 1981, pp. 239-243.

N. Wirth, "Toward a Discipline of Real-Time Programming," *CACM*, Vol. 20, No. 8, Aug. 1977, pp. 577-583.

M.H. Woodbury and K.G. Shin, "Workload Effects on Fault Latency for Real-Time Computing Systems," *Proc. Real-Time Systems Symp.*, IEEE CS Press, Los Alamitos, Calif., Dec. 1987, pp. 188-197.

M.L. Wright, M.W. Green, and P.F. Cross, "An Expert System for Real-Time Control," *IEEE Software*, Vol. 3, No. 2, March 1986, pp. 16-24.

J. Xu and L. Parnas, "Scheduling Processes with Release Times, Deadlines, Precedence, and Exclusion Relations," *IEEE Trans. Software Engineering,* Vol. 16, No. 3, March 1990, pp. 360-369.

V. Yodaiken, "A Logic-Free Method for Compositional Specification," *Proc. ICCI*, Springer-Verlag LNCS Series, New York, 1990.

V. Yodaiken, "The Algebraic Feedback Product of Automata," *WAV 1990* (Springer-Verlag LNCS series and longer version in ACM/AMS Series).

V. Yodaiken and K. Ramamritham, "Specifying and Verifying a Real-Time Priority Queue with Modal Algebra," *Proc. Real-Time Systems Symp.*, IEEE CS Press, Los Alamitos, Calif., Dec. 1990, pp. 300-310.

V. Yodaiken and K. Ramamritham, "Mathematical Models of Real-Time Scheduling," in *Foundations of Real-Time Computing: Formal Specifications*, Andre van Tilborg, ed., Kluwer Academic Publishers, New York, 1992, pp. 55-85.

W. Zhao, "A Heuristic Approach to Scheduling Hard Real-Time Tasks with Resource Requirements in Distributed Systems," doctoral dissertation, Univ. of Massachusetts, Amherst, Mass., Feb. 1986.

W. Zhao and K. Ramamritham, "Distributed Scheduling Using Bidding and Focussed Addressing," *Proc. Real-Time Systems Symp.*, IEEE CS Press, Los Alamitos, Calif., Dec. 1985, pp. 103-111.

W. Zhao and K. Ramamritham, "Simple and Integrated Heuristic Algorithms for Scheduling Tasks with Time and Resource Constraints," *J. Systems and Software,* Vol. 7, 1987, pp. 195-205.

W. Zhao and K. Ramamritham, "Virtual Time CSMA Protocols for Hard Real-Time Communication," *IEEE Trans. Software Engineering,* Vol. SE-13, No. 8, Aug. 1987, pp. 938-952.

W. Zhao, K. Ramamritham, and J.A. Stankovic, "Scheduling Tasks with Resource Requirements in Hard Real-Time Systems," *IEEE Trans. Software Engineering*, Vol. SE-12, No. 5, 1987, pp. 567-577.

W. Zhao, K. Ramamritham, and J.A. Stankovic, "Preemptive Scheduling Under Time and Resource Constraints," *IEEE Trans. Computers*, Vol. C-36, No. 8, Aug. 1987, pp. 949-960.

W. Zhao and J.A. Stankovic, "Performance Analysis of FCFS and Improved FCFS Scheduling Algorithms for Dynamic Real-Time Computer Systems," *Proc. Real-Time Systems Symp.*, IEEE CS Press, Los Alamitos, Calif., Dec. 1989, pp. 156-165.

W. Zhao, J.A. Stankovic, and K. Ramamritham, "A Window Protocol for Transmission of Time Constrained Messages," *IEEE Trans.Computers*, Vol. C-39, No. 9, Sept. 1990, pp. 1186-1203.

H. Zhou and K. Schwan, "Dynamic Scheduling for Hard Real-Time Systems Toward Real-Time Threads," *Proc. Eighth IEEE Workshop on Real-Time Operating Systems and Softwar*, May 1991.

Author Profiles

John A. Stankovic

Krithi Ramamritham

John A. Stankovic received the B.S. degree in electrical engineering and the M.S. and Ph.D. degrees in computer science from Brown University, Providence, RI, in 1970, 1976, and 1979, respectively.

He is a professor of computer science at the University of Massachusetts at Amherst. His research interests include scheduling on local area networks and multiprocessors, developing flexible, distributed, hard real-time systems, and experimental studies on distributed database protocols. He has held visiting positions in the Computer Science Department at Carnegie-Mellon University, at INRIA in France, and at the Scuola Superiore S. Anna in Pisa, Italy. He received an Outstanding Scholar Award from the School of Engineering at the University of Massachusetts, the Meritorious Service Award from the IEEE, and is a Fellow of the IEEE.

He is co-founder and co-editor-in-chief for *Real-Time Systems Journal,* served four years as a member of the Editorial Board for *IEEE Transactions on Computers,* and was a Guest Editor for a special issue of *IEEE Transactions on Computers on Parallel and Distributed Computing.* He is a member of the ACM, the IEEE executive committee for distributed systems, the advisory board for the Computer Society of India's *Journal of Computer Science and Informatics,* and Sigma Xi.

Krithi Ramamritham received the Ph.D. degree from the University of Utah, Salt Lake City, in 1981. Since then he has been with University of Massachusetts at Amherst where he is currently a professor in the department of computer science. During 1987-1988 he was a Science and Engineering Research Council (U.K.) Visiting Fellow at the University of Newcastle upon Tyne, U.K., and a Visiting Professor at the Technical University of Vienna, Austria.

He is a director of the Spring project whose goal is to develop scheduling algorithms, operating system support, architectural support, and design strategies for distributed real-time applications.

His other research interests include enhancing the performance of database applications that require transaction support through the use of semantic information about the objects, operations, transaction model, and the application.

He has served on numerous program committees for conferences and workshops devoted to databases and real-time systems. He is an editor for *Real-Time Systems Journal* and the *Distributed Systems Engineering Journal* and has co-authored two IEEE tutorial texts on hard real-time systems. He is a member of the IEEE and ACM

Other titles from
IEEE Computer Society Press

Current Research in Decision Support Technology
edited by Robert W. Blanning and David R. King

This tutorial presents recent studies on DSS and identifies research issues of current interest that offer significant promise for further development. The areas covered explore the use of expert systems in DSS construction, recent research on logic modeling and integration, and group DSS and the determination of the organizational impact of DSS on understanding organizational information processing and decision-making.

Sections: Introduction, Advanced Decision Modeling and Model Management, Knowledge-Based Decision Support, Organizational Issues in DSS Development.

256 pages. 1993. Hardcover. ISBN 0-8186-2807-3. Catalog # 2807-01 — $45.00   Members $35.00

Groupware:
Software for Computer-Supported Cooperative Work
edited by David Marca and Geoffrey Bock

Investigates the task of designing software to fit the way groups interact in specific work situations and emphasizes the technical aspects involved in the development of software within the bounds of strong social and organizational factors. The book provides a guide to the computer-supported cooperative work field, highlights key trends and ideas, and covers the perspective of work as a cooperative and social endeavor being done by groups, not just individuals.

Sections: Introduction, Groups and Groupware, Conceptual Frameworks, Design Methods, Enabling Technologies — System-Related, Enabling Technologies — UI-Related, Computer Supported Meetings, Bridging Time and Space, Coordinators, What Makes for Effective Systems.

592 pages. 1992. Hardcover. ISBN 0-8186-2637. Catalog # 2637-01 — $75.00   Members $45.00

Information Systems and Decision Processes
edited by Edward A. Stohr and Benn R. Konsynski

This book focuses on DSS and vital issues in the application of information technology to decision making, and introduces some promising new directions for research. It contains the collaborative studies of DSS researchers and explains the potential opportunities and problems in the application of information systems to the decision process in organizations.

Sections: Review and Critique of DSS, Decision Processes, Behavioral Decision Theory and DSS, Group Decision Support Systems, Organizational Decision Support Systems, Technology Environments to Support Decision Processes, Model Management Systems, Research Challenges, Research Approaches in ISDP.

368 pages. 1992. Hardcover. ISBN 0-8186-2802-2. Catalog # 2802-04 — $45.00   Members $35.00

Fault-Tolerant Software Systems:
Techniques and Applications
edited by Hoang Pham

A collection of 12 papers investigating the rapidly growing field of software fault-tolerant computing. It provides a concise overview of the latest theories and techniques to reveal the recent directions of research, and to stimulate more research in this field.

Papers: Definition and Analysis of Hardware and Software Fault-Tolerant Architectures, An Environment for Developing Fault-Tolerant Software, Assuring Design Diversity of N-Version Software, Modeling Execution Time of Multi-Stage N-Version Software, Performance Analysis of Real-Time Software Supporting Fault-Tolerant Operation, Reliability Analysis Fault-Tolerant Systems.

128 pages. 1992. Softcover. ISBN 0-8186-3210-0. Catalog # 3210-05 — $35.00 Members $25.00

 IEEE COMPUTER SOCIETY

▼   **To order call toll-free: 1-800-CS-BOOKS**   ▼

▼   **Fax: (714) 821–4641**   ▼

10662 Los Vaqueros Circle   **Los Alamitos, CA   90720-1264**   **Phone: (714) 821–8380**

Other titles from
IEEE Computer Society Press

Codes for Detecting and Correcting Unidirectional Errors
edited by Mario Blaum

This collection of papers presents state-of-the-art theory and practice for codes that correct or detect unidirectional errors. The text begins with a selection of four papers providing an introduction to the field that includes applications. It also features key papers demonstrating the best results in each subject related to unidirectional errors.

Sections: Unidirectional Errors, Codes for Detecting Unidirectional Errors, Codes for Correcting Unidirectional Errors, Codes for Correcting *t*-Symmetric Errors and Detecting All Unidirectional Errors, Codes for Correcting and Detecting Combinations of Symmetric and Unidirectional Errors, Codes for Detecting and/or Correcting Unidirectional Burst Errors, Codes for Detecting and/or Correcting Unidirectional Byte Errors.

224 pages. 1993. Hardcover. ISBN 0-8186-4182-7. Catalog # 4182-03 — $44.00 Members $35.00

The Cache Coherence Problem in Shared-Memory Multiprocessors:
Hardware Solutions
edited by Milo Tomasevic and Veljko Milutinovic

Provides an insight into the nature of the cache coherence problem and the wide variety of proposed hardware solutions available today. Its chapters discuss the shared-memory multiprocessor environment, the cache coherence problem and solutions, directory cache coherence schemes, and scalable schemes for large multiprocessor systems, and evaluate different hardware coherence solutions.

Sections: Introductory Issues, Memory Reference Characteristics in Parallel Programs, Directory Cache Coherence Protocols, Snoopy Cache-Coherence Protocols, Coherence in Multilevel Cache Hierarchies, Cache Coherence Schemes in Large-Scale Multiprocessors, Evaluation of Hardware Cache Coherence Schemes.

448 pages. 1993. Hardcover. ISBN 0-8186-4092-8. Catalog # 4092-01 — $62.00 Members $50.00

Bridging Faults and IDDQ Testing
edited by Yashwant K. Malaiya and Rochit Rajsuman

Includes an overview and 17 key papers on recent developments and the major issues regarding bridging faults and the use of IDDQ testing. Some of the selections presented in this text discuss analytical models, test generation procedures, and fault coverage under various situations. Other articles cover the basics of bridging faults and reveal the limitations of conventional logic testing.

Papers: Detecting I/O and Internal Feedback Bridging Faults, Limitations of Switch-Level Analysis for Bridging Faults, IDDQ Benefits, A New Approach to Dynamic IDDQ Testing, High-Quality Tests for Switch-Level Circuits Using Current and Logic Test Generation Algorithms, Constraints for Using IDDQ Testing to Detect CMOS Bridging Faults, Fault Location with Current Monitoring, Built-In Current Testing.

136 pages. 1992. Softcover. ISBN 0-8186-3215-1. Catalog # 3215-05 — $35.00 Members $25.00

Readings in Computer-Generated Music
edited by Dennis Baggi

This tutorial contains 12 articles that cover applications of computer technology to music and focus on the significant effort towards improving musical quality at the levels of tools, compositional strategies, representational models, and abstract methodologies. Its topics range from compositional models and languages to express music, to systems for sound modeling and interpretive performance.

Papers: Formula – A Programming Language for Expressive Computer Music, Tonal Context by Pattern Integration Over Time, Sound Synthesis by Dynamic Systems Integration, AlgoRhythms: Real-Time Algorithmic Composition for a Microcomputer, Composition Based on Pentatonic Scales: A Computer-Aided Approach, An Expert System for the Articulation of Bach Fugue Melodies.

232 pages. 1992. Hardcover. ISBN 0-8186-2747-6. Catalog # 2747-01 — $45.00 Members $35.00

 IEEE COMPUTER SOCIETY

▼   **To order call toll-free: 1-800-CS-BOOKS**   ▼

▼   **Fax: (714) 821–4641**   ▼

10662 Los Vaqueros Circle   Los Alamitos, CA   90720-1264   Phone: (714) 821–8380